OXFORD MONOGRAPHS IN
PRIVATE INTERNATIONAL LAW

GENERAL EDITOR: P. B. CARTER QC
*Emeritus Fellow of
Wadham College, Oxford*

INTELLECTUAL PROPERTY AND PRIVATE INTERNATIONAL LAW

OXFORD MONOGRAPHS IN
PRIVATE INTERNATIONAL LAW

The aim of the series is to publish work of high quality and originality in a number of important areas of private international law. The series is intended for both scholarly and practitioner readers.

ALSO IN THIS SERIES

Declining Jurisdiction in Private International Law
JAMES J. FAWCETT

Foreign Law in English Courts
Pleading, Proof and Choice of Law
RICHARD FENTIMAN

FORTHCOMING TITLES INCLUDE

Insolvency in Private International Law
IAN FLETCHER

Autonomy in International Contracts
PETER NYGH

INTELLECTUAL PROPERTY AND PRIVATE INTERNATIONAL LAW

JAMES J. FAWCETT
*Professor of International Commercial Law,
University of Nottingham*

PAUL TORREMANS
*Lecturer in Law,
University of Leicester*

CLARENDON PRESS · OXFORD
1998

Oxford University Press, Great Clarendon Street, Oxford OX2 6DP
www.oup.co.uk
Oxford New York
Athens Auckland Bangkok Bogotá Buenos Aires Calcutta
Cape Town Chennai Dar es Salaam Delhi Florence Hong Kong Istanbul
Karachi Kuala Lumpur Madras Madrid Melbourne Mexico City Mumbai
Nairobi Paris São Paolo Singapore Taipei Tokyo Toronto Warsaw
and associated companies in
Berlin Ibadan

Oxford is a trade mark of Oxford University Press

Published in the United States
by Oxford University Press Inc., New York

© *Fawcett & Torremans 1998*

First published 1998

All rights reserved. No part of this publication may be reproduced,
stored in a retrieval system, or transmitted, in any form or by any means,
without the prior permission in writing of Oxford University Press.
Within the UK, exceptions are allowed in respect of any fair dealing for the
purpose of research or private study, or criticism or review, as permitted
under the Copyright, Designs and Patents Act 1988, or in the case of
reprographic reproduction in accordance with the terms of the licences
issued by the Copyright Licensing Agency. Enquiries concerning
reproduction outside these terms and in other countries should be
sent to the Rights Department, Oxford University Press,
at the address above

British Library Cataloguing in Publication Data
Data available

Library of Congress Cataloging in Publication Data
Fawcett, J. J.
Intellectual property and private international law /
J. J. Fawcett, Paul Torremans.
p. cm.—(Oxford monographs in private international law)
Includes bibliographical references and index.
1. Conflict of laws—Intellectual property—Great Britain.
2. Conflict of laws—Intellectual property. I. Torremans, Paul.
II. Title. III. Series.
KD685.I54F39 1998 340.9'48'0941—dc21 98–26752
ISBN 0–19–826214–0

1 3 5 7 9 10 8 6 4 2

Typeset by Hope Services (Abingdon) Ltd.
Printed in Great Britain
on acid-free paper by
Biddles Ltd., Guildford and King's Lynn

General Editor's Preface

When in 1990 in the course of a critical commentary upon the holding in *Tyburn Production Ltd* v *Conan Doyle* [1991] Ch. 75 I advocated 'the construction of a much needed private international law of intellectual property' (61 B.Y.I.L. 202), I was, of course, advocating satisfaction of an obvious need. In the years that have elapsed since then, although some, albeit piecemeal, progress has been made, that need has become even more pressing. This has largely been as a result of advances in technology, both actual and prospective.

Historically the impact of private international law upon intellectual property issues was slight. This may have been in part due to the 'territorial' approach adopted by private international lawyers. The physical location of non-physical phenomena presented difficulty. Even in the immediate post-Beale era response to the criteria of 'closest connection', 'proper law', 'governmental interest analysis', etc., has not been free from difficulty.

However, whatever the explanation of the past failure of private international law to meet the need to accommodate problems in the area of intellectual property, that need is compelling. What is required is a comprehensive pattern of legal rules individually tailored to deal appropriately with a wide and diverse variety of issues. Whether this is to be satisfactorily achieved by statutory intervention alone is, especially in the light of the likelihood of continuing and fairly rapid development, doubtful. There is certainly room for creative judicial activity, which is now facilitated by the currently emerging flexible and justice orientated approach to private international law generally. Moreover, legal writing obviously has an important part to play in the achievement of the objective. The avowed aim of *Oxford Monographs in Private International Law* is to publish works of originality and quality on a number of important and developing areas of private international law. I think that both practitioners and academics will regard this volume as not only providing a detailed and illuminating analysis of the present position but as also constituting a major contribution to the long overdue evolution of a comprehensive and sophisticated private international law of intellectual property.

Wadham College, Oxford P. B. CARTER
1 May, 1998

Authors' Preface

This book is concerned with the application of the rules of private international law to intellectual property cases. Private international lawyers have largely ignored this topic, and it has been left to intellectual property lawyers to discuss this. This is a pity. It is a topic which raises unique questions for the private international lawyer which deserve an answer, and at the same time tells us much about the rules of private international law that are being applied. The aim of the book is to fill this gap in the literature. The emphasis in the book is on private international law rather than on intellectual property law. Nonetheless, it is hoped that intellectual property lawyers will find much to interest them here.

The book is divided up into sections to reflect the classic issues in private international law: jurisdiction; choice of law; and recognition and enforcement of foreign judgments. Within each section, there are chapters to reflect the major issues that arise in relation to intellectual property: the creation of intellectual property rights; the ownership of such rights; the commercial exploitation of such rights by means of licensing and other agreements; and the protection of such rights by means of the tort of infringement and complementary causes of action.

A proper understanding of how jurisdictional and choice of law problems arise requires some knowledge of the substantive law background. Moreover, when it comes to the application of the rules of private international law, it is necessary to characterise the issue and the cause of action and, as regards the latter, to identify the constituent elements thereof. There are limitations on jurisdiction which apply in relation to certain types of intellectual property right but not others. The approach adopted, therefore, is to start the treatment of each new issue with a discussion of the substantive law background. This is followed by a discussion of how jurisdictional or choice of law problems arise. Most of the book, though, is taken up with the discussion of the relevant rules of private international law and their application in the context of intellectual property law. A major theme of the book is the extent to which there are special rules of private international law for this area and whether there should be such rules. Alternative private international law solutions will be considered by looking at law in other jurisdictions, such as the United States, France, Germany, Austria, Switzerland and the Netherlands. Where appropriate, proposals will be put forward for a better solution.

We have relied upon the help and guidance of friends and colleagues in preparing this book and would like particularly to thank Professor

John Adams, Michael Bowman, Professor W R Cornish, Professor Hector MacQueen, David Ormerod, Dr Harry Duintjer Tebbens and Irini A Stamatoudi for her invaluable research assistance. Especial thanks are due to P B Carter, the General Editor of the Oxford Monographs in Private International Law, for his encouragement and many helpful comments on the text. All errors are, of course, our responsibility.

The law is stated as at 31 December 1997.

Nottingham and Leicester JAMES J. FAWCETT
PAUL TORREMANS

Contents

General Editor's Preface	v
Authors' Preface	vii
Table of Cases	xi
Table of Legislation	xxxv
Table of Conventions and Treaties	xlvii

SECTION I JURISDICTION

	Preliminary remarks	1
1	Creation and validity of intellectual property rights: jurisdiction	5
2	Entitlement to the grant and ownership of intellectual property rights: jurisdiction	49
3	Contracts in relation to the exploitation of intellectual property rights: jurisdiction	73
4	Infringement: preliminary matters	119
5	Infringement: jurisdiction under the European Community/European Free Trade Association rules	139
6	Infringement: jurisdiction under the traditional rules	239
7	Jurisdictional issues in relation to European Community rights	317
8	Complementary torts and other causes of action: jurisdiction	359

SECTION II THE APPLICABLE LAW

	Preliminary remarks	455
9	Choice of law elements in the intellectual property conventions	459
10	Creation, scope and termination of intellectual property rights: the applicable law	483
11	Contracts in relation to the exploitation of intellectual property rights: the applicable law	543
12	Infringement: the applicable law	595
13	Complementary torts and other causes of action: the applicable law	649

SECTION III RECOGNITION AND ENFORCEMENT OF FOREIGN JUDGMENTS

Preliminary remarks 721

14 Recognition and enforcement of foreign judgments relating to
    intellectual property 723

Selected Bibliography 743

Index 747

Table of Cases

Australia

Akai Pty Ltd *v* People's Insurance Co Ltd (1996) 141 ALR 374,
High Ct 107
Best Australia Ltd and others *v* Aquagas Marketing Pty Ltd
and others (1988) 83 ALR 217, Federal Ct 246, **260**, 262
Dagi and others *v* The Broken Hill Pty Co Ltd and another
(No 2) [1997] 1 VR 428 284
Evers *v* Firth (1987) 10 NSWLR 22 ....268, 269
McKain *v* RW Miller & Co (SA) Pty Ltd (1991) 174 CLR 1 606
Potter *v* The Broken Hill Pty Co Ltd (1906) 3 CLR 479, High Ct;
affg [1905] VLR 612, Supreme Ct, Victoria 43, 44, **282–4**, 285, 288,
293, 297, 302, 408, **609**
Steinhardt (Norbert) and Son Ltd *v* Meth and another (1960)
105 CLR 440, High Ct 284, 285, 288, 297, 302, 305, **603**,
605, **608–9**, 617, 623
Stevens *v* Head (1993) 176 CLR 433 606
Usines de Melle and Firmin Boinot's Patent, Re [1954] CLR 42,
High Ct 165
Waterhouse *v* Australian Broadcasting Corp (1989) 86 ACTR 1 689
West Clothing Co Pty Ltd *v* Sail America Foundation for
International Understanding [1988] WAR 119 ....**103**

Austria

Case 4 Ob 345/82 [1984] GRUR Int 453, judgment of 28 June 1983,
Supreme Ct 521
Case 4 Ob 370/85 [1986] 6 EIPR D-91, judgment of 29 October 1985,
Supreme Ct 247, 410
Case 4 Ob 312/86 [1987] GRUR 259, judgment of 25 March 1986,
Supreme Ct 301
Case 4 Ob 86/88 [1989] 6 EIPR D-95, judgment of 11 October 1988,
Supreme Ct 410
Case 4 Ob 19/91 [1992] ECC 456; [1991] GRUR Int 386, judgment of
28 May 1991, Supreme Ct 504
Case 4 Ob 44/92 [1994] ECC 526; [1994] IPRax 380, judgment of
16 June 1992, Supreme Ct 505
Case 4 Ob 118/94 28 (1997) IIC 574, judgment of 22 November 1994,
Supreme Ct 550

Hotel Sacher (Case 4 Ob 408/85) [1986] GRUR Int 735, judgment of 14
  January 1986, Supreme Ct 518, 519
Hotel Video [1986] GRUR Int 728, judgment of 17 June 1986,
  Supreme Ct 512
Oberlandesgericht, Graz [1991] GRUR Int 386, judgment of
  6 December 1990 504
Oberlandesgericht, Vienna [1990] GRUR Int 537, judgment of
  30 November 1989 505
Oberlandesgericht, Vienna [1991] GRUR Int 925, judgment of
  27 June 1991 505
Stefanel [1988] GRUR Int 72, judgment of 5 May 1987, Supreme Ct **563**

Belgium
Always/Regina [1993] 4 IER 22, judgment of 27 May 1983, CA 597
De Bloos (A) Sprl v Société en commandité par actions Bouyer JT
  1977, 637; Jur Belg 1977, 348; Pas b 1978, II, 8; D Series I-5.1.1–B 6,
  judgment of 3 May 1977, Cour d'Appel, Mons..87
Hof van Cassatie – Cour de Cassation, judgment of 24 February 1938
  [1938] Pas I 66 554
Knauer & Co Maschinenfabrik v Callens JT 1978, D Series I-5.1.1–B 8,
  judgment of 6 April 1978 87
SA Jouets Eisenmann v Geobra Brandstatter GmbH & Co KG and
  Big Spielwaren Fabrik Dipl Ing Ernst A Bettag [1985] ECR 246,
  judgment of 4 January 1983, Commercial Ct of Liège............................74

Benelux Court
MB v Mattell (Case A 92/3) (Barbie-pop II) judgment of 26 March 1993
  [1993] BIE 260 (No 66); [1993] NJ 328...218
Renault v Reynocar and Reynotrade (Cases A 93/1 & A 93/2)
  judgment of 13 June 1994 [1995] BIE 23 (No 7) 218
Union/Union Soleure [1984] BIE 137, judgment of 20 May 1983............596
Verkade [1980] BIE 117–118 218

Canada
Composers, Authors and Publishers Association of Canada Ltd v
  International Good Music Inc et al (1963) 37 DLR (2d) 1, Supreme
  Ct...247–8
Empire-Universal Films Ltd et al v Rank et al [1948] OR 235,
  Ontario CA 100, 103
Jenner v Sun Oil Co [1952] 2 DLR 526, Ontario High Ct...............402–3, 678
Kaverit Steel and Crane Ltd et al v Kone Corp et al (1992) 87 DLR (4th)
  129 108
Kornberg v Kornberg (1991) 76 DLR (4th) 379 109

Sterling Software International (Canada) Inc *v* Software Recording Corp
of America and others [1994] ILPr 43, Ontario **107**

European Union
Numerical List

Joined Cases 56 & 58/64: Consten and Grundig *v* Commission [1966]
ECR 299; [1966] CMLR 418 419
Case 24/67: Parke, Davis & Co Ltd *v* Probel, Reese, Beintema-
Interpharm and Centrapharm [1968] ECR 55; [1968]
CMLR 68 ....419, **420–1**
Case 78/70: Deutsche Grammophon GmbH *v* Metro-SB-Grossmarkte
GmbH & Co KG [1971] ECR 487; [1971] CMLR 631 ....137, 421
Joined Cases 6 & 7/73: Commercial Solvents *v* Commission [1974]
ECR 223; [1974] 1 CMLR 309 420
Case 15/74: Centrafarm *v* Sterling Drug [1974] ECR 1147 137
Case 16/74: Centrafarm *v* Winthrop [1974] ECR 1183 137
Case 51/75: EMI Records Ltd *v* CBS United Kingdom Ltd [1976]
ECR 811; [1976] 2 CMLR 235 421
Case 12/76: Tessili *v* Dunlop [1976] ECR 1473 ....78, 85, 433
Case 14/76: Établissements de Bloos *v* Société en Commandite par
Actions Bouyer [1976] ECR 1497; [1977] 1 CMLR 60 ....77, 87, 169, 433
Case 21/76: Handelskwekerij Bier BV *v* Mines de Potasse
d'Alsace SA [1978 QB 708; [1976] ECR 1735 ....**152–5**, 166, 168, 169,
248, 250, 373, 381, 392, 397, 400, 401, 403, 410, 415, 439
Case 29/76: LTU *v* Eurocontrol [1976] ECR 1541 ....31, 34
Case 42/76: De Wolf *v* Cox [1976] ECR 1759; [1977] 2 CMLR 43 727
Case 73/77: Sanders *v* Van der Putte [1977] ECR 2383 ....16, 213
Case 33/78: Établissements Somafer *v* Saar-Ferngas AG [1978]
ECR 2183; [1979] 1 CMLR 490 ....85, 169, 170
Case 143/78: De Cavel *v* de Cavel [1979] ECR 1055 ....125, 225, 726
Case 258/78: LC Nungesser KG *v* Commission [1982] ECR 2015;
[1983] 1 CMLR 278 419
Case 125/79: Bernard Denilauler *v* SNC Couchet Frères [1980]
ECR 1553 ....216, **224–5**, 727
Case 139/80: Blanckaert and Willems *v* Trost [1981] ECR 819;
[1982] 2 CMLR 1 169
Case 38/81: Effer SpA *v* Kantner [1982] ECR 825 ....74, 77, 150, 205
Case 34/82: Martin Peters Bauunternehmung GmbH *v* Zuid
Nederlandse Aannemers Vereniging [1983] ECR 987 ....85, **432**
Case 288/82: Duijnstee *v* Goderbauer [1983] ECR 3663 ....**16–19**, 22, 61,
62, 64, 204, 213
Case 178/83: Firma P *v* Firma K [1984] ECR 3033 726

Case 193/83: Windsurfing International Inc *v* Commission [1986]
ECR 611; [1986] 3 CMLR 489 419
Case 220/84: As-Autoteile Service GmbH *v* Mahle [1985] ECR 2267 16
Case 266/85: Shenavai *v* Kreischer [1987] ECR 239 .... 78, 82
Case 402/85: Basset *v* Sacem [1987] ECR 1747 421
Case 144/86: Gubisch Maschinenfabrik KG *v* Giulio Palumbo [1987]
ECR 4861 .... **177**
Case 145/86: Hoffmann *v* Krieg [1988] ECR 645 .... 213, 339, 727, 729, 731
Case 158/86: Warner Brothers Inc *v* Christiansen [1988] ECR 2605 .... **466**
Case 218/86: Sar Schotte GmbH *v* Parfums Rothschild Sarl [1987]
ECR 4905 .... 169, 170, 243
Case 9/87: SPRL Arcado *v* SA Haviland [1988] ECR 1539 .... 77, 432
Case 53/87: Consorzio italianio della componentistica di ricambio per
autoveicoli and Maxicar *v* Régie des Usines Renault [1988] ECR 6039;
[1990] 4 CMLR 265 421
Case 189/87: Athanasios Kalfelis *v* Bankhaus Schröder, Munchmeyer,
Hengst & Co [1988] ECR 5565 .... 172, 372, 373, 378, **433–9**
Case 238/87: AB Volvo *v* Erik Veng (UK) Ltd [1988] ECR 6211;
[1989] 4 CMLR 122 .... 420, 421
Case 220/88: Dumez France and Tracoba *v* Hessische Landesbank
(Helaba) and others [1990] ECR I–49 .... 144, 163, 250, 441
Case C–365/88: Kongress Agentur Hagen GmbH *v* Zeehaghe BV
[1990] ECR I–1845 144
Joined Cases C–241 & 242/91P: Radio Telefis Eireann (RTE) and
Independent Television Publications Ltd (ITP) *v* Commission
[1995] ECR I–743; [1995] CMLR 718; [1995] FSR 530 .... 421, 422, 486
Case C–288/92: Custom Made Commercial Ltd *v* Stawa Metallbau
GmbH [1994] ILPr 516; [1994] ECR I–2913 .... 85, 115
Case C–314/92: Ladenimor SA *v* Interconfinanz SA (removed from the
register) 186
Case C–406/92: Owners of the Cargo Lately Laden on Board the
Ship Tatry *v* The Owners of the Ship Maciej Rataj [1994] ECR I-5439;
[1995] ILPr 81 .... 37, 60, 61, 177, 181–3
Case C–68/93: Shevill and others *v* Presse Alliance SA [1995] 2 AC 18;
[1995] 2 WLR 499; [1995] ECR I–415 .... 143, 144, 150, **153–4**, 155,
156, 158, **161–4**, **167**, 169, 205, 251, 328, 371, 376, 378, **394–405**, 411, 448
Case C–341/93: Danvaern Production A/S *v* Schuhfabriken Otterbeck
GmbH & Co [1995] ECR I–2053 212
Case C–346/93: Kleinwort Benson Ltd *v* City of Glasgow District
Council [1995] 3 WLR 866 435
Case C–364/93: Marinari *v* Lloyds Bank plc and another (Zubaidi
Trading Co, Intervener) [1996] 2 WLR 159 .... 158, 163, 166, 250, 329,
377, 393, 414, 425, 441

Case C–432/93: SISRO v Ampersand Software BV 733
Case C–439/93: Lloyd's Register of Shipping v Soc Campenon Bernard
  [1995] ECR I–961 169
Case C–136/94: Beta-Film 152
Case C–106/95: Mainschiffahrts-Genossenschaft eG (MSG) v Les
  Gravieres Rhenanes Sarl [1997] 3 WLR 179 78
Case C–251/95: Sabel BV v Puma AG, Rudolf Dassler Sport decision of
  11 November 1997, unreported 597
Case C–269/95: Francesco Benincasa v Dentalkit Srl [1997] ILPr 559 90
Case C–383/95: Rutten v Cross Medical Ltd [1997] All ER (EC) 121 64
Case C–391/95: Van Uden Maritime BV, agissant sous le nom
  Van Uden African Line v Kommanditgesellschaft in Firma
  Deco-Line ea (pending) 216, 218, 220, 223

Alphabetical List
AB Volvo v Erik Veng (UK) Ltd (Case 238/87) [1988] ECR 6211;
  [1989] 4 CMLR 122 .... 420, 421
As-Autoteile Service GmbH v Mahle (Case 220/84) [1985] ECR 2267 16
Basset v Sacem (Case 402/85) [1987] ECR 1747 421
Benincasa (Francesco) v Dentalkit Srl (Case C–269/95) [1997]
  ILPr 559 90
Beta-Film (Case C–136/94) 152
Blanckaert and Willems v Trost (Case 139/80) [1981] ECR 819;
  [1982] 2 CMLR 1 169
Centrafarm v Sterling Drug (Case 15/74) [1974] ECR 1147 137
Centrafarm v Winthrop (Case 16/74) [1974] ECR 1183 137
Commercial Solvents v Commission (Joined Cases 6 & 7/73)
  [1974] ECR 223; [1974] 1 CMLR 309 420
Consorzio italianio della componentistica di ricambio per autoveicoli
  and Maxicar v Régie des Usines Renault (Case 53/87) [1988]
  ECR 6039; [1990] 4 CMLR 265 421
Consten and Grundig v Commission (Joined Cases 56 & 58/64)
  [1966] ECR 299; [1966] CMLR 418 419
Custom Made Commercial Ltd v Stawa Metallbau GmbH
  (Case C–288/92) [1994] ILPr 516; [1994] ECR I–2913 .... 85, 115
Danvaern Production A/S v Schuhfabriken Otterbeck GmbH & Co
  (Case C–341/93) [1995] ECR I–2053 212
De Cavel v de Cavel (Case 143/78) [1979] ECR 1055 .... 125, 225, 726
De Wolf v Cox (Case 42/76) [1976] ECR 1759; [1977] 2 CMLR 43 727
Denilauler (Bernard) v SNC Couchet Frères (Case 125/79)
  [1980] ECR 1553 .... 216, **224–5**, 727
Deutsche Grammophon GmbH v Metro-SB-Grossmarkte GmbH & Co
  KG (Case 78/70) [1971] ECR 487; [1971] CMLR 631 .... 137, 421

Duijnstee *v* Goderbauer (Case 288/82) [1983] ECR 3663 ....**16–19**, 22, 61, 62, 64, 204, 213
Dumez France and Tracoba *v* Hessische Landesbank (Helaba) and others (Case 220/88) [1990] ECR I–49..............................144, 163, 250, 441
Effer SpA *v* Kantner (Case 38/81) [1982] ECR 825 ....74, 77, 150, 205
EMI Records Ltd *v* CBS United Kingdom Ltd (Case 51/75) [1976] ECR 811; [1976] 2 CMLR 235..421
Établissements de Bloos *v* Société en Commandite par Actions Bouyer (Case 14/76) [1976] ECR 1497;[1977] 1 CMLR 60...............77, 87, 169, 433
Établissements Somafer *v* Saar-Ferngas AG (Case 33/78) [1978] ECR 2183; [1979] 1 CMLR 490..85, 169, 170
Firma P *v* Firma K (Case 178/83) [1984] ECR 3033...................................726
Gubisch Maschinenfabrik KG *v* Giulio Palumbo (Case 144/86) [1987] ECR 4861 ....**177**
Handelskwekerij Bier BV *v* Mines de Potasse d'Alsace SA (Case 21/76) [1978] QB 708; [1976] ECR 1735 ....**152–5**, 166, 168, 169, 248, 250, 373, 381, 392, 397, 400, 401, 403, 410, 415, 439
Hoffmann *v* Krieg (Case 145/86) [1988] ECR 645......213, 339, 727, 729, 731
Kalfelis (Athanasios) *v* Bankhaus Schröder, Munchmeyer, Hengst & Co (Case 189/87) [1988] ECR 5565 .....172, 372, 373, 378, **433–9**
Kleinwort Benson Ltd *v* City of Glasgow District Council (Case C–346/93) [1995] 3 WLR 866 435
Kongress Agentur Hagen GmbH *v* Zeehaghe BV (Case C–365/88) [1990] ECR I–1845 144
Ladenimor SA *v* Interconfinanz SA (Case C–314/92) removed from the register 186
Lloyd's Register of Shipping *v* Soc Campenon Bernard (Case C–439/93) [1995] ECR I–961..169
LTU *v* Eurocontrol (Case 29/76) [1976] ECR 1541..................................31, 34
Maciej Rataj, The. *See* Owners of the Cargo Lately Laden on Board the Ship Tatry *v* The Owners of the Ship Maciej Rataj (Case C–406/92)
Magill. *See* Radio Telefis Eireann and Independent Television Publications Ltd *v* Commission (Joined Cases C–241 & 242/91P)
Mainschiffahrts-Genossenschaft eG (MSG) *v* Les Gravieres Rhenanes Sarl (Case C–106/95) [1997] 3 WLR 179 78
Marinari *v* Lloyds Bank plc and another (Zubaidi Trading Co, Intervener) (Case C–364/93) [1996] 2 WLR 159 ....158, 163, 166, 250, 329, 377, 393, 414, 425, 441
Mines de Potasse d'Alsace. *See* Handelskwekerij Bier BV *v* Mines de Potasse d'Alsace SA (Case 21/76)
Nungesser (LC) KG *v* Commission (Case 258/78) [1982] ECR 2015; [1983] 1 CMLR 278..419

Table of Cases xvii

Owners of the Cargo Lately Laden on Board the Ship Tatry *v* The
  Owners of the Ship Maciej Rataj (Case C–406/92) [1994]
  ECR I-5439; [1995] ILPr 81 ....37, 60, 61, 177, 181–3
Parke, Davis & Co Ltd *v* Probel, Reese, Beintema-Interpharm and
  Centrapharm (Case 24/67) [1968] ECR 55; [1968] CMLR 68....419, **420–1**
Peters (Martin) Bauunternehmung GmbH *v* Zuid Nederlandse
  Aannemers Vereniging (Case 34/82) [1983] ECR 987......................85, **432**
Radio Telefis Eireann (RTE) and Independent Television Publications
  Ltd (ITP) *v* Commission (Joined Cases C–241 & 242/91P)
  [1995] ECR I–743; [1995] CMLR 718; [1995] FSR 530 ....421, 422, 486
Rutten *v* Cross Medical Ltd (Case C–383/95) [1997] All ER (EC) 121 64
Sabel BV *v* Puma AG, Rudolf Dassler Sport (Case C–251/95)
  decision of 11 November 1997, unreported 597
Sanders *v* Van der Putte (Case 73/77) [1977] ECR 2383 ....16, 213
Sar Schotte GmbH *v* Parfums Rothschild Sarl (Case 218/86)
  [1987] ECR 4905 ....169, 170, 243
Shenavai *v* Kreischer (Case 266/85) [1987] ECR 239 ....78, 82
Shevill and others *v* Presse Alliance SA (Case C–68/93)
  [1995] 2 AC 18; [1995] 2 WLR 499; [1995] ECR I–415............143, 144, 150,
      153–4, 155, 156, 158, **161–4, 167**, 169, 205, 251,
      328, 371, 376, 378, **394–405**, 411, 448
SISRO *v* Ampersand Software BV (Case C–432/93) 733
SPRL Arcado *v* SA Haviland (Case 9/87) [1988] ECR 1539 ....77, 432
Tessili *v* Dunlop (Case 12/76) [1976] ECR 1473 ....78, 85, 433
Van Uden Maritime BV, agissant sous le nom Van Uden African
  Line *v* Kommanditgesellschaft in Firma Deco-Line ea
  (Case C–391/95) pending..216, 218, 220, 223
Warner Brothers Inc *v* Christiansen (Case 158/86) [1988] ECR 2605......**466**
Windsurfing International Inc *v* Commission (Case 193/83)
  [1986] ECR 611; [1986] 3 CMLR 489 419

Finland
Salamander AG *v* (1) TOO VITL (2) Kissol Ltda 7 March 1996
  S 95/1952; [1996] 12 EIPR D-354, Helsinki CA.......................................292

France
Almax International [1992] JCP éd G II 21780; [1992] Clunet 148,
  Cour d'Appel, Paris..470
Arregui Mendizabal and Cuenca Sanchez *v* Régie Nationale des
  Usines Renault [1986] PIBD 387, iii-125, judgment of 7 October
  1985, Cour de Cassation..148
Bragance (Anne) *v* Olivier Orban and Michel de Grèce (1989) 142 RIDA
  301, judgment of 1 February, Cour d'Appel, Paris..........511, **517, 549–50**

Braillecellen II [1994] BIE No 111, 395; [1995] 3 EIPR D-73, 28 January
   1994, Cour d'Appel, Paris..225, 729, **730**
Busuioo Ionesco (Dimitri) *v* Sté Metro Goldwyn Mayer and
   Sté Romania Films (1978) 96 RIDA 179, judgment of 14 February,
   Tribunal de Grande Instance, Paris...510
Charlie Chaplin (1959) ICP II 11134, Cour de Paris; (1963) ICP II 11134,
   Cour de Cassation..**588**
Coca Cola Co *v* Bernard Carant & Cie [1986] PIBD 387, iii-123, judgment
   of 5 July 1985, Tribunal de Grande Instance, Paris................................148
Cour d'Appel, Paris, judgment of 6 July 1989 [1990] Receuil
   Dalloz Sirey 152; [1989] Revue Critique de Droit International
   Privé 706...503
Cour de Cassation, judgment of 5 December 1910 [1911] Rec
   Sirey I 129..554
Cour de Cassation [1944] Rec Sirey I 107, 1 February 1944......................589
Cour de Cassation [1964] Revue Critique de Droit International Privé
   513, 28 May 1963..589, 590
Cour de Cassation, judgment of 29 April 1970 [1971] Revue Critique de
   Droit International Privé 270..510
Cour de Cassation, judgment of 28 May 1991 [1991] Revue Critique de
   Droit International Privé 752..503
Friedman (Leopold) *v* SA Galba Films (1976) 88 RIDA 115, judgment of
   15 December 1975, Cour de Cassation...508
Gaf Corp *v* Soc Amchem Products [1977] Receuil Dalloz Sirey 511,
   judgment of 28 April 1976, Cour d'Appel, Paris............................519, 521
Hantarex SpA *v* SA Digital Research [1993] ILPr 501, Cour d'Appel.
   Paris 94
Herscovici (Charly) and another *v* Société Karla and another [1992]
   ECC 209, Tribunal de Grande Instance, Paris 149, **179**, **181–2**, 186
Huston (John) *v* La Cinq [1991] 149 RIDA 197, judgment of 28 May
   1991, Cour de Cassation...502, **503**, **510–11**, **586**
Ideal Clima SpA and others *v* SA Ideal Standard Gaz Pal 1982,
   Somm, 378; D Series I.5.3–B 13, Cour d'Appel, Paris 150, **154**, 156,
                                                                                              162, 373–5, 378, 411
Kid [1964] D 677; [1964] Revue Critique de Droit International
   Privé 513, judgment of 28 May 1963, Cour de Cassation......................586
Masseaut and another *v* Interidées [1996] Revue Critique de Droit
   International Privé 90, Cour d'Appel, Paris 470
Meyer (Gilbert) *v* La Société Charles Wednesbury Ltd [1996] ILPr 299,
   Cour d'Appel, Paris..**84**
Mobile Parking *v* Copega [1970] Propriété Industrielle Bulletin
   Documentaire III-131, judgment of 17 December 1969,
   Cour d'Appel, Paris..521

Montforts (A) GmbH & Co *v* Dudon SA, judgment of 2 June 1988,
  Note Hurt, Clunet 1990, 147; D Series I-5.1.1–B 27 84
Radio Monte Carlo *v* SNEP (1990) 144 RIDA 215, judgment of
  19 December 1989 164
SA des Établissements Salik et SA Diffusal *v* SA J Esterel 1982 Revue
  Critique de Droit International Privé 135; D Series I-16.4–B 2 ....20, 91
SA Galba Films *v* Friedman, SARL Capital Films, Pernot and Société
  Les Films La Boétie (1975) 83 RIDA 106, judgment of 24 April 1975,
  Cour d'Appel, Paris...**508**
SARL La Rosa *v* Sté Almax International SpA [1992] La Semaine
  Juridique 21780, judgment of 14 March 1991, Cour d'Appel,
  Paris 510, 512
Soc Toho Cy Ltd *v* Soc Film d'art et Soc Prodis (1961) 33 RIDA 112,
  judgment of 3 June 1961, Cour d'Appel, Paris...512
Société Fox-Europa *v* Société Le Chant du Monde (1960) 28 RIDA 120,
  judgment of 22 December, Cour de Cassation **499**
Thomasson [1972] Revue Critique de Droit International Privé 482,
  Cour d'Appel, Lyon 470
Tribunal de Grande Instance de la Seine [1975] GRUR Int 443
  (reprint) 18 June 1955 589
Tribunal de Grande Instance, Paris, judgment of 14 February 1977
  (1978) 97 RIDA 179 510
Tribunal de Grande Instance, Paris, judgment of 21 September 1983
  (1984) 120 RIDA 156 510
Tribunal de Grande Instance, Paris, judgment of 23 November 1988
  [1989] Receuil Dalloz Sirey 342 [1989] Revue Critique de Droit
  International Privé 372...503
Wegmann *v* Société Elsevier Science Ltd [1997] ILPr 760, Cour de
  Cassation..150, 154, **162**, 167, 168

Germany
BGH BGHZ 40, 391, 20 December 1963..688
BGH [1981] NJW 1606f...200
Bundesgerichtshof [1965] GRUR Int 504, judgment of
  21 October 1964 ....552, 590
Bundesgerichtshof [1993] GRUR Int 257, judgment of 17 June 1992 506
Bundesgerichtshof [1994] NJW 262, judgment of 26 October 1993 580
District Ct of Düsseldorf [1962] GRUR Int 256, 4 August 1961................567
District Ct of Stuttgart [1956–57] IPR Rspr No 29,
  14 March 1957 ....567, **568**
Effer *v* Kantner [1983] ECC 1, judgment of 13 May 1982,
  Bundesgerichtshof 74
Epilady (1993) 24 IIC 803 597

Jurisdiction in Tort and Contract, Re (Case I ZR 201/86) [1988] ECC 415,
  Federal Supreme Ct **150–1**, 154, 209, 373, 374
Landesgericht Düsseldorf, judgment of 27 October 1966 [1968]
  GRUR 101 242
Landesgericht Mannheim (Case 702/80) [1980] GRUR 935 151
Landesgericht Stuttgart, judgment of 14 October 1975,
  Case No 3 O 112/75; D Series I-6-B1 33
Mietz v Intership Yachting Sneek BV [1996] ILPr 661, Federal
  Supreme Ct 221, 224
Oberlandesgericht Hamm, judgment of 3 October 1978–9 U 278/77;
  D Series I-5.3– B9 ....154, 166, 413, 423, **424–5**
Oberlandesgericht München, judgment of 29 April 1954 Schulze
  Rechtsprechung zum Urheberrecht Vol V, No 8 549

Ireland
An Bord Tráchtala v Waterford Foods plc [1994] FSR 316 ......369, 387, 654,
  656, 659, 665, 679
Ferndale Films Ltd v Granada Television Ltd and another
  [1994] ILPr 180, Supreme Ct **81–2**
Mitchelstown Co-operative Society Ltd T/A CMP Dairy v Société des
  Produits Nestlé SA, Chambourcy Food Company Ltd and Nestlé
  (Ireland) Ltd [1989] ILRM 582 103
Olympia Productions Ltd v Cameron Mackintosh (Overseas) Ltd,
  Cameron Mackintosh Ltd [1992] ILRM 204 ....**80**, 89
Schmidt (Norburt) v Home Secretary of the Government of the United
  Kingdom, the Commissioner of the Metropolitan Police and David
  Jones [1995] 1 ILRM 301 ....**423**
Stuart (Carl) Ltd v Biotrace Ltd [1994] ILPr 554; [1993] ILRM 632,
  High Ct 85, **86–8**

Italy
Adda Construzioni Elettromagnetiche SpA v Alsthom SA and Delle
  Alsthom SA [1992] Riv Dir Int Priv Proc 332, Tribunale di Lodi, 13
  February 1991 No 20; [1994] 2 EIPR D-30, No 10704, Supreme Ct 28
  October 1993 ....154, 373, 374, **392–3**, 411, 414, **416**
Candy SpA v Schell and Stoecker Reinshagen GmbH Foro Pad 1979,
  I, 225; Note; Magelli; Riv dir int priv proc 1980, 429, Tribunale di
  Monza, 28 September 1979 ....154, **166**, 413, 423, **424–5**
Judgment [1957] GRUR Int 443 589
Judgment 2754 of 29 July 1958 [1959] Revista di diritto internazionale
  333, Supreme Ct 495
Motte (JA) v Tecno SpA 1981 Riv dir int priv proc 913;
  D Series I-16.1–B 3, Tribune di Milano **91**, 94, 111, **207–8**

Société de Droit Italien Ernesto Stoppani SpA v Sarl Stoppani France
[1997] ILPr 759 78

Japan
Case NE-619/89, 24 (1993) IIC 391, judgment of 16 September 1991,
Tokyo High Ct 549

Netherlands
Alnati [1967] Ned Jur 16 (No 3) Hoge Raad 13 May 1966 582
ARS v Organon 1995 IER 8; 1995 GRUR Int 253, Hague CA,
3 February 1994 218
Baars Kaas/Westland [1986] BIE No 21 690
Bijzondere Afdeling van de Octrooiraad, 19 November 1981 [1982]
Bijblad bij de Industriëlle Eigendom 321 524
Chiron Corp v Akzo Pharma-Organon Technica-UBI 1994 IER, No 24,
150, Hague District Ct, 22 July 1994; Case No 94/1341, Hague CA,
1 December 1994 ....174, 219–21
EBES [1990] ILPr 246 151
Forge et Coutellerie Dubois NV and Wolpa Plastics v Fantu Food BV
and Reinders D Series I-5.3–B 1, Arrondissementsrechtbank
Arnhem, 3 July 1975 ....373, 375, 411
Geobra Brandstätter GmbH & Co KG v Big Spielwarenfabrik
Dipl Ing Ernst A Bettag NJ 1979, No 146, Arrondissementsrechtbank
Amsterdam, 15 June 1977 ....154, 373, 374, 377, **413**
Hacker Kuchen GmbH v Bosma Huygen Meubelimpex BV
(Case 14.197) [1992] ILPr 379, Supreme Ct..**88**
Interlas v Lincoln Supreme Ct, 24 November 1989, 1992 NJ, No 404,
1597 with comments, Verkade, 1991 BIE, No 23, 86 ....**218**, 220
Isopad v Huikeshoven NJ 1992, 422, note Schultsz; NIPR 1992,
no 121, judgment of 1 November 1991 88
Jucotex v Belconi (the LEOPARD case) [1980] BIE 115 (No 32)
Arrondissementsrechtbank Rotterdam, 19 June 1979 218
Lips BV v Van Gunsteren [1985] Bijblad bij de Industriëlle
Eigendom 96, Rechtbank Den Bosch, 2 February 1979 ....524, **525**
Monopoly/Anti-Monopoly [1978] BIE 39, Hoge Raad,
24 June 1977 596
NV Gebr Van Zijverden v GF Mens [1973] BIE 99 (No 24),
Arrondissementsrechtbank Haarlem, February 18 1971 ....125, 247
Philips v Hemogram 1992 BIE No 80, 323; [1992] IER No 17, 76,
Hague District Ct, 30 December 1991 ....219, 292
United Feature Syndicate Inc v Van der Meulen Sneek BV [1990]
Bijblad Industriële Eigendom 329, Arrondissementsrechtbank
Leewarden, 1 March 1989 501

Van Uden Africa Line *v* Kommanditgesellschaft in Firma
  Deco-Line, Peter Determann KG [1996] ILPr 269, Supreme
  Ct 218, 220, **223–4**, 225, 227, 228
Voerderhek [1992] BIE 315 (No 78) Hague District Ct,
  28 August 1990 218

New Zealand
Atkinson Footwear Ltd *v* Hodgskin International Services Ltd and
  another (1994) 31 IPR 186, HC **285–6**, 302

Norway
Saba Molnlycke AS *v* Procter & Gamble Scandinavia Inc
  [1997] ILPr 704, Tonsberg CA 373, 377, **413**

Spain
Menadiona SA *v* Pfizer Inc Supreme Court (First Chamber) 28 January
  1994 Aranzadi 572; [1994] 8 EIPR D-204 45

Sweden
Hogsta Domstolen (SO 48) 23 February 1994 [1994] Nytt Juridiskt
  Arkiv 81; 1995 European Current Law 106 ....33, 53
Nordic Water Products AB *v* Sven H [1995] ILPr 766, Supreme Ct 56

Switzerland
Court of Appeals Zürich [1969] AWD 329, 20 November 1968 567
Federal Ct [1976] JdT I 519 561
Obergericht Zürich (1968) 67 Blätter für zürcherische Rechtsprechung
  118, judgment of 29 November 1968 564
Stipa *v* Dixi BGE 94 II 355f 562
Supreme Ct [1993] GRUR Int 972, judgment of 27 November 1991 132
Togal [1977] GRUR Int 208; BGE 94 II 362, judgment of 22 April 1975,
  Bundesgericht 562

United Kingdom
A Ltd *v* B Bank and Bank of X [1997] FSR 165 279
Aas *v* Benham [1891] 2 Ch 244 430
ABKCO Music & Records Inc (Body Corporate) *v* Music Collection
  International Ltd and another [1995] RPC 657, CA 125, 144, **148**,
                    157, 247, 248, 601, **603–4**, 621, 632, 633, 635, 639, 640
Acrow (Automation) Ltd *v* Rex Chainbelt Inc and another
  [1971] 1 WLR 1676 ....**98**
Ad-lib Club Ltd *v* Glanville [1972] RPC 673 363
Adams *v* Cape Industries plc [1990] Ch 433 ....242, 243, 734, 738

Advanced Portfolio Technologies Inc *v* Ainsworth [1996]
  FSR 217 ....**385–6**, 438
Agrafax Public Relations Ltd *v* United Scottish Society Inc [1995]
  ILPr 753 102
Aiglon Ltd and L'Aiglon SA *v* Gau Shan Co Ltd [1993]
  1 Lloyd's Rep 164 ....95, 186, 188
Airbus Industries GIE *v* Patel and others (1998) *The Times*, 6 April, HL;
  Affg [1997] ILPr 230..**276–7**
Albert (Prince) *v* Strange (1849) 2 De Gex & Sim 652 430
Alexander (Phillip) Securities and Futures Ltd *v* Bamberger and
  others [1997] ILPr 73...96, 189
Alloway *v* Phillips [1980] 1 WLR 888..489
Amber Size & Chemical Co Ltd *v* Menzel [1913] 2 Ch 239........................429
American Cyanamid *v* Ethicon [1975] AC 375 226
Amersham International plc *v* Corning Ltd and another [1987]
  RPC 53 ....**268–9**, **272**, 273, **274**, 309
Amin Rasheed Corp *v* Kuwait Insurance Co [1984] AC 50 ....261, 554
Anderson *v* Liebig's Extract of Meat Co Ltd (1881) 45 LT (NS) 757........390
Angelic Grace, The [1995] 1 Lloyd's Rep 87 ....96, 189
Annabel's (Berkely Square) Ltd *v* G Schock [1972] RPC 838....................364
Apple Corps Ltd and another *v* Apple Computer Inc and others [1992]
  FSR 431 ....43, 44, 287, **520**, 550, 587, 588
Arab Monetary Fund *v* Hashim (No 9) (1994) *The Times*, 11 October.....599
Assunzione, The [1954] 1 All ER 278 554
Athlete's Foot Marketing Associates Inc *v* Cobra Sports Ltd [1980]
  RPC 343 363
Atkinson Footwear Ltd *v* Hodgkin International Services Ltd and
  another (1995) 31 IPR 186 125
Attorney-General *v* Guardian Newspapers [1987] 1 WLR 1248...............527
Attorney-General *v* Guardian Newspapers (No 2) [1990] 1 AC 109;
  [1988] 5 All ER 545...429, 430, 440
Attorney-General *v* Observer Newspapers (1986) 136 NLJ 799................527
Attorney-General for Canada *v* Attorney-General for Ontario [1937]
  AC 326, PC..460
Babanaft International Co SA *v* Bassatne and another [1990] 1 Ch 13....227
Badishe Anilin and Soda Fabrik *v* H Johnson & Co (1897)
  14 RPC 919 121
Badische Anilin und Soda Fabrik *v* The Basle Chemical Works,
  Bindschedler [1898] AC 200, HL..**258**, **602**, 621
Baghlaf Al Safer Factory Co BR for Industry Ltd *v* Pakistan National
  Shipping Co and another (1997) *The Times*, 17 December 107
Balkanbank *v* Taher and others (No 2) [1995] 1 WLR 1067 ....216, 223
Banco, The [1971] P 137...461

Bank of Scotland *v* Seitz 1990 SLT 584 78
Barclays Bank plc *v* Glasgow City Council [1994] 2 WLR 466 .... **434–5**
Barings plc (in Administration) and another *v* Coopers & Lybrand)
 a Firm) and others [1997] ILPr 576, CA; affg [1997]
 ILPr 12 .... 102, 249, 257
Bata *v* Bata [1948] WN 366; 92 Sol Jo 574, CA 402, 403
Baume & Co *v* AH Moore Ltd [1958] Ch 907; [1958]
 2 All ER 113 367
BBC *v* Talbot Motor Co Ltd [1981] FSR 228 363
Beecham Group plc and another *v* Norton Healthcare Ltd and
 others [1997] FSR 81 .... 228, **249–51**, 252, **254**, 259, **314**, **445–7**
Beloit Technologies Inc and Beloit Walmsley Ltd *v* Valmet Paper
 Machinery Inc and Valmet Paper Machinery (UK) Ltd [1996]
 FSR 718 273
Berkeley Administration Inc *v* McClelland (No 2) [1995] ILPr 201 181
Berkeley Administration Inc *v* McClelland and others [1996]
 ILPr 772, CA 176
Blohn *v* Desser [1962] 2 QB 116; [1961] 3 All ER 1 735
Boardman *v* Phipps [1967] 2 AC 46 430
Boissevain *v* Weil [1950] AC 327; [1950] 1 All ER 728; affg [1949]
 1 KB 482; [1949] 1 All ER 146 581
Bollinger (J) *v* Costa Brava Wine Co Ltd [1960] Ch 262; [1959]
 3 All ER 800 365
Bollinger (J) *v* Costa Brava Wine Co Ltd (No 2) [1961] 1 All ER 561;
 [1961] 1 WLR 277 365
Boss Group Ltd *v* Boss France SA [1996] 4 All ER 970; [1990]
 2 Lloyd's Rep 112, CA 77, 78, 80, **84–6**
Boston Scientific Ltd and others *v* Cordis Corp (1997) Ch, CA,
 not yet reported 39, 142
Bovril Ltd *v* Bodega Co Ltd (1916) 33 RPC 155 367
Boys *v* Chaplin [1971] AC 356, HL 196, 295–7, 305, 607, 610,
  626–9, **631–2**, 637
British Airways Board *v* Laker Airways Ltd [1985] AC 58;
 revsg [1984] QB 142, CA 110, 277, 460, 695, 697
British Association of Aesthetic Plastic Surgeons *v* Cartwright
 [1987] RPC 549 364
British Nylon Spinners Ltd *v* Imperial Chemical Industries Ltd [1953]
 1 Ch 19 .... 165, **490–1**, 495, 496, **519**
British South Africa Co *v* Companhia de Mocambique [1893] AC 602,
 HL 280, 283, 284, 286–9, 297, 538
Brodin *v* A/R Seljan 1973 SC 213 640
Buchanan (James) & Co Ltd *v* Babco Forwarding and Shipping (UK) Ltd
 [1978] AC 141 461

Burlands Trade Mark, In re; Burland *v* Broxburn Oil Co
(1889) 41 Ch D 542 ....254, **255**, 261, **265**
Burrough (James) Distillers plc *v* Speymalt Whisky Distributors Ltd
1989 SLT 561 ....369, 387, **605–6**, **609**, 610, **611**, 617, **653**,
656, 665–7, 679, 682
Burrough (James) Distillers plc *v* Speymalt Whisky Distributors Ltd
[1991] RPC 130..136
Cadbury Schweppes Pty Ltd *v* Pub Squash Co Pty Ltd [1981]
1 All ER 213; [1981] 1 WLR 193, PC...365
Camera Care *v* Victor Hasselblad AB and another [1986]
ECC 373, CA 423, **425**
Camilla Cotton Oil Co *v* Granadex SA [1976] 2 Lloyd's Rep 10 294
Campbell Connelly & Co Ltd *v* Noble [1963] 1 WLR 252;
[1963] 1 All ER 237..**497**, **516**, **548–9**
Cape (Jonathan) Ltd *v* Consolidated Press Ltd [1954] All ER 253;
[1954] 1 WLR 1313 125
Carrick *v* Hancock (1895) 12 TLR 59 734
Castanho *v* Brown and Root (UK) Ltd [1981] AC 557 301
Catnic Components Ltd *v* Hill & Smith Ltd [1982] RPC 183....................122
Channel Tunnel Group Ltd *v* Balfour Beatty Construction Ltd
[1993] AC 334 216
Chaplin *v* Boys. *See* Boys *v* Chaplin
Chappell & Co Ltd and others *v* Redwood Music Ltd; Redwood Music
Ltd *v* Francis, Day & Hunter Ltd and another [1981] RPC 337, HL;
revsg sub nom Redwood Music Ltd *v* B Feldman & Co Ltd and
others [1979] RPC 385, CA; revsg sub nom [1979] RPC 1 549
Chelsea Man Menswear Ltd *v* Chelsea Girl Ltd [1987] RPC 189 363
Chemische Fabrik Vormals Sandoz *v* Badische Anilin und Soda
Fabriks (1904) 90 LT 733, HL(E)..102, 103, 254, 257
Chiron Corp *v* Evans Medical Ltd and others [1996] FSR 863 ...19, 171, 201
Chiron Corp and others *v* Organon Teknica Ltd (No 2)
[1993] FSR 567, CA **585**, **599**, 600, **641**
Chiron Corp and others *v* Organon Teknica Ltd (No 10)
[1995] FSR 325 ....172, **220–1**, **227**
Church of Scientology of California *v* Metropolitan Police Commissioner
(1976) 120 Sol Jo 690, CA...676, **677–8**
Citi-March Ltd and another *v* Neptune Orient Lines Ltd and others
[1996] 1 WLR 1367 104
Coco *v* AN Clark (Engineers) Ltd [1969] RPC 41, High Ct...**426–7**, 429, 527
Coin Controls Ltd *v* Suzo International (UK) Ltd and others
[1997] 3 All ER 45.........................39, 62, **91–2**, 147, **149**, 173, 174, 178, 179,
183, 191, 193–5, 201, 202, **204–6**, 207–9,
211, 214, 217, 282–5, 295–8, 309, 310, 737

Colgate-Palmolive Ltd *v* Markwell Finance Ltd [1989] RPC 497 367
Commissioners of Inland Revenue *v* Muller & Co's Margarine Ltd
    [1901] AC 217 ....363, 376, 493, 661
Connelly *v* RTZ Corp plc [1997] 3 WLR 373 ....38, **271–2**
Consortio del Prosciutto di Parma *v* Marks & Spencer plc
    [1991] RPC 351..362
Continental Bank NA *v* Aeakos Compañia Naviera SA [1994]
    1 WLR 588, CA 96, 182, 189, 443
Copin *v* Adamson (1874) LR 9 Ex Ch 345 735
Cordoba Shipping Co Ltd *v* National State Bank, Elizabeth,
    New Jersey (The 'Albaforth') [1984] 2 Lloyd's Rep 91, CA 196, 264
Cordova Land Co *v* Victor Bros Inc [1966] 1 WLR 793 393
Crédit Suisse Fides Trust SA *v* Cuoghi [1997] 3 WLR 871................**215, 216**
De Beers Abrasive Products Ltd *v* International General Electric Co
    of New York Ltd [1975] 2 All ER 599; [1975] 1 WLR 972 390
Dean *v* Macdowell (1878) 8 Ch D 345 430
Def Lepp Music and others *v* Stuart-Brown and others
    [1986] RPC 273.................................125, **258**, 285, 288, 295–7, 300, **301**, 302,
                    305, 602–3, 607, **608**, 609–11, 617, 620, **624**, 655, 663, **691–3**
Diamond *v* Bank of London and Montreal Ltd [1979] QB 333 393
DR Insurance Co *v* Central National Insurance Co and others [1996]
    1 Lloyd's Rep 74..102
Draper *v* Trist & Tristbestos Brake Linings Ltd (1939) 56 RPC 429.........368
Drummond's Patent, Re (1889) 6 RPC 576...25
Dunhill (Alfred) Ltd and another *v* Sunoptic SA and another [1979]
    FSR 337, CA **387**, 636, **663**, 665, 666, 682, **685**, 689
Dunlop Rubber Co Ltd *v* Dunlop [1921] 1 AC 367 402
Egon Oldendorff *v* Liberia Corp [1995] 2 Lloyd's Rep 64..........................553
El Amria, The [1981] 2 Lloyd's Rep 119, CA...107
Electric Furnace Co *v* Selas Corp of America [1987] RPC 23,
    CA 106, 171, **245–6, 259–60**, 262–4
Eleftheria, The [1970] P 94 107
EMI Record Ltd *v* Modern Music Karl-Ulrich Walterbach GmbH [1992]
    1 QB 115; [1992] 1 All ER 616; [1991] 3 WLR 663....................................**727**
Eras EIL Actions and Bastone & Firminger *v* Nasima Enterprises (1996)
    20 May, unreported 249
Evans (Joseph) & Sons *v* John G Stein & Co (1904) 12 SLT 462...............**405**
Evans Marshall & Co Ltd *v* Bertola SA [1973] 1 WLR 349.....................**104–5**
Exchange Telegraph Co Ltd *v* Gregory & Co [1898] 1 QB 147.................427
Exchange Telegraph Co Ltd *v* Howard (1906) 22 TLR 375........................430
Faccenda Chicken *v* Fowler [1987] Ch 117; [1986]
    1 All ER 617..**428–9**, 528
Feyerick *v* Hubbard (1902) 71 LJKB 509 735

Table of Cases xxvii

First National Bank of Boston *v* Union Bank of Switzerland and others
 [1990] 1 Lloyd's Rep 32 294
Fleetwood Mac Promotions Ltd *v* Clifford Davis Management Ltd [1975]
 FSR 150 ....**657**
Fort Dodge Animal Health Ltd and others *v* Akzo Nobel NV and another
 (1997) not yet reported, CA 19, 39, 92, 93, 142, 150, **174**, 179,
                    189, 191, **193**, 194, 195, 201, 204, **206–7**, 208–11,
                    213, 214, 216, 217, 226, 228, 231, 309, 310, 312, 737
Foster *v* Driscoll [1929] 1 KB 470 578
Fraser *v* Evans [1969] 1 QB 349; [1969] 1 All ER 8 ....428, 430, 527
Fraser *v* Thames Television Ltd [1984] 1 QB 44; [1983] 2 All ER 101 429
GAF Corp *v* Amchem Products Inc [1975] 1 Lloyd's Rep 601,
 CA 42, **67–9**, 270
Gamlestaden plc *v* Casa de Suecia SA and Hans Thulin [1994]
 1 Lloyd's Rep 433 94
Garden Cottage Foods *v* Milk Marketing Board [1984] AC 130 423
Gascoine *v* Pyrah [1994] ILPr 82 172
Granada Group Ltd *v* Ford Motor Co Ltd [1973] RPC 49.........................364
Grant (William) & Sons Ltd *v* Glen Catrine Bonded Warehouse Ltd
 1995 SLT 936 ....369, **654**, 666
Grupo Torras SA and Torras Hostench London Ltd *v* Sheikh Fahad
 Mohammed Al-Sabah and others [1995] 1 Lloyd's Rep 374, QBD;
 [1996] 1 Lloyd's Rep 7, CA 102, 151, 175
Guaranty Trust Co of New York *v* Hannay & Co [1975] 2 KB 536..........294
Guccio Gucci SpA *v* Paolo Gucci [1991] FSR 89 366
Halcon International Inc *v* The Shell Transport and Trading Co and
 others [1979] RPC 97..173
Harrods (Buenos Aires) Ltd, Re [1992] Ch 72, CA...........38, 65, **95–6**, **186–9**,
                                                                                                        190, 194, 195, **335**
Harrods Ltd *v* R Harrod Ltd (1924) 41 RPC 74..364
Hawke Bay Shipping Co Ltd *v* The First National Bank of Chicago
 (The 'Efthimis') [1986] 1 Lloyd's Rep 244...273
Hayter (John) Motor Underwriting Agencies Ltd *v* RBHS Agencies Ltd
 [1977] FSR 285 366
Henry *v* Geoprosco [1976] QB 726; [1975] 2 All ER 702 735
Hivac Ltd *v* Park Royal Scientific Instruments Ltd [1946] Ch 169;
 [1946] 1 All ER 350...428
House of Spring Gardens Ltd *v* Waite [1991] 1 QB 241; [1990] 2 All ER
 990 ....150, 736
Improver Corp *v* Remington Consumer Products Ltd [1990] FSR 181;
 [1989] RPC 69...**122**, 597
Intel Corp *v* General Instrument Corp and others (1990) unreported,
 available through Lexis..264

Intercontex and another *v* Schmidt and another [1988]
FSR 575 ....**382**, 387, **654**, **660**, 661–3
Interdesco SA *v* Nullifire Ltd [1992] 1 Lloyd's Rep 180 728
International Business Machines Corp and another *v* Phoenix
International (Computers) Ltd [1994] RPC 251 ....**637**, 689
Israel Discount Bank of New York *v* Hadjipateras [1984] 1 WLR 137 736
Jacobson *v* Frachon (1928) 138 LT 386 738
Jif Lemon. *See* Reckitt & Colman Products Ltd *v* Borden Inc
Johnson *v* Coventry Churchill International Ltd [1992]
3 All ER 14...**626**, 628
Johnson & Johnson's Application [1991] RPC 1 25
Johnston *v* Orr Ewing (1882) 7 App Cas 219..368, 654
Kakkar and others *v* Szelke and others [1989] 1 FSR 225, CA......**53–4**, **56–7**
Kalman and another *v* PCL Packaging (UK) Ltd and another [1982]
FSR 406 ....121, **145–6**, **244–5**, 258
Kinahan *v* Kinahan (1890) 45 Ch D 78 ....254, 255, **261**, 265
Kitechnology BV and others *v* Unicor GmbH Plastmaschinen and
others [1994] ILPr 568...............................154, 166, **217**, **434**, 439, **440–4**, 446
Kleinwort Benson Ltd *v* Glasgow City Council [1996] 2 All ER 257;
[1996] QB 678...372, 382, 432, **435**, 437
Kleinwort Benson Ltd *v* Glasgow City Council [1997] 3 WLR 923,
HL 77, 432, **436–9**
Kroch *v* Rossell et Cie [1937] 1 All ER 725, CA.................................402, **406–7**
Kurz *v* Stella Musical Veranstaltungs GmbH [1992] Ch 196......................94
Kuwait Oil Tanker Co SAK and another *v* Al Bader and others [1997]
1 WLR 1410 99
Kwok Chi Leung Karl *v* Commissioner of Estate Duty [1988]
1 WLR 1035 489
LA Gear Inc *v* Gerald Whelan & Sons Ltd [1991] FSR 670 ....**178**, **184–5**,
191, 285, 302, 378, **379–80**, 609, **659**
Ladbroke *v* William Hill [1964] 1 All ER 465; [1964] 1 WLR 273 125
Lecouturier and others *v* Rey and others [1910] AC 262, HL.......165, **492–3**,
495, 497, **520**, 521, 522
Lego Systems Aktieselskab *v* Lego M Lemelstrich Ltd [1983]
FSR 155 ....**364**
Levey (A) *v* Henderson-Kenton (Holdings) Ltd [1974] RPC 617.............363
Librarie du Liban Inc *v* Pardoe Blacker Ltd and others (unreported,
available through Lexis) 280, 296, 300, 305
Linda, The [1988] 1 Lloyd's Rep 175 ....185, 210
Lonrho plc *v* Fayed [1991] 3 WLR 188, HL 145, 264, 607
Lubrizol Corp and another *v* Esso Petroleum Co Ltd and others (No 1)
[1992] RPC 281..149, 309, 310
Lyne *v* Nicholls (1906) 23 TLR 86 390

Macaulay (A) (Tweeds) Ltd v Independent Harris Tweed
  Producers Ltd [1961] RPC 184 ....**383**
McDonald's Hamburgers Ltd v Burgerking (UK) Ltd [1986] FSR 45 391
Mackinnon v Donaldson, Lufkin and Jenrette Securities Corp and
  others [1986] 1 Ch 482 228
Mahavir Minerals Ltd v Cho Yang Shipping Co Ltd (The 'MC Pearl')
  [1997] 1 Lloyd's Rep 566 107
Malone v Commissioner of Police [1979] 2 All ER 620................................527
Mann (ED & F) (Sugar) Ltd v Yani Haryanto (No 2) [1991] 1 Lloyd's
  Rep 429 738
Marshall v Marshall (1888) 38 Ch D 330......................................254, 261, **265**
Marshall (Thomas) (Exports) Ltd v Guinle [1979] 1 Ch 227;
  [1978] 3 All ER 193...427
Matthews v Kuwait Bechtel Corp [1959] 2 QB 57 ....655, 699
Maxim's Ltd v Dye [1977] FSR 364...**363**, 388
Mead Corp and another v Riverwood Multiple Packaging Division of
  Riverwood International Corp [1997] FSR 484......................................147
Mecklermedia Corp and another v DC Congress GmbH [1997] 3 WLR
  479..............168, **180–1**, 184, 185, **372**, 373, **376**, 377, 379, **380**, 382, **659**, 664
Medway Packaging Ltd v Meurer Maschinen GmbH & Co KG
  [1990] ILPr 234; [1990] 2 Lloyd's Rep 112, CA.....................78, 80, **83–6**, 88
Mercedes Benz AG v Leiduck [1995] 3 WLR 718..215
Metall und Rohstoff AG v ACLI Metals (London) Ltd
  [1984] 1 Lloyd's Rep 598 273
Metall und Rohstoff AG v Donaldson Lufkin and Jenrette Inc
  [1990] 1 QB 391...145, 264, 607, 618, 672
Midland Bank plc v Laker Airways Ltd [1986] QB 689..............................278
Mike Trading and Transport Ltd v R Pagnan and Fratelli (The 'Lisboa')
  [1980] 2 Lloyd's Rep 546 110
Minster Investments Ltd v Hyundai Precision and Industry Co Ltd
  [1988] 2 Lloyd's Rep 621 ....155, 374,
 437
Modus Vivendi Ltd v The British Products Sanmex Co Ltd and another
  [1996] FSR 790 ....373, **374–6**, 377, 382, 658
Mölnlycke AB and another v Procter & Gamble Ltd and others
  [1992] 1 WLR 1112 ....19, 143, **147**, 150, 155, 156, 162, 175,
  191, **228–30**, 305, **600**
Monro (George) Ltd v American Cyanamid and Chemical Corp
  [1944] KB 432..**403**
Morison and Moat (1851) 9 Hare 241; 68 ER 492...528
'Morocco Bound' Syndicate Ltd v Harris [1895] 1 Ch 534 ....**300**, 301, 305
Morton-Norwich products Inc and others v Intercen Ltd
  [1978] RPC 501..**146**

Multinational Gas and Petrochemical Co *v* Multinational Gas and
  Petrochemical Services Ltd [1983] Ch 258 ....106, 265
Napp Laboratories *v* Pfizer Inc [1993] FSR 150 ....19, 25
Neste Chemicals SA *v* DK Line SA [1994] 3 All ER 180 216
New York Life Insurance Co *v* Public Trustee [1924] 2 Ch 101 489
News Group Ltd *v* Mirror Group Ltd [1989] FSR 126..............................124
Newsweek Inc *v* BBC [1979] RPC 441...**366**
Nile Rhapsody, The [1994] 1 Lloyd's Rep 382....................................186, 187
North (James) & Sons Ltd *v* North Cape Textiles Ltd and another
  [1984] 1 WLR 1428, CA **255–6**, 261, 264, 384
Nouvion *v* Freeman (1889) 15 App Cas 1..735
Novelli *v* Rossi (1831) 2 B & Ad 757..734
Novello & Co Ltd *v* Hinrichsen Edition Ltd and another [1951]
  1 Ch 595...165, **494**, 495, 501
Oppenheimer *v* Cattermole [1976] AC 249 635
Organon Teknika Ltd *v* Hoffmann-La Roche AG [1996] FSR 383...........201
Pall Corp *v* Commercial Hydraulics (Bedford) Ltd and others
  [1988] FSR 274 ....37, 273
Parmiter *v* Coupland (1840) 6 M & W 105 405
Pearce *v* Ove Arup Partnership Ltd and others [1997] 2 WLR 779;
  [1997] 3 All ER 31 ....19, 39, 142, 150, 156, **157**,
                162, 171, 172, 176, 186, 191, **192–4**, 195, 282,
                283, 285, 289, 290, 296, **610**, 612, **617**
Pemberton *v* Hughes [1899] 1 Ch 781 734
Phillips *v* Eyre (1870) LR 6 QB 1 ....297, 302, 305, 607
Phonogram Ltd *v* Def American Inc (1994) *The Times*, 7 October 272
Phrantzes *v* Argenti [1960] 2 QB 19..635
Pillai and another *v* Sarkar (1994) *The Times*, 21 July.........................406, **408**
Pioneer Container, The [1994] 2 AC 324, PC 107
Plastus Kreativ AB *v* Minnesota Mining and Manufacturing Co and
  another [1995] RPC 438....................121, 133, 201, 227, 264, 269, 271, 272,
                285, **290**, 292–4, **303**, 309
Po, The [1991] 2 Lloyd's Rep 206, CA 95, 186, 187
Poiret *v* Jules Poiret Ltd and AF Nash (1920) 37 RPC 177 526
Procea Products Ltd *v* Evans and Sons Ltd (1951) 68 RPC 210................368
Puschner *v* Tom Palmer (Scotland) Ltd and another [1989]
  RPC 430 ....171, 245, 260, **262**
Ralli Bros *v* Compañia Naviera Sota y Aznar [1920] 2 KB 287.................578
Rank Film Distributors *v* Lanterna Editrice Srl [1992] ILPr 58,
  Commercial Ct **79**, 95
Ratcliffe *v* Evans [1892] 2 QB 524 ....**389**
Raychem Corp *v* Thermon (UK) Ltd and another
  [1989] RPC 423..258

Reckitt & Colman Products Ltd *v* Borden Inc [1990] 1 All ER 873; [1990] 1
  WLR 491 ....362, **366**, 367, 368
Red Sea Insurance Co Ltd *v* Bouygues Sa and others [1995]
  1 AC 190, PC 296, 606, **607**, 609, 611, 618, 624, 629
Redwood Music Ltd *v* Francis, Day & Hunter Ltd.
  See Chappell & Co Ltd and others *v* Redwwod Music Ltd;
  Redwood Music Ltd *v* Francis Day & Hunter Ltd and another
Regazzoni *v* KC Sethia (1944) Ltd [1956] 2 QB 490 578
Republic of Haiti and others *v* Duvalier and others [1990]
  1 QB 202..216, 227
Reuter (RJ) Co Ltd *v* Mulhens [1954] 1 Ch 50, CA 165, **376–7**, **493**, 495,
                                                                   519–20, 526, 661
Rey *v* Lecouturier [1908] 2 Ch 715...44, **69–70**
Rossano *v* Manufacturer's Life Insurance Co [1963] 2 QB 352.................490
Royal Baking Powder Co *v* Wright, Crossley & Co (1901) 18 RPC 95 390
S & W Berisford plc *v* New Hampshire Insurance Co [1990]
  QB 631..96, 187
Sadler *v* Robins (1808) 1 Camp 253 735
Salomon *v* Commissioners of Customs and Excise [1967] 2 QB 116.......461
Saltman *v* Campbell [1963] 3 All ER 413n..429
Salvesen *v* Administrator of Austrian Property [1927] AC 641 734
Sarrio SA *v* Kuwait Investment Authority [1997] 3 WLR 1143, HL;
  revsg [1997] ILPr 481 ....183, 185, 267, 338
Sayers *v* International Drilling Co NV [1971] 1 WLR 1176.......................640
Schibsby *v* Westenholz (1870) LR 6 QB 155 734
Schneider *v* Eisovitch [1960] 2 QB 430 636
Seaconsar Far East Ltd *v* Bank Markazi Jomhouri Islami Iran [1994]
  1 AC 438; [1993] 3 WLR 756, HL..........................40, 41, 101, 102, 144, 149,
                                                                   151, 243, 244, 246, 256, 257
Seager *v* Copydex Ltd (No 1) [1967] 2 All ER 415;
  [1967] 1 WLR 923 ....430, 527
Shapiro *v* La Morta (1924) 40 TLR 201 391
Sheraton Corp of America *v* Sheraton Motels Ltd [1964] RPC 202 526
Shevill *v* Presse-Alliance SA [1996] 3 All ER 929, HL................................**398**
Simon Engineering plc *v* Butte Mining plc [1997] ILPr 599......................110
Siskina, The [1979] AC 210 ....252, 255, 446
SISRO *v* Ampersand Software BV [1994] ILPr 55, CA 729, 732
Smith Kline & French Laboratories Ltd and others *v* Bloch [1983]
  1 WLR 730 ....**109–10**
Société Commerciale de Reassurance and others *v*
  Eras International Ltd and others (No 2) [1995] 2 All ER 278 189
Société Nationale Industrielle Aerospatial *v* Lee Kui Jak
  [1987] AC 871 ....109, 275, 386

Sohio Supply Co *v* Gatoil (USA) Inc [1989] 1 Lloyd's Rep 588 109
Source Ltd *v* TUV Rheinland Holding AG and others [1997]
  3 WLR 365...**435–9**
South Carolina Insurance Co *v* Assurantie NV [1987] AC 24 ....269, 277
South Hetton Coal Co Ltd *v* North-Eastern News Association Ltd
  [1894] 1 QB 133..395, 396
South India Shipping Corp Ltd *v* Export-Import Bank of Korea [1985]
  1 WLR 585..242
Spiliada Maritime Corp *v* Cansulex Ltd [1987]
  1 AC 460, HL 38, 41, 42, 105, 252, **259**, 261, 263, 264, **267–8**, 271–3, 293
Spycatcher. *See* Attorney-General *v* Guardian Newspapers (No 2)
Stannard *v* Reay [1967] RPC 589..363
Star Industrial Co Ltd *v* Yap Kwee Kor [1976] FSR 256..........................**526**
Stephens *v* Avery [1988] Ch 449; [1988] 2 All ER 477 427
Stringfellow *v* McCain Foods (GB) Ltd [1984] RPC 501............................368
Svendborg *v* Wansa [1997] 2 Lloyd's Rep 183...110
Symbol Technologies Inc *v* Opticon Sensors Europe BV (No 1)
  [1993] RPC 211..25, **180**, 311
Szalatnay-Stacho *v* Fink [1947] KB 1 ....**677**
Taitinger SA *v* Allbev Ltd [1994] 4 All ER 75..365
Tesam Distribution Ltd *v* Schuh Mode Team GmbH and
  Commerzbank AG [1990] ILPr 149 ....144, 150, 151
Toepfer International GmbH *v* Société Cargill France [1997]
  2 Lloyd's Rep 98...96, 189
Tolley *v* JS Fry Ltd [1931] AC 333, HL...**395**
Tournier *v* National Provincial & Union Bank of England [1924]
  1 KB 461...427
Tracomin SA *v* Sudan Oil Seeds Co Ltd [1983] 3 All ER 137;
  [1983] 1 WLR 1026 735
Tyburn Productions Ltd *v* Conan Doyle [1991] Ch 75 ...43, 282, **284–6**, 288,
        289, 290, 291, 293–5, 298, 299, **302**, 303, 388, 609, 661, 667
Unilever plc *v* Chefaro Proprietaries Ltd and another
  [1994] FSR 135, CA 147, **229–30**, 243
Unilever plc *v* Gillette (UK) Ltd [1989] RPC 583................147, 171, 243, **245**,
                                                                                                             263, **313**
United States *v* Inkley [1989] QB 255; [1988] 3 All ER 144........................737
Vallée *v* Dumergue (1849) 4 Ex Ch 290..735
Vervaeke *v* Smith [1983] 1 AC 145, HL..736, **738**
Virgin Aviation *v* CAD Aviation (1990) *The Times*, 2 February 185
Vitkovice Horni a Hutni Tezirstvro *v* Korner [1951] AC 869...................257
Vokes Ltd *v* Heather (1945) 62 RPC 135 528
Volvox Hollandia, The [1988] 2 Lloyd's Rep 361 294
WAC Ltd *v* Whillock 1990 SLT 213..152

Wagamama [1995] FSR 713 596
Wagg (Helbert) & Co Ltd, Re [1956] Ch 323 635
Walker (John) & Sons Ltd v Douglas Laing & Co Ltd
  1993 SLT 156 ....369, 654
Walker (John) & Sons Ltd v Douglas McGibbon & Co Ltd
  [1975] RPC 506..369, 654, 666
Walker (John) & Sons Ltd and others v Henry Ost & Co Ltd
  and another [1970] 2 All ER 106 ....**368**, 369, 387, 654, 656, 658, 659, **692**
Warnink (Erven) BV v J Townsend & Sons (Hull) Ltd [1979] AC 731;
  [1979] 2 All ER 927 361–2
Washburn and Moen & Co v The Cunard Steamship Co and
  JC Parkes and Sons (1889) 5 TLR 592..**253**, 311
Waterhouse v Reid [1938] 1 KB 743..446
White v Mellin [1895] AC 154 ....389, 390
White Horse Distillers Ltd v Gregson Associates Ltd and others (1983)
  LS Gaz 2844...368, 654, 666
Wilderman v FW Berk and Co Ltd [1925] 1 Ch 116....................**491**, 495, **519**
William Grant & Sons International Ltd v Marie Brizard et Roger
  International SA [1997] ILPr 391..87, 95
Williams Electronics Inc v Rene Pierre SA and others (unreported,
  available through Lexis) 254
Williams (JB) Co v H Bronnley Co Ltd (1909) 26 RPC 765 366
Wombles Ltd v Wombles Skips Ltd [1977] RPC 99 364
Woodward v Hutchins [1977] 2 All ER 751; [1977] 1 WLR 760................427
X v Y [1988] 2 All ER 648...429
X v Y [1990] 1 QB 220..215
Yorkshire Tannery and Boot Manufactury (Ltd) v The Eglinton
  Chemical Co (Ltd) (1884) 54 LJ Ch 81 ....**99–100**

United States of America
Acrison Inc v Control and Metering Ltd et al 730 F Supp 1445
  (NE ILL 1990) 251
Bensusan Restaurant Corp v King (US DC for SDNY) [1997]
  2 EIPR D 55 159
Corcovado Music Corp v Hollis Music 981 F 2d 679 (2d Cir 1993)..........516
Creative Technology Ltd v Aztech System Pte Ltd 61 F 3d 696
  (9th Cir 1995) **270–1**
Honeywell Inc v Metz Apparatewerke 509 F 2d 1137
  (7th Cir 1975) **232**
Honeywell Inc v Metz Apparatewerke 647 F 2d 200 (DC 1981) 251
Huchel v Sybron Corp 212 USPQ 133 (SD Tex 1980) 246
Interface Biomedical Laboratories v Axiom Medical Inc 600
  F Supp 731; 225 USPQ 146 (EDNY 1985)..251

ITSI TV Productions Inc *v* California Authority of Racing Fairs
785 F Supp 854 (ED Cal 1992) 280, 293
Laker Airways Ltd *v* Sabena, Belgian World Airlines 731 F 2d 909
(DC Cir 1984) 278
London Film Productions Ltd *v* Intercontinental Communications Inc
580 F Supp 47 (US DC SDNY 1984) 292, 298, 299
Loucks *v* Standard Oil Co of New York 224 NY 99 (1918) 634
Maritz Inc *v* Cybergold Inc (US DC for Ed of Miss) [1997] 2EIPR D 56;
40 USPQ 2d 1729 159
Neidhart *v* Neidhart SA 184 USPQ 393 488
Packard Instrument Co *v* Beckman Instruments Inc 346 F Supp 408
(US DC ND Illinois, ED 1972) 298, 299
Robert Stigwood Group Ltd *v* O'Reilly 530 F 2d 1096 (2d Cir);
cert denied 429 US 848 (1976) 301
Stein Associates Inc *v* Heat and Control Inc 748 F 2d 653 (1984) **278–9**
Subafilms Ltd *v* MGM Pathe Communications Co (1994) 30 USPQ 2d
1746, (9th Cir), CA 125
Texaco Inc *v* Pannzoil 729 SW 2d 768 689
Vanity Fair Mills *v* T Eaton Co 234 F 2d 633 (2d Cir 1956) 293, 298, 299

Table of Legislation

Austria
Private International Law Statute (IPR – Gesetz) 499, 565, 576, 589
    Art 34(1) 500, 501, 507, 518, 519
        (2) **515**, 524
    Art 44 515
    Art 48(2) 711

Belgium
Civil Code—
    Art 1382 ....415, 652
    Art 1383 652
Eenvormige Beneluxwet van 198 maart 1962 op de merken [1969]
    Belgisch Staatsblad 14 October 480
Wet betreffende de handelspraktijken, 14 July 1991 [1991] Belgisch
    Staatsblad, 29 August 1991
    Art 94 409
Wet betreffende het auteursrecht en de naburige rechten, 30 June 1994
    [1994] Belgisch Staatsblad 19297 (Copyright Act) 500

European Union
Treaties
EC Treaty (Treaty of Rome) 423
    Arts 30, 36 ....136, 583
    Art 85 ....**416–7**, 418, 419, 422–5, 583, 694, 697
        (1), (2) 418, 422
        (3) 418
    Art 86 ....416, 419–25, 583, 694, 697
    Art 100a 584
Directives
Council Directive 89/104/EC (Trade Marks) [1989] OJ L40/1—
    Art 5 124
Council Directive 91/205/EEC (Protection of Computer Programs)
    [1991] OJ L122/42—
    Preamble 584
    Art 6 584
Council Directive 92/100/EEC (Rental and Lending Rights) [1992] OJ
    L346/61—
    Preamble 584

Art 4 584
Council Directive 93/83/EEC (Satellite Broadcasting) [1993]
    OJ L248/15 ....162, 248, 505
    Art 1(2)(b) 158, 248, 505, 622
        (d) 505
Council Directive 93/98/EEC (Protection of Copyright) [1993]
    OJ L290/9 507
Council Directive 96/9/EC (Databases) [1996] OJ L77/20 ......130, 528, 529
    Art 3(1), (2) 130
    Art 6(1) 130
    Art 7(1), (4) 131

Regulations
Community Design Regulation [1994] OJ C29/40 (Draft) 2, 3, 342,
                                                                                                        357, 537
    Art 29 536
        (1) 534, 536
        (2)–(4) 536
    Arts 30–34 536
    Art 35 536
        (1)–(3) 536
        (4) 537, 538
    Art 36 536
    Art 83(3) 343
    Art 86 343
        (3) 343
        (5) 152, 168
    Art 87(2) 161
    Art 88(3) 536
    Art 89 536
    Art 90(2)–(4) 536
    Arts 92, 93 535
    Arts 94, 95 536
    Art 99(1)–(3) 344
    Title X 343
Council Regulation 2100/94 (Community Plant Variety Rights
    Regulation) [1994] OJ L227/1 ....2, 3, 152, 349, 350–2, 356, 357, 537
    Arts 6, 20 356
    Art 21 ....356, 537
    Arts 94–100 351
    Art 94 537
        (1)–(3) 537
    Art 98 355

Art 101	350, 351, 357
(1)	352, 355, 357
(2)	351, 354, 355, 358
(a)	**352**, 353, 355
(b), (c)	**353**
(3)	161, 168, **354**, 355, 358
Art 102	350, 351, 357
(1)	351, 355
(2)	354
(3)	353
Arts 103, 104	351
Art 105	351, 356
Art 106	351
(1)	356
(2)	**356**

Council Regulation 40/94/EC (Community Trade Mark Regulation) [1994] OJ L11/1 ....2, 3, 124, 345, 351–4, 356–358, 480, 532, 536

Art 1	532
(2)	331
Art 9	532
(3) 2nd sent	325, 327, 332, 333
Arts 10–13	532
Art 14	532
(2)	532
Art 16	534
(2), (3)	534
Arts 17–20	534
Art 21	534, 535, 538
Art 22	534
Art 23	534
(2)	534
(4)	535
Art 24	534
Art 29(1)	534
Art 54	333
Arts 57–63	318
Art 90	341, 346, 740
(1)	320, 322, 323, 326, 328, 329, 332–5, 338–40
(2)	322, 326, 339, 341
(c)	322, 325, 326
Art 91	322
Art 92	320, **322**, 334, 346
(a)	351

```
        (c) .................................................................................................333
        (d) ..........................................................................................332, 346
    Art 93 ..............................................................323, 329, 331, 334, 341, 343, 346
        (1) ..................................................................322–5, 327–30, 340, 341
        (2) .........................................................322, 324, 325, 327–30, 335, 340, 341
        (3) ..................................................322, 324, 325, 327–30, 335, 340, 341, 343, 354
        (4) .............................................................322, 325, 327, 328, 333, 340
            (a) ..................................................................................................324
            (b) ..................................................................................................325
        (5) ...........................................................152, 168, 325–30, 335, 340, 341
    Art 94 ....................................................................................................335, 346
        (1) ..........................................................................................327, 340, 355
        (2) ................................................................................161, 327, 328, 340, 355
    Art 95 ..............................................................................................................533
        (1), (2) ..............................................................................................................331
        (3) ..................................................................................................................333
    Art 96 ..............................................................................................322, 346, 533
        (1), (2), (7) ..........................................................................................................332
    Art 97 ......................................................................................................533, 535
        (2) ..................................................................................................................480
    Art 98 ......................................................................................................346, 533
        (1) ................................................................................................................**341**
    Art 99 ......................................................................................................346, 357
        (1) ..........................................................................................................339, 533
        (2) ..................................................................................................................340
    Art 100 ....................................................................................................334, 346
        (1), (2) ........................................................................................................333, 334
    Art 101(1) ................................................................................................................322
    Art 102 ....................................................................................................................320
        (1), (2) ..................................................................................................................321
    Art 103 ....................................................................................................................321
    Art 104 ....................................................................................................................320
    Art 105 ....................................................................................................................336
        (1) .......................................................................................336, 338, 339, 344
            (a) ........................................................................................................**336**, 337
            (b) ..................................................................................................336, **337**, 338
        (2), (3) ..............................................................................................338, 339, 344
    Art 106(2) ..............................................................................................................534
    Art 107(1) ..............................................................................................................533
        (2) ..........................................................................................................533, 534
    Arts 126–130 ........................................................................................................318
    Title VI, Section 5 ................................................................................................318
    Title X ........................319, 321–3, 325, 328–30, 332, 343, 351, 532, 533, 740
```

Section 1 320
Section 2 321
Section 3 321
Commission Regulation 240/96/EC (Transfer of technology agreements)
  [1996] OJ L31/2 418

France
Civil Code—
  Art 1382 ....415, 652
  Art 1383 652

Germany
Civil Code—
  § 32 424
UrheberGesetz..516

Italy
Civil Code—
  Art 204 416
  Art 2598(2) 411
Law 218 of 31 May 1995 [1995] Gazzetta Officiale 128 (3 June 1995) 495

Netherlands
Code of Civil Procedure 223
  Art 126(1) 220
Patent Law (Rijksoctrooiwet)—
  Art 10 525

Spain
Basic Law on jurisdiction—
  Art 22.1 45
Unfair Competition Law 1986—
  Art 3 670

Switzerland
Private International Law Statute 1987—
  Art 15 719
    (1) **713**
  Arts 17–19 ....713, 719
  Art 109 46
    (1) 45, **46**, 47, 71
    (2) 47
    (3) 46, **47**

Art 110 47
    (1) 47
    (2) 644
Art 122(1) **562**
Art 133(1) 713
    (3) 698, **712**, 713
Art 135(2) 719
Art 136 ....450, 705–7, 711, 713, 718
    (1) 711, 717
    (2) **712**
Art 137 ....**719**
Unfair Competition Statute 1986 ....409, 711
    Art 3 674
    Art 5(a) 698
    Art 6 698
    Art 133(1) 688
    Art 136 688

United Kingdom
Administration of Justice Act 1920 739
Arbitration Act 1996—
    s 9(1), (4) 108
Civil Jurisdiction and Judgments Act 1982 ....223, 739
    s 9(1) 2
    ss 16, 17 26
    s 25 ....215–17, 226, 227, 252, 255, 272, 312, 313, 340, 373, 381
        (1) 215
        (2) 215, 227, 313
    s 30 283
        (1) 280, 281, 286, 289
    s 32 738
    s 33 735
    Sch 4 ....26, 152, 328, 374, 435
    Sch 5 26
        para 2 ....**26**
    Sch 8 152
        para 2 256
            (14) 27, 45, 62
        para 10 256
Civil Liability (Contribution) Act 1978 599
Companies Act 1985 241
    s 690A 241
    ss 690B, 691 242

s 694A(2)	241
(3)	242
s 695	242
s 725(1)	241
Sch 21A, para 3(e)	241
para 13	241
Consumer Protection Act 1987	599
Contracts (Applicable Law) Act 1990	456, 551, 589
s 2(2)	639
(3)	551
Sch 1	639
Art 12	497
Sch 3A	544
Copyright Act 1956	258, 603
s 1(2)	604, 608, 635
s 31(4)	604, 608, 635
Copyright, Designs and Patents Act 1988	8, 124, 125, 127, 131, 476, 499, 501, 503, 510, 513, 539, 599, 608
ss 1–5B	500
s 1	7, 498
(3)	498
s 3(2)	7, 500
(5)	8
s 6	504
(4)	505
s 9	510
(1)	509
(2)(a)	509
s 11(1)	511
(2)	514
ss 12–15	507
s 12(2)	9, 507
(6)	508
s 13A(2)	507
(a)	507
(4)	508
s 13B(2)	507
(7)	508
s 14(2)	507
(3)	508
Pt I, Ch II (ss 16–27)	131
s 16(1)	125, 131, 494, 495, 498
(2)	147, 604

(3)(a)	125
s 17	**494**
(2)–(5)	126
s 18	126
s 19(3)	126
s 20	126
s 21(1), (2)	126
ss 22–26	127
s 27	127
Pt I, Ch 3 (ss 28–76)	506
ss 78, 79, 81	503
s 90(1)	516
ss 94, 95	516
ss 115, 149	27
Pt I, Ch IX (ss 153–162)	498, 501
Pt II (ss 180–212)	127
s 197	127
s 213	8
Pt III, Ch II (ss 226–235)	131
ss 226–228	128
s 226(1), (3), (4)	128
s 227(1)	129
(a), (b)	128
(c)	129
s 228(2), (3)	129
s 233	128
(1)	128
s 253	132
(3)	132
ss 287–229	27
Defamation Act 1952—	
s 3(1)	**391**
Emergency Powers (Defence) Act 1939	581
Employment Protection (Consolidation) Act 1978—	
s 141	581
s 153(5)	581
Employment Rights Act 1996	
s 196	581
s 204(1)	581
Foreign Judgments (Reciprocal Enforcement) Act 1933	739
Foreign Limitation Periods Act 1984	199
Law Reform (Personal Injuries) Act 1948—	
s 1(3)	599

Patents Act 1949	122
Patents Act 1977	131–3, 478, 491, 492, 599, 600
s 1(1)(a), (b)	6, 520
(c)	7, 520
ss 2, 3	6, 520
s 4	7, 520
s 5	491
ss 7, 8	523
ss 12, 14–21	518
s 14	492
(1)(b)	7
(2)	6
s 15(1)(d)	7
s 17	7, 492
(3)	8
s 18	7, 492
(3)	8
s 25(1)	521
(3)	7
ss 37, 39	523
s 40	524, 525, 586
(4)	586, 587
s 41	586
s 42	586, 587
s 43	586
(2)	586
(b)	587
(4)	586
s 44	584, 585, 599
(1)	585, 599, 641
(3)	585, 641
ss 60–71	131
s 60	120, 121, 131, 145, 492
(1)	120, 121, 245
(a), (b)	**120**, 146
(c)	**120**
(2)	120, 121, 146, 245
(5)	121
s 62(1)	130
s 70	132
(4)	132
s 71	132
s 72	8, 27

s 73	8
s 82(3)	53, 54, 56
ss 89A, 89B	530
Private International Law (Miscellaneous Provisions) Act 1995	654
Pt III	148, 598, 606, 612–18, 624, 628, 633, 634, 636, 640, 643–5, 655–7, 659, 663, 669–76, 680, 683, 690–3, 695, 696, 699, 700, 704, 706, 707, 709
s 9(1)	598, 612
(2)	**612**, 613, 615, 655
(3)	617
(5)	**641**
(6)	**618**, 659
s 10	598, 616, 618
s 11	601, 604, 606, 619, 620, 623, 624, 627, 629, 638, 640, 643–6, 658, 660, 668, 684
(1)	**619**, 621, 623, 625, 658–60, 685, 692
(2)	**619–20**, 621, 660, 686, 701
(a)	620, 622, 661, 662, 685, 686
(b)	620, 622, 660–2, 685, 686, 701
(c)	620, 622, 629, 660–2, 685, 686, 693, 702
s 12	619, 623–5, 627–32, 638, 643–5, 647, 657, 663, 668, 715–18, 720
(1)	**625**
(2)	**625**, 629, 630, 664, 693, 717
s 13	606, 617, 683
(1)	**670**, 675
(2)	683
(a)	**670**, 675
(b)	**670**, 671, **675**
s 14	618, 623, 633, 639
(1)	606, 612
(2)	598, 606, 612, **616**, 617, 618, 633, 644, 658, 682, 691, 692, 694, 696, 700, 703
(3)(a)(i)	**634**
(ii)	636, 696
(b)	**636**, 637
(4)	598, 612, **638**, 639, 644, 647, 668
Protection of Trading Interests Act 1980—	
s 5(2)	697, 737
Registered Designs Act 1949	129, 492, 599
s 1(2), (2)	7
s 3	492
(5)	8

s 7	131, **279**
(1), (2)	129
(3)	130
(4)(a), (b)	130
s 9(1)	130
ss 14, 16	492
s 20	27
s 26	132
(2A)	132
s 45	27
State Immunity Act 1978	279
s 3	45
s 7	70, 112
(a)	**45**
Trade Marks Act 1938—	
s 32	27
s 66(1)	27
Trade Marks Act 1994	131, 493, 599
s 1(1)	7, 493
ss 3–5	7
s 9(1)	123
ss 10–14	131
s 10	122
(1)	122, 123
(2)	123, 596
(a), (b)	123
(3)	123
(5)	123
(6)	123, 124
s 21	132
(1)	132
s 32	7, 492
ss 37–41	518
s 37	492
(3), (4)	8
s 40	492
s 43	9
s 45	521
s 46	8
(1)	521
s 47	22
s 56	364
s 60	522

ss 75, 76..........8
Trading with the Enemy Act 1916..........491
Rules of the Supreme Court—
Ord 10..........25
Ord 11, r 1(1)..........26, 40, 41, 67, 68, 97, 100, 101, 103, 105, 111, 112,
..........117, 144, 145, 149, 180, 243, 244, 248, 255, 256,
..........258, 259, 263, 265, 266, 268, 269, 289, 301, 309,
..........310, 313, 316, 381, 382, 393, 404, 443, 445, 447
    (b)..........67, **100**, 215, 254, 256, 264, 446
    (c)..........**99**, 106, 175, 253, 254, 264, 314, 383
    (d)..........41, 97, 102, 444, 446
        (i)..........**97**, 105
        (ii)..........**97**
        (iii)..........**98**, 105
        (iv)..........**98**, 105, 446
    (e)..........41, 67, 97, **98**, 101, 444
    (f)..........41, 133, **244**, 245–52, 257, 264, 314–16, 381, 393,
..........402, 403, 405, 406, 408, 411, 414, 423, 425, 444,
..........445, 448, 451–3
    (g)..........253, 383
    (h)..........402
    (t)..........446
  (2)..........215
    (a)..........25, 26, 341
r 4(1)..........103
  (d)..........100
r 8A..........215

United States of America
Constitution..........232
Restatement, Second, Conflict of Laws..........716
  s 145..........644, 688, 709
  ss 149, 150..........673, 716
  s 151..........671, 673

Table of Conventions and Treaties

Accession Convention of Austria, Finland and Sweden to the Brussels
   Convention [1977] OJ C15/1 ....1, 2, 544
Berne Convention 1886 ....14, 269, 300, 462, 472, 476, 477, 480,
                                                                   481, 499, 502, 508, 512
   Art 2 ....471, 500
       (1), (2) 500
       (6) 471
       (7) 24, 29, 470
   Art 2bis 471, 500
   Art 3 ....462–5, 501
       (1) 463, 464
          (a), (b) 463
       (2) 463
       (3) 463, 464, 471
       (4) 471
   Art 4 ....464, 465
   Art 5 ....12, 13, 465, 467, 469, 475, 476
       (1) **12**, 466–9, 473, 474
       (2) **13**, 467, 473, 474, 498, 501, 504
       (3) 466, 468, 472, 473, 499, 501
       (4) 464, 471
   Art 6bis 471
       (3) 502
   Art 7 471
       (1) 471, 507
       (8) 470, 471, 507
   Art 7bis 471
   Art 8 ....471, 472
   Arts 9–11 471
   Art 11bis 471, 505
   Arts 11ter, 12, 14 471
   Art 14bis 471
       (2) 511, 513
          (b)–(c) 513
   Art 14ter 471
       (1), (2) 471
   Art 15 471
   Art 16 468

  (1) 471
 Art 18 471
 Art 19 472
 Art 21 471
Brussels Convention on Jurisdiction and the Enforcement of
 Judgments in Civil and Commercial Matters 1968.....1, 3, 6, 14, 17, 25,
   26, 30, 34, 38, 45, 46, 55, 61, 68, 70, 141, 175, 186, 188–91, 209, 225,
   230, 232, 235, 247 257, 258, 270–2, 286, 290, 301, 305, 306, 320, 333,
   346–8, 351, 352, 355, 356, 370, 559, 684, 702, 706, 725, 730, 733, 740
 Preamble 2
 Art 1 ....2, 30, 142, 215
 Art 2 ....16, **31,** 32, **33**, 38, 41, 47, 63, 65, 76, 79–81, 82, 89,
   ....92, 95, 96, **142**, 143, 161, 162, 187, 188, 192, 194,
   ....196–8, 208, 212, 214, 217, 219, 221, 222, 225,
   ....226, 234, 237, 289, 322, 323, 329, 371, 373, 375,
   ....380, 397, 431, 442
 Art 3 ....31, 142, 329
 Art 4 ....31, 142, 322
 Art 5 ....16, 31, 33, 41, 77, 85, 143–5, 149, 150, 196, 230,
   ....234, 335, 371, 372, 404, 432
  (1) **33**, 63, 64, 77–85, 87–90, 92, 95, 96, 113–17, 188,
   ....224, 227, 322, 382, 432, 434–9, 442
  (2) 326
  (3) 133, 142, 147, 148, 150–7, 161–4, 166–8, 171, 188,
   ....197, 198, 205, 206, 208, 217, 219, 221, 222, 225,
   ....226, 229, 231–4, 237, 244, 247–52, 257, 314–16,
   ....322, 325–7, 329, 330, 371–8, 381–3, 392, 397–400,
   ....403, 406, 410, 415, 423–5, 432–41, 444, 448, 451–3,
  720
  (4) 322
  (5) **34**, 63, 77, 92, 150, **169**, 170, 208, 212, 322–4, 330
 Art 6 ....16, 31, 33, 41, 63, 77, 143–5, 196, 230, 234, 326,
   ....328, 330, 335, 371–3
  (1) 33, **34**, 92, 143, 148, **170**, 171, 173–6, 179, 183,
   ....184, 192, 193, 197, 198, 208, 212, 219, 221, 222,
   ....225, 226, 230, 326, 332, 371, 378, 442
  (2) 326
  (3) **34**, **212**, 213, 326
 Arts 7–12 31
 Art 8 329
 Section 4 (Arts 13–15) 90
 Art 13 31
  (3) 90

Art 14	31, 329
Art 15	2, 31
Art 16	2, 15, 16, 22, 24, 25, 31, 60, 62, 213, 217, 431, 729
(1)	34, 35, 175, 190
(a)	32, **34**, 35
(3)	343
(4)	11, **15**, 16–24, 26, 28–33, 35, 39–44, 46–8, 51, 54, 61–3, 65, 66, 91–4, 111, 112, 142, 176, 184, 189, 190, 195, 198, 201–6, 208, 210–14, 292, 298, 307–12, 321, 729, 731
Art 17	16, 25, 31, **36**, 42, 58, 63, 64, 78, 94–6, 104, 182, 189, 322–6, 328, 329, 335, 340, 431, 441, 446
(5)	65
Art 18	31, **36**, 63, 322–5, 328, 329, 335, 340
Art 19	16, 22, 23, 92, 93, 189, 202, **203**, 204, 206–8, 210–14, 308, 310, 312
Art 20	341
Art 21	**36**, 37, 60, 61, 65, 95, **177**, 178, 179, 181–3, 185, 266, 267, 285, 319, 330, 334, 336, 337, 343, 357, 378
Art 22	**37**, 65, 95, 177, 179, 180, 183–5, 210, 212, 266, 267, 334, 336–9, 357, 380
(1)	**182**
(2)	184, **185**
(3)	37, 183, 186
Art 23	23, 24
Art 24	152, **214**, 215–18, 220–7, 231, 319, 322, 339, 342, 345, 350, 357, 373
Art 25	725, 726
Art 26	725, **727**
Art 27	332, 728, 732
(1)	16, 212, 728, 729
(2)	726, 728, 730
(3)	339, 730
(4), (5)	731
Art 28	22, 729, 731, 732
Art 31	725, 732
Arts 32–34, 36	732
Art 37(1)	732
Arts 38–40	732
Arts 52, 53	323
Art 57	2, 11, 54
(1)	28
(3)	2, 320, 321

Title II, Section 3	114, 329
Section 4	329
Protocol	
Art V D	24
Community Patent Convention 1976	347, 358
Art 38	536
Art 77(1)	356, 357
(2)	356
Community Patent Convention 1989	2, 3, 18, 357, 480
Art 3	345
(2)(a), (b)	345
(3), (4)	345
Art 18	357
Art 34(1), (2)	356
Art 66	347, 348
Art 67	347, 348
(a)	347
(b)	347, 348
Art 68(1)	**348**
(3)	348
Art 69(2)	328
(4)(b)	18
Art 70	347
Art 72	349
Art 73	348
(1)	**348**
(2)	**349**
Art 86	24
Pt VI	345–7
Annex	346
Protocol on Litigation	319, 336, 347–9, 357, 358
Art 13	346
(1)	346
Art 14	346
(3)	346
(5)	152, 168
Art 15	346, 347
Art 17	346
(2)	161
Art 18(1)	349
Art 34	346
(1)	349
Arts 35, 36	346

Art 37	345
Pt II	345
European Patent Convention 1973	2, 3, 11, 18, 20, 21, 27, 29, 40, 52, 53, 136, 200, 318, 479, 486, 524, 530, 545, 637, 740
Arts 1–3	27
Arts 29, 30	121
Art 34	535
Art 60	52, 58, 530
(1)	18, 52, 57, 531
2nd sent	348
(3)	52
Art 61	52, 531
Art 69	121, 597
Arts 96, 100, 101	530
Arts 106, 107	27
Art 167	53
Protocol on Jurisdiction and the Recognition of Decisions in respect of the Right to the Grant of a European Patent	2, 21, 51, 52, 54, 60, 62, 63, 66, 597, 740, 741
Art 1	59
(1)	**52**, 53, 54
(2)	52
(3)	53
Art 2	52, 55, **56**, 57–60
Art 3	52, 55, **57**, 58–60
Art 4	18, 52, 55, 56, **57**, 58–60
Art 5	52, 55–60
(1)	**58**, 59
(2)	**59**
Art 6	52, 55, 57, 58, **59**, 60
Art 7	60
Art 8	60
(1)	**60**
(2)	61
Art 9	531
(1), (2)	740
Art 10	531
(a), (b)	740
Art 11(1)	54
Protocol on the Settlement of Litigation concerning the Infringement and Validity of Community Patents [1989] OJ L401/1	
Art 26, 32	535
Greek Accession Convention 1982	1

Hague Arrangement 1925 21
Hague Convention on the Law Applicable to Products Liability
  1972 ....645, 687
Hague Convention on the Taking of Evidence Abroad in Civil and
  Commercial Matters 230
Lugano Convention [1988] OJ L391/9 ....1, 3, 17, 26, 30, 31, 34, 38, 45,
            46, 55, 65, 68, 70, 142, 175, 186, 188–190, 209, 225, 230, 232, 235, 247,
                  257, 258, 270–2, 286, 301, 306, 347, 351, 352, 356, 370, 730, 733
    Art 1 ....2, 30, 215
    Art 2 ....16, **31**, **33**, 47, 63, 76, 79, 80, **142**, 143, 197, 198,
                        208, 212, 214, 234, 237, 352, 355, 371, 373, 431, 442
    Arts 3, 4 142
    Art 5 ....16, 77, 143–5, 234, 371, 372, 404, 432
        (1) **33**, 63, 64, 77–81, 113–17, 188, 351, 354, 355, 432, 434, 442
        (3) 197, 198, 205, 206, 208, 217, 231, 233, 234, 237, 244,
                        248–52, 257, 314–16, 351, 354, 355, 371–5, 381–3,
                        406, 410, 413, 415, 423–5, 432–4, 444, 448, 451–3
        (4) 351, 355
        (5) **34**, 63, 77, 170, 208, 212, 355
    Art 6 ....16, 63, 77, 143–5, 234, 355, 371–3
        (1) **34**, 95, 143, **170**, 183, 184, 188, 197, 198, 208, 212, 371, 442
        (3) **34**, **212**, 213
    Art 16 ....3, 15, 16, 22, 24, 25, 60, 62, 213, 217, 351, 431
        (1) 18, 175, 190
            (a) 32, **34**
        (2), (3) 18
        (4) 11, **15**, 16–24, 39–44, 46–8, 51, 54, 61–3, 65, 66, 112, 142, 176,
                        184, 190, 195, 198, 201–6, 208, 210–14, 298, 307–12
        (5) 18
    Art 17 ....3, 16, 25, 42, 58, 63, 64, 78, 104, 351, 354, 355, 431, 442, 446
    Art 18 ....63, 351, 354, 355
    Art 19 ....16, 22, 23, 202, **203**, 204, 206–8, 210–14, 308, 310, 312
    Art 21 ....**36**, 37, 61, 65, 95, **177**, 178, 179, 181–3, 185, 266, 267, 357
    Art 22 ....**37**, 65, 95, 177, 179, 180, 183–5, 210, 212, 266, 267, 357
        (1) **182**
        (2) 184, **185**
        (3) 37, 183, 186
    Art 23 ....23, 24
    Art 24 ....152, **214**, 215–17, 231, 357, 373
    Art 27(1) 212
    Art 28 22
    Arts 52, 53 353
    Art 54B 352

Art 57	11, 54
(3)	2
Title II, Section 3	114
Madrid Agreement Concerning the International Registration of Marks 1891	21, 479, 480
Art 3	546
Art 4	23
Art 6	546
Protocol Relating to the Madrid Agreement Concerning the International Registration of Marks 1989	479, 480
Art 4	23
Montevideo Convention 1889	475
Art 2	475
Paris Convention for the Protection of Industrial Property 1883	477–81, 491, 539
Art 2	477
(1)	**12**, 13, 477
(2)	477
(3)	13, 14, 477, 518
Art 3	477
Art 4	523
(1), (2)	518
Art 4A(1)	517
Art 4C	518
Art 4bis	24, 29, 478, 523
Art 6(1), (2)	478
(3)	518
Art 6bis	364
Art 6quarter(1)	522
Art 6quinquies	546
Art 6septies	522
Art 10bis	**409**, 410, 451, 478, 707
Patent Co-operation Treaty	479, 530
Resolution of the Institute of International Law on the Conflict of Laws Rules on Unfair Competition	451, 705–7, 709, 715
Art I	705, 707
(2)	680, 698
(4)	674
(6)	706
Art II	**708**, 709, 710
(1)	711, 717
Art III	**709**, 710, 713
Art IV	709, **710**

Art V 369, 708, 710, 711
Art VII...710
Rome Convention for the Protection of Performers, Producers of Phono-
    grams and Broadcasting Organisations 1961 ....127, 476, 477, 481
    Arts 2, 4–6 476
Rome Convention on the Law Applicable to Contractual Obligations
    1980 ....456, 525, 544, 546, 548, 551, 555, 560,
                                                          569, 576, 577, 589, 592, 593
    Art 1 551
        (1) 546
        (2) 551
    Art 2 552
    Art 3 ....548, 552, 553, 556, 578, 590
        (1), (2)...553
        (3) 578
    Art 4 ....554, 556, 558, 566, 571, 575, 578, 590, 591
        (1) 557, 572, 576, 590, 591
            2nd sent..557
        (2) 556, 559, 561, 562, 570–2, 575, 576, 590–2
        (3) 557, 559
        (5) 556, 558, 561–3, 568–72, 574–6, 590, 591
    Art 5 578–80
    Art 6 ....64, 515, 524, 531, 579, 580, 586, 587
    Art 7 ....579, 580
        (1) 579, 580, 639
        (2) 578, **580**, 581, 582, 584, 587, 590
    Art 8 588
    Art 9 ....588, 590
        (1), (2)...588
    Art 10 552
    Art 12 497
    Art 16 587
    Art 21 531
Spanish and Portuguese Accession Convention 1989 (San Sebastian
    Convention)...1, 58, 64, 337, 544
TRIPS Agreement (Agreement on Trade-related Aspects of Intellectual
    Property Rights)...480, 538
    Art 2 480
    Art 3 481
        (1), (2)...481
    Art 9 480
United Kingdom, Irish and Danish Accession Convention
    1978 ....1, 21, 24, 58, 151, 222

SECTION I

JURISDICTION

Preliminary Remarks

I	Jurisdiction under the European Community/European Free Trade Association rules and the traditional rules	1
	1. When will the Brussels and Lugano Conventions apply?	2
	(a) The Brussels Convention	2
	(b) The Lugano Convention	3
	2. When will the traditional rules apply?	3
II	Jurisdictional issues	3
III	Jurisdiction and the applicable law	3

I
JURISDICTION UNDER THE EUROPEAN COMMUNITY/EUROPEAN FREE TRADE ASSOCIATION RULES AND THE TRADITIONAL RULES

In a case involving a foreign element the first thing that a court has to decide is whether it has jurisdiction. This refers to 'the question of whether an English court will hear and determine an issue upon which its decision is sought'.[1] The jurisdiction of the English courts is complicated by the fact that there are two different sets of jurisdiction rules. The first is the EC/EFTA rules, the source of which is the Brussels and Lugano Conventions.[2] The second is the traditional English rules on jurisdiction.

---

[1] Cheshire and North, p 179.

[2] The Brussels Convention of 1968, which was entered into by the original six Member States of the EEC, has been amended by four subsequent Accession Conventions: the United Kingdom, Irish and Danish Accession Convention of 1978; the Greek Accession Convention of 1982; the Spanish and Portuguese Accession Convention of 1989 (the San Sebastian Convention); the Accession Convention of Austria, Finland and Sweden to the Brussels Convention, set out in [1997] OJ C15/1. This book is written on the assumption that the latter, which has been signed by all 15 Member States, has received the requisite number of ratifications and is in force. The Accession Convention of Austria, Finland and Sweden does not amend the current version of the Brussels Convention (ie as amended by the three Accession Conventions, and set out in SI 1990/2591, Schedule 1) on any point of importance. The Lugano Convention is contained in [1988] OJ L391/9.

1. When Will the Brussels and Lugano Conventions Apply?

(a) THE BRUSSELS CONVENTION

First, the Convention, according to its preamble, is only concerned with the international jurisdiction of Contracting States, and will not apply where there is no foreign element.

Secondly, this Convention does not affect certain other Conventions on jurisdiction or recognition or enforcement which Contracting States have in the past, or will in the future, enter into, or statutes implementing them.[3] Two such Conventions, which are particularly important in the context of intellectual property rights, are the European Patent Convention and the Community Patent Convention. The European Patent Convention, which is concerned with national rights, has its own special rules dealing with disputes arising during the examination and application process, which will be discussed in chapter 1. The European Patent Convention also has a Protocol on Jurisdiction and the Recognition of Decisions in respect of the Right to the Grant of a European Patent (Protocol on Recognition), which will be discussed in chapter 2. The Community Patent Convention, which looks unlikely to come into force, is concerned with Community rights, and will be considered in chapter 7.

Thirdly, jurisdictional provisions in EC Regulations on Community property rights (ie the Community trade mark Regulation, the Community plant variety rights Regulation, and, in the future, the Community design Regulation – which is at present in draft form only) will take precedence over the Brussels Convention.[4] These provisions will be examined in chapter 7, where jurisdiction in relation to Community rights will be considered.

Fourthly, the matter must be within the scope of the Convention, ie a civil and commercial matter.[5]

Fifthly, when it comes to bases of jurisdiction, the defendant must be domiciled in an EC Contracting State (ie one of the 15 EC countries).[6] Even if he is not, jurisdiction may be allocated to the courts of an EC Contracting State by virtue of Article 16 (exclusive jurisdiction) or Article 17 (an agreement conferring jurisdiction on the courts of a EC Contracting State) of the Convention.

---

[3] Article 57 of the Brussels Convention, and the Civil Jurisdiction and Judgments Act 1982, s 9(1).

[4] Article 57(3) of the Brussels Convention.

[5] Article 1 of the Conventions; Cheshire and North, pp 288–289.

[6] Austria, Belgium, Denmark, Finland, France, Germany, Greece, Ireland, Italy, Luxembourg, Netherlands, Portugal, Spain, Sweden, United Kingdom. This book is written on the assumption that the Accession Convention of Austria, Finland and Sweden to the Brussels Convention has received the requisite number of ratifications and is now in force.

(b) THE LUGANO CONVENTION

The first four points made above apply equally to the Lugano Convention. The difference comes in relation to the fifth point. When it comes to bases of jurisdiction, the Lugano Convention applies where the defendant is domiciled in an EFTA Contracting State (ie one of the three EFTA States).[7] Even if he is not, jurisdiction may be allocated to the courts of an EFTA Contracting State under Articles 16 or 17 of that Convention.

2. When Will the Traditional Rules Apply?

The traditional English rules on jurisdiction will apply in the situation where the Brussels and Lugano Conventions do not apply. However, other international Conventions containing jurisdiction rules (ie the European Patent Convention and the Community Patent Convention if it were ever to come into force) will take priority over the traditional rules, as will the above mentioned EC Regulations.

II
JURISDICTIONAL ISSUES

Although there are many fundamental differences between the two sets of jurisdictional rules, it is possible to identify three basic issues that have to be considered under both sets of rules in order to determine whether a court has jurisdiction. First, whether there is a basis of jurisdiction. Secondly, whether, even though there is a basis of jurisdiction, the court will decline to exercise that jurisdiction. This may involve the exercise of a discretionary power, as happens with the well known common law doctrine of *forum non conveniens*, or a mechanical rule, as happens under the Brussels and Lugano Conventions. Thirdly, whether there is a subject matter limitation in relation to jurisdiction. This is particularly important in intellectual property cases, where there is a limitation in cases concerning foreign rights.

III
JURISDICTION AND THE APPLICABLE LAW

If a court decides that it possesses jurisdiction, then the next thing that it has to decide is the law applicable to that case, ie which State's law

---

[7] Iceland, Norway and Switzerland.

governs. The position is further complicated in the context of intellectual property because an English judge will have to decide whether the substantive law contained in the English intellectual property statutes is intended to apply even though a foreign law governs. Nonetheless, it can be seen that private international law involves a two stage process. The two stages of jurisdiction and the applicable law are not entirely separate and, increasingly, a finding as to the applicable law is reached at the jurisdictional stage of the process.[8] But what is fundamental to the private international lawyer is that this jurisdictional stage has to be gone through. Understanding of the two stage process is not helped by the fact that reported cases normally deal with either jurisdiction or the applicable law, but not with both.

It is important to emphasise the methodology point at this preliminary stage. Many problems have been created by the fact that intellectual property lawyers are not entirely familiar with the methodology of private international law. Conflicts lawyers, on the other hand, tend to be baffled by the complexity of the national and international intellectual property law.

[8] See Fawcett, (1991) 44 *Current Legal Problems* 39.

1

Creation and Validity of Intellectual Property Rights: Jurisdiction

I	Introduction	6
II	The substantive law background	6
	1. How is an intellectual property right created?	6
	(a) Patents, trade marks and registered designs	6
	(b) Copyright and design right	7
	2. Revocation of a registered intellectual property right	8
	3. How does litigation arise?	8
	(a) Registration linked litigation	8
	(b) Revocation linked litigation	9
	(c) Infringement linked litigation	9
	(d) A negative declaration	10
III	How jurisdictional problems arise	10
IV	Jurisdictional provisions	11
	1. Introduction	11
	2. Special jurisdictional rules	11
	(a) Are there special jurisdictional rules in the intellectual property Conventions?	12
	(b) Article 16(4) of the Brussels and Lugano Conventions	15
	(c) The European Patent Convention 1973	27
	3. Jurisdictional rules of general application	28
	(a) When do the jurisdictional rules of general application apply?	28
	(b) Will recourse be had to these rules?	29
	(c) The EC/EFTA rules	30
	(d) The traditional rules	39
V	An alternative solution: Article 109 Swiss PIL Statute	46
	1. Scope of the provision	46
	2. Bases of jurisdiction	46
	3. A subject matter limitation on jurisdiction	47
	4. Comparison with the traditional English rules	47

I
INTRODUCTION

The creation of certain intellectual property rights requires the successful completion of a registration procedure, whilst the creation of other intellectual property rights does not. Once a right is supposedly created, the issue of its validity arises. Were all the criteria met or should the right never have been granted? The creation issue is also closely linked to the scope of the intellectual property right, because the content of the right is determined by the outcome of the creation process.

After a brief introduction to the relevant substantive provisions, the jurisdictional provisions that apply to these issues will be examined. Both the traditional English common law rules and the provisions of the Brussels Convention will be examined.

A number of special rules apply specifically to these issues. Special rules in the intellectual property conventions might influence the normal jurisdictional rules. The private international law provisions on jurisdiction also contain specific rules for intellectual property rights. Finally, there are special jurisdictional rules in relation to the creation of supra-national intellectual property rights.

II
THE SUBSTANTIVE LAW BACKGROUND

1. How is an Intellectual Property Right Created?

(a) PATENTS, TRADE MARKS AND REGISTERED DESIGNS

No one receives a patent or any form of patent protection at the moment when they think of a marvellous new invention. Nor do they receive a patent when they write the invention down or when they make or use the invention. For a product or a process to be patented a patent application needs to be lodged with the appropriate Patent Office.[1] In the application, the invention must be described and the scope of the exclusive rights that are claimed must be laid down.[2] The examination of the application focuses on the three requirements of novelty,[3] meaning that the invention must be new; inventive step,[4] meaning that the invention must present a

---
[1] For more details, see Holyoak and Torremans, *Intellectual Property Law*, Butterworths (1995) chapter 3 and *Terrell on the Law of Patents*, Sweet and Maxwell, (14th edn, 1994) pp 13–16 and 104–142.
[2] Patents Act 1977, s 14(2).
[3] Patents Act 1977, ss 1(1)(a) and 2.
[4] Patents Act 1977, ss 1(1)(b) and 3.

clear departure from the existing level of knowledge and not be obvious; and capability of industrial application[5]. A patent is only granted if the Patent Office arrives at the conclusion that all requirements for patentability are met.[6] Obtaining and maintaining in force a patent also requires the payment of the relevant fees.[7]

The same applies, *mutatis mutandis*, to trade marks and registered designs. In a trade mark application, the applicant must demonstrate that the sign can be represented graphically and that it is capable of distinguishing the undertaking's goods or services from other goods or services.[8] When applying to register the sign as a trade mark, the applicant has to provide a representation of the mark and a statement that the mark is being used or that the bona fide intention to use the mark exists.[9] These requirements are reflected in the absolute grounds for a refusal to register the sign as a trade mark.[10] For example, marks that are devoid of any distinctive character and marks that are contrary to accepted principles of morality cannot be registered. There are also relative grounds for refusal of registration which add another requirement. A mark which is identical with an earlier mark shall not be registered in relation to the same goods or services as those in relation to which the earlier mark is registered. And a mark which is identical to an earlier mark shall not be registered in relation to similar goods or services if the public is likely to be confused. Obviously, the opposite rule exists as well. A similar mark shall not be registered in relation to identical goods or services if the public is likely to be confused.[11] A registered design must be new and such an aesthetic design must have eye appeal. A design is defined as 'features of shape, configuration, pattern or ornament applied to an article by an industrial process'.[12]

The registration of an intellectual property right will also determine the scope of the right. The entry in the register will create the right, but, at the same time, the description of the right in the register will determine the scope of the right. The entry in the register determines what is protected and what is not.

(b) COPYRIGHT AND DESIGN RIGHT

Copyright does not require any formalities.[13] It comes into existence when a work is fixated or recorded in any permanent way.[14] No application,

---

[5] Patents Act 1977, ss 1(1)(c) and 4.   [6] Patents Act 1977, ss 17 and 18.
[7] See, eg Patents Act 1977, ss 14(1)(b), 15(1)(d) and 25(3).
[8] Trade Marks Act 1994, s 1(1).   [9] Trade Marks Act 1994, s 32.
[10] Trade Marks Act 1994, ss 3 and 4.   [11] Trade Marks Act 1994, s 5.
[12] Registered Designs Act 1949, s 1(1) and (2), for more details, see Holyoak and Torremans, n 1 above, chapter 20.
[13] For more details concerning substantive copyright, see Holyoak and Torremans, n 1 above, chapter 9.   [14] See eg Copyright Designs and Patents Act 1988, ss 1 and 3(2).

examination or registration system exists for original literary, artistic, musical and dramatic works, films, sound recordings, broadcasts, cable programmes and the typographical arrangements of published editions. The Copyright Designs and Patents Act 1988 also introduced a design right for functional designs along the same lines.[15] The latter right could be called an unregistered design. A design is defined as 'the design of any aspect of the shape or configuration (whether internal or external) of the whole or part of an article'.[16]

2. Revocation of a Registered Intellectual Property Right

Only those intellectual property rights that have formally been granted and registered by the Patent Office can be revoked. The Comptroller may revoke a patent upon the application of any person, for example, on the basis that the invention is not a patentable invention, or on the basis that the patent was granted to a person who was not entitled to it, or on the basis that the specification of the patent does not disclose the invention clearly enough for it to be performed by a person skilled in the art.[17] Trade marks are normally revoked for reasons of non use.[18]

3. How Does Litigation Arise?

(a) registration linked litigation

Any application for the registration of a trade mark, patent or registered design can obviously be refused by the Registrar.[19] The applicant has a right to appeal against such a refusal. During the examination procedure the Registrar may suggest that the application be amended.[20] This may give rise to litigation if the applicant does not agree to the suggested amendment, especially as the sanction for the applicant's refusal to amend the application is the refusal of the application. The appeal procedure may eventually reach the courts. For example, Section 76 of the Trade Marks Act 1994 specifies that any decision made by the Registrar under the Act can be the subject of an appeal in the High Court.[21] The litigation will take place between the applicant and the Registrar. This kind of litigation, of course, does not arise in relation to copyright and the (unregistered)

---

[15] For more details on substantive design law, see Holyoak and Torremans, n 1 above, chapter 21.
[16] Copyright Designs and Patents Act 1988, s 213.
[17] See Patents Act 1977, ss 72 and 73.   [18] See Trade Marks Act 1994, s 46.
[19] See Patents Act 1977, s 18(3); Trade Marks Act 1994, s 37(4); Copyright Designs and Patents Act 1988 s 3(5).
[20] See Patents Act 1977, ss 17(3) and 18(3); Registered Designs Act 1949, s 3(5); Trade Marks Act 1994, s 37(3) and (4).
[21] Or the Court of Session in Scotland, see Trade Marks Act 1994, s 75.

design right, since the creation of these rights does not involve any registration, examination or administrative procedure.

(b) REVOCATION LINKED LITIGATION

An alleged infringer may try to get the registered intellectual property right out of the way by filing an application for its revocation. On the other hand, any revocation procedure is almost bound to be opposed by the owner of the intellectual property right that forms the object of the procedure. Litigation is bound to be the result.

(c) INFRINGEMENT LINKED LITIGATION

The alleged infringer of an intellectual property right may try to escape by challenging the validity of the intellectual property right by way of defence. The validity of an intellectual property right can also be challenged by way of a counterclaim in such cases. In some cases, the alleged infringer will argue that the term of protection of the intellectual property right has expired, for example because the author of the poem that has been copied died 75 years ago while the term of protection is only life of the author plus 70 years,[22] or that the intellectual property right has lapsed, for example because the renewal fee for the trade mark was never paid after the initial ten year period had expired.[23] It is simply impossible to infringe a right which no longer exists. It is, for example, a prerequisite for copyright infringement, in our earlier example, that copyright protection for the poem still exists. Most cases are slightly different, though, in that it is argued that the intellectual property right is not valid and should never have been granted or never came into existence because the essential requirements for the registration of creation were not met. The argument is that the allegedly infringed patent should never have been granted because the invention was obvious and did not involve an inventive step. Or that a telephone directory which has been copied was not protected by copyright, because the originality requirement was not met, only original literary works attracting copyright protection.

In each of these cases, the validity of the intellectual property right is challenged. Was copyright or an (unregistered) design right ever created, did the term of protection of the intellectual property right expire, or should a patent, a trade mark or a registered design ever have been granted? The influence on the jurisdictional issue of the fact that there is,

[22] See Copyright, Designs and Patents Act 1988, s 12(2).
[23] See Trade Marks Act 1994, s 43.

at the same time, an infringement issue to be dealt with will also have to be examined.[24]

(d) A NEGATIVE DECLARATION

The creation, the scope and the validity of an intellectual property right can also form the object of a negative declaration. This technique allows the party who wants to undertake a potentially infringing activity to ask the court to determine in advance, by way of an *ex parte* application, whether that activity would infringe the intellectual property right. To take an earlier example, would the new telephone directory infringe the copyright in the old directory, this is assuming that the latter one attracted copyright in the first place? Similarly, would the production of a new similar product infringe an existing product patent?

III
HOW JURISDICTIONAL PROBLEMS ARISE

If there is no valid intellectual property right in place, a potentially infringing activity by a competitor can be carried out without incurring the risk of infringement litigation and damages. Clarifying the validity and the precise scope of existing intellectual property rights is an important point when a decision to go ahead with major investments is made. For example, if a French company is considering the construction of a plant in the United Kingdom in which a new product that is to be marketed in the United Kingdom is to be produced, it might want certainty about the validity and the scope of potentially conflicting UK patents and trade marks before committing itself to the investment. Which national court will have jurisdiction to hear the case?

Obviously, the issue whether a valid intellectual property right has been created and exists will often arise as a preliminary point in cases of alleged infringement. For example, an English company cannot infringe the copyright in a film in Germany and in Italy if a valid right did not exist in the first place in these countries. Should the preliminary point be litigated in England, in Germany, or in Italy? Would the outcome be the same if a registered trade mark was at issue?

Litigation can also take place between the applicant and the Registrar if the Registrar refuses an application for the registration of an intellectual property right or when he suggests that the application should be amended. Can an overseas applicant in such a case sue the Registrar and

---

[24] Chapters 5 and 6, below pp 201–214 and 307–312, deal with infringement and validity.

the UK Patent Office abroad? Can an English applicant who applied for the registration of an intellectual property right abroad in such a case sue in the High Court in London a foreign Patent Office and/or its Registrar?

An application for a negative declaration will also give rise to problems. Before a decision can be made as to whether or not a proposed activity will infringe an intellectual property right, the issue whether or not the intellectual property right has validly been created and continues to exist will normally have to be addressed. The jurisdictional issue arises particularly sharply in the situation where intellectual property rights in more than one jurisdiction are involved. Can one court deal with all these issues and rights? Which court should that be? The court of the country where the right is located, or alternatively, the court of the domicile of the defendant? And who is the defendant when a negative declaration is applied for?

IV
JURISDICTIONAL PROVISIONS

1. Introduction

Jurisdiction in relation to the creation and validity of intellectual property rights is unusual in that there are special jurisdictional rules dealing with this. The first and most important of these is contained in Article 16(4) of the Brussels and Lugano Conventions. As will be seen, this provision does not cover all cases of jurisdiction in respect of creation or validity of intellectual property rights. The second, and much more limited, special rule is contained in the European Patent Convention 1973. In cases that are not covered by these special rules, recourse will have to be had to jurisdictional rules of general application contained in the Brussels and Lugano Conventions or to the traditional English rules on jurisdiction.

2. Special Jurisdictional Rules

Before turning to examine Article 16(4) of the Brussels and Lugano Conventions and the European Patent Convention, it is important to see whether there are any special jurisdictional rules in the intellectual property conventions. If there are, they will take precedence over the jurisdiction rules contained in the Brussels and Lugano Conventions, including Article 16(4).[25]

---

[25] See Article 57 of the Brussels and Lugano Conventions, discussed above, p 2.

(a) ARE THERE SPECIAL JURISDICTIONAL RULES IN THE INTELLECTUAL PROPERTY CONVENTIONS?

(i) The traditional view

The only provisions that are of interest in the present context to be found in the international intellectual property conventions are those that deal with national treatment. The Paris Convention stipulates that 'nationals of any country of the Union shall, as regards the protection of intellectual property, enjoy in all the other countries of the Union the advantages that their respective laws now grant, or may hereafter grant, to nationals . . . '.[26] The Berne Convention uses the following terms: 'authors shall enjoy, in respect of works for which they are protected under this Convention, in countries of the Union other than the country of origin, the rights which their respective laws do now or may hereafter grant to their nationals . . . '.[27] Historically, many authors derived from these provisions a strictly territorial approach towards jurisdiction and concluded that 'a limitation of international jurisdiction must be accepted in the sense that legal protection may be claimed only before the national courts on the basis of the national copyright or industrial property right'.[28] For our present purposes, this would mean that exclusive jurisdiction would be given to the courts of the State which grants national treatment and under whose laws the intellectual property right was granted or created. Thus, the UK courts would have exclusive jurisdiction to deal with a case concerning the grant of a UK trade mark, for example a case between the Registrar who refused to register a trade mark and the applicant. And the same courts would also have exclusive jurisdiction to decide whether a certain telephone directory attracts copyright in the United Kingdom.

(ii) Rejection of the traditional view

It is submitted that such a wide ranging territoriality principle cannot be derived from any of the provisions of the various Conventions and that this principle must consequently be rejected.[29] National treatment does not determine which court has jurisdiction, it operates solely at the choice of law level by determining that the same substantive provisions will be applied to foreigners and nationals in relation to intellectual property rights.[30] This interpretation is supported by the text of the Conventions.[31]

---

[26] Article 2(1).   [27] Article 5(1).   [28] Ulmer, pp 9–10.
[29] See Cornish, 'The Significant but Limited Scope of the IP Conventions', IP and PIL conference, Cambridge, 24 February 1996 and Koumantos, 'Copyright and PIL in the Face of the International Diffusion of Works', WIPO Symposium on the Future of Copyright and Neighbouring Rights, 1994, pp 233–234.   [30] See also Cornish, n 29 above.
[31] This point of view seems also to be shared by Ricketson, whose discussion of Article 5 of the Berne Convention focuses entirely on choice of law and the definition of the concept of the country of origin, p 195 *et seq.*

The Berne Convention further defines national treatment by stipulating that 'the extent of protection, as well as the means of redress afforded to the author to protect his rights, shall be governed exclusively by the laws of the country where protection is claimed' and by describing the scope of national treatment as 'the enjoyment and the exercise of these rights'.[32] When the Berne Convention refers to the scope of protection, ie how these rights can be enjoyed and exercised, this is a clear indication that what is being referred to is choice of the applicable law, especially as the Article stipulates that these issues shall be 'governed by the law', etc. The only doubt that could arise concerns the meaning of 'means of redress'. This does not allocate jurisdiction though. This is clear when the wording of earlier drafts and the wording of the equivalent paragraph in the Paris Convention is considered. The relevant passages '. . . [A]uthors . . . shall enjoy the same rights of protection . . . as nationals',[33] '[authors] will have . . . the same recourse to law against infringement of their rights'[34] and '[n]ationals of any country of the Union shall . . . have . . . the same legal remedy against any infringement of their rights'[35] all avoid any reference to jurisdiction and focus on the applicable law and its remedies to which equal access is included in the definition of national treatment. And the discussion which led to the adoption of the final wording of Article 5 of the Berne Convention focused entirely on the definition of the country of origin concept. Once again, jurisdiction was never mentioned. An example will illustrate this interpretation of Article 5 more clearly. If my poem enjoys copyright protection in a foreign country in the same way as a poem written by a local poet that right become worthless unless I can act against infringement in the same way as the local poet can. National treatment therefore grants me access to the courts in the same way as the local authors and I am also entitled to the same remedies. The latter points are essential elements in any national copyright which I can invoke in the same way as the local author can. What national treatment does not determine is to which court I have to turn in order to see my rights applied.

The role which the provisions of the international intellectual property conventions can play in relation to the determination of the court that can take jurisdiction in cases relating to the creation or validity of intellectual property rights seems almost negligible or non-existent. Confirmation of this point can be found in Article 2(3) of the Paris Convention which mentions specifically that the convention rules do not deal with jurisdiction

---

[32] Article 5(2) Berne Convention, see the similar wording of Article 2(1) of the Paris Convention 1883.
[33] ALAI Draft of 1883, Actes 1884, 7; quoted by Ricketson, p 195.
[34] Federal Council Programme, submitted to the 1884 Diplomatic Conference, Actes 1884, 11; quoted by Ricketson, n 31 above, p 196.
[35] Paris Convention 1883, Article 2(1).

and that this issue is reserved for 'the provisions of the laws of each of the countries of the Union'.[36]

(iii) Recourse to the rules of private international law

Ricketson seems to suggest that it is for the provisions of the private international law of each individual country to determine freely which rule on jurisdiction it will operate in relation to the creation and the validity of copyright. He clearly rejects an overlap between the country whose law is applicable and the (exclusive) jurisdiction of the courts of that country.[37] It is submitted that this is indeed the case and that this rule applies to all intellectual property rights and not just to copyright, because all conventions contain similar provisions. This solution is also in line with the approach that is taken in private international law. The private international law rules of jurisdiction must be applied unless there are specific jurisdictional provisions in the substantive law conventions.

(iv) Is there any restriction on the jurisdiction rule in relation to creation and validity?

In the absence of binding provisions in the conventions, national legislatures are able to create a jurisdiction rule in their national system of private international law; a jurisdiction rule which will apply to all cases which are international in nature. Is there any restriction on the rule to be adopted in cases of creation and validity?

One could take the point of view that the national jurisdiction rule can be based on any criterion and that there exists a complete freedom as to the contents of that provision. Arguably, this is wrong. The jurisdiction rule should not take the nationality of any of the parties as its criterion, as this would violate the national treatment principle by not treating foreigners and nationals in the same way. The latter interpretation relies on a wide interpretation of national treatment and the applicable law. It does not restrict the obligation to treat foreigners as nationals in relation to intellectual property rights to the provisions of the statutes that deal explicitly with intellectual property, but expands it to all provisions of the national law that may have an influence in the intellectual property area.[38] All these provisions, including those in private international law, should deal in the same way with foreigners and nationals.[39] It is submitted that such

---

[36] Paris Convention 1883, Article 2(3).

[37] Ricketson, n 31 above, p 226, with references to Ulmer, *Intellectual Property Rights and the Conflict of Laws*, Kluwer (1978) p 10 and Desbois, Françon and Kerever, *Les Conventions internationales du droit d'auteur et des droits voisins*, Dalloz (1976) p 152 *et seq*.

[38] This view was rejected in the discussion regarding droit de suite which certain countries had incorporated in separate statutes which were not headed 'copyright', a discussion that took place before the Brussels revision of the Berne Convention; see Ricketson, p 208 and Ladas, p 268.

[39] This view was advocated by Ladas, *The International Protection of Literary and Artistic Property*, (1938), p 268.

an approach would go too far and needs to be refined. The international intellectual property rights conventions only deal with matters relating to the creation or the acquisition of intellectual property rights, their scope, duration and termination.[40] No other elements are dealt with in their provisions. It is therefore logical to assume that the national treatment principle is also limited to these matters and would, for example, not apply to the taxation of intellectual property royalties.[41] It is arguable though that the creation of intellectual property rights must, for these purposes, include the issue of which court has jurisdiction in these matters. The creation of the intellectual property right is the central issue, not the jurisdictional point.

Of course, from an English perspective, even the private international law jurisdictional rules exclude nationality as a criterion. This is, however, not the case in many other systems of private international law. Many of these do not have special rules on creation and validity of intellectual property rights and they deal with these issues under their general rules. Nationality may be an important connecting factor under these general jurisdictional rules. We now turn to the existing rules of national private international law.

(b) ARTICLE 16(4) OF THE BRUSSELS AND LUGANO CONVENTIONS

This provides that the following courts shall have exclusive jurisdiction, regardless of domicile:

in proceedings concerned with the registration or validity of patents, trade marks, designs, or other similar rights required to be deposited or registered, the courts of the Contracting State in which the deposit or registration has been applied for, has taken place or is under the terms of an international convention deemed to have taken place.

(i) Justification of Article 16(4)

There are two justifications for Article 16(4). The first is that this provision is based on the sovereign power of the forum, in that the grant of a national patent is an exercise of national sovereignty.[42] This theme is also to be found in international conventions on intellectual property.

The second justification is one that applies to all of the five heads of Article 16 and not just to paragraph (4). The justification for Article 16 as a whole is in terms of the interests of the proper administration of justice, all five heads deal with '. . . matters which, because of their particular difficulty or complexity, require that the court having jurisdiction should be

---

[40] See Ulmer, n 37 above, pp 1–3 and 28–35. [41] See Ricketson, n 31 above, pp 208–210.
[42] See the Jenard Report, [1979] OJ C59, p 36.

particularly familiar with the relevant national law. . .'.[43] In other words, jurisdiction is allocated to the State whose law will be applied. There is a concern therefore with litigational convenience.[44] This common thread is equally applicable to paragraph (4). The Court of Justice in the leading case on Article 16(4), *Duijnstee* v *Goderbauer*,[45] has justified this particular provision on the basis that the exclusive jurisdiction '. . . conferred upon the courts of the Contracting State in which the deposit or registration has been applied for is justified by the fact that those courts are best placed to adjudicate upon cases in which the dispute itself concerns the validity of the patent or the existence of the deposit or registration'.[46] The law applicable to the issue of creation of intellectual property rights is that of the State of registration or deposit,[47] and it is for this reason that the courts of the Contracting State in which registration or deposit occurred are best placed to try the case. It has been questioned whether a justification in terms of convenience is really very convincing in the light of the harmonisation of patent law, and the fact that the parties are unable to choose the place of trial in Article 16(4) cases,[48] and that the true justification is in terms of public policy.[49] This cannot be referring to public policy as used in Article 27(1) of the Brussels Convention, which provides a defence to recognition of foreign judgments. It must be referring to policy rather than public policy as strictly understood, but what policy justifies Article 16(4) if it is not that of litigational convenience and the proper administration of justice?

(ii) Interpretation of Article 16(4)

Looking at the scheme of the Convention, Article 16, as a whole, can be seen to be an exception to the general and special bases of jurisdiction set out in Articles 2, 5 and 6, and, accordingly, it has, normally, been narrowly interpreted. This is equally true in respect of Article 16(4).[50]

(iii) Scope of Article 16(4)

(a) *Regardless of domicile*

So strong is the desire to allocate jurisdiction under Article 16 that it applies regardless of domicile. It is an exception to the normal rule under

---

[43] Advocate General Lenz in Case 220/84 *As-Autoteile Service GmbH* v *Malhe* [1985] ECR 2267 at 2271. See also Case 73/77 *Sanders* v *van der Putte* [1977] ECR 2383.
[44] See Tritton and Tritton, [1987] 12 *EIPR* 349 at 350, who describe the rule in Article 16(4) as being one of convenience.
[45] Case 288/82 [1983] ECR 3663. [46] Ibid, at 3676. [47] See below, pp 487 *et seq*.
[48] Article 16 takes precedence over Article 17, which is discussed below, p 36.
[49] See Wadlow, (1985) 10 *ELR* 305, 310. There is support for this view in the comments in the Jenard Report, n 42 above, at p 38 in relation to Article 19.
[50] See Advocate General Rozes in the *Duijnstee* case, n 45 above, at 3683.

(b) *Proceedings concerned with registration or validity*

(i) Duijnstee *v* Goderbauer

Article 16(4) is limited to proceedings concerned with registration or validity of patents, etc. The meaning of 'registration or validity' was elucidated by the Court of Justice in *Duijnstee* v *Goderbauer*.[51]

The case concerned a dispute between the liquidator, Duijnstee, of Belgium, in the winding up of a company, whose registered office was in the Netherlands, and Goderbauer, a former employee from the Netherlands who made a patented invention whilst employed by the company. The company had taken action to transfer to its name the application for a patent in the Netherlands. The company went into liquidation. Duijnstee applied to a Dutch court for an interlocutory injunction requiring Goderbauer to transfer to it the patents applied for or granted in 22 countries besides the Netherlands, including five Contracting States to the Brussels Convention. This claim was dismissed. Goderbauer, in turn, applied to the Dutch courts, claiming that he had a lien over the patents and applications for patents both in the Netherlands and abroad. Duijnstee counterclaimed in the same terms as his application for an interlocutory injunction. The Dutch court dismissed both claim and counterclaim. On appeal to the Supreme Court of the Netherlands, that court was concerned that the courts of other Contracting States had exclusive jurisdiction under Article 16(4) and, therefore, it lacked jurisdiction. One of the questions referred to the Court of Justice was whether the expression 'proceedings concerned with the registration or validity of patents' included a dispute such as the present one.

The Court of Justice held that an independent Community meaning must be given to this expression, and that this did not include a dispute between an employee for whose invention a patent had been applied for or obtained and his employer, where the dispute relates to their respective rights in that patent arising out of the contract of employment. In reaching this decision, the court employed two lines of reasoning. The first was to look at the justification for Article 16(4). The outcome of the case depended exclusively on the question of who owned the patents and this had to be determined on the basis of the legal relationship which existed between the parties. Neither the validity of the patents nor the legality of their registration in the various countries was disputed. Accordingly, there was no special reason to confer exclusive jurisdiction on the courts of the

---

[51] N 45 above.

Contracting State in which the patent was applied for or granted. The second line of reasoning was that the European Patent Convention[52] and the Community Patent Convention[53] make a clear distinction between jurisdiction in disputes concerning the right to the patent, especially where the patent concerns the invention of an employee, and jurisdiction in disputes concerning the registration or validity of a patent.

If Article 16(4) had applied the result would have been that there would have had to be separate actions in the Netherlands and in the five other Contracting States over the ownership of the various patents. As it is, Article 16(4) would not prevent the Dutch courts from trying an action in respect of the patents registered in other Contracting States. This is a good result in terms of consolidating litigation in one Contracting State. There may still be problems in enforcing the judgment if the defendant refused to assign the patents. It has been suggested that separate actions would have to be brought in each State.[54]

(ii) *What is covered*

Two rather different types of proceedings are covered within the expression 'proceedings concerned with the registration or validity' of patents etc. The first is proceedings concerned with the registration of patents, etc. The second is proceedings concerned with the validity of patents, etc. Before looking at these two different types of proceedings, a word is needed on the phrase 'proceedings concerned with'. It is noticeable that paragraphs (1), (2) and (3) of Article 16 are differently worded,[55] all referring to 'proceedings which have as their object'. It is arguable that the former phrase is a wider one than the latter, which in turn could lead to an argument that the exception in paragraph (4) should be interpreted more generously than the exceptions in paragraphs (1), (2) and (3). However, there is nothing to suggest that this change in wording is so intended.[56] Moreover, as has been seen, the same narrow interpretation has been given to paragraph (4) as to the other heads of Article 16.

Proceedings concerned with registration. According to the *Duijnstee* case,[57] such proceedings are concerned with the legality of their registration, the existence of the deposit or registration. The same case also states that Article 16(4) covers proceedings concerned with '. . . existence or lapse of a patent or an alleged right of priority by reason of an earlier deposit'.[58] An action by an applicant to challenge the Registrar's decision to refuse the

---

[52] See Article 4 of the Protocol on Recognition attached to the European Patent Convention, discussed below, pp 57–58, and Article 60(1) of the Convention itself.
[53] See Article 69(4)(b) of the Community Patent Convention.
[54] See Wadlow, n 49 above, at 308.   [55] But not Article 16(5).
[56] There is nothing in the Jenard Report to suggest this. See generally, O'Malley and Layton, p 537.
[57] N 45 above, at 3677.   [58] N 45 above, at 3677.

registration of a patent for lack of inventive step will come within Article 16(4), as will an action for cancellation in the registry of trademarks or designs.[59] What is required is a direct link with the activities of the intellectual property office as the functioning of a public service.[60] The same idea has been expressed in terms of Article 16(4) covering 'that which affects the validity of the actions taken by the public authorities in reviewing and granting the rights in question'.[61]

Proceedings concerned with validity. Again, according to the *Duijnstee* case,[62] Article 16(4) includes within its scope proceedings concerned with the 'validity' of a patent, etc. A petition for revocation of a patent alleging invalidity will come within Article 16(4).[63] This was shown in *Napp Laboratories v Pfizer Inc.*[64] The English courts had exclusive jurisdiction under Article 16(4) in respect of a revocation petition, concerning the validity of a patent granted in an unspecified Contracting State, which had been served on a company in New York.[65] To give a final example, Advocate General Rozes in the *Duijnstee* case referred to unity of the invention as coming within Article 16(4).[66]

(iii) *What is not covered*

We also know from the *Duijnstee* case what is not covered by the expression 'proceedings concerned with the registration or validity' of patents, etc. Actions for the infringement of patents etc are governed by the general rules of the Convention and not by Article 16(4).[67] Neither is an action for a declaration of non-infringement within this provision.[68] The position where validity is raised as a defence to infringement is particularly problematic and will be considered later after jurisdiction in respect of infringement has been discussed.[69] We also know that the expression does not cover disputes concerning the right to a patent where what is involved is an invention of an employee. Doubtless, the same will be true even if it is not an invention of an employee.[70] It has been suggested that issues which

---

[59] See Ulmer, p 16. [60] See Holleaux, Foyer and de la Pradelle, p 385, para 831.
[61] Trooboff, in McLachlan and Nygh at p 140. He is summarising the views of Gautier, (1991) 80 *RCDIP* 400.
[62] N 45 above, at 3677.
[63] See Advocate General Rozes in the *Duijnstee* case, n 45 above, at 3683.
[64] [1993] FSR 150. See also *Chiron Corp v Evans Medical Ltd and others* [1996] FSR 863 at 866; *Fort Dodge Animal Health Ltd and Others v Akzo Nobel NV and Another* [1998] FSR 222.
[65] Service of the petition is discussed below, pp 25–26. [66] N 45 above, at 3683.
[67] *Ibid*, at 3677. This follows the Jenard Report, n 42 above, at p 36. See also *Molnlycke AB and Another v Procter & Gamble Ltd and Others* [1992] 1 WLR 1112 at 1117; *Chiron Corp v Evans Medical Ltd and Others*, n 64 above at 866; *Pearce v Ove Arup Partnership Ltd and Others* [1997] 2 WLR 779 at 785; *Fort Dodge Animal Health Ltd and Others v Akzo Nobel NV and Another* [1998] FSR 222.
[68] *Chiron Corp v Evans Medical Ltd and Others*, n 64 above, at 866–867.
[69] See below, pp 202–210. [70] See chapter 2 at p 61–62.

arise by virtue of the transfer of a right by contract or license are not covered, even though there may be a change in the registration of the right.[71] In this situation, the public authorities play no administrative role but are merely recording the actions of the transferor and transferee. This is a distinction recognised by French law. The Cour d'Appel, Paris, in *SA des Etablissements Salik et SA Diffusal v SA J Esterel*,[72] held that Article 16(4) did not apply to an action concerned solely with breaches of a licensing agreement, without the validity of that agreement or of the trade mark being affirmed or contested by any party. The limited situations where Article 16(4) is relevant in relation to licensing agreements are discussed in chapter 3.[73]

(c) *Patents, trade marks, designs, or other similar rights required to be deposited or registered*

Article 16(4) only applies to 'patents, trade marks, designs, or other similar rights required to be deposited or registered'. The common theme is that all of these rights are required to be deposited or registered. The first three specified rights (patents, trade marks, designs) are easily identified. There is more of a problem of identification with the fourth and residual category of 'other similar rights required to be deposited or registered'. The Jenard Report gives, as an example, rights protecting fruit and vegetable varieties.[74]

Article 16(4) will not apply to rights that are not required to be registered or deposited. It is a matter for national law to decide whether national rights have to be registered or deposited.[75] As far as English law, and indeed that of other EC States, is concerned, Article 16(4) will not apply to copyrights, even though an action is concerned with the validity of a copyright. Again, as far as English law is concerned, it will not apply to performers' rights or to unregistered designs, or to confidential information.[76]

(d) *European patents*

Article 16(4) can apply in relation to European patents under the European Patent Convention.[77] This is subject to the proviso that the special rules on jurisdiction dealing with the right to the grant of a patent, contained in the

---

[71] Gautier, n 61 above.
[72] Revue Critique de Droit International Privé, 1982, p 135; D Series I-16.4–B2.
[73] See below, pp 91–94.   [74] N 42 above, at p 36.
[75] See O'Malley and Layton, p 541.
[76] On this last example, see Tritton and Tritton, n 44 above, at 350.
[77] See below, p 24.

Protocol on Recognition attached to that Convention,[78] take precedence over the provisions contained in the Brussels and Lugano Conventions. However, the right to the grant of a patent usually involves the issue of ownership and this is a different issue from that of registration or validity and so Article 16(4) would not apply anyway. In the rare situation where the right to the grant of a European patent involves an issue other than ownership it is arguable that there are proceedings concerned with registration. In this situation, the Protocol on Recognition would apply rather than Article 16(4). Moreover, as will be seen the European Patent Convention contains special rules dealing with cases arising during the application and examination process. These too will apply rather than Article 16(4).

(e) *Deposit or registration has been applied for, etc*

Article 16(4) presupposes that the deposit or registration has been applied for, has taken place or is under the terms of an international convention deemed to have taken place. It adds some width to the provision by making it clear that it can apply to proceedings concerned with registration or validity brought at the early stage, where national law allows this, where there has been a patent application but the patent has not yet been granted. This takes account of the fact that under most national laws, such as those of Germany and the United Kingdom, the grant of a patent is subject to a prior examination.[79] The Schlosser Report explains that such national laws are there so as to reduce the risk of a patent being granted and the correctness of the grant being subsequently challenged.[80] It is easy enough to say when deposit or registration has been applied for or taken place, but when is this deemed to have taken place? This refers, for example, to the system of international registration of trade marks under the Madrid Agreement of 1891, as revised, and international registration of industrial designs under the Hague Arrangement of 1925, as revised. The Jenard Report explains that under this system 'the deposit of a trade mark, design or model at the International Office in Berne through the registry of the country of origin has the same effect in the other Contracting States as if that trade mark, design or model had been directly registered there'.[81]

---

[78] See below, pp 52–61.
[79] See the Jenard Report, n 42 above.
[80] [1979] OJ C59, at 123. This is the Report on the UK/Irish/Danish Accession Convention to the Brussels Convention.
[81] See the Jenard Report, n 42 above, at p 36.

(f) *An EC/EFTA Contracting State*

The deposit or registration must have been applied for, etc in an EC/EFTA Contracting State. It follows that Article 16(4) will not apply, for example, in a case concerning the validity of a patent registered in the United States.

(iv) Exclusive jurisdiction

Jurisdiction under Article 16(4) is exclusive in the sense that a Contracting State other than the one that has jurisdiction under it is deprived of jurisdiction, even though it has jurisdiction under some other basis such as the defendant's domicile in that Contracting State. This provision, like the other heads of Article 16, operates as a basis of jurisdiction, allocating jurisdiction to the courts of a Contracting State, but also as a subject matter limitation on jurisdiction, preventing courts in other Contracting States from trying the case. The courts of Contracting States are required by Article 19 to declare of their own motion that they do not have jurisdiction when they are seised of a claim which is principally concerned with a matter over which the courts of another Contracting State have exclusive jurisdiction by virtue of Article 16. The *Duijnstee*[82] case decided that this requirement applies to Contracting States regardless of their own rules of procedure, which may require the jurisdictional point to be raised by one of the parties, and regardless of what steps have been taken by the defendant. Moreover, a court which is being asked to recognise a judgment granted in another Contracting State will refuse to do so if it conflicts with Article 16.[83] This an exception to the normal rule that the recognising court cannot review the jurisdiction taken by the court in the Contracting State in which the judgment was granted.

(v) Allocation to the courts of the Contracting State in which the deposit or registration has been applied for, etc

Article 16(4) allocates jurisdiction to the courts of one Contracting State. When it comes to identifying which Contracting State this is, three alternative connecting factors are used. The first is the State in which the registration or deposit has been applied for, for example in the situation in which an applicant launches an appeal against the Registrar's decision to refuse the registration of a patent for lack of novelty. The second is the State in which the registration or deposit has taken place, for example when the validity of a registered trade mark is challenged by the owner of an earlier mark.[84] The third is the State in which the registration or deposit is, under the terms of an international convention, deemed to have taken

---

[82] N 45 above.   [83] Brussels and Lugano Conventions, Article 28.
[84] See Trade Marks Act 1994, s 47.

place. The only problem in identifying the relevant Contracting State will arise in relation to this third alternative. As has been seen, it applies, for example, to the Madrid Agreement and Protocol system of international registration of trade marks. A single application for the registration of a trade mark in a number of countries can be made under this system. When granted, both Article 4 of the Agreement and the Protocol make it clear that these trade marks should be dealt with as if one individual application per Contracting State had been made in each of the Contracting States covered by the single application.[85] If we assume that the single application covers France, the Benelux countries and the United Kingdom this means that once the trade mark has been registered for the United Kingdom this registration is deemed to have taken place in the United Kingdom.[86] These three alternatives apply to different situations and there is no case which is covered by more than one of them. The upshot is that there is always only one Contracting State whose courts will have exclusive jurisdiction.

(vi) Parallel applications

Often, parallel patent applications are launched in a number of countries, for example, for a single invention. Substantive intellectual property law requires one application per country or the equivalent under an international convention. Article 16(4) clearly deals separately with each national application. Exclusive jurisdiction is granted to a court for each application or for the intellectual property right that was granted as a result of such an application. No other court can take jurisdiction and even the court which has taken jurisdiction for one application of one right (the one relating to its own country) on the basis of Article 16(4), has to decline jurisdiction in relation to other parallel applications concerning other Contracting States.[87] This does not involve overlapping exclusive jurisdiction and, accordingly, the provisions designed to deal with this phenomenon[88] will not apply.

In the situation where parallel patent applications are launched in a number of countries, the same issue may arise in each of those countries concerning the creation of the intellectual property right in question. Likewise, the validity of the right may be contested on the same grounds in the various countries. In these situations, it could be argued that a single court should deal with the whole issue. Nonetheless, any such suggestion should be rejected. Admittedly, the intellectual property conventions

---

[85] Madrid Agreement Concerning the International Registration of Marks 1891, Article 4 and Protocol Relating to the Madrid Agreement Concerning the International Registration of Marks 1989, Article 4.
[86] See also the example in the Jenard Report, n 42 above, at p 36.
[87] See Article 19, discussed below, p 203.
[88] See Article 23, discussed below, p 24.

institute a link between the various applications in terms of priority dates, but this is as far as the link goes. National treatment clearly implies the creation of national rights that are limited in scope to the territory of the granting State. The national examination procedures apply their national rules and are conducted independently in each country. The intellectual property rights that are eventually granted are also fully independent from one another.[89] What happens to one parallel right has no influence whatsoever on the other parallel rights. This is a clear policy reason not to put them together for the purposes of jurisdiction relating to their creation either. Accordingly, the approach adopted by Article 16(4) in relation to parallel rights can be seen to be the correct one to adopt.

(vii) Application in relation to European patents

There was a problem in applying Article 16(4) in relation to European patents. Take the following example. There has been the grant of a European patent (UK), a European patent (France) and a European patent (Italy). An issue arises as to the validity of each of these national patents. Arguably, the German courts would have exclusive jurisdiction in relation to all three national patents on the basis that Germany is the Contracting State in which the registration has taken place. To avoid this,[90] Article V D was introduced[91] into the Protocol attached to the Brussels Convention.[92] This provides that 'the courts of each Contracting State shall have exclusive jurisdiction, regardless of domicile, in proceedings concerned with the registration or validity of any European patent granted for that State', provided that this is not a Community patent.[93] In the above example, the UK courts would have exclusive jurisdiction in relation to the European patent (UK), the French courts in relation to the European patent (France), and the Italian courts in relation to the European patent (Italy). This result is a logical and inevitable consequence of the idea that a European patent is a bundle of national patents. The drawback with this is that it would be very inconvenient to have three separate actions, which may come to different conclusions on the issue of validity. However, Article 23 of the Brussels and Lugano Conventions prevents this happening. This provides that, where more than one Contracting State is allocated jurisdiction under Article 16, any court other than the one first seised shall decline jurisdiction.

---

[89] See Paris Convention 1883, Article 4bis; Berne Convention 1886, Article 2(7).
[90] See Anton & Beaumont, para 7.21.
[91] By the 1978 UK/Danish/Irish Accession Convention to the Brussels Convention.
[92] See the Schlosser Report, n 80 above, at 123.
[93] Article 86 of the Community Patent Convention provides for a transitional period for the grant of a patent for one or more Contracting States. This is not a Community patent and so Article V D can apply. See the Schlosser Report, n 80 above.

(viii) Service out of the jurisdiction

In the *Napp Laboratories* [94] case, Hoffmann J held that a petition for revocation of a patent must be served personally on the respondent.[95] With a foreign defendant this means service out of the jurisdiction. There was an attempt to avoid this in *Symbol Technologies Inc v Opticon Sensors Europe BV (No 1)*,[96] where service was effected on English patent agents whose address for service appeared in the register of UK patents. Aldous J held that this address for service could not be taken as an agreement by the patentee to dispense with the requirements for personal service. Petitions had to be served personally in accordance with Order 10 of the Rules of the Supreme Court. The position is otherwise when it comes to trade marks, and an address entered in the register of trade marks has been held to be a proper address for the service, which does not have to be made personally.[97] There is no logical justification for this difference, which can only be regarded as an historical anomaly which requires an amendment to the Rules of the Supreme Court.[98]

In cases where the jurisdiction of the English courts is based on the Brussels Convention, a writ can be served out of the jurisdiction without the leave of the court by virtue of Order 11, rule 1(2)(a). This requires that either the defendant is domiciled in a Contracting State or the proceedings begun by the writ are ones to which Article 16 or 17 apply. In the *Napp Laboratories* case, the petitioners were entitled to serve a petition for revocation on the respondent in New York without the leave of the court since the jurisdiction of the English court was based on Article 16(4), which of course applies regardless of the defendant's domicile.

There is though a further requirement under Order 11, rule 1(2)(a) that 'no proceedings between the parties concerning the same cause of action are pending in the courts of any other part of the United Kingdom or of any other Convention territory'. In the *Symbol Technologies* case, Opticon issued in the High Court a petition for the revocation of two European patents. Symbol issued a summons in the Patents County Court alleging infringement of the two European patents. Symbol argued that the latter proceedings represented proceedings concerning the same cause of action as the revocation proceedings. Service could not, therefore, be effected without leave. Aldous J rejected this argument. He doubted that a dispute as to the validity of a patent could be a cause of action, but assuming that it could be, infringement and validity were two different causes of action.

---

[94] N 64 above; see, generally, Reynolds, [1993] 6 *EIPR* 218.
[95] *Re Drummond's Patent* (1889) 6 RPC 576 was not followed.   [96] [1993] RPC 211.
[97] *Johnson & Johnson's Application* [1991] RPC 1.
[98] See the *Symbol* case, n 96 above, at 214–215.

In the case of service of a writ out of the jurisdiction without leave, the writ must be indorsed with a statement that the claim is one that the court has power to determine. Hoffmann J held that this requirement of indorsement does not apply in relation to a petition. If the terms of rule 1(2)(a) are not met, service out of the jurisdiction will have to come within Order 11, rule 1(1),[99] and leave of the court for this will be necessary.[100] There is no head of rule 1(1) dealing specifically with revocation of UK patents, or indeed with intellectual property rights generally. There may be difficulty bringing the case within one of the other heads.

(ix) Allocation of jurisdiction within the United Kingdom

The Brussels and Lugano Conventions allocate jurisdiction to the courts of Contracting States. The United Kingdom is the Contracting State to the Conventions and there is, therefore, the problem of whether the courts of England, Scotland or Northern Ireland are to have jurisdiction. Section 16 of the Civil Jurisdiction and Judgments Act 1982 solves the problem by introducing a modified version of the Brussels Convention,[101] which allocates jurisdiction within the United Kingdom. The terms of the Modified Convention are, with a few exceptions, the same as those of the Brussels Convention. One important difference though is that the former does not contain any equivalent of Article 16(4). If it had contained such a provision the result would have been that in all cases where Article 16(4) of the Brussels Convention allocated jurisdiction to the United Kingdom, the Modified Convention would have allocated jurisdiction to the English courts since UK intellectual property rights are registered in England, not in Scotland or Northern Ireland. The courts in Scotland and Northern Ireland are, therefore, not precluded from trying cases concerning the registration or validity of patents, etc. It is important to note though that jurisdiction cannot be grounded on the bases of jurisdiction contained in the Modified Convention. Section 17 of the Civil Jurisdiction and Judgments Act 1982 gives effect to Schedule 5 of that Act, which expressly excludes from the provisions of the Modified Convention 'Proceedings concerned with the registration or validity of patents, trade marks, designs or other similar rights required to be deposited or registered'.[102] The result is that, in principle, an English court will apply traditional national rules on jurisdiction to determine whether it will try the case,[103] and, unlike in

---

[99] Discussed below, pp 40–42.
[100] In multi-defendant cases leave may be required for one defendant but not for another (because the terms of r 1(2)(a) are met), see SI 1996/2892.
[101] Contained in Schedule 4 of the 1982 Act. The latest version of Sch 4 is contained in SI 1993/603.
[102] Paragraph 2 of Schedule 5.
[103] See Kaye, p 990. These rules are discussed below, pp 39–45.

Scotland,[104] there is no special jurisdictional rule providing for jurisdiction (non-exclusive jurisdiction) in cases principally concerned with the registration in the United Kingdom or validity in the United Kingdom of patents, etc. The various intellectual property statutes dealing with patents, trade marks and registered designs contain provisions on what types of action various courts can try but do not as such allocate jurisdiction within the United Kingdom.[105]

(c) THE EUROPEAN PATENT CONVENTION 1973

Normally, intellectual property rights are granted separately by each country. They are only valid in and their scope is limited to the country which granted them. Some recently created systems depart from that system and are truly supranational in nature. The territorial scope of the intellectual property rights these systems provide for is wider than one country and, ideally, a single intellectual property right is granted. Issues relating to jurisdiction concerning the creation of the rights and its validity arise as usual in two different forms. First of all, during the granting procedure and, secondly, in the course of an infringement case.

Most of these systems are concerned with Community rights, and will be considered in chapter 7. The European Patent Convention 1973 is different in that it did not create a fully supranational system. It only created a single application and examination system for patents, while afterwards a bundle of national patents is granted rather than a single supranational European Patent.[106]

Nonetheless, the European Patent Convention 1973 has established its own judicial system to deal with cases arising during the application and examination process. Article 106 provides that decisions reached by the Receiving Section, the Examining Divisions, the Opposition Decisions and the Legal Division of the European Patent Office which is conducting the application and examination process can be the subject of an appeal by '[a]ny party to proceedings adversely affected by [such] a decision'.[107] This appeal is dealt with by one of the Boards of Appeal of the European Patent Office which operate as an internal court against whose decisions

---

[104] See Sch 8 para 2 (14) of the Civil Jurisdiction and Judgments Act 1982, quoted below, p 45. See also Anton, p 269; Aird and Jameson, *The Scots Dimension to Cross-Border Litigation* (1996), pp 71–72.

[105] See O'Malley and Layton, p 1110, referring to Patents Act 1977, s 72; Trade Marks Act 1938, ss 32 and 66(1); Registered Designs Act 1949, ss 20 and 45; Copyright, Designs and Patents Act 1988, ss 115, 149 and 287–289.

[106] See Convention on the Grant of European Patents (European Patent Convention) 1973, Articles 1 to 3.

[107] See Convention on the Grant of European Patents (European Patent Convention) 1973, Article 107.

no further appeal is possible. This means, for example, that the applicant whose application has been turned down can appeal to the Board of Appeal, but so also can the competitor of a successful applicant that opposed the grant of the patent in front of the Opposition Division on the basis of an earlier patent they hold and whose opposition has been rejected.

The convention creates the impression that this is the only system and that no other court has jurisdiction in this respect. How does this system interact with the provisions of the Brussels Convention and, in particular, what, if any, is the influence of the exclusive jurisdiction rule contained in Article 16(4) of the Brussels Convention? It is submitted that the system contained in the European Patent Convention should be seen as provisions in a convention to which the Contracting States to the Brussels Convention are members and which governs jurisdiction in relation to a particular issue. In such a case, Article 57(1) of the Brussels Convention results in the non-applicability of the provisions of the Brussels Convention, including Article 16(4), and leads to the application of the jurisdiction rules contained in the other convention. The reason behind this rule is that a specialist convention deals with a narrow topic, for which special jurisdiction rules that deviate from the general rules contained in the Brussels Convention might be appropriate . In our case, Article 57(1) leads to the exclusive jurisdiction of the Boards of Appeal of the European Patent Office, because this is the system provided by the specialised convention, whilst at the same time ruling out any application of Article 16(4) of the Brussels Convention.[108]

Once the examination procedure is over and a bundle of national patents has been granted the situation which is created is identical to the one described above in relation to national patents and the same solution as the one described there is applicable to jurisdiction issues. The special Convention system ceases to operate in that situation and a bundle of national patents is all that is left. This solution is particularly applicable to cases of alleged patent infringement in which the validity issue is raised by way of defence or counterclaim.

3. JURISDICTIONAL RULES OF GENERAL APPLICATION

(a) WHEN DO THE JURISDICTIONAL RULES OF GENERAL APPLICATION APPLY?

The jurisdictional rules of general application will apply in all cases of creation and validity of intellectual property rights falling outside the special

---

[108] See also the further comments on the non-applicability of Article 16(4) to similar Community Trade Mark cases. These comments apply *mutatis mutandis* also to European Patent Cases.

jurisdictional rules, ie Article 16(4) and the special jurisdictional rule in the European Patent Convention.[109] Cases in relation to creation and validity of rights fall outside Article 16(4) for two reasons. First, because of the nature of the right, for example it involves the validity of a copyright or other unregistered right. Secondly, because the right is registered outside an EC/EFTA Contracting State, for example it involves the validity of a US patent.

(b) WILL RECOURSE BE HAD TO THESE RULES?

In the situation where the jurisdictional rules of general application apply it is questionable how often recourse will be had to them. In examining this, it is important to distinguish between locally created rights and foreign created rights.

(i) Locally created rights

We are concerned here with a situation, which could well arise, where, for example, there is a dispute over whether an English copyright in a work has been created. The plaintiff wishes to bring the action in England, which looks to be an appropriate forum in the circumstances. If the defendant is foreign, recourse will have to be had to the jurisdictional rules of general application. As will be seen, there may be some difficulty, both under the EC/EFTA rules and the traditional English rules of jurisdiction, in finding a basis of jurisdiction in such a case.

(ii) Foreign created rights

We are concerned here with the situation where, for example, there is a dispute over the creation or validity of a French copyright or a US patent. Let us assume that the defendant is not English. In practical terms, the best place to bring such an action is in the State where the right was created, not in England. The intellectual property conventions have clearly put in place a system which results in the granting of national rights.[110] The scope of these rights is limited to the territory of each State and foreign applicants are given the same bundle of rights as nationals in each Contracting State. Cases concerning the creation and validity of intellectual property rights are, in such a system, logically and best brought before the courts of the State which granted them or in which they have been applied for. If the plaintiff is able to bring the action before the French or US courts, there is little to be gained by suing in England, apart from the fact that it may be

---

[109] The jurisdictional rules of general application will also apply in cases involving licensing agreements, see chapter 3 below, infringement, see chapters 5 and 6 below, and protection by complementary torts, see chapter 8.
[110] See Paris Convention 1883, Art 4bis; Berne Convention 1886, Article 2(7).

more convenient for an English plaintiff to sue in his home State. Moreover, it is likely that an English judgment would not be recognised in France or the United States, or any other country, on public policy grounds. The creation of intellectual property rights as exclusive economic rights, or monopoly rights should one prefer that cruder expression, clearly touches on the rules regulating competition in the market. Public policy lurks under the surface in such cases. The upshot of all of this is that English courts are unlikely to be troubled by actions involving the creation or validity of foreign rights, subject to one exception, which is examined below.

If the English courts were to be faced with such cases, as will be seen, the jurisdiction rules of general application are such that there may be difficulty in finding a basis of jurisdiction and, under the traditional English rules, there is a subject matter limitation on jurisdiction in relation to foreign rights.

The one exceptional situation where an English court could be faced with an action involving the validity of a foreign right is where there is a claim for infringement during the course of which the defendant raises the issue of the validity of that right. The question then, inevitably, arises of whether the English court has jurisdiction in relation to the issue of validity. Recourse will have to be had to the rules of general application to determine this.[111]

(c) THE EC/EFTA RULES

(i) When do the EC/EFTA rules apply?

The question of when the Brussels and Lugano Conventions apply has already been examined.[112] A key factor is whether the defendant is domiciled in a Contracting State. Thus a dispute over the validity of a UK copyright, where the defendant is French, falls to be dealt with by the rules of general application in the Brussels Convention (Article 16(4) does not apply). There are though two particular problems in relation to the application of these Conventions in the context of creation and validity cases.

(a) *A civil and commercial matter*

The Conventions apply in civil and commercial matters.[113] Is, for example, an appeal against a decision of the Registrar not to grant a patent such a

---

[111] In the situation where validity is raised in the context of infringement the position is complex. It is arguable that the court trying the infringement issue should, in certain circumstances, be able to also try the issue of validity even though it has no jurisdiction in relation to that issue, see below, pp 208–209.

[112] See above, pp 2–3.   [113] Article 1 of the conventions.

matter? Doubts could be raised in the light of the decision of the Court of Justice in *LTU* v *Eurocontrol*,[114] where it was held that a Community meaning had to be given to this concept and that it did not apply to the situation where a public authority was acting in the exercise of its powers. The grant of a patent involves the intervention of the Patent Office, which could be described as a public authority. Nonetheless, such doubts are unfounded because Article 16(4) makes it clear that the issue of registration or validity of a patent, etc comes within the scope of the Convention.

(b) *Patents registered outside the EC/EFTA States*

It has been suggested that cases involving patents registered outside the EC Contracting States are not only excluded from Article 16(4) of the Brussels Convention but also from the operation of the other bases of jurisdiction in that Convention.[115] The Brussels Convention is said to be irrelevant and national bases of jurisdiction will apply instead. This extraordinary view is said to be justified by commonsense and by analogy with Article 4 of the Convention. This provision states that national rules of jurisdiction apply in relation to defendants domiciled outside the EC Contracting State (subject to Article 16). If it is followed and the traditional English rules on jurisdiction are applied, what would doubtless happen is that the English courts, even though they might have jurisdiction over the defendant, a writ having been served on the defendant, would decline to try the case on the ground of *forum non conveniens*,[116] ie that the clearly appropriate forum was the foreign State where the patent is registered.

There are four strong objections that can be made to this suggestion. The first is that it ignores the wording of the Brussels Convention. Article 2 is perfectly clear: 'persons domiciled in a Contracting State shall, whatever their nationality, be sued in the courts of that State'. The Convention goes on to provide that persons domiciled in a Contracting State can, in certain circumstances, be sued in the courts of some other Contracting State. However, Article 3 provides this can only be done by virtue of the bases set out in Sections 2 to 6 (Articles 5–18). No exception to these rules is made for patents registered outside the EC Contracting States. Any attempt to use traditional English bases of jurisdiction against a defendant domiciled in an EC Contracting State in a case involving a patent registered outside the EC would be a breach of Article 3. Not to allow a plaintiff to base jurisdiction on Article 2 would also be a breach of that provision, likewise not

[114] Case 29/76 [1976] ECR 1541.
[115] Tritton and Tritton, n 44 above, at 351. This suggestion, although made in relation to the Brussels Convention, would, if correct, apply equally to the Lugano Convention.
[116] See below, pp 42–43, 267–274.

to allow a plaintiff to rely on any of the other bases of jurisdiction contained in the convention would be a breach of the Article relied upon.

The second is that if the convention were to be interpreted to allow for such an exception, the matter would not end there. The same argument could be made in relation to proceedings which have as their object rights *in rem* in immovable property situated outside an EC/EFTA Contracting State. Yet it has never been suggested that there is any such exception. Indeed, writers assume that the Brussels or Lugano Convention, albeit not Article 16(1)(a) thereof, will apply.[117]

Thirdly, the reasoning used to justify the suggestion that the Brussels Convention is irrelevant in cases involving, say, a US patent will not apply in cases where Article 16(4) does not operate for some other reason, such as the fact that the issue in the case does not concern registration or validity. The Brussels Convention will still be relevant. But this means distinguishing between different situations where Article 16(4) does not apply, which is a rather curious thing to do.

Fourthly, if the real object of the exercise is to enable the English courts to refuse to try cases involving patents registered outside the EC Contracting States, this can be achieved without taking the heretical line that there is no jurisdiction under the Brussels Convention. As will be seen later, an English court which has jurisdiction under Article 2 of the Brussels Convention can, nonetheless, in certain circumstances decline jurisdiction on the ground of forum non conveniens.[118]

(ii) **Bases of jurisdiction**

The bases of jurisdiction under the Brussels and Lugano Conventions are best discussed in detail in the contexts of licensing agreements and infringement of intellectual property rights.[119] Disputes as to jurisdiction are common in these contexts, there are no special rules as to jurisdiction and recourse, therefore, has to be made to the jurisdictional rules of general application contained in the conventions, and there is plenty of case law authority. In contrast, jurisdictional disputes in relation to creation and validity will often come within the special rule contained in Article 16(4), cases falling outside this rule will be relatively rare, and there is a dearth of authority on the operation of the bases of jurisdiction of general application in the context of creation and validity. At this stage, it is sufficient to mention briefly those bases of jurisdiction that might apply in cases of creation and validity of intellectual property rights falling outside the special jurisdictional rules dealing with these issues.

---

[117] See Hartley, p 66; Cheshire and North, *Private International Law* 11 ed 1987, p 328.
[118] See below, p 38.   [119] See below, chapters 3 and 5.

(a) ARTICLE 2

Article 2 is entitled general jurisdiction and states that:

persons domiciled in a Contracting State shall, whatever their nationality, be sued in the courts of that State.

As a simple example, a Swedish court has taken jurisdiction under Article 2 of the Lugano Convention in an action brought by a Swedish company to challenge a Swedish employee's attempt to lodge an application for a patent in another country.[120]

(b) *Articles 5 and 6*

In certain circumstances, trial is permitted in the courts of a Contracting State other than the one in which the defendant is domiciled. This is what is known as 'special jurisdiction' and is dealt with in Articles 5 and 6 of the conventions. Article 5 sets out seven different situations where special jurisdiction is allowed, and Article 6 sets out five such situations. If Article 5 or 6 applies, the plaintiff is given a choice of fora. He can sue, by virtue of Article 2, in the Contracting State where the defendant is domiciled or in some other Contracting State or States, by virtue of Articles 5 and 6. However, there is no head of Article 5 or 6 dealing specifically with creation or validity of intellectual property rights. Moreover, many of the heads of Articles 5 and 6 are obviously irrelevant in such cases. The ones that may be relevant are as follows.

(i) *Article 5(1)*

This is concerned with matters relating to a contract and, in these matters, provides for jurisdiction 'in the courts for the place of performance of the obligation in question'. It is not easy to envisage circumstances where the issue of creation or validity of an intellectual property right will involve a matter relating to a contract. Of course, a contractual dispute can arise in the context of the creation of a patent or other registrable right. An example is where a patent agent sues for his fees in relation to work involved in the creation of the right.[121] But such a case does not raise the issue of creation or validity of the right, and should be regarded as a straightforward contractual dispute, to which Article 5(1) would, naturally, apply.[122]

[120] Hogsta Domstolen (SO 48), 23 February 1994 [1994] *Nytt Juridiskt Arkiv* 81. Presumably, Article 16(4) did not apply because there was a dispute over the ownership of the patent. The other State may also not have been a Contracting State to the Lugano Convention.
[121] See Landgericht Stuttgart, Judgment of 14 October 1975, Case No 3 O 112/75; D Series I-6-B1. Jurisdiction was taken under Article 6(1).
[122] See the discussion of jurisdiction in relation to contracts for the exploitation of intellectual property rights, below, pp 77–90, for details of how this provision operates.

The issue of creation of the right does not depend on the contractual relationship between the parties, in the way that the issue of ownership of a right can do so.[123]

(ii) *Article 5(5)*

This states that a defendant domiciled in one Contracting State may be sued in another Contracting State 'as regards a dispute arising out of the operations of a branch, agency or other establishment, in the courts for the place in which the branch, agency or other establishment is situated'.

(iii) *Article 6*

Article 6(1) deals with multi-defendant cases and provides that a person domiciled in a Contracting State may also be sued 'where he is one of a number of defendants, in the courts for the place where any one of them is domiciled'. Article 6(3) deals with counterclaims and provides for jurisdiction 'on a counterclaim arising from the same contract or facts on which the original claim was based, in the court in which the original claim is pending'.

(c) Does Article 16(1) apply?

Article 16(1)(a) provides that 'in proceedings which have as their object rights *in rem* in immovable property or tenancies of immovable property, the courts of the Contracting State in which the property is situated' shall have exclusive jurisdiction, regardless of domicile. At first sight, this provision would appear to be totally irrelevant in the present context. However, it has been said that if copyright is treated as an immovable then Article 16(1) will apply.[124] This raises two questions. First, is copyright an immovable for the purposes of the Brussels and Lugano Conventions? Secondly, even if it is, do cases raising the issue of creation of an intellectual property right have as their object rights *in rem* in this immovable property?

Turning to the first question, the concept of 'immovable property' should be given an independent Community meaning.[125] In determining this definition, it is necessary to look at the objectives and scheme of the conventions and at 'the general principles which stem from the corpus of the national legal systems'.[126] The scheme of the conventions is that jurisdiction in respect of the creation of patents and other registrable rights will

---

[123] See below, pp 63–64.
[124] Arnold, [1990] 7 *EIPR* 254 at 260. See also Jooris, [1996] 3 *EIPR* 127, 137–139.
[125] See, generally, Cheshire and North, pp 282–283, and more specifically in relation to immovable property O'Malley and Layton, p 525.
[126] Case 29/76 *LTU v Eurocontrol* [1976] ECR 1541.

normally come within Article 16(4). If copyrights are classified as immovable property so, in principle, must be patents and other registrable rights. As a matter of classification of property into movables and immovables, there is no justification for differentiating between these different types of intellectual property rights. Yet patents and other registrable rights are designed to come within Article 16(4). There is then a clash between Articles 16(4) and 16(1). The intention of the drafters of the Brussels Convention must have been that patents and other registrable rights should be regarded as falling outside Article 16(1), in which case copyright should also be so regarded. When it comes to the corpus of national legal systems, English law classifies copyright as an intangible movable.[127] A leading continental lawyer has described intellectual property rights as intangible products of the mind, and, because they have no corporeal qualities, different from immovable property.[128] Moreover, it is clear from the Jenard and Schlosser Reports that the only thing envisaged by the expression 'immovable property' is land,[129] and there is no suggestion in any of the decisions of the Court of Justice in relation to Article 16(1) that anything more than this is intended. This is borne out by the reference in Article 16(1)(a) to tenancies of immovable property. Finally, the nature of intellectual property rights is very different from land.[130] Indeed, as will be seen later on in this book, the two cannot even be regarded as being analogous.[131] This suggests that it would be wrong to adopt the same immovable classification for intellectual property rights as is adopted for land.

Turning to the second question, even if, contrary to what has been argued above, it is accepted that copyright is immovable property, it is by no means clear that a case of, for example, validity of a copyright would have as its object rights *in rem* in that immovable property. Do the proceedings have as their object a right which is enforceable against the whole world, in which case the requirement is met, or merely a right which is enforceable against a particular person, in which case it is not? It is easy enough to answer this question where the proceedings have as their object the rectification of a register: the requirement is met. But, of course, copyrights are not registered and so the identification of the proceedings as ones which have as their object a right *in rem* is much more difficult. If the issue of validity arises in the context of a defence to an infringement action this requirement would not appear to be met.

---

[127] Dicey and Morris, pp 979–980; Jooris, n 124 above, at 138; below, pp 487–494.
[128] K Troller, *International Encyclopaedia of Comparative Law* Vol III, chapter 22 at p 3, who also suggests that they are different from movable property for this reason.
[129] The Jenard Report, n 42 above, at p 35; the Schlosser Report, n 80 above, at pp 121–122; O'Malley and Layton, p 525.
[130] See below, p 496.
[131] See below, p 287.

(d) Article 17

This provision[132] is concerned with the situation where the parties 'have agreed that a court or the courts of a Contracting State are to have jurisdiction to settle any disputes which have arisen or which may arise in connection with a particular legal relationship'. If one or more of the parties is domiciled in a Contracting State, the effect of such an agreement is to give exclusive jurisdiction to the court or courts of the Contracting State agreed upon. There is unlikely to be such an agreement between the parties in cases where the dispute is over the creation of intellectual property rights.[133]

(e) Article 18

This provides that '... a court of a Contracting State before whom a defendant enters an appearance shall have jurisdiction'. It does not appear to involve any special difficulties in cases concerning the creation or validity of intellectual property rights.

(iii) Declining jurisdiction

(a) Under the Brussels and Lugano Conventions

Article 21 deals with the problem of *lis pendens*. This is defined in Article 21 as 'Where proceedings involving the same cause of action and between the same parties are brought in the courts of different Contracting States'. In this situation, 'any court other than the court first seised shall of its own motion stay its proceedings until such time as the jurisdiction of the court first seised is established'. Where the jurisdiction of the court first seised is established, 'any court other than the court first seised shall decline jurisdiction in favour of that court'. Although this is a mechanical (as opposed to discretionary) rule, it is not without its problems.[134]

One requirement that could cause particular problems in the present context is that the proceedings are brought before the courts of different Contracting States. Is this requirement met in the situation where a petition for revocation is brought before the English courts and a notice of opposition is lodged before the European Patent Office, seeking revocation of the patent on the ground of invalidity? This raises the question of whether an action brought before the European Patent Office is one

---

[132] It is examined in more detail below, p 94.
[133] Compare the position in relation to ownership of an invention, below, pp 64–65.
[134] See, generally, Cheshire and North, pp 327–329; Article 21 is discussed more fully in the context of infringement, see below, pp 177–182.

brought before the 'courts' of a Contracting State. In other words, is the European Patent Office a 'court' for the purposes of Article 21, or does this refer merely to national courts? The meaning of 'courts' should be the same under the Brussels and Lugano Conventions, regardless of the provision involved.

Another requirement that could cause difficulties under Article 21 is that the cause of action is the same in both sets of proceedings. This requirement would obviously be met in the situation where both sets of proceedings are for revocation on the ground of invalidity. But what if there are proceedings in England for infringement, to which a defence of invalidity is raised, and the other set of proceedings is brought before the European Patent Office for revocation of the patent on the same ground of invalidity?[135] If the English court is first seised, then it is submitted that the European Patent Office should stay its proceedings under Article 21 (this is assuming that it is a 'court' for the present purposes and that it applies the Brussels Convention). This is what would happen in the analogous situation where, in multi-party litigation, the parties in both sets of proceedings are not precisely the same.[136] On the other hand, again applying the same analogy, if the European Patent Office is first seised, it is submitted that the English court is not precluded under Article 21 from trying the infringement issue, but it would have to stay its proceedings in relation to the invalidity defence. Whatever Article 21 says, it would then be impracticable to try the infringement issue until the European Patent Office had ruled on the validity of the patent. Is the cause of action the same where there are parallel actions concerning, for example, the validity of the UK copyright and the French copyright in a work? These are different national rights and the traditional view is that the cause of action is not the same.

Article 22 deals with the situation where the cause of action in the two sets of proceedings is not the same but is related. Related actions are ones not falling within the definition of *lis pendens* but which 'are so closely connected that it is expedient to hear and determine them together to avoid the risk of irreconcilable judgments resulting from separate proceedings'.[137] Any court other than the court first seised may, rather than must, while the actions are pending at first instance, stay its proceedings. This gives a discretion to stay proceedings.[138]

---

[135] See the facts of *Pall Corp* v *Commercial Hydraulics (Bedford) Ltd and Others* [1988] FSR 274, discussed below, pp 272–273.
[136] See the decision of the Court of Justice in Case C-406/92 *The Maciej Rataj* [1994] ECR I-5439.
[137] Article 22(3), discussed below, pp 183–185.
[138] For the criteria for the exercise of the discretion, see below, chapter 5 p 185.

(b) Using the doctrine of forum non conveniens

The Brussels and Lugano Conventions contain no general discretionary power to decline jurisdiction on the basis of *forum non conveniens* (there is some other available forum, having competent jurisdiction, which is the appropriate forum for trial of the action, ie in which the case may be tried more suitably for the interests of all the parties and the ends of justice[139]). Nonetheless, the Court of Appeal in *Re Harrods (Buenos Aires) Ltd*[140] held that an English court had the power to stay its own proceedings on this basis in the situation where the alternative forum for trial was a non-Contracting State to the Brussels Convention, in the instant case Argentina. It was accepted though that there was no such power where the alternative forum was a Contracting State.

The effect of the decision in *Re Harrods* in creation cases is that if, for example, a Japanese plaintiff were to sue an English domiciled defendant in England in respect of the creation of a Japanese patent, the English court would have power to stay the English proceedings on the ground of *forum non conveniens*, even though the English court's jurisdiction is based on Article 2 of the Brussels Convention. An English court, applying that doctrine to such facts, may well conclude that the clearly appropriate forum for trial is Japan, and therefore grant a stay of the English proceedings.[141] Ascertaining whether there is a clearly more appropriate forum abroad involves looking at connecting factors 'and these will include not only factors affecting convenience or expense (such as availability of witnesses), but also other factors such as the law governing the relevant transaction . . ., and the place where the parties respectively reside or carry on business'.[142] In a case involving the creation of an intellectual property right, the single most important connecting factor should be regarded as that of where the right has been created or is sought to be created. In the above example this is Japan. Furthermore, Japanese law would govern the issue of creation.[143] Finally, albeit of less importance than the other two factors, the plaintiff is Japanese.

(iv) A subject matter limitation on jurisdiction

Under the Brussels and Lugano Conventions, there is no direct subject matter limitation on jurisdiction in cases involving the issue of creation of foreign intellectual property rights. However, it should be remembered

---

[139] See *Spiliada Maritime Corpn* v *Cansulex Ltd* [1987] AC 460 at 476 (per Lord Goff); discussed below, pp 267–272. See also *Connelly* v *RTZ Corpn plc* [1997] 3 WLR 373.
[140] [1992] Ch 72.
[141] The doctrine of *forum non conveniens* is examined in more detail in the context of infringement below, pp 267–274.
[142] *Spiliada Maritime Corpn* v *Cansulex Ltd* [1987] AC 460 at 478.
[143] See below, pp 517–522.

that when Article 16(4) operates it not only gives the courts of one Contracting State jurisdiction, but also, because this is exclusive jurisdiction, it deprives the courts of other Contracting States of jurisdiction. To this extent, there can be said to be a subject matter limitation on jurisdiction, albeit in an indirect form, in proceedings concerned with the registration or validity of patents, etc, in respect of patents, etc deposited or registered, or applied for, in another Contracting State. Thus, an English applicant cannot sue in England the Swiss Patent Office after the Swiss Registrar has turned down the defendant's application for a Swiss patent. The Swiss courts have exclusive jurisdiction in relation to the registration of the patent by virtue of Article 16(4). Under the traditional English rules, there is a well known subject matter limitation on jurisdiction in relation to the validity or infringement of foreign intellectual property rights.[144] The effect of this is essentially the same as Article 16(4). It differs though in that it is a direct limitation on jurisdiction. This common law limitation on jurisdiction cannot be applied in Brussels and Lugano Convention cases.[145]

(d) THE TRADITIONAL RULES

(i) When do the traditional rules apply?

The traditional rules on jurisdiction apply in creation and validity cases in the situation where neither the special jurisdictional rules nor the rules of general application contained in the Brussels and Lugano Conventions apply.[146] Such cases will be relatively rare because of the width of the scope of the Brussels and Lugano Conventions, and, in particular, of Article 16(4). An example of such a case would be where an English plaintiff wishes to bring an action in England against a New York defendant for a declaration that the latter has no US copyright. Another example would be where an English petitioner petitions in England for revocation of a Canadian patent against an Ontario respondent on the ground of invalidity. As has been seen, in such cases the plaintiff would be better off bringing the action in the State in which the right was created. Moreover, if trial is sought in England when it comes to applying the traditional rules there may be problems in finding a basis of jurisdiction and, even more fatal, there is the subject matter limitation on jurisdiction in respect of actions concerning foreign intellectual property rights. This limitation is going to

---

[144] See below, pp 283–299.
[145] See *Pearce v Ove Arup Partnership Ltd and Others* [1997] 2 WLR 779; *Coin Controls Ltd v Suzo International (UK) Ltd and Others* [1997] 3 All ER 45; *Fort Dodge Animal Health Ltd and Others v Akzo Nobel NV and Another* [1998] FSR 222; below, pp 190–196. See also *Boston Scientific Ltd and Others v Cordis Corpn*, Ch and CA (1997) Unreported as yet.
[146] See above, pp 11–28, 30–32.

reduce even further the number of creation and validity actions brought in England under the traditional rules. An example of an action that could be brought in England under the traditional rules would be where there is a dispute between two US companies in relation to the creation or validity of a UK copyright. The Brussels and Lugano Conventions, including Article 16(4), would not apply,[147] neither would the subject matter limitation on jurisdiction under the traditional rules in respect of actions concerning foreign intellectual property rights.

(ii) Bases of jurisdiction

The traditional bases of jurisdiction are best discussed in detail in the contexts of licensing agreements and infringement, for the same reasons, given above,[148] as the EC/EFTA bases of jurisdiction are best discussed in these contexts.

(a) *Service of a writ within the jurisdiction*

The normal rules on service of writs within the jurisdiction will operate.[149] This basis of jurisdiction is unlikely to be of any use in creation cases. If, for example, an English applicant wishes to sue in England the Japanese Patent Office after the Japanese Registrar has turned down the defendant's application for a Japanese patent, he will be unable to serve a writ within the jurisdiction. An overseas intellectual property office is not present within the jurisdiction. Neither will it agree to being served within the jurisdiction. It is doubtful whether its national intellectual property law gives it authority to agree to submit itself to the jurisdiction of a foreign court. If the defendant is domiciled in England, the EC/EFTA rules will apply; the issue of creation and validity of rights is a civil and commercial matter and thus within the scope of the Brussels and Lugano Conventions.[150]

(b) *Service of a writ out of the jurisdiction*

(i) *The heads of Order 11, rule 1(1)*

The onus is on the plaintiff to establish a good arguable case that one of the heads of rule 1(1) is satisfied.[151] It is to be noted that, although Order 11, rule 1(1) sets out 21 alternative heads, going from 1(1)(a) to 1(1)(u), there is no head dealing specifically with the issue of creation and validity of intellectual property rights, or indeed with any other issue in relation to

---

[147] Neither would the special jurisdictional rule in the European Patent Convention 1973.
[148] At p 32.   [149] See Cheshire and North, pp 183–190; below, pp 241–243.
[150] See above, pp 30–31.
[151] *Seaconsar Far East Ltd v Bank Markazi Jomhouri Islami Iran* [1994] 1 AC 438.

such rights. This contrasts markedly with the Brussels and Lugano Conventions, which, of course, have Article 16(4). The absence of a special head in rule 1(1) to deal with intellectual property does not matter as much in infringement cases since they can be brought within the tort head,[152] or in cases involving licensing agreements, since they can be brought within one of the contract heads.[153] But it can cause much more of a problem where the cause of action concerns the creation and validity of intellectual property rights.

(ii) *A serious issue to be tried*

The plaintiff has to establish that there is a serious issue to be tried on the merits.[154] This requirement will be discussed in more detail in relation to infringement.[155] It does not appear to raise any particular problems in relation to creation and validity of intellectual property rights.

(iii) *The exercise of the discretion*

Order 11, rule 1(1) is a discretionary form of jurisdiction. The courts may, rather than must, allow service of a writ out of the jurisdiction. This requirement will be examined in detail in infringement cases.[156] However, it does need to be briefly discussed in the present context because it represents an obstacle to service out of the jurisdiction that is going to be particularly difficult to surmount in creation and validity cases.

The criterion for the exercise of the Order 11 rule 1(1) discretion is that of *forum conveniens*. The burden of proof is on the plaintiff to show that England is the appropriate forum for trial, and that this is clearly so.[157] When ascertaining whether this is so the same criteria will be applied as in declining jurisdiction on the basis of *forum non conveniens*.[158] As has already been seen,[159] the single most important connecting factor in a creation case should be that of where the right has been created; another important factor will be that of the applicable law.

If you apply these criteria to typical cases of creation and validity under the traditional English rules it is important to distinguish between two different scenarios. The first scenario involves an intellectual property right from abroad (outside the EC/EFTA Contracting States – otherwise Article 16(4) of the Brussels and Lugano Conventions would apply where it is a registered right). The defendant will not be domiciled in an EC/EFTA Contracting State, otherwise Article 2, 5 or 6 of the Brussels Convention,

---

[152] Order 11, rule 1(1)(f); see below, pp 244–253.
[153] Order 11, rule 1(1)(d) and (e); see below, pp 97–98.
[154] The *Seaconsar* case, n 151 above.   [155] See below, pp 256–258.
[156] See below, pp 259–266.
[157] *Spiliada Maritime Corpn v Cansulex Ltd* [1987] AC 460 at 481.
[158] See above, p 38, and in more detail below, pp 267–274.   [159] See above, p 38.

rather than the traditional English rules, would apply. The fact that it is a foreign intellectual property right means that it is unlikely that the plaintiff would want to bring the action in England in the first place. Moreover, there is the subject matter limitation on jurisdiction in relation to foreign intellectual property rights under the traditional English rules. However, if it were to come before the English courts, and it is suggested below[160] that the subject matter limitation on jurisdiction under the traditional rules should be abolished, it is going to be very difficult for the plaintiff to establish that England is the clearly appropriate forum. Not only is it a foreign right and a foreign defendant, but also the applicable law will be that of the foreign State where the right was created.

The second scenario is where the English courts are faced, under the traditional English rules, with the issue of creation or validity of a UK intellectual property right. If the right in question is a copyright, Article 16(4) will not apply, and, if the defendant is domiciled outside the EC/EFTA Contracting States, neither will most other bases of jurisdiction in the Brussels and Lugano Conventions.[161] In this situation, where it is a UK right and English law applies in relation to it, these will be strong factors indicating that England is the clearly appropriate forum. Nonetheless, even in this situation a court may decide, looking at the circumstances as a whole, that the appropriate forum is abroad.[162]

(iii) Declining jurisdiction

Even though an English court has jurisdiction to try an action, a writ having been served on the defendant under the above rules, it has a discretion to stay the action on the basis of *forum non conveniens*. This doctrine will be examined in more detail in relation to infringement actions.[163] In outline though, the burden of proof is on the defendant to show that there is another available forum which is clearly or distinctly more appropriate than the English forum.[164] If this is shown, the court will move on to the second stage, which is to consider the requirements of justice.[165] As has already been seen,[166] ascertaining whether there is a clearly more appropriate forum for trial abroad involves looking at connecting factors. The same considerations will apply as in cases of *forum conveniens*, but with the difference that now the burden of proof is on the defendant. The single most important connecting factor should be regarded as being that of where the right is created; another important factor will be that of the applicable law. If the sole or principal issue in a case is that of validity or

---

[160] At pp 283–299, 314–315.
[161] However, Article 17 could apply.
[162] See *GAF Corp* v *Amchem Products Inc* [1975] 1 Lloyd's Rep 601; a case concerned with the issue of ownership, discussed below, p 67.
[163] See below, pp 267–274.
[164] The *Spiliada* case, n 157 above, at 474.
[165] See Cheshire and North, pp 226–230.
[166] See above, p 38.

creation of a foreign right the natural forum must be regarded as being the State where the right was created abroad. It is hard to envisage circumstances where the English court would not decline jurisdiction.[167]

(iv) Subject matter limitations on jurisdiction

(a) Foreign rights

Under the traditional English rules, there is the well known subject matter limitation on jurisdiction in relation to foreign intellectual property rights. Most of the authorities on this are cases involving the infringement of such rights, and these cases and the limitation generally are discussed in detail in chapter 6 on infringement. However, this limitation is not confined to proceedings for infringement. The leading modern authority is *Tyburn Productions Ltd v Conan Doyle*.[168] The plaintiff sought a declaration from the English courts that the defendant had no rights under the copyright, unfair competition and trade mark laws of the United States to entitle her to prevent distribution of a film, and an injunction preventing the defendant from so asserting. Vinelott J refused these claims. He held that an English court lacks jurisdiction to adjudicate in actions raising questions as to the validity or infringement of patent rights, copyrights, rights of trade mark and other intellectual property rights. This case was cited by counsel in *Apple Corps Ltd v Apple Computer Inc*[169] as authority for the proposition that the courts of one country will not, as a general rule, pronounce upon the validity of intellectual property rights granted by another country. This statement was, seemingly, approved by Ferris J.

Undeniably, there is a subject matter limitation on jurisdiction where the issue in a case concerns the validity of foreign intellectual property rights. What if the issue concerns some aspect, not of validity but of the creation of such rights? An example would be where there is an issue concerning the registration of rights abroad (outside an EC/EFTA Contracting State).[170] Does the limitation still apply? The rationale of the limitation,[171] which in the English cases is based on an analogy with foreign land and a distinction between local and transitory actions,[172] would suggest that it should do so. The High Court of Australia have justified the limitation on the different basis of what is essentially the Act of State doctrine.[173]

---

[167] Compare the position where the action is for infringement of a foreign right, below pp 294–295. For the situation where validity arises in the context of infringement see below, pp 307–312.
[168] [1991] Ch 75, discussed more fully below, pp 284–290.   [169] [1992] FSR 431, 470.
[170] Article 16(4) of the Brussels and Lugano Conventions will apply in proceedings concerned with the registration of patents, etc registered in EC/EFTA States.
[171] See below, pp 287–288.
[172] There was also a reluctance to grant negative declarations.
[173] *Potter v The Broken Hill Pty Co Ltd* (1906) 3 CLR 479.

O'Connor J said that 'the grant of a foreign patent is a document evidencing an act of the foreign State'.[174] If it is the grant of the patent that is so significant, it must follow that the limitation will apply whenever this is in issue. Moreover, one policy justification that can be given for the limitation, in terms of it being convenient that the State in which the right was created should decide on its validity, is equally applicable to issues in relation to creation.[175]

There is also case law authority in favour of the proposition that the limitation applies to creation cases. That this is so is indicated by comments made by Ferris J in *Apple Corps Ltd* v *Apple Computer Inc*,[176] where he said that the English court has no power 'to pronounce for or against a challenge to any such mark [he was referring to an Australian or German mark] under the relevant law in any way which operates *in rem*'.[177] When he refers to challenging the mark, this comment is made in the context of preceding remarks about cancellation of a mark on grounds of non-use and of widening the scope of a mark. More generally, *Rey* v *Lecouturier*[178] suggests that the limitation is not confined to the issues of validity and infringement, but also extends to deny the English courts' jurisdiction to determine what ought to be the entry in the register of trademarks abroad where this depended on the ownership of the mark.

It is noticeable that this limitation on jurisdiction is wider in a number of respects than the indirect limitation on jurisdiction contained in Article 16(4) of the Brussels and Lugano Conventions. First, it is not confined to patents and other registrable rights, it also applies to copyrights. Secondly, it applies not just to the issues of validity and registration of rights but also to infringement and, seemingly, to the issue of who owns the right.

It is to be hoped that the English courts will take the first opportunity available to them to get rid of this unwarranted subject matter limitation on their jurisdiction. It is argued, later on,[179] that this limitation is wrong in principle and that there are strong policy reasons against it. Admittedly, there are reasons why an English court should be loathe to try a case relating to the creation or validity of foreign intellectual property rights,[180] but they can, and no doubt would, avoid doing so by the use of the flexible doctrine of *forum non conveniens*. This is a much better way of dealing with the problem than by having a blanket exclusion of all actions relating to the creation and validity of foreign intellectual property rights.[181]

One effect of this limitation on jurisdiction is that, where there are parallel actions, for example, in the United Kingdom and the United States between the same parties concerning, respectively, the validity of the UK

---

[174] *Potter* v *The Broken Hill Pty Co Ltd* (1906) 3 CLR 479 at 514.
[175] See below in relation to infringement, p 290.   [176] N 169 above.
[177] *Ibid*, at 470.   [178] [1908] 2 Ch 715; discussed below, pp 69–70.
[179] See below, pp 283–299.   [180] See below, pp 290–291.   [181] See below, pp 293–294.

and US copyright in a work, there is no question of the English court being able to try the issue of the validity of the US copyright, even though it has jurisdiction over the person of the defendant.

(b) State immunity

The State Immunity Act 1978 provides that a foreign State is immune from the jurisdiction of the English courts, except as provided for in the Act. One important exception is contained in Section 3 which provides that a foreign State is not immune as respects any proceedings relating to a commercial transaction entered into by that State. Consistently with this, Section 7 of the Act goes on to provide that:

A State is not immune as respects proceedings relating to –
  (a) any patent, trade mark, design or plant breeders' rights belonging to the State and registered or protected in the United Kingdom or for which the State has applied in the United Kingdom.

(v) Criticism of the traditional English rules

The basic criticism of the traditional English rules is that, in cases of creation and validity, it is unjustifiably difficult to obtain jurisdiction in England. First, there is the unwarranted subject matter limitation on jurisdiction in relation to cases concerning the validity or infringement of foreign intellectual property rights. Secondly, there is no special rule which would give the English courts jurisdiction on the basis that the case concerns the registration or validity of an English right. The basis of jurisdiction is the normal one that a writ has been served on the defendant, and where this is a foreign defendant this may be difficult. This, of course, contrasts with the position under the Brussels and Lugano Conventions. More importantly, it also contrasts with the position under many national rules of jurisdiction. Both Swiss[182] and Spanish[183] national rules contain such a provision basing jurisdiction on local intellectual property rights. Coming closer to home, so do the Scottish national rules on jurisdiction, ie the traditional Scottish rules. These contain a provision stating that a person may be sued 'in proceedings principally concerned with the registration in the United Kingdom or the validity in the United Kingdom of patents, trade marks, designs or other similar rights required to be deposited or registered, in the Court of Session.'[184]

---

[182] See Article 109(1) of the Swiss Private International Law Statute of 1987, discussed below, pp 46–48.
[183] Article 22.1 of the Basic Law on jurisdiction; *Menadiona SA v Pfizer Inc* Supreme Court (First Chamber) 28 January 1994 Aranzadi 572, p 727; [1994] 8 *EIPR* D-204, 205.
[184] Civil Jurisdiction and Judgments Act 1982, Sch 8, para 2(14).

V
AN ALTERNATIVE SOLUTION: ARTICLE 109 SWISS PIL STATUTE

Switzerland is a Contracting State to the Lugano Convention and will apply the terms of that convention in all cases coming within its scope. In cases coming outside that convention, Switzerland will apply its traditional rules on jurisdiction as set out in the Swiss private international law statute of 1987. This has a special rule dealing with jurisdiction in intellectual property cases. Article 109(1) states that:

> Lawsuits on intellectual property rights are subject to the jurisdiction of the Swiss courts at defendant's domicile or, if there is none, at the place where protection is sought; lawsuits on the validity or the registration of intellectual property rights abroad are excepted.

It is possible to analyse this rule in terms of its scope, the bases of jurisdiction, and a subject matter limitation on jurisdiction. This will allow a comparison to be made with the rules on jurisdiction in the Brussels and Lugano Conventions.

1. Scope of the Provision

Article 109 applies to 'lawsuits on intellectual property rights'. This gives an exceptionally wide scope to Article 109. This can be seen in two respects. First, it covers 'lawsuits on' intellectual property rights, without any restriction on the issue in dispute. It is clearly intended to cover lawsuits on the validity or registration of intellectual property rights.[185] But, presumably, it would cover a lawsuit in respect of the ownership of intellectual property rights, not, as Article 16(4) of the Brussels and Lugano Conventions does, just those on validity or registration. Secondly, it applies to 'intellectual property rights'. Again, unlike Article 16(4), there is no restriction as to the type of right involved. Accordingly, it would cover not just registrable rights, such as patents, but also unregistrable rights, such as copyrights.

2. Bases of Jurisdiction

Article 109(1) provides that the Swiss courts have jurisdiction if one of two alternative bases of jurisdiction is satisfied. The first is that the defendant

---

[185] See the subject matter limitation on jurisdiction, discussed below p 47, and Article 109(3).

is domiciled in Switzerland. The second, which applies in the situation where the defendant is not so domiciled, is that Switzerland is the place where protection is sought.

The first basis of jurisdiction is, of course, the same as that contained in Article 2 of the Brussels and Lugano Conventions. The second basis of jurisdiction means that Switzerland would have jurisdiction in cases where there is, for example, a Swiss trade mark or copyright.[186] Article 16(4) of the Brussels and Lugano Conventions makes a similar allocation of jurisdiction, but Article 109(1) is wider in the two respects mentioned above under scope. This second basis of jurisdiction should be read in conjunction with Article 110, which deals with the applicable law. Paragraph 1 of this Article states that 'Rights in intellectual property are governed by the law of the country for which protection of those rights is sought'. It is convenient that jurisdiction should be allocated to Switzerland in circumstances where it will apply its own law.

3. A SUBJECT MATTER LIMITATION ON JURISDICTION

The last part of Article 109(1) contains an express limitation on the jurisdiction of the Swiss courts. They have no jurisdiction in lawsuits on the validity or the registration of intellectual property rights abroad. This is to the same effect as the indirect limitation on jurisdiction contained in Article 16(4) of the Brussels and Lugano Conventions. Like that provision, it is limited to cases where the issue is that of validity or registration. This means that the Swiss courts have jurisdiction on the basis of the defendant's domicile in Switzerland, even though the lawsuit is about, for example, the ownership of foreign intellectual property rights.[187] Unlike Article 16(4), Article 109(1) applies to 'intellectual property rights', not just to 'patents, trade marks, designs, or other similar rights required to be deposited or registered'. It follows that the limitation in Article 109(1) could apply to copyrights and other unregistered rights.

4. COMPARISON WITH THE TRADITIONAL ENGLISH RULES

So far, the comparison has been between, on the one hand, the Swiss special rules on jurisdiction in intellectual property cases and, on the other

---

[186] Article 109(3) provides that 'If the defendant is not domiciled in Switzerland, jurisdiction for lawsuits on validity or registration of intellectual property rights in Switzerland lies with the Swiss courts at the seat of the registered agent or, if there is none, at the seat of the Swiss registration authority'. For allocation of jurisdiction within Switzerland in multi-defendant cases, see Article 109(2).

[187] The allocation of jurisdiction to Switzerland on the basis that it is a Swiss right, see above, covers a wider range of issues than are covered under the limitation in respect of foreign rights. This is different from Article 16(4).

hand, the EC/EFTA rules. One other comparison that can be made is between these Swiss national rules on jurisdiction and the English national rules on jurisdiction, ie the English traditional rules on jurisdiction. Two points can be made in favour of the Swiss approach. First, by having special rules to deal with intellectual property cases it enables the Swiss courts to have jurisdiction in intellectual property cases involving the issue of creation and validity, when this may not be possible under the traditional English rules. Secondly, the Swiss national rules are not dissimilar from those contained in the Brussels and Lugano Conventions. The same is not true of the traditional English rules on jurisdiction. The gap between jurisdiction in relation to creation and validity of intellectual property rights under the EC/EFTA regime and the traditional English rules is enormous. At least under the former there is a special rule on jurisdiction contained in Article 16(4). The English position contrasts with that in Scotland, where, because its national rules are closely modelled on the Brussels Convention, the gap is very narrow.

2
Entitlement to the Grant and Ownership of Intellectual Property Rights: Jurisdiction

I	Introduction	49
II	How disputes arise	50
III	How jurisdictional problems arise	50
IV	Jurisdictional provisions	51
	1. Introduction	51
	2. Special jurisdictional rules	52
	(a) The Protocol on Recognition attached to the European Patent Convention	52
	(b) Article 16(4) of the Brussels and Lugano Conventions	61
	3. Jurisdictional rules of general application	62
	(a) When do the jurisdictional rules of general application apply?	62
	(b) The EC/EFTA rules	63
	(c) The traditional rules	66
V	An alternative solution: Article 109 Swiss PIL Statute	71

I
INTRODUCTION

An issue which is linked to the creation of intellectual property rights is that of their ownership. Which court will have jurisdiction to hear the case when the ownership of an intellectual property right is disputed? Are the special jurisdictional rules that apply to the creation of intellectual property rights also applicable to the issue of ownership of intellectual property rights?

There is, however, more than one aspect of the ownership issue that needs to be addressed. First, there is the question of first ownership of an intellectual property right. In the case of a registered right, this is the question of who is entitled to the grant of such a right. For an unregistered right, one has to determine who becomes the first owner of the right upon its creation. Secondly, statutory provisions can provide for an automatic transfer of ownership. Thirdly, the ownership of an intellectual property right, or at least of certain aspects of it, can be transferred contractually. The jurisdictional aspects of the first two points will be examined in this chapter, whilst the third point will be dealt with in the context of the next chapter.

II
HOW DISPUTES ARISE

Patents are awarded on a first to file basis, but it is assumed that the inventor will be the one to apply and the one to be granted the patent. Disputes concerning ownership can arise when someone gets hold of the information and applies in his own name before the inventor can apply. More frequent though are disputes between employers and employees. An employee can apply for a patent on the basis that he made the invention in his or her own spare time. The employer might claim the ownership of such a patent if the invention was made in the course of employment. The crucial issue is often then whether the invention was made in the course of employment or not. Similar problems arise in relation to copyright works that are created by employees. Who owns the copyright in these works?

At a later stage in their existence, intellectual property rights can be assigned. Afterwards, disputes concerning the ownership of the right can arise between the assignor and the assignee. No one can assign what he does not own. Partial assignments are also possible.

III
HOW JURISDICTIONAL PROBLEMS ARISE

Complex research programmes are often carried out by an international team of researchers. The invention that results from such a research programme is then patented in a series of countries. For example, a team of Swedish, British and Japanese researchers might invent a machine that converts the energy that is released through the movement of gletchers into electricity. The Swedish members of the team file a patent application with the Swedish patent office, the British members file a patent application with the European patent office and the Japanese members of the team assign their rights in the invention to Mitsubishi Heavy Industries Ltd. Which court will have jurisdiction to hear the case, if the British members of the team argue that they too are jointly entitled to the grant of the

Swedish patent, or if the Swedish members of the team, similarly, argue that they too are entitled to the grant of the European patent? And what about a dispute relating to each of the applications if the Japanese members of the team argue that they only assigned the rights in a Japanese patent to Mitsubishi?

Another type of case arises when a television program or a computer program is created in the course of employment. In the situation where an English employee creates such a programme in England, whilst being employed by an English company, a jurisdictional issue is unlikely to arise. However, copyright will also be created abroad in countries whose laws might be different on the point of employee ownership. Which court will have jurisdiction to hear the case when the ownership of the French copyright in such a programme is in dispute? Similar issues arise when an employer applies abroad for a patent in an invention made by one of his employees.

IV
JURISDICTIONAL PROVISIONS

1. Introduction

The Protocol on Recognition attached to the European Patent Convention contains special jurisdictional rules dealing with the issue of the right to the grant of a European patent.[1] The special jurisdictional rule contained in Article 16(4) of the Brussels and Lugano Conventions also has to be considered. It is arguable that there is such a strong link between the creation of an intellectual property right and at least its first owner that the jurisdiction rules concerning the creation of such rights should also apply to the issue of ownership. In many cases, this would mean the application of Article 16(4) of the Brussels and Lugano Conventions. However, as has been seen, this provision does not operate in the context of ownership. It may operate though in the context of entitlement to the grant of an intellectual property right in those rare cases where the issue of ownership is not raised. There are then these two special jurisdictional rules dealing with entitlement to grant and ownership. In cases raising these issues but falling outside these two special rules, recourse will have to be had to jurisdiction rules of general application contained in the Brussels and Lugano Conventions and to the traditional English rules on jurisdiction.

---

[1] See, generally, Tritton, pp 776–778.

2. Special Jurisdictional Rules

(a) THE PROTOCOL ON RECOGNITION ATTACHED TO THE EUROPEAN PATENT CONVENTION

Particular problems in relation to ownership arise in the context of the European Patent Convention. The issue is who is entitled to the grant of the bundle of national patents at the end of the single application procedure. Who should become the first owner of these national patents and how do we deal with disputes concerning that issue? Article 60 of the European Patent Convention lays down the rule that the inventor or his successor in title shall be entitled to the grant of the patent[2] and the European Patent Office will assume that the applicant is the inventor.[3] Problems arise when the applicant is not the inventor or when at least that point is in dispute. Article 61 provides a solution for the situation which arises when a decision that the original applicant was not the inventor has been reached, but refers to a Protocol to the Convention for the procedure to be followed in reaching that decision. The Contracting States thought this issue was part of the single application process and that it would be undesirable to deal with it separately in each State. This could have lead to conflicting judgments concerning the issue of who was the inventor and should have been the first owner of the patent. A first step towards avoiding such an undesirable situation is the recognition of each other's decisions, but in order for the Contracting States to agree to that there must be a certain uniformity in terms of jurisdiction, hence the jurisdictional provisions in the Protocol on Recognition.

(i) When does the Protocol on Recognition apply?

(a) *The right to the grant of a European patent*

Article 1(1) of the Protocol on Recognition states that

> the courts of the Contracting States shall, in accordance with Articles 2 to 6, have jurisdiction to decide claims, against the applicant, to the right to the grant of a European patent in respect of one or more of the Contracting States designated in the European patent application.

For the purposes of the Protocol, the term 'courts' includes authorities which, under the national law of a Contracting State, have jurisdiction to decide the claims referred to in paragraph (1).[4] The term 'Contracting

---

[2] Paragraph 1. This then goes on to discuss choice of law issues which will be returned to later, below pp 530–531.
[3] Article 60(3).
[4] Article 1(2).

State' refers to a Contracting State which has not excluded application of the Protocol.[5] Article 1(1) will not apply in a case concerning an application for a patent in a country which is not a party to the European Patent Convention.[6]

Section 82 of the Patents Act 1977, implementing the Protocol on Recognition, states in paragraph (3) that 'This section applies to a question arising before the grant of a European patent whether a person has a right to be granted a European patent, or a share in any such patent ...'. There are two obvious differences in the wording of this provision, when compared with Article 1(1) of the Protocol on Recognition. The first is that Section 82(3) makes it clear that the stage in the process of the grant of a European patent being referred to is that 'before the grant'. Secondly, Section 82(3) expressly applies not only to whether a person has a right to be granted a European patent, but also to whether a person has a right to be granted a share in a European patent. The construction of Section 82(3) arose before the Court of Appeal in *Kakkar and Others* v *Szelke and Others*.[7]

A dispute arose between two medical research teams from English universities in relation to an invention on which they had collaborated. The plaintiffs were three members of one team and the trustees of an English charitable trust which supported their work, the defendants were three members of the other research team and two Swedish companies. The first three defendants had filed European applications for the invention, but then assigned their interests in the invention and the patent applications to the fifth defendant. The fifth defendant was recorded as applicant for the European patents. The plaintiffs sought a declaration that the fifth defendant held the European Patent Application on constructive trust for itself and for the charitable trust. They conceded that the other declarations that they had sought, that they be named as co-inventors in the European patent application, and that the charitable trust was entitled to be granted a patent together with the fifth defendant, fell within Section 82(3), with the result that the English courts lacked jurisdiction since the applicant had its principal place of business in Sweden, which was, accordingly, the place for trial. They argued though that Section 82(3) was only concerned with the right to be named as grantee (in other words it was concerned with form rather than with substance), not with the beneficial interest in or under the patent when granted, and therefore the declaration sought was outside this provision.

The Court of Appeal (Parker LJ dissenting) rejected this argument. According to Lord Justice Lloyd, what mattered was the right to the

---

[5] Article 1(3). For exclusion of the Protocol see Article 167 of the Convention.
[6] See,eg the decision of a Swedish court in Hogsta Domstolen (SO 48) 23 February 1994 [1994] *Nytt Juridiskt Arkiv* 81; 1995 *European Current Law* 106.
[7] [1989] 1 FSR 225.

patent, not the right to be named as grantee. What must be looked at was the substance of the question that arose in the claim, not at the procedure by which a patent is granted, and that this was as to who was the true owner of the invention. If a question of ownership was within Section 82(3), so also must be a question as to who was entitled to the fruits of the invention. Nicholls LJ decided the case on the basis that the plaintiffs were claiming that the charitable trust was entitled to be granted 'a share' in the European patents. The result in the case was that the English courts had no jurisdiction in relation to the declaration sought and trial would have to take place before a Swedish court, which would have to consider matters of English law in relation to constructive trusts. The more appropriate court to consider this would be an English court.

(b) *Regardless of the residence of the applicant*

There is no requirement in Article 1(1) that the applicant or the party claiming the right to a European patent be resident in a Contracting State. To this extent, this provision resembles Article 16(4) of the Brussels and Lugano Conventions. This is not to say that the residence of the two parties is irrelevant under the Protocol on Recognition. As will be seen,[8] there are different bases of jurisdiction depending on where the applicant and the party claiming the right to the grant are resident.

(c) *Relationship with the Brussels and Lugano Conventions*

It has already been seen that the jurisdiction rules contained in the Protocol on Recognition take precedence over the jurisdiction rules in the Brussels and Lugano Conventions. The latter Conventions acknowledge this,[9] as does the Protocol on Recognition.[10] Where the issue is in respect of the right to the grant of a European patent the Protocol on Recognition will apply. If the jurisdictional issue in relation to a European patent is something other than this narrow issue then the Brussels or Lugano Convention will apply.[11] If the issue, other than that of the right to the grant of a European patent, relates to the registration or validity of a European patent then the provision in the Brussels or Lugano Convention that will apply will be Article 16(4).[12]

---

[8] Below, pp 56–57. [9] Article 57. [10] Article 11(1).
[11] This is assuming that it is a situation where one of these Conventions applies rather than traditional rules on jurisdiction, see above, p 51.
[12] See above, pp 15–27.

(ii) Bases of jurisdiction

(a) *Complex rules*

The bases of jurisdiction are set out in Articles 2–6 of the Protocol on Recognition. These are complex rules, particularly when it is born in mind that they are only dealing with one narrow issue. There are five different rules on jurisdiction. They use three different connecting factors: the residence or principal place of business of the applicant; the residence or principal place of business of the party claiming the right to the grant of the European patent; the Contracting State where the employee is mainly employed. Jurisdiction is not just based on connecting factors. It is also based on an agreement that the court or courts of a particular Contracting State shall decide on such a dispute. Moreover, in one specific situation jurisdiction is allocated exclusively to the German courts.

(b) *Five different situations*

These jurisdictional rules do not provide alternative bases of jurisdiction. A plaintiff is not given an opportunity to forum shop as is allowed, in certain circumstances, under the Brussels and Lugano Conventions. The five rules on jurisdiction are all concerned with different situations. Thus, Article 2 deals with the situation where the applicant has his residence or principal place of business in a Contracting State. Article 3 deals with the situation where the applicant has his residence or principal place of business outside the Contracting States, but the party claiming the right to the grant of the European patent has his residence or principal place of business within one of the Contracting States. Article 4 deals with the situation where the subject matter of a European patent application is the invention of an employee. Article 5 deals with the situation where the parties to a dispute concerning the right to the grant of a European patent have concluded an agreement to the effect that a court or courts of a particular Contracting State shall decide on such a dispute. Finally, Article 6 deals with the situation where none of the other Articles applies. As far as Articles 2 and 3 are concerned, this means that neither party has his residence or principal place of business within one of the Contracting States.

(c) The five rules

(i) The applicant's residence, etc in a Contracting State

Article 2 states that:

Subject to Articles 4 and 5, if an applicant for a European patent has his residence or principal place of business within one of the Contracting States, proceedings shall be brought against him in the courts of that Contracting State.[13]

One of the problems with using residence as a connecting factor is that the residence of a party can change over time. This raises the question of the precise point at which we are concerned to identify the applicant's residence. Is it at the time when the applicant applies for a European patent, when the dispute arises or when the dispute comes to trial? There is no answer in the Protocol on Recognition. However, in other areas of jurisdiction in private international law what we are concerned with is residence at the moment of commencement of the proceedings.[14] If it were at the time of the trial, a defendant could thwart the jurisdiction of the English courts by moving abroad after the commencement of proceedings.

This uncertainty leads on to another problem. Over a period of time, the application may be assigned to another person. This is what happened in the *Kakkar* case.[15] The original applicants assigned their interest in the invention and in the patent applications to the fifth defendant, a Swedish company. It was conceded by counsel that as from the date of the assignment, or at the latest from when the change of applicant was recorded by the European Patent Office as effective, the English courts, if the claims were within Section 82(3), ceased to have jurisdiction. Instead, the Swedish courts would have jurisdiction under Article 2 since the Swedish applicant had its principal place of business there. As has been seen, the argument in the case was confined to the issue of whether the claims for constructive trust came within Section 82(3). The Court of Appeal was prepared to proceed on this basis. However, Parker LJ said that he was not to be taken as accepting 'the proposition that, if this court has jurisdiction at the time when the application is made, that jurisdiction is lost because the applicant has chosen to assign his rights in the application to an applicant with a residence in a relevant Contracting State. It may be that this is so, but I do not regard it as being by any means self-evident.'[16] He pointed out that this would involve two consequences. First, that an assignment would pass to the assignee a right which the assignor did not have, namely a right to object to the jurisdiction of the court here and insist on trial in his

---

[13] This provision appears to have been used by the Swedish Supreme Court to support their jurisdiction in a case concerning the right to patent applications lodged abroad by a Swedish domiciled applicant: *Nordic Water Products AB* v *Sven H* [1995] ILPr 766.
[14] See Cheshire and North, pp 630–631.   [15] N 7 above.   [16] *Ibid*, at 231.

own country. Secondly, there might be a constantly shifting jurisdiction if there were successive assignments. He went on to comment that both of these consequences appear somewhat strange. The facts of the case concerned an assignment made before the present action was brought. Parker LJ was also concerned about the situation where there was an assignment after an action was brought. He asked whether the English courts would be deprived of jurisdiction in mid process. It would be truly bizarre if this were to be allowed. As mentioned above, the time that is relevant for jurisdiction in private international law is that of the commencement of proceedings, not the date of the trial.

(ii) *The residence, etc within one of the Contracting States of the party claiming the right to the grant of the European patent*

Article 3 states that:

Subject to Articles 4 and 5, if an applicant for a European patent has his residence or principal place of business outside the Contracting States, and if the party claiming the right to the grant of the European patent has his residence or principal place of business within one of the Contracting States, the courts of the latter State shall have exclusive jurisdiction.

This provision applies in the situation where the applicant has his residence or principal place of business outside the Contracting States. An example would be where the applicant, who pretends to be the inventor is a resident in Japan or is a Japanese company with its headquarters and principal place of business in Tokyo. In this situation, exclusive jurisdiction is given to the courts of the place of residence or principal place of business of the party claiming the right to the grant if that place is situated within the territory of one of the Contracting States. The allocation of exclusive jurisdiction, subject to Articles 4 and 5, has the effect of depriving the courts of any other Contracting State of jurisdiction which they might have under Articles 2 or 6. However, given that Articles 2,3 and 6 are all dealing with different situations it is hard to see how the courts of another Contracting State could have jurisdiction under both Article 3 and either Article 2 or 6.

(iii) *The Contracting State where the employee is mainly employed*

Article 4 states that:

Subject to Article 5, if the subject matter of a European patent application is the invention of an employee, the courts of the Contracting State, if any, whose law determines the right to the European patent pursuant to Article 60, paragraph 1, second sentence, of the Convention [the Contracting State where the employee is mainly employed], shall have exclusive jurisdiction over proceedings between the employee and the employer.

This rule is best regarded as an exception to the normal rules, set out above. It is concerned with employee inventions. Article 60 of the European Patent Convention contains a choice of law rule for such cases and the protocol gives exclusive jurisdiction to the court of the Contracting State, if any, whose laws will apply to the dispute. This exception only applies to proceedings between the employer and the employee and where the applicable law under the Convention rule is that of a Contracting State. The jurisdiction allocated under Article 4 is, subject to the rule dealing with jurisdiction agreements contained in Article 5, exclusive jurisdiction. This means that the courts of other Contracting States are deprived of jurisdiction even though they might otherwise have had it under Articles 2, 3 or 6.

(iv) *Jurisdiction agreements*

Article 5 is the second exception to the normal rules set out in Articles 2 and 3, and allows the parties to deviate from these rules by means of a jurisdiction agreement. Article 5 has one general provision, set out in paragraph 1, and a special provision for the situation where the parties are an employee and his employer. Article 5(1) states that:

If the parties to a dispute concerning the right to the grant of a European patent have concluded an agreement, either in writing or verbally with written confirmation, to the effect that a court or the courts of a particular Contracting State shall decide on such a dispute, the court or courts of that State shall have exclusive jurisdiction.

For this provision to operate, two conditions must be met: first, the parties must have agreed that a court or the courts of a particular Contracting State shall decide on such a dispute; secondly, that certain requirements of form are satisfied – the agreement must be either in writing or verbal with written confirmation. This same requirement as to form is to be found in the equivalent provision in the Brussels and Lugano Conventions (Article 17).[17]

The concern under the latter Conventions is that the agreement does not go unnoticed by one of the parties.[18] No doubt this is also the rationale of the requirement contained in Article 5(1). In ascertaining whether the requirement of writing or confirmation in writing has been satisfied, it is submitted that the decisions of the Court of Justice in relation to Article 17 of the Brussels and Lugano Conventions should be consulted as persuasive authority.

---

[17] The original version of the Brussels Convention contained the same requirement as to form. The latest version, as amended by the 1978 UK/Danish/Irish and the 1989 Spanish/Portuguese Accession Conventions, sets out additional ways in which the formal requirement can be satisfied, see Cheshire and North, pp 319–320.

[18] See Cheshire and North, pp 317–319.

The effect of an agreement coming within Article 5 is to allocate exclusive jurisdiction to the court or courts agreed upon. This means that the courts of other Contracting States are deprived of jurisdiction, even though they might otherwise have had it under the rules contained in Articles 2, 3, 4 or 6.

Paragraph 2 is concerned with the situation where the parties who have concluded an agreement are an employee and his employer. It provides that in this situation 'paragraph 1 shall only apply in so far as the national law governing the contract of employment allows the agreement in question'. This provision will take precedence over the provision on employee inventions contained in Article 4.

(v) Allocation of jurisdiction to the German courts

Article 6 is the provision that applies where none of the other Articles apply. It states that:

In cases where neither Articles 2 to 4 nor Article 5, paragraph 1, apply, the courts of the Federal Republic of Germany shall have exclusive jurisdiction.

Jurisdiction in this situation, where neither party has his residence or principal place of business in a Contracting State and so Articles 2 and 3 will not apply, and neither of the other two bases of jurisdiction apply, is allocated to the German courts on the basis that the only link with the Contracting States is that the application is in front of the European Patent Office which is located in Munich, Germany. The allocation of exclusive jurisdiction to the German courts is curious since this provision operates in the situation where none of the other Articles operate, and so, presumably, the courts of no other Contracting State have jurisdiction anyway.

(d) *The hierarchy of rules*

Articles 2, 3, 4 all start off by stating what other rules they are subject to and Article 6 makes it clear that it is subject to all the other bases of jurisdiction. Article 5 is the one provision which is not subject to any of the other provisions. The hierarchy of rules, starting with the most important and working downwards, is therefore as follows: Article 5, Article 4, Article 2, Article 3, Article 6.

(e) *The examination of jurisdiction*

The courts of Contracting States before which claims referred to in Article 1 (ie in respect of the right to the grant of a European patent) are brought are required of their own motion to decide whether they have jurisdiction pursuant to Articles 2 to 6.[19] This requirement that the courts must act on their own motion is also to be found in relation to Article 16 of the Brussels and Lugano Conventions. It is very different from the normal position under English law whereby the courts only act after submissions by the parties.

(f) *No definition of residence/principal place of business*

There is no definition of the key concepts of residence/principal place of business. The forum in which a claim is brought will have to apply its own definition. These definitions may differ from one Contracting State to another. However, the practical impact of such differences will be reduced because, as will be seen shortly, the Protocol on Recognition contains a *lis pendens* rule which will preclude a situation in which courts in different Contracting States take jurisdiction in respect of the same claim on the basis that, under their national definitions, the defendant has his residence in that State.

(iii) Declining jurisdiction

Article 8 contains a *lis pendens* rule, which is modelled closely on an earlier version of Article 21 of the Brussels Convention.[20] Paragraph 1 of Article 8 states that:

In the event of proceedings based on the same claim and between the same parties being brought before courts of different Contracting States, the court to which a later application is made shall of its own motion decline jurisdiction in favour of the court to which an earlier application was made.

This is a mechanical rule, and as such is very different from the discretionary rule of *lis alibi pendens* under the traditional English rules on jurisdiction.[21] The court to which an earlier application is made takes priority, and the court to which a later application is made must of its own motion decline jurisdiction. This rule is easy to operate since it will be readily apparent when an application for the right to the grant of a European patent is made to a court.

For Article 8 to operate there are three requirements. First, the two sets of proceedings must be based on the same claim. Secondly, the parties to both sets of proceedings must be the same. The meaning of 'the same parties' has been examined by the Court of Justice in *The Maciej Rataj*[22] in rela-

---

[19] Article 7.
[20] Ie prior to the latest version containing the amendments introduced by the 1989 Spanish/Portuguese Accession Convention.
[21] See Cheshire and North, pp 231–234.
[22] Case C-406/92 *The Owners of the Cargo Lately Laden on Board the Ship Tatry* v *The Owners of the Ship Maciej Rataj* [1994] ECR I-5439; discussed below, pp 181–182.

tion to the Brussels Convention and this case should be treated as being of persuasive authority in the present context. Thirdly, the two sets of proceedings must be brought before the courts of different Contracting States.

One problem that can arise with this rule is that where the jurisdiction of the court which was applied to first is challenged. There is a danger that if the courts of the Contracting State applied to second decline jurisdiction and the court applied to first decides that it lacks jurisdiction, then both actions would have been dismissed and starting an action afresh may run into time bar problems. Paragraph 2 seeks to resolve this problem by providing that in the event of the jurisdiction of the court to which an earlier application is made being challenged, 'the court to which a later application is made shall stay the proceedings until the other court takes a final decision'. Article 21 of the Brussels and Lugano Conventions deals with the problem slightly differently by providing that the court second seised must of its own motion stay its proceedings until such time as the jurisdiction of the court first seised is established. Once it has been, the court seised second must then decline jurisdiction.

(b) ARTICLE 16(4) OF THE BRUSSELS AND LUGANO CONVENTIONS

We are concerned here with patents, etc.[23] This can include European patents. Of course, if the issue is that of the right to the grant of a European patent, the Protocol on Recognition will apply. The Court of Justice in *Duijnstee* v *Goderbauer*[24] has established that Article 16(4) does not cover disputes concerning the right to a patent where what is involved is an invention of an employee. The same will be true even if it is not an invention of an employee. A dispute over the ownership of a patent, etc does not concern either the registration of the patent or its validity, as required under Article 16(4).[25] It is true that a decision as to ownership might lead to a change in the name of the owner in the appropriate register, indeed under English law ownership may be challenged by a motion to rectify the register, but this should not be enough to bring the case within the expression 'proceedings concerned with the registration', etc.[26] It has already been seen that, where rights are transferred, the mere change in registration is not enough to bring issues arising from the transfer within Article 16(4) because the public authorities are only recording the transfer, not playing an administrative role.[27] Moreover, Advocate General Rozes, in the *Duijnstee* case, stated that Article 16(4) covered only disputes which are principally concerned with the registration or validity of a

---

[23] See above, p 20. [24] Case 288/82 [1983] ECR 3663; discussed above, pp 17–20.
[25] See above, pp 19–20. [26] But compare Wadlow, (1985) 10 *ELR* 305, at 308.
[27] See above, pp 19–20.

patent.[28] This interpretation is supported by a comment in the Jenard Report in relation to Article 16 as a whole.[29] It is submitted that proceedings in relation to ownership are not principally concerned with registration, etc.[30]

Disputes as to the right to the grant of a patent, etc[31] would also appear to be excluded in so far as they raise the matter of ownership. But what if the dispute as to the right to the grant of a patent, etc is not in relation to the ownership, but relates to some other matter? For example, the applicant for a grant is a national of a State which has not entered into any of the intellectual property conventions. In such circumstances, there would appear to be proceedings concerned with the registration of a patent, etc, with the result that Article 16(4) applies, and exclusive jurisdiction is allocated to the courts of the Contracting State in which the deposit or registration has been applied for, has taken place or is, under the terms of an international convention, deemed to have taken place.

3. JURISDICTIONAL RULES OF GENERAL APPLICATION

(a) WHEN DO THE JURISDICTIONAL RULES OF GENERAL APPLICATION APPLY?

The jurisdictional rules of general application will apply in all cases of entitlement to grant and ownership falling outside the Protocol on Recognition and outside Article 16(4) of the Brussels and Lugano Conventions. An example would be a dispute over the ownership of a Japanese patent. As regards the Brussels Convention, the Jenard Report makes it clear that intellectual property related cases falling outside Article 16(4) follow the normal rules of the Brussels Convention.[32]

A case raising the issue of the right to the grant of a patent can fall outside the Protocol on Recognition because of the nature of the right. For

---

[28] N 24 above, at 3687. The Scots traditional rules on jurisdiction, based on the Brussels Convention, have a parallel provision to Article 16(4), but it refers to 'proceedings principally concerned with' etc, see Civil Jurisdiction and Judgments Act 1982, Schedule 8, para 2(14).

[29] [1979] OJ C59, at p 34: ' the matters referred to in this Article [Article 16] will normally be the subject of exclusive jurisdiction only if they constitute the principal subject-matter of the proceedings of which the court is to be seised'.

[30] Whether a dispute is 'principally concerned' with validity arises in the situation where this is raised as a defence to a claim for breach of a licensing agreement or infringement, see below pp 91–92 and pp 202–210. In the context of infringement/validity 'principally concerned' has been very widely defined to mean 'not arising incidentally': *Coin Controls Ltd v Suzo International (UK) Ltd* [1997] 3 All ER 45. It is submitted below, pp 204–206, that this interpretation is wrong; but even if right it could be argued that proceedings in relation to ownership only raise registration incidentally.

[31] We are talking here about patents other than European patents – otherwise the Protocol on Recognition would apply to the issue of the right to the grant.

[32] N 29 above, at p 36.

example, the patent may be a US patent, or it may be a French patent rather than a European patent (France). Likewise, this special rule will not apply where the right in question is a trademark or design. Article 16(4) will not apply if the right to grant raises the matter of ownership, as it commonly does.

When it comes to disputes relating to the ownership of rights, these will come within the Protocol on Recognition if this issue arises at the stage of the grant of the right and concerns a European patent. The Protocol on Recognition will not apply if the issue of ownership arises after the grant of a European patent, for what has then been granted is a bundle of national rights. Naturally, neither will it apply where what is in question is the ownership of a right other than a European patent. Cases raising the issue of ownership will fall outside Article 16(4).

(b) THE EC/EFTA RULES

(i) When do the EC/EFTA rules apply?

The same comments apply as in the previous chapter[33] and need not be repeated here.

(ii) Bases of jurisdiction

For the reasons given in the previous chapter,[34] the bases of jurisdiction under the Brussels and Lugano Conventions are best discussed in the contexts of licensing agreements and infringement of intellectual property rights. Nothing needs to be added to what was said in outline in the previous chapter in relation to jurisdiction under Articles 2, 5(5), 6 and 18. In the context of ownership, though, a little more needs to said about Articles 5(1) and 17.

(a) *Article 5(1)*

There are two situations that commonly occur where the ownership of an intellectual property right will involve a matter relating to a contract, and thus come within the scope of Article 5(1). The first is where an intellectual property right is assigned and the issue of ownership arises under that contract. As was mentioned in the last chapter, Article 5(1) allocates jurisdiction to 'the courts for the place of performance of the obligation in question'. The meaning of this concept is examined in detail in chapter 3 in the context of contracts for the commercial exploitation of intellectual property rights.

---

[33] See above, pp 30–32.   [34] See above, p 32.

The second is where there is a dispute between an employer and an employee over the ownership of an invention, and the dispute relates to their respective rights in that invention arising out of the contract of employment. This was the situation that arose in the *Duijnstee* case. Many employment contracts contain clauses concerning the ownership of intellectual property rights.

The 1989 Spanish/Portuguese Accession Convention added a separate provision to Article 5(1) to deal with matters relating to individual contracts of employment.[35] In these matters, the place of performance of the obligation in question is 'that where the employee habitually carries out his work'.[36] This means that jurisdiction is normally allocated to the Contracting State whose law may well be applicable under the Rome Convention on the law applicable to contractual obligations of 1980.[37] Article 5(1) goes on to provide that 'if the employee does not habitually carry out his work in any one country, the employer may also be sued in the courts for the place where the business which engaged the employee was or is now situated'.

This special rule for matters relating to individual contracts of employment had not been introduced at the time when the *Duijnstee* case was decided. Would the special rule apply if such facts were to happen now? Did that case involve 'matters relating to individual contracts of employment'? On the surface, the answer would be no, because it involved a dispute between a liquidator of the company and a former employee. But looking beneath the surface, the dispute related to the respective rights of the employer and employee in the patent arising out of their contract of employment and, accordingly, involved a matter relating to an individual contract of employment.

(b) *Article 17*

In cases of entitlement and grant, there is one situation where the parties may well 'have agreed that a court or the courts of a Contracting State are to have jurisdiction to settle any disputes which have arisen or which may arise in connection with a particular legal relationship', thereby bringing the case within Article 17.[38] This is the one that arose in the *Duijnstee* case, ie there is a dispute between an employer and an employee over the ownership of an invention, and the dispute relates to their respective rights in that invention arising out of the contract of employment. In matters relat-

---

[35] These are to be contrasted with collective agreements between employers and workers' representatives see the Jenard and Moller Report, [1990] OJ C189/57, p 73.
[36] For the identification of this place when the employment is performed in several Contracting States see Case C-383/95 *Rutten* v *Cross Medical Ltd* [1997] All ER (EC) 121.
[37] See Article 6 of the Rome Convention, and below, p 524.
[38] See, generally, above, p 36.

ing to individual contracts of employment, Article 17(5) of the Brussels Convention provides that the agreement on jurisdiction will only take effect if it is entered into after the dispute has arisen or[39] if it is invoked by the employee as plaintiff.

(iii) Declining jurisdiction

(a) *Under the Brussels and Lugano Conventions*

Articles 21 (*lis pendens*) and 22 (related actions) of the Brussels and Lugano Conventions have been examined in the previous chapter.[40] There do not appear to be any particular problems in applying these provisions in cases of entitlement to grant and ownership.[41]

(b) *Using the doctrine of* forum non conveniens

The effect of the decision in *Re Harrods (Buenos Aires) Ltd*[42] in cases of entitlement to grant and ownership is the same as in cases of creation and validity of intellectual property rights. Thus, to take the same example given in the latter context,[43] but now applying it to a dispute concerning ownership, if a Japanese plaintiff were to sue an English domiciled defendant in England in respect of the ownership of a Japanese patent, the English court would have power to stay the English proceedings on the ground of *forum non conveniens*, even though the English court's jurisdiction is based on Article 2 of the Brussels Convention. Applying that doctrine to such facts, an English court may well conclude that the clearly appropriate forum for trial is Japan and, accordingly, grant a stay of the English proceedings. An important connecting factor, albeit perhaps not as important as in a case of creation, will be that of where the right has been created, ie Japan. Another important factor will be that of the governing law; this will be Japanese law.[44] Finally, albeit of less importance, the plaintiff is Japanese.

(iv) A subject matter limitation on jurisdiction?

As has been seen, Article 16(4) does not apply in a case of ownership of patents, etc. It follows that there is no subject matter limitation under the Brussels and Lugano Conventions preventing the courts in one Contracting State from trying a case concerned with the ownership of patents, etc deposited or registered, or applied for in another Contracting

---

[39] There is no such alternative under the Lugano Convention.
[40] See above, pp 36–37.
[41] Compare the position in cases of creation and validity.
[42] [1992] Ch 72; discussed above, p 38.
[43] See above, p 38.
[44] See below, pp 522–525.

State.[45] This contrasts with the position under the traditional rules on jurisdiction, where it seems that there is a subject matter limitation on jurisdiction in cases involving the ownership of foreign intellectual property rights. The only situation where Article 16(4) will operate, and thus, when exclusive jurisdiction has been allocated to the courts of another Contracting State, act as a subject matter limitation on jurisdiction is the unusual one where there is an issue as to the right to grant of a patent etc which does not raise the matter of ownership.

(c) THE TRADITIONAL RULES

(i) When do the traditional rules apply?

The traditional rules on jurisdiction apply in cases of entitlement to grant and ownership of intellectual property rights in the situation where neither of the special rules (contained in the Protocol on Recognition and in Article 16(4) of the Brussels and Lugano Conventions) nor the rules of general application contained in the Brussels and Lugano Conventions apply. Such cases will be relatively rare. An example would be where there is a dispute between two US companies in respect of the ownership of a UK patent. It is not a European patent and so the Protocol on Recognition would not apply, neither would Article 16(4) (the issue is as to ownership) nor any other basis of jurisdiction in the Brussels or Lugano Convention (the defendant is domiciled outside an EC/EFTA Contracting State).

(ii) Bases of jurisdiction

As has already been said,[46] the traditional bases of jurisdiction are best discussed in detail in the contexts of licensing agreements[47] and infringement.[48]

(a) *Service of a writ within the jurisdiction*

The normal rules on service of writs within the jurisdiction will apply. There are no special problems in applying these rules to cases of entitlement to grant and ownership of intellectual property rights.

---

[45] Compare the position in cases of creation and validity, above, pp 38–39.
[46] See above, pp 40.
[47] See below, pp 97–106, 241–266.
[48] See below, pp 241–266.

(b) Service of a writ out of the jurisdiction

(i) The heads of Order 11, rule 1(1)

No specific head dealing with entitlement to grant and ownership. There is no head of Order 11, rule 1(1) dealing specifically with the issues of entitlement to grant and ownership of intellectual property rights, or indeed with any other issue in relation to such rights. As a result there can be real problems in finding a basis of jurisdiction. This is illustrated by *GAF Corp v Amchem Products Inc*,[49] a rare example of a reported case on the use of Order 11, rule 1, in the context of the ownership of intellectual property rights.

Both the plaintiffs and defendants were two US companies, which entered into a contract under which the plaintiffs were to send chemicals for testing by the defendants. The defendants made patent applications and were granted patents in the United States, Germany, Great Britain and France in relation to certain of these chemicals. The plaintiffs brought an action in England claiming, *inter alia*, (i) a declaration that they were entitled to beneficial interests in the English patent, (ii) an order directing the defendants to assign the patent to the plaintiffs, (iii) an injunction which, *inter alia*, sought to restrain the defendants from assigning the patent other than to the defendants. The defendants being outside the jurisdiction, the plaintiffs sought to rely on Order 11, rule 1, claiming that the case came within both a contract head and the injunction head. The former required there to have been a 'breach committed within the jurisdiction of a contract made ... out of the jurisdiction'.[50] The latter required that 'an injunction is sought ordering the defendant to do or refrain from doing anything within the jurisdiction ...'.[51]

Megarry J held that, as regards paragraph (i) of the claim, the action was not one for breach of contract but one more akin to an action by beneficiaries against a trustee in respect of breach of fiduciary obligation. Paragraph (ii) of the claim could be complied with by effecting an assignment anywhere in the world and not merely within the jurisdiction, and, accordingly, did not come within the injunction head. Neither did paragraph (iii) of the claim. The relief sought therein was, essentially, incidental or ancillary; when the judgment was given in the action, the injunction, if granted at all, would only be of limited operation and probably of short duration. The result was that service of notice of the writ out of the jurisdiction was set aside.[52]

[49] [1975] 1 Lloyd's Rep 601.
[50] Order 11, rule 1(g); now Order 11, rule 1(1)(e).
[51] Order 11, rule 1(i); now Order 11, rule 1(1)(b).
[52] The Court of Appeal dismissed an appeal, basing their decision on the *forum conveniens* discretion, see below pp 68–69.

The contract heads. In the not uncommon situation where there is a dispute between an employer and an employee over the ownership of an invention, and the dispute relates to their respective rights in that invention arising out of the contract of employment, it is likely that the plaintiff will be able to avail himself of one of the contract heads of Order 11, rule 1(1). These are discussed more fully in the next chapter, where jurisdiction in relation to contracts concerning the exploitation of intellectual property rights is examined.

(ii) *A serious issue to be tried*

There do not appear to be any particular problems for the plaintiff in establishing that there is a serious issue to be tried on the merits in cases of entitlement to grant and ownership of intellectual property rights.

(iii) *The exercise of the discretion*

When applying the *forum conveniens* criteria[53] to cases of entitlement to grant and ownership of intellectual property rights it is important to separate out two different scenarios. The first is where it is a foreign right. The law applicable to ownership will be that of the foreign State where the right was created.[54] The defendant will be from outside the EC/EFTA, otherwise the Brussels or Lugano Convention would apply. Such a case is unlikely to arise before the English courts because of the subject matter limitation on jurisdiction in relation to foreign rights.[55] However, if it were to arise, and it is suggested below that this unjustifiable subject matter limitation on jurisdiction should be abolished,[56] the plaintiff would have considerable difficulty in establishing that England is the appropriate forum for trial and that this is clearly so.

The second scenario is where it is a UK right. This is much more likely to arise because the subject matter limitation on jurisdiction in respect of foreign intellectual property rights will not operate. English law will apply to the issue of ownership of a UK right. The fact that it is a UK right and that English law is applicable are strong factors indicating that England is the clearly appropriate forum. Nonetheless, even in this situation, it is not inconceivable that the court may decide that the *forum conveniens* is abroad. This is what happened in the *GAF* case. This was decided long before the Brussels Convention came into force in the United Kingdom. But if it were to arise now, this would still be a case to be decided under the traditional rules. Megarry J, at first instance, said, *obiter*, that the appropriate forum was the US court. The Court of Appeal upheld the first instance decision, deciding the case solely on the basis of the exercise of the *forum conveniens* discretion. The Court of Appeal[57] agreed with

[53] See above, pp 41–42.   [54] See below, pp 522–525.   [55] See below, pp 283–299.
[56] At pp 314–315.   [57] N 49 above, at 608–609.

Megarry J that the appropriate forum for trial was the US Court. The connections with the US included the fact that both parties were US corporations, the law governing their contract was that of Delaware or Pennsylvania, factual evidence related to events that took place in the United States, there were proceedings between the same parties pending, which had gone some considerable distance, in the US in respect of the UK patent, all relevant documents and witnesses were based in the United States.

(iii) Declining jurisdiction

When it comes to the application of the *forum non conveniens* criteria[58] in cases of entitlement to grant and ownership, we can take as an example the facts of the *GAF* case,[59] ie a dispute between two US companies in respect of the ownership of a UK patent. This was a case involving service of a writ out of the jurisdiction. In theory, after the service of the writ abroad there could be an application for a stay on the basis of forum non conveniens. In practice, this is unlikely to occur because for leave to serve out of the jurisdiction to have been granted, the English court will have already decided that England is the clearly appropriate forum for trial. The defendant will then not be able to establish that the clearly appropriate forum for trial is abroad. An application for a stay is much more likely to arise where the service of the writ has been effected within the jurisdiction. Looking at the connecting factors in the *GAF* case, the patent is a UK patent and English law will be applicable to the issue of ownership of the right. These are strong connections with England, although perhaps the factor of where the right is created should not be regarded as being as important in ownership cases as in cases where the issue is that of creation of the right.[60] Nonetheless, as has been seen,[61] the Court of Appeal held on the facts that the appropriate forum for trial was the United States. A stay of the English proceedings would then be granted unless the plaintiff can establish that there are circumstances by reason of which justice requires that a stay should nevertheless not be granted.

(iv) Limitations on jurisdiction

(a) *Foreign rights*

Does the subject matter limitation on jurisdiction in cases where the issue concerns validity, infringement and, seemingly, the creation of foreign intellectual property rights also apply in cases where the issue is as to the ownership of such rights? *Rey v Lecouturier*[62] suggests that it does. A

---

[58] See above, pp 42–43.
[59] N 49 above and text accompanying.
[60] See above, pp 42–43.
[61] See above, pp 68–69.
[62] [1908] 2 Ch 715.

representative of an order of monks brought an action in England to restrain a liquidator, in whom the property of the monks was vested by virtue of a French statute, from using the word 'Chartreuse' and to expunge the name of the liquidator's representative from the register of English trade marks. The Court of Appeal held that the name of the liquidator's representative must be expunged from the register of English trade marks. During the course of the judgment, attention focused on French judgments as to who was entitled to the property of the order of monks, and thus whether the French statute affected their property. Buckley LJ said that the French court was adjudicating on the monks' business, including its trade marks, as carried on in France, 'but that [French] Court had no jurisdiction to determine what ought to be the entries in the register of trade marks in England . . .'.[63] If the French courts had no such jurisdiction, it is implicit that neither would an English court if faced with foreign rights. Accordingly, Buckley LJ can be taken as supporting the proposition that an English court has no jurisdiction to determine what ought to be the entry in the register of trade marks abroad where this is dependent on the issue of the ownership of the mark. If the issue of ownership arose in some context other than that of entries in a register, the limitation would doubtless still apply.

(b) *State immunity*

The exception to the principle of State immunity in respect of proceedings relating to patents, etc belonging to the State[64] will operate where there are proceedings concerning the entitlement to grant and ownership of such rights.

(v) Criticism of the traditional English rules

The basic criticism of the operation of the traditional English rules in cases of entitlement to grant and ownership of intellectual property rights is that it is unjustifiably difficult to obtain jurisdiction in England. This is the same criticism levelled at the application of the traditional English rules in cases of validity and creation of such rights. First, there is the unwarranted subject matter limitation on jurisdiction which seemingly extends to cases concerning entitlement to grant and ownership. Secondly, there is no special rule which would give the English courts jurisdiction on the basis that the case concerns entitlement to grant or ownership of an English right. Of course, the Brussels and Lugano Conventions do not contain such a basis of jurisdiction so that this criticism of the traditional English rules must be rather muted. Nonetheless, the English position contrasts with that under Swiss national law.

[63] [1908] 2 Ch 715 at 731.   [64] State Immunity Act 1978, s 7; quoted above, p 45.

V
AN ALTERNATIVE SOLUTION: ARTICLE 109 SWISS PIL STATUTE

This provision has been examined in detail in the previous chapter.[65] The limitation on jurisdiction in respect of foreign intellectual property rights under Article 109(1) of the Swiss Private International Law Statute is limited to cases where the issue is that of registration or validity. This means that the Swiss courts have jurisdiction on the basis of the defendant's domicile in Switzerland, even though the lawsuit concerns foreign intellectual property rights if the issue in question is that of ownership of such rights. Moreover, Article 109(1) allocates jurisdiction to the Swiss courts where there is a lawsuit on a Swiss intellectual property right. Presumably, this would cover a lawsuit concerning entitlement to grant or ownership of such a right.

---

[65] See above, pp 46–48.

3

Contracts in Relation to the Exploitation of Intellectual Property Rights: Jurisdiction

I	Introduction	73
II	The substantive law background	74
III	How jurisdictional problems arise	75
IV	Jurisdictional provisions	76
	1. Introduction	76
	2. The EC/EFTA Rules	76
	(a) Bases of jurisdiction	76
	(b) Declining jurisdiction and restraining foreign proceedings	95
	3. The traditional rules	97
	(a) Bases of jurisdiction	97
	(b) Declining jurisdiction and restraining foreign proceedings	106
	(c) Limitations on jurisdiction	111
	4. Specific aspects of transfer of technology contracts	112
	5. Anti-trust issues	113
V	Reform	113
	1. The EC/EFTA rules	113
	(a) Criticism of the existing law	113
	(b) Special jurisdictional rules or reform of the jurisdictional rules of general application?	114
	(c) Reform of Article 5(1)	115
	2. The traditional rules	117

I
INTRODUCTION

There are two types of contract in relation to intellectual property. Our analysis is only concerned with contracts for the exploitation of intellectual property rights. It is not concerned with contracts where the intellectual property right is not the central element. For example, this chapter will not deal with the issues arising from a contract between the inventor and a patent agent in which the latter is instructed to file an application for a patent.[1]

II
THE SUBSTANTIVE LAW BACKGROUND

The owner of an intellectual property right is, obviously, free to exploit the right himself. In many cases, however, that exploitation is, at least partially, carried out by third parties. In such cases, a contract for the exploitation of the intellectual property right is concluded between the owner of the right and the party that will exploit the right.

A contract for the exploitation of intellectual property rights can take various forms. The most common forms are licences and assignments. Distribution agreements, joint-ventures, franchising agreements, etc can also play a role, but most of these include either a licence or an assignment.

A licence contract is essentially a contract that grants the licensee the right to do something that would normally amount to an infringement of the intellectual property right. For example, a patent licence grants the licensee the right to produce the patented product, whilst this would normally be an infringement of the patent. A copyright licence allows the reproduction of a chapter of a book. Once more, this would normally amount to copyright infringement. Licence contracts can be restricted in their territorial scope and in time. It is quite common, for example, for a licence to be granted for a single country and for a period of ten years.

An assignment is similar to the sale of the intellectual property right. It normally involves a transfer of ownership of the intellectual property right. However, assignments can be partial. This means that not the whole right is transferred. In practice, they are often also restricted in time. That implies that after a certain time the right reverts to its original owner. The assignment may also be restricted in its territorial scope. For example, the author of a novel can assign the right to make a movie on the basis of the novel, but he can also assign the right to exploit the work outside the United Kingdom for a period of 25 years.

A distribution agreement, typically, grants someone the right to distribute goods or services in a certain territory. The goods or services are often

---

[1] See, eg the Judgment of 13 May 1982 of the German Bundesgerichtshof, *Effer* v *Kantner*, [1983] ECC 1 and Case 38/81 *Effer* v *Kantner* [1982] ECR 825; see also the judgment of 4 January 1983 of the Commercial Court in Liège (Belgium), *SA Jouets Eisenmann* v *Geobra Brandstatter GmbH & Co KG and Big Spielwaren Fabrik Dipl Ing Ernst A Bettag*, [1985] ECC 246.

linked to intellectual property rights and most of these contracts are restricted in time.

Traditionally, licences are more commonly used in relation to patents and trade marks, whilst assignments are more common in relation to the exploitation of copyright. The boundaries between the two types of contract have become vague though. A partial assignment with a limited territorial scope and which is also limited in time, has become very similar to a licence.

III
HOW JURISDICTIONAL PROBLEMS ARISE

Jurisdictional problems can arise fairly easily, because the majority of licences and assignments are concluded between, on the one hand, licensors and assignors in one country, and, on the other hand, licensees and assignees in another country. Two examples can be given to illustrate the point. First, a British licensor may grant a licence to produce (and market) its patented product in China to a Chinese licensee. Secondly, a British author may assign the right to make a TV series on the basis of his novel to an American production company. Both contracts can be breached, for example because the Chinese licensee fails to pay the agreed royalty or because the author signs a second contract with another production company in which he purports to assign the same right. Which court will have jurisdiction in these situations? The court of the country of the licensor/assignor, the court of the country of the licensee/assignee and the court of the country of the place of performance are just a few potential fora.

The exploitation of intellectual property rights also gives rise to more complicated contractual patterns. Rights that are registered, such as patents and trade marks, are registered locally. Often, a subsidiary of the owner of the original rights is set up to own and administer the intellectual property rights in the foreign country in which exploitation is to take place. That subsidiary then enters into an exploitation contract with the local licensee. In this scenario, jurisdictional problems only arise if the foreign partner attempts to sue the parent company, separately or jointly with the administration subsidiary. The need to do so may arise, in practice, because most of these administration subsidiaries do not have a lot of assets. The administration subsidiary may, in a number of cases, administer intellectual property rights in a number of countries. In such cases, the jurisdictional problems which have been mentioned in relation to a normal licence will arise.

Transfer of technology contracts may be even more complicated. A local intellectual property administration subsidiary may own the patent and trade mark rights and it may licence them to the local licensee. A separate subsidiary, located in another country, may rent the machinery for the plant to the licensee. That machinery may include patented technology and the mould to apply the trade mark. A third subsidiary, often located in a tax haven, then buys the finished products from the licensee 'in the mould'. This system results in the fact that the licensee at no stage owns any product that incorporates the trade mark or the patented technology. The finished product is then sold to yet another subsidiary which will distribute and sell it. In this final transaction between subsidiaries, the price of the product is raised substantially. This neatly allows the group of companies to locate most of the profits in the tax heaven. Disputes that arise from such a complex chain of contracts, obviously, give rise to complex jurisdictional issues. They often involve multi-defendant cases.

IV
JURISDICTIONAL PROVISIONS

1. Introduction

There are no special jurisdictional rules for contracts in relation to the exploitation of intellectual property rights. What must be applied then are rules of general application: the EC/EFTA rules and the traditional English rules on jurisdiction.[2] There are, though, under these different regimes, certain provisions dealing specifically with contracts. These provisions are concerned with contracts generally, rather than specifically with contracts in relation to the exploitation of intellectual property rights, though they apply equally to the latter. It is on these contract provisions that the rest of this chapter will tend to concentrate.

2. The EC/EFTA Rules

(a) BASES OF JURISDICTION

(i) General jurisdiction

As has been seen,[3] Article 2 of the Brussels and Lugano Conventions allows a plaintiff to bring an action against the defendant in the Contracting State in which the latter is domiciled. There are no special

---

[2] See above, pp 2–3.   [3] See above, p 33.

difficulties in applying this provision in cases concerning contracts relating to the exploitation of intellectual property rights.

(ii) Special jurisdiction: Articles 5 and 6

When it comes to trial in the courts of a Contracting State other than the one in which the defendant is domiciled, the most important provision in the present context is Article 5(1). Other provisions that might be utilised are Articles 5(5)[4] and 6.[5] There are no particular difficulties in applying these last two provisions to disputes concerning contracts relating to the exploitation of intellectual property rights.

(iii) Article 5(1)

(a) *The provision*

It has already been mentioned,[6] that a defendant can be sued in a Contracting State other than his domicile 'in matters relating to a contract, in the courts for the place of performance of the obligation in question'. When trial takes place in England, a plaintiff, who seeks to rely on this provision, has to establish a good arguable case that its terms have been met.[7]

The Court of Justice has given a Community meaning to the concept of 'matters relating to a contract'.[8] This, according to one case, can include a claim for damages for wrongful repudiation, being based on a failure to fulfil a contractual obligation to give reasonable notice of termination.[9] Jurisdiction may be invoked by the plaintiff even where there is a dispute between the parties over the existence of the contract on which the claim is based.[10] However, a majority of the House of Lords has held that a claim for restitution of moneys paid under a purported contract subsequently accepted by both parties as being void *ab initio* did not fall within Article 5(1) of the Modified Convention.[11] The claim was based on the principle of unjust enrichment, not on a particular contractual obligation.

The Court of Justice, in *de Bloos* v *Bouyer*, held that the obligation in question is referring not to any obligation under the contract but to the contractual obligation forming the basis of the legal proceedings; the one which the contract imposes on the defendant, the non-performance of which is relied upon by the plaintiff.[12] In the situation where the claim is

---

[4] See above, p 34.   [5] See above, p 34.   [6] See above, p 33.
[7] See *Boss Group Ltd* v *Boss France SA* [1996] 4 All ER 970.
[8] See Dicey and Morris, pp 356–357.
[9] Case 9/87 *SPRL Arcado* v *SA Haviland* [1988] ECR 1539.
[10] Case 38/81 *Effer* v *Kantner* [1982] ECR 825.
[11] *Kleinwort Benson Ltd* v *Glasgow City Council* [1997] 3 WLR 923; discussed below, pp 432–433.
[12] Case 14/76 *Etablissements de Bloos* v *Société en Commandite par Actions Bouyer* [1976] ECR 1497.

based on several different obligations to be performed in different States, the judge is required to identify the principal obligation on which the plaintiff's action is based and jurisdiction is to be determined in accordance with this.[13]

The Court of Justice has not given a community definition to the concept of 'the place of performance' of the obligation in question. Instead, it has held that the national court before which the matter is brought 'must determine in accordance with its own rules of conflict of laws what is the law applicable to the legal relationship in question and define in accordance with that law the place of performance of the contractual obligation in question'.[14] This is not as daunting as might appear at first sight. First, if neither party pleads and proves foreign law, then the English court will apply English law.[15] Secondly, it has been said that the same general approach towards determining the place of performance operates throughout the EC.[16] This approach is as follows.[17] Effect is normally given to an express stipulation as to the place of performance in the contract.[18] In the absence of any such stipulation, it may be possible to imply a choice by the parties. This is a question of contractual interpretation. If this does not produce an answer, each Contracting State has residual rules which determine the place of performance. It is at this stage that the question of the applicable law may become vital. For example, the English rule on where a debtor has to pay a creditor is different from the German rule.[19] Under the former law, the debtor must seek out the creditor; under the latter, the creditor must normally seek out the debtor.

There may be an obligation which is to be performed in several different Contracting States. In this situation, the English court has jurisdiction if the obligation relied upon fell to be performed in England, even if it also fell to be performed elsewhere.[20]

---

[13] Case 266/85 *Shenavai* v *Kreischer* [1987] ECR 239.
[14] Case 12/76 *Tessili* v *Dunlop* [1976] ECR 1473 at 1485.
[15] Compare the position in Italy, see *Société De Droit Italien Ernesto Stoppani SpA* v *Sarl Stoppani France* [1997] ILPr 759.
[16] Kennett, *1995 Yearbook of European Law*, p 193 at p 196.
[17] Kennett, *Ibid* at 196 *et seq*; O'Malley and Layton, pp 396–401.
[18] But see Case C-106/95 *Mainschiffahrts-Genossenschaft eG (MSG)* v *Les Gravières Rhénanes Sarl* [1997] 3 WLR 179: an oral agreement on the place of performance which is designed not to determine the place where the person liable is actually to perform the obligations incumbent on him, but solely to establish that the courts for a particular place have jurisdiction, is not governed by Article 5(1) but by Article 17.
[19] See Forsyth and Moser, (1996) 45 *ICLQ* 190 at 193.
[20] The *Boss* case, n 7 above, at 975–976; discussed below, p 84. See also *Medway Packaging Ltd* v *Meurer Maschinen GmbH & Co KG* [1990] 2 Lloyd's Rep 112 at 117, CA; discussed below, pp 83–84. But compare the Inner House in Scotland in *Bank of Scotland* v *Seitz* 1990 SLT 584.

(b) Application to intellectual property contracts

(i) *Licenses*

Licensee's obligations. Let us start with the situation where the licensor is suing the licensee for the breach of one of his obligations under the licence. The licensee has an obligation to pay royalties to the licensor; normally, these will be payable in the State where the latter resides. If, for example, an English licensee fails to pay royalties to a French licensor, the latter will be able to sue the former in France by virtue of Article 5(1). Alternatively, of course, it could sue in England by virtue of Article 2. The obligation to pay for a licence arose in the English Commercial Court in *Rank Film Distributors* v *Lanterna Editrice Srl*.[21] The plaintiffs granted the first defendants an exclusive licence to exploit certain films in Italy and elsewhere. Payment was to be by instalments, the third of which was by way of a bank guarantee, which was not paid. The plaintiffs brought an action for payment against an Italian company, which took over the rights and obligations of the original licensee, and an Italian bank. After some argument at the trial, it was held by Saville J that, as a matter of contractual interpretation, the third instalment was payable in London. Accordingly, the English court had jurisdiction under Article 5(1).

The licensee may have an obligation to allow the licensor to check his accounts so that the latter can collect a royalty in respect of the product manufactured. The natural place of performance of this obligation is the Contracting State in which the accounts are to be checked. This could be specified in the licensing agreement as being where the accounts are kept, which presumably would be where the product is manufactured or where the licensee is domiciled. Difficult questions can be raised as to the precise nature of the obligation imposed by the licensing agreement. Take, for example, the obligation imposed on the licensee of labelling the product as being manufactured and sold under licence by the licensor. Is the essence of this obligation the fixing of the label on the product when it is manufactured, the place of performance of which doubtless would be where the product is manufactured, or is it ensuring that the product has the label on it when sold, the place of performance of which doubtless would be where the product is sold? The latter place may be different from where the product was manufactured. The better view is to regard the obligation as being to ensure that the product has the label attached to it when sold.

Licensor's obligations. We now move on to the situation where the roles are reversed and the licensee is suing the licensor for breach of one of his obligations. The latter may have agreed to grant an exclusive and sole licence to the former, but has failed to grant the right. This was the

---

[21] [1992] ILPr 58.

situation that arose in the Irish case of *Olympia Productions Ltd* v *Cameron Mackintosh (Overseas) Ltd, Cameron Mackintosh Ltd*.[22] The plaintiff owned the Olympia Theatre in Dublin and claimed it had a sole and exclusive right to perform the musical 'Les Miserables' in Ireland. It wished to sue in Ireland the three English defendants for specific performance of the contract. Costello J held that the obligation forming the basis of the plaintiff's claim was to grant a right to perform, ie an intellectual property right. This obligation would be performed by the execution of a valid legal document by which exclusive distribution rights are granted. The execution of this document would take place in England, not in Ireland. Accordingly, the Irish courts had no jurisdiction under Article 5(1). The plaintiff would have to sue in England, using Article 2.

Once a sole and exclusive right has been granted, the licensor will be under an obligation not to grant the same right to another person. It is not easy to say where a negative obligation like this is to be performed.[23] The *Olympia* case would suggest that it is where the licensor resides and executes the document granting the right to another. Thus, if the Irish plaintiff in that case had complained that the sole and exclusive rights granted to it, assuming that such rights had been granted, had been broken by the grant in England to another of performance rights in Ireland, it would not be able to sue the English defendants in Ireland by virtue of Article 5(1). In contrast, the Court of Appeal in *Medway Packaging Ltd* v *Meurer Maschinen GmbH & Co KG*[24] regarded the negative obligation not to supply goods to another in breach of an exclusive distribution agreement as being performed in more than one State, for reasons which are neither fully explained nor obvious. As will be seen, on the facts of the case, performance was in, first, the State of the grantor's residence and, secondly, the State whose area is covered by the distribution agreement and where the distributor was resident. If you apply this analogy, it could be argued that the negative obligation not to grant a right to another person is performed not only where the licensor resides and executes the document granting the right to another but also where the territory is that is covered by the grant. It is submitted though that it makes much more sense to regard the obligation not to grant a licence to another person as being performed where the licensor resides and executes the document granting the right to another.

It might be thought, from these examples, that Article 5(1) is of little use to licensees who wish to sue in their home State a licensor domiciled in another Contracting State. But this is not always so. It all depends on the

---

[22] [1992] ILRM 204.
[23] See the *Medway* case at first instance [1990] ILPr 234 at 240, discussed below, p 83.
[24] N 20 above; see also the *Boss* case, n 7 above. Both cases are discussed and criticised below, pp 84–86.

obligation, the breach of which is relied upon by the licensee. Take the example of a French company granting to an English company rights in relation to England under an exclusive license. If the licensor operates in England in breach of the obligation of exclusivity, the place of performance of this obligation, presumably, is England and the licensee will be able to sue in England using Article 5(1). Moreover, it has been argued that the license need not specifically refer to England; that exclusivity should cover all States where the parties expect the license to be effective, ie is capable of being registered.[25] Thus, in a case where it was alleged that a Portuguese licensor itself attempted to register an infringing trade mark in France in breach of a licence granted to a French plaintiff, it has been suggested that the French courts should have jurisdiction even though France was not specifically referred to in the license.[26] If the obligation of the licensor that has been broken is that of helping with the quality control of a product manufactured under the licence, the place of performance of this obligation is, presumably, where the licensee manufactures the product. This will not necessarily be in the same Contracting State as where the licensee is domiciled.

(ii) *Distribution agreements*

Distributor's obligations. Let us start with the obligations imposed on the distributor who is granted the distribution rights. Two such obligations were considered in the context of Article 5(1) by the Irish Supreme Court in *Ferndale Films Ltd* v *Granada Television Ltd and Another*.[27] The plaintiff company, which made the film 'My Left Foot', brought an action in Ireland for breach of contract against the first defendant, a company registered and domiciled in England, which had been granted world wide distribution rights for the film, except for the United Kingdom and Ireland. The first defendant contested the jurisdiction of the Irish court, alleging that it would have to be sued in England by virtue of Article 2 of the Brussels Convention. Carney J, at first instance, treated the case as one where the core obligation under the distribution agreement was to pay money and, since this was to be paid in Ireland, there was jurisdiction by virtue of Article 5(1). The appeal by the defendant was allowed by the Irish Supreme Court. Blayney J, giving the judgment of that Court, accepted the argument of the defendant that there was no plea in the statement of claim of any sums having actually been received and not properly distributed and therefore no breach of the obligation to pay money in Ireland. He took the view that the plaintiff's statement of claim complained, principally, of two breaches of obligation, first, failing to use all reasonable endeavours

---

[25] Gautier, (1991) 80 *RCDIP* 400. See also Trooboff, in McLachlan and Nygh at pp 139–140 and 143–144.
[26] Gautier, N 25 above.
[27] [1994] ILPr 180.

to ensure the proper distribution and exploitation of the film throughout the distribution territory and secondly, failing properly to collect sums due and owing in respect of the distribution of the film. He followed the case law of the Court of Justice[28] on Article 5(1) stating that in this situation, where reliance is placed on the breach of two obligations, it is necessary to identify the principal obligation and then determine whether this obligation was to be performed in Ireland. He came to the conclusion that the main thrust of the statement of claim was that the defendant failed to perform the first of these obligations. This obligation was not to be performed in Ireland. Accordingly, the Irish courts lacked jurisdiction under Article 5(1).

A distributor is given distribution rights for certain territory. Commonly, a locally domiciled distributor will be appointed for the territory in question. The obligations of the distributor will frequently be specifically related to the territory over which the distribution rights have been granted, and will be performed there. As a consequence, it is going to be relatively easy to identify the place of performance of the obligation in question. More significantly, it will often be the case that Article 5(1) will be of no use to a grantor who wishes to sue the distributor in a Contracting State other than the one in which the latter is domiciled. To take an example, a distributor, domiciled in State A, is under an obligation to use its best endeavours to improve the goodwill of the grantor, who is domiciled in State B, in State A, the territory for which it is given distribution rights. No doubt, the place of performance of this obligation will be State A. The result is that the grantor cannot use Article 5(1) to sue in State B for breach of this obligation, since this is not the place of performance of the obligation in question. It will be necessary to sue the distributor in State A, using Article 2. The same result will apply if the obligation broken by the distributor was not to compete in the specified territory (State A), or to achieve certain sales targets in State A or to store products under certain conditions in State A, or meet the labelling requirements of State A.

It would be otherwise, and the grantor may be able to employ Article 5(1) so as to sue in a Contracting State other than the one in which the distributor is domiciled, in the situation where the obligation of the distributor is to send to the grantor an inspection report on each shipment received by the distributor. The place of performance of this obligation would doubtless be where the grantor resides,[29] enabling the latter to bring an action there, using Article 5(1). Similarly, if the obligation in question is not to sell outside the specified territory, doubtless the place of performance of this obligation will be in the territory where the product is sold in breach of the obligation. The place of performance is more difficult to

---

[28] See the *Shenavai* case, n 13 above and text accompanying.
[29] Unless it is said that merely posting the report is enough.

identify where the obligation is phrased in terms of not exporting a product. Is the place of performance where the product is exported from or where it is exported to? There is a similar problem in identifying the place of performance of the obligation not to assist any other party to copy products. Where does the assistance take place? Is it where the copy is made or where the information is sent from, ie where the distributor resides?

Grantor's obligations in relation to a sole and exclusive agreement. We now move on to look at the situation where the grantor is being sued by the distributor for breach of one of his (the grantor's) obligations. The most common situation that has come before the courts is where the distributor claims that the grantor has appointed another as distributor in breach of a sole and exclusive distribution agreement. The agreement itself often will not spell out what the obligations of the grantor are in respect of such an agreement. This has led to considerable discussion in the courts, both in England and abroad, as to what the grantor's obligation or obligations are, and consequently as to where the obligation or obligations are to be performed. The obligation of the grantor has been variously described as an obligation: to supply the distributor; not to supply anyone else; to give the distributor reasonable notice before terminating the agreement; and to continue the exclusive distributorship. The grantor is regarded by the English and Irish courts as being under more than one of these obligations. This means that it has been necessary to identify the principal obligation. In contrast, Belgian, French and Dutch courts have referred to just one obligation.

An obligation to supply the distributor. Both English and French courts have discussed this obligation. In *Medway Packaging Ltd* v *Meurer Maschinen GmbH & Co KG*, Hobhouse J referred to this first obligation, and indeed to two other obligations.[30] The English plaintiff grantee sued the German defendant grantor for breach of an exclusive distribution agreement, appointing it a sole distributor of the defendant's machinery in the United Kingdom. Hobhouse J held that the defendant's obligations under what was an informal and undefined agreement were: (i) in Germany, to sell goods to the plaintiff at a discount; (ii) arguably, not during the currency of the agreement to sell goods to any other UK importer; (iii) arguably, to give the plaintiff reasonable notice before terminating the agreement. As regards this first obligation, this was to be performed in Germany because the goods were sold on terms which were ex-works in Germany. There was no jurisdiction under Article 5(1) if reliance was placed on this obligation. However, as will be seen, jurisdiction was possible by relying on the other two obligations. It was on these two obligations that the Court of Appeal[31] focused its attention, identifying the

[30] [1990] ILPr 234. [31] [1990] 2 Lloyd's Rep 112.

principal obligation, when upholding the judgment at first instance. Indeed, the Court of Appeal did not appear to be concerned with the obligation to supply, seemingly on the basis that supply was dealt with under separate sales contracts.[32]

Similar reasoning was applied more recently by the Court of Appeal in *Boss Group Ltd* v *Boss France SA*.[33] The plaintiff English company sought a negative declaration in England that no contract of distributorship of its products in France existed between it and the defendant French distributor. Saville LJ[34] said that the plaintiff could be said to be under two obligations, again in respect of an undefined agreement: an obligation to supply the distributor and a negative obligation not to supply anyone else. As regards the first obligation, the products were delivered to the defendant ex-works England. The obligation, therefore, fell to be performed in England. Accordingly, there was jurisdiction under Article 5(1). If the French distributor were to complain in France about a breach of the distribution agreement, and the French court were to apply this reasoning, it would not be able to sue in France on the basis of an obligation to supply, since this was to be performed in England. As will be seen, reliance was also placed by the Court of Appeal on the negative obligation not to supply anyone else. Whichever of the two obligations was regarded as the principal one, there was jurisdiction under Article 5(1).

The grantor can protect itself from being sued in a Contracting State other than its domicile for breach of the obligation to supply by ensuring that the place of supply is in its home State. If, on the other hand, the place of supply is in the distributor's home State, then the grantor will be subject to the jurisdiction of the courts of that State. This is illustrated by the decision of the Cour d'Appel, Paris, in *Gilbert Meyer* v *La Société Charles Wednesbury Ltd*.[35] The plaintiff French domiciled company had acted as exclusive agent for the defendant English company for a number of years and complained that the latter had broken their agreement. The defendant's products were delivered to the French plaintiff. The Cour d'Appel, Paris, had jurisdiction under Article 5(1). The defendant was under an obligation to supply the plaintiff with its products, the place of performance of this obligation was France.

A negative obligation not to supply anyone else. We now return to look in more detail at this obligation. Hobhouse J in the *Medway* case referred to what was, arguably, an obligation not, during the currency of the agreement, to sell goods to any other UK importer. He pointed out that this was a negative obligation and that the problem with this was that it may not

---

[32] [1990] 2 Lloyd's Rep 112 at 116. [33] [1996] 4 All ER 970.
[34] *Ibid*, at 975–976.
[35] [1996] ILPr 299. See also Judgment of 2 June 1988, *A Montforts GmbH & Co* v *Dudon SA* Note Huet, Clunet 1990, 147; D Series I-5.1.1–B 27.

involve performance or may have no clear place of performance.[36] Moreover, the attribution of a location to an act of repudiation is essentially arbitrary. Nonetheless, he went on to hold that the obligation not to supply any other United Kingdom distributor is an obligation which the plaintiff grantee can say has to be performed in England as much as in Germany. In other words, it was an obligation which had more than one place of performance. The English courts had jurisdiction since England was one of the places in which this obligation was to be performed. The Court of Appeal agreed with this analysis.[37] Lord Justice Fox, with whom Lord Justices Parker and Ralph Gibson concurred, said that the grant of an exclusive right of distribution in England carries with it an obligation on the part of the grantor so to act in England and Germany as to respect fully the rights of the grantee under the distribution agreement. Neither Fox LJ nor Hobhouse J explained how it could be said that the obligation was to be performed in England, when the German grantor sold its goods ex-works in Germany. The explanation may lie in the fact that a distinction was drawn in the Court of Appeal between the distribution agreement itself and the sales contracts made in pursuance of this agreement.[38] But if the negative obligation is one not to supply another, as Lord Justice Fox accepted, it is surely relevant to look at the contract of supply. Whatever complaints there are about the process of reasoning, there is surely nothing wrong with the result in the *Medway* case. Article 5 has been justified on the basis that jurisdiction is allocated to an appropriate forum.[39] If an English exclusive distributor is complaining about another English distributor being appointed for the United Kingdom then it is hard to deny that England is an appropriate forum for trial.

The Court of Appeal in the *Boss* case used similar reasoning. The grantor was said to be under a negative obligation not to supply anyone else. This latter obligation was held to be probably performable everywhere, including both in England and France. This meant that the English courts had jurisdiction under Article 5(1). The result in the case cannot be justified. The English court should not be trying a case involving the distribution of a product in France by a French company. This is what happens when you combine a negative declaration with a negative obligation. The use of a negative declaration in the *Boss* case has rightly been criticised[40] What is objectionable is the fact that this obligation is said to be performable

---

[36] N 30, at 240. See also *Carl Stuart Ltd v Biotrace Ltd* [1994] ILPr 554 at 558–559, discussed below, pp 87–88.

[37] N 31, at 117.   [38] N 31 above, at 116.

[39] See the Jenard Report, p 22; the *Tessili* case, n 14 above; Case 33/78 *Etablissements Somafer v Saar-Ferngas AG* [1978] ECR 2183; Case 34/82 *Peters v Zuid Nederlandse Aannemers Vereniging* [1983] ECR 987. It may not be the forum which has the closest connection with the dispute: Case C-288/92 *Custom Made Commercial Ltd v Stawa Metallbau GmbH* [1994] ILPr 516.

[40] See, generally, the criticism by Forsyth, [1996] *Lloyd's MCLQ* 329.

'everywhere'. It is noticeable that the obligation was phrased in rather different terms from that in the *Medway* case. In that case, by referring to not selling to any other English distributor, it limited the place of performance to two States, England and Germany. An obligation not to supply *anyone* has a dramatic effect on where the obligation is to be performed, ie *everywhere*. How this comes about and what it actually means is not entirely clear. Does this mean anywhere in the EC where the supply could potentially take place? This would give the plaintiff far too wide a choice of fora. It would make much more sense to limit it to where the supply actually takes place, in other words, where the breach takes place. Even so, in a case of an action for breach of the distribution agreement, it could mean an English court having jurisdiction because the supply to a new distributor for France took place in England, even though the dispute was between a German grantor and a French distributor in relation to distribution in France. The result is that jurisdiction is being allocated to a State which is not an appropriate one for trial.

In the Irish case of *Carl Stuart Ltd* v *Biotrace Ltd*,[41] Barron J expressed the negative obligation in rather different terms. He referred to an obligation not to permit any other distributor to sell its goods within the jurisdiction, and to the fact that the breach of this obligation may occur in a number of ways. The defendant may sell the goods to another in a particular country, he may enter into an agreement with a foreign parent of a local subsidiary. In this latter situation, he pointed out that the place where the breach occurs would depend on where the document was executed.[42] Clearly unhappy at allocating jurisdiction on this basis, he went on to base his decision on a positive obligation to continue the distribution agreement, which is examined below.

An obligation to give the grantee reasonable notice before terminating the agreement. Hobhouse J in the *Medway* case referred to what was, arguably, an obligation to give the plaintiff grantee reasonable notice before terminating the agreement. This obligation was also to be performed in England. The Court of Appeal agreed with this analysis. Lord Justice Fox said[43] that, unless there is some provision to the contrary in the contract, a requirement to give notice to an English company carrying on business in England must be interpreted as an obligation to give notice at the company's place of business in England. The company can waive this by way of a concession. The upshot was that this obligation was to be performed in England. He went on to add that this could reasonably be regarded as the principal obligation in the present case. This was because it is the giving of proper notice which brings the whole contract to an end. In contrast, Lord Gill, in the Court of Session, appears not to have accepted the argu-

---

[41] [1994] ILPr 554. [42] *Ibid*, at 558–559. [43] N 31 above, at 116.

ment of counsel that the Scots grantor was under an obligation to give due notice of termination of an exclusive distribution agreement to the French grantee and that this obligation fell to be performed in France.[44]

The Belgian courts have likewise based their jurisdiction under Article 5(1) on this obligation. After the Court of Justice, in the famous case of *De Bloos v Bouyer*,[45] gave its preliminary ruling, that the obligation in question was the one forming the basis of the legal proceedings, it referred back to the Belgian courts the question of the identity of that obligation in the situation where a Belgian exclusive distributor was seeking dissolution of its contract with a French supplier and damages for the supplier's unilateral repudiation without notice. The Cour d'Appel, Mons, held that the basis of the dispute was the obligation to give a period of notice.[46] To that obligation corresponded the right of the exclusive distributor to continue to make use of the rights under the exclusive distributorship contract within the area covered by the contract during the period of notice. It was in that area, in this case Belgium, that the obligation was to be performed. Accordingly, the Belgian courts had jurisdiction. This obligation to give a period of notice has been described as a manifestation of the continuing existence of the supplier's fundamental contractual obligation to respect the exclusive rights of the distributor in his area.[47] It is noticeable that, under Belgian law, this obligation has to be performed in the country where the exclusive agreement was to be carried out.[48] In the situation where, for example, an English company is exclusive distributor for Belgium, the obligation would be performed in Belgium. In contrast, under the English approach, it would be performed at the company's place of business in England.

An obligation to continue the exclusive distributorship. This obligation formed the basis of the decision of Barron J in the Irish High Court in *Carl Stuart Ltd v Biotrace Ltd*.[49] The plaintiff sought to enforce an exclusive distributorship for Ireland, granted by a company with a registered office in the United Kingdom. Barron J, after referring to the difficulties in fixing the place of performance of a negative obligation, said that it was necessary to look to the right to which such obligation corresponds and upon which the proceedings are based. The plaintiff sought to establish: (i) the

---

[44] *William Grant & Sons International Ltd* v *Marie Brizard Et Roger International SA* [1997] ILPr 391, 402.

[45] N 12 above.

[46] Judgment of 3 May 1977, *A De Bloos Sprl* v *Société en commandité par actions Bouyer* JT 1977, 637; Jur Belg 1977, 348; Pas b 1978, II, 8; D Series I-5.1.1–B 6.

[47] Judgment of 6 April 1978, *Knauer & Co Maschinenfabrik* v *Callens* JT 1978, D Series I-5.1.1–B 8.

[48] Judgment of 19 January 1984, *Carl Freudenberg KG* v *Bureau RV Van Oppens SARL* JT 1984, 637; D Series I-5.1.1–B 21.

[49] [1993] ILRM 632.

right to continue as exclusive distributor of the defendant's products; and (ii) the right to continued supply of these products. Barron J sought to identify the principal obligation to which the proceedings relate, and came to the conclusion that it was the former obligation. This obligation could only be performed in Ireland. Presumably, this was because the distributorship related to Ireland. Consequently, the Irish court had jurisdiction under Article 5(1). The good thing about this decision is that, seemingly, it homes in on the Contracting State to which the distribution agreement relates, which, it is submitted, is a much more significant connection than where sale or delivery to the distributor take place. It also avoids all the problems associated with a negative obligation.

Essentially, the same process of reasoning was adopted by the Supreme Court of the Netherlands[50] in an earlier case concerning a concession agreement. That court described the main obligation in an exclusive concession agreement as being a positive one, to enable the Dutch concessionaire to deal in the foreign grantor's products in the Netherlands to the exclusion of others. This was perhaps not very surprising since counsel for the concessionaire pleaded the case on the basis of a single obligation by the grantor to maintain the concession, rather than on the basis, as in the English cases, of several obligations. It was explained that this main obligation was to be performed in the Netherlands because the concessionaire had his place of business in the Netherlands and this was the country to which the concession applied. In another case, where the nature of the obligation was not pleaded as clearly, the same Dutch court again put the emphasis on the positive obligation to maintain the concession, even though a lower court regarded the relevant obligation as being a negative one not to terminate the concession.[51]

The Irish and Dutch view of the obligation in question has much to commend it. It is to be regretted that the English courts have taken a different view. Lord Justice Fox in the *Medway* case, whilst accepting that an agreement for an exclusive agency is to be performed by procuring that a certain state of affairs continues to exist, was insistent that the nature of the obligation is a negative one.[52]

Other obligations of the grantor. The grantor may be under an obligation to provide promotional literature to the distributor free of charge. The place of performance of this is normally going to be where the distributor resides, enabling him, by virtue of Article 5(1), to bring an action in his home State against a grantor domiciled abroad for breach of this obligation.

[50] *Hacker Kuchen GmbH* v *Bosma Huygen Meubelimpex BV (Case 14.197)* [1992] ILPr 379.
[51] Judgment of 1 November 1991, *Isopad* v *Huikeshoven* NJ 1992, 422, note Schultsz; NIPR 1992, no 121. See, generally, on both cases Pellis [1993] NILR 239.
[52] N 31, above at 117. See the discussion above at pp 84–86.

(iii) *Assignments*

Assignee's obligations. Let us start with the obligations of the assignee. The most obvious obligation is to pay a lump sum to the assignor. Normally, the place of performance of this obligation will be where the assignor resides. This means that, in the event of the assignee failing to pay, the assignor will be able to sue in its home State by virtue of Article 5(1). Alternatively, by virtue of Article 2, the assignor can sue in the Contracting State where the assignee is domiciled. In short, the position is analogous to that where a licensee fails to pay royalties. As with licences and distribution agreements, there can be problems in identifying the place of performance of an obligation because of the very nature of that obligation. For example, the assignee may be under an obligation to accept a joint venture, the assignment being part of this. Where is the place of performance of such an obligation? Is it where the joint venture is to operate, or where the assignee is to execute documents or do other acts in pursuance of the joint venture?

Assignor's obligations. We now move on to look at the assignor's obligations. The assignor is under an obligation to transfer a proprietary right. Applying the analogy of the *Olympia* case,[53] the place of performance of this obligation is where the assignor would execute the document of transfer, ie where he is domiciled. The result is that the assignee, who complains that the right has not been transferred, will be unable to use Article 5(1) in order to sue in a Contracting State other than the one in which the assignor is domiciled. The assignor may be under an obligation to alter the name appearing in the register in which the right is registered. The place of performance of this obligation undoubtedly will be where the right is registered. Thus, if an English company assigns a French patent to a German company, and fails in its obligation to alter the name in the register, the German company can sue in France to force it to do so. Neither party may come from France. Nonetheless, Article 5(1) allocates jurisdiction to an appropriate forum, given that this is a French patent. There is the usual problem that with some obligations it is difficult to identify the place of performance. For example, the assignor may be in breach of the obligation guaranteeing that the right is valid in the first place or the obligation guaranteeing that the right is free of licences. Where is the place of performance of such obligations? It is arguable that these guarantees are linked to the assignment itself and so are given when the assignor executes the document of transfer. The place of performance is, therefore, where the document is executed, ie where the assignor is domiciled.

---

[53] N 22 above and text accompanying.

(c) Employment contracts

Article 5(1) provides that, in matters relating to individual contracts of employment, the place of performance of the obligation in question 'is that where the employee habitually carries out his work, or if the employee does not habitually carry out his work in any one country, the employer may also be sued in the courts for the place where the business which engaged the employee was or is now situated'. It is hard to envisage this provision coming into play in a contract for the exploitation of intellectual property rights, such as a license or assignment. However, it would come into play in the more general context of contracts relating to intellectual property. For example, it would be relevant where an employee who made an invention applies for compensation under his contract of employment.

(iv) Consumer contracts (Articles 13–15)

Section 4 (Articles 13–15) contains special jurisdictional rules in relation to consumer contracts. For these special jurisdictional rules to apply there has to be a contract concluded by a consumer (ie a person who concludes a contract for a purpose outside his trade or profession[54]). Normally, with contracts for the exploitation of intellectual property rights this will not be the case. For example, the Court of Justice has held that a German plaintiff, who entered into a franchise agreement for the purpose of setting up a business (under which agreement he was authorised to exploit the right to use a trade mark within a particular geographical area) was not a consumer.[55] However, you could have a software license and the licensee plans to use the software for private purposes falling outside his profession. You would then have a contract concluded by a consumer. There is, though, an additional requirement which has to be satisfied before these special jurisdictional rules can apply. This is that the contract is of a type listed in Article 13. This includes a contract for the supply of goods or for the supply of services, provided that certain other conditions are met.[56] It is doubtful whether a contract for a software license can be so categorised. The upshot is that the special jurisdiction rules in relation to consumer contracts will not apply to such a contract, or, indeed, to any other contract for the exploitation of intellectual property rights.

---

[54] Article 13.
[55] Case C-269/95 *Francesco Benincasa v Dentalkit Srl* [1997] ILPr 559.
[56] Article 13(3).

(v) Does Article 16(4) apply?

(a) *The normal position*

In chapter 1, it was seen that Article 16(4), by allocating exclusive jurisdiction to courts of one Contracting State, acts as a subject matter limitation on the jurisdiction of the courts of other Contracting States. However, this provision is limited to proceedings concerned with the registration or validity of patents, etc. At first sight, it would appear to have no relevance to contractual disputes, even though the contract relates to intellectual property rights. As has previously been mentioned,[57] the Cour d'Appel, Paris, in *SA des Etablissements Salik et SA Diffusal v SA J Esterel*,[58] held that Article 16(4) did not apply to an action concerned solely with breaches of a licensing agreement, without the validity of that agreement or of the trade mark being affirmed or contested by any party.

(b) *A defence of invalidity*

What is interesting about the decision in the *Salik* case is that it gives an indication as to when Article 16(4) would be relevant in a contract case. There is the implication that if the validity of that agreement or of the trade mark is affirmed or contested by any party Article 16(4) would apply. The invalidity of a right registered in an EC/EFTA Contracting State may be raised, in effect, as a defence to a claim for the payment of royalties. This is what happened in *JA Motte v Tecno SpA*,[59] a case decided by the Tribunale di Milano. The owner of a patent registered in France brought proceedings before the Tribunale di Milano against an Italian company for the payment of royalties owed by the latter under a contract for the exclusive use of the patent in Italy. The Italian company objected that the patent was void for lack of novelty, the contract for its exclusive use was void as lacking in object, and the claim for royalties should be dismissed. The court dismissed the claim. It held that it had no jurisdiction with respect to the defendant's application for a declaration that the patent was void. Because of Article 16(4), only the French courts could decide on the validity of the patent.

The same approach has been applied by Laddie J in the High Court in England in *Coin Controls Ltd v Suzo International (UK) Ltd and Others*.[60] This was an infringement case where it was plain that the validity of the three European patents involved was going to be raised. The learned judge held

---
[57] See above, p 20.
[58] *Revue Critique de Droit International Privé*, 1982, p 135; D Series I-16.4–B2.
[59] *Rivista di Diritto Internazionale Privato e Processuale* 1981, p 913; D Series I-16.4–B3.
[60] [1997] 3 All ER 45; discussed below, pp 204–206.

that Articles 19[61] and 16(4) meant that the court had no jurisdiction over the whole of the claim, including the infringement part. This decision was expressly affirmed by the Court of Appeal in *Fort Dodge Animal Health Ltd and Others* v *Akzo Nobel NV and Another*.[62]

Nonetheless, it is arguable that these decisions are wrong and that if the question of validity is raised merely as a defence, then this does not preclude jurisdiction in the Contracting State in which the claim for the payment of royalties, or infringement, is brought. This view is based on the wording of Article 19, and its requirement that a court of a Contracting State only has no jurisdiction when it is seised of a claim which is *principally concerned* with validity. It is submitted that when validity is raised merely as a defence to a claim for royalties the claim is not *principally concerned* with validity. This argument is considered in more detail in the context of infringement.[63] What is needed is a decision of the Court of Justice to eliminate the uncertainty in this area. There is a reference to the Court of Justice from the Court of Appeal in the *Fort Dodge* case which should end the uncertainty, at least where validity is raised in the context of infringement.

We must now examine the situation where Articles 19 and 16(4) do not preclude jurisdiction (ie the above argument is accepted, or it is a case involving an unregistered right, or one registered outside the EC/EFTA Contracting States). Does the court with jurisdiction in relation to the cause of action for payment of royalties also have jurisdiction in relation to the validity defence? A court which has jurisdiction to try the claim for the payment of royalties on the basis of Article 2 (domicile of the defendant), Article 5(5) (branch, agency or other establishment), or Article 6(1) (a multi-defendant case) would also have jurisdiction to try the issue of validity in the situation where Article 16(4) does not come into play.[64] There is a problem, though, where jurisdiction is based on Article 5(1). The wording of this provision would not cover a cause of action for validity. However, there is a strong argument of principle that, where validity is raised as a mere defence, no independent basis of jurisdiction should be necessary for the trial of this defence.[65] It is also important, as a matter of policy, that the issue of the claim for the payment of royalties and the issue of validity should not be split between the courts of different Contracting States.[66]

(c) *A counterclaim for revocation*

Where the invalidity issue arises by way of a counterclaim for revocation, this is a cause of action in its own right. If you treat the counterclaim for

[61] Set out below, p 203.
[62] [1998] FSR 222.
[63] See below, p 203.
[64] See above, p 29.
[65] See below, pp 208–209.
[66] See below, p 209.

revocation as separate proceedings, which you should do given that this is a cross action, the proceedings are *principally concerned* with validity. If the case concerns a right registered in another EC/EFTA Contracting State, Articles 19 and 16(4) will apply to preclude jurisdiction in relation to the counterclaim for revocation. Does it also preclude the claim for the payment of royalties? There is a suggestion, in infringement cases, that the claim for infringement is also precluded where there is a counterclaim for revocation.[67] But this is based on the close relationship between validity and infringement under English patent law. Moreover, there is general uncertainty over the position in infringement cases in the situation where there is a counterclaim for revocation. The better view is that a claim for the payment of royalties should not be precluded by a counterclaim for revocation.

In the situation where Article 16(4) does not apply, for example it concerns an unregistered right or one registered outside the EC/EFTA Contracting States, there would need to be a basis of jurisdiction in relation to this cause of action for revocation. The same difficulties arise in infringement cases where there is a counterclaim for revocation, and have been the subject of some discussion. The discussion in that context is equally applicable in the present context.[68]

(d) *Separate revocation proceedings*

We are concerned here with the situation where there is a claim for royalties in Contracting State A and the defendant petitions for revocation of the right in Contracting State B where it is registered. The courts of Contracting State B have exclusive jurisdiction to try the petition for revocation. Does this mean though that the courts in Contracting State A are precluded from trying the claim for royalties because of Articles 19 and 16(4)? The case law dealing with the analogous situation where there is a claim for infringement and separate revocation proceedings[69] suggests that they are so precluded. But to say that the courts of Contracting State A are *principally concerned* with a matter not even raised in the litigation in that State, but only raised in separate revocation proceedings in another Contracting State gives an extraordinarily wide interpretation to Article 19. The better view is that they are not so concerned and, accordingly, not precluded from trying the royalties claim.

(e) *The validity of the agreement is contested*

The *Salik* case could be read literally as suggesting that Article 16(4) can come into play in the situation where the validity of the licence agreement

[67] See below, pp 210–211.   [68] See below, pp 211–212.   [69] See below, pp 213–214.

is contested. If this is contested on the basis that the patent is invalid, as happened in the *Motte* case, then Article 16(4) does indeed become relevant, but this is because of the invalidity of the patent being raised. If the validity of the licence is raised without any question arising as to the validity of the patent then Article 16(4) can have no relevance.

(v) Article 17

Brief mention has previously been made of exclusive jurisdiction under Article 17.[70] This basis of jurisdiction is particularly significant where there is a contactual dispute. The parties may well have inserted a choice of jurisdiction clause within the contract and have thereby 'agreed that a court or the courts of a Contracting State are to have jurisdiction to settle any disputes which have arisen or which may arise in connection with a particular legal relationship', as specified by Article 17. Certain formalities have to be satisfied for Article 17 to apply.[71] It has been held, by Hoffmann J, that a clause conferring non-exclusive jurisdiction on the English courts comes within Article 17 so as to give jurisdiction to the English courts.[72] An exclusive jurisdiction clause protects the licensor from the risk of being sued in several countries by a licensee who has been granted a licence for an area covering several countries.[73] On the other hand, it forces the licensor (and the licensee) to sue in one country when he might prefer the option of suing in some other country where the defendant has assets.

There do not appear to be any particular difficulties in applying Article 17 in cases involving contracts in relation to the exploitation of intellectual property rights. A simple illustration of its application in this context can be seen in the decision of the Cour d'Appel, Paris, in *Hantarex SpA v SA Digital Research*.[74] A French importer and distributor of software and computer diskettes, brought a claim in the French courts for royalties against its Italian licensee. The French court had jurisdiction because of a jurisdiction clause in the licence agreement conferring non-exclusive jurisdiction on 'the Paris Courts'.

---

[70] See above, p 36.
[71] The agreement must be in writing or evidenced in writing, or in a form which accords with practices which the parties have established between themselves, or in a form which accords with a trade usage. See, generally, Cheshire and North, pp 318–320.
[72] *Kurz v Stella Musical Veranstaltungs GmbH* [1992] Ch 196; followed in *Gamlestaden PLC v Casa De Suecia SA and Hans Thulin* [1994] 1 Lloyd's Rep 433.
[73] Lefever, (1988) 132 SJ 980. [74] [1993] ILPr 501.

Exploitation of IP rights: jurisdiction 95

(b) DECLINING JURISDICTION AND RESTRAINING FOREIGN PROCEEDINGS

(i) Declining jurisdiction

(a) *Under the Brussels and Lugano Conventions*

There are no special difficulties in applying the provisions on lis pendens and related actions[75] in cases concerning contracts relating to the exploitation of intellectual property rights.[76]

(b) *Using the doctrine of* **forum non conveniens**

(i) *Does the* Re Harrods (Buenos Aires) *doctrine apply where jurisdiction is based on Articles 5(1) or 17?*

The application of the *Re Harrods (Buenos Aires)* doctrine has already been examined.[77] One question that arises in the context of contracts is whether that doctrine extends to cases where jurisdiction is based, not on Article 2 of the Brussels Convention, but on Article 5(1) or Article 17. The principle enunciated by the Court of Appeal appears to be applicable, regardless of the basis of jurisdiction. Indeed, it has been accepted that the principle in *Re Harrods* applies equally to cases where the jurisdiction of the English courts is based on Article 6(1) of the Lugano Convention.[78] It is important to note that where the jurisdiction of the English courts is based on Article 5(1), there will necessarily be a strong connection with another Contracting State. This provision only operates to allocate jurisdiction to one Contracting State where the defendant is domiciled in another Contracting State. Accordingly, there will be an alternative forum in a Contracting State. However, the case may involve connections with a third State outside the EC and the defendant may claim that the alternative forum is outside the EC. If this is the only forum put forward by the defendant, the Court of Appeal has held that there is a discretion to stay on the basis of *forum non conveniens*.[79] Nonetheless, this situation is very different from that facing the court in the *Re Harrods* case where the United Kingdom was the only EC Contracting State with which there were connections and the alternative forum was Argentina. Similarly, where an

---

[75] Articles 21 and 22 are discussed above, pp 36–37.
[76] For an example of the use of Article 21 see *William Grant & Sons v Marie Brizard*, n 44 above. For an example of an unsuccessful attempt to use the related actions provision in Article 22, see *Rank Film Distributors v Lanterna Editrice Srl*, N 21 above.
[77] See above, p 38.
[78] See *Aiglon Ltd and L'Aiglon SA v Gau Shan Co Ltd* [1993] 1 Lloyd's Rep 164, this was obiter since it was a case involving a Contracting State as the alternative forum.
[79] *The Po* [1991] 2 Lloyd's Rep 206.

English court has exclusive jurisdiction under Article 17, it must be the case that one of the parties is domiciled in a Contracting State. If this is outside the UK, there will be an alternative forum in an EC Contracting State. Of course, there may be connections with a third State outside the EC and if the only forum put forward by the defendant is this State, there is a power to stay. But again, the situation is very different from that facing the court in the *Re Harrods* case. It is submitted that it would be best if the *Re Harrods* doctrine were to be confined to the situation where jurisdiction is based on Article 2 , as happened in the case itself.

(ii) *Application of the* forum non conveniens *criteria*

Even if the present position is maintained so that, as a matter of principle, the doctrine can apply where jurisdiction is based on these other provisions, when it comes to applying the *forum non conveniens* criteria the outcome is fairly predictable. The defendant will be very hard pressed to show that the clearly appropriate forum is the alternative forum from outside the EC. If there is an agreement on trial in England, this would appear to be the natural forum for trial. If the English court's jurisdiction is based on Article 5(1), two of the most important connecting factors, the defendant's domicile and the place of performance of the obligation in question, will not be with the alternative forum, if any, outside the EC. It should also be noted that there is judicial support for the idea that the English courts should be reluctant to stay proceedings when jurisdiction has been allocated to the United Kingdom under the Brussels Convention.[80]

(ii) Restraining foreign proceedings

An English court will issue an injunction restraining a party from continuing with proceedings brought in another Contracting State in breach of an exclusive jurisdiction clause conferring exclusive jurisdiction on the English courts under Article 17.[81] It will do, likewise, where the proceedings have been brought in another Contracting State in breach of an English arbitration clause.[82] Moreover, where interlocutory injunctions have been issued in England restraining foreign defendants from continuing with proceedings in another Contracting State and they have notice of this before obtaining judgments in actions relating to the same cause of action in their home courts, the resulting foreign judgments will be refused recognition under the Brussels Convention as being contrary to public policy.[83]

---

[80] *S & W Berisford plc* v *New Hampshire Insurance Co* [1990] QB 631 at 645–646.
[81] *Continental Bank NA* v *Aeakos Compañía Naviera SA* [1994] 1 WLR 588.
[82] *The Angelic Grace* [1995] 1 Lloyd's Rep 87. See also *Toepfer International GmbH* v *Société Cargill France* [1997] 2 Lloyd's Rep 98.
[83] *Phillip Alexander Securities and Futures Ltd* v *Bamberger and Others* [1997] ILPr 73.

3. THE TRADITIONAL RULES

(a) BASES OF JURISDICTION

(i) Service of a writ within the jurisdiction

There are no special difficulties in respect of serving a writ on the defendant[84] in cases where the dispute concerns a contract relating to the exploitation of intellectual property rights. Indeed, this basis of jurisdiction is not concerned with the nature of the cause of action.

(ii) Service of a writ out of the jurisdiction

(a) *The heads of Order 11, rule 1(1)*

(i) *The contract heads*

Order 11, rule 1(1) contains two separate heads dealing with contractual disputes. The first of these is rule 1(1)(d), which sets out four different alternatives, the second is rule 1(1)(e). Neither head is concerned with the type of contract involved. Thus, for example, they apply in exactly the same way to a licensing contract as to a sale of goods contract. Neither head is concerned with the obligation, the breach of which is relied upon by the plaintiff. The upshot is that there are no special difficulties in applying these heads to licensing agreements, distribution agreements or assignments. It is, though, worth looking briefly at the content of these heads and commenting on their practical importance in cases involving contracts relating to the exploitation of intellectual property rights.

Order 11, rule 1(1)(d). Service of a writ out of the jurisdiction is permissible with the leave of the court where 'the claim is brought to enforce, rescind, dissolve, annul or otherwise affect a contract, or to recover damages, or obtain other relief in respect of the breach of a contract' in the following cases:

(i) Where the contract 'was made within the jurisdiction.' There are no particular difficulties in applying this provision to contracts relating to the exploitation of intellectual property rights.
(ii) Where the contract 'was made by or through an agent trading or residing within the jurisdiction on behalf of a principal trading or residing out of the jurisdiction.' Likewise, there are no particular difficulties in applying this provision to contracts relating to the exploitation of intellectual property rights.

---

[84] See above, p 40.

(iii) Where the contract 'is by its terms, or by implication, governed by English law.' The question of what law governs a contract is considered in chapter 11. Suffice it to say at this stage that, subject to certain limitations, the parties are free to choose the law governing their contract. It is common for licensing and distribution agreements to contain a choice of law clause, which does precisely this. Where English law is chosen as the governing law, the result is that it will be possible to bring an action before the English courts involving a foreign defendant. A simple example is *Acrow (Automation) Ltd v Rex Chainbelt Inc and Another*.[85] The plaintiffs, an English company, entered into a licensing agreement with a US company, SI, under which they were granted the exclusive right to manufacture in England equipment for conveying goods. The agreement was expressed to be 'read and construed in accordance with English law'. The US licensor purported to terminate the agreement. It also directed other US companies, the defendants, not to supply to the plaintiffs equipment essential to the manufacture. This was in breach of an implied term of the licence agreement. The English courts had jurisdiction to grant an injunction restraining SI from, *inter alia*, doing anything to impede the plaintiffs in manufacturing the equipment. Despite the injunction, SI continued to give instructions to the defendant companies not to supply the plaintiffs. This was a contempt of court. The Court of Appeal granted an injunction restraining the defendants from obeying such instructions.

(iv) Where the contract 'contains a term to the effect that the High Court shall have jurisdiction to hear and determine any action in respect of the contract.' It is common for licensing and distribution contracts to contain a choice of jurisdiction clause, sometimes combined with a choice of law clause and sometimes on its own. If the choice of jurisdiction clause selects the English High Court, it is possible to bring an action against a foreign defendant before that court using sub-paragraph (iv).

Order 11, rule 1(1)(e) – A breach committed within the jurisdiction. Service of a writ out of the jurisdiction is permissible with the leave of the court where:

... the claim is brought in respect of a breach committed within the jurisdiction of a contract made within or out of the jurisdiction, and irrespective of the fact, if such be the case, that the breach was preceded or accompanied by a breach committed out of the jurisdiction that rendered impossible the performance of so much of the contract as ought to have been performed within the jurisdiction.

There are no particular difficulties in applying this provision to contracts relating to the exploitation of intellectual property rights.

[85] [1971] 1 WLR 1676.

(ii) The multi-defendant head

Rule 1(1)(c) provides that service of a writ out of the jurisdiction is permissible with the leave of the court where:

... the claim is brought against a person duly served within or out of the jurisdiction and a person out of the jurisdiction is a necessary or proper party thereto ...

It is a precondition of leave to serve a writ on a defendant out of the jurisdiction under this head that another defendant has already been served within or outside the jurisdiction.[86] There is a danger with this provision of the improper joining of defendants.[87] Both the first and second defendants are at risk. The plaintiff may bring a spurious claim against the first defendant, who is subject to jurisdiction, solely in order to join the 'real' defendant who is outside the jurisdiction. Alternatively, the first defendant may be the 'real' defendant and an action against the second defendant may be bound to fail. To meet these concerns, safeguards have been provided for both defendants.

A real issue. At one time, the first defendant was protected by a requirement that the action against him must have been properly brought. This also protected the second defendant from being subjected to jurisdiction in cases of abuse of the provision. The properly brought requirement was not met in *The Yorkshire Tannery and Boot Manufactory (Ltd) v The Eglinton Chemical Co (Ltd)*,[88] a case involving a licensing agreement. The plaintiff English company was granted a licence by a Scots domiciled company to use certain patent processes relating to tannery, and undertook in return to pay certain royalties. The plaintiff sought to set aside the licence agreement on the basis that it had been induced to enter into it by fraud and misrepresentation. It added on an English resident defendant and sought leave to serve out of the jurisdiction against the Scots defendant, using the multi-defendant head.[89] Pearson J discharged the order granted for service out of the jurisdiction. He said: 'I cannot think that it is the intention of this Rule of Court to bring into this country an action which was properly a Scotch action, simply because some person who had some trifling interest in the matters in dispute, and who was not a principal defendant, was made a defendant and was resident here.'[90]

The properly brought requirement has been omitted from this latest version of the multi-defendant head. Nonetheless, there is a requirement

---

[86] *Kuwait Oil Tanker Co SAK and Another v Al Bader and Others* [1997] 1 WLR 1410.
[87] See Fawcett, (1995) 44 *ICLQ* 744.   [88] (1884) 54 LJ Ch 81.
[89] Order 11, rule 1(1)(g), a predecessor of the present provision.
[90] N 88 above, at 83. There was an additional problem in the case. The first defendant must have been 'duly served', but the English defendant was only served several days after leave for service out of the jurisdiction was sought. However, the court does have power retrospectively to validate the leave for service out of the jurisdiction: *Kuwait Oil Tanker Co SAK and Another v Al Bader and Others* [1997] 1 WLR 1410.

under Order 11, rule 4(1)(d) that the plaintiff's application for service out of the jurisdiction under the multi-defendant head must be supported by an affidavit stating the grounds for his belief that there is a real issue between it and the first defendant, ie the one who is subject to jurisdiction after being duly served. It is implicit from this that the plaintiff has to establish that there is a real issue between it and the first defendant. If the facts of the *Yorkshire Tannery* case were to arise now, the same result could be reached by the use of the real issue requirement.

A necessary or proper party. It must also be shown that the second defendant, who is to be served out of the jurisdiction is 'a necessary or proper party'. This requirement will not be met if the claim against the second defendant is bound to fail.

(iii) *The injunction head*

Rule 1(1)(b) provides that service of a writ out of the jurisdiction is permissible with the leave of the court where:

... an injunction is sought ordering the defendant to do or refrain from doing anything within the jurisdiction (whether or not damages are also claimed in respect of a failure to do or the doing of that thing).

This provision is useful where, for example, a plaintiff which has been granted sole and exclusive distribution rights over a territory seeks an injunction restraining foreign grantor defendants from acting in breach of the agreement by distributing the work itself within that territory, or licensing that work for distribution within that territory, or granting a licence to distribute within that territory.[91] The advantage of using this head is that it also enables service out of the jurisdiction on foreign defendants who have in some way interfered with the rights of the plaintiff, but are not parties to the distribution or licensing contract and hence fall outside the contract heads. The nature of the cause of action against such defendants does not matter as long as there is one. It could be a cause of action, for example, in tort for conspiracy or inducement of breach of contract.[92]

Nonetheless, there are few reported cases of this head being used in relation to contracts relating to the exploitation of intellectual property rights. Doubtless, this is because of the width of the contract heads. It is often preferable to use the latter. First, there is a requirement under the injunction head that an injunction is sought ordering the defendant to do

---

[91] See *Empire-Universal Films Ltd et al* v *Rank et al* [1948] OR 235. Service out of the jurisdiction was refused by the Ontario Court of Appeal because of the defective nature of the affidavit, see below, pp 103–105.

[92] There is a tort head of Order 11, rule 1(1), discussed below, pp 244–253, which could be used instead of the injunction head.

or refrain from doing anything in England. There is no such limitation under the contract heads. Secondly, the injunction head requires that the substantial relief sought is an injunction. The contract heads are not so confined; they can operate in the situation where the substantial relief sought is damages.

(b) A serious issue to be tried

According to Lord Goff, who gave the judgment of the House of Lords in *Seaconsar Far East Ltd v Bank Markazi Jomhouri Islami Iran*, the plaintiff has to establish that there is a serious issue to be tried in that there is 'a substantial question of fact or law or both, arising on the facts disclosed by the affidavits, which the plaintiff bona fide desires to try . . .'.[93] This is a lesser standard of proof than the 'good arguable case' standard that was formerly applied when considering the merits of the plaintiff's claim. This new lesser standard undoubtedly leads to considerable complexity because of the different standard of proof when the plaintiff has to establish that a head of Order 11, rule 1(1) is satisfied.

(i) *The complexity arising from the different standards of proof for merits and heads*

The standard of proof applicable when the plaintiff has to establish that the head of Order 11, rule 1(1) is satisfied is that of a good arguable case. When considering the merits of the plaintiff's claim it is, of course, the lesser standard of a serious issue. What then complicates things is that, with certain heads of rule 1(1), in order to establish that the head is satisfied, it may be necessary to go into the merits of the case. The standard of proof applicable in such circumstances remains that of a good arguable case. In so far as the merits have already been gone into at the stage of establishing a head of rule 1(1), it is no longer necessary to make a separate enquiry into the merits of the case once the head has been established. As a result of the *Seaconsar* case, it is necessary to look at each head of rule 1(1) and ascertain whether the merits have to be gone into to establish that the terms of the head are satisfied. The heads that will commonly arise in disputes involving contracts relating to the exploitation of intellectual property rights will now be examined.

The contract heads. The position with regard to Order 11, rule 1(1)(e) is straightforward. In order to come within this head, the plaintiff must establish a good arguable case in relation to the three elements of contract, breach and place of breach. This involves going into the merits of the case. Once the terms of the head have been established, no separate issue will

[93] [1994] 1 AC 438 at 452.

arise on the merits of the plaintiff's claim to which a lower standard of proof is applied.[94]

The position with regard to paragraph (d) is more complex.[95] In order to come within sub-paragraph (i), the plaintiff has to establish a good arguable case that there was a contract and that such a contract was made within the jurisdiction. In order to come within sub-paragraph (ii), (iii) or (iv), the plaintiff must establish a good arguable case that the relevant contract exists. But once the terms of the sub-paragraph have been established, a separate issue arises as to the merits of the plaintiff's claim in relation to that contract. The lower standard of proof applies to this.[96] So, for example, if the plaintiff's cause of action is based on breach of contract, the plaintiff has to establish that there is a serious issue to be tried in relation to this breach.

The multi-defendant head. It was argued by counsel, in *Grupo Torras SA and Torras Hostench London Ltd* v *Sheikh Fahad Mohammed Al Sabah and Others*,[97] that the plaintiff had to show a good arguable case on the merits against the defendants duly served within the jurisdiction. However, this aspect of the defendants' submission was rejected by Mance J as being contrary to Lord Goff's approach in the *Seaconsar* case.[98] This conclusion is surely right, but for a different reason: it is because the wording of Order 11, rule 4(1)(d), which provides the safeguard for the defendant duly served, merely refers to a belief that there is 'a real issue', rather than a good arguable case, to be tried in relation to this defendant. Establishing that the second defendant, out of the jurisdiction, is a necessary or proper party under the head has not been regarded as raising questions on the merits. Accordingly, the plaintiff has to establish a good arguable case that the second defendant is a necessary or proper party.[99] The merits will then be gone into as a separate exercise after the head has been established, and the standard is that of a serious issue on the merits.[100]

The injunction head. The wording of this head does not suggest that any enquiry into the merits is necessary in order to come within its terms. This view is accepted implicitly by the House of Lords in the *Seaconsar* case, in which the judgment of Lord Davey in an earlier House of Lords case,[101]

---

[94] The *Seaconsar* case, N 93 above, at pp 453–454. See also *Agrafax Public Relations Ltd* v *United Scottish Society Inc* [1995] ILPr 753.

[95] The *Seaconsar* case, N 93 above, at 454–455.

[96] Ibid. See, eg *DR Insurance Co* v *Central National Insurance Co and Others* [1996] 1 Lloyd's Rep 74 at 80.

[97] [1995] 1 Lloyd's Rep 374. Appeals to the Court of Appeal were dismissed: [1996] 1 Lloyd's Rep 7.

[98] N 97 above, at 380. There was no discussion of this point in the Court of Appeal.

[99] *Barings plc (In Administration) and Another* v *Coopers & Lybrand (A Firm) and Others* [1997] ILPr 576, 585 CA.

[100] See Chadwick J, at first instance, in the *Barings* case, [1997] ILPr 12 at 23–24.

[101] *Chemische Fabrik Vormals Sandoz* v *Badische Anilin & Soda Fabriks* (1904) 90 LT 733 at 735.

involving patent infringement and the injunction head, was approved. There, Lord Davey accepted that it was necessary to go into the merits because of the general requirement that applies for all heads of Order 11, rule 1 that the deponent believes that this plaintiff has a good cause of action.[102] This suggests, by inference, that it is not necessary to go into the merits in order to establish that the terms of the head are met.

(ii) *Establishing liability*

Establishing that there is a serious issue on the merits does not raise any particular problems in disputes relating to contracts for the exploitation of intellectual property rights.[103] An example of where this requirement was not satisfied in the context of a licensing agreement is the Western Australian case of *West Clothing Co Pty Ltd* v *Sail America Foundation For International Understanding*.[104] The plaintiff licensee complained that the US licensor was in breach of a warranty in the exclusive licence agreement that the licensor had not assigned, granted or let any licence or any right whatever to any third party, and sued for breach of contract in the Western Australian courts. The plaintiff sought leave for service out of the jurisdiction. This was refused. Franklyn J held that the plaintiff was relying on an assignment to a third party prior to the licence contract made with the plaintiff. Accordingly, there was no breach of contract. The claim would have to be for fraudulent misrepresentation, but he was not satisfied that the statement of claim supported this.

(c) *The exercise of the discretion*

(i) Forum conveniens

The criteria for the exercise of the discretion have already been examined in chapter 1.[105] The same factors of appropriateness, such as those of convenience or expense, the applicable law, the place where the parties reside or carry on business, will apply to disputes concerning contracts relating to the exploitation of intellectual property rights as to any other dispute. The fact that the grant of leave would result in a multiplicity of proceedings in England and abroad has been regarded as a ground for exercising the discretion in favour of the defendant.

---

[102] See Order 11, r 4(1), which deals with the contents of the affidavit required for the grant of leave under rule 1(1). This requires a statement 'that in the deponent's belief the plaintiff has a good cause of action'.

[103] Compare the position in relation to infringement, below, pp 257–258.

[104] [1988] WAR 119. See also *Empire-Universal Films Ltd et al* v *Rank et al* [1948] OR 235 (distribution agreement); *Mitchelstown Co-operative Society Ltd T/A CMP Dairy* v *Société des produits Nestle SA, Chambourcy Food Company Ltd and Nestle (Ireland) Ltd* [1989] ILRM 582 (licensing agreement).

[105] See above, p 41.

Are there any additional connecting factors which are special to this type of contract? One such factor is the territory over which a distribution agreement extends. If the right to distribute a product relates to just one State, it is submitted that this constitutes an important connection with that State. The same can be said in respect of a licensing agreement. Another relevant connecting factor is that the contract relates to the exploitation of an intellectual property right which was created in a particular country. For example, the fact that the contract relates to the exploitation of a French patent, constitutes a connection with France. But how important a connecting factor is this? It has been argued above,[106] that where the dispute relates to the creation of an intellectual property right, the single most important connecting factor should be regarded as that of where the right has been created. Likewise, in infringement cases,[107] this constitutes an important factor, given that the substantive law of infringement is normally territorially limited to local rights. However, what we are now concerned with are contractual disputes, the contract being for the exploitation of intellectual property rights. The place where the right was created is of much less significance in relation to such disputes. Accordingly, the great weight given to this factor in creation and infringement cases should not be given to it in contract cases.

One further factor that needs to be mentioned, because it is commonly found in contracts of all types, is that of an agreement by the parties as to jurisdiction. If the parties have conferred jurisdiction on the courts of an EC/EFTA Contracting State, the case is likely to come within Article 17 of the Brussels or Lugano Convention.[108] But what if they have agreed on trial in, say, New York or, for some other reason, Article 17 does not operate as a basis of jurisdiction?[109] The English court will be reluctant to allow service out of the jurisdiction and will need very strong reasons to allow one of the parties to go back on his word. The court is particularly unlikely to allow service out of the jurisdiction where it is an exclusive jurisdiction clause.

Nonetheless, we are dealing with the exercise of a discretionary power in relation to the particular facts of the case, and there is a well known example of where service out of the jurisdiction was allowed despite the fact that the parties had agreed on trial before the Spanish courts, prior to the coming into force of the Brussels Convention. This was the case of *Evans Marshall & Co Ltd* v *Bertola SA*.[110] The plaintiffs, an English company, entered into what was really a distributorship agreement, but was

---

[106] At p 41.   [107] See below, pp 269–270.   [108] See above, p 94.
[109] Eg the formalities have not been met or both parties are domiciled outside the EC/EFTA.
[110] [1973] 1 WLR 349. See also as an example, *Citi-March Ltd and Another* v *Neptune Orient Lines Ltd and Others* [1996] 1 WLR 1367 – a shipping case.

referred to in the trade as an agency agreement, with the first defendants, a Spanish company, to act as their sole agents in England for the sale of their sherry. The first defendants purported to appoint the second defendants, another English firm, as their agents. The plaintiffs issued a writ claiming against the first defendants for breach of the agreement and against both defendants for, *inter alia*, conspiracy. The contract provided that disputes should be submitted to the Barcelona Court of Justice. Nonetheless, various heads of Order 11, rule 1 were satisfied.[111] The Court of Appeal upheld the first instance decision granting leave for service out of the jurisdiction. The case was regarded as exceptional because of the close connections with England. The substance of the claim related to the marketing of sherry in England. The essential witnesses were English. The second defendants were English and the first defendant brought about an action against the second defendant by appointing it as agent.[112] Moreover, according to Kerr J, the Spanish procedure was extremely slow compared with the English and the Spanish courts would not grant interlocutory relief.[113]

(ii) *The significance of the particular head*

Lord Goff, in the *Spiliada* case,[114] pointed out that the circumstances specified under the different heads vary greatly, and that this affects the court's willingness to exercise the discretion in favour of allowing service out of the jurisdiction.

The contract heads. If the parties have agreed on trial in England, the courts have been very willing to allow service out of the jurisdiction under Order 11, rule 1(1)(d)(iv). There would have to be strong reasons not to allow this, this is because the parties should abide by their agreement. In contrast, the mere fact that a contract was made in England, although coming within a head of Order 11, ie rule 1(1)(d)(i), does not in itself constitute much of a connection with England. After all, the State where a contract was made may be fortuitous. It follows that there should be a much more cautious attitude towards the exercise of the discretion where this head is being used. Lord Goff, in the *Spiliada* case, also said that the importance to be attached to any particular head may vary from case to case.[115] This is particularly so where the head in question is (d)(iii). The fact that English law governs the contract is, in some cases, of very great importance, and in others of little importance. It all depends on the circumstances of the case. In the *Spiliada* case itself, the fact that English law governed was said to be by no means an insignificant factor since the dispute was, *inter alia*, as to the nature of the obligation under the contract.

---

[111] *Ibid*, at 360.   [112] *Ibid*, at 375–376.   [113] *Ibid*, at 364.
[114] [1987] AC 460 at 481.   [115] *Ibid*.

The multi-defendant head. There is a distinct unwillingness to allow service of a writ out of the jurisdiction in cases where jurisdiction is based on this head.[116] This is because of the lack of connection between the claim and the English forum. This results in an even greater reluctance to exercise the discretion than is normal. On the other hand, in *The Electric Furnace Co v Selas Corpn of America*,[117] which concerned an infringement action, it was made clear that it was not the case that leave will never be given under this head unless it is strictly necessary. The wording of paragraph (c) gives the lie to any such suggestion since it includes cases where a defendant out of the jurisdiction is a *proper* party and not just a *necessary* party.

The injunction head. In cases where jurisdiction is based on this head, one important consideration that has been taken into account by the courts is whether the injunction can be effectively enforced in this country. This is clear from infringement cases, which are examined in chapter 6.[118]

(b) DECLINING JURISDICTION AND RESTRAINING FOREIGN PROCEEDINGS

(i) Declining jurisdiction

The English courts have power to stay their proceedings in three different situations: first, where the doctrine of *forum non conveniens* applies; secondly, where there is a foreign choice of jurisdiction clause; and thirdly, where there is an agreement on arbitration.

(a) *Forum non conveniens*

The criteria for the exercise of the discretionary power to decline jurisdiction on the ground of *forum non conveniens* have already been examined in chapter 1.[119] The same considerations apply as in cases of *forum conveniens*. What has been said in that context concerning contracts relating to the exploitation of intellectual property rights[120] is equally applicable here. One further factor to mention is that of *lis alibi pendens* and, more generally, that of where there is a multiplicity of proceedings in different States, ie where the parties or issue are not the same. *Lis alibi pendens*, and more generally a multiplicity of proceedings, is treated as a facet of *forum non conveniens*. It is very undesirable to have concurrent actions in England and abroad, and so this factor operates in favour of staying the English proceedings.

An example of the exercise of the *forum non conveniens* discretion in the context of a licensing agreement can be seen in the Ontario case of *Sterling*

---

[116] *Multinational Gas and Petrochemical Co v Multinational Gas and Petrochemical Services Ltd* [1983] Ch 258.
[117] [1987] RPC 23 at 32 (*per* Slade LJ).
[118] See below, p 265.
[119] See above, pp 42–43.
[120] See above, pp 103–105.

Software International (Canada) Inc v *Software Recording Corpn of America and Others*.[121] The plaintiff, a Canadian company which was a subsidiary of a United States company, commenced proceedings in Ontario against the defendants, two Texan companies. The dispute arose out of a complicated series of contracts pertaining to the use and licensing of computer software. There was a major issue of whether the plaintiff had misappropriated any of the property of the defendants. Roberts J, applying the Canadian doctrine of *forum non conveniens*, which is very similar to the English doctrine, granted a stay of the Ontario proceedings. The factors that led to this were as follows: the core issue was the interpretation of a contract entered into in Texas and governed by Texan law; the two defendants were Texan companies; there were concurrent proceedings in respect of the same major issue in Texas involving, *inter alia*, these parties;[122] the plaintiff was a wholly owned subsidiary of a US corporation; the defendants had given undertakings which went a considerable way towards meeting the interlocutory relief sought by the plaintiff; in a commercial action involving companies of international experience it was not a major hardship on the Canadian plaintiff that some of its witnesses are situate in Ontario. Finally, should any of the cause of action in the Ontario proceedings be unable to proceed in Texas, they may be pursued in Ontario at the conclusion of the Texan proceedings.

(b) Foreign jurisdiction clauses

There is a *prima facie* rule under English law that an action brought in England in breach of an agreement to submit to a foreign jurisdiction will be stayed.[123] The parties are expected to honour their contractual obligations. However, the power to stay is discretionary and the courts will allow the English action to continue if it considers that the ends of justice will be better served by a trial in this country.[124] The criteria for the exercise of this discretion[125] are the same factors of appropriateness as are considered under the doctrine of *forum non conveniens*. Nonetheless, there is a vital difference between these two discretionary grounds for a stay of the English proceedings. In cases involving a foreign jurisdiction clause, the burden is on the plaintiff to show why a stay should not be granted. In

---

[121] [1994] ILPr 43.
[122] Roberts J pointed out that the Texan proceedings were commenced first. This is of no significance under English law.
[123] See Cheshire and North, pp 234–236; Dicey and Morris, pp 433–436.
[124] See, eg *Mahavir Minerals Ltd* v *Cho Yang Shipping Co Ltd (The 'M C Pearl')* [1997] 1 Lloyd's Rep 566; *Baghlaf Al Safer Factory Co BR for Industry Ltd* v *Pakistan National Shipping Company and Another* (1997) *Times* 17 December. See also *Akai Pty Ltd* v *People's Insurance Co Ltd* (1996) 141 ALR 374 HC of Australia.
[125] See *The Eleftheria* [1970] P 94 at 110; affirmed by the CA in *The El Amria* [1981] 2 Lloyd's Rep 119; affirmed by the Privy Council in *The Pioneer Container* [1994] 2 AC 324.

cases of *forum non conveniens*, it is the other way round and the defendant must show that the clearly appropriate forum is abroad. The upshot is that the principles in respect of the former discretionary power are loaded in favour of a stay; under the latter discretionary power they are loaded in favour of trial continuing in England.

In any contractual dispute, it is important to see whether the parties have agreed on a foreign choice of jurisdiction clause. This is as important with contracts relating to the exploitation of intellectual property rights as it is with any other type of contract.

(c) Arbitration agreements

A contract may well contain an agreement as to arbitration. A party to an arbitration agreement against whom legal proceedings are brought (whether by way of claim or counterclaim) in respect of a matter which under the agreement is to be referred to arbitration may (upon notice to the other parties to the proceedings) apply to the court in which the proceedings have been brought to stay the proceedings so far as they concern that matter.[126] The staying of the proceedings is mandatory unless the court is satisfied that the arbitration agreement is null and void, inoperative, or incapable of being performed.[127]

The operation of an arbitration agreement in the context of contracts for the exploitation of intellectual property rights can be seen in the Alberta case of *Kaverit Steel and Crane Ltd et al v Kone Corpn et al*.[128] A licensing and distribution agreement provided for the settlement of disputes in accordance with the Rules of Conciliation and Arbitration of the International Chamber of Commerce. The distributor commenced an action in Alberta alleging a breach of the exclusive distributorship by the licensor. The latter sought a stay and a reference to arbitration. Cooke J, at first instance, refused the stay on the grounds that some of the issues in the action fell outside the scope of the arbitration clause, and some of the parties to the action were not parties to the arbitration agreement. The Alberta Court of Appeal allowed the appeal. It held that the fact that the action raised issues that were not arbitrable was not a sufficient ground for declining to enforce the arbitration clause or for declaring it inoperative. All the issues that arose between the licensor and the distributor, who were both parties to the arbitration agreement, that rested upon the existence of the contract, which was a matter that was arbitrable, should be stayed and referred to arbitration.

---

[126] Arbitration Act 1996, s 9(1).   [127] Arbitration Act 1996, s 9(4).
[128] (1992) 87 DLR (4th) 129.

(ii) Restraining foreign proceedings

An English court also has a discretionary power, in certain limited circumstances, to issue an injunction restraining a party from commencing or continuing as plaintiff with foreign proceedings.[129] This power must be exercised with caution because of the obvious comity problems inherent in its use. The categories where this power has been exercised will now be examined.

(a) Trial is available in England and abroad

In such cases, the English court will 'generally speaking, only restrain the plaintiff from pursuing proceedings in the foreign court if such pursuit would be vexatious or oppressive'.[130] This test, generally, presupposes that England is the natural forum for trial. Having so concluded, it must be decided whether pursuit of the proceedings abroad would be vexatious or oppressive. When applying this criterion, the court is ultimately concerned with the ends of justice. This involves considering the position of both parties. It has to be shown that there would be injustice to the defendant (abroad) if the plaintiff is allowed to pursue the foreign proceedings. There is no such injustice if the defendant is being sued abroad in a State with which there are very real connections. Thus, in *Kornberg v Kornberg*,[131] there was no oppression in bringing proceedings abroad because part of the property in dispute was situated there and the defendant was permanently resident there.

If the proceedings have actually been commenced abroad, this will operate as a factor in favour of restraining the foreign proceedings. In deciding whether the continuance of foreign proceedings would be vexatious or oppressive, the Court of Appeal, in *Sohio Supply Co v Gatoil (USA) Inc*,[132] was influenced, *inter alia*, by the undesirability of having concurrent proceedings in two different proceedings in two different jurisdictions involving the same subject matter.

There are no special difficulties in applying this test to contractual disputes arising out of the exploitation of intellectual property rights. A well known example of restraining foreign proceedings that arose in this context is *Smith Kline & French Laboratories Ltd and Others v Bloch*.[133] The defendant in the English proceedings, Dr Bloch, was an English research worker who entered into an agreement with an English pharmaceutical company,

---

[129] See Cheshire and North, pp 241–250.
[130] *Société Nationale Industrielle Aerospatial v Lee Kui Jak* [1987] AC 871 at 896.
[131] (1991) 76 DLR (4th) 379.
[132] [1989] 1 Lloyd's Rep 588. The action was brought in breach of an English exclusive jurisdiction clause.
[133] [1983] 1 WLR 730.

a subsidiary of a US company, licensing it to use his information worldwide in exchange for a royalty on worldwide sales of drugs developed from the ideas of Dr Bloch. The English company decided to discontinue further development work. In a classic example of forum shopping, Dr Bloch commenced proceedings in Philadelphia against both the English subsidiary and its US parent claiming damages, *inter alia*, for breach of contract. The two companies sought an injunction in the English courts restraining Dr Bloch from continuing the Philadelphia proceedings. This was granted at first instance and the Court of Appeal dismissed an appeal against this. The case was decided at a time when the criteria for the exercise of the discretion were different from those used now. Applying these now obsolete criteria, it was said that England was the natural forum for trial. The dispute was between an English resident and an English company. It was an English contract governed by English law. There were a large number of witnesses who were all in England. Under the present criteria, it would still be necessary to show that England was the natural forum for trial. It was also said that Dr Bloch would not be deprived of any legitimate personal or juridical advantage by being compelled to discontinue the American proceedings. Under the present criteria, this would still be relevant when considering the ends of justice.[134] What is different now is that it would have to be shown that there would be injustice to the English and US companies if Dr Bloch were to be allowed to pursue the foreign proceedings.

(b) *Trial is available in alternative fora abroad (but not in England)*

This situation is much more likely to arise in infringement cases, where traditional subject matter limitations in relation to jurisdiction come into play, than in contract cases, and so the criteria for the grant of an injunction in this situation will be examined in the context of jurisdiction in infringement cases.[135]

(c) *The bringing of proceedings abroad is an invasion of a legal or equitable right not to be sued there*

Such a right not to be sued abroad may be contractual in nature. Thus, an injunction may be granted to prevent a party from pursuing proceedings brought abroad in breach of an exclusive jurisdiction clause providing for trial before the English courts.[136] An agreement for the commercial exploitation of intellectual property rights may well contain such a clause.

---

[134] See *Simon Engineering PLC* v *Butte Mining plc* [1997] ILPr 599.
[135] See below, pp 276–277.
[136] *Mike Trading and Transport Ltd* v *R Pagnan and Fratelli (The Lisboa)* [1980] 2 Lloyd's Rep 546; *British Airways Board* v *Laker Airways Ltd* [1985] AC 58 at 81; *Svendborg* v *Wansa* [1997] 2 Lloyd's Rep 183, judgment of Clarke J affirmed by CA.

(d) *The bringing of the proceedings abroad would be unconscionable*

There are few reported cases coming within this category. It is more likely to come into play in infringement cases, and accordingly, the criteria for the grant of an injunction in cases coming within this category will be examined in more detail in that context.[137]

(c) LIMITATIONS ON JURISDICTION

(i) Subject matter limitations on jurisdiction

(a) *Under the traditional rules on jurisdiction*

The subject matter limitation on jurisdiction in relation to foreign intellectual property rights under the traditional English rules[138] only applies to actions raising questions as to the validity or infringement of such rights. It follows that an action, for example, for breach of a licensing agreement in which the validity of the right is not in issue will be unaffected by this limitation. But what if the validity of the right is, in effect, raised as a defence to the action in contract, as happened in the *Motte* case.[139] That was a case decided under Article 16(4) of the Brussels Convention, but the same scenario could arise entirely under the traditional rules. An example would be where an English company sues a New York company for the payment of royalties in relation to a US patent, basing jurisdiction on one of the contract heads of Order 11, rule 1(1) and the defendant alleges that the patent is invalid. Will the traditional subject matter limitation on jurisdiction prevent the English courts from trying the validity issue? This question does not appear to have arisen to date. It is submitted that the traditional subject matter limitation on jurisdiction should only operate where the action is *principally* concerned with validity of the right. Whatever the uncertainties over the meaning of *principally* concerned under the EC/EFTA rules,[140] in the present context it should mean *mainly* concerned. Where validity of the right is merely raised as a defence to an action for breach of contact, it cannot be said that the action is *mainly* concerned with validity and the limitation on jurisdiction will not prevent the English courts from trying the validity issue.

Is a basis of jurisdiction needed in relation to the validity defence? In the situation where contractual jurisdiction is based on service of a writ within the jurisdiction there is no difficulty because this is also a basis of jurisdiction for validity jurisdiction. The difficulty comes where

---

[137] See below, p 277.
[139] N 59 above and text accompanying.
[138] Discussed above, pp 43–45.
[140] See below, pp 202–208.

contractual jurisdiction is based on one of the contract heads of Order 11, rule 1(1). The wording of these heads is such that they cannot be regarded as a basis of jurisdiction for validity. However, it is submitted that the English courts should be able to try the validity defence without having any independent basis of jurisdiction in relation to this defence.[141]

On the other hand, if the defendant counterclaims, seeking revocation of the right, this is a separate cause of action and these proceedings are *principally* (ie *mainly*) concerned with validity and the limitation would prevent trial of this issue in England. Of course, there is a question whether this much criticised traditional limitation on jurisdiction should be extended to affect contract actions in this way. If, as is argued in this book,[142] the subject matter limitation on jurisdiction in relation to foreign intellectual property rights is abolished, this whole problem of validity of a right being raised in the context of a contract action disappears. The fact that this traditional limitation on jurisdiction has the potential for affecting contract actions as well as infringement actions gives an extra impetus for its abolition.

(b) *Article 16(4) of the Brussels and Lugano Conventions*

It is important to note that this provision could come into play even where the jurisdiction of an English court in a contract action is based on the traditional bases of jurisdiction. An example would be where an English company sues a New York company for the payment of royalties in relation to a French patent, basing jurisdiction on one of the contract heads of Order 11, rule 1(1), and the defendant alleges that the patent is invalid. The defendant then claims that the English court lacks jurisdiction over the validity issue because the French courts have exclusive jurisdiction in relation to this issue by virtue of Article 16(4). The question of whether this provision applies in relation to contract actions has already been examined in the context of jurisdiction under the Brussels Convention.[143] What was said there is equally applicable in the present context.

(ii) State immunity

The exception to State immunity as respects proceedings relating to UK patents, etc[144] would doubtless include contractual disputes relating to the commercial exploitation of such patents, etc.

4. Specific Aspects of Transfer of Technology Contracts

Transfer of technology contracts are subject to the same rules. What complicates things slightly is the fact that such contracts, typically, include

---

[141] See below, pp 208–209.
[142] See below, pp 314–315.
[143] See above, pp 91–94.
[144] State Immunity Act 1978, s 7, set out above, p 45.

aspects that relate to the exploitation of several intellectual property rights. The identification of the various elements and connecting factors will, as a result, in practice, be somewhat more difficult.

5. Anti-Trust Issues

Contracts in relation to the exploitation of intellectual property rights can include exclusivity clauses and other clauses that restrict competition. The jurisdictional rules that have been outlined above, will, obviously, not stop the competition law authorities from enforcing their competition law rules. The provisions concerning jurisdiction in relation to competition law are not contractual in nature.

V
REFORM

1. The EC/EFTA Rules

(a) criticism of the existing law

(i) Article 5(1)

Much of this chapter has been taken up with a discussion of Article 5(1) of the Brussels and Lugano Conventions, and most of the criticism of the present law is concerned with this provision. Application of this provision in cases of exploitation of intellectual property rights leads to uncertainty and to the plaintiff being given an excessively wide choice of fora.

(a) *Uncertainty*

There is uncertainty, for example, over what a grantor's obligations are in relation to a sole and exclusive distribution agreement and, consequently, as to where this obligation is to be performed. Is the obligation of the grantor: to supply the distributor, not to supply anyone else, to give the distributor reasonable notice before terminating the agreement, or to continue the exclusive distributorship? Is the grantor under just one of these obligations, as courts in Continental States have suggested, or several of them, as the English courts have suggested? If the latter, which is the principal obligation? There is also uncertainty, for example, over where the negative obligation not to supply any one else is to be performed. Is this literally everywhere? Is this anywhere in the EC where supply could potentially take place? Is it where supply actually takes place, ie where the breach takes place?

(b) *An excessively wide choice of fora*

The combination of negative obligations with a wide interpretation as to where such obligations are to be performed means that the plaintiff may have an excessively wide choice of fora in which to sue under Article 5(1).

(ii) Raising the issue of validity

The other major criticism of the existing law is that a defendant, seemingly, can thwart jurisdiction in a State which has a basis of jurisdiction in relation to a contractual claim for the payment of royalties by raising the issue of validity of the right (registered in another Contracting State) in respect of which the license was granted.

(b) SPECIAL JURISDICTIONAL RULES OR REFORM OF THE JURISDICTIONAL RULES OF GENERAL APPLICATION?

The Brussels and Lugano Conventions acknowledge the need for special jurisdictional rules for certain types of contract. Thus, Article 5(1) contains a special rule for identifying the place of performance of the obligation in question in matters relating to individual contracts of employment. Even more radically, Section 3 of Title II of the Conventions contains special rules for consumer contracts and matters relating to insurance (which would cover, but are not confined to, contractual disputes between the policy-holder and the insurer), whereby exclusive jurisdiction is granted to certain Contracting States and recourse cannot be had to other bases of jurisdiction. Underlying and justifying these special jurisdictional rules is a very clear policy objective of protecting the weaker party, ie the employee, the consumer and the insured/policy-holder. However, in contracts for the exploitation of intellectual property rights there is no obvious party which can be identified as the weaker party. Both parties, typically, will be commercial organisations. To be sure, one party may be in a stronger economic position than another but in one case this could be the licensee/distributor/assignee, whereas in another case it could be the licensor/grantor/assignor. It follows that there is no strong policy reason, in terms of protecting the weaker party, for having special jurisdictional rules for contracts for the exploitation of intellectual property rights.

It has been seen that the major problem that arises, where Article 5(1) is applied in cases of exploitation of intellectual property rights, is that of uncertainty, but this is more to do with the weaknesses in that provision than with any special difficulties raised by such cases. The basic concepts of the obligation and its place of performance cause difficulties in relation to many types of contract, as testified by the considerable body of case law on Article 5(1). It is submitted, therefore, that any reform in the law should be focused on Article 5(1) rather than on the introduction of special jurisdictional rules for cases of exploitation of intellectual property rights.

(c) REFORM OF ARTICLE 5(1)

(i) Suggestions for reform

Article 5(1) has been a much criticised provision[145] and the Diplomatic Conference to be held in 1998 to review the operation of the Brussels and Lugano Conventions will doubtless look at the operation of this provision with particular care.[146] A number of suggestions for reform have been made.

A Working Group of the European Group on Private International Law (a group of eminent academics but with no official standing) has come up with the radical suggestion that Article 5(1) be deleted.[147] As an alternative, they have suggested that a more appropriate connecting factor may be the place of delivery of the item in question, or, in the case of services, the place where a service is carried out.[148]

Hill has suggested that there should be two basic principles.[149] The first principle is that 'if the dispute between the parties is centred on the question whether the performance of the party who undertakes the characteristic obligation is defective or in conformity with the terms of the contract, the courts for the place of performance of the characteristic obligation should have jurisdiction'.[150] The second principle is that 'if the substance of the dispute is not centred on the performance of the characteristic obligation, special jurisdiction should be conferred on the courts of the Contracting State whose law is the applicable law so long as that Contracting State also has – at least – a minimum factual connection with the dispute'.[151]

A number of writers have suggested that there should be an autonomous community meaning for the 'place of performance',[152] rather than, as at the moment, a definition which refers to the applicable law. This autonomous interpretation is supported by Advocate General Lenz in *Custom Made Commercial Ltd* v *Stawa Metallbau GmbH*.[153]

As regards the problem where there is more than one place of performance, it has been suggested that a restrictive interpretation should be

---

[145] See, eg Hill, (1995) *ICLQ* 591.
[146] See the Consultation Paper on the operation of the Brussels and Lugano Conventions issued by the Lord Chancellor's Department and the Scottish Courts Administration, pp 10–14.
[147] *Ibid*, para 32.   [148] *Ibid*.   [149] (1995) 44 *ICLQ* 591 at 617–619.
[150] *Ibid*, at 617.   [151] *Ibid*, at 618.
[152] See Kennett, n 16 above; Anton & Beaumont, p 101; Hill, n 145 above, at 618.
[153] Case C-288/92 [1994] ECR I-2913, 2934.

adopted with regard to negative obligations so as 'to ensure that the distributor will not be subject to the jurisdiction of a wide range of courts other than the courts of its domicile and, in particular, that the supplier cannot sue the distributor in the supplier's home jurisdiction on no better basis than a diffusely localised negative obligation'.[154]

(ii) Operation in cases of exploitation of intellectual property rights

A number of general comments can be made in relation to each of these suggestions. But of especial importance, in the present context, is the question of how they would operate in cases involving the exploitation of intellectual property rights.

Starting with the suggestions of the Working Group of the European Group on Private International Law, the deletion of Article 5(1) would certainly get rid of the present uncertainty inherent in the use of this provision. But, in the absence of some other basis of special jurisdiction, this would result in the plaintiff having to sue in the defendant's domicile. Why should the plaintiff be denied the option of an alternative forum in a contractual dispute when he would still have this in a dispute relating to tort or delict? As regards their alternative suggestion, which looks to the place of delivery or to where a service is carried out, this is of no use at all in contracts for the exploitation of intellectual property rights. There is no delivery of any item and no service rendered. The practical effect is that the plaintiff would end up having to sue in the defendant's domicile.

Hill's suggestions are somewhat complicated. Moreover, they would not solve the problem of uncertainty in cases of exploitation of intellectual property rights. The first principle continues to focus on the concept of an obligation, it merely differs from the present law as to which obligation this is. But how can you identify the characteristic obligation when it is unclear, for example, what a grantor's obligations are in relation to a sole and exclusive licence? Even if you can identify precisely what the obligations of each party are, it is very difficult to identify the characteristic obligation when, as in licenses, distribution agreements and assignments, each party may be under numerous different obligations. The second principle focuses on the applicable law; but in contracts for the exploitation of intellectual property rights, if the parties have not chosen a governing law, there is considerable uncertainty over which law governs the contract. The rules on the law applicable in the absence of choice do not work well in respect of anything other than the most simple contracts for the exploitation of intellectual property rights.[155]

An autonomous meaning for the place of performance would be useful in the situation where there is no agreement by the parties (express or

---

[154] Forsyth, n 40 above, at 333.   [155] See below, pp 556–577.

implied) as to this place. As has been seen, in this situation there can be national differences in the rule identifying the place of performance. This is apparent in cases involving the obligation to give the grantee reasonable notice before terminating a distribution agreement. However, differences as to where the obligation is to be performed commonly relate back to differences over what the obligation is regarded as being in the first place. Moreover, there would be a period of uncertainty whilst the Court of Justice identifies and gives an autonomous meaning to the place of performance for particular obligations.

A restrictive interpretation of negative obligations would produce the desired effect of avoiding the excessively wide choice of fora that can arise under the present law.

2. The Traditional Rules

It has been seen that there are no particular difficulties in applying the traditional rules on jurisdiction to contracts for the exploitation of intellectual property rights. When it comes to finding a basis of jurisdiction, the contract heads of Order 11, rule 1(1) do not refer to an obligation to perform and thus avoid the difficulties that arise under Article 5(1) of the Brussels and Lugano Conventions. The discretionary element under the traditional rules is exercised on the basis of flexible criteria which operate as effectively in cases of exploitation of intellectual property rights as in any other case.

4
Infringement: Preliminary Matters

I	Introduction	119
II	Substantive law	120
	1. What constitutes an infringement?	120
	(a) Patents	120
	(b) Trade marks	122
	(c) Copyright	124
	(d) Rights in performances	127
	(e) Designs	127
	(f) Databases	130
	2. The elements of infringement	131
	(a) An act of infringement – The territorial limitation on liability	131
	(b) No requirement of damage	132
	(c) Prevention of infringement allegations	132
	(d) Are the elements of infringement necessarily defined by English law?	133
III	How do jurisdictional problems arise?	134
IV	Infringement of parallel rights: is the cause of action the same?	135
	1. The old fashioned view	135
	2. The better view	136

I
INTRODUCTION

As has been discussed above, intellectual property rights are granted on a national basis, along the lines of the national intellectual property statutes. It is quite normal though for these intellectual property rights to be exploited internationally. This gives rise to jurisdictional problems in infringement cases.

Chapters 5 and 6 deal with jurisdictional provisions and their application in infringement cases. Before turning to these provisions, there are some preliminary matters that need to be discussed. What constitutes an infringement of an intellectual property right? What are the elements of infringement? How do jurisdictional problems arise? Is the cause of action the same in cases involving the infringement of parallel rights? The first two of these questions are a matter for the substantive law of infringement, and it is to that topic that we will turn first.

II
SUBSTANTIVE LAW

1. What Constitutes an Infringement?

(a) PATENTS

(i) The basic rule

Under English law, the essence of what constitutes patent infringement[1] is found in Section 60 of the 1977 Patents Act. It contains slightly different provisions for product and for process patents. The following actions are infringements according to Section 60(1), at least if they are undertaken by the infringer without the permission of the patentholder:

(a) where the invention is a product, he makes, disposes of, offers to dispose of, uses or imports the product or keeps it whether for disposal or otherwise;
(b) where the invention is a process, he uses the process or he offers it for use in the United Kingdom when he knows, or it is obvious to a reasonable person in the circumstances, that its use there without the consent of the proprietor would be an infringement of the patent;
(c) where the invention is a process, he disposes of, offers to dispose of, uses or imports any product obtained directly by means of that process or keeps any such product whether for disposal or otherwise.

Section 60(2) adds that there is also an infringement in the situation where the unauthorised disclosure takes place of an essential element of the invention such that the recipient will be able to put the invention into effect. This section applies to both product and process inventions, but it does not apply to the supply of a staple commercial product unless it is supplied with a view to inducing an infringement. These provisions in Section 60(2) relate to what is commonly described as indirect infringement, ie where the act of infringement consists of enabling another to infringe.

(ii) The territorial requirement

The fact that patents granted under the 1977 Act are national UK patents, the territorial scope of which is limited to the United Kingdom, restricts

---

[1] For more details see Holyoak and Torremans, *Intellectual Property Law*, Butterworths (1995), chapter 5 and Young, Watson, Thorley and Miller, *Terrell on the Law of Patents*, Sweet & Maxwell (14th ed, 1994), chapter 6.

the effectiveness of Section 60. In cases of direct infringement only actions within the United Kingdom can lead to its application.[2] Section 60(1) mentions specifically that the alleged infringer must do 'any of the following things in the United Kingdom'. Section 60(2) mirrors that when it is stated there that the offer to supply or the actual supply have to take place 'in the United Kingdom' and that it must be intended to put 'the invention into effect in the United Kingdom'. This means that the sale of an infringing article does not infringe the UK patent if the sale entirely takes place abroad, nor does the offer to dispose of such an article outside the United Kingdom, even if that offer was made inside the jurisdiction.[3] Nothing, though, excludes the fact that these activities are infringing activities in relation to foreign parallel patents under the provisions of the relevant foreign patent law. That law can be *de facto* similar to the UK's 1977 Act.[4]

(iii) Defences

Section 60(5) of the 1977 Act provides statutory defences. This means that certain acts which would in normal circumstances constitute an infringement do not count as infringements if the requirements of the subsection are met. Suffice it to highlight here acts that are done privately for non-commercial purposes and acts that are done for experimental purposes.[5]

(iv) A purposive interpretation

Patent infringement cases often centre around the precise definition of what is protected. What exactly is the subject matter of the patent? This subject matter can be found in the specifications and the claims of the patent. These contain technical and scientific information and their interpretation has given rise to serious problems. The lawyer's literal interpretation approach is not suited to this task since the specifications and claims were not written primarily or exclusively as legal documents, while a purely purposive interpretation would create legal uncertainty and give an exorbitantly wide scope of protection to the patentholder. In the past, the United Kingdom favoured a more literal approach, whilst other European countries, such as Germany, tended to favour a far more purposive approach. The protocol to Article 69 of the European Patent Convention forms the basis for the new balanced approach. The latter approach has been the subject of a whole series of (recent) cases. It is

---

[2] See *Plastus Kreativ AB* v *Minnesota Mining and Manufacturing Co and Another* [1995] RPC 438.
[3] *Kalman* v *PCC Packaging (UK) Ltd* [1982] FSR 406; see also *Badische Anilin and Soda Fabrik* v *H Johnson & Co* (1897) 14 RPC 919.
[4] This will certainly be the case in Europe as most provisions are based on and implement Articles 29 and 30 of the European Patent Convention.
[5] Four further defences complete the list in the Patents Act 1977, s 60(5).

beyond the scope of a book on private international law to go into all the details of these cases. Instead, reference can simply be made to the test which was established in *Catnic Components Ltd v Hill & Smith Ltd*[6] and which was rephrased by Hoffman J, as he then was, in *Improver Corpn v Remington Consumer Products Ltd*[7] in the following terms:

The proper approach to the interpretation of English patents registered under the Patents Act 1949 was explained by Lord Diplock in *Catnic Components Ltd v Hill & Smith Ltd*. The language should be given a 'purposive' and not necessarily a literal construction. If the issue was whether a feature embodied in an alleged infringement which fell outside the primary, literal or a contextual meaning of a descriptive word or phrase in the claim ('a variant') was nevertheless within its language as properly interpreted, the court should ask itself the following three questions:

(1) Does the variant have a material effect upon the way the invention works? If yes, the variant is outside the claim. If no –
(2) Would this (ie that the variant had no material effect) have been obvious at the date of publication of the patent to a reader skilled in the art. If no, the variant is outside the claim. If yes –
(3) Would the reader skilled in the art nevertheless have understood from the language of the claim that the patentee intended that strict compliance with the primary meaning was an essential requirement of the invention. If yes, the variant is outside the claim.

On the other hand, a negative answer to the last question would lead to the conclusion that the patentee was intending the word or phrase to have not a literal but a figurative meaning (the figure being a form of synecdoche or metonymy) denoting a class of things which included the variant and the literal meaning, the latter being perhaps the most perfect, best-known or striking example of the class.

(b) TRADE MARKS

(i) **The basic rule**

The essential provision on trade mark infringement is now found in Section 10 of the Trade Marks Act 1994.[8] The obvious infringement case occurs when a sign which is identical to a registered trade mark is used without the authorisation of the trade mark owner in relation to goods or services which are identical with those goods or services for which the sign is registered as a trade mark.[9] Infringements also occur in two cases, which are slightly different, if one other requirement is met. In the first case, the difference is found in the fact that the sign is used in relation to

---

[6] [1982] RPC 183. [7] [1990] FSR 181 at 189.
[8] For a more detailed analysis of the provisions on trade mark infringement see Holyoak and Torremans, n 00 above, chapter 23 p 318 *et seq* and Annand and Norman, *Blackstone's Guide to the Trade Marks Act 1994*, Blackstone Press (1994), chapter 9.
[9] Trade Marks Act 1994, s 10(1).

similar rather than identical goods or services. This means that the use of a sign which is identical with the trade mark on the register also constitutes an infringement when this use takes place in relation to goods or services that are similar to the goods and services for which the sign has been registered as a trade mark.[10] In the second and opposite case, the goods or services in relation to which the sign is used are identical to those for which the sign has been registered as a trade mark, whilst the sign itself is similar, rather than identical, with the sign that has been registered as a trade mark.[11] The extra requirement, in both cases, is that a likelihood of confusion on the part of the public exists.[12] In the final and third scenario that deviates fully from the original obvious infringement case, the infringing act is the unauthorised use of an identical or a similar mark in relation to totally different goods, but additionally it must be shown that the trade mark has a reputation in the United Kingdom and that the distinctive character or the repute of the mark will be harmed by such a use.[13] All infringement cases rely on the use of the sign in the course of trade.[14]

Section 10(5) contains some examples of what constitutes the use of a sign that has been registered as a trade mark. Affixing the sign to goods or their packaging and offering or selling goods under the sign are easy examples. Further clarification is provided by examples such as the import or export of goods under the sign and the use of the sign on any business papers or in advertising.

What are similar goods or services and what are similar signs? The definition of similarity is a matter of fact. The test is whether the public is likely to be confused.

Section 9(1) of the Trade Marks Act 1994 makes it clear that trade mark rights are territorially limited in scope. This is clear from the wording of the section: 'The proprietor of a registered trade mark has exclusive rights in the trade mark which are infringed by use of the trade mark in the United Kingdom without his consent'.

(ii) Additional details

Two further points merit attention. Firstly, Section 10(5) extends the normal infringement rules and secondly, the comparative advertising exception in Section 10(6) exempts certain potentially infringing uses of a trade mark. Starting with the first point, Section 10(5) introduces a right to act against anyone who applies a trade mark to labels or packages of goods, business papers or advertising material if that person either knew or else had reason to believe that the use of the mark was not authorised by its proprietor. Apart from the person who makes the decision to infringe, any

---

[10] Trade Marks Act 1994, s 10(2)(a).
[11] Trade Marks Act 1994, s 10(2)(b).
[12] Trade Marks Act 1994, s 10(2).
[13] Trade Marks Act 1994, s 10(3).
[14] Trade Marks Act 1994, s 10(1), (2) and (3).

person who helps that person implement the decision, for example by printing the trade mark on the packaging of the goods, will now also be liable if the other requirements of the subsection are met.

Moving on to the second point, Section 10(6) authorises certain forms of comparative advertising. The use by anyone of a mark to identify any goods or services as being those of the proprietor of the mark will no longer give rise to trade mark infringement, at least in so far as the use is in accordance with honest industrial and commercial practices and does not take unfair advantage of, or is detrimental to, the repute or distinctive character of the mark without due cause.[15]

(iii) Infringement of a Community trade mark

Within the European Union, we now also have a Community trade mark.[16] Under this system, one trade mark is granted for the whole of the Community. There is no need to go into detail concerning the substantial infringement provisions relating to the Community trade mark, as they are identical to those found in the Trade Marks Act 1994 which were analysed above. This is the result of a European directive which undertook the partial harmonisation of national trade mark laws, including the law on infringement.[17]

(c) COPYRIGHT

Historically, copyright was the right to make copies, and making unauthorised copies constituted copyright infringement. This is still the rule on which the provisions of the Copyright, Designs and Patents Act 1988 are based,[18] but these provisions are far more sophisticated than the old rule. In particular, a distinction is drawn between primary and secondary infringement.

(i) Primary infringement

(a) *The basic rule*

One way or the other, all forms of primary infringement involve copying, whether through reproduction or through performance of the work.

---

[15] See *News Group Ltd* v *Mirror Group Ltd* [1989] FSR 126. This case was decided in the absence of an equivalent to the Trade Marks Act 1994, s 10(6).

[16] Council Regulation (EC) No 40/94 of 20 December 1993 on the Community Trade Mark [1994] OJ L11/1.

[17] First Council Directive (EC) No 104/89 of 21 December 1988 to approximate the laws of the Member States relating to trade marks [1989] OJ L40/1, see Article 5.

[18] For a more detailed analysis see Holyoak and Torremans, n 1 above, chapter 14 and Laddie, Prescott and Vitoria, *The Modern Law of Copyright*, Butterworths (2nd ed, 1995), pp 80–116, 244–248, 402–420, 435–438, 465–470 and 490.

According to Section 16(1), the rights of the copyright owner are infringed if:

(i)   the work is copied;
(ii) copies of the work are issued to the public;
(iii) the work is performed, shown or played in public;
(iv) the work is broadcasted or included in a cable programme service and;
(v)   an adaptation is made of the work or any of the above is done in relation to an adaptation.

It is an infringement not only to do these acts without the consent of the copyright owner, but also to authorise someone else to do them without that consent. It is clear though that the idea is not protected by copyright and can be copied freely. The alleged infringer must also have copied the whole work or at least a substantial part of it.[19] The definition of a substantial part is based on a qualitative rather than on a quantitative basis.[20]

(b) *Territorial scope*

Section 16(1) also contains a clear rule concerning its territorial scope. The infringing acts must take place in the United Kingdom.[21] Two examples will clarify the importance of this provision. When infringing copies of a brochure are printed in the United Kingdom for export only and use, for example, as promotional literature in the United States there will be an infringement under the UK Copyright Act. What matters is that copies are made in this country, the fact that they are exclusively made for export and use abroad does not change this.[22] On the other hand, if someone authorises an American printer to print the brochures in the United States for distribution there, no infringement action can be brought under the provisions of the Copyright, Designs and Patents Act 1988, even if the authorisation has been given in the United Kingdom.[23] Only an authorisation to perform an infinging act in the United Kingdom will be actionable.[24]

---

[19] Copyright, Designs and Patents Act 1988, s 16(3)(a).
[20] See *Ladbroke* v *William Hill* [1964] 1 All ER 465 at 469; [1964] 1 WLR 273 at 276, *per* Lord Reid.
[21] See *Jonathan Cape Ltd* v *Consolidated Press Ltd* [1954] All ER 253, [1954] 1 WLR 1313; *Def Lepp Music* v *Stuart-Brown* [1986] RPC 273; *Atkinson Footwear Ltd* v *Hodgkin International Services Ltd and Another* (1995) 31 IPR 186.
[22] This rule is also found in the copyright laws of many other countries, see, eg the Dutch example in *NV Gebr Van Zijverden* v *GF Mens*, judgment of the President of the Arrondissementsrechtbank (District Court) in Haarlem, 18 February 1971, [1973] BIE 99.
[23] The same rule exists in US Copyright law, see *Subafilms Ltd* v *MGM Pathe Communications Co*, Court of Appeals Ninth Circuit, (1994) 30 USPQ 2d 1746.
[24] See *ABKCO Music & Records Inc* v *Music Collection International Ltd and Another* [1995] RPC 657, at 660 *per* Hoffmann LJ (as he then was).

(c) Specific forms of primary infrigement

Attention will now be turned to each of the specific forms of primary infringement. First of all, the various types of copyright works can be infringed by being copied. Original literary, artistic, dramatic and musical works are copied through reproduction in any material form, irrespective of the medium or the means used.[25] For artistic works, this includes making a three dimensional copy of a two dimensional work and vice versa.[26] Films, television broadcasts and cable programmes are copied when they are reproduced or when a substantial part is reproduced.[27] As regards the final type of copyright work, copying a typographical arrangement of a published edition involves making a facsimile copy of that arrangement.[28]

Secondly, copyright is also infringed when copies of a work of any category are issued to the public. Copies are only issued to the public when they are put into circulation for the first time. Copies of the work should not previously have been put into circulation in the United Kingdom or elsewhere. An exception is made for sound recordings, films and computer programs. They are also issued to the public when copies are rented to the public.[29]

Thirdly, the copyright in literary, dramatic and musical works can be infringed when these works are performed, showed or played in public. It is also an infringement of copyright to play or show a sound recording, film, broadcast or cable programme in public.[30] This kind of infringement arises, for instance, when background music is played in a shop or restaurant.

Fourthly, copyright in literary, dramatic, musical and artistic works as well as sound recordings, films, broadcasts and cable programmes is infringed when these works are broadcast or included in a cable programme service.[31]

The final form of primary infringement is making an adaptation of a literary, dramatic or musical work.[32] Examples are adapting a novel into a play, making an arrangement of a musical work or the translation of a literary work into a foreign language.[33]

We now turn to the secondary infringement of copyright.

---

[25] Copyright, Designs and Patents Act 1988, s 17(2).
[26] Copyright, Designs and Patents Act 1988, s 17(3).
[27] Copyright, Designs and Patents Act 1988, s 17(4).
[28] Copyright, Designs and Patents Act 1988, s 17(5).
[29] Copyright, Designs and Patents Act 1988, s 18.
[30] Copyright, Designs and Patents Act 1988, s 19(3).
[31] Copyright, Designs and Patents Act 1988, s 20.
[32] Copyright, Designs and Patents Act 1988, s 21(1).
[33] The making of an adaptation or doing any other restricted act to an adaptation, for example including it in a broadcast, is also an act restricted by the copyright in the work and will constitute an infringement, see Copyright, Designs and Patents Act 1988, s 21(2).

(ii) Secondary infringement

Secondary infringement is no longer concerned with the act of copying, but operates at the stage at which persons are dealing commercially with copies of works that attract copyright. An important difference from primary infringement is that the alleged infringer must have had knowledge or reason to believe that his activity is a secondary infringement of copyright. This means, in practice, that it should have been obvious to the defendant, as a reasonable person, that his activity would infringe copyright. The importation into the United Kingdom of an infringing copy of the copyright work, possessing an infringing copy in the course of a business, selling it, letting it for hire, offering or exposing it for sale or hire and providing the means to make infringing copies of the work are obvious examples of secondary infringement.[34] The references in Section 27 to importation and proposed importation into the United Kingdom when 'infringing copies' are defined make it clear that the scope of the secondary infringement provisions is also limited to the United Kingdom.

(d) RIGHTS IN PERFORMANCES

Traditional copyright often does not protect the performers and those with recording rights in performances, since they are often not the authors of the works that are performed. The Copyright, Designs and Patents Act 1988 remedied that problem by introducing, in its Part II, specific rights in performances which were granted to performers and those who have acquired the right to record the performance.[35]

When turning to the infringement of these rights in performances it can be said, in general terms, that the rights in performances are infringed whenever a performance is exploited without the consent of the performer or whenever the performance is recorded without the consent of the person who owns the exclusive recording right. The essential point is the consent of the owners of the rights in the performance.[36]

(e) DESIGNS

(i) Unregistered designs

How is an unregistered design infringed? This design right was introduced by the Copyright, Designs and Patents Act 1988, so it comes as no

---

[34] For a full list see Copyright Designs and Patents Act 1988, ss 22–26.

[35] These provisions were introduced in implementation of the Rome Convention for the Protection of Performers, Producers of Phonograms and Broadcasting Organisations 1961; for more details concerning rights in performances see Holyoak and Torremans, n 1 above, chapter 16.

[36] See Copyright, Designs and Patents Act 1988, s 197.

surprise that, in relation to design right infringement, a distinction is also made between primary and secondary infringement. The relevant substantive law provisions are found in Sections 226 to 228 of the Copyright, Designs and Patents Act 1988.

(a) *Primary infringement*

Starting then with primary infringement, the owner of the design right is given the exclusive right to reproduce the design for commercial purposes. As a result, the design right will, first of all, be infringed by anyone making an article to that design without the licence of the owner of the design right, and by anyone making a design document that records the design for the purpose of enabling someone to make articles to this design, once again if this is done without the licence of the design right owner. Primary infringement extends to the situation where someone authorises someone else to do one of these two things.[37]

A design can be reproduced directly or indirectly. However, indirect reproduction will still infringe, even if the intervening acts themselves do not infringe the design right.[38]

Does the intention of the infringer matter? Not a lot, as innocent infringement is possible. This can be derived indirectly from Section 233 of the 1988 Act. If at the time of the infringement the defendant was unaware, and had no reason to believe, that a design right subsisted in the design, the plaintiff will not be entitled to damages against the defendant. But other remedies remain available, which means that there will be infringement even though it could be called innocent infringement.[39]

(b) *Secondary infringement*

That brings us to the second form of design right infringement, which is called secondary infringement. In addition to the primary infringement cases, the design right will also be infringed if a person does any of the following acts in relation to an infringing article without the licence of the owner of the design right. First of all, importing the article into the United Kingdom for commercial purposes.[40] Secondly, there will be a secondary infringement if such a person has the article in his possession for commercial purposes.[41] Thirdly, the design right will be infringed if such a person sells, hires, or offers or exposes for sale or hire, the article in the

---

[37] Copyright, Designs and Patents Act 1988, s 226(1) and (3).
[38] Copyright, Designs and Patents Act 1988, s 226(4).
[39] Copyright, Designs and Patents Act 1988, s 233(1).
[40] Copyright, Designs and Patents Act 1988, s 227(1)(a).
[41] Copyright, Designs and Patents Act 1988, s 227(1)(b).

course of a business.⁴² An action for secondary design infringement can only be successful if it is proven that the defendant knew or had reason to believe that the article was an infringing article.⁴³ This additional requirement of knowledge is identical to the one found in copyright.

(c) What is an infringing article?

Regardless of whether it is a primary or secondary infringement, one additional issue requires further clarification. What is an infringing article? An article is such if the making of the article to the design constituted an infringement of the design right in the design.⁴⁴ Articles which have been imported into the United Kingdom, or are proposed to be imported into it, and the making of which would have constituted an infringement of the design right (or a breach of an exclusive licence agreement), had the articles been made in the United Kingdom, are also infringing articles.⁴⁵

(ii) Registered designs

Registered designs involve eye appeal and are novel aesthetic designs that are registered in respect of certain articles to which they are applied by an industrial process. The Registered Designs Act 1949 gives the registered owner of a design the exclusive right to do certain things in relation to articles which embody the design and in respect of which the design has been registered. According to the provisions of the 1949 Act, the owner has the exclusive right to make or import these articles for sale or for hire or for use for the purposes of a trade or business. He also has the exclusive right to sell, hire or offer or expose these articles for sale or hire. Articles to which a design, which is not substantially different from the registered design, has been applied are covered by extension.⁴⁶

It is easy to derive from these provisions what will constitute an infringement of a registered design. Indeed, anyone who does any of the above mentioned acts without the consent or licence of the owner of the registered design infringes the rights in the registered design.⁴⁷ The finding of infringement can only be avoided if the design used is substantially different from the registered design.

A couple of other forms of infringement of a registered design also figure in the Registered Designs Act 1949. They have in common the fact that all of them lead indirectly to an article that embodies the registered design. According to these provisions, it is an infringement of a registered design:

---

⁴² Copyright, Designs and Patents Act 1988, s 227(1)(c).
⁴³ Copyright, Designs and Patents Act 1988, s 227(1).
⁴⁴ Copyright, Designs and Patents Act 1988, s 228(2).
⁴⁵ Copyright, Designs and Patents Act 1988, s 228(3).
⁴⁶ Registered Designs Act 1949, s 7(1).   ⁴⁷ Registered Designs Act 1949, s 7(2).

(i) to make anything for enabling an infringing article to be made anywhere;[48]
(ii) to do anything in relation to a kit which would infringe if it were done to the assembled article;[49]
(iii) to make anything for enabling a kit to be made or assembled anywhere if the assembled article embodies the design,[50]

if in each case this is done without the licence of the owner of the registered design. In essence, this removes the possibility of working with parts of the article which can be assembled.

It should be noted that no damages can be awarded if the defendant can show that at the time of the infringement he was unaware of the registration of the design and had no reasonable grounds for supposing that the design was registered.[51] This provision bears a strong similarity to Section 62(1) of the Patents Act 1977. Apart from this provision, the intention of the alleged infringer is not relevant.

(f) DATABASES

A special system for the protection of databases was introduced by the European Union through its Database Directive.[52] The implementation of this Directive by the Member States will result in a two tier system of protection comprising copyright and a *sui generis* right.

(i) The copyright aspect

Copyright will exist in 'databases which, by reason of the selection or arrangement of their contents, constitute the author's own intellectual creation'.[53] But this copyright does not extend to the contents of the database, which might be the subject of one or more separate copyrights. This would, for example, be the case if the database contained a collection of poems which are themselves protected as original literary works. The copyright in these poems is unaffected by the creation of a copyright in the database as such.[54]

The Directive's rules on copyright infringement bear strong similarities to the existing copyright infringement rules and warrant no further comments in this context apart from the fact that, obviously, they do not extend to the acts necessary for the normal access to and use of the database by its lawful user.[55]

---

[48] Registered Designs Act 1949, s 7(3).
[49] Registered Designs Act 1949, s 7(4)(a).
[50] Registered Designs Act 1949, s 7(4)(b).
[51] Registered Designs Act 1949, s 9(1).
[52] EP and Council Directive No 9/96 on the legal protection of databases [1996] OJ L77/20.
[53] Article 3(1) of the Directive.
[54] Article 3(2) of the Directive.
[55] Article 6(1) of the Directive.

(ii) The *sui generis* aspect

On top of the copyright protection, a new *sui generis* right has been created. This right will exist independently, and might thus exist even in those cases that are not covered by copyright.[56] The requirements for the right to be granted to the maker of a database are that a qualitatively and/or quantitatively substantial investment in either the obtaining, the verification or the presentation of the contents of the database is shown. This *sui generis* right is really a right to act against unfair extraction and re-utilisation. The maker of the database can prevent the extraction and/or the re-utilisation of the whole or a substantial part of the contents of the database. Whether a part is substantial will be evaluated qualitatively and/or quantitatively.[57]

2. THE ELEMENTS OF INFRINGEMENT

As will be seen,[58] certain bases of jurisdiction are founded on typical elements of a tort: a wrongful act and consequent damage. This raises the question of what the elements of the tort of infringement are.

(a) AN ACT OF INFRINGEMENT – THE TERRITORIAL LIMITATION ON LIABILITY

A successful action can be brought whenever one of the infringing acts which are specified in the various intellectual property statutes[59] occurs. However, the Patents Act 1977[60] and the Copyright, Designs and Patents Act 1988[61] clearly restrict their infringing acts to acts committed in the United Kingdom. Although this is not the case for the Trade Marks Act 1994, there is little reason to doubt that Parliament intended the potentially infringing use of a sign, which has been registered as a trade mark, to take place in the United Kingdom. The UK trade mark which is granted under the Act is only valid in the territory of the United Kingdom. It is a property right which is created by law and it must be assumed that the legislative jurisdiction of Parliament is restricted to the territory of the United Kingdom, especially if, as in this case, the text of the statute does not indicate that Parliament attempted to rule extraterritorially as well.

---

[56] Article 7(4) of the Directive.
[57] Article 7(1) of the Directive.
[58] See below, pp 142–175 and 244–253.
[59] See Registered Designs Act 1949, s 7; Patents Act 1977, ss 60–71; Copyright, Designs and Patents Act 1988, Part I, Chapter II and Part III, Chapter II; Trade Marks Act 1994, ss 10–14.
[60] Patents Act 1977, s 60, as discussed above.
[61] Copyright, Designs and Patents Act 1988, s 16(1), as discussed above.

(b) NO REQUIREMENT OF DAMAGE

It is important to note that the statutory provisions do not require any presence, let alone evidence, of damage. It is assumed that any infringing act constitutes a wrong which will eventually give rise to negative consequences and damage. Damage might consist of loss of market-share, sales and earnings, negative impact on business goodwill, etc. Such an action for damages would be brought after the infringing act was committed. If damage is effectively shown, that is, of course, reflected in the damages that are awarded.

An action can also be brought before the infringing products are marketed, to prevent any damage from occurring. Such an action would normally result, *inter alia*, in an injunction being issued.

A rightholder can also threaten to bring infringement proceedings against a third party unless they stop the allegedly infringing activity. There can be cases where there is no real ground for the threat, where no writ is issued and where such a threat is used unfairly to undermine lawful commercial activities by the third party. This is especially the case when potential customers are also sent warning letters. In such a case, the third party involved can bring an action and obtain a remedy for groundless threats of infringement proceedings. This could result in a declaration to the effect that the threats are unjustifiable, an injunction against the continuance of the threats or even damages in cases where any loss occurred as a consequence of the groundless threats.[62]

(c) PREVENTION OF INFRINGEMENT ALLEGATIONS

The Patents Act 1977 allows for an action for a negative declaration. Before undertaking an important commercial venture, a third party might want to be sure that its activity will not infringe an existing patent.[63] The third party can contact the rightholder and ask for an acknowledgement, that the activity will not infringe the patent. When the rightholder fails or refuses to give such acknowledgement an action can be brought and the court is asked to provide a negative declaration, ie a declaration that the activity or the proposed activity will not infringe the patent.[64] Such a neg-

[62] Registered Designs Act 1949, s 26; Patents Act 1977, s 70; Copyright, Designs and Patents Act 1988, s 253 (only for designs, there is no corresponding copyright provision) and Trade Marks Act 1994, s 21; Certain types of alleged infringement are excluded from the scope of these provisions, see Registered Designs Act 1949, s 26(2A); Patents Act 1977, s 70(4); Copyright, Designs and Patents Act 1988, s 253(3) and Trade Marks Act 1994, s 21(1).

[63] Certain foreign patent Acts contain also a provision in relation to a positive declaration, which essentially confirms the validity of the patent, In terms of jurisdiction rules this is then treated in the same way as an infringement action, see Swiss Supreme Court, judgment of 27 November 1991, [1993] GRUR Int 972.

[64] Patents Act 1977, s 71.

Infringement: preliminary matters

ative declaration can only cover acts done in the United Kingdom. This is the logical consequence of the fact that the patents granted under the 1977 Act have a territorial scope that is restricted to the United Kingdom. A negative declaration is, indeed, a declaration that a specific act will not infringe that UK patent.[65]

(d) ARE THE ELEMENTS OF INFRINGEMENT NECESSARILY DEFINED BY ENGLISH LAW?

Up to here, this chapter has been concerned with English substantive law. However, for jurisdictional purposes, the elements of the tort are not necessarily to be determined by reference to English law. When defining the scope of Article 5(3) of the Brussels Convention, the Court of Justice has given a Community meaning to the concept of 'matters relating to tort, delict or quasi-delict',[66] avoiding a reference to the law of the forum or to the law of the country whose law is applicable to the tort. Instead, it has looked for the common core of the laws of the Member States on this point. This approach is easy to apply in infringement cases when identifying the elements of the tort at the next stage of determining the place of the harmful event under Article 5(3). Most European laws on infringement are rather similar. This is due to the fact that they are all based on the same international Convention rules and on the same EC Directives. The alternative approach would be to concentrate on the law being relied upon. Thus, if an attempt is made to sue in an English court, relying on a foreign applicable law (the infringement having taken place abroad), the elements of the infringement, and the definition of what constitutes an infringement, should be determined under the foreign substantive intellectual property law. This should not raise too many practical problems given the similarity in the European laws on infringement. However, in general, the Court of Justice, understandably, has been reluctant to go into the applicable law at the jurisdictional stage, and to do so is inconsistent with the approach adopted in relation to defining the scope of Article 5(3).

When it comes to jurisdiction under the traditional English rules, the English courts have defined the elements of the tort under the tort head of Order 11, rule 1, of the Rules of the Supreme Court by refence to English law. It is not clear whether this was because it was the law of the forum or because it was the applicable law. English courts are now going to be faced with actions where the plaintiff relies on a foreign applicable law.[67] In this situation, it would be appropriate to use the second of the two approaches outlined above and to identify the elements of the tort by reference to the

---

[65] See *Plastus Kreativ AB* v *Minnesota Mining and Manufacturing Co and Another* [1995] RPC 438.
[66] See below, pp 150–153.   [67] See below, ch 12.

foreign applicable law. With a tort like infringement it would be possible to adopt the first approach, but this would not be possible in relation to many other torts where there is not the similarity between national definitions of the tort that is found with infringement.

III
HOW DO JURISDICTIONAL PROBLEMS ARISE?

Normally, intellectual property rights are exploited internationally. Accordingly, litigation quite often involves an international element too. Jurisdictional problems can arise in infringement cases in a wide variety of different circumstances. A good starting point is the case where an overseas intellectual property right, for example a Belgian patent, is infringed abroad. The alleged infringer may be domiciled in England and all of his assets might be found within this jurisdiction. Can the patent-owner sue in England?

It is easy to find a slightly more complex scenario in which parallel intellectual property rights exist in England and in one or more states abroad, for example the invention has been patented in all Member States of the European Union. Can the whole case be litigated in the English courts if the alleged infringer commits infringing acts in all countries involved, for example by producing and/or marketing infringing goods in all countries of the European Union? Does it matter whether the infringer is domiciled or resident in England?

There might also be more than one defendant. An English parent company might, allegedly, have infringed a UK trade mark by selling goods under a confusingly similar mark, while its German subsidiary might have done the same in Germany, allegedly infringing the German parallel trade mark. Can the English court hear the whole case? Does the answer change if the German company is only an agent or if it is a licensee?

If infringement of an intellectual property right takes place in England, can the plaintiff also serve writs on a second defendant abroad for discovery purposes if that defendant holds vital evidence? A foreign company or individual may have authorised the infringing act or conspired with the English defendant to infringe the intellectual property right. This can occur when a foreign parent company keeps a tight control over the operations of its subsidiary in Britain. The potential second defendant could even have provided assistance, for example by printing labels abroad which contain the trade mark which is later affixed to the goods in the UK. That trade mark may or may not be registered abroad too.

There are also multi-plaintiff cases. Different persons or companies might hold the intellectual property right in the various countries involved. And combined multi-defendant and multi-plaintiff cases are bound to arise too. Which rules on jurisdiction apply to these cases? Are they different from the rules which apply to most standard cases?

Questions of where the plaintiff can litigate and how many separate but parallel cases need eventually be brought are not purely academic, but, on the contrary, very practical ones which are of huge importance. Effective enforcement of intellectual property rights is a vital element in relation to their commercial value and importance. Private international law rules have a vital role to play if intellectual property rights are to be enforced effectively in order for them to be capable of fulfilling their economic function adequately.

IV
INFRINGEMENT OF PARALLEL RIGHTS: IS THE CAUSE OF ACTION THE SAME?

Foreign infringement cases, especially the multi-plaintiff and multi-defendant ones, raise another interesting problem. Does the same cause of action exist between the parties if an intellectual property right is infringed both in England and abroad?

1. THE OLD FASHIONED VIEW

Intellectual property rights such as trade marks, patents and copyright are granted nationally and it is said that they are strictly territorial in scope. It could, therefore, be argued that what happens in practice is that different intellectual property rights are infringed in the various jurisdictions involved. For example, let us assume that an English company owns trade mark X in the United Kingdom, France and Germany. This would mean that there are three different intellectual property rights, ie a UK trade mark X, a German trade mark X and a French trade mark X. The infringer who markets his own goods under the trade mark X in all countries involved would infringe the UK trade mark through his marketing activity in the UK, the German trade mark through his marketing activity in Germany and the French trade mark through his marketing activity in France. The UK mark is only valid in the United Kingdom, though, and would not be infringed by the marketing activity in Germany and in France, and the same would apply, *mutatis mutandis*, to the German and the French trade mark. It could further be assumed that the trade marks might be owned by different companies in the various countries, for example by different subsidiaries of the same parent-company or by companies that are related in some other way. This would result in there not being the same cause of action between the parties when the whole infringement case is brought in England. The infringement in Britain of the British trade mark is one cause of action, whilst the infringement in France of the French trade mark is a separate and different cause of action, especially when the plaintiffs are different too.[68] This could provide another argument for the English court not to deal with the whole case, and to refuse to take jurisdiction in respect of the foreign infringement aspects. Patents that have been granted under the European Patent Convention 1973 raise an interesting issue in this respect. There is no single European patent, but all the national patents in the bundle have been granted as a result of a single application. The similarities between these patents are much higher than those between other parallel rights. Even adopting the old fashioned view, the argument, that the infringement of these patents still does not give rise to the same cause of action, becomes open to doubt, because is relies exclusively on the formalistic point that they are a bundle of national patents rather than a single patent. The fact that the rules that underpin the system are almost entirely identical is ignored completely, whilst maybe it should carry a great deal of weight.

2. The Better View

It is submitted that it would be wrong to adopt this old fashioned view. Any kind of property right is regulated independently and slightly differently in each jurisdiction, but it is generally accepted that property rights in tangible movable goods are recognised across the borders of the legal systems. This is because the essential characteristics of the right are the same in any legal system. When it comes to intellectual property rights, what matters is that parallel national intellectual property rights have the same essential content. Accordingly, their international infringement involves the same cause of action. This is based on the analysis taken by the Court of Justice in its case law in relation to Articles 30 and 36 of the EC Treaty. These cases are concerned with the doctrine of exhaustion of intellectual property rights. The Court accepted the argument that national intellectual property rights should be seen as parallel rights whenever they cover the same invention in relation to patents, whenever they cover the same trade mark in relation to overlapping categories of goods or services and whenever copyright covers the same work. When the intellectual property right in one Member State is used and, for exam-

---

[68] See *James Burrough Distillers plc* v *Speymalt Whisky Distributors Ltd* [1991] RPC 130.

ple, the patented product is put on the market in that Member-State by the patent-owner or by a third party with his consent, there is not only exhaustion of the national patent in that Member State but also all parallel patents in all other Member States are exhausted.[69] Within the European Union, parallel intellectual property rights can no longer be treated as being completely unrelated and independent. The Court has said repeatedly that putting the product involved on the common market for the first time and fighting infringement of the right are at the core of the specific subject matter of an intellectual property right.[70] Infringement issues are at the heart of the right and form part of the essence of it. In the situation where there is infringement of UK and foreign parallel intellectual property rights, the essence of the rights involved is the same. Accordingly, the cause of action must be the same.

---

[69] See, eg Case 15/74 *Centrafarm* v *Sterling Drug* [1974] ECR 1147; Case 16/74 *Centrafarm* v *Winthrop* [1974] ECR 1183 and Case 78/70 *Deutsche Grammophon v Metro* [1971] ECR 487; for further details see Holyoak and Torremans, n 1 above, pp 91–100, 232–237 and 331–337.

[70] See, eg Case 15/74 *Centrafarm* v *Sterling Drug* [1974] ECR 1147; see also Holyoak and Torremans, n 1 above, pp 91–100, 232–237 and 331–337.

5

Infringement: Jurisdiction Under the European Community/European Free Trade Association Rules

I	Introduction	141
II	When do the rules apply?	141
III	Bases of jurisdiction	142
	1. General jurisdiction: Article 2	142
	(a) Advantages in using this provision	143
	(b) Disadvantages	143
	2. Special jurisdiction: Articles 5 and 6	144
	(a) The threshold requirement	144
	(b) Article 5	149
	(c) Article 6	170
	3. Exclusive jurisdiction: Article 16	175
	(a) Article 16(1)	175
	(b) Article 16(4)	176
IV	Abuse of process	176
V	Declining jurisdiction	177
	1. Under the Brussels and Lugano Conventions	177
	(a) *Lis pendens*	177
	(b) Related actions	182
	2. Using the doctrine of *forum non conveniens*	186
	(a) *Re Harrods (Buenos Aires) Ltd*	186
	(b) Altering the facts	187
	3. Restraining foreign proceedings	188
	(a) A non-Contracting State	188
	(b) A Contracting State	189
VI	No subject matter limitations on jurisdiction	190
	1. The position under the Conventions	190
	2. Judicial misunderstanding	191
	3. The point is now settled	191
	(a) The *Pearce* case	192
	(b) The *Coin Controls* case	193
	(c) The *Fort Dodge* case	193

	4.	Foreign rights created outside the EC/EFTA Contracting States	193
	5.	Infringements committed outside the EC/EFTA Contracting States	195
	6.	Difficulties in establishing a basis of jurisdiction against the person	196
VII	Forum shopping	196
	1.	The choice of fora	197
	2.	The advantages to be obtained	198
		(a) A personal advantage	198
		(b) Procedural advantages	198
		(c) A substantive law advantage	199
		(d) Other advantages	200
VIII	Infringement and validity	201
	1.	The nature of the problem	201
	2.	A defence of invalidity	202
		(a) Do Articles 19 and 16(4) preclude infringement jurisdiction?	202
		(b) Is a basis of jurisdiction necessary in relation to the invalidity issue?	208
		(c) A complication: separate revocation proceedings	210
	3.	A counterclaim for revocation	210
		(a) Do Articles 19 and 16(4) preclude infringement jurisdiction?	210
		(b) The necessity of a basis of jurisdiction in relation to the counterclaim	211
		(c) Recognition of a revocation order	212
	4.	Separate revocation proceedings	213
		(a) Do Articles 19 and 16(4) preclude infringement jurisdiction?	213
		(b) Is a basis of jurisdiction necessary in relation to the infringement issue?	214
IX	Provisional measures	214
	1.	Article 24	214
	2.	Infringement cases	217
X	Cross-border injunctions	218
	1.	The Dutch position	218
		(a) The kort-geding procedure	219
		(b) The basis of jurisdiction	219
		(c) The willingness to grant cross-border injunctions	220
	2.	Foreign reaction	220
	3.	Are the Dutch courts acting improperly under the Brussels Convention?	221

		(a) Do Articles 2, 5(3) and 6(1) permit cross-border injunctions?	221
		(b) Is a provisional measure within Article 24 being granted?	222
		(c) Can a provisional measure have extra-territorial effect?	224
		(d) Recognition and enforcement	225
	4.	The English position	225
		(a) Do the English courts have power to grant a cross-border injunction?	225
		(b) Will the English courts be willing to grant cross-border injunctions?	227
		(c) Will the English courts enjoin the Dutch proceedings?	228
XI	International discovery		228
	1.	The need to join a foreigner as a substantive defendant	228
	2.	Difficulties involved	229
		(a) Determining which company to join	229
		(b) Establishing liability	229
		(c) Satisfying the jurisdictional criteria	230
	3.	A different approach	230
XII	Reform		231
	1.	Criticism of the existing law	231
	2.	An alternative solution	232
	3.	Reform of the jurisdictional rules of general application	232
	4.	Special jurisdictional rules	233
		(a) Independent jurisdictional rules	233
		(b) Within the framework of existing jurisdictional rules	234

I
INTRODUCTION

In this chapter, the law relating to jurisdiction under the EC/EFTA rules and its application in infringement cases will be examined.

II
WHEN DO THE RULES APPLY?

It has already been seen that, broadly speaking, the jurisdiction rules in the Brussels Convention apply[1] where the matter is within the scope of the

[1] See, generally, Cheshire and North, pp 286–292.

Convention, ie it is a civil and commercial matter,[2] and, when it comes to bases of jurisdiction, the defendant is domiciled in an EC Contracting State.[3] Likewise, when it comes to the Lugano Convention, its jurisdiction rules apply[4] where the matter is within the scope of the Convention, ie it is a civil and commercial matter,[5] and, when it comes to bases of jurisdiction, the defendant is domiciled in an EFTA Contracting State.[6] It is clear that intellectual property matters are intended to come within the scope of these Conventions because of the presence of Article 16(4).[7] Even without this provision, there can be no doubt that an action for infringement, being an action in tort,[8] is a civil and commercial matter. That infringement is a civil and commercial matter has been confirmed by Lloyd J in *Pearce v Ove Arup Partnership Ltd and Others*.[9] Moreover, the Court of Appeal in *Fort Dodge Animal Health Ltd and Others v Akzo Nobel NV and Another*,[10] has held that Article 5(3) applies in infringement cases.

III
BASES OF JURISDICTION

Infringement is not within the exclusive jurisdiction provision in Article 16(4)[11]. It is necessary, therefore, to turn to other provisions in the Conventions to provide a basis of jurisdiction. There is no special provision dealing solely with infringement but a number of bases of jurisdiction of general application are available for use in infringement cases.

1. GENERAL JURISDICTION: ARTICLE 2

Article 2 of the Conventions states that:

persons domiciled in a Contracting State shall, whatever their nationality, be sued in the courts of that State

The expectation under the Conventions is that, normally, persons should be sued in the courts of the Contracting State where they are domiciled. Clearly, this provision can apply in infringement cases.[12]

---

[2] Article 1
[3] Articles 3 and 4. The rules on declining jurisdiction do not require that the defendant is domiciled in a Contracting State.
[4] See, generally, Cheshire and North, p 341.   [5] Article 1
[6] Articles 3 and 4. The rules on declining jurisdiction do not require that the defendant is domiciled in an EFTA Contracting State.
[7] See above, pp 15–27.   [8] See below, p 150.   [9] [1997] 2 WLR 779.
[10] [1998] FSR 222. The questions that were referred to the Court of Justice also relate to another case concerning the same points: *Boston Scientific Ltd and Others v Cordis Corpn*.
[11] See above, p 19.   [12] See the *Fort Dodge* case, n 10 above.

Infringement: Jurisdiction under the EC/EFTA rules

(a) ADVANTAGES IN USING THIS PROVISION

There are two major advantages to the plaintiff in an infringement action in using this provision, as opposed to basing jurisdiction on special jurisdiction under Articles 5 and 6.

First, it can be used to consolidate in one Contracting State a number of claims arising out of the infringement in different States of parallel rights.[13] Thus, for example, a plaintiff can sue in England an English domiciled defendant following infringements in the United States, Germany and Japan of the plaintiff's patents registered in those three States. This is assuming that it is the same defendant responsible for each infringement. The important role that Article 2 plays in centralising litigation in one State has been acknowledged by Advocate General Darmon in *Shevill and Others* v *Presse Alliance SA*,[14] a case concerning multi-State defamation. He pointed out that the courts of the State of the defendant's domicile have unlimited jurisdiction in the sense that they can try cases arising out of unlawful acts in another State, or other States.[15]

Secondly, there is no need to go into the merits of the case at the jurisdictional stage of the proceedings as long as jurisdiction is based on Article 2.[16] Under English law, this is necessary where jurisdiction is based on special jurisdiction under Article 5 or 6 of the Conventions.[17]

(b) DISADVANTAGES

First, whatever the cause of action, there is the inherent disadvantage in using Article 2, that the plaintiff, rather than suing in its home State, will have to pursue the defendant to the Contracting State in which that person is domiciled. Secondly, it is very common for the plaintiff to wish to bring an infringement action against two or more defendants, domiciled in different States, even when the infringement only takes place in one State. If, as is natural, the plaintiff wishes to sue all the defendants together in a single action in one Contracting State, resort will have to be made to other provisions in the Conventions.[18]

---

[13] Compare the difficulties under Articles 5 and 6, below pp 167–168, 172–173.
[14] Case C-68/93 [1995] 2 WLR 499, discussed below pp 396–399.
[15] *Ibid* at 522, 524. See also Advocate General Léger at 532 and the decision of the Court of Justice at 540.
[16] See *Mölnlycke AB and Another* v *Procter & Gamble Ltd and Others*, [1992] 1 WLR 1112 at 1120. But see the doctrine of abuse of process, discussed below, p 176.
[17] See below, p 145.
[18] See, in particular, Article 6(1) of the Brussels and Lugano Conventions, discussed below, pp 170–175.

2. Special Jurisdiction: Articles 5 and 6

Jurisdiction under Articles 5 and 6 is 'special' in that trial is allowed in the courts of a Contracting State other than the one in which the defendant is domiciled. Special jurisdiction is 'based on the existence of a particularly close connecting factor between the dispute and courts other than those of the State of the defendant's domicile, which justifies the attribution of jurisdiction to those courts for reasons relating to the sound administration of justice and the efficacious conduct of proceedings'.[19]

(a) THE THRESHOLD REQUIREMENT

(i) A serious issue on the merits

With special jurisdiction, whether under Article 5 or 6, there is a threshold requirement which the plaintiff has to satisfy before the defendant can be subjected to jurisdiction. The plaintiff's case must establish that there is a serious issue on the merits to be tried.[20] This is a lesser standard of proof than that of a good arguable case, which previously applied.[21] This threshold requirement is not to be found in the Conventions themselves. Its origin lies in the traditional English rules on jurisdiction in cases where there is an application for service of a writ out of the jurisdiction under Order 11, rule 1(1) of the Rules of the Supreme Court.[22] This requirement has been applied by way of analogy in the very different context of the Brussels Convention.[23] Questions of the standard and burden of proof, doubtless, are ones of procedure. The Conventions are not concerned with such questions except in so far as they prejudice their effectiveness.[24] The English threshold requirement does not appear to lead to such prejudice. Certainly, there can be no objection, in principle, to the English courts having a threshold requirement that necessitates an examination of the merits since this may have to be done anyway at the later stage of determining whether the terms of a head of Article 5 have been met.[25] There is authority that, at this later stage, the standard of proof as to the merits is a matter for national courts as part of determining their own jurisdiction.[26]

---

[19] Case C-220/88 *Dumez France and Tracoba* v *Hessische Landesbank (Helaba) and Others* [1990] ECR I-49 at 79–80.
[20] *ABKCO Music & Records Inc* v *Music Collection International Ltd and Another* [1995] RPC 657.
[21] *Tesam Distribution Ltd* v *Schuh Mode Team GmbH and Commerzbank AG* [1990] IL Pr 149 at 166.
[22] See *Seaconsar Far East Ltd* v *Bank Markazi Jomhouri Islami Iran* [1994] 1 AC 438; discussed below, p 256.
[23] The *Tesam* case, n 21 above, the *ABKCO* case, n 20 above.
[24] Case C-365/88 *Kongress Agentur Hagen GmbH* v *Zeehaghe BV* [1990] ECR I-1845, 1866.
[25] See below, pp 150–151.
[26] Case C-68/93 *Shevill* v *Presse Alliance SA* [1995] 2 WLR 499 at 528 (Advocate General Darmon).

The threshold requirement is particularly significant in infringement cases because of the difficulty of establishing liability under English law in such cases due to the territorial limitations on liability contained in the relevant English statutes.

(ii) Establishing liability

(a) *The applicable law*

Any enquiry as to the merits can raise questions regarding the applicable law even at the jurisdictional stage of the action.[27] The question of when an English court will apply a foreign law in infringement cases is one of considerable complexity, which will be considered in detail later on.[28] For the purposes of the present discussion though, it is important to look separately at two different situations: first, where English law applies; secondly, where a foreign law applies.

(b) *English law applies*

(i) *An act of infringement*
A plaintiff who wishes to establish liability for infringement under English law will have to show that the defendant has committed one of the acts of infringement described earlier.[29] It may be alleged that a foreign defendant has committed an individual act of infringement or, more commonly, that this person is a joint tortfeasor.

(ii) *The territorial limitation on liability*
Patents. As has been explained in chapter 4, under the English law of patent infringement [30] there is a requirement that the act must have been committed in the United Kingdom. In the event of an act of patent infringement being committed abroad, it is impossible to satisfy the threshold requirement as to liability, and it follows that there is no jurisdiction under Articles 5 and 6 of the Brussels or Lugano Convention. The same is true under the traditional English rules where jurisdiction is based on Order 11, rule 1(1) of the Rules of the Supreme Court, and cases decided in this latter context can be used to show the relationship between jurisdiction, the establishment of liability and the need for a local act of infringement. *Kalman and Another v PCL Packaging (UK) Ltd*[31] is a good illustration.

---

[27] See *Metall und Rohstoff AG v Donaldson Lufkin and Jenrette Inc* [1990] 1 QB 391, overruled on a different point in *Lonhro plc v Fayed* [1991] 3 WLR 188.
[28] See below, chapter 12.
[29] See above, pp 120–134.
[30] See the Patents Act 1977, s 60.
[31] [1982] FSR 406.

The first defendants (PCL), an English company, obtained two allegedly infringing filters from the second defendants (BC), a US corporation. The plaintiffs sued PCL for infringement by, *inter alia*, importation, and obtained leave to serve BC out of the jurisdiction relying on torts committed within England. It was alleged that BC had: first, offered to dispose or disposed of infringing apparatus contrary to Section 60(1)(a) of the Patents Act 1977; secondly, offered for use in the United Kingdom a process with knowledge that its use would be an infringement contrary to Section 60(1)(b); and thirdly, knowingly supplied PCL with the means for putting the invention of the patent into effect in the United Kingdom contrary to Section 60(2).

Falconer J decided that the plaintiffs had no cause of action against BC and set aside the writ and service out of the jurisdiction. As regards the first of the allegations, it was held that 'disposal' includes selling and that, since the sale of the filters had taken place in the United States, and property had passed there, BC had no further rights which they could 'dispose' of in the United Kingdom. Neither was there an offer to dispose since this requires an offer made in the United Kingdom to dispose of the filters within the jurisdiction. The argument that the airline which carried the filters into the United Kingdom was disposing of them for these purposes was rejected. The second allegation was regarded as a complete non-starter, for what was offered to PCL was the sale of filters in the United States, not the use of a process in the United Kingdom. The third allegation likewise failed since there was no supply in the United Kingdom to PCL by BC or offer to supply.

Similarly, in *Morton-Norwich Products Inc and Others* v *Intercen Ltd*,[32] there was no infringing sale *in England* by the Dutch defendant, who put the goods aboard an aircraft in Rotterdam, at which point the property passed to the English buyers. The sale took place in The Netherlands. However, it was said that the Dutch defendant remained in possession of the goods for trade purposes until they were actually handed over to the consignee in England, and that such possession could constitute an infringement which would be committed *in England*. This is a rare example where it was possible to show that a foreign defendant committed an individual act of infringement in England.

With the more common allegation of joint infringement, once this has been established, there is no difficulty in showing that the act of infringement occurred in England. For example, A is an English company, which has plainly committed an act of infringement in England by marketing an infringing product there, and B is the foreign manufacturer. If B is a joint tortfeasor then there is an act of infringement committed by B (albeit

---

[32] [1978] RPC 501.

jointly) in England. *Mölnlycke A B and Another* v *Procter & Gamble Ltd and Others*[33] is a good illustration.

The first plaintiff, a Swedish company, which was the registered proprietor of a patent relating to disposable nappies, and the second plaintiff, an English company which was the exclusive licensee under the patent, brought an action in England against two companies in a well known multinational group for infringement of the UK patent. The first defendant was an English company, the second defendant the American parent company. The plaintiffs, for the purpose of obtaining discovery of relevant documents, sought to join as a third defendant a German domiciled company in the group, referred to as GmbH. In order to establish the liability of GmbH it had to have committed an act of infringement in England.[34]

The Court of Appeal affirmed the decision at first instance granting leave to join the German company.[35] The plaintiffs had shown a good arguable case[36] that GmbH and the first defendant had a common design, with or without the second defendant, to market the infringing products in England. This established the liability of GmbH for an act of infringement in England.

However, it is not always possible to establish that there has been infringement by common design, even where the companies are within the same group of companies. The foreign company must have done some act in furtherance of the common design.[37] It must have taken part in the primary act of infringement. Material 'which merely shows that the foreign and domestic defendants are closely associated with each other, or which shows that the parent regards itself and its subsidiaries as a single economic unit throws no light on the issue of who took part in the acts alleged to infringe the patent'.[38] Evidence that merely shows that what the parent was doing was looking on with approval at what its subsidiaries were doing in the local market is not enough.[39]

Copyrights. If liability is to be imposed under Section 16(1) of the Copyright, Designs and Patents Act 1988[40] for doing acts restricted by the copyright, these acts must be carried out within the United

---

[33] [1992] 1 WLR 1112. See also under the traditional rules *Unilever plc* v *Gillette (UK) Ltd* [1989] RPC 583.

[34] N 33 above, at 1118, 1123.

[35] This was on the basis of Article 5(3) of the Brussels Convention, discussed below, p 155; see, generally, at 1117.

[36] The standard of proof for establishing the threshold requirement is now that of a serious issue on the merits; see above p 144.

[37] *Unilever plc* v *Chefaro Proprietaries Ltd* [1994] FSR 135 at 138.

[38] *The Mead Corpn and Another* v *Riverwood Multiple Packaging Division of Riverwood International Corpn* [1997] FSR 484 at 490. See also *Coin Controls Ltd* v *Suzo International (UK) Ltd* [1997] 3 All ER 45, 49–51.

[39] The *Mead* and *Coin Controls* cases, n 38 above.   [40] See above, p 125.

Kingdom.[41] The more difficult question has arisen of whether infringement by authorising another to do acts of infringement within the United Kingdom is similarly limited territorially so that the authorisation has to be given within the United Kingdom. This question arose in *ABKCO Music Records Inc (Body Corporate)* v *Music Collection International Ltd and Another*.[42] It was alleged that the first defendant, an English company, had infringed the plaintiff's copyright by manufacturing and issuing to the public copies of certain sound recordings, and that the second defendant, a Danish company, had done so by authorising or directing, counselling or procuring the acts of the first defendant by granting it a licence. The Court of Appeal held that it was enough that the restricted act authorised by the Danish defendant was done within the United Kingdom, even though the authorisation itself was given outside. It followed that the plaintiff satisfied the threshold requirement, under Articles 5(3) and 6(1) of the Brussels Convention, that there was a serious issue to be tried on the merits. Accordingly, the Danish company was subject to jurisdiction in England, it having previously accepted that the plaintiff's case fell within the terms of these Articles.

Trade Marks. It will be recalled that there is a territorial limitation on liability in relation to trade marks, as there is with patents and copyrights. A similar restriction exists in France. Nevertheless, importation and marketing in France of goods that had been labelled in Britain with the Coca Cola trade mark without the consent of the trade mark's owners was held to amount to trade mark infringement in France and the Tribunal de Grande Instance (District Court) in Paris took jurisdiction on that basis,[43] even if the labelling in Britain was not an infringement of French trade mark law.

(c) *A foreign law applies*

The recent introduction of statutory tort choice of law rules[44] means that a plaintiff in an action brought in England may now be able to establish liability on the basis of actionability under the law of the country abroad in which the events constituting the tort occurred. When it comes to establishing liability under a foreign law, the question will arise of whether there has been an infringement of an intellectual property right according

---

[41] See *ABKCO Music & Records Inc* v *Music Collection International Ltd and Another* [1995] RPC 657. For a borderline example in which importation of goods that were in transit was held to provide a sufficient link with the territory on the basis that importation can be a form of infringement, see *Arregui Mendizabal and Cuenca Sanchez* v *Régie Nationale des Usines Renault*, French Cour de Cassation, judgment of 7 October 1985, [1986] PIBD 387, iii-125.

[42] N 41 above.

[43] *The Coca Cola Company* v *Bernard Carant & Cie*, judgment of 5 July 1985, [1986] PIBD 387, iii-123.

[44] See the Private International Law (Miscellaneous Provisions) Act 1995, Part III, discussed below pp 612–640.

to the law of that country. Thus, in *Coin Controls Ltd* v *Suzo International (UK) Ltd*,⁴⁵ there were allegations of joint tortfeasance in respect of infringements in, *inter alia*, Spain and Germany. Laddie J held that whether a number of parties were liable for joint tortfeasance had to be determined in accordance with Spanish and German law. The existence of international conventions in relation to patents and copyrights ensures that, normally, the same definition of infringement will apply in the foreign country as is applied in England. It may also be that the law of the foreign country in question territorially limits liability. This happens, for example, under French law. The Tribunal De Grande Instance (District Court), in Paris has held that a claim in respect of the sale and importation *in Great Britain* of sweaters which infringed the copyright in an artistic work was unfounded.⁴⁶ However, usually, there will be no difficulty in establishing liability under a foreign law in this respect, since the normal reason why the English court is applying foreign law in the first place is because the events constituting the tort occurred there.

(d) *Validity of the right*

Establishing liability may also mean considering whether a patent or other intellectual property right is valid and any other defence to infringement.⁴⁷ Such matters do not have to be considered in detail since all that is being decided at the jurisdictional stage is whether there is a serious issue on the merits to be tried. A choice of law question may arise as to which State's law is applied to determine the validity of the right.⁴⁸

(b) ARTICLE 5

If trial of an infringement action is sought in England, the plaintiff has to show a good arguable case that the terms of Article 5 are satisfied. This is a higher standard of proof than that under the threshold requirement as to the merits. It is though the same standard of proof that has been laid down by the English courts when it comes to establishing, under the traditional rules on jurisdiction, that the terms of the heads of Order 11, rule 1(1) of the Rules of the Supreme Court⁴⁹ have been satisfied. This English standard of proof can not be regarded as being so high that it threatens the effectiveness of the Conventions.⁵⁰

---

⁴⁵ [1997] 3 All ER 45.
⁴⁶ *Charly Herscovici and Another* v *Société Karla and Another* [1992] ECC 209.
⁴⁷ *The Lubrizol Corpn and Another* v *Esso Petroleum Co Ltd and Others (No 1)* [1992] RPC 281. This was an Order 11, rule 1(1) case.
⁴⁸ See below, pp 484–538. ⁴⁹ The *Seaconsar* case, n 22 above; discussed below, p 256.
⁵⁰ See above, p 144.

Article 5 sets out seven situations where the defendant can be sued in a Contacting State other than that of his domicile. The two that are relevant in infringement cases are contained in Article 5(3) and (5).

Article 5(3)

in matters relating to tort, delict of quasi-delict, in the courts for the place where the harmful event occurred

(i) Is infringement within the scope of Article 5(3)?

Infringement of an intellectual property right is characterised as tortious in common law jurisdictions[51] and as delictual in civil law systems;[52] accordingly, it falls within the scope of Article 5(3). In *Mölnlycke AB and Another v Procter & Gamble Ltd and Others*, Dillon LJ, in the Court of Appeal, said that 'It is not in doubt that patent infringement falls within the rubric in Article 5(3), "matters relating to tort, delict or quasi-delict" '.[53] The same point was made in relation to copyright infringement by Lloyd J in *Pearce v Ove Arup Partnership Ltd and Others*.[54] This decision was affirmed by the Court of Appeal in *Fort Dodge Animal Health Ltd and Others v Akzo Nobel NV and Another*.[55] There are French decisions applying Article 5(3) in respect of the infringement of copyright[56] and a German one in respect of infringement of trade mark rights.[57]

(ii) Denial of the existence of a tort

The defendant may deny the existence of a tort. This cannot in itself deprive the national court of its jurisdiction under Article 5(3).[58] An enquiry will have to be made into the merits of the plaintiff's claim, in order 'to verify, on the basis of the evidence adduced by the plaintiff, whether the defendant did or did not commit an act which might render him liable . . .'.[59] Thus, in an Article 5(3) case decided in Germany,[60] involving the alleged infringement of a trade mark, it was argued that there was no tort since the infringing conduct was not unlawful, being

---

[51] *House of Spring Gardens Ltd v Waite* [1991] 1 QB 241 at 253 (copyrights); *Mölnlycke AB and Another v Procter & Gamble Ltd and Others* [1992] 1 WLR 1112 at 1117 (patents).
[52] von Bar, *Internationales Privatrecht* (1991), Vol II, at p 518.
[53] N 33 above at 1117.   [54] [1997] 2 WLR 779; discussed below, p 192.
[55] [1998] FSR 222.
[56] See the decision of the Cour d'Appel Paris in *Ideal Clima SpA and Others v SA Ideal Standard* Gaz Pal 1982, Somm, 378; D Series I-5.3–B13, and of the Cour de Cassation in *Wegmann v Société Elsevier Science Ltd* [1997] IL Pr 760.
[57] *Re Jurisdiction in Tort and Contract (Case I ZR 201/86)* [1988] ECC 415.
[58] Advocate General Darmon in Case C 68/93 *Shevill and Others v Presse Alliance* [1995] 2 WLR 499 at 529. See in relation to the existence of a contract: Case 38/81 *Effer SpA v Kantner* [1982] ECR 825; *Tesam Distribution Ltd v Schuh Mode Team GmbH and Commerzbank AG* [1990] IL Pr 149.
[59] The *Shevill* case, n 26 above, at 528.
[60] *Re Jurisdiction in Tort and Contract (Case I ZR 201/86)* [1988] ECC 415.

authorised by a contractual agreement between the parties. It was held by the German Federal Supreme Court that the court with jurisdiction as to tort must also consider this matter.

If trial takes place in England, this raises a very important question: do you treat a denial of infringement as being merely a denial of liability under the threshold requirement, or as a denial of the terms of Article 5(3)? As a result of the *Seaconsar* case,[61] this distinction matters because of the different standards of proof in these two different contexts: the standard of proof is that of a serious issue on the merits, in the former context; a good arguable case, in the latter. In *Grupo Torras SA and Torras Hostench London Ltd* v *Sheikh Fahad Mohammed Al-Sabah and Others*,[62] which was admittedly not an infringement case, the defendants denied that there was any conspiracy which would justify proceedings under Article 5(3). Mance J held that there was a serious case for arguing that there was such a conspiracy.[63] The denial of the existence of the tort of conspiracy was treated as a denial of the threshold requirement rather than as a denial of the terms of Article 5(3). This was the approach adopted by the Court of Appeal in *Tesam Distribution Ltd* v *Schuh Mode Team GmbH*,[64] a case decided before the *Seaconsar* decision was given.

(iii) Threatened wrongs

Article 5(3) refers to the place where the harmful event *occurred*. The use of the past tense strongly suggests that this provision cannot be used as the basis of jurisdiction in an action to prevent a threatened wrong.[65] The point is, however, not entirely free from doubt and some writers[66] have taken the opposite view. Unfortunately, the Schlosser Report[67] is rather ambiguous on this point,[68] and can be used to support both viewpoints. It

---

[61] N 22 above.   [62] [1995] 1 Lloyd's Rep 374.
[63] *Ibid*, at 450. This test was accepted by the Court of Appeal, although this point was not raised on appeal: [1996] 1 Lloyd's Rep 7 at 13.
[64] [1990] IL Pr 149 at 154.
[65] See Kaye, pp 570–571; Cheshire and North, p 300. A Dutch court has used this reasoning to deny jurisdiction under Article 5(3), *EBES* [1990] IL Pr 246. However, German Courts might take the opposite view. In a case based on the patent law provision which creates a ground of action for groundless threats of infringement proceedings the Landesgericht Mannheim (Case 702/80, [1980] GRUR 935) has applied Article 5(3). But maybe this case should not be seen as an ideal example, since this provision could be seen as a provision that is creating a separate right of action.
[66] See O'Malley and Layton, p 429; Collins, p 60; Dicey and Morris, p 363; Vitoria *et al*, paras 10–503. See also Betlem, (1996) 4 *European Review of Private Law* 159, 162–163 who distinguishes pollution cases from infringement cases and argues that threatened wrongs should come within Article 5(3) in the former.
[67] [1979] OJ C59. This accompanied the UK, Irish and Danish Accession Convention to the Brussels Convention.
[68] Para 134: 'There is much to be said for the proposition that the courts specified in Article 5(3) should also have jurisdiction in proceedings whose main object is to prevent the imminent commission of a tort.'

was hoped that the present uncertainty would be resolved by the Court of Justice when the German Federal Supreme Court in the *Beta-Film* case referred to it the issue of whether Article 5(3) can be used in relation to threatened wrongs.[69] This hope was dashed when the request for a reference was withdrawn and the case was removed from the Court register.

If Article 5(3) cannot be so used this is a very serious omission as far as intellectual property cases are concerned, since it is not uncommon for the plaintiff to seek an injunction to restrain a threatened infringement. The position is much more satisfactory when it comes to the infringement of Community intellectual property rights. The Community patent Convention,[70] the Community Trade Mark Regulation,[71] and the proposed Community Design Regulation,[72] all allocate jurisdiction to the Contracting State in which an act of infringement was committed *or threatened*. Moreover, Article 5(3) of the Modified Convention,[73] which allocate jurisdiction within the United Kingdom, is worded so as to cover threatened wrongs.

Nonetheless, the courts of an EC/EFTA State are not entirely powerless to deal with threatened wrongs. Article 24 of the Brussels or Lugano Conventions, which is concerned with provisional, including protective, measures, can be invoked in such cases.[74]

(iv) The place where the harmful event occurred

(a) *The definitional problem and the solution provided by the Court of Justice*

There is a well recognised problem in identifying 'the place where the harmful event occurred' in cases, such as those involving environmental damage by pollution, where the act which initiated the damage occurs in one State, but the resulting damage takes effect in another State. The Court of Justice, in *Handelskwekerij Bier Bv* v *Mines de Potasse d'Alsace SA*,[75] solved this definitional problem by holding that Article 5(3) was intended to cover both the place where the damage occurred and the place of the event giving rise to it, where the two are not identical. The plaintiff has the option of suing in either Contracting State. Underlying this wide interpretation of Article 5(3) were two important considerations.[76] First, special

---

[69] Case C-136/94.   [70] [1989] OJ L401/1, Protocol on Litigation, Article 14(5).
[71] [1994] OJ L11/1, Article 93(5).
[72] [1994] OJ C29/40, Article 86(5). But compare the Community Plant Variety Rights Regulation [1994] OJ L227/1.
[73] Contained in Civil Jurisdiction and Judgments Act 1982, Sch 4; as amended by SI 1993/603. See *WAC Ltd* v *Whillock* 1990 SLT 213. See also rule 2(10) of the Scots traditional rules on jurisdiction contained in Schedule 8 of the 1982 Act, as amended by SI 1993/603.
[74] See below, p 217.   [75] Case 21/76 [1978] QB 708, [1976] ECR 1735.
[76] *Ibid*, at 1747.

jurisdiction is justified on the basis of a particularly close connecting factor between a dispute and the court which may be called upon to hear it with a view to the efficacious conduct of the proceedings. Both the place of the event giving rise to the damage and the place where the damage occurred can constitute a significant connecting factor. Secondly, Article 5(3) is designed to give the plaintiff a choice of suing in a forum other than the State of the defendant's domicile. In an appreciable number of cases, the place of the event giving rise to the damage coincides with the State of the defendant's domicile. Allocating jurisdiction to the place where the damage occurred ensures the element of choice. At the same time, to deny jurisdiction to the place of the event giving rise to the damage would exclude a helpful connecting factor.

The *Mines de Potasse d'Alsace* case involved physical damage. In other cases, what is involved is non-material or non-pecuniary damage. It has been argued that, in such cases, the harmful event should be defined in terms of a single State and the distinction in *Mines de Potasse d'Alsace* should not be applied.[77] However, this argument was rejected by the Court of Justice in *Shevill and Others* v *Presse Alliance SA*.[78] This case concerned defamation which is actionable under English law without proof of damage, ie without proof of financial loss. What has been damaged though is the plaintiff's reputation. The Court of Justice regarded defamation as a tort involving non-material or non-pecuniary damage. It was said by Advocate General Léger[79] that the solution, in the present case, of defamation was indistinguishable from that in *Mines de Potasse d'Alsace* in that there was a geographical separation between the causal event and the place where the damage occurred. The Court of Justice concluded that the distinction adopted in the *Mines de Potasse d'Alsace* case must apply equally in the case of loss or damage other than physical or pecuniary, in particular to injury to reputation.[80] The Court of Justice then went on to identify the place of the event giving rise to the damage and the place where the damage occurred in the case of multi-State distribution of libel through the press.[81]

(b) *Infringement actions*

In infringement actions, it is not always clear where the harmful event has occurred. For example, if an allegedly infringing product was made in Germany and then imported and sold in England is the place of the harmful event in Germany or England? As yet, there is no decision of the Court of Justice specifically on the interpretation of Article 5(3) in relation to

---

[77] See Case C-68/93 *Shevill and Others* v *Presse Alliance SA* [1995] 2 WLR 499 at 518–519 (*per* Advocate General Darmon).
[78] *Ibid*.   [79] *Ibid*, at 532.   [80] *Ibid*, at 540.   [81] See below, pp 396–399.

infringement. Nonetheless, there is considerable authority to the effect that the definition adopted in the *Mines de Potasse d'Alsace* case should be applied to infringement cases.

First, as has been seen, the Court of Justice in the *Shevill* case turned its back on the idea of having special definitions of the place of the harmful event for particular torts. The same definition applies regardless of whether it is a case of non-material or material loss, and of whether it is a case of non-financial or financial loss. It might have been better if the Court of Justice had divided up torts in terms of the type of damage required and only applied the *Mines de Potasse d'Alsace* case in relation to material or financial damage. But it did not do so. Indeed, Advocate General Léger clearly regarded an action for infringement of a trade mark as being essentially the same as one for defamation in that both torts involved non-material or non-pecuniary damage.[82]

Secondly, there is a national decision in France specifically dealing with infringement which applies the *Mines de Potasse d'Alsace* definition. In *Ideal Clima SpA and Others* v *SA Ideal Standard*,[83] the Cour d'Appel, Paris, in a case concerning an action for infringement of copyright and unfair competition brought by a French company against a company whose seat was in Italy, following the display of a radiator in Paris, held that under Article 5(3), proceedings could be brought either in the State in which the radiator was displayed for commercial purposes, France, or in the State where the damage was suffered. There is also the decision of the Cour de Cassation in *Wegmann* v *Société Elsevier Science Ltd*,[84] which applies the principles in the *Shevill* case to the directly analogous situation of copyright infringement arising out of publications distributed in several Contracting States.

Thirdly, there are Dutch,[85] German[86] and Italian[87] cases which accept that the definition in the *Mines de Potasse d'Alsace* case applies in cases involving unfair competition.[88] There is a similar English decision[89] involving breach of confidence, which is a complementary tort to infringe-

---

[82] See Case C-68/93 *Shevill and Others* v *Presse Alliance SA* [1995] 2 WLR 499 at 530.

[83] Gaz Pal 1982, Somm, 378; D Series I-5.3–B13. See also *Re Jurisdiction in Tort and Contract Case I ZR 201/86*, [1988] ECC 415, which followed the *Mines de Potasse* case on a point as to the width of claims coming within Article 5(3).

[84] N 56 above; discussed below, pp 162–163.

[85] Arrondissementsrechtbank, Amsterdam, Judgment of 15 June 1977, *Geobra Brandstätter GmbH & Co KG* v *Big Spielwarenfabrik Dipl Ing Ernst A Bettag* NJ 1979, No 146, Note: Schultsz; Note: Verheul, NILR 1978, 87.

[86] Oberlandesgericht Hamm, Judgment of 3 October 1978 – 9 U 278/77.

[87] Tribunale di Monza, Judgment of 28 September 1979, *Candy SpA* v *Schell and Stoecker Reinshagen GmbH* Foro pad 1979, I, 225, Note: Magelli; Riv dir int priv proc 1980, 429. See also Italian Supreme Court, 28 October 1993 No 10704.

[88] See below, pp 410–411.

[89] *Kitechnology BV and Others* v *Unicor GmbH Plastmaschinen and Others* [1994] ILPr 568; discussed below, pp 439–441.

ment. It would be very undesirable to apply a different definition in cases involving infringement, given that an action will not uncommonly be based on both infringement and unfair competition.

The major authority going the other way is the English Court of Appeal decision in *Mölnlycke AB and Another v Procter & Gamble Ltd and Others*.[90] In this case, the infringement relied on in the statement of claim was the marketing in the United Kingdom by the first defendant of nappies manufactured by the third defendant, referred to as GmbH, in Germany. It was held that it was not in doubt that the harmful event was the marketing of the infringing nappies in England; accordingly, the harmful event occurred in England.[91] This defines the place of the harmful event in terms of the place where the act of infringement occurred.[92] The *Mines de Potasse d'Alsace* case was not cited by the Court and there was no attempt to follow the definition adopted in that decision. Application of the definition adopted by the Court of Justice, in fact, allocates jurisdiction to the place where the act of infringement occurred. The crucial difference is in relation to the place where damage occurred. The *Mölnlycke* case would suggest that in an infringement case a court does not have jurisdiction, under Article 5(3), on the basis that the damage occurred in that Contracting State, whereas the *Mines de Potasse d'Alsace* definition allows jurisdiction on this basis. This is not the first English case to ignore the *Mines de Potasse d'Alsace* definition and adopt a special definition for the place where the harmful event occurred. This happened in an earlier case involving negligent misstatement.[93] The case was a complex one where the event giving rise to the liability could be said to have occurred in one of several States. The *Mines de Potasse d'Alsace* definition was thought to be not particularly helpful in such circumstances and Steyn J preferred to look for 'where in substance the cause of action in tort arises, or what place the tort is most closely connected with'.

These English cases were decided before the *Shevill* case[94] and it is now much harder to adopt a special definition of the place of the harmful event for a particular tort in the light of that decision. The *Mölnlycke* case is a weak authority in that there is no discussion of the definitional problem or the *Mines de Potasse d'Alsace* case, and no consideration of the Continental authorities on infringement. Moreover, at the end of the day, it does not expressly reject the basing of jurisdiction in infringement cases on damage occurring in England.

It is submitted that the weight of authority is strongly in favour of applying the *Mines de Potasse d'Alsace* definition to infringement cases. The

[90] [1992] 1 WLR 1112. [91] *Ibid*, at 1117.
[92] Cornish seems to adopt the same approach, see Cornish, p 79 note 81.
[93] *Minster Investments Ltd v Hyundai Precision and Industry Co Ltd* [1988] 2 Lloyd's Rep 621.
[94] See above, n 77.

156   *Intellectual Property and Private International Law*

next two subsections will, therefore, seek to identify the place of the event giving rise to the damage and the place where the damage occurred in such cases.

(c) *The place of the event giving rise to the damage*

It is submitted that, normally, this will be where the act of infringement occurred. There is though a possible exception, whereby, in circumstances analogous to those in the *Shevill* case, the place of the event giving rise to the damage is where the defendant has its establishment.

(i) *Where the act of infringement occurred*

There can be no doubt that, in most cases, the place of the event giving rise to the damage is the place where the act of infringement occurred. This is supported by the *Ideal Clima* case,[95] the *Mölnlycke* case[96] in so far as it allocated jurisdiction to this place, and by *Pearce v Ove Arup Partnership Ltd and Others*.[97]

Patents. There is normally no difficulty in ascertaining where an act of infringement of a patent occurred. Typical acts of infringement, such as a disposal of a product or offering to dispose of a product, are confined to one State in the sense that you do not have part of the disposal in State A and another part of the same disposal in State B.[98] The classic scenario that frequently comes before the English courts is that of a product manufactured abroad by A, a foreign manufacturer, which is marketed in England by B, an English company. Usually, there is no question but that there is an act of infringement committed by B in England. The real issues are whether A is liable as a joint infringer[99] and whether there is some basis of jurisdiction over A. These two questions are interrelated. Establishing a case of joint infringement not only satisfies the threshold requirement of liability but also means that there is jurisdiction over the foreign defendant on the basis of an act of infringement committed in England in respect of which that person is a joint tortfeasor. The *Mölnlycke* case[100] serves as a simple example. In that case, it was possible to show an act of infringement in England, the marketing of the nappies, but the German manufacturer could only be liable for this by virtue of the doctrine of joint infringement and likewise could only come within Article 5(3) if this was shown.

Copyrights. Identifying the place where the act of infringement takes place is also not normally going to pose any problem. The place where the

---

[95] See above, n 56.   [96] See above, n 33.
[97] [1997] 2 WLR 779; discussed below.
[98] Of course, there may be two separate infringements: a disposal in State A and a separate disposal in State B.
[99] See above, p 147.   [100] See above, n 33.

act of copying a work, or issuing copies to the public, or performing a work in public is going to be self-evident. In the *Pearce* case,[101] the plaintiff alleged that two Dutch defendants had infringed his copyright in architectural plans for a building, drawn up in England, by copying them in designing a building in the Netherlands. It was also alleged that the civil engineers retained for the construction of the building and the owner of the building infringed his copyright. Lloyd J said, *obiter*, that it would be possible to bring the action in the Netherlands as the place where the harmful event occurred.[102]

There is a problem though where what is alleged is infringement by authorising another to do acts of infringement within the United Kingdom. In *ABKCO Music & Records Inc v Music Collection International & Another*,[103] the authorisation was given in Denmark by a Danish company and this led to acts of infringement in England – manufacturing and selling compact disks – by an English Company. Was the Danish company subject to the jurisdiction of the English courts? An appeal against the service of a writ on that defendant was dismissed. The argument in the case centred on the threshold requirement rather than on the terms of Article 5(3).[104] However, Lord Justice Hoffmann did say, in relation to this provision, that: 'It is well established that in the case of torts or crimes which include in their definition a described consequence, the English courts can assert jurisdiction on the grounds that consequence took place, or was intended to take place in England . . . It does not matter that the acts which preceded that consequence all took place abroad . . . It is I think sufficient that the definition of the tort requires an act and that that act is performed within the United Kingdom, however it may be linked to the preliminary act performed abroad.'[105] Thus the crucial act for the purpose of jurisdiction was the act of infringement that took place in the UK rather than the act of authorisation abroad.

Infringement of copyright by broadcasting raises a particularly difficult problem in locating the place where the act of infringement occurred. A satellite broadcast may originate, for example, in England where a signal is emitted from a ground station towards the satellite (England could be described as the country of the up-link[106]) and then the signal from the satellite may be received in many countries (what has been described as the foot print of the satellite[107]), for example in the Netherlands, Germany, Belgium and France. It is not clear whether the act of broadcasting occurs

---

[101] N 97 above.   [102] *Ibid*, at 784.   [103] [1995] RPC 657.
[104] See above, p 148.
[105] At 660. See also at 664 (per Neill LJ). Both judges were using conflicts jurisdiction cases to help them decide whether to impose a territorial limitation on liability under the relevant English statute.
[106] See Ginsburg, (1995) 42 *Journal of the Copyright Society of the USA* 318, 335.
[107] *Ibid*.

in the State of origin or that of reception. The State of origin solution has the virtue that it only allocates jurisdiction to a single State, whereas the State of reception solution would lead to a multiplication of competent fora, which is something that the Court of Justice, when interpreting the Brussels Convention, has been concerned to avoid.[108] Moreover, there is support for the State of origin theory in the very different context of determining which State's rules on the protection of copyright are to be applied.[109] Finally, the Satellite Broadcasting Directive, in effect, defines the act of broadcasting as 'the act of introducing ... of the programme-carrying signals intended for reception by the public into an uninterrupted chain of communication leading to the satellite and down towards the earth'.[110] This is not a rule of private international law in the strict sense. Nonetheless, by fixing upon the origin of the broadcast rather than its reception, it determines what the jurisdictional rule should be. It is submitted, in the light of these arguments, that a State of origin solution should be adopted. The same jurisdictional problem arises with terrestrial broadcasting or cable transmission, and the same solution should be adopted.

Of course, the problem of locating the place where the act of infringement occurred in cases of infringement of copyright by satellite broadcasting is avoided if in such cases the *Shevill* approach is applied and the place of the event giving rise to the damage is regarded as being where the defendant has its establishment.[111]

Infringement over the internet. Infringement over the internet is most likely to arise in cases of breach of copyright.[112] For example, an English company operates a world wide web server on the internet and puts on the net pirated material infringing a German copyright.[113] However, it is also possible to have an infringement of a patent or a trade mark over the internet.[114] An example of the former would be where a computer network user situated in France logs onto the network, accesses a machine that is physically situated in England, and runs software that would infringe an English patent.[115] An example of the latter would be where a German company advertises goods on the net thereby infringing a French trade mark.

[108] The *Shevill* case, n 82 above at 524 (*per* Advocate General Darmon); Case C-364/93 *Marinari* v *Lloyd's Bank plc and Another* [1996] 2 WLR 159 at 170–171.
[109] See the EC Green Paper, *Copyright and Related Rights in the Information Society*, discussed below.
[110] EC Council Directive 93/83/EEC of 27 September 1993 on the co-ordination of certain rules concerning copyright and rights related to copyright applicable to satellite broadcasting and cable retransmission, [1993] OJ L248/15, Article 1(2)(b).
[111] See below, pp 162–163.
[112] See, generally, Ginsburg, (1995) 95 *Colum L Rev* 1466.
[113] See Perritt, (1996) 41 *Villanova L Rev* 1 at 4–6.
[114] See in relation to patents, Burk, (1993) 68 *Tulane L Rev* 1. [115] *Ibid* at 39.

Such cases present an especially difficult problem in localising the place where the act of infringement occurred. Indeed, it has been argued by American writers that, in internet cases, jurisdiction should not be based on the act of infringement or indeed on any territorial connection.[116] But under the present law you cannot avoid territorial connections, and if the place of the event giving rise to damage is defined in terms of where the act of infringement occurred it is necessary to localise this place. The difficulty with this lies in the fact that it is exceedingly hard to say where the act of infringement occurred when there is a whole sequence of events between the original uploading (input) of information and its eventual display on a screen in another country.[117] The sequence of events is as follows: uploading of information; digitisation of the work; storage of the digitised form of the work; conversion of the digitised form of the work into the carrying signal; transmission of the carrying signal; reception of the carrying signal in the receiving machine; downloading (storage of information in the memory of the machine); screen display and, possibly, print out of display material. Innumerable countries may be involved. The transmission in a simple case will go from a computer in country A to a computer in country B. In a more complex case, it may go via a number of intermediate computers located in countries C and D. The carrying signal may be received in virtually every country in the world. A signal may be received in country A but printed out in country B. Underlying this problem of localising the place where the act of infringement occurred is the fact that the substantive law of infringement does not specify sufficiently clearly what the act of infringement is. Thus, in an infringement of copyright case it is copying. But such a loose concept does not help you identify where this occurred in a complicated case involving a whole sequence of events involving connections with perhaps many different countries.

In internet cases, the act of infringement could, and perhaps should, be regarded as being truly multi-national. But, for jurisdictional purposes, it is necessary artificially to locate this act in a particular State. If you try to do this, the act of infringement could be said to have occurred in any one of the States in which one of the events making up this complicated sequence occurred. Nonetheless, it is submitted that the only two really significant events in the whole sequence are the uploading of the information and its eventual downloading. These are the two constants which will

---

[116] See below, pp 236–237. But there are US cases applying normal jurisdictional principles to infringement over the internet, see *Bensusan Restaurant Corpn* v *King* (US DC for SDNY) [1997] 2 *EIPR* D 55, *Maritz Inc* v *CyberGold Inc* (US DC for ED of Miss) [1997] 2 *EIPR* D 56, 40 USPQ 2d 1729. See also Dutson, [1997] *JBL* 495 at 496.

[117] I am greatly indebted to J A L Sterling, Senior Visiting Fellow, Queen Mary and Westfield College, University of London, who presented a paper entitled 'Copyright and conflict of laws: some problems raised by Internet' at the Fordham University/King's College, London Seminar on 31 January 1996.

be there whenever there is infringement litigation. The route that the information takes in between can vary greatly from case to case, depending, for example, on whether a server is used in a third country, and should not operate to form a basis of jurisdiction. In the case, for example, where the route is via a server in a third State it would be absurd to allocate jurisdiction to the State where this may be quite fortuitously located.

Of the two alternatives, the place of uploading and that of downloading, there are strong arguments in favour of the former. First, it leads to a single act of infringement. In contrast, the place of downloading will lead to multiple acts of infringement since the information may be downloaded in numerous different States. Secondly, it concentrates on the act of the defendant, which is appropriate given that what is being sought to be established is jurisdiction over that defendant. In contrast, the place of downloading concentrates on the act of the retriever or receiver of the information, not that of the defendant. Thirdly, the analogy could be drawn with that other area where it is very difficult to localise the place where infringement occurred, satellite broadcasting. The place of uploading in internet cases is analogous to that of the place of origin in broadcasting cases. The drawback with a place of uploading solution is that it could lead to manipulation.[118] 'Cyberpirates will simply make sure they . . . locate their services in, a country having an extremely lax intellectual property regime'.[119]

There are two arguments in favour of the place of downloading. The first is based on an acknowledgment of the role of the retriever in internet cases. The position is very different from in broadcasting cases.[120] In such cases, there is an active broadcaster and a passive receiver. In internet cases there are two active parties.[121] One person puts the information on the web but the person eventually receiving that information often has to take positive steps to access it, particularly where information is placed on a server, and will not receive it unless he does so. He is a retriever rather than a receiver. This leads then to the argument that it is the downloading, ie the retrieval, that is the truly significant event and that the act of infringement occurs in the place where this takes place. This difference between satellite broadcasting and internet cases cannot be denied. But that merely leaves you with the acknowledgment that there are two active parties in internet cases. It does not produce an argument for preferring the acts of the retriever to those of the uploader. The second argument is that, as a matter of substantive law, it is arguable that the downloading constitutes the copying in a case of copyright infringement.

---

[118] See Ginsburg, n 106 above, at 336.   [119] *Ibid.*
[120] See, generally, Geller, (1996) 20 *Columbia-VLA Journal of Law and the Arts* 571, 595–596.
[121] See, generally, Geller, *ibid*; Perritt, n 113 above, at 20–21.

It is submitted that, in cases of infringement over the internet, the policy arguments for adopting a place of uploading rule are stronger than those for adopting a place of downloading rule, and, accordingly, the act of infringement should be regarded as being committed in the State where the uploading of the information occurred.[122]

Of course, the problem of locating the place where the act of infringement occurred in cases of infringement over the internet is avoided if in such cases the *Shevill* approach is applied and the place of the event giving rise to the damage is regarded as being where the defendant has its establishment.[123]

(ii) *Multiple acts of infringement*

Cases of multiple acts of infringement committed in different States, such as where an infringing product is marketed in England, France and Germany, are common. It is not clear whether the fact that a court of a Contracting State has jurisdiction under Article 5(3) on the basis of an act of infringement committed in that State also means that it has jurisdiction in relation to the separate acts of infringement committed in other Contracting States. This point has been clarified in the jurisdiction rules contained in the Protocol on Litigation of the Community Patent Convention,[124] the Community Trade Mark Regulation,[125] and the proposed Regulation on Community Design.[126] In all three Community instruments, it is provided that a court whose jurisdiction is based on a local act of infringement shall have jurisdiction only in respect of acts of infringement committed or threatened within the territory of that State. This is a territorial limitation on jurisdiction. Such a limitation should also be applied equally in relation to the infringement of national intellectual property rights. There is some support for this approach in the *Shevill* case.[127] There, the Court of Justice, in the context of defamation, imposed a territorial limitation on jurisdiction based on damage in the forum so that there was no jurisdiction in relation to damage suffered in another Contracting State. There must be a distinct likelihood that the same approach would be adopted in relation to jurisdiction based on an act of infringement. Moreover, it has to be borne in mind that Article 5(3) is an exception to Article 2 and, normally, should be used restrictively. If jurisdiction on the basis of an act of infringement under Article 5(3) is confined to local infringements, the plaintiff can always consolidate the litigation in

---

[122] This was the conclusion reached by Kaufmann-Kohler in her paper, 'Global Communication-Universal Jurisdiction', presented at a conference entitled 'Internet: Which court decides, which law applies', held at the University of Utrecht on 28 June 1997.
[123] See below, pp 162–163.   [124] See Article 17(2).   [125] See Article 94(2).
[126] See Article 87(2). See also Article 101(3) of the Regulation on Community plant variety rights.
[127] Case C-68/93 *Shevill and Others* v *Presse Alliance SA* [1995] 2 WLR 499; discussed below.

respect of all the infringements, wherever they take place, by suing under Article 2. To allow jurisdiction in relation to acts of infringement abroad involves undermining Article 2. In conclusion, it is doubtful whether, when jurisdiction under Article 5(3) is based on a local act of infringement, there is also jurisdiction under that provision in relation to acts of infringement committed abroad.[128]

(iii) *Where the defendant has its establishment*

In the *Shevill* case, which concerned libel by a newspaper article distributed in several Contracting States, the Court of Justice held that the place of the event giving rise to the damage was that where the publisher of the newspaper in question was established.[129] This idea was applied by the French Cour de Cassation in the *Wegmann* case,[130] which concerned the directly analogous situation where there was infringement of copyright by counterfeiting involving publications distributed in several Contracting States. It was held that the victim could pursue its claim for damages either before the courts of the place where the author of the counterfeiting has its establishment, which, following the *Shevill* case, have jurisdiction to deal with the whole damage, or, under the damage part of Article 5(3), before the courts of the Contracting States where the counterfeited goods are distributed, which, again following the *Shevill* case, have jurisdiction to deal only with the damage suffered in that State.

The circumstances in the *Wegmann* case were directly analogous to those in the *Shevill* case. Are there any other circumstances in infringement cases in which the *Shevill* approach, with its definition of the place of the event giving rise to the damage in terms of where the defendant has its establishment, should be adopted? Simple cases of infringement, such as the *Pearce*, *Molnlycke* and *Ideal Clima* cases, are very different from the *Shevill* case, and in such cases, a definition in terms of the place where the act of infringement occurred should continue to be applied. On the other hand, cases of infringement by satellite broadcasting or over the internet are complex, involving the multi-State dissemination of information. It is arguable that such cases are sufficiently analogous to the *Shevill* case for the approach in that case to apply, thereby avoiding the difficulty in ascertaining where the act of infringement occurred. However, as has been seen, the latter problem is not insoluable. Moreover, adoption of a definition in terms of where the defendant has its establishment does not fit in with the Satellite Broadcasting Directive with its emphasis on the place of origin of the broadcast,[131] nor does it fit in with the position in relation to the question of which State's rules on the protection of copyright are to be

---

[128] See Brinkhof, [1994] *EIPR* 360 at 364.
[129] N 82 above, at 540. This is discussed further below, p 397.   [130] N 56 above.
[131] See above, pp 157-158.

applied.[132] Finally, as will be seen,[133] it is not easy to apply the *Shevill* definition of damage, under the damage part of Article 5(3), to cases of infringement by satellite broadcasting or over the internet. In such cases, it is submitted that the place of the event giving rise to the damage should be defined in terms of where the act of infringement occurred. For the same reasons, the definition of damage adopted in the *Shevill* case should not be adopted in cases of infringement by satellite broadcasting or over the internet.

(d) *The place where the damage occurred*

(i) *The definitional problem and the solution adopted by the Court of Justice*

There is, normally, no difficulty in ascertaining where damage occurs in cases of personal injury or physical damage to property. Problems have, however, arisen in cases where the damage is financial harm, since this may occur in more than one State. In *Dumez France and Tracoba* v *Hessische Landesbank (Helaba) and Others*,[134] the Court of Justice held that the place where the damage occurred 'can be understood only as indicating the place where the event giving rise to the damage, and entailing tortious, delictual or quasi-delictual liability, directly produced its harmful effects upon the person who is the immediate victim of that event'.[135] This case involved the plaintiffs, parent companies with head offices in France, who were indirect victims, suffering damage to their assets in France as the indirect consequence of the harm initially suffered in Germany by the direct victims, their German subsidiary companies, after the German defendants cancelled certain bank loans. The Court of Justice held that the French courts had no jurisdiction under Article 5(3) to hear an action brought by the French plaintiffs against the German defendants.

In the subsequent case of *Marinari* v *Lloyds Bank Plc (Zubaidi Trading Company, Intervener)*,[136] the situation was simpler; there was only one victim. The Italian domiciled plaintiff was arrested and promissory notes were sequestrated in England. On his release, the plaintiff brought an action in Italy, *inter alia*, for compensation for the damage he claimed to have suffered as a result of his arrest, the breach of several contracts and injury to his reputation. The Court of Justice held that the place of damage was to be interpreted as not referring to the place where the victim claimed to have suffered financial loss consequential upon initial damage arising and suffered by him in another Contracting State. The policy underlying this decision was to keep Article 5(3) within certain bounds so as to avoid multiplication of competent fora. If this provision were to be extended

[132] See above, p 158. [133] See below, p 167. [134] Case 220/88 [1990] ECR 49.
[135] *Ibid*, at 80. [136] Case C-364/93 [1996] 2 WLR 159.

beyond the particular circumstances which justified it, it would allow the plaintiff the option, in effect, of suing in the State of his own domicile.

In the *Shevill* case, the Court of Justice held that, in the case of international libel through the press, damage 'occurs in the places where the publication is distributed, when the victim is known in these places'.[137]

(ii) *Infringement cases*

It has been suggested that damage in infringement of copyright cases can only occur where copyright is protected.[138] The argument is that 'the very territorial character of copyright implies that it can only be infringed where it is protected. The jurisdiction of the English courts would hence be excluded when a foreign copyright is infringed, because it could in no way be that the damage were suffered in England'.[139] This appears to confuse the issues of liability and the basis of jurisdiction. It also fails to answer the crucial question of what is meant by damage in infringement cases. In infringement cases, there is no material damage. Neither is evidence of financial loss required as part of the cause of action. Accordingly, it is exceedingly difficult to identify what the damage is, in any meaningful way, in such cases. Instead, it becomes necessary to artificially invent a concept of damage for the purpose of Article 5(3). What, arguably, could be said to be damaged is the intellectual property right itself. Damage would therefore occur in the place in which the damage to the intellectual property right was sustained.[140] Alternatively, it could be argued that, in the situation where there is evidence of direct economic loss to the plaintiff, damage occurs in the place in which such loss was suffered. These two alternative solutions will now be examined.

The place in which damage to the intellectual property right was sustained. It is not immediately obvious where this is. There are two possible alternatives: first, the State in which the intellectual property is situated; secondly, the State in which the intellectual property right is infringed.

The first alternative is difficult to apply. The intellectual property right is, presumably, situated where the property is situated. But it is by no means obvious where intellectual property, being intangible, is situated. English courts apply the law of the forum in order to ascertain the *situs* of property.[141] According to Dicey and Morris, rule 114, 'patents and trade-

---

[137] N 82 above, at 540.
[138] Jooris, [1996] 3 *EIPR* 127,139–140.
[139] *Ibid*, at 140.
[140] The Court of Appeal in Paris applied this principle to take jurisdiction on the basis of Article 5(3) of the Brussels Convention in a case where the reception in France of the signal of Radio Monte Carlo that had been broadcast from abroad caused damage to the rights of the owners of the rights in the phonograms that were broadcast. No royalties for broadcasting in France had been paid. *Radio Monte Carlo* v *SNEP*, judgment of 19 December 1989, (1990) 144 RIDA 215.
[141] This is a connecting factor and an English court will apply English law to define such factors.

marks are situate in the country where they can be effectively transferred under the law governing their creation'.[142] The High Court of Australia, in a case involving an application in Australia for the extension of the terms of letters patent granted in Australia, and the question of the law governing the devolution of a company's interest in the patent, held that the patent was to be regarded as being situated in Australia.[143] Likewise, in the House of Lords, Lord Loreburn regarded trade marks registered in England as being situated in that country, with the result that this property had to be regulated and disposed of in accordance with the law of England.[144] Similarly, Wyn-Parry J has held[145] that an English copyright was situated in England with the result that the English courts would not give effect to a foreign confiscatory law in relation to this copyright.

However, a question mark hangs over the use of this rule in infringement jurisdiction cases in that it requires reference to the law governing the creation of the property and is based on choice of law, not jurisdiction, cases. It is arguable that a different, and simpler, definition of the situation of intellectual property should be adopted in the context of jurisdiction. According to which, an intellectual property right is situated in the State in which it was created. With patents, trade marks and registered designs, this would be where the property is registered. The analogy can be drawn with shares, which are another form of intangible property. Shares that 'are transferable only by an entry in the register are deemed to be situated in the country where the register or branch register is kept'.[146] This proposed rule is not incompatible with the cases mentioned above, which are cited by Dicey and Morris in support of rule 114. It would lead to the desirable result that the State which has jurisdiction in relation to the issue of validity of an intellectual property right would also have jurisdiction in relation to the issue of infringement. This rule would work well enough in cases where the property is only registered in one State, but not where there are parallel registrations in, say, six European States. Would there be damage in each of these States, with the result that each State has jurisdiction? It cannot be suggested seriously that infringement of, for example, a French patent in France actually causes damage to the parallel patent registered in Italy. There would have to be a special rule for such cases of parallel registration.

---

[142] At p 934.
[143] *In Re Usines De Melle and Firmin Boinot's Patent* [1954] CLR 42 at 48. See also *British Nylon Spinners Ltd v Imperial Chemical Industries Ltd* [1953] 1 Ch 19 at 26 – refusal to recognise a US extraterritorial assertion of jurisdiction.
[144] *Lecouturier and Others v Rey and Others* [1910] AC 262 at 273. See also *R J Reuter Co Ltd v Mulhens* [1954] Ch 50 at 96 – whether property was vested in the custodian of enemy property.
[145] *Novello & Co Ltd v Hinrichsen Edition Ltd and Another* [1951] 1 Ch 595 at 604.
[146] Cheshire and North, pp 823–824.

It is, at first sight, more satisfactory to adopt the second alternative, according to which an intellectual property right is damaged in any place in which that right is infringed. This place is easy to identify; it is the place in which the act of infringement occurred. However, this solution gives no wider jurisdiction than is allowed under the act of infringement rule. The two parts of the *Mines de Potasse d'Alsace* definition would never operate as alternatives, as was intended in certain circumstances, but would coincide.

The place in which direct economic loss was suffered. In many cases an act of infringement will cause direct economic loss to the plaintiff. Indeed, the plaintiff may seek not merely an injunction to restrain the infringement but also damages, and/or loss of profits, and/or an account of profits. It is not usually hard to identify what the loss is. If, for example, the defendant sells an infringing product this will result in a loss of sales. Damage is, therefore, sustained in the place in which the sales are lost. This will be the place in which the infringing product is sold. This view of 'damage' is supported by the Tribunale di Monza in *Candy SpA v Schell and Stoecker Reinshagen GmbH*,[147] an Article 5(3) case concerned with breach of competition rules rather than with infringement. Since the damage had occurred in Germany, the Italian court had no jurisdiction. No relevance was to be attached to the place where that damage brought about the specific reduction in the assets of the victim. However, a German court[148] has taken a different view. The Oberlandesgericht Hamm held that if the close factual connection assumed by the Court of Justice in the *Mines de Potasse d'Alsace* case to exist between the harmful event and the occurrence of damage did not in fact exist, the courts at the place where financial damage ensued could not be regarded as particularly closely connected with the tort. This was a case involving financial loss in the State of the plaintiff's domicile, which was different from the State where the harmful event occurred.

The major flaw with the direct economic loss solution is that, in some cases, there will be an infringement but no direct economic loss will be suffered by the plaintiff. For example, an injunction is sought prior to the infringing products being marketed in order to prevent damage. Moreover, the place in which sales are lost will be the same as that in which the act of infringement was committed.

Any company which has had its intellectual property right infringed will suffer not only a direct loss of sales but also an indirect loss of profits as a result of this. This indirect damage will be sustained in the place in which the company has its seat. The Court of Justice, in the *Marinari* case,[149] has made it clear that the courts of the Contracting State in which

---

[147] Foro pad 1979, I, 225, Note: Magelli; Riv Dir int priv proc 1980, 429.
[148] Judgment of 3 October 1978 – 9 U278/77.
[149] Above n 136. See also *Kitechnology BV and Others v Unicor GmbH Plastmaschinen and Others* [1994] IL Pr 568 – a case on breach of confidence, discussed below.

such indirect damage has been sustained do not have jurisdiction under Article 5(3).

The places where the publication is distributed. In the *Wegmann* case, which, as has been seen, was directly analogous to the *Shevill* case, the Cour de Cassation adopted the same definition for damage as in that case. The French courts had jurisdiction to hear a claim for compensation for the damage suffered because of counterfeiting, partly carried out in France, as a result of the distribution of publications published in Great Britain, in so far as they only dealt with the damage suffered in France.

If, contrary to what is argued above, the approach in the *Shevill* case towards defining both the place of the event giving rise to the damage and the damage itself is applied to cases of infringement by satellite broadcasting or over the internet, then, when it comes to identifying the damage in such cases, it has to be decided what the publication is and where this is distributed. This points to the danger of trying to apply the *Shevill* approach in a different context. Nonetheless, it could be argued that the damage occurs in the places where the information is received. The courts of such a place would only be able to deal with the damage suffered in that Contracting State.

(iii) *Multiple damage*

Does a court of a Contracting State which has jurisdiction under Article 5(3) on the basis of local damage also have jurisdiction in relation to damage which has occurred in other Contracting States? This is a parallel problem to that of multiple acts of infringement, discussed above.[150] However, when it comes to multiple damage, it is helpful to look at the area of multi-State defamation where the Court of Justice has been faced with this problem. In *Shevill and Others v Presse Alliance SA*,[151] the Court of Justice held that the plaintiff was able, under the place where the damage occurred part of Article 5(3), to bring an action before the courts of each Contracting State in which the publication was distributed and where the victim claims to have suffered injury to his reputation but these courts only have jurisdiction to rule in respect of the harm caused in the State of the court seized. The Court of Justice justified this rule in terms of the sound administration of justice, which is the underlying basis of Article 5(3). It was said that 'the Courts of each Contracting State in which the defamatory publication was distributed and in which the victim claims to have suffered injury to his reputation are territorially the best placed to assess the libel committed in the State and to determine the extent of the corresponding damage'.[152] The corollary to this is that such courts are not best placed to assess libel committed in another State and to determine the extent of the corresponding

[150] See above, pp 161–162.   [151] Case C-68/93 [1995] 2 WLR 499.
[152] *Ibid*, at 540.

damage. In infringement cases, the same argument, based on territoriality, should be applied and a court which has jurisdiction on the basis of damage occurring in that State should not have jurisdiction in relation to damage occurring in another Contracting State. As has just been seen, this is what the French Cour de Cassation did in the *Wegmann* case. The French courts had jurisdiction under the damage part of Article 5(3), but could only deal with the damage suffered in France. In contrast, if the infringement of copyright action is brought, using the place of the event giving rise to the damage part of Article 5(3), before the courts of the place where the author of the counterfeiting has its establishment, these courts have jurisdiction to deal with the whole damage.

Adoption of the principle in relation to multiple damage in the *Shevill* case would have profound implications in parallel infringement cases. As Jacob J has pointed out, it 'would mean that a plaintiff could not forum shop around Europe for a Europe wide injunction. He could only seek such an injunction in the state of the source of the allegedly infringing goods or piratical activity'.[153] However, he refused to say whether the *Shevill* case was to be applied to cases of multiple damage arising from parallel infringements.

(e) *A special definition for infringement cases*

There are strong arguments, in principle, which could be put to the Court of Justice in an infringement case, as to why a special definition of the place of the harmful event should be adopted in such cases, rather than applying the definition in the *Mines de Potasse d'Alsace* case.

First, in infringement cases, there is no requirement of damage of any sort to be shown. This is different from defamation, where damage to reputation is an element of the tort.[154]

Secondly, it is extremely difficult, in infringement cases, to identify what the damage is and where this takes place. As has been seen, there are no entirely satisfactory solutions to these problems.

Thirdly, that infringement is different is recognised in the Community instruments in relation to Community patents,[155] trade marks[156] and designs,[157] where international jurisdiction is allocated to the State in

---

[153] *Mecklermedia Corpn and Another v DC Congress GmbH* [1997] 3 WLR 479, 488.

[154] Under English law, all that has to be shown is the likelihood of damage to reputation.

[155] See Article 14(5) of the Protocol on Litigation of the Community Patent Convention; discussed below.

[156] See Article 93(5) of the Community Trade Mark Regulation; discussed below pp 325–326.

[157] See Article 86(5) of the proposed Community Design Regulation. See also Article 101(3) of the Council Regulation on Community Plant Variety Rights which refers to the place where the harmful event occurred, but this contemplates an act of infringement.

which the act of infringement was committed or threatened. The distinction drawn in the *Mines de Potasse d'Alsace* case between the wrongful act and the ensuing damage is not used.

Fourthly, the *Mines de Potasse d'Alsace* definition is concerned with the situation where the place where the causal event occurred coincides with the place of the defendant's domicile (at least in an appreciable number of cases), and there is then a need for the alternative of the place of damage. In infringement cases, the position is very different. In the common scenario of a foreign defendant manufacturing an infringing product abroad which is marketed in England, the causal event is the marketing of the product in England. This does not coincide with the defendant's domicile, and the plaintiff has the necessary choice of fora.

Fifthly, the place where the damage arose has been justified as a potential forum because of the particularly close connecting factor between the dispute and the courts other than those of the State of the defendant's domicile. In infringement cases, it is questionable whether there is such a close connection in relation to the place of damage, in whatever way this is defined.

Sixthly, many of the above arguments show that infringement is different from defamation and that the *Shevill* case should not, therefore, operate to preclude a special rule in the former area.

The obvious special rule to have would be one which allocates jurisdiction to the place where the act of infringement occurred, as happens in relation to Community patents, trade marks and designs. The plaintiff would have a choice of suing either in this place or in the State of the defendant's domicile. Since the two often do not coincide the plaintiff normally would have a real choice of two fora in which to bring the action.

Article 5(5)

as regards a dispute arising out of the operations of a branch, agency or other establishment, in the courts for the place in which the branch, agency or other establishment is situated

There are two requirements under this provision. First, the defendant domiciled in a Contracting State must have a 'branch, agency or other establishment' in another Contracting State. A 'branch, agency or other establishment' has been defined by the Court of Justice[158] in terms of the typical characteristics of a branch office. The branch, etc must: (i) have a fixed permanent place of business; (ii) be subject to the direction and

---

[158] Case 14/76 *De Bloos* v *Bouyer* [1976] ECR 1497, [1977] 1 CMLR 60; Case 33/78 *Somafer* v *Saar-Ferngas* [1978] ECR 2183, [1979] 1 CMLR 490; Case 139/80, *Blanckaert and Willems* v *Trost* [1981] ECR 819, [1982] 2 CMLR 1; Case 218/86 *Sar Schotte GmbH* v *Parfums Rothschild SARL* [1987] ECR 4905; Case C-439/93 *Lloyd's Register of Shipping* v *Soc Campenon Bernard* [1995] ECR I-961.

control of the parent; (iii) have a certain autonomy; and (iv) act on behalf of and bind the parent.[159] Secondly, the dispute must arise out of the operations of the branch, etc. This requirement is satisfied, *inter alia*, where there is a non-contractual action arising from the activities of the branch, etc.

This is a very useful provision in infringement cases. It would allow, for example, an action to be brought in England against a French manufacturing company which markets an infringing product in England through its English branch office. The branch office cannot be sued as a defendant since it is not a separate legal entity. It follows that the principle of joint infringement does not help in this situation. The French manufacturing company, however, can be sued in England by virtue of Article 5(5), provided that the dispute arises out of the operations of the branch.[160] If the branch, for example, markets the infringing product this requirement will be satisfied. On the other hand, if the French manufacturer merely happens to have a branch office in England which plays no part in the infringement Article 5(5) will not come into play.

Article 5(5) is less useful in the common situation where a subsidiary company is set up in order to market a product manufactured abroad. The subsidiary is a separate legal entity and may be sued alongside its foreign parent. The problem in relation to Article 5(5) is that a typical subsidiary company will act for itself and not on behalf of its foreign parent, and thus cannot be regarded as an 'establishment' within Article 5(5). It may, however, be possible to subject the foreign parent to jurisdiction under Article 5(3) by establishing that parent and subsidiary are joint tortfeasors. In rare cases a subsidiary company may act on behalf of the parent as if it were a branch, and Article 5(5) will then apply. Equally, if a parent company acts on behalf of, and as an extension of, its subsidiary Article 5(5) will apply.[161]

(c) ARTICLE 6

A person domiciled in a Contracting State may also be sued:

(1) Where he is one of a number of defendants, in the courts for the place where any one of them is domiciled

This is the only provision in the Brussels and Lugano Conventions which is specifically geared to multi-party litigation.[162] A plaintiff who wishes to pursue an action for infringement against, for example, an English domiciled company which markets an infringing product and a Belgian domi-

---

[159] See Cheshire and North, pp 303–305. [160] See the *Somafer* case, above n 158.
[161] See the *Sar Schotte* case, above n 158.
[162] See, generally, Fawcett, (1995) 44 ICLQ 744.

ciled company which manufactured that product, is able to proceed against both companies in either England or Belgium. It is a particularly useful basis of jurisdiction in infringement cases, given that multi-defendant litigation is so common in such cases. A simple example of the operation of Article 6(1) can be seen by looking at the English case of *Pearce v Ove Arup Partnership Ltd and Others*.[163] In this case, the English court had jurisdiction under Article 6(1) in relation to a claim for breach of a Dutch copyright in respect of architectural plans for a building brought by an English plaintiff against four defendants, the first of whom was domiciled in the United Kingdom, the second may have been so domiciled and the third and fourth were domiciled in the Netherlands. Article 6(1) is also useful in cases involving a declaration of non infringement. It was used successfully in *Chiron Corpn v Evans Medical Ltd and Others*,[164] where a worldwide exclusive licensee under a patent was held to be a proper party to an action for a declaration of non infringement brought against the proprietor of a patent. Instead of using Article 6(1) on its own, a plaintiff will often argue in the alternative, that the forum has jurisdiction by virtue of Article 5(3) and/or Article 6(1).

(i) Reasons for multi-defendant litigation in infringement cases

It is worth asking why plaintiffs in infringement cases take the trouble to sue a foreign party, whether individually or jointly, when there is an English party available to be sued, without getting involved with the complexities of private international law. One reason is so as to obtain discovery of documents held by the foreign company.[165] A second reason is that the foreign manufacturer knows best how technical equipment works and can, therefore, assist in an infringement action.[166] A third, and even more fundamental reason, is that if the plaintiff proceeds against a manufacturer abroad, it is stopping the infringement at its source. A fourth reason is that it can be useful to pursue a remedy for damages against one defendant and an account of profits against another.[167] A fifth, and final, reason is that obtaining a judgment against two defendants in respect of which the plaintiff has a good cause of action will enable it to choose against which of the defendants it will seek to enforce its judgment.[168]

---

[163] N 54 above. The case raised important issues in relation to subject matter limitations on jurisdiction, discussed below p 192, and abuse of process, discussed below, p 176.
[164] [1996] FSR 863.
[165] *Unilever plc v Gillette (UK) Ltd* [1989] RPC 583 at 601. International discovery is discussed below, pp 228–230.
[166] *Puschner v Tom Palmer (Scotland) Ltd and Another* [1989] RPC 430 at 440.
[167] *The Electric Furnace Co v Selas Corpn of America* [1987] RPC 23 at 33.
[168] *Ibid*.

(ii) Requirements

(a) *The requisite connection between the various actions*

There must exist between the various actions brought by the same plaintiff against the different defendants a connection of such a kind that it is expedient to hear them together to avoid irreconcilable judgments.[169] Judgments may be irreconcilable because they involve contradictory findings of facts, or contradictory legal conclusions drawn from those facts, or contradictory remedies.[170] This requirement is designed to uphold the principle that the defendant should normally be sued in the Contracting State in which that person is domiciled and to ensure that an action should not be brought against a number of defendants solely with the object of ousting the jurisdiction of the courts of the State in which one of the defendants is domiciled.

(i) *Joint tortfeasors*

The connection requirement is clearly met in the situation where the defendants are joint tortfeasors. In infringement cases, it is not difficult to show, for example, that an English company, which markets an infringing product, and the foreign manufacturers, are joint tortfeasors by virtue of having a common design.[171] In the *Pearce* case, the requirement was not discussed but it would clearly be met. It was a simple case where all four defendants were alleged to have infringed in the Netherlands the plaintiff's Dutch copyright.

(ii) *Multiple infringements*

Are the actions against the various defendants sufficiently connected if they are based on multiple infringements taking place in different States? For example, an English defendant is alleged to have infringed the plaintiff's UK intellectual property right in England and a Dutch defendant is alleged to have infringed the same right in the Netherlands, for example by authorisation of the infringement. The law on infringement in European countries is very similar and this reduces the risk of irreconcilable judgments. Nonetheless, there is an obvious risk of inconsistent findings of fact. This is likely to happen, given that the procedures for discovering the facts are different in each State.[172] There is also a risk of different legal conclusions being drawn from the facts. For example, in a

---

[169] Case 189/87 *Kalfelis v Schröder, Munchmeyer, Hengst & Co* [1988] ECR 5565.
[170] See *Gascoine v Pyrah* [1994] IL Pr 82; Fawcett, n 162 above, pp 751–752.
[171] See above.
[172] *Chiron Corpn and Others v Organon Teknika Ltd (No 10)* [1995] FSR 325 at 338.

copyright infringement case, the English and Dutch courts might have different views as to what constitutes substantial copying and may reach inconsistent findings on whether there has been an infringement. In such circumstances, Article 6(1) would be applicable.

(iii) *Parallel rights*

Are the actions against the various defendants sufficiently connected if they are based on parallel intellectual property rights? For example, an English defendant is alleged to have infringed the plaintiff's UK copyright and a German defendant the plaintiff's German copyright. The two actions may raise substantially identical issues.[173] The better view is that the essence of the rights is the same and the cause of action in both actions is the same.[174] It follows that the two actions are sufficiently connected for the purpose of Article 6(1). However, Laddie J took a different view, in *obiter dicta*, in *Coin Controls Ltd v Suzo International (UK) Ltd and Others*.[175] He adopted the old fashioned view[176] that actions for infringement of parallel rights are based on different rights. The actions would not be based on the same facts and there would not appear to be a risk of inconsistent findings of fact or of inconsistent legal conclusions drawn from those facts. It follows, therefore, that Article 6(1) would not apply.[177]

(iv) *European patents*

The position may well be different where there is a European patent. Even if the old fashioned view of parallel rights, that these are different rights, is adopted, there is a strong case for treating European patents differently. If, for example, the English defendant is alleged to have infringed the European patent (UK) and a German defendant the European patent (Germany) (in respect of the same invention) there could be irreconcilable judgments since both actions are, in effect, concerned with the same patent. This was the view taken by Laddie J, in *obiter dicta*, in the *Coin Controls* case. He said that European patents for the United Kingdom, Spain and Germany were identical and, therefore, infringement claims brought in relation to each of them were related. He went on to say that it would be otherwise if they began life as an EPC application but were subject to different amendments in different countries after grant. Moreover,

---

[173] *Halcon International Inc v The Shell Transport and Trading Co and Others* [1979] RPC 97 at 117 (substantially identical issues as to obviousness in relation to parallel patents).

[174] See chapter 4, pp 135–137.

[175] [1997] 3 All ER 45, 61–62. Jurisdiction was refused because it was plain that validity was going to be raised by the defendants, see below, pp 204–206.

[176] See above, pp 135–136.

[177] See Brinkhof, [1994] *EIPR* 360 at 364, who thinks the jurisdiction of the judge is questionable. See also O'Sullivan, [1996] 12 *EIPR* 654, 657.

the President of a District Court in the Netherlands has allowed the use of Article 6(1) in such circumstances.[178]

The alternative, and much less convincing, approach is to apply the old fashioned view of parallel rights, even to European patents. The argument is that, since a European patent merely consists of a bundle of national patents, it is no different from any other litigation involving parallel rights and the courts of each Contracting State would be giving judgment in relation to a different patent and there would be no risk of irreconcilable judgments. This was the view taken by the Court of Appeal in the *Fort Dodge* case.[179] In this case, there were claims brought against UK domiciled appellants, who were only alleged to have infringed a European patent (UK), and a claim brought against a Dutch appellant, alleged to have infringed a European patent (Netherlands). The Court of Appeal held that there was no risk of irreconcilable judgments if the claims against the UK and Dutch appellants were heard in different countries. However, the Court accepted that the law was not clear on this point and that they would be referring to the Court of Justice the question of how Article 6 should apply to the dispute.

Does it make any difference if the infringement claims concern infringements that took place in different countries? In the *Coin Controls* case, there were allegations, *inter alia*, of infringement of the European patent (UK) in the United Kingdom, the European patent (Spain) in Spain, and the European patent (Germany) in Germany. Nonetheless, the crucial point in deciding that these claims were related was said to be that the patents were identical.[180] Similarly, in the *Fort Dodge* case, the UK appellants were alleged to have infringed the European patent (UK) in the United Kingdom, whereas the Dutch appellant was alleged to have infringed the European patent (Netherlands) in the Netherlands. This does not appear to have influenced the Court of Appeal, which based its decision on the view that the patents were different.

(b) *Additional requirements*

The English courts have added on additional requirements to be satisfied before Article 6(1) can be used,[181] requirements that are found in the multi-defendant provision under the English traditional rules on jurisdic-

---

[178] *Chiron Corpn* v *Akzo Pharma-Organon Technika-UBI*. The Hague District Court, 22 July 1994, 1994 IER, No 24,150. On appeal, only upheld with respect to those defendants with a serious risk of infringement, The Hague Court of Appeals, 1 December 1994, Case No 94/1341. See also the paper by Judge Brinkhof entitled *Transborder Injunctions and the Kortgeding* presented at the Herchel Smith Seminar on Intellectual Property and Private International Law: New Directions, at Cambridge on 24 February 1996.

[179] N 55 above.   [180] N 175 above, at 61–62.

[181] See Fawcett, above n 162, pp 752–754.

tion[182] and have been introduced, by way of analogy, into this different context. There must be a valid claim against the defendant domiciled in the forum. Also, the second defendant must be a necessary or proper party to the action against the first defendant. This latter requirement was introduced in the well known infringement case of *Mölnlycke AB and Another v Procter & Gamble Ltd and Others*[183] and was not satisfied in respect of a German corporate defendant which was added merely in order to obtain discovery of documents.[184]

The introduction of these two additional requirements means that, in order to establish that the case comes within Article 6(1), it may be necessary to go into the merits of the case. A denial of the validity of the claim against the first defendant obviously necessitates this, as does a denial that the second defendant is a necessary or proper party when this is based on an allegation that the claim against that defendant is bound to fail. This raises the difficulty that has already been encountered in respect of other bases of jurisdiction under the Brussels and Lugano Conventions, of the standard of proof to be satisfied by the plaintiff when it is necessary to go into the merits of the case in order to establish a basis of jurisdiction.[185] The same difficulty arises in relation to the multi-defendant basis of jurisdiction under the traditional rules on jurisdiction, where it has been held that the plaintiff merely has to establish a serious issue on the merits in relation to the liability of the first defendant.[186]

3. Exclusive Jurisdiction: Article 16

(a) ARTICLE 16(1)

Article 16(1) of the Conventions, which allocates exclusive jurisdiction 'in proceedings which have as their object rights in rem in immovable property' to 'the courts of the Contracting State in which the property is situated', will not apply in infringement proceedings.[187] There are two reasons for this. First, as has already been seen,[188] the intellectual property rights that have been infringed should not be classified as immovable property for the purposes of the Brussels and Lugano Conventions. Secondly, even if the above point is not accepted, it cannot be seriously suggested that infringement proceedings have as their object rights *in rem*

---

[182] Order 11, rule 1(1)(c) of the Rules of the Supreme Court, discussed below, pp 253–254.
[183] [1992] 1 WLR 1112.   [184] *Ibid*, at 1116–1117; see below, pp 228–229.
[185] See above, p 151.
[186] *Grupo Torras SA and Torras Hostench London Ltd v Sheikh Fahad Mohammed Al-Sabah and Others* [1995] 1 Lloyd's Rep 374 at 380, discussed below. An appeal on other grounds was dismissed by the Court of Appeal without discussion of this point: [1996] 1 Lloyd's Rep 7.
[187] See Jooris, n 138 above, at 137–139.   [188] See above chapter 1, at pp 34–35.

in immovable property.[189] The upshot is that a UK court cannot use this provision to take jurisdiction in an infringement action on the basis that it is a UK right that has been infringed. Equally importantly, a UK court is not precluded from taking jurisdiction, if it has a basis of jurisdiction, on the ground that a foreign intellectual right has been infringed and the courts of a foreign Contracting State have exclusive jurisdiction under this provision.[190]

(b) ARTICLE 16(4)

It has already been seen that Article 16(4) of the Conventions does not apply in infringement proceedings.[191] The upshot is that a UK court cannot use this provision to take jurisdiction in an infringement action on the basis that it is a UK registered right that has been infringed. Equally importantly, a UK court is not precluded from taking jurisdiction, if it has a basis of jurisdiction, on the ground that a foreign registered intellectual property right has been infringed and the courts of a foreign Contracting State have exclusive jurisdiction under this provision.

IV
ABUSE OF PROCESS

In *Pearce* v *Ove Arup Partnership Ltd and Others*,[192] the English court had jurisdiction under Article 6(1) of the Brussels Convention in relation to a claim for infringement of a Dutch copyright. Nonetheless, Lloyd J, at a preliminary stage of the action, struck out the claim as an abuse of process. On consideration of the evidence presented, the plaintiff's claim was purely speculative and was bound to fail. This ground for dismissing the claim would apply regardless of the basis on which the English court has jurisdiction. The Brussels and Lugano Conventions say nothing about abuse of process. However, the Conventions are not concerned with questions of procedure except in so far as they prejudice their effectiveness.[193] The doctrine of abuse of process can be legitimately regarded as being concerned with procedure. That the use of the English doctrine of abuse of process is not inconsistent with the provisions of the Brussels Convention has been confirmed by the Court of Appeal in a separate case.[194]

---

[189] See *Pearce* v *Ove Arup Partnership Ltd and Others* [1997] 2 WLR 779 at 785. See also Jooris, n 138 above, at 138–139.
[190] See the *Pearce* case, n 189 above, discussed below, p 192.   [191] See above, p 19.
[192] [1997] 2 WLR 779.   [193] N 24 above and text accompanying.
[194] *Berkeley Administration Inc* v *McClelland and Others* [1996] IL Pr 772. The Court of Appeal applied the test of whether the abuse of process doctrine rendered 'virtually impossible or excessively difficult' the exercise of rights under Community law.

V
DECLINING JURISDICTION

1. Under the Brussels and Lugano Conventions

We are concerned here with Articles 21 (*lis pendens*) and 22 (related actions). These provisions can apply even where the defendant is domiciled outside an EC/EFTA Contracting State. In other words, they can apply even where jurisdiction is based on traditional national rules on jurisdiction.

(a) LIS PENDENS

Article 21 of the Brussels and Lugano Conventions states that:

Where proceedings involving the same cause of action and between the same parties are brought in the courts of different Contracting States, any court other than the court first seised shall of its own motion stay its proceedings until such time as the jurisdiction of the court first seised is established.

Where the jurisdiction of the court first seised is established, any court other than the court first seised shall decline jurisdiction in favour of that court.

For Article 21 to apply, there must be proceedings in the courts of different Contracting States. This causes no particular problem in infringement cases. More problematical are the requirements in relation to the cause of action and the parties.

(i) The same cause of action

For Article 21 to apply, the two sets of proceedings must involve the same cause of action. The cause of action 'comprises the facts and the rule of law relied on as the basis of the action'.[195] In the leading case of *Gubisch Maschinenfabrik KG v Giulio Palumbo*,[196] the Court of Justice was faced with two actions: one for rescission of a contract, the other for its enforcement. It was held that the two proceedings were based on the same cause of action, that is they were based on the same contractual relationship. There is also a separate requirement, which does not appear in the English language version of the Conventions, that the subject matter of the proceedings must be the same. The Court of Justice held that, because the same question of whether the contract was binding lay at the heart of the two actions, the subject matter was the same.[197] It is not required that the two claims be entirely identical.

---

[195] Case C-406/92 *The Maciej Rataj* [1995] All ER (EC) 229, 254.
[196] Case 144/86 [1987] ECR 4861.   [197] *Ibid*, at 4876.

The operation in infringement cases of these two requirements raises a number of questions. First, is the cause of action and subject matter the same in the situation where there are parallel registrations of, for example, a patent in two different Contracting States and the patentee brings parallel infringement actions in each State in respect of the locally registered patent? The decision of Mummery J in *LA Gear Inc v Gerald Whelan & Sons Ltd*,[198] although not directly on the point, strongly suggests that the answer should be in the negative. The case involved concurrent actions in England and Ireland. In the English proceedings, there was a claim for infringement of a UK registered trade mark, coupled with a claim for passing-off. In the Irish proceedings, the statement of claim referred to the existence of a trade mark, but there was no allegation of infringement of the UK trade mark by the defendant. Mummery J doubted whether the Irish court would have jurisdiction to try such an allegation. There was though an allegation of passing off. The learned judge concluded that the cause of action was not the same in both sets of proceedings. As regards infringement, it is implicit in the judgment that what would be required for the cause of action to be the same would be that the claims in both States involve allegations of infringement of the UK trade mark. The cause of action was not the same in relation to passing-off because different acts were relied upon.[199] This must be right. What Article 21 does is to concentrate the litigation in one State, thereby avoiding the expense and inconvenience of concurrent litigation and the risk of irreconcilable judgments. If there is no alternative forum abroad which can try the infringement action in relation to the UK trade mark, declining jurisdiction in England would be manifestly unfair to the plaintiff. Neither was the subject matter the same. The subject matter of the English action was a trade mark registered in the United Kingdom, and the claimed goodwill and reputation in the mark located in the United Kingdom. The subject matter of the Irish action was the goodwill and reputation claimed by the plaintiff for its mark in Ireland. The result in the case was that Article 21 did not apply.

The *Coin Controls* case contains *obiter dicta* which support the view expressed above in respect of parallel national rights. It will be recalled that Laddie J did not regard claims in respect of such rights as even being related, the claims being materially different. Both of these cases adopt the old fashioned view under intellectual property law that, where parallel rights have been infringed, the cause of action is different in each action.

Secondly, is the answer any different where the two actions concern a European patent? For example, one action is in relation to the European patent (UK), the other in relation to the European patent (Germany). It can be strongly argued that the subject matter of the two actions is the same.

[198] [1991] FSR 670.   [199] See below, p 379.

But is the cause of action the same? The better view is that the patents are identical,[200] and the cause of action is the same.[201] Even if you accept the old fashioned view in relation to parallel rights, it is possible to regard European patents as being different, as Laddie J did in the *Coin Controls* case.

The alternative, and much less convincing, view is that since a European patent consists of a bundle of national rights, neither the subject matter nor the cause of action is the same. The Court of Appeal, in the *Fort Dodge* case, treated European patents as being no different from other parallel rights.[202] This was in the context of whether there would be irreconcilable judgments under Article 6(1), but if the reasoning in that case was applied in the present context, it would lead to the conclusion that neither the subject matter nor the cause of action is the same. The question of how European patents should be regarded may be cleared up by the Court of Justice following the reference in relation to Article 6 to that Court from the Court of Appeal in *Fort Dodge*.

Thirdly, is the cause of action and subject matter the same if, for example, the English proceedings involve an infringement in England and the French proceedings involve an infringement in France? Allied to this, is the question of whether the acts of infringement on which the proceedings are based have to be the same. Both of these questions arose before the District Court of Paris in *Charly Herscovici and Another* v *Société Karla and Another*.[203] It was held that the subject matter of the two sets of proceedings was not the same because the Belgian action was concerned with dealings in Belgium whereas the French action was concerned with acts in France, by one defendant, relating to importing and selling, and acts in France, Italy and England, by another defendant, in relation to manufacturing and exporting. This conflates the two questions but suggests that not only must the infringements take place in the same State but also the acts of infringement relied upon must be the same. In the *Coin Controls* case, the various European patents were regarded as identical but they were infringed in different Contracting States. The claims were regarded as being related for the purpose of Article 6(1). The decision would no doubt be the same for the purpose of Article 22.[204] This is the appropriate provision to use rather than Article 21.

Fourthly, is the cause of action and subject matter the same in the situation where there is an infringement action in one Contracting State and proceedings in relation to the revocation of the same intellectual property

---

[200] See the *Coin Controls* case, n 175 above.
[201] But not if it concerns infringements taking place in different Contracting States, see below.
[202] N 55 above; discussed above, p 174.   [203] [1992] ECC 209.
[204] Discussed below, pp 182–185.

right in another Contracting State?[205] It is arguable that the subject matter of the two actions is the same in that it is the same intellectual property right, for example a French patent, that underlies both actions. Any infringement action presupposes that there is a valid intellectual property right. Admittedly, the claims are not identical but this is not required. The argument that the subject matter is the same becomes even stronger if the infringement action also involves the defence that the intellectual property right is invalid. The more difficult question is whether the cause of action is the same. In *Symbol Technologies Inc v Opticon Sensors Europe BV (No 1)*,[206] Aldous J doubted whether a dispute as to the validity of a patent could be a cause of action, but assuming that it could be, said that infringement and validity were two different causes of action. The case involved a petition before the High Court for revocation of two European patents and the issue was whether this petition had been properly served. The argument that the petition could not now be served out of the jurisdiction under Order 11, rule 1, because proceedings between the same parties concerning the same cause of action were now pending in the courts of the United Kingdom, ie an infringement action before the Patents County Court, was rejected.

Fifthly, is the cause of action and the subject matter the same in the situation where there is an infringement action in one Contracting State and proceedings for a declaration of non-infringement in another Contracting State? It would appear that they are.[207] This means that an action for a declaration of non-infringement can be used to pre-empt infringement proceedings in a less favourable forum.[208] It can also be used to slow down infringement proceedings by bringing the action for a declaration of non-infringement before slow moving courts in a State such as Italy.[209] Of course, if the proceedings for a declaration of non-infringement are based on allegations of invalidity the position is essentially the same as in the previous paragraph.

Sixthly, is the cause of action and the subject matter the same in the situation where there is an infringement action in one Contracting State and proceedings in relation to a complementary tort, such as unfair competition , in another Contracting State? In *Mecklermedia Corpn and Another v DC Congress*,[210] Jacob J held that the cause of action was not the same where there was an action in Germany for infringement of a German trade mark and an action in England for passing-off. Hardly any of the facts relevant to the passing-off action, such as goodwill and damage in England would

---

[205] On the question of whether the actions are related for the purpose of Article 22, see below, pp 183–184.
[206] [1993] RPC 211.
[207] See O'Sullivan, n 177 above, at 657.
[208] *Ibid*.
[209] See Franzosi [1997] 7 *EIPR* 382.
[210] [1997] 3 WLR 479, 488.

be relevant in the German action. And many of the facts and all the law relied upon in the German action would not be relevant in England.

Seventhly, is the cause of action and subject matter the same in the situation where in one set of proceedings there are, for example, claims for infringement, passing off, and breach of confidence, and in the other set of proceedings the claim is merely for infringement and passing off? An analogous problem has arisen in cases of multi-party litigation when it comes to satisfying the other requirement under Article 21 – that the parties must be the same. Application of the reasoning adopted by the Court of Justice,[211] in that context, leads to the conclusion that if the proceedings in the court second seised involve two claims and the proceedings in the court first seised involve an additional claim the former court must decline jurisdiction. In the converse situation, the court second seised will not decline jurisdiction in relation to the additional claims that have come before it.

(ii) The same parties

The two sets of proceedings must also be between the same parties. In the *Mecklermedia* case,[212] Jacob J held that this requirement was not met where the English action involved the plaintiff and defendant, whereas the German action involved the defendant and the plaintiffs' German licensees. A licensee is 'a wholly different enterprise which happens to be working with the plaintiff'.[213] On the other hand, a wholly owned subsidiary might be regarded as the same party as the parent.[214]

This requirement causes particular difficulties in cases of multi-party litigation. Are the parties the same if, for example, A sues B and C in an infringement action in England, but B, C and D sue A in an infringement action in Germany? This problem arose in *Charly Herscovici and Another v Société Karla and Another*.[215] The case involved proceedings, in Belgium, the court seised first, and France, the court seised second, for infringement of copyright. In the Belgian proceedings, Herscovici (the owner of reproduction rights) and Van Berg sued Karla (a company with a registered office in France which offered for sale the infringing sweaters). In the French proceedings, Herscovici and ADAGP (a copyright management society) sued Karla and Krizia (the Italian manufacturer of the infringing sweaters). It was held that the parties were not identical and, therefore, Article 21 would not apply.

However, since then the Court of Justice, in *The Maciej Rataj*,[216] has given a ruling on the operation of the concept of 'the same parties' in cases

---

[211] Case C-406/92 *The Owners of the Cargo Lately Laden on Board the Ship Tatry v The Owners of the Ship Maciej Rataj* [1994] ECR I-5439; [1995] IL Pr 81; discussed below, pp 181–182.
[212] N 153 above. [213] N 153 above, at 488.
[214] *Ibid*. See also *Berkeley Administration Inc v McClelland (No 2)* [1995] IL Pr 201, 211.
[215] N 203 above. [216] N 211 above.

of multi-party litigation. It held that the second court seised is required to decline jurisdiction only to the extent to which the parties to the proceedings before it are also parties to the action previously commenced; it does not prevent the proceedings from continuing between the other parties. The result is that if there is an additional party in the proceedings in the court seised second that court will not decline jurisdiction in relation to that additional party. Following this decision, if the facts of the *Charly Herscovici* case were to arise now, the French court, being seised second, would have to decline jurisdiction under Article 21 in relation to the claim by Herscovici against Karla because these parties were also parties to the action before the Belgian courts who were seised first, but not in relation to the claim by ADAGP against Krizia. This assumes that the latter, if sued on its own, is subject to the jurisdiction of the French court by virtue of the Brussels Convention. Being an Italian company, there may be difficulties over this.

(iii) Must the court second seised always give way to that first seised?

The operation of this mechanical rule, whereby the court other than the court first seised has to stay its proceedings or decline jurisdiction in favour of that court, will not normally involve any particular problems in infringement cases. However, one issue that may arise in such cases is that of whether the court second seised has to give way to the court first seised when it disapproves of the assertion of jurisdiction by that court. Given the disapproval by English judges of the Dutch practice of granting cross border interlocutory injunctions using their Kort-geding procedure this issue may well arise sooner rather than later. In principle, an English court should not examine the basis of jurisdiction or procedures of the courts of another Contracting State. However, the Court of Appeal, in *Continental Bank NA v Aeakos Compañía Naviera SA*,[217] held that, if the court second seised has jurisdiction conferred on it by the agreement of the parties under Article 17 of the Brussels Convention, this takes priority over Article 21.

(b) RELATED ACTIONS

(i) A stay of proceedings

Article 22(1) of the Brussels and Lugano Conventions states that:

Where related actions are brought in the courts of different Contracting States, any court other than the court first seised may, while the actions are pending at first instance, stay its proceedings.

[217] [1994] 1 WLR 588.

Article 22 deals with the situation where the cause of action is not the same in the two actions but the actions are related. According to paragraph 3, actions are deemed to be related 'where they are so closely connected that it is expedient to hear and determine them together to avoid the risk of irreconcilable judgments resulting from separate proceedings'. The question whether actions are related should be determined in a broad commonsense manner bearing in mind the objective of Article 22, namely to improve co-ordination of the exercise of judicial functions within the Community and to avoid conflicting and contradictory decisions,[218] and the width of its terms.[219] The concept of actions being so closely connected that it is expedient to hear and determine them together to avoid a risk of irreconcilable judgments covers a wide range of circumstances and, in deciding whether there is such a risk, no distinction is properly to be drawn between the primary or essential issues necessary to establish a cause of action and other matters not essential to the court's conclusion.[220] The actions may be so related in the situation where neither the cause of action nor the parties are the same.[221] Any court other than the court first seised may, rather than must, while the actions are pending at first instance, stay its proceedings. This gives a discretion to stay proceedings.

(a) Are the actions related?

(i) Is there a risk of irreconcilable judgments?

What has already been said, in the context of Article 6(1), about the risk of irreconcilable judgments in infringement cases is equally applicable here. There is a risk of irreconcilable judgments if the same intellectual property right has been infringed in two different States. The same can be said where there are separate actions for infringement and revocation.[222] A finding of infringement will be irreconcilable with a finding of invalidity. What if the two actions involve parallel rights? There is the old fashioned view that, in litigation involving parallel rights, the actions are based on different rights and there would not be a risk of irreconcilable judgments.[223] However, the better view is that the essence of the rights is the same, and that, accordingly, there is a risk of irreconcilable judgments.[224] The position is somewhat clearer in the situation where the two actions

---

[218] *The Maciej Rataj* n 211 above, at pp 5457–5458, 5473, 5478 and 5479; *Sarrio SA* v *Kuwait Investment Authority* [1997] 3 WLR 1143, at 1147, HL.
[219] The *Sarrio* case, n 218 above.   [220] The *Sarrio* case, *ibid*.
[221] The *Sarrio* case, *ibid*.
[222] O'Sullivan, n 177 above, at 658; Tritton, para 13.024.
[223] See the *obiter dicta* in the *Coin Controls* case, n 175 above; O'Sullivan, n 177 above, at 658; Tritton, para 13.025.
[224] It has been argued, above p 173, that the cause of action is the same which could bring Article 21 into play.

relate to parallel European patents. Laddie J said, *obiter dicta*, that the claims were related for the purpose of Article 6(1), and the answer would no doubt be the same for the purpose of Article 22. Finally, there has been held to be no risk of irreconcilable judgments where the action in one Contracting State was for passing off and the action in the other Contracting State was for trade mark infringement.[225]

(ii) *Is it expedient to hear and determine the two actions together?*

The further difficulty is over the requirement that it is expedient to hear and determine the two actions together. According to Mummery J, this presupposes that there is a court in one Contracting State which is able to hear and determine both sets of proceedings together in that one country.[226] This is very problematic in the situation where the actions in two different Contracting States are, respectively, for infringement and revocation.[227] The court with infringement jurisdiction, and this will probably be the one first seised, will not have jurisdiction in relation to revocation because the courts of the Contracting State with revocation jurisdiction will have exclusive jurisdiction by virtue of Article 16(4), in cases coming within the scope of that provision. The upshot is that the actions are not related, Article 22 will not apply, and there will have to be separate proceedings, even though there is the risk of irreconcilable judgments.

The requirement that it is expedient to hear and determine both sets of proceedings together in a single action has also been seen as causing a problem in an infringement case involving the parallel registration of a patent in two different Contracting States. In *LA Gear Inc* v *Gerald Whelan & Sons Ltd*[228] Mummery J accepted that the two sets of proceedings were related in the broad sense that they were between the same parties and concerned the activities of the defendant in two different countries in dealing in footwear which it was alleged wrongly bore the plaintiff's mark without the plaintiff's consent. However, 'it would not be possible, let alone expedient, for the two sets of proceedings to be heard and determined together in one country'.[229] If the English proceedings for infringement of a UK registered trade mark were stayed, the plaintiff would be prevented from pursuing this matter altogether because of the doubts as to whether the Irish courts would have jurisdiction in respect of a claim for infringement of a UK trade mark. It is submitted, however, that this problem is more apparent than real. It is doubtful whether an Irish court, at least where its jurisdiction is based on the Brussels Convention – as

---

[225] The *Mecklermedia* case, n 153 above; see below p 379.
[226] *L A Gear Inc* v *Gerald Whelan & Sons Ltd* [1991] FSR 670. But compare O'Malley and Layton, p 644. Declining jurisdiction under Article 22(2), discussed below p 185, does require that the court first seised has jurisdiction over both actions.
[227] See O'Sullivan, n 177 above.   [228] [1991] FSR 670.   [229] *Ibid*, at 675–676.

appears to have been the situation in the *LA Gear* case, can refuse to try a case on the ground that it concerns a UK intellectual property right. It will be seen that, in more recent cases, the English courts have denied that they have any such power of refusal when they have been faced with Brussels Convention cases (ie their jurisdiction is based on the Brussels Convention) involving the infringement of a foreign intellectual property right.[230] It follows that it may be possible to find a Contracting State in which a court can try proceedings involving the infringement of parallel rights, at least where its jurisdiction is based on the Brussels or Lugano Convention. The problem will arise though where the jurisdiction of the Irish court, or indeed an English court, is based on its traditional rules on jurisdiction[231] because of the subject matter limitation in respect of foreign intellectual property rights.[232]

(b) *The exercise of the discretion to stay*

When it comes to the exercise of the discretion to stay proceedings, there is authority stating that this is not a *forum non conveniens* discretion and that, normally, a stay should be granted in order to avoid irreconcilable judgments.[233] Nonetheless, Jacob J, in the *Mecklermedia* case, which involved an English action for passing off, appears to have adopted a *forum non conveniens* approach. He said that 'normally the most convenient forum for deciding an English trade mark or passing off case is this court'.[234]

(ii) Declining jurisdiction

The question of whether a court in one Contracting State can try all the infringement litigation also arises under Article 22(2). This provides that:

A court other than the court first seised may also, on the application of one of the parties, decline jurisdiction if the law of that court permits the consolidation of related actions and the court first seised has jurisdiction over both actions.

Under this provision, a court may decline jurisdiction, as opposed to merely staying its proceedings.[235] The use of Article 22(2) in the context of

---

[230] See below, pp 190–193.
[231] Articles 21 and 22 can still apply in this situation. There is no requirement that jurisdiction has to be based on the bases set out in the Conventions.
[232] See below, pp 283–299.
[233] *The Linda* [1988] 1 Lloyd's Rep 175 at 179. See also *Virgin Aviation* v *CAD Aviation* (1990) *Times*, 2 Feb.
[234] N 153 above, at 491. For further discussion of this point in the context of passing-off, see below, p 380.
[235] For the additional requirements that have to be satisfied for declining jurisdiction as opposed to staying proceedings see O'Malley and Layton, pp 641–643. The House of Lords in the *Sarrio* case, n 218 above at 1149–1150, declined jurisdiction.

infringement arose in the *Charly Herscovici* case,[236] where the Paris District Court did not think that the Belgian and French actions were sufficiently closely connected to be regarded as being related under Article 22(3).

2. Using the Doctrine of *Forum Non Conveniens*

(a) *re harrods (buenos aires) ltd*

There is no general discretionary power to decline jurisdiction on the basis of *forum non conveniens* to be found in the Brussels and Lugano Conventions themselves. This would suggest that, where an English court's jurisdiction is based on the Brussels or Lugano Convention, this jurisdiction cannot be declined on the basis of *forum non conveniens*. However, the Court of Appeal, in the controversial decision in *Re Harrods (Buenos Aires) Ltd*,[237] held that an English court has power to stay its own proceedings on the ground of *forum non conveniens* in the situation where the alternative forum is a non-Contracting State to the Brussels Convention, in the instant case Argentina. On the other hand, it was accepted that there was no such power in the situation where the alternative forum is another Contracting State.[238] The reasoning of the Court of Appeal was that the Brussels Convention was intended to regulate jurisdiction as between Contracting States and not as between a Contracting and a non-Contracting State.[239] Hence, the vital importance attached to whether the alternative forum is a Contracting State or not. This case has, generally, been welcomed by English writers[240] and has been followed subsequently.[241] However, it is open to criticism partly on the basis that it misunderstands the Convention, but, more fundamentally, on the basis that it leads to a lack of harmonisation in the law of jurisdiction in the EC,[242] since English courts may decline jurisdiction in circumstances where courts in other Contracting States, which lack a doctrine of *forum non conveniens*, would have to try the case. These are serious criticisms and it is questionable whether the Court of Justice would uphold the principle established in the *Re Harrods* case.[243]

---

[236] N 203, above at 212. [237] [1992] Ch 72.
[238] See also *Aiglon Ltd and L'Aiglon SA v Gau Shan Co Ltd* [1993] 1 Lloyd's Rep 164; *Pearce v Ove Arup Partnership Ltd and Others* [1997] 2 WLR 779 at 789.
[239] Following Collins, (1990) 106 *LQR* 535.
[240] Briggs, (1991) 107 *LQR* 180; Kaye, [1992] *JBL* 47.
[241] See *The Po* [1991] 2 Lloyd's Rep 206; *The Nile Rhapsody* [1994] 1 Lloyd's Rep 382.
[242] See Cheshire and North, pp 333–334; Gaudemet-Tallon in *Declining Jurisdiction*, at pp 178–179; Duintjer Tebbens, in Sumampouw *et al* (eds), *Law and reality—Voskuil Essays* (1992), 47.
[243] The decision was originally referred to the Court of Justice (Case C-314/92 *Ladenimor SA v Intercomfinanz SA*)but the action was settled and this has been removed from the register. The Court of Appeal has subsequently refused to refer the same issue to the Court of

The effect of the decision in *Re Harrods* in infringement cases is that if, for example, a New York plaintiff were to sue an English domiciled defendant in England for the infringement, in New York, of the plaintiff's US patent, relying on the application of US law,[244] the English court would have power to stay the English proceedings on the basis of *forum non conveniens*, even though the English court's jurisdiction is based on Article 2 of the Brussels Convention. An English court, applying that doctrine to such facts, may well conclude that the clearly appropriate forum for trial is New York, and, accordingly, grant a stay of the English proceedings.[245]

(b) ALTERING THE FACTS

Two questions arise if the facts are altered so that they are not on all fours with the *Harrods* case.[246] First, is there power to stay the English proceedings in a case where there are connections with three States so that there are two alternative fora to England? To complicate matters, one of the alternative fora may be a Contracting State, the other a non-Contracting State. For example, a New York plaintiff brings an action in England against an English defendant, who authorised in the United States an act of infringement in France in respect of the plaintiff's US patent.[247] Does it make any difference if only New York is put forward by the defendant as the alternative forum to England? As was previously mentioned,[248] the Court of Appeal has held that there is a discretion to stay the English proceedings on the basis of *forum non conveniens* in this latter situation.[249] However, there is then the separate question of exercising this power, ie whether it is possible for the defendant to show that the clearly appropriate forum is that of the non-Contracting State in such circumstances.[250] It is by no means obvious, on the above facts, that New York is the clearly appropriate forum for trial, given that the act of direct infringement was not committed there and the defendant is not domiciled there. It must also be remembered that there is judicial[251] support for the idea that the English courts should be reluctant to stay proceedings when jurisdiction has been allocated to England under the Brussels Convention.

Justice: *The Nile Rhapsody* [1994] 1 Lloyd's Rep 382. This was because of the expense and delay that such a reference would occasion.

[244] See chapter 12 below, pp 623–624.
[245] The doctrine of *forum non conveniens* is discussed below, pp 267–272.
[246] See Cheshire and North, pp 333–334.
[247] The plaintiff may seek to rely on the application of US law on the basis of the indirect infringement in the US by way of authorisation, see generally below, chapter 12 pp 621–624.
[248] See chapter 3, at pp 95–96.   [249] *The Po* [1991] 2 Lloyd's Rep 206.
[250] The Court of Appeal in *The Po*, *ibid*, upheld the first instance decision that the defendant had failed to show that Brazil was the clearly more appropriate forum.
[251] *S & W Berisford plc v New Hampshire Insurance Co* [1990] QB 631 at 645–646.

Secondly, is there power to stay English proceedings in a case where the English courts' jurisdiction is not based, as it was in *Re Harrods*, on Article 2 of the Brussels Convention, but on some other provision that can be used in infringement cases? For example, it is based on Article 5(3) following an act of infringement in England in respect of the New York plaintiff's UK patent by a defendant domiciled in France. As was previously mentioned in the context of Article 5(1) of the Conventions,[252] the principle enunciated by the Court of Appeal appears to be applicable regardless of the basis of jurisdiction. Moreover, it has been accepted that the principle in *Re Harrods* applies equally to cases where the jurisdiction of the English courts is based on Article 6(1) of the Lugano Convention.[253] On the above facts, there remains the additional difficulty, discussed above, of the fact that there are two alternative fora, France and New York, to England. It would be best if *Re Harrods* were to be confined to cases where jurisdiction is based on Article 2. Even if this does not happen, it is inconceivable that, on applying the forum non conveniens criteria, a stay of English proceedings would be granted when the only connection with New York is that the plaintiff was resident there.

3. Restraining Foreign Proceedings

The English courts have power, in certain limited circumstances, to grant an injunction to restrain proceedings in another State. It is important when considering this topic to consider whether the State in question is a non-Contracting or Contracting State.

(a) A NON-CONTRACTING STATE

We are dealing here with the situation where an English court has jurisdiction under the Brussels or Lugano Convention and the plaintiff in the English proceedings wishes to restrain a party from commencing or continuing proceedings in a non-Contracting State. By granting an injunction, the English court is, in effect, upholding the principle under the Convention that defendants domiciled in a Contracting State are to be sued there. The problem is very different from that of staying English proceedings where, in a sense, the Conventions are being undermined. It follows that, as far as the Conventions are concerned, there can be no objection, in principle, to the grant of an injunction in such circumstances.

---

[252] See above, pp 95–96.
[253] See the *Aiglon* case, n 238 above, a case involving a Contracting State as the alternative forum.

One of the bases under English law for granting an injunction restraining foreign proceedings has to be established.[254] One such basis is that the bringing of proceedings abroad is an invasion of a legal or equitable right not to be sued there.[255] What *Re Harrods* establishes is that there is no 'right' to be sued in the Contracting State in which the defendant is domiciled, at least not in the situation where the alternative forum is a non-Contracting State. Accordingly, an injunction restraining proceedings in a non-Contracting State will not be granted merely because the action was brought outside the Contracting State in which the defendant was domiciled.[256]

(b) A CONTRACTING STATE

This situation is very different. An English court which seeks to restrain proceedings in another Contracting State surely needs some authority under the Brussels or Lugano Convention to do so. There is no such authority under the Convention. Moreover, if one applies the analogy of *Re Harrods*, this is intra EC litigation since the alternative forum is a Contracting State. Such litigation is dealt with by the Convention. It is submitted that there is no power to grant an injunction in such circumstances.

However, this is not the view that the English courts have taken. The Court of Appeal, in a much criticised decision, has issued an injunction restraining Greek proceedings[257] in the situation where the English courts had exclusive jurisdiction under Article 17 of the Brussels Convention. This has been followed in a case where an injunction was granted to restrain Italian proceedings brought in breach of an English arbitration clause.[258] The policy has been to make the parties abide by their agreement. Finally, in the most recent case, the Court of Appeal considered that it had power to grant an injunction restraining companies from continuing with infringement proceedings in the Netherlands. Nonetheless, it refused to do so, even though it had come to the conclusion that the Dutch courts had no jurisdiction because of Articles 19 and 16(4) and that the English courts had exclusive jurisdiction.[259] The Court accepted that the matter of jurisdiction was not clear and a reference

---

[254] See below, pp 275–279.   [255] See, Cheshire and North, pp 247–248.
[256] *Société Commerciale de Reasssurance and Others* v *Eras International Ltd and Others (No 2)* [1995] 2 All ER 278, 298–299.
[257] *Continental Bank NA* v *Aeakos Compañía Naviera SA* [1994] 1 WLR 588. Criticised by Bell, (1994) 110 *LQR* 204; Rogerson, (1994) 53 *CLJ* 241.
[258] *The Angelic Grace* [1995] 1 Lloyd's Rep 87. See also *Toepfer International GmbH* v *Société Cargill France* [1997] 2 Lloyd's Rep 98. For refusal to recognise a foreign judgment obtained after notice of the anti-suit injunction see *Phillip Alexander Securities and Futures Ltd* v *Bamberger and Others* [1997] IL Pr 72, discussed above in chapter 3 at p 96.
[259] The *Fort Dodge* case, n 55 above; discussed below, pp 206–207.

would have to be made to the Court of Justice. The Court of Appeal held that, in the light of this, it would be wrong to conclude that the Dutch claim was vexatious and grant a final injunction restraining the Dutch proceedings at this time.

VI
NO SUBJECT MATTER LIMITATIONS ON JURISDICTION

1. THE POSITION UNDER THE CONVENTIONS

The Brussels and Lugano Conventions contain no subject matter limitations on jurisdiction in relation to the infringement of foreign intellectual property rights or infringements abroad,[260] and the Dutch courts have taken jurisdiction under the Brussels Convention in such infringement cases.[261] This stands in marked contrast to the position under the traditional English rules on jurisdiction where, although there may be a basis of jurisdiction in respect of the defendant, there are subject matter limitations in respect of both foreign intellectual property rights and infringements abroad.[262] This also contrasts with the position under Article 16(4) of the Conventions, which prohibits a court in one Contracting State from adjudicating on the issue of validity of a patent, etc registered in another Contracting State,[263] and Article 16(1), which precludes a court in one Contracting State from adjudicating in proceedings which have as their object rights *in rem* in immovable property situated in another Contracting State. As has been seen, neither Article 16(4) nor 16(1) apply to infringement proceedings.[264]

For the English courts to introduce subject matter limitations in relation to foreign intellectual property rights and infringements abroad would be in breach of the Conventions, and, in particular, of the provision on which jurisdiction is based, which gives the plaintiff the right to bring an action in the Contracting State which has been allocated jurisdiction under that provision.[265]

---

[260] See, generally, Jooris, [1996] 3 *EIPR* 127.
[261] See below, pp 218–219. German writers accept that there is jurisdiction under the Brussels Convention in cases of infringement of foreign patents: Meibom and Pitz, [1997] 8 *EIPR* 469 at 470.
[262] See below, pp 283–306. [263] See above, pp 15–24.
[264] See above, pp 175–176.
[265] According to English law this right is subject to the principle in *Re Harrods (Buenos Aires)*, discussed above, pp 186–188.

2. Judicial Misunderstanding

Nonetheless, there are some judicial comments which can be read as suggesting that there are subject matter limitations akin to those under the traditional English rules on jurisdiction. In *Mölnlycke AB and Another v Procter & Gamble Ltd and Others*,[266] Dillon LJ said that 'from the nature of a UK patent, proceedings for infringement of a UK patent can only be brought in a UK court, in the present case the English court, and could only be founded on infringement in England. The German court could entertain an action for infringement of the comparable German patent, but could not entertain a claim for infringement of an English patent. Conversely, the English court could not entertain a claim for the infringement of a German patent'.[267]

It is submitted that the assertion that there is a limitation on jurisdiction in relation to foreign intellectual property rights is plainly wrong as regards the Brussels Convention. What Dillon L J also appears to have been referring to was the different matter of whether, once there is jurisdiction, a *successful* action can be brought in England in relation to foreign intellectual property rights infringed abroad. Certainly, there was much concern with establishing liability in the *Mölnlycke* case.[268] At that time, the English tort choice of law rules made it impossible to bring a successful action in England in relation to a foreign intellectual property right that had been infringed abroad. The recently introduced statutory tort choice of law rules mean that this is no longer so.[269]

Equally perplexing are the comments of Mummery J in *LA Gear Inc v Gerald Whelan & Sons Ltd*,[270] where the traditional jurisdictional limitation in relation to foreign intellectual property rights was mentioned with approval in a Brussels Convention case. However, this was not used to deny the jurisdiction of the English courts. It was merely a comment made in relation to proceedings afoot in Ireland.

3. The Point is Now Settled

The point is now settled, at least as regards foreign rights created in EC/EFTA Contracting States and infringements committed in such States,[271] following a trio of English decisions.[272]

---

[266] [1992] 1 WLR 1112.   [267] *Ibid*, at 1118.   [268] See above, p 147.
[269] See below, pp 623–624.
[270] [1991] FSR 670 at 674.
[271] For the position where the foreign right is created outside the EC/EFTA Contracting States, see below, pp 193–195.
[272] *Pearce v Ove Arup Partnership Ltd and Others* [1997] 2 WLR 779; *Coin Controls Ltd v Suzo International (UK) Ltd and Others* [1997] 3 All ER 45; *Fort Dodge Animal Health Ltd and Others v Akzo Nobel NV and Another* [1998] FSR 222 CA. See, generally on the first two

(a) THE *PEARCE* CASE

Pearce v *Ove Arup Partnership Ltd and Others*[273] is, seemingly, the first case where an English court had to decide whether the subject matter limitation in respect of foreign intellectual property rights under the traditional English rules applied in a Brussels Convention case. A basis of jurisdiction (Article 6(1)) under the Convention was satisfied in relation to both the UK and Dutch defendants. However, it was argued that the claim for infringement was not justiciable in England because it related to a Dutch copyright. Lloyd J rejected this argument. He held that, in these circumstances, the Convention required the English courts to accept jurisdiction. To decide otherwise would 'impair the effectiveness of the Convention by frustrating the operation of the basic rule in Article 2' and any limitation in relation to foreign intellectual property rights had to 'give way in order to allow the jurisdictional rules of the Convention to have their proper effect'.[274] This decision is very much to be welcomed. It is consistent with the position taken by Dutch and German courts which have taken jurisdiction under the Brussels Convention in cases of infringement of other Contracting States' intellectual property rights.[275]

What can be criticised though about the *Pearce* case are some unfortunate comments made by the judge which show a basic misunderstanding of the nature of the limitation on jurisdiction in relation to foreign intellectual property rights. He said that this was not a rule as to jurisdiction but concerned non justiciability. This then raises the question of what is meant by non justiciability[276] and how does this differ from jurisdiction? This would be to go down a blind alley. It is submitted that the true position is that the limitation in relation to foreign intellectual property rights is a jurisdictional rule, a subject matter limitation in relation to jurisdiction. The distinction drawn by Lloyd J is a dangerous one to draw because it leads on to the argument put by the defendants that, because it was not a jurisdiction rule, it could be applied when operating the Brussels Convention. Fortunately, Lloyd J did not accept this latter argument.

The case can also be criticised because of the failure to understand the choice of law aspect of the case. It was said that if the limitation in relation to foreign rights was overcome this would also overcome the common law requirement in international tort cases of double actionability.[277] But this is a choice of law requirement and it is entirely illogical to think that this

---

cases: Briggs, (1997) 113 *LQR* 364; Cohen, [1997] 7 *EIPR* 379; Dutson, (1997) 46 *ICLQ* 918; Fentiman, [1997] *CLJ* 503; Inglis and Gringras, [1997] 8 *EIPR* 396; Tugendhat, (1997) 113 *LQR* 360.

[273] N 272 above.
[275] For the Dutch position see below, pp 218–219.
[276] On which see Briggs, n 272 above at 366.
[274] *Ibid*, at 790.
[277] See below, pp 606–611.

can be satisfied by removing a subject matter limitation on jurisdiction. The result of this misunderstanding was that there was no proper discussion of the question of the applicable law or of its significance at the jurisdictional stage of the action. As will be seen later,[278] the double actionability rule is not met where a foreign intellectual property right has been infringed abroad. The significance of this at the jurisdictional stage is that the threshold requirement,[279] that there is a serious issue to be tried on the merits, is not satisfied and jurisdiction is not possible against the Dutch defendants under Article 6(1).

(b) THE *COIN CONTROLS* CASE

The decision in the *Pearce* case was approved and followed shortly afterwards by Laddie J in another Brussels Convention case, *Coin Controls Ltd v Suzo International (UK) Ltd and Others*.[280] In this case, there were allegations, *inter alia*, of infringement of a Spanish patent in Spain and infringement of a German patent in Germany. The same argument, as in the *Pearce* case, that these claims were not justiciable in England was firmly rejected.[281]

(c) THE *FORT DODGE* CASE

In *Fort Dodge Animal Health Ltd and Others v Akzo Nobel NV and Another*,[282] Laddie J, at first instance, reaffirmed the view he had taken in the *Coin Controls* case that the *Pearce* case was correctly decided. The Court of Appeal, in *Fort Dodge*, upheld the decision at first instance. The *Fort Dodge* case involved a Dutch court taking infringement jurisdiction under the Brussels Convention against, *inter alia*, companies domiciled in the United Kingdom. The Court of Appeal raised no objection to the fact that this was in respect of a European patent (UK), which had been infringed in the United Kingdom. Objection was made though to the Dutch assertion of jurisdiction on the ground that the validity of the patent was raised.[283]

4. FOREIGN RIGHTS CREATED OUTSIDE THE EC/EFTA CONTRACTING STATES

The *Pearce*, *Coin Controls* and *Fort Dodge* cases all concerned the infringement of rights created in EC/EFTA Contracting States. What if the case

---

[278] See below, pp 609–611. [279] See above, pp 144–149. [280] [1997] 3 All ER 45.
[281] *Ibid*, at 59. However, the learned judge ended up refusing to try the case because the issue of validity was going to be raised by the defendants, see below pp 204–206.
[282] [1998] FSR 222. [283] See below, pp 206–207.

concerns the infringement of a right created outside the EC/EFTA Contracting States, for example a Japanese patent?[284] The Brussels Convention may apply. If the defendant is domiciled in England, jurisdiction would be based on Article 2 the defendant being domiciled in England. It is submitted that the principle set out in the three above cases is equally applicable in this situation,[285] and the English court has no right to apply its traditional subject matter limitations on jurisdiction and refuse to try the case on the basis that it concerns the infringement of a foreign intellectual property right created outside the EC/EFTA Contracting States. The operation of Article 2 would be frustrated, which is what concerned Lloyd J in the *Pearce* case, if the English courts were to act in this way. Moreover, Lloyd J was, in part, influenced by the fact that the Dutch courts will try actions concerning the infringement of foreign intellectual property rights.[286] The Dutch courts do not, in fact, distinguish between rights created in EC/EFTA Contracting States and those created outside these States.[287] Finally, Laddie J, in the *Coin Controls* case, referred to the principle established by the *Pearce* case that the courts of a Contracting State had to entertain and determine foreign infringement proceedings.[288] He did not qualify or limit this by referring to rights created in the EC/EFTA Contracting States.

Of course, if the right was created outside the EC/EFTA Contracting States, in say Japan, it may well be argued that the alternative forum for trial is Japan. The principle in *Re Harrods (Buenos Aires)*[289] would apply, and jurisdiction could be declined on the basis of *forum non conveniens*. But the use of this discretionary power to decline jurisdiction is a very different matter from having a blanket subject matter limitation on jurisdiction in respect of the infringement of foreign intellectual property rights created outside the EC/EFTA Contracting States.

Admittedly, there is an argument that can be made,[290] by way of analogy with the principle in the *Re Harrods* case, that in cases where the right is created outside the EC/EFTA Contracting States, the Conventions are not concerned with this situation and there is nothing to stop the English courts using its traditional subject matter limitation on jurisdiction in relation to foreign intellectual property rights. A number of objections can be

---

[284] Lloyd J in the *Pearce* case, n 272 above at 789–790, said that he did not have to decide this question.
[285] See Briggs, n 272 above, at 366; Dutson, n 272 above, at 921. Compare Fentiman, n 272 above, at 504 in relation to infringements committed outside EC/EFTA Contracting States.
[286] N 272 above, at 788. See also Dutson, n 272 above, at 921.
[287] See below, p 219.
[288] N 280 above at 59. See also the *Fort Dodge* case at first instance.   [289] N 237 above.
[290] See Dutson, n 272 above, at 921. See also Cornish, 2.77 who distinguishes rights created in EC/EFTA Contracting States from those created outside and advocates taking jurisdiction in the former but not the latter.

made to this line of reasoning. First, as has been mentioned, the principle adopted in the three English cases is equally applicable to cases where it is a right created outside the EC/EFTA Contracting States. Secondly, the *Re Harrods* case has been subject to strong criticism and it is questionable whether it should be used to establish another principle under which an English court would be refusing to try a case when the courts in other Contracting States may be willing to try the case, as indeed the Dutch courts are in relation to foreign intellectual property rights, regardless of whether these rights are created within or outside the EC/EFTA Contracting States. Moreover, the Brussels and Lugano Conventions, although silent on the topic of *forum non conveniens*, contain subject matter limitations on jurisdiction; this is what Article 16(4) is. For the English courts to apply additional subject matter limitations in Brussels or Lugano Conventions cases flies in the face of the Conventions. If they are prepared to do this, why not go the whole way and introduce additional English type bases of jurisdiction in Brussels or Lugano Conventions cases? This, of course, would be unthinkable and so should be the introduction of English traditional subject matter limitations on jurisdiction. Thirdly, the traditional limitation on jurisdiction in relation to foreign intellectual property rights is itself open to criticism, both in terms of principle and policy,[291] and the better view is that it should be abolished. Fourthly, the doctrine of *forum non conveniens* can be used to decline jurisdiction and so a blanket subject matter limitation on jurisdiction is not necessary, and indeed allows the matter to be dealt with in a flexible way, which a blanket subject matter limitation on jurisdiction does not.

5. Infringements Committed Outside the EC/EFTA Contracting States

The *Pearce, Coin Controls* and *Fort Dodge* cases were all concerned with infringements committed within the EC/EFTA Contracting States. What if the infringement is committed outside the EC/EFTA Contracting States? Is it still possible to apply the traditional subject matter limitation in relation to infringements committed abroad, even though the English court's jurisdiction is based on the Brussels or Lugano Convention? The arguments are precisely the same as those set out above in relation to the infringement of rights created outside the EC/EFTA Contracting States. The conclusion is the same too. An English court has no right to apply a traditional subject matter limitation on jurisdiction in Brussels or Lugano Conventions cases. However, it may be possible to decline jurisdiction on the basis of *forum non conveniens*, applying *Re Harrods (Buenos Aires)*.

[291] See below, pp 286–293.

6. Difficulties in Establishing a Basis of Jurisdiction Against the Person

Although there are no subject matter limitations in relation to infringements abroad or foreign intellectual property rights, when it comes to establishing a basis of jurisdiction against the person there can be difficulty in such circumstances. It has to be remembered that there is the threshold requirement in cases of special jurisdiction under Articles 5 and 6, that there is a serious issue on the merits to be tried.[292] If the action will fail, and this is likely if there is an act of infringement abroad in respect of a UK intellectual property right[293] or there is an act of infringement in England in respect of a foreign intellectual property right,[294] then the threshold requirement cannot be established and the English courts have no jurisdiction under these Articles. However, an action based, for example, on infringement in France of a French copyright, will succeed.[295]

VII
FORUM SHOPPING

It is not uncommon to find references to forum shopping in the literature on infringement.[296] 'Forum shopping' is not a term of art.[297] It describes the scenario of 'a plaintiff by-passing his natural forum and bringing his action in some alien forum which would give him relief or benefits which would not be available to him in his natural forum'.[298] What the natural forum is will depend on the facts of the case. In complex cases, there may be no natural forum for trial; instead, there may be a number of natural fora for trial. In infringement cases, it is arguable that the natural State in which to bring an action is where the right was created and infringed.[299] Of course, the act of infringement may have occurred in a different State from the one in which the right was created. There would then appear to be two natural fora for trial.[300] Moreover, if in a Brussels or Lugano

---

[292] Compare the position where jurisdiction is based on Art 2, above p 143.
[293] The foreign law will normally apply, see below p 623, and this is unlikely to provide redress in respect of a foreign right.
[294] English law will normally apply, see below p 623, and this does not provide redress in respect of foreign rights.
[295] See below, pp 623–624.
[296] See Adams, [1995] 10 *EIPR* 497; O'Sullivan, [1996] 12 *EIPR* 654.
[297] *Boys* v *Chaplin* [1971] AC 356 at 401 (*per* Lord Wilberforce).
[298] *Cordoba Shipping Co Ltd* v *National State Bank, Elizabeth, New Jersey (The Albaforth)* [1984] 2 Lloyd's Rep 91 at 97, CA.
[299] See, generally, O'Sullivan, n 177 above, at 662.
[300] But whichever law is applied it is unlikely to provide redress, see below, p 623.

Conventions case the plaintiff brings an action in the Contracting State where the defendant is domiciled, it is arguable that this is the natural forum, or at least a natural forum, as far as the Conventions are concerned. It may be inappropriate to use the term 'forum shopping' in most cases of infringement. At the end of the day, though, nothing hinges on whether the conduct of the plaintiff is to be described as forum shopping or not. What is important to realise is that in cases coming within the EC/EFTA rules the plaintiff may have a considerable choice of fora in which to bring the action, and that there are advantages to be gained from bringing the action in one Contracting State rather than another.

1. The Choice of Fora

Even in a simple case, where merely one defendant is being sued and jurisdiction is based on the defendant's domicile, the plaintiff may be given a choice of fora. This is due to the fact that the Conventions do not define the meaning of domicile; they merely provide for which Contracting State's definition is to be used. Differences in the definition of domicile used in the different Contracting States can result in the plaintiff having a choice of fora even if suing merely one defendant. For example, the plaintiff may be able to proceed against the defendant in Germany where the company has its seat, under the German definition, or in France, where the company has its seat under the different French definition.[301]

Infringement cases are usually more complex, often involving many defendants. In multi-defendant cases, the choice of fora given to the plaintiff is widened out even further. If jurisdiction is based on Article 6(1), the plaintiff is given the choice of suing both defendants in either of the Contracting States in which one of them is domiciled. If one of the defendants is domiciled in two Contracting States and the other is domiciled in a third Contracting State, the plaintiff has a choice of three fora.

As an alternative to using Article 6(1), the plaintiff in an infringement case may use Article 5(3) and this too may give a wide choice of fora. The plaintiff, by being able to sue in the Contracting State in which the act of infringement took place, as an alternative to suing in the Contracting State of the defendant's domicile, will have a minimum of two alternative fora. Of course, if the defendant is domiciled in two different Contracting States, there will be a minimum of three alternative fora. If the damage takes place in a fourth Contracting State the plaintiff will have a choice of four alternative fora – two by virtue of Article 2 and two further fora by virtue of Article 5(3).

---

[301] See O'Malley and Layton, *European Civil Practice* (1989), paras 50.25, 51.25.

Moreover, under the Brussels and Lugano Conventions, there are no subject matter limitations on jurisdiction in relation to foreign intellectual property rights infringed abroad.[302]

When the plaintiff is choosing from these alternative fora there is no need to worry about the enforcement in other Contracting States of any judgment that may be obtained. Under the Conventions, any judgment obtained will be recognised and enforced on a semi-automatic basis in other Contracting States.

One final point to note though is that the one Contracting State where the plaintiff cannot automatically bring an infringement action is that where the right was created. It is not like cases where the issue is that of registration or validity of registrable rights, where jurisdiction, indeed exclusive jurisdiction, is allocated by Article 16(4) to the Contracting State where registration has taken place. Infringement is treated differently under the Conventions. It is only going to be possible to bring the infringement action in the Contracting State where the right was created if, coincidentally, one of the bases of jurisdiction under the Conventions, in practice this is likely to be Articles 2, 5(3), or 6(1), is satisfied.

2. THE ADVANTAGES TO BE OBTAINED

The advantages to be obtained from bringing an action in one Contracting State rather than another may be personal, procedural, substantive, other advantages or all of these. Before turning to look at each of these advantages, it is worth pointing out that international patent litigation in Europe normally takes place in Germany, the United Kingdom, Italy, France, Switzerland, or the Netherlands.[303]

(a) A PERSONAL ADVANTAGE

A plaintiff may well regard it as an advantage to bring an action in the Contracting State in which he is domiciled.

(b) PROCEDURAL ADVANTAGES

There are numerous differences in the procedural rules of different countries which can lead to advantages in selecting trial in one Contracting State rather than another and include such matters as: pre-trial discovery; costs; expense of litigation; the possibility of making a payment into court;

---

[302] See above, pp 190–196.
[303] Voet, (1997) 68 *Managing Intellectual Property* 16. For the advantages of such litigation being held in Germany see Jaekel, *ibid* at 20–23; in England, Freeland and Cook, *ibid* at 28–31; in the Netherlands, Hoyng and Eijsvogels, *ibid* at 24–27.

delay in obtaining trial; limitation periods;³⁰⁴ the availability of interlocutory injunctions, Anton Piller orders or their equivalent, Mareva injunctions or their equivalent.

To give some examples of the operation of these factors in infringement cases, there is evidence that patent litigation costs in England, generally, are higher than those in Continental countries.³⁰⁵ Germany is also a country to avoid if minimising costs is essential.³⁰⁶ If a quick preliminary injunction is required, the Netherlands is a good country for trial,³⁰⁷ as is Germany.³⁰⁸ Preliminary injunctions are, of course, also available in the United Kingdom.

In infringement actions, which can raise complex technical issues, a very important consideration is that of pre-trial discovery. Perhaps the biggest difference to be found in the procedural rules of common law States, when compared with those in civil law States, is in respect of pre-trial discovery, ie the process by which one party is able to inspect the files and records and talk to the employees of the other party. In common law States, pre-trial discovery is available,³⁰⁹ and enables a plaintiff to build up a case as the action proceeds; in civil law States, such as Germany,³¹⁰ it is not available.

Anton Piller orders or their equivalent are available in a number of European States, such as the United Kingdom, France, Italy, but normally not in Germany, Austria or the Netherlands.³¹¹

(c) A SUBSTANTIVE LAW ADVANTAGE

(i) The nature of the advantage

There are two sorts of advantage to be obtained from having one law applied rather than another. The first and most obvious is that there may be an infringement under the law of one Contracting State but not under the law of another. The substantive law of infringement in Europe is often derived from the same international conventions. The law is largely harmonised. It follows that there is normally no advantage to be gained from having the substantive law of one country applied rather than that of another. Nonetheless, the harmonisation is not total and differences in the

---

³⁰⁴ An English court will no longer apply domestic law in respect of limitation periods. Instead, it will apply the law which governs the substantive issue according to the English choice of law rules: Foreign Limitation Periods Act 1984.
³⁰⁵ Adams, (1995) 10 *EIPR* 497 at 499; Bouju, *Patent Infringement Litigation Costs* (1988) – a study for the EC Commission; Freeland and Cook, n 303 above.
³⁰⁶ Voet, (1997) 68 *Managing Intellectual Property*, 14–16. But compare Jaekel, *ibid* at 20–23.
³⁰⁷ Voet, n 306 above.   ³⁰⁸ *Ibid*.
³⁰⁹ Park and Cromie, pp 135–143 (England), 98–105 (Australia), 115–122 (Canada), 221–228 (US).
³¹⁰ Park and Cromie, p 180.   ³¹¹ See Voet, n 306 above; Adams, n 305 above at 501.

law of infringement remain.[312] For example, under the European Patent Convention, Contracting States are left to decide what constitutes an infringement and experience with litigation of essentially the same issue being tried in different States shows that in difficult borderline cases there may be a different result depending on which substantive law is applied.[313] Under English law, there may be some difficulty in establishing infringement because of the literal interpretation given to claims. German or Dutch law may take a broader view, and regard something as an infringement which would not be so regarded under English law.[314]

The second and more subtle advantage from having one law apply rather than another is that, if this is local law, this avoids having to plead and prove foreign law.

(ii) Tort choice of law rules

A plaintiff who wishes to gain a substantive law advantage is going to have to take into account the choice of law position. The plaintiff will have to obtain trial in a forum whose tort choice of law rule will lead to the application of the substantive law which is most favourable to him. Given that tort choice of law rules are not harmonised in Europe, this introduces an extra layer of complexity for the plaintiff when deciding on the best place for trial. Some States may have tort choice of law rules which are inherently unattractive to forum shoppers because they are uncertain. This is a criticism that can be levelled at the English statutory tort choice of law rules when applied in infringement cases.[315] Other countries have choice of law rules which may be attractive because of their pro-plaintiff stance. Thus, under German law, if the defendant acts in one State and the plaintiff suffers harm in another it is the duty of the judge to establish *ex officio* which law is more favourable for the plaintiff and to apply only that law.[316]

(d) OTHER ADVANTAGES

There are other advantages to be gained from trial of an infringement action in one Contracting State rather than another, which relate very much to the facts of the case and which do not fall within any of the other categories. Thus, the plaintiff is going to find it advantageous to bring proceedings in the Contracting State where all the infringement litigation, for example involving parallel infringements or revocation proceedings and

---

[312] See O'Sullivan, n 177 above, at 661–662; below, pp 596–597.
[313] O'Sullivan, n 177 above, at 661.
[314] Voet, n 306 above. See also chapter 12 below, pp 596–597.   [315] See below, p 643.
[316] BGH [1981] NJW 1606f. There are exceptions to this rule, see Fawcett, (1993-I) 238 *Hague Recueil des Cours* 13 at 203–204.

infringement, can be consolidated.[317] In the UK, France, Belgium and Italy the same court is able to try the issues of infringement and validity.[318] However, in Germany validity must be challenged in a separate court from the one trying the issue of validity.[319] Likewise, it may be advantageous to bring proceedings in the Contracting State where the defendant has assets, to avoid the expense of having to enforce the judgment abroad.[320]

VIII
INFRINGEMENT AND VALIDITY

1. THE NATURE OF THE PROBLEM

Some jurisdictional cases are concerned solely with the issue of infringement without the issue of validity being raised at all,[321] and the rules outlined earlier in this chapter will apply. Of course, as a matter of substantive law, validity and infringement are two sides of the same coin.[322] Under English law, the view has often been expressed that it is not possible to infringe an invalid patent claim.[323] However, what we are concerned with are the rules on jurisdiction under the Brussels and Lugano Conventions. These rules clearly distinguish the issues of infringement and validity and have separate rules for each issue.[324] Moreover, you cannot deal with jurisdiction on the basis of suspicions as to what defence might run.[325] The fact that the defendant can challenge validity does not mean that he will do so.[326] Naturally, there is always the possibility that the issue of validity may be raised in the future by some amendment to the writ. But such a theoretical possibility should be ignored.[327]

Other cases are concerned solely with the issue of validity, for example there is a petition for revocation of a patent on this ground. In such cases, if a patent, trade mark, design or other similar right has been deposited or registered in a Contracting State to the Brussels or Lugano Conventions, Article 16(4) of that Convention will apply to give exclusive jurisdiction to the courts of the Contracting State of registration or deposit.[328]

---

[317] See O'Sullivan, n 177 above, at 662–663.   [318] Voet, n 306 above.
[319] Ibid.   [320] Ibid.
[321] See, eg *Plastus Kreativ AB* v *Minnesota Mining and Manufacturing Co* [1995] RPC 438.
[322] *Chiron Corpn* v *Evans Medical Ltd and Others* [1996] FSR 863.
[323] *Organon Teknika Ltd* v *Hoffmann-La Roche AG* [1996] FSR 383 at 384; the *Fort Dodge* case, n 282 above.
[324] See chapter 1 at p 19.
[325] See *Coin Controls Ltd* v *Suzo International (UK) Ltd and Others*, n 280 above, at 60.
[326] Ibid.
[327] *Chiron Corpn* v *Evans Medical Ltd*, n 322 above, at 872.   [328] See above, pp 15–24.

But what if the validity of a patent, etc is raised during the course of an action for infringement, or it is plain that it is going to be put in issue?[329] Can the court before which the infringement action is brought, and which has a basis of jurisdiction in respect of infringement, try this action when the issue of validity is raised before it? If it can try the issue of infringement can it also try the issue of validity? Or must it give up both issues to be tried before the courts of the Contracting State which have validity jurisdiction under Article 16(4)? But can these courts try both issues or must they be split between courts in different Contracting States? The position is very straightforward under the jurisdiction rules in relation to Community intellectual property rights, which will be examined in the chapter 7.[330] The same court will try both issues. But when it comes to national intellectual property rights the position is far from clear. In finding an answer, it is important to distinguish three different situations. The first is where invalidity is raised as a defence to infringement. The second is where it is raised by way of a counterclaim for revocation. The third is where there are separate proceedings for revocation brought in a Contracting State other than the one where the infringement action was brought.

2. A Defence of Invalidity

It is common for the validity of a patent, etc to be raised as a defence to a claim for infringement, the obvious point being that a person cannot have infringed an invalid intellectual property right that should never have been granted. Let us assume that the Contracting State in which the patent, etc is deposited or registered is different from the Contracting State in which the action for infringement is brought, and which has a basis of jurisdiction in relation to infringement. Can the courts of the latter Contracting State try the issue of infringement if validity is raised as a defence? If so, can they also try the defence of invalidity?

(a) do articles 19 and 16(4) preclude infringement jurisdiction?

The first thing to be said is that this question only arises if the issue of validity brings Article 16(4) into play in the first place. If the patent, etc has been registered outside a Contracting State to the Brussels or Lugano Conventions, Article 16(4) will not apply anyway and there is no limitation on jurisdiction preventing the court which has a basis of jurisdiction in relation to infringement from trying the infringement claim. Similarly,

---

[329] The latter was treated in the *Coin Controls* case as being equivalent to actually raising the defence.
[330] See below, pp 321–323.

there is no limitation on jurisdiction if Article 16(4) is inapplicable because the case involves a copyright or unregistered design.

Let assume though that it is a patent etc registered in a Contracting State and Article 16(4) comes into play. There is a strong argument based on the wording of the Conventions that this does not preclude infringement jurisdiction in another Contracting State. Unfortunately, there are cases which misguidedly have taken the opposite view.

(i) The argument based on the wording of the Conventions

Writers of great eminence have suggested that the courts of a Contracting State which has jurisdiction to try the infringement action are not prevented from doing so where the defence of invalidity is raised.[331] It is submitted that this view is correct and is supported by an examination of Article 19 of the Conventions. Article 19 states that 'Where a court of a Contracting State is seised of a claim which is principally concerned with a matter over which the courts of another Contracting State have exclusive jurisdiction by virtue of Article 16, it shall declare of its own motion that it has no jurisdiction.' The matter of validity is undeniably for the exclusive jurisdiction of another Contracting State in situations where Article 16(4) applies. But is a 'claim' concerned with the matter of a defence raised thereto? Even if one assumes that it is, is a claim for infringement to which invalidity is raised as a defence *principally concerned* with the matter of validity? The Jenard Report says that these words 'have the effect that the court is not obliged to declare of its own motion that it has no jurisdiction if an issue which comes within the exclusive jurisdiction of another court is raised only as a preliminary or incidental matter'.[332] This looks to be merely an example of a situation where a claim is not principally so concerned, and a pretty obvious example at that. It does not define these words, nor give an example of what does come within their ambit. The dictionary meaning of 'principally' is 'mainly'. A claim for infringement to which validity is raised as a defence is mainly concerned with infringement or, perhaps more accurately, equally concerned with both infringement and validity. It is certainly not mainly concerned with validity. The result is that the court in which the infringement action is brought, and which has a basis of jurisdiction in relation to infringement, does not have to declare that it lacks jurisdiction in relation to infringement.

---

[331] See Dicey and Morris, p 386, n 79; Wadlow, (1985) 10 *E L Rev* 305, 313–314. But see to the contrary Newman at p 5 in chapter 1, of *The Option of Litigation in Europe*, eds Carey Miller and Beaumont; Cornish, GRUR Int 1996 Heft 4285 at 289.

[332] [1979] OJ C59, p 1 at p 39.

(ii) Cases going the other way

(a) Coin Controls Ltd *v* Suzo International (UK) Ltd and Others

Unfortunately, Laddie J, in *Coin Controls Ltd* v *Suzo International (UK) Ltd and Others*,[333] has taken the opposite view. The case concerned an action brought in England for the infringement of three European patents: a European patent (UK); a European patent (Spain); and a European patent (Germany). It was plain that validity was to be put in issue. Laddie J held that the English court had no jurisdiction, not only in relation to the validity part but over the whole of the claim, ie including the infringement part. The learned judge said that he could see no reason to give a narrow linguistic interpretation to the words 'principally concerned', and that 'something which is a major feature of the litigation is not incidental and is therefore a matter with which the action is principally concerned'.[334] What is remarkable about this is the interpretation of 'principally concerned' as meaning 'not arising incidentally'. He relied upon the wording of the Jenard Report, quoted above, to explain this interpretation, treating these words as a definition rather than as an example. A number of criticisms can be made of this decision; a decision which it appears the Dutch courts regard as being wrong.[335] Even though validity is in issue the Dutch courts can still grant interlocutory relief.

First, it does not fit in with various provisions and principles established by the Court of Justice. It is hard to believe that the drafters of the Brussels Convention used the word 'principally' in Article 19 when what they actually meant was the very different, and much wider concept, of 'not arising incidentally'. Such an extraordinary interpretation can only be justified by the clearest explanation in the Jenard Report, but, as has been seen, there is no such clear explanation. Moreover, one thing that Laddie J does not appear to have considered is Article 16(4). Like the other provisions of Article 16, this will only operate where the proceedings are *principally* concerned with validity, etc.[336] If the action for infringement is brought in the Contracting State where a patent is registered and invalidity is raised as a defence, is it really right that this State has exclusive jurisdiction in relation to a mere defence of invalidity? This is the logical consequence of the definition adopted by Laddie J. Neither does the learned judge take into account the attitude under the Convention towards infringement. The intention is that general bases of jurisdiction will apply, such as Article

---

[333] [1997] 3 All ER 45. [334] *Ibid*, at 60.
[335] See Laddie J in the *Fort Dodge* case at first instance [1998] FSR 222.
[336] See generally, Anton & Beaumont, *Civil Jurisdiction in Scotland*, para 7.05. See, specifically, in respect of Article 16(4) the Advocate General in Case 288/82 *Duijnstee* v *Goderbauer* [1983] ECR 3663.

5(3).[337] But this intention can be defeated merely by the defendant raising the issue of validity. Furthermore, by denying the validity of the intellectual property right, the defendant is denying that the tort of infringement has been committed. But, it is well established by the Court of Justice that a simple denial of the existence of a tort by the defendant does not prevent a court from having jurisdiction under Article 5(3) of the Brussels or Lugano Conventions.[338]

Secondly, it can lead to a proliferation of litigation, a point noted with some concern by Laddie J.[339] The court in which the action for infringement is brought, and which also has a basis of jurisdiction in relation infringement, may well also have jurisdiction in relation to passing off, but if it is required to hand the whole of the infringement/validity proceedings over to the court with validity jurisdiction the result will be that trials of these complementary torts will take place in different Contracting States. Another aspect of this proliferation is that with European patents granted for, say, three different countries, essentially the same issue of validity will have to be tried in three different Contracting States. Whilst not happy with these consequences, Laddie J thought that this did not alter the meaning of the Brussels Convention and the real crux of the matter was that intellectual property litigation had not been thought out properly in the Convention.[340]

Thirdly, Laddie J also noted that his decision allows the defendant to thwart jurisdiction in the Contracting State in which the action for infringement was brought, and which has a basis of jurisdiction in relation to infringement, by simply raising the issue of validity. This allows the defendant to forum shop by deciding whether to attack validity.

Fourthly, the whole of the proceedings is handed over to the courts of the Contracting State or States where the patent, etc was registered. There are dangers with this. First, the latter courts may say that Article 16(4) does not apply to give them validity jurisdiction because the issue of validity only arises as a defence to an infringement action. The dispute is, accordingly, not principally concerned with validity. In other words, it adopts a different definition from that adopted by Laddie J. Of course, even if Article 16(4) does not apply, the courts of the Contracting State(s) where the patent, etc was registered may still have jurisdiction in relation to validity.[341] The second and even greater danger is that the courts with validity jurisdiction do not have infringement jurisdiction. It is clear under the Conventions that, as far as infringement is concerned, the general

---

[337] See chapter 1 above, p 19.
[338] Case 38/81 *Effer SpA* v *Kantner* [1982] ECR 825 at 838 (Advocate General Reischl); Case C-68/93 *Shevill and Others* v *Presse Alliance SA* [1995] 2 WLR 499 at 528 (Advocate General Darmon).
[339] N 333 above at 62.   [340] *Ibid*.   [341] See above, pp 28–45.

bases of jurisdiction, ie other than Article 16(4) are intended to apply. It follows that a court with validity jurisdiction under Article 16(4) cannot automatically take infringement jurisdiction. It is going to have to have a basis of jurisdiction for infringement. Often, the courts of the Contracting State(s) where the patent, etc was registered will have infringement jurisdiction.[342] But if they do not, the result seemingly is that no court can try the infringement litigation. How is a plaintiff to avoid this happening? The plaintiff could bring an action for a declaration of the validity of the patent, etc in the Contracting State with validity jurisdiction under Article 16(4) and then follow this up with an infringement action in a Contracting State whose courts have jurisdiction in relation to infringement, with no fear of a defence of invalidity being raised. But this certainly complicates things for the plaintiff and it means an undesirable splitting of the litigation with the issues of validity and infringement being tried in separate Contracting States.

(b) *The* Fort Dodge *case*

The decision of Laddie J in the *Coin Controls* case was expressly affirmed by the Court of Appeal in *Fort Dodge Animal Health Ltd and Others* v *Akzo Nobel NV and Another*.[343]

An infringement action was brought in the Netherlands by a Dutch company and its wholly owned subsidiary against, *inter alia*, three companies domiciled in England in respect of a European patent (UK). Subsequently, these defendants (appellants in the English proceedings) petitioned the English Patents Court for revocation of this patent. They also intended to rely on a 'Gillette' defence, ie that the patent is invalid if the alleged infringing acts fall within the ambit of the claims. It was argued by the appellants that the only court which had jurisdiction to determine whether the appellants had infringed the UK patent is the English Patents Court. Accordingly, so they argued, the prosecution of the claim in the Dutch courts was vexatious and should be restrained by injunction.

The Court of Appeal held that the infringement claim by the respondents (the plaintiffs in the Dutch action) in respect of acts carried out in the United Kingdom is principally concerned with validity of the UK patent and, therefore, by virtue of Articles 19 and 16(4) the claim falls within the exclusive jurisdiction of the UK Court. However, the Court of Appeal

---

[342] It is arguable that it would have jurisdiction under Article 5(3) because the intellectual property right has been damaged in the State in which it is situated: see above pp 164–165. The Maxwell Report, *The Report of the Scottish Committee on Jurisdiction and Enforcement* (1980), at 5.172, was of the view that in most cases the court that had jurisdiction in relation to validity would also have infringement jurisdiction.

[343] [1998] FSR 222.

accepted that the position under the Brussels Convention in relation to this point was not clear and that a ruling should be sought from the Court of Justice. In the meantime, they were not prepared to grant an injunction enjoining the Dutch proceedings.

The following criticisms can be made of the decision in so far as it deals with infringement and validity under the Brussels Convention. First, the reasoning of the Court of Appeal was based on the close relationship between the issues of infringement and validity under the English law of patents, according to which it is said to be impossible to infringe an invalid patent. But is it right when interpreting the Brussels Convention to rely solely on a substantive law point? Moreover, if the substantive law is to be considered should this be the substantive law of only one EC Contracting State?

Secondly, there was no discussion of the meaning of the words 'principally concerned' under Article 19. Moreover, none of the four arguments, listed above, in favour of a different view were considered even though some of them were mentioned in the *Coin Controls* case. These four points are equally valid in the context of the *Fort Dodge* case.

Thirdly, the Court of Appeal is, in effect, creating a new form of exclusive jurisdiction in infringement cases (in the sense that Contracting States other than the one in which the right was registered are precluded from trying the issue of infringement), at least in infringement cases where validity is raised, which, according to the Court of Appeal, is invariably the case. But the Brussels Convention sets out all the bases of exclusive jurisdiction and these do not include a provision dealing with infringement. Moreover, the Jenard Report contemplates that infringement can be tried in some Contracting State other than the one in which registration occurred.

Fourthly, it extends *Coin Controls* by applying the principles in that case to the situation where validity is raised, not by way of defence before the court in which the infringement action is brought, but in the context of separate revocation proceedings brought in another Contracting State. This aspect of the case is discussed below.[344]

(c) JA Motte v Tecno Spa

In *JA Motte* v *Tecno SpA*,[345] the Tribunale di Milano, in an action for the payment of royalties in relation to a patent registered in France, held that it had no jurisdiction with respect to the defendant's application for a declaration that the patent was void, only the French courts being able to

---

[344] At pp 213–214.
[345] *Rivista di Diritto Internazionale Privato e Processuale* 1981, p 913; D Series I-16.4 – B3; discussed above p 91.

decide this because of Article 16(4). The brief report of the case does not explain the reasoning adopted in the case, neither does it refer to Article 19. As an authority, therefore, it is not as strong as the *Coin Controls* or *Fort Dodge* cases. Nonetheless, the result supports those decisions.

(iii) The need for a decision of the Court of Justice

What is needed is a decision of the Court of Justice on the position under Article 19 where an infringement action raises the defence of invalidity. The reference from the Court of Appeal in the *Fort Dodge* case will provide this.

(b) IS A BASIS OF JURISDICTION NECESSARY IN RELATION TO THE INVALIDITY ISSUE?

It is now necessary to discuss the situation where Articles 19 and 16(4) do not preclude infringement jurisdiction. The case may concern a copyright or other unregistered right, or it concerns a right registered outside an EC/EFTA Contracting State, or it concerns a right registered in an EC/EFTA Contracting State but, contrary to the *Coin Controls* and *Fort Dodge* cases, the matter of a mere defence is not regarded as being principally concerned with validity. Can the court with infringement jurisdiction also try the issue of validity when this arises as a defence?

A court which has infringement jurisdiction on the basis of Article 2 (domicile of the defendant), Article 5(5) (branch, agency or other establishment), or Article 6(1) (a multi defendant case) would also have jurisdiction to try the issue of validity since these are bases of jurisdiction to try that issue in the situation where Article 16(4) does not apply.[346] Moreover, the fact that a court with infringement jurisdiction tries the issue of validity would not affect its infringement jurisdiction. As has already been seen, denying the validity of the intellectual property right is denying that the tort of infringement has been committed. But a simple denial of the existence of a tort by the defendant does not prevent a court from having jurisdiction under Article 5(3) of the Conventions.

However, there is a problem where infringement jurisdiction is based on Article 5(3). The wording of this provision would not cover a cause of action for validity. In order to deal with this situation, it is vital to decide whether an independent basis of jurisdiction is needed before the court with infringement jurisdiction can try the defence of invalidity.

There is a strong case that, as a matter of principle, the court which has infringement jurisdiction should also be able to try the validity issue without having to have any independent basis of jurisdiction in respect of this

---

[346] See above, pp 32–34.

issue, ie of automatically being able to try the validity issue by virtue of having infringement jurisdiction. There are two arguments in favour of this. The first is the close relationship between the two issues. As Laddie J has said, the two issues 'are so closely interrelated that they should be treated for jurisdiction purposes as one issue or claim'.[347] The second is based on the idea that the defence of invalidity to an infringement action is treated like any other defence to any other tort claim. After all, in actions in respect of other torts the court which has jurisdiction to try the plaintiff's claim will also be able to try any defence to that claim. Thus, the court which has jurisdiction to try an action for infringement is also able to try a contractual defence, alleging that the conduct is authorised, to that claim, even though under the Brussels and Lugano Conventions the rules in relation to special jurisdiction for an action in contract are different from those for an action in tort.[348] It is, of course, true that invalidity is different from other defences to other torts in that it can arise as a cause of action in its own right, but when it is raised as a defence it is not arising in this way.

Moreover, it is desirable, as a matter of policy, that the court of the Contracting State with infringement jurisdiction should also try the defence of invalidity. It is in the interest of the good administration of justice that all aspects of a claim be heard before the same court in the same Contracting State. The desirability of this has been recognised in relation to Community intellectual property rights and this is no less desirable in relation to national intellectual property rights. However, it has to be admitted that this is not a view that is universally accepted. Courts in the United States have been very unwilling to try infringement cases raising the issue of the validity of foreign intellectual property rights, and have, commonly, dismissed such actions.[349]

If the courts of the Contracting State in which the action for infringement is brought were unable to try the issue as to validity, that issue would have to be tried abroad in a Contracting State which has jurisdiction in relation to that issue. This would involve splitting the issues of infringement and validity between the courts of different Contracting States. This is a course of action which Laddie J has described as having 'nothing to commend it and is only likely to result in an unhelpful proliferation of proceedings'.[350] The plaintiff would be able to avoid this split by bringing the action in the first place in the Contracting State with validity jurisdiction, provided, of course, that the courts of that State also have infringement jurisdiction.

---

[347] *Coin Controls*, n 333 above, at 61. See also the *Fort Dodge* case, n 343 above.
[348] *Re Jurisdiction in Tort and Contract* (Case I ZR 201/86) [1988] ECC 415, a decision of the German Federal Supreme Court.
[349] See below, p 293.   [350] *Coin Controls*, n 333 above, at 61.

(c) A COMPLICATION: SEPARATE REVOCATION PROCEEDINGS

If, as is suggested above, the court in which the action for infringement is brought, and which has a basis of jurisdiction in relation to infringement, is not precluded from trying this issue and is also able to try the defence of invalidity, it has to be admitted that there is a complication in that there may be separate revocation proceedings brought in the Contracting State in which the patent, etc is registered, and whose courts have exclusive jurisdiction under Article 16(4).[351] When it comes to declining jurisdiction under Article 22 of the Brussels and Lugano Conventions, these revocation proceedings would be 'related' to those brought earlier in respect of the defence of invalidity in the Contracting State with infringement jurisdiction. The only question would then be whether the court second seised would exercise its discretion to stay its proceedings. Normally, it should do so in order to avoid irreconcilable judgments,[352] although it has been questioned whether the court seised of revocation proceedings would stay these proceedings in favour of the court with infringement jurisdiction which was also determining the issue of validity.[353]

This problem did not arise in the *Fort Dodge* case because the Court of Appeal came to the conclusion that the Dutch courts lacked jurisdiction. Moreover, the defence of invalidity had not yet been raised in the Netherlands.

3. A COUNTERCLAIM FOR REVOCATION

The validity of a patent, etc may arise in an infringement action in a different way. This is where the defendant counterclaims for revocation of the patent, etc in question. This is different from the situation where validity arises by way of a defence in that a counterclaim is a cross-action not a mere defence, and an action for revocation is a cause of action in its own right.[354]

(a) DO ARTICLES 19 AND 16(4) PRECLUDE INFRINGEMENT JURISDICTION?

There may well be problems in relation to Articles 19 and 16(4) if the case concerns a patent, etc registered in another Contracting State.[355] Is the court in which the action for infringement is brought, and which has a basis of jurisdiction in relation to infringement, seised of a claim which is principally concerned with a matter over which the courts of another

---

[351] See Wadlow, n 331 above, p 314.   [352] See *The Linda* [1988] 1 Lloyd's Rep 175.
[353] Tritton and Tritton, [1987] 12 *EIPR* 349 at 352.   [354] See below, p 311.
[355] Floyd and Purvis [1995] 3 *EIPR* 110 at 111 assert that Article 16(4) will preclude jurisdiction without going into the reasoning for this.

Contracting State have exclusive jurisdiction? If so, Article 19 operates and the court in which the infringement action is brought, and which has a basis of jurisdiction in relation to infringement, has to declare that it lacks jurisdiction over the claim.

If you regard the 'claim' as being proceedings combining an action for infringement and a counterclaim for revocation, it seems that the claim is as much concerned with infringement as with revocation. Nonetheless, applying the test in the *Coin Controls* case, the question is whether validity arises not incidentally. The obvious answer is that it does not so arise[356] and, therefore, the claim is principally concerned with a matter over which the courts of another Contracting State have exclusive jurisdiction by virtue of Article 16(4). It follows that the court in which the infringement action is brought, and has a basis of jurisdiction in relation to infringement, is unable to try the claim for infringement and the counterclaim. The claim has to be passed over to the Contracting State with validity jurisdiction. The reasoning in the *Fort Dodge* case supports this conclusion. It is, of course, arguable that the *Coin Controls* and *Fort Dodge* cases are wrong. A more natural interpretation of the Convention would be that you are concerned with whether the claim is 'mainly' concerned with validity, in which case the court would not have to give up its infringement jurisdiction.

On the other hand, if, as seems more appropriate, you focus on the fact that the proceedings for infringement/counterclaim for revocation actually consist of cross-actions, and treat the counterclaim for revocation as the 'claim' for the purpose of Article 19, it is undeniable that this 'claim' is principally concerned with the validity of the patent, etc and exclusive jurisdiction as regards this counterclaim is allocated to the Contracting State in which the deposit or registration has taken place. Is the court in which the infringement claim is brought, and which has a basis of jurisdiction in relation to infringement, also deprived of jurisdiction in relation to that claim? The reasoning in the *Fort Dodge* case would suggest that it is. If separate revocation proceedings abroad preclude infringement jurisdiction,[357] so also must local counterclaim proceedings. There is the uncertainty though over whether this decision is correct.

(b) THE NECESSITY OF A BASIS OF JURISDICTION IN RELATION TO THE COUNTERCLAIM

What of cases falling outside the scope of Article 16(4),[358] for example where it is the validity of a copyright that is in issue or a right registered

---

[356] But see Jooris, n 260 above, at 145, who says that a counterclaim in infringement proceedings only arises incidentally for the purpose of Article 16.
[357] See below, pp 213–214.   [358] See above, pp 28–29.

outside the EC? What if, contrary to what is argued above, it is decided that Articles 19 and 16(4) do not preclude infringement jurisdiction in the courts of the Contracting State in which the action for infringement is brought, and which has a basis of jurisdiction in relation to infringement? Can the court with infringement jurisdiction also try the counterclaim? It is going to have to have some positive basis of jurisdiction to try the counterclaim for invalidity, given that this is a separate cause of action.

Article 6(3) of the Brussels and Lugano Conventions provides jurisdiction in relation to counterclaims. This states that 'A person domiciled in a Contracting State may also be sued . . . (3) on a counterclaim arising from the same contract or facts on which the original claim was based, in the court in which the original claim is pending'. Article 6(3) is intended to establish the conditions under which a court has jurisdiction to hear a claim which would involve a separate judgment or decree.[359] The counterclaim must be related to the original claim.[360] A closer connection is required between the two than is necessary to establish that actions are related under Article 22.[361] It has been argued that this provision will not apply since a counterclaim for revocation is not based on the same facts as an infringement action. 'Infringement is necessarily based on facts occurring after publication of the patent application, while validity will normally depend on facts occurring before the application was made, at least 18 months before'.[362] It has also been argued that Article 6(3) should not operate to give counterclaim jurisdiction because this would mean allowing it to derogate from Article 16(4).[363] However, it would not be so derogating in situations falling outside the scope of Article 16(4), or if it is accepted that this provision does not preclude jurisdiction. As an alternative to basing jurisdiction on Article 6(3), it may be possible to base jurisdiction on Articles 2, 5(5) or 6(1).

(c) RECOGNITION OF A REVOCATION ORDER

One further matter that needs to be addressed is whether a revocation order granted by a court in the Contracting State with infringement jurisdiction will be recognised in other Contracting States. Clearly, it will not be if the courts of another Contracting State have exclusive jurisdiction under Article 16(4). It also has been suggested,[364] that, even where this is not the situation, recognition would probably be refused on the ground of public policy.[365] However, this concept is only used in exceptional

---

[359] Case C-341/93 *Danvaern Production A/S* v *Schuhfabriken Otterbeck GmbH & Co* [1995] ECR I-2053. It does not cover set-off as a defence.
[360] The Jenard Report, n 332 above at p 28.
[361] O'Malley and Layton, p 453; Dicey and Morris, p 372.   [362] Wadlow, n 331 above.
[363] Tritton and Tritton, [1987] 12 *EIPR* 349 at 351.
[364] Wadlow, n 331 above at p 313.   [365] Article 27(1).

cases,[366] and normally (Article 16 is an exception) cannot be used to review the jurisdiction of the judgment granting State. It cannot be used to review an assertion of jurisdiction on the basis of Article 6(3).

4. SEPARATE REVOCATION PROCEEDINGS

We are concerned here with the situation where the validity of a registered right is raised in the context of separate proceedings for revocation. For example, an infringement action is brought in Contracting State A in respect of a patent registered in Contracting State B. Subsequently, a petition for revocation is brought in Contracting State B.

(a) DO ARTICLES 19 AND 16(4) PRECLUDE INFRINGEMENT JURISDICTION?

It will be recalled that, in the *Fort Dodge* case, the issue of validity arose both in the context of separate revocation proceedings brought in England, where the patent was registered, and in the context of a defence to infringement, which was presumably going to be raised in the Netherlands. However, the Court of Appeal did not appear to be concerned about the context in which the issue of validity arose or the Contracting State in which it arose (ie whether it arose in the Contracting State in which the infringement action was brought or the Contracting State where the right was registered). Moreover, the reasoning of the Court, being based on the close relationship between the issues of infringement and validity under English law, is equally applicable in either context. It is submitted, therefore, that if the issue of validity had arisen solely in the context of separate revocation proceedings, the decision of the Court of Appeal would have been exactly the same: the Dutch courts lacked infringement jurisdiction because of Articles 19 and 16(4).

But is this right? To say that the Dutch claim is principally concerned with a matter not even raised in the Dutch litigation, but only raised by way of separate revocation proceedings brought in another Contracting State, gives an extraordinarily wide interpretation to Article 19. Yet this provision is there to back up Article 16. The latter is an exception to the normal rules on jurisdiction and, as such, has normally been given a restrictive interpretation by the Court of Justice.[367]

What is needed is a decision of the Court of Justice dealing with the situation where validity is raised in the context of separate revocation proceedings. The reference to the Court of Justice in the *Fort Dodge* case should provide this.

[366] Case 145/86 *Hoffmann* v *Krieg* [1988] ECR 645.
[367] See, eg Case 288/82 *Duijnstee* v *Goderbauer* [1983] ECR 3663; Case 73/77 *Sanders* v *Van der Putte* [1977] ECR 2383.

If the Dutch courts are not precluded from trying the issue of infringement, this then raises the question of whether the Dutch courts can consider the issue of validity. This depends on the context in which this issue arises. If separate revocation proceedings are brought in the Netherlands, the Dutch courts will have to declare on their own motion that they have no jurisdiction because of Articles 19 and 16(4). If, on the other hand, the issue of validity arises by way of a defence to the infringement action, then the situation is as explained above.[368] The Dutch courts may well regard themselves as having jurisdiction to consider the validity defence. Laddie J has said that the Dutch courts regard *Coin Controls* as being wrong.[369]

(b) IS A BASIS OF JURISDICTION NECESSARY IN RELATION TO THE INFRINGEMENT ISSUE?

If the *Fort Dodge* case is correct and the Dutch courts are precluded from trying the infringement issue, can the English courts try it? The English courts have exclusive jurisdiction in relation to the revocation proceedings, but they are going to need some basis of jurisdiction in relation to infringement. The Court of Appeal, in *Fort Dodge*, referred to the English court having exclusive jurisdiction over infringement. But there is no basis of exclusive jurisdiction for infringement cases under the Brussels or Lugano Conventions. The English courts would have jurisdiction to try the infringement action on the facts of the case because the defendants were domiciled in England. But this is under Article 2, which does not provide for exclusive jurisdiction. The only sense in which the jurisdiction of the English courts can be described as being exclusive is that, if the Court of Appeal is correct about the Dutch courts not having jurisdiction, all Contracting States, other than the UK, are precluded from trying the case.

IX
PROVISIONAL MEASURES

1. ARTICLE 24

Article 24 of the Brussels and Lugano Conventions states that:

Application may be made to the courts of a Contracting State for such provisional, including protective, measures as may be available under the law of that State, even if, under this Convention, the courts of another Contracting State have jurisdiction as to the substance of the matter.

---

[368] See above, pp 202–208. [369] *Fort Dodge* at first instance, [1998] FSR 222.

This provision permits an application to be made to the courts of a Contracting State, which does not have jurisdiction in relation to the substance of the action, for such provisional measures as are available under the laws of that State. The English common law rule is that an ancillary order is only available where the English courts have jurisdiction over the main action. This would have rendered Article 24, which is concerned with the situation where the injunction granting State lacks jurisdiction on the merits, of no practical effect in England. Section 25 of the Civil Jurisdiction and Judgments Act 1982 was therefore passed. This provides that English courts can grant interim relief where proceedings: (a) have been or are to be commenced in a Contracting State to the Brussels or Lugano Convention other than the United Kingdom, or in another part of the United Kingdom; and (b) are proceedings whose subject matter is within the scope of the Convention under Article 1 (whether or not that or any other Convention has effect in relation to the proceedings). There is no requirement under this section that the defendant is domiciled in a Contracting State to the Brussels or Lugano Conventions.[370] A recent Order in Council[371] has greatly extended the scope of Section 25. The proceedings referred to now include proceedings commenced or to be commenced otherwise than in a Brussels or Lugano Contracting State. Moreover, proceedings whose subject matter is not within the scope of Article 1 are now included. However, on an application for interim relief under Section 25(1) the court may refuse to grant that relief if, in the opinion of the court, the fact that the court has no jurisdiction apart from this section in relation to the subject matter of the proceedings in question makes it inexpedient for the court to grant it.[372] The Court of Appeal has said that the expediency or otherwise of granting relief should be the focus of the court's attention.[373]

The twin themes brought out in the English cases in relation to Section 25 are that the English courts lack jurisdiction as to the substance and that the provisional measure is in support of proceedings in a foreign State which has such jurisdiction. Lord Mustill, in the House of Lords, has said that the English 'court does not engage itself at all in the resolution of the

---

[370] In cases where the defendant is so domiciled, service of a writ abroad is possible without the leave of the court: Order 11, rule 1(2). In cases where the defendant is not so domiciled it has been held that the plaintiff can seek the leave of the court for service abroad under Order 11, rule 1(1)(b) : *X* v *Y* [1990] 1 QB 220. See also *Mercedes Benz AG* v *Leiduck* [1995] 3 WLR 718 at 732. Subsequently, the Rules of the supreme Court have been amended so that service of an originating summons out of the jurisdiction claiming interim relief under Section 25(1) is permissible with the leave of the court under Order 11, rule 8A: SI 1997/415.

[371] SI 1997/302. See also for service of the originating summons out of the jurisdiction, SI 1997/415.

[372] Section 25(2).

[373] *Crédit Suisse Fides Trust SA* v *Cuoghi* [1997] 3 WLR 871. The considerations in relation to expediency are discussed by Lord Bingham at p 882.

dispute, but merely seeks to make the resolution of the dispute by the foreign court more effective. It is a free-standing item of ancillary relief'.[374] The role of the English court has been described by the Court of Appeal as ancillary to and supportive of the foreign court seised with the substantive proceedings.[375] An obvious example of such ancillary relief is the grant by the English courts of a Mareva injunction, preserving assets, pending a decision by a French court, whose judgment subsequently will be enforced in England under the Brussels Convention.[376] There is no requirement under Section 25 that the proceedings in the foreign Contracting State must have actually started at the time when the provisional measure is sought.[377] It merely requires that the foreign proceedings have been or 'are to be commenced'. This is understandable given that the grant of a Mareva injunction may be a matter of urgency before assets can be removed out of the jurisdiction. Section 25 is more restrictive than Article 24 under which it does not matter at all whether substantive proceedings on the main issue have or will be started, as long as the possibility of substantive proceedings exists under national law.[378]

One noticeable feature of Section 25 is that it requires the provisional measure to be used in support of *foreign* proceedings. Whilst Article 24 certainly allows a provisional measure in support of foreign proceedings, it is not confined to this situation. It does not preclude a provisional measure in support of proceedings as to the substance in the same Contracting State.[379] However, an English court which has jurisdiction as to the substance of the matter doubtless has the power to grant provisional measures by virtue of this fact and does not need to rely on Section 25.[380]

When it comes to recognition and enforcement of provisional measures, the Court of Justice has held that an *ex parte* provisional and protective measure is not enforceable in other Contracting States under the Brussels Convention since Title III of the Convention does not cover decisions resulting from proceedings which by their very nature neither allow the defendant to state his case nor give him an opportunity to do so.[381]

---

[374] *Channel Tunnel Group Ltd* v *Balfour Beatty Construction Ltd* [1993] AC 334 at 365. See also *Neste Chemicals SA* v *DK Line SA* [1994] 3 All ER 180 at 187–188; *Balkanbank* v *Taher and Others (No 2)* [1995] 1 WLR 1067 at 1073.

[375] *Crédit Suisse Fides Trust SA* v *Cuoghi*, n 373 above. See also the *Fort Dodge* case, n 343 above.

[376] See, eg *Republic of Haiti* v *Duvalier* [1990] 1 QB 202.

[377] See Anton & Beaumont's, *Civil Jurisdiction in Scotland*, para 7.46.

[378] See the opinion of Advocate General Léger in Case C-391/95 *Van Uden Maritime BV, agissant sous le nom Van Uden African Line* v *Kommanditgesellschaft in Firma Deco-Line ea*, discussed below pp 223–224.

[379] See the *Van Uden* case, n 378 above.

[380] There is no requirement that the terms of Section 25 must also be satisfied in this situation, see below, pp 226–227.

[381] Case 125/79 *Denilauler* v *SNC Couchet Frères* [1980] ECR 1553.

2. Infringement Cases

Article 24 is particularly useful in infringement cases, where the grant of an injunction is a normal remedy. It allows a court of a Contracting State which lacks a basis of jurisdiction under the Brussels or Lugano Conventions[382] to grant injunctive relief preventing infringement pending the determination of the substantive dispute in another Contracting State. *Kitechnology Bv and Others* v *Unicor GmbH Plastmaschinen and Others*[383] is an example of how useful Article 24 and Section 25 can be. This case involved an action for injunctive relief brought against two German defendants to prevent breaches of confidence. Millett J, at first instance, would have been prepared to grant the interlocutory injunction sought by the plaintiffs pending the determination of the substantive dispute in Germany, even if, contrary to his view, the court had no jurisdiction under Article 5(3) of the Brussels Convention. The Court of Appeal held that Article 5(3) could not be relied upon but allowed the plaintiffs to seek interlocutory relief anyway.

In infringement cases, one specific situation where the forum court may well lack jurisdiction is in relation to threatened wrongs. It has already been seen[384] that there is a serious doubt as to whether Article 5(3) of the Brussels or Lugano Conventions can be used to prevent a threatened wrong in England. However, it was assumed by the Lord Chancellor, Lord Hailsham, when discussing in Parliament the Civil Jurisdiction and Judgments Bill, that Section 25 could be used to prevent a threatened wrong in England.[385] To take a practical example, a French domiciled defendant threatens to infringe a patent in England. The French courts have jurisdiction under Article 2 of the Brussels Convention in respect of the substance of the matter. An interlocutory injunction can be granted in England, in support of the French action preventing this threatened wrong in England.

Another specific situation where the forum may lack jurisdiction is where validity is raised as a defence to the infringement action, this is assuming, for the sake of argument, that the *Coin Controls* case was rightly decided.[386] Laddie J, in that case, accepted that the powers granted by Article 24 were very wide and were not limited by Article 16.

As has been mentioned, it is also possible under Article 24 (but not Section 25) to grant a provisional measure in support of local final proceedings. In the *Fort Dodge* case, the Court of Appeal said that since the Dutch courts lacked jurisdiction in relation to the final proceedings for infringement they, therefore, also lacked jurisdiction to grant a provisional

---

[382] These are set out above, pp 142–175.
[383] [1994] IL Pr 568.
[384] Above, pp 151–152.
[385] Hansard HL Deb, Vol 426, cols 712–716 (21 January 1982); Hartley, pp 125–126.
[386] For criticism of the case see above, pp 204–206.

measure in support of them. However, the Dutch courts may not agree that they lack jurisdiction over the final proceedings. Moreover, the effect of the Advocate General's opinion in the *Van Uden* case is that the grant of a provisional measure in the Netherlands could be regarded as being in support of English proceedings for infringement because there is the possibility of such proceedings under English law.

X
CROSS-BORDER INJUNCTIONS

1. The Dutch Position

In 1989, the Dutch Supreme Court granted a prohibitory injunction in relation to an infringement in the Benelux territories of Benelux trade marks.[387] This is what is known as a cross-border injunction,[388] ie one which operates extra-territorially in respect of the infringement abroad of foreign intellectual property rights. This was an obvious development in the area of Benelux trade marks. As a result of the Benelux trade mark Treaty, a uniform Benelux trade mark law has been introduced in the three Member States and a trade mark is necessarily granted for the whole Benelux territory. National enforcement procedures remained in operation, but the decision of the Court necessarily affects the mark as such and thus it applies to the whole of the Benelux territory.[389] The Benelux Court, which ultimately rules on matters of interpretation of the uniform law, accepted that this principle also applies to interim measures and injunctive relief.[390] Since 1989, there has been a series of first instance decisions[391] and a Hague Court of Appeals (Gerechtshof) decision[392] granting such injunctions in cases involving the infringement of a European patent.

---

[387] *Interlas* v *Lincoln* Supreme Court, 24 November 1989, 1992 NJ, No 404, 1597 with comments, Verkade, 1991 BIE, No 23,86.

[388] See, generally, Bertrams, (1995) 20 IIC 619; Meibom and Pitz, [1997] 8 *EIPR* 469.

[389] The rule that a judgment applies in principle in the whole Benelux was laid down positively in Cases A 93/1 and A 93/2 *Renault* v *Reynocar and Reynotrade*, Benelux Court, judgment of 13 June 1994, [1995] BIE 23 (No 7). Earlier cases dealt with the point in a negative way only, see *Verkade* [1980] BIE 117–118.

[390] In as far as the national procedural rules of the Member-State in which the application is pending allow for that type of interim measure, see Case A 92/3 *MB* v *Mattel* (Barbie-pop II) Benelux Court, judgment of 26 March 1993, [1993] BIE 260 (No 66) and [1993] NJ 328. See also *Jucotex* v *Belconi* (the LEOPARD case), President of the Arrondissementsrechtbank (district court) of Rotterdam, judgment of 19 June 1979, [1980] BIE 115 (No 32, the case refers to Article 24 of the Brussels Convention).

[391] See, eg the *Voerderhek* decision. The Hague District Court, 28 August 1990, 1992 BIE, No 78,315. See the cases cited by Bertrams, above n 388, at p 620 n 6.

[392] *ARS* v *Organon* Hague Court of Appeals, 3 February 1994, 1995 IER 8; 1995 GRUR Int 253.

Infringement: Jurisdiction under the EC/EFTA rules 219

This, obviously, involves a major expansion of the technique, since no single intellectual property right is involved. A bundle of national rights is granted in the European patent system and this is not done on the basis of a uniform law, but on the basis of substantially harmonised national laws. The link between the single right and the single enforcement procedure is no longer present. Cross-border injunctions have been refused on the basis that the infringement or threat of infringement had not been substantiated. A cross-border injunction has been granted against American defendants in relation to a European patent.[393] Such injunctions have been granted in relation to European patents, parallel patents (including US, Australian and Canadian patents[394]) and Benelux trade marks, but not in relation to copyright. Moreover, such injunctions have been granted not only in relation to infringements in Europe but world-wide.

(a) THE KORT-GEDING PROCEDURE

The procedure used in the Dutch cross-border injunction cases has been the Kort-geding procedure. This has been described as 'a shortened procedure reserved for provisional measures taken by the President of the court in urgent cases'.[395] This is a summary procedure, but which operates as an alternative to principal proceedings. There is no obligation to commence the latter, which are slower and more expensive. Although interim in nature, the procedure, in practice, often gives a final solution. This comes about because, in most cases, the interim injunction is granted for an indefinite period of time and the defendant chooses not to challenge the injunction.[396] The President may refuse to grant the injunction on the basis that the matter is not urgent or that it is too complex for an interim decision. For an injunction to be granted, there must have been an infringement according to the applicable law.

(b) THE BASIS OF JURISDICTION

In recent years, the Kort-geding jurisdiction of the Dutch courts in the cross-border injunction infringement cases has been based on Articles 2, 5(3) and 6(1) of the Brussels Convention.[397] As regards defendants

---

[393] *Chiron Corp* v *Akzo Pharma-Organon Technika-UBI* The Hague District Court, 22 July 1994, 1994 IER, No 24, 150. On appeal, only upheld in relation to those defendants with a serious risk of infringement, The Hague Court of Appeals, 1 December 1994, Case No 94/1341.

[394] *Philips* v *Hemogram* The Hague District Court, 30 December 1991, 1992 BIE, No 80, 323, 1992 IER, No 17, 76. This involved, *inter alia*, an Australian patent.

[395] Brinkhof, [1994] 8 *EIPR* 360 at 361, n 4.

[396] See also generally, Bertrams, (1995) 26 *IIC* 618; Freudenthal and Van Der Velden in chapter 15 of *Declining Jurisdiction* at pp 334–335.

[397] This point is made in a paper by Judge Brinkhof entitled *Transborder Injunctions and the Kort Geding* presented at the Herchel Smith Seminar on Intellectual Property and Private International Law: New Directions at Cambridge on 24 February 1996.

domiciled outside the EC, jurisdiction has been based on national rules of jurisdiction (Article 126 (1) of the Dutch Code of Civil Procedure).[398] It important to note, though, that Kort-geding jurisdiction is not dependent on the bases of jurisdiction under the Brussels Convention, even where the defendant is domiciled in an EC/Contracting State. Article 24, in effect, operates like a basis of jurisdiction and allows recourse to national rules of jurisdiction, including exorbitant bases of jurisdiction prohibited under the Brussels Convention.[399] Thus, a Dutch court in a Kort-geding case involving a contractual dispute has taken jurisdiction under the Netherlands Code of Civil Procedure on the basis of the claimant's Dutch residence, even though the defendant was a company registered in Germany.[400]

(c) THE WILLINGNESS TO GRANT CROSS-BORDER INJUNCTIONS

Even if national courts have power to grant such injunctions, and this issue will be examined below, they may be unwilling to do so. The Dutch courts have been willing. Their justification for this is that it consolidates litigation in one State, and quickly lets the parties know where they stand. The alternative is for a plaintiff, whose rights have been infringed by unlawful actions of a cross-border nature, to seek a series of injunctions in different States.[401] A further justification is that since the law of infringement and validity is the same in various European States the decision of the Dutch court regarding the grant of an injunction should be applied to those States as well.[402] This explains why cross-border injunctions have been granted in cases concerning European patents and Benelux trade marks, where the law of infringement and validity is the same, but not in cases of copyright, where it is not.

2. Foreign Reaction

Practitioners in England have viewed these Dutch developments with consternation. There is a natural fear that the Netherlands will become the European centre for international infringement litigation, and that the Patents Court in England will lose business. Concern also has been raised about the Dutch Kort-geding procedure, in particular whether it provides the defendant with adequate time in which to respond. There has been judicial criticism in England of the Dutch position. In *Chiron Corpn and*

---

[398] See *Chiron Corpn* v *Akzo Pharma-Organon Technika-UBI*, above, n 393.
[399] See the *Van Uden* case, below, pp 223–224. [400] Ibid.
[401] See *Interlas* v *Lincoln*, n 387 above.
[402] *Chiron Corpn and Others* v *Organon Teknika Ltd (No 10)* [1995] FSR 325 at 338.

Others v *Organon Teknika Ltd (No 10)*,[403] Aldous J was aware that, in the present international patent litigation, a Dutch court had granted cross-border injunctions relating to other European States, but not the United Kingdom. He was critical of the idea that a Dutch court should grant such an injunction in relation to the United Kingdom. This was for two reasons. First, since the procedure for ascertaining the facts and scientific evidence are different in England and the Netherlands, factual findings are unlikely to be the same. The Dutch court would be deciding on the grant of an injunction in England on the basis of one set of facts whereas the English court would make their decision on the basis of a different set of facts. Secondly, the considerations taken into account by an English court when deciding whether to grant an injunction would not be the same as those taken into account by a Dutch court. Thus, the Dutch court could not decide if the grant of an injunction in England would be appropriate.

German courts have expressed a more general concern about the growth of the use of the Kort-geding procedure in the Netherlands, not just in infringement cases, and, if this comes within Article 24 of the Brussels Convention,[404] about the possibilities this opens up of by passing the normal jurisdictional rules in the Brussels Convention.[405]

3. Are the Dutch Courts Acting Improperly Under the Brussels Convention?

(a) do articles 2, 5(3) and 6(1) permit cross-border injunctions?

It has been seen[406] that Article 2 allows jurisdiction as to the merits in relation to acts of infringement of foreign rights committed abroad, as does Article 5(3). Thus, jurisdiction can be based under Article 5(3) on damage within the forum, even though the act of infringement of a foreign right occurred abroad. Neither is there anything in principle to stop Article 6(1) from applying in cases involving the infringement of foreign rights abroad, although there is a query over whether this provision can be used in a case involving the infringement of parallel rights.[407] The position though is somewhat clearer in the case of the infringement of parallel European patents,[408] and the Dutch courts were right to rely on Article 6(1) in this situation,[409] since there is a risk of irreconcilable judgments if there are separate actions in the designated European States.

---

[403] Ibid.   [404] See below, pp 222–224.
[405] See the decision of the German Federal Supreme Court in *Mietz* v *Intership Yachting Sneek BV* [1996] IL Pr 661.
[406] See above, pp 190–196.   [407] See above, p 173.   [408] See above, pp 173–174.
[409] See, eg *Chiron Corpn* v *Akzo Pharma-Organon Technika–UBI*, above n 393.

(b) IS A PROVISIONAL MEASURE WITHIN ARTICLE 24 BEING GRANTED?

If the Dutch courts were granting a final injunction after a full trial on the merits, there would be no criticism of the Dutch practice, provided, of course, that the Dutch courts have jurisdiction as to the substance. But what is granted is an interim injunction following summary proceedings. Is this a provisional measure within Article 24 of the Brussels Convention?

(i) Why this matters

In the situation where jurisdiction is based on Article 24, for example a Dutch court which has no jurisdiction over the substance of the dispute uses national rules of procedure to grant an injunction in support of a German action, then to come within Article 24 there has to be a provisional measure within the meaning of that Article. In this situation, the normal rules on jurisdiction under the Brussels Convention are being by-passed.

In the situation where there is jurisdiction as to the substance based on Articles 2, 5(3) or 6(1), the question then arises of whether it is also necessary to come within Article 24, because an interim injunction is being granted. If the Netherlands court has jurisdiction under the Brussels Convention, it could grant a final injunction after normal proceedings. Is it right to impose possible extra requirements because an interim injunction is being granted? In the past, Dutch writers have disagreed over this.[410]

What there is general agreement on, in the Netherlands, is that the grant of an interim injunction using the Kort-geding procedure falls within Article 24.[411] But is this so? There are two major queries in relation to this.

(ii) The queries

First, does Article 24 encompass the situation where, in practice, the grant of the interim injunction in an infringement case will often be determinative of the dispute? This means that the injunction is not actually being used in support of further proceedings either in the Netherlands or abroad. This is a point that concerns Brinkhof, who contemplates that there may have to be a guarantee of normal proceedings to come within Article 24.[412] However, according to the Schlosser Report, 'No doubt Article 24 is applicable when courts have an application for provisional protective measures before them, even if their decision has, in practice, final effect.'[413] In principle, all that should be needed is that there is the

---

[410] Compare Brinkhof, n 395 above, at 362 and Bertrams, n 388 above, at 628.
[411] Brinkhof, *ibid*, Bertrams, *ibid*. See also Freudenthal and Van Der Velden, n 396 above, at 335.
[412] Above, n 395, at pp. 363–364.
[413] [1979] OJ C59 at 111. This Report accompanied the UK/Danish/Irish Accession Convention to the Brussels Convention.

possibility of a further action being brought as to the substance of the matter in the Netherlands. There is much to be said for this view. As Saville L J pointed out in *Balkanbank* v *Taher and Others (No 2)*,[414] 'To the litigants concerned, nice legal jurisdictional distinctions between proceedings for the purpose of resolving the merits of the disputes between the parties (so-called substantive proceedings) and ancillary proceedings for interim relief (which themselves of course are likely to raise disputes which the court has to a degree to resolve on the merits) are likely to have little or no meaning or sense'.[415] One question remains, though, if an interim injunction can be granted which, in practice, is determinative of the dispute how much detail on the merits should be gone into?

Secondly, does the Kort-geding procedure come within Article 24? The aspect of a 'mini' trial of the substantive dispute under the Kort-geding procedure has been criticised as being outside Article 24.[416] Another feature of the Kort-geding proceedings which may raise a problem is that Presidents of some District Courts have accepted claims for the payment of money.[417] But it has been suggested that interim payments of money are outside the scope of Article 24.[418] Nonetheless, if it is an interim injunction that is being granted, this criticism is not applicable.

(iii) References to the Court of Justice

The Dutch Supreme Court, in *Van Uden Africa Line* v *Kommanditgesellschaft In Firma Deco-Line, Peter Determann KG*,[419] has referred a number of questions to the Court of Justice in relation to the Dutch practice, in the context of a case where the plaintiff sought in Dutch summary proceedings provisional payment of sums due under a contract. The defendant was a company registered in Germany and the Kort-geding jurisdiction of the Dutch courts was based on the plaintiff's residence in the Netherlands under the Netherlands Code of Civil Procedure. The questions include: whether the relief granted under the Dutch Kort-geding procedure constitutes a provisional or protective measure within Article 24; does it make any difference whether substantive proceedings on the main issue are, or may become, pending; does it make any difference that the interim relief sought is an order requiring performance of an obligation to pay a sum of money; if it is a provisional measure, does the summary court have jurisdiction to hear the case if it has jurisdiction under national rules, even where those rules

---

[414] [1995] 1 WLR 1067.
[415] *Ibid*, at 1073. The result in the case was that once a Mareva injunction had been granted an English court could consider a counterclaim by the defendant even though this involved going into the merits of the case.
[416] See Adams, (1995) 10 *EIPR* 497 at 498.
[417] Freudenthal and Van Der Velden in *Declining Jurisdiction* at 334, n 44.
[418] Collins, *Essays*, pp 38–39; *Civil Jurisdiction and Judgments Act 1982*, p 99.
[419] [1996] IL Pr 269, pending in the Court of Justice as case 391/95.

are exorbitant rules of jurisdiction outlawed by the Brussels Convention in cases coming within that Convention, or is its jurisdiction conditional on the fulfilment of more specific conditions, for example that the relief sought from that court must take effect, or be capable of taking effect in the Contracting State in question?

In response to these questions, Advocate General Léger has given his opinion that the Dutch Kort-geding procedure does indeed constitute a provisional or protective measure within Article 24; it does not matter at all whether substantive proceedings on the main issue have or will be started, as long as the possibility of substantive proceedings exists under national law; it does not make any difference that the interim relief sought is an order requiring performance of an obligation to pay a sum of money; the summary court does have jurisdiction to hear the case even where this is based on an exorbitant national basis of jurisdiction outlawed by the Brussels Convention.[420] It is submitted that, from the point of view of private international law, all of this makes perfect sense and there is nothing under Article 24 to limit its use in any of the ways raised under these questions. There is an interesting limitation mentioned in that substantive proceedings must be possible. The fact that the Kort-geding procedure often resolves the matter without recourse to full proceedings on the substantive issue is because the defendant chooses not to take the matter further. Provided that the defendant has the opportunity to do so there can be no objection to the grant of the provisional measure using this summary procedure.

The German Federal Supreme Court has also referred to the Court of Justice the question of whether the Kort-geding procedure constitutes a provisional measure within the meaning of Article 24.[421]

(c) CAN A PROVISIONAL MEASURE HAVE EXTRA-TERRITORIAL EFFECT?

A further question arises in respect of the Dutch position. Can a provisional measure under Article 24 have extra-territorial effect?[422] In *Bernard Denilauler v Snc Couchet Frères*,[423] Advocate General Mayras said that he was not adopting the view that no provisional or protective measure can have extra-territorial effect.[424] However, what he was concerned with was the question of whether a judgment concerning the measure could be enforceable under the Convention in another Contracting State, and in what circumstances this would be so. Perhaps more to the point, no criti-

---

[420] The Advocate General rightly adds that jurisdiction in relation to interim measures can also be based on any of the other provisions of the Brussels Convention (Article 5.1 in *Van Uden*). The nature of the proceedings is irrelevant in relation to the application of the main jurisdictional provisions of the Convention.
[421] The *Mietz* case, n 405 above.
[422] See generally, Collins, *Essays*, chapter 8.
[423] Case 125/79 [1980] ECR 1553.
[424] *Ibid*, at 1576. See Adams, (1995) 10 *EIPR* 497.

cism was made of the fact that the case involved a French court making an order authorising the freezing of the defendant's assets in a bank in Frankfurt as security. Neither was there any criticism, in another Court of Justice case,[425] of the fact that a French court froze furniture and other effects in a flat in Frankfurt. Finally, this question was specifically addressed by Advocate General Léger in the *Van Uden* case, who gave his opinion that the measure granted by the judge under Article 24 can have extra-territorial effect. This is to be welcomed. It means that a plaintiff can go to the courts of one Contracting State and obtain an interlocutory injunction preventing infringement in several different Contracting States, rather than having to go to these different Contracting States and seek a series of separate injunctions.

(d) RECOGNITION AND ENFORCEMENT

Will the injunction be recognised and enforced in other Contracting States? Under the Brussels and Lugano Conventions, judgments granted in one Contracting State are recognised in other Contracting States on a semi-automatic basis. A 'judgment', for these purposes, includes an injunction. The Dutch Kort-geding procedure is not an *ex parte* one and so the rule which precludes the recognition of *ex parte* orders will not operate. Would recognition of a cross-border injunction be contrary to public policy in the State in which recognition is sought? This defence to recognition is only to be used in exceptional cases and it is doubtful if this is such a case. This is supported by a decision of the Paris Court of Appeals which has held that recognition of a Dutch cross-border injunction would not be contrary to public policy.[426]

4. THE ENGLISH POSITION

(a) DO THE ENGLISH COURTS HAVE POWER TO GRANT A CROSS-BORDER INJUNCTION?

In order to grant an injunction as the substantive remedy in a case, the English courts will need a basis of jurisdiction as to the substance. However, it has been seen that Articles 2, 5(3) and 6(1) can be used in relation to infringements abroad of foreign intellectual property rights. The grant of the injunction requires that a successful action has been brought

---

[425] Case 143/78 *de Cavel* v *de Cavel* [1979] ECR 1055.
[426] *Braillecellen II* 28 January 1994, 1994 BIE No. 111, p 395, with comment by Verkade, see also [1995] 3 *EIPR* D-73. The case is discussed further below, chapter 14, p 730. It should be noted that the French Courts were not in a position to grant measures similar to those granted by the Dutch Courts.

in England in the same way that an award of damages would require this. This raises the issue of the applicable law. Under the common law double actionability rule, a successful action, normally, could not be brought in England in respect of an infringement that took place abroad.[427] The abolition of that rule now means that a successful action can be brought in England where the infringement took place abroad, at least where it is a foreign right that has been infringed.[428] This removes a major obstacle to the grant of cross-border injunctions.[429]

The position is very different where the injunction is in support of foreign proceedings. It is then possible to use Section 25 of the Civil Jurisdiction and Judgments Act 1982 to grant interim relief. There is, obviously, no requirement that the English court has jurisdiction as to the substance. Article 24 and Section 25 are the basis of jurisdiction for the grant of the interim injunction. Neither will there be any enquiry as to whether a successful action can be brought in England. Section 25, even though recently extended, still requires that proceedings have been or are to be commenced in a foreign State. There is no question under this provision of interim relief being granted in support of proceedings in England as to substance. Nor is it possible to grant interim relief where the mere possibility of substantive proceedings exists; the foreign proceedings must have been or are to be commenced.

What happens if an English court has jurisdiction as to the substance which is based on Articles 2, 5(3) or 6(1) but the plaintiff for reasons of speed seeks an interlocutory injunction? This is an interim measure. Is it necessary to come within Article 24 and Section 25, even though there is jurisdiction over the substance? If it is necessary, the English courts are not authorised by Section 25 to grant interim relief except in the situation where they are acting in support of foreign proceedings, and certainly cannot act in the way that the Dutch courts have done by using interim proceedings to back up a possible local action as to substance. This whole question is perhaps somewhat academic, at least as regards patent infringement. An English court will only grant an interlocutory injunction where the balance of convenience test in *American Cyanamid* v *Ethicon*[430] is satisfied. Money tends to be an adequate remedy in patent infringement cases and so interlocutory injunctions are relatively uncommon in such cases.[431] Thus, in the *Fort Dodge* case,[432] interim relief, in the form of an injunction restraining the respondents from continuing the Dutch proceedings, pending the decision of the Court of Justice on the jurisdictional issues, was refused. It was said that any harm suffered in the meantime could be compensated by the award of damages. On the other hand, inter-

---

[427] See below, pp 607–610.
[429] See Kempner and Fricker, [1996] 7 *EIPR* 377.
[431] Kempner and Fricker, n 429 above, at 378.
[428] See below, pp 623–624.
[430] [1975] AC 375.
[432] N 343 above.

locutory injunctions are relatively common in copyright infringement cases and so the question becomes a real one in that context. There is though an answer now to this. Advocate General Léger, in the *Van Uden* case, gave his opinion that if there is jurisdiction under Article 5(1) of the Brussels Convention additional requirements in relation to provisional measures cannot be added on, which clearly means that Article 24 does not have to be complied with.

(b) WILL THE ENGLISH COURTS BE WILLING TO GRANT CROSS-BORDER INJUNCTIONS?

Even though the English Courts have the power to grant cross-border injunctions, will they be willing to do so? It is not unknown for the English courts to grant injunctions restraining a person from doing an act abroad. English judges have been prepared to grant, pursuant to section 25 of the Civil Jurisdiction and Judgments Act 1982, pre-judgment[433] Mareva injunctions in relation to assets world wide. The effect of such injunctions is that the defendants are restrained from disposing of assets abroad. It is, though, only appropriate to grant such interlocutory injunctions in rare cases.[434] The English courts are also prepared, in certain limited circumstances, to restrain a person from commencing or continuing with proceedings abroad. It is recognised though that this raises comity of nations problems, and that this power must be exercised with caution.[435] When it comes to the protection of intellectual property rights, cross-border injunctions have been granted in passing off cases.[436]

However, when it comes to infringement, what little judicial discussion there has been shows a distinct unwillingness to grant cross-border injunctions. In *Chiron Corpn and Others v Organon Teknika Ltd (No 10)*,[437] Aldous J referred to the fact that a Dutch court had not only granted an injunction in relation to a Dutch patent but also granted cross-border injunctions in relation to corresponding patents in other European countries. He went on to say that 'At one time I wondered whether it would be right for this court to do the same as the Dutch court, but have concluded that it would not be right for this court to grant an injunction which had an effect outside the United Kingdom'.[438] As has been seen, the learned judge was very critical of the notion that a Dutch court should grant an injunction which had an effect in the United Kingdom.[439]

---

[433] *Republic of Haiti and Others v Duvalier and Others* [1990] 1 QB 202. See also *Babanaft International Co SA v Bassatne and Another* [1990] 1 Ch 13 at 30–32.
[434] See Section 25(2) discussed above p 215. [435] See Cheshire and North, p 242.
[436] See below, p 387. [437] [1995] FSR 325.
[438] *Ibid*, at 338. See also *Plastus Kreativ AB v Minnesota Mining and Manufacturing Co* [1995] RPC 438; discussed below.
[439] See above, p 221.

(c) WILL THE ENGLISH COURTS ENJOIN THE DUTCH PROCEEDINGS?

Now that Advocate General Léger, in the *Van Uden* case, has given the green light to the Dutch use of the Kort-geding procedure in infringement cases, it is hard to envisage an English court enjoining Dutch proceedings. Uncertainty remains in the situation where validity of the right is raised during infringement litigation, but this will be resolved if and when the reference from the Court of Appeal in the *Fort Dodge* case comes before the Court of Justice. It is important to note though that, in the meantime, the Court of Appeal was not prepared to grant an injunction enjoining Dutch proceedings, even though they considered that the Dutch courts lacked jurisdiction because of the issue of validity being raised.[440] Interestingly, the Court of Appeal said that they did not believe that consideration of the procedures adopted by the Dutch courts to resolve patent disputes was material to the issue before them and it was not appropriate for an English court to voice any opinion upon them.

XI
INTERNATIONAL DISCOVERY

International discovery is of great practical importance in infringement cases and so brief mention must be made of the law relating to this.

1. THE NEED TO JOIN A FOREIGNER AS A SUBSTANTIVE DEFENDANT

It has been held that an English court should not, save in exceptional circumstances, require a foreigner who was not a party to an English action, to produce documents outside the jurisdiction.[441] The result is that it is not uncommon to find that foreigners have been joined as a party to an English action solely in order to obtain discovery against them, not because of any intention to obtain recovery against them. One of the leading cases on jurisdiction in relation to infringement illustrates this.

In *Mölnlycke AB and Another* v *Procter & Gamble Ltd and Others*,[442] the plaintiffs, having failed to obtain certain documents from the US parent company, the second defendant, sought to add on the German manufacturers, referred to as GmbH, of the infringing nappies, as a third defendant. As has been seen,[443] the Court of Appeal granted leave to do so. The

---

[440] See the discussion on restraining foreign proceedings, above pp 189–190.
[441] *Mackinnon* v *Donaldson, Lufkin and Jenrette Securities Corpn and Others* [1986] 1 Ch 482.
[442] [1992] 1 WLR 1112. See also *Beecham Group plc and Another* v *Norton Healthcare Ltd and Others* [1997] FSR 81; discussed below.
[443] See above, pp 146–147.

fact that the plaintiffs' only purpose in joining GmbH was to obtain discovery of relevant documents did not make it an abuse of process or improper for the plaintiff to rely on Article 5(3) of the Brussels Convention since the English court had power to control the process of discovery in English proceedings and could prevent oppressive demands against a party who had been joined in such circumstances.[444]

2. Difficulties Involved

The *Mölnlycke* case might suggest that there is little difficulty in joining on a foreign defendant for the purpose of discovery. Indeed, Hoffmann J, at first instance in the *Mölnlycke* case, said that 'it will almost invariably be the case that a member of the group which is sufficiently involved in the alleged infringement to have documents which are discoverable will also be sufficiently involved to give rise to at any rate an arguable case that it is a joint tortfeasor'.[445] However, such optimism has been shown to be misplaced. There can be difficulties in determining which company to join, establishing the liability of that company, and satisfying the jurisdictional criteria.

(a) DETERMINING WHICH COMPANY TO JOIN

There may be a practical problem in ascertaining which company in a group was responsible for research and development and thus deciding which company to join as an additional defendant.

(b) ESTABLISHING LIABILITY

In order to join a foreign defendant as a party, it has to be shown that there is a serious issue on the merits that this person or body is liable for infringement. That it is not always possible to establish this was shown in *Unilever plc v Chefaro Proprietaries Ltd and Another*.[446] The plaintiff company brought an action for patent infringement against the first defendant, a British registered company. The first defendant alleged that the patent was invalid on the ground that the essential features of the invention were obvious. The plaintiff sought to join a Dutch company, the ultimate holding company of the first defendant, as second defendant in the hope of obtaining documents relating to the research and development of the allegedly infringing product so as to show the subject matter of the patent

---

[444] N 442 above at 1123.
[445] This statement was quoted with approval by Dillon LJ in the Court of Appeal, n 442 above, at 1123.
[446] [1994] FSR 135.

was not obvious to them. The Court of Appeal held that there was insufficient evidence that the Dutch company was a party to a common design to commit the acts alleged to constitute infringement, and therefore could not be joined as a substantive defendant.[447]

(c) SATISFYING THE JURISDICTIONAL CRITERIA

The jurisdictional criteria which have to be met in respect of a foreign defendant are no different just because the reason for wishing to join that defendant is in order to obtain discovery. However, in such cases there may be problems in satisfying these criteria. This is shown by the *Mölnlycke* case. There was an attempt to join the German defendant using the multi-defendant provision in Article 6(1) of the Brussels Convention, which requires that the second defendant is a necessary or proper party to the action against the first defendant. Dillon LJ seemingly took the view that this requirement was not satisfied. He said that if the plaintiffs relied only on Article 6, it would be improper to join the German defendant merely to obtain discovery,[448] the point being that discovery could be obtained from that defendant in Germany by an application there under the Hague Convention on the Taking of Evidence Abroad in Civil or Commercial matters. In other words, the German defendant was not a necessary or proper party. There was, however, no problem if the plaintiffs relied on the tort head of Article 5 of the Brussels Convention, which can always be used in multi-defendant cases and contains no such requirement.

3. A Different Approach

Lord Justice Hoffmann, as he then was, criticised the necessity of having to establish that a person or body is a substantive defendant when the purpose of this is not to obtain a final judgment against this additional defendant, but in order to obtain discovery. He also commented on the practical problem of determining which company to join. He thought that the 'logical solution . . . is that discovery of research and development documents should be available against a multi-national on a group basis'.[449] However, he admitted that such a radical change in the law would require legislative change. If it involves taking jurisdiction under the Brussels or Lugano Conventions, it would need an alteration to those Conventions.

---

[447] See above, pp 146–147, in relation to establishing a common design.
[448] N 442 above at 1116–1117. [449] N 446 above at 143.

XII
REFORM

1. CRITICISM OF THE EXISTING LAW

The most notable feature of the existing law under the EC/EFTA rules is the absence of special jurisdictional rules to deal with infringement cases. This contrasts markedly with the position where the proceedings are concerned with registration or validity of patents, etc.[450] Infringement cases have to be dealt with by the application of general rules relating to jurisdiction, in particular the tort provision in Article 5(3) of the Brussels and Lugano Conventions. But infringement cases are particularly complex when compared with many other torts. The use of jurisdiction rules of general application is unsatisfactory for the following reasons.

First, it leads to uncertainty. There is uncertainty over where the act of infringement occurred for the purpose of the tort jurisdiction rule and, indeed, whether this concept should be replaced in certain circumstances by a rule which looks to where the defendant has its establishment. This uncertainty is particularly acute in cases of infringement of copyright over the Internet and by satellite broadcasting. There is uncertainty in cases of multiple acts of infringement, some committed locally and others abroad, over whether Article 5(3) allows jurisdiction over the foreign acts of infringement. There is also uncertainty over the position where invalidity is raised during infringement litigation. This involves a major problem given that there are different jurisdiction rules under the Brussels and Lugano Conventions for the issues of validity and infringement. The Court of Justice may eliminate at least some of this uncertainty following the referral by the Court of Appeal in the *Fort Dodge* case. Finally, there is uncertainty over the role of Article 24 of the Brussels and Lugano Conventions in cases where there is the grant of a cross border injunction, although this uncertainty is in the process of being solved by the Court of Justice.

Secondly, it leads to the use of an inappropriate connecting factor. Damage is not part of the cause of action for infringement cases and a concept of damage has to be artificially created for the purpose of Article 5(3). It follows that it is inappropriate to base jurisdiction on the concept of damage, as happens under the tort jurisdiction rule.

Thirdly, Article 5(3) gives inadequate protection to the holder of the right that has been infringed. Infringement cases can involve threatened wrongs. But the tort jurisdiction rule is not framed in such a way as to deal with this.

---

[450] See above chapter 1.

2. AN ALTERNATIVE SOLUTION

It is worth looking at the position in countries outside the EC/EFTA bloc to see how they deal with infringement cases. It is normal for countries to apply their jurisdictional rules of general application to such cases. These rules, although different from those contained in the Brussels and Lugano Conventions, will not necessarily produce a different result. This is illustrated by looking at one of the leading US cases on infringement, *Honeywell Inc v Metz Apparatewerke*.[451] The Court of Appeals, 7th Circuit, held that Metz, a German manufacturer of electronic flash equipment, which allegedly infringed the US patents of the plaintiff company, which had its principal place of business in Illinois, was subject to jurisdiction in Illinois under that State's long arm statute. The latter provides for jurisdiction if a tortious act, which includes the concept of injury, took place there. Metz was said to have actively induced the infringement which took place in Illinois where injury was suffered. It did so by entering into a distribution agreement with US distributors. The essence of this was Metz's intention to invade the US market (it even provided instruction booklets in English), being fully aware of the plaintiff's patents. If faced with this situation, an English court could assert jurisdiction against Metz on the basis of a common design between the local distributor and Metz leading to an act of infringement by the latter in England, this would then come within Article 5(3) of the Brussels Convention. What is unfamiliar to European lawyers is the discussion in the case of whether the due process requirements under the American Constitution were satisfied. The requisite minimum contacts with Illinois were established. By entering into the agreement for distribution in the United States, Metz promoted American sales and ensured that infringement would take place causing injury to the plaintiff. It made no difference that Metz sold the equipment FOB Germany. To take this into account would allow a foreign manufacturer to insulate itself from jurisdiction.

3. REFORM OF THE JURISDICTIONAL RULES OF GENERAL APPLICATION

It has been seen that, in infringement cases, the application of the jurisdictional rules of general application does not work well. But this can be seen as being as much due to weaknesses in the jurisdictional rules as to special features of infringement cases. Thus, the uncertainty over localising the act of infringement applies not only in relation to infringement cases but in

---

[451] 509 F 2d 1137 (7th Cir 1975). See, generally, on the US position, Trooboff, chapter 8 in McLachlan and Nygh.

relation to any complex situation. The inappropriateness of basing jurisdiction on the concept of damage applies to certain other torts, for example defamation. The weakness in not dealing with threatened wrongs is there in relation to other torts. For a private international lawyer, the solution is obvious: reform the jurisdiction rules. The opportunity to do so is presented by the Diplomatic Conference in 1998 to review the operation of the Brussels and Lugano Conventions. At the very least, Article 5(3) could be redrafted to clearly encompass threatened wrongs. But is it possible to redraft Article 5(3) in such as way as to get rid of all of the present uncertainties, and to do so in such a way that it gives an appropriate answer regardless of the tort involved. There is much to be said for leaving the definition as it is at the moment, deliberately vague, so as to allow for development on a case by case basis. Drafting appropriate rules is much easier if you concentrate solely on infringement. It is important, therefore, to consider the option of special jurisdictional rules for such cases.

4. Special Jurisdictional Rules

The weaknesses in the present law could be solved by having special rules of jurisdiction for infringement cases.[452] This is a solution that is likely to appeal to intellectual property lawyers. It is not as radical a suggestion as may appear at first sight. There are such rules in relation to Community intellectual property rights. These are contained within the framework of substantive law rules, rather than within the framework of a private international law convention. These special jurisdictional rules dealing with the infringement of Community rights will be examined in detail in chapter 7.

If there are to be special jurisdictional rules dealing with the infringement of national intellectual property rights, it has to be decided whether these should be independent rules or contained within the framework of existing jurisdictional rules.

(a) INDEPENDENT JURISDICTIONAL RULES

This would be a very radical approach to adopt. Nonetheless, the special jurisdictional rules dealing with the infringement of community rights are independent of existing private international law rules, though not independent of substantive law rules. Independent jurisdictional rules dealing with the infringement of national rights could be contained in an EC Convention on private international aspects of intellectual property rights, which could deal with issues other than just infringement.

[452] See generally, Trooboff, chapter 8 in McLachlan and Nygh, at p 154; Tugendhat, (1997) 113 *LQR* 360 at 364.

(b) WITHIN THE FRAMEWORK OF EXISTING JURISDICTIONAL RULES

(i) The advantages of the approach

This would be a much less radical approach to adopt. Articles 2, 5 and 6 would remain unaltered. The only exception would be that a special rule would be added to Article 5(3) defining the place where the harmful event occurred in infringement cases. The Diplomatic Conference reviewing the operation of the Lugano and Brussels Conventions in 1998 could recommend this. From there, it could lead to world wide reform. The Hague Conference on private international law is working on a General Convention on Recognition and Enforcement of judgments. This is based on the Brussels Convention. It has been suggested that this Hague Convention should have special provisions to deal with infringement cases.[453] Alternatively, it would be possible for the Court of Justice to use the flexibility of the terms of Article 5(3) to introduce such a definition. However, so far that Court has used the same basic concepts of the place of the event giving rise to the damage and the resulting damage in a complex case of multi-State defamation,[454] and so is unlikely to depart from this approach in infringement cases.

(ii) The suggested rules

(a) *Additions to Article 5(3)*

(i) *The place where the act of infringement has been committed or threatened*

In infringement cases, the place where the harmful event occurred should be defined as being where the act of infringement has been committed or threatened.[455] This basis of jurisdiction is to be found in relation to the infringement of Community rights.[456] This would get rid of the inappropriate connecting factor of damage and deal effectively with threatened wrongs. It would not solve the uncertainty over where the act of infringement occurred. This would have to be left to the Court of Justice to solve as cases present themself to that Court.

(ii) *Local acts only*

It should also be provided, for the sake of clarification, that in cases of multiple acts of infringement, some committed locally and others committed abroad, a court will only have jurisdiction under Article 5(3) in relation to local acts committed or threatened. This provision is to be found in the

---

[453] Trooboff, n 452 above.
[454] See below, pp 396–399.
[455] See, generally, Tritton, para 13.010.
[456] See below, pp 325–326.

special rules in relation to Community rights.[457] Of course, it will still be possible to consolidate the litigation in one State by bringing the action in the State where the defendant is domiciled.

(b) A special rule for where invalidity is raised during the course of infringement litigation

This would still leave the uncertainty over the position where invalidity is raised during the course of infringement litigation. There is no such uncertainty in relation to the infringement of Community rights.[458] We can look briefly at the example of Community trade marks[459] to see how this has been achieved. A system of national Community trade mark courts has been set up. These courts have exclusive jurisdiction not only in respect of infringement but also in respect of counterclaims for revocation or for a declaration of invalidity. The rules on international jurisdiction apply in relation to all such proceedings. There are no separate bases of international jurisdiction for, on the one hand, infringement and, on the other hand, counterclaims for revocation or for a declaration of invalidity. This achieves the desirable result that the same court in the same Member State deals with both issues.

Under the Brussels and Lugano Conventions there are, of course, separate bases of jurisdiction for validity and infringement. This works perfectly satisfactorily where a case raises just the issue of validity or just the issue of infringement. However, where invalidity is raised during the course of infringement proceedings there is not only uncertainty but also the possibility of the two issues being split between the courts of different Contracting States. It is manifestly desirable that the courts in one Contracting State should be able to try both issues.[460] This can be achieved by adding a special jurisdictional rule for infringement cases giving the courts of the Contracting State with infringement jurisdiction (on whatever basis) the power to try the issue of invalidity when this arises during the course of the infringement litigation. It would not matter how the issue of invalidity was raised. It could be raised as a defence or by way of a counterclaim or even by way of separate revocation proceedings,[461] provided that invalidity was raised during the course of the infringement litigation. If the courts in one Contracting State are to try both issues, it would be possible to achieve this by giving the court with validity jurisdiction the power to try the issue of infringement. However, it is submitted that chanelling both issues into the courts of the Contracting State with

---

[457] See below, pp 325–328, 343, 346.   [458] See below, pp 318–358.
[459] See below, pp 321–326.   [460] See above, p 209.
[461] In this last situation, the courts of the Contracting State with validity jurisdiction should also be able to try the revocation proceedings.

validity jurisdiction would unnecessarily widen out infringement jurisdiction, allocating it to the courts of a Contracting State other than one with jurisdiction under the normal bases of jurisdiction that operate in infringement cases.

If the issue of validity is raised before the commencement of infringement proceedings and, in the light of the decision on validity, there are subsequent infringement proceedings, it may well be that the two issues are tried before the courts of different Contracting States, depending on whether the courts of the Contracting State with validity jurisdiction also, coincidentally, have infringement jurisdiction.

(iii) What about infringement over the internet?

(a) *Should territorial connections be used at all?*

There is an argument that, in cases of infringement over the internet, jurisdiction should not be based on territorial connections at all. The internet ignores territorial boundaries. Users do not realise that they are crossing State boundaries, and no one can stop a person from abroad from accessing a site. It has been suggested that everything takes place in cyberspace, and that there should be a separate jurisdiction for cyberspace.[462]

This is all pretty unconvincing stuff. There is a danger of becoming carried away by the excitement of the new technology. Cyberspace is not outer space. In internet cases, there are territorial connections with various States. The plaintiff and defendant will be resident/domiciled in particular States. The uploading and the downloading will take place in States. Computers are used and these will be situated in States, it is even possible to consider software as being located in a State. Moreover, if you reject the use of territorial connections what is jurisdiction to be based on? There is, though, a question of which territorial connection should be used in internet cases.

(b) *Which territorial connection should be used?*

In theory, it would be possible to base jurisdiction on any of the territorial connections mentioned in the previous paragraph. However, in reality, the choice is between a special rule based on the act of infringement (place of uploading or downloading) or one based on a personal connecting factor (the plaintiff's or defendant's domicile/residence). A rule based on where computers are located does not work well because you quickly face the problem that the information may be routed via a server located in a

---

[462] See generally, Burnstein, (1996) 29 *Vanderbilt Journal of Transnational Law* 75, who is concerned about choice of law rather than jurisdiction. See also Perritt, n 113 above, at 100–103.

country which has no connection with the parties or the uploading or downloading.

Of the realistic alternatives then, is it right in internet cases to base jurisdiction on the act of infringement? Admittedly, there is the problem over localising this act. But this problem is not confined to internet cases, it is simply a question of degree in that the problem is particularly difficult in such cases. But then it is also very difficult to locate the act of infringement in cases of satellite broadcasting. Moreover, the alternatives of the domicile/residence of the plaintiff or defendant are unworkable in the European context. A special rule for internet cases, if it is to come within the framework of existing rules, would have to operate alongside Article 2 of the Brussels and Lugano Conventions. The Conventions already have a rule in Article 2 allocating jurisdiction to the State of the defendant's domicile. The Court of Justice has rejected the allocation of jurisdiction to the State of the plaintiff's domicile under Article 5(3). We are left then with a special rule based on the act of infringement. The only thing that is needed is clarification of where this is to be localised. It is submitted, for the reasons given above,[463] that in cases of infringement over the internet this should be regarded as being located in the State where the uploading (input) of the information took place.

---

[463] At pp 158–161.

6

Infringement: Jurisdiction Under the Traditional Rules

I	Introduction	241
II	Bases of jurisdiction	241
	1. Service of a writ within the jurisdiction	241
	(a) Presence within the jurisdiction	241
	(b) The advantages of service within the jurisdiction	243
	2. Service of a writ out of the jurisdiction	243
	(a) The heads of Order 11, rule 1(1)	244
	(b) A serious issue to be tried	256
	(c) The exercise of the discretion	259
III	Declining jurisdiction and restraining foreign proceedings	266
	1. *Forum non conveniens*	267
	(a) The role of *forum non conveniens*	267
	(b) The principles to be applied when exercising the discretion	267
	(c) A stay pending a decision abroad in relation to validity	272
	(d) A multiplicity of proceedings	273
	2. Restraining foreign proceedings	275
	(a) Trial is available in England and abroad	275
	(b) Trial is available in alternative fora abroad (but not in England)	276
	(c) The bringing of proceedings abroad is an invasion of a legal or equitable right not to be sued there	277
	(d) The bringing of the proceedings abroad would be unconscionable	277
IV	State immunity	279
V	Subject matter limitations in relation to jurisdiction	279
	1. Foreign immovable property	280
	(a) The exclusionary rule in relation to foreign immovable property	280
	(b) The classification of intellectual property rights	281
	2. Foreign intellectual property rights	283
	(a) Origin and development of the limitation	283

		(b)	Policy considerations	290
		(c)	The solution: the doctrine of *forum non conveniens*	293
		(d)	Confusion between jurisdiction and choice of law	295
		(e)	Should different foreign intellectual property rights be treated the same?	298
		(f)	Should different issues be treated the same?	299
	3.	Infringements abroad		299
		(a)	The authorities	300
		(b)	Policy considerations	303
		(c)	The solution: the doctrine of *forum non conveniens*	304
		(d)	Confusion between jurisdiction and choice of law	305
		(e)	Can a successful action be brought?	305
	4.	Intra-UK cases		306
VI	Forum shopping			306
	1.	The choice of fora		306
		(a)	Within Europe	306
		(b)	Outside Europe	307
	2.	The advantages to be obtained		307
VII	Infringement and validity			307
	1.	The significance of Article 16(4)		307
	2.	A defence of invalidity		308
		(a)	No problem under the present law	308
		(b)	The problem if there is jurisdiction in relation to foreign intellectual property rights	310
	3.	A counterclaim for revocation		311
	4.	Separate revocation proceedings		312
VIII	Interim relief			312
IX	International discovery			313
	1.	The need to join a foreigner as a substantive defendant		313
	2.	Difficulties involved		314
	3.	A different approach		314
X	Reform			314
	1.	Criticism of the existing law		314
	2.	Reform of the jurisdictional rules of general application		315
	3.	Special jurisdictional rules		315
		(a)	Within the framework of existing rules	315
		(b)	The suggested rules	315

I
INTRODUCTION

In the situation where the EC/EFTA rules, outlined in the previous chapter, do not apply, recourse must be had to the traditional rules on jurisdiction. These rules are more complicated than the EC/EFTA rules. It is not simply a question of finding a basis of jurisdiction in respect of a foreign defendant, it also has to be asked whether the English court will exercise its discretionary powers to stay the action. Moreover, in infringement cases, there are subject matter limitations in relation to jurisdiction which do not exist under the EC/EFTA rules.

II
BASES OF JURISDICTION

1. Service of a Writ Within the Jurisdiction

(a) presence within the jurisdiction

(i) The rules

The English courts are competent to try an action *in personam* in the situation where there has been service of a writ on a defendant present within the jurisdiction.[1] Mere transient presence of an individual will suffice. With corporate defendants, it is necessary to see if a company is registered in England under the Companies Act 1985. If so, service of the writ can be effected by sending it to the registered office of the company.[2] With a foreign company the position is more complicated.

The Companies Act 1985, as amended,[3] distinguishes between foreign companies which have a branch in Great Britain and those that have established a place of business, which is not a branch, in Great Britain.

A limited company which is incorporated outside the United Kingdom and Gibraltar, and has a branch[4] in Great Britain is required to register with the registrar of companies the names and addresses of all persons resident in Great Britain authorised to accept on the company's behalf service of process in respect of the business of the branch.[5] Process in respect of the carrying on of the business of a branch is sufficiently served if addressed to any such person and is left at or sent by post to that address.[6]

---

[1] See Cheshire and North, pp 183–188.   [2] Companies Act 1985, s 725(1).
[3] See SI 1992/3179.   [4] For the interpretation of branch see Schedule 21A, para 13.
[5] Section 690A and Schedule 21A, 3(e).   [6] Section 694A(2).

Where a company fails to comply with its statutory obligations to so register, or if all the persons named are dead or have ceased to reside in Great Britain, or refuse to accept service on the company's behalf, or for any other reason cannot be served, a document may be served on the company in respect of the carrying on of the business of the branch by leaving it at, or sending it by post to, any place of business[7] established by the company in Great Britain.[8]

A company incorporated elsewhere than in Great Britain which establishes a place of business in Great Britain (this does not include a limited company which is incorporated outside the United Kingdom and Gibraltar, and has a branch in the United Kingdom[9]) is required to file with the registrar of companies the names and addresses of some one or more persons resident in Great Britain authorised to accept service of process on its behalf.[10] If a company fails to comply with its statutory obligations, or if the persons on the register are dead or no longer resident here, or refuse to accept service on the company's behalf, or for any reason cannot be served, the writ may be served on the company by leaving it at, or sending it by post to, 'any place of business established by the company in Great Britain'.[11] There may, of course, be some argument over whether the foreign company has *established a place of business* in Great Britain. There is no rigid list of requirements for this but it is relevant to see, *inter alia*, whether there are staff in England, premises and a person who can bind the foreign company contractually.[12] A typical branch office will have these characteristics, but branches are subject to the rules set out in the previous paragraph. More to the point, an independent commercial agency may have these characteristics. It is important to note that there is no requirement that the dispute has to relate to the activities of the business carried on at the place of business which has been established in Great Britain. This contrasts with the position in relation to branches where the provisions on service are dealing with service *in respect of the carrying on of the business of the branch*.

(ii) Application in infringement cases

In infringement cases, it will often not be possible to serve a writ within the jurisdiction.[13] A common scenario, in such cases, is that where there is a

---

[7] For a Dutch comment on this issue, see REPdR [1986] *Intellectuele Eigendom & Reclamerecht* 47.
[8] Section 694A(3).   [9] Section 690B.   [10] Companies Act 1985, s 691.
[11] Companies Act 1985, s 695.
[12] *Adams* v *Cape Industries plc* [1990] Ch 433 at 530–531. See also *South India Shipping Corpn Ltd* v *Export-Import Bank of Korea* [1985] 1 WLR 585.
[13] For a German example of a case where no problem arose in suing a defendant that was present in the jurisdiction in relation to the infringement of a foreign patent, see the judgment of 27 October 1966 of the Landsgericht in Düsseldorf, [1968] GRUR 101.

foreign corporate manufacturer of an infringing product. The plaintiff wishes to sue that company in England. The defendant has sought to penetrate the English market by setting up a subsidiary company in England which will market the product.[14] This is not a branch and so the provisions on branches cannot be used. Moreover, it is doubtful whether the foreign defendant can be regarded as having established a place of business in Great Britain when it carries on business here by means of a subsidiary company. Under English company law principles, the foreign parent and English subsidiary are separate legal entities. Normally, the English subsidiary will be carrying on its own business rather than that of the parent. The upshot is that the foreign parent cannot be subjected to jurisdiction by virtue of service of a writ on its English subsidiary.[15]

(b) THE ADVANTAGES OF SERVICE WITHIN THE JURISDICTION

It is always advantageous to the plaintiff to serve the writ within the jurisdiction wherever possible. First, service in such cases is effected as of right, whereas the court's permission is needed for service of a writ out of the jurisdiction.[16] However, after the writ has been served within the jurisdiction the defendant may be able to obtain a stay of the English proceedings on the basis of *forum non conveniens*.[17] The onus will be on the defendant to show that there is a clearly more appropriate forum for trial abroad.

Secondly, because service within the jurisdiction does not require the court's permission, there is no necessity to go into the merits of the case at the jurisdictional stage. An examination of the merits is required in all cases of service of a writ out of the jurisdiction under Order 11, rule 1(1),[18] and is a very noticeable feature in infringement cases.

2. SERVICE OF A WRIT OUT OF THE JURISDICTION

A judge faced with a question of leave to serve proceedings out of the jurisdiction under Order 11, rule 1(1) of the Rules of the Supreme Court has to be satisfied: first, that there is a good arguable case that one of the heads (paragraphs) of rule 1(1) is satisfied; secondly, that there is a serious issue to be tried on the merits; thirdly, that the discretion should be exercised to allow service of a writ out of the jurisdiction.[19]

---

[14] See, eg *Unilever plc v Gillette (UK) Ltd* [1989] RPC 583; *Unilever plc v Chefaro Proprietaries Ltd and Another* [1994] FSR 135.
[15] See the *Adams* case, n 12 above. For an unusual example where a parent acted on behalf of its subsidiary see Case 218/86 *Sar Schotte GmbH v Parfums Rothschild* [1987] ECR 4905; see above, p 170. See, generally, Fawcett, (1988) 37 *ICLQ* 645.
[16] See below, p 259.   [17] See below, pp 267–274.   [18] See below, pp 256–258.
[19] *Seaconsar Far East Ltd v Bank Markazi Jomhouri Islami Iran* [1993] 3 WLR 756 at 767 (*per* Lord Goff).

(a) THE HEADS OF ORDER 11, RULE 1(1)

As previously mentioned,[20] the onus is on the plaintiff to establish a good arguable case that one of the heads of rule 1(1) is satisfied.[21] Three of these are particularly relevant in infringement cases: the tort head; the multi-defendant head; and the injunction head.

(i) The tort head

Rule 1(1)(f) provides that service of a writ out of the jurisdiction is permissible with the leave of the court when:

> the claim is founded on a tort and the damage was sustained, or resulted from an act committed, within the jurisdiction.

It is well established that an action for infringement is tortious[22] and thus 'the claim is founded on a tort' within the wording of paragraph (f).

This is a very widely drafted provision, for it allows an English court to take jurisdiction if either the damage was sustained or an act, from which the damage resulted, was committed in England. It was drafted in this way so as to bring jurisdiction under the English traditional rules into line with Article 5(3) of the Brussels Convention, as interpreted by the Court of Justice.[23]

(a) *An act, from which the damage resulted, was committed in England*

In infringement cases, the relevant act is undoubtedly the act of infringement. What is required, therefore, is that an act of infringement was committed in England.

(i) *Patents*

It has already been seen[24] that, normally, there is no problem in ascertaining where an act of patent infringement was committed. The more specific question of whether an act of patent infringement was committed *in England* has not infrequently been discussed by the courts, but in the context of establishing liability[25] rather than in that of establishing that the tort head of Order 11, rule 1(1), is satisfied. *Kalman and Another v PCL Packaging (UK) Ltd and Another*[26] is a good example. This was an Order 11 case, in which there was much discussion in the judgment of whether liability had been established, as is necessary in all such cases because of the requirement that there is a serious issue to be tried on the merits. Having decided

---

[20] See above, p 40.   [21] The *Seaconsar* case, *ibid*.   [22] See above, p 150.
[23] Article 5(3) is discussed above, pp 150–169. Article 5(3) of the Lugano Convention is identically worded.
[24] See above, p 156.   [25] See above, pp 145–149.   [26] [1982] FSR 406.

that there was no liability under Section 60(1) and (2) the 1977 Patents Act on the part of the US defendant, there having been no act of individual infringement committed by the defendant in the United Kingdom,[27] it was held that the tort head of Order 11, rule 1(1) was not satisfied.[28] The result was that Falconer J set aside the writ and service against the US defendant, struck out the statement of claim as against that defendant, and granted a declaration that the court had no jurisdiction over that defendant in respect of the subject matter of the action or the relief claimed.

The pattern is the same in the Order 11 cases involving allegations of joint infringement. The emphasis in these cases has been upon establishing liability which requires an act of infringement *in England*. Once this has been established the courts have taken it for granted that the tort head of Order 11, rule 1(1) is satisfied in respect of the foreign defendant. What you have is an obvious act of infringement, such as marketing an infringing product, committed in England by an English defendant in respect of which the foreign defendant is a joint tortfeasor, and can, accordingly, be regarded as having committed an act of infringement in England. This is illustrated by one of the leading cases on joint infringement, *Unilever plc v Gillette (UK) Ltd*.[29]

The plaintiff, which was the proprietor of a European patent (UK) for an antiperspirant, commenced infringement proceedings against an English defendant (GUK) complaining of the importation into the United Kingdom from the United States of an antiperspirant (Apache). The plaintiff then sought leave to join as defendant[30] the US parent (Boston) of GUK, which sold Apache to GUK, and serve a writ out of the jurisdiction on it. It was argued that Boston was a joint infringer with GUK.

The Court of Appeal held that the plaintiffs had established a good arguable case of a common design,[31] and leave to serve out of the jurisdiction was granted. The tort head of Order 11 was referred to by Falconer J at first instance.[32] It was not specifically referred to in the Court of Appeal, although Mustill LJ did say that if GUK and Boston were joint tortfeasors the case would fall within Order 11.[33] One important point to note is that if there is an act of infringement in England, not only is there a basis of jurisdiction but also the subject matter limitation on jurisdiction in respect of infringements abroad will not apply.[34]

Similarly, in *The Electric Furnace Co v Selas Corpn of America*,[35] the first defendant was a US company engaged in the design and manufacture of

---

[27] See above, p 146. An allegation of joint tortfeasance was also rejected.
[28] At 424.   [29] [1989] RPC 583.
[30] This was done so as to try to force Boston to disclose certain technical documents. See below, p 313.
[31] See above, pp 146–147.   [32] At 588.   [33] At 601.
[34] See below, pp 299–306. Also Trooboff, in McLachlan and Nygh, pp 128–132.
[35] [1987] RPC 23. See also *Puschner v Tom Palmer (Scotland) Ltd and Another* [1989] RPC 430.

furnaces for use in steel plants. Acting in collaboration, the first defendant designed and the second defendant, a UK company, made and installed a furnace, in the United Kingdom, which allegedly infringed the plaintiff's patent. Slade LJ, in the Court of Appeal, said that, in such circumstances, the action was unquestionably founded on a tort committed within the jurisdiction under the tort head of Order 11.[36] An application for discharge of an order granting leave to serve a writ out of the jurisdiction on the first defendant was rejected at first instance, and the appeal against this was dismissed.

The same principles apply in Australia.[37] In the United States, some States have interpreted their long-arm statute to focus on the tortious act. The relevant act in infringement cases has been held to be the sale of infringing products.[38] A foreign supplier which sells to a US distributor is subject to jurisdiction because of its involvement in the act of infringement in the United States. The foreign supplier could be liable for inducing infringement.

The above English cases were decided at a time when the standard of proof in Order 11 cases, both for establishing liability and establishing that the tort head of Order 11 was satisfied, was that of a good arguable case. This is no longer so. Following the House of Lords decision in *Seaconsar Far East Ltd v Bank Markazi Jomhouri Islami Iran*,[39] a plaintiff only has to show that there is a serious issue on the merits to be tried. On the other hand, it is necessary to show a good arguable case that the head of Order 11 is satisfied. It follows that the fact that a plaintiff has shown that there is a serious issue on the merits that a foreign defendant is liable for having committed (either individually or jointly) an infringement *in England* does not automatically establish that there is a good arguable case that the tort head of Order 11 is satisfied on the basis that the defendant has committed an act of infringement *in England*. Fortunately, one other change introduced by the *Seaconsar* case relates to the order in which the different requirements under Order 11 are dealt with. Prior to the *Seaconsar* case, it was normal for liability to be established first and the head of Order 11 second. The House of Lords has reversed this order. As a result, it may well be that attention will now focus on whether an act of infringement (individual or joint) has been committed *in England* by the defendant for the purpose of satisfying the tort head of Order 11. Once a good arguable case to this effect has been shown, this will necessarily establish that there is a

---

[36] N 35 above, at pp 30–31.

[37] See *Best Australia Ltd and Others v Aquagas Marketing Pty Ltd and Others* (1988) 83 ALR 217.

[38] See, generally, Wille, (1991) 90 *Mich L Rev* 658, 668; *Huchel v Sybron Corp* 212 USPQ 133 (SD Tex 1980).

[39] [1993] 3 WLR 756; see below, p 256.

serious issue to be tried on the merits under English law that a foreign defendant is liable for having committed an infringement *in England*.[40]

(ii) *Copyrights*

It has been seen earlier[41] that there is, normally, no difficulty in ascertaining the State where the act of copyright infringement takes place.[42] It has also been seen that there is a problem where the alleged act of infringement is that of the authorisation abroad of an act of infringement in the United Kingdom. In the *ABKCO* case,[43] which discussed this problem, the Court of Appeal regarded the problem and solution thereto, as being the same regardless of whether it was a case brought under Article 5(3) of the Brussels Convention or Order 11, rule 1(1)(f).[44]

In complex cases involving infringement of copyright by satellite broadcasting there is, of course, a very real difficulty in identifying what the act of infringement is and where this takes place.[45] With satellite broadcasting, the act of infringement is committed either in the State of origin or in the State of reception. It has been argued that, as far as the Brussels and Lugano Conventions are concerned, a State of origin rule, should be adopted. However, when it comes to Order 11 there is authority in relation to broadcasting, unlike in Brussels and Lugano Convention cases, and this supports a State of reception rule.

The leading case is *Composers, Authors and Publishers Association of Canada Ltd* v *International Good Music Inc et al*,[46] a decision of the Supreme Court of Canada, decided under the old tort head of Order 11, applicable in Canada, which required that a tort was committed within the jurisdiction.

One of the defendants was a company incorporated in the State of Washington, where it had its head office, which operated a radio and television station in that State whose primary object was to transmit programmes for reception in Canada. It was alleged that this company had committed a tort in British Columbia by the transmission of programmes, beamed at Canada, in which musical works, in respect of which the plaintiff had a copyright, were played.

---

[40] For the problem where the defendant denies that there has been an infringement, see below, pp 307–311.

[41] See above, pp 156–157.

[42] For an example of a case where jurisdiction was established on the basis of the fact that a publicity folder that was to be distributed abroad was printed in the Netherlands, see the judgment of 18 February 1971 of the President of the Arrondissementsrechtbank (district court) in Haarlem, [1973] BIE 99 (No 24). Compare also the Austrian unfair competition case that focuses on the reception in Austria of telexes that had been sent from abroad, Judgment of 29 October 1985 of the Austrian Supreme Court (Case 4 Ob 370/85), [1986] 6 EIPR D-91.

[43] *ABKCO Music & Records Inc* v *Music Collection International Ltd and Another* [1995] RPC 657; discussed above.

[44] *Ibid*, at 660, 664–665.   [45] See above, pp 157–158.   [46] (1963) 37 DLR (2d) 1.

The Supreme Court of Canada held that a tort had been committed in Canada. This was on the basis that the musical works had been communicated there. This accepted that it is the reception of the broadcast that is the crucial element for this purpose, not its original transmission.

An English court may be tempted to apply this definition. A State of reception rule allows an English plaintiff to bring an action in England against a foreign broadcaster on the basis of the reception of the broadcast in England. A State of origin rule is of little practical use to English plaintiffs in this respect. If the broadcast is transmitted from England, it is likely that the defendant is present in England and a writ can be served within the jurisdiction anyway. It is arguable that the real need is to have the ability, under Order 11, rule 1(1), to serve a writ out of the jurisdiction on foreign broadcasters.

Nonetheless, Order 11, rule 1(1)(f) is designed to introduce into the traditional rules of jurisdiction the rule to be found in Article 5(3) of the Brussels and Lugano Conventions, as interpreted in the *Mines de Potasse* case. It makes sense then for any interpretation adopted for the latter to also be adopted for the former. This policy is supported by the Court of Appeal in the *ABKCO* case. Moreover, the need to found jurisdiction under the place of acting rule is nowadays perhaps not so urgent given that there is the alternative of founding jurisdiction on the basis that the damage was sustained in England. This alternative was not available under the old tort head of Order 11, which was the head being discussed in the *Composers* case. Finally, the Satellite Broadcasting Directive,[47] by defining the act of broadcasting, in effect, in terms of the origin of the broadcast rather than its reception, determines what the jurisdictional rule should be. It is submitted, therefore, that in cases of satellite broadcasting the act from which the damage resulted should be regarded as being committed in England if this was the State of origin of the broadcast.

(iii) *Infringement over the internet*

The same difficulty in localising the act of infringement of a copyright, patent or trade mark over the internet arises under the traditional rules as under the EC/EFTA rules. Should the same solution be adopted whereby the infringement is regarded as occurring in the place of uploading? The arguments for applying the same solution in Order 11, rule 1(1)(f) cases as in Article 5(3) cases are set out above in the context of satellite broadcasting, and apply equally to internet cases. It is submitted, therefore, that in cases of infringement over the internet the act from which the damage

---

[47] EC Council Directive 93/83/EEC of 27 September 1993 on the co-ordination of certain rules concerning copyright and rights related to copyright applicable to satellite broadcasting and cable retransmission, [1993] OJ L248/15, Article 1(2)(b). The Directive is discussed below in the context of choice of law, chapter 10 pp 504–506.

resulted should be regarded as being committed in England if this was the State where the information was uploaded.

(b) *Damage was sustained in England*

(i) *The nature of the problem*

As has been seen when discussing Article 5(3) of the Brussels and Lugano Conventions, it is normally easy to identify the State in which damage was sustained in cases of material damage. It is the State in which the victim was injured or died, or the State in which property was damaged. There can be a problem in cases of financial damage, which may involve damage in more than one State. Nonetheless, damage there clearly is and the only difficulty is identifying where it took place. In infringement cases, the problem is more fundamental because it is by no means clear what the damage is in such cases, let alone where it was sustained.

Although the tort head has been worded in its current form since 1987, there is a shortage of authority, generally, on the meaning of damage. There is some authority for the proposition that the damage caused must be direct and not indirect. This was so decided by Jacob J in *Beecham Group plc and Another* v *Norton Healthcare Ltd and Others*,[48] in the context of the tort of detention and wrongful interference. The learned Judge said that a mere effect on the plaintiff's financial position in England, for example because it is a company damaged by the tort abroad, is not enough. On the facts of the case, the direct damage to the plaintiff was caused by the sale in England of the product by the English importer not the wrongful interference by the defendant Slovenian manufacturer and supplier. As a result, the case did not come within rule 1(1)(f).[49]

There is even less authority on the meaning of damage in the context of infringement. This is not surprising. What rule 1(1) (f) allows for is the conferring of jurisdiction on the English courts in the situation where damage was sustained in England as the result of an act committed abroad. But, in infringement cases, there is authority to the effect that there is a subject matter limitation on jurisdiction in relation to acts of infringement committed abroad.[50] Moreover, it will normally be impossible to establish liability under English law in this situation, with the result that the separate

---

[48] [1997] FSR 81 at 97–98. He was following the decision of Rix J in *The Eras EIL Actions and Bastone & Firminger* v *Nasima Enterprises* (Unreported) 20 May 1996. But compare *Barings plc and Another* v *Coopers & Lybrand (A Firm) and Others* [1997] IL Pr 12, 24–25 – massive losses incurred by Singapore subsidiary leading to collapse of whole group of companies, damage held to be sustained in England because of losses in value of English subsidiaries; affd by CA without discussion of this point, [1997] IL Pr 576.

[49] It was possible, though, to bring the case within the multi-defendant head.

[50] See below, pp 299–303.

requirement, that there is a serious issue on the merits to be tried, will not be satisfied.[51] As the law stands at the moment then, there is little point in a prolonged discussion which seeks to identify whether damage was sustained in England since the English courts do not have jurisdiction under the traditional rules unless an act of infringement occurred in England, and jurisdiction can then be taken on that basis. However, if, as is suggested later on,[52] the current subject matter limitation on jurisdiction in relation to foreign infringements is removed, jurisdiction on the basis of damage sustained in England comes into its own. The following discussion is in anticipation of this.

(ii) *Considerations when fixing upon a definition*

The English courts are entirely free to develop their own concept of damage for the purpose of Order 11, rule 1(1)(f). One option, though, that is not available is to ignore the concept of damage altogether. This is different from the position in relation to Article 5(3) of the Brussels and Lugano Conventions, where one option is to ignore the concept of damage and to revert to the actual wording of the provision and look for the place where the harmful event occurred. The English courts will have to apply the concept of damage in infringement cases, even though it is inappropriate to use this concept in such cases.

In fixing upon the best definition, it is important to recall that jurisdiction on the basis that damage was sustained in England is designed to be an alternative to jurisdiction on the basis that an act, from which damage resulted, was committed in England. There is an argument for saying that damage for the purpose of rule 1(1)(f) should be defined in exactly the same way as it is in relation to Article 5(3). This, in effect, was what Jacob J was doing in the *Beecham* case. After all, the wording of the former is based on the interpretation of the latter provision in the *Mines de Potasse d'Alsace* case. However, it is important to note that the principles of interpretation of the Conventions, as laid down by the Court of Justice,[53] are very different from the principles adopted by English courts when interpreting the traditional English rules of jurisdiction. For example, interpretation of Article 5(3) takes into account the sound administration of justice and the efficacious conduct of proceedings, and the desire to avoid the multiplication of courts of competent jurisdiction. This latter consideration does not apply when the only issue is whether the English courts have jurisdiction. Neither do those decisions of the Court of Justice[54] apply which prohibit the conferring of jurisdiction on the basis of indirect eco-

---

[51] It may be possible to establish liability according to the foreign law of the State where the act of infringement took place, see below p 623.
[52] See below, p 316.   [53] See above, pp 152–153.
[54] The *Dumez* case, p 163 n 134 above; the *Marinari* case, p 163 n 136 above.

nomic loss occurring in the forum. It could, therefore, be decided that damage was sustained in England if indirect economic loss occurred there.

(iii) *The options*

When it comes to ascertaining whether damage was sustained in England for the purpose of Order 11, rule 1(1)(f), most of the same options apply as those already examined[55] when discussing the place where the damage occurred under Article 5(3) of the Brussels and Lugano Conventions, with the one addition of an indirect economic loss rule. It follows that jurisdiction in England could be based on the fact that:

(i) damage to the intellectual property right was sustained in England; or
(ii) direct economic loss to the plaintiff was sustained in England; or
(iii) indirect economic loss to the plaintiff was sustained in England.

The first of these options involves further definitional problems. The second, whilst normally easy to ascertain (it is where sales are lost[56]), does not cater for cases where there is no such loss and does not provide any wider jurisdiction than that conferred by the act of infringement limb of rule 1(1)(f). The third option is, normally, easy to ascertain. For example, an English incorporated company which has lost sales in New York, where the act of infringement occurred, will suffer indirect economic loss in England by way of lost profits. In its favour, it does at least confer a wider jurisdiction on the English courts than that already conferred under the act of infringement limb of rule 1(1)(f). Moreover, there is authority in the United States to the effect that injury in infringement cases takes place where the plaintiff resides or does business.[57] However, it goes against the decision of Jacob J in the *Beecham* case, albeit not in the context of infringement, and it means that the definition of damage for rule 1(1)(f) purposes would be different from that used in relation to Article 5(3) of the Brussels and Lugano Conventions. Neither does it cater for cases where there is no such loss. These are strong reasons for not adopting this third option. Neither of the other two options is entirely satisfactory and serves to bring

---

[55] See above, pp 163–169. It is submitted that a definition in terms of the places where the publication is distributed, derived from the decision of the Court of Justice in the multi-State defamation case of *Shevill* v *Presse Alliance SA* Case C-68/93 [1995] ECR I-415, is not appropriate under the traditional English rules.

[56] For US authority in support of injury at the place where sales are lost, see *Interface Biomedical Laboratories* v *Axiom Medical, Inc* 600 F Supp 731, 225 USPQ 146 (EDNY 1985). See generally, Wille, n 38 above, at 667–668.

[57] *Acrison, Inc* v *Control and Metering Ltd et al* 730 F Supp 1445 (NE ILL 1990); *Honeywell, Inc* v *Metz Apparatewerke* 647 F 2d 200 (DC 1981). See generally, Wille, n 38 above, at 666–667. The reasoning is that this is where the intellectual property right is injured. These cases can therefore equally support the first of the alternatives.

home the point that it is inappropriate to base jurisdiction on the concept of damage in infringement cases.

(c) *Multiple acts of infringement and multiple damage*

The same problem in relation to multiple acts of infringement and multiple damage arises under the tort head of Order 11, rule 1(1) as arises under Article 5(3) of the Brussels and Lugano Conventions.[58] It is doubtful whether an English court which has jurisdiction under the tort head on the basis of an act of infringement committed within the jurisdiction also has jurisdiction under that head in relation to other acts of infringement committed abroad. Order 11, rule 1(1) is regarded as being an 'exorbitant' or 'extraordinary' basis of jurisdiction.[59] It has been said that if the construction of the Order is at all doubtful it should be resolved in favour of the defendant.[60] For the same reason, it is doubtful whether an English court which has jurisdiction on the basis of damage committed within the jurisdiction also has jurisdiction under the tort head in relation to other damage sustained abroad. Moreover, even if technically the tort head is satisfied, there would be difficulties when it comes to the exercise of the *forum conveniens* discretion. It would be very hard for the plaintiff to establish that England is the clearly appropriate forum for trial if the substance of the action was concerned with acts of infringement committed, or damage sustained, abroad.[61] Indeed, the presence of this discretionary element means that the precise question of whether, in such circumstances, there is jurisdiction under the tort head may never be addressed, instead the court may simply decide that England is not the *forum conveniens*.

(d) *Threatened wrongs*

Rule 1(1)(f) is phrased in the past tense and, therefore, does not appear to cover threatened wrongs. Nonetheless, rather surprisingly, Jacob J has said that it is reasonably clear that under this provision 'it makes no difference whether or not the damage has occurred or is merely threatened'.[62] What is certain though is that a plaintiff who wishes to obtain a *quia timet* injunction to prevent such a wrong can use the injunction head of Order 11.[63] Furthermore, in cases where proceedings have been or are to be commenced abroad, it is possible, by virtue of Section 25 of the Civil

---

[58] See above, pp 161–162, 167–168.
[59] *Spiliada Maritime Corpn* v *Cansulex Ltd* [1987] 1 AC 460 at 481.
[60] *The Siskina* [1979] AC 210.
[61] See below, pp 270–271. Cf the position in relation to defamation, below p 408.
[62] *Beecham Group plc and Another* v *Norton Healthcare Ltd and Others* [1997] FSR 81 at 97.
[63] See below, p 256.

Infringement: Jurisdiction under the traditional rules   253

Jurisdiction and Judgments Act 1982, for an English court to grant an interlocutory injunction preventing a threatened wrong in England.[64]

(ii) The multi-defendant head

As has previously been mentioned,[65] rule 1(1)(c) provides that service of a writ out of the jurisdiction is permissible with the leave of the court where 'the claim is brought against a person duly served within or out of the jurisdiction and a person out of the jurisdiction is a necessary or proper party thereto.'

(a) *Application in infringement cases*

This is the only head of Order 11, rule 1(1) which deals specifically with multi-defendant cases.[66] With international infringement actions, it is common practice to bring the proceedings against more than one defendant. Typically, the two defendants will be the foreign manufacturer or supplier of the infringing product and the English seller. Rule 1(1)(c) looks tailor made to deal with this scenario. The English defendant will have been duly served within the jurisdiction and the foreign defendant is a necessary or proper party to that action. A simple example is *The Washburn and Moen, & C, Company* v *The Cunard Steamship Company and J C Parkes and Sons*.[67]

The plaintiffs, an American company, were the owners of a patent for making barbed wire. The second defendants, J C Parkes and Sons, a firm which carried on business in Ireland, had bought from another American firm wire which, it was alleged, infringed the plaintiffs' patent. This wire was consigned to the second defendants on board a ship belonging to the first defendants who landed the wire at Liverpool from where it was to be transhipped to Ireland. The plaintiffs obtained an injunction against the first defendants restraining them from parting with the wire. The question was whether the second defendants could be added as a party to the action and served with a writ out of the jurisdiction.

Stirling J held that they could since they were 'necessary or proper parties' to the action brought against the first defendants.

(b) *Safeguards against misuse*

It has previously been mentioned[68] that the plaintiff's application for service out of the jurisdiction under the multi-defendant head must be

---

[64] See above, p 217.   [65] See above, p 99.
[66] See Fawcett, (1995) 44 *ICLQ* 744 at 746–749.
[67] (1889) 5 TLR 592. The case was concerned with an earlier version of the multi-defendant head, r 1(1)(g). This was differently worded from the present provision.
[68] See above, pp 99–100.

supported by an affidavit stating the grounds for his belief that there is a real issue between it and the first defendant, who is subject to jurisdiction, and that it is implicit from this that the plaintiff has to establish that there is a real issue between it and the first defendant. This involves going into the merits of the claim. Thus, in *Williams Electronics Inc v Rene Pierre SA & Others*,[69] leave to serve a French company out of the jurisdiction under the multi-defendant head was refused because of the failure to produce adequate evidence that the English importers (the party served within the jurisdiction) knew that the making of the articles in question by the French defendant constituted an infringement of copyright.

It must also be shown that the second defendant, who is to be served out of the jurisdiction, is 'a necessary or proper party'. This requirement was met in *Beecham Group plc and Another v Norton Healthcare Ltd and Others*.[70] The plaintiff brought an action for patent infringement against an English importer of medicinal tablets, manufactured and supplied by a Slovenian company. This company was refusing to give discovery of the production process. The plaintiff sought to join the Slovenian company as a defendant and for leave to serve out of the jurisdiction. Jacob J held that the two defendants were involved in a common design to manufacture and import the product into the United Kingdom. The Slovenian defendant was a necessary or proper party under rule 1(1)(c). Moreover, without proper discovery against the Slovenian defendant justice could not be done between the plaintiff and the first defendant, which was subject to jurisdiction. This requirement will not be met, though, if the claim against the second defendant is bound to fail.

(iii) **The injunction head**

It has also previously been mentioned[71] that rule 1(1)(b) provides that service of a writ out of the jurisdiction is permissible with the leave of the court where ' an injunction is sought ordering the defendant to do or refrain from doing anything within the jurisdiction (whether or not damages are also claimed in respect of a failure to do or the doing of that thing)'.

(a) *Application in infringement cases*

There is a number of late 19th Century and early 20th Century cases[72] involving trade mark or patent infringement which discussed an earlier

---

[69] Unreported, except through Lexis.   [70] [1997] FSR 81 at 86.
[71] See above, pp 100–101.
[72] See *Marshall* v *Marshall* (1888) 38 Ch D 330; *In re Burland's Trade-Mark, Burland* v *Broxburn Oil Co* (1889) 41 Ch D 542; *Kinahan* v *Kinahan* (1890) 45 Ch D 78; *Chemische Fabrik Vormals Sandoz* v *Badische Anilin und Soda Fabriks* (1904) 90 LT 733 HL(E).

version of this head. One such case was *Re Burland's Trade-Mark, Burland v Broxburn Oil Company*.[73] The plaintiff, who had registered a trade mark in England, sought an injunction to restrain a Scots corporation from infringing its trademark by selling in England infringing articles. Chitty J refused to discharge an order granting leave to serve the writ out of the jurisdiction. More modern examples are comparatively rare and invariably involve an allegation that several heads of rule 1(1), one of which is the injunction head, are satisfied. In *James North & Sons Ltd v North Cape Textiles Ltd and Another*,[74] which involved an action for passing-off, trade mark infringement, and inducing breach of contract, the plaintiffs only resorted to the injunction head once their attempt to use a contract head of Order 11, rule 1(1) had failed.

(b) Why this provision is seldom used in infringement cases

There are three factors which explain why this head is not commonly used in infringement cases.[75] First, there is a requirement that an injunction is sought ordering the defendant to do or refrain from doing anything *in England*, which means that there must have been an infringement *in England*, or at least the threat of an infringement *in England*.[76] In the situation where there is such an infringement, the tort head of Order 11, rule 1(1) also will apply. The latter provision will not apply, though, in the case of threatened wrongs, whereas the injunction head can be used.

Secondly, the injunction head requires that the substantial relief sought is an injunction. The advantage of using the tort head is that it is not so confined; it can operate in the situation where the substantial relief sought is damages. It may be possible, though, to use the injunction head even though the grant of an injunction is coupled with a claim for an account of profits. This is suggested by the decision in *Kinahan v Kinahan*,[77] where it was argued, against using this head, that the injunction was only a small part of the relief claimed because an account of profits was wanted besides. It was held that the latter claim flowed from the injunction and, therefore, it was a case falling within the injunction head.[78]

Thirdly, the injunction head only applies where a permanent injunction is sought. It cannot be used in the case of an interlocutory injunction.[79] In

---

[73] (1889) 41 Ch D 542. [74] [1984] 1 WLR 1428.
[75] For reasons why this provision is not commonly used in contractual disputes, see above, pp 100–101.
[76] The *James North* case, n 74 above, at 1434 (*per* Dunn LJ). [77] (1890) 45 Ch D 78.
[78] *Ibid*, at 84. The order for service out of the jurisdiction was discharged on *forum conveniens* grounds.
[79] *The Siskina* [1979] AC 210; *James North & Sons Ltd v North Cape Textiles Ltd and Another* [1984] 1 WLR 1428. For jurisdiction to grant interlocutory injunctions see the Civil Jurisdiction and Judgments 1982, s 25, discussed below, pp 312–313.

infringement cases, speed in obtaining an injunction is vital and it is common practice to seek such an injunction. Accordingly, this limitation on the use of rule 1(1)(b) is, in practical terms, a major one.

(c) *Threatened wrongs*

The situation where the injunction head comes into its own is where an injunction is sought to restrain threatened wrongs. There is some uncertainty over whether the tort head covers this situation, whereas the injunction head clearly does. This latter point was established in *James North & Sons Ltd v North Cape Textiles Ltd and Another*,[80] where the Court of Appeal held that the injunction head was wide enough to cover an action for a permanent injunction to restrain threatened breaches of contract committed within the jurisdiction. Scots law reaches the same result by a slightly different route. The Scots traditional rules on jurisdiction have a special rule dealing with injunctions in relation to threatened wrongs. This states that a person may be sued 'in proceedings for interdict, in the courts for the place where it is alleged that the wrong is likely to be committed'.[81]

(b) A SERIOUS ISSUE TO BE TRIED

(i) The standard of proof

As has previously been mentioned,[82] according to the House of Lords in the *Seaconsar* case,[83] the plaintiff has to establish that there is a serious issue to be tried in that there is 'a substantial question of fact or law or both, arising on the facts disclosed by the affidavits, which the plaintiff bona fide desires to try . . .'.[84] In contrast, the standard of proof applicable when the plaintiff has to establish that the head of Order 11 rule 1(1) is satisfied is that of a good arguable case, a higher standard. This means that it is necessary to ask whether the merits of the case have to be gone into in order to satisfy the terms of the head of rule 1(1). If so, the plaintiff has to show a good arguable case as to the merits, and the merits will not be gone into again at the jurisdictional stage of the action. If not, the examination of the merits will only arise after the terms of the head have been satisfied and the plaintiff will only have to establish that there is a serious issue to be tried on the merits.

---

[80] [1984] 1 WLR 1428.
[81] Schedule 8, rule 2 (10) Civil Jurisdiction and Judgments Act 1982. See Anton, pp 196–198.
[82] See above, pp 101–103. [83] N 19 above.
[84] *Seaconsar Far East Ltd* v *Bank Markazi Jomhouri Islami Iran* [1993] 3 WLR 756 at 763.

(a) The tort head

What if the defendant denies that there has been an infringement? A denial that a tort has taken place could be construed as going to the head of rule 1(1) since, as has already been seen, under paragraph (f) the claim has to be founded on a tort. However, Lord Goff in the *Seaconsar* case approved[85] the judgment of Lord Tucker in *Vitkovice Horni a Hutni Tezirstvro v Korner*[86] and, in the latter case, it was said, in relation to the tort head, that the standard of proof for establishing negligence was a lesser one than that for establishing that the negligence occurred within the jurisdiction (which clearly goes to establishing the terms of the head).[87]

Establishing that an act of infringement has been committed within the jurisdiction can raise issues which go to the merits of the case,[88] and, in such circumstances, the standard of proof required of the plaintiff is, presumably, that of a good arguable case.

(b) The multi-defendant head

It has already been seen,[89] that the plaintiff only has to show that there is a real issue to be tried on the merits in relation to the first defendant, duly served within or out of the jurisdiction. The plaintiff has to establish a good arguable case that the second defendant is a necessary or proper party. The merits will then be gone into as a separate exercise.

(c) The injunction head

It has already been seen,[90] that it is not necessary to go into the merits in order to establish that the terms of this head are met, and that the authority for this is a case involving patent infringement.[91]

(ii) Establishing liability

The position in relation to establishing liability is the same in Order 11, rule 1(1) cases as it is in Brussels/Lugano Conventions cases.[92] If liability is based on English law, first there has to be an act of infringement according to English law, and, secondly, it is normally also necessary, because of the territorial limitation on liability, that this was committed in England.

---

[85] *Ibid*, at 766. [86] [1951] AC 869 at 889.
[87] See also *Barings plc and Another v Coopers & Lybrand (A Firm) and Others* [1997] IL Pr 12, 25–26; affirmed by CA without discussion of this point, [1997] IL Pr 576.
[88] See above, p 101.   [89] See above, p 102.   [90] See above, pp 102–103.
[91] *Chemische Fabrik Vormals Sandoz v Badische Anilin und Soda Fabriks* (1904) 90 LT 733 at 735; approved in the *Seaconsar* case.
[92] See above, pp 145–149.

When it comes to establishing the first of these two requirements, it has been held that a mere assertion of infringement of a patent is not enough. There has to be sufficient detail for an understanding of the facts on which the claim of infringement is based.[93] Doubtless, though, the same level of detail would be required if this matter arose in the context of the Brussels or Lugano Convention.

There is a number of Order 11 cases where, in order to establish liability, what had to be shown was that the act of infringement occurred in England so as to satisfy a territorial limitation on liability under English law. A simple example, in relation to patents, is *The Badische Anilin Und Soda Fabrik v The Basle Chemical Works, Bindschedler*,[94] which involved the infringement in Switzerland of an English patent by a Swiss resident. The House of Lords held that the writ ought not to have been served out of the jurisdiction. There was no right of action against the defendant since what he did in Switzerland was perfectly lawful because 'our patent law does not extend beyond this country. Acts which here would be infringements of the patent are no infringement if they are done in a country which is not within the ambit of the patent'.[95]

A similar case in relation to copyright is *Def Lepp Music & Others v Stuart Brown*.[96] The case involved alleged infringement of a UK copyright in a tape recording by acts committed outside the United Kingdom. It was held that copyright under English law is strictly defined in terms of territory. The intangible right is to do things in the United Kingdom and only acts in the United Kingdom constitute infringement. Accordingly, there was no breach of the UK copyright in the tape and no liability under the Copyright Act 1956. An attempt to establish liability on the basis that wrongs had been committed abroad also failed. This raised a choice of law point, and involved the application of the common law tort choice of law rule.[97] Under the first limb of the old double actionability rule, the plaintiff had to establish that the act was actionable as a tort according to English law. The acts complained of, having been committed abroad, were not actionable as a tort according to English law. The upshot was that a successful action could not be brought in England for the infringement. The plaintiffs had failed to show that the case was a proper one for service out of the jurisdiction. Accordingly, the Vice-Chancellor, Sir Nicholas Browne-Wilkinson, set aside service on the foreign defendants.

---

[93] *Raychem Corpn v Thermon (UK) Ltd and Another* [1989] RPC 423.

[94] [1898] AC 200. See also *Kalman and Another v PCL Packaging (UK) Ltd and Another* [1982] FSR 406; above, pp 244–245.

[95] [1898] AC 200 at 206.

[96] [1986] RPC 273. The case also concerned a subject matter limitation in relation to jurisdiction, see below, p 301.

[97] See below, p 608. There are now statutory tort choice of law rules, see below pp 612–640.

Infringement: Jurisdiction under the traditional rules 259

(c) THE EXERCISE OF THE DISCRETION

The fact that service of a writ out of the jurisdiction under Order 11, rule 1(1) is a discretionary form of jurisdiction requiring the leave of the court has already been touched upon in previous chapters. The exercise of this discretion will now be examined in detail.

(i) General considerations

An application for leave under rule 1(1) is made *ex parte*. Full and fair disclosure of all the facts is therefore necessary. However, even if there is a material non-disclosure, if this is inadvertent and not serious, the court need not discharge the order.[98] In infringement cases, as with other causes of action, there can be an allegation of non-disclosure of material facts. Thus, in *The Electric Furnace Co v Selas Corpn of America*,[99] it was argued that the *ex parte* order should be discharged on the basis that a letter from the British Steel Corporation, explaining why the operation of a furnace installed in the UK did not infringe the plaintiff's patent, had not been disclosed. This argument was rejected in the Court of Appeal. It was said that it would be unreasonable to expect a plaintiff preparing his evidence to anticipate all the arguments, or all the points, which might be raised in his case. To amount to a failure to make a full and fair disclosure, an innocent omission must be of such weight that it may mislead the court in exercising its jurisdiction and its discretion whether or not to grant leave.[100] Non-disclosure relates to the merits of the case, but discussion of the merits takes place at an earlier stage, when the court is considering whether the plaintiff has established that there is a serious issue to be tried on the merits.[101] This means that the discussion of non-disclosure under the full and fair disclosure principle tends to be rather cursory.

(ii) *Forum conveniens*

As has previously been mentioned,[102] the criterion for the exercise of the Order 11 rule 1(1) discretion is that of *forum conveniens*. The principles to be applied when exercising this discretion were set out by Lord Goff in the House of Lords in the leading case in this area, *Spiliada Maritime Corpn v Cansulex Ltd*.[103] The basic principle is that the court has 'to identify the forum in which the case can be suitably tried for the interests of all the parties and for the ends of justice'.[104] This involves identifying the appropriate forum for trial and examining whether justice will be obtained in the alternative forum abroad. The same principle underlies the exercise of the

---

[98] *Beecham Group plc and Another v Norton Healthcare Ltd and Others* [1997] FSR 81 at 89.
[99] [1987] RPC 23. See also the *Beecham* case, n 98 above.
[100] N 99 above, at 29.   [101] See above, p 256.   [102] See above, pp 41–42.
[103] [1987] AC 460.   [104] *Ibid*, at 480.

discretion to stay English proceedings on the basis of *forum non conveniens*,[105] and cases decided in the latter context are of assistance in the present context.

(a) An alternative forum abroad

The exercise of the *forum conveniens* discretion presupposes that there is an obvious alternative forum abroad. If not, it is proper to allow service of the writ out of the jurisdiction. This aspect of the *forum conveniens* discretion is of great importance in infringement cases. In *The Electric Furnace Co v Selas Corpn of America*,[106] the plaintiffs brought an action in England against a United States defendant and a UK defendant in respect of infringement of the plaintiffs' UK patent in the United Kingdom. When it came to the exercise of the *forum conveniens* discretion, the Court of Appeal held that, as regards the US defendant, 'the courts of this country [England] are not only the appropriate forum, but the only possible forum'.[107] The appeal against a refusal to set aside the order for service out of the jurisdiction was, therefore, dismissed. It was not explained why England was the only possible forum. The assumption must have been that a court in the United States would either not have jurisdiction or would not exercise jurisdiction in a case involving a UK patent which had been infringed in the United Kingdom. There was certainly concern that if trial were not allowed here the US defendant might escape 'Scot free' despite having committed a tort.

The process of reasoning was more explicit in the Federal Court of Australia in *Best Australia Ltd and Others* v *Aquagas Marketing Pty Ltd and Others*,[108] where Wilcox J pointed out that the plaintiff could not litigate in New Zealand the question whether a New Zealand company had infringed an Australian patent. It followed that there was no other jurisdiction in which the claim could be fully litigated and the court could not properly decline to hear the case.

The only danger with this approach is that of assuming that a foreign court would be unable to try the case, just because an English court would not do so in those circumstances. There is a well known instance of an American court exercising jurisdiction in a case involving the infringement of a foreign copyright.[109] Japanese courts are prepared to try actions relating to the infringement of foreign patents.[110] Finnish courts are prepared to try actions relating to the infringement of foreign trade marks,[111]

---

[105] See below, pp 267–274.
[106] [1987] RPC 23. See also *Puschner* v *Tom Palmer (Scotland) Ltd and Another* [1989] RPC 430 at 440 '... this is a United Kingdom patent ... In effect the patent can only be litigated in this country'.
[107] *Op cit*, at 31.   [108] (1988) 83 ALR 217.   [109] See below, p 292.
[110] See below, p 292.   [111] See below, p 292.

and the Dutch courts have granted interlocutory injunctions in relation to the infringement of foreign intellectual property rights which have been infringed outside the Netherlands.[112]

(b) *The appropriate forum*

The burden of proof is on the plaintiff to show that England is the appropriate forum for trial, and that this is clearly so.[113] 'The court must take into account the nature of the dispute, the legal and practical issues involved, such questions as local knowledge, availability of witnesses and their evidence and expense.'[114] Other considerations include the question of the applicable law (if English law is applicable this may point towards England as the appropriate forum), whether the parties have agreed to trial abroad (the parties should be kept to their agreement), and whether trial in England will lead to a multiplicity of proceedings with concurrent actions, involving the same parties and issues, taking place in England and abroad (this would suggest that the discretion should be exercised against allowing service out of the jurisdiction).

It is worth pausing to examine how some of these considerations operate in infringement cases.

(i) *Expense and convenience*

It saves money for the parties and is convenient if all the litigation involving the parties can be heard in one State; if this is England, this will be a factor in favour of exercising the discretion to allow service out of the jurisdiction. However, it may not be a decisive factor. Thus, in *Kinahan* v *Kinahan*,[115] two applications were brought in England by the same plaintiff: one for infringement of the plaintiff's English trade mark; the other to expunge from the register the defendant's similar trade mark. Kekewich J discharged an order allowing service out of the jurisdiction in the infringement action because of the strong Irish connections, despite the other English action.

(ii) *Witnesses*

When it comes to proving that there was an act of infringement committed in England, it will be witnesses here who will have to be used.[116] More generally, the evidence will be here.[117] Infringement cases can raise

---

[112] See above, p 219.
[113] *Spiliada Maritime Corpn* v *Cansulex Ltd* [1987] AC 460 at 481.
[114] *Amin Rasheed Corpn* v *Kuwait Insurance Co* [1984] AC 50 at 72 (*per* Lord Wilberforce).
[115] (1890) 45 Ch D 78. See also *Marshall* v *Marshall* (1888) 38 Ch D 330 involving an application to register a trade mark and an action for infringement.
[116] *In re Burland's Trade-Mark, Burland* v *Broxburn Oil Company* 1889 41 Ch D 542 at 545.
[117] *James North & Sons Ltd* v *North Cape Textiles Ltd* [1984] 1 WLR 1428 at 1433.

difficult technical questions, for example about whether equipment infringes a patent. *Puschner v Tom Palmer (Scotland) Ltd*[118] involved an action for infringement of a UK patent. The two defendants were the UK seller of infringing equipment and the Austrian manufacturer. Aldous J said, obiter, that the foreign manufacturer would best know how the equipment worked and would be able to assist the court. There must, therefore, be some advantage in having it as a party to the action.[119] On the other hand, if the parties are from different countries they may well produce expert witnesses from their respective countries to testify on technical issues. The convenience of the witnesses will then be a neutral factor.[120]

(iii) *Consolidation of litigation in multi-defendant cases*

International infringement actions very frequently involve two or more defendants. In multi-defendant cases, there is a concern to concentrate litigation in one State so that, instead of having two actions in different States, there is a single action in one State binding on all the parties concerned. If England is the only State in which several defendants can be joined together in a single action, this factor operates as an important one in favour of trial taking place in England.[121]

(iv) *The applicable law*

It has already been seen[122] that the applicable law is relevant in infringement cases at the stage of determining whether there is a serious issue on the merits to be tried. It is also very relevant when it comes to the exercise of the *forum conveniens* discretion. Thus, in *The Electric Furnace Co v Selas Corpn of America*,[123] it was said that 'where it is a tort committed in this country, properly governed by the laws of this country, with the country as the obviously proper place for trial, it might well be a serious departure from the demands of justice and, I venture to think, of international comity if leave to serve abroad were refused . . .'.[124] In infringement cases, it will be unusual for an English court to be faced with a case involving a foreign applicable law. If the act of infringement was committed in England then, normally, English law will apply.[125] If it was committed abroad, then the subject matter limitation on jurisdiction will operate.[126]

---

[118] [1989] RPC 430.   [119] *Ibid*, at 440.
[120] See *Best Australia Ltd and Others v Aquagas Marketing Pty Ltd and Others* (1988) 83 ALR 217 at 223.
[121] See Fawcett, (1995) 44 *ICLQ* 744 at 759–760; Beaumont in chapter 10 of Fawcett (ed), *Declining Jurisdiction*.
[122] See above, pp 145–149.   [123] [1987] RPC 23.   [124] *Ibid*, at 36.
[125] The general rule on the applicable law may be displaced, but this will be rare in infringement cases, see below, pp 630–633.
[126] See below, p 299.

(v) *Parallel proceedings*

A person who has registered an intellectual property right in a number of different States will often end up bringing parallel infringement actions in each one of these States. The avoidance of a multiplicity of proceedings in different States normally operates as a factor against exercising the discretion to allow service out of the jurisdiction. However, it should not do so in parallel infringement cases. The courts in many foreign States will refuse to try an action relating to foreign intellectual property rights that have been infringed abroad. To deny jurisdiction in England would not lead to a concentration of the actions in one State abroad. Instead, what it would lead to is a denial of justice to the plaintiff, with no State trying the infringement action in relation to the UK patent.

(c) *Injustice abroad*

If substantial justice will not be done abroad, the court may well exercise its discretion in favour of allowing service out of the jurisdiction even though there are strong connections with the alternative forum abroad. It is not easy to show that there will be positive injustice abroad. What is easier to show is that the trial abroad will deprive the plaintiff of some advantage that would be obtained from trial in England. However, the advantage to the plaintiff factor has been downgraded in importance by the *Spiliada* case, where Lord Goff said that the court should not be deterred from refusing leave in Order 11 cases simply because the plaintiff will be deprived of an advantage, such as higher damages or a more generous limitation period, provided that the court is satisfied that substantial justice will be done in the available appropriate forum abroad.[127]

In multi-defendant cases, whether involving infringement or some other cause of action, it is not necessary to show that the plaintiff will actually obtain some advantage from joining a foreign defendant to the action. Potential advantages, of the sort already mentioned,[128] will be readily assumed.[129] However, adding on a second defendant at a late stage of the proceedings may cause injustice to the first defendant because it may lead to an adjournment of the trial date whilst the second defendant prepares its evidence. If there is likely to be delay and the second defendant is only being added on for the purpose of discovery of documents, then fairness may well dictate that leave should not be granted for service out of the jurisdiction.[130] The stage at which it was first attempted to join the second defendant may then become crucial. Adding on further defendants may also increase costs,

---

[127] [1987] 1 AC 460 at 482–484.
[128] See above, p 171.
[129] *The Electric Furnace Co v Selas Corpn of America* [1987] RPC 23 at 33–34.
[130] *Unilever plc v Gillette (UK) Ltd* [1989] RPC 583 at 611.

although if the defendants are in the same group of companies and are represented by the same lawyers this may not be significant.[131]

In infringement cases, one question that may arise is whether the plaintiff will be able to obtain abroad a remedy which is as effective as that obtained from the English courts.[132]

(d) *The significance of the particular head of Order 11*

The different heads vary greatly in the extent of the connection with England that is required. This affects the willingness of the court to exercise the discretion to allow service of the writ out of the jurisdiction.[133] It is important, therefore, to examine the attitude of the courts towards the exercise of the discretion in relation to the three heads of rule 1(1) that are particularly relevant in infringement cases.

(i) *The tort head*

It has often been said that 'the jurisdiction in which a tort has been committed is *prima facie* the natural forum for the determination of the dispute'.[134] The fact that a tort had been committed in a particular State constituted a strong connection with that State. Moreover, if a tort was committed in England, the English court applied English law. This presumption did not evolve in infringement cases, nonetheless it has been applied in such cases.[135] The wording of the presumption should be altered now that tort choice of law rules have been put on a statutory basis. The governing law depends on where the events constituting the tort or delict in question occurred. This means that if the events constituting the tort or delict in question occurred in England, then this is, *prima facie* the natural forum for trial. In infringement cases the event constituting the tort is the act of infringement, and if this act occurred in England the presumption should operate.

(ii) *The multi-defendant head*

In contrast to the distinct willingness to exercise the discretion to allow service of a writ out of the jurisdiction in cases based on the tort head, it

---

[131] *Intel Corpn* v *General Instrument Corpn and Others* 11 May 1990 (unreported except through Lexis).

[132] *James North & Sons Ltd* v *North Cape Textiles Ltd and Another* [1984] 1 WLR 1428 at 1433. See also *Plastus Kreativ AB* v *Minnesota Mining and Manufacturing Co* [1995] RPC 438 at 447.

[133] *Spiliada Maritime Corpn* v *Cansulex Ltd*, above n 127 at 481.

[134] *Cordoba Shipping Co Ltd* v *National State Bank, Elizabeth, New Jersey, The Albaforth* [1984] 2 Lloyd's Rep 91 at 94 (*per* Ackner L J), 96 (*per* Robert Goff LJ). Applied in *Metall und Rohstoff AG* v *Donaldson Lufkin and Jenrette Inc* [1990] 1 QB 391; overruled on a different point in *Lonrho plc* v *Fayed* [1991] 3 WLR, 188, HL.

[135] *The Electric Furnace Co* v *Selas Corpn of America* [1987] RPC 23 at 36 (*per* Sir John Megaw); quoted above.

(iii) *The injunction head*

As previously mentioned,[138] in cases where jurisdiction is based on the injunction head, one important consideration that has been taken into account by the courts is whether the injunction can be effectively enforced in this country. In *Re Burland's Trade-Mark, Burland v Broxburn Oil Co*,[139] the plaintiff brought an action for the infringement of its registered trademark against the defendant, a company with a registered office in Scotland but with a number of branch offices in England. The defendant was carrying on a considerable amount of business in this country. The injunction could, therefore, be effectively enforced by sequestration here and leave to serve the writ out of the jurisdiction was granted.

This should be contrasted with the earlier case of *Marshall v Marshall*,[140] where the injunction could not be enforced in England against the defendant himself, but only against his agents in England who were not primarily responsible. The defendant being a Scotsman, it was the Scots courts that could enforce its orders against the defendant himself; therefore leave to serve the writ out of the jurisdiction was refused. Understandably, leave was also refused in a case[141] where the defendant, a company with its registered office in Belfast, had no agents or depots in England, but merely supplied occasional customers in England direct from Belfast.

(iv) *Actions based on more than one head*

It is common, in infringement cases, to base jurisdiction on a number of different heads of Order 11 rule 1(1). This raises an interesting, and as yet unanswered, question when it comes to the exercise of the *forum conveniens* discretion. If, for example, jurisdiction is based on the tort head (in respect of which there is a willingness to exercise the discretion to give leave to serve out of the jurisdiction) and the multi-defendant head (in respect of which there is a lack of willingness to exercise the discretion), what is the court's attitude to be towards the exercise of the discretion? Is it to take the most favourable attitude, the least favourable attitude, or a broadly neutral view? If jurisdiction in an infringement case could be based on the tort head alone, it does seem wrong to do anything other than to adopt the favourable attitude towards the exercise of the discretion

---

[136] See above, pp 106.
[137] See *Multinational Gas and Petrochemical Co v Multinational Gas and Petrochemical Services Ltd* [1983] Ch 258.
[138] See above, pp 106.   [139] (1889) 41 Ch D 542.   [140] (1888) 38 Ch D 330.
[141] *Kinahan v Kinahan* (1890) 45 Ch D 78.

which applies for that head, even if the plaintiff has invoked, as an alternative, the multi-defendant head, in respect of which a less favourable attitude prevails.

(e) *Foreign intellectual property rights and infringements abroad*

Existing subject matter limitations on jurisdiction,[142] in relation to these two types of infringement action, mean that there has been no discussion of the use of Order 11 rule 1(1) to obtain jurisdiction over the person in such actions. However, if, as is suggested below, these subject matter limitations were to be abolished, the question would then arise of where the appropriate forum is in cases involving foreign intellectual property rights and or acts of infringement committed abroad. It would be very difficult to establish that the clearly appropriate forum is England in such cases. On the contrary, there is a strong argument that the natural forum for trial is the foreign State in which the intellectual property right is created, particularly if the act of infringement is also committed there.[143]

III
DECLINING JURISDICTION AND RESTRAINING FOREIGN PROCEEDINGS

An English court, even though it has jurisdiction following the service of a writ, can decline to exercise that jurisdiction by granting a stay of the English proceedings.[144] A stay will be granted in three situations: where the doctrine of *forum non conveniens* applies; where there is a foreign choice of jurisdiction clause; where there is an agreement on arbitration. In infringement cases, there is unlikely to be an agreement between the infringer and infringee[145] in relation to the place of trial or arbitration and, therefore, concentration will be upon the doctrine of *forum non conveniens*. Before turning to examine this doctrine, it is important to note that Articles 21 and 22 of the Brussels and Lugano Conventions,[146] apply to cases of concurrent litigation in two EC/EFTA Contracting States, even though the jurisdiction in both of these States is based on traditional national rules on jurisdiction. If the requirements of Articles 21 or 22 are met, jurisdiction will be declined under this provision. On the other hand, it is possible to have concurrent litigation in two EC/EFTA Contracting States which does

---

[142] See below, pp 283–306.
[143] See below, pp 269–271.
[144] See Dicey and Morris, chapter 12.
[145] There may be a choice of jurisdiction or arbitration clause in a licensing agreement, see above, pp 107–108.
[146] Discussed above, pp 177–186.

not satisfy the requirements of either of these provisions, for example the cause of action is not the same in the two actions and they are not related. In this situation, where jurisdiction is based on the traditional English rules and Articles 21 and 22 do not apply, recourse can be had to the doctrine of *forum non conveniens*, despite the fact that there is concurrent litigation in another Contracting State to the Brussels or Lugano Conventions.[147] This situation will seldom arise due to the wide interpretation given to Article 22.[148]

1. FORUM NON CONVENIENS

(a) THE ROLE OF *FORUM NON CONVENIENS*

In common law jurisdictions, the doctrine of *forum non conveniens* performs a number of roles. It is the antidote to excessively wide bases of jurisdiction; it is concerned to avoid contradictory judgments; prevents forum shopping; and provides flexibility.[149] In infringement cases, the role of *forum non conveniens* is, necessarily, a rather limited one. The subject matter limitations on jurisdiction adopted by many States in cases involving foreign intellectual property rights and acts of infringement committed abroad mean that excessively wide assertions of jurisdiction are not normally a problem. Neither is the risk of contradictory judgments. Nor is forum shopping much of a problem[150] since a plaintiff will often have no choice of fora, and, normally, will gain no substantive law advantage from forum shopping, given that the law of infringement of many countries is substantially the same, being derived from the same international conventions. However, this still leaves the role of providing flexibility so as to allow in a whole range of considerations, ignored by certain traditional bases of jurisdiction, which are encompassed by the notions of appropriateness and justice.

(b) THE PRINCIPLES TO BE APPLIED WHEN EXERCISING THE DISCRETION

The leading English case on *forum non conveniens*, *Spiliada Maritime Corpn v Cansulex Ltd*,[151] has already been discussed in relation to the *forum conveniens* discretion. Lord Goff set out the basic principle that:

a stay will only be granted on the ground of *forum non conveniens* where the court is satisfied that there is some other available forum, having competent jurisdiction,

---

[147] *Sarrio SA v Kuwait Investment Authority* [1997] IL Pr 481; reversed by the House of Lords without discussion of this point, [1997] 3 WLR 1143.
[148] The *Sarrio* case in the House of Lords, n 147 above; discussed above, p 183.
[149] Fawcett (ed) *Declining Jurisdiction*, pp 19–21.   [150] See below, pp 306–307.
[151] [1987] AC 460.

which is the appropriate forum for trial of the action, ie in which the case may be tried more suitably for the interests of all the parties and the ends of justice.[152]

This involves a two stage process: first, determining whether there is a clearly more appropriate forum abroad; secondly, consideration of the requirements of justice.

(i) A clearly more appropriate forum abroad

As has previously been mentioned,[153] the burden of proof is on the defendant to show that there is another available forum which is clearly or distinctly more appropriate than the English forum.[154] If this is shown, the court will move on to the second stage, which is to consider the requirements of justice. In order to establish that there is a clearly more appropriate forum abroad, the defendant has to show two things: first, that there is another available forum abroad; secondly, that this is clearly or distinctly more appropriate than the English forum.

(a) *Another available forum*

This requirement is more obvious in the present context than it is in relation to the *forum conveniens* discretion, for it is going to be impossible to establish that there is a clearly more appropriate forum for trial abroad in the absence of an alternative forum abroad, whereas it is possible to show that England is the clearly appropriate forum for the purpose of Order 11 rule 1(1), without going into this. In cases involving a UK intellectual property right, it may be hard to find a foreign forum which is able, or willing, to try the case. In the absence of an alternative forum abroad, any application for a stay of the English proceeding is, in effect, seeking to prevent the action being tried at all, and a stay will not be granted on the basis of the doctrine of *forum non conveniens*.[155]

In *Amersham International plc v Corning Ltd and Another*,[156] it was argued that the 'alternative forum' was the European Patent Office.

The plaintiff was granted a European patent in respect of a number of countries, including the UK. The plaintiff brought an action in England alleging that the two defendants had infringed its patent. The second defendant, subsequently, lodged a notice of opposition at the European Patent Office, seeking revocation of the patent. The defendants then sought a stay of the English infringement proceedings pending determination of that opposition.

Falconer J refused to grant a stay of proceedings. Only the issue of validity could be litigated before the European Patent Office. Proceedings for

---

[152] [1987] AC 460 at 476.
[154] The *Spiliada* case, n 152 above, at 474.
[156] [1987] RPC 53.
[153] See above, p 42.
[155] *Evers v Firth* (1987) 10 NSWLR 22.

infringement could not be brought before that court. It followed that the European Patent Office could not be considered to be an alternative forum.

This does not mean that the English courts are completely powerless to grant a stay in such a case. It may be possible to do so under the courts' inherent jurisdiction to prevent injustice. The defendant has to show that the plaintiff's conduct in bringing the action is, in the circumstances, unconscionable and thus unjust.[157] The English courts can restrain foreign proceedings using this criterion;[158] it would be highly anomalous if they were unable to stay their own proceedings using the same criterion.

(b) Which is clearly more appropriate than the English forum

When determining whether the foreign forum is clearly more appropriate than the English forum, the same considerations apply as are applied when exercising the *forum conveniens* discretion in Order 11, rule 1(1) cases.[159]

(i) Is it a UK or foreign right?

In infringement cases arguably the most important connection of all is concerned with whether it is a UK or foreign intellectual property right. In the case of patents, trade-marks and registered designs, it is easy to ascertain this. One merely looks to see where the right was registered. If there are parallel registrations, the one that matters is the one on which the plaintiff's action is based. With unregistered rights, such as copyright, finding the State with which there is the relevant connection is more difficult. The Berne Convention gives a definition of when copyright is established. Other countries which are parties to that Convention then give parallel protection. Nonetheless, cases do refer to, for example, UK copyright or US copyright. When ascertaining the natural forum for trial, the important thing is whether the plaintiff is relying on UK copyright or that of a foreign country.

If the case concerns a UK intellectual property right, this constitutes a very significant connection with England. Moreover, in the case of a UK registered right, an English court will have jurisdiction to try the issue of validity if, as commonly happens, this arises during the course of the infringement litigation. It is clearly desirable that the same court should, if possible, try both the issue of infringement and that of validity.[160]

Nonetheless, it is not impossible, in a case relating to a UK intellectual property right, to show that the clearly appropriate forum is abroad. This

---

[157] *Evers v Firth* (1987) 10 NSWLR 22.
[158] *South Carolina Insurance Co v Assurantie NV* [1987] AC 24.
[159] See above, pp 259–264.
[160] See *Plastus Kreativ AB v Minnesota Mining and Manufacturing Co* [1995] RPC 438 at 447.

was shown in *GAF Corpn* v *Amchem Products Inc*,[161] where, as has already been seen,[162] the Court of Appeal held that the appropriate forum for an action in which the plaintiff claimed to be beneficially entitled to a UK patent was the United States.

The English courts will seldom be faced with an application for a stay of proceedings on the basis of *forum non conveniens* in a case involving a foreign intellectual property right. The reason for this is very simple. The English courts have no jurisdiction in such a case because of the subject matter limitation on jurisdiction in relation to foreign intellectual property rights. The issue, therefore, does not arise of whether the English courts should refuse to exercise their jurisdiction and grant a stay of action. Without this jurisdictional limitation, *forum non conveniens* might become more of a live issue in infringement cases, as it is in the United States.

The one situation where an English court may be faced with an application for a stay of proceedings on the basis of *forum non conveniens*, in a case involving a foreign intellectual property right, is that where jurisdiction is founded on the Brussels or Lugano Conventions and the defendant argues that the alternative forum is in a non-Contracting State. There is no subject matter limitation on jurisdiction in relation to foreign intellectual property rights when jurisdiction is based on the Brussels or Lugano Conventions.[163] But there is power to decline jurisdiction under the doctrine of *forum non conveniens* in the above circumstances.[164]

(ii) *Did the act of infringement take place in England or abroad?*

Another important factor in determining whether there is another available forum which is clearly more appropriate than the English forum is going to be the question of where the act of infringement took place. Because of a separate subject matter limitation on jurisdiction in relation to intellectual property rights that have been infringed abroad, the English courts will, normally, only be faced with cases involving infringements in England. In this situation, the presumption that England is, *prima facie*, the natural forum for trial[165] will operate. If the case also involved a UK intellectual property right, it would be even harder for the defendant to establish that the clearly appropriate forum was abroad. It is worth noting though, by way of comparison, that in the United States the Ninth Circuit, applying the US doctrine of *forum non conveniens*,[166] dismissed an action based on allegations of infringement of a US copyright in the United

---

[161] [1975] 1 Lloyd's Rep 601. This was an Order 11 case.
[162] See above, pp 67–69, where the factors taken into account by the Court of Appeal are discussed.
[163] See above, pp 190–196.   [164] See above, pp 186–188.   [165] See above, p 264.
[166] This is different from the English doctrine, see Fawcett in *Declining Jurisdiction*, pp 14–16.

States.[167] Both parties were Singaporean, the work originated there and was first published outside the United States.

The one situation where an English court could be asked to decline jurisdiction in relation to an action involving an infringement abroad is, again, where jurisdiction is based on the Brussels or Lugano Conventions, which contain no such limitation, and the alternative forum for trial is a court in a non-Contracting State to one of these Conventions. The fact that the act of infringement was committed abroad would constitute a strong connection with that State. Moreover, Aldous J, in *Plastus Kreativ AB v Minnesota Mining and Manufacturing Co*,[168] was of the view that if an act of infringement was committed abroad, it was appropriate that trial should be held there, because the local court could look at the particular acts in the context in which they are carried out, as long as the foreign court could provide an appropriate remedy. Finally, the law of that foreign State would normally be applicable, which would suggest that trial should take place there. Proving the foreign law will be expensive, although the growing harmonisation of the substantive intellectual property laws of different countries means that English lawyers will be able to understand foreign intellectual property laws.

Normally, though, what the English courts are dealing with is a UK intellectual property right which has been infringed in England. In such circumstances, England would look to be the natural forum for trial.

(ii) The requirements of justice

If there is some other available forum which, *prima facie*, is clearly more appropriate for the trial of the action, the court will, ordinarily, grant a stay unless there are circumstances by reason of which justice requires that a stay should nevertheless not be granted.[169] Once it has been shown that there is a clearly more appropriate forum for trial abroad, the burden of proof shifts to the plaintiff to justify coming to England.[170] Lord Goff elaborated on this second stage in the House of Lords case of *Connelly v RTZ Corpn Ltd*.[171] He said that there was a general principle that 'if a clearly more appropriate forum overseas has been identified, generally speaking the plaintiff will have to take that forum as he finds it, even if it is in certain respects less advantageous to him than the English forum. He may, for example, have to accept lower damages, or do without the more generous English system of discovery. The same must apply to the system of court procedure, including the rules of evidence, applicable in the foreign forum . . . Only if the plaintiff can establish that substantial justice cannot

---

[167] *Creative Technology, Ltd v Aztech System Pte Ltd* 61 F 3d 696 (9th Cir 1995).
[168] [1995] RPC 438 at 447; discussed below, p 290.
[169] The *Spiliada* case n 152 above, 478.   [170] *Ibid*, at 476.
[171] [1997] 2 WLR 373.

be done in the appropriate forum, will the courts refuse to grant a stay'.[172] On the facts of the case, substantial justice could not be done in the appropriate forum, Namibia. The case could not be tried at all without the benefit of financial assistance; this was available in England by way of legal aid or a conditional fee, but not in Namibia. It is also submitted that there would be injustice in having trial abroad if there is no appropriate remedy in that State.[173]

One important point to note is that a stay of English infringement proceedings does not necessarily leave the plaintiff completely unprotected. If the stay is granted pending trial abroad, there is the possibility of obtaining an interlocutory injunction pending this decision, even where trial is to take place in a non-Contracting State to the Brussels or Lugano Conventions.[174] However, it would be unusual for an English court to pre-empt any ruling of the foreign court by making such an order.

(c) A STAY PENDING A DECISION ABROAD IN RELATION TO VALIDITY

In the *Amersham* case,[175] Falconer J went on to discuss the question of a stay of the English proceedings on the assumption that he was wrong and that the European Patent Office could be regarded as being an alternative forum. However, he came to the conclusion that a stay of proceedings should still not be granted. This was a pre-*Spiliada* case, nonetheless it is interesting as an example of the factors that can be relevant to the exercise of the discretion in infringement cases.

In reaching his conclusion, the learned judge was influenced by five factors. First, revocation of a European patent should, primarily, be a matter for the national court of the designated State and, when validity is put in issue in infringement proceedings, the intention is that both issues should be litigated in the court of the designated State. Secondly, it is convenient, desirable, and the usual practice, for infringement and validity to be decided in the same proceedings. Thirdly, if a stay is granted pending the outcome of the opposition proceedings in the European Patent Office, and the stay is subsequently lifted, the plaintiff's infringement claim will have been delayed for four to five years and possibly longer. Fourthly, the question of expense to the parties was of little or no significance in the instant case; both parties were very substantial organisations for whom the costs of the litigation were small in comparison with what was at stake financially. Fifthly, speculation as to a possible multiplicity of suits in the

---

[172] [1997] 2 WLR 373 at 384–385.

[173] *Plastus Kreativ AB* v *Minnesota Mining and Manufacturing Co* [1995] RPC 438 at 447, a case involving subject matter limitations on jurisdiction discussed below, p 290.

[174] See Section 25 of the Civil Jurisdiction and Judgments Act, discussed below, pp 312–313. See also *Phonogram Ltd* v *Def American Inc The Times*, 7 October 1994.

[175] N 156, above, at 58–59.

future, with the plaintiff suing for infringement in other States, would be ignored.

In the subsequent case of *Pall Corpn v Commercial Hydraulics (Bedford) Ltd and Others*, [176] Whitford J, when faced with essentially the same circumstances, also refused the grant of a stay of the English proceedings. He thought that it was in the interests of justice that the issues of infringement and validity be tried together, which they would be in England. There was one material difference on the facts of the case from those in the *Amersham* case, which made it even less likely that a stay would be granted. The defendants were not prepared to be bound by the decision of the European Patent Office on the validity issue. In the event of failure before that Office, they wanted to maintain their right to contest the issue of validity all over again in the English infringement proceedings. This duplication would involve unnecessary expense and delay.

The impression given by the *Amersham* and *Pall* cases is that the English courts are reluctant to stay English proceedings pending a decision by the European Patent Office. This is not surprising given the length of time it takes that body to reach a conclusion (four to five years). This impression of reluctance is confirmed in a third and more recent case, where, a stay of an English appeal, pending a decision of the European Patent Office, was refused by the Court of Appeal.[177]

(d) A MULTIPLICITY OF PROCEEDINGS

The English courts, when exercising their discretionary powers to decline jurisdiction, have been influenced by the undesirability of having a multiplicity of proceedings in different States. This concern is not confined to cases of what are, technically, *lis alibi pendens*[178] and is there even though the cause of action or the parties are different in the English and foreign proceedings. Indeed, the English courts do not have a separate doctrine of *lis alibi pendens* under their traditional rules on jurisdiction. What they have is the flexible doctrine of *forum non conveniens* which can take into account the fact that there is a multiplicity of litigation in England and abroad. This factor is one that operates powerfully in favour of the English court staying its own proceedings. Infringement actions often lead to a multiplicity of litigation in different States. For example, a plaintiff may

---

[176] [1988] FSR 274. The judgment was given after the *Spiliada* case; nonetheless, the old outmoded language of judicial advantage to the plaintiff was still used.

[177] *Beloit Technologies Inc and Beloit Walmsley Ltd v Valmet Paper Machinery Inc and Valmet Paper Machinery (UK) Ltd* [1996] FSR 718. In this case, the plaintiff, seeking a stay, had earlier agreed to prosecute the English appeal with due diligence.

[178] See *Metall und Rohstoff AG v ACLI Metals (London) Ltd* [1984] 1 Lloyd's Rep 598; *Hawke Bay Shipping Co Ltd v The First National Bank of Chicago, The Efthimis* [1986] 1 Lloyd's Rep 244. See, generally, Fawcett (ed) *Declining Jurisdiction*, pp 29–31.

bring an infringement action in England to protect his UK patent and parallel actions in the United States and Australia to protect his United States and Australian patents. As has already been seen,[179] the old fashioned view is that the cause of action is not the same in each State and so there is not a situation of what is technically *lis alibi pendens*. Neither may the defendant be the same in each State. Nonetheless, this multiplicity of litigation can be considered under the doctrine of *forum non conveniens*. However, this presupposes that there is an alternative forum abroad in which all the litigation can be consolidated. If there is a forum abroad, for example in the United States, which is prepared to adjudicate on the infringement of foreign intellectual property rights which have been infringed abroad, then the consolidation of litigation factor should operate as a powerful consideration in favour of a stay of the English proceedings. On the other hand, if, as is often the case, there is no such alternative forum abroad, then a stay of the English proceedings should not be granted.

The weight to be attached to the possibility of a multiplicity of litigation arising in the future was considered in the *Amersham* case.[180] It was said that the plaintiff, having brought an action in England for infringement of its European patent (UK), might sue the second defendant in each of the States in which the plaintiff had parallel European patents. It was argued that it would be sensible not to have the validity issue litigated in a number of jurisdictions, but to have it litigated in the European Patent Office. This argument was given very short shrift by Falconer J, who said that 'mere speculation of a possible multiplicity of suits occurring at some time in the future is to be ignored and I do ignore it'.[181] But what if the plaintiff had already commenced actions for infringement in several different States so that multiplicity of litigation was the reality not mere speculation? It is hard to deny that it would be desirable to have the validity issue settled by one action before the European Patent Office. If the European patent was held to be invalid, this would settle the issue of infringement in all States. If, on the other hand, the European patent was held to be valid, it would still be necessary for the plaintiff to pursue the infringement actions in separate European States, since the European Patent Office could not consider a claim for infringement. There would be a strong case for an English court encouraging the parties to litigate the validity issue before the European Patent Office and awaiting the decision of the Office in relation to the validity of the patent, before proceeding with the infringement action.

---

[179] See above, p 135.   [180] [1987] RPC 53.   [181] *Ibid*, at 59.

2. Restraining Foreign Proceedings

It will be recalled[182] that the English courts have a discretionary power to issue an injunction restraining a party from commencing or continuing as plaintiff with foreign proceedings. In infringement cases, often there will be no possibility of proceedings being brought abroad. As has been seen, in cases involving the infringement of UK intellectual property rights, there may well not be an alternative forum abroad which has jurisdiction to try the action, and so the question of restraining foreign proceedings does not arise. It would arise, though, if a foreign court was prepared to try such an action. More obviously, it would also arise in the situation where a foreign court is considering a case involving infringement of a local intellectual property right.

The various categories of case where injunctions restraining foreign proceedings, and the application of the principles developed by the courts to infringement cases, will now be considered.

(a) TRIAL IS AVAILABLE IN ENGLAND AND ABROAD

We are dealing here with the rather unusual situation where, for example, a UK patent has been infringed in England but a US court is available as an alternative forum. In cases where a remedy for a particular wrong is available both in England and abroad, it will be recalled that the English court will 'generally speaking, only restrain the plaintiff from pursuing proceedings in the foreign court if such pursuit would be vexatious or oppressive',[183] and that, generally, the English court must have first concluded that England is the natural forum for trial. Since the court is ultimately concerned with the ends of justice, account must also be taken of the plaintiff's position, and he will not be deprived of advantages in the foreign forum of which it would be unjust to deprive him.

In infringement cases, it will not be difficult to establish that England is the natural forum for trial. The subject matter limitations on jurisdiction under English law mean that, in order for the English court to have jurisdiction, the case will necessarily involve a UK intellectual property right which has been infringed in the United Kingdom.

It has also to be shown that there would be injustice to the defendant if the plaintiff is allowed to pursue the foreign proceedings. There is no such injustice if the defendant is being sued abroad in a State with which there are very real connections. In infringement cases, there are unlikely to be strong connections with the alternative forum abroad. Two of the

---

[182] See above, pp 109–111.
[183] *Société Nationale Industrielle Aerospatial* v *Lee Kui Jak* [1987] AC 871 at 896.

strongest connections are necessarily going to be with England : the fact that it is a UK intellectual property right; and that this was infringed in England.

It is important in infringement cases, as with any other case,[184] to see whether proceedings have actually commenced abroad. If they have, this is a factor in favour of restraining the foreign proceedings.

(b) TRIAL IS AVAILABLE IN ALTERNATIVE FORA ABROAD (BUT NOT IN ENGLAND)

In this category, the English courts do not have jurisdiction over the substantive proceedings and, accordingly, when granting an injunction restraining foreign proceedings, are not protecting their own jurisdiction. Nonetheless, the power to grant an injunction is not confined to cases where the English court is so acting. The basic question is whether an injunction is necessary to prevent injustice. In the leading case, an injunction restraining the English plaintiffs from prosecuting further their proceedings in Texas was granted by the Court of Appeal in the situation where the conduct of the plaintiffs, in suing in Texas, was clearly oppressive and caused significant injustice to the defendant.[185] There was one forum, India, which was the appropriate forum; another forum, France, which was an appropriate forum; the plaintiffs were seeking to sue in Texas which was clearly inappropriate. In these circumstances, the conduct of the plaintiffs was, *prima facie*, oppressive. There was oppression and injustice, which seemed to be treated as the same thing, in having trial in Texas, because it involved trial in an inappropriate forum; it involved trial in a forum which would apply the strict liability law of Texas; there would be significant injustice to the defendant in relation to any contribution claim that it would want to make. It was necessary to weigh against this any legitimate advantage that the plaintiffs gained by suing in Texas. It was said that any advantage obtained by suing in a manifestly inappropriate forum, *prima facie*, is not legitimate.[186] The only legitimate advantage that the plaintiffs would gain in trial in Texas was that the delay in trial was less than in India, but the extent of the disparity was uncertain and of limited importance.

Applying these principles to infringement, what we are concerned with is the situation where, for example, a Canadian patent has been infringed in Canada, which is the clearly appropriate forum in which to bring

---

[184] See above, pp 109–110, in relation to contractual disputes.

[185] *Airbus Industries GIE* v *Patel and Others* [1997] IL Pr 230. The House of Lords allowed an appeal by the defendants [1998] 2 WLR 686. As a general rule, an anti-suit injunction would not be granted unless there was a sufficient interest in, or connection with, England to justify that interference.

[186] *Ibid*, at 248.

infringement proceedings. Nonetheless, the English plaintiff brings the proceedings in the US, and a court there takes jurisdiction. The US court is clearly inappropriate for trial. An application is made to the English courts for an injunction restraining the English plaintiff from continuing with the US proceedings. The conduct of the plaintiff is, *prima facie*, oppressive, and any advantage obtained by the plaintiff is, *prima facie*, not legitimate. It would appear that, *prima facie*, an injunction will be granted.

(c) THE BRINGING OF PROCEEDINGS ABROAD IS AN INVASION OF A LEGAL OR EQUITABLE RIGHT NOT TO BE SUED THERE

This category encompasses the situation where the bringing of the action abroad constitutes a breach of contract. This ground is unlikely to apply in infringement cases.

(d) THE BRINGING OF THE PROCEEDINGS ABROAD WOULD BE UNCON-SCIONABLE

The English courts can grant an injunction restraining foreign proceedings 'if the bringing of the suit in the foreign court is in the circumstances so unconscionable that in accordance with our principles of a "wide and flexible" equity it can be seen to be an infringement of an equitable right of the applicant'.[187] Unconscionable conduct encompasses the situation where the defendant has a right not to be sued because a defence is available to him under English law, such as promissory estoppel. There are very few reported cases where it has been possible to show that the bringing of the proceedings abroad would be unconscionable. Caution is said to be very necessary in cases where the court is being asked to restrain the proceedings in the only State in which the plaintiff can obtain a remedy.

In infringement cases, it is important to differentiate between the infringement of a foreign intellectual property right and the infringement of a UK right.

(i) Infringement of a foreign intellectual property right

We are dealing here with a situation that is quite likely to arise. Trial is available in a foreign State because it is a local intellectual property right that has been infringed in that State. Trial is not available in England because of subject matter limitations in relation to jurisdiction. It seems very unlikely that an English court would restrain foreign proceedings which relate to an intellectual property right granted in that State. It surely

---

[187] *British Airways Board* v *Laker Airways Ltd* [1985] AC 58 at 95. See also *South Carolina Insurance Co* v *Assurantie NV* [1987] AC 24.

(ii) Infringement of a UK intellectual property right

What if the foreign proceedings relate to a UK intellectual property right? If this was infringed in the United Kingdom, the English court would have jurisdiction and the restraint of the foreign proceeding could be based on the ground of vexation or oppression, rather than unconscionability. But if the infringement took place abroad, for example there was foreign authorisation of infringement, the English court would not have jurisdiction. The only available forum may be abroad in the State where the infringement occurred. If jurisdiction is taken abroad, this would be in circumstances where an English court, faced with those facts, would not take jurisdiction. That of itself should not be enough for the grant of an injunction restraining the foreign proceedings. Nevertheless, it is perhaps pertinent to point out that in the leading example of a restraint of foreign proceedings on the basis of unconscionability, *Midland Bank plc* v *Laker Airways Ltd*,[188] there was an element of disapproval of the assertion of jurisdiction in the United States.

(iii) Infringement of parallel rights

In infringement cases, it is not uncommon to have parallel infringement actions in relation to parallel intellectual property rights. Take a simple example. There is an infringement action in England in respect of a UK patent, and a parallel action is about to start or has already started in the United States in respect of the parallel US patent. Essentially, what we are now concerned with is the situation, where an English court, which has no jurisdiction in relation to the US patent, is being asked to restrain those proceedings. What is said above,[189] concerning the infringement of foreign intellectual property rights when trial is not available in England, is equally applicable in the present context, and it seems very unlikely that an English court would grant an injunction restraining the foreign proceedings. There does not appear to be any English authority on this point. There is, though, authority in the United States.

Courts in the United States have 'the discretionary power to enjoin a party from pursuing litigation before a foreign tribunal but can exercise that power only if the parties and issues are the same, and resolution of the domestic action will dispose of the foreign action'.[190] In *Stein Associates Inc* v *Heat and Control Inc*,[191] there were parallel proceedings in the United States and England. The US proceedings were for infringement of US

---

[188] [1986] QB 689. [189] See above, p 277.
[190] *Laker Airways Ltd* v *Sabena, Belgian World Airlines* 731 F2d 909 (DC Circ, 1984).
[191] 748 F2d 653 (1984).

patents and the English proceedings were for infringement of British patents. The US Court of Appeals, Federal Circuit, upheld the decision of the District Court judge to deny the motion to enjoin the defendant's effort to enforce its British patents in Great Britain. It was held that the issues were not the same in the two sets of proceedings. Moreover, resolution of the US action would not dispose of the British action since 'Only a British court, applying British law, can determine validity and infringement of British patents'.[192] The resolution of whether the US patents were valid could have no binding effect on the decision of the British courts.

IV
STATE IMMUNITY

The State Immunity Act 1978 provides that a foreign State is immune from the jurisdiction of the English courts, except as provided for in the Act. One exception in relation to rights registered in the United Kingdom has already been considered.[193] There is a further exception, again concerned with proceedings which are by their nature commercial, in relation to infringement. Section 7 of the Act provides that:

A State is not immune as respects proceedings relating to:

. . . (b) an alleged infringement by the State in the United Kingdom of any patent, trade mark, design, plant breeders' rights or copyright . . .

Thus, if a foreign sovereign State X is sued for infringement of a UK patent relating to a type of security paper for bank notes by keeping for disposal and disposing in England of the currency of State X, which is printed on this paper, it will not enjoy immunity from suit.[194]

V
SUBJECT MATTER LIMITATIONS
IN RELATION TO JURISDICTION

An English court may be incompetent to try a case, despite the fact that a writ has been served on the defendant, because of a limitation in relation to the subject matter of the dispute. One such limitation is in respect of foreign immovable property. However, as will be seen, intellectual property

---

[192] *Ibid*, at 658.   [193] See above, pp 45, 112.
[194] *A Ltd v B Bank and Bank of X* [1997] FSR 165 at 171, 174. Neither will a commercial bank in England which has disposed of the currency in question enjoy immunity from suit.

rights are classified as movable property and so this limitation will not apply. In intellectual property cases, there are two clear subject matter limitations in relation to jurisdiction.[195] The first is in respect of foreign intellectual property rights. The second is in respect of acts of infringement committed abroad. This distinction between subject matter jurisdiction and personal jurisdiction, and its operation in intellectual property cases, is also to be found in Australia,[196] whose law has influenced the development of English law, New Zealand,[197] and the United States.[198]

A defendant may raise one of these subject matter limitations to deny that the English court has jurisdiction. But what if the parties are both content to have trial in England? Will the English court, on its own motion, examine its jurisdiction and declare that it has no jurisdiction in the event of one of these subject matter limitations being applicable? Normally, English courts do not act on their own motion. However, Vinelott J, in an unreported case,[199] did precisely this. He held that he had to be satisfied that the court had jurisdiction to resolve a question involving a US copyright allegedly infringed in the United States, despite the fact that neither party was concerned to argue the jurisdiction point. He said that 'it is trite law that parties cannot by agreement confer a jurisdiction which the court would not otherwise have'.

1. FOREIGN IMMOVABLE PROPERTY

(a) THE EXCLUSIONARY RULE IN RELATION TO FOREIGN IMMOVABLE PROPERTY

At common law, an English court had no jurisdiction to adjudicate upon trespass to or any other tort to, the right of property in, or the right to possession of, foreign immovables, ie foreign land. This rule derived from the House of Lords' decision in *British South Africa Co v Companhia de Mocambique*.[200] The rule has been restricted by Section 30(1) of the Civil Jurisdiction and Judgments Act 1982, getting rid of its most criticised aspect, so that an English court can entertain proceedings for trespass to, or any other tort affecting, immovable property 'unless the proceedings are principally concerned with a question of title to, or the right to possession of, that property'.

---

[195] See, generally, Austin, (1997) 113 *LQR* 321.
[196] See below, pp 283–284.
[197] See below, pp 285–286.
[198] See generally Trooboff, in Mclachlan and Nygh, chapter 8; *ITSI TV Productions Inc v California Authority of Racing Fairs* 785 F Supp 854, 864 (ED Cal 1992).
[199] *Librarie du Liban Inc v Pardoe Blacker Ltd and Others* (Unreported).
[200] [1893] AC 602.

(b) THE CLASSIFICATION OF INTELLECTUAL PROPERTY RIGHTS

The effect of Section 30(1) would be dramatic if intellectual property rights were classified as immovable property, for there would then be statutory authority limiting jurisdiction in the situation where the proceedings are principally concerned with a question of title to, or the right to possession of, that property, but allowing jurisdiction in an infringement action where this is not the case. This raises the question of how intellectual property rights should be classified for jurisdictional purposes.

(i) Arguments of principle and policy

It has been argued that intellectual property rights should be classified as immovable property for jurisdictional purposes.[201] This is on the basis, *inter alia*, that intellectual property rights are much less movable than things such as debts.[202] In answer to this policy argument, it has been said that the reason why some intellectual property rights can be moved less readily than other intangibles is because of their special treatment in private international law and, thus, this argument is no basis for characterisation.[203] It has also been argued, in favour of an immovable characterisation, that such rights have a *situs* and are *in rem*.[204] But then so do other intangible movables, such as debts, have a *situs*. A third possible argument is that land is classified as an immovable. Intellectual property rights have been regarded as analogous to foreign land; indeed, it is on this basis that the subject matter limitation on jurisdiction in relation to foreign land has been extended to foreign intellectual property rights.[205] Accordingly, intellectual property should also be classified as immovable property. The answer to this is that: first, as will be shown,[206] there is no real analogy between land and intellectual property rights; and secondly, even if you accept, for the sake of argument, that the two are analogous, a court which says the two are analogous is doing something very different from actually classifying intellectual property rights as immovables. After all, instead of applying an analogy a court could have actually classified such rights as immovables and then applied the subject matter limitation in relation to foreign immovables.

The arguments in favour of an immovable classification are unconvincing. Moreover, there are strong arguments of principle and policy against such a classification. First, there is an argument of principle. The nature of

---

[201] Arnold, [1990] 7 *EIPR* 254 at 258. For a detailed and convincing refutation see Austin, (1997) 113 *LQR* 321, 325–327.

[202] See Arnold, n 201 above at 258.   [203] Austin, n 195 above at 327.

[204] See Forsyth in a paper entitled 'Intellectual Property and Private International Law : Issues of Title', presented at the Herchel Smith Seminar on Intellectual Property and Private International law: New Directions, held at Cambridge University on 24 February 1996.

[205] See below, pp 283–284.   [206] See below, p 287.

intellectual property rights is very different from land, so different that they cannot be regarded as analogous.[207] Secondly, and here we move on to policy, under the EC/EFTA rules on jurisdiction an immovable classification is not adopted for intellectual property rights.[208] It is surely not sensible to adopt a different classification for the purposes of the traditional rules. Thirdly, under English private international law, intellectual property rights are classified as movable property for the purposes of choice of law.[209] Again, it would not be sensible to adopt a different classification in the area of jurisdiction. Fourthly, the effect of an immovable classification would be to stultify the development of the law by introducing a statutory limitation on jurisdiction, when what is needed is to introduce new flexibility so as to allow the doctrine of *forum non conveniens* to operate so that jurisdiction can be declined where appropriate.

(ii) **What do the cases say?**

So much for arguments of principle and policy, but what do the cases say? There does not appear to be any case law authority adopting an immovable characterisation. It is important to repeat that the subject matter limitation in relation to foreign intellectual property rights, which will be examined next, is based on an *analogy* between foreign land and such rights, not on a classification of such rights as being immovable property.[210] Thus, in *Potter* v *Broken Hill Pty Co Ltd*, a decision of the High Court of Australia, Griffith C J[211] said that both rights are the creation of the State and the title to each devolves according to the law imposed by that State;[212] nonetheless he described a patent as being, in some respects, analogous to immovable property, rather than characterising it as being immovable property. Moreover, as will be seen, it was not part of the reasoning of the leading English case on the subject matter limitation in respect of foreign intellectual property rights, *Tyburn Productions Ltd* v *Conan Doyle*,[213] or of any of the authorities on which that case relied, that intellectual property was to be classified as immovable property.

Even more importantly, we now have authorities rejecting an immovable classification, cases which specifically address the issue of whether Section 30 operates as a limitation on jurisdiction in cases relating to for-

---

[207] See below, p 287.   [208] See above, chapter 1 pp 34–35.
[209] See below, chapter 10, pp 487–498.
[210] *Pearce* v *Ove Arup Partnership Ltd and Others* [1997] 2 WLR 779 at 782–783. See also *Coin Controls Ltd* v *Suzo International (UK) Ltd and Others* [1997] 3 All ER 45, at 54.
[211] (1906) 3 CLR 479 at 494.
[212] N 211 above, at p 494. It was also recognised, though, that intellectual property rights are intangible whereas land is obviously not, *ibid*. A'Beckett J in his dissenting judgment in the *Potter* case in the Supreme Court of Victoria, [1905] VLR 612 at 636, pointed out that patents are short lived, no two are alike and determination of a dispute as to one involves no adjudication affecting rights as to others.
[213] [1991] Ch 75, discussed below pp 284–290.

eign intellectual property rights. In *Pearce* v *Ove Arup Partnership Ltd and Others*,[214] Lloyd J, after reviewing the authorities, said that it was difficult to regard foreign intellectual property as immovable property under English conflict of laws rules and seemed to accept that, accordingly, Section 30 would not so operate.[215] In *Coin Controls Ltd* v *Suzo International (UK) Ltd and Others*, Laddie J was even more emphatic.[216] He said that 'intellectual property rights are not accurately described as immovables', and, accordingly, Section 30 would not apply.[217]

2. Foreign Intellectual Property Rights

(a) origin and development of the limitation

(i) The extension in Australia of the exclusionary rule in relation to foreign land to patents

The common law exclusionary rule in the *Mocambique* case was extended in Australia to patents. In *Potter* v *The Broken Hill Pty Co Ltd*,[218] the Supreme Court of Victoria regarded the *Mocambique* case as being decided on the basis of a distinction between 'local' and 'transitory' actions (a transitory action is one in which the facts relied on as the foundation of the plaintiff's case have no particular connection with a particular locality; with a local action there is such a connection),[219] and that this reasoning was equally applicable in relation to foreign patent rights. The case involved an action brought in the State of Victoria alleging infringement in New South Wales of a New South Wales patent by a Victorian company, carrying on mining in New South Wales. It was held that an action for the infringement of a patent is a local action. The reasoning underlying this is concerned very much with the territorial nature of intellectual property rights.[220] The courts will not exercise jurisdiction over rights which are by their nature local.[221] A violation of the right of monopoly claimed could only take place within the territory where the monopoly existed.[222] Accordingly, the Victorian Court had no jurisdiction to deal with the action.

This decision was affirmed by the High Court of Australia.[223] However, the distinction between local and transitory actions was not regarded as

[214] N 210 above. [215] *Ibid*, at 782–783. [216] [1997] 3 All ER 45.
[217] *Ibid*, at 54. [218] [1905] VLR 612.
[219] The *Mocambique* case, n 200 above, 618. See, generally, Lee, (1995) 32 *Colum J Transnational Law* 607, 616 *et seq*.
[220] See Trooboff in McLachlan and Nygh, pp 125–127; the *Coin Controls* case, n 216 above.
[221] *Per* Lord Herschell in the *Mocambique* case.
[222] N 218 above, 638. See the decision of the High Court of Australia (1906) 3 CLR 479 at 492 (*per* Griffith CJ). See also the *Coin Controls* case, n 216 above, at 53.
[223] N 211 above.

being to the point.[224] Instead, the reasoning of the High Court was based on what was essentially the Act of State doctrine,[225] according to which an English court will not enquire into a sovereign act done within the territory of a foreign State.[226] Nonetheless, there was still seen to be an analogy with foreign land. Griffith CJ said that:

> ... the right of creating a title to such property as land, being vested in the ruler, that is in the sovereign power, of the country, controversies relating to such property can only be decided in the State in which the property is situated. The reason appears equally applicable to patent rights, which ... are created by a similar exercise of the sovereign power.[227]

More recently, the *Potter* case was followed by the High Court of Australia in *Norbert Steinhardt and Son Ltd* v *Meth and Another*,[228] where Fullagar J said that 'no action could be maintained in England for an infringement of an Australian patent, or in Australia for an infringement of an English patent ...'[229]

(ii) The English limitation : *Tyburn Productions Ltd* v *Conan Doyle*

The *Potter* and *Norbert Steinhardt* cases were followed and, indeed, extended to intellectual property rights other than patents, in the leading English case of *Tyburn Productions Ltd* v *Conan Doyle*.[230]

The plaintiff, a UK company which produced and wished to distribute in the United States a television film featuring Sherlock Holmes and Dr Watson, was concerned that the defendant, the only surviving child of the late author Sir Arthur Conan Doyle, would repeat previous assertions that she had the copyright in these two famous characters. The plaintiff, therefore, sought from the English courts a declaration that the defendant had no rights under the copyright, unfair competition or trade mark laws of the United States to entitle her to prevent the distribution and an injunction to prevent her from so asserting.

Vinelott J refused these claims and struck out the writ as disclosing no cause of action. He considered that the distinction between transitory and local actions was fundamental to the *Mocambique* case and not merely an historical prologue to the decision, and that actions raising questions as to the validity or infringement of patent rights, copyrights, rights of trademark and other intellectual property rights are to be regarded as being local actions. He found support for this limitation on jurisdiction in the

---

[224] *Ibid*, at 500 (*per* Barton J). But compare *Dagi and Others* v *The Broken Hill Pty Co Ltd and Another (No 2)* [1997] 1 VR 428 at 441.
[225] There was a reluctance by some of the judges to use this term, see O'Connor J at 513. But compare Griffith CJ at 496.
[226] See Dicey and Morris, p 110.   [227] (1906) 3 CLR 479 at 496–497.
[228] (1960) 105 CLR 440, the case is discussed below, p 603.   [229] *Ibid*, at 443.
[230] [1991] Ch 75; Carter, (1990) 61 *BYBIL* 400; Arnold, [1990] 7 *EIPR* 254.

aforementioned High Court of Australia decisions in *Potter*[231] and *Norbert Steinhardt*,[232] and in the English case of *Def Lepp Music* v *Stuart Brown*.[233]

One point that comes out strongly in the judgment of Vinelott J is a reluctance to grant a negative declaration. Even if the validity of the rights had been justiciable in the English courts, the learned judge said that he would not have been prepared to grant the negative declaration requested.[234] The claims raised complex issues which may require a survey of the laws of each of the States in the United States and there was no evidence that the decision of the English courts would be treated as binding on any of the States of the United States.

The decision in the *Tyburn* case was applied by Mummery J in *LA Gear Inc* v *Gerald Whelan & Sons Ltd*,[235] which concerned a trade mark. However, this was not a case involving a limitation on the jurisdiction of the English courts but one concerning declining jurisdiction under Article 21 of the Brussels Convention. The *Tyburn* decision was relevant to this in so far as it explained, in this case, the absence of an allegation of infringement of a UK trade mark in parallel Irish proceedings. This assumes, of course, that Irish law is the same as English on this point, and there was no evidence to the contrary on this point. In *Plastus Kreativ AB* v *Minnesota Mining and Manufacturing Co and Another*,[236] Aldous J regarded submissions of the defendants which relied on the *Tyburn* case as having considerable force 'based, as they are, upon the considered judgment of Vinelott J and the established Law',[237] but found it unnecessary to decide this subject matter limitation point and did not do so. In *Pearce* v *Ove Arup Partnership Ltd and Others*,[238] Lloyd J, whilst deciding that the limitation in relation to foreign intellectual property rights would not apply in cases coming under the Brussels Convention, implicitly accepted that the limitation would apply in cases coming under the traditional rules on jurisdiction. The same point was made explicitly in *Coin Controls Ltd* v *Suzo International (UK) Ltd and Others*,[239] another Brussels Convention case. There is a very odd remark by Lloyd J, in the *Pearce* case, that this limitation is not a rule as to jurisdiction, although Lloyd J acknowledges that it precludes an English court from hearing an action.[240] What it is, of course, is a subject matter limitation on jurisdiction rather than being concerned with jurisdiction over the person.

The *Tyburn* case has also been followed in New Zealand. In *Atkinson Footwear Ltd* v *Hodgskin International Services Ltd and Another*,[241] the plaintiff sought an injunction in New Zealand preventing the defendants from

---

[231] N 211 above.
[232] N 228 above.
[233] N 96 above.
[234] N 230 above at 88–89.
[235] [1991] FSR 671 at 674; discussed above.
[236] [1995] RPC 438; discussed below.
[237] *Ibid*, at 446–447.
[238] N 210 above.
[239] N 216 above.
[240] *Ibid*, at 790.
[241] (1994) 31 IPR 186, HC.

importing in Australia footwear which allegedly infringed its copyright. Tipping J refused to extend the ambit of the injunction beyond New Zealand. He examined the territorial scope of the New Zealand copyright law, holding that this only grants protection within New Zealand. He went on to say that 'an assertion that acts done or threatened to be done outside New Zealand constitute an infringement of the copyright law of another country is not justiciable in the New Zealand courts; nor is an infringement of copyright under foreign law actionable under New Zealand law'.[242]

(iii) Criticism of the decision in the *Tyburn* case

It has been objected that 'Underlying the jurisdictional prohibition is a series of premises associated with the territoriality of intellectual property rights which do not bear detailed scrutiny'.[243] More specifically, the following criticisms can be made of the *Tyburn* case, and the reasoning it employed.

First, the exclusionary rule in *Mocambique* was followed, but that rule has been the subject of much criticism, and has been 'partially eroded by judicial decision, . . . is often circumvented by equity . . .'.[244] It has, eventually, been limited by statute.[245] Moreover, the law relating to jurisdiction has changed so much, particularly during the 1980s,[246] since the *Mocambique* case was decided, that it is dangerous to rely on such an old case.

Secondly, the exclusion of jurisdiction in relation to foreign land has been justified on the basis that 'any judgment *in rem* that might be given would be totally ineffective unless it were accepted and implemented by the authorities in the *situs*'.[247] This justification does not apply in relation to a judgment in infringement proceedings. Such a judgment will be recognised and enforced in Contracting States to the Brussels and Lugano Conventions, subject to possible defences. It is doubtful whether recognition could be refused on the ground of public policy.[248] When it comes to enforcement of the judgment in non-Contracting States, the judgment will be one *in personam*[249] and does not present the problems that a judgment in relation to foreign land presents.

---

[242] (1994) 31 IPR 186, HC at 190.
[243] Austin, n 195 above at 323. See also the criticisms by Fentiman, [1997] *CLJ* 503 at 505.
[244] Carter, n 230 above at 402.
[245] See Civil Jurisdiction and Judgments Act 1982, s 30(1).
[246] See below, pp 289, 293.   [247] Cheshire and North, p 254.   [248] See above, p 225.
[249] Even if validity is raised it will be a judgment in personam unless it settles the destiny of the res itself and binds all persons claiming an interest in the property. The mere fact that the judgment concerns a *res* does not make it a judgment *in rem*: Cheshire and North, pp 362–365.

Thirdly, intellectual property rights have been regarded as being analogous to land. However, Ferris J has warned that 'It may be dangerous to press too far the analogy between a trade-mark right, or other item of intellectual property, and land',[250] and a leading Australian writer has described this analogy as being 'highly artificial'.[251]

At one time, there was perhaps some justification for this analogy. Land is linked to sovereignty and the sovereign territory of States. Courts clearly do not want to interfere with titles to foreign land, that area is reserved for the courts of the nation in whose territory the land is situated. Originally, patents, being the ultimate example of intellectual property rights, were granted as a Royal Privilege. It is easy to observe the same link with sovereignty and the exercise of the executive power of a State, and an English court would not want to interfere with the sovereignty and the exercise of the executive power of another State. This policy argument, which underlies the *Mocambique* rule, may have been valid in relation to intellectual property rights until the beginning of the 20th century, but clearly modern intellectual property rights can no longer be seen as Royal Privileges or even as the exercise of the executive power of the State. They are, in the words of the statutes, personal rights, which can be dealt with commercially. They are tools of business and commercial policy. The interference of several government agencies in economic life is not exceptional at all and the normal legal rules apply to their activities. There is no reason to treat intellectual property differently in this respect. Even the argument that intellectual property rights institute monopolies and that competition policy is an area which each State deals with independently is not convincing. This may be true when intellectual property statutes are drafted. States determine which rules they need to implement, their views on competition policy and the scope of monopolies. But things are different when it comes to applying these rules in individual patent, trade mark or copyright cases. The sovereignty rule might apply when rules are drafted, but it clearly does not apply when these rules are not changed but simply applied to the individual case before the court. At least it does not seem to matter when it comes to other competition law related issues in commercial conflict of laws cases, where it is never argued that the English court should not have subject matter jurisdiction.

Fourthly, what the limitation excludes are actions and there is no obvious analogy between an action for infringement, where all that may be in dispute is whether there was an act of infringement, and an action which is concerned with the title to foreign land.[252]

Fifthly, it was assumed that the *Mocambique* case was based on a distinction between local and transitory actions when, in fact, the case

---

[250] *Apple Corps Ltd and Another* v *Apple Computer Inc and Others* [1992] FSR 431, at 470.
[251] Nygh, at 119. [252] See Austin, n 195 above, at 331.

dispelled the idea that the exclusion in relation to foreign land ever rested on a technical rule of procedure.[253] The distinction between local and transitory actions has been described as 'outmoded and analytically dubious'.[254] Moreover, it is a distinction that is shrouded in mystery. It is by no means clear why an action for infringement of foreign intellectual property rights is to be classified as local. Is it, as has been suggested,[255] because the right is the creation of a local statute or agency? In which case, it can be objected that all property rights are local.[256] Or is it because of the territorial nature of intellectual property rights?[257] This is probably the better view, but it means that complex issues are raised in order to ascertain whether the action is local or transitory. One obvious issue is: what is the territorial extent of the substantive law?[258] You then have the issue of which State's substantive law are we looking at? There is a foreign element in the *Tyburn* case. The question of the applicable law has to be considered in working out whether it is a local or transitory action.[259] But the significance of choice of law rules, when considering the subject matter limitation on jurisdiction, was not explained in the *Tyburn* case. Presumably, if the applicable law provides a cause of action, even in respect of infringement of a foreign intellectual property right, it is, arguably, a transitory action, not a local one, and the limitation on jurisdiction will not apply.

Sixthly, the cases relied on by Vinelott J are weak authorities. The two decisions of the High Court of Australia are, of course, not binding in England. Moreover, the *Potter* case[260] was not, in fact, based on the distinction between local and transitory actions. The *Norbert Steinhardt*[261] case was not concerned with jurisdiction over the person or subject matter jurisdiction, but with what, in Australia, has been described as a preliminary or threshold jurisdictional rule prior to determination of the applicable substantive law.[262] As far as English law is concerned, it was dealing with what we would regard as a tort choice of law rule.[263] Also, it was concerned with an Australian patent, rather than a foreign one. As regards the *Def Lepp Music* case,[264] this did not involve the subject matter limitation in respect of foreign intellectual property rights; it was concerned with the infringement of a UK copyright. Admittedly, there are comments by the

---

[253] See Cheshire and North, pp 253–254. see also Jooris, [1996] 3 EIPR 127 at 129–130.
[254] Carter, [1990] *BYBIL* 400–402.   [255] See Austin, n 195 above, at 328–329.
[256] Ibid.
[257] See Trooboff, n 220 above, at 125–127; see also above for case law support for this, n 222 and text accompanying.
[258] Trooboff, n 220 above.   [259] Trooboff, n 220 above, at 126.   [260] N 211 above.
[261] N 228 above.   [262] See Nygh, pp 342–344.
[263] See below, p 297. See also Mcleod, *The Conflict of Laws* p 560, where the case is cited as authority for the proposition that 'no action may be brought in Canada for the infringement of a foreign patent by acts occurring in the foreign country'. This statement appears in the chapter on tort choice of law.
[264] See above, n 96 .

Vice-Chancellor supporting a subject matter limitation in respect of foreign acts of infringement.[265] But, ultimately, the issue was whether the case was a proper one for service out of the jurisdiction under Order 11, rule 1(1) of the Rules of the Supreme Court when what was involved was an action that was bound to fail once the common law tort choice of law rules were applied to the facts of the case.

Seventhly, the *Tyburn* case itself was a weak authority. The legal proceedings were instituted after the Convention came into force in the United Kingdom. The defendant was an English resident, no doubt also domiciled in the United Kingdom and, presumably, the English court's jurisdiction was based on Article 2 of the Brussels Convention.[266] No mention of the Brussels Convention is made in the law report of the case. If jurisdiction was based on this Convention, the question should have been asked whether a common law limitation on jurisdiction can be applied in such cases. We now know that it cannot.[267]

Eighthly, insufficient attention was paid to Section 30(1) of the Civil Jurisdiction and Judgments Act 1982.[268] With Parliament so recently concerned to limit the exclusionary rule in the *Mocambique* case, it is hard to justify the judicial extension of that rule, in the *Tyburn* case, to the completely new area of foreign intellectual property rights. More specifically, in the *Mocambique* case, the distinction between local and transitory actions was raised in connection with a claim which, by the time it reached the House of Lords, was solely for damages for trespass to foreign land and did not involve any issue as to title. Now that such a claim is allowed by virtue of Section 30(1) of the Civil Jurisdiction and Judgments Act 1982, it would have been easy, in *Tyburn*, to distinguish the *Mocambique* case.[269] Further, following the passing of Section 30(1), we now have the bizarre situation whereby the limitation in cases involving foreign intellectual property rights is wider than that in cases involving foreign land. An action for trespass to foreign land which does not involve any issue of title to the land can now be heard by the English courts, whereas an action for infringement of a foreign intellectual property right, which does not involve any issue as to the title to the right but merely, for example, the question of whether there has been an act of infringement, cannot be heard.

---

[265] See below, p 301.
[266] Lloyd J raises a doubt, which misunderstands when the Convention applies, as to whether the Convention would apply on the facts: the *Pearce* case, n 210 above, at 787–788.
[267] See above, p 190.
[268] See Floyd and Purvis, [1995] EIPR 110 at 112 where it is suggested that the modification of the *Mocambique* rule by Section 30(1) has the effect that that rule no longer prevents an action for infringement of a foreign patent. This overstates the position. See also Jooris, [1996] 3 *EIPR* 127, 143.
[269] See Floyd and Purvis, n 268 above.

Ninthly, the real issue is whether, on policy grounds, a court should refuse to try an action in respect of the infringement of a foreign intellectual property right.[270] The policy considerations in favour of and against having this limitation in relation to jurisdiction were ignored in the *Tyburn* case. These considerations are very much affected by recent developments in private international law, which were also ignored. These policy considerations will now be considered.

(b) POLICY CONSIDERATIONS

(i) In favour of the limitation

In *Plastus Kreativ AB v Minnesota Mining and Manufacturing Co*,[271] Aldous J came to the conclusion that the court had no jurisdiction to hear a claim for a declaration that the plaintiffs' activities did not constitute infringement of the defendants' French or German patents. This was on the ground that there had been no claim by the defendants that the plaintiffs had infringed the German or French patents or intended to do so. The learned judge found it unnecessary to decide the more interesting legal point raised by Counsel for the respective parties of whether the limitation in the *Tyburn* case would preclude jurisdiction. Counsel for the plaintiffs argued, in the light of the introduction of the Brussels Convention and the harmonisation of patent law in Europe, that it would not do so.

However, Aldous J expressed the view that he would not welcome the task of having to decide whether a person had infringed a foreign patent. He gave two reasons for this. First, a finding of infringement involves the public having to pay higher prices than if no such monopoly existed, and the public abroad are more likely to respect a decision which affects them in this way if it comes from a local court. Secondly, for an infringement, there has to be a valid patent. It is convenient that infringement, like validity, should be decided in the State in which the intellectual property right arises. In terms of policy, what Aldous J was concerned with was the reaction of members of the public to a monopoly and the desirability of the same court trying the twin issues of infringement and validity. As regards the former, it has been questioned whether this provides a sufficient basis for distinguishing intellectual property rights from other intangibles.[272] As regards the latter, though, it is possible to achieve this objective in an entirely different way. This is by allowing an English court which has infringement jurisdiction to try a defence of invalidity.[273]

Lloyd J, in *Pearce v Ove Arup Partnership and Others*,[274] gave a different policy reason for judicial reluctance to try cases of infringement of foreign

---

[270] See Carter, n 254 above. [271] [1995] RPC 438. [272] Austin, n 195 above, at 333.
[273] See below, pp 308–310. [274] [1997] 2 WLR 779 at 788.

intellectual property rights. This is because of the problem of having to decide, possibly in the absence of national decisions, what some unclear provision of foreign law means.[275] But this is hardly a convincing reason for retaining the limitation. It is tantamount to saying that we should not try any case where, at the choice of law stage, foreign law is applicable.

A final policy justification that has been given is the problem of enforcement.[276] It is admitted, though, that this is more of a problem with a finding as to validity than with infringement as such.[277] In fact, the finding that is difficult to enforce is one of invalidity, in which case the infringement action will fail anyway and, accordingly, there is no question of any other State having to enforce an injunction or damages.

(ii) Against the limitation

First, it is unfair to plaintiffs who, despite having jurisdiction over the person in respect of the defendant, are unable to bring an action in England and instead are forced to go abroad for trial. It is unusual for this to happen in private international law, where there are relatively few subject matter limitations on jurisdiction. In the past, this would not have mattered. The common law tort choice of law rules were such that even if an infringement action could be brought in England in respect of a foreign intellectual property right, this action would be unlikely to be successful. But with the introduction of statutory tort of law rules this has now changed, so that, if there is jurisdiction, an action in respect of the infringement abroad of a foreign intellectual property right can succeed. The sole obstacle to a plaintiff obtaining a remedy in England in respect of such an infringement is the subject matter limitation in relation to jurisdiction in respect of foreign intellectual property rights.[278] In infringement cases, this effectively cancels out the benefit for plaintiffs produced by the statutory tort choice of law rules. The upshot is that the *Tyburn* case is going to come in for much closer scrutiny and criticism than it has in the past.[279]

Secondly, the limitation prevents the consolidation in one State (ie England) of litigation concerning the infringement of parallel intellectual property rights. This is particularly noticeable in relation to European patents. Given that a bundle of national rights is granted, it follows that each designated State would have to be treated separately for the purpose of the subject matter limitation in the *Tyburn* case. Thus, with a European patent granted in respect of the UK, France and Germany, the application of the subject matter limitation would mean that a court in the United Kingdom would have no jurisdiction in relation to the French and German

---

[275] See, generally, Arnold, n 230 above, at 258.   [276] *Ibid.*   [277] *Ibid.*
[278] And the subject matter limitation in respect of infringements abroad, discussed below.
[279] See, eg Dicey and Morris, *Fourth Supplement*, pp 231–232.

patents.[280] If these other States apply the same subject matter limitation, the plaintiff would be forced to bring three separate actions in three different States. It is in the interests of both parties and the efficient administration of justice that this should be avoided.

Thirdly, the limitation is not in the interests of the English courts in that it unnecessarily rules out England as a venue for international litigation concerning intellectual property rights. Putting it bluntly, the English courts and lawyers are losing out on business. Courts abroad are not always so unwise. The Dutch courts are happy to adjudicate upon infringements concerning foreign intellectual rights that have been infringed abroad, and have granted injunctions not only in respect of intellectual property rights granted in other EC/EFTA Contracting States but also in respect of those granted in other States.[281] In Finland, the Helsinki Court of Appeal has taken jurisdiction in a case involving the infringement of trade marks registered in Brazil and Russia.[282] Moving outside Europe to the United States, although the concept of subject matter jurisdiction is well known and applied, at least in patent and trademark cases, there is a well known example of a court taking jurisdiction in a case concerning the infringement of a British copyright in Chile and other South American countries.[283] It also appears that Japanese courts are prepared to try actions relating to the infringement of foreign patents.[284]

Fourthly, the limitation has the effect of widening the gap between the traditional rules on jurisdiction and those under the EC/EFTA rules, which contain no such subject matter limitation,[285] and in respect of which it is not possible to apply this traditional limitation.[286]

Fifthly, the limitation is unnecessary in that an English court can use the doctrine of *forum non conveniens* to decline jurisdiction where it considers it appropriate in cases involving the infringement of foreign intellectual property rights.[287]

---

[280] See the *Plastus Kreativ AB* case, n 271 above.

[281] See *Philips v Hemogram* The Hague District Court, 30 December 1991, 1992 BIE, No 80, 323, 1992 IER, No 17,76. For the Dutch position see above, pp 218–219.

[282] *Salamander AG v (1) TOO VITL (2) Kissol Ltda* 7 March 1996 S 95/1952; [1996] 12 *EIPR* D-354.

[283] *London Film Productions Ltd v Intercontinental Communications Inc* 580 F Supp 47 (US District Court SDNY 1984). But compare the *ITSI* case, n 198 above, which is also concerned with a foreign copyright.

[284] Takeda, *Patent Litigation in Japan, Foreign Patent Litigation* (Practising Law institute 1983).

[285] See above, p 190. Article 16(4) is, in effect, a limitation in relation to actions concerned with the registration or validity of foreign patents, trade marks, designs, or other similar rights, but does not apply to infringement.

[286] See above, pp 191–193.

[287] See, generally, Fentiman, n 243 above at 506; Austin, n 195 above at 323, 336–338. Austin, at 323 and 335–336, would also employ a general principle, used in respect of cases involving foreign land, that the courts will not act where they cannot grant an appropriate

Sixthly, the infringement of foreign rights often arises in the context of parallel rights. As has been seen,[288] the better view under intellectual property law is that, where there are separate proceedings for infringement of parallel rights, the cause of action is the same. It is hard then to see the objection to taking jurisdiction in relation to an action for the infringement of a foreign right, at least where it is a parallel right.

It is submitted that the policy considerations against the limitation outweigh these in favour of the limitation.

(c) THE SOLUTION: THE DOCTRINE OF *FORUM NON CONVENIENS*

At the time when the *Potter* case was decided in Australia there was no doctrine of *forum non conveniens* which could be used to stay actions when the natural forum for trial was abroad. Since the development of this doctrine in the 1970's and 1980's, culminating in the *Spiliada* case in 1986, it is possible to use it to deal with cases of infringement of foreign intellectual property rights. In the United States, it is not unknown for courts to decline jurisdiction on *forum non conveniens* grounds in cases involving the infringement of foreign intellectual property rights.[289] Unfortunately, this possibility was not considered by Vinelott J in the *Tyburn* case.

(i) **The virtues of this solution**

The use of the doctrine of *forum non conveniens*, rather than having a blanket limitation on jurisdiction, allows the interest of the plaintiff in having trial in England to be considered, as well as the interests of the defendant, and the public interest in allowing the trial of international litigation to take place in England. More generally, it allows in a consideration of all the connections with the alternative fora, factors of litigational convenience, and the interests of justice.

The doctrine of *forum non conveniens* can deal very effectively with the concern raised by Vinelott J in the *Tyburn* case and by Aldous J, in the *Plastus Kreativ AB* case, in relation to granting a negative declaration. The fact that a negative declaration is sought before the English courts is one of the relevant factors in exercising the *forum non conveniens* discretion.[290] There is a number of instances of where there were concurrent proceedings pending abroad and a negative declaration was sought in

---

remedy. It is submitted that this perpetuates the false analogy with foreign land and unnecessarily complicates matters.

[288] See above, chapter 4, pp 136–137.
[289] See *Vanity Fair Mills v T Eaton Co* 234 F 2d 633 (2d Cir 1956); the *ITSI* case, n 198 above; Trooboff, n 220 above, at 152–153.
[290] See Beaumont in chapter 10 of Declining Jurisdiction, ed Fawcett, p 219. See generally Dicey and Morris, pp 406–408; Collins: Essays, pp 274–288; Bell, (1995) 111 *LQR* 674.

England.[291] This was regarded as forum shopping and the English proceedings were stayed. It has been said that a negative declaration will hardly ever be granted.[292] The question is asked of whether the grant of the declaration would serve any useful purpose.[293] The same principles apply where the negative declaration is sought in England to pre-empt litigation abroad.[294]

Moreover, the use of the doctrine of *forum non conveniens* is a much better way of dealing with the concerns raised by Aldous J, in the *Plastus Kreativ AB* case,[295] in relation to the reaction of the public to a decision concerning a monopoly and the desirability of the issues of validity and infringement being tried before the same court, than a blanket limitation on jurisdiction. Both of these considerations can be taken into account, and the proper weight attached to them in the light of the circumstances of the case. After all, the significance to be attached to the desirability of the same court trying the validity and the infringement issues, rather than splitting them up amongst different States, is going to depend on whether the issue of validity is actually raised or clearly going to be raised in the instant case. For example, in the *Plastus Kreativ AB* case, there was no dispute over the validity of the patent. When discussing jurisdiction in relation to acts of infringement committed abroad, Aldous J was also concerned about whether a foreign court could provide an appropriate remedy. This is obviously a matter which can be taken into consideration when exercising a flexible *forum non conveniens* discretion, but is not one that can be properly dealt with by a rigid subject matter limitation on jurisdiction.

(ii) Application in cases involving foreign intellectual property rights

The fact that a case concerns a foreign intellectual property right will be a powerful factor suggesting that the clearly appropriate forum is abroad, and doubtless often will lead to a stay being granted. Take the facts of the *Tyburn* case itself. The defendant, probably, would have been able to establish that the clearly appropriate forum for trial was in the United States; the case concerned US copyright and its infringement in the United States. Accordingly, a stay would normally be granted. The plaintiff might seek to justify trial in England on the basis, and this was not denied, that the negative declaration sought could not be obtained in the United States. But it must be very doubtful, given the reluctance of English judges to grant negative declarations, that this would be sufficient to satisfy the court that, in the interests of justice, a stay should not be granted. On the

---

[291] See *First National Bank of Boston v Union Bank of Switzerland and Others* [1990] 1 Lloyd's Rep 32; *The Volvox Hollandia* [1988] 2 Lloyd's Rep 361.

[292] *Camilla Cotton Oil Co v Granadex SA* [1976] 2 Lloyd's Rep 10 at 14 (*per* Lord Wilberforce), quoting Lord Sterndale in *Guaranty Trust Co of New York v Hannay & Co* [1915] 2 KB 536.

[293] The *Camilla* case, n 292 above, at 14; the *First National Bank* case, n 291 above, at 36.

[294] Beaumont, n 290 above. [295] N 271 above.

contrary, the fact that a negative declaration is sought may be seen as a form of pre-emptive forum shopping and lead to a stay of the English proceedings.

Nonetheless, there may still be circumstances where an English court thinks it right not to decline jurisdiction, even though the case concerns the infringement of foreign intellectual property rights. It has been suggested[296] that one such case would be where one English company markets products in various countries and owns copyrights, designs and trade marks in respect of them. Another English company enters the same markets with products which infringe these rights. In essence one English company has harmed another and an English court should try the case. This is the great virtue of the doctrine of *forum non conveniens*; it provides the flexibility to allow an action commenced in England to continue, which a blanket subject matter limitation on jurisdiction does not.

(d) CONFUSION BETWEEN JURISDICTION AND CHOICE OF LAW

To the private international lawyer, one of the most perplexing aspects of the cases involving the infringement of foreign intellectual property rights is the widespread confusion between the basic concepts of jurisdiction and choice of law.

(i) Examples of confusion

In the *Coin Controls* case,[297] Laddie J said of the double actionability rule in *Chaplin* v *Boys*[298] that 'this common law rule prevented infringement of foreign intellectual property rights being litigated here'.[299] He relied on the *Def Lepp* case as authority for this proposition. However, it is submitted that this misunderstands that decision. This is not surprising, given that the reasoning in that case is often hard to follow. The real importance of that case, in the present context, is that it supports the existence of a subject matter limitation on jurisdiction in relation to infringements committed abroad.[300] As far as the relationship between choice of law and jurisdiction is concerned, the Vice-Chancellor, Sir Nicholas Browne-Wilkinson made it clear that, as a matter of principle, even if the double actionability rule had been satisfied, which it was not on the facts of the case, this could not get round this subject matter limitation on jurisdiction,[301] thus separating correctly the two issues of jurisdiction and choice of law. Even more fundamentally, Laddie J appears to treat the first limb of the double actionability rule in *Chaplin* v *Boys*, which requires

---

[296] See Austin, n 195 above, at 337. [297] N 210 above.
[298] [1971] AC 356, discussed below, p 607.
[299] N 297 above, at 52. The same confusion is evident in the *Tyburn* case, n 230 above.
[300] See below, p 301. [301] N 96 above, at 276, quoted below, p 305.

actionability by English law, as if it were a jurisdictional rule, despite the fact that Lord Wilberforce, in the case[302] itself, was explicit that this was a choice of law rule. That this is so has been confirmed by the Privy Council in *Red Sea Insurance Co Ltd v Bouygues SA and Others*.[303] Clearly, a choice of law rule cannot deprive an English court of jurisdiction that it would otherwise have.[304] All it can do is tell us whether an action would be successful if the English courts were to have jurisdiction to try the case.

The confusion gets even worse because it has been assumed by some that the so called limitation on jurisdiction imposed by the double actionability rule is the same as the subject matter limitation in respect of foreign intellectual property rights. This has led to the suggestion that if the double actionability rule is satisfied then so is the subject matter limitation. This appears to have been the view of Vinelott J in the unreported case of *Librarie du Liban Inc v Pardoe Blacker Ltd and Others*. The learned judge held that an English court had jurisdiction to grant an interlocutory injunction to restrain a number of defendants, English and American,[305] from doing acts (publishing certain books) in the United States which would constitute an infringement of the plaintiff's US copyright. The authority for this startling proposition was said to be the common law rule in *Chaplin v Boys*,[306] the suggestion being that the English courts would have jurisdiction if the acts complained of abroad would be a wrong if committed in England. But a choice of law rule cannot give jurisdiction to the English courts, when they would not otherwise have this, any more than it can deprive an English court of jurisdiction. Again, all it can do is to indicate whether an action would be successful if the English courts were to have jurisdiction to try the case.

The same equation of the double actionability rule and the subject matter limitation can be found in the *Pearce* case,[307] but here it worked the other way round. In this case, Lloyd J decided that if the limitation in relation to foreign intellectual property rights was overcome, it would also remove any problems presented by the double actionability choice of law rule.[308] Clearly, satisfaction of a jurisdictional rule cannot mean that you have, automatically, also satisfied the choice of law rule. Lloyd J not only misunderstands the common law tort choice of law rule, which he thought was a rule which precluded an English court from hearing an action,[309]

---

[302] [1971] AC 356, 385–387. See also *Def Lepp Music v Stuart-Brown* [1986] RPC 273 at 276. Dicey and Morris, pp 1488–1489.

[303] [1995] 1 AC 190 at 198.

[304] This statement has to be qualified by remembering that application of the tort choice of law rule may show that there is no serious issue to be tried on the merits, see above pp 145–149, 258. There is nothing to suggest that this is what Laddie J had in mind in the *Coin Controls* case.

[305] The US defendants had submitted to the jurisdiction of the English court.

[306] [1971] AC 356; discussed below p 607.   [307] N 210 above.   [308] *Ibid*, at 783.

[309] *Ibid*, at 790.

but also misunderstands the nature of the subject matter limitation on jurisdiction.

To his credit, Laddie J, in the *Coin Controls* case, at least did not confuse the double actionability rule with the subject matter limitation on jurisdiction. He said that 'The *Mocambique* rule [by which he meant the subject matter limitation on jurisdiction in relation to foreign intellectual property rights] has nothing to do with double actionability. It is a principle of public policy based on the undesirability of our courts adjudicating on issues which are essentially foreign and local'.[310]

(ii) The reasons for confusion

Why is there this confusion over the concepts of jurisdiction and choice of law, which is also sometimes to be found in the literature on intellectual property?[311] A number of reasons can be given for this. First, the defendant was protected both by the subject matter limitation on jurisdiction and, until its recent replacement in England by new statutory tort choice of law rules, by the common law double actionability rule.[312] Secondly, the latter was unusual for a choice of law rule in being double limbed. Thirdly, considerable reliance has been placed on Australian cases, and in that country there has been a tendency to regard the tort choice of law rule in *Chaplin* v *Boys*, and the earlier rule in *Phillips* v *Eyre*, as being threshold jurisdictional rules.[313] There are indications of this misguided view in the Supreme Court of Victoria in the *Potter* case,[314] and in the High Court of Australia in the *Norbert Steinhardt* case.[315] Fourthly, the jurisdictional limitation is also unusual in that it is concerned with a subject matter limitation rather than being concerned with jurisdiction over the person. The two types of jurisdiction are often not clearly separated. Moreover, when it comes to jurisdiction over the person, the applicable law is relevant to establishing liability for the purpose of satisfying the threshold requirement.[316] Fifthly, the subject matter limitation is based on the distinction between local and transitory actions. When determining whether it is a local or transitory action, the question has been asked: is the wrong actionable under English law?[317] This is the same question that is asked under the first limb of the double limbed choice of law rule.

(iii) An end to confusion

Now that tort choice of law has been put largely on a statutory basis,[318] with the result that the rule in *Chaplin* v *Boys* no longer applies in

[310] N 216 above, at 53.
[311] Drysdale and Silverleaf, *Passing Off Law and Practice* 2nd ed (1995), paras 4.50–4.54; Jooris, n 268 above at 144.
[312] See Austin, n 195 above, at 321.
[313] Nygh, pp 342–344.
[314] N 218 above.
[315] N 228 above.
[316] See above, pp 145–149.
[317] See the *Def Lepp* case, below, p 608.
[318] See below, pp 612–640.

infringement cases, the confusion caused by the common law double actionability rule should also disappear. There is an encouraging sign of this in the *Coin Controls* case where Laddie J held that, since the abolition of the common law double actionability rule, it can no longer be used to prevent proceedings being brought in England to enforce foreign rights.[319] It would, of course, have been even better if he had pointed out that a choice of law rule cannot prevent the English courts from having jurisdiction in the first place.

(e) SHOULD DIFFERENT FOREIGN INTELLECTUAL PROPERTY RIGHTS BE TREATED THE SAME?

Even if, contrary to what is argued here, one accepts that there should be an exclusion in relation to foreign intellectual property rights, there is a question of whether this should apply to copyrights. Counsel for the plaintiff, in the *Tyburn* case, did not seek to distinguish between different intellectual property rights. Nonetheless, there is an argument that copyrights are different from patents, which is what the Australian cases relied on in *Tyburn* were dealing with, in that they do not have to be registered. The point has also been made that the historical background to the law of patents is quite different from that of copyright, which suggests that there should be no extension of the limitation to this area.[320] Moreover, it is important to recall that Article 16(4) of the Brussels and Lugano Conventions distinguishes between different intellectual property rights. It is only concerned with those rights which are required to be deposited or registered, and, accordingly, does not apply to copyrights. Finally, in the United States, a distinction has been drawn between infringement of a foreign copyright and other rights which have to be registered on the basis that in the former 'there is . . . no need to pass upon the validity of acts of foreign government officials'.[321] Thus, jurisdiction was taken in a case concerning the infringement of a British copyright in various South American States,[322] but declined in a case concerning infringement of a trade mark in Canada under Canadian law, a trade mark which Canadian officials had seen fit to grant.[323]

The counter argument to this is that, although the way in which patents and copyrights come into existence is very different, once created there is an important similarity. A patent gives a monopoly which is effective for

---

[319] N 210 above, at 52.   [320] Nygh, p 119. See also Fentiman, n 243 above at 505.

[321] Nimmer, 3 *Nimmer on Copyright* (1982), para 1703. Approved in the *London Film Productions* case, n 283 above.

[322] The *London Film Productions* case, *ibid*.

[323] The *Vanity Fair Mills* case, n 289 above. Followed in the patent infringement case of *Packard Instrument Company* v *Beckman Instruments Inc* 346 F Supp 408 (US District Court ND Illinois, ED 1972).

a particular territory, likewise, the rights of a copyright owner are territorially limited.[324] This territoriality point is significant when it comes to applying the distinction between local and transitory actions. If you apply that distinction, then it is hard to deny that a copyright is local, just as a patent is.

Rather than trying to distinguish between different intellectual property rights, it would be better to accept that *Tyburn* is a wrong decision and that there should be no limitation in respect of any foreign intellectual property rights.

(f) SHOULD DIFFERENT ISSUES BE TREATED THE SAME?

There is support in the United States case law for the idea that, in a straightforward case where all that is in issue is whether there has been an infringement of a foreign right, there is no objection to the assertion of jurisdiction.[325] On the other hand, if the existence or validity of the right is raised by one of the parties, and the right has been granted by foreign government officials (ie it is a foreign registered right), a US court should dismiss the infringement claim.[326] But this too does not address the fundamental point that *Tyburn* is a wrong decision and there should be no limitation in respect of foreign intellectual property rights, whatever the issue.

3. INFRINGEMENTS ABROAD

If a foreign intellectual property right has been infringed abroad,[327] there is the well established, albeit suspect, limitation on jurisdiction in relation to foreign intellectual property rights, as set out above, so that the existence of a second limitation in relation to infringements abroad is of no practical importance, unless and until, as is suggested, the first limitation is abolished. However, if there is an act of infringement committed abroad in respect of a UK intellectual property right, it is of vital importance to ascertain whether there is this second limitation.

---

[324] See, though, Koumantos, (1988) 24 *Copyright* 415 at 417 who asserts that the history of the principle of territoriality shows that it does not concern copyright.
[325] See the *London Film Productions* case, n 283 above.
[326] *Ibid*. See also the *Vanity Fair Mills* case, n 289 above; the *Packard* case, n 323 above.
[327] For infringement of copyright on the high seas, see Copinger and Skone James, paras 11–32.

(a) THE AUTHORITIES

(i) The *Morocco Bound* case

'*Morocco Bound' Syndicate, Ltd* v *Harris*[328] is an early authority which, seemingly, supports the proposition that there is a limitation in relation to acts of infringement committed abroad. The plaintiffs had English rights in the form of the sole right to represent a musical dramatic work in the United Kingdom. Kekewich J held that an English court has no jurisdiction to restrain a threatened copyright infringement in Germany by a defendant who was a British subject and was to be treated as in England. In so far as the judgment is referring to English rights, it appears to support the limitation. However, the learned judge went on to point out that the work was also entitled to protection in other States by virtue of the Berne Convention. Accordingly, he was also being asked to enforce German law, but he said that the plaintiff should bring his action in Germany with a view to protecting his German rights from infringement there. A denial of jurisdiction in relation to foreign intellectual property rights that have been infringed abroad is explicable by virtue of the limitation in relation to such rights. The decision can also be seen as one which was largely concerned with the difficulties relating to enforcement of the injunction if it were to be granted. Kekewich J said that 'If these defendants are not in *England*, they may set any such judgment at defiance, and unless they come to England there will be no means of enforcing it against them'.[329] Arguably, it was for this reason that the injunction sought was not granted.[330]

In *Def Lepp Music and Others* v *Stuart-Brown and Others*,[331] the Vice-Chancellor (Sir Nicholas Browne-Wilkinson) described the decision in *Morocco Bound* as being a puzzling one,[332] and found it impossible to derive any useful guidance from it. However, he went on to say, in relation to the grant of injunctions, that 'the English court does have jurisdiction to enforce rights under English law by granting injunctions against a person within the jurisdiction restraining him from doing acts outside the jurisdiction, although in many cases the court would be reluctant to exercise such jurisdiction'.[333]

The *Morocco Bound* case was also distinguished in *Librarie du Liban Inc* v *Pardoe Blacker Ltd and Others*,[334] partly on the basis that the US defendants had submitted to the jurisdiction and had also agreed, in US proceedings, that any order of the English courts should be made an order of the New

[328] [1895] 1 Ch 534.
[329] At p 538. See also the unreported case of *Librarie du Liban Inc* v *Pardoe Blacker Ltd*.
[330] See Copinger and Skone James 1971 11th ed, p 234 at n 8.
[331] [1986] RPC 273. [332] *Ibid*, at 277. [333] *Ibid*.
[334] Unreported, except through Lexis; discussed above p 296.

York courts. There was, therefore, no problem in relation to enforcement of the English injunction, if granted.

As regards this matter of the enforcement of the injunction, it should be noted that, in recent years, the English courts have been prepared to grant injunctions restraining a party from commencing or continuing proceedings abroad. There may be practical problems in relation to such an injunction, but the courts will not consider the possibility that a foreign defendant will not obey this injunction.[335] There does, of course, need to be jurisdiction in respect of this foreign defendant, which means that a writ will have to be served out of the jurisdiction on the person under Order 11, rule 1(1) of the Rules of the Supreme Court.

(ii) The *Def Lepp* case

Despite his reservations about the *Morocco Bound* case, the Vice-Chancellor, in the *Def Lepp* case, made certain remarks suggesting that there is a limitation in respect of acts of infringement committed abroad. The reasoning underlying this limitation was said to be that the UK copyright law did not extend to acts abroad.[336] This, presumably, means that it is a local action.[337] The *Def Lepp* case has been given as authority, in Copinger and Skone James, for the proposition that 'A claim that acts done outside the United Kingdom constitute an infringement of UK copyright is not maintainable because only acts done in the United Kingdom constitute infringement, direct or indirect, of such copyright'.[338] The reasoning looks to be the same as that found in the United States.[339] But why, even at the jurisdictional stage, should you look automatically at what UK substantive law says? The tort was committed abroad, there is accordingly an issue as to the applicable law. Moreover, the authority of the case is weakened by the fact that these comments were made in the context of whether there was jurisdiction over the defendant under Order 11, rule 1(1). There was a failure to separate out the issues of subject matter jurisdiction and personal jurisdiction.[340]

---

[335] *Castanho v Brown and Root (UK) Ltd* [1981] AC 557.

[336] Compare the views of the Austrian Supreme Court in relation to patents (German patent not infringed by acts in Austria), judgment of 25 March 1986 (case 4 Ob 312/86), [1987] GRUR 259.

[337] But compare Dutson, [1997] *JBL* 495 at 496–497 who regards subject matter limitations as being derived from territorial limitations in the substantive statutory law. This view is not supported by the case law generally on subject matter limitations or by the position under the Brussels and Lugano Conventions. It confuses the issues of jurisdiction and the applicable law.

[338] Paras 11–31.

[339] See below, pp 302–303 and see also Toraya (1985) 70 Cornell Law Review 1165 and *Robert Stigwood Group Ltd v O'Reilly*, 530 F2d 1096, 1100–01 (2d Cir), cert denied, 429 US 848 (1976).

[340] See Trooboff, n 220 above, pp 127–128.

(iii) The *Tyburn* case

The *Def Lepp* case was decided before *Tyburn*.[341] The latter case is of considerable importance in relation to this second limitation. For if you apply the distinction between transitory and local actions, it must be the case that an action in respect of an act of infringement abroad of a UK intellectual property right is a local action. Redress is only available if such a right is infringed in the United Kingdom and the facts that have to be relied on by the plaintiff have a particular connection with a particular locality.[342]

This was the view of Mummery J in *LA Gear Inc v Gerald Whelan & Sons Ltd*.[343] Applying the *Tyburn* case, he said that 'An action for infringement of it [a UK trade-mark] is local and not transitory in nature. In other words the acts of infringement relied upon must take place within the United Kingdom'.[344] However, as this was not a case involving, on its facts, a limitation on the jurisdiction of the English courts, these were only *obiter dicta*. Moreover, as has already been seen, the reasoning in the *Tyburn* case is open to strong criticism.

(iv) Australian and New Zealand authority

In Australia, this exception is regarded as being well established.[345] The authority cited for it is the *Norbert Steinhardt* case, which involved the infringement of an Australian patent in England. The High Court of Australia held that there was no cause of action justiciable in Australia. However, as has been seen, this was a case decided on the basis of the first limb of the rule in *Phillips v Eyre*, which is regarded in Australia as a jurisdictional rule, but which is regarded in English law as being a tort choice of law rule. Nonetheless, the New Zealand *Atkinson Footwear* case[346] clearly supports the exception.

(v) United States authority

In the United States, subject matter jurisdiction is concerned not only with whether it is a local or foreign right but also with whether the infringement was committed at home or abroad.[347] Subject matter jurisdiction is tied in with the territorial nature of intellectual property rights. If the plaintiff brings the action in State A and the law of that State affords rights to the plaintiff that extend to the conduct of the defendant abroad, then State A is authorised to hear the action.[348] It would, of course, still need personal jurisdiction in relation to the particular defendant. Ascertaining whether the law of State A affords such rights is an example of the sort of com-

---

[341] N 230 above.
[342] See *Potter v The Broken Hill Pty Co Ltd* [1905] VLR 612 at 638.   [343] [1991] FSR 670.
[344] *Ibid* 674.   [345] See Nygh, p 119.   [346] Discussed above pp 285–286.
[347] See, generally, Trooboff, n 220 above, at 125–128.
[348] Trooboff, n 220 above, at 127–128.

plexity that you get if you rely on the distinction between local and transitory actions.

(b) POLICY CONSIDERATIONS

(i) In favour of the limitation
Aldous J, in *Plastus Kreativ AB* v *Minnesota Mining and Manufacturing Co*,[349] when discussing the *Tyburn* case, expressed the view that 'it would not normally be right for the courts of this country to decide a dispute on infringement of a foreign patent in respect of acts done outside this country provided there is an adequate remedy in the relevant country'.[350] The reason for this is that the foreign court 'is able to look at the particular acts in the context in which they are carried out'.[351] He accepted, though, that if there was not an adequate remedy in the other State, then it might be appropriate that action be taken in a State in which there was an appropriate remedy. The flexibility to take into account the question of whether there is an adequate remedy in a foreign State, in cases of an infringement abroad, cannot be achieved by a blanket limitation on jurisdiction, but only by the use of the discretion to stay English proceedings on the ground of *forum non conveniens*.

(ii) Against the limitation
There are six policy considerations against having this limitation. The first five are the same as the first five policy considerations already mentioned as considerations against the limitation in relation to foreign intellectual property rights. The remaining one is new.

First, it is unfair to plaintiffs. In the past, even if there was jurisdiction, an action based on an infringement abroad would have failed at the choice of law stage. This is no longer true. The type of action which will succeed at the choice of law stage is one where a foreign intellectual property right has been infringed abroad in that country and there is actionability under that country's law. There is no point in removing the limitation in relation to foreign intellectual property rights unless the limitation in relation to infringement committed abroad is also removed.[352]

Secondly, multiple infringements (whether involving a single intellectual property right or parallel rights) taking place in many different States are increasingly common. A person may set up in business supplying to many countries pirated copies of books, records or films, or shipping

---

[349] [1995] RPC 438.   [350] *Ibid*, at 447.   [351] *Ibid*.
[352] But compare Cornish, para 2–76 who supports the continued use of the subject matter limitation on jurisdiction in relation to acts abroad despite the new tort choice of law rules.

products with counterfeit trade-marks.³⁵³ What is needed is one State in which the litigation can be consolidated. If jurisdiction is available against such a person in England, the English courts ought to be able to try actions involving infringements abroad.

Thirdly, the limitation unnecessarily rules out England as a venue for international litigation concerning intellectual property rights.

Fourthly, the limitation has the effect of widening the gap between the traditional rules on jurisdiction and those under the EC/EFTA rules, which contain no such subject matter limitation.

Fifthly, the limitation is unnecessary in that an English court can use the doctrine of *forum non conveniens* to decline jurisdiction, where it considers it appropriate, in cases involving infringements that took place abroad.

Sixthly, modern methods of communication, such as satellite broadcasting and the Internet, have meant that fixing the infringement in one State has become increasingly difficult, if not downright unrealistic. A subject matter limitation on jurisdiction based on the place of infringement looks to be equally unrealistic.

It is submitted that, as with the limitation in relation to foreign intellectual property rights, the policy considerations against the limitation greatly outweigh those in its favour.

(c) THE SOLUTION : THE DOCTRINE OF *FORUM NON CONVENIENS*

As with the subject matter limitation in relation to foreign intellectual property rights, the solution to this second limitation is to use the doctrine of *forum non conveniens* to decline jurisdiction when the clearly more appropriate forum is abroad.

(i) The virtues of this solution

These are the same as those discussed earlier in relation to the use of *forum non conveniens* as the solution to the limitation in relation to foreign intellectual property rights. In particular, the flexibility of the doctrine means that it is possible to take into account the concern of Aldous J that the foreign court is able to look at the particular act in the context in which it is carried out.

(ii) Application in cases involving acts of infringement committed abroad

As has been seen,³⁵⁴ the fact that an intellectual property right has been infringed abroad will be a strong factor indicating that this is the clearly

---

³⁵³ See Minutes of evidence taken before the Special Public Bill Committee on the Private International Law (Miscellaneous Provisions) Bill, *HL Paper* 36 (1995), Annex by Cornish, p 65.

³⁵⁴ See above, p 271.

appropriate forum for trial. However, where there have been multiple infringements taking place in many States there may be no natural forum for trial; accordingly, a stay will be refused.

(d) CONFUSION BETWEEN JURISDICTION AND CHOICE OF LAW

In *Librarie du Liban Inc v Pardoe Blacker Ltd and Others*,[355] when deciding that the court had jurisdiction in relation to an act of infringement in the United States, *Morocco Bound* was distinguished, partly at least, on the basis that it was decided before the introduction of the rule in *Chaplin v Boys*. The same confusion between jurisdiction and choice of law is noticeable in relation to this limitation as it is in relation to the limitation in respect of foreign intellectual property rights.[356] But, as the Vice-Chancellor pointed out in the *Def Lepp* case, when it was argued that the English courts could take subject matter jurisdiction in relation to foreign acts of infringement if the tort choice of law rule was satisfied, 'No common law rule of international law can confer on a litigant a right under English law that he would not otherwise possess'.[357]

(e) CAN A SUCCESSFUL ACTION BE BROUGHT?

It is clear that any action brought in England for infringement of a UK right and based on the application of the foreign law of the place where the act of infringement was committed, is likely to fail. For that foreign law will probably contain a territorial limitation on liability; accordingly, the infringement will not be actionable under that law. Thus, in the *Def Lepp Music* case, after discussing the English common law tort choice of law rule, Sir Nicholas Browne-Wilkinson expressed the view that '. . . a *successful* action cannot be brought in England for alleged infringement of UK copyright by acts done outside the Kingdom'.[358] Similarly, in *Mölnlycke AB v Procter & Gamble Ltd*,[359] it was said that 'proceedings for infringement of a UK patent . . . could only be *founded* on infringement in England'.[360] This is the explanation of the decision of the High Court of Australia in the *Norbert Steinhardt* case. Applying the rule in *Phillips v Eyre*, there was no actionability under English law (the law of the place abroad where the tort was committed) in relation to Australian patents. Neither was there any actionability under Australian law in relation to infringements abroad. The effect of this is that the subject matter limitation on jurisdiction in

---

[355] Unreported (except through Lexis). [356] See, eg Dutson, n 337 above.
[357] N 96 above, at 276. [358] [1986] RPC 273 at 276–277. Emphasis added.
[359] [1992] 1 WLR 1112
[360] *Ibid*, at 1118 (*per* Dillon LJ). Emphasis added. This was a Brussels Convention case, discussed above at p 155.

relation to infringements abroad is not of crucial importance if the case involves a UK intellectual property right, since even if there is jurisdiction the action is unlikely to succeed.

On the other hand, if there is jurisdiction, a successful action can now be brought in relation to the infringement abroad of an intellectual property right of that State. If the limitation in relation to foreign intellectual property rights disappears, it is vital that this second limitation in relation to foreign acts of infringement also disappears with it, thereby allowing the plaintiff to take the benefit of the recently introduced statutory tort choice of law rules.

4. Intra-UK Cases

The two subject matter limitations arise out of the territorial limits to UK intellectual property rights. There is no limitation if litigation arises within the United Kingdom in relation to a UK intellectual property right. Thus, an English patentee can sue a New South Wales resident in England following infringement of his UK patent in Scotland provided that there is jurisdiction over the person. Similarly, in Canada, patents can be enforced throughout that country and there is no limitation as regards the province in which the infringement occurred.[361]

VI
FORUM SHOPPING

1. The Choice of Fora

(a) WITHIN EUROPE

In cases coming with the traditional rules on jurisdiction, it is for each EC/EFTA State to determine its own jurisdiction. Each State tends to have its own exorbitant forms of jurisdiction, albeit different forms, which may allow it to adjudicate in actions involving defendants domiciled outside a Contracting State to the Brussels or Lugano Conventions. A more significant difference between European States is as to whether they have subject matter jurisdiction in infringement actions. England is not the State to go to for trial in a complex case involving the infringement in different States of parallel intellectual property rights, since it will only adjudicate in relation to a UK right infringed in England. In contrast, the Dutch courts have opened the door to such actions.[362] The Netherlands is a State in which

---

[361] Mcleod, *Conflict of Laws* p 560.   [362] See above, pp 218–219.

actions involving parallel rights from anywhere in the world can be consolidated.

(b) OUTSIDE EUROPE

It is, of course, a question for the private international law of, for example, New South Wales, to determine whether it has jurisdiction to adjudicate in an infringement action brought by a foreign plaintiff. The usual question will arise of whether there is jurisdiction over the person, but in an infringement action, there is the equally important question of whether the forum has subject matter jurisdiction. Australian courts do not have jurisdiction in an infringement action that relates to a UK patent.[363] This limitation on jurisdiction operates to deny a foreign plaintiff the opportunity to forum shop in Australia. The position is the same in Canada.[364] On the other hand, a US court has taken jurisdiction in a case involving infringement of a foreign copyright and Japanese courts have jurisdiction in cases of infringement of foreign patents.[365]

2. THE ADVANTAGES TO BE OBTAINED

The personal, procedural, substantive and other advantages to be obtained from trial in one European State rather than another have already been discussed and what has previously been said[366] need not be repeated. When it comes to forum shopping outside Europe, one country where much international patent litigation is held is the United States. There are numerous differences between trial in the United States of a claim for infringement and trial in European States which are civil law jurisdictions, and even between trial in the United States and trial in England.[367]

VII
INFRINGEMENT AND VALIDITY

1. THE SIGNIFICANCE OF ARTICLE 16(4)

It is important to realise that Article 16(4) of the Brussels and Lugano Conventions may be raised even where the jurisdiction of an English court in an infringement action is founded on the traditional bases of

---

[363] See above, pp 283–284; Nygh, p 119.
[364] Mcleod, *Conflict of Laws*, p 560.
[365] See above, p 292.
[366] See above, pp 198–201.
[367] See, generally Adamo, (1997) 68 *Managing Intellectual Property* 17–19.

jurisdiction. An example would be where an English company sues a New York company for infringement of a French patent, basing jurisdiction on the establishment of a place of business (other than a branch) in England. The defendant alleges that the patent is invalid. Quite apart from the traditional limitation on jurisdiction in relation to foreign intellectual property rights, the defendant may claim that the English court lacks jurisdiction over the validity issue because the French courts have exclusive jurisdiction in relation to this issue by virtue of Article 16(4). The difficulties involved under the EC/EFTA rules where the issues of infringement and validity arise in the same case have been examined in the previous chapter. In examining this matter in the present context it is important, as it was under the EC/EFTA rules, to distinguish between cases where invalidity is raised as a defence to infringement, where it arises by way of a counterclaim for revocation, and where it arises by way of separate revocation proceedings brought in a State other than the one in which the infringement action is brought.

2. A Defence of Invalidity

(a) no problem under the present law

The difficult problem that arises in relation to jurisdiction under the EC/EFTA rules of whether the court in which an action for infringement is brought, and which has a basis of jurisdiction in relation to infringement, is, by virtue of Articles 19 and 16(4) of the Conventions, deprived of jurisdiction when a defence of invalidity is raised in respect of an intellectual property right registered in another Contracting State, does not arise under the traditional rules. The English courts will only try infringement actions in respect of UK intellectual property rights. It follows that an English court which has jurisdiction in relation to infringement will not be faced with the argument that the courts of another Contracting State have exclusive jurisdiction under Article 16(4) in respect of the validity issue and, therefore, Article 19 applies to deprive the English courts of jurisdiction over the whole of the claim including the infringement part.[368]

But can an English court which has infringement jurisdiction also try the issue of validity? The answer to this is probably going to be yes. First, it is arguable that it has exclusive jurisdiction in relation to validity by virtue of Article 16(4), in cases coming within the scope of that provision. It is a UK registered right. The only query is whether the claim for infringement to which validity is raised as a defence is *principally* concerned with validity, as is required under Article 16(4). According to the definition adopted

---

[368] For jurisdiction over validity under the traditional rules in cases falling outside the scope of Article 16(4), see above pp 38–45.

by Laddie J in the *Coin Controls* case,[369] it is, although this decision can be criticised,[370] and is, arguably, wrong. Secondly, even if Article 16(4) does not apply (for example, it is an unregistered UK right or, with a UK registered right, it is accepted that a mere defence is not principally concerned with validity), an English court may still have validity jurisdiction on some other basis.[371] Thirdly, there is a strong argument of principle that the English court should be able to try a defence without having to have any independent jurisdiction in relation to validity.[372] The upshot is that, where a UK right has been infringed, an English court which has infringement jurisdiction is also likely to be able to try the validity issue.

The desirability of the same court trying both the issue of validity and that of infringement was mentioned by Aldous J in *Plastus Kreativ AB v Minnesota Mining and Manufacturing Co*,[373] where this consideration was given as a reason why English courts should not try cases involving infringement abroad of a foreign patent. This consideration may also be relevant when exercising the *forum non conveniens* discretion. As has already been seen in the *Amersham* case,[374] where English courts could consider the infringement claim and the defence of lack of validity, but the European Patent Office could only consider revocation of the patent on grounds of invalidity, Falconer J, when refusing a stay of the infringement proceedings, said that the 'convenient and, indeed, desirable course, and the usual practice, is for both infringement and validity to be tried and decided in the same proceedings'.[375] Even more fundamentally, the European Patent Office was not an alternative forum for the purpose of a stay of proceedings. Finally, the thrust of the *Fort Dodge* case[376] is that the same court should try the issues of infringement and validity, because of the close relationship between the two issues.

The stage at which the issue of validity will be considered by the court will vary depending on whether it is an Order 11, rule 1(1) case or not. In the situation where a writ has been served within the jurisdiction, this issue will be considered when the merits of the infringement claim are considered. The position is different in the situation where a writ has to be served out of the jurisdiction. The issue of invalidity is relevant at the stage in Order 11, rule 1(1) proceedings, where the plaintiff has to show that there is a serious issue to be tried on the merits. In *The Lubrizol Corpn and Another v Esso Petroleum Co Ltd and Others (No 1)*,[377] the judge, Hugh Laddie QC, made the valuable point that the parties do not need to engage

---

[369] [1997] 3 All ER 45; discussed above, pp 204–206.
[370] See above, pp 204–206.
[371] See above, pp 38–45.
[372] See above, pp 208–209.
[373] [1995] RPC 438 at 447, discussed above, p 290.
[374] N 156 above.
[375] N 156 at 58.
[376] *Fort Dodge Animal Health Ltd and Others v Akzo Nobel NV* [1998] FSR 222; discussed above, pp 206–207.
[377] [1992] RPC 281 at 289.

in detailed disputes as to infringement or validity in an Order 11 application. On the facts of the case, the defence of invalidity was enough to prevent the plaintiff from establishing his case on the merits.

(b) THE PROBLEM IF THERE IS JURISDICTION IN RELATION TO FOREIGN INTELLECTUAL PROPERTY RIGHTS

If, as is suggested, the English courts drop the present subject matter limitation in relation to foreign intellectual property rights exactly the same problems, ie whether Articles 19 and 16(4) will preclude infringement jurisdiction and whether a basis of jurisdiction is needed in relation to validity, will arise as occur, at the present time, under the EC/EFTA rules.[378]

Little more needs to be said about the first of these problems. The position is exactly the same as under the EC/EFTA rules. It is unclear whether an English court is precluded from infringement jurisdiction by Articles 19 and 16(4) in the situation where the right is registered in another Contracting State to the Brussels or Lugano Conventions. The *Coin Controls* and *Fort Dodge* cases say that it is, but a decision of the Court of Justice is needed on this point.

As regards the second problem, where the infringement jurisdiction is based on service of a writ within the jurisdiction, there is no difficulty because this is also a basis of jurisdiction for validity litigation.[379] The difficulty comes where infringement jurisdiction is based on the injunction or tort heads of Order 11, rule 1(1). The wording of these heads is such that they cannot be regarded as a basis of jurisdiction for validity litigation.[380] However, as has been argued above,[381] it is submitted that the English court should be able to try the validity defence without having any independent basis of jurisdiction in relation to this issue. Validity is raised as a defence, it is not an action for revocation on the ground of invalidity. Furthermore, it is manifestly undesirable to split up the infringement and validity issues so that each issue is tried in a different State.

Of course, although the English court has jurisdiction it may decline this on the ground of *forum non conveniens*. As has been seen, normally this is what would happen in cases of infringement of foreign intellectual property rights. The fact that validity of a foreign right is raised as a defence will be an important additional factor in favour of granting a stay of the English proceedings. This factor is balanced out, though, by another factor, the desirability of not splitting up the issues of infringement and validity amongst different States. This leaves us back where we started with the

---

[378] See above, pp 302–309. [379] See above, p 40.
[380] Arguably, it would be different if the multi-defendant head were used.
[381] See above, pp 208–209.

position of normally declining jurisdiction in relation to infringement of foreign intellectual property rights. An example was given earlier of an infringement action where jurisdiction should not be declined.[382] It is submitted that this should still be so even if validity is raised as a defence.

3. A Counterclaim For Revocation

It has been mentioned in the previous chapter that a counterclaim is very different from a mere defence. It is a cross-action, and an action for revocation is a cause of action in its own right. This cause of action is not the same as that in infringement proceedings. This point was crucial in *Symbol Technologies Inc v Opticon Sensors Europe BV (No 1)*[383] where, as has been seen, Aldous J held that the two causes of action in separate proceedings for revocation and infringement were not the same. If there are separate proceedings in England for validity and for infringement, there has to be jurisdiction in relation to both sets of proceedings.[384] It is submitted that the position is the same even if there are no separate proceedings. If there is a counterclaim for revocation in infringement proceedings, the English court would need jurisdiction in relation to both causes of action. However, under the English traditional rules, there is no difficulty in obtaining jurisdiction in respect of a counterclaim. A person who brings an infringement action in England submits to the jurisdiction of the court, and this gives it jurisdiction in relation to a counterclaim.[385]

There is a complicating factor in that it is a counterclaim for revocation. This raises the question of whether Article 16(4) of the Brussels and Lugano Conventions will operate to preclude jurisdiction. Under the existing law, it will not do so. The effect of the subject matter limitation on jurisdiction in relation to foreign intellectual property rights is that an English court will only have infringement jurisdiction where it is a UK right. Article 16(4) will only preclude jurisdiction where it is a right registered in another Contracting State. Indeed, if it is a UK registered right an English court will have exclusive jurisdiction in relation to revocation proceedings by virtue of Article 16(4) independently of any counterclaim. With unregistered rights, or those registered outside the EC/EFTA Contracting States, Article 16(4) will not apply anyway.

What happens if this subject matter limitation disappears, and there is an action for infringement of a foreign intellectual property right to which there is a counterclaim for revocation? Can the English court try the revocation proceedings? In cases where Article 16(4) of the Brussels and

---

[382] See above, p 295. [383] [1993] RPC 211; discussed above, p 180.
[384] See, for an example of such a situation, *The Washburn and Moen, & C, Company v The Cunard Steamship Company and J C Parkes and Sons* (1889) 5 TLR 592, discussed above p 253.
[385] See Dicey and Morris, p 310.

Lugano Conventions applies, the answer must be no. Article 16(4) allocates exclusive jurisdiction to the Contracting State in which the patent or other registered right is registered and, if it is registered in another Contracting State, Article 19 of the Conventions will preclude the jurisdiction of the English courts in relation to the revocation proceedings. Moreover, any revocation order granted by an English court in breach of Article 16(4) will not be recognised and enforced in other Contracting States.[386] In contrast, where there are unregistered rights or those registered outside the EC/EFTA Contracting States, Article 16(4) will not operate to preclude jurisdiction over the revocation proceedings.

4. SEPARATE REVOCATION PROCEEDINGS

A factual situation analogous to that encountered in the *Fort Dodge* case[387] could arise under the traditional rules. For example, a Japanese company brings an action in Japan against an English company for infringement of its UK patent. The English company petitions in England for revocation of the UK patent. The English company seeks an injunction from the English court enjoining the Japanese proceedings. The English court has exclusive jurisdiction in relation to the revocation proceedings by virtue of Article 16(4) of the Brussels Convention. On the other hand, since Japan is not a party to the Brussels Convention, the question of whether the Japanese court can try the infringement action and determine the validity of the patent is one of Japanese law. The English court cannot say that the Japanese court is precluded from trying these two issues. The question of whether the English court should issue the injunction sought will be determined by the straightforward application of the principles on restraining foreign proceedings set out above.[388]

VIII
INTERIM RELIEF

It was seen, in the previous chapter, that Section 25 of the Civil Jurisdiction and Judgments Act 1982 allows an English court to grant interim relief in support of proceedings which have been or are to be brought in a foreign State, and that this has recently been extended to include a non-Contracting State to the Brussels or Lugano Convention. This is an extension which could have a significant impact in infringement cases.

Section 25 allows an English court which lacks jurisdiction as to the substantive infringement proceedings to grant interim relief by way of an

---

[386] See above, p 212.   [387] See above, pp 206–207.   [388] See above, pp 275–279.

interlocutory injunction preventing the infringement pending the determination of the substantive dispute abroad. Take the example of where a Japanese defendant company, which has established a place of business (other than a branch) in England and has assets in England, infringes the plaintiff's US copyright in New York. Under the traditional rules on jurisdiction, the English courts lack jurisdiction over the substantive infringement proceedings because of the subject matter limitations on jurisdiction. Accordingly, the plaintiff brings the infringement action in New York. The effect of Section 25, as extended, is that the English courts have power to grant an interlocutory injunction in England prohibiting the infringement pending the trial of the New York proceedings. This does not necessarily mean that such an injunction will be granted, but there is at least power to do so, which there was not in the past. When it comes to the exercise of this power, it has been seen[389] that Section 25(2) provides that the court may refuse to grant interim relief if, in the opinion of the court, the fact that the court has no jurisdiction apart from this section in relation to the subject matter of the proceedings in question makes it inexpedient for the court to grant it. Moreover, in relation to the specific example above, it has to be remembered that there does seem to be some reluctance in England to grant cross border injunctions in infringement cases.[390]

IX
INTERNATIONAL DISCOVERY

1. THE NEED TO JOIN A FOREIGNER AS A SUBSTANTIVE DEFENDANT

The need to join a foreigner as a substantive defendant in order to obtain discovery has already been mentioned.[391] An example involving the traditional rules where this was done, and there was no intention of obtaining recovery against the defendant, is *Unilever plc v Gillette (UK) Ltd*.[392] The plaintiff company had tried to obtain discovery against a subsidiary company in the Gillette group of companies. After this application failed, it sought to join as defendant the ultimate parent company, a US company, in order to obtain disclosure of certain technical documents. There was held to be a good arguable case of liability in respect of the US company and service of a writ out of the jurisdiction under Order 11, rule 1 of the Rules of the Supreme Court was granted.

---

[389] See above, pp 215–216.   [390] See above, p 227.   [391] See above, pp 228–229.
[392] [1989] RPC 583; discussed above p 245.

2. Difficulties Involved

As has previously been mentioned, there can be difficulties in determining which company to join, establishing the liability of that company, and satisfying the jurisdictional criteria. An example where the jurisdictional criteria were met is *Beecham Group plc and Another v Norton Healthcare Ltd and Others*.[393] Here, it was possible to show that a Slovenian manufacturer of medicinal tablets was a necessary and proper party, for the purpose of Order 11, rule 1(1)(c) to an action for patent infringement brought against an English importer, the two defendants being involved in a common design to manufacture for import and to import. The object of joining the Slovenian defendant was to obtain discovery and this was now possible.

3. A Different Approach

The different approach recommended by Lord Justice Hoffmann, as he then was, would be as effective in cases where jurisdiction is based on the traditional rules as it is in cases where jurisdiction is based on the EC/EFTA rules.[394] However, he admitted that such a radical change in the law would require legislative change.

X
REFORM

1. Criticism of the Existing Law

Much of what was said in the previous chapter in relation to reform is equally applicable in the present context. Obviously, the same criticisms can be made of the application of the tort head of Order 11, rule 1(1) in infringement cases as were made of Article 5(3) of the Brussels and Lugano Conventions, as interpreted by the Court of Justice.[395] The two provisions are to the same effect. In other words, the tort head of rule 1(1) leads to uncertainty, involves the use of an inappropriate connecting factor (damage), and, arguably, does not provide adequate protection in cases of threatened wrongs. There is the same uncertainty over the position where invalidity is raised during the course of the infringement litigation.

There is, though, one additional criticism that can be made of the traditional rules on jurisdiction that cannot be levelled at the EC/EFTA rules. Under the traditional rules, there are the well known subject matter

---

[393] [1997] FSR 81.   [394] See above, p 230.   [395] See above, p 231.

limitations on jurisdiction in respect of foreign intellectual property rights and foreign acts of infringement. In other words, there are special rules dealing with infringement: limitations which are unjustifiable and undesirable in policy terms,[396] leading to unfairness to the plaintiff; preventing the consolidation of litigation in one State in cases of multiple acts of infringement; unnecessarily ruling out England as a venue for international litigation; and widening the gap between the traditional rules on jurisdiction and the EC/EFTA rules.

2. Reform of the Jurisdictional Rules of General Application

There is the possible option of seeking to reform the traditional rules themselves, which would affect other torts, rather than introducing special jurisdictional rules for infringement cases. The arguments in respect of adopting such an approach have been considered already in the context of reform of the EC/EFTA rules. There is, though, an additional important factor that has to be borne in mind in the context of the traditional rules. There are, at the moment, special rules for infringement cases in the form of the subject matter limitations on jurisdiction. This suggests that reform needs to focus on special rules for infringement cases.

3. Special Jurisdictional Rules

(a) within the framework of existing rules

It is unrealistic to imagine that English law would ever adopt, under the traditional rules on jurisdiction, independent jurisdictional rules for infringement cases. What we are talking about, then, is the introduction of special jurisdictional rules within the framework of existing jurisdictional rules. This is very much easier to effect in the context of the traditional rules than it is in the context of the EC/EFTA rules. It can be done unilaterally, without the agreement of other EC/EFTA States. Amendments to Order 11 of the rules of the Supreme Court are easily and frequently made. The common law subject matter limitations on jurisdiction could be departed from by a judge at first instance or overruled by the Court of Appeal.

(b) the suggested rules

The tort head of Order 11, rule 1(1) should be amended to bring it into line with the suggested rule in respect of Article 5(3) of the Brussels and

[396] See above, pp 286–293, 303–304.

316   *Intellectual Property and Private International Law*

Lugano Conventions.[397] After all, at the moment, the two provisions are to the same effect. Rule 1(1)(f) would have to provide that, in infringement cases, service of a writ out of the jurisdiction is permissible where the act of infringement has been committed or threatened within the jurisdiction. When it comes to localising the place where the act of infringement occurred in those complex cases of satellite broadcasting and over the internet, the same definitions should be adopted as under the EC/EFTA rules.[398] Again, to be consistent with the special rules suggested in relation to Article 5(3), it should be provided for the sake of clarification that, in cases of multiple acts of infringement, some committed locally and others abroad, a court will only have jurisdiction under rule 1(1)(f) in relation to local acts. If the subject matter limitations on jurisdiction at common law are abolished, it will be possible to consolidate jurisdiction in England by basing jurisdiction on service of a writ within the jurisdiction or by using some head of Order 11, rule 1(1) other than the tort head.

The common law subject matter limitations on jurisdiction should not be followed by judges at first instance and, when an opportunity presents itself, should be abolished by the Court of Appeal. The flexible doctrine of *forum non conveniens* should be used to decline jurisdiction, where appropriate, in cases involving foreign intellectual property rights and/or foreign acts of infringement.

This would still leave the uncertainty over the position where invalidity is raised during the course of the infringement litigation, as there still would be under the EC/EFTA rules.

The effect of these suggested reforms would be to bring the traditional rules on jurisdiction into line with the EC/EFTA rules, and into line with the special rules dealing with the infringement of Community rights. This would greatly simplify the law.

---

[397] See above, pp 234–235.   [398] See above, pp 236–237.

7

Jurisdictional Issues in Relation to European Community Rights

I	Introduction	318
II	Trade marks	318
	1. The substantive law background	318
	2. How jurisdictional problems arise	318
	3. Jurisdictional provisions	319
	(a) Other disputes (ie other than in relation to infringement, etc)	320
	(b) Infringement, etc	321
III	Designs	342
	1. The substantive law background	342
	2. How jurisdictional problems arise	342
	3. Jurisdictional provisions	343
IV	Patents	344
	1. The substantive law background	344
	2. How jurisdictional problems arise	344
	3. Jurisdictional provisions	345
	(a) The Protocol on Litigation	345
	(b) Part VI of the Community Patent Convention	346
V	Plant Variety Rights	349
	1. The substantive law background	349
	2. How jurisdictional problems arise	350
	3. Jurisdictional provisions	350
	(a) The proceedings	351
	(b) Relationship with the Lugano and Brussels Conventions	351
	(c) Bases of jurisdiction	352
	(d) Infringements committed abroad	355
	(e) A plea of invalidity	356
	(f) Declining jurisdiction	356
	(g) Provisional, including protective measures	357
	(h) Summary of similarities and differences	357

I
INTRODUCTION

In this chapter, the jurisdictional rules concerning the infringement of European Community rights, and other disputes in relation to such rights, will be considered. The Community rights in question are trade marks, designs, patents and plant variety rights. The most developed jurisdictional rules are to be found in the area of Community trade marks, and, it has been proposed that what has been adopted there should operate as the model for designs and is likely to be the model for patents. Accordingly, the discussion will start, and deal in most detail, with trade marks.

II
TRADE MARKS

1. The Substantive Law Background

The Community trade mark system is fully supra-national in nature. A single application, which necessarily covers the whole of the Community, is filed with the Office for the Harmonisation in the Internal Market (Trade Marks and Designs), which is situated in Alicante in Spain, and this Office grants a single Community Trade Mark if the examination procedure has been concluded successfully. All decisions of the Office can be the subject of an appeal to the Boards of Appeal of the Office. These Boards of Appeal have exclusive jurisdiction. The system has been copied from the European Patent Convention, but one important addition has been made. The decisions of the Boards of Appeal can be the subject of a further appeal to the Court of Justice of the European Communities.[1]

2. How Jurisdictional Problems Arise

Because the Community Trade Mark, necessarily, covers the whole of the Community, the international element is, necessarily, present, which means that jurisdictional issues will arise. Essentially, jurisdictional problems arise in three ways. First, there are the obvious actions for infringement and validity. The Regulation has put in place a system which comprises a limited number of specially designated Community trade mark courts per Member State, both at first and at second instance, and the

---

[1] Council Regulation (EC) 40/94 of 20 December 1993 on the Community Trade Mark, [1994] OJ L11/1, Title VI, Section 5 and Articles 57–63 and 126–130.

Court of Justice of the European Communities as the ultimate appeal court. As the right applies to the whole of the Community, which of these courts will have jurisdiction to hear infringement and validity cases? Allegedly infringing acts can take place in more than one Member State and the alleged infringer could be domiciled in yet another Member State. If the registration of the right is the connecting factor, any court in the Community could have jurisdiction. Or do we look at the place where the alleged infringement took place, or do we turn to the domicile of the alleged infringer? Which court will deal with a case where the defendant has no domicile in any of the Member States? Could its establishment or place of business in the Community offer an alternative solution? In all these circumstances, which are similar to those described in relation to national trade mark infringement cases,[2] it will be critical to determine whether or not the Brussels Convention applies. Any alternative solution will also have to include an equivalent to Article 24 of the Brussels Convention. Which courts will have jurisdiction to take interim measures? Do we restrict that power to the court that is dealing with the infringement case, or do we, potentially, allow almost any court to offer assistance in this area?

Secondly, similar jurisdictional problems arise in disputes concerning Community trade marks that are not infringement or validity related, such as disputes in relation to the creation or ownership of such marks. Will the same rules apply to determine jurisdiction? And will these matters also be reserved for the specially designated Community trade mark courts?

A third way in which jurisdictional issues arise is related to the fact that the Regulation does not abolish national trade marks. This means that infringement actions that involve the same cause of action could be brought between the same parties in different Member States. One action could be based on a Community trade mark, another could be based on a national mark. How is this issue of conflicting jurisdiction to be addressed? Should a variant of the *lis alibi pendens* rule in Article 21 of the Brussels Convention apply?

3. JURISDICTIONAL PROVISIONS

Title X of the Community Trade Mark Regulation is concerned with jurisdiction and procedure in legal actions relating to Community trade marks.[3] By and large, its provisions have been copied from those contained in the Protocol on Litigation annexed to the Agreement Relating to Community Patents of 1989.[4] Most of Title X concerns disputes relating to

---

[2] See above Chs 5 and 6.   [3] See, generally, Tritton, paras 3.052–3.056.
[4] For differences see below, pp 345–346.

the infringement and validity (arising during the course of an infringement action) of Community trade marks (hereinafter referred to as infringement, etc).[5] However, it does say something, albeit in a rather oblique way, about other disputes that can arise in respect of Community trade marks and it is to these that we will turn first.

(a) OTHER DISPUTES (ie OTHER THAN IN RELATION TO INFRINGEMENT, ETC)

(i) Application of the Brussels Convention

Section 1 of Title X is entitled Application of the Convention on Jurisdiction and Enforcement. Within this section, Article 90(1) provides that, unless otherwise specified in the Regulation, the Brussels Convention[6] shall apply to proceedings relating to Community trade marks and applications for Community trade marks, as well as to proceedings relating to simultaneous and successive actions on the basis of Community trade marks and national trade marks (hereinafter collectively referred to as proceedings relating to Community trade marks, etc). This gives a very wide definition to the proceedings concerning Community trade marks to which the Brussels Convention applies. It applies: first, to proceedings relating to Community trade marks; secondly, to proceedings relating to applications for Community trade marks; and thirdly, to proceedings relating to simultaneous and successive actions on the basis of Community trade marks and national trade marks. It follows that the Brussels Convention will apply not only to proceedings for infringement, etc but also to other disputes, such as those concerning the creation of Community trade marks and their validity (arising during the granting procedure). Disputes in relation to the right to a grant and the ownership of such rights will also be covered, as doubtless will contractual disputes in relation to the commercial exploitation of such rights.

The application of the Brussels Convention is subject to what is said elsewhere in the Regulation. In other words, it excludes the rules in the Brussels Convention in cases covered by the Regulation's own system. This approach is fully in line with Article 57(3) of the Brussels Convention, which allows for the provisions of the Convention to be superseded by rules on jurisdiction which are contained in an act of the institutions of the

---

[5] See Article 92 for the jurisdiction of Community trade mark courts over infringement and validity, below p 322.

[6] This is referring to the Brussels Convention as amended by the subsequent Accession Conventions. Unlike the United Kingdom, not all Contracting States to the Convention operate the latest version. In such States the version rendered applicable by the Regulation is the one currently in force in that State: Article 104 of the Community Trade Mark Regulation.

Community dealing with a particular matter. A Council Regulation which contains special rules on jurisdiction for cases relating to the special matter of Community trade marks meets the requirements laid down in Article 57(3). However, the rest of Title X is concerned almost exclusively[7] with infringement, etc. It lays down no bases of international jurisdiction in relation to other disputes. It follows that, in relation to these other disputes, the Brussels Convention will apply unaffected by the Regulation.

Section 3 of Title X is concerned with the jurisdiction of national courts in relation to other disputes. It provides that, within the Member State whose courts have jurisdiction under this provision, those courts have jurisdiction for actions other than those for infringement, etc which would have jurisdiction in the case of actions relating to a national trade mark registered in that State.[8] If no court has jurisdiction under this provision, such action may be heard before the courts of the Member State in which the Office has its seat.[9] A national court which is dealing with an action relating to a Community trade mark, other than ones for infringement and validity (arising during the infringement action) is required to treat the trade mark as valid.[10]

(ii) Which provisions will apply?

In principle, all the provisions of the Brussels Convention can apply to 'other disputes'. None of its provisions are excluded from application in respect of such disputes.[11] There is a question, though, of whether Article 16(4) of the Brussels Convention[12] can apply to supra national rights such as the Community trade mark. This provision undoubtedly applies to national applications put before a national intellectual property office or, whatever nature the application and examination procedure may have been, an intellectual property right with the same nationally limited effects.[13] The argument against its application in the case of supra national rights is that, when it comes to such rights, the Community would have to be a Contracting State to the Brussels Convention, which it clearly is not.[14]

(b) INFRINGEMENT, ETC

Section 2 of Title X is entitled 'disputes concerning the infringement and validity of Community trade marks'.

---

[7] But see Article 102, discussed below, which is concerned with the jurisdiction of national courts in relation to disputes other than for infringement and validity.
[8] Article 102(1).   [9] Article 102(2).   [10] Article 103.
[11] Compare the position in respect of infringement, etc.
[12] Discussed above, pp 15–27.   [13] See Gothot et Holleaux, notes 155–156.
[14] See Huet, (1994) *Journal du Droit International* 623 at 627–628.

(i) Community trade mark courts and their exclusive jurisdiction over infringement, etc

Member States are required to designate in their territories national courts of first and second instance to act as Community trade mark courts.[15] Article 92 provides that the Community trade mark courts shall have exclusive jurisdiction:

(a) for all infringement actions and – if they are permitted under national law – actions in respect of threatened infringement relating to Community trade marks;
(b) for actions for declaration of non-infringement, if they are permitted under national law;
(c) for all actions brought as a result of acts referred to in Article 9(3), second sentence [ie reasonable compensation claimed in respect of matters arising after the date of publication of a Community trade mark application];
(d) for counterclaims for revocation or for a declaration of invalidity of the Community trade mark . . .[16]

An appeal to the community trade mark courts of second instance shall lie from judgments of the Community trade mark Courts of first instance in respect of proceedings arising from the actions and claims referred to in Article 92.[17]

(ii) Relationship with the Brussels Convention

The Brussels Convention will apply to disputes concerning infringement, etc by virtue of Article 90(1). This, of course, is unless otherwise specified in the Regulation. And Article 90(2) goes on to specify that, in the case of proceedings for infringement, etc, certain provisions in the Brussels Convention shall not apply, and that others shall apply. It states that Articles 2, 4, 5(1), (3), (4), (5) and 24 shall not apply, whereas Articles 17 and 18 shall apply.[18] Most of the provisions that are excluded have the common element that there is the same or some equivalent provision under Title X.[19] If resort is made to the Brussels Convention, the provisions in Title II thereof, which are applicable to persons domiciled in a Contracting State, are also applicable to persons who do not have a domicile in any Member State but have an establishment therein.[20]

(iii) The definition of domicile/an establishment

The jurisdiction provisions in Title X make extensive use of the concepts of domicile[21] and an establishment.[22] Title X does not define the meaning of

---

[15] Article 91.   [16] Pursuant to Article 96.   [17] Article 101(1).
[18] This is subject to the limitations in Article 93(4) of the Regulation, discussed below, pp 324–325.
[19] See below. There is however no equivalent of Article 5(4) of the Brussels Convention.
[20] Article 90(2)(c).   [21] See Articles 93(1), (2), (3).
[22] See Articles 90(2)(c), 93(1), (2), (3).

'domicile'. However, the effect of Article 90(1) is that Articles 52 and 53 of the Brussels Convention, which are concerned with the concept of domicile, will apply to proceedings relating to Community trade marks, etc. This is not as helpful as, at first sight, might appear to be the case. Articles 52 and 53, with one exception,[23] do not provide a definition of domicile as such. They merely tell us which State's definition of that concept is to be applied.

Neither is 'establishment' defined in Title X. However, guidance on the meaning of this concept can be found in the case law in relation to Article 5(5) of the Brussels Convention, according to which jurisdiction is allocated to the court 'for the place in which the branch, agency or other establishment is situated'. An 'establishment' encompasses a branch office, or agency. As has already been seen,[24] a branch, etc can be identified by virtue of certain characteristics laid down by the Court of Justice. There is an argument against allowing reference to this case law since Article 5(5) is excluded from operation in proceedings for infringement, etc of Community trade marks, etc. But the reason for this may well be because of the use of the concept of an establishment in various places in Title X. It is submitted, therefore, that reliance can be placed on the case law on Article 5(5).

(iv) Bases of jurisdiction

The bases of jurisdiction in proceedings for infringement, etc are derived from two sources. First, Article 93 sets out a number of bases of jurisdiction (including the incorporation of Articles 17 and 18 of the Brussels Convention). Secondly, Article 90(1), more generally, incorporates any other basis of jurisdiction contained in the Brussels Convention which has not been specifically excluded in the Regulation. The combined effect of these Articles is that there are the six following bases of jurisdiction.

(a) *Defendant's domicile/an establishment*

Article 93(1) provides that proceedings for infringement, etc 'shall be brought in the courts of the Member State in which the defendant is domiciled or, if he is not domiciled in any of the Member States, in which he has an establishment'. This is analogous to Article 2 of the Brussels Convention. The use of the concept of an establishment as an alternative in the situation where the defendant is not domiciled in any of the Member States, has wide ranging implications. Thus, a New York incorporated company with an establishment in France can be sued there for infringement, etc of a Community trade mark. What Article 93(1) does not allow,

[23] Article 53 provides that a company is domiciled where it has its seat.
[24] See above, pp 169–170.

unlike Article 5(5) of the Brussels Convention, is for the plaintiff to bring an action against a French company in England on the basis of its English establishment. The defendant is domiciled in a Member State and the establishment alternative, therefore, does not operate. When this alternative does operate, it is noticeable that there is no requirement, as there is under Article 5(5) of the Brussels Convention, that the dispute arises out of the operations of the establishment.

(b) *Plaintiff's domicile/an establishment*

Article 93(2) deals with the situation where the defendant is neither domiciled nor has an establishment in any of the Member States. In this situation, 'such proceedings shall be brought in the courts of the Member State in which the plaintiff is domiciled or, if he is not domiciled in any of the Member States, in which he has an establishment'. This would allow a French domiciled plaintiff to sue a Japanese domiciled defendant in France for infringement.

(c) *The seat of the Office*

In some proceedings, neither the defendant nor the plaintiff will be so domiciled or have such an establishment. Article 93(3) states that 'such proceedings shall be brought in the courts of the Member State where the Office has its seat'. The extent of the connection with this State (ie Spain) is bound to be very limited. Neither party will be domiciled or have an establishment there, and the act of infringement may have taken place outside this Member State. However, this provision does ensure that there are courts in one Member State which will have jurisdiction in respect of infringement, etc of a Community trade mark.

(d) *Articles 17 and 18 of the Brussels Convention*

(i) *Article 17*

Article 93(4)(a) provides that, notwithstanding paragraphs (1) to (3), Article 17 of the Brussels Convention 'shall apply if the parties agree that a different Community trade mark court shall have jurisdiction'. An agreement which satisfies the requirements of Article 17[25] will give exclusive jurisdiction to the Community trade mark court selected by the parties. This means that the courts of other Member States have no jurisdiction. The plaintiff is therefore unable to sue, for example, under Article 93(1) in the Member State in which the defendant is domiciled.

---

[25] Cheshire and North, pp 314–322.

Article 17 jurisdiction overrides jurisdiction under Article 93(1)(2)(3). According to Article 17, even if the requirements in relation to the agreement are satisfied, it can only give exclusive jurisdiction if one or more of the parties is domiciled in a Contracting State to the Brussels Convention. In the case of proceedings for infringement, etc it is enough if one of the parties has an establishment in any Member State.[26]

(ii) *Article 18*

Article 93(4)(b) provides that, notwithstanding paragraphs (1) to (3), Article 18 of the Brussels Convention 'shall apply if the defendant enters an appearance before a different Community trade mark court'. Article 18 does not give exclusive jurisdiction. It follows that the inclusion of this basis of jurisdiction provides the plaintiff with an alternative forum for trial to the one specified in Article 93(1)(2)(3). It seems that in order for Article 18 to apply, the defendant must be domiciled in a Contracting State to the Brussels Convention. In the present context, it would be enough that the defendant has an establishment there, even if domiciled in a non-Contracting State.[27]

(e) *A local act of infringement*

Article 93(5) provides that actions for infringement, etc, with the exception of actions for a declaration of non-infringement of a Community trade mark, '... may also be brought in the courts of the Member State in which the act of infringement has been committed or threatened ...'.[28] This provision allows the plaintiff to sue in an alternative Member State from the one whose courts have been allocated jurisdiction under Article 93(1) to (3). It also allows the plaintiff to sue in an alternative forum to the Community trade mark court which has jurisdiction by virtue of Article 18 of the Brussels Convention. What is less clear is whether the plaintiff can use this provision in the situation where the parties have agreed that a Community trade mark court shall have jurisdiction and Article 17 of the Brussels Convention applies, so as to give that court exclusive jurisdiction. Article 93(5) is phrased in terms that proceedings may *also* be brought, and the order of paragraphs in Article 93, with the reference to Article 17 of the Brussels Convention coming in paragraph (4), ie preceding paragraph (5), might suggest that the plaintiff can do so. As against this, it would be odd to insert a provision in Title X which gives exclusive jurisdiction and then take away its exclusive effect. Moreover, Article 93(5) is the equivalent in Title X to Article 5(3) of the Brussels Convention, and, according to that

---

[26] Article 90(2)(c). [27] *Ibid.*
[28] Or in which an act within the meaning of Article 9(3), second sentence, (see above, p 322) has been committed.

Convention, exclusive jurisdiction under Article 17 overrides Article 5(3) jurisdiction.

Given that Article 93(5) is analogous to Article 5(3) of the Brussels Convention, the English courts would be justified in introducing a requirement that the plaintiff establish that there is a serious issue to be tried on the merits, as they have done in respect of the latter provision.

(f) *Other bases of jurisdiction contained in the Brussels Convention*

As has been seen, Article 90(2) specifically excludes many of the bases of jurisdiction contained in the Brussels Convention from applying in the case of proceedings for infringement, etc. A number of the other bases of jurisdiction under the Brussels Convention, although not specifically excluded, are, by virtue of their content, inapplicable in cases of infringement, etc. An obvious example is Article 5(2) which is concerned with maintenance. This does not leave very much from the Brussels Convention which can be used as a basis of jurisdiction in cases of infringement, etc of a Community trade mark. However, it does leave Article 6. It is not specified in the Regulation that this provision does not apply. According to Article 90(1), it can therefore be used as a basis of jurisdiction.

Article 6(1) is dealing with the situation where there are two or more defendants domiciled in different Contracting States to the Brussels Convention. In the case of proceedings for infringement, etc of Community trade marks, this provision would also apply to persons who do not have a domicile in any Member State but have an establishment therein.[29] It means, for example, that if one defendant is a Japanese domiciled company with an establishment in France, and the other is a New York domiciled company with an establishment in Germany, both defendants can be sued together in either France or Germany. An agreement conferring exclusive jurisdiction under Article 17 of the Brussels Convention will override jurisdiction under Article 6. In cases involving third party proceedings or a counterclaim, Article 6(2) or 6(3) can apply.

(v) Extent of jurisdiction: acts or threats of infringement abroad

In considering whether a Community trade mark court has jurisdiction in relation to acts or threats of infringement committed abroad, it is important to separate out the different bases on which jurisdiction can be taken.

---

[29] Article 90(2)(c).

(a) *Jurisdiction is based on Article 93(1) to (4): no territorial limitation*

Article 94(1) of the Regulation provides that a Community trade mark court whose jurisdiction is so based 'shall have jurisdiction in respect of: acts of infringement committed or threatened within the territory of any of the Member States'.[30] This allows jurisdiction in respect of an act of infringement committed abroad; for example, an action can be brought under Article 93(1) in France, where the defendant is domiciled, in respect of an act of infringement committed in Germany. Equally importantly, it allows the consolidation of litigation in one Member State following multiple acts of infringement (actual or threatened) committed in several different Member States. Thus, an infringement action can be brought in England, where the defendant is domiciled, in respect of acts of infringement committed in England, France and Germany.

It is logical to treat the Member States as one unit given that what is granted under the Regulation is a single Community trade mark rather than a bundle of national trade marks. What of the situation where there is jurisdiction over the defendant by virtue of Article 93(1) to (4), but the act of infringement was committed *outside* the territory of any of the Member States, for example in New York? It is implicit in Article 94(1) that there is no jurisdiction in such circumstances. In such circumstances, Article 94(1) can be said to contain a territorial limitation on jurisdiction, the territory being that of the Member States as a whole.

There is no requirement under Article 94(1) of the Regulation, unlike under Article 5(3) of the Brussels Convention, that the defendant is domiciled in a Member State. Thus, for example, a plaintiff could bring an action in England for infringement of a Community trade mark against a New York domiciled defendant following an act of infringement committed by that person in England.

(b) *Jurisdiction is based on Article 93(5): a territorial limitation*

Article 94(2) states that 'A Community trade mark court whose jurisdiction is based on Article 93(5) shall have jurisdiction only in respect of acts committed or threatened within the territory of the Member State in which that court is situated'. Jurisdiction under Article 93(5) is based on a local act of infringement or threat thereof. This provision clarifies the position where there are multiple acts, or threats, of infringement, one or more act(s) being committed locally and another, or other, act(s) being committed abroad. In this situation, a Community trade mark court has no jurisdiction in relation to the act or acts committed abroad. This very strict

---

[30] There is also jurisdiction in relation to acts within the meaning of Article 9(3), second sentence, committed within the territory of any of the Member States.

territorial limitation on jurisdiction has been explained by Advocate General Darmon in the following terms: 'we appear here to be on the fringes of civil matters, so that it seems preferable to adhere, within certain limits, to the concept of territoriality'.[31] The problem with this approach is that it leads to fragmentation of litigation. If the plaintiff wishes to bring an action which consolidates in one Contracting State the litigation in respect of all of the acts of infringement, both local and foreign, it is necessary to base jurisdiction on Article 93(1) to (4).

(c) *Residual jurisdiction based on the Brussels Convention*

Article 94 says nothing about the situation where, by virtue of Article 90(1), there is residual jurisdiction based on the Brussels Convention. This is understandable. It is, after all, a matter of Brussels Convention law. The question of whether there is jurisdiction in respect of acts of infringement committed abroad when jurisdiction is based on Article 6 of the Brussels Convention has already been examined in the context of infringement of national rights.[32] What was said there is equally applicable in the present context.

(vi) **Allocation of jurisdiction within the UK**

Title X, in a number of instances,[33] allocates jurisdiction to the courts of a Member State. This raises a problem for the United Kingdom. The Member State for the purpose of the Regulation is the United Kingdom. Accordingly, a plaintiff would not know whether he is able to bring his action in England, Scotland or Northern Ireland. United Kingdom legislation is needed to allocate jurisdiction within the United Kingdom, as was done when the Brussels Convention was implemented.[34] There is no problem of allocating jurisdiction within the United Kingdom in the situation where Articles 17 or 18 of the Brussels Convention are being relied upon since these articles allocate jurisdiction to an obviously identifiable Community trade mark court, rather than to a court of a Member State.

(vii) **Comparison with the Brussels Convention**

There is a number of similarities and differences between the bases of jurisdiction contained in the Regulation and those contained in the Brussels Convention.

---

[31] Case C-68/93 *Shevill* v *Presse Alliance* [1995] 2 WLR 499. He referred to Article 69(2) of the Community Patent Convention, which is in the same terms as Article 94(2) of the Community Trade Mark Regulation. In the *Shevill* case, a somewhat similar limitation was introduced in relation to defamation involving multi-State publication, see below, pp 397–398.
[32] See above p 172–173.
[33] See Article 93(1), (2) and (5).
[34] See Civil Jurisdiction and Judgments Act 1982, Schedule 4.

(a) Similarities

First, both sets of rules follow the same scheme of having, in effect, a general rule based on a personal connecting factor and then, as an alternative, a special rule based on the cause of action. Secondly, as a result of this scheme, both sets of rules allow scope for forum shopping by the plaintiff.

Thirdly, certain bases of jurisdiction under the Brussels Convention are directly incorporated into Title X. Articles 17 and 18 of the Brussels Convention are incorporated into Article 93 of the Regulation, and there is the residual jurisdiction based on the Brussels Convention as provided for by Article 90(1) of the Regulation.

Fourthly, several of the bases of jurisdiction under Title X are either the same as, or similar to, provisions under the Brussels Convention. Thus, Article 93(1) of the Regulation is the same as Article 2 of the Brussels Convention. Article 93(5) (a local act of infringement) of the former is analogous to Article 5(3) of the latter, albeit not identical in that Article 5(3) uses the wider concept of the place of the harmful event.[35]

(b) Differences

First, there is a major difference as to when the jurisdiction rules apply. The Brussels Convention, normally, requires the defendant to be domiciled in a Contracting State, although there are a number of important exceptions to this. There is no such requirement under the Regulation when jurisdiction is based on Article 93 (2), (3) or (5).[36]

Secondly, Title X uses the plaintiff's domicile as a connecting factor whereas the Brussels Convention, normally, does not.[37] Indeed, the Brussels Convention treats the plaintiff's domicile as an exorbitant form of jurisdiction outlawing its national use in cases where the Convention applies,[38] and the Court of Justice has been concerned to interpret the Convention so as to avoid allocating jurisdiction to this State.[39]

Thirdly, in certain circumstances, Title X allocates jurisdiction specifically to the courts of the Member State where the Office has its seat, ie Spain, whereas the Brussels Convention does not refer to a designated State in this way.

---

[35] See above, pp 150–153.
[36] If jurisdiction is based on Article 93(1) the defendant's establishment can be used as an alternative to domicile. It is a matter of Brussels Convention law whether Articles 17 and 18 of that Convention require the defendant to be domiciled in a Contracting State.
[37] But see Section 3 of Title II of the Brussels Convention (jurisdiction in matters relating to insurance), Article 8, and Section 4 (jurisdiction over consumer contracts), Article 14.
[38] Article 3.
[39] Case C-364/93 *Marinari* v *Lloyd's Bank plc and Another* [1996] 2 WLR 159.

Fourthly, even where there are bases of jurisdiction in Title X which are analogous to those in the Brussels Convention there can be important differences in detail. Thus, under Article 93(5) of the Regulation, there is no possibility of suing in the Member State in which the damage occurred, which is possible by virtue of the wider wording of Article 5(3) of the Brussels Convention.

Fifthly, there is no real equivalent in the Regulation of Article 5(5) of the Brussels Convention. It is true that the concept of an establishment is used in Title X, but there is no possibility of suing a defendant domiciled in one Member State, in another Member State in which the defendant has a branch, agency or other establishment, as allowed under Article 5(5) of the Brussels Convention. Article 93(1) only allows an action to be brought in the Member State in which the defendant has an establishment if that defendant is not domiciled in any of the Member States.

(viii) Forum shopping

(a) A choice of fora

Under Title X, a plaintiff may have a choice of many different Member States in which to bring the action,[40] assuming, of course, that there is no exclusive jurisdiction agreement. These are:

(i) the Member State the courts of which have jurisdiction by virtue of: Article 93(1) (defendant's domicile, etc); or, if not within this, Article 93(2) (plaintiff's domicile, etc); or, if not within either of the above, Article 93(3) (seat of the Office, ie Spain);
(ii) the Member State in which the defendant has entered an appearance before a different Community trade mark court;
(iii) the Member State in which the act(s) of infringement has (have) been committed or threatened;
(iv) the Contracting States to the Brussels Convention whose courts have jurisdiction by virtue of Article 6 of that Convention.

To take an example, A, domiciled in France, is a joint infringer with B, domiciled in Germany. Both A and B enter an appearance before an Italian Community trade mark court. The act of infringement was committed in Belgium. France, Germany, Italy and Belgium all have jurisdiction, and the plaintiff could proceed against A and B in any of these States. If acts of infringement were also committed in the Netherlands and Luxembourg, proceedings could be brought in either of these two States, although juris-

---

[40] The plaintiff cannot proceed in more than one Member State because of Article 21 of the Brussels Convention, discussed below.

diction will be territorially limited to the local act of infringement and will not encompass the acts of infringement committed abroad.

(b) *The benefit to be gained from forum shopping*

In proceedings brought for infringement, etc of a Community trade mark, what benefits are there to be gained from forum shopping? The personal and procedural advantages to be gained from bringing an action in one EC Contracting State rather than another have already been examined in the context of the infringement of national rights,[41] and what is said there is equally applicable in the present context. There will, though, be no substantive law advantage to be gained from bringing an action for infringement, etc of a Community trade mark in one Member State rather than another, given that the substantive law is the same in each Member State.

(ix) Revocation/invalidity

In a case of alleged infringement of a Community trade mark, the validity of the mark can be raised by way of a counterclaim or as a defence to the infringement action. However, the validity of a Community trade mark may not be put in issue in an action for a declaration of non-infringement.[42] A successful action for a counterclaim has the result that the Community trade mark itself will be invalidated for the whole of the Community.[43] It is different with a defence of invalidity. If this defence is successful, no infringement will have taken place, but the mark itself will remain unaffected.

(a) *Counterclaims*

A defendant to an action for infringement who wishes to put in issue the validity of the Community trade mark can do so by a counterclaim for revocation or for a declaration of invalidity. The Community trade mark courts have to treat the Community trade mark as valid unless this is done.[44] Any Community trade mark court which has international jurisdiction to try an infringement claim also has jurisdiction to try the counterclaim for revocation or for a declaration of invalidity. The bases of international jurisdiction set out in Article 93 apply in relation to all proceedings for infringement, etc, and, as has been seen, the Community trade mark courts have exclusive jurisdiction not only in respect of all infringement actions (this can take the form of a simple infringement case, or an action to counter threatened trade mark infringement, or an action for the payment of damages on the basis of the facts mentioned in Article

---

[41] See above, pp 198–201.   [42] Article 95(2).   [43] Article 1(2).   [44] Article 95(1).

9(3), second sentence, of the Regulation) but also for counterclaims for revocation or for a declaration of invalidity. This is a welcome innovation, ending the uncertainty and the possible need to split the infringement action from the counterclaim for revocation, which exists in relation to the infringement of national trade marks. The ability of the same court to try both the action for infringement and the counterclaim for revocation or for a declaration of invalidity will operate regardless of the basis of international jurisdiction under Title X. It follows that even where a Community trade mark court bases jurisdiction on Article 6(1) of the Brussels Convention, it will have exclusive jurisdiction to try both the infringement action and the counterclaim for revocation or for a declaration of invalidity.

Community trade mark courts have jurisdiction to deal with all cases where a counterclaim is made, whatever ground for revocation or invalidity is invoked. This conclusion is unavoidable when Articles 92(d), 96(1) and (2) are read together. This goes against all common sense and it might have been preferable to leave it to the exclusive jurisdiction of the Office for the Harmonisation in the Internal Market (Trade Marks and Designs) in Spain to invalidate a Community Trade Mark for the whole of the Community. At the moment, it is only an option for the Community trade mark courts to refer the counterclaim to the Office.[45]

There are three exceptional situations in which the Community trade mark court is unable to deal with the counterclaim for revocation or invalidity.[46] First, this is so if another organ has already reached a final decision concerning the invalidation or revocation of the Community trade mark. Three further requirements need to be met for this exception to apply, at least if the earlier decision rejected the request to revoke or invalidate the Community trade mark.[47] The final decision needs to be one between the same parties, it must be based on the same grounds and it must have the same object. The Regulation provides an interesting example in which the other organ that has already reached a decision is the Office. A Community trade mark court will be unable to proceed with the identical case if the Office has already reached a final decision.[48] This is a normal *res judicata* rule, it applies logically to both the situation where there is a counterclaim and that where there is a defence of invalidity, although the text of the Regulation only refers to the former situation. It is also logical that this exception should apply if the earlier decision between the parties has been reached by another Community trade mark court.[49]

---

[45] Article 96(7). [46] Huet, (1994) *Journal du Droit International* 623, at 631–632.
[47] *Ibid* at 631. [48] Article 96(2).
[49] Unless, of course, the earlier decision should not be recognised because one of the grounds for non recognition contained in Article 27 of the Brussels Convention is met (the Brussels Convention is applicable by virtue of Article 90(1) of the Regulation); see also Huet, n 46 above, at 631, n 35.

There is no reason, on the other hand, to hold on to the three further requirements in the situation where the Office or a Community trade mark court has revoked or invalidated the Community trade mark.[50] In this situation, the mark is deemed to have never existed[51] and the possibility of reaching a decision to the contrary would render the whole system nonsensical.

The second exceptional situation is where the action for infringement, etc[52] is being heard before one Community trade mark court but the validity of the Community trade mark is already in issue before another Community trade mark court. In this situation, the former court is, normally, required to stay its proceedings.[53]

The third exceptional situation is where an application for revocation or for a declaration of invalidity is being heard before the Office but the validity of the Community trade mark is already in issue on account of a counterclaim before a Community trade mark court. In this situation, the Office is, normally, required to stay its proceedings.[54]

(b) *Invalidity as a defence*

Article 95(3) of Title X contemplates that, in an action for infringement or threatened infringement,[55] a plea relating to revocation or invalidity of the Community trade mark may be submitted otherwise than by way of a counterclaim. This provision makes a plea of invalidity by way of a defence admissible. It is submitted that this would be so even where jurisdiction is based on the Brussels Convention.[56]

A different approach is taken from that in relation to counterclaims as regards the grounds of invalidity. In cases where invalidity is raised as a defence the Community trade mark court only has jurisdiction if the defendant in the main action argues that the Community trade mark should be revoked because the mark has not been put to genuine use or that the mark should be invalidated because the defendant possesses an earlier mark.[57]

---

[50] This is possible in a main action or on the basis of a counterclaim.
[51] Article 54.   [52] Other than an action for a declaration of non-infringement.
[53] Article 100(1); discussed below.
[54] Article 100(2); discussed below, p 334.
[55] Or under Article 92(c) in an action brought as a result of acts referred to in Article 9(3), second sentence.
[56] By virtue of Articles 93(4) and 90(1).   [57] Article 95(3).

(x) Declining jurisdiction

(a) *Proceedings relating to Community trade marks*

(i) *Specific rules on related actions*

Article 100 of the Regulation sets out specific rules on related actions. Article 100(1) is concerned with the situation where a Community trade mark court is hearing an action for infringement, etc,[58] but the validity of the Community trade mark is already in issue before another Community trade mark court on account of a counterclaim or where an application for revocation or a declaration of invalidity has already been filed at the Office. In this situation, the Community trade mark court[59] hearing the action for infringement, etc, of its own motion after hearing the parties or at the request of one of the parties and after hearing the other parties, is required to stay the proceedings, unless there are special grounds for continuing the hearing.

Article 100(2) is concerned with the situation where the Office is hearing an application for revocation or for a declaration of invalidity and the validity of the Community trade mark is already in issue on account of a counterclaim before a Community trade mark court. In this situation, the Office, of its own motion after hearing the parties or at the request of one of the parties and after hearing the other parties, is required to stay the proceedings before it, unless there are special grounds for continuing the hearing. There is, though, an exception to this. One of the parties to the proceedings before the Community trade mark court may request a stay of those proceedings, and that court may, after hearing the other parties to these proceedings, grant this. In this instance, the Office will continue the proceedings pending before it. The Community trade mark court will subsequently deal with the main action for infringement once the Office has reached a decision on the revocation or invalidity issue.

(ii) *Articles 21 and 22 of the Brussels Convention*

Articles 21 (*lis pendens*) and 22 (related actions) of the Brussels Convention[60] are not specified in the Regulation as not applying, and therefore, by virtue of Article 90(1) of the Regulation, can be applicable to actions for infringement, etc of a Community trade mark. This will be so regardless of whether jurisdiction is based on Article 93 of the Regulation

---

[58] For the purpose of this provision this means an action referred to in Article 92, other than an action for a declaration of non-infringement.

[59] For the situation where the European Patent Office has to stay its proceedings, see Article 100(2).

[60] See above, pp 177–186.

or on the residual jurisdiction under the Brussels Convention as provided for by Article 90(1) of the Regulation.

(iii) *Is there a discretionary power to decline jurisdiction?*

We are concerned here with the question of whether an English court can apply the principle in *Re Harrods (Buenos Aires) Ltd*[61] and, in cases where the alternative forum is a non-Contracting State to the Brussels Convention, decline jurisdiction on the basis of *forum non conveniens*. This would undoubtedly involve an extension of that principle in the sense that it would be applied in a different context. However, the Community Trade Mark Regulation can be said to be concerned with jurisdiction within the Community in that it binds EC Member States, and the reasoning of the Court of Appeal in the *Re Harrods* case would therefore appear to be equally applicable in this new context. On the other hand, those, like the authors of this book, who are critical of the decision would not want to see it extended to any new area.

The analogy with *Re Harrods* becomes more strained if jurisdiction under the Regulation is not based on the defendant's domicile, which was the basis of jurisdiction in that case, but on some other basis. It has already been seen[62] that there is a serious question over whether the principle in *Re Harrods* should be extended to encompass cases where jurisdiction is based on Articles 5 or 6 of the Brussels Convention.[63] The same doubt will arise if jurisdiction under the Regulation is based on Article 93(2), (3) or (5). It will arise also if jurisdiction under the Regulation is based on Articles 17, 18 or 6 of the Brussels Convention.

Even if it is accepted, which is doubtful, that the English courts have the power to decline jurisdiction on the ground of *forum non conveniens* in cases involving the infringement, etc of a Community trade mark, it is questionable whether a stay of English proceedings will ever be granted under that doctrine. It will not be easy for the defendant to establish that the clearly appropriate forum for trial is in a State outside the EC Member States. There will always be a strong connection with the Community in that it will be a Community trade mark that is the subject of the litigation. Moreover, that Community trade mark will have been infringed within the territory of the Member States.[64] In most cases, in order for there to be jurisdiction in the first place one of the parties, usually the defendant, will be domiciled in a Member State. Even if it is one of those rare cases where both parties are domiciled outside the Member States, this may not be

---

[61] [1992] Ch 72; discussed above, p 186. [62] See above, p 188.
[63] At the moment, the principle is applicable, seemingly, regardless of the basis of jurisdiction, see above, p 188.
[64] See Article 94, discussed above, pp 327–328.

enough to establish that the State of common domicile is the clearly more appropriate forum for trial.

(b) Simultaneous and successive civil actions on the basis of Community trade marks and national trade marks

Article 105 in Title XI sets out a series of provisions dealing with such actions.[65] In cases involving such actions, but which fall outside Article 105, recourse can be had to the provisions on declining jurisdiction in the Brussels Convention.

(i) Article 105

Simultaneous actions. Article 105(1) deals with the situation where 'actions for infringement involving the same cause of action and between the same parties are brought in the courts of different Member States, one seized on the basis of a Community trade mark and the other seized on the basis of a national trade mark'. It does so by introducing two rules on declining jurisdiction. The first is concerned with identical proceedings and is analogous to Article 21 of the Brussels Convention; the second is concerned with similar proceedings and is in some ways analogous to Article 22 of the Brussels Convention.

Identical proceedings. Article 105(1)(a) states that:

the court other than the court first seized shall of its own motion decline jurisdiction in favour of that court where the trade marks concerned are identical and valid for identical goods or services.

This rule is analogous to Article 21 of the Brussels Convention in that it only applies where the subject matter of the proceedings is the same, ie the trade marks concerned are identical and valid for identical goods or services. If this is not the case this provision will not apply but Article 105(1)(b) – the similar proceedings provision – may well apply. It is also, of course, required that the actions for infringement involve the same cause of action and are between the same parties. If this is not the case Article 105(1) will not apply but there is the possibility of using the related actions provision contained in Article 22 of the Brussels Convention.[66]

Article 105(1)(a) is also analogous to Article 21 of the Brussels Convention in that it adopts the mechanical solution whereby the court second seized must give way to the court first seized.

What if the jurisdiction of the court first seized is challenged? There is a danger that the court second seized will decline jurisdiction and, subse-

---

[65] There are no such provisions in the Protocol on Litigation attached to the Community Patent Convention.
[66] See below.

quently, the court first seized decides that it has no jurisdiction. Both actions have been dismissed. To meet this danger, Article 105(1)(a) goes on to state that 'The court which would be required to decline jurisdiction may stay its proceedings if the jurisdiction of the other court is contested'. This discretionary power to stay proceedings is not an entirely satisfactory solution to the problem. The Spanish/Portuguese Accession Convention to the Brussels Convention[67] changed the wording of Article 21 so that the court seized second must of its own motion stay its proceedings until such time as the jurisdiction of the court first seized is established. Once it has been, the court seized second must then decline jurisdiction. This is a much better solution to the problem. It is a pity that Article 105(1)(a) follows the old wording of Article 21 of the Brussels Convention rather than the new improved wording.

Similar actions. Article 105(1)(b) states that:

the court other than the court first seized may stay its proceedings where the trade marks concerned are identical and valid for similar goods or services and where the trade marks concerned are similar and valid for identical or similar goods or services.

This provision is analogous to Article 22 of the Brussels Convention in that, like that provision, it does not require the subject matter of the two actions to be the same. It is enough that the trade marks concerned are similar and valid and that this is for similar goods or services. There is no need for the trade marks to be identical or for the goods or services to be so. It follows that any of the following permutations can come within the provision:

(i) identical and valid trade marks for similar goods or services;
(ii) similar and valid trade marks for identical goods or services;
(iii) similar and valid trade marks for similar goods or services.

This provision is also like Article 22 of the Brussels Convention in that it uses the mechanical rule giving priority to the court seized first. It also confers on the court second seized a discretionary power to stay its proceedings. What are the criteria for the exercise of this discretion? Arguably, the criteria should be the same as for the exercise of the discretion under Article 22 of the Brussels Convention.[68]

Article 105(1)(b) is, however, different from Article 22 of the Brussels Convention in one important respect, in that it requires that the actions for

---

[67] See SI 1990/2591, Schedule I. This includes the amendments introduced by the Spanish/Portuguese Accession Convention to the Brussels Convention (the San Sebastian Convention) [1989] OJ L285/1.
[68] See above, p 185.

infringement involve the same cause of action and the same parties. If either of these requirements is missing, Article 105(1) will not apply but there is the possibility of using Article 22 of the Brussels Convention.[69] The essential requirement under that provision is that the two actions are related and this is defined in terms of whether there is a risk of irreconcilable judgments. This concept of related actions is not used under Article 105(1)(b).

Successive actions. Article 105(2) deals with a different situation, that where the court hearing an action for infringement on the basis of a *Community* trade mark is faced with the fact that a final judgment has been given on the merits and between the same parties on the basis of an identical *national* trade mark valid for identical goods or services. In this situation, the court hearing an action for infringement on the basis of a Community trade mark is required to reject the action. The earlier judgment creates a cause of action estoppel.

This situation will not arise very often. If the two actions are being tried concurrently, the court second seized is required to decline jurisdiction in favour of the court first seized and doubtless will do so before a judgment is granted in the court first seized. What is envisaged is the situation where the two actions are not being tried concurrently, a final judgment on the merits is granted in relation to a national trade mark and then an action is brought for infringement on the basis of a Community trade mark. It should be noted that the requirements for the operation of Article 105(2) are very stringent: the cause of action must be the same; the parties must be the same; the trade marks (one Community, the other national) must be identical; the goods or services must be identical.

The converse situation could also arise, ie the court hearing an action for infringement on the basis of a national trade mark is faced with a final judgment on the merits in relation to an identical Community trade mark. Exactly the same rule applies in this converse situation, and according to Article 105(3), the court hearing the action for infringement on the basis of a national trade mark is required to reject the action. The same stringent requirements apply as for Article 105(2).

(ii) *The Brussels Convention*

Article 90(1) of Title X, when dealing with the relationship with the Brussels Convention, states that this will apply not only to proceedings relating to Community trade marks but also to proceedings relating to simultaneous and successive actions on the basis of Community trade marks and national trade marks, unless otherwise specified in the Regulation.

---

[69] Article 22 can apply even though both the cause of action and the parties are different, see *Sarrio SA v Kuwait Investment Authority* [1997] 3 WLR 1143, HL, discussed above, p 183.

Simultaneous actions. Article 22 of the Brussels Convention is not specified as not applying under the Regulation and, therefore, can be applied by virtue of Article 90(1).[70] Article 22 can apply in a number of situations where Article 105(1) will not apply because the parties, or the cause of action, or both, are not the same.

Successive actions. In cases where Article 105(2) and (3) do not apply, for example because the cause of action is not the same, the court hearing an action for infringement will not reject the action and will end up giving a judgment. There may then be two irreconcilable judgments,[71] one granted on the basis of a Community trade mark, the other on the basis of a national trade mark. Article 27(3) of the Brussels Convention is applicable by virtue of Article 90(1) of Title X. This provides that a judgment granted in another Contracting State to that Convention shall not be recognised if the judgment is irreconcilable with a judgment given in a dispute between the same parties in the State in which recognition is sought. The judgment given in the recognising State takes priority, regardless of whether it was the first judgment to be granted.

(xi) Provisional, including protective measures

(a) *Measures available in the forum*

Article 24 of the Brussels Convention, which is concerned with provisional and protective measures, does not apply where there are proceedings for infringement, etc relating to Community trade marks.[72] Instead, Article 99(1) of the Regulation, which is substantially the same as Article 24 of the Brussels Convention, deals with such measures in relation to Community trade marks. The Regulation allocates jurisdiction to the Community trade mark courts of a Member State in respect of the substance of infringement actions, etc. Nonetheless, Article 99 allows an application to be made to the courts of a Member State, including Community trade mark courts, for such provisional, including protective, measures in respect of a Community trade mark or Community trade mark application as may be available under the law of that State in respect of a national trade mark, even if, under the Regulation, a Community trade mark court of another Member State has jurisdiction as to the substance of the matter. This would allow a French court to grant the provisional measures available under French law even though a German court has jurisdiction as to the substance of the matter. It would not preclude, though, a French court

---

[70] Article 90(2) which lists articles of the Brussels Convention which do and do not apply does not mention this article.
[71] Judgments are irreconcilable when they entail legal consequences that are mutually exclusive: Case 145/86 *Hoffman* v *Krieg* [1988] ECR 645.
[72] Article 90(2).

granting provisional measures in support of a French court as to the substance of the matter.

What provisional measures are available under English law in the situation where a foreign court has jurisdiction over the substance of the matter? At common law, the answer is none.[73] Section 25 of the Civil Jurisdiction and Judgments Act 1982[74] was introduced to ensure that in Brussels Convention cases an English court can grant interim relief in respect of proceedings in another Brussels Convention Contracting State. However, the wording of Section 25 is not designed to cover Community trade marks, and would need to be extended to cover such cases.[75] Moreover, the wording of Section 25 would not allow an English court to grant a provisional measure in support of proceedings as to the substance of the matter brought in England. Doubtless, though, an English court has the power to grant such measures, not by virtue of Section 25, but by virtue of the fact that it has jurisdiction as to the substance of the matter.[76]

(b) *Extra-territorial application*

Article 99(2) enables a Community trade mark court to grant provisional measures which 'are applicable in the territory of any Member State'. So, for example, a French Community trade mark court could grant an interlocutory injunction restraining acts of infringement of a Community trade mark in Germany and Italy.

This power to grant measures which have extra-territorial effect only applies where the granting court has jurisdiction under the bases set out in Article 93(1), (2), (3) or (4) (domicile/an establishment, the seat of the Office, Articles 17 and 18 of the Brussels Convention). The conferring of jurisdiction as to the trial of the substance of the matter in relation to acts of infringement committed in other Member States only applies where jurisdiction is based on Article 93(1) to (4).[77] In order to be consistent with this, it is understandable that the power to grant provisional measures should be limited likewise. In contrast, if jurisdiction is based on Article 93(5) (a local act or threat of infringement) there is no jurisdiction to grant extra-territorial provisional measures. Again, this is consistent with the rule in relation to jurisdiction as to the substance of the matter.[78] Neither does Article 99(2) provide jurisdiction to grant extra-territorial provisional measures in the situation where jurisdiction as to the substance of the matter is based on the Brussels Convention, as provided for by Article 90(1) of the Regulation.

[73] See above, p 215.
[74] See above, pp 215–216.
[75] It has been extended to cover proceedings commenced outside the EC/EFTA Contracting States.
[76] See above, p 216.
[77] Article 94(1), discussed above.
[78] Article 94(2), discussed above.

Moreover, the power to grant provisional measures which have extra-territorial effect is limited to the territory of the EC Member States. Thus, for example, an English court could not grant a provisional measure in relation to an act of infringement in the United States.

Finally, the jurisdiction to grant provisional measures which have extra-territorial effect in the territory of other Member States is subject to any necessary procedure for recognition and enforcement pursuant to Title III of the Brussels Convention.

(xii) Safeguarding the rights of the defendant

Article 20 of the Brussels Convention, which requires a court of a Contracting State to examine its jurisdiction where the defendant does not enter an appearance and lays down minimum standards in relation to notice, is not excluded by Article 90(2) or by any other provision in the Regulation. Accordingly, Article 20 applies to safeguard the rights of the defendant in proceedings relating to Community trade marks, etc. This will be so, regardless of whether jurisdiction is under Article 90 or 93 of the Regulation.

(xiii) Sanctions

Article 98(1) provides that 'where a Community trade mark court finds that the defendant has infringed or threatened to infringe a Community trade mark, it shall, unless there are special reasons for not doing so, issue an order prohibiting the defendant from proceeding with the acts which infringed or would infringe the Community trade mark'. Given the bases of jurisdiction under the Regulation, this could mean, for example, an English court, which has jurisdiction on the basis of the plaintiff's domicile in England, granting an injunction to prevent a New York defendant from infringing a Community trade mark in Germany. The English court would have to take such measures in accordance with English law as are aimed at ensuring that the injunction is complied with.[79]

(xiv) Procedure for service of the writ

In so far as jurisdiction under the Regulation is based on the Brussels Convention, then the English courts can use the procedure for service of the writ abroad introduced for such cases.[80] A similar procedure will need to be introduced for cases where jurisdiction is based on Article 93(1), (2), (3) or (5) of the Regulation.

---

[79] Article 98(1).
[80] See Order 11 rule 1 (2)(a) of the Rules of the Supreme Court; Cheshire and North, pp 324–325.

III
DESIGNS

1. THE SUBSTANTIVE LAW BACKGROUND

The troubled Draft Community Design Regulation will eventually put in place a unitary system of design protection. The idea is that, parallel to any existing national design rights, a system of Community Design Rights, that would be valid for the whole of the Community, will be established. These would be registered designs and the system would be administered by a Community Design Office, which is to be attached to the existing Community Trade Mark Office[81] in Alicante in Spain.

2. HOW JURISDICTIONAL PROBLEMS ARISE

Because the Community Design Right would, necessarily, cover the whole of the Community, the international element is necessarily present, which means that jurisdictional issues will arise. The position is very similar to that described earlier in relation to the Community trade mark. Essentially, jurisdictional problems arise in three ways. First, there are the obvious actions for infringement and validity. The Regulation will put in place a system which comprises a limited number of specially designated courts and the Court of Justice of the European Communities as ultimate appeal court. As the right applies to the whole of the Community, which of these courts will have jurisdiction to hear infringement and validity cases? Allegedly infringing acts can take place in more than one Member State and the alleged infringer could be domiciled in yet another Member State. If the registration of the right is the connecting factor, any court in the Community could have jurisdiction. Or do we look at the place where the alleged infringement took place, or do we turn to the domicile of the alleged infringer? Which court will deal with a case where the defendant has no domicile in any of the Member States? Could its establishment or place of business in the Community offer an alternative solution? In all these circumstances, it will be critical to determine whether or not the Brussels Convention applies. Any alternative solution will also have to include an equivalent to Article 24 of the Brussels Convention. Which courts will have jurisdiction to take interim measures? Do we restrict that power to the court that is dealing with the infringement case, or do we, potentially, allow almost any court to offer assistance in this area?

---

[81] Officially, Office for the Harmonisation of the Internal Market (Trade Marks and Designs).

Secondly, similar jurisdictional problems will arise in disputes concerning Community design rights that are not infringement or validity related, such as those in relation to the creation or ownership of such rights. Will the same rules apply to determine jurisdiction? And will these matters also be reserved for the specially designated courts?

A third way in which jurisdictional issues arise is related to the fact that the Regulation will not abolish national design rights. This means that infringement actions that involve the same cause of action could be brought between the same parties in different Member States. One action could be based on a Community design, another could be based on a national design. How is this issue of conflicting jurisdiction to be addressed? Should a variant of the *lis alibi pendens* rule in Article 21 of the Brussels Convention apply?

3. JURISDICTIONAL PROVISIONS

Title X[82] of the Draft Community Design Regulation deals with jurisdiction and procedure in legal actions relating to Community designs. Its terms are closely modelled on Title X of the Community Trade Mark Regulation. Indeed, most of the provisions are identical. There are, though, a few differences.

First, when it comes to the relationship of Article X of the Draft Community Design Regulation to the Brussels Convention, there is an additional provision[83] concerned with actions for a declaration of invalidity of an unregistered Community design or for counterclaims for a declaration of invalidity of a Community design raised in connection with an action for infringement or threatened infringement. Proceedings in respect of such an action or claim comply with Article 16(3)[84] of the Brussels Convention if they are brought before any Community Design Court having international jurisdiction as specified under Article 86 of the Regulation.[85]

Secondly, jurisdiction is allocated to the courts of the Member States where the Office is *situated*[86] rather than to where it has its *seat*. This represents a difference in terminology, but it does not represent any difference in substance.

---

[82] [1994] OJ C29/20.   [83] Article 83(3) of Draft Community Design Regulation.
[84] This provides that 'in proceedings which have as their object the validity of entries in public registers, the courts of the Contracting State in which the register is kept' have exclusive jurisdiction.
[85] Article 86 uses the same bases of jurisdiction as Article 93 of the Community Trade Mark Regulation, discussed above, pp 323–326.
[86] Compare Article 86(3) of the Draft Community Design Regulation with Article 93(3) of the Community Trade Mark Regulation.

Thirdly, as regards parallel actions on the basis of Community designs and national design rights, there is a *lis pendens* provision which applies where the latter right provides simultaneous protection with the former.[87] This is similar to a provision to be found in the Community Trade Mark Regulation,[88] but there is no requirement under the Draft Community Design Regulation that the designs are identical.

Fourthly, the provisions concerning successive actions[89] apply where the Community Design Court or other court is hearing an action not only for infringement but also for threatened infringement.[90]

IV
PATENTS

1. THE SUBSTANTIVE LAW BACKGROUND

If it ever comes into existence, the Community Patent system will offer a single patent for the whole of the Community. For the time being at least, this system would co-exist with a system of national patents. The new system will be an improvement on the current European Patent Convention, where a common filing and examination system still results in the grant of a bundle of national patents.

2. HOW JURISDICTIONAL PROBLEMS ARISE

Because the Community Patent will cover the whole of the Community, the international element is necessarily present, which means that jurisdictional issues will arise. Essentially, jurisdictional problems will arise in two ways. First, there are the obvious actions for infringement and validity. Here the opposition procedure before the Community Patent Office and the actions in the national courts will have to co-exist. And as the right applies to the whole of the Community, which of the national courts will have jurisdiction to hear infringement and validity cases? Allegedly infringing acts can take place in more than one Member State and the alleged infringer could be domiciled in yet another Member State. If the registration of the right is the connecting factor, any court in the Community could have jurisdiction, or do we look at the place where the

---

[87] Article 99(1).
[88] Compare Article 105(1) of the Community Trade Mark Regulation, discussed above, pp 336–338.
[89] Article 99(2), (3).
[90] Compare Article 105(2), (3) of the Community Trade Mark Regulation which does not cover the hearing of actions for threatened infringement.

alleged infringement took place; or do we turn to the domicile of the alleged infringer? Which court will deal with a case where the defendant has no domicile in any of the Member States? Could its establishment or place of business in the Community offer an alternative solution? In all these circumstances, it will be critical to determine whether or not the Brussels Convention applies. Any alternative solution will also have to include an equivalent to Article 24 of the Brussels Convention. Which courts will have jurisdiction to provide interim measures? Do we restrict that power to the court that is dealing with the infringement case, or do we, potentially, allow almost any court to offer assistance in this area?

Secondly, similar jurisdictional problems arise in disputes concerning Community Patents that are not infringement or validity related. Ownership disputes, for example between employers and their employees, are obvious examples of such disputes. Will the same rules apply to determine jurisdiction?

3. Jurisdictional Provisions

Under the current proposals, rules on jurisdiction in relation to Community Patents are derived from two sources. First, Part II of the Protocol On The Settlement Of Litigation Concerning The Infringement And Validity Of Community Patents (Protocol on Litigation)[91] annexed to the Agreement Relating To Community Patents of 15 December 1989 contains provisions on international jurisdiction. The Protocol only applies to proceedings initiated after the entry into force of the Agreement Relating To Community Patents.[92] The provisions in Part II of the Protocol are similar to those found in the original Community Patent Convention[93] but represent an improved version thereof. Secondly, Part VI of the Community Patent Convention contains rules on international jurisdiction and procedure in actions relating to Community patents other than those governed by the Protocol on Litigation. The Court of Justice has jurisdiction to give preliminary rulings concerning the interpretation of the provisions on jurisdiction in the Protocol and in Part VI.[94]

(a) THE PROTOCOL ON LITIGATION

The Protocol on Litigation contains substantially the same provisions as the Community Trade Mark Regulation. Indeed, the latter copied the

---

[91] [1989] OJ L401/34.   [92] Article 37.   [93] [1976] OJ L17/18.
[94] Article 3 of the Agreement relating to Community patents. The House of Lords must request a ruling, if it considers that a decision on the question is necessary to enable it to give a judgment: Article 3(2)(a) and (3). The Court of Appeal may so request: Article 3(2)(b) and (4).

former, in relation to the following: the proceedings in respect of which the Community patent courts have exclusive jurisdiction;[95] the relationship with the Brussels Convention;[96] the bases of jurisdiction;[97] territorial jurisdiction over acts or threats of infringement committed abroad;[98] a counterclaim for revocation;[99] specific rules on related actions;[100] provisional and protective measures, including extra-territorial application thereof;[101] and sanctions.[102] In relation to these matters, everything that was said earlier when the Community Trade Mark Regulation was being discussed is equally relevant now, as is everything said earlier in relation to the definition of domicile/an establishment;[103] allocation of jurisdiction within the UK;[104] comparison with the Brussels Convention;[105] forum shopping;[106] declining jurisdiction;[107] safeguarding the rights of the defendant;[108] and the procedure for service of the writ.[109]

At the same time, there are certain differences between the Protocol on Litigation and the Community Trade Mark Regulation. The former only deals with disputes concerning infringement and validity, not with other disputes;[110] it is only concerned with the situation where invalidity is raised by way of a counterclaim for revocation;[111] and it contains no provisions on simultaneous and successive civil actions on the basis of Community rights and national rights.[112]

(b) PART VI OF THE COMMUNITY PATENT CONVENTION

(i) Scope

Part VI of the Community Patent Convention is concerned with jurisdiction and procedure in actions relating to Community patents other than

[95] Article 15 of the Protocol, see Article 92 of the Regulation, discussed above, p 322.
[96] Article 13 of the Protocol, see Article 90 of the Regulation, discussed above p 322. An Annex to the Agreement relating to Community patents contains a Declaration whereby the Governments of the EC Member States express their willingness to enter into negotiations with the EFTA States concerning jurisdiction in respect of Community patents.
[97] Articles 14 and 13(1) of the Protocol, see Article 93 of the Regulation, discussed above, pp 323–326. Article 14(3) of the Protocol on Litigation refers to where the Common Appeal Court has its seat.
[98] Article 17 of the Protocol, see Article 94 of the Regulation, discussed above.
[99] Article 15 of the Protocol, see Articles 96 and 92(d) of the Regulation, discussed above.
[100] Article 34 of the Protocol, see Article 100 of the Regulation, discussed above.
[101] Article 36 of the Protocol, see Article 99 of the Regulation, discussed above, pp 339–341.
[102] Article 35 of the Protocol, see Article 98 of the Regulation, discussed above, p 341.
[103] See above, p 323. [104] See above, p 328. [105] See above, p 329.
[106] See above, pp 330–331. See, generally, Young and Birss, [1992] 10 *EIPR* 361.
[107] See above, pp 334–336. [108] See above, p 341. [109] See above, p 341.
[110] See above, pp 320–322.
[111] The Regulation on Community trade marks has provisions dealing with the situations where there is a counterclaim for a declaration of invalidity and where there is a defence of invalidity, see above, p 322.
[112] See above, pp 336–338.

those governed by the Protocol on Litigation. Part VI does not list what actions these are, although it clearly contemplates that actions relating to compulsory licences and to the right to a patent come within its scope.[113] Guidance on the scope of Part VI can also be derived from seeing what the Protocol does and does not cover. The Protocol does not say directly what proceedings are governed by its provisions. However, in Article 15 it lists the actions in respect of which the Community patent courts of first instance have exclusive jurisdiction. These are actions for infringement, etc, and are clearly within the scope of the Protocol.

(ii) Relationship with the Brussels Convention

Article 66 provides that, unless otherwise specified in the Community Patent Convention, the Brussels Convention, as amended by the Accession Conventions, applies to actions relating to Community patents, other than those to which the Protocol applies. Unlike the Protocol, there is no specification of provisions under the Brussels Convention which do not apply, or of those that do.

Nothing is said about the Lugano Convention. The Declaration in relation to this Convention[114] is only concerned with the Protocol on Litigation, and therefore it seems that no attempt will be made to enter into negotiations with EFTA States concerning jurisdiction in relation to Community patents other than those governed by the Protocol.

(iii) Bases of jurisdiction

(a) *Exclusive jurisdiction*

In certain clearly defined circumstances, Article 67 allocates jurisdiction exclusively to the courts of a specified Contracting State. The grant of exclusive jurisdiction means that the courts of no other Contracting State can try the case, even if they appear to have a basis of jurisdiction under some other provision.

(i) *Compulsory licenses*

Article 67(a) states that in actions relating to compulsory licenses in respect of Community patents, the courts of the Contracting State, the national law of which is applicable to the licence, shall have exclusive jurisdiction.

(ii) *The right to a patent*

Article 67(b) states that in actions relating to the right to a patent in which an employer and employee are in dispute, the courts of the Contracting

---

[113] See Articles 67 and 70. [114] See above, n 96.

State under whose law the right to a European patent is determined in accordance with Article 60(1), second sentence, of the European Patent Convention, shall have exclusive jurisdiction. Article 67(b) goes on to provide that any agreement conferring jurisdiction shall be valid only in so far as the national law governing the contract of employment allows the agreement in question.

(b) *The Brussels Convention*

In cases falling outside the scope of the exclusive jurisdiction provision in Article 67, resort will have to be made to the jurisdictional provisions in the Brussels Convention. An example would be an action relating to the right to a patent in which it is not an employer and an employee in dispute. Which of the bases of jurisdiction in the Brussels Convention would apply in this situation?

(c) *The German courts*

Article 68(3) provides that where no court has jurisdiction under Articles 66 and 67, actions may be heard before the courts of the Federal Republic of Germany.

(iv) Allocation of jurisdiction within the United Kingdom

Article 68(1) states that 'Within the Contracting State whose courts have jurisdiction under Articles 66 and 67, those courts shall have jurisdiction which would have jurisdiction *ratione loci* and *ratione materiae* in the case of actions relating to a national patent granted in that State'.

(v) Stay of proceedings

Article 73 is concerned with a stay of proceedings by a national court which is faced with proceedings before the European Patent Office. It is divided up to reflect two situations: the first is that prior to the grant of the Community patent; the second is that after the grant of the Community patent.

(a) *Prior to the grant of the Community patent*

Article 73(1) states that 'If the decision in an action before a national court relating to a European patent application which may result in the grant of a Community patent, other than an action governed by the Protocol on Litigation, depends upon the patentability of the invention, that decision may be given only after the European Patent Office has granted a Community patent or refused the European patent application'. An almost identical provision is to be found in the Protocol on Litigation.[115] The grant of a stay of proceedings is mandatory rather than discretionary.

(b) *After the grant of the Community patent*

Article 73(2) deals with this situation. It states that 'Where an opposition has been filed or a request for the limitation or an application for the revocation of a Community patent has been made, the national court may, at the request of one of the parties and after hearing the other parties, stay proceedings relating to the Community patent, in so far as its decision depends upon validity'. It is noticeable with this provision that the national court *may* grant a stay, ie this is a discretionary power. At the request of one of the parties, the court shall instruct that the documentary evidence of the opposition, limitation or revocation proceedings be communicated to it, in order to give a ruling on the request for a stay of proceedings. There is a similar provision in the Protocol on Litigation, albeit wider in that it also allows for a stay where the validity of the Community patent is already in issue before another Community patent court.[116]

(vi) Validity

A national court which is dealing with an action relating to a Community patent, other than the actions governed by the Protocol, is required to treat the patent as valid.[117]

V
PLANT VARIETY RIGHTS

1. The Substantive Law Background

Living material and its protection give rise to difficult issues in an intellectual property context. Moral arguments are easily drawn into the debate and the opinion that such material should never be the subject of an exclusive commercial right is shared by a significant part of society. More specifically, plant varieties have explicitly been excluded from patent protection, at least for the time being. It was, on the other hand, felt that the growing economic importance of the European biotechnology industry required that some form of protection should be granted. This protection eventually took the form of the Community Plant Variety Right.[118] This is an exclusive right in a plant variety, and its use

---

[115] Article 18(1).   [116] Article 34(1); discussed above.   [117] Article 72.
[118] Council Regulation 2100/94 on Community plant variety rights.

and reproduction, that applies in the whole of the Community in respect of distinct, homogeneous, stable and new varieties for which a variety denomination exists. The Community plant variety system is a registration system which is administered by a Community Plant Variety Office.

2. How Jurisdictional Problems Arise

Because the Community plant variety right, necessarily, covers the whole of the Community the international element is necessarily present, which means that jurisdictional issues will arise. Essentially, jurisdictional problems arise in two ways. First, there are the obvious actions for infringement and validity. As the right applies to the whole of the Community, which national courts will have jurisdiction to hear infringement and validity cases? Allegedly infringing acts can take place in more than one Member State and the alleged infringer could be domiciled in yet another Member State. If the registration of the right is the connecting factor, any court in the Community could have jurisdiction, or do we look at the place where the alleged infringement took place, for the whole case or only in respect of the infringements alleged to have been committed in the territory of the Member State concerned; or do we instead turn to the domicile of the alleged infringer? Which court will deal with a case where the defendant has no domicile in any of the Member States? Could its establishment or place of business in the Community offer an alternative solution? In all these circumstances, it will be critical to determine whether or not the Brussels Convention applies. Any alternative solution will also have to include an equivalent to Article 24 of the Brussels Convention. Which courts will have jurisdiction to take interim measures? Do we restrict that power to the court that is dealing with the infringement case, or do we, potentially, allow almost any court to offer assistance in this area?

Secondly, similar jurisdictional problems arise in disputes concerning Community plant variety rights that are not infringement or validity related. Entitlement and ownership claims in relation to the Community plant variety right are the obvious examples of such disputes. Will the same rules apply to determine jurisdiction?

3. Jurisdictional Provisions

Articles 101 and 102 of the Community Plant Variety Rights Regulation deal with jurisdiction and procedure in legal actions relating to civil law claims.[119] These provisions, whilst bearing some resemblance in places to

---

[119] See, generally, Tritton, para 6.042.

those contained in Title X of the Community Trade Mark Regulation, are distinctively different and need to be set out in some detail.

(a) THE PROCEEDINGS

The proceedings in respect of which Articles 101 and 102[120] apply are those relating to actions in respect of the claims referred to in Articles 94 to 100. This includes actions for infringement but, unlike the Community Trade Mark Regulation, not actions for threatened infringement.[121] It is, however, worth noting that an infringement of a Community plant variety right can be committed by an early act, such as an offering for sale. It also includes an action claiming entitlement to a Community plant variety right.

(b) RELATIONSHIP WITH THE LUGANO AND BRUSSELS CONVENTIONS

(i) The Lugano Convention

Article 101(1) provides that the Lugano Convention[122] shall apply to proceedings for infringement, etc.[123] There is no qualification to this of the type found in the Community Trade Mark Regulation, which applies the Brussels Convention 'Unless otherwise specified in this Regulation'. This would suggest that all the provisions of the Lugano Convention apply. This impression is confirmed by the fact that the bases of jurisdiction set out in Article 101(2) are described as being 'complementary' to the Lugano Convention. Furthermore, whilst the Community Trade Mark Regulation goes on to specifically exclude many of the provisions in the Brussels Convention, the Plant Variety Rights Regulation does not, with one exception,[124] specifically exclude any of the provisions of the Lugano Convention. In common with the Community Trade Mark Regulation, the Plant Variety Rights Regulation specifically provides that certain provisions do apply. Article 102(2) of the latter provides that 'Notwithstanding Article 101 of this Regulation, Articles 5(1), 17 and 18 of the Lugano Convention shall apply'. Of course, reliance can only be placed on a provision in the Lugano Convention if the terms of that Convention are met. It has been seen already that the bases of jurisdiction under the Lugano Convention (with the exception of Articles 16 and 17) only apply in the

---

[120] And Articles 103 to 106.
[121] Compare Article 92(a) of the Community Trade Mark Regulation.
[122] See above, pp 1 and 3.
[123] Ie actions in respect of the claims referred to in Articles 94 to 100.
[124] Article 102(1) provides that actions for claiming entitlement pursuant to Article 98 of the Regulation shall not be considered to fall under the provisions of Article 5(3) and (4) of the Lugano Convention.

situation where the defendant is domiciled in an EFTA Contracting State.[125]

(ii) The Brussels Convention

The Community Plant Variety Rights Regulation says nothing about the relationship between its provisions on international jurisdiction and those contained in the Brussels Convention. This is in sharp contrast to the Community Trade Mark Regulation, which contains a provision dealing with this. The Community Plant Variety Rights Regulation, of course does deal with the relationship between the Regulation and the Lugano Convention, which the Community Trade Mark Regulation does not. The Lugano Convention tells EC Contracting States when they are to apply, on the one hand, the Brussels Convention and, on the other hand, the Lugano Convention.[126] By incorporating the Lugano Convention into the Regulation, the latter is also, indirectly, incorporating the Brussels Convention in those cases where, according to the Lugano Convention, the former Convention applies.

Does this mean that all of the Brussels Convention is incorporated in cases of infringement, etc of a Community plant variety right? This would be consistent with the position under the Regulation in relation to the Lugano Convention.

(c) BASES OF JURISDICTION

In actions for infringement, etc, the following bases of jurisdiction are applicable.

(i) Defendant's domicile (seat)/an establishment

Article 101(2)(a) provides that proceedings for infringement, etc shall be brought in the courts:

of the Member State or another Contracting Party to the Lugano Convention in which the defendant is domiciled or has his seat or, in the absence of such, has an establishment.

This provision is basically the same as that found in the Community Trade Mark Regulation. There are, though, some differences.

First, it allocates jurisdiction to the courts of a Member State of the European Union but makes clear that the courts of the Contracting Parties to the Lugano Convention which are not Member States of the European Union (ie the three EFTA States) also have jurisdiction under Article 2 of

---

[125] See above.
[126] See Article 54B of the Lugano Convention; Cheshire and North, p 341.

the Lugano Convention in cases of infringement, etc involving defendants domiciled or with their seat in EFTA States.

Secondly, it uses the concept of domicile as a connecting factor, as does the Community Trade Mark Regulation. Unlike the latter, though, it provides, as an alternative, the concept of a seat, to be used with a corporate defendant. The domicile or seat of a party is determined pursuant to Articles 52 and 53 of the Lugano Convention,[127] which tells us which State's definition of domicile or seat is to be used. It is, in fact, unnecessary to mention as a separate alternative the defendant's seat since Article 53 provides that the seat of a company is treated as its domicile. Domicile and seat are one and the same thing as far as corporate defendants are concerned.

Thirdly, if the defendant is not domiciled or has no seat in an EU Member State or in a Contracting Party to the Lugano Convention, the defendant can nonetheless be sued in one of these States if it has an establishment there. There is a similar provision in the Community Trade Mark Regulation. However, what is odd about this provision is that it purports to give the courts of an EFTA State jurisdiction when the jurisdiction of the courts of such a State must be derived from the Lugano Convention, which does not allocate jurisdiction on the basis of an establishment in a Contracting State to that Convention.

(ii) Plaintiff's domicile (seat)/an establishment

Article 101(2)(b) provides that, if this condition (in Article 101(2)(a)) is not met in any of the Member States or Contracting Parties, proceedings for infringement, etc shall be brought in the courts:

> of the Member State in which the plaintiff is domiciled or has his seat or, in the absence of such, has an establishment.

This is a very similar provision to one found in the Community Trade Mark Regulation, the only real difference being the reference to the seat in the case of a company as an alternative to domicile in the case of an individual. The Lugano Convention does not allocate jurisdiction to the State of the plaintiff's domicile and so there is no reference to that Convention.

(iii) The Member States in which the seat of the Office is located

Article 101(2)(c) provides that if this condition (in Article 101(2)(b)) is also not met in any of the Member States proceedings for infringement etc shall be brought in the courts:

> of the member States in which the seat of the Office is located.

---

[127] Article 102(3).

This provision is, essentially, the same as that contained in the Community Trade Mark Regulation.[128]

(iv) The courts for the place where the harmful event occurred

Article 101(3) provides that:

> Proceedings relating to actions in respect of claims for infringement may also be brought in the courts for the place where the harmful event occurred.

This parallels a provision in the Community Trade Mark Regulation, and allows the plaintiff the option of suing in a State other than that allocated jurisdiction under Article 101(2). Whilst the former provision refers to the State in which the act of infringement was committed, the latter provision refers instead to the place where the harmful event occurred. This, of course, is the wording adopted in Article 5(3) of the Lugano Convention. If the place in question is in a Member State of the EU Article 101(3) will apply. If the place is in a Contracting State to the Lugano Convention, which is not a Member State of the EU (ie an EFTA State), Article 5(3) of that Convention will apply, provided, as required by this provision, that the defendant is domiciled in a Contracting State to the Convention. There is no problem in allocating jurisdiction within the United Kingdom under this provision because the courts of the place in question will be easily identifiable as being in England, Scotland, or Northern Ireland.

The difficulty in infringement cases with using the concept of the place where the harmful event occurred is the uncertainty over whether this is referring simply to the place where the act of infringement occurred or whether it is referring both to this place and to the place where the resulting damage occurred. If the latter, the plaintiff is given a choice of suing in either State. It is submitted that, for the purpose of Article 101(3), the place where the harmful event occurred should be regarded as being the State where the act of infringement occurred. This view is supported by the next sentence of Article 101(3), which limits jurisdiction to 'infringements alleged to have been committed in the territory of the Member State to which it belongs'. That provision, which will be examined latter, is concerned with acts of infringement. Whilst primarily concerned to prevent jurisdiction in relation to infringements abroad, it also prevents jurisdiction being asserted on the basis of local damage.

(v) Articles 5(1), 17 and 18 of the Lugano Convention

These provisions[129] are expressly preserved by Article 102(2) of the Regulation. Presumably, they are specifically mentioned because there is no equivalent to them under Article 101(2) or (3), and so they are provi-

---

[128] Article 93(3).
[129] They are discussed above, pp 36, 77–78, 94. See also Cheshire and North, pp 343–344.

sions that a plaintiff may wish to rely on instead of those contained in these paragraphs.

(vi) Other bases of jurisdiction contained in the Lugano Convention

Given that Article 101(1) categorically states that the Lugano Convention shall apply to proceedings for infringement, etc, it is open to the plaintiff to rely on bases of jurisdiction other than those (Articles (5(1), 17 and 18) specified above. The two provisions in the Lugano Convention which are most useful to the plaintiff, Articles 2 and 5(3) are, in effect, subsumed within Article 101(2)(a) and (3). However, this still leaves the multi-defendant basis of jurisdiction contained in Article 6. It also leaves Article 5(5). This enables a plaintiff to sue, for example, in Switzerland on the basis that the Icelandic defendant has a branch office in Switzerland provided that the dispute arises out of the operations of this branch.

The only limitation on the use of the bases of jurisdiction contained in the Lugano Convention is set out in Article 102(1), which states that actions for claiming entitlement[130] cannot be considered to fall under Article 5(3) (the tort head) or 5(4) (a civil claim for damages or restitution based on an act giving rise to criminal proceedings) of the Lugano Convention.

(vii) Bases of jurisdiction contained in the Brussels Convention

Given that the Regulation appears to incorporate indirectly the Brussels Convention, presumably any of the bases of jurisdiction under that Convention can be used, provided that the terms of that Convention are met.

(d) INFRINGEMENTS COMMITTED ABROAD

(i) Jurisdiction is based on Article 101(2) (domicile (seat)/an establishment, seat of the Office)

In this situation, Article 101(2) provides that the competent courts shall have jurisdiction in respect of infringements alleged to have been committed in any of the Member States. This parallels a provision found in the Community Trade Mark Regulation.[131]

(ii) Jurisdiction is based on Article 101(3) (the place where the harmful event occurred)

In this situation, it is provided that 'the court shall have jurisdiction only in respect of infringements alleged to have been committed in the territory of the Member State to which it belongs'. This is the same territorial limitation as is found in the Community Trade Mark Regulation.[132]

[130] Article 98.   [131] Article 94(1).   [132] Article 94(2).

(iii) Jurisdiction is based on the Lugano or Brussels Conventions

The Regulation says nothing about this. The same problem arises in relation to the Community Trade Mark Regulation and is addressed there.[133]

(e) A PLEA OF INVALIDITY

Article 105 provides that a 'national court or other body hearing an action relating to a Community plant variety right shall treat the Community plant variety right as valid'. There is also a rule, which will be examined next, on stay of proceedings where there are related actions in the Office and in a national court which raise the issue of validity.

(f) DECLINING JURISDICTION

(i) Specific rules on stay of proceedings

Article 106(2) provides that:

> Where an action relates to a Community plant variety right that has been granted and in respect of which proceedings for revocation or cancellation pursuant to Articles 20 (Nullity of Community plant variety rights) or 21 (Cancellation of Community plant variety rights) have been initiated [before the Office], the proceedings may be stayed in so far as the decision depends upon the validity of the Community plant variety right.

This is a badly drafted provision. It refers to 'the proceedings' being stayed. This could be read as giving the Office a discretionary power to stay its proceedings,[134] whereas the provision makes more sense if what is intended is that the national court hearing the action has the discretionary power to stay its proceedings pending the decision of the Office on the validity of the Community plant variety right. Interpreted in this way, the provision is very similar to one found in the original version of the Community Patent Convention,[135] on which Article 106(2) appears to be based.[136]

The only other provision in relation to stay of proceedings is Article 106(1). This is concerned with actions relating to claims for entitlement to a Community plant variety right. Where the decision in such an action depends upon the protectability of the variety,[137] a decision may not be

---

[133] See above, p 328.
[134] See Article 34(2) of the latest version of the Community Patent Convention.
[135] Article 77(2) [1976] OJ L17/18. See Article 34(1) of the latest version of the Community Patent Convention, discussed above.
[136] This view is reinforced if you compare Article 106(1) of the Community Plant Variety Rights Regulation with Article 77(1) of the original Community Patent Convention.
[137] Pursuant to Article 6.

given before the Office has decided on the application for a Community plant variety right. This provision parallels one to be found in the Community Patent Convention.[138]

(ii) Articles 21 and 22 of the Lugano Convention

These provisions will apply by virtue of Article 101(1), and if the argument above[139] is accepted so will Articles 21 and 22 of the Brussels Convention.

(g) PROVISIONAL, INCLUDING PROTECTIVE MEASURES

There is no provision in the Regulation dealing with this, unlike under the Community Trade Mark Regulation.[140] This is an example of how the Community Plant Variety Rights Regulation, because of its brevity, resembles the original Community Patent Convention more than its successor or the similarly worded Community Trade Mark Regulation. Of course, it is possible to resort to Article 24 of the Lugano Convention, which is concerned with provisional measures and, if the argument above is accepted, Article 24 of the Brussels Convention.

(h) SUMMARY OF SIMILARITIES AND DIFFERENCES

The rules relating to international jurisdiction contained in the Community Trade Mark Regulation, the Draft Community Design Regulation and the Protocol on Litigation attached to the Community Patent Convention, are all very similar. In contrast, those contained in the Community Plant Variety Rights Regulation are in a number of respects very different. If we take as the point of comparison the Community Trade Mark Regulation, and compare that with the Community Plant Variety Rights Regulation it can be seen that, first, the latter is extremely brief when compared with the former. Secondly, nearly all the provisions of the Lugano Convention can be used alongside those contained in Articles 101 and 102 of the Community Plant Variety Rights Regulation; under the Community Trade Mark Regulation most of the jurisdictional provisions of the Brussels Convention are specifically excluded. Thirdly, the relationship between the Brussels Convention and the Community plant variety rights Regulation is not even mentioned. Fourthly, actions for threatened infringement of Plant Variety Rights are not actionable under the Community Plant Variety Rights Regulation. Fifthly, there are no rules in the Community Plant Variety Rights Regulation on counterclaims or provisional measures, and it says very little about invalidity. One of the

---

[138] Article 18, see also Article 77(1) of the original Community Patent Convention.
[139] See above, p 352.   [140] Article 99.

essential features of the Community Trade Mark Regulation is, of course, that Community trade mark courts have jurisdiction in relation to infringement and validity.

This is not to say that there are no similarities between these different sets of rules. First, the bases of jurisdiction introduced in Article 101(2), (3) of the Community Plant Variety Rights Regulation are largely the same as those contained in the Community Trade Mark Regulation. Secondly, the territorial scope of jurisdiction under these provisions is the same. Thirdly, the provisions on stay of proceedings under the Community Plant Variety Rights Regulation have parallels under the Community Trade Mark Regulation.

The overall impression is that the provisions on international jurisdiction in the Community Plant Variety Rights Regulation bear a much stronger resemblance to the brief provisions in the original version of the Community Patent Convention than to the much more detailed and satisfactory provisions in the Community Trade Mark Regulation or the Protocol on Litigation attached to the Community Patent Convention.

8

Complementary Torts and Other Causes of Action: Jurisdiction

I	Introduction	361
II	Passing-off	361
	1. Substantive law	361
	(a) Goodwill	363
	(b) Misrepresentation	365
	(c) Damage	367
	(d) Enabling passing-off	368
	2. How jurisdictional problems arise	369
	3. Jurisdictional provisions	370
	(a) The EC/EFTA rules	370
	(b) The traditional rules	381
III	Malicious falsehood	388
	1. Substantive law	389
	(a) A false statement	389
	(b) A derogatory statement	390
	(c) Malice	390
	(d) Damage	391
	2. How jurisdictional problems arise	391
	3. Jurisdictional provisions	392
	(a) The EC/EFTA rules	392
	(b) The traditional rules	393
IV	Defamation	394
	1. Substantive law	394
	(a) A recent example of defamation	394
	(b) The elements of the tort	394
	(c) No territorial limits on the harmful activity	395
	(d) Protection of a professional or business reputation	395
	2. How jurisdictional problems arise	396
	3. Jurisdictional provisions	396
	(a) The EC/EFTA rules	396
	(b) The traditional rules	402
V	Unfair competition	409
	1. Substantive law	409

	2.	How jurisdictional problems arise	410
	3.	Jurisdictional provisions	410
		(a) The EC/EFTA rules	410
		(b) The traditional rules	414
VI	Wider Continental protection in delict		415
	1.	Substantive law	415
	2.	How jurisdictional problems arise	415
	3.	Jurisdictional provisions	415
		(a) The EC/EFTA rules	415
		(b) The traditional rules	416
VII	Breach of competition rules		416
	1.	Substantive law	416
		(a) Article 85 EEC	416
		(b) Article 86	419
		(c) Actions for breach of competition law	421
	2.	How jurisdictional problems arise	422
	3.	Jurisdictional provisions	423
		(a) The EC/EFTA rules	423
		(b) The traditional rules	425
VIII	Breach of confidence		426
	1.	Substantive law	426
		(a) Elements of the action for breach of confidence	426
		(b) Classification of breach of confidence	430
	2.	How jurisdictional problems arise	431
	3.	Jurisdictional provisions	431
		(a) The EC/EFTA rules	431
		(b) The traditional rules	443
IX	Reform		447
	1.	Criticism of the existing law	448
	2.	Comparison with infringement	449
	3.	Reform of the jurisdictional rules of general application	449
	4.	Special jurisdictional rules	449
		(a) The preliminary questions	449
		(b) The suggested rules	452

I
INTRODUCTION

There is a wide variety of causes of action under English and foreign law which are complementary to the tort of infringement.[1] In this chapter, we will be examining these other causes of action: ie passing-off; malicious falsehood; defamation; unfair competition; wider Continental protection in delict; breach of competition rules; breach of confidence. Most of these causes of action are tortious. Passing-off, which is often used in combination with a trade mark infringement action, is the most obvious example to start with. In many continental legal systems, this area is taken up by the tort of unfair competition. Whilst not identical, there is an overlap between the common law and the continental civil law approaches. This overlap will be examined from a comparative point of view.

II
PASSING OFF

1. SUBSTANTIVE LAW

The standard passing-off case is concerned with the situation where a trader tries to rely on the goodwill or established reputation of another trader and where the public will be confused and think it is acquiring the goods of the latter. The first trader passes his goods off as if they were the goods of the other trader. The leading case, *Erven Warnink B V v J Townsend & Sons (Hull) Ltd*,[2] provides a good example of this practice. Warnink had developed a substantial amount of goodwill in a drink based on a mixture of spirits and eggs. The defendants produced a drink that blended Cyprus sherry and dried eggs which was cheaper and they marketed it as 'Keeling's old English Advocaat'. The argument was that the public would confuse both products and could be duped into buying the defendants' inferior product by their use of the brand name. The defendants sought to rely on the plaintiff's established reputation and pass off their drink as the plaintiff's product.

That case, as interpreted in later judgments, laid down a five stage test for passing-off. Lord Diplock identified the following requirements:

---

[1] See, generally, Troller, *International Encyclopedia of Comparative Law*, Vol III, chapter 34–14.
[2] [1979] AC 731; [1979] 2 All ER 927.

(1) a misrepresentation (2) made by a trader in the course of trade (3) to prospective customers of his or ultimate consumers of goods or services supplied by him, (4) which is calculated to injure the goodwill of another trader . . . and (5) which causes actual damage to a business or goodwill of the trader by whom the action is brought.[3]

This test was later simplified and reduced to a three stage test. Lord Oliver formulated this approach, which did not fundamentally change the essence of passing-off, as follows in the *Jif Lemon* case:

First, he must establish a goodwill or reputation attached to the goods or services which he supplies in the mind of the purchasing public by association with the identifying 'get-up' (whether it consists simply of a brand name or a trade description, or the individual features of labelling or packaging) under which his particular goods are offered to the public, such that the get-up is recognized by the public as distinctive specifically of the plaintiff's goods or services. Secondly, he must demonstrate a misrepresentation (whether or not intentional) leading or likely to lead the public to believe that goods or services offered by him are the goods or services of the plaintiff. Whether the public is aware of the plaintiff's identity as the manufacturer or supplier of the goods and services is immaterial, as long as they are identified with a particular source which is in fact the plaintiff. For example if the public is accustomed to rely upon a particular brand name in purchasing goods of a particular description, it matters not at all that there is little or no public awareness of the identity of the proprietor of the brand name. Thirdly, he must demonstrate that he suffers or, in a *quia timet* action, that he is likely to suffer damage by reason of the erroneous belief engendered by the defendant's misrepresentation that the source of the defendant's goods or services is the same as the source of those offered by the plaintiff.[4]

When dealing with a case where an Italian consortium of producers of Parma ham unsuccessfully tried to stop the defendant from selling genuine Parma ham without their official approval Nourse L J summarised the new test as a simple trinity of:

(1) the goodwill of the plaintiff in his goods;
(2) a misrepresentation by the defendant leading to confusion; and
(3) damage to the plaintiff.[5]

The claim was bound to fail in that case since there was no misrepresentation of the origin of the ham. Each of the three components of the test warrants some additional comments.[6]

[3] [1979] AC 731 at 742; [1979] 2 All ER 927 at 932–933.
[4] *Reckitt & Colman Products Ltd* v *Borden Inc* [1990] 1 All ER 873 at 880; [1990] 1 WLR 491 at 499.
[5] *Consortio del Prosciutto di Parma* v *Marks & Spencers plc* [1991] RPC 351.
[6] For a more detailed analysis of the case law concerning passing-off see Holyoak and Torremans, *Intellectual Property Law*, Butterworths (1995) pp 339–372.

(a) GOODWILL

(i) **Existence of goodwill**

The plaintiff is, first of all, required to show the existence of goodwill and this depends often on factual considerations. When a business is set up it will take some time to develop its goodwill. A speedy build up of a substantial trade and high profile publicity will assist in establishing goodwill quickly.[7] Established goodwill does not necessarily disappear when the business to which it is attached stops trading. The lapse of time is not the main factor involved. The only issue is whether the goodwill has lapsed or not. The fact that people confuse the new business with the old one will be a powerful argument to demonstrate that the latter's goodwill has not (yet) lapsed.[8] It would be unfair, in these circumstances, to allow the new business to seize that goodwill for its own purposes and to allow the dilution of the existing goodwill which the original owner might still want to use at a later stage.[9]

(ii) **The location of goodwill and its geographical extent**

An inevitable problem linked to goodwill is its location and its geographical extent. As early as 1901, the House of Lords established a geographical link between goodwill and the place where business is carried on.[10] If goodwill exists somewhere in England because the plaintiff carries out his business there it is now readily accepted that any injunction to protect that goodwill against passing-off will extend to the whole of England and Wales.[11] One should, however, not rush to the conclusion that the absence of any business activity in England will lead to the absence of any goodwill here. Goodwill in the jurisdiction can, in such a case, also arise from the fact that the trader involved has a reputation in this country. The *Maxim's* case provides a clear example.[12] Although this famous restaurant is located in Paris, the name 'Maxim's' has an international reputation which also exists in this country. That led the judge to conclude that goodwill existed in this country and that the defendant should not be allowed to capitalise upon this goodwill by calling his Norwich bistro 'Maxim's'. A reputation will, in practice, only exist if the use of the name in this country could lead to confusion in the mind of consumers.[13] Only

---

[7] See *Stannard* v *Reay* [1967] RPC 589 and *BBC* v *Talbot Motor Co Ltd* [1981] FSR 228.
[8] See *Ad-lib Club Ltd* v *Glanville* [1972] RPC 673.
[9] See *A Levey* v *Henderson-Kenton (Holdings) Ltd* [1974] RPC 617.
[10] *Commissioners of Inland Revenue* v *Muller & Co's Margarine Ltd* [1901] AC 217; see also Derenberg, (1978) 68 *Trade Mark Reporter* 387.
[11] *Chelsea Man Menswear Ltd* v *Chelsea Girl Ltd* [1987] RPC 189.
[12] *Maxim's Ltd* v *Dye* [1977] FSR 364.
[13] *The Athlete's Foot Marketing Associates Inc* v *Cobra Sports Ltd* [1980] RPC 343 provides a good example of a case where that requirement was not met and the passing-off action failed.

well-known foreign marks are protected that way, in implementation of Article 6bis of the Paris Convention for the Protection of Intellectual Property 1883. This point of law has now been codified in Section 56 of the Trade Marks Act 1994. An injunction can now be obtained by the owner of a well-known foreign trade mark against any use in the United Kingdom of a mark

> identical or similar to his mark, in relation to identical or similar goods or services, where the use is likely to cause confusion.

This right goes even slightly further as it arises irrespective not just of whether the claimant has any business but also irrespective of the existence of any goodwill in the UK, though the mark must be 'well-known'.

(iii) Trade-related goodwill

The courts see passing-off as a trade related offence and not any kind of goodwill will be protected, but only goodwill created by trade. The boundaries of this category have been drawn reasonably clearly. First of all there must be trade. In the absence of any trading activity no protectable goodwill can arise.[14] Secondly, there must be trade by both parties to the same customers and in the same or at least broadly similar fields of activity. This is commonly referred to as the common field of activity requirement.[15] This level of broad similarity being required is the subject of greatest uncertainty or discretion in this area. The common field of activity requirement became less clear after *Lego Systems Aktieselskab* v *Lego M Lemelstrich Ltd*.[16] The plaintiffs were well known manufacturers of toy plastic bricks and their action was directed against the sale by the defendants of Lego brand water sprinklers and other gardening irrigation equipment. An injunction was granted although it could be doubted whether a common field of activity existed. The court seems to operate a more flexible rule here because the Lego toy manufacturers possessed a great fame and it attached great weight to the assumption that would be made by customers of the sprinkler-firm that they were buying products made by the Danish toy brick firm. In cases where the trader's goodwill is exceptionally great, goodwill will extend beyond their sole trading field into other areas of activity.

---

[14] See *British Association of Aesthetic Plastic Surgeons* v *Cartwright* [1987] RPC 549, the association was not trading and therefore no protectable goodwill existed.

[15] See *Granada Group Ltd* v *Ford Motor Co Ltd* [1973] RPC 49; *Wombles Ltd* v *Wombles Skips Ltd* [1977] RPC 99; *Annabel's (Berkely Square) Ltd* v *G Schock* [1972] RPC 838 and *Harrod's Ltd* v *R Harrod Ltd* (1924) 41 RPC 74.

[16] [1983] FSR 155.

(iv) Collective goodwill

Normally, this goodwill in trade will be owned by a single trader, but this is not a requirement. Collective goodwill can be generated by a group of traders and, in such cases, each of them is allowed to rely on that collective goodwill when bringing a case in passing off. The champaign industry has brought a series of successful passing-off actions. In each of these actions, they relied on the collective goodwill in the name 'champagne' which is shared by all producers of that type of sparkling wine from the 'Champagne' region in France.[17]

(v) Less obvious types of goodwill

In the previous paragraphs, reference has been made to goodwill in a brand name, company name or a distinctive product description such as 'champagne'. Whilst these are the obvious examples, it is submitted that goodwill can extend towards more peripheral parts of the plaintiff's trading activity. *Cadbury Schweppes Pty Ltd* v *Pub Squash Co Pty Ltd*[18] seems to suggest that protectable goodwill can arise in an advertising campaign and in more general imagery associated with the product. This extension will only happen, though, if such material has become part of the goodwill of the product. That will be the case if the product has derived from the advertising a distinctive character which the market recognises. The additional material needs, at least, to be original and innovative and lead to distinctiveness. Obviously, all the other requirements for passing-off need to be met as well and it is to these requirements that we now turn, noting in passing that Cadbury Schweppes' claim failed, *inter alia*, because no misrepresentation was found.

(b) MISREPRESENTATION

Misrepresentation means, essentially, that the defendant represents his goods or services in such a way as if they were those of the plaintiff and that, in the mind of the consumer, a false belief of connection between the two products is created. Confusion is, necessarily, the result of such a misrepresentation.

(i) The use of a similar get-up

There are various types of misrepresentation. The most common example is found in those cases where confusion arises because of a similar get-up

---

[17] See *J Bollinger* v *Costa Brava Wine Co Ltd* [1960] Ch 262, [1959] 3 All ER 800; *J Bollinger* v *Costa Brava Wine Co Ltd (No 2)* [1961] 1 All ER 561, [1961] 1 WLR 277; *Taitinger SA* v *Allbev Ltd* [1994] 4 All ER 75.
[18] [1981] 1 All ER 213; [1981] 1 WLR 193, PC.

being used for competing products. In practice, this means that strong similarities are found in the packaging and the presentation of the product. But passing-off will only arise if the appearance of the product is not dictated by its function.[19] The most striking passing-off case in this area is the successful *Jif Lemon* case.[20] The defendant in that case started selling lemon juice in yellow lemon shaped containers, something the plaintiffs had been doing for many years. There were several differences between the two containers, but the overall appearance was similar. It was emphasised in this case that the fact that there was a strong likelihood of confusion in the marketplace was essential. Passing-off will only arise when the consumer will be confused between the two products and, in establishing this fact, factors such as the type of consumer involved[21] and the circumstances in which the consumer buys the type of product involved have to be taken into account.[22]

(ii) The name as a source of confusion

Another type of misrepresentation is based on the fact that the name which is being used is the source of potential confusion. The use of an identical or similar name in the same or in a related field of activity might lead to confusion if the original user has acquired a strong reputation and a substantial amount of goodwill in the name. Passing-off will prevent the use of a name in such cases even though the defendant might be using his own name.[23] Once again, the defendant should not be allowed to capitalise upon the goodwill established by the plaintiff. Once more, customer confusion is the key requirement. Passing-off will only arise if the customer would buy the defendant's product bearing the name at issue while thinking that he was buying the plaintiff's original. An example of a case where no such confusion could arise is *Newsweek Inc v BBC*.[24] The publishers of the international news magazine tried unsuccessfully to prevent the use of 'Newsweek' as the title of a BBC current affairs television programme. The Court of Appeal argued that since the BBC would broadcast the programme with their usual logos there would be no risk of confusing it with the plaintiffs' publication.

---

[19] *J B Williams Co v H Bronnley Co Ltd* (1909) 26 RPC 765.
[20] *Reckitt & Colman Products Ltd v Borden Inc* [1990] 1 All ER 873; [1990] 1 WLR 491.
[21] Eg when dealing with insurance firms, specialist brokers are less likely to get confused between two similar names than the ordinary citizen, see *John Hayter Motor Underwriting Agencies Ltd v RBHS Agencies Ltd* [1977] FSR 285.
[22] Eg much more attention will be paid to high price purchases such as a car than to low price staple purchases such as lemon juice or flour. In the latter case, people might also be in a noisy environment and being in a hurry, etc. All these factors will influence the likelihood of confusion.
[23] See *Guccio Gucci SpA v Paolo Gucci* [1991] FSR 89, in this case Paolo Gucci was stopped from selling clothes under his own name.
[24] [1979] RPC 441.

(iii) A different version of the original product

Misrepresentation is also present in exceptional cases where the product itself seems to be that of the plaintiffs. A multinational company might sell, in various countries, the same product, bearing the same mark and the same get-up, but of different quality. The problem then arises when parallel import results in the low quality version being put on the market in which the original producer markets the high quality version of the product. It was held, in such a case, that Colgate-Palmolive could use passing-off to stop the sale in Britain of low quality toothpaste it had originally marketed in Brazil and which had been put on the market in Britain by a parallel importer.[25] Once more, consumer confusion and the fact that the parallel importer was capitalising upon Colgate-Palmolive's established goodwill were essential factors.

(iv) Intention is not required

One other important point in relation to the misrepresentation requirement remains to be made. The emphasis on customer confusion leads to the conclusion that the intention of the defendant is of no importance. All that needs to be shown is that the misrepresentation is likely to harm the plaintiff's goodwill and interests. Even an innocent defendant, who does not intend to cause harm, can be liable[26] if he is responsible for the misrepresentation at issue.[27]

(c) DAMAGE

Damage represents the final requirement for passing-off. The plaintiff has to show damage,[28] or the likelihood of damage in cases where injunctive relief is sought. How, though, can damage to goodwill resulting from the misrepresentation be shown? The easy cases are those where the plaintiff can show a decline in sales or in business in general as a result of the defendant's activities. In such cases, it is relatively easy to quantify the damage and to eliminate other contributing factors, such as a change in consumer taste or a general decline of the economy. But often it will be difficult to pinpoint the exact loss of trade, especially because the plaintiff does not really want to wait until the full extent of the damage materialises before bringing an action. He rather wants to act as soon as possible. Moreover, other interfering economic factors and the impact of legitimate

---

[25] *Colgate-Palmolive Ltd* v *Markwell Finance Ltd* [1989] RPC 497.
[26] See, eg *Baume & Co* v *AH Moore Ltd* [1958] Ch 907 at 916; [1958] 2 All ER 113 at 116.
[27] On the latter point see *Bovril Ltd* v *Bodega Co Ltd* (1916) 33 RPC 155; a defendant who makes no representation at all, let alone a misrepresentation, cannot be liable.
[28] *Reckitt & Colman Products Ltd* v *Borden Inc* [1990] 1 All ER 873 at 880; [1990] 1 WLR 491 at 499, *per* Lord Oliver.

competition may be hard to discount. The courts do not require the exact quantification of damage in such cases, but at least the likelihood of damage resulting from the misrepresentation needs to be shown.[29] When inferring the risk of damage, the scope of the goodwill of the plaintiff and the way in which confusion may arise will be of importance to the court. Feared loss of goodwill did not suffice in *Stringfellow v McCain Foods (GB) Ltd*[30] in the absence of any evidence that there was a decline in the nightclub business of the plaintiff as a result of the fact that the defendants marketed their new brand of long thin oven chips under the name 'Stringfellows' while advertising it on television with a disco scene.

It is clear from this analysis of passing-off that many cases can also be brought under the law of trade marks. When a registered trade mark is involved, the case is, in practice, often brought both under passing-off and trade mark law. But passing-off is wider in scope. There are not just the cases in which the mark has not been registered as a trade mark, there are also all those cases, described above, where the misrepresentation is not concerned with a mark at all. It has to be conceded, though, that the recent reform of trade mark law in 1994 has resulted in more cases being able to be brought under the definition of a trade mark, and with a registered right offering more certainty and stronger protection[31] this has reduced the importance of passing-off. It may, for example, now be possible to register the shape of containers as trade marks. *Jif Lemon* and similar cases could become trade mark cases as a result of this change.

(d) ENABLING PASSING-OFF

It is a tort to enable another person to pass off abroad, as in the Scotch whisky cases. One of the leading English cases is *John Walker & Sons Ltd and Others v Henry Ost & Co Ltd*.[32] Foster J held that it is a tort for an English defendant to sell in England single malt whisky, bottles, labels and cartons to an Ecuadorian defendant when the former not only knew that the latter was going to add local cane spirit to the whisky and sell it as Scotch whisky in Ecuador, but also intended that the whisky supplied should be mixed, bottled and have labels attached to it describing it as Scotch whisky. It is not entirely clear what the elements of this tort are. *Walker v Ost* appears to lay down a requirement that the defendant knows and intends that the equipment supplied is to be used for passing-off

---

[29] See *Draper v Trist & Tristbestos Brake Linings Ltd* (1939) 56 RPC 429 and *Procea Products Ltd v Evans and Sons Ltd* (1951) 68 RPC 210.
[30] [1984] RPC 501.
[31] The trade mark owner is at least better placed to stop an alleged infringer without having to go to court.
[32] [1970] 2 All ER 106. See also *Johnston v Orr Ewing* (1882) 7 App Cas 219; *White Horse Distillers Ltd v Gregson Associates Ltd and Others* 1983 LS Gaz 2844.

abroad. But the Scottish decisions on enabling passing-off do not even mention this.[33] What both English and Scots cases agree on, though, is that the tort of passing-off is completed in the forum by supplying another with the means to pass off.[34] There is no need to show an actual passing-off abroad in the sense of the elements of the tort of passing-off. It follows that there is no need to show goodwill abroad or, indeed, in England.

It has been argued that the tort of enabling passing-off abroad was a device used to avoid the unjust common law tort choice of law rules which applied in respect of foreign torts, and that continuing this tort, which disregards the substantive laws of foreign territories, would undermine the spirit of the recently introduced statutory tort choice of law rules, which largely abolish the common law rules.[35] However, this ignores the fact that this tort has an important function in allowing the plaintiff to stop the passing-off abroad at its source by stopping the supplier of the means of passing-off. Other countries see the need for such a tort. German law, for example, has a delict concerned with preparatory acts in relation to unfair competition.[36] Moreover, it fits in with the law of copyright where you can have an infringement by authorising someone to infringe copyright.

2. How Jurisdictional Problems Arise

The issue whether an English court has jurisdiction to hear a passing-off case will arise when a foreign defendant engages in commercial activity in England which involves a misrepresentation leading to customer confusion and damage to the established goodwill of the (English) plaintiff. Or in a multi-defendant case, where one of the defendants may be a foreign individual or company. Another aspect of jurisdiction is the question: what happens if goodwill which may exist in more than one jurisdiction is damaged in other countries as a result, for example, of the defendant advertising his products on satellite television channels whose signal can be received all over Europe?[37] Does the English court have jurisdiction to deal with the whole case, maybe on the basis that the misrepresentation and the broadcast originate in the jurisdiction? Or is the court's jurisdiction restricted to a misrepresentation in England, leading to customer

---

[33] See *John Walker & Sons Ltd* v *Douglas McGibbon & Co Ltd* [1975] RPC 506; *John Walker & Sons Ltd* v *Douglas Laing & Co Ltd* 1993 SLT 156; *William Grant & Sons Ltd* v *Glen Catrine Bonded Warehouse Ltd* 1995 SLT 936.

[34] *Walker* v *Ost* [1970] 2 All ER 106, at 116; *James Burrough Distillers plc* v *Speymalt Whisky Distributors Ltd* 1989 SLT 561, at 564. See also the Irish case of *An Bord Trachtala* v *Waterford Foods plc* [1994] FSR 316, at 320.

[35] Rodger 1996 *SLT* 105 at 108.

[36] Troller, *International Encyclopedia of Comparative Law*, pp 34–11. See also Article V of the Resolution of the Institute of International Law, discussed below, pp 710–711.

[37] Eg one of the Sky television channels, broadcasted from Britain but to be received all over Europe via satellite.

confusion in England and to damage to the goodwill the plaintiff had acquired in England? The plaintiff may, eventually, have to bring separate actions in all countries involved. That leads us to the question of what kind of alternative for passing-off there is in other legal systems. This issue will be discussed in this chapter at a later stage, when our attention will turn to the tort of unfair competition.[38]

Another interesting situation is that in which a foreign plaintiff sues an English defendant for enabling passing-off abroad. This could, for example, be the case when an English defendant has provided an Italian company with the means to pass-off cheap whisky as Scottish single malt whisky in Italy. The plaintiff is Scottish. Could an English court take jurisdiction in such a situation?

3. Jurisdictional Provisions

(a) THE EC/EFTA RULES

(i) When do the Brussels and Lugano Conventions apply?

The circumstances in which the Conventions apply have already been examined and little more needs to be added.[39] There is, though, one important aspect of this question that needs to be considered in passing-off cases. According to the preamble, the Conventions are only concerned with the international jurisdiction of Contracting States. In a typical case of enabling passing-off the defendant will be local. If the plaintiff is domiciled abroad there is a foreign element and this requirement is met. But what if, as commonly occurs, the plaintiff is also local? As has been seen, the tort is completed in the forum by supplying another with the means of passing-off and there is no need to show an actual passing-off abroad, in the sense of the elements of the tort of passing-off. Even if there is a requirement, which is questionable, that the defendant knows and intends that the equipment supplied is to be used for passing-off abroad, this knowledge and intention could be formed locally. Nonetheless, there is a significant foreign element in these cases, namely that there will be or already has been a passing-off abroad. Moreover, it is strongly arguable that this foreign element would be enough to raise a choice of law problem.[40] If so, it would be very odd to say that there is no issue of international jurisdiction.

(ii) Bases of jurisdiction

There are no special jurisdictional rules in the Brussels and Lugano Conventions relating to passing-off or, more broadly, to unfair competi-

[38] See below, p 409–414. [39] See above, pp 2–3. [40] See below, pp 656–657.

tion. It is, therefore, necessary to use the provisions on general jurisdiction contained in Article 2 and special jurisdiction contained in Articles 5 and 6.

Little needs to be said in respect of Article 2. This provision will commonly be used in cases of enabling passing-off. The typical defendant will be domiciled locally and jurisdiction will, accordingly, be based on this provision; assuming, of course, that there is a foreign element in the case in the first place.

Considerably more needs to be said in relation to Articles 5(3) and 6(1), and it is on these provisions that the discussion of bases of jurisdiction will focus.

Articles 5(3) and 6(1)

(i) Passing-off and unfair competition

There are English authorities on the application of Article 5(3) of the Brussels Convention in passing-off cases. It is tempting just to look at these cases. There is, however, a considerable number of decisions of Continental courts on the application of the Convention in unfair competition cases, including cases where the act of unfair competition looks very similar to what would be regarded in England as passing-off. Such authorities should not be ignored when applying the EC/EFTA rules in passing-off cases. Of course, it would be wrong for jurisdictional purposes to treat passing-off under English law as simply a type of unfair competition. The object of the Brussels Convention is not to unify the rules of substantive law and procedure of the different Contracting States, but to determine which court has jurisdiction.[41] It has been said in relation to Article 5(3) that '. . . it is not the function of the European court . . . to stipulate whether tortious or any other form of liability ought to exist in a particular fact situation and reference must always be made to the applicable national law in order to determine the characteristics of the liability, if any, which is the subject of the national court proceedings . . .'.[42] We are concerned with passing-off under English law. Nonetheless, the Court of Justice, when interpreting the Brussels Convention, is also concerned with the effectiveness of the Convention. The definition of the place of the harmful event under Article 5(3) adopted by the Court of Justice in cases of multi-State defamation[43] will apply regardless of whether it is a defamation case brought under the French law of defamation or under the different English law. Equally, the same definition of this concept should apply

---

[41] Case C-68/93 *Shevill v Presse Alliance SA* [1995] 2 WLR 499 at 541; discussed below, pp 396–399.
[42] Kaye, *Civil Jurisdiction and Enforcement of Foreign Judgments*, at p 564.
[43] See the *Shevill* case, n 41 above.

regardless of whether what is relied upon is the English tort of passing-off or the Continental delict of unfair competition, particularly where this takes the form of unfair competition by means of passing-off.

(ii) *The threshold requirement*

It will be recalled that before Articles 5 or 6 can be used as a basis of jurisdiction in England, a threshold requirement has to be satisfied by the plaintiff, ie that there is a serious issue to be tried on the merits. This is concerned with establishing liability. This threshold requirement applies in passing-off cases brought under Article 5(3), as it does in infringement cases.[44] If English law applies, it means that the plaintiff has to establish that there is a serious issue to be tried on the merits in relation to the trinity of elements for passing-off. Of course, a plaintiff who wishes to bring an action for passing-off often will of necessity seek to rely on English law, given the absence of this nominate tort in civil law systems. However, this does not mean that the issue of choice of law can be ignored.[45] The defendant could raise the argument that the tort was committed abroad and under the foreign law there is no tort of passing-off and, therefore there is no serious issue to be tried on the merits before an English court. One puzzling aspect of *Mecklermedia Corpn and Another* v *DC Congress GmbH*[46] is that counsel when establishing liability for jurisdictional purposes set out to show that there was goodwill *in England*, a misrepresentation *in England*, that caused damage *in England*. Jacob J treated this as being what the plaintiff had to show. Is this emphasis on England necessary in every case where liability has to be established, thereby imposing territorial limitations on liability, or was it simply that in this particular case it was argued in this way so as to make it clear that English law would apply, the tort having been committed in England? The answer is not clear.

(iii) *Article 5(3)*

Is an action for passing-off within the scope of Article 5(3)? Article 5(3) applies in 'matters relating to tort, delict or quasi-delict'. This concept should be given a Community meaning.[47] Jurisdiction is not allocated under the Convention by virtue of a cause of action.[48] It follows that the fact that, under English law, an action for passing-off is undoubtedly one in tort does not necessarily mean that it would come within the scope of Article

---

[44] See, eg *Mecklermedia Corpn and Another* v *DC Congress GmbH* [1997] 3 WLR 479, at 481–484.
[45] As seems to have happened in the *Mecklermedia* case, ibid.
[46] [1997] 3 WLR 479 at 481–484.
[47] Case 189/87 *Kalfelis* v *Bankhaus Schröder Munchmeyer Hengst & Co* [1988] ECR 5565; discussed below pp 433–439.
[48] *Kleinwort Benson Ltd* v *Glasgow City Council* [1996] 2 All ER 257 at 273.

5(3). Nonetheless, there are at least two English authorities deciding that passing-off does indeed come within Article 5(3)[49] and it is difficult to see how else a passing-off action could be classified for jurisdictional purposes than as a tort. Moreover, French,[50] Dutch,[51] German,[52] Italian[53] and Norwegian[54] courts have accepted that an action for unfair competition comes within the scope of Article 5(3).[55] This comes as no surprise, for it is uncontroversial in Continental countries that unfair competition is a delict. In some of these Continental cases, the acts of unfair competition involved look very similar to what in England would be regarded as passing-off. It would be very odd to treat a case of passing-off under English law differently and as not coming within Article 5(3).

Threatened passing-off. It will be recalled that there is considerable uncertainty over whether Article 5(3) can be used in cases of threatened wrongs.[56] It follows that if the plaintiff wishes to obtain an injunction to prevent a threatened passing-off, it may be safer to try and found jurisdiction on some other basis, such as Articles 2 or 6, where there is no such problem. Moreover, it may be possible to obtain such an injunction by virtue of Article 24 and Section 25 of the Civil Jurisdiction and Judgments Act 1982.[57]

The place where the harmful event occurred. In the passing-off cases of *Modus Vivendi Ltd v The British Products Sanmex Co Ltd and Another*[58] and *Mecklermedia Corpn and Another v DC Congress GmbH* Knox J and Jacob J, respectively, applied the definition in the *Mines de Potasse d'Alsace* case.[59] It follows that, in such cases, the plaintiff has, by virtue of Article 5(3), a choice of suing either in the place of the event giving rise to the damage, or in the place where the damage occurred, where the two are not

---

[49] *Modus Vivendi Ltd v The British Products Sanmex Co Ltd and Another* [1996] FSR 790; *Mecklermedia Corpn v DC Congress*, n 44 above.

[50] *Ideal Clima SpA and Others v SA Ideal Standard* Judgment of 15 June 1982, Cour d'Appel Paris, Gaz Pal 1982, Somm, 378; D-Series I-5.3-B13.

[51] *Forge et Coutellerie Dubois NV and Wolpa Plastics v Fantu Food BV and Reinders Arrondissementsrechtbank* (District Court) Arnhem Judgment of 3 July 1975 D series I-5.3-B1; *Geobra Brandstätter GmbH & Co KG v Big Spielwarenfabrik Dipl Ing Ernst A Bettag Arrondissementsrechtbank* (District Court) Amsterdam Judgment of 15 June 1977. NJ 1979, No 146, note: Schultz; Note: Verheul, NILR 1978, 87.

[52] *Re Jurisdiction in Tort and Contract* (Case IZR 201/86) Bundesgerichtshof (German Federal Supreme Court) [1988] ECC 415.

[53] *Adda Construzioni Elettromagnetiche SPA v Alsthom SA and Delle Alsthom SA* (Tribunale di Lodi, 13 February 1991 No 20), [1992] Riv Dir Int Priv Proc 332; No 10704 Italian Supreme Court, 28 October 1993, [1994] 2 EIPR D-30.

[54] *Saba Molnlycke AS v Proctor & Gamble Scandinavia Inc* [1997] ILPr 704.

[55] Nearly all of these cases pre-date the decision of the Court of Justice in the *Kalfelis* case, n 47 above, with its arguably very wide interpretation of the scope of Article 5(3) covering non-tortious actions, see below pp 433–438.

[56] See above, pp 151–152.   [57] See above, pp 214–218.   [58] N 49 above.

[59] Case 21/76 *Bier BV v Mines de Potasse D'Alsace SA* [1978] QB 708; discussed above, pp 152–153.

identical. Moreover, many of the Continental authorities[60] on unfair competition, including ones involving acts which look very similar to what we in England would regard as passing-off, have applied this approach.

The place of the event giving rise to the damage – the English approach. The leading English authority is the *Modus Vivendi* case. The plaintiff manufactured and sold in Hong Kong and China butane gas refills. The first defendant, a Scots domiciled company, filled cans in Scotland and exported them in the plaintiff's livery to Hong Kong and China. The plaintiff brought an action in England alleging passing-off and sought to rely on Article 5(3) of the Modified Version of the Brussels Convention,[61] which applies in intra-UK cases. Knox J held that the event giving rise to the damage occurred in Scotland. This was because what the defendant did, ie filled the cans which had offending material on them, was in Scotland. The act of passing-off was undeniably in Hong Kong and China where there was the illicit incursion into the plaintiff's goodwill by way of a misrepresentation that the cans were those of the plaintiff rather than those of the defendant, but this played no part in determining what the event was that gave rise to the damage and where this occurred. The problem with the approach adopted by Knox J is that the plaintiff will end up suing in the State where the defendant is domiciled and Article 5(3) fails to provide an alternative forum in which the plaintiff can sue.[62] The real argument in the case, in fact, was over whether the event giving rise to the damage occurred in England. The plaintiff argued that it did on the basis that the offending cans were produced by an English company (a sub-contractor) and the cans with the offending material on them were sent to Hong Kong from English ports. Knox J rejected this argument. He did not think it appropriate to dissect the events relied upon so as to find an element occurring within the State where jurisdiction was sought. He preferred to look at where in substance the cause of action arose,[63] and this was in Scotland. The accident of transport through England was of relatively trivial importance. This part of the judgment which emphasises the strong connection with a State which justifies its jurisdiction under Article 5(3) is to be welcomed.

The place of the event giving rise to the damage – the Continental approach. Many of the Continental cases on unfair competition are of little assistance in defining the place of the event giving rise to the damage since they involve acts which are very different from that involved in a case of

---

[60] See the *Ideal Clima* case n 50 above; the *Geobra* case n 51 above; *Re Jurisdiction in Tort and Contract* n 52 above; No 10704 Italian Supreme Court, 28 October 1993, n 53 above.

[61] See the Civil Jurisdiction and Judgments Act 1982, Sch 4.

[62] But it may be possible to sue in the State where the damage occurred, see below, pp 375–378.

[63] Following Steyn J in *Minster Investments Ltd v Hyundai Precision and Industry Co Ltd* [1988] 2 Lloyd's Rep 621 at 624.

passing-off. Indeed, they often involve what, under English law, are different torts from that of passing-off. Nonetheless, there are some examples of unfair competition which look very similar to what in England would be regarded as being the tort of passing-off. These Continental cases adopted a very different definition for the place of the event giving rise to the damage than that adopted in England in the *Modus Vivendi* case. They have held that the place of the event giving rise to the damage is that where the act of unfair competition by way of passing-off was committed.[64] Thus, the District Court in Arnhem, using Article 5(3), held that it had jurisdiction against a German company following the harmful act of its marketing in the Netherlands of imitation containers made of cheaper synthetic materials.[65] The Cour d'Appel, Paris, has held that an action for infringement of copyright and unfair competition could be brought in France under Article 5(3) against a company whose seat was in Italy, following the display for commercial purposes of a radiator, which was a copy of one of the plaintiff's designs, in Paris.[66] What is noticeable about this case is that there are two causes of action, infringement of copyright and unfair competition. The same Contracting State has jurisdiction under Article 5(3) in relation to both because the acts of infringement and unfair competition occur in the same Contracting State.

If this Continental approach is adopted, in most cases there will be no difficulty in ascertaining the *place* where the act of passing-off occurred. In the example just given, it is where the radiator was displayed in Paris. The act of passing-off may occur outside the forum. To take an example, if Scotch whisky is shipped to Italy, mixed with local spirit by the Italian defendant, and sold as genuine Scotch whisky the act of passing-off will take place in Italy, the place where the imitation whisky is sold. Neither is there damage in England to the English plaintiff. Article 5(3) will not apply.[67] Nonetheless, there is always the possibility of proceeding in England against an English defendant, who supplied the means of passing-off, on the basis of Article 2 of the Brussels Convention.

The place where the damage occurred. One view, supported by the English case law, is that this is where the goodwill is damaged; another view, for which there is some Continental case law support in unfair competition cases, is that this is where business is lost.

Where goodwill is damaged. In the *Modus Vivendi* case, Knox J held that the place where the damage occurred in a case of passing-off was the place where the passing-off was effected. This was in Hong Kong or China, seemingly because this was where the illicit incursion into the plaintiff's

---

[64] Essentially, the same rule applies under the traditional English rules on jurisdiction, see below, pp 381–382.
[65] The *Forge* case, n 51 above. [66] The *Ideal Clima* case, n 50 above.
[67] The damage will have occurred in Italy, see below, pp 375–378.

goodwill, by way of misrepresentation that the goods were those of the plaintiff rather than those of the defendant, occurred. This would be so regardless of whether inferior goods or those of adequate quality were sold there. The implicit suggestion is that what is damaged in a passing-off case is the goodwill of the plaintiff.

Knox J rejected a definition in terms of the place where the loss to the plaintiff was suffered, equating this with where sales fall, which in turn he equated with the place where damage was suffered. Knox J was influenced in this by the opinion of Advocate General Leger in the defamation case of *Shevill v Presse Alliance SA*.[68] The latter had spoken out against basing jurisdiction on the place where damage was suffered because this is generally suffered by the victim at his domicile.

More recently, Jacob J in *Mecklermedia Corpn and Another v DC Congress GmbH*,[69] took jurisdiction under Article 5(3) in a passing-off case brought against a German defendant on the ground that damage was suffered in England by the plaintiffs, a US company and its English subsidiary. This was on the basis that the plaintiffs' goodwill in England was damaged. The plaintiffs established that there was a serious issue that they owned a goodwill in England, that the activities in Germany and Austria of the defendant would mislead the public in England, and that the plaintiffs' goodwill in England would be damaged by this misrepresentation.[70] The defendant argued that Germany was the place of the harmful event. Jacob J rejected this argument saying that 'So far as the English tort of passing-off is concerned, the harm is to the goodwill in England, and is the effect on the reputation in England. That is a direct effect on the plaintiffs' claimed English property.'[71]

If damage is concerned with damage to goodwill, this leads on to the question: where does the damage to goodwill take place? This must be where the goodwill is situated. It is not as easy to ascertain where goodwill is situated as it is to ascertain where an intellectual property right, at least one which has been registered, is situated. Nonetheless, as has been mentioned, it is still possible to do so. According to Lord Lindley, 'goodwill is inseparable from the business to which it adds value, and, in my opinion, exists where the business is carried out'.[72] He went on to say that if the business is carried on in several countries, there may be several businesses each one having a goodwill of their own. This was the approach adopted by the Court of Appeal in *R J Reuter Co Ltd v Mulhens*.[73] The German defendants' business consisted of the manufacture of '4711' prod-

---

[68] Case 68/93 [1995] 2 AC 18.   [69] N 44 above.
[70] It was assumed that liability would be under English law, with seemingly no discussion of the choice of law issue.
[71] N 44 above, at 486–487.
[72] *Commissioners of Inland Revenue v Muller & Co's Margarine Ltd* [1901] AC 217 at 235.
[73] [1954] Ch 50, 95–96, CA.

ucts, containing secret essences, and their marketing in many countries, of which Great Britain was one. The goodwill in question was that attached to the British business of the defendants. It was held that this goodwill did possess a locality and that locality was Britain, not Germany or any of the other countries in which the products were marketed.

Of course, goodwill can be international and the question presumably will then be: which goodwill is the plaintiff relying on for his cause of action?

Where business is lost. As has been seen, as a matter of substantive law, damage to goodwill can be evidenced by a loss of sales. This would suggest that, the damage occurs where business is lost. There is Dutch authority supporting the view that, in cases of unfair competition, the damage for the purpose of Article 5(3) is that of loss of business and that this is where sales are lost.[74] Similarly, in an unfair competition case a Norwegian court has held that under Article 5(3) the damage was the loss of sales.[75] Moreover, once it is accepted that goodwill is situated where business is carried on, it is but a short step from there to saying that damage occurs where business is lost. But this is precisely what Knox J was against having as a basis of jurisdiction. It is submitted that his assumption that this would lead to jurisdiction being allocated to the plaintiff's domicile was erroneous. It all depends on how one identifies where business, ie sales, is lost. The place where sales are lost should be determined ignoring technicalities of where the plaintiff made a contract of sale, but by reference to where the plaintiff's product is marketed. So, for example, if an English company sells its goods to a middle man in England who then exports them to Italy, where there is an imitation product which reduces demand for the plaintiff's product, the loss of sales should be regarded as being in Italy rather than in England. The upshot is that a definition in terms of loss of business and loss of sales does not mean, as Knox J thought, that jurisdiction is being allocated to the State where the plaintiff is domiciled.

In the above example, the plaintiff will also suffer a loss of profit from the loss of sales in Italy. If the plaintiff's business is centred on England, this is where the loss will be felt. However, according to the Court of Justice in the *Marinari* case,[76] jurisdiction under Article 5(3) cannot be founded on indirect damage. The result is that, on these facts, the English courts will have no jurisdiction on the basis of damage occurring in England.

Which is the better approach? Both approaches, when applied to the facts of the *Modus Vivendi* or *Mecklermedia* cases, produce the same result. The State where the goodwill was damaged and where the business was lost,

---

[74] *Geobra Brandstätter GmbH v Big Spielwarenfabrik* n 51 above.
[75] The *Saba Molnlycke* case, n 54 above; discussed below, p 413.
[76] Case C-364/93 *Marinari v Lloyd's Bank plc and Another* [1996] 2 WLR 159.

if this is defined as suggested above, are one and the same. Under both approaches, the plaintiff is able to sue in some Contracting State other than the one where the defendant is domiciled. It is submitted, though, that, conceptually, the loss of business approach makes more sense.

Multiple acts of passing-off and multiple damage The same problem arises with passing-off as with infringement.[77] Does a court of a Contracting State which has jurisdiction under Article 5(3) on the basis of a local act of passing-off[78] or local damage also have jurisdiction in relation to additional acts of passing-off or damage committed abroad. It has been suggested earlier, when discussing infringement, that it is doubtful whether it does so. In particular, it has been pointed out that Article 5(3), normally, should be used restrictively and that there is support in the *Shevill* case[79] for a restrictive view in relation to damage abroad. These same arguments apply in the context of passing-off.[80] Moreover, it would be very undesirable to adopt a different position for passing-off from that suggested for infringement, given that it is not uncommon for proceedings to be brought which are based on both causes of action.[81]

(iv) *Article 6(1)*

Cases of passing-off not infrequently involve two defendants. Article 6(1) is as useful in such cases as it is in those of infringement.[82] Returning to the above example, if an English company exports whisky, bottles and labels to the Italian company which adds 'local spirit' to the whisky, bottles it up and sells it in Italy as genuine Scotch whisky, Article 6(1) enables jurisdiction to be taken in England against the Italian company. There is the requisite connection between the claims[83] against the separate English and Italian defendants since they are joint tortfeasors in respect of the passing off in Italy. There is, of course, a separate tort committed in England by the English defendant which supplies the means for the passing-off abroad. If the claim against the English defendant were to be based solely on this, it is questionable whether such a claim is sufficiently closely connected with the claim against the Italian defendant to come within Article 6(1). It is doubtful whether there is a risk of irreconcilable judgments, if the two claims are heard apart.

[77] See above, pp 161–162, 167–168.
[78] This is assuming that the Continental approach towards defining the place of the event giving rise to the damage is adopted. The problem is not likely to arise under the English approach which concentrates on where the cause of action arose.
[79] Case C-68/93 *Shevill and Others* v *Presse Alliance SA* [1995] 1 WLR 499.
[80] The argument based on an analogy with the infringement of Community intellectual property rights cannot be used in relation to passing-off.
[81] See, eg *Ideal Clima SpA and Others* v *SA Ideal Standard* n 50 above; *L A Gear Incorporated* v *Gerald Whelan & Sons Ltd* [1991] FSR 670 discussed above, pp 178, 184–185.
[82] See above, pp 180–181.
[83] See Case 189/87 *Kalfelis* v *Schroder* [1988] ECR 5565; discussed above, p 172.

(iii) Declining jurisdiction

(a) *Lis pendens*

Much has already been said about this matter in the context of infringement proceedings, and does not need to be repeated.[84] Some interesting questions arise though in passing-off cases in relation to the requirements under Article 21 that the cause of action and the subject matter are the same in the two sets of proceedings, and that the parties are the same.

(i) *Is the cause of action and the subject matter the same?*
First, is the cause of action and the subject matter the same where there is an action for infringement in another Contracting State and an action for passing-off in England? In *Mecklermedia Corpn and Another* v *DC Congress*, Jacob J held that in this situation the cause of action was not the same.[85]

Secondly, is the cause of action and the subject matter the same where actions for passing off are brought in two common law States but different acts are relied upon? This is the situation that arose in *LA Gear Inc* v *Gerald Whelan & Sons Ltd*.[86] The claim in the English proceedings was in respect of import of footwear into the United Kingdom and sales and offers for sale in the United Kingdom, while in the Irish proceedings there were allegations of passing-off by reason of sales and offers for sale in Ireland and re-exporting goods from Ireland to the United Kingdom. Mummery J held that different acts were relied upon, giving rise to different causes of action. Neither was the subject matter of the English and Irish proceedings the same. The subject matter of the English proceedings was the trade mark registered in the United Kingdom and claimed goodwill and reputation of the plaintiff's mark located in the United Kingdom. The allegation being that that mark had been infringed and that goodwill and reputation had been damaged by acts of infringement committed in the United Kingdom. The subject matter of the Irish proceedings was the goodwill and reputation claimed by the plaintiff for its mark in Ireland and which it alleged had been damaged by acts of passing-off committed by the defendant in Ireland.

Thirdly, is the cause of action and subject matter the same if one set of proceedings is brought in England for passing-off and the other set is brought in another Contracting State for unfair competition? If the acts relied upon in each action are the same, for example the marketing of imitation goods in the one State, then the subject matter is undeniably the same. It is submitted that the cause of action is also the same. This is

---
[84] See above, pp 177–182.
[85] N 44 above at 488. See chapter 5, pp 180–181, for why this was so.
[86] [1991] FSR 670; discussed above p 178.

supported by the decision of Mummery J in the *L A Gear* case in so far as that case, by deciding that there are different causes of action if different acts are relied upon, suggests that the cause of action is the same if the same acts are relied upon. However, differences in the scope of trade mark protection mean that an action for passing-off in England may be performing a much wider role than the unfair competition action brought in another Contracting State. In turn, this will mean that in some cases the acts on which the respective claims for passing-off and unfair competition are brought are not the same.

(ii) *Are the parties the same?*

In the *Mecklermedia* case, Jacob J held that the parties were not the same where the English action involved the plaintiffs and the defendant, and the German action involved the defendant and the plaintiffs' German licensees.[87]

(b) Related actions

It is helpful again to look at the *Mecklermedia* case. Jacob J held that the infringement action in Germany and the passing off action in England were not related actions within the meaning of Article 22.[88] There was no risk of irreconcilable judgments in the two Contracting States.

Further difficulty was caused by the additional requirement that it is expedient to hear and determine the two actions together. This raised the question of whether the German courts could hear the passing-off action. There was some uncertainty over this.[89] This seems curious. The German courts would, presumably, have jurisdiction under Article 2, the defendant being domiciled in Germany, at least under our definition of domicile but doubtless also under the German definition. The German courts cannot in a Brussels Convention case impose subject matter limitations on jurisdiction, any more than an English court can do so in respect of foreign intellectual property rights.[90]

Moreover, even if the actions came within Article 22, Jacob J would not have exercised the discretion under this provision to decline jurisdiction. This was on the basis that 'normally the most convenient forum for deciding an English trade mark or passing-off case is this court'.[91] A German court would have to import both the evidence and the law. This treats the discretion as being akin to a *forum non conveniens* discretion, which is very dubious.

---

[87] N 44 above, at 488. See above, chapter 5, p 181, for why this was so.
[88] N 44 above, at 489.
[89] N 44 above, at 490–491.   [90] See above, pp 190–193.   [91] N 44 above, at 491.

(b) THE TRADITIONAL RULES

(i) Bases of jurisdiction

The position under the traditional rules is the same as that under the EC/EFTA rules in that there are no special jurisdictional provisions dealing with passing-off. If a writ cannot be served within the jurisdiction it is necessary to resort to service out of the jurisdiction under Order 11, rule 1(1) of the Rules of the Supreme Court, and as with an action for infringement, the three heads that will be most commonly used are the injunction, multi-defendant and tort heads.

(a) *The tort head*

In a passing-off action, the claim is undoubtedly founded on a tort and this comes within the scope of Order 11, rule 1(1)(f); the plaintiff can therefore sue in England if either the damage was sustained or resulted from an act committed within the jurisdiction. As is well known, the wording of the tort head was designed to follow Article 5(3), as interpreted by the *Mines de Potasse d'Alsace* case. But in defining the 'damage' and the 'act', the approach is very different from that adopted in relation to Article 5(3) of the Brussels and Lugano Conventions. What we are concerned with is the cause of action. We are not concerned with a Community definition or with Continental ideas of unfair competition.

(i) *Threatened passing-off*

It will be recalled that there is some uncertainty over whether rule 1(1)(f) can be used in cases of threatened wrongs.[92] It follows that a plaintiff who wishes to obtain an injunction to prevent a threatened passing-off is better to use some other basis of jurisdiction, such as the injunction head of rule 1(1), which does not involve this problem. Moreover, it may be possible to obtain interim relief by virtue of Section 25 of the Civil Jurisdiction and Judgments Act 1982.[93]

(ii) *An act of passing-off committed within the jurisdiction*

Of the elements of the tort[94] (the goodwill of the plaintiff in his goods; a misrepresentation by the defendant leading to confusion; damage to the plaintiff), the only one that can be regarded as being an act from which damage resulted, is the act of misrepresentation by the defendant. An English court, therefore, has jurisdiction if the act of misrepresentation occurred in England. When it comes to the stage of ascertaining the applicable law, the rule that was adopted at common law was concerned with

---

[92] See above, pp 252–253.   [93] See above, pp 214–218.   [94] See above, p 362–368.

where the tort was committed and for the tort of passing-off this was where the act of misrepresentation took place.[95] Although the tort choice of law rules are now put on a statutory basis, it is submitted that, for passing-off, the crucial factor in determining the governing law should remain that of where the act of misrepresentation occurred.[96] Adoption of the same rule for jurisdictional purposes leads to the desirable result[97] that an English court which has jurisdiction on the basis of the misrepresentation being made in England, is then able to apply the English law of passing-off.

Normally, there will be no difficulty in determining whether an act of misrepresentation occurred in England. However, this will not always be so. In *Intercontex and Another* v *Schmidt and Another*,[98] the misrepresentation was contained in invoices sent by the defendants in Germany to the plaintiff's customers outside the United Kingdom. Gibson J held that the misrepresentation was made where the invoices were received outside the United Kingdom. The mere receipt of letters and monies within the United Kingdom resulting from the misrepresentation was held to be no part of the tort. This was decided in the context of determining the applicable law, in order to establish a good arguable case on the merits for the purpose of obtaining injunctive relief.

(iii) *Damage was sustained within the jurisdiction*

The same difficulty arises here as under Article 5(3) of the EC/EFTA rules of whether damage should be regarded as having been sustained where goodwill was damaged or business was lost. It is submitted that the better view is that damage should be regarded as having been sustained in England if business was lost there. Business is lost where sales are lost and this place should be ascertained by reference to where the plaintiff's product is marketed.[99] English cases which take a different view[100] were decided under the Brussels Convention or Modified Convention, not under the traditional rules where the matter can be decided on principle rather than precedent.

(iv) *Multiple acts of passing-off and multiple damage*

The same problem in relation to multiple acts of passing-off and multiple damage arises under the tort head of Order 11, rule 1(1) as arises under

---

[95] *Intercontex and Another* v *Schmidt and Another* [1988] FSR 575 at 578; discussed below p 382.
[96] See below, p 662.
[97] Cf *Kleinwort Benson Ltd* v *Glasgow City Council* [1996] 2 All ER 257 at 271 *per* Roch LJ (an Article 5(1) case).
[98] N 95 above. [99] See above, pp 377–378.
[100] The *Modus Vivendi* case, n 49 above and text accompanying, and *Mecklermedia* case, n 44 above and text accompanying.

Article 5(3) of the Brussels and Lugano Conventions. It is doubtful whether an English court which has jurisdiction under the tort head on the basis of an act of passing-off committed within the jurisdiction also has jurisdiction under that head in relation to acts of passing-off committed abroad. The reasons for this have already been examined in the context of infringement and need not be repeated here.[101] It would also be very hard for the plaintiff to establish that England is the clearly appropriate forum for trial if the substance of the action was concerned with acts of passing-off committed, or damage sustained, abroad.[102]

(b) The multi-defendant head

The leading case on the use of this head in relation to passing-off is *Macaulay (A) (Tweeds) Ltd* v *Independent Harris Tweed Producers Ltd*.[103]

The plaintiffs, a group of Scottish tweed manufacturers, sued an English retailer of clothing for passing-off in relation to the sale in England of tweed jackets labelled 'Harris Tweed'. They joined as defendants a number of Scottish tweed manufacturers. The second defendant was a rival association which had authorised the use of the labels complained of, and had advertised that label in England. The third, fourth, and fifth defendants were named in the advertisements as suppliers of tweed under the label.

Cross J refused to set aside service out of the jurisdiction on the Scottish defendants. The terms of the multi-defendant head[104] were satisfied. The Scottish defendants were necessary or proper parties to the action against the English defendant. If the Scottish defendants had been resident within the jurisdiction, they could have been joined as defendants to the same action against the English defendant. The position of the second defendant was regarded as being clear and it could not be suggested that this defendant was not a proper party. The position of the other defendants was different on the facts. Nonetheless, there was a sufficient connection between the action against the first defendant and the third, fourth, and fifth defendants to justify their all being made defendants to a single action, and, if resident in England, they too could have been joined as defendants to the action against the English defendant.

---

[101] See above, p 252.
[102] See above, pp 259–266, 271. Cf the position in relation to defamation, see below, pp 406–408.
[103] [1961] RPC 184.
[104] Order 11, rule 1(1)(g). This was an earlier, and differently worded, version from the current provision contained in Order 11, rule 1(1)(c); see Cheshire and North, pp 193–195.

(c) The injunction head

An injunction is commonly sought as a form of relief in passing-off cases. One advantage[105] in using this particular head, as opposed to the tort head, is that it applies regardless of whether the cause of action is in tort, contract or anything else. It is, therefore, extremely useful in cases, and these are not uncommon, which are founded on several different causes of action. For example, in *James North & Sons Ltd* v *North Cape Textiles Ltd and Another*,[106] service of a writ out of the jurisdiction was granted in an action brought under the injunction head for passing-off, trade mark infringement, and inducing breach of contract. The same point also can be made in relation to the multi-defendant head.

(ii) The discretionary element

(a) Forum conveniens/Forum non conveniens

When it comes to the exercise of the *forum conveniens* discretion to allow service of a writ out of the jurisdiction, and the discretion to stay English proceedings on the basis of *forum non conveniens* following the service of a writ (usually within the jurisdiction), the normal criteria will apply. The criteria are the same regardless of the cause of action, and have already been examined in the context of infringement of intellectual property rights.[107] When it comes to applying these criteria in the context of a passing-off action there are certain considerations that are of particular importance.

(i) *The applicable law*

It is submitted that the same rule should apply under the new statutory tort choice of law rules as under the old common law rules to the effect that, in general, in passing-off cases, the applicable law depends on where the act of misrepresentation took place.[108] If this occurred in England, normally English law will apply. The fact that local law governs constitutes a powerful consideration in favour of trial taking place in England. It has frequently been said that if a tort is committed in England, then England is, *prima facie*, the natural forum for trial.[109] Underlying this presumption was the common law tort choice of law rule that if a tort was committed in England, then English law was applicable. Under the new statutory tort choice of law rules, the governing law no longer depends on where the tort was committed; instead, as a general rule, it depends on where the events

---

[105] For other advantages, including in relation to threatened wrongs see above.
[106] [1984] 1 WLR 1428.   [107] See above, pp 259–274.   [108] See below, p 662.
[109] See above, p 264.

constituting the tort or delict in question occurred. The terminology has changed and the language of the presumption is no longer apt. Nonetheless, the thrust of the presumption remains the same, and the link between the applicable law and the identification of the appropriate forum for trial is a strong one. It is submitted that if the act of misrepresentation occurred in England, then this is, *prima facie*, the natural forum for trial.

(ii) *Multiple acts of passing-off*

Unlike with infringement,[110] there is no subject matter limitation on jurisdiction in relation to acts of passing-off committed abroad.[111] The fact that an English court is able to adjudicate on all the claims, both local and foreign, is an important consideration pointing towards England as the appropriate forum for trial.[112]

(iii) *Where the goodwill is situated*

Under English law, goodwill is an essential element of the cause of action and the question of where this is situated[113] must be regarded as an important consideration. If the plaintiff is relying on goodwill in England this will constitute a strong connection with this country. Conversely, if the plaintiff is relying on goodwill abroad and actionability under the law of that country, this will constitute a strong connection with that country. If the plaintiff is relying on goodwill in more than one country, the situation of the goodwill becomes a neutral factor, although the fact that all the claims can be heard before an English court becomes an important consideration pointing towards trial in England.

(iv) *The relief sought*

In the passing-off case of *Advanced Portfolio Technologies Inc v Ainsworth*,[114] Harman J, in determining that England was the *forum conveniens*, attached considerable importance to the relief sought. This was an injunction and an 'injunction which is a remedy *in personam* is most aptly sought against a defendant where he resides', which in this case was in England. It was also pointed out that the defendant conducted at least part of his business in England. A stay of the English proceedings was refused, despite the fact that there was a concurrent action in New York involving the same parties and subject matter.

(b) *Restraining foreign proceedings*

The same criteria[115] apply for restraining foreign proceedings for passing-off as for any other cause of action. In so far as these criteria require that

---

[110] See above, pp 299–306. [111] See below, pp 386–388. [112] See, generally, p 387.
[113] See above, pp 363–364. [114] [1996] FSR 217. [115] See above, pp 275–277.

England is the natural forum before an injunction restraining foreign proceedings can be granted, the same comments apply in relation to restraining foreign proceedings as have just been made in relation to *forum non conveniens*. Apart from this, there do not appear to be any considerations that are of particular importance in relation to passing-off. It is worth noting though that one of the few reported cases where an injunction has been granted restraining foreign proceedings involved an action for passing-off.

This was the *Advanced Portfolio Technologies*[116] case, in which Harman J dealt with the problem of concurrent proceedings in New York and England, involving the same parties and subject matter, by issuing an injunction restraining the plaintiff from bringing or proceeding with an action in New York, rather than by staying the English proceedings. This solution to the problem of parallel proceedings is the one frequently adopted by US courts when faced with a case of *lis alibi pendens*;[117] whereas English courts, normally, would solve the problem by staying their own proceedings.

The injunction was granted on the basis of the criterion of vexation and oppression set out in the *Société Nationale Industrielle Aerospatiale* case.[118] It is not enough to show that England is the natural forum for trial. Generally speaking, it also has to be shown that pursuing proceedings in the foreign court would be vexatious or oppressive. The *Advanced Portfolio Technologies* case involved a plaintiff which had commenced proceedings against the same defendant in both England and New York. The plaintiff now wanted trial only in New York; the defendant wanted trial only in England. Having decided that England was the *forum conveniens* and refused the plaintiff's application to stay the English proceedings, Harman J went on to hold that there would be substantial injustice to the defendant in requiring him to fight on two fronts. There was evidence from the defendant that there would be delay in coming to trial in New York and that this would adversely affect the defendant's business resources, which would become exhausted. The oppression to the defendant was not outweighed by any legitimate juridical advantage to the plaintiff in having trial in New York.

(iii) No subject matter limitations in relation to jurisdiction

The fundamental difference between jurisdiction under the traditional rules in an action for passing-off and in one for infringement of an intellectual property right is that there are no subject matter limitations on

---

[116] N 114 above.
[117] See Fawcett in *Declining Jurisdiction*, pp 40–41, and Del Duca and Zaphiriou in *Declining Jurisdiction*, pp 418–427.
[118] *Société Nationale Industrielle Aerospatiale* v *Lee Kui Jak* [1987] AC 871, discussed above.

jurisdiction in the case of the former, whereas there are well known limitations in relation to the latter.[119] An English court can try an action for passing-off, provided that there is jurisdiction over the person of the defendant. It does not matter that the action is in respect of foreign goodwill (ie goodwill that is situated abroad) or acts of passing-off committed abroad.

(a) *The authorities*

Surprisingly, there appears to be no discussion in the passing-off cases of this phenomenon. Nonetheless, the absence of any such limitations can not be in any doubt. For there are numerous instances of English,[120] Scots[121] and Irish[122] judges trying cases involving foreign acts of passing-off. Admittedly, these cases were concerned with the question of the applicable law and did not discuss jurisdiction. But, if there had been a limitation on jurisdiction in relation to foreign acts of passing-off, the judges would have refused to try the case in the first place, and would never have got on to the choice of law stage of the action.

(b) *Consolidation of litigation*

The absence of any subject matter limitations allows for the consolidation of litigation in England. It is possible to bring a single action in England in relation to multiple acts of passing-off, committed in numerous foreign States. For example, in *Alfred Dunhill Ltd and Another* v *Sunoptic SA and Another*,[123] the Court of Appeal was prepared to grant an interlocutory injunction restraining acts in the nature of passing-off in the United Kingdom and Switzerland. A wider injunction encompassing other countries would have been granted on proof of acts of attempted passing-off actionable under the local law of those countries. A world wide injunction is, in theory, a possibility but, in practice, would not happen since it would require the above evidence in relation to each country in the world. If limitations on jurisdiction were to be imposed what it would mean would be splitting up the action between England and abroad or finding a foreign court which can try the whole of the action.

---

[119] See above.
[120] *John Walker & Sons Ltd and Others* v *Henry Ost & Co Ltd and Another* [1970] 2 All ER 106; *Alfred Dunhill Ltd and Another* v *Sunoptic SA and Another* [1979] FSR 337; *Intercontex and Another* v *Schmidt and Another* [1988] FSR 575.
[121] *James Burrough Distillers plc* v *Speymalt Whisky Distributors Ltd* 1988 SLT 562.
[122] *An Bord Tráchtala* v *Waterford Foods plc* [1994] FSR 316.
[123] N 120 above at 368–369.

(c) Why is passing-off treated differently, and should it be?

It is interesting to speculate on the reasons why passing-off is treated so differently from infringement of an intellectual property right. The English and Scots passing-off cases referred to above were all decided before *Tyburn Productions Ltd v Conan Doyle*,[124] the leading English case introducing subject matter limitations in relation to jurisdiction in infringement actions. The different treatment of the two areas may simply, therefore, be a matter of timing.

In the light of the *Conan Doyle* case, the question must be addressed of whether territorial limitations on jurisdiction should be introduced in the area of passing-off. There is an argument in favour of doing so. The distinction between local and transitory actions lies at the heart of the decision in *Conan Doyle*. It appears that an action based on an act of passing-off committed abroad is a local one. If you take the classic situation in the *Maxim's* case of a well known foreign restaurant which wishes to prevent an English restaurant from using the same name, the plaintiff, if relying on English law, has to establish that it has goodwill, ie a business reputation, in *England* to be protected.[125] This means that the facts relied on as the foundation of the plaintiff's case must have a particular connection with England; with the consequence that the action is a local one.

Against this, it has to be remembered that the reasoning in the *Conan Doyle* case is open to heavy criticism, and produces results which are undesirable in terms of policy.[126] It has been suggested above[127] that the subject matter limitations in relation to jurisdiction in infringement cases should be dropped. It would be folly to extend the application of such dubious limitations to another area, that of passing-off.

III
MALICIOUS FALSEHOOD

Trade marks are quite often linked to goodwill and the reputation of a trader or a company. It is clear, however, that goodwill and reputation can also exist independently from any trade mark and even in cases where there is no trade mark. In such cases, other legal tools can be used to protect that reputation. For the protection of the reputation of an individual the law of defamation,[128] to which we will return in a later stage,[129] is quite

---

[124] [1991] Ch 75; discussed above, pp 284–290.
[125] See *Maxim's Ltd v Dye* [1977] FSR 364; discussed above, p 363.
[126] See above. [127] Above, pp 314–315. [128] Ie libel and slander.
[129] See below, pp 394–396.

Complementary torts and other causes of action: jurisdiction 389

often used, while the reputation of businesses is protected through malicious falsehood.[130]

1. SUBSTANTIVE LAW

Unwarranted negative comments in relation to businesses are not necessarily defamatory and although they cause damage it might not be possible to say that they affect your business reputation in a negative way.[131] Any cause of action that could be successful in relation to businesses should, therefore, exclude the defamation aspect. For example, someone might allege that the plaintiff's business has ceased to exist. While this statement may be inaccurate or false, it may be difficult to call it defamatory and to show a negative impact on the plaintiff's business reputation. The case involving these facts allowed the court to lay down the requirements for the related tort of malicious falsehood. In *Ratcliffe* v *Evans*,[132] Bowen LJ found the statements to be actionable stating that:

> an action will lie for written or oral falsehoods, not actionable *per se* nor even defamatory, where they are maliciously published, where they are calculated in the ordinary course of things to produce, and where they do produce, actual damage.

These requirements were confirmed by the House of Lords in *White* v *Mellin*,[133] but one additional requirement was added. It was also necessary for the plaintiff to establish that special damage had been suffered. Putting a notice on the wrapper stating that a competing brand of baby food in which you have an interest is more nutritious does not reveal any denigration of the plaintiff's baby food and no special damage resulting from this activity was proved. The claim failed but the case highlights the four following requirements in relation to a malicious falsehood claim. First, it is necessary to show that the defendant has made a false statement. Secondly, this statement must be derogatory of the plaintiff's goods or business. Thirdly, this statement must have been made with malice. Fourthly, this statement must have resulted in damage to the plaintiff.

(a) A FALSE STATEMENT

Falsity is the first and rather simple requirement. The statement must not be true. In this respect, there is no difference between defamation and malicious falsehood. But in contrast with defamation cases, it is for the

---

[130] Malicious falsehood is sometimes also referred to as slander of goods or injurious falsehood.
[131] For more details on the substantive law of malicious falsehood see Holyoak and Torremans, n 6 above, at pp 373–377.
[132] [1892] 2 QB 524 at 527.   [133] [1895] AC 154.

plaintiff to prove falsity,[134] rather than for the defence to justify the truth of the statement or the information.

(b) A DEROGATORY STATEMENT

The statement must not simply be false though, it must also be denigrating. The statement must be derogatory and harm the reputation of the plaintiff's goods or business. *White v Mellin* illustrates this clearly. Suggesting that your product is of a superior quality is not derogatory. Things would have been different if the statement had alleged that your competitor's product was harmful to children's health. In deciding whether or not a statement is derogatory, the context in which it is made will play an important role. For example, even if most people simply do not understand it, highly technical information which is false, in alleging the technical inferiority of the plaintiff's goods, will be derogatory if the experts in the field for whom the information is meant would so understand it.[135] Other statements may, at first sight, be harmless, but the context in which they are made can make them derogatory. Whilst, at first sight, there is, for example, nothing wrong with an inaccurate statement that one newspaper's circulation is 20 times lower than the circulation of another newspaper, this may become derogatory if the statement is made by a competitor because it would seriously undermine the possibility of the newspaper with the allegedly low circulation attracting advertisements.[136]

(c) MALICE

Malice is the third requirement, and this element is really at the core of this tort. In marked contrast with the tort of defamation, where malice is not an issue, the plaintiff has to prove malice on behalf of the defendant. Obviously, this greatly reduces the impact of the tort since the action will fail if the defendant can demonstrate that his statement was merely based on an accidental mistake rather than on deliberate malice. How then is malice defined? Although the courts are able to identify the presence of malice on the basis of the facts of each case, they have not yet defined it exhaustively. At an early stage, it was defined as the absence of any 'just cause or excuse',[137] but this far from rigorous definition has now been abandoned. Other definitions refer to intentionally or recklessly made

---

[134] *Anderson v Liebig's Extract of Meat Co Ltd* (1881) 45 LT (NS) 757.
[135] *De Beers Abrasive Products Ltd v International General Electric Co of New York Ltd* [1975] 2 All ER 599; [1975] 1 WLR 972.
[136] See *Lyne v Nicholls* (1906) 23 TLR 86.
[137] *Royal Baking Powder Co v Wright, Crossley & Co* (1901) 18 RPC 95 at 99, *per* Lord Bankes.

statements,[138] and at least a reckless indifference as to whether harm may be caused to the interests of the plaintiff.[139]

(d) DAMAGE

Originally, the plaintiff had to bring evidence of harm to his business to satisfy the special damage requirement. In most cases, this is no longer required following the Defamation Act 1952, s 3(1) which establishes, in respect of this tort, that special damage is not necessary if the words used are:

calculated to cause pecuniary damage to the plaintiff and are published in writing or other permanent form

or alternatively are

calculated to cause pecuniary damage to the plaintiff in respect of any office, profession calling, trade or business.

It is submitted that most cases in which the plaintiff has been able to prove malice in the first place will fall within the scope of this provision.

2. How Jurisdictional Problems Arise

In this respect, there seems to be no difference between the tort of malicious falsehood and that of defamation, which will be discussed below. One or more elements of the tort could have been committed abroad and multi-defendant cases can arise in both contexts.

The various elements of the tort of malicious falsehood might have taken place in different countries. For example, the false statement may have been made in France, while the impact on the plaintiff's reputation took place primarily in England. Malicious falsehood, in all its components, can also take place in more than one country. Can one bring a single action covering all instances of malicious falsehood? And in which jurisdiction can one do so? A rather obvious case in which a jurisdictional problem can arise is that in which there is more than one defendant. Where can one bring such a multi-defendant case if the defendants are not domiciled, resident, etc in a single jurisdiction?

---

[138] *Shapiro v La Morta* (1924) 40 TLR 201 at 203, *per* Atkin LJ.
[139] *McDonald's Hamburgers Ltd v Burgerking (UK) Ltd* [1986] FSR 45 at 61, *per* Whitford J.

3. JURISDICTIONAL PROVISIONS

(a) THE EC/EFTA RULES

Article 5(3)

There are no reported English cases on the operation of Article 5(3) in relation to malicious falsehood. However, there is Continental authority in relation to unfair competition involving acts which might well come within the ambit of the English tort of malicious falsehood. The Supreme Court of Italy, in a decision of 28 October 1993,[140] involving an action for unfair competition, following the spreading of false and disparaging information discrediting an Italian company on foreign markets, took jurisdiction on the basis of Article 5(3). The *Mines de Potasse d'Alsace* distinction was applied, allowing the plaintiff the option of suing either in the place of the event giving rise to the damage or in the place where the damage occurred.

(a) *The place of the event giving rise to the damage*

In the decision of the Supreme Court of Italy of 28 October 1993, it was held that the place of the event giving rise to the damage was the place where the false and disparaging information was spread by the English defendant company. This occurred in England. Accordingly, the Italian Court had no jurisdiction on this basis.

(b) *The place where the damage occurred*

As we know, damage for the purpose of Article 5(3) is referring to direct damage, not indirect. In the case of unfair competition by means of malicious falsehood, damage will take the form of lost business. Where does this occur? The answer is where sales are lost, to be ascertained by reference to where the plaintiff's product is marketed.[141] For example, if a Dutch company cancels an order with an English company as a result of a false statement concerning the latter, and if goods would have been exported to the Netherlands if the order had not been cancelled, there is a loss of sales in the Netherlands.

In this example, the lost sales will undoubtedly result in lost profits in England, where the plaintiff company is incorporated. However, this constitutes an indirect loss and there is no jurisdiction under Article 5(3) on the basis of such a loss occurring in the forum. Admittedly, the Italian Supreme Court, in their decision of 28 October 1993, took jurisdiction in Italy on the basis of the economic loss suffered there by the Italian plaintiff company, following the loss of reputation and reduction of sales in

---

[140] N 53 above.   [141] See above in relation to passing-off, pp 375–378.

England, where the false information was spread. But this decision can no longer stand in the light of the judgment of the Court of Justice in the *Marinari* case.[142]

(b) THE TRADITIONAL RULES

The position is essentially the same as that in respect of passing off. The only matter that needs brief discussion is the application of the tort head of Order 11, rule 1(1) in relation to malicious falsehood.

(i) The tort head

In an action for malicious falsehood, the claim is undeniably founded on a tort and thus comes within the scope of the tort head of Order 11, rule 1(1). As with passing-off, in defining the 'act' and the 'damage' under this provision what we are concerned with are the requirements of the cause of action for malicious falsehood.

(a) *An act of malicious falsehood committed within the jurisdiction*

It is submitted that, if you look at the elements of the cause of action under English law, it is the making of the false and denigrating statement which constitutes the act from which the damage resulted. Service of a writ out of the jurisdiction is, accordingly, permissible if the false statement was made in England. There may be difficulties sometimes in ascertaining where a false and denigrating statement was made. For example, if a Californian company writes and posts a letter in California which is delivered to a Japanese company, telling it that an English company has ceased to exist, is the false and denigrating statement, contained in the letter, made in California or in Japan? It is submitted that a misstatement is made in the State in which it is communicated. In the above example, this would be in Japan, where the letter is received. Support for this view can be found in English authority on service of a writ out of the jurisdiction following a fraudulent misrepresentation made in England.[143]

(b) *Damage was sustained within the jurisdiction*

Identification of the 'damage' is more difficult with malicious falsehood than in the case of passing-off, given that, with the former, there is no requirement that special damage (ie distinct evidence of harm to the plaintiff's business) has to be established. Nonetheless, damage is not irrelevant

---

[142] N 76 above; discussed above p 377.
[143] *Diamond* v *Bank of London and Montreal Ltd* [1979] QB 333 at 350 (*per* Stephenson L J). See also *Cordova Land Co* v *Victor Bros Inc* [1966] 1 WLR 793 at 801.

to establishing the tort. As has been seen, the defendant's acts must be calculated to cause pecuniary damage. In the light of this, it is submitted that damage for the purposes of the tort head should be equated with loss of business. This adopts the same solution as has been reached for jurisdiction under the traditional rules in relation to passing-off and has the virtue that, if a plaintiff brings an action in respect of both passing-off and malicious falsehood, he will be able to sue in England in respect of both claims provided that he has lost business in England. Business is lost where sales are lost and this should be ascertained by reference to where the plaintiff's product is marketed.[144] Adopting a different definition for 'damage' in malicious falsehood cases from that adopted for passing-off could lead to an undesirable splitting of the claims with the English courts only having jurisdiction in respect of one claim but not the other.

IV
DEFAMATION

1. SUBSTANTIVE LAW

(a) A RECENT EXAMPLE OF DEFAMATION

Assume you are a decent honourable person working for a bureau de change. You grasp the opportunity to work abroad and are enjoying the experience. Then your bureau de change is raided by police as part of an investigation into drugs and money laundering activities. Although there is not the slightest indication or allegation that you are in any way involved, your name and picture appear in a newspaper report of the raid. Copies of that newspaper are sold all over the country in which you are working, but some copies also find their way to your home country. Your reputation as a decent honourable person is at least put in serious doubt. This is roughly what happened in the *Shevill v Press Alliance SA*[145] case. We will return to the private international law aspects of this case, but its facts are also a perfect example of a defamation case.

(b) THE ELEMENTS OF THE TORT

Without going into too much detail of the English law of defamation,[146] a few important requirements can be highlighted. First, false information or false statements that are made in public or that are made public form the

---

[144] See above, pp 377–378.   [145] Case C-68/93, [1995] ECR I-415; [1995] 2 WLR 499.
[146] For more details see Holyoak and Torremans, n 6 above, at pp 372–373.

starting point. Accurate information, even if it reflects in an extremely negative or harsh way on someone, can never form the basis for a successful defamation claim.[147] Secondly, that false information or these false statements must affect the reputation of the person about whom they are made negatively. They must be derogatory in nature and/or effect. The information published by the newspaper was false in so far as it implied at least indirectly, by mentioning her name and picture in relation to the raid, that Fiona Shevill was linked to criminal activities. Her reputation as a decent honourable person was at least put into serious doubt as a result. What is important to note though is that the focus is on the negative impact on someone's reputation; there is no need to show actual damage of any kind. The existence of damage is simply implied and no evidence is required.

(c) NO TERRITORIAL LIMITS ON THE HARMFUL ACTIVITY

For present purposes, it is also important to know that there are no territorial limits regarding the harmful activity. In the *Shevill* case, the false negative information was published abroad. Elements of the tort can take place in various jurisdictions, without affecting the possibility of bringing an action in defamation in England. There is no rule that all elements constituting the tort must have taken place inside the jurisdiction. This is an important difference between defamation and an action to stop the infringement of intellectual property rights such as trade marks, patents and copyright.

(d) PROTECTION OF A PROFESSIONAL OR BUSINESS REPUTATION

The *Shevill* case deals with the private personal reputation of an individual, but it is clear that the tort of defamation also extends its coverage to the professional or business reputation of an individual. Indeed, this can be derived from *Tolley v J S Fry Ltd*[148] where the plaintiff, a (genuinely) amateur golfer was appalled to discover that a likeness of him was appearing in newspaper adverts for the defendants' chocolate bars, accompanied by a banal limerick comparing the excellence of Tolley's golf with the superb quality of the defendants' product. Tolley complained because he felt that his status as an amateur would be hopelessly compromised in the minds of readers as they would assume that, contrary to the then rules, he must have lent his name to the adverts in exchange for some financial remuneration. The House of Lords accepted this line of argument and found that the adverts amounted to defamation by innuendo.

---

[147] See *South Hetton Coal Co Ltd v North-Eastern News Association Ltd* [1894] 1 QB 133.
[148] [1931] AC 333.

Although there may be other and better routes to try in most cases, defamation can be used in cases where a business reputation is falsely impugned.[149] This amounts to a back-door method of protecting a trading reputation against false allegations. Cases of this nature have been few and far between and not always accompanied by success, but it seems reasonably clear that such a cause of action exists.

2. How Jurisdictional Problems Arise

The *Shevill* case demonstrates graphically how jurisdictional problems in relation to defamation claims arise. The various elements of the tort of defamation took place in different countries. Thus, the information was published in France, while the impact on the plaintiff's reputation took place primarily in England. Defamation in all its components can also take place in more than one country. Can a plaintiff bring a single action in one country covering all instances of defamation that took place in several countries? And in which jurisdiction can the plaintiff do so? A final rather obvious case is that in which the defamatory activity has been undertaken by more than one defendant. Where can one bring such a multi-defendant case if the defendants are not domiciled, resident, etc in a single jurisdiction?

3. Jurisdictional Provisions

(a) THE EC/EFTA RULES

(i) The defamation rules

(a) *Multi-state distribution of libel through the press*

It is important to observe at the outset that the leading case on jurisdiction in relation to defamation, the decision of the Court of Justice in *Shevill* v *Presse Alliance SA*,[150] was dealing with a very specific and complex situation; that of multi-State distribution of libel through the press. It is also important to note that this was not a case of one business defaming a business competitor. Admittedly, some of the plaintiffs were businesses, but the defendant was the publisher of a newspaper, not a rival business. The facts of the case were as follows.

The first plaintiff was an English resident working at a bureau de change in Paris. The second plaintiff was a company operating bureaux de change in England. The third plaintiff was a French company operating

---
[149] See *South Hetton Coal Co Ltd* v *North-Eastern News Association Ltd*, n 147 above.
[150] N 145 above; discussed by Carter in McLachlan and Nygh, chapter 7, at pp 118–121.

bureaux de change in France. The fourth plaintiff was a Belgian holding company which controlled the second and third plaintiffs. The plaintiffs alleged that an article which appeared in 'France Soir', published by the defendant, a company incorporated under French law whose registered office was in Paris, suggested that they were part of a drug-trafficking network for which they had laundered money. The newspaper article was distributed in several Contracting States. The plaintiffs brought proceedings in England for libel. The defendant sought an order dismissing or staying the proceedings on the ground that they had to be brought in the Contracting State of the defendant's domicile under Article 2 of the Brussels Convention, and that the English courts did not have jurisdiction under Article 5(3) since no harmful event had occurred in England. The House of Lords sought guidance from the Court of Justice, *inter alia*, on the interpretation of 'the place where the harmful event occurred', with a view to establishing which courts had jurisdiction to hear an action for harm caused to the victim following distribution of a defamatory newspaper article in several Contracting States.

There is an obvious difficulty in applying the *Mines de Potasse d'Alsace* definition, or at least that part of which allocates jurisdiction to the place where the damage occurred, in defamation cases, given that in such cases there is no physical or pecuniary loss.[151] Nonetheless, the Court of Justice held that the definition in the *Mines de Potasse d'Alsace* case applied equally in the case of loss or damage other than physical or pecuniary. In particular, it applied to injury to the reputation and good name of a natural or legal person due to a defamatory publication. Accordingly, the plaintiffs had the option of suing either in the courts for the place where the damage occurred or in the courts for the place of the event which gave rise to and was at the origin of that damage.

It was held that, in the case of a libel by a newspaper article distributed in several Contracting States, the place of the event giving rise to the damage 'can only be the place where the publisher of the newspaper in question is established, since that is the place where the harmful event originated and from which the libel was issued and put into circulation'.[152] The court of this place has jurisdiction to hear an action for damages for all the harm caused by the unlawful act. The only query about this rule is that it may not always be clear where a publisher is established.

As regards the place where the damage occurred, it was held that, in the case of an international libel through the press, damage 'occurs in the places where the publication is distributed, when the victim is known in these places'.[153] This is the place where the injury to the honour, reputation and good name of a natural or legal person occurs.

[151] See generally, Carter, n 150 above, at p 106. [152] [1995] 2 WLR 499, at 540.
[153] *Ibid*.

However, each Contracting State in which the defamatory publication was distributed and in which the victim claims to have suffered injury to his reputation only has jurisdiction to rule on the injury caused in that State to the victim's reputation.[154] This may lead to a splitting up of the action. In the situation where the plaintiff has a reputation in six different Contracting States, and this is injured by distribution of the same defamatory article in each of these States, the plaintiff would have to bring actions in all six Contracting States in order to recover for the full harm caused by the defendant. It is, though, always open to the plaintiff to bring the entire claim in the Contracting State of the defendant's domicile, under Article 2, or in the Contracting State where the publisher of the defamatory publication is established, under Article 5(3), where this is different.

Under English law, the publication of a defamatory statement is presumed to be harmful to the person defamed without specific proof thereof. In the light of this, the House of Lords also referred to the Court of Justice a number of questions: does the phrase 'harmful event' include this situation? in deciding whether or where a harmful event has occurred, is the local court to decide this otherwise than by reference to its own rules? what standard of proof should the local court require of the plaintiff that the conditions of Article 5(3) are met? The Court of Justice pointed out that the object of the Convention was not to unify the rules of substantive law and procedure of the different Contracting States, but to determine which court has jurisdiction. The fact that, under the national law applicable to the main proceedings, damage is presumed in libel actions does not preclude the application of Article 5(3). The criteria for assessing whether the event in question is harmful and the evidence required of the existence and extent of the harm alleged by the victim of the defamation are not governed by the Convention but by the substantive law determined by the national conflict of laws rules of the court seised, provided that the effectiveness of the Convention is not thereby impaired. The case was then referred back to the House of Lords for a further hearing.[155] There, rather surprisingly, it was argued that Article 5(3) would not apply in a libel case where the plaintiff relied solely on the presumption of harm. The House of Lords, in the light of the abundantly clear decision in the Court of Justice, rejected this argument. Where English law presumed that the publication of a defamatory statement was harmful to the person defamed, without specific proof thereof, that was sufficient for the application of Article 5(3). The plaintiffs, in their pleadings, had made a case entitling them to inquiry as to the harm which they alleged they had suffered[156] in England; it followed

---

[154] Ibid.   [155] See [1996] 3 All ER 929.
[156] The plaintiffs averred that 'By reason of the aforesaid publication the plaintiffs and each of them have been gravely damaged in their characters, credit and reputation and

that they could invoke the jurisdiction of the English courts under Article 5(3).

(b) Application of Shevill *in other cases of defamation*

In working out the implications of the *Shevill* case, it is important to note that international defamation can arise in a wide variety of different circumstances. The *Shevill* case was a complex one, involving as it did, defamatory material distributed through the press in a number of Contracting States. It is possible to think of equally or even more complex cases involving broadcasting or defamation over the internet. Should the definition of the place of the harmful event adopted in the *Shevill* case be applied for such other complex cases? There are also simple cases in which there is no multi-State distribution or reception; the cause of action involves only two Contracting States, such as where an allegedly defamatory letter is sent from one Contracting State to another. Should the *Shevill* definition be applied in this very different situation? In order to answer these questions, it is necessary to look separately at complex and simple cases.

(i) *Complex defamation*

Broadcasting. International defamation by broadcasting is different from the situation dealt with in the *Shevill* case. It does not involve the press; nor, according to the law of some States, does it involve libel, instead the defamation is classified as slander. On the other hand, it does involve the same complexity in that a broadcast may be received in numerous Contracting States in the same way that a newspaper may be so distributed.

It is easy to apply the *Shevill* definition in cases of broadcasting. The place of the event giving rise to the damage can be regarded as being that where the broadcaster of the programme in question is established. There may be problems over ascertaining where a broadcaster is established, as indeed there may be in relation to the publisher of a newspaper. It is submitted that it would be preferable to allocate jurisdiction to the courts of the place of origin of the broadcast. This place is easy to identify. Also, this can be regarded as being the place where the harmful event originated and from which the libel or slander was issued and put into circulation. Moreover, the adoption of a place of origin rule would mean that Article 5(3) would operate in the same way in cases of defamation by broadcasting as it is suggested[157] it should operate in cases of infringement of copyright by broadcasting.

brought into public scandal, ridicule, hatred and contempt. The first plaintiff has also suffered great distress, hurt feelings and embarrassment.'

[157] See above, pp 157–158.

Finally, in many cases, the place of origin will doubtless be the same as the place where the broadcaster is established.

The place where the damage occurred is that where the broadcast is received, when the victim is known there. It is in that place that the injury to the honour, reputation and good name of a natural or legal person occurs. The courts of that place would only have jurisdiction to rule on the injury caused there to the victim's reputation.

Defamation over the internet. The complexity involved in cases of defamation over the internet can be seen from the following example. Information is uploaded by a Spaniard whilst staying with a friend in Italy, the information is downloaded in Germany, by means of an internet server in England, and injures the reputation of a French company. The very real problems in operating Article 5(3) in relation to the internet have been examined previously[158] in relation to infringement of intellectual property rights. When it comes to ascertaining the place of the event giving rise to the damage, it is not possible to follow the *Shevill* case to the letter. The place where the harmful event originated and from which the libel or slander was issued and put into circulation cannot be regarded as being the place where the *publisher* is established because there is no publisher. Even if a company uses the internet as a bulletin board and puts a message on it defaming a rival business there is no publisher or broadcaster in the sense of a body whose business it is to publish or broadcast. This in itself should not be fatal. You could adopt a definition in terms of the place where the author of the defamation is established. More importantly, though, Article 5(3) should operate in the same way in cases of defamation over the internet as it is suggested it should operate in cases of infringement over the internet.[159] Accordingly, it is submitted that the place where the harmful event originated and from which the libel or slander was issued and put into circulation is the place of uploading (input) of the defamatory information.

As regards the place where the damage occurred, the place where the injury to the reputation of the plaintiff occurs is, presumably, where information placed on the internet is read. Following the *Shevill* case, it is required that the victim is known in that Contracting State in order for its courts to have jurisdiction. The plaintiff may have the option of suing in many different Contracting States. However, forum shopping is discouraged by the limitation in *Shevill* that the courts of the place of injury would only have jurisdiction to rule on the injury caused there to the victim's reputation, not in relation to injury caused in other Contracting States.

(ii) *Simple defamation*

There can be little doubt that the definition of the place where the harmful event occurred adopted by the Court of Justice in the *Mines de Potasse*

[158] See above, pp 158–161. [159] See above, p 161.

d'Alsace case would be applied by that Court to simple cases of defamation. The *Mines de Potasse d'Alsace* definition has been applied consistently by the Court of Justice regardless of the tort involved. Having applied it already to the area of defamation, it is very hard to envisage that Court not doing so again in another, more simple, case of defamation.

The more difficult matter is whether, when it comes to defining the place of the event giving rise to the damage and the place where the damage occurred, the definitions adopted in *Shevill* should be applied. The definitions adopted in that case were concerned specifically with multi-State distribution of libel through the press, and look to be inappropriate in cases of simple defamation. Thus, reference to the place where the *publisher* is established is clearly not apposite in a case where an individual defendant writes a defamatory letter. Neither is reference to the place where the publication is *distributed* appropriate. Moreover, in simple cases, the difficulty which arises in complex cases, and was discussed in the *Shevill* case, of whether, following distribution in a number of Contracting States, a court which has jurisdiction on the basis of local damage should also have jurisdiction in relation to damage suffered in the other Contracting States, does not arise.

Nonetheless, the *Shevill* case is useful in that it tells us that the place of the event giving rise to the damage is the one where the harmful event originated and from which the libel was issued and put into circulation. In a case of simple defamation involving, for example, a letter written and posted in Germany and received and read in England, the place of the event giving rise to the damage is that where the allegedly libellous letter is written and posted, ie Germany. The *Shevill* case is also useful in that it makes clear that the place where the damage occurred is the one where the victim claims to have suffered injury to his reputation. In the above example of the defamatory letter, this would be the place where the allegedly defamatory letter is read, ie in England.

(ii) Would different rules be adopted for defamation of a business competitor?

Let us assume that the plaintiff brings an action based on the English law of defamation, but the case involves defamation of a business competitor. Would the Court of Justice apply the principles set out in the *Shevill* case in this very different situation? The position is uncertain. In theory, it would be possible for the Court of Justice to introduce a different rule for defamation of a business competitor. However, there is nothing in the *Shevill* case to suggest that its principles should be departed from in such a case. Moreover, the Court of Justice has not been keen to act in such a way. In the *Shevill* case itself, the Court was not prepared to depart from the principles in the *Mines de Potasse* case, even though the situation facing them was very different. The likelihood is that the fact that there is defamation of a business competitor would probably not be enough to lead to a departure from the *Shevill* principles.

If the plaintiff brings an action based on the law of unfair competition taking the form of defamation of a business competitor, it is to the jurisdictional rules in relation to unfair competition that one must turn,[160] rather than to the rules on defamation.

(b) THE TRADITIONAL RULES

English law characterises defamation of a business competitor as simply being defamation, and what we are concerned with under the traditional rules on jurisdiction is how English law characterises a matter. The fact that some Continental countries adopt an unfair competition classification is irrelevant.

There are no special jurisdictional rules for defamation, although there are special choice of law rules.[161] If a writ has to be served out of the jurisdiction it may be possible to use the injunction head.[162] More commonly though, since defamation is undeniably a tort, resort will be had to the tort head of Order 11.

(i) The tort head of Order 11

(a) *The old head*

Prior to 1987, the tort head required that the tort was committed in England.[163] There was some case law deciding whether the tort of defamation was committed in England for the purpose of service of the writ out of the jurisdiction.[164] In *Bata* v *Bata*,[165] defamatory letters were written by the defendant in Switzerland and posted to England. The Court of Appeal held that publication was the material element that completed the tort of libel, and the cause of action had arisen in England. Leave to serve the writ out of the jurisdiction was granted. In *Kroch* v *Rossell et Cie*,[166] publication was held to have taken place in England after a small number of copies of a foreign newspaper were sold here. These cases involved libel. The Canadian case of *Jenner* v *Sun Oil Co*[167] was the leading authority on slander. The defendants were the owners of a radio station and it was alleged that they had defamed the plaintiff by remarks broadcast from the United

---

[160] See below, pp 410–414.   [161] See below, pp 673–678.
[162] See, eg *Dunlop Rubber Co Ltd* v *Dunlop* [1921] 1 AC 367.
[163] Order 11 rule 1(1)(h) of the old rules of the Supreme Court.
[164] See Carter, n 150 above, at pp 109–111. This also contains a useful comparative survey.
[165] [1948] WN 366, 92 Sol Jo 574.   [166] [1937] 1 All ER 725.
[167] [1952] 2 DLR 526.

States but heard in Ontario. The Ontario High Court held that the tort had been committed in Ontario and granted leave for service out of the jurisdiction.

(b) The new head

(i) An inappropriate test

As is well known, the new tort head[168] is differently worded so that service of a writ out of the jurisdiction may be granted if 'the damage was sustained, or resulted from an act committed, within the jurisdiction'. This wording, being based on a distinction between a wrongful act and the subsequent damage, is appropriate for torts such as negligence, which require damage as part of the cause of action. But such a distinction is not easy to apply in relation to a tort such as defamation which, under English law, does not require actual damage as part of the cause of action. Indeed, *Bata v Bata* refused to follow the leading case on negligence under the old tort head, the *George Monro* case,[169] regarding it as irrelevant when considering the very different area of defamation. In the *Jenner* case, *George Monro* was described as a case 'where damage arose within the jurisdiction as a result of an alleged wrongful act (negligence) committed within the jurisdiction. For reasons that I shall later express, I do not think this class of case can be regarded as decisive authority in this application'.[170] This judicial view, that defamation is different and not suitable for analysis in terms of a wrongful act and consequent damage, has been ignored in the interest of having one single all embracing tort head. Following the adoption of the new tort head, we are now forced to apply this distinction, and ascertain whether damage was sustained in England or resulted from an act committed in England. There is a lack of authority, in general, on the application of these criteria under the new tort head, and in particular in relation to defamation, so this will be no easy task.

(ii) Application of the Shevill case?

The tort head of Order 11 was altered to bring this basis of jurisdiction into line with Article 5(3) of the Brussels Convention, as interpreted by the *Mines de Potasse d'Alsace* case. The *Shevill* case is a clear authority from the Court of Justice in relation to the interpretation of Article 5(3) in a case of defamation. There is a lack of English authority in relation to the interpretation of the new tort head of Order 11 in relation to defamation. In the light of these three facts, there is a temptation to apply the rules

---

[168] Order 11, rule 1(1)(f).
[169] *Monro (George) Ltd v American Cyanamid and Chemical Corpn* [1944] KB 432.
[170] N 167 above at 535.

introduced in the *Shevill* case when interpreting the new tort head in the context of defamation. However, this temptation should be resisted. The Community approach towards interpretation of bases of jurisdiction under the Conventions is so different from that under the traditional English rules on jurisdiction that interpretations arrived at in the former context cannot be regarded as reliable in the latter context. Moreover, any head of Order 11 operates in conjunction with the *forum conveniens* discretion which is there to ensure that England only takes jurisdiction when it is the clearly appropriate forum for trial. There is no such discretion under the Conventions. Instead, the Court of Justice interprets Article 5 so as to ensure that jurisdiction is allocated to an appropriate forum. What is more, applying the *forum conveniens* discretion to the tort head, as interpreted in the light of *Shevill*, could lead to some very curious results. For example, in a case of multi-State distribution of libel if the English court only has jurisdiction in relation to the damage in England, there is the possibility of a multiplicity of actions in England and abroad. In such circumstances, an English court would be likely to say that England was inappropriate as the forum and refuse leave for service of the writ out of the jurisdiction. The upshot of all of this is that the English courts should seek to develop their own jurisprudence when applying the tort head in cases of defamation.

(iii) *An act committed within the jurisdiction*

With a simple case of defamation by letter, the act from which the damage results could be regarded as being either the writing and posting of the letter or its publication in the State in which the letter is received and read. The publication of a libel is the last event necessary for the cause of action.[171] However, the new tort head requires an act to have been committed, and presumably by a person. The person in question, doubtless, is the defendant. Publication of a libel is not an act committed by the defendant. The last act so committed is the writing and posting of the letter, and it is submitted that this should be regarded as the act from which the damage results. With a complex case of multi-State distribution of libel through the press, the last act committed by the defendant is sending off the copies of the newspaper to various countries. The State where the act is committed is therefore the State from which the copies are sent rather than the State or States where they are received. With a case of broadcasting, the relevant act is that of transmitting the allegedly defamatory programme. This act is committed in the State of origin of the transmission rather than in the State of reception. With a case of defamation over the internet, the relevant act is that of uploading the information and transmitting it.

---

[171] See Webb and North, (1965) 14 *ICLQ* 1314 at 1359.

Complementary torts and other causes of action: jurisdiction 405

The act is the same regardless whether it is a case of defamation of a business competitor or not and thus there is no justification for applying a different definition in the former case from that adopted in the latter.

(iv) *Damage was sustained within the jurisdiction*
When it comes to determining what the damage is in a defamation case, the two possible alternatives are injury to the reputation or loss of business.

Injury to reputation. This view of damage is justified by looking at the definition of the tort of defamation under English law. A defamatory statement is one 'which is calculated to injure the reputation of another . . .'.[172] Identifying damage in the light of the definition of the tort of defamation is supported by the Scots case of *Joseph Evans & Sons* v *John G Stein & Co*,[173] which is a rare example of a case of international defamation in a business context, although not of a competitor. The case concerned allegedly defamatory letters sent by a Scots buyer of a pump to the English Corporate suppliers. Under Scots law, there was actionability on the basis of injury to feelings. It was held, in the First Division, that it was only when the letters were delivered at Wolverhampton to the English company that damage by way of injury to the 'feelings' of the English company was done.[174]

A rule that looks to the injury to the reputation of the plaintiff has the great virtue of being easy to apply. In a simple case where a defamatory letter is received in England and the plaintiff's reputation is injured here, the tort head of Order 11 will be satisfied. This rule is equally workable in complex cases. If a foreign newspaper is published in England by being sold here and the plaintiff has a reputation here that is injured then again the tort head will be satisfied. The same is true if a broadcast transmitted from abroad is received in England and the plaintiff's reputation here suffers, or if defamatory information on the internet appears on a screen in England and the plaintiff's reputation here suffers.

The question will then arise in these complex cases that was addressed by the Court of Justice in the *Shevill* case, of whether the English Court also has jurisdiction in relation to the damage to reputation sustained abroad. It is doubtful whether it does so.[175] But even if it does, the fact that there is damage to reputation abroad is an important consideration militating against the exercise of the discretion to allow service out of the jurisdiction.[176]

Loss of business. Alternatively, the damage could be regarded as being the loss of business to the plaintiff, as it is in cases of unfair competition. In

---
[172] *Parmiter* v *Coupland* (1840), 6 M & W 105 at 108 (*per* Parke B).
[173] (1904) 12 SLT 462.
[174] *Ibid* at 463.
[175] See the discussion in relation to passing-off, above, pp 382–383.
[176] See below, pp 259–266.

cases of defamation of a business competitor, normally there will be such loss, and the plaintiff will want this to be reflected in the damages awarded. This is adopting the definition of damage suggested in relation to jurisdiction under Article 5(3) of the Brussels and Lugano Conventions.

There is, though, a number of powerful arguments against this solution. Under the traditional rules on jurisdiction, it is the cause of action that is vital, at least in cases under the tort head, and proof of actual damage is not part of the cause of action for libel. Moreover, it cannot be argued under English law that defamation of a business competitor is a type of unfair competition, where loss of business is the essence of the damage.

Accordingly, it is submitted that, on the basis of principle, policy and of what little authority there is, the damage in a case of defamation, whether of a business competitor or not, should be regarded as that of injury to the reputation of the plaintiff.

(ii) The discretionary element

The normal criteria for *forum conveniens* and *forum non conveniens* apply. But there is a number of considerations which merit a special mention in cases of international defamation.

(a) *Connections with the alternative fora*

In determining the appropriate forum, the court will consider not only matters of litigational convenience but also the connections that the parties and the cause of action have with the alternative fora. One connection that is particularly important in complex cases of defamation relates to where the plaintiff has a reputation.

(i) *No reputation in England*

The significance of this was shown by the decision of the Court of Appeal in *Kroch* v *Rossell et Cie*.[177]

The plaintiff, described as a foreign gentleman, brought actions for libel against the separate publishers of a Belgian and a French newspaper. Both defendants were foreign. A very small number of each newspaper was sold and distributed in England. Technically, this constituted publication of the alleged libel within the jurisdiction. The old tort head of Order 11 was satisfied. However, the substantial publication of both newspapers took place in Belgium and France, where very large numbers were sold. The plaintiff produced no evidence of any reputation, or indeed any associations with England. It was held that, looking at the substance of the case, leave to serve out of the jurisdiction should have been refused.

---

[177] N 166 above. See also *Pillai and Another* v *Sarkar* (1994) Times Law Reps 411.

(ii) *A multi-state reputation*

There are indications in the *Kroch* case that it might have been otherwise if the plaintiff had a reputation here to be defamed, was known here or traded here. It was accepted that the sale of a very few copies might do serious harm. If the English court took jurisdiction against the foreign defendants the question would then arise of whether it would also have jurisdiction in relation to the loss of reputation suffered in Belgium and France as a result of the publication of the newspapers in those countries. It is arguable that, in principle, there is no jurisdiction under the tort head in respect of the damage, in the form of loss of reputation, suffered abroad.[178] The *Kroch* case does not answer this point one way or the other. What it does suggest, though, is that this issue may never come before the courts. Instead, attention is likely to focus on the discretionary element of *forum conveniens* rather than on the precise scope of the tort head. In a case involving publication and loss of reputation in England and abroad, the English court could come to the conclusion that the substance of the case is more concerned with the latter State than the former, and that, accordingly, England is not the clearly appropriate forum for trial. In gauging this, it would be important to look at the number of copies of the newspaper sold and the extent of the plaintiff's reputation in each country.

Of course, it is always possible for a plaintiff to rely solely on the reputation in England, and ignore, for the purposes of the English proceedings, the injury to reputation abroad. However, as will be seen, this may lead to a multiplicity of actions in different States, which is something that English courts are concerned to avoid and is a factor militating against trial in England.

(b) *Where the tort is committed*

The principle that if a tort is committed in England, *prima facie* this is the natural forum for trial[179] continues to operate in the area of defamation.[180] This is because, unlike with other torts, the applicable law still depends on the common law rule which looks to where the tort was committed.[181]

(c) *The applicable law*

When it comes to defining where the tort of defamation is committed for the purpose of this choice of law rule, the position is clear: this is where the publication takes place.[182] The fact that an English court has jurisdiction

---
[178] See the discussion in relation to passing-off, above, p 383. [179] See above, p 264.
[180] Compare the position in relation to passing-off, above, pp 384–385.
[181] See below, pp 674–678.
[182] This would be under the common law rules, see below, pp 677–678.

under the tort head of Order 11 does not necessarily mean that the publication took place in England. For example, if the defendant wrote and posted a defamatory letter in England which was received and read in New York there would be jurisdiction in England on the basis of the defendant's wrongful act here. However, the tort would have been committed in New York, the State of publication, with the result that New York law would apply. This would be a factor suggesting that England is not the clearly appropriate forum for trial and the discretion should not be exercised to allow service of the writ out of the jurisdiction. It would be otherwise in the situation where jurisdiction under the tort head was based on damage occurring in England, since injury to the plaintiff's reputation will normally occur in the State of publication. The English court would apply English law with the result that, *prima facie*, this would be the natural forum for trial.

(d) *Avoidance of a multiplicity of actions in different States*

This is an important consideration in complex cases of multi-State distribution or reception of defamatory material. In *Pillai and Another* v *Sarkar*,[183] it was held that India was clearly the more appropriate forum for trial rather than England when the English language periodical containing the allegedly defamatory material had a circulation of 73,000 in India and a mere 15 in England. This was so even though the plaintiffs confined their claim for damages to the injury allegedly suffered in England. The defendant would still face an action in India in relation to the injury suffered there. French J referred to a trial in England as being oppressive for this very reason. The result was that the writ served on the defendant whilst present for a short time in England was set aside.

(iii) No subject matter limitations on jurisdiction

With defamation, unlike with infringement of foreign intellectual property rights,[184] there are no subject matter limitations in relation to jurisdiction. If there is jurisdiction over the defendant, there is nothing, in principle, to prevent jurisdiction in respect of acts of defamation committed abroad or damage to reputation abroad. Even if, contrary to what is argued in this book,[185] one accepts that the distinction between local and transitory actions is still a valid one, it is clear that an action for libel is a transitory one. In *Potter* v *The Broken Hill Pty Company Ltd*[186] Hodges J, in the Supreme Court of Victoria, gave libel as an example of such an action. He said that 'In transitory actions, such as an action for libel published in France, the cause of action is the publication of the defamatory matter, and

[183] (1994) Times Law Reps 411.
[184] See above, pp 279–306.
[185] See above, pp 287–288.
[186] [1905] VLR 612.

the plaintiff obtains redress, not because it is published in France, but because it is published'.[187]

V
UNFAIR COMPETITION

1. Substantive Law

Passing-off and malicious falsehood are typical common law torts. They are not found as such in civil law systems. Most of the latter systems have a tort of unfair competition. This tort is defined less precisely and covers a wide variety of matters. There are huge differences between what is covered by the various national rules on unfair competition and it is beyond the scope of this book to discuss them in any great detail. Suffice it to say that, apart from what is covered by the tort of passing-off, things as diverse as unfair advertising and selling at a loss can be included. Other unfair competition statutes even include things such as the violation of business secrets,[188] something English law would approach under breach of confidence. Most national legislations seem to include elements such as the fact that the consumer will be mislead and that there is damage or at least likelihood of damage.[189]

It is useful to refer, in the present context, to Article 10bis of the Paris Convention for the Protection of Industrial Property 1883. According to this provision, all Member States undertake to offer protection against unfair competition which is defined as any act of competition which is contrary to honest practices in industrial or commercial matters. Interestingly enough, paragraph three of Article 10bis gives some core examples of unfair competition. These are:

– all acts of such a nature as to create confusion by any means whatever with the establishment, the goods, or the industrial or commercial activities, of a competitor;
– false allegations in the course of trade of such a nature as to discredit the establishment, the goods, or the industrial or commercial activities, of a competitor;
– indications or allegations the use of which in the course of trade is liable to mislead the public as to the nature, the manufacturing process, the characteristics, the suitability for their purpose, or the quantity, of the goods.

Any unfair competition legislation is supposed to cover these three points and one can also clearly see how, in the absence of a tort of unfair

---

[187] *Ibid*, at 638.   [188] Swiss Statute on Unfair Competition of 1986, see below, p 698.
[189] See, eg Article 94 of the Belgian 'Wet betreffende de handelspraktijken' of 14 July 1991, [1991] *Belgisch Staatsblad*, 29 August 1991.

competition, English law uses mainly passing-off to cover the first point, while defamation and malicious falsehood may assist in covering the other points. It is beyond the scope of this book to examine in detail whether of not the existing provisions of English law fully cover all points of Article 10bis or whether a tort of unfair competition should be introduced in some kind of format to ensure that all obligations under Article 10bis are met.

2. How Jurisdictional Problems Arise

Although, in most cases, all elements constituting the tort will be located in one jurisdiction, this is not necessarily so. Advertising, for example, can originate in another country. Would it be sufficient for a court to take jurisdiction if the advertising had the effect of disturbing fair competition in the country where the advert appears? In Austria, the court seemed to be happy to found its jurisdiction in a case where telexes advertising certain services were sent from abroad on the basis that writings were received within the jurisdiction.[190] Multi-defendant cases are the other obvious example of cases where jurisdictional problems arise.

3. Jurisdictional Provisions

(a) THE EC/EFTA RULES

There has already been some discussion of the jurisdictional rules in relation to the broad delict of unfair competition when examining the equivalent English torts of passing-off, malicious falsehood and defamation. But, given that, in Continental States, unfair competition is a delict in its own right, and, indeed, goes wider than these English torts, it is important to look at the jurisdictional position with regard to it. Moreover, the English courts, because of recent changes in the English tort choice of law rules,[191] are now likely to be faced with actions based on, for example, breach of the Swiss law of unfair competition.

Article 5(3)

One matter that needs to be re-examined is the application of Article 5(3) of the Brussels and Lugano Conventions in an action for unfair competition. As has already been mentioned,[192] Continental authorities establish that an action for unfair competition comes within the scope of Article 5(3) and that the distinction in the *Mines de Potasse d'Alsace* case is applied

---

[190] Austrian Supreme Court, 29 October 1985, case 4 Ob 370/85, [1986] 6 *EIPR* D-9; see also Austrian Supreme Court, 11 October 1988, case 4 Ob 86/88, [1989] 6 *EIPR* D-95.
[191] See below, pp 612–640.   [192] See above, pp 371–373.

Complementary torts and other causes of action: jurisdiction 411

when ascertaining the place where the harmful event occurred. Applying this distinction, where is the place of the event giving rise to the damage? Where has the damage occurred?

(a) The place of the event giving rise to the damage

It is impossible to provide a single definition for this place because of the way in which the concept of unfair competition encompasses a number of very different acts. Moreover, there is no agreement in Contracting States on what these acts are. What you have to have is a series of definitions, which depend on the type of unfair competition being relied upon. This, in turn, involves identifying which Contracting State's law of unfair competition is being relied upon. This was the approach adopted by the Italian Supreme Court in a case[193] where the action was based on unfair competition under Article 2598(2) of the Italian Civil Code, which is concerned with the diffusion of information discrediting competitors. When unfair competition takes the form of passing-off, the place of the event giving rise to the damage has been held to be that where the marketing of the imitation product occurred.[194] When it takes the form of spreading false and disparaging information, it has been held to be the place where this is spread.[195] There does not appear to be any authority on unfair competition taking the form of defamation of a business competitor. The position is, accordingly, somewhat uncertain. Do you apply the analogy of defamation? This would mean that, in a case of multi-State distribution of libel, the place of the event giving rise to the damage is the place where the distributor of the libel is established.[196] Given that what we are concerned with is unfair competition and not defamation proper, this would look to be inappropriate. It is submitted that it would be much better to concentrate on the act of unfair competition. If you regard this act as referring to an act by the defendant, the last such act is the posting of the letter, or the sending off of the newspapers, or the transmission of the broadcast containing the defamatory statement. The place of the event giving rise to the damage is, therefore, the place where the letter was posted from, or the place where the newspapers were sent from, or the place where the broadcast was transmitted from.[197] There also appears to be no authority in relation to unfair competition in the form of improper advertising. Again, it would be best to concentrate on the act of unfair competition. An advert

[193] See Italian Supreme Court, 28 October 1993 No 10704, [1994] 2 *EIPR* D-30.
[194] Judgment of 3 July 1975, *Forge et Coutellerie Dubois NV and Wolpa Plastics v Fantu Food BV and Reinders* D Series I-5.3-B1; discussed above. See also *Ideal Clima SpA and Others v SA Ideal Standard* Judgment of 15 June 1982, Gaz Pal 1982, Somm, 378; D Series I-5.3-B13.
[195] No 10704 Supreme Court of Italy, 28 October 1993 [1994] 2 *EIPR* D-30.
[196] See *Shevill and Others v Presse Alliance SA* [1995] 2 WLR 499; discussed above.
[197] The place is the same as that where an act of defamation takes place for the purpose of Order 11, rule 1(1)(f), see above, pp 404–405.

could be placed on the internet giving rise to unfair competition over the internet. Localising the act of unfair competition in the place of uploading the information would be consistent with the position that has been recommended above in relation to defamation and infringement over the internet.

(b) *The place where the damage has occurred*

The two alternatives for defining this place are as follows: the place where damage to a particular relationship was sustained; the place where direct economic loss to the plaintiff was sustained. These two alternatives will now be examined.

(i) *The place where damage to a particular relationship was sustained*

It has been argued that the damage immediately resulting from an act of unfair competition is to the relationship between the victim and someone else, such as the customer, supplier or employee.[198] The precise relationship that is damaged, and hence the place where this occurred, will depend on the form that the unfair competition takes. Thus, with unfair competition by means of passing-off, the damage immediately resulting from this act is, presumably, the damage to the relationship with the customer. Doubtless, the same is true with improper advertising.

However, with some forms of unfair competition the damage most immediately resulting from the act does not appear to be damage to a particular relationship. Thus, with unfair competition which takes the form of disparagement of a business or its products, the damage immediately resulting from the act of disparagement is surely to the victim's reputation. This will occur even before the relationship with another is affected. Similarly, if the act was one of improper appropriation and disclosure of trade secrets, what has been damaged, as an immediate result of this act, is the confidentiality of the information.

The major drawback, though, with a definition in terms of the place where damage to a particular relationship was sustained is that it involves focusing on the form of unfair competition, and, doubtless, this may take place in different Contracting States, depending on the form in question. Moreover, if the plaintiff bases the action on several different forms of unfair competition, this could result in jurisdiction being allocated to the courts of different Contracting States, each of which would only deal with one aspect of the action.

---

[198] Dyer, (1988) *Hag Rec* 376, 409–413.

(ii) *The place where direct economic loss to the plaintiff was sustained*

In most instances, the direct economic loss to the plaintiff will take the form of a loss of sales. There is support in Norway for a definition in terms of the place where sales are lost. In *Saba Molnlycke AS v Proctor & Gamble Scandinavia Inc*,[199] the Norwegian plaintiffs brought an action in Norway for compensation for a decline in the sale of its nappies in Norway as a consequence of the broadcasting of the Swedish defendant's commercial to consumers in Norway. The Tonsberg Court of Appeal held that it had jurisdiction under Article 5(3) of the Lugano Convention on the basis that the damage, the decline in sales, had been sustained in Norway. The decline in sales was to be considered as the immediate and directly damaging effect of the unfair competition by way of the improper advertising.

In a case of unfair competition in the form of passing-off, the direct economic loss, likewise, is the loss of sales.[200] This will take place in the State where the sales are lost, ie where the competitor confuses customers into buying his product. This can be seen from the decision of the District Court of Amsterdam in *Geobra Brandstätter GmbH v Big Spielwarenfabrik*.[201] The plaintiff German company sought an injunction restraining the defendant German company from marketing in the Netherlands its 'Playbig' dolls, being too similar to the plaintiff's own 'Playmobil' dolls, and damages. The defendant manufactured the offending dolls in Germany and also delivered them in Germany to the Dutch importer. It was accepted, by the District Court, that the damage in relation to the Dutch market occurred in the Netherlands, where business was lost. However, on the facts, jurisdiction could not be based on this because the plaintiff had previously opted to sue in Germany on the basis that this was the place of the event giving rise to the damage.

This view of 'damage' is also supported by an Italian decision in relation to the operation of Article 5(3) in the context of the breach of competition rules.[202]

However, with certain forms of unfair competition, the direct economic loss will be other than loss of sales. Thus, in a case of trade disparagement, which results in the victim losing a supplier, the direct economic loss is the cost to the victim of losing the supplier.

---

[199] [1997] ILPr 704. [200] See Dyer, n 198 above, at p 414.
[201] Judgment of 15 June 1977, NJ 1979, No 146, Note: Schultsz; Note: Verheul, *NILR* 1978, 87.
[202] Tribunale di Monza, Judgment of 28 September 1979, *Candy SpA v Schell and Stoecker Reinshagen GmbH* Foro pad. 1979, I, 225, Note: Magelli; Riv dir int priv proc 1980, 429. But compare Oberlandesgericht Hamm, Judgment of 3 October 1978 – 9U 278/77, D-Series I-5.3 – B9; below.

Given the judicial support for a definition in terms of the place where direct economic loss was sustained, it is submitted that this is the definition that should be applied.

As has previously been mentioned, there is support in the decision of the Italian Supreme Court of 28 October 1993[203] for defining the place where the damage has occurred in terms of the place where indirect economic loss to the plaintiff was sustained. However, this case was decided before the decision of the Court of Justice in the *Marinari*[204] case, which precludes jurisdiction on the basis of indirect loss suffered in the forum, and should no longer be followed. Nonetheless, it has to be admitted that an indirect loss rule has one great virtue in cases of unfair competition in that it means that the place of damage will be the same regardless of the form of unfair competition. The indirect loss will be the loss of profits to the victim and, probably, this takes place where the victim has its seat.

(b) THE TRADITIONAL RULES

If an action is brought in England based on a foreign State's law of unfair competition there would be jurisdiction against a defendant domiciled in a non-EC/EFTA Contracting State under the tort head of Order 11, rule 1(1) if the damage resulted from an act of unfair competition committed in England or the damage was sustained in England. There is no English cause of action in unfair competition which can be looked to in order to determine what the act of unfair competition was. The same approach has to be adopted as that used in relation to jurisdiction under the EC/EFTA rules: it is necessary to focus on the particular State's law of unfair competition that is being relied upon, and the type of unfair competition under that law. In cases of unfair competition over the internet, the same solution should be adopted as in cases under the EC/EFTA rules.[205] As regards the damage, there is no English concept of damage in relation to unfair competition. It is submitted that the same definition of damage should be adopted as under the EC/EFTA rules, and that damage resulting from unfair competition is sustained in the State in which the plaintiff sustains direct economic loss. It follows that service of a writ out of the jurisdiction should be permissable under the tort head if, for example, sales are lost in England as the result of unfair competition in the form of passing-off.

---

[203] No 10704. [1994] 2 *EIPR* D-30; discussed above, pp 392–393.
[204] Case C-364/93 *Marinari* v *Lloyd's Bank plc and Another* [1996] 2 WLR 159.
[205] See above, pp 411–412.

VI
WIDER CONTINENTAL PROTECTION IN DELICT

1. Substantive Law

Most continental civil law systems do not opt for the literal interpretation of statutory provisions. Purposive interpretation of statutory provisions makes it possible to have a wide general provision concerning liability in delict. The ultimate example of such a provision is found in Article 1382 of the French and Belgian Civil Codes. These articles incorporate the principle that whoever causes damage through his fault, should repair the damage. This sweeping liability rule is supplemented by a similar rule that imposes the same liabilty in cases where the damage arises as a result of negligent behaviour. The general nature of this type of rule means that it can also be used in intellectual property related areas. One example of such a situation might be the spreading of inaccurate and/or defamatory information. A civil action could then be brought on the basis of these general delictual provisions.[206]

2. How Jurisdictional Problems Arise

Returning to the above example, it is easy to imagine a case where the inacurate or defamatory information is spread abroad, whilst the damage arises in the jurisdiction. In general, the by now well-known pattern of multi-defendant cases and elements of the tort or delict occurring in different jurisdictions applies also to this delict.

3. Jurisdictional Provisions

(a) THE EC/EFTA RULES

Article 5(3), obviously, will apply in relation to cases involving wider Continental protection in delict. It is also clear that the *Mines de Potasse d'Alsace* definition will operate. When it comes to defining the place of the event giving rise to the damage and the place where the damage occurred, it is submitted that the same definitions should be adopted as those in cases of unfair competition. Given that certain acts qualify both as unlawful acts in delict and as unfair competition, it is important that the

---

[206] Obviously, an eventual criminal prosecution remains also possible. The two types of action do not exclude each other.

jurisdictional position should be the same in respect of both; otherwise jurisdiction would depend solely on how the case is pleaded. The decision of the Italian Supreme Court of 28 October 1993[207] illustrates this point. It will be recalled[208] that that case involved unfair competition by spreading false and disparaging information about an Italian company in foreign countries. Jurisdiction was available either in the Contracting State where the disparaging information was spread or where the damage was suffered.[209] However, the claim for damages in that case could, equally, qualify as compensation for unlawful acts under Article 204 of the Italian Civil Code.

(b) THE TRADITIONAL RULES

It is submitted that the same approach should apply as that, outlined above,[210] in relation to jurisdiction under the traditional rules in cases of unfair competition.

VII
BREACH OF COMPETITION RULES

1. SUBSTANTIVE LAW

Articles 85 and 86 of the Treaty of Rome deal with competition law and neither of these articles contains an exception for a specific area, such as intellectual property. Intellectual property must, therefore, be subject to the rules on competition in the European Union. The impact of Article 85 on intellectual property will be discussed first and then attention will be turned to Article 86.

(a) ARTICLE 85 EEC

(i) The provision

Article 85 of the Treaty consists of three paragraphs:

1. The following shall be prohibited as incompatible with the common market: all agreements between undertakings, decisions by associations of undertakings and concerted practices which may affect trade between Member States and which have as their object or effect the prevention, restriction or distortion of competition within the common market, and in particular those which:

   (a) directly or indirectly fix purchase or selling prices or any other trading conditions;

---

[207] No 10704.
[209] See above, pp 392–393.
[208] See above, pp 392–393.
[210] At p 414.

(b) limit or control production, markets, technical development, or investment;
(c) share markets or sources of supply;
(d) apply dissimilar conditions to equivalent transactions with other trading parties, thereby placing them at a competitive disadvantage;
(e) make the conclusion of contracts subject to acceptance by the other parties of supplementary obligations which, by their nature or according to commercial usage, have no connection with the subject of such contracts.

2. Any agreements or decisions prohibited pursuant to this Article shall be automatically void.

3. The provisions of paragraph 1 may, however, be declared inapplicable in the case of:

- any agreement or category of agreements between undertakings;
- any decision or category of decisions by associations of undertakings;
- any concerted practice or category of concerted practices;

which contributes to improving the production or distribution of goods or to promoting technical or economic progress, while allowing consumers a fair share of the resulting benefit, and which does not:

(a) impose on the undertakings concerned restrictions which are not indispensable to the attainment of these objectives;
(b) afford such undertakings the possibility of eliminating competition in respect of a substantial part of the products in question.

(ii) Analysis of the provision

This Article will now be analysed briefly.[211] Paragraph 1 outlaws a number of deals because they are anti-competitive, and paragraph 2 sanctions this by declaring them void. Paragraph 3 contains an exception. When a number of requirements are met, a deal, which would normally fall foul of paragraph 1, will be exempted and paragraph 1, and consequently paragraph 2 as well, will not be applied to it.

(a) *Paragraph 1*

With which deals is paragraph 1 concerned? The obvious category consists of the agreements concluded between undertakings. These will be affected if they have as their object, or simply as their effect, the prevention of competition, the restriction of competition or the distortion of competition within the Common Market. If it were to stand on its own, this provision could easily be circumvented by avoiding a formal agreement. Competition could, nevertheless, still be affected if the parties were to co-ordinate their actions and replace competition by co-ordination. The same effect could be reached by replacing an agreement with a decision of an

---

[211] A detailed analysis is found in Whish, *Competition Law*, Butterworths (3rd ed, 1993), chapter 7.

association of undertakings. The drafters of the Treaty avoided this risk by including both concerted practices and decisions of associations of undertakings as separate categories which are covered by Article 85. A last additional requirement is that trade between Member States must be affected for Article 85 to operate. Small deals which do not affect trade between Member States are not important enough, because they will not have a substantial influence on competition at Community level. National competition authorities may nonetheless decide to pick up these deals and scrutinise them under national competition law.

(b) *Paragraph 2*

When a deal is caught by Article 85(1), the sanction provided by Article 85(2) is that it is automatically void. No declaratory decision by a court or competition authority is necessary and, in law, we act as if the deal never existed. The deal will not bind anyone and no-one will be able to rely upon it.

(c) *Paragraph 3*

Exemptions which effectively place the deal outside the scope of Article 85(1) can be granted under the authority of Article 85(3) if four conditions, two positive and two negative, are met. These conditions are applied cumulatively, all four need to be met at any one time. First, the anticompetitive deal must provide a contribution to the improvement of the production or distribution of goods or to promoting technical or economic progress. Secondly, it must also allow consumers a fair share of the resulting benefit. Thirdly, no restrictions which are not indispensable to the attainment of these objectives can be imposed and fourthly, there should be no possibility of eliminating competition in respect of a substantial part of the products in question. If these four requirements are met an individual exemption can be granted. In practice, this is done by submitting the deal to the Commission, which executes the Community's competition law, as an application for an individual exemption. This individual process is a fairly lengthy one and it causes a lack of legal certainty since the parties to a deal do not know in advance which restrictive clauses will be acceptable to the Commission. In order to solve these problems, and to avoid being unable to cope with a flood of applications, the Commission has issued block exemptions.[212] These take the form of a Regulation and contain lists of acceptable and non-acceptable clauses. Agreements that

---

[212] See, eg Commission Regulation 240/96 on the application of Article 85(3) of the Treaty to certain categories of transfer of technology agreements [1996] OJ L31/2.

stay within the limits set out by the block exemption are automatically exempted and no further application or other procedure is required.

(d) *Application to intellectual property agreements*

The next issue to address, now that we know what Article 85 is all about, is whether agreements concerning intellectual property are caught by it. Licence contracts, or eventually assignments, can restrict to a considerable extent competition between the licensor and the licensee or between licensees.[213] Exclusive licences are prime examples of this, as the emergence of a competitor on a certain market, be it another licensee or the licensor, is precluded.[214] On the other hand, there is no provision in the Treaty which provides an exception for the intellectual property area. The conclusion must, accordingly, be that Article 85 applies unreservedly to intellectual property agreements.[215]

(b) ARTICLE 86

(i) Abuse of a dominant position

This Article prohibits the abuse of a dominant position. The first matter that must be examined is what constitutes a dominant position for the purposes of the Treaty. It is beyond the scope of this book to discuss all the issues related to the technical application of Article 86 in detail and it will be necessary to restrict our comments to a couple of essential points.[216] Dominance should not exist in an abstract way, but in the context of a market, and three aspects are important. A position needs to be dominant in the relevant product market, it needs to be dominant in the relevant geographical market, and the market is also restricted in time when considering the issue of dominance. The determination of the relevant product market raises issues such as the interchangeability and substitutability of products, while in many cases the relevant geographical and temporal market are more obvious to determine. Once a dominant position has been established, Article 86 requires that that dominant position is held in a substantial part of the Common Market.

But dominance as such is not sufficient for the purposes of Article 86 as there also needs to be an abuse of that dominant position. Article 86 does

---

[213] See, eg Case 193/83 *Windsurfing International Inc* v *Commission* [1986] ECR 611 and [1986] 3 CMLR 489.
[214] See Case 258/78 *LC Nungesser KG* v *Commission* [1982] ECR 2015 and [1983] 1 CMLR 278.
[215] See Cases 56 and 58/64 *Consten and Grundig* v *Commission* [1966] ECR 299 and [1966] CMLR 418 and Case 24/67 *Parke, Davis & Co Ltd* v *Probel* [1968] ECR 55 and [1968] CMLR 68.
[216] A more detailed approach is found in Whish, n 211 above, chapter 8.

not contain an exhaustive list of what would amount to an abuse, but it gives charging unfair prices, limiting production and discrimination as obvious examples of abuse.

A last important preliminary point in relation to Article 86 is that it will only apply if there is an effect on inter-State trade.[217] The Court has held that this requirement will be satisfied where conduct brought about an alteration in the structure of competition in the Common Market.[218]

(ii) Application in the context of intellectual property

It will be necessary to discuss the case law in detail to discover what may amount to an abuse of a dominant position in the context of intellectual property. It is clear that monopoly rights, such as intellectual property rights, can lead to a dominant position, but an abuse of a dominant position involves a certain action and a certain use of rights. It is, therefore, correct to assume that, as in relation to the free movement of goods, the existence of intellectual property rights as such cannot amount to an abuse of a dominant position[219] and neither can certain uses of these rights. Attention must be focused on what constitutes an abusive use or exercise of an intellectual property right. As with the free movement of goods, the existence and the normal use of intellectual property rights will not be affected since only the abusive use of intellectual property rights for a purpose which is unrelated to intellectual property, namely the distortion of competition and the distortion of the free movement of goods, will be targeted by the Treaty provisions. In fact, many of these elements are already found in various forms in one of the earliest intellectual property judgments of the Court of Justice.

The Court indicated, for the first time, that Article 86 could interfere with intellectual property rights in its *Parke Davis* judgment of 1968 when it ruled that the existence of the intellectual property rights granted by a Member State is not affected by the prohibition contained in Article 86 of the EEC Treaty and that, in the absence of any abuse of a dominant position, the exercise of such rights cannot of itself fall under Article 86:

Although a patent confers on its holder a special protection within the framework of a State, it does not follow that the exercise of the rights so conferred implies the existence of the three elements mentioned (the existence of a dominant position on the single market or on a substantial part thereof, abuse of that dominant position and a negative effect on trade between Member States). It could only do so if the

---

[217] See *Ibid*, at 247–248.
[218] Cases 6 and 7/73 *Commercial Solvents* v *Commission* [1974] ECR 223 and [1974] 1 CMLR 309.
[219] See Case 238/87 *Volvo* v *Erik Veng (UK) Ltd* [1988] ECR 6211 (at paragraph 8) and [1989] 4 CMLR 122.

utilisation of the patent could degenerate into an improper exploitation of the protection.[220]

In this first case, the Court found that a higher sale price for the patented product, as compared with that of the unpatented product coming from another Member State, does not necessarily constitute an abuse of a dominant position. The possibility of asking a higher price for the product as a result of the patent protection was seen as being the normal result of the existence of that patent protection. And even if, in this first case, no abuse of a dominant position was found, it opened the way for a series of other cases.

Article 86 has been applied in relation to intellectual property rights on a number of occasions.[221] The existence of the right in itself is no abuse, but it can, potentially, be exercised or used in an abusive way. It is beyond the scope of this work to discuss the case law of the Court of Justice in detail, but the following examples illustrate clearly the approach taken. A whole series of cases was concerned with collecting societies that occupy a dominant position vis-à-vis their members, who are obliged to work with them if they are to collect their royalties effectively, and vis-à-vis the users, who have only one source to buy a licence from. That dominant position is based on the existence of intellectual property rights and can, of course, give rise to abuse. For example, certain members can be discriminated against or unjustifiably high licence charges can be imposed on users.[222]

Other cases deal with the refusal of a company, that occupies a dominant position due to the existence of an intellectual property right, to grant a licence. Could such a refusal constitute an abuse of a dominant position and could the remedy be the 'compulsory' grant of a licence?[223] Unless exceptional circumstances are present, such a refusal was held not to constitute an abuse of the company's dominant position.

(c) ACTIONS FOR BREACH OF COMPETITION LAW

Most actions for breach of competition law are started by the Commission of the European Communities. The Commission has indeed been given

---

[220] Case 24/67 *Parke, Davis & Co* v *Probel, Reese, Beintema-Interpharm and Centrapharm* [1968] ECR 55, [1968] CMLR 47, in relation to trade marks see Case 51/75 *EMI Records Ltd* v *CBS United Kingdom Ltd* [1976] ECR 811, [1976] 2 CMLR 235 and in relation to copyright see Case 78/70 *Deutsche Grammaophon GmbH* v *Metro-SB-Grossmarkte GmbH & Co KG* [1971] ECR 487, [1971] CMLR 631.

[221] For more details see Holyoak and Torremans, at pp 115–116 and 237–245.

[222] For a recent example see Case 402/85 *Basset* v *Sacem* [1987] ECR 1747.

[223] See and compare the approaches in Case 53/87 *Consorzio italiano della componentistica di ricambio per autoveicoli and Maxicar* v *Régie des usines Renault* [1988] ECR 6039, [1990] 4 CMLR 265; Case 238/87 *AB Volvo* v *Erik Veng (UK) Ltd* [1988] ECR 6211, [1989] 4 CMLR 122 and Cases C-241/91P and C-242/91P *Radio Telefis Eireann (RTE) and Independent Television Publications Ltd (ITP)* v *Commission of the European Communities* [1995] CMLR (Antitrust Reports) 718.

the task of enforcing the Community's competition policy. Private parties are also allowed to bring a case, although often they file a complaint with the Commission and leave it to the Commission to initiate the proceedings. In many cases, Article 85 is raised by the defendant in a case where the plaintiff attempts to enforce a contract or sues for breach of contract. The defendant then argues that the contract cannot be enforced, and he cannot be liable for damages as a result of breach of contract, because the contract is void on the basis that its provisions are in breach of Article 85. Private actions on the basis of Article 86 have also been brought by parties that had allegedly been the victim of an abuse of a dominant position, for example because they had been refused a licence.

The competition law provisions have a peculiar territorial scope. Any agreement that affects trade between Member States, and any conduct that produces effects within the Community, is caught by the provisions of competition law. The fact that some of the parties are established outside the Community is irrelevant in this respect.

2. How Jurisdictional Problems Arise

Article 85 applies to intellectual property agreements. Many of these contracts are international in nature. Technology is licensed for exploitation in a third country or copyright permission is granted for the production and marketing of a local language version of a work. Whenever the parties are established in different countries, a choice between two or more potential fora becomes possible. Elements of the allegedly infringing conduct might also have taken place in different countries.

A dominant position might be held in more than one country, but the effects of its abuse might be felt particularly in one country. Elements of the abusive conduct can also take place in different countries.

In many cases, competition law will not be the main issue. Often, Articles 85 and/or 86 are (only) raised as a defence. The typical case is the one where a licensor attempts to enforce a licence contract against a licensee who finds himself in breach of its provisions, but who argues that the contract cannot be enforced because it restricts competition and is, therefore, in breach of Article 85(1) and void under Article 85(2). Or Article 86 can be raised by an infringer of an intellectual property right to argue that the refusal to grant him a licence under which his acts would have been permitted constituted an abuse of dominant position.[224] In those situations, the jurisdictional issue will have been addressed before the competition law point is raised.

---

[224] See, eg Cases C-241/91P and C-242/91P *Radio Telefis Eireann (RTE) and Independent Television Publications Ltd (ITP)* v *Commission of the European Communities* [1995] ECR I-743 and [1995] CMLR (Antitrust Reports) 718.

The fact that competition law is enforced by the competition law authorities is another important factor. On top of the court cases between private parties, the Commission will take action against infringers of Articles 85 and 86 and its decisions will be open to an appeal before the Court of Justice. This alternative route remains outside the scope of private international law. The Commission will take jurisdiction on the basis of the fact that the effects of the allegedly infringing conduct are felt within the Community.

3. Jurisdictional Provisions

(a) THE EC/EFTA RULES

As with the other forms of tortious protection previously discussed in this chapter, the focus of discussion will be on Article 5(3) of the Brussels and Lugano Conventions.

(i) Is an action for breach of competition rules within the scope of Article 5(3)?

There can be no real doubt that such an action falls within the scope of Article 5(3). This has been accepted without discussion by the Tribunale di Monza in Italy[225] and by the Oberlandesgericht Hamm in Germany.[226] If one is looking for a basis for this, it can be found in the view that any actionable breach of Community law which gives rise to a claim in damages should be categorised as a tort/delict, being a breach of statutory duty.[227] This view has been accepted by Geoghegan J in the High Court in Ireland in *Norburt Schmidt* v *Home Secretary of the Government of the United Kingdom, the Commissioner of the Metropolitan Police and David Jones*.[228] The case involved allegations of false imprisonment and breach of rights of free movement pursuant to the Treaty of Rome. It was accepted that actionable breaches of EC law which give rise to a claim for damages were 'matters relating to a tort' within the meaning of Article 5(3) of the Brussels Convention. The same tortious classification has been adopted by the English Court of Appeal in a breach of competition rules case involving the application of the tort head of Order 11.[229]

---

[225] Judgment of 28 September 1979, *Candy SpA* v *Schell and Stoecker Reinshagen GmbH*, n 202 above.
[226] Judgment of 3 October 1978–9 U 278/77.
[227] *Garden Cottage Foods* v *Milk Marketing Board* [1984] AC 130.
[228] [1995] 1 ILRM 301.
[229] *Camera Care Ltd* v *Victor Hasselblad AB and Another* [1986] ECC 373; discussed below.

(ii) The place of the event giving rise to the damage

It is submitted that this is the place where the breach of competition law is alleged to have been committed. It is submitted that, in an Article 85 case, it will be where the prohibited agreement was entered into, or the prohibited decisions made or the prohibited concerted practices adopted. In an Article 86 case, it will be where the actions and use of rights constituting an abuse of a dominant position took place. Authority for this can be found in the judgment of 3 October 1978 of the Oberlandesgericht Hamm.[230] The German plaintiff imported BMW cars from Belgium, taking advantage of the price discrepancy between Belgium and Germany. The defendant, the Belgian subsidiary of BMW, issued a circular forbidding its Belgian dealers to re-export BMW cars. The plaintiff brought an action in Germany in respect of the damage it claimed to have suffered as a result of the export prohibition. It was held that the German courts lacked jurisdiction. It was said that the only place where the breach of competition law was alleged to have been committed was Belgium, where the cartel agreement and the refusal to deliver had taken place.[231]

(iii) The place where the damage has occurred

It is submitted that damage caused by a breach of competition rules occurs in the place where direct economic loss to the plaintiff was sustained, ie where business is lost. This view of 'damage' is supported by the Tribunale di Monza in *Candy SpA v Schell and Stoecker Reinshagen GmbH*.[232] The plaintiff Italian company alleged that the German undertakings engaged in unfair competitive practices in Germany, with the intention of eliminating it from the German market. It was held that, for the purpose of Article 5(3), the place where the damage occurred meant the place where the harmful circumstances came about, and that this consisted in the loss of business sustained by the plaintiff as a result of the unlawful conduct of the defendants. Since the damage had occurred in Germany, the Italian court had no jurisdiction. A definition of damage in terms of lost business would mean the adoption of the same rule as that recommended in relation to passing-off, malicious falsehood and unfair competition. This would result in the courts of the same Contracting State having jurisdiction, based on damage sustained there, in the situation where the plaintiff brings allegations of breach of competition rules and unfair competition. There is a close relationship between these actions which makes

---

[230] 9 U 278/77, D-Series I-5.3–B9.
[231] This was in the context of whether there was jurisdiction under para 32 of the German Code of Civil Procedure which requires identification of the district where the unlawful act was committed. However, it was accepted that there was no intention under Article 5(3) of amending the law as stated in para 32.
[232] N 202 above.

it particularly undesirable that they should be tried in different Contracting States.

In the *Candy* case, it was said that no relevance was to be attached to the place where the damage in question brought about the specific reduction in the assets of the victim. Thus, the Court rejected a definition of the place where the damage has occurred in terms of the place where indirect economic loss to the plaintiff was sustained. Likewise, this view of damage was rejected by the Oberlandesgericht Hamm.[233] The effects on the plaintiff's trade and finances of the breach of competition law in Belgium were felt in Germany. It was accepted that jurisdiction was available in the place where the harmful event was committed or the place where the damage occurred,[234] but not where further harmful consequences ensued. Jurisdiction could not be established at a place which was unconnected with the commission of the tort except through the arbitrary fact that financial loss had occurred there. Most recently of all, there is, of course, the decision of the Court of Justice in the *Marinari* case, to the effect that jurisdiction under Article 5(3) cannot be founded on indirect damage.

(b) THE TRADITIONAL RULES

The familiar issue arises of whether the tort head of Order 11 can be used. In *Camera Care Ltd v Victor Hasselblad*,[235] the Court of Appeal was prepared to assume, for the purpose of service of a writ out of the jurisdiction under Order 11 rule (1) of the Rules of the Supreme Court,[236] that an action based on breach of Articles 85 and 86 of the Treaty of Rome was capable of constituting a tort in English law. Accordingly, it could come within the tort head of that Order.

Under the tort head, an English court will have jurisdiction against a foreign defendant if the damage resulted from a breach of competition rules committed in England. It is submitted that, in an Article 85 case, this breach will have been committed in England if the prohibited agreement was entered into there, or the prohibited decisions were made there, or the prohibited concerted practices were adopted there. In an Article 86 case, the breach will have been committed in England if the actions and use of rights constituting an abuse of a dominant position took place there. In other words, the position is the same as under the EC/EFTA rules.

---

[233] N 202 above.
[234] It is arguable, on the facts that the German courts had jurisdiction on the basis of direct damage, ie lost sales, sustained there.
[235] [1986] ECC 373 at 377–378.
[236] Sir Roger Ormrod was careful to say that it was unnecessary and inappropriate to decide whether breaches of Arts 85 and 86 can be categorised as a tort in English private law: *ibid* at 380.

An English court also will have jurisdiction under the tort head if the damage resulting from the breach of competition rules was sustained in England. It is submitted that the damage occurs in England if there is direct economic loss, ie business is lost, there. Again, the position is the same as under the EC/EFTA rules.

VIII
BREACH OF CONFIDENCE

In English law, the action for breach of confidence is wide in scope and can cover things as different as, on the one hand, secret know-how detailing how best to work a patented process and, on the other hand, salient details about the private life of a showbusiness celebrity. The first example can be seen as forming part of a wider category of intellectual property related items which could be called trade secrets. That group could also include know-how concerning the marketing of certain products, business strategy details, etc. Attention will be focused on the trade secret side of breach of confidence, but it will be seen that the law does not really distinguish between the various types of confidential information. Most of the following comments will, therefore, apply to any action for breach of confidence.

1. SUBSTANTIVE LAW

(a) ELEMENTS OF THE ACTION FOR BREACH OF CONFIDENCE

The elements of the modern breach of confidence action[237] were laid down in *Coco v A N Clark (Engineers) Ltd*.[238] Confidential plans for a new moped engine were at issue. It was alleged that the defendant, who had acquired the confidential information while examining the potential for co-operation with the plaintiff, was using the information for its own purposes, having decided not to pursue the co-operation with the plaintiff. In the High Court, Megarry J laid down the rule detailing three essential aspects of the action for breach of confidence.[239] First, the information must be, in itself, of a confidential character. Secondly, the imparting of the information must be in circumstances or on an occasion of confidence. Thirdly and finally, the information must be used in an unauthorised way and so as to cause detriment to the plaintiff. The action in *Coco* v *Clark* failed because the latter two requirements were not met.

---

[237] For a more detailed approach see Holyoak and Torremans, n 6 above, chapter 25.
[238] [1969] RPC 41.
[239] [1969] RPC 41 at 47.

(i) When is information confidential?

An objective test is used to determine whether information is confidential or not. Would an ordinary reasonable man almost instinctively recognise that the information was not intended for the public domain? Would an ordinary reasonable man recognise that the information should not be spread beyond those persons who have to know of the facts in question? The beliefs of the owner of the information as a subjective factor have only a limited influence. The subjective belief that certain information is confidential in nature is only taken into account in so far as it is reasonable. It is, therefore, not likely that the views of the reasonable man will be contradicted.[240]

It is clear that the private, or at least restricted, nature of the information is an essential element if it is to become confidential. Information about facts which happened in public simply cannot become confidential.[241] On the other hand, the fact that more than two people know a secret will not be able to change the confidential nature of the information.[242]

(ii) The occasion of confidence

Once it has been established that the information is confidential in nature, a second and fully independent requirement needs to be met. The information must have been passed on on an occasion of confidence. The circumstances in which it was past on must, in other words, give rise to an obligation of confidence. Whether or not this was the case will be determined by means of an objective test involving the normal reasonable man's judgment. In *Coco v Clark*, Megarry J formulated the test as follows:

> it seems to me that if the circumstances are such that any reasonable man standing in the shoes of the recipient of the information would have realised that upon reasonable grounds the information was being given to him in confidence, then this should suffice to impose upon him the equitable obligation of confidence.[243]

Confidentiality clauses are quite often included in contracts. If there is an express clause to this effect in the contract, the information will obviously have been passed on on an occasion of confidence,[244] but an express confidentiality clause is not always required. The courts are sometimes prepared to read an implied confidentiality clause into the contract. Indeed, some contracts cannot exist and result in a workable relationship between the parties without an implied obligation of confidentiality.[245] Obvious

---

[240] *Thomas Marshall (Exports) Ltd v Guinle* [1979] 1 Ch 227; [1978] 3 All ER 193.
[241] See *Woodward v Hutchins* [1977] 2 All ER 751; [1977] 1 WLR 760.
[242] See *Stephens v Avery* [1988] Ch 449; [1988] 2 All ER 477, *per* Sir Nicholas Browne-Wilkinson V-C at 454 and 481.
[243] [1969] RPC 41 at 47–48.
[244] See *Exchange Telegraph Co v Gregory & Co* [1896] 1 QB 147.
[245] See *Tournier v National Provincial & Union Bank of England* [1924] 1 KB 461.

examples are the doctor-patient relationship and a contract between a manufacturer of a revolutionary new product and its advertising agency. It is equally clear, though, that a contract can also explicitly deny the existence of an obligation of confidentiality.[246]

Confidential information passing between employer and employee

Contracts of employment and the employer-employee relationship present a special case due to the inevitably large amount of confidential information that passes between employer and employee – information about working methods, manufacturing processes, etc. Even though express terms are often found in employment contracts, the courts, in any event, clearly regard the employee as being under a duty of fidelity towards his employer throughout the course of the employment relationship and will use this to enforce the obligation of confidentiality. Secret information that is passed on to the employee in the course of employment is almost inevitably passed on on an occasion of confidence due to the duty of fidelity that the employee is under.[247]

The duty of fidelity may, of course, change when the employee leaves his employment. The employee's duties of confidentiality, while diminishing, do not disappear entirely. It may well be that the contract itself has laid down stipulations as to future conduct, perhaps restricting the nature and location of subsequent work in order to avoid the risk of prejudicial competition or limiting the use that may be made of information learnt during the period of employment. Leaving aside the issue whether such terms could be in restraint of trade and not upheld by the court, the law of confidence may also intervene, irrespective of any contractual provisions. The rules in relation to the post-employment situation were laid down in *Faccenda Chickens* v *Fowler*,[248] where a sales manager, upon leaving the company, set up a rival operation involving a fleet of vans selling fresh chickens. It was alleged that, in doing so, he was using confidential information gained during his employment.

A distinction was made in this case between three types of information. First, there is non-confidential information. This information, for example the look of the vans, is accessible from the public domain. The employee is always free to disclose this information. Secondly, there is the category of trade secrets. These will remain confidential and the employee is not free to disclose them even after leaving his employment. An example could be secret manufacturing processes. In determining whether certain information is a trade secret, consideration should be given to the following: the

---

[246] See *Fraser* v *Evans* [1969] 1 QB 349; [1969] 1 All ER 8.
[247] See *Hivac Ltd* v *Park Royal Scientific Instruments Ltd* [1946] Ch 169; [1946] 1 All ER 350.
[248] [1987] Ch 117; [1986] 1 All ER 617.

nature of the employment; habitual handling of confidential information giving rise to a higher burden on the employee because its importance is more likely to be realized; the nature of the information and the aura of secrecy (or otherwise) which surrounds it; whether the employer has stressed the secret nature of the information; and whether the information is separate or forms an inevitable part of the employee's package of skills which he is entitled to take to his next post. The latter point refers to the third intermediate category. This information is confidential during the period of employment, but it loses its confidential nature once that period of employment has ended. The contents of this category have been described as all elements forming part of the package of skills which the ex-employee brings to the workplace. Obvious examples include the information concerning basic plant or tool operating techniques, or customer information remembered by the ex-employee after he has finished employment. It is clear from the description of these three categories that the category of trade secrets is a restricted one, and in most cases, the ex-employee will not be hindered by an obligation of confidence.

When confidential information is passed on to a third party, that third party is also bound by the obligation of confidence,[249] as long as it is clear when the third party receives the information that it is confidential in nature.[250]

(iii) Unauthorised use of confidential information

This requirement first of all pre-supposes that the information concerned is used. The information gained must at least be usable.[251] However, this might not be sufficient as such. There is also the issue of detriment suffered by the plaintiff. The law is not very clear on this issue,[252] but it is submitted that it is not necessary to show any other detriment than that created by the disclosure of the information *per se*. Of course, evidence of further harm will strengthen the plaintiff's case and damages might only become available if further harm is proved. An injunction though should be available without there being evidence of further harm.

The requirement of unauthorised use is met when the information is used. The law does not require any specific form of use or any intention on behalf of the defendant. What is in the mind of the defendant is not

---

[249] See *Saltman* v *Campbell* [1963] 3 All ER 413n.
[250] See *Fraser* v *Thames Television Ltd* [1984] 1 QB 44; [1983] 2 All ER 101.
[251] See *Amber Size & Chemical Co Ltd* v *Menzel* [1913] 2 Ch 239 and *Fraser* v *Thames Television Ltd* [1984] 1 QB 44; [1983] 2 All ER 101.
[252] See the different views expressed by Megarry J in *Coco* v *A N Clark Engineers Ltd* [1969] RPC 41 at 48 (detriment is an essential part of breach of confidence) and Rose J in *X* v *Y* [1988] 2 All ER 648 (special detriment in the use of the information is unnecessary) and the different approaches taken by the Law Lords in *Spycatcher* [1990] 1 AC 109; [1988] 5 All ER 545.

relevant and subconscious or innocent use of confidential information will also result in the requirement being met.[253]

(b) CLASSIFICATION OF BREACH OF CONFIDENCE

The classification of the action for breach of confidence will determine which jurisdiction rules and, eventually, choice of law rules are applicable to such cases. It is important, therefore, to discuss briefly the nature of an action for breach of confidence in substantive intellectual property law. An obligation of confidence can be created by a clause in a contract. If such an obligation of confidence is subsequently breached, the action that is brought is an action for breach of contract. It is obvious that such an action is classified as contractual. The real classification problem arises, however, in those instances where the breach of confidence is non-contractual.

The action of breach of confidence has its roots in equity. Lord Denning MR argued, in *Fraser v Evans*, that what is involved is an equitable jurisdiction based 'not so much on property or on contract, but rather on good faith'.[254] On the other hand, it must be admitted that it is not clear whether the nature of the action is solely equitable. A certain vagueness surrounds the issue and the concepts involved, and the House of Lords declined to deal with the issue head on in the *Spycatcher* case.[255] It has been suggested that confidential information is really some form of property as it can be licensed, assigned, taxed, etc.[256] The courts have never endorsed this approach without reservations, and often property and equity are mentioned jointly.[257] The main problem with this approach is that a normal property right can be restored fully after having been infringed, while confidentiality cannot be restored once the information has been disclosed publicly without there being any breach of an obligation of confidence.[258] Although clearly showing strong similarities with property rights, it cannot be said that breach of confidence provides some form of property in the information concerned. That property aspect is rather a pre-requisite, the essence of the action is found in the confidentiality aspect and more specifically in the obligation to maintain the confidential nature of the information. The essential element is the destruction of the confidential nature of the information. This rather points towards a tortious classifica-

---

[253] *Seager v Copydex Ltd (No 1)* [1967] 2 All ER 415; [1967] 1 WLR 923.
[254] [1969] 1 All ER 8 at 11, see also *Seager v Copydex (No 1)* [1967] 2 All ER 415 at 417.
[255] *Attorney-General v Guardian Newspapers (No 2)* [1990] 1 AC 109.
[256] See Goff & Jones on *Restitution* (4th ed) p 679 *et seq.*; see also *Prince Albert v Strange* (1849) 2 De Gex & Sim 652, *Dean v Macdowell* (1878) 8 Ch D 345, *Aas v Benham* [1891] 2 Ch 244, *Exchange Telegraph Co Ltd v Howard* (1906) 22 TLR 375 *per* Buckley LJ, *Boardman v Phipps* [1967] 2 AC 46 at 107 *per* Lord Hodson.
[257] See, eg *Fraser v Evans* [1969] 1 QB 349; *Seager v Copydex Ltd (No 1)* [1967] 2 All ER 415 and [1967] 1 WLR 923.
[258] Coleman, *The Legal Protection of Trade Secrets*, Sweet & Maxwell (1992), p 48 *et seq.*

tion. It could be argued that the nature of the action for breach of confidence is the tort of the misappropriation of a trade secret or any other confidential information.[259] The destruction of the confidential nature of the information must be the commission of a wrong. Thus, the action for breach of confidence must, arguably, somehow be tortious in nature. It may be, though, that non-contractual breach of confidence does not fit within any existing category and should be regarded as being *sui generis*. In conclusion, the outcome of this exercise must be that the classification of the action for breach of confidence as a matter of substantive law remains uncertain.

2. How Jurisdictional Problems Arise

A further important issue that arises, in the present context, is whether the various elements of the breach of confidence action need to have been located inside the jurisdiction. This does not seem to be the case. The chances of success of the action for breach of confidence do not depend on the territorial location of the elements required. In this respect, the action for breach of confidence resembles the torts of passing-off, malicious falsehood and defamation, rather than the formal intellectual property rights such as patents, trade marks and copyright. This means that jurisdictional issues will arise whenever elements of the breach of confidence take place in different countries. For example, the confidential information may have been acquired in one country, it may have been used in a second country and the damage may have arisen in a third country. In many breach of confidence cases, there is also more than one defendant. Jurisdictional issues will also arise whenever these defendants are not resident, established or domiciled in the same country.

3. Jurisdictional Provisions

(a) The EC/EFTA Rules

An action for breach of confidence brings into play a wider range of bases of jurisdiction under the Brussels and Lugano Conventions than is the case in a straightforward action in tort or delict, such as one for unfair competition.

(i) Article 2

It is always possible, subject to Articles 16 and 17, for the plaintiff to bring the action in the Contracting State of the defendant's domicile.

---

[259] See North [1972] *JSPTL* 149.

(ii) Article 5

Under English law, the cause of action may be based on a contractual obligation of confidence, or a non-contractual obligation, or on both. But under Article 5 of the Conventions, what is important is not the classification of the cause of action under English law, but whether it is a matter relating to a contract within the meaning of Article 5(1) or a matter relating to a tort, delict or quasi-delict within the meaning of Article 5(3).

(a) *Article 5(1)*

According to Article 5(1) of the Brussels and Lugano Conventions, a defendant can be sued in a Contracting State other than that of his domicile 'in matters relating to a Contract, in the courts for the place of performance of the obligation in question'.

(i) *Matters relating to a contract*

The Court of Justice has held that 'the concept of matters relating to a contract should be regarded as an independent concept which for the purpose of the application of the Convention, must be interpreted by reference chiefly to the system and objectives of the Convention, in order to ensure that it is fully effective'.[260] Those objectives include 'legal certainty, consistency and avoidance of parallel proceedings, and the avoidance of possibly conflicting decisions in different jurisdictions'.[261] The rationale of Article 5 is that there should be, in certain clearly defined situations, 'a particularly close connecting factor between a dispute and the court which may be called upon to hear it, with a view to the efficacious conduct of the proceedings'.[262]

Guidance on the scope of Article 5(1) can also be found in the judgment of the Court of Justice in *SPRL Arcado* v *SA Haviland*,[263] in which it was held that a claim for damages for wrongful repudiation of an agreement was a matter relating to a contract, being based on the failure to fulfil a contractual obligation to give reasonable notice of termination. The defendant's argument that this was a claim based on quasi-delict was rejected. In *Kleinwort Benson Ltd* v *Glasgow City Council*,[264] a majority of the House of Lords, Lords Mustill and Nicholls dissenting, held that a claim for restitution of moneys paid under a purported contract subsequently accepted by both parties as being void *ab initio* did not fall within Article 5(1) of the Modified Convention. It was said that a claim can only come within this

---

[260] Case 34/82 *Martin Peters Bauunternehmung GmbH* v *Zuid Nederlandse Aannemers Vereniging* [1983] ECR 987 at 1001.
[261] See *Kleinwort Benson Ltd* v *Glasgow City Council* [1996] 2 All ER 257 at 273.
[262] The *Martin Peters* case, n 260 above, at 1002. [263] Case 9/87 [1988] ECR 1539.
[264] [1997] 3 WLR 923.

provision if it is based on a particular contractual obligation. The claim for restitution was based upon the principle of unjust enrichment, not on a particular contractual obligation.

In the light of these decisions, it is submitted that an action for breach of confidence based on a contractual obligation of confidence is clearly a matter 'relating to a contract'.

(ii) *The place of performance of the obligation in question*

The plaintiff is able to sue in the courts for the place of performance of the obligation in question. The obligation in question is the one forming the basis of the legal proceedings; the one which the contract imposes on the defendant, the non-performance of which is relied upon by the plaintiff.[265] In an action for breach of confidence, the obligation in question is the defendant's obligation to maintain the confidence; it is a negative obligation not to misuse the information.

Where is the place of performance of this obligation? The court 'must determine in accordance with its own rules of conflict of laws what is the law applicable to the legal relationship in question and define in accordance with that law the place of performance of the contractual obligation in question'.[266] It is not easy to identify the place of performance of a negative obligation. But if you concentrate on the obligation in question as being the one whose non-performance is relied on by the plaintiff, the place of this non-performance is that where the confidence is broken by misusing the confidential information. For example, it is the place where rival equipment is produced or a press conference given.

(b) *Article 5(3)*

If, as a matter of substantive law, a claim for non-contractual breach of confidence is classified as tortious then clearly this is a matter relating to a tort, delict or quasi delict and Article 5(3) comes into play. However, given the uncertain classification of such a claim, the major question that arises is whether Article 5(3) can still apply even though, as a matter of substantive law, the claim is not classified as being tortious. In other words, how wide is the scope of Article 5(3)?

(i) *The scope of Art 5(3)*

The Kalfelis *case.* The starting point of this discussion is the decision of the Court of Justice in *Kalfelis* v *Schröder*.[267] The Court of Justice gave an

[265] Case 14/76 *De Bloos* v *Bouyer* [1976] ECR 1497.
[266] Case 12/76 *Tessili* v *Dunlop* [1976] ECR 1473 at 1485.
[267] Case 189/87 *Athanasios Kalfelis* v *Bankhaus Schröder, Münchmeyer, Hengst and Co and Others* [1988] ECR 5565.

autonomous Community definition to the concept of 'matters relating to tort, delict or quasi delict'. In the first key passage, it was said that this 'must be regarded as an independent concept covering all actions which seek to establish the liability of a defendant and which are not related to a "contract" within the meaning of Article 5(1)'.[268] Read literally, this gives an extremely wide definition to the concept. The case, on its facts, involved a claim for unjust enrichment. Such a claim, according to this literal reading, would come within the scope of Article 5(3), assuming, of course, that it does not come within the community concept of a contractual matter. More importantly from the point of view of intellectual property, it would encompass an action for breach of confidence based on a non-contractual obligation, although not one based on a contractual obligation since this would involve a matter relating to a contract.[269]

The picture is clouded by a further statement of the Court of Justice in the second key passage, which is set out in the next paragraph of their judgment, that 'a court which has jurisdiction under Article 5(3) over an action in so far as it is based on tort or delict does not have jurisdiction over that action in so far as it is not so based'.[270] This could be read as flatly contradicting the wide interpretation of the scope of Article 5(3), and adopting a narrow interpretation, according to which the scope of this provision is confined to torts as strictly understood. It would not cover an action for non-contractual breach of confidence which is classified as other than tortious.

It was not long before the English Courts were faced with these two seemingly inconsistent statements.

Uncertainty in England. In *Barclays Bank plc v Glasgow City Council*,[271] the Court of Appeal was faced with the issue of whether restitutionary claims come within the scope of Article 5(3). It concluded that it is not easy to reconcile the two passages in the *Kalfelis* case, and referred to the Court of Justice the question whether Article 5(3) has an extended meaning in relation to such claims. Essentially, the same question arose subsequently in *Kitechnology BV and Others v Unicor GmbH Plastmaschinen and Others*.[272] This time, the action was for breach of confidence, based on the existence of both contractual and non-contractual duties of confidentiality. The Court of Appeal held that the issue raised as to the scope of Article 5(3) was indistinguishable, in principle, from that raised in relation to restitutionary claims and earlier referred to the Court of Justice. Accordingly, it was impossible to express a concluded view on this issue.[273]

---

[268] Case 189/87 *Athanasios Kalfelis v Bankhaus Schröder, Münchmeyer, Hengst and Co and Others* [1988] ECR 5565 at 5585.
[269] See above, p 432. [270] N 268 above, at 5585. [271] [1994] 2 WLR 466.
[272] [1994] ILPr 568. [273] *Ibid*, at 580.

A decision from the Court of Justice was eagerly awaited. However, those expecting an answer to the present uncertainty have been disappointed. The Court of Justice[274] has declined to give a ruling on the referral from the Court of Appeal in the *Barclays Bank* case. This was on the ground that it had no jurisdiction to do so since that case was an intra-UK one involving interpretation of Article 5(3) of the Modified Version of the Brussels Convention contained in the Civil Jurisdiction and Judgments Act 1982,[275] not a case on the Brussels Convention itself.

Reconciling the statements in Kalfelis. In the absence of a decision from the Court of Justice, the English courts have sought to reconcile the two key passages from the *Kalfelis* case, quoted above, which have caused the difficulty.

Differing views in the Court of Appeal. Leggatt LJ, in a dissenting judgment in *Kleinwort Benson Ltd* v *Glasgow City Council*,[276] the resumed appeal before the Court of Appeal following the decision of the Court of Justice declining to give a preliminary ruling, reconciled the two key passages in *Kalfelis* in the following way. He said that[277] the first key passage was concerned with the question whether the phrase 'matters relating to tort, delict or quasi-delict' must be given an independent meaning or not, whereas the second key passage was concerned with the different question of whether a court which has jurisdiction by virtue of Article 5(3) may adjudicate on the action in so far as it is not based on tort/delict. He concluded that an action based on unjust enrichment is not so based and is, accordingly, outside Article 5(3). This gives a narrow interpretation to the scope of Article 5(3), confining it to torts as strictly understood. It puts the emphasis on the second key passage. The comments of Leggatt LJ are all *obiter* since Lord Justices Roch and Millett came to the conclusion that an action to recover money paid under a contract which was a nullity because of a recipient's lack of capacity to enter into the transaction was 'a matter relating to a contract' within Article 5(1). It was unnecessary for them to discuss Article 5(3), Roch LJ did not do so at all and Millett LJ said that he preferred to express no opinion on the scope of this provision.[278]

In contrast, a differently constituted Court of Appeal, in *Source Ltd* v *TUV Rheinland Holding AG and Others*,[279] after referring to the *Kalfelis* case, held that 'matters relating to tort, delict or quasi-delict' meant 'all actions which seek to establish the liability of a defendant and which are not related to a contract within the meaning of Article 5(1)'. This regards the first key passage in the *Kalfelis* case as laying down the scope of Article 5(3). Although the second key passage is cited, there is no discussion of the problems that this causes and no attempt to reconcile the two key

---

[274] Case C-346/93 *Kleinwort Benson Ltd* v *City of Glasgow District Council* [1995] 3 WLR 866.
[275] See Schedule 4. [276] [1996] 2 All ER 257. [277] *Ibid*, at 266–267.
[278] *Ibid*, at 276. [279] [1997] 3 WLR 365.

passages. The Court of Appeal did not dissent from the view of counsel for the plaintiffs that 'liability', in this context means liability for damage which would exclude, apparently, a cause of action for unjust enrichment.[280]

The House of Lords adopts a narrow interpretation. A majority of the House of Lords, Lords Mustill and Nicholls dissenting, in the *Kleinwort Benson* case,[281] reversed the decision of the Court of Appeal in relation to Article 5(1) and held that a claim for restitution of moneys paid under a purported contract subsequently accepted by both parties as being void *ab initio* did not fall within Article 5(1) of the Modified Convention. More interesting in the present context, their Lordships were unanimous that a claim based on unjust enrichment did not fall within Article 5(3).

Lord Hutton gave the fullest judgment on this point.[282] He started by pointing out that the questions referred to the Court of Justice for a preliminary ruling made it clear that the first key passage was concerned with whether an independent meaning should be given to the term 'tort', and the second key passage was concerned with whether unjust enrichment would come within Article 5(3). This is the same approach towards reconciling the statements as used by Leggatt LJ in the Court of Appeal. He went on to say that 'liability' under the first key passage referred to liability within the scope of Article 5(3), namely liability in 'tort, delict or quasi-delict'. Adding these words to the first key passage, it now reads as follows: 'The term "matters relating to tort, delict or quasi-delict" used in Article 5(3) of the Convention must be regarded as an independent concept covering all actions which seek to establish the liability [in tort, delict or quasi-delict] of a defendant and which are not related to a "contract" within the meaning of Article 5(1)'. This addition highlights the fact that nothing is said about the width of the concept of 'tort, delict or quasi-delict'. The second key statement does this and makes it clear that a claim based on unjust enrichment is not covered.

The judgment of Lord Goff is less satisfactory because he made no attempt to reconcile the two key passages. Nonetheless, he too thought that unjust enrichment fell outside Article 5(3). He said that to argue to the contrary was based on a misreading of the first key passage in the *Kalfelis* case, and that Leggatt LJ was right to reject the argument.[283] This looks to support the judgment of Lord Hutton. He also said that the argument that unjust enrichment fell within Article 5(3) was impossible to reconcile with the words of Article 5(3) 'if only because a claim based on unjust enrichment does not, apart from exceptional circumstances, presuppose either a harmful event or a threatened wrong'.[284] Lord Hutton made the same point.[285] This is a different line of reasoning from that based on an inter-

---

[280] [1997] 3 WLR 365.
[281] [1997] 3 WLR 923.
[282] *Ibid*, at 957–958.
[283] *Ibid*, at 935.
[284] *Ibid*.
[285] *Ibid*, at 958.

pretation of the *Kalfelis* case. The difference can be seen if you think of a claim for non-contractual breach of confidence which is not classified as tortious. Such a claim involves a harmful event and thus would come within Article 5(3) if this was the only criterion for the scope of this provision. On the other hand, applying the *Kalfelis* case, if the claim is not classified as tortious it falls outside Article 5(3). It seems that Lords Goff and Hutton were laying down two requirements. First, it must be a tort in the strict sense; secondly, there must be a harmful event or a threatened wrong. If so, the second requirement appears to be superfluous. If it is tortious in the strict sense, then there will be a harmful event or threatened wrong.

Lord Clyde said the argument that unjust enrichment was within Article 5(3) was based on a misunderstanding of the first key passage in the *Kalfelis* case.[286] Lords Mustill[287] and Nicholls[288] said that, on Article 5(3), they agreed with the views of the other three Law Lords.

Concurrent actions in contract and tort. The *Source* case adds a further twist to the saga. The case involved allegations of breach of contract and breach of a duty of care in failing to exercise reasonable skill and care in the preparation and supply of reports as to the quality of goods purchased by the plaintiffs. It was held that both causes of action were excluded from the scope of Article 5(3) because both related to a contract within Article 5(1).[289] This follows Dicey and Morris.[290] Staughton LJ, Waite and Aldous LJJ concurring, said[291] that 'a claim which may be brought under a contract or independently of a contract on the same facts, save that the contract does not need to be established, is, in my judgment, excluded' from the scope of Article 5(3). This goes further than was necessary on the facts in front of the court. It makes clear that if the cause of action in the *Source* case had only been pleaded in tort, as opposed to tort and contract, the matter would still be regarded as related to a contract because the parties have a contractual relationship and the claim could have been brought under the contract. What Article 5(3) is concerned to exclude are matters related to a contract rather than causes of action in contract.[292]

Is this decision affected by the House of Lords' judgment in the *Kleinwort Benson* case? The *Source* case was not referred to by the Law Lords. This is not surprising: the *Source* case was dealing with a very different situation. Nonetheless, following *Kleinwort Benson*, there is some uncertainty over whether the *Source* case was correctly decided. It is doubtful whether the court with jurisdiction under Article 5(1) can try the

[286] *Ibid*, at 947–948. [287] *Ibid*, at 936. [288] *Ibid*, at 940.
[289] *Ibid*, at 371. But compare *Minster Investments Ltd v Hyundai Precision & Industry Co Ltd* [1988] 2 Lloyd's Rep 621.
[290] At p 362. [291] N 279 above, at 371.
[292] N 279 above, at 371–372. See also *Kleinwort Benson Ltd v Glasgow City Council* [1996] QB 678 at 698.

tort claim. The majority of the House of Lords gave a narrow interpretation to the scope of this provision. Moreover, Lord Goff[293] said that the view of Advocate General Darmon in the *Kalfelis* case, that where there were concurrent claims in contract and tort both would be channelled into Article 5(1), had been rejected by the Court of Justice in that case. Lord Clyde[294] also thought that the *Kalfelis* case did not adopt this view. Lords Goff and Clyde both appear to envisage that concurrent claims may have to be split amongst the courts of different Contracting States, and that this can be avoided by bringing the whole claim in the Contracting State in which the defendant is domiciled. Can the tort part of the claim be tried in the place of the harmful event under Article 5(3)? If, as the House of Lords requires, you home in on the second key passage in the *Kalfelis* case defining the scope of Article 5(3), this can be read as excluding from the scope of this provision a concurrent action in tort and contract. This is consistent with the overall interpretation of *Kalfelis* adopted in the *Source* case. But if the tort part of the concurrent claim in contract and tort cannot be tried in the place of the harmful event under Article 5(3), then the House of Lords needs to rethink its view on channelling of actions under Article 5(1), at least in the situation where there are concurrent actions in tort and contract. Otherwise, you get the result that the tort part does not come under either Article 5(1) or Article 5(3), which is revolting to common sense. It is one thing to say that restitution does not fall within either provision but to conclude that a tort claim does not do so, simply because it is concurrent with a contract claim, cannot be right.

Application in cases of breach of confidence. The first situation to be considered is where there is no contractual relationship between the parties. The claim has to be based on non-contractual breach of confidence. If, as a matter of substantive law, a claim for non-contractual breach of confidence is classified as tortious, then Article 5(3) will apply.

The second situation is where there is no contractual relationship between the parties. If, as a matter of substantive law, the claim for non-contractual breach of confidence is not classified as tortious then Article 5(3) will not apply because of the interpretation given to the *Kalfelis* case by the House of Lords in the *Kleinwort Benson* case. If, as can happen,[295] the plaintiff brings an action for passing-off and for non-contractual breach of confidence, jurisdiction is allocated to the courts of the place where the harmful event occurred in relation to the former but not in relation to the latter. Splitting the litigation in this way is not in the interests of the parties or the good administration of justice.

The third situation is where there is a contractual relationship between the parties and the claim is for both contractual and non-contractual

---

[293] N 281 above, at 930. [294] *Ibid*, at 946.
[295] See, eg *Advanced Portfolio Technologies Inc v Ainsworth* [1996] FSR 217.

breach of confidence. Let us assume that the non-contractual part is classified, as a matter of substantive law, as tortious. The contractual part of the claim is clearly excluded from the scope of Article 5(3), as is the tortious part, according to the *Source* case. Moreover, following the *Kleinwort Benson* case in the House of Lords, it appears that the tort part of the claim cannot be channelled within Article 5(1).

The fourth situation is where there is a contractual relationship between the parties and the claim is for both contractual and non-contractual breach of confidence. Let us assume that the non-contractual part is classified as being other than tortious. The contractual part of the claim is clearly excluded from the scope of Article 5(3), as is the non-contractual part as a result of the interpretation given to the *Kalfelis* case by the House of Lords in *Kleinwort Benson*.

The fifth situation is where there is a contractual relationship between the parties but the plaintiff's claim is based solely on non-contractual breach of confidence. According to the *Source* case, this situation is to be treated the same as that where the claim is for both contractual and non-contractual breach of confidence. In other words, if the non-contractual part of the claim is classified as tortious, then situation three applies. If it is classified as other than tortious, then situation four applies.

(ii) *The place where the harmful event occurred*

In the situation where claims based on non-contractual duties of confidentiality come within the scope of Article 5(3) (ie the first of the situations listed above), it is necessary to ascertain the place where the harmful event occurred. There was lengthy discussion in the *Kitechnology* case, in the Court of Appeal, of the question of whether, even if non-contractual claims come within the scope of Article 5(3), the plaintiffs could show that the harmful event had occurred in England. On the assumption that Article 5(3) applied, it was accepted by the Court of Appeal that the definition in the *Mines de Potasse* case would operate. The English courts would, therefore, have jurisdiction if either England was the place of the event giving rise to the damage or the damage occurred in England.

The place of the event giving rise to the damage. It is submitted that the event giving rise to the damage is the use of the confidential information in an unauthorised way. If you look at the substantive law of breach of confidence, this is the only element that consists of an act by the defendant. To give some examples, it is telling the press the confidential information that a doctor has aids, rather that its subsequent publication, that constitutes the event giving rise to the damage. It is the production of the TV series which is based on someone else's ideas, told in confidence to the producers. If, in the first example, the press are told in England, or, in the second example, the programme is produced in England, there is jurisdiction by virtue of Article 5(3), over a defendant domiciled in another Contracting State.

A definition in terms of the use of the confidential information in an unauthorised way is supported by comments made in the Court of Appeal in the *Kitechnology* case. The complaint against the defendants was that they had used the plaintiffs' confidential information in order to develop and manufacture equipment for the manufacture of composite pipe, manufacture and deal in such pipes, and had disclosed the plaintiffs' confidential information by supplying equipment embodying the whole or part thereof to third parties. It was accepted by the Court of Appeal that it was these activities that constituted the events giving rise to the damage, but that since there was no evidence that any of the alleged activities complained of had taken place in England, there was no jurisdiction on this basis.[296]

The place where the damage occurred. Damage, for this purpose, could be defined in terms of the confidentiality of the plaintiff's information, the plaintiff's commercial interests, or direct economic loss to the plaintiff.

Confidentiality of the plaintiff's information. This treats confidential information almost as a type of property which has been damaged by the breach of the duty of confidentiality. This is the thing that most obviously and directly has been damaged by the defendant's activities. It fits in with the English concept of detriment, according to which mere disclosure of confidential information itself constitutes a detriment.[297]

Where does this damage occur? Does it occur in every Contracting State in which the information was capable of being exploited by the plaintiff, or only in the Contracting State(s) in which the defendant has actually exploited or disclosed the information? Millett J, at first instance, in the *Kitechnology* case,[298] adopted the first of these two alternatives taking jurisdiction on the basis that the destruction of the confidential nature of information caused damage to the owner in his ability to exploit that information in his domestic market in England. The Court of Appeal rejected the assertion of jurisdiction on this basis. It was pointed out that there was no evidence and no suggestion that the defendants had publicised the information either in England or elsewhere, or that they had breached the alleged confidentiality otherwise than by exploiting it in Germany.[299] This could be read as implicitly accepting that damage in the form of the confidentiality of the plaintiff's information being breached takes place in the Contracting State(s) in which the defendant has actually exploited or disclosed the information. However, what the Court of

---

[296] N 272 at 581.
[297] See the *Spycatcher* case: *Attorney-General* v *Guardian Newspapers No 2* [1990] 1 AC 109 at 256 (*per* Lord Keith).
[298] [1994] ILPr 560.
[299] *Ibid* at 582.

Appeal appears to have preferred was a concept of damage based on the fact that the defendant's commercial interests have suffered.

The effect on the plaintiff's commercial interests. The Court of Appeal, in the *Kitechnology* case, accepted that jurisdiction could be based on damage directly caused to the plaintiffs' commercial interests in England. However, on the facts of the case, there was no evidence that the plaintiffs' commercial interests had suffered in *England*. It would have been otherwise if the defendants were alleged to have imported into England pipes or machinery which they had produced in breach of confidence in Germany or elsewhere. The commercial interests of the plaintiffs would also be adversely affected if the value of their rights as licensor had been reduced, but this again would have required imports into England.

Direct economic loss. The advantage of basing jurisdiction on direct economic loss suffered in the forum is that the same rule applies in relation to various forms of tortious protection of intellectual property rights. This means that a plaintiff who brings an action based on unfair competition and breach of confidence will be able to proceed, in respect of both claims, before the courts in the one Contracting State. Where direct economic loss is established, ie by loss of business, there is no doubt that it is also possible to say that the plaintiff's commercial interests have been adversely affected. It follows that the adoption of the definition of damage preferred by the Court of Appeal would come close to the adoption of a direct economic loss rule. However, the two are not necessarily the same. It may be possible to show that the plaintiff's commercial interests have been adversely affected without proof of direct economic loss. Indeed, the examples given by the Court of Appeal of damage to the plaintiff's commercial interests involve this situation. Thus, a mere showing of import of goods produced in circumstances involving a breach of confidence would be enough.

The Court of Appeal, in the *Kitechnology* case, accepted that, for the purpose of Article 5(3), damage does not include indirect damage,[300] a point subsequently decided definitively by the Court of Justice in the *Marinari* case.[301] On the facts of the *Kitechnology* case, there may have been indirect repercussions in England from the defendants' activities abroad, but this was not enough to found jurisdiction.

Conclusion. The *Kitetechnology* case, in the Court of Appeal, indicates that damage occurs in the Contracting State where there is damage directly caused to the plaintiff's commercial interests in that State.

---

[300] *Ibid* at 581; following Case 220/88 *Dumez France and Tracoba* v *Hessiche Landesbank* [1990] ECR 49.
[301] N 76 above.

(iii) Article 17

A contract which establishes the duty of confidentiality may contain an agreement on jurisdiction. An agreement coming within Article 17[302] confers exclusive jurisdiction on the courts of the Contracting State chosen by the parties, provided that one of them is domiciled in an EC/EFTA Contracting State.

(iv) Consolidating the litigation

From the plaintiff's point of view, the vital thing is to be able to bring the action in respect of both contractual and non-contractual matters before the courts of one Contracting State. Indeed, it is not in the interests of either party that the claims should be split between courts in different Contracting States. The plaintiff can consolidate the litigation if he relies upon Article 2 or 6(1) (but probably not Article 5(1)[303]) of the Brussels or Lugano Convention, or if Article 17 applies.

(a) *Article 2*

It is always possible, subject to Articles 16 and 17 of the Conventions, to bring an action before the courts of the Contracting State of the defendant's domicile, which can consider the whole of the action regardless of whether it involves a contractual or non-contractual matter or both.

(b) *Article 6(1)*

Likewise, if Article 6(1) applies, the court can consider the whole of the action regardless of whether it involves a contractual or non-contractual matter or both.

(c) *Article 17*

The courts of the Contracting State on which jurisdiction is conferred by virtue of Article 17 will be able to try the whole of the action, in respect of both contractual and non-contractual matters, provided that the agreement as to jurisdiction covers such matters. It is a question of construction whether an agreement as to jurisdiction under Article 17 includes the claims or causes of action upon which the plaintiff relies.[304] An agreement as to jurisdiction may be construed so as to cover not only claims in con-

---

[302] See Cheshire and North, pp 315–322. [303] See above, pp 437–438.
[304] The *Kitechnology* case, n 272 above, at 575.

tract but also claims in tort,[305] or non-contractual claims for breach of confidence.[306]

In the *Kitechnology* case, the first and second defendants entered into two jurisdiction agreements, one of which provided that 'the parties hereto thereby submit to the exclusive jurisdiction of the English courts'. The action for breach of confidence was based on contractual and non-contractual duties of confidentiality. There was no definition of the kinds of dispute agreed to be so referred. Nonetheless, the Court of Appeal came to the conclusion that 'the express jurisdiction clauses in the present case include not only claims for breach of the relevant contract, but also other claims which are so closely connected with them that the parties can properly be taken to have intended that they should be decided by the same tribunal.'[307] Applying this test, it was decided that the English courts had exclusive jurisdiction over claims alleging misuse of confidential information by the first and second defendants, regardless of whether the claims were formulated in contract or otherwise. Seemingly, it would have been different if the non-contractual claim had stood on its own. It was said that the non-contractual claims must be connected with the contract, which postulates that there is a contractual claim.[308] There was a further difficulty in relation to the scope of the submission. Was it limited to claims in respect of the confidential information made available to the first and second defendants in 1988/89, around the time of the agreements being entered into, or were further developments covered? The plaintiffs were allowed to redraft their statement of claim to clarify this.[309]

(b) THE TRADITIONAL RULES

(i) The heads of Order 11, rule 1(1)

If a writ has to be served out of the jurisdiction under Order 11, rule 1(1), the cause of action is crucial if, as commonly happens, reliance is to be placed on the tort or contract heads. It is important to distinguish three situations: the first is where an action for breach of confidence is based on a contractual obligation; the second is where it is based on a non-contractual obligation; the third is where it is based on both contractual and non-contractual obligations.

(a) *A contractual obligation*

In the situation where an action for breach of confidence is based on a contractual obligation, the case may well come within one of the contract

[305] *Continental Bank NA v Aeakos Cia Naviera SA* [1994] 1 WLR 588, CA.
[306] The *Kitechnology* case, n 272 above.   [307] *Ibid*, at 576.   [308] *Ibid*.
[309] *Ibid* at 576–577.

heads of Order 11, rule 1(1)[310] and the plaintiff can seek the court's permission for service of the writ out of the jurisdiction on a foreign defendant.

(b) *A non-contractual obligation*

(i) *The tort head*

The tort head of Order 11 rule 1(1) requires that 'the claim is founded on a tort'.[311] Given the uncertainty in the substantive law on the classification of non contractual breach of confidence, there must be a serious doubt over whether such a claim can be so classified.

Nonetheless, if, as a matter of substantive law, a claim for non-contractual breach of confidence is classified as tortious then, clearly, the claim is founded on a tort and the tort head can be used. The English courts will have jurisdiction under this head if there was an act of breach of confidence within the jurisdiction or damage was sustained within the jurisdiction. Applying the analogy of the position under Article 5(3) of the Brussels and Lugano Conventions, it is submitted that an act of breach of confidence is committed within the jurisdiction if confidential information is used in an unauthorised way in England. Again, applying the analogy of Article 5(3), it is submitted that damage is sustained within the jurisdiction if there was damage to the plaintiff's commercial interests in England.

What if confidential information is regarded as a form of property? The better view is that it should not be so regarded. However, if this were to happen, what you would have would be tortious damage to property. This would not affect the identification of the act of breach of confidence; this could still be regarded as the use of the confidential information in an unauthorised way. It could affect, though, the identification of the damage. The argument could be made that damage was to property and this was sustained where the property (ie the confidential information) was situated. This would be difficult to identify. Moreover, it would be taking a very different line from that taken in the *Kitechnology* case in relation to Article 5(3).

If, as a matter of substantive law, a claim for non contractual breach of confidence is classified as equitable or as being *sui generis*, then it appears that the tort head of Order 11, rule 1(1) cannot be used in a case involving such an action. There is no authority to suggest that a tort under this jurisdictional provision means anything other than a tort as strictly understood.

[310] Order 11, rule 1(1)(d) and (e); discussed above. [311] Order 11, rule 1(1)(f).

In some circumstances, it may be possible to come within the scope of the tort head of rule 1(1) by framing the cause of action as one of detention and wrongful interference. This is what happened in *Beecham Group plc and Another v Norton Healthcare Ltd and Others*.[312] The English plaintiff brought an action for breach of confidence and interference with goods against the English importer and the Slovenian supplier/manufacturer of medicinal tablets, claiming that the latter had come by a confidential production strain allegedly stolen from the plaintiffs and was the user and receiver of this stolen property. The claim for wrongful interference with the plaintiff's property was undoubtedly tortious and, accordingly, came within the scope of the tort head of rule 1(1). However, service out of the jurisdiction under this head was not possible because the Slovenian defendant had committed no act of wrongful interference in England, neither had this defendant directly caused damage in England. The direct damage to the plaintiff would be caused by the sale of the finished product in England by the English defendant, not the manufacture and use (wrongful interference) of the plaintiff's property in Slovenia.[313]

(ii) *The multi-defendant head*

Of the other heads of Order 11, rule 1(1), the multi-defendant head can be used in an action for non-contractual breach of confidence provided that the defendant out of the jurisdiction is a necessary or proper party to the claim brought against the person duly served within or out of the jurisdiction. In the *Beecham* case, it was possible to use this head to obtain leave to serve the Slovenian defendant out of the jurisdiction. The latter was a necessary and a proper party to the proceedings for breach of confidence against the English defendant. The Slovenian defendant was the supplier and a participant in a common design with the English defendant and was deeply concerned with the marketing of the tablets in England. The Slovenian defendant was a necessary and proper party in a patent infringement action brought against the English defendant. If the Slovenian defendant were not a necessary and proper party to the breach of confidence claim 'it would mean that a foreigner with stolen confidential information could get his products into the United Kingdom without our courts being able to touch him and without his United Kingdom customer being able to defend the proceedings properly'.[314]

(iii) *The injunction head*

The injunction head can be used if 'an injunction is sought ordering the defendant to do or refrain from doing anything within the jurisdiction (whether or not damages are also claimed in respect of a failure to do or

[312] [1997] FSR 81. [313] *Ibid* at 97–98. [314] *Ibid* at 97.

the doing of that thing)'.[315] It was not possible to use this head in the *Beecham* case in respect of the Slovenian defendant because, although an injunction was sought in relation to this defendant, it was the English defendant that was going to be doing all the relevant acts within the jurisdiction.[316] According to Jacob J, the mere fact that the defendants had a common design did not mean that they were both planning to do something here.

(iv) *The constructive trustee head*

The constructive trustee head can be used where 'the claim is brought for money had and received or for an account or other relief against the defendant as constructive trustee, and the defendant's alleged liability arises out of acts committed, whether by him or otherwise, within the jurisdiction'.[317] Under English law, a holder of confidential information will hold any profit made from misuse of that information as a constructive trustee, provided that the information can be regarded as property.

(c) Both contractual and non-contractual obligations

If the plaintiff can manage to obtain jurisdiction on the basis of service of the writ within the jurisdiction, he can consolidate the litigation in England, relying upon the breach of both contractual and non-contractual obligations. If service of the writ has to be effected out of the jurisdiction, it may be necessary to split the claims with the result that the contractual part of the action can be heard in England, but not the non-contractual part. If service abroad is permissible under the contract head, the action being in contract, the plaintiff is not allowed to add on a claim for breach of a non-contractual obligation when leave to serve a writ out of jurisdiction would not have been given for this.[318] It is to be noted that an English choice of jurisdiction clause, which does not satisfy the requirements for jurisdiction under Article 17 of the Conventions,[319] even if it is worded so as to encompass non-contractual disputes, will not enable such claims to be tried in England by virtue of Order 11, rule 1(1)(d)(iv).[320] This allows for service of a writ out of the jurisdiction where the contract 'contains a term to the effect that the High Court shall have jurisdiction to hear and determine any action in respect of the contract'. But like all the other sub-heads of rule 1(1)(d), it only applies where 'the claim is brought to enforce, rescind, dissolve, annul or otherwise effect a contract, or to recover dam-

---

[315] Order 11, rule 1(1)(b).   [316] N 312 above, at 96–97.   [317] Order 11, rule 1(1)(t).
[318] *Waterhouse* v *Reid* [1938] 1 KB 743; *The Siskina* [1979] AC 210.
[319] Eg neither of the parties is domiciled in an EC/EFTA Contracting State.
[320] Compare the position under Article 17, and see the *Kitechnology* case, discussed above, p 443.

ages or obtain other relief in respect of the breach of contract'. A non-contractual claim, even if added on to a contractual claim cannot be so regarded.

(ii) The forum conveniens discretion

The *Beecham* case is a good illustration of the *forum conveniens* factors that can be involved in a breach of confidence claim. Jacob J listed seven such factors. First, all the relief claimed (including an injunction against importation) related to activity planned for or intended to take place in the United Kingdom. Secondly, there was jurisdiction over the English defendant and it could not defend the case without the presence of the Slovenian defendant. Thirdly, the question of what organism was used by the Slovenian defendant was already in issue on the patent side of the case. Fourthly, the Slovenian defendant was acting in concert with the English defendant. Fifthly, in substance the Slovenian defendant wanted to do business in England – to have their tablets sold in England. They could hardly complain if the English court claimed jurisdiction in respect of that. Sixthly, it was not suggested that there was any procedural advantage in proceedings in Slovenia. Whereas here the plaintiff had all the advantages of discovery and interrogatories which English procedure provided. Seventhly, the case was well on the way to trial in England. The learned judge thought that these reasons (particularly the first, second, third and fifth) militated strongly in favour of the United Kingdom being the *forum conveniens* and leave would be given for service out of the jurisdiction.[321] On the facts, it was an obvious case for an English court to try. As Jacob J pointed out it would be unfortunate for an English court to decline jurisdiction 'in a case where a foreign manufacturer, using stolen information, was using a United Kingdom importer to get his tainted product onto the United Kingdom market. And all the more so when the information was stolen from this country in the first place'.[322]

IX
REFORM

There are no special EC/EFTA or traditional rules as to jurisdiction in relation to passing-off, malicious falsehood, defamation, unfair competition, wider Continental protection in delict, breach of competition rules or breach of confidence. The question then is whether special rules should be

---

[321] N 312 above, at 99. The case concerned an application for leave to amend a statement of claim and so the question was whether leave would be granted if an application under Order 11 were made now.
[322] *Ibid*, at 99.

introduced. Before answering this, it is necessary to examine what is wrong under the existing law.

1. CRITICISM OF THE EXISTING LAW

The problems in relation to all of these causes of action tend to focus round Article 5(3) of the Brussels and Lugano Conventions and the tort head of Order 11, rule 1(1). These problems are particularly acute in England because of the lack of a substantive law of unfair competition, resulting in the substantial number of different complementary causes of action that may be used.

The first criticism of the existing law is its uncertainty. With many of these causes of action, it is not clear what the damage is for the purpose of Article 5(3) and the tort head of Order 11, rule 1(1), and where it occurs. There is uncertainty over whether Article 5(3) and rule 1(1)(f) can be used in cases of non-contractual breach of confidence because of the uncertain classification of this cause of action as a matter of substantive law. There is uncertainty over the application of Article 5(3) to certain forms of unfair competition.

Secondly, jurisdiction will depend on which cause of action is used. This is because, for example, the place of the event giving rise to the damage has been defined differently in cases of passing-off from in cases of unfair competition even where it takes the form of passing-off. Even more striking is the fact that, under Article 5(3), an action for defamation of a business competitor will probably raise the principles in the *Shevill* case, whereas an action for unfair competition in the form of defamation of a business competitor probably will not. In short, with complementary torts there is a lack of uniformity as to jurisdiction. There are two reasons why uniformity is desirable in relation to all the causes of action dealt with in this chapter. First, it recognises that they all have something in common; namely, they are all complementary to the tort of infringement. Secondly, it is convenient that there should be the same jurisdictional result, regardless of which cause of action is relied upon, particularly when a claim may be based upon parallel causes of action.

The third criticism is that the inappropriate connecting factor of damage is used in defamation cases, where, although it is possible to identify damage, this is much more contrived than in cases where the tort has as one of its constituent elements physical damage or pecuniary loss. Even worse, the definition of damage used in defamation cases is, according to the *Shevill* case, concerned with an abstract matter of lost reputation. But in cases of defamation of a business competitor, the motivation behind the action will be that of lost sales. Nonetheless, under the present law, the inappropriate *Shevill* definition of damage will probably apply to a case of defamation of a business competitor. In contrast, the tort of unfair competition, which can take the form of defamation or disparagement of a competitor in relation to his business, has damage as one of its constituent elements and, accordingly, this is an appropriate connecting factor for jurisdictional purposes. Moreover, in cases of unfair competition, including cases where this takes the form of defamation of a business competitor, it is possible to adopt a definition of damage which focuses on lost business, which reflects the commercial reality.

2. Comparison with Infringement

Although the present law is open to criticism, to give the matter some perspective it should be noted that, from a jurisdictional point of view, there are two clear advantages in basing an action on one of these complementary causes of action rather than on infringement. First, there is none of the uncertainty you get when invalidity is raised as a defence to infringement. Secondly, under the traditional rules, there are no subject matter limitations in relation to jurisdiction. For example, jurisdiction is available in respect of acts of passing-off committed abroad or damage to goodwill situated abroad, provided that there is jurisdiction over the defendant.

3. Reform of the Jurisdictional Rules of General Application

It has been suggested, in the context of infringement, that probably the best option for reform is to have special jurisdiction rules for infringement cases, rather than attempt the much more difficult task of reform of the jurisdictional rules of general application, thereby affecting other causes of action. What we now have to discuss, therefore, are special jurisdictional rules for complementary torts and other causes of action. This does not necessarily mean having a special rule for each separate cause of action, since it would be possible to have a rule just for unfair competition, as widely defined.

4. Special Jurisdictional Rules

(a) THE PRELIMINARY QUESTIONS

(i) Rules for different causes of action or just for unfair competition?
It is important to separate out jurisdiction under the EC/EFTA rules and jurisdiction under the traditional English rules.

(a) The EC/EFTA rules

There is a number of compelling reasons why there should be one special rule in relation to unfair competition, rather than a series of rules for the different complementary torts.

First, Continental Contracting States are familiar with the concept of unfair competition, but not with the separate English nominate torts of passing-off, malicious falsehood and defamation. It would be much more difficult for them to accept a series of special rules based on these alien causes of action than a single rule based on unfair competition. At the same time it would be possible to define 'unfair competition' in such a way as to make clear that it encompasses these English nominate torts.[323]

Secondly, having a single special rule for unfair competition would greatly simplify the law.

Thirdly, having a special jurisdictional rule for unfair competition, as widely defined, would achieve uniformity as to jurisdiction. It would mean the same result in relation to jurisdiction, regardless of the cause of action.

Fourthly, it would enable the concept of 'damage' to be used as a connecting factor. This would be an appropriate connecting factor, given the significance of this concept in the substantive law of unfair competition. It would also allow this concept to be defined in a way that reflects commercial reality.

Fifthly, there has been much discussion in Europe of special choice of law rules for unfair competition and there are precedents available for such rules,[324] including a provision within the Swiss Private International Law Statute of 1987.[325] A special jurisdictional rule would complement these developments.

(b) The traditional rules

When it comes to the traditional English rules on jurisdiction, the position is more complicated. It would be possible to introduce a series of special rules for the separate causes of action dealt with in this chapter. However, this would not address the lack of uniformity under the present law and would also open up a gap between the position under the EC/EFTA rules and that under the traditional rules. It would be much better, under the traditional rules, to adopt the special rule for unfair competition developed for use under the EC/EFTA rules.

---

[323] See below, pp 707–708. [324] See below, pp 707–713.
[325] Article 136; discussed below, pp 711–713.

(ii) Independent rules or within the framework of existing rules?

It would be possible to have independent jurisdictional rules dealing with unfair competition, which could be contained in an EC Convention. This Convention could deal solely with unfair competition and operate in parallel with an EC Convention dealing with infringement and other issues or as part of one big Convention on private international law aspects of intellectual property rights. Having independent rules in a Convention would allow space for the introduction of a definition of unfair competition. Fixing upon such a definition is not as difficult as might be thought and there are various precedents available both in national laws and under international agreements.[326] For example, there is a Resolution of the Institute of International Law on the Conflict of Laws Rules on Unfair Competition. This is concerned with choice of law and adopts the definition of unfair competition set out in Article 10*bis* of the Paris Convention for the Protection of Industrial Property,[327] ie 'any act of competition contrary to honest practice in industrial or commercial matters'. It then supplements this basic definition by giving examples of such acts.[328] This definition is extremely wide and would, doubtless, cover situations coming within the English nominate torts of passing off, malicious falsehood and defamation. Moreover, given that there are in existence independent choice of law rules for unfair competition,[329] to do the same for jurisdictional rules is not quite as revolutionary as might at first sight appear.

A less radical approach would be to introduce special rules within the framework of existing jurisdictional rules. This solution has the virtue of familiarity. Moreover, the problems at the moment are largely in relation to the tort head under the EC/EFTA rules and the English traditional rules. It would be possible to simply alter Article 5(3) of the Brussels and Lugano Conventions and Order 11, rule 1(1)(f), inserting a special rule for unfair competition. The mechanism for effecting this change would, though, be different in the case of alterations to Article 5(3) from that of alterations to rule 1(1)(f).[330] The latter can be altered fairly easily. Alterations to the Conventions are a more difficult matter. However, the Diplomatic Conference to be held in 1998 to review the operation of the Brussels and Lugano Conventions could recommend the addition to Article 5(3) of a special rule for unfair competition.

---

[326] See below, pp 707–708. [327] See above, pp 409–410. [328] See below, p 409.
[329] See below, pp 707–713. [330] See above, p 315.

(b) THE SUGGESTED RULES

(i) Unfair competition

The suggested rule to replace Article 5(3) and Order 11, rule 1(1)(f) in unfair competition cases, as widely defined, would be the same regardless of whether it would operate as part of independent rules or within the framework of existing rules. The same rule should also be adopted under the EC/EFTA rules and the traditional rules on jurisdiction.

(a) *Where the act of unfair competition occurred*

The suggested rule is that jurisdiction should be available in the State where the act of unfair competition occurred. Unfair competition, of course, can take many different forms. It would be important to look at which form, and which country's law, was being relied upon by the plaintiff. There is, at the moment, some guidance from Continental courts in relation to the place of the event giving rise to the damage under Article 5(3) in cases involving certain forms of unfair competition.[331] Such cases can be used to determine where the act of unfair competition occurred. However, there is no such guidance in respect of unfair competition in the form of defamation of a business competitor or improper advertising.[332] A special rule could resolve this uncertainty. Looking at some of the common forms of unfair competition, it is submitted that the act of unfair competition should be regarded as taking place in the following States: where it takes the form of passing-off, in the State where the imitation product was marketed; where it takes the form of spreading false and disparaging information, in the State where the false and disparaging statement is spread; where it takes the form of defamation of a business competitor, in the State from which the letter is posted, or from which copies of the newspaper are sent, or from which the broadcast is transmitted; when it takes the form of improper advertising, in the State where the advert was placed.

(b) *Where the resulting damage occurred*

Jurisdiction should also be available in the State where the resulting damage occurred. This is an appropriate connecting factor to use in cases of unfair competition. Identification of the place where the damage occurred is much easier than that of the place where the act of unfair competition occurred; it is submitted that this should be defined, as it is under the pre-

---

[331] See above, pp 411–412.
[332] See the suggestions for appropriate rules, above, pp 411–412.

sent law,[333] in terms of the place where the plaintiff has suffered direct economic loss, ie, normally, where he has lost sales.[334]

(ii) Non-contractual breach of confidence

Breach of confidence, as arguably the one action that does not lie in tort, not surprisingly raises different problems from those encountered in relation to all the other actions. In so far as the action is based on contract, it raises the possibility, under both the EC/EFTA and the traditional rules, of bases of jurisdiction geared to contract being used. In cases where there is no contractual relationship between the parties, it is suggested that the law should be changed so that Article 5(3) is available in relation to actions for breach of confidence based on non-contractual obligations even if these are not classified as tortious. Under the traditional rules on jurisdiction, Order 11, rule 1(1)(f) should be extended to cover this situation.

---

[333] See above, pp 412–414.   [334] For an exception, see above, p 413.

SECTION II

THE APPLICABLE LAW

Preliminary Remarks

I Choice of law rules	455
II Mandatory rules of the forum	456

I
CHOICE OF LAW RULES

Once a court has decided that it possesses jurisdiction, it must move on to the next stage of determining the law applicable to that case, ie which State's substantive law governs. This is of vital importance. To illustrate this, we can take the example of unfair competition. The plaintiff complains that disparaging remarks have been made about his product. Under Swiss substantive law, there is an actionable tort of unfair competition, whereas under English law there is not. It follows that the plaintiff will recover damages if Swiss law is applied, but fail to do so (at least for breach of unfair competition law) if English law is applied. In order to determine whether English substantive law or that of a foreign State applies, resort has to be made to choice of law rules. Choice of law rules are expressed in terms of juridical categories, such as tort and contract, and connecting factors, such as the place where a contract was made or where a tort was committed.[1] To take an example, there is a choice of law rule that succession to immovable property is governed by the law of the *situs*. The juridical category is succession to immovable property, the connecting factor is the *situs*.[2] There are different choice of law rules for different juridical categories. The choice of law rules for contract are very different from those for tort, and both of these are very different from those for property. The first step in the process of ascertaining the applicable law is, therefore, to classify, or, as it is sometimes called, characterise the cause of action, ie allocate the question raised in a particular case to its correct legal category.[3] Once this has been done, it is possible to move on to the next step of applying the appropriate choice of law rule. It is not only important to classify the cause of action, it is also important to classify the precise issue arising before the court. The significance of the issue can be seen by looking at the contract choice of law rules. If the issue is that of formal validity of a contract, a different choice of law applies from that where the issue is that of capacity to contract. The choice of law rule is different again where the issue is that of interpretation of the contract. Application of the

---

[1] Dicey and Morris, p 34.   [2] *Ibid*.   [3] Cheshire and North, p 44.

appropriate choice of law rule enables the court to ascertain the applicable substantive law.

In intellectual property cases, the process of classification can raise some difficult problems. Is there an existing category of choice of law rules within which the issues of creation, scope and termination of intellectual property rights fit? It is questionable whether these issues fit properly within the category of property. Moreover, a property classification raises the question, familiar to us from the discussion of jurisdiction, of whether intellectual property is immovable property. With contracts in relation to the exploitation of intellectual property rights, which issues are contractual, and thus for the contract choice of law rules, and which are concerned with the right itself, and thus for the choice of law rules that deal with creation? How is infringement of intellectual property rights, which is a statutory cause of action, to be classified for choice of law purposes? Is it tortious? If not, what is it? Moving on to causes of action which are complementary to infringement, how is breach of confidence to be classified? All of these questions will be examined in the following chapters.

Finally, a brief word needs to be said about the sources of the English choice of law rules. There is no single source. The property choice of law rules are largely based on case law. The contract choice of law rules are now largely Europeanised, and are contained in the Rome Convention on the law applicable to contractual obligations of 1980, implemented in the United Kingdom by the Contracts (Applicable Law) Act 1990. The fact that we are dealing here with harmonised European law adds an extra dimension to the issue of classification. In contrast, tort choice of law has not been Europeanised. After recent reform, this is now largely put on a statutory basis. Case law, statutes and EC Conventions on private international law are standard sources of rules on private international law. However, two further possible sources of choice of law rules are special to intellectual property. These are the international conventions and the European Community Regulations and Directives on intellectual property. These need to be examined to see whether they contain any direct or indirect choice of law rules. This will be done in chapter 9.

II
MANDATORY RULES OF THE FORUM

A court may end up applying local substantive law, not because it is the governing law under a choice of law rule, but because it is what is called a mandatory rule. The Law Commissions have described mandatory rules of the forum as substantive rules which 'are regarded as so important that as a matter of construction or policy they must apply in any action before a court of the forum, even where the issues are in principle governed by a foreign law selected by a choice of law rule'.[4] The statutory choice of law rules in relation to contracts and torts both contain provisions preserving the mandatory rules of the forum. The concept is most highly developed in contract cases and, in chapter 11, which is concerned with the applicable law in relation to contracts for the exploitation of intellectual property rights, the difficult question of the identification of mandatory rules will be examined in detail. This concept is particularly likely to come into play in intellectual property cases because of the links between intellectual property law and competition law and because of the fact that the substantive law is territorially limited in its scope, protection only being provided in respect of local rights and, normally, only in respect of local infringements as well.

---

[4] Law Commission Working Paper No 87 (1984), para 4.5.

9

Choice of Law Elements in the Intellectual Property Conventions

I	Introduction	460
	1. How do choice of law issues arise?	460
	2. Why look at international Conventions?	460
	3. No straightforward answers in the Conventions	461
II	The Berne Convention 1886	462
	1. Qualification rules	462
	(a) The scope of the Convention	462
	(b) How choice of law problems arise	465
	2. Which law applies to qualifying works?	466
	(a) Does the qualification rule include a choice of law?	466
	(b) Determination of the applicable law	467
	3. National treatment	468
	4. Restrictions on the application of the law of the protecting country	469
	(a) A role for the law of the country of origin	469
	(b) Minimum protection granted by substantive rules	471
	5. An alternative interpretation	472
	(a) Bilateralisation of the unilateral conflict rules	472
	(b) A restrictive interpretation of Article 5(2)?	473
III	The Rome Convention 1961	476
	1. Qualification	476
	2. National treatment and the law of the protecting country	476
IV	Paris Convention for the protection of industrial property 1883	477
	1. National treatment	477
	2. The law of the protecting country	477
V	International co-operation agreements	479
VI	Supra-national intellectual property rights	479
VII	The TRIPs Agreement	480
	National treatment	480

I
INTRODUCTION

1. How Do Choice of Law Issues Arise?

Intellectual property rights have been regulated internationally by many Conventions. These Conventions are the obvious places to start the search for choice of law rules. They might contain a harmonised uniform set of rules for the protection of intellectual property rights. It will soon become clear that such a system, that removes the need for choice of law rules, never was a realistic goal for the draftsmen of these Conventions, but maybe the Conventions contain choice of law rules or elements that may facilitate the choice of such rules. When the Conventions deal, for example, with the exclusive rights that are granted to the patentholder, they might, in the absence of a single harmonised rule that covers this substantive point, contain a rule which decides which national patent law will decide which exclusive rights the French owner of a German patent will receive when he applies in Germany on the back of his original French patent. If the connecting factor is the origin of the patent, French law might be applied, while German law might be applied if the connecting factor is the place of registration of the patent. Do the relevant Conventions contain a choice of law rule to solve this issue?

2. Why Look at International Conventions?

A preliminary point that should retain our attention, though, is concerned with the justification for looking at the Conventions. From a theoretical perspective, we could point out that English law does not allow us to look at and give value to international Conventions, because such Conventions do not have force of law[1] in the absence of implementing legislation. Maybe our analysis ought to focus immediately on the relevant domestic statutes, while leaving the provisions of the Conventions temporarily on one side, before coming back to them when interpretative difficulties arise. It is suggested that there are good reasons to depart from this approach and discuss the provisions of the Conventions first, since most domestic statutes are, in part, based on these Conventions and are supposed to implement their provisions.

Intellectual property is almost international by definition. The vast majority, for example, of patents, such as those for new drugs, are

---

[1] See, eg *Att-Gen for Canada* v *Att-Gen for Ontario* [1937] AC 326, PC and *British Airways Board* v *Laker Airways Ltd* [1985] AC 58, at 83; Dicey and Morris, *The Conflict of Laws*, Stevens (11th ed, 1987), at p 8.

exploited worldwide. The same goes for copyright. It may well be that copies of this book will be sold in many different countries. It is vital, in this context, that the owner of the patent in a new drug can stop a foreign company from copying the drug, while the owners of the copyright in this book might also want to claim royalties for each copy that is sold abroad. On the other hand, most national intellectual property statutes seem to ignore the international dimension. They only contain substantive rules. The national statutes are supposed to be the national implementation of the provisions of the Conventions. Parliament has taken upon itself an obligation under public international law to implement the Conventions. If we accept that it lived up to its obligation when it drafted the national intellectual property statutes,[2] we are allowed to turn to the Conventions' provisions for clarification on how to interpret the domestic provisions in an international context. We suggest that it is worthwhile to discuss first, in detail, which system is concealed in the provisions of the Conventions. This will guide our discussion in the next chapter of the national rules of private international law in relation to the creation, scope and termination of intellectual property rights, which should be in conformity with these private international law related provisions. And as the provisions of the Conventions are implemented in various countries, a desirable uniform interpretation[3] can only be achieved if proper attention is paid to the provisions of the Conventions. A uniform set of conflicts rules would also be beneficial for the international exploitation of intellectual property rights.

All the international Conventions which will be analysed below have been implemented by statute. The text of the Conventions, though, was not included in these statutes, but that no longer stops the courts from looking at these Conventions when interpreting the provisions of the statute, even if the statute does not refer to the Conventions and even if it is not ambiguous.[4]

3. NO STRAIGHTFORWARD ANSWERS IN THE CONVENTIONS

However, the Conventions do not address the issue straightforwardly, and it is fair to say, in advance, that they do not contain any specific and complete choice of law rules. They only address the issue partially. Good examples are the national treatment rules in most of the Conventions. They are not complete choice of law rules that are needed to solve the choice of law issues, but their obligation to treat nationals and foreigners in the same way gives a first indication of the situations in which the

---

[2] Dicey and Morris, n 1 above, at p 10.   [3] Dicey and Morris, n 1 above, at p 9.
[4] *Ibid*; *James Buchanan & Co Ltd* v *Babco Forwarding and Shipping (UK) Ltd* [1978] AC 141, at 152 *per* Lord Wilberforce; *Salomon* v *Commissioners of Customs and Excise* [1967] 2 QB 116, at 141 and *The Banco* [1971] P 137, at 151 both *per* Lord Denning MR.

domestic national law will apply.⁵ Private international lawyers could turn this into a unilateral conflicts rule and try to bilateralise it afterwards. We now turn to the analysis of these 'partial' Convention rules.

II
THE BERNE CONVENTION 1886

1. QUALIFICATION RULES

The Berne Convention deals with copyright and it does not require any registration or other formalities for copyright to exist. An important issue is to know which authors and which works will qualify for protection under the Convention's provisions, because in spite of the large number of countries adhering to the Berne Union not all countries are Member States. Intellectual property lawyers are familiar with this point and describe it as qualification. An author or a work has to meet the qualification requirements before any copyright can be granted. These requirements are really criteria of eligibility for protection. The Convention provides for a number of connecting factors which link the author and/or his work to a Member State. Protection can be claimed if one of these connecting factors is satisfied.

(a) THE SCOPE OF THE CONVENTION

These provisions, primarily, determine the scope of the Convention. 'The factors linking the author to a *country* of the Union are in no respect connecting principles as regards the applicability of the *law* of that country.'⁶ When confronted with a work, the first issue that is to be determined is whether it comes within the scope of the Berne Convention and will, as such, attract copyright protection. This is what is being done at this qualification stage. Once the work comes within the scope of the Berne Convention, the Convention will guarantee it a minimum level of protection.

(i) **The relevant connecting factors**

(a) *Nationality*

The nationality of the author is the first connecting factor that is mentioned in Article 3 of the Convention. Copyright protection is granted to all the

---

⁵ See Locher, *Das Internationale Privat- und Zivilprozessrecht der Immaterialgüterrechte aus urheberrechtlicher Sicht*, Schulthess Polygraphischer Verlag (1993), at p 7.
⁶ Boytha, (1988) 24 *Copyright* 399, at 407.

works of an author who is a national of one of the Member States of the Berne Union. These works even include works which are published in a country that is not a Member State and unpublished works.[7] The nationality rules have been revised at the Stockholm Revision Conference.

Authors who have their habitual residence in a Member State are now assimilated to nationals if they do not possess the nationality of one of the Member States.[8] The connecting factor can now be redefined as nationality or habitual residence. The Convention does not deal with the issue when nationality or habitual residence is determined. Does the existing work of an author who abandons his nationality of a non-Member State in favour of that of a Member State, or who at least becomes habitually resident in a Member State, qualify for protection from that moment onwards, for example? And does it lose its protection when the author gives up the nationality of and habitual residence in a Member State? All these issues are left to the national courts and the law that they will apply, although they may wish to be guided by the Report on the Work of the Main Committee at the Stockholm Revision Conference which seems to prefer that the existence of nationality or habitual residence is determined at the time when the work was first made available to the public.[9] This interpretation is to be supported as it creates legal certainty for the users of the work. They can determine at the time when the first use of the work becomes possible whether they have to take account of copyright, and that certainty cannot be undermined by later changes in the nationality or habitual residence of the author of which users are not necessarily aware and which they cannot reasonably be expected to keep track of.

(b) *First publication of the work in a Member State*

First publication of the work in a Member State forms the second connecting factor that is mentioned in Article 3. Simultaneous publication in a non-Member State and in a Member State within a 30-day period is assimilated to first publication in a Member State.[10] This connecting factor operates independently and no further requirements, for example related to nationality, have to be satisfied. The Convention defines what amounts to publication by describing published works as 'works published with the consent of their authors, whatever may be the means of manufacture of the copies, provided that the availability of such copies has been such as to satisfy the reasonable requirements of the public, having regard to the nature of the work'.[11] It needs to be added, though, that the scope of this second

---

[7] Article 3(1)(a) Berne Convention.   [8] Article 3(2) Berne Convention.
[9] Report on the Work of the Main Committee I, paras 29 and 30, Stockholm Conference 1967. This does not even have to involve first publication as defined by the Convention.
[10] Article 3(1)(b) Berne Convention.   [11] Article 3(1)(3) Berne Convention.

connecting factor is restricted significantly by the fact that the Convention goes on to exclude from the definition of publication '[t]he performance of a dramatic, dramatico-musical, cinematographical or musical work, the public recitation of a literary work, the communication by wire or the broadcasting of a literary or artistic work, the exhibition of a work of art and the construction of a work of architecture'.[12]

(c) Headquarters or habitual residence of the maker of a cinematographic work

Article 4 of the Convention adds two narrow connecting factors, which can apply even when the criteria of Article 3 are not met. The first of these is that the authors of a cinematographic work will enjoy protection if the maker of that cinematographic work has either his headquarters or his habitual residence in a Member State.

(d) Headquarters or habitual residence of architects, etc

Article 4 goes on to provide the same protection to authors of works of architecture if the work has been erected in a Member State and to authors of artistic works that have been incorporated in a building or another structure that is located in a Member State. This is the second narrow connecting factor.

(ii) Which connecting factor takes priority?

The above four connecting factors establish a link between the work and a Member State of the Berne Union. A connecting factor will indeed select a particular Member State each time it is applicable. That Member State is the country of origin of the work. There are, of course, cases in which more than one connecting factor is applicable and as it is desirable to determine a single country of origin for each work, the Convention contains rules as to which connecting factor will take priority.[13] It is necessary to determine first of all whether a work has been first published in a Member State. If that is the case, the country of first publication will be the country of origin of that work, regardless of the fact that the author of the work may be a national of another Member State or that he may be habitually resident in another Member State. In cases of simultaneous publication, priority is given to the Member State whose legislation grants the shortest term of protection. It is obvious that the country of origin will be the Member-State country in those cases in which the other country of simultaneous publication is a non-Member State. Only if the work has not been published or

---

[12] Article 3(1)(3) Berne Convention.   [13] Article 5(4) Berne Convention.

if it has been published in a non-Member State, without there being any simultaneous publication in a Member State, does the Convention turn to nationality and habitual residence. Even then, the two narrow connecting factors that are contained in Article 4 take priority if their requirements are met. The preference for the work-orientated publication connection is fully justifiable and has been summarised neatly by Schack in the following terms:

> ... the author's right in his published work becomes a distinct subject of legal relations, separated from the person in whom it has been vested; the work-orientated connection (with a particular country) corresponds to this fact. The personal statute[14] of the author is largely unknown to the public, to which it is the use of the work that comes into prominence.[15]

It is indeed much easier for those using the copyright work to determine where it was first published. This enhances legal certainty and it facilitates the exploitation of the work.

(b) How Choice of Law Problems Arise

Once the work comes within the scope of the Berne Convention and is given an entitlement to protection, the next step is to know the exact format the protection will take in each of the Member States and it is only here that the real choice of law issue arises. After having dealt with qualification in Articles 3 and 4, the Convention turns to this next step in Article 5.

Qualification only leads to a distinction between two categories of works: those works that come within the scope of the Convention and those works that fall outside that scope. The Convention no longer deals with the latter category of works, but we now have to see how it will deal with those works that come within its scope. One option, which would have excluded all choice of law problems, would have been the introduction of a harmonised uniform statute on copyright, but the Convention did not chose that option. The Convention contains instead guidelines for the provisions of the national copyright statutes and an attempt to create an international system of copyright protection is made through rules that guarantee works some form of protection in all Member States. The next step is to detemine which law will apply to the exact format of that

---

[14] Which depends on factors such as nationality or habitual residence.
[15] Translated from German by Boytha (1988) 24 *Copyright* 399, at 408); the original German quote '... dass ein solches Urheberrecht ein von der Person seines Trägers losgelöster selbständiger Gegenstand des rechtsverkehrs ist. Die Person des Urhebers tritt demgegenüber zurück. Dieser Tatsache entspricht eine werkbezogene Anknüpfung. Das Personalstatut des Urhebers ist der Öffentlichkeit weitgehend unbekannt; für sie steht die Nutzung des Werkes im Vordergrund.' has been taken from Schack, *Zur Anknüpfung des Urheberrechts im internationalen Privatrecht*, Duncker & Humblot (1979), at p 50.

protection, as there are differences between the copyright statutes of the Member States. Choice of law issues that arise include the question what amounts to a work and the question of which exclusive rights are given to the owner of the copyright in the work. Does the creation have to be original, and does 'original' mean 'of artistic value', before a creation amounts to a work and before it will be given copyright protection? A clear example of a situation in which it does matter which national copyright law is applicable is found in the *Warner Brothers Inc v Christiansen* case[16] that came before the Court of Justice. The case was concerned with the rental of a videocassette that contained the latest James Bond movie 'Never Say Never Again'. At that time, English copyright law did not give the owner of the copyright in the work any right in the rental of the work (financial compensation whenever the cassette is hired by a customer at a videoshop), while the Danish copyright statute provided the owner with a right to authorise or refuse rental and a right to a royalty whenever the cassette was hired out. Mr Christiansen bought the cassette in London and used it for rental in his shop in Denmark. Could Warner Brothers stop him from doing so? And could they claim royalties? It is obvious that the answer to these questions will be different depending on whether English or Danish copyright law is applied.[17]

2. WHICH LAW APPLIES TO QUALIFYING WORKS?

(a) DOES THE QUALIFICATION RULE INCLUDE A CHOICE OF LAW?

The qualification round left us with the country of origin of the work. The work is, first of all, granted protection in that country. This protection in granted under the provisions of the domestic law of the country of origin. These provisions apply in the same way to an author who is not a national of that country, but whose work has that country as its country of origin, as they do to national authors.[18] It is perhaps tempting to derive from this rule the proposition that the work will enjoy the same copyright protection in all other Member States because the full level of protection has now been determined,[19] but this interpretation is irreconcilable with the presence and the wording of Article 5(1). Article 5(1) takes us, indeed, one step further once we have determined that the work qualifies and once the level of protection in the country of origin has been determined. On the back of these first two steps, the Convention goes on to grant the work

---

[16] Case 158/86 [1988] ECR 2605.
[17] This example leaves on one side the exhaustion issue that arose in this context in the Court of Justice.
[18] Article 5(3) Berne Convention.
[19] See, eg Koumantos, [1979] *Il Diritto di Autore* 616 and (1988) 24 *Copyright* 415; H Schack, *Zur Anknüpfung des Urheberrechts im internationalen Privatrecht*, Duncker & Humblot (1979).

protection in all other Member States. The level of protection in all those States is not to be determined by the law of the country of origin. That law is not even referred to in Article 5(1). Instead, the text of that Article refers to the fact that the work will in each of these countries benefit from the same level of protection that is granted to national authors[20] under their respective laws. Also the fact that there was a need to add another specific rule in Article 5(1) demonstrates that another law or other laws will be applicable outside the country of origin.

(b) DETERMINATION OF THE APPLICABLE LAW

How will this applicable law or laws be determined? Article 5(2) points towards the law of the protecting country (*lex loci protectionis*) when it provides that '. . . apart from the provisions of this Convention, the extent of protection, as well as the means of redress afforded to the author to protect his rights, shall be governed by the laws of the country where protection is claimed'. This law of the protecting country is the law of the country in which the work is being used,[21] in which the exploitation of the work takes place.[22] This follows from the logic of the Convention. What is being determined in Article 5 is the substantive level of protection for those works that have previously qualified for protection under the Convention. The substantive right and the conditions under which the work can be used have to be determined first. The Convention was not concerned primarily with enforcement, it set out to establish an international comprehensive legal system of lawful uses of works. Obviously, once the content and the extent of the right in a particular country have been defined, the infringing acts follow logically, as do the sanctions that go with them. All this constitutes a unity.[23] The alternative minority interpretation, that the law of the protecting country refers to the country where the author is involved in legal proceedings[24] and the suggested link with the law of the forum, cannot be accepted in the light of these facts. Neither can the law of the protecting country be seen as an application of the law of the place

---

[20] This reference to nationality needs to be seen in the light of the heavy emphasis the original version of the Convention placed on nationality as a connecting factor (eg habitual residence was only added in 1967).
[21] See Ulmer, *Intellectual Property Rights and the Conflict of Laws*, Kluwer & Commission of the European Communities (1978), at p 11.
[22] See also Ginsburg [1994] *La Semaine Juridique* 49 (Doctrine 3734).
[23] See the expertise ('Stellungname des Max-Planck-Institut für ausländisches und internationales Patent-, Urheber- und Wettbewerbsrecht zur Ergänzung des Internationalen Privatrechts ausservertragliche Schuldverhältnisse und Sachen') of the Max Planck Institute for Foreign and International Patent, Copyright and Competition Law, [1985] GRUR Int 105, at 106.
[24] See Koumantos, [1979] *Il Diritto di Autore* 616, at 635–636 and (1988) 24 *Copyright* 415, at 426.

where the tort was committed (*lex loci delicti commissi*) rule,[25] as we are not, primarily, concerned with infringement, but rather with any form of exploitation or use of the copyright work.

Where would all this lead us in a practical case? If, for example, a book was first published in Germany, it will be protected under German copyright law in Germany because this is the country of origin of the work. When copies of the book are subsequently sold in England, English law will be applicable, for example, to the issue whether the sale of copies of the work forms part of the exclusive right of the copyright owner, because it constitutes the law of the protecting country.[26] English law will also apply to the infringement issue when substantial parts of the book are copied in England and this will even be the case if the Dutch defendant is sued in the Dutch court of his domicile. If the infringing works are to be seized, this seizure should take place according to the English law of the protecting country. The latter point is the logical solution and is expressly contained in Article 16 of the Berne Convention.

3. National Treatment

Articles 5(1) and 5(3) add an additional instrument of protection by securing national treatment for the foreign author both in the country of origin and in the country where protection is sought. National treatment is enjoyed for each work which qualifies for protection under the Convention. This comes on top of the fact that the law of the protecting country applies in each case.[27]

The difference between the situation in the protecting country and that in the country of origin is that Article 5(1) requires that, in the protecting country, the substantive harmonised rights that are contained in the Convention itself are applied to foreign works on top of the national treatment that is given to them and of the law of the protecting country that is applied to them. Article 5(3) contains no such rule in relation to the country of origin. This leads to two conclusions. First, the substantive rights granted by the Convention cannot be claimed, as such, in the country of origin and the domestic works could eventually be given a lower level of protection. And secondly, the Convention does not regulate the situation where the country of origin is dealing with a work whose author is a national of the country of origin or is habitually resident in that country.

---

[25] See Koumantos, (1988) 24 *Copyright* 415, at 426.
[26] Compare Plaisant's summary in *Juris-Classeur*, Fasc 23, N 37: '... l'oeuvre donne naissance à un droit d'auteur dans chaque pays où elle est exploitée, et ce droit est exclusivement régi par la loi de ce pays ...'.
[27] In the country of origin the domestic law is in ultimate analysis also the law of the protecting country, see Boytha, n 6 above, at 409.

Returning to national treatment, it can be seen that Article 5 of the Convention applies this principle, in practice, by granting the same rights to foreign authors as to national domestic authors. The use of the word 'rights' has certain implications. In practice, it means that the author is given a separate right in each protecting country, and one in the country of origin as well. These rights are identical to the national right which each country grants to its own authors. These various rights which the author is granted are independent of each other and the author ends up with a bundle of national (copy-)rights. International exploitation of the work, such as the international distribution of computer programs or films, will have to take all these separate national rights into consideration. Another implication of the use of the term 'right' is the exclusion of *renvoi* and private international law in general. The author is granted rights, whereas rules of private international law do not grant rights to the national and/or the foreign author. They just determine the jurisdiction of the courts and the applicable law. Any use of renvoi would, indeed, have made the practical operation of this area of law in cases of international exploitation, such as those mentioned above, unduly complicated and burdensome. The normal exploiter would be unable to determine quickly which rights he had to take into account.[28]

The undeniable consequence of this analysis is that the proposition, that the national treatment requirement is also met solely by applying the same choice of law rules to all creators,[29] has to be rejected. This clearly does not go far enough. The same substantive 'rights' have to be given to the creators.

4. Restrictions on the Application of the Law of the Protecting Country

(a) A role for the law of the country of origin

The Member States to the Berne Convention were not prepared to agree to full national treatment without retaining some corrective mechanism in the situation when one of them offered much lower national standards of protection. The old principle of reciprocity, which had blocked the efficient international protection of copyright works, was not abandoned fully. In this exceptional situation, the law of the protecting country is still applied, but it is applied as amended in the light of the extent of protection granted by the law of the country of origin (*lex loci originis*). The existence of some form of protection under the law of the country of origin does not become the most important point that is decisive for the grant of any

---

[28] Article 5(1) Berne Convention; see also Boytha, n 6 above, at 410.
[29] As advocated by Walter (1976) 89 *RIDA* 45, at 47.

protection in the other Member States under their respective laws (of the protecting country). The law of the country of origin operates at a later stage to take away or reduce the protection that is available under the law of the protecting country.[30]

A first example of this approach is found in Article 2(7) in relation to industrial design and models. The Convention leaves it to its individual Member States to decide whether or not they will offer a special regime of protection for industrial design and models. Irrespective of the situation in the country of origin, the law of the protecting country will apply. No foreign author is entitled to any right that does not exist nationally under the law of the protecting country.[31] This special situation arises when the country of origin grants protection only under a special regime and excludes general copyright protection. In such a case, the work will only receive the special protection which is available in the protecting country. If no special regime exists, though, it will receive copyright protection as an artistic work.[32] The alternative would have been no protection at all, but that would have been an unduly harsh decision, especially as the Convention aims to expand the international protection of works. That major aim should not be jeopardised due to the lack of agreement on harmonising to a greater extent the area of industrial design and models.

A second and even clearer example deals with the term of copyright protection. This matter of the duration of the right granted to the author clearly comes under the law of the protecting country. But some Member States may grant, under their national laws, a longer term of protection than the minimum term imposed by the Convention. This improvement in the protection of authors and their works should not be stopped by the unwillingness of other Member States to join this development, whilst the Member States that extend the duration of the protection might not want to grant this extension to foreign authors without receiving anything in exchange for its own authors.[33] The Convention provides for the application of the law of the protecting country to the issue of the term of protection, but it allows Member States to limit the term of protection to the term granted in the country of origin.[34] Such a rule might also encourage other

---

[30] See See Bergé [1996] *Revue Critique de Droit International Privé* 93 (annotation of the judgment of 19 September 1994 of the Court of Appeal Paris, *Masseaut and Another* v *Interidées*, reported immediately above on pp 90–93), at 95.

[31] *Ibid*.

[32] See in France judgment of 12 October 1971 of the Court of Appeal Lyon, *Thomasson*, [1972] *Revue Critique de Droit International Privé* 482 (with annotations by Françon); judgment of 14 March 1991 of the Court of Appeal Paris, *Almax International*, [1992] *JCP* éd G II 21780 (with annotations by Ginsburg) and [1992] *Clunet* 148 (with annotations by Pollaud-Dulian).

[33] Ulmer, n 21 above, at 29, goes as far as to state that this involves a partial reference to the law of the country of origin on top of the basic reference to the law of the protecting country in conflict of law terms.

[34] Article 7(8) Berne Convention; see also Ginsburg, n 22 above, at 49.

Member States to grant a longer term of protection, as their own authors will want to benefit from the extended protection abroad and they may put pressure on their national authorities. The rule does not apply when the term of protection under the law of the protecting country is shorter than the one granted by the law of the country of origin. In the latter case, the basic rule that the law of the protecting country governs the term of protection applies without restrictions. More importantly, this rule only touches upon the term of certain rights and not upon the existence or grant of these rights. This means that Article 7(8) cannot be used to argue that the term of protection should be reduced to zero in cases where there is no identical right in the country of origin.[35]

A third example concerns the provision on the *droit de suite*.[36] This right, basically, gives the author of an original work of art or a manuscript a right to share in the return of any later sale of the original copy of the work. The law of the protecting country is applicable, as the right is integrated into copyright by Article 14ter of the Berne Convention.[37] In practice, this means that the author will only be granted a *droit de suite* if the law of the protecting country creates one, which is not obligatory under the Convention, and the extent of the *droit de suite* will be the extent given to it by the provisions of the *lex loci protectionis*. This is all just an application of the normal rule. There is, though, an additional requirement in respect of the *droit de suite* that is to be given to a foreign author in the situation where the law of the protecting country contains a *droit de suite*: the law of the country to which the author belongs must permit this.[38] In the situation where no *droit de suite* can be claimed in the latter country, the author will not be entitled to a *droit de suite*.[39] Once more, a reciprocity rule is added to the principle of national treatment and the applicability of the law of the protecting country.[40]

(b) MINIMUM PROTECTION GRANTED BY SUBSTANTIVE RULES

The Berne Convention also imposes a minimum level of protection through the introduction of certain substantive rules.[41] Examples of the latter include the standard minimum term of protection for the life of the author plus 50 years (Article 7(1)) and the exclusive right for authors of

---

[35] The independence of the rights is not affected; see also Boytha, n 6 above, at 411.
[36] Article 14ter Berne Convention.
[37] See Doutrelepont, *Le droit et l'objet d'art: le droit de suite des artistes plasticiens dans l'union européenne. Analyse juridique, approche économique*, Bruylant and LGDJ (1996), at pp 69–74.
[38] Article 14ter(2) Berne Convention.
[39] See Ulmer, n 21 above, at 29.
[40] See also Katzenberger [1983] *IPRax* 158, at 160.
[41] See, eg Articles 2, 2(6), 2bis, 3(3)(4), 5(4), 6bis, 7, 7bis 8, 9, 10, 11, 11bis, 11ter, 12, 14, 14bis, 14ter(1), 15, 16(1), 18 and 21 Berne Convention.

literary and artistic works to authorise translations of their work during that term of protection (Article 8). This move should not be seen as restricting the application of the law of the protecting country.[42] When the law of the protecting country goes further and offers a higher level of protection than the minimum level set out in the Convention, the law of the protecting country applies unreservedly and without any restriction.[43]

5. An Alternative Interpretation

(a) bilateralisation of the unilateral conflict rules

Problems arise because the Berne Convention does not contain specific and clear choice of law provisions. Its provisions could be seen as unilateral conflict rules[44] which only determine when domestic law applies to foreigners. These rules leave open the question of which law will be applied when the domestic law is not applicable. The next step then is to examine how these unilateral conflict rules can be turned into multilateral or true choice of law rules which would also deal with the latter issue.[45] This can generally be done by means of bilateralising the unilateral choice of law rule. Thus, if the rule is that all works produced nationally are protected by the domestic law, then this rule can be bilateralised, leading to the conclusion that the applicable law is the law of the country where the work was produced.[46] Accordingly, the country of origin becomes the main connecting factor and the applicable law is the law of the country of origin. Under the Berne Convention, the unilateral choice of law rule is found in Article 5(3), which leads to the application of the law of the country of origin.

Special rules which lead to the application of other laws in relation to specific issues should then be seen as exceptions to this basic choice of law rule. In relation to issues of infringement of the author's rights, the law of the country where the infringement takes place should, exceptionally, be

---

[42] Bergé, n 30 above, at 98 argues, in this respect, that the original importance in the Berne Convention of the law of the country of origin was based upon the fact that a right could only be exercised in a third State once it had been granted in the State of origin. A certain logic leads in such a situation to the law of the country of origin defining the content of the right. That logic is no longer valid after the various revisions of the Berne Convention granted more and more minimum substantive rights. The rights in a third country depend now to a far lesser extent on the law of the country of origin than they do on the minimum substantive rules. These minimum rules form, *de facto*, part of the law of the protecting country. All this clearly reduces the strenght of the arguments that favour the choice of the law of the country of origin as the applicable law.

[43] Article 19 Berne Convention.

[44] These rules answer the question, 'When does the system of law of which the statute forms part apply?', Dicey and Morris, n 1 above, at p 17.

[45] On the distinction between unilateral and multilateral conflict rules, see *ibid*.

[46] See Koumantos, (1988) 24 *Copyright* 415, at 418.

applied and the law of the country of which the author is a national should be applied to the issue of the content of moral rights[47] and to the issue of unpublished works for which, in the absence of any publication, no country of origin can be determined in the normal way.[48]

If it is accepted that the correct interpretation of the provisions of the Berne Convention is to start from the unilateral rule in Article 5(3) and bilateralise it to arrive at a basic choice of law rule that the law of the country of origin is normally the applicable law,[49] then the national treatment rule and the rule in Article 5(2) must be given a different interpretation to the one given above. National treatment means that foreigners are assimilated to nationals. If one emphasises and sticks to this principle and ignores the use of the word 'right' in Article 5(1), one can arrive at the conclusion that complete assimilation includes subjecting foreigners to the rules of private international law,[50] although these rules, strictly, do not grant any rights. This would mean that the national treatment rule does not influence the determination of the applicable law, but rather stipulates only that the law applicable to foreigners and nationals should be determined in the same way by the law of the forum when a dispute arises.[51]

(b) A RESTRICTIVE INTERPRETATION OF ARTICLE 5(2)?

(i) The arguments in favour

Turning to Article 5(2), an attempt can be made to give this provision a restrictive interpretation. According to the wording of the Convention, the main rule in Article 5(2) is that there will be no formalities for the enjoyment and the exercise of the rights that are granted on the basis of the Berne Convention. Directly linked to that is then the rule in the same Article of the Convention that the existence of protection will be independent from the existence of protection in the country of origin. This independence could be restricted to the formalities point, as that point is made in the first part of the sentence in which the independence point is mentioned. Protection in all other Member States would then, following such a restrictive interpretation, exist independent of formalities that might be required in the country of origin. The third rule in Article 5(2) then refers to the application of the law of the country where protection is claimed in relation to the extent of protection and the means of redress. The use of the word 'consequently' seems to indicate that this flows from the two

---

[47] At least if one accepts that they are linked to the author's personality rights, rather than constituting an element of copyright; see Koumantos, (1988) 24 *Copyright* 415, at 427.
[48] In the absence of publication, an identification of the country of first publication, leading to the determination of the law of the protecting country, is impossible.
[49] See Schack, [1985] *GRUR Int 523*, at 525.   [50] See Schack, n 15 above, at 33.
[51] Koumantos, (1988) 24 *Copyright* 415, at 419 and 426–427.

previous rules, but that link is denied by those who advocate this alternative interpretation of Article 5(2).[52] They deny any proper meaning to the connecting word 'consequently'.[53] In their view, the applicability of the law of the protecting country is by no means a consequence of the first two paragraphs of Article 5. According to this view, a general choice of law rule pointing towards the law of the protecting country does not exist.

More important, in their view, is the full text of this third rule. The law of the country where protection is claimed applies to two issues, the means of redress and the extent of protection. The meaning of the latter term is seen as different from the word 'right' or the words 'extent of rights'.[54] It seems to assume that a right exists and that its scope, term and owner have been defined. Extent of protection would then refer to the sanctions that are available for the infringement of this right. This is different also from the conditions under which protection is made available, as it refers only to the consequences of copyright infringement.[55] 'Means of redress' refers, in this view, solely to rules of procedure in relation to the means available for the copyright owner to bring a claim in the courts of a country.[56] Article 5(2) and its reference to the country where protection is claimed can, in this interpretation, be seen as a provision dealing with the situation where infringement of copyright takes place. Any reference to rules of procedure must clearly lead to the law of the forum being the law of the country where protection is claimed and that would fit in with the interpretation given to the term 'extent of protection'.[57] This view leads to the conclusion that Article 5(2) does not contain a general conflict of laws rule, which deals with more than just sanctions and enforcement, and that the only remaining general rule must be that the law of the country of origin is applicable.[58] However, it is necessary to add that both points require the bilateralisation of the unilateral conflicts rules that are contained in the Convention.

(ii) The arguments against this restrictive interpretation

It is submitted that this restrictive interpretation cannot be accepted. The text of Article 5(2) is clearly not confined only to dispute related situations. For example, the term 'enjoyment of right' cannot be restricted to cases where the right is in dispute, it must also include the conditions under which peaceful enjoyment of the right can take place. There is also the interpretation given to the national treatment provision and the word 'right'. Rules on private international law are not 'rights' granted to the author and cannot be included. And national treatment does not go

---

[52] See, eg Schack, n 15 above, at 28 and Koumantos, (1988) 24 *Copyright* 415, at 424.
[53] Koumantos, *ibid*, at 424.
[54] Schack, n 15 above, at 28–29.
[55] Schack, *ibid*, at 30.
[56] Schack, *ibid*, at 28–29.
[57] Schack, *ibid*, at 30.
[58] Koumantos, (1988) 24 *Copyright* 415, at 424.

further, according to Article 5 itself, than the grant of certain rights. It is submitted that the interpretation outlined above[59] is more in conformity with the text and purpose of Article 5.

It might be argued that the alternative restrictive interpretation has the advantage that it would lead to the application of the law of the country of origin to a work, irrespective of the place of its exploitation. Thus, the same law would govern the work all over the territory of the Member States of the Berne Union. Even if one were to accept, for the sake of argument, that this outcome would not be affected seriously by the many exceptions to the law of the country of origin rule that are contained in the Convention, it must be doubted whether the application of a single law to a work is really an advantage. Indeed, it would lead to a situation where different copyright systems would govern different works in the same country, depending on their respective countries of origin. This, in turn, would lead to substantial problems for those who exploit these rights, as they need to know the country of origin of each work and they need to have a detailed level of knowledge of a, potentially, very large number of national copyright regimes.

This is clearly born out by the experiences under the Montevideo Convention. This Convention was signed in 1889 and its membership was not limited to American States, as several European States became members too. Article 2 is relevant for the purpose of the present analysis. It gives rights to authors which they enjoy in each Member State and it does so on the basis of the country of first publication of the work (the law of the country of origin). This law should be applied *ex officio* by the judge hearing the case and Member States undertake to exchange copies of their respective laws. Nevertheless, it is fair to say that the system never worked and the Convention has, in practical terms, been abandoned and most Member States have now joined the Berne Convention.[60]

The law of the country of origin approach, which in relation to the Berne Convention is the outcome of the restrictive interpretation outlined in the previous paragraphs, might initially seem attractive from a theoretical point of view. It is clear, however, that it causes great practical problems and it is based on an interpretation of the text of the Berne Convention which is, arguably, wrong[61] or at least artificial in nature.

---

[59] See above, p 466–469. [60] See Boytha, n 6 above, at 406.
[61] See also Bergé's point that the influence of the law of the country of origin is declining, n 30 above.

III
THE ROME CONVENTION 1961

The Rome Convention for the Protection of Performers, Producers of Phonograms and Broadcasting Organisations 1961 deals, as its title indicates, with the rights in performances and those of broadcasting organisations. These rights are closely linked to traditional copyright and, in the UK, the implementing provisions are found in the Copyright, Designs and Patents Act 1988. It is, therefore, not surprising that the Convention's provisions which touch upon the conflict of laws are very similar to those of the Berne Convention. The interpretation advocated above in that context applies here too. The present analysis will, therefore, be restricted to a brief overview of the relevant provisions.

1. Qualification

Article 4, which needs to be read in conjunction with Articles 5 and 6 of the Convention, deals with the issue of qualification. The starting point is always the performance, and special rules apply for performances which are incorporated in a phonogram and performances which are not fixed on a phonogram but which are carried by a broadcast.

2. National Treatment and the Law of the Protecting Country

Performers will be entitled to national treatment. In practice, this means that foreign performers will be treated the same way as national performers in relation to performances that take place, or are broadcast, or first recorded on the territory of that country. Foreign producers of phonograms are to be treated the same way as national producers in relation to phonograms that are first recorded or first published in that country and foreign broadcasting organisations are to be treated the same way as broadcasting organisations which have their headquarters in that country in relation to broadcasts that are transmitted from transmitters that are located in that country.[62]

Article 2 makes it also clear that the basic rule is that the domestic law of the country where protection is claimed will be applied. Following the interpretation given above in relation to the almost identically worded provision in Article 5 of the Berne Convention, this must mean that the applicable law will be the law of the protecting country, the law of the country where the right in the performance is used. This conclusion is

---

[62] Article 2 Rome Convention 1961, see also Article 4.

IV
PARIS CONVENTION FOR THE PROTECTION OF INDUSTRIAL PROPERTY 1883

This Convention deals mainly with patents and trade marks, but also with unfair competition and industrial designs. For the purposes of the present analysis, though, it is not necessary to distinguish between the various rights involved, as the relevant provisions, ie Articles 2 and 3, apply to all the rights without distinction.

1. National Treatment

Foreign nationals are given the same rights as own nationals.[63] The national treatment principle applies here too. Article 2(1) specifies that foreign nationals are entitled to the same advantages. However, is this necessarily a reference to the substantive domestic law? It is submitted that it must indeed be interpreted as referring to national trade mark, patent, etc laws, because the text of Article 2(3) makes it clear that the provision does not apply to rules of jurisdiction and procedure. In respect of the latter point, the law of the forum applies. The fact that this forms the subject of a special rule, which is phrased in terms of an express reservation or exception, indicates clearly that the law of the forum is not generally applicable. It must be added that, on top of the national treatment rule, the parties concerned are also entitled as a minimum standard to those substantive rights which the Paris Convention itself provides for.[64]

2. The Law of the Protecting Country

The fact that Article 2(2) not only covers the use of intellectual property rights in contentious circumstances, but also in non-contentious circumstances, becomes even clearer when it is pointed out that a distinction is made between protection and remedies against infringement. This brings us back to the line of argument that was pursued in relation to the Berne Convention.[65] Each country applies its domestic law to foreign and

---

[63] The term 'national' is defined widely, as Article 3 Paris Convention also includes those persons who have a real and effective industrial or commercial establishment in the Member State concerned, while not having the nationality of that State.
[64] Article 2(1) Paris Convention. [65] See above p 466–469.

national parties alike. The law of the protecting country is applicable.[66] This is almost self-evident for those rights for which a registration is in operation. If A applies for the registration of his patent in Germany and in the United Kingdom, it seems logical to assume that national treatment means that the German authorities will apply German law in examining A's application, while the Patents Act 1977 will be applied by the UK Patent Office. Government agencies always operate under their own national law and always apply their own national procedure.[67] Article 2 does not distinguish between the phase of the application procedure and the phase after the grant of the patent and it can thus be assumed that, in the latter phase as well, German patent law will apply in Germany, whilst UK patent law will apply in the United Kingdom.

This system leads to a patchwork of national protections. Articles 4bis and 6(2) reinforce that conclusion by stipulating that the various national rights are independent of each other.[68] What happens to one of them has no influence on the other rights. If one national patent is revoked, that fact, as such, has no influence on all other parallel patents in other Member States of the Paris Union. It seems to follow, logically, from this system that the national legislations only apply within their respective national territories. If one State's legislation would also extend to another State, the rule in Article 2, which dictates that the law of the latter country should be applicable there as the law of the protecting country, would be infringed. The territorial scope of national intellectual property statutes and the rights granted under these statutes are restricted to the territory of the State concerned. This is the territoriality principle that has been derived from the text of Article 2.

The application of the law of the protecting country, as a general rule,[69] also extends to the non-registration rights. The law of the protecting country applies in relation to the protection against unfair competition which the Member States, by becoming a Party to the Convention, undertook to provide.[70] But, as this issue will only arise in a contentious case, the law of the protecting country is, almost necessarily, also the law of the forum.

---

[66] See Ulmer, n 21 above, at 55–56 and 66.
[67] This is confirmed by Article 6(1) Paris Convention in relation to trade mark applications.
[68] See Ulmer, n 21 above, at 56.
[69] See Ulmer, *ibid*, at 55–56 and 66.   [70] Article 10bis Paris Convention.

V
INTERNATIONAL CO-OPERATION AGREEMENTS

When co-operation agreements concerning the international application, examination and registration process apply, the identification of the law of the protecting country can cause problems.[71] Examples of such agreements are the Madrid Agreement and the Protocol to it concerning the international registration of trade marks, and the Patent Co-operation Treaty and the European Patent Convention in relation to patents.

This kind of agreement results in the grant of national intellectual property rights, which means that, after grant, the normal rule concerning the application of the law of the protecting country does not cause problems. Indeed, the situation is identical to the one resulting from a strictly national application and all these agreements operate within the scope of the Paris Convention. However, the harmonised single application process rules might present differences from the national ones. In the situation where the issue arises before the intellectual property right is granted, this might cause problems. The law of the protecting country must clearly be the law of the country for which protection is requested. This flows from the rules under the Paris Convention which are still applicable. But in cases where an international application is involved, the law of the protecting country includes, or is at least to be taken as it would have been after it had been amended by, the text of the co-operation treaty. It might, indeed, be the case that the co-operation agreements also contain substantive provisions which regulate the problem with which we are concerned. Ulmer suggested that 'where protection may be claimed in a State by virtue of both a national and an international application, to the extent to which the provisions differ, those provisions are to be regarded as the rules of the protecting country which apply in respect of the right claimed by virtue of the application',[72] and it is suggested that this is the appropriate solution.

VI
SUPRA-NATIONAL INTELLECTUAL PROPERTY RIGHTS

How is the law of the protecting country to be determined in relation to a supra-national intellectual property right? Two examples of such

---

[71] See Ulmer, n 21 above, at 59–66. [72] Ulmer, *ibid*, at 67 and 100–101.

supra-national rights come to mind. The Benelux trade mark system was put in place by a Convention to which a Uniform Trade Mark Act was attached. This Act has been implemented in the three countries concerned.[73] Also, the European Community now operates a single Community trade mark, the scope of which extends to the whole territory of the Community.[74]

It is important to note that these supra-national rights fit in with the Paris Convention and the Madrid Agreement and the Protocol to it and are, for these purposes, treated as if they constituted a right granted by one Member State. The applicable law of the protecting country is, therefore, the law common to those countries or the uniform law, as contained in the Regulation or the Benelux Trade Marks Act. It may, of course, be that the uniform law refers to the national law on a few points.[75] This does not mean that the uniform law is no longer the law of the protecting country. The uniform law is applicable and it is only when applying its provisions that certain rules of national law may also be taken into account by way of supplement.[76]

A similar system will operate under the Community Patent Convention, should that Convention ever come into force.[77]

VII
THE TRIPS AGREEMENT

The Agreement on Trade-related Aspects of Intellectual Property Rights was concluded in 1994 and covers all the intellectual property rights that were discussed earlier. Its provisions refer specifically to the Paris and Berne Conventions and Member States are required to implement all Articles of those Conventions which were discussed above in relation to private international law, and this is irrespective of whether or not the individual Member State concerned has signed up to these Conventions.[78]

NATIONAL TREATMENT

The agreement covers all intellectual property rights that come within the scope of the agreement. The agreement also contains the national treat-

---

[73] See, for example, for Belgium Eenvormige Beneluxwet van 19 maart 1962 op de merken, [1969] *Belgisch Staatsblad* 14 October.

[74] Council Regulation (EEC) 40/94 of 20 December 1993 on the Community trade mark [1994] OJ L11/1.

[75] See, eg Article 97(2) Council Regulation (EEC) 40/94 of 20 December 1993 on the Community trade mark [1994] OJ L11/1.

[76] See Ulmer, n 21 above, at 67.   [77] *Ibid*.   [78] Articles 2 and 9 TRIPs Agreement.

ment rule.[79] Under this rule, foreigners are given the same protection as nationals. The interesting feature of this rule is that the term 'protection' has been defined fairly precisely in a note to Article 3. It is said to include 'matters affecting the availability, acquisition, scope, maintenance and enforcement of intellectual property rights as well as those matters affecting the use of intellectual property rights specifically addressed in this Agreement'. This means that the same substantial rights are to be granted to foreigners and nationals. This can only be achieved through the application of the law of the protecting country.

The definition of protection does not refer solely to the contentious exercise of intellectual property rights in the context of infringement procedures and remedies. Non-contentious use is also included, otherwise the availability and acquisition issue, for example, would not have been included in the definition. This means that the alternative restrictive interpretation which was discussed above,[80] and which refers to the application of the law of the country of origin and/or the law of the forum, is no longer sustainable, as this relies on the restriction of the scope of the term protection to contentious issues only. The fact that there is no such restriction is reinforced by the second paragraph of Article 3 of the TRIPs Agreement, which provides a specific exception to the rule that the law of the protecting country is applicable. This exception relates to administrative and judicial procedural issues. The law of the forum can be applied, within firm limits, to these issues, but, of course, such an exception would not have been necessary if, as a general rule, the law of the forum was already the applicable law.

It must be emphasised that the TRIPs Agreement, being the most recent Agreement and indirectly incorporating the relevant articles of the Paris and Berne Conventions, has a decisive influence on the interpretation issue. It is now clear that all Convention provisions must be interpreted as adhering to the general rule that the law of the protecting country is the applicable law. Specific issues may, exceptionally, be governed by a different law, but only on the basis of a specific provision in the TRIPs Agreement,[81] or on the basis of a specific provision in any of the other Convention if that provision has been sanctioned by the TRIPs Agreement.[82] Any alternative interpretation favouring the application of the law of the country of origin or the law of the forum as a general rule is no longer acceptable as it would be in breach of Article 3 of the TRIPs Agreement.[83]

[79] Article 3 TRIPs Agreement.
[80] See above p 472–475.
[81] See, eg Article 3(2) TRIPs Agreement.
[82] See, eg Article 3(1) TRIPs Agreement.
[83] And as even more countries have now signed up to the TRIPs Agreement than there are Contracting States to the Paris, Berne and Rome Conventions, the alternative interpretation is no longer acceptable, because all these countries undertook to implement the provisions of the TRIPs Agreement when they signed up to it.

10

Creation, Scope and Termination of Intellectual Property Rights: the Applicable Law

I	Introduction	484
II	How choice of law problems arise	486
III	Intellectual property as property	487
	1. The wrong title?	487
	2. A property characterisation	488
	3. Property choice of law rules	489
	(a) The situs of intellectual property rights	489
	(b) The nature of intellectual property rights	496
	(c) The assignment of rights	496
	(d) Property rules are not sufficient	497
IV	Copyright	498
	1. The creation of the right	499
	(a) The types of works that will be protected	500
	(b) Fixation in a material form	500
	(c) The qualification requirement	501
	(d) Formalities	501
	2. The scope of the right	501
	(a) Moral rights	502
	(b) Broadcasting	504
	(c) Satellite broadcasting	504
	(d) Exceptions to the rights	506
	(e) Civil remedies	506
	3. Termination of the right	507
	4. Validity of the right	508
	5 Authorship, ownership of right and works created by employees	509
	(a) Authorship of copyright works	509
	(b) First ownership of copyright works	511
	(c) Article 14bis(2) in more detail	513
	(d) Ownership of copyright in works created by employees	513
	6. Transferability of the right	515

V	Patents and trade marks		517
	1. The registration system		517
	2. The law of the protecting country		518
		(a) No clear answers in the case law	519
		(b) To which issues is the law of the protecting country applied?	520
	3. Ownership of rights		522
		(a) Trade marks	522
		(b) Patents	522
VI	Other intellectual property rights		525
	1. Widening the categories		525
	2. Tortious protection of intellectual property rights		525
		(a) Goodwill	526
		(b) Business reputation	526
		(c) Goodwill and reputation	527
	3. Breach of confidence		527
	4. The *sui generis* right in relation to databases		528
VII	Rights created by international Conventions		529
	1. The Patent Co-operation Treaty		530
	2. The European Patent Convention		530
VIII	Community rights		532
	1. The Community Trade Mark		532
		(a) Article 14	532
		(b) Title X	532
		(c) Substantive rules in the Regulation	533
		(d) National law provisions	534
	2. The Community Patent		535
	3. The Community Design Right		535
	4. The Community Plant Variety Right		537
IX	Conclusions and alternative approaches		538

I
INTRODUCTION

The international intellectual property Conventions are mainly and almost exclusively concerned with the creation of the various intellectual property rights, the scope and content of these rights and their termination. We will now have to consider what effect the private international law related provisions of these Conventions, which we analysed in the previous chapter, have in this area. It needs to be emphasised once more, though, that the choice of law rules in the Conventions are not comprehensive.[1] As was outlined in the previous chapter, they do not provide a complete conflict of laws rule which addresses all issues. National treatment does mean, though, that foreign works, inventions or marks can rely on the domestic intellectual property laws of the country where protection is sought. This means that rules contained in the Conventions will be relevant in relation to the issues of creation, scope and termination of intellectual property rights[2] which are addressed in this chapter. On the points that are not fully covered by the rules in the Conventions, choice of law rules of general application will be used to address these points. Attention will also be paid to related issues such as that of authorship and (first) ownership of intellectual property rights.

From a conflicts point of view, the issues that are being dealt with in this chapter could be characterised as the property aspects of intellectual property rights. They can, in that respect, be separated neatly from the contractual aspects that are raised by contractual dealings with intellectual property rights, once the latter have been created. The application of the property choice of law rules to intellectual property would then have to be the main focus of this chapter. The existing case law and the specific provisions of the intellectual property statutes would have to be analysed to see whether they amend the property choice of law rules.

There is, however, a shortage of relevant case law in this area, neither do the intellectual property statutes contain many relevant provisions. It will, also, be shown that the application of the property choice of law rules to intellectual property rights is problematical due to the specific nature of intellectual property and the differences from other types of property.

An alternative model will, therefore, be suggested. This model is based on the few existing English cases, the relatively numerous foreign cases, and the few relevant statutory provisions. It also takes the guidance that is provided by the provisions of the international Conventions into account, as our national systems are supposed to implement these Conventions.

In the jurisdiction part of this book, we dealt with Community rights in a separate chapter, because many special jurisdiction rules surround these rights. This is not so in relation to choice of law. Community rights will, therefore, be included in this chapter.

A final introductory comment which needs to be made is that this chapter will mainly consider those intellectual property rights which can be said to grant positive rights to their owners. An exclusive right, such as the exclusive right to use the patented process, or the exclusive right to copy the work, need to be at the heart of the right concerned. Negative rights, such as that to object to unfair competition or any of the equivalent English

---

[1] Ulmer, *Intellectual Property Rights and the Conflict of Laws*, Kluwer & Commission of the European Communities (1978), at pp 9–10.
[2] *Ibid.*

torts (eg malicious falsehood, passing-off), are mainly relevant and mainly raise choice of law issues at the infringement stage and they will, therefore, be discussed in detail at that appropriate stage. Issues relating, for example, to the nature of secret know-how and the *situs* of goodwill will, however, be discussed in this chapter.

II
HOW CHOICE OF LAW PROBLEMS ARISE

How do choice of law problems arise in this context? This can be clarified by looking at a few practical examples. Inventions are patented in more than one country to facilitate their international exploitation. This is often done via the use of the Paris Convention based right of priority. Copyright works are, also, exploited internationally. For example, famous rock groups release their CDs simultaneously in many countries. This raises the issue of the creation of intellectual property rights in each country.

National patent laws differ on the issue whether and under what conditions certain biotechnological inventions are patentable. For example, the United States and most European countries have different views on which inventions are not patentable because they are contrary to public policy or morality. Let us assume that the US Patent Office has granted a patent for a genetically modified animal. Which law would the European Patent Office apply to decide whether or not to grant a parallel European patent when the American patentholder uses his right of priority to apply for such a patent? Application of US law, as the law of the country of origin, and European law,[3] as the law of the protecting country, might well lead to a different outcome.

English copyright law has a different, slightly lower, originality criterion for the creation of copyright than most continental European countries. The *Magill* case, in the Court of Justice,[4] has made it clear, for example, that listings of TV programmes are granted copyright protection in the UK, because enough skill and labour is involved for them to be original works, whilst it is doubtful whether French copyright law would grant copyright to TV listings that are created in France, because they lack originality. This means, in practice, that the English listings will only be granted copyright protection in France if the law of the country of origin applies to the creation of copyright. Does it?

---

[3] The EPC, as implemented, or the relevant provisions of the national patent laws of the Member States. The details of the system are irrelevant for current purposes.

[4] Joined Cases C-241/91P and 242/91P *Radio Telefis Eireann and Independent Television Publications Ltd v EC Commission*, [1995] ECR I-743, [1995] 4 CMLR 718 and [1995] FSR 530.

Substantive copyright and patent law differ also on the issue of the ownership of rights that arise in an employer-employee relationship. Different solutions might be reached depending on the law that is chosen. Does the choice of law rule take account of the law applicable to the contract of employment? Or, do we apply the law of the protecting country for each intellectual property right?

Moral rights are only granted to authors. The director of a film is, at least, a co-author of a film in most European copyright laws, but he is not an author under US copyright law. Which law applies to the authorship issue when the director of an American film attempts to stop the release in Europe of a colourised version of the film?

These are just a few practical examples of situations in which choice of law issues arise concerning the existence, creation, scope, ownership, validity, duration and termination of intellectual property rights. We now turn to the theoretical analysis of the choice of law issues that are involved.

III
INTELLECTUAL PROPERTY AS PROPERTY

1. The Wrong Title?

It could be argued forcefully that the title of this chapter is wrong. That argument treats intellectual property rights as a form of property and, as a result, property choice of law rules would simply have to be applied to intellectual property. It is submitted that this approach overlooks the special characteristics of intellectual property rights. These special characteristics would require that the property choice of law rules are departed from on (too) many occasions and their application to intangible rights, such as intellectual property rights, would be particularly cumbersome. We submit that the international nature of intellectual property rights and their exploitation, and the other special characteristics of intellectual property rights, require a *sui generis* regime for intellectual property rights. Intellectual property rights are, in most aspects, different from the standard type of property, thus a modified or *sui generis* regime in relation to choice of law is equally called for. This *sui generis* regime is based on the various relevant provisions in our intellectual property statutes and on those in the Conventions. First of all, we will outline the characterisation for the purposes of choice of law issues, which could lead us to the property choice of law rules. This will be followed by an analysis of the property rules and their application to intellectual property rights. Once the property rules have been analysed and rejected as a solution, we will return to the suggested *sui generis* system that is tailored to the needs of intellectual property rights.

2. A Property Characterisation

From a conflict of laws point of view, characterisation of the issue is an important tool. A major distinction is that between contractual and non-contractual issues.[5] Copyright is created without registration or any other formality, while its scope, duration and way of termination are determined by statutory provisions. Clearly, no contract is involved. An application for registration is required for the creation of a patent or a trade mark. These rights are granted by the Patent Office upon registration. Once more their scope, duration and way of termination are determined by statutory provisions. The grant of these rights cannot be considered to involve a contract between the applicant and the Patent Office. The issues of creation, scope and termination are clearly non-contractual. Things change once the intellectual property right has been created, and contracts play a prominent role in its exploitation. Licence contracts, authorising third parties to carry out acts in exploiting the right that would normally infringe the exclusive right of the owner of the intellectual property right, are clearly contractual in nature. The same goes for transfers of the ownership and assignments of the intellectual property right.

The non-contractual category could be divided further into two categories. Issues relating to the infringement of intellectual property rights should be classified as tort cases, while what is left would then concern the intellectual property right as a form of property. A division of the issues over these three categories, contract, tort and property, would be useful from a conflicts point of view as our legal system has a choice of law rules for each of them. It would allow the conflicts lawyers to apply their existing choice of law rules to intellectual property problems.[6]

A number of problems arise, though. First of all, which issues fall within which category? To take just one example, is the issue part of the property right if copyright entitles authors and performers of works to an equitable remuneration when copies of the work or registrations of the performance are exploited commercially through rental, or is it more related to the contractual exploitation of the work or performance? Secondly, there may be situations in which two categories are relevant. Which conflict rule will be applied in such a situation?[7] Before returning

---

[5] For a practical example in relation to intellectual property see the US case *Neidhart v Neidhart SA* 184 USPQ 393.

[6] See Fentiman, 'The Range of Conflicts Problems', Paper delivered at the Herchel Smith Seminar on Intellectual Property and Private International Law: New Directions, Cambridge 24 February 1996.   [7] *Ibid*.

in more detail to the problems that are raised by a property characterisation, let us first analyse how the property choice of law rules are applied to intellectual property.[8]

3. Property Choice of Law Rules

English law, and English private international law with it, knows more than one type of property. The first issue, therefore, which retains our attention is that of the nature of property, and more in particular the nature of intellectual property. Dicey and Morris suggest the following choice of law rule to determine the nature of property: '[t]he law of a country where a thing is situate (*lex situs*) determines whether . . . the thing itself is considered an immovable or a movable'.[9] However, this rule does not solve the problem until a preliminary point is addressed. Where is a thing situate? An answer to this question is required before we can proceed.

(a) THE SITUS OF INTELLECTUAL PROPERTY RIGHTS

(i) The Dicey and Morris property approach

According to Dicey and Morris, 'the *situs* of things is determined as follows: . . . choses in action generally are situate in the country where they are properly recoverable or can be enforced'.[10]

The *situs* of land is determined according to a different rule, but we submit, as Dicey and Morris argue,[11] that intellectual property cannot be put in the same category as land. This conclusion is based on a number of cases which we will analyse below. This is consistent with the position in relation to jurisdiction, where it has already been seen that intellectual property rights should be classified as movable property.[12] Apart from the cases and the parallel with jurisdiction, there is a third argument to reject any suggestion that intellectual property rights should be classified as immovable property. The nature of these rights is very different from that of immovable property. It has been demonstrated above that the nature of both is not even analogous.[13] None of these arguments obscures the fact that classification is done for a certain purpose. In this case, intellectual property rights have to be classified for the purposes of choice of law.

---

[8] For a comprehensive treatment of this issue in relation to copyright, see Raynard, *Droit d'auteur et conflits de lois*, Litec (1990), 743pp, who argues that copyright is a form of property for the purposes of private international law.

[9] Dicey and Morris, *The Conflict of Laws*, Sweet & Maxwell (12th ed, 1993), Rule 113, at p 915.

[10] *Ibid*, Rule 114, at 922; the editors refer to *New York Life Insurance Co v Public Trustee* [1924] 2 Ch 101 at 109; *Alloway v Phillips* [1980] 1 WLR 888 and *Kwok Chi Leung Karl v Commissioner of Estate Duty* [1988] 1 WLR 1035.

[11] *Ibid*, Rule 114, at 922.   [12] See above chapter 1, pp 34–35 and chapter 6, pp 281–283.

[13] See above, chapter 6, pp 281–282.

But how is a situation to be ascribed to intangibles? Because the *situs* is used as a connecting factor, all references must be interpreted according to the law of the forum.[14] The provisions of the law of the forum will, therefore, be used to determine where the intellectual property right, as a chose in action, can be recovered properly or can be enforced. The recovery and the enforcement concepts have legal connotations, though, and the law of the forum may have to refer to foreign law to determine the relevant place. Important differences are found between the various choses in action. This means, by implication, that the rule will have to be refined for each type of chose in action.[15] The Dicey and Morris rule has already indicated this through the use of the word 'generally'.

(a) Patents

(i) *The transfer of the right*

Where is a patent situate? The grant of a patent results in statutory rights being given to the patentholder. 'By English law [a patent] confers certain monopoly rights, exercisable in England, on its proprietor.'[16] This *dictum* of Evershed MR in *British Nylon Spinners Ltd* v *Imperial Chemical Industries Ltd* stresses the importance of the fact that a British patent confers rights, statutory monopoly rights, which can be exercised in Britain. This leads to the conclusion that the right can be enforced in Britain and must, therefore, be situate in Britain. Dicey and Morris interpret the term 'exercise' restrictively, and they arrive at the rule that 'patents ... are situate in the county where they can be effectively transferred under the law governing their creation'.[17] It is submitted that this must be wrong, but, before returning to that issue, it should be explained how the peculiar facts of this case lead to this conclusion concerning the interpretation of the case.

In this case, the American company du Pont de Nemours had agreed to assign certain (British) patents to ICI. In turn, ICI had agreed contractually with British Nylon Spinners that the latter would be granted a right to be granted a licence under these patents, whenever they choose to exercise that right. As a result of a US antitrust action, du Pont de Nemours was obliged to undo the assignment contract with ICI, and British Nylon Spinners tried to stop ICI from co-operating, as they would, in turn, become unable to exercise their contractual rights. The case really turned upon the extra-territorial impact in Britain of the US antitrust judgment, whether an English Court should recognise such a judgment, and upon

---

[14] See *Rossano* v *Manufacturer's Life Insurance Co.* [1963] 2 QB 352, at 379–380.
[15] Dicey and Morris, n 9 above, at pp 923–924.
[16] *British Nylon Spinners Ltd* v *Imperial Chemical Industries Ltd* [1953] 1 Ch 19, at 26, *per* Evershed MR.
[17] Dicey and Morris, n 9 above, at p 934.

the assignment and licence contracts.[18] In such circumstances, the exercise of the rights seems to be restricted to assignments and licences, that is to the transfer of the rights. This is not correct. The contractual transfer of rights is only one way to exercise patents. The patentholder can also opt to exploit the patented invention itself, whilst using the patents to stop third parties from doing the same. The *dictum* in *British Nylon Spinners Ltd* v *Imperial Chemical Industries Ltd* does not focus on the contractual exercise of the patents. All it justifies is a focus on the exercise of the patents, but that is only due to the fact that the facts of the case were exclusively concerned with that aspect, rather than with, for example, the creation of the patents.

The misleading focus on the exercise of the rights granted under a patent is strengthened by the other case that could be said to touch upon the *situs* issue. *Wilderman* v *Berk*[19] is, primarily, concerned with the exact scope of patent rights, but, because parallel British and German patents for improvements in electrolytic cells were involved, the situs of the English patent, which had allegedly been infringed, became relevant too. The product, the importation of which in Britain allegedly infringed the British patent, had been manufactured in Germany by means of a process that involved at some stage the use of machinery that incorporated the patented technology. The German manufacturer was entitled to that use on the basis of the German parallel patent, but the British patent was owned by a third company. The different ownership of the patents had been caused by the forced assignment of the patent in the United Kingdom, as a result of the Trading with the Enemy Act 1916 and the circumstances during World War I. On the basis of these facts, the *situs* of the patent seems, once again, to be linked to the place where it can be transferred. Or is it better to say: 'where the exclusive rights that are granted by it can be exercised', even if the plaintiff was not successful in this case?

(ii) *The law governing the creation of the right*

Dicey and Morris do not simply refer to the transfer of rights. They link the *situs* of a patent to the 'country where [it] can be effectively transferred under the law governing their creation'.[20] The question which law governs the creation of a patent remains unanswered. This is clearly not a factual issue. It also has its importance. The Patents Act 1977 accepts that a foreign patentholder can use its right of priority, which it acquired as a result of an earlier application abroad in a Paris Convention country, to apply for a British patent up to twelve months after the date of the original application.[21] Which law will govern the creation of such a British

---

[18] *British Nylon Spinners Ltd* v *Imperial Chemical Industries Ltd*, n 16 above.
[19] [1925] 1 Ch 116.   [20] Dicey and Morris, n 9 above, at p 934.
[21] Patents Act 1977, s 5.

patent? Will it be the UK's Patents Act 1977, because the right is granted in, and for, the United Kingdom, or will it be the law of the country of the original application? These laws may differ substantially. The Dicey and Morris approach can be understood if one accepts that choses in action, for example debts, are, typically, created as a result of a contractual transaction. The law of the contract could then be said to govern their creation. This is not the case for patents and other intellectual property rights. The emphasis on the contractual transfer of the rights is, as we argued above,[22] accidental, dependant on the peculiar set of facts in these cases, and misplaced. A patent is created by the grant of an exclusive right by the Patent Office, through an entry in the Patent Register. Such an entry is only made once the examination of the inventor's application has been concluded successfully.[23] The grant of statutory rights cannot be treated as the conclusion of a contract between the inventor and the Patent Office. To give just one example, the rights of the inventor have their effects against third parties,[24] rather than against the Patent Office. Privity of contract is a rather different concept.

(b) *Registered designs*

Registered design rights are similar to patents in this respect. Similar procedures for application, registration and assignment and licensing are found in the Registered Designs Act 1949.[25] The comments made in relation to patents apply to registered designs as well, especially in the absence of any relevant case law.

(c) *Trade marks*

Where is a trade mark situate? Dicey and Morris apply the same rule to trade marks as they do to patents.[26] Considering that trade marks are also granted as a result of an application and examination process[27] and that their transfer is not as important and dominant in their exploitation as it may seem, it is submitted that the comments made in relation to patents also apply to trade marks.[28] Let us now turn to the case law, though, to see whether analysis of this confirms this point of view.

In *Lecouturier* v *Rey*,[29] the trade mark for Grande Chartreuse liquor had been assigned in France when the Chartreuse monks were forced to cease their activity and leave the country. The main issue in this case was

---

[22] See above, pp 490–491. [23] Patents Act 1977, ss 14, 17 and 18.
[24] See, for example, the provisions on infringement, Patents Act 1977, s 60 *et seq*.
[25] See, for example, *ibid*, ss 3, 14 and 16.
[26] Dicey and Morris, n 9 above, at p 934.
[27] See, for example, Trade Marks Act 1994, ss 32, 37 and 40. [28] See above pp 490–491.
[29] [1910] AC 262.

whether the decision of the French court to this effect had also transferred the ownership of the British trade mark. Dicey and Morris[30] refer to Lord Loreburn's comments in the House of Lords to support their interpretation. Lord Loreburn stated that 'this property . . . [the trade mark] which has come into question in this appeal is property situated in England, and must therefore be regulated and disposed of in accordance with the law of England'.[31] His Lordship accepted, as a fact, that the trade mark was situate in England and it followed, in his view, that it could only be transferred under English law. It is submitted that this does not necessarily answer the question where the property is situate. The Dicey and Morris interpretation of the judgment relies heavily on the comments in this case that trade marks are linked to business goodwill.

That link is also present, in a prominent way, in *Reuter* v *Mulhens*.[32] This case is concerned with the rights in the mark 4711 for Eau de Cologne. As a result of the special legislation on enemy property in World War II, the German manufacturer had lost his UK trade mark, which had been assigned to an English company. Both parties alleged that they were entitled to use the mark in the United Kingdom after the war and accused each other of infringement. The Court of Appeal ruled that business goodwill is attached to trade or business[33] and is situate in the country where the premises, through which the owner of the mark carries out his business in relation to which there is goodwill, are located.[34] That business must be distinct and severable from any business abroad. The Trade Marks Act 1994 no longer links trade marks to business goodwill in such an explicit way. The main concept is now that a trade mark is a sign that distinguishes goods or services.[35] Business goodwill should, therefore, not be relied upon so heavily when determining the *situs* of a trade mark.

Both cases involve the non-voluntary assignment of a trade mark. This is not the typical way in which trade mark rights are exercised, nor does it address the issue of which law governs the creation of trade mark rights. The case law does not solve, therefore, the problems raised in relation to the Dicey and Morris rule.

(d) *Copyright*

Where is a copyright situate? Dicey and Morris refrain from including copyright straightforwardly in the patent and trade mark rule, or in any

---

[30] Dicey and Morris, n 9 above, at p 934.
[31] *Lecouturier* v *Rey* [1910] AC 263, at 273.   [32] [1954] 1 Ch 50.
[33] The Court (*ibid*, at 96) approved and followed in this respect the observations of Lord Lindley in *Commissioners of Inland Revenue* v *Muller & Co's Margarine Ltd* [1901] AC 217, at 235.
[34] See also Derenberg 68 (1978) *Trade Mark Reporter* 387, at 390.
[35] See Trade Marks Act 1994, s 1(1).

other rule,[36] and refer the reader to *Novello v Hinrichsen*,[37] another World War II non-voluntary expropriation case. That case demonstrates strongly that there are problems attached to a non-voluntary assignment of copyright in Nazi Germany. It makes also clear that a German copyright owner got his English copyright back as soon as he lost his enemy status. The German and British copyrights in the works are clearly, *de facto*, dealt with as separate rights, but the case lends little or no support to the theory that the *situs* of copyright should be linked to the effective transfer of the right.

(ii) Problems arise

This analysis clearly demonstrates that the application of the traditional property approach, as it has been outlined by Dicey and Morris, to intellectual property is problematical. It is submitted that a *sui generis* approach, that is closely linked to certain property principles, would be a better solution. But before we discuss the alternative in more detail, it is necessary to return to the principles that underpin intellectual property.

(iii) An alternative approach

(a) *Intellectual property rights as restrictions on competition*

Intellectual property rights are restrictions on competition in furtherance of competition.[38] The fact that intellectual property rights are exclusive monopoly rights is clearly very important. Desbois put it very convincingly in relation to copyright: 'les droits d'auteur ne sont rien d'autre qu'une restriction arbitrairement apportée à l'exploitation des oeuvres de l'esprit, à la liberté du commerce; chaque Etat apprécie souverainement l'opportunité d'instituer de telles entraves et les forge à sa guise: peu importe la teneur de la législation du pays d'origine'.[39] Nobody is allowed to make copies without the consent of the copyright-owner, as long as copyright exists.[40] Desbois argues that this is a restriction on free competition in the marketplace. The same can be said about the exclusive right of the patentholder to use the patented invention for 20 years and the entitlement of the owner of a registered trade mark to the exclusive use of the mark. Desbois is also right in suggesting that competition rules in the ter-

---

[36] Dicey and Morris, n 9 above, at 914 (note 95).   [37] [1951] 1 Ch 595.
[38] See Lehmann [1989] *IIC* 1 and Holyoak and Torremans, *Intellectual Property Law*, Butterworths (1995), pp 13–19.
[39] 'Copyright is nothing but an arbitrary restriction on the exploitation of works of the mind and on the freedom of trade. Every State decides in a sovereign way whether or not such restrictions should be created and moulds them to its own needs. The wording of the law of the country of origin has no influence on this process.' (translation by the authors); Desbois, 'Les droits d'auteur et le droit international privé français', in *Festschrift GS Marikadis*, Athens (1966), 29–46, at 38.
[40] See, for example, Copyright, Designs and Patents Act 1988, ss 16(1) and 17.

ritory of a State are the exclusive competence of that State. These rules are considered to form part of the public policy of each State. No State will allow that a foreign state regulates competition and allows restrictions on competition on the territory of their State.

The law of each State should, in each State, on the basis of these public policy considerations, govern the creation and the scope of each right that restricts competition. All intellectual property rights come within this category. A good example is found in the UK's Copyright, Designs and Patents Act 1988 where it is stipulated that 'the owner of the copyright in a work has . . . the exclusive right to do the following acts in the United Kingdom'.[41] The territorial scope of the exclusive right, that restricts competition, is restricted to the United Kingdom. This confirms the theory set out earlier in this paragraph.

(b) Registration and exercise

All this results in the creation of one patent, trade mark or copyright per country. Would it not seem logical then to link the *situs* of the intellectual property right concerned to the country in which it is created, and in the territory of which it can be exercised? A patent or a trade mark should be situate in the country where the application is filed and the Patent Office of which has, at the end of its examination, decided that the application meets all criteria and that, on that basis, a restriction on competition should be allowed by granting the patent or the trade mark. Registration in a country is the fact that links the intangible right that needs registration to a *situs*.[42] Rights, such as copyright, that do not need registration, present, at first sight, more problems, but the public policy argument links them to a single country. They too should, therefore, be situate in the country in respect of which they have been granted, and in which the exclusive right can be exercised.[43] This is also the approach that has been taken in Italy. The Italian Supreme Court has held that the law applicable to copyright was the law of the place of use of the copyrighted asset[44] and that choice in favour of the law of the country of utilisation has been copied in its statutory provisions on private international law.[45] It is also important to add that this solution is in no way contradicted by the cases[46] that Dicey and Morris invoke in support of their solution. They deal almost exclusively with non-voluntary assignments of intellectual property

---

[41] Copyright, Designs and Patents Act 1988, s 16(1).
[42] See also Kloss [1985] 1 *EIPR* 15.   [43] See *ibid*.
[44] Judgment 2754 of 29 July 1958, [1959] *Revista di diritto internazionale* 333.
[45] Law 218 of 31 May 1995, [1995] *Gazzetta Officiale* 128 (3 June 1995).
[46] *Lecouturier* v *Rey* [1910] AC 262, *British Nylon Spinners Ltd* v *Imperial Chemical Industries Ltd* [1953] 1 Ch 19, *Reuter* v *Mulhens* [1954] 1 Ch 54, *Wilderman* v *Berk* [1925] 1 Ch 116, *Novello* v *Hinrichsen* [1951] 1 Ch 595.

rights[47] and, in those situations, both solutions lead to the same conclusion. It is submitted, though, that the solution outlined in this paragraph does not give rise to the problems that the Dicey and Morris solution creates.

The registration requirement for certain intellectual property rights, and the fact that intellectual property rights are statutory exclusive rights, point towards another important difference between intellectual property and other choses in action. The latter type of property is, typically, created by contract. For example, a debt can be created in a contract between a bank and a customer. Intellectual property rights are, as was shown above,[48] not created by contract. The State grants exclusive statutory rights, that, primarily, have effect against third persons. There is no contract between the State and the person that is granted the right. The link with the law of the contract for the creation of the rights is, therefore, not applicable to intellectual property. In the cases listed by Dicey and Morris,[49] this distinction did not arise, as they all dealt with assignments and licences and the creation issue was undisputed, and never raised.

(b) THE NATURE OF INTELLECTUAL PROPERTY RIGHTS

Once it has been determined where a chose in action is situate, the law of the *situs* will determine whether the thing should be considered as a moveable or as an immoveable.[50] It has been argued forcefully above that intellectual property rights should be considered as movables and this discussion will not be re-opened here.[51] Suffice it to say that Dicey and Morris deal with the assignment of intellectual property rights in the chapter on the transfers of movables and it is submitted that this is correct.[52]

No foreign State should classify intellectual property rights as immovable property. The nature of intellectual property rights is very different from that of land. As has been seen in the context of jurisdiction, there is no analogy between the two.[53] Moreover, the authors do not know of any foreign State which classifies intellectual property as immovable property. On the contrary, there is evidence of a movable classification being adopted.[54]

(c) THE ASSIGNMENT OF RIGHTS

Dicey and Morris do not suggest clearly which law governs the scope of an intellectual property right. They determine the *situs* and the nature of

---

[47] However, *British Nylon Spinners* v *ICI*, n 16 above, involves the voluntary assignment and licencing of patents.
[48] See above p 492.
[49] Dicey and Morris, n 9 above, at p 934.
[50] *Ibid*, Rule 113, at p 915.
[51] See above, pp 34–35 and 281–283.
[52] Dicey and Morris, n 9 above, chapter 24.
[53] See above, pp 34–55.
[54] See, eg Van Hecke and Lenaerts, *Internationaal Privaatrecht*, Story-Scientia, (2nd ed, 1989), chapter 30.

property and then they turn immediately towards the transfers of movables. Whether an intellectual property right is capable of being assigned, or not, is, in their view, governed by the law governing the creation of the intellectual property right.[55] As with the rule on the *situs* of intellectual property rights, no suggestion concerning the rule that allows the identification of the law governing the creation of intellectual property rights is made. As has been argued above,[56] this is not simply a factual matter. It is submitted, though, that the rule on the capability of assignment is correct. This is borne out by the judgment in *Campbell Connelly* v *Noble*,[57] in which it was said that the matter was governed by US copyright law. This is a logical conclusion in a case where a renewable copyright in the US had been assigned, before the actual renewal period had started, in a contract that was governed by English law. It could also be argued, that the reference to the law of the place where the right was created, and the distinction which Dicey and Morris draw on the assignment point between debts (or choses in action that are created contractually) and intangibles (such as intellectual property rights), lend support to our alternative approach in relation to the property aspect of intellectual property, rather than to the Dicey and Morris approach.[58]

It could also be argued that Article 12 of the Rome Convention 1980,[59] upon which the Dicey and Morris rule[60] is based, is relevant to this issue. This argument needs to be rejected, as it is based on the prerequisite that the right that is assigned is created by contract. It has been demonstrated above that this is not the case for intellectual property rights.[61] This means that intellectual property rights as such, and this includes the issue whether or not they are assignable, fall outside the scope of the Rome Convention 1980.[62] Article 12 cannot, therefore, apply to them. The Rome Convention 1980 only becomes applicable when existing intellectual property rights become the object of a contractual transaction.[63] These matters will be discussed in the next chapter.

(d) PROPERTY RULES ARE NOT SUFFICIENT

We have demonstrated that the application of the property rules to intellectual property rights does not work satisfactorily. Some issues are not

---

[55] Dicey and Morris, n 9 above, Rule 120(2), at 979.
[56] See p 489 above.　　　　　　　　　　　　　　[57] [1963] 1 WLR 252, at 255.
[58] The 11th illustration to Rule 121 in the 11th edition makes this even clearer, as it refers explicitly to registration in relation to trade marks; see *Lecouturier* v *Rey*, n 29 above.
[59] In force in the United Kingdom through the Contracts (Applicable Law) Act 1990, see Schedule 1, Article 12.
[60] Dicey and Morris, n 9 above, Rule 120, at p 979.　　　[61] See above, p 492.
[62] See the Giuliano-Lagarde Report to the Convention [1980] OJ C282/10.
[63] See also Dicey and Morris, n 9 above, at pp 979–980.

addressed. Others are addressed with some difficulty. In the next part of this chapter, an alternative approach, that is based on the international intellectual property Conventions and the provisions of the UK's intellectual property statutes, will be considered in more detail. It will also be shown that such an approach is fully in line with the *dicta* in the existing case law. Let us, therefore, now consider the creation, scope and termination issues in greater detail, looking separately at copyright, patents, trade marks, etc.

IV
COPYRIGHT

The Copyright, Designs and Patents Act 1988 does not contain a true choice of law rule. Section 1 immediately sets off to define the various types of work that will attract copyright protection. These are substantive rules, but a peculiar rule, that is of interest to the choice of law analysis, has been added to it. Copyright will, according to this rule, only be granted if the work also meets the qualification requirement,[64] either through the author or through the country of first publication. This means, in broad terms, that the work will be granted copyright protection if the author is a British citizen, domiciliary or resident, or if the work is first published[65] in Britain.[66] The system is then expanded to other countries, of first publication or of which the author is a national, etc, by means of an Order in Council.[67] This system addresses the point whether or not a work will be protected in the United Kingdom, but the statute does not determine which law will govern that protection. A work of a Belgian author, that was first published in Belgium, should be protected in the United Kingdom, but should that protection be governed by Belgian or by British copyright law? In terms of substantive rules, the UK's Copyright, Designs and Patents Act 1988 stipulates that 'the owner of the copyright in a work has . . . the exclusive right to do the following acts in the United Kingdom'.[68] It could be argued that such a system equally expects all other systems to restrain their territorial scope to the territory of their own country. Does this go further, though, than the scope of the protection?

The Berne Convention, on which all this is based, does not just grant national treatment, Article 5(2) adds to this the additional substantive

---

[64] Copyright, Designs and Patents Act 1988, s 1(3).   [65] Or broadcast.
[66] See Copyright, Designs and Patents Act 1988, ss 153–162.
[67] For more detail on the qualification rules, see Holyoak and Torremans, n 38 above, chapter 10.
[68] Copyright, Designs and Patents Act 1988, s 16(1).

rights which are granted in the Convention itself. An exception to this minimal rights rule is formed by the level of protection in the country of origin of the works that originate there. Article 5(3) does not mention the additional substantive rights in relation to these works and, in general, their level of protection is left entirely to the domestic law of the country of origin. In practice, a second exception might arise in those countries, such as the UK, that do no give direct effect to international conventions, as individual parties will not be able to invoke the provisions in the Convention that grant them these additional substantive rights in the absence of national implementing legislation. With this in mind, we can now turn to the particular implications of this regime.

We will look at issues such as the creation of the right, the scope of the right, the duration of the right,[69] the assignability of the right, etc.

1. THE CREATION OF THE RIGHT

The Copyright, Designs and Patents Act 1988 does not contain any detailed guidance on the issue of the applicable law. Whilst the provisions that were discussed in the previous paragraphs decide whether a work will be protected or not, no indication is to be found that would address the issue of which law should govern that protection. The creation of copyright leads to an exclusive right that restricts competition. It would, therefore, seem to follow that the UK's public policy dictates that the creation of a copyright that will be exercisable in the United Kingdom will be governed by the provisions of the Copyright, Designs and Patents Act 1988. Protection will be sought in the United Kingdom; therefore, the 1988 Act should apply as the law of the protecting country.

The Berne Convention also leads to the application of the law of the protecting country[70] to issues related to the creation of copyright, as these

---

[69] In a wide ranging approach that can be used as a first starting point Von Bar, 108 (1988) *UFITA* 27, refers for the three latter issues to the law of the country where the right has been used, which is also the approach of the Austrian Private International Law Statute.

[70] Holleaux has argued that the French Cour de Cassation decided, in a case where he was the judge-rapporteur, that the existence, creation and scope of copyright in France was governed by French law, as the law of the protecting country. See Judgment of 22 December of the French Cour de Cassation, *Société Fox-Europa* v *Société Le Chant du Monde* (1960) 28 *RIDA* 120, annotated by Holleaux at 121 *et seq*. The very short text of the judgment mentioned the fact that the composers whose music had been used in a film also enjoyed copyright protection in the USSR, the country of origin. This gave rise to the argument that the law of the country of origin was the applicable law, while the law of the protecting country was only concerned with the enforcement of the rights that had been granted by the law of the country of origin. See, eg Desbois, 'Les Droits d'Auteur et le Droit International Privé Français', in *Festschrift GS Marikadis*, Athens (1966), p 29 *et seq*, at p 34. The Berne Convention did not apply in this case.

issues form part of the non-contractual 'property' category.[71] Which issues, though, are related to the creation of copyright?[72]

(a) THE TYPES OF WORKS THAT WILL BE PROTECTED

Rules on the types of works that will be protected are a first example of rules that relate to the creation of copyright. Article 2 of the Berne Convention restricts itself to stating the principle that 'literary and artistic works', which include 'every production in the literary, scientific and artistic domain', will be protected, and Article 2bis allows for certain limitations without obliging Member States to introduce them. The precise definition of the types of works that will be protected and the decision whether or not to introduce any limitation is left to the Member States and their domestic legislation.[73] Even if they are not large, differences exist between the laws of the Member States. Whether a work comes within a category of works that will be protected and, if so, in which category of works will be determined by the law of the protecting country.

(b) FIXATION IN A MATERIAL FORM

Copyright is not simply created because a work comes within one of the categories of works that are protected. On top of this, fixation in some material form[74] may be required. Article 2(2) of the Berne Convention leaves it up to the Member States to decide whether or not to introduce this additional requirement. The UK, for example, has decided to introduce this additional requirement,[75] while many other countries in the European Union have decided not to do so.[76] Whether or not this additional requirement is applicable is also an issue related to the creation of copyright and thus the issue will be decided under the law of the protecting country.

---

[71] Issues such as whether copyright exists and what its content is in each case are governed by the law of the country where the copyright work is exploited, see Siehr's argument in 108 (1988) *UFITA* 9, at 18 and the reference to Article 34, para 1 of the Austrian Private International Law Statute: 'The creation, content and extinction of rights in intangible property shall be judged according to the law of the state in which an act of use or violation occurs.'

[72] See Ulmer, n 1 above, at pp 34–35.

[73] Compare, in this respect, Article 2(1) of the Berne Convention and Copyright, Designs and Patents Act 1988, ss 1–5B.

[74] This does not mean that publication is required. Unpublished works that are fixated in some material form, for example because the work has been put in writing, are protected fully.

[75] Copyright, Designs and Patents Act 1988, s 3(2).

[76] Eg Belgium, see the recent Copyright Act: Wet betreffende het auteursrecht en de naburige rechten, 30 June 1994, [1994] *Belgisch Staatsblad* 19297.

Creation, scope and termination of IP rights: the applicable law 501

(c) THE QUALIFICATION REQUIREMENT

The qualification requirement also needs to be met if copyright is to be created. Article 3 of the Berne Convention contains fairly detailed rules which do not leave a lot of discretion to the Member States, nonetheless minor differences exist between the domestic legislations of the Member States. It is the law of the protecting country which determines the precise qualification requirements[77] which have to be met if copyright is to be created.

(d) FORMALITIES

Registration or other formalities would have been another example of an issue related to the creation of copyright if formalities had not been ruled out by Article 5(2) of the Berne Convention. On a point of detail, it can be mentioned here that the ban in Article 5(2) only applies to works that originate in another country of the Berne Union. Member States could, for example, require that works that originate in their territory, and for which their law is the law of the country of origin in application of Article 5(3) of the Berne Convention, are registered. A foreign author who first publishes his work in such a country will have to register his work before copyright in it is created, because here the law of the protecting country, which is applicable to creation issues is the law of that country as protection is sought there.[78]

2. THE SCOPE OF THE RIGHT

Once copyright has been created it is important to know what the content of the exclusive right will be. How far will the protection and the restriction of competition extend? Logically speaking, this issue is inextricably linked with the decision to grant copyright, as it determines what exactly is being granted. The issue should, therefore, be decided under the same applicable law. The law of the protecting country should apply.[79] The law of the place where the right is used has to decide whether the right exists and what its content is.[80] There is, however, no specific provision in the Copyright, Designs and Patents Act 1988 that deals with this issue.

---

[77] For the United Kingdom, see Copyright, Designs and Patents Act 1988, Chapter IX.
[78] For the discussion on the relationship between the law of the protecting country and the law of the country of origin in such cases, see the previous chapter.
[79] See *Novello & Co Ltd v Hinrichsen Edition Ltd and Another* [1951] 1 Ch 595 and see also Article 34, para 1 of the Austrian Private International Law Statute, n 71 above, that contains the same rule and Schack 108 (1988) *UFITA* 51.
[80] See Walter (1976) 89 *RIDA* 45, at 51 and, for an example, see the judgment of 1 March 1989 of the Arrondissementsrechtbank (Dutch court of first instance) in Leewarden, *United Feature Syndicate Inc v Van der Meulen Sneek BV* [1990] Bijblad Industriële Eigendom 329, the

This choice of law point is important, in practice, as the Berne Convention does not define the scope of protection in a rigid way. It rather sets minimum standards. While it is generally accepted that the copyrightholder has the exclusive right to reproduce the work and make public representations of the work, certain national legislations add to this the exclusive right for the copyrightholder to distribute copies of the work.[81]

(a) MORAL RIGHTS

Whether one sees moral rights as an integral part of copyright or as separate rights, the precise content of the moral rights that are granted is also determined by the law of the protecting country.[82] Either they are just part of the scope of the copyright that has been granted, or, if they are seen as independent rights, they come into being automatically through the creation of the copyright. It is logical, in these circumstances, to accept that they are governed by the same rule, for reasons of uniformity. The applicability of the law of the protecting country is confirmed by Article 6bis (3) of the Berne Convention which states explicitly that the means of redress in relation to moral rights are governed by the law of the protecting country. The specific means of redress for each moral right are linked so strongly to the moral right concerned that it would make no sense to separate them in terms of the applicable law.

Moral rights could also be seen as personality rights that are linked to the person of the author of the work. From a choice of law point of view, they could then be classified as forming part of the personal law of the author. An alternative, in copyright terms, could be the law of the country of origin, because the latter is closely linked to the author. The common law approach to substantive copyright and moral rights, which is based on the commercial exploitation of the work rather than on the author, has never gone down this path. It is, therefore, submitted that this choice of law approach is to be rejected.

We have argued elsewhere that moral rights should be seen as fundamental rights that protect the author against the abuse of his work.[83] From that point of view, the UK's approach to moral rights should form part of its public policy. This would have important implications in a situation where the case is litigated in the United Kingdom, but where the law of the

scope of copyright in the Garfield dolls in the Netherlands was determined by Dutch law (law of the protecting country), rather than under US law.

[81] Ulmer, n 1 above, at 36.
[82] The term 'rights' in the Berne Convention includes both pecuniary and moral rights, see Ginsburg 17 (1993) *Columbia-VLA Journal of Law and the Arts* 395, at 405 and see also the analysis of the John Huston Case, pp 503 and 510–511 below.
[83] Holyoak and Torremans, n 38 above, chapter 13; see also Stamatoudi [1997] *Intellectual Property Quarterly* 478.

protecting country is not the Copyright, Designs and Patents Act 1988. Rather than applying the law of the protecting country, the court would be obliged to apply the UK's provisions on moral rights, if the standard of moral rights protection in the law of the protecting country would be lower than the one in the Copyright, Designs and Patents Act 1988. It needs to be stressed that this approach does not replace the choice of law rules and the law of the protecting country altogether. Public policy considerations, and eventually the application of the law of the forum, can only be considered at a later stage[84].

Mandatory rules, however, operate in a slightly different way. These rules are directly applicable[85] and the choice of law process is not followed at all. The provisions on moral rights of the forum are directly applicable, irrespective of the content of the law of the protecting country, if they are mandatory rules. This is the approach that was taken by the French Court de Cassation[86] in the *John Huston* case[87]. It is submitted that the nature of moral rights, as rights that come only into operation when the copyright work is used abusively, does not justify the latter approach. The traditional law of the protecting country, plus public policy of the forum in exceptional cases, is far more suitable.[88] The same law would then also be applied to all issues that form part of the scope of copyright.

The applicability of the United Kingdom's substantive provisions on moral rights has certain interesting implications. A foreign author, who is not resident in the United Kingdom and whose work is first published abroad, will not have the right to be identified, unless he asserts that right in the format prescribed by Section 78 of the Copyright, Designs and Patents Act 1988.[89] The fact that a similar assertion requirement is unheard off in the author's country, or in the country of first publication,

---

[84] See Ginsburg and Sirinelli, 15 (1991) *Columbia-VLA Journal of Law and the Arts* 135, at 139.

[85] In French legal terminology these rules are refered to as 'règles d'application immédiate', which characterises them very well.

[86] Different decisions were reached at first instance and upon appeal, see Judgment of 23 November 1988 of the Tribunal de Grande Instance de Paris, [1989] *Recueil Dalloz Sirey* 342 (Jurisprudence), annotated by Audit and [1989] *Revue Critique de Droit International Privé* 372, annotated by Gautier; Judgment of 6 July 1989 of the Cour d'Appel de Paris, [1990] *Recueil Dalloz Sirey* 152 (Jurisprudence), annotated by Audit and [1989] *Revue Critique de Droit International Privé* 706, annotated by Gautier; Judgment of 28 May 1991 of the Cour de Cassation, [1991] *Revue Critique de Droit International Privé* 752, annotated by Gautier. In this case, French law was both the law of the protecting country and the law of the forum, but that does not influence our conclusions. The related issue concerning the law applicable to the authorship issue will be returned to later (see below, pp 510–511).

[87] For an in depth analysis of the case see Ginsburg and Sirinelli, n 84 above (an English translation of the judgment is attached as an appendix); Ginsburg and Sirinelli [1991] 150 RIDA 3; see also Ginsburg 36 (1988–1989) *Journal of the Copyright Society of the USA* 81 and Ginsburg 17 (1993) *Columbia-VLA Journal of Law and the Arts* 395.

[88] See Ginsburg and Sirinelli, (1991) 150 RIDA 3, at 21.

[89] The exceptions to moral rights will also apply, see Copyright, Designs and Patents Act 1988, ss 79 and 81.

is irrelevant in this respect. This conclusion, though correct, could seem rather bizarre, especially as it may be doubted whether the United Kingdom's assertion requirement is in compliance with the no-formalities rule in the Berne Convention.[90]

(b) BROADCASTING

Broadcasting the work is, in general, also part of the exclusive right that is given to the copyrightholder. When it is claimed, for example, that royalties are due in the United Kingdom in relation to a planned broadcast, the law of the protecting country, in our example UK copyright law, should be used to define what amounts to a broadcast and whether the planned activity comes within the scope of that definition.[91] The definition of what amounts to a broadcast should also include the determination of the place where the exploitation takes place. It should also determine where broadcasting takes place and only if that place is within the United Kingdom in our example will the proposed activity be broadcasting for the purposes of the law of the protecting country. The latter point is particularly relevant as many broadcasts can be received in more than one country. There is a general agreement on considering the point of emission of the signal as the place where the broadcast takes place[92] and defining broadcasting as a transmission by wireless telegraphy.[93]

(c) SATELLITE BROADCASTING

Satellite broadcasting presents us with an even more complex picture.[94] Does the broadcasting take place in the country of the up-link where the signal is emitted from the ground station towards the satellite or does it also take place wherever the signal from the satellite is received? The latter area covers, traditionally, many countries and is described as the foot-print of the satellite. Does it matter that certain countries or parts of countries do not come intentionally within the foot-print of the satellite, but are only there for unavoidable technical reasons?

---

[90] English courts are not entitled to verify this point, but see Article 5(2) Berne Convention and Stamatoudi, n 83 above, at 503–504.

[91] This includes the determination whether a broadcast that can be received in the protecting country is an unintentional spill-over broadcast or a deliberate targeting of the audience in the protecting country from abroad. Only in the latter case will the copyright law of the protecting country apply and will copyright permission from the rightholders in that country be necessary. See Judgment of 28 May 1991 of the Austrian Supreme Court (Case 4 Ob 19/91), [1992] *European Commercial Cases* 456 and [1991] *GRUR Int* 920, see also judgment of 6 December 1990 of the Oberlandesgericht in Graz, [1991] *GRUR Int* 386.

[92] See Ulmer, n 1 above, at p 14.

[93] See, eg Copyright, Designs and Patents Act 1988, s 6.

[94] See Dietz (1989) 20 *IIC* 135–150.

The Berne Convention, in Article 11bis, speaks of broadcasting as communication to the public, but one has to turn to the law of the protecting country to see how this principle has been translated into national law, as this issue is part of the scope of copyright. The wording of the Convention could lead one to the conclusion that both emission and reception are essential elements and that the copyright law of the emission country and the copyright laws of the countries inside the footprint of the satellite should be applied cumulatively.[95] This is called the 'Bogsch Theory'.[96] The opposing theory is called the emission theory and it has now been adopted by the UK[97] and the whole of the European Union. Communication to the public is deemed to occur solely in the country where the signal is emitted to the satellite.[98]

The Satellite Broadcasting Directive states that 'communication to the public by satellite means the act of introducing, under the control and responsibility of the broadcasting organisation, of the programme-carrying signals intended for reception by the public into an uninterrupted chain of communication leading to the satellite and down towards the earth'.[99] An exception to this rule is provided for the situation where communication takes places from the territory of a non-Member State (third country) which does not provide the required minimum level of protection. In that case, the act of communication is deemed to have occurred in the Member State of the Union in which the uplink ground station is situated or in the Member State in which the broadcasting organisation has its principal establishment if there is no use of an up-link ground station situated in a Member State.[100]

The rule contained in the Directive is, sensu stricto, not a rule of private international law,[101] but it has a determinative effect on choice of law matters. The rightholder can only invoke his exclusive right if broadcasting takes place and by defining broadcasting the Directive assures that this will only take place in one country. That country's law is the only law of the protecting country under which the rightholder can make a successful

---

[95] This approach was taken by the Austrian Supreme Court, Judgment of 16 June 1992 (Case 4 Ob 44/92), [1994] *European Commercial Cases* 526 and [1994] *IPRax* 380; see also the judgments of 30 November 1989 and 27 June 1991 of the Oberlandesgericht in Vienna, [1990] *GRUR Int* 537 and [1991] *GRUR Int* 925 respectively.

[96] See Ficsor [1990] *International Business Lawyer* 258.

[97] Copyright, Designs and Patents Act 1988, s 6(4).

[98] See Karnell [1990] *International Business Lawyer* 263.

[99] EC Council Directive 93/83/EEC of 27 September 1993 on the co-ordination of certain rules concerning copyright and rights related to copyright applicable to satellite broadcasting and cable retransmission, [1993] OJ L248/15, Article 1(2)(b), see also Kern [1993] 8 *EIPR* 276.

[100] EC Council Directive 93/83/EEC of 27 September 1993 on the co-ordination of certain rules concerning copyright and rights related to copyright applicable to satellite broadcasting and cable retransmission, [1993] OJ L248/15, Article 1(2)(d).

[101] See Hohloch [1994] *IPRax* 387, at 391, note 52.

claim, or that country is the only country where protection can be claimed. According to the definition, no broadcasting takes place in any other country involved and, in the absence of any copyright activity, no protection can be claimed in these countries. So, to a certain extent, the law of the uplink country is singled out as the applicable law while any other law is, in practical terms, ruled out.

(d) EXCEPTIONS TO THE RIGHTS

Restrictions placed on the exclusive right modify the content of the latter. So, if all issues relating to the content of the exclusive right granted by copyright are to be governed by the law of the protecting country, exceptions to the rights granted to the copyrightholder form the next issue in this category. The precise scope of the rights granted is, indeed, only to be determined when these exceptions are also taken into account. For example, the rightholder's exclusive right to make copies of the work is restricted by the exceptional right of the user to make a copy for personal use. Further exceptions might exist for reporting current events, research and private study, etc.[102] The same exceptions, obviously, also play a role as defences against copyright infringement.

(e) CIVIL REMEDIES

Civil remedies are the final issue in this category. The availability of damages and injunctions restraining further encroachments on the exclusive rights of the rightholder make the rights effective. This includes the issue of who can sue, for example whether a licensee can sue independently for copyright infringement or whether he needs to rely on the copyrightowner to do so. They determine the real scope of the right involved and should, therefore, come under the law of the protecting country.[103] The parties cannot use the law of the contract to change the rights to sue which each of them has, in so far as that change is to have effect against third parties.[104] The traditional procedural restrictions apply though in the situation where the law of the protecting country is not equally the law of the forum. For example, the quantification of damages issue will be governed by the law of the forum.[105]

[102] For a full catalogue of these exceptions under UK law see Copyright, Designs and Patents Act 1988, Chapter 3 (ss 28–76).
[103] See, for an example in the case law, the judgment of 17 June 1992 of the German Bundesgerichtshof (Supreme Court), [1993] *GRUR Int* 257 and see Ulmer, n 00 above, pp at 35.
[104] See the judgment of 17 June 1992 of the German Bundesgerichtshof (Supreme Court), n 103 above.
[105] See Cheshire and North, *Private International Law*, Butterworths (12th ed, 1992), chapter 6 and more specifically at p 95.

3. TERMINATION OF THE RIGHT

This issue is important because the Berne Convention only sets out a minimum term of protection of life of the author plus fifty years.[106] Member States are free to introduce longer terms of protection into their legislation. The European Union countries have used this flexibility to introduce a 70 years after the death of the author term of protection as a general rule, although other shorter terms of protection apply to some categories of works.[107] The Copyright, Designs and Patents Act 1988[108] has introduced the 70 year after the death of the author term for literary, dramatic, musical and artistic works[109] and, for example, for films[110] whilst a fifty year term from release[111] or broadcast applies to sound recordings[112] and broadcasts[113] respectively. The term of protection could thus be different depending on which law is applicable.

The question of which law should be applicable to the issue of the termination of copyright becomes easier to answer when it is considered that what is really involved is the term of copyright and that the question can be reformulated as meaning: for how long is the exclusive right created? Looking at it this way, it seems logical to opt for the same applicable law as the one that is applicable to the creation issues. The law of the protecting country will therefore govern the duration and the termination of the right.[114] This solution also fits in well with the public policy idea that the country that authorises a restriction on competition may only wish to do so if its legislation can also determine the length in time of the restriction.

One special situation should be looked at in more detail. The Berne Convention restricts the length of the term of protection which Member States' legislation grants to foreign works to the term granted in the country of origin of the work, but it also gives Member States the option to deviate from this rule.[115] The United Kingdom has decided, in application of the Directive, to impose such a restriction on the length of the term of certain works. The restriction applies to works, the country of origin[116] of

---

[106] Article 7(1) Berne Convention.
[107] In general, see EC Council Directive 93/98/EEC of 29 October 1993 harmonising the term of protection of copyright and certain related rights, [1993] OJ L290/9.
[108] Sections 12 to 15.   [109] Section 12(2).   [110] Section 13B(2).
[111] Or from the end of the calendar year in which the recording was made if the recording was not released during that period, see s 13A(2)(a).
[112] Section 13A(2).   [113] Section 14(2).
[114] See also Article 34, para 1 of the Austrian Private International Law Statute, n 00 above, which contains the same rule; Schack, [1985] *GRUR Int* 523 and Ulmer [1983] *GRUR Int* 109.
[115] Article 7(8) Berne Convention.
[116] The first (country of origin) limb of the rule has not been retained in relation to sound recordings and broadcasts and cable programmes.

which is not a Member State of the European Economic Area[117] and the author of which is not a national of such Member State.[118] The term of protection is, initially, still governed by the law of the protecting country. But the substantive rule only imposes a maximum length of the term of protection that is equal to that granted to domestic works. The specific length of the term of copyright protection for such works is then referred back to the term granted by the law of the country of origin.

France has used the option left open by the Berne Convention in a similar way. The Court of Appeal in Paris ruled that a series of American Buster Keaton films that were no longer protected by copyright in their country of origin, the United States, were not entitled to copyright protection under the law of the protecting country, France. The films were not entitled to the normal longer French term of protection, because they were no longer in copyright in the country of origin and continuing copyright protection in the country of origin is a prerequisite for protection in France.[119]

4. VALIDITY OF THE RIGHT

The question concerning the validity of the right is answered by looking at the criteria for the creation of the right. The test is whether the criteria for the creation of the right were present at the time the right allegedly came into existence. If the answer is in the negative the right is, and never was, valid. Such cases arise frequently before the courts. Alternatively, the criteria might have been met at the time the right came into existence, but they are now no longer met. In that case, the right is no longer valid. Apart from the issue of the expiry of the term of copyright, situations involving the latter alternative will hardly ever arise in relation to copyright.

The strong link with the creation of the right militates strongly in favour of the application of the same choice of law rules in both cases. It is suggested that the issue of validity should also be governed by the law of the protecting country.[120]

The fact that the validity point often arises in an infringement context, where, typically, an alleged infringer argues, as a defence or by way of counterclaim, that the right is not valid in the first place and that therefore

---

[117] The areas of co-operation between the EU and the EFTA countries include intellectual property. The EU zone could, therefore, be expanded to the EEA zone.
[118] See Copyright, Designs and Patents Act 1988, ss 12(6), 13A(4), 13B(7) and 14(3).
[119] Judgment of 24 April 1975 of the Cour d'Appel de Paris, *SA Galba Films v Friedman, SARL Capital Films, Pernot and Société Les Films La Boétie* (1975) 83 *RIDA* 106; the decision was appealed unsuccessfully in the French Cour de Cassation, see judgment of 15 December 1975, *Léopold Friedman v SA Galba Films* (1976) 88 *RIDA* 115, annotated by Françon.
[120] See Caldwell 6 (1976) *Denver Journal of International Law and Policy* 191, at 199, who refers in this respect to Rabel's, *The Conflict of Laws*, (1950), at p 295.

it cannot be infringed, constitutes a factor which complicates matters slightly. It could be argued that the whole infringement issue, including the validity point, should be governed by the same law. This might seem attractive from a practical point of view, but it is submitted that this argument needs to be rejected. Apart from the fact that the two points arise in the same proceedings, there is no substantive link between the two points, while there is, as demonstrated above, a strong link between validity and the creation and existence of the right. Moreover, it makes no sense to apply a different law to the same validity point depending on whether it arise independently or in the course of infringement proceedings. In the latter case, the validity of the right should be determined as a preliminary point on the basis of the law of the protecting country. The situation in which the validity point arises should have no influence on the choice of law rule.[121]

5. AUTHORSHIP, OWNERSHIP OF RIGHT AND WORKS CREATED BY EMPLOYEES

(a) AUTHORSHIP OF COPYRIGHT WORKS

Authorship could be said to be a factual matter. The author of a work is the person who creates it: the writer, painter or sculptor, etc. The Copyright, Designs and Patents Act 1988 sets off, in Section 9(1), by restating that rule. However, it does not stop there. A set of legal fictions follow. For example, the author of a film is taken to be the person who makes the necessary arrangements for the making of the film.[122] English law has, traditionally, referred to the producer in this respect, but other legal systems have traditionally (also) referred to the director. A different person could be designated as author, according to the choice of the applicable law.[123]

Two obvious laws could be chosen as the law applicable to the issue of authorship. The law of the protecting country is an obvious candidate, if the function of copyright is to reward the author. It could seem logical to apply the law that authorises the restriction and that determines its scope to the authorship issue if that reward is to take the form of a restriction on competition. After all, the author could well be the beneficiary of the right that is created. The law of the country of origin could be an alternative, though. The author is also the first point of contact for those parties that are interested in the worldwide exploitation of the copyright in the work. Such a worldwide exploitation has become the norm, for example on the internet, and it is important that the same starting point is available on a worldwide scale. The logical aim of identifying the same author for the

[121] See also below, chapter 12, p 642.   [122] Section 9(2)(a).
[123] See generally, Seignette [1990] *Informatierecht/AMI* 195.

same work in every jurisdiction can be achieved if the issue of authorship were to be governed by the law of the country of origin, as each work has one country of origin only. It is submitted that the latter solution is the better option.[124] It would facilitate the international exploitation of the work, eliminates the artificial situation in which a single work could have different authors in different countries and the English case law, as well as the statute and the Convention, do not preclude it.

Apart from being used often to identify the owner of the copyright, the definition of authorship is also used to identify the beneficiary of moral rights. The Copyright, Designs and Patents Act 1988 grants to the 'author' of the work the right to be identified and the right to object to derogatory treatment. If someone is not identified as the author, he cannot be granted moral rights from a substantive law point of view. It has been argued above that moral rights touch public policy and it must, therefore, follow that the identification of the author, only for the purposes of the attribution of moral rights,[125] must also touch upon public policy. The provisions of Section 9 *et seq* of the Copyright, Designs and Patents Act 1988 should apply whenever the law of the country of origin grants an insufficient level of protection for moral rights, as compared with the level offered by the provisions of the law of the forum.

The French Cour de Cassation applied the French authorship rules as mandatory rules for the purpose of the identification of the author of the film 'Asphalt Jungle'. John Huston was, in his capacity as director, not the author under the law of the country of origin,[126] the United States. Under US law, he was, therefore, not entitled to moral rights protection. The French Cour de Cassation argued that lack of moral rights protection in the United States would lead to a French Court being obliged to deny moral rights protection in France. This was unacceptable from a French public policy point of view. The problem was solved through the mandatory application[127] of the French rules on authorship, according to which Huston was an author. This meant that he was entitled to moral rights pro-

---

[124] See Judgment of 29 April 1970 of the French Cour de Cassation, [1971] *Revue Critique de Droit International Privé* 270, at 271; Judgment of 14 March 1991 of the Cour d'Appel de Paris [1992] *La Semaine Juridique* 21780 (Jurisprudence); Judgment of 21 September 1983 of the Tribunal de Grande Instance de Paris, (1984) 120 *RIDA* 156; Judgment of 14 February 1977 of the Tribunal de Grande Instance de Paris, (1978) 97 *RIDA* 179; and see generally Ginsburg 36 (1988–1989) *Journal of the Copyright Society of the USA* 81, at 98–99 and Ginsburg and Sirinelli 15 (1991) *Columbia-VLA Journal of Law and the Arts* 135, at 141.

[125] See Ginsburg 36 (1988–1989) *Journal of the Copyright Society of the USA* 81, at 98–99.

[126] It has been suggested that authorship for moral rights purposes is determined by applying the provisions of the law of the country of origin, see judgment of 14 February of the Tribunal de Grande Instance de Paris (first instance court), *Dimitri Busuioo Ionesco* v *Sté Metro Golwyn Mayer and Sté Romania Films* (1978) 96 *RIDA* 179. This decision can no longer stand in the light of the Cour de Cassation's (supreme court) decision in the *John Huston* case.

[127] Concerning the distinction between mandatory rules and public policy, see above, p 503, the same comments apply in this case.

tection in France. It needs to be stressed, though, that the *Huston* ruling is restricted in scope to the moral rights and authorship for the purposes of moral rights issues.[128] The public policy argument does not apply to any other issue and the normal choice of law rules can then be applied to the authorship issue.[129]

(b) FIRST OWNERSHIP OF COPYRIGHT WORKS

The Copyright, Designs and Patents Act 1988 contains only a substantive rule on ownership. The author is supposed to be the first owner of the copyright in the work.[130] The case law has never addressed the issue of choice of law in relation to the first ownership of copyright. Finally, the Berne Convention contains one detailed rule on ownership. Article 14bis (2) determines that the law of the protecting country will govern the issue of ownership in relation to cinematographic works. It is important to trace back the history of this rule to see what implications it has. The original version of the Convention contained no rule at all concerning ownership. In practice, almost no real problems arose because most legal systems considered the creator of a work to be the author of a work and the author to be the first owner of the copyright in the work and cases on co- and joint authorship are relatively rare. Differences did however arise in relation to the ownership of copyright in a cinematographic work. One could, primarily, look towards the maker of the film or, alternatively, to the individual creator of contributing parts of the work.

Article 14bis(2) was introduced during the Stockholm Revision Conference of the Berne Convention to deal with these specific differences. There are no explicit indications that the Member States wanted to introduce an exception for cinematographic works to the general rule on ownership, but there are no indications to the contrary either. All that is known is that the Member States could not agree who was to be the author of a cinematographic work. In the absence of an agreement as to who, in substantive law, was the author of a film, the point was addressed from a choice of law point of view. The rule that the issue will be governed by the law of the protecting country means that all Member States can continue to apply their own (different) substantive rules, without any of them having to give way. The choice of law rule confirms and continues the disagreement in the area of substantive law. The general point concerning the first ownership of copyright was not necessarily raised, but why would

---

[128] See Ginsburg and Sirinelli (1991) 150 *RIDA* 3, at 19.
[129] On the difference in approach between moral rights and pecuniary rights, see also Judgment of 1 February 1989 of the Cour d'Appel de Paris, *Anne Bragance* v *Olivier Orban and Michel de Grèce* (1989) 142 *RIDA* 301.
[130] Copyright, Designs and Patents Act 1988, s 11(1).

the draughtsmen restrict the application of the rule to one category of works if the same rule was already applicable to all other works? If the latter had been the case, a note mentioning that the same rule would also apply to cinematographic works would have been sufficient.

That brings us to the general rule. Which law should be applied to the issue of ownership?[131] At first sight, there seems to be a strong link between the grant of the copyright and the issue of to whom it is granted. It may make sense to apply the same law of the protecting country to both issues.[132] This would also result in a situation where a single choice of law rule deals with the issue of ownership in relation to all types of works. It is submitted, however, that upon closer analysis, these arguments are not convincing. Other arguments point towards the law of the country of origin.[133] The exploitation of copyright works, to an increasing extent, takes place at international level. For example, literary works, photographs and films are disseminated and exploited over the internet. The internet does not know any borders and it would create enormous practical difficulties and costs if the first ownership of these works was given to different persons in different countries. A choice of law rule that links the first ownership of copyright to the law of the country of origin would solve this problem.[134] The copyright in each work would have a single (first) owner. The latter would be able to sell the rights for the worldwide exploitation of the work and the buyer would have certainty that he would be dealing with the real rightholder.[135] It would also make sense to apply the same law to the issues of authorship and first ownership, because most legal systems would have a substantive rule that makes the author the first owner of the copyright in the work.

This discussion is not entirely academic in nature, because, although most legal systems operate the same general ownership rule, there are differences between the provisions in the various national copyright regimes which deal with issues such as co- and joint authorship and authorship in relation to films and sound recordings.

---

[131] See, generally and from a US point of view, Nimmer [1973] *GRUR Int* 12.

[132] For an example, but admittedly one in relation to cinematographic works (but outside the scope of the Berne Convention) see the judgment of 17 June 1986 of the Austrian Supreme Court, *Hotel Video* [1986] *GRUR Int* 728

[133] See also Drobnig 40 (1976) *RabelsZ* 195, at 198–202.

[134] See Schack, n 114 above and see Judgment of 14 March 1991 of the Court d'Appel de Paris, *SARL La Rosa v Sté Almax International SPA*, [1992] *La Semaine Juridique* 21780 (Jurisprudence), in which the Paris Court of Appeal applied this approach, even if the Italian law of the country of origin granted the rights to a company, whereas French substantive law would rule out such an option. The fact that the author is a company does not offend against French public policy, see Judgment of 3 June 1961 of the Cour d'Appel de Paris, *Soc Toho Cy Ltd v Soc Film d'art et Soc Prodis* (1961) 33 *RIDA* 112.

[135] See Ginsburg's annotations under the judgment of 14 March 1991 of the Court d'Appel de Paris, *SARL La Rosa v Sté Almax International SPA*, [1992] *La Semaine Juridique* 21780 (Jurisprudence), at p 5.

(c) ARTICLE 14BIS(2) IN MORE DETAIL

Article 14bis(2) does not simply determine that the ownership of copyright in a cinematographic work is governed by the law of the protecting country, it also provides for certain exceptions and rules on formalities. Certain countries may include certain contributors to a film amongst the owners of the copyright in the film. If these contributions were made on the basis of a specific undertaking to do so,[136] the normal Article 14bis(2) rule is that these owners of copyright cannot object to the 'reproduction, distribution, public performance, communication to the public by wire, broadcasting or any other communication to the public, or the subtitling or dubbing of texts, of the work'. This is subject to a stipulation to the contrary.[137] However, authors of scenarios, dialogues and musical works that are created for the making of a film are exempted from this rule, unless there is a national legislative provision to the contrary.[138] The form of the undertaking concerned, ie whether a written agreement or a written text with the same legal effect is required, is to be determined by the law of the country where the maker of the film has his headquarters or habitual residence.[139] This is a sensible move, as it will enable the maker of a film to settle the legal position in one agreement which satisfies the formal rules of his own domestic law and the coverage of which is worldwide. The application of the different provisions of the various laws of the protecting countries would have given rise to great practical problems.

These problems come back in through the back door, though, as the same Article 14bis(2) also states that the law of the protecting country may require a written agreement. The result is the more or less cumulative application of the law of the protecting country and the law of the country where the maker of the film has his headquarters or habitual residence to this issue. Clearly, the Member States were not prepared to give up control over the issue via the law of the protecting country, especially as a foreign law over which they have no control might indirectly interfere with the distribution of the ownership of certain rights and the resulting royalty income. This solution is clearly undesirable. A harmonised substantive rule on formalities would have been a far better solution.

(d) OWNERSHIP OF COPYRIGHT IN WORKS CREATED BY EMPLOYEES

The provisions of the Copyright, Designs and Patents Act 1988 depart from the normal first ownership rule in the situation where a literary, musical or artistic work is made by an employee in the course of his

[136] For example if a script or screen-play has been commissioned from an author.
[137] Article 14bis (2)(b) Berne Convention.   [138] Article 14bis (2)(d) Berne Convention.
[139] Article 14bis (2)(c) Berne Convention.

employment. Subject to an agreement to the contrary, the employer becomes the first owner of the copyright in the work, rather than the employee-author.[140] This change is, of course, a change in the substantive law. The statute is silent on the choice of law point. Would it be advisable to follow the change in substantive copyright law and change the choice of law rule too?

It would, of course, be possible to apply the same choice of law rule to works created by employees and works created outside an employer-employee relationship. The application of the law of the country of origin would have the advantage that the same law would be applicable to all issues concerning ownership. A choice in favour of the law of the protecting country would, however, seem to have the advantage that the copyright industry in a given country would always be able to apply the same law. This is not a valid argument. Such an approach would create great practical difficulties for the international use and exploitation of works created by employees. Let us take the example of a manual containing operating instructions and useful tips for the use of a video-camera. The manufacturers clearly want to market their product, accompanied by the manual, in as many countries as possible. Applying the law of the protecting country would mean applying as many different laws as there are countries in which the product is marketed and, because of the differences in national laws, the manufacturers might in a number of countries be selling a manual in which they do not own the copyright, whilst they might own the copyright in the country of production. This situation is clearly undesirable. This seems to point to the application of the law of the country of origin to the issue of employee-ownership.

A matter which needs also to be considered is the employment relationship as set out in the contract of employment.[141] If the employee retains the copyright and becomes the owner of the rights that flow from it, the exploitation of these rights might provide him with an extra income, whilst the extra royalty cost for the use of the work in which the employee owns the copyright will be taken into account by the employer. This might influence the determination of the salary of the employee in the contract of employment. This establishes a close link with the contract of employment and provides an argument for applying the same law to both that contract and the issue of employee ownership of copyright. Maybe the issue ought to be characterised as an employment-related contractual issue. Such a solution would also eliminate the problem highlighted above[142] in relation to the law of the protecting country approach. One law would then govern the ownership issue, irrespective of the place of exploitation of the work. Which law would be applicable in such a situation though? After

---

[140] Copyright, Designs and Patents Act 1988, s 11(2).
[141] See Drobnig, n 133 above, at 202–203.　　[142] See above, pp 512–513.

the entry into force of the EC Convention on the Law Applicable to Contractual Obligations 1980 (the Rome Convention) there is no longer any doubt on this point. Article 6 of the Convention allows the parties to choose the applicable law and it determines that, in the absence of a choice of law by the parties, the law of the place where the employee habitually carries out his work is applicable. In the situation where the employee does not habitually carry out his work in any one country that rule is replaced by a rule applying 'the law of the country in which the place of business through which he [the employee] was engaged is situated'. The employee will also be able to rely on the mandatory rules of the law that would govern the contract in the absence of a choice of law by the parties, even if the parties have made such a choice.

It is submitted that the link with the employment relationship and the contract of employment is stronger than the link with the general copyright ownership rule. Accordingly, a contractual characterisation is preferable[143] and the choice of law rule contained in Article 6 of the Rome Convention 1980 should be applied to the issue of employee ownership. This solution has also been adopted in the Austrian Private International Law Statute.[144]

6. Transferability of the Right

We are not concerned here with the actual transfer of the right. Before a transfer of a right enters the picture, there is a preliminary issue which needs to be addressed. This is the issue of whether the right can be transferred in the first place. Does the issue of the scope of the right which is granted also include the issue of whether the rightholder is able to transfer the right to another party? Once more, the statutory provisions remain silent on this point.

This transferability issue is linked with the grant of the right, rather than with the transfer of the right by means of a contract. Transferability and assignability are closely linked to the issue of what can be assigned, for example pecuniary rights and moral rights or pecuniary rights only, and with the scope of the right.[145] It would clearly not be desirable to apply the law of the contract to it and allow the parties to choose a law which allows the transfer of the right at their convenience. It is, therefore, submitted that the issue of transferability should be governed by the law which governs

---

[143] See Ulmer 41 (1977) *RabelsZ* 479, at 507–509.
[144] Article 34, para 2: 'For intangible property rights arising from the activity of an employee within the framework of his employment relationship, the conflicts rule governing the employment relationship (Article 44) shall be determinative for the relationship between the employer and the employee.'
[145] De Boer [1977] *WPNR* Nr 5412 p 674, at 707.

the creation and the scope of the right.[146] The choice of law rule should thus result in the application of the law of the protecting country.[147] This solution has been approved in *Campbell Connelly & Co Ltd v Noble*.[148] In this case, the proper law of the contract (English law) was *de facto* applied to determine whether the contract had validly transferred the copyright in a popular tune, but only after the assignability issue had been determined under the law of the protecting country (US law). Whether the US copyright could be assigned had to be decided as a preliminary point and that issue was governed by the law of the protecting country.[149]

The issue of transferability assumes practical importance due to the fact that some legal systems allow for the transfer of the copyright itself, while others do not. For example, the UK's Copyright, Designs and Patents Act 1988 allows the transfer of copyright,[150] whilst the German UrheberGesetz rules out any such transfer. The German Act only provides the opportunity to grant licences to carry out some form of activity which would otherwise have amounted to copyright infringement. In contrast, the view is held, almost unanimously, that moral rights are not transferable, and so no choice of law problem arises.[151]

Up to now, we have been concerned primarily with the transfer of the right by contract during the lifetime of the rightholder. Similar problems arise though after the death of the author. These are of less practical importance in terms of private international law. This is because the rules in the various legal systems are very similar in this respect and allow for the transfer of copyright and moral rights by testamentary disposition. In the absence of a will, a statutory transfer regime is, generally, provided for.[152]

In the final analysis, there is no reason not to apply the law of the protecting country to the issue of transferability of rights, regardless of the situation in which it arises.[153] The boundaries of the issue need to be taken into account, though. Assignability is restricted to the question whether or not the right can be assigned. Whether and under what conditions a transfer or assignment occurred is a matter for the law of the contract, if the law

---

[146] See Dicey and Morris, n 9 above, Rule 120(2), at 979.

[147] Contra: Schack, n 114 above, who argues that the law of the country of origin should govern this issue, because that would mean that the same law applied in every jurisdiction and this would facilitate the worldwide commercial exploitation of copyright works. It is submitted that this suggestion is to be rejected as a not feasible one, as the issue of assignability is strongly linked with the public policy of each country.

[148] [1963] 1 WLR 252, at 255.

[149] A similar result was reached in an American case in which the law of the contract was Brazilian law, see *Corcovado Music Corpn v Hollis Music*, 981 F2d 679 (2d Cir 1993).

[150] See s 90(1).

[151] See, eg Copyright, Designs and Patents Act 1988, s 94.

[152] See, eg for the United Kingdom, Copyright, Designs and Patents Act 1988, ss 90(1) and 95.

[153] See *Campbell Connelly & Co Ltd v Noble* [1963] 1 WLR 252, at 255.

of the protecting country allows the principle of an assignment or a transfer of right[154]. This approach was followed by the Court of Appeal in Paris in *Anne Bragance v Olivier Orban and Michel de Grèce*.[155] The contract between Anne Bragance, who had helped Michel de Grèce with the writing of his book, and the latter was governed by US (New York) law and included a transfer of all aspects of copyright to Michel de Grèce. This included both the moral and the pecuniary aspects of copyright. Due to the publication of the book in France, French law was the law of the protecting country. The French court ruled that moral rights are not assignable under French law and it was therefore impossible for the contract and the law of the contract to transfer these rights effectively. Pecuniary rights are, on the contrary, assignable under French law and the assignment was valid under the law of the contract.[156] In practical terms, the outcome of the case was as follows. Anne Bragance gained the right to be identified as an author on every (French) copy of the book, but she did not gain any further pecuniary compensation, as she had effectively assigned all her pecuniary rights.

V
PATENTS AND TRADE MARKS

It serves no useful purpose to repeat anything which was outlined in previous paragraphs in relation to copyright and, accordingly, comments in this section will be restricted to those points where differences appear.

1. THE REGISTRATION SYSTEM

The main differences between copyright, on the one hand, and patents and trade marks, on the other hand, is that the latter require registration before they come into existence. Upon the filing of an application, a trade mark or a patent is registered by the Patent Office. Whether or not the application forms the subject of an examination and the level of the examination vary from country to country. This application and registration system is organised per country. Normally, one application is made per country and eventually, after a national examination procedure, a national patent or trade mark is granted.[157] The rights that are granted are valid for the country in

---

[154] See Ginsburg 17 (1993) *Columbia-VLA Journal of Law and the Arts* 395, at 408
[155] Judgment of 1 February 1989 of the Cour d'Appel de Paris, (1989) 142 *RIDA* 301.
[156] The public policy argument that was invoked in relation to moral rights was not invoked in relation to pecuniary rights, even if the specific arrangement would not have been permissible under French law. See Ginsburg 17 (1993) *Columbia-VLA Journal of Law and the Arts* 395, at 414.
[157] See Article 4(A)(1) Paris Convention.

which the application was brought and in which they were granted. When applying for a patent or a trade mark, once an initial application has been made, the applicant can invoke a right of priority (over other applications) of twelve and six months respectively.[158] Nevertheless, after grant the national rights are fully independent from one another.[159] International co-operation at the application and examination stages exists, as do certain supra-national rights. We will discuss their implications separately.

What are the choice of law implications of this registration procedure? The involvement of a government agency, ie the patent office, has clear implications. Government agencies only apply their own national procedural law.[160] Not only is the procedure, *sensu strictu*, governed by that law, but so also are the tests that are applied during that procedure. Any authority to act which the governmental agency may have, only arises from the application of its domestic law. Without the application of that law, the agency has no power to do anything whatsoever.[161] This approach is approved of in Article 2(3) of the Paris Convention, in which an express reservation is made, as a result of which judicial and administrative procedures are reserved for the domestic law of the agency. Since protection in each country is sought through a national application for and registration of the right, the domestic law of the government agency is also the law of the protecting country. It seems, after all, logical that an application to the UK Patent Office, which will eventually lead to the grant of a UK patent or trade mark, is governed by the procedure contained in the UK's Patents Act 1977[162] and Trade Marks Act 1994.[163] The Patents Act also contains an indication in Section 12 that this conclusion must be right. If a patent application can be made abroad 'under the law of any country other than the United Kingdom' that should, *a contrario*, mean that the provisions of the Patents Act must be applied to the procedural issues of a British application.

2. The Law of the Protecting Country

Here there are no important differences from copyright.[164] The law of the protecting country should be applied to the acquisition,[165] the scope,[166]

---

[158] Article 4(C) Paris Convention.   [159] Articles 4(1), 4(2) and 6(3) Paris Convention.

[160] For a parallel with the procedural rules that are applied necessarily by the English Courts, see Dicey and Morris, n 9 above, Rule 17, at p 169.

[161] There is, in this respect, a direct link with the jurisdiction issue. See Van Hecke and Lenaerts, *Internationaal Privaatrecht*, Story Scientia, (2nd ed, 1989), at p 16.

[162] See, ie ss 14–21 and the corresponding provisions of the Patent Rules.

[163] See, ie ss 37–41 and the corresponding provisions of the Trade Mark Rules.

[164] See Ulmer, n 1 above, at pp 68–70.

[165] See also Article 34, para 1 of the Austrian Private International Law Statute, n 71 above, that contains the same rule and the judgment of 14 January 1986 of the Austrian Supreme Court (Case 4 Ob 408/85), *Hotel Sacher*, [1986] *GRUR Int* 735.

[166] *Ibid.*

the transferability[167] and the termination[168] of patents[169] and trade marks.[170] This is, in essence, the law of the country in which the relevant application for registration has been filed.[171]

(a) NO CLEAR ANSWERS IN THE CASE LAW

The existing case law does not contain very clear and explicit *dicta* on this point, but certain conclusions can, nevertheless, be derived from it. *Wilderman* v *Berk*[172] deals with parallel German and British patents. Tomlin J did not address the choice of law issue, but de facto he applied English law to determine the scope of protection when dealing with the alleged infringement through importation into Britain. The main problem with this case is the fact that the judge did not clarify why he applied English law. Did he do so because it was the law of the forum, or because it was the law of the protecting country? As the case did not mention which patent was applied for first, English law could even have been the law of the country of origin, the country of the first original application. *British Nylon Spinners* v *ICI*[173] is more helpful. Evershed MR ruled out every foreign interference with the statutory rights of the patentholder.[174] That leads inevitably to the conclusion that the only law that is not excluded is the law of the country in which the registration has been filed. The law of the protecting country must be the applicable law, but the problem with the case is that the only point that was really to be decided was whether the US interference with rights in a British patent would be tolerated. The case did not deal with the patent itself and it is not clear to which issues the choice of law rule should be applied.

British Nylon Spinners is helpful on another point too. The case made it clear that the application for and the scope of a British patent touch upon the public policy of the UK.[175] This means that the law of the protecting country should be applied. The case confirms the argument which was put forward in the copyright context.[176]

In *Reuter* v *Mulhens*,[177] the trade mark rights in the name 4711 for Eau de Cologne are linked to the existence of goodwill. It is clear that the Court of

---

[167] See Dicey and Morris, n 9 above, Rule 120(2), at p 979.
[168] See also Article 34, para 1 of the Austrian Private International Law Statute, n 71 above, that contains the same rule and the judgment of 14 January 1986 of the Austrian Supreme Court (Case 4 Ob 408/85), *Hotel Sacher*, [1986] *GRUR Int* 735.
[169] See *Wilderman* v *F W Berk and Company Ltd* [1925] 1 Ch 116 and *British Nylon Spinners Ltd* v *Imperial Chemical Industries Ltd* [1953] 1 Ch 19.
[170] See, in relation to trade marks, *R J Reuter Co Ltd* v *Mulhens* [1954] 1 Ch 50.
[171] For a French example see Judgment of 28 April 1976 of the Cour d'Appel de Paris, *Gaf Corporation* v *Soc Amchem Products* [1977] *Recueil Dalloz Sirey* 511 (Jurisprudence), annotated by Mousseron at p 513 *et seq*, see especially p 514.
[172] [1925] 1 Ch 116. [173] [1953] 1 Ch 19. [174] *Ibid*, at 26.
[175] *Ibid*. [176] See above, pp 501–506. [177] [1954] 1 Ch 50.

Appeal derived that link from the substantive English law. The Court determined, on that basis, whether or not goodwill existed, what the scope of protection was and whether the right was assignable. In the presence of rights in Germany (the country of origin for the registered mark) and Britain, this must be seen as an indication either that the law of the forum or the law of the protecting country should be applied. Unfortunately, the choice of law point was not raised in the case and English law was both the law of the forum and the law of the protecting country. *Lecouturier* v *Rey*[178] addressed the issue whether a British parallel trade mark could be assigned by a decision of a French court that assigned the French parallel trade mark. The House of Lords decided that it could not. Two of the three speeches focus on the extraterritorial aspects of the French decision. Lord Loreburn added, though, that the regulation and disposal of British trade marks should be governed by English law.[179] His speech supports the argument that the creation, scope and assignability of trade marks are governed by the law of the protecting country.

Apple Corps v *Apple Computer*[180] was concerned with a delimitation contract between the Apple trade mark of the record company and that of the computer company, but Ferris J seemed to suggest that the scope and validity of trade marks that are registered in many countries are, first of all not governed by the English law of the forum or of the contract, whilst, secondly, they are governed by their relative laws. It may seem that the 'relative' law is the law of the protecting country, or in this case the law of the country of registration for each mark, but the case did not address the point clearly. It did rule, however, that a delimitation contract and its law of the contract did not influence the issues of scope and validity. Contracts in relation to intellectual property rights, which will be discussed in the next chapter, need to be separated from the rights themselves.

(b) TO WHICH ISSUES IS THE LAW OF THE PROTECTING COUNTRY APPLIED?

(i) Acquisition of the right

In practical terms, this means that the law of the protecting country will cover areas such as the requirements for registration and protection. For example, in relation to patents the concepts of novelty,[181] inventive step[182] and capability of industrial application[183] will be covered. The fact that, at the application stage, a right of priority was created by a previous appli-

---

[178] [1910] AC 262. [179] *Ibid*, at 273. [180] [1992] FSR 431.
[181] Patents Act 1977, ss 1(1)(a) and 2, see Holyoak and Torremans, n 38 above, at pp 47–56.
[182] Patents Act 1977, ss 1(1)(b) and 3, see Holyoak and Torremans, n 38 above, at pp 56–67.
[183] Patents Act 1977, ss 1(1)(c) and 4, see Holyoak and Torremans, n 38 above, at pp 67–70.

cation abroad does not change this. The law of the country of origin has no influence.[184]

The acquisition process is concerned with the creation and the existence of the right. A nullity claim contains an argument that the right should never have been created and should never have existed. It is, therefore, logical that the law of the protecting country should also be applied to the issue of nullity.[185]

(ii) Scope of the right

The scope of the right includes such issues as the content[186] and limits of the right[187] and the claims to be asserted in infringement cases. Examples are the right for the patentholder to manufacture the patented product or to use the patented process. Whilst these are generally accepted in almost all legal systems, additional rights to control importation and distribution are not found in the laws of all protecting countries. Further examples in relation to which domestic laws differ are the limits of these exclusive rights. One could think in terms of the honest concurrent use of a trade mark or the use of patented technology for private and/or non-commercial purposes.

(iii) Termination of the right

Issues such as the term and the rules on the termination of patents and trade marks should also be governed by the law of the protecting country. This includes such things as the twenty year term for patent protection,[188] the surrender of a trade mark[189] or the revocation on the basis on the non-use of a trade mark during a five year period.[190] Further examples will arise from the rules concerning the effects of the failure to pay fees.

(iv) Validity and transferability of the right

Issues of validity of a patent[191] or a trade mark and issues relating to the transferability of those rights[192] should also be governed by the law of the

---

[184] See Judgment of 28 April 1976 of the Cour d'Appel de Paris, *Gaf Corn* v *Soc Amchem Products* [1977] *Recueil Dalloz Sirey* 511 (Jurisprudence), French law was applied irrespective of the law of the country of origin, the USA.

[185] See Judgment of 17 December 1969 of the Cour d'Appel de Paris, *Mobile Parking* v *Cogepa* [1970] *Propriété Industrielle Bulletin Documentaire* III-131, at 132; the public policy argument was raised in this patent case, because nullity concerns the grant and existence of an exclusive right that restricts competition.

[186] For an Austrian example concerning trade marks, see Judgment of 28 June 1983 of the Supreme Court (Case 4 Ob 345/82), [1984] *GRUR Int* 453, annotated by Wirner.

[187] See *Lecouturier* v *Rey* [1910] AC 262, at 270.

[188] See, eg for the UK, Patents Act 1977, s 25(1).

[189] See, eg for the UK, Trade Marks Act 1994, s 45.

[190] See, eg for the UK, Trade Marks Act 1994, s 46(1).

[191] See Caldwell, n 120 above, at 199, who refers in this respect to Ernst Rabel's *The Conflict of Laws*, (1950), at p 295.

[192] See Dicey and Morris, n 9 above, Rule 120(2), at p 979.

protecting country. The issue of transferability includes rules on the possibility of registering such a transfer on the Patent or Trade Mark Registers. It also includes the issue whether a trade mark can be transferred as such or whether it can only be transferred together with the business or the goodwill to which the mark belongs.[193]

3. Ownership of Rights

(a) TRADE MARKS

There are no special choice of law rules in relation to this issue. Article 6septies of the Paris Convention just introduces a substantive rule which allows the proprietor of the mark to oppose an application for the registration of the mark made by an agent or representative without his authorisation. The proprietor can also apply for the cancellation of the registration or ask for it to be assigned to him. The latter option is only available in the situation where the law of the country in which the registration took place allows it. The UK has chosen to implement all aspects of this provision. This implementation is found in Section 60 of the Trade Marks Act 1994. Returning to the wider issue, it can be observed that the law of the place of registration is the law of the protecting country anyway. Apart from that, the law of the protecting country applies, as it did in relation to copyright. Although the case was mainly concerned with the assignability of the trade mark, the House of Lords seemed to assume, in *Lecouturier* v *Rey*, that the issue of trade mark ownership is also governed by the law of the protecting country.[194]

(b) PATENTS

(i) Applications by non-authorised persons
Similar ownership problems arise in relation to patents. A first series of important issues can be referred to as issues concerning applications by non-authorised persons. The law of the protecting country should govern the issue of who is entitled to the patent, as this is closely linked to the grant and the creation itself of the patent. Certain systems operate a first to invent rule, whereby the inventor is necessarily the one who will get the patent. Other systems, such as the one in operation in the United Kingdom, work on a first to file basis. However, the latter systems, normally, have a presumption that the applicant will be the inventor or a person authorised by him and they provide mechanisms for the inventor to reclaim his rights at the various stages of the application and granting

---

[193] See Article 6quater(1) Paris Convention.   [194] [1910] AC 262, at 273.

procedure if the original application was made by a non-authorised person. In the United Kingdom, the Patents Act 1977 deals with these issues in Sections 7, 8 and 37. These issues of the rights of the inventor to the patent and the legal position in the situation where the application for a patent is made by a non-authorised person will be addressed through the application of the law of the protecting country.

The latter situation, that confronts the inventor with a non-authorised person, is, in fact, an example of a wider category of cases in which two or more parties claim to be entitled to a patent. The situation in which several parties claim the patent on the basis that they have made the same invention independently of one-another is also within this category and will thus be governed by the same law.[195] The law of the protecting country determines not only under what conditions the right is granted but also to whom it is granted and who is entitled to the right. Certain discrepancies between the various national systems could result from this approach, but this must be acceptable in the light of the choice made in the Paris Convention in favour of a strictly territorial scope and full independence for the nationally granted patents.[196] A last issue which does not concern full ownership, will also be governed by the same law of the protecting country, because it is closely related to ownership. This is the issue of the right of the inventor to be mentioned in his capacity as inventor in any patent application, notification or in the patent itself.[197] This issue arises regularly in cases where the right to patent the invention is given to a third party. An employee's invention often presents a good example of such a situation and it is to that issue that we now turn.

(ii) **Employee's inventions**

The second important issue is the ownership of employee's inventions. National laws differ widely on this point and this gives great practical importance to the choice of law rule. In the United Kingdom, the relevant substantive provisions are found in Section 39 *et seq* of the Patents Act 1977, but no choice of law rule has been included. Which law will decide whether the employee or the employer will own the patent in a specific case or whether they are joint-inventors?[198]

A number of authors have argued that there is no reason to deviate from the general rule according to which the law of the protecting country applies.[199] They link the ownership issue strictly to the scope of the right itself and advocate the application of the same rule to ownership issues

---

[195] See Ulmer, n 1 above, at pp 70–72. [196] Articles 4 and 4bis Paris Convention.
[197] See Ulmer, n 1 above, at p 101.
[198] See Bremer [1985] *Bijblad Industriële Eigendom* 165.
[199] See, eg Batiffol, *Le conflit des lois en matière des contrats* (1938), at p 183 and Wolff, *Traité élémentaire du droit international privé*, at p 183.

both inside and outside the context of employment. In contrast, the majority view rejects this argument and gives precedence to the link with the employment relationship[200] and contract.[201] This view[202] has the strong advantage that the ownership issue is assessed uniformly and according to one law, even if the patent is exploited internationally and many parallel patents are applied for.

Now that the EC Rome Convention on the Law Applicable to Contractual Obligations 1980 has entered into force the rule supported by the majority view has been refined slightly by that Convention.[203] The parties are free to choose the applicable law for their employment contract. If they have made a choice of law, the law that has been chosen will also apply to the ownership issue. This law can only be put aside in cases where a mandatory rule overrides it. This mandatory rule has to be found in the law of the forum or in the law of the country in which the employee habitually carries out his work in performance of the contract. In the situation where the employee does not habitually carry out his work in any one country, the law of the country in which the place of business through which he was engaged is situated is applied.

This leaves us with the question of whether rules on employee ownership are mandatory in nature. It is submitted that the ownership issue itself is not. Eugen Ulmer seems to disagree, as he prefers not to allow the parties the freedom to choose the law applicable to this issue.[204] His suggestion, that the free choice by the parties should be excluded, has been incorporated in the equivalent provision of the European Patent Convention.[205] Leaving that Convention on one side for the time being, it can be observed that Dutch courts have repeatedly held that the Dutch rules on this point are not mandatory.[206] This conclusion, though, does not apply to the substantive rule concerning the possibility of the employee obtaining compensation in cases where the ownership of the patent was given to the employer.[207] It is submitted that this substantive rule is mandatory as it deals with an issue of social justice. This view is supported

---

[200] On the characterisation issue, see Straus, [1984] *GRUR Int* 1, at 2 and Ulmer, n 1 above, at p 507.

[201] See, eg Bodenhausen, [1942] *Propriété industrielle* 110; Godenhielm [1957] *GRUR Int* 155; Ulmer, n 1 above, at 507–510; G Van Hecke and K Lenaerts, n 54 above, at 313–314 and Troller, *Das internationale Privat- und Zivilprozessrecht im gewerblichen Rechtsschutz und Urheberrecht*, Basel (1952), at 193 note 20.

[202] This view is also found in Article 34, para 2 of the Austrian Private International Law Statute, n 71 above.

[203] See Article 6 Rome Convention 1980.   [204] Ulmer, n 1 above, at p 73.
[205] See below, pp 530–531.

[206] Bijzondere Afdeling van de Octrooiraad, 19 November 1981, [1982] *Bijblad bij de Industriële Eigendom* 321; see also *Lips BV v Van Gunsteren*, Rechtbank Den Bosch, 2 February 1979, [1985] *Bijblad bij de Industriële Eigendom* 96.

[207] See, eg for the UK, Patents Act 1977, s 40.

Creation, scope and termination of IP rights: the applicable law 525

by the Dutch decision of *Lips BV* v *Van Gunsteren*.[208] In the course of his employment by Lips, Van Gunsteren had made an invention. It was not disputed that Lips owned the patent, but Van Gunsteren claimed compensation for the parallel patent that Lips had obtained in the United Kingdom. The Court of first instance in *Den Bosch* ruled that the Dutch equivalent[209] to the UK's Section 40 of the Patents Act 1977 was mandatory and needed to be applied irrespective of all other circumstances.

If the parties have not included a choice of law clause in the contract of employment, the Rome Convention determines the applicable law. This is done by using the same rule as the one used in relation to mandatory rules and this leads us to the law of the country in which the employee habitually carries out his work in performance of the contract. In the situation where the employee does not habitually carry out his work in any one country, this leads us instead to the law of the country in which the place of business through which he was engaged is situated.

VI
OTHER INTELLECTUAL PROPERTY RIGHTS

1. Widening the Categories

In order to simplify the analysis and the examples slightly, the discussion in the previous pages centred around copyright, on the one hand, and patents and trade marks, on the other hand. But as Ulmer has indicated,[210] the rules which apply in relation to patents and trade marks apply also to all other industrial property rights which form the subject of an application and registration procedure. This list includes patents, design rights, trade marks, utility models and plant variety rights. All rights which do not form the subject of registration can be assimilated to copyright. The unregistered design right is a prime example of this.

2. Tortious Protection of Intellectual Property Rights

That brings us to the link between intellectual property and tort. The rights that arise here could be called negative rights. The rightholder can use tort law to stop certain things only. We do not intend to discuss the substantive law of torts such as passing-off or malicious falsehood[211] or the tort

---

[208] *Lips BV* v *Van Gunsteren*, n 206 above.
[209] Article 10 of the patent law ('Rijksoctrooiwet'). [210] Ulmer, n 1 above, at p 100.
[211] See Holyoak and Torremans, n 38 above, pp 339–377; Carty [1995] *JBL* 139; Martin [1995] *JBL* 70 and Mostert [1989] 12 *EIPR* 440.

choice of law rules[212] in this chapter. What is important, for our current purposes, is that the substantive law of passing-off, for example, refers to goodwill and/or reputation.[213] Often, goodwill and/or reputation replace the registered trade mark, in practice. Goodwill and reputation will be looked at separately.

(a) GOODWILL

What is the *situs* of goodwill in the absence of a registration system? This does not create problems, as goodwill is clearly *de facto* linked to the business to which it is attached.[214] It is, therefore, logical to localise the goodwill in the country where the business premises are situate.[215] The cases that were discussed in relation to trade marks[216] support this, far more than they support the rule in relation to the *situs* of trade marks. We submit, therefore, that, as Dicey and Morris argue, 'the goodwill of a business is situate in the country where the premises are to which the goodwill is attached'.[217] The link between the place of business and goodwill was also emphasised by Lord Diplock in *Star Industrial Co Ltd* v *Yap Kwee Kor*, when his Lordship stated that goodwill 'is local in character and divisible; if the business is carried on in several countries, separate goodwill attaches to it in each'.[218] This quote deals mainly with substantive issues, but it also makes clear that goodwill is divided territorially per country. It is, therefore, submitted that the law of the place where goodwill is situate is also the law of the protecting country. That law will govern the issue whether goodwill exists, what the scope of that goodwill is and who will be the (first) owner of it.

(b) BUSINESS REPUTATION

As a matter of substantive law, reputation is considered to be a weaker requirement.[219] In the absence of goodwill, one can still enjoy a reputation. This can be established through international advertising or through the fact that one has customers in the jurisdiction, even if one has no place of business there.[220] The choice of law rule cannot, therefore, rely on the link with the place of business. The goodwill solution cannot be applied. It is,

---

[212] See below, ch 12.
[213] The debate over whether goodwill is required or whether reputation is sufficient is irrelevant for private international law purposes.
[214] See Derenberg, n 34 above, at 390.
[215] Dicey and Morris, n 9 above, at p 933.
[216] See especially *Reuter* v *Mulhens*, n 32 above, at 96.
[217] Dicey and Morris, n 9 above, at p 933.   [218] [1976] FSR 256, at 269.
[219] See Martin, n 211 above.
[220] See *Poiret* v *Jules Poiret Ltd and A F Nash* (1920) 37 RPC 177 and see also *Sheraton Corpn of America* v *Sheraton Motels Ltd* [1964] RPC 202.

however, submitted that the copyright solution can be applied. The existence of a business reputation would then be governed by the law of the country where the alleged reputation can be invoked. If a business reputation is relied upon in England, English law will determine whether such a reputation exists. Logically speaking, the same law will also determine the scope and extent of the reputation, and the issue of ownership.

(c) GOODWILL AND REPUTATION

These solutions for goodwill and reputation fit in well with the public policy argument in favour of the law of the protecting country. The existence of goodwill or a reputation allows the owner to restrict their free use and this involves a restriction on competition. This touches upon the public policy of the forum; as was argued earlier.[221]

In this respect, goodwill and reputation are dealt with in the same way as any other form of intellectual property. This property aspect has important implications when tort choice of law issues arise. The link between damage to property, the law of the protecting country and tort choice of law will be addressed when we analyse the rules on tort choice of law.[222]

3. BREACH OF CONFIDENCE

Before attempting to characterise the action for breach of confidence for the purposes of choice of law, we need to analyse it briefly from a substantive law point of view. Under English law, three main elements are involved. First, the information involved must be of a confidential character. Secondly, the imparting of the information must occur in circumstances or on an occasion of confidence. And finally, the information must be used in an unauthorised way and so as to cause detriment to the plaintiff.[223] The information involved can be very different in nature. It can be a trade secret, or secret technical know-how, but it could also be information about the private life of an individual. The main problem in this area is that it is very difficult to characterise the action and to determine its nature.[224]

Could breach of confidence be characterised as damage to property? Can we deduce from indications such as the fact that confidential information can be assigned, inherited, licensed, etc that confidential information is a property right?[225] It has been argued elsewhere that this is not

---

[221] See above, p 495.   [222] See below, ch 12.
[223] See *Coco v A N Clark (Engineers) Ltd* [1969] RPC 41.
[224] See Holyoak and Torremans, n 38 above, at pp 382–383.
[225] See *Seager v Copydex Ltd* [1967] 1 WLR 923; *Fraser v Evans* [1969] 1 QB 349; *Malone v Commissioner of Police* [1979] 2 All ER 620; *A-G v Observer Newspapers* (1986) 136 NLJ 799; *A-G v Guardian Newspapers* [1987] 1 WLR 1248, at 1264 and see also Ricketson (1978) 11 *Melbourne University Law Review* 289.

correct.[226] Once the confidential information has been disclosed publicly without a breach of any obligation of confidence, confidentiality cannot be restored, while any other form of property can be restored. Moreover, cases such as *Morison and Moat*[227] indicate very clearly that equity is involved. The plaintiff in the action has an equitable right not to see the confidential information disclosed.[228]

The discussion concerning the nature of the action for breach of confidence and the nature of a potential right in the confidential information has not yet reached a final conclusion in substantive law.[229] It is not suggested that this discussion be finalised here. The negative character of the right not to see the information disclosed is important. The essence of the right is not simply found in an imperfect property right, but also in the equitable right of action, that is given to the plaintiff. The action for breach of confidence shows, in this respect, strong similarities with the action for the infringement of a patent. This hints towards a tortious influence. The fact that the action does not confer a positive right property right eliminates the need to determine the law under which the right is created, the law that determines the scope, duration and ownership of the right. No further problems arise in relation to issues that are discussed in this chapter.

In conclusion, the classification in substantive law of the action for breach of confidence is still unclear. A straightforward property classification has to be rejected, though. The action does, however, arise in another context too. Often, a confidentiality clause is included in a contract.[230] The fact that one of the parties that is bound by the clause does not respect the confidence gives in such a situation, rise to an action for breach of confidence. If such an action is brought as an action for breach of contract (ie a breach of the confidentiality clause), the contractual characterisation should prevail and the contract choice of law rules should be applied.[231]

4. The *Sui Generis* Right in Relation to Databases

The Database Directive[232] grants a *sui generis* right to object to the unauthorised extraction and re-utilisation of all or part of the material that is contained in the database, irrespective of the decision to grant copyright

---

[226] Holyoak and Torremans, n 38 above, at 382–383; see also Coleman, *The Legal Protection of Trade Secrets*, Sweet & Maxwell (1992), at p 48 *et seq*.
[227] (1851) 9 Hare 241; 68 ER 492.
[228] See Holyoak and Torremans, n 38 above, at 382–383.
[229] *Ibid*.
[230] See, eg *Vokes Ltd v Heather* (1945) 62 RPC 135 and *Faccenda Chicken v Fowler* [1987] Ch 117.
[231] See ch 11 below.
[232] Council Directive 96/9/EEC of 11 March 1996 on the legal protection of databases [1996] OJ L77/20.

protection for the structure of the database. The Directive does not contain rules on choice of law.

It is submitted that the choice of law rules that are applicable to copyright should apply. The aim of the Directive is to provide an adequate level of intellectual property right protection for the maker of a database. To fulfil this aim the Directive uses two instruments: copyright in the structure of the database, and, amongst other things, because the works that are included may already be protected by a copyright owned by a third party and this right is to be left unaltered, a *sui generis* right in the contents of the database. The slightly weaker nature of the latter is a deliberate attempt to get the balance of protection right. The aim of the Directive is to be met through the combination of both instruments. It would, therefore, be logical to grant (first) ownership of both instruments to the same person. In terms of choice of law, this can be guaranteed by applying the same choice of law rule to both instruments. The specific way in which the two instruments are combined in the substantive law is an attempt to get the balance of protection right. The potential distortion of that balance can be avoided if the same choice of law rule is applied to the issue of the scope of both rights. The same choice of law rule will, in relation to a single database, lead to the applicability of a single substantive law. That will, in turn, allow for the aims of the Directive to be met.

The substantive rules on copyright in the Directive are in no way different from the standard copyright rules. There is, therefore, no reason to suggest that a different choice of law rule should be applied to copyright in relation to databases. This leads us to the conclusion that the copyright choice of law rules, that were analysed above, should also apply to the *sui generis* right in relation to databases.

VII
RIGHTS CREATED BY INTERNATIONAL CONVENTIONS

Intellectual property rights can be created strictly on the basis of domestic national law, or they can be created, at least partially, on the basis of the provisions of an international Convention which facilitates the application and examination process. Before going into the detail of these Conventions, we need to clarify what we mean by the law of the protecting country in the situation where intellectual property rights are created by international Conventions. Normally, it is the domestic law, but in the latter situations it is the domestic law as modified by the international Convention.

1. The Patent Co-operation Treaty

An example of such a modification is found in the application of the Patent Co-operation Treaty, where an international application and an international search can replace their national equivalents to a certain extent. In such cases, the relevant provisions of the Patent Co-operation Treaty are to be considered as forming part of the law of the protecting country, which is determined on the basis of the country for which the patent concerned is eventually granted. This point has already been fully explained in relation to copyright[233] and it applies here in the same way.[234] Sections 89A and 89B of the Patents Act 1977 give effect to this system in the United Kingdom. During the international phase of the application for a UK patent, the provisions in the Patent Co-operation Treaty are made applicable to issues such as publication, search, examination and amendment. In this situation, the Treaty provisions replace the normal provisions of the Act.

2. The European Patent Convention

This Convention is another good example of the principle which is outlined in the previous paragraph. A single application and examination leads to the grant of a bundle of national patents. In relation to each of these patents, the law of the protecting country is the combination of the substantive provisions of the Convention and the existing domestic law for those points with which the Convention does not deal. The Convention does not contain any specific rules on choice of law.

Without wishing to discuss the Convention's provisions in detail, two points require some attention. First, in procedures before the European Patent Office the applicable provisions are those contained in the Convention, both in relation to substance and in relation to procedure.[235] At this stage, in a unified system, the European level replaces the national level. The provisions of the Treaty then become the law of the protecting country in so far as the single procedure applies.

Secondly, the Convention contains specific rules in relation to the ownership of inventions made by employees.[236] These rules will apply to all such situations in relation to European Patents and any deviating national rule is excluded. The general rule is that the patent will be owned by the inventor. The specific rules which operate in relation to jurisdiction in relation to this issue have already been outlined.[237] Turning to the law

---

[233] See pp 498–499 above.
[234] See also Ulmer, n 1 above, at 100–101 (Article G(2) of the Proposed Rules).
[235] See, eg Articles 96 and 100–101.   [236] Article 60 EPC.
[237] See above chapter 00, pp 00.

applicable to an employee's invention, the Convention specifies that 'the right to the European patent shall be determined in accordance with the law of the State in which the employee is mainly employed'. If such a State cannot be determined, an alternative rule states that 'the law to be applied shall be that of the State in which the employer has his place of business to which the employee is attached'.[238] In those cases where these rules deviate from the rules contained in Article 6 of the Rome Convention 1980, the EPC rule should be applied. This is because the Rome Convention considers itself to be the general provision (*lex generalis*) which gives way to the specific provision (*lex specialis*) which is contained in Conventions, such as the EPC, which deal with particular specialist topics.[239] In addition to this provision, Article 61 offers substantive rules that deal with the situation once the rightful owner has been identified.

The difference in approach between the Rome Convention 1980 solution for non-European (UK) patents, which includes the freedom for the parties to choose the applicable law, and the European Patent Convention solution for European (UK) patents, which rules out the freedom for the parties to choose the applicable law, is to be regretted. It would be desirable for the same solution to apply to all patents that are valid in the United Kingdom. It could be argued that the freedom to choose the applicable law would lead, in practice, to a standard clause which an employer would impose upon all its employees.[240] This would destroy the purpose of the free choice option. It is submitted, however, that mandatory rules would take over when necessary and solve the problem. This means that the choice of law option should be retained for those cases where a standard clause would not be inserted, or where both parties agree that a different law, that has more appropriate or detailed provisions on this point, should apply. It has even been argued that the European Patent Convention approach does not necessarily exclude a choice of law by the parties.[241] This argument sees the Convention provision as a reference to a whole legal system. The parties would be free to choose the applicable law if the provisions of that legal system allowed a free choice of the applicable law by the parties. It is submitted, though, that the wording of the provisions of the Convention do not support this renvoi option.[242]

---

[238] Article 60(1) EPC; the procedure to indentify the inventor-rightful owner will not take place before the European Patent Office, but before national courts; their judgments are recognised in the other Contracting States under the rules of the Protocol on Jurisdiction and Recognition of Decisions in Respect of the Right to the Grant of a European Patent (Articles 9 and 10).
[239] Article 21 of the Rome Convention 1980.
[240] See Ulmer, n 1 above, at pp 508–509.   [241] Straus, n 200 above, at 6.
[242] See Ulmer, n 1 above, at p 508.

VIII
COMMUNITY RIGHTS

1. THE COMMUNITY TRADE MARK

The Community trade mark provides a single trade mark for the whole territory of the European Community. The law of the protecting country contains the substantive rules of the Community Trade Mark Regulation[243] and those rules of national law to which the Regulation explicitly refers on certain points.

The Regulation sets out the substantive rules relating to (Community) trade marks, including amongst other issues the requirements for registration and the grounds for refusal. The rules of the Regulation form the applicable law.[244]

(a) ARTICLE 14

The first provision which is of special relevance in relation to choice of law is found in Article 14. This Article starts with the basic rule that the scope and effects of a (Community) trade mark are governed by the provisions of the Regulation, as outlined in its Articles 9 to 13. Although it is not strictly relevant for our discussion in this chapter, for reasons of completeness it might be added that the same provision goes on to state that those aspects of trade mark infringement which are not covered by these provisions, such as for example the remedies issue, are governed in each Member State by the provisions of the national law of that Member State in the same way as they apply to the infringement of national trade marks. Actions for unfair competition and civil liability in relation to national trade marks have traditionally been brought in a number of Member States. Article 14(2) makes it clear that these actions can now also be brought in relation to a Community trade mark and that the same provisions of national law will be applicable.

(b) TITLE X

Title X of the Regulation contains further general private international law rules, including rules dealing with choice of law. The latter rules merit further attention in the present context. Not only will the Office for the Harmonisation in the Internal Market (Trade Marks and Designs)[245] apply the provisions of the Regulation in all its procedures, the Community

---

[243] Council Regulation 40/94/EC of 20 December 1993 [1994] OJ L11/1.
[244] See Article 1.   [245] Ie the European Trade Mark Office in Alicante, Spain.

trade mark courts will also do this.²⁴⁶ In other words, the provisions of the Regulation are the applicable law. There is one important exception to this rule. Each Community trade mark court will apply its national law to those matters that are not covered by the Regulation. And the national law is to include the national rules on private international law. Renvoi is, therefore, not excluded if the relevant national law operates this principle. It is almost needless to add that the national Community trade mark courts will also apply their own procedural rules as the law of the forum, even if these rules might have been affected and modified slightly by the provisions of Title X of the Regulation.²⁴⁷

Article 98 deals specifically with sanctions. When a Community trade mark court arrives at the conclusion that a case of infringement or threatened infringement has been established, it will normally order the defendant to refrain from proceeding with the acts concerned. This is the substantive rule contained in the Regulation and it is necessarily applicable. This substantive rule is supplemented by a reference to the national law of the country in which the court is located. The court will apply the law of the forum so as to take measures which are aimed at ensuring that the prohibition is complied with. The applicable law in relation to sanctions is the law of the Member State where the acts of infringement or threatened infringement were committed. This reference to the law of the place of the tort (*lex loci delicti*) includes its private international law rules, renvoi is, therefore, possible in appropriate cases.

Courts which are asked to grant provisional and protective measures will equally apply their national law in this respect and make those measures which are available in respect of national trade marks available in cases involving Community trade marks.²⁴⁸

(c) SUBSTANTIVE RULES IN THE REGULATION

Certain details concerning substantive rules may be mentioned here. Community trade mark courts are supposed to treat the Community mark as valid unless the validity of the mark is raised by a counterclaim for revocation or for a declaration of invalidity. These are the only ways in which the validity point can be raised and such a counterclaim can only be based on the grounds for revocation or invalidity provided for in the Regulation. Any reference to national law is explicitly ruled out on this point.²⁴⁹ Earlier rights are another issue which receives attention in two Articles: 107(1) and 107(2). Such an earlier right may apply to a particular locality. Eventually, the owner of such a right might prohibit the use of the Community trade mark in that area.²⁵⁰ The Regulation allows for such a

---

[246] Article 97. [247] Ibid. [248] Article 99(1). [249] Articles 95 and 96.
[250] Article 107(1).

prohibition, but only in as far as the law of the Member State concerned so permits. This is another example of a case where the applicable law is the Regulation, but that applicable law contains, in relation to a specific point, a reference to the national law of the Member State concerned. This becomes clear when it is seen that the Regulation adds further substantive provisions which limit the possibility of invoking an earlier right if there has been a five year period of acquiescence in the use of the Community mark in that area.[251]

(d) NATIONAL LAW PROVISIONS

Even though the provisions of the Regulation, in general, form the applicable law, this does not, of course, rule out the possibility of bringing a case under national civil, administrative or criminal law in appropriate cases. In these cases, the relevant national law provisions will be applicable. European law might also be applicable if a case is brought under Community law, for example a case under EC competition law provisions.[252]

The Regulation contains some additional references to the domestic law of the Member States. Article 23 deals with 'effects vis-à-vis third parties'. Any legal act in relation to Community trade marks will only have effects against third parties that did not know about these acts after they have been entered into the Community Trade Mark Register.[253] These effects against third parties are governed by the law that has been determined in accordance with Article 16. Article 16 contains the principle that, as an object of property, any Community trade mark shall be dealt with in the same way as a national trade mark of the Member State in which the proprietor of the mark has his seat or domicile or, in the absence of either of these two, an establishment.[254] If the proprietor does not even have an establishment in the Community, the trade mark shall be dealt with in the same way as a national trade mark of the Member State in which the Community Trade Mark Office is established.[255] These rules will lead to the law of one of the Member States. Effects vis-à-vis third parties that result from a bankruptcy or insolvency are governed by the law of the

---

[251] Article 107(2), knowledge of the use during the five year period is also required and the Community trade mark should not have been applied for in bad faith anyway.
[252] Article 106(2) of the Community Trade Mark Regulation.
[253] This provision is, according to Article 23(2), subject to an exception in relation to situations where the whole undertaking is transferred or where any other universal succession takes place.
[254] Article 29(1) of the Regulation. Article 16(3) contains a special rule for joint holders. All rules are subject to Articles 17 to 24.
[255] Article 16(2) of the Regulation. The office has been established as the Office for the Harmonisation of the Internal Market (Trade Marks and Designs) in Alicante, Spain.

Member State in which the bankruptcy or insolvency proceedings are first brought.[256] These provisions may also affect the commercial exploitation of the Community trade mark.

2. THE COMMUNITY PATENT

The Community trade mark system is also, *mutatis mutandis*, envisaged for the Community patent, should it ever come into existence.[257] The new Green Paper[258] does not explicitly suggest the introduction of new choice of law rules, but changes cannot be excluded in the light of the substantial changes that are suggested in terms of substantive law.

3. THE COMMUNITY DESIGN RIGHT

The draft Regulation on the Community Design,[259] which sets out to create a single design right for the Community, contains one Article that is entitled 'Applicable Law'. This is Article 92, which is modelled on Article 97 of the Community Trade Mark Regulation. The main principle that is contained in Article 92 is that the Community Design will, in principle, be governed by the provisions of the Regulation and that these provisions will be the ones that will be applied by the Community design courts. However, the draftsman recognised that, eventually, matters that are not covered by the provisions of the Regulation might arise. When confronted with such a situation, the Community design courts will apply their own national law, ie the domestic law of the country in which the Community design court that is dealing with the matter, and has jurisdiction to do so, is established. This is particularly important in the absence of a complete harmonisation of the rules on infringement, despite the efforts towards this aim that are made, for example, in Article 93 of the Regulation.[260] Reference to domestic law is to be taken to include all provisions on private international law. This means that the possibility of *renvoi* is deliberately left open.

In terms of procedure, the Community design courts will follow the traditional rule in private international law which states that the court will

---

[256] Article 23(4) of the Regulation. This rule will only apply until common rules for the Member State in this area come into force. See also Article 21 of the Regulation.

[257] See Convention for the European Patent for the Common Market and the Protocol on the Settlement of Litigation concerning the Infringement and Validity of Community Patents [1989] OJ L401/1; especially Article 34 of the Convention and Articles 26 and 32 of the Protocol.

[258] Commission of the European Communities, *Green Paper on the Community Patent and the Patent System in Europe*, COM(97) 314 final.

[259] [1994] OJ C29/20.

[260] Scordamaglia, in Franzosi (ed), *European Design Protection: Commentary to Directive and Regulation Proposals*, Kluwer Law International (1996), at p 365.

always apply its own national procedural rules. This rule is qualified slightly by the rule that the Regulation may, on certain points, lay down different procedural rules.[261] In such circumstances, these have to be applied. This is normal practice, because the draft Regulation will automatically become part of the national laws of the Member States.

The draft Regulation contains, in addition to these fundamental rules on choice of law, two other Articles that might be relevant in this context and that may also affect the commercial exploitation of the right. First, Article 29 contains the principle that, as an object of property, any Community design right shall be dealt with in the same way as a national design right of the Member State in which the holder has his seat or domicile or, in the absence of either of these two, an establishment.[262] This rule applies in accordance with the entries in the Community Design Register whenever a registered Community design right is concerned.[263] If the holder does not even have an establishment[264] in the Community, the right shall be dealt with in the same way as a national design right of the Member State in which the Community Design Office will be situated.[265] These rules will lead to the law of one of the Member States. That law will be applied to the property questions that arise in relation to the (registered or unregistered) Community design right.[266]

Secondly, Article 35 deals with 'effects vis-à-vis third parties'. These effects are governed by the law that has been determined in accordance with Article 29.[267] As regards registered Community design rights, any transfer of the right or any right *in rem* will only have effects against third parties that did not know about these acts after these acts have been entered into the Community Design Register.[268] Effects vis-à-vis third par-

---

[261] See, in particular, Articles 88(3), 89, 90(2), 90(3), 90(4), 94 and 95 of the Draft Community Design Regulation.

[262] Article 29(1) of the Draft Regulation. Article 29(3) contains a special rule for joint holders. All rules are subject to Articles 30 to 34 and the seat, domicile or establishment needs to be present at the relevant date (ie the date on which an act which deals with the Design right as an object of property is carried out).

[263] Article 29(2) of the Draft Regulation.

[264] Article 29 is closely modelled on its equivalent in the Community Trade Mark Regulation. See Hoyng, in Franzosi (ed), *European Design Protection: Commentary to Directive and Regulation Proposals*, Kluwer Law International (1996), at p 185. The difference that is pointed out by that author is wrong in as far as it relates to the Community Trade Mark Regulation. The different provision is, in reality, found in Article 38 of the Community Patent Convention.

[265] Article 29(4) of the Draft Regulation. The office should normally become a division of the Office for the Harmonisation of the Internal Market (Trade Marks and Designs) in Alicante, Spain, which already operates as the Community Trade Mark Office.

[266] See, eg Article 36 of the Draft Regulation.

[267] Article 35(1) of the Draft Regulation.

[268] Article 35(2) of the Draft Regulation. This provision is, according to Article 35(3), subject to the exception in relation to situations where the whole undertaking is transferred or where any other universal succession takes place.

ties that result from a bankruptcy or insolvency shall be governed by the law of the Member State in which the bankruptcy or insolvency proceedings are first brought.[269]

The Draft Regulation is currently awaiting the final approval of the European Parliament. The outcome of this process is uncertain. It is, however, unlikely that any changes will be made to the choice of law provisions at this late stage. The uncertainty rather concerns the question whether or not the draft as a whole will meet with the approval of the Parliament and whether it will ever become more than a draft.

4. THE COMMUNITY PLANT VARIETY RIGHT

The Community Plant Variety Right Regulation[270] creates a *sui generis* regime of protection for plant varieties at Community level. In the light of the special nature of this right, it must have seemed rather obvious to the draftsman that this right would be governed by the provisions of the Regulation. This may explain the rather minimalist way in which choice of law issues are dealt with in the Regulation.

Article 94 deals with the 'supplementary application of national law regarding infringement'. The word 'supplementary' indicates that, in all normal cases, the provisions of the Regulation will form the applicable law and this is explicitly confirmed by Article 94(3). Article 94 deals first of all in paragraph 1 with restitutionary claims for gains made at the expense of the rightholder as a result of the infringement of his right. These restitutionary claims are governed by the national law of the court that deals with the infringement case. Private international law rules and the possibility of renvoi are explicitly included. Secondly, Article 94(2) makes it clear that the solution in Article 94(1) will also apply to claims that arise in respect of the performance of restricted acts in the time between the publication of the application for the grant of a Community plant variety right and the eventual disposal of that request.

When it comes to the property aspects of the right, Article 21 of the Regulation contains a reference to the law of the country in which the rightholder has a seat, domicile or establishment at the time of the registration of the right. This provision is very similar to the one that is found in the Draft Community Design Regulation.[271] However, the Plant Variety Regulation contains specific rules for the transfer of the right, rather than a reference to the national law of a Member State. The solution that will apply in a bankruptcy or insolvency situation is very similar to the one

---

[269] Article 35(4) of the Draft Regulation. This rule will only apply until common rules for the Member States in this area come into force.
[270] Regulation 2100/94, [1994] OJ L227/1.   [271] See above, p 536.

that is found in Article 21 of the Community Trade Mark Regulation[272] and in Article 35(4) of the Draft Community Design Right Regulation.[273]

IX
CONCLUSIONS AND ALTERNATIVE APPROACHES

International exploitation of intellectual property rights is now the rule, rather than the exception. The existing intellectual property Conventions have created a system of protection in each country, but that protection is based on one right per country. Such a system can only operate smoothly if all these rights are, for example, granted to the same (first) owner, have the same scope of protection and offer the same term of protection. Ideally, that situation would be reached through an international harmonisation of substantive intellectual property law. The difficulties in achieving a modest level of harmonisation through the conclusion of the GATT-WTO TRIPs Agreement[274] have shown clearly, however, that this approach will not lead to a complete solution in the foreseeable future.

In the absence of a complete harmonisation of the substantive law of intellectual property, a system of choice of law rules remains the best solution. We have shown, in this chapter, that the current UK rules are underdeveloped to take account of the specific characteristics of intellectual property rights. Property based rules are not sufficient. There is, on the other hand, nothing in the existing case law that would stop the development of a complete set of choice of law rules along the lines suggested in this chapter. These suggestions are based on the International Intellectual Property Conventions and on the wider experience which other European countries have in this area. They reached that level of experience because they never experienced jurisdiction problems of the sort caused by the *Moçambique* rule[275] and because they did not know the double actionability rule for tort choice of law cases.[276] Many cases that were never even brought in England came before the foreign courts and were given a solution that was often fully satisfactory.

Our proposed set of choice of law rules starts by taking into account the fact that most intellectual property rights are still granted on a country per country basis. Subject to the effects of the partial international harmonisa-

---

[272] See above, p 535. The trade mark version adds a possibility of making an entry in this respect in the Community Trade Mark Register.
[273] See above, p 537.
[274] See Blakeney, *Trade Related Aspects of Intellectual Property Rights: A Concise Guide to the TRIPs Agreement*, Sweet & Maxwell (1996).
[275] See above, p 280.
[276] See above, pp 295–298 and ch 12 below.

tion of the substantive rules on intellectual property, each country grants national domestic intellectual property rights that are effective in the territory of that country. Even if those national rights are based on an international right of priority that is applied under certain international intellectual property Conventions, such as the Paris Convention 1883, by all Member States, the right that is granted is a national intellectual property right. It seems, therefore, logical to suggest that each national domestic intellectual property law will govern the conditions on which an intellectual property right is created in that country. For example, if I apply for patent protection in France for my invention which I originally made in the United Kingdom, French law will determine exactly under which conditions a French patent will be granted. This issue is governed by the law of the protecting country, ie the law of the country for which intellectual property protection is sought. This approach is not limited to one kind of intellectual property right. It can be applied to all types of intellectual property right, irrespective of the need to register a number of these rights. For example, in relation to copyright the law of the protecting country will apply to the issue of which types of work will be protected by copyright. In that sense, the provisions of the Copyright, Designs and Patents Act 1988 will determine, in each case, whether or not copyright protection will be granted in the United Kingdom for a particular type of work and whether or not a particular work comes within one of these categories.

These issues could be said to relate to the creation of the intellectual property right. Once the right is created, the issue of its scope arises. Most rights will have parallel rights, for example for the same invention or trade mark, in existence in a number of other countries. It would therefore make sense, in the light of the international exploitation of these (parallel) intellectual property rights, to apply the same law to the issue of the scope of the right. That would guarantee that the rightholder would effectively have exactly the same exclusive rights in the whole territory that is covered by all the parallel rights. This view starts from the practical side of things and cannot be reconciled with the legal reality that all rights are granted nationally on a country by country basis by virtue of application of the fundamental international intellectual property Conventions. If we agree that rights are created nationally until the moment on which we might in the future decide to change the international intellectual property Conventions on this point, it must follow that the law of the country that allows the creation of an exclusive right in these particular circumstances must also govern the scope of that right. One cannot allow the creation of a restriction on competition, which is the effect of the creation of intellectual property rights, without determining at the same time how far that restriction will go. We have submitted, therefore, that the scope of an intellectual property right should also be governed by the law of the protecting country, as this is the law of the country that allows the exclusive right as a restriction on competition. A similar reasoning can and should be followed to determine the law applicable to the issue of the duration or the termination of the intellectual property right. Once more, the law of the protecting country should be retained as the law applicable to that issue.

Whether or not an intellectual property right is valid is a matter that involves an answer to the question whether all the requirements for the grant or the creation of the right were met. The issue of validly, therefore, presents a strong link with the issue of creation and grant of the intellectual property right. It makes sense to apply the same law of the protecting country to both issues.

However, the same link with the creation of a restriction on competition no longer exists in relation to the issue of ownership. It may be important to grant the exclusive right to the correct person, but other considerations are equally important. Intellectual property is almost by definition exploited internationally, but protection is granted on a national basis and relies on parallel rights. Any form of international exploitation would be improved if the ownership issue was resolved in a uniform way. It must be easy to determine who owns the rights in each country and situations where parallel rights are involuntarily, through the operation of different applicable laws, owned by different parties are to be avoided. We have suggested on this basis that this issue of ownership should not be governed by the law of the protecting country, but that the link with the country in which the mark, invention or copyright work was originally created should prevail. Rights that are created in the course of employment present a link with the law that is applicable to the employment relationship and it seems logical that that law should also govern the issue of the ownership of intellectual property rights that are created in the course of employment.

A more radical alternative to our suggestion would be the introduction of a system of choice of law rules that would be based on the application of the law of the country of origin to almost all issues. Certain authors[277] have advocated such a system to overcome the fact that the intellectual property Conventions are based on national treatment and the grant of national intellectual property rights. Under this alternative, all emphasis is placed on the fact that each invention, mark or work on which a patent, trade mark or copyright is based is created in one place. That is normally the country in which protection is first sought. The applications for and the grant of subsequent parallel rights are then just a technical way of extend-

---

[277] See, eg Schack, *Zur Anknüpfung des Urheberrechts im internationalen Privatrecht*, Duncker & Humblot (1979).

ing the cover of the original protection. That protection should then be governed worldwide by the law of the country of origin, because the system has its strongest link with that country. However, this harmonisation through the back door comes with a number of problems. For example, the public policy considerations linked to the grant of exclusive intellectual property rights, that restrict competition, are ignored completely.[278] It is submitted, therefore, that this alternative is not feasible in practice, although it would present a number of practical advantages for the international exploitation of intellectual property rights, as we have shown in the previous paragraphs. On top of this are the objections to such an alternative that were made in the previous chapter. This alternative is not supported by the provisions of the international intellectual property Conventions and would even involve conflict with certain provisions of these Conventions. Accordingly, this alternative solution cannot be accepted.

[278] See above, p 495.

11

Contracts in Relation to the Exploitation of Intellectual Property Rights: The Applicable Law

I	Introduction	543
II	Contractual issues distinguished from other issues	545
	1. Industrial property rights	545
	(a) Issues relating to the right	545
	(b) Contractual aspects of the transfer	546
	(c) Restrictions for transfer of technology agreements	547
	(d) Formalities	547
	2. Copyright	547
III	How questions as to the applicable law arise	549
IV	The Rome Convention on the Law Applicable to Contractual Obligations	551
	1. When does the Rome Convention 1980 apply?	551
	2. The applicable law	552
	(a) The law is chosen by the parties	552
	(b) The applicable law in the absence of choice	554
	3. Limitations on the applicable law	577
	(a) Mandatory rules	577
	(b) Mandatory rules: summary	587
	(c) Public policy/ordre public	587
	4. A particular issue: formal validity	588
	5. Alternative approaches	590
V	Conclusion	591

I
INTRODUCTION

In this chapter, we are concerned with contracts in relation to the exploitation of intellectual property rights. These contracts take various forms,[1] such as, for example, licences and assignments, on the one hand, and more

---

[1] See above, chapter 3, at p 74.

complex forms, such as distribution contracts and transfer of technology agreements, that involve more than a simple transfer of intellectual property rights, on the other hand. We do not propose however to deal separately with each of these types of contract, as they all have in common the fact that they involve a transfer of certain rights to do certain acts which would otherwise have constituted an infringement of the intellectual property right in question. Any such transfer can, irrespective of the type of contract, be subject to restrictions of time and scope, so it is submitted that the transfer is the essential point. When our discussion is based on the example of a licence it is, therefore, submitted that the same discussion and analysis would equally apply to assignments and other formats.

However, it is generally recognised that there is a distinction between copyright and neighbouring rights, on the one hand, and industrial property rights on the other hand. Different types of contract are used in both cases and in copyright there is no registration requirement. This means that the issue whether or not contracts in relation to registered intellectual property rights need also be registered does not arise in relation to copyright. We will analyse contracts in relation to both types of intellectual property rights separately and we start our analysis by considering contracts in relation to industrial property rights.

The main instrument in relation to contract choice of law is now the European Community Convention on the Law Applicable to Contractual Obligations of 1980 (the Rome Convention 1980).[2] We will have to analyse its impact in this area in detail. Its provisions will be the starting point of the analysis. It should be noted from the outset that, although the Rome Convention has certain special rules for particular types of contract (ie contracts in relation to immovable property, carriage of goods, consumer contracts, employment contracts), it contains no special rules in relation to contracts for the exploitation of intellectual property rights.

But before starting our examination of the Rome Convention 1980, the scope of the contract choice of law problem in cases in relation to intellectual property rights has to be defined.

---

[2] EEC Convention on the Law applicable to Contractual Obligations, [1980] OJ L266/1, which came into force on 1 April 1991 (the 'Rome Convention 1980') (The Convention is now also in force regarding Spain and Portugal, the Accession Convention was signed in Funchal on 18 May 1992 and entered into force on 1 September 1993. For the text of the Funchal Convention see [1992] OJ L333/1; for additional comments on the Convention see Gaudemet-Tallon, [1993] *RTD eur* 61; the Funchal Convention is now scheduled to the Contracts (Applicable Law) Act 1990 as Schedule 3A: SI 1994/1900); A further accession convention was signed with Austria, Finland and Sweden on 29 November 1996. This Convention is awaiting ratification and is not yet in force at the time of writing; see below for a discussion of the applicability and the influence of the Rome Convention on International Intellectual Property Contracts.

II
CONTRACTUAL ISSUES DISTINGUISHED FROM OTHER ISSUES

1. INDUSTRIAL PROPERTY RIGHTS

Industrial property rights present a double aspect under private international law. Certain issues can be qualified as being part of the industrial property right as such, while other issues should rather be qualified as contractual issues.[3] As we are in this chapter only dealing with contractual issues, it is important in order to define its scope to summarise the issues being treated as part of the industrial property right as such and which,[4] accordingly, fall outside the scope of this chapter.

(a) ISSUES RELATING TO THE RIGHT

Industrial property rights are still national rights and, in most countries, administrative formalities have to be fulfilled if someone wants to be granted an industrial property right.[5] The rights grant protection for the territory of the granting state, the protecting country. It is logical that the law of the protecting country governs the industrial property right as such.[6] We do not intend to repeat our analysis of the previous chapters, but this implies, for example, that the law of the protecting country governs the following issues.

Which exclusive industrial property rights can be obtained? Some countries do not accord certain plant breeding rights as patents or do not accord protection to colours, smells or sounds as trade marks. The law of the protecting country determines what can be protected and under which right. Who can obtain such an exclusive industrial property right? This not only raises the problem of the situation of foreigners. Another issue that is raised concerns the question whether the right is owned by the inventor or creator of its subject matter or simply by the person who registers it. When and how an industrial property right originates and when and how

---

[3] See Van Hecke and Lenaerts *Internationaal Privaatrecht* Story-Scientia (2nd ed, 1989) at pp 312–313, see also Ulmer *Intellectual Property Rights and the Conflict of Laws*, Kluwer and the Commission of the European Communities (1978) at p 87, who distinguishes between contractual effects and effects *in rem*, but recognises that this does not represent an appropriate solution.

[4] Walter, (1976) 89 *RIDA* 45, at 59.

[5] Even under the European Patent Convention only a bunch of national patents is granted.

[6] See for a more substantial analysis of this point Ulmer 'Fremdenrecht und internationales Privatrecht im gewerblichen Rechtsschutz und Urheberrecht' in Holl and Klinke (eds) *Internationales Privatrecht, Internationales Wirtschaftsrecht* Carl Heymanns Verlag (1985) p 257 ff.

it terminates are issues which are equally determined by the law of the protecting country.[7]

The answer to the question whether an industrial property right can be assigned, or whether licensing agreements may be concluded in respect of them, is equally given by the law of the protecting country. Some countries do not accept the partial assignment of an industrial property right. A registration requirement is also frequently found.[8] And any claim arising from the industrial property right which a licensee may assert in the event of the infringement of his rights is governed by the same law of the protecting country.[9] This clearly restricts in a serious way the number of issues that are governed by the law of the licence contract, issues that can be chosen freely by the parties.

However, it has to be taken into account as well that the law of the protecting country may refer to the law of the country of origin of the industrial right for the solution of a specific problem.[10] Two examples in relation to trade marks are: Article 6quinquies of the Paris Convention, which contains an exception advantaging the law of the country of origin to the rules concerning the validity of the trade mark (the 'telle quelle'-trade mark) and Articles 6–3 of the of Madrid agreement, which relies on the continuation of the protection in the country of origin for the duration of five years.

(b) CONTRACTUAL ASPECTS OF THE TRANSFER

The fact that the Rome Convention 1980 came into force on 1 April 1991 constitutes an important development for the choice of law problem concerning contracts. Industrial property rights as such do not fall within the scope of the Convention, as they do not imply any contractual obligation.[11] An Article in the original preliminary draft had expressly so provided, but it was considered to be superfluous. However, this does not result in the Convention being irrelevant in the context of industrial property rights and licences, because an international industrial property licence contract meets the requirements laid down in Article 1(1) of the Convention. Such a licence contract does indeed create contractual obligations in a situation involving a choice of law between the laws of different countries. This leads us to the conclusion that industrial property licence contracts fall within the scope of the Rome Convention 1980 and

---

[7] Van Hecke and Lenaerts, n 3 above, at pp 311–312.
[8] Ulmer, n 3 above, at p 90 and Van Hecke and Lenaerts, n 3 above, at p 312.
[9] Ulmer, n 3 above, at p 91.
[10] Van Hecke and Lenaerts, n 3 above, at p 313.
[11] See Giuliano and Lagarde 'Report on the Convention on the Law applicable to contractual obligations' [1980] OJ C 282/1 at 10.

that we will have to examine how the Convention's provisions should be applied to such contracts.[12]

Mandatory rules may restrict the applicability of the law of the protecting country[13] or the law of the contract. This is an issue to which we will return at length later on in this chapter.

(c) RESTRICTIONS FOR TRANSFER OF TECHNOLOGY AGREEMENTS

A last limitation to be mentioned is the trend which existed in developing countries to subject all transfer of technology agreements imperatively to the law and to the jurisdiction of the receiving country.[14] In doing so, these countries did not distinguish between the industrial property right as such and the purely contractual aspects of the transfer. One has the impression that this trend is on the decline because most companies reacted by suspending the transfer of technology to the countries which incorporated such provisions in their laws.[15]

(d) FORMALITIES

The issue of the formal validity of international industrial property licence contracts has given rise to different approaches. But it should first of all be stressed that the formalities required by the law of the protecting country, an issue which we have already mentioned,[16] and the issue of the formal validity of the licence contract are different matters. The latter issue will be discussed at length towards the end of this chapter.

2. COPYRIGHT

Contracts in relation to copyright differ slightly from those in relation to industrial property rights. As regards the latter, licences are the most common type of contract; whereas with copyright assignments are more common. This means that most contracts in relation to copyright contain two elements. First, there is the determination of the rights and duties of the parties and, secondly, there is the transfer of proprietary rights, ie the copyright or part of it. Both elements warrant separate attention in relation

---

[12] See Beier [1982] *IIC* 162 at 165.   [13] See also above, pp 495, 503 and 510.
[14] See the UNCTAD Study *The Role of Trademarks in Developing Countries* UN Document with Sales No E 79IID5, for the practice in Latin American Countries in the seventies see Freitag in [1976] *GRUR Int* 328 and [1978] *GRUR Int* 162, Beier, n 12 above, at 167–168 and, in general, Blakeney *Legal Aspects of the Transfer of Technology to Developing Countries* ESC Publishing (1989) at chapter 7.
[15] On the latter point see Beier in Holl and Klinke (eds) *Internationales Privatrecht, Internationales Wirtschaftsrecht* Carl Heymanns Verlag (1985) p 287 at pp 288–290.
[16] See above, pp 501 and 518.

to choice of law. It must be emphasised, though, that the second aspect can be absent from certain copyright contracts in which there is only a non-exclusive transfer of rights. These contracts are pure licences, in the sense that they only authorise someone to do an act which would otherwise be an infringement. The rights of the copyright owner are unaffected in such a case and no transfer of proprietary rights is effected.[17]

Let us first consider the transfer of proprietary rights. Here, the non-contractual issues have to be separated from the contractual ones. For the former, we can refer back to the chapter on the creation of rights. The law applicable to most non-contractual issues is the law of the protecting country. It is worth listing briefly the items that fall within this category. First of all, the issue of whether or not a copyright is assignable in whole or in part is covered. This also includes the related issue of whether exclusive or non-exclusive rights to exploit a copyright work may be granted. A second issue that is covered is whether or not grantees of exclusive rights are independently entitled to remedies in the case of copyright infringement by third parties and in which cases, if at all, an assignment or grant of rights is, in principle, effective against third parties that have subsequently been assigned or granted conflicting rights by the author or his successor in title. Thirdly and finally, the issue of the register for cinematographic works is covered. The law of the protecting country will determine whether such a register exists and whether and in which circumstances it is necessary to register agreements in relation to cinematographic reproduction and adaptation rights and other rights in relation to cinematographic works for them to be valid, or, eventually, even just for them to be effective against third parties.[18]

What is left is the determination of the rights and obligations of the parties inside the framework and borderlines that are provided by the non-contractual provisions of the law of the protecting country. These contractual aspects are governed by the Rome Convention 1980. The starting point here is once again Article 3 of the Convention. The parties are free to determine the applicable law. That route presents no problems and the choice of the parties is, normally, respected.

The distinction between the contractual aspect, ie the determination of the rights and duties of the parties, and the transfer of proprietary rights has been recognised by the courts. In *Campbell Connelly v Noble*, the High Court had to determine whether the agreement by which the world rights in the song 'The very thought of you' had been assigned to a British music publisher by the British composer of the song also covered the renewal of copyright in the United States. The Court distinguished between, on the one hand, the question whether and under which circumstances the

---

[17] Ulmer, n 3 above, at pp 44–45.   [18] *Ibid*, at pp 46–47.

renewal of copyright could be assigned, which was governed by the law of the protecting country, ie US copyright law, and, on the other hand, the interpretation of the contract as to whether the renewal of copyright was included amongst the rights that were given to the music publisher. The latter issue was decided under the law of the contract, ie in that case English law.[19]

III
HOW QUESTIONS AS TO THE APPLICABLE LAW ARISE

Contracts in relation to intellectual property rights are not uncommon. The copyright in a song, for example, is often assigned to a music publisher or a record company. One can, of course, assign only the UK copyright in the song, but one could also assign the US copyright as well as the UK copyright to a record company.[20] In either case, the parties may be established in yet different countries. Which law will determine the rights and obligations to the contract? This includes issues such as what rights exactly did the assignor assign to the assignee and which obligations did the assignee accept in return?

Should all these contractual issues also be governed by the law that governs the copyright as such? There are no obvious reasons why, in relation to intellectual property rights, the contractual freedom of the parties to choose the applicable law should not be respected,[21] as the parties can only transfer or assign whatever is assignable or transferable and the latter issues are not governed by the law chosen by the parties, but by the law of the protecting country.[22] Obviously, there is also a rule to determine the law applicable to the contract in the absence of a choice made by the parties.

A good copyright example is the case where a French ghostwriter assigned the copyright in the book she co-authored to her co-author in a

---

[19] *Campbell Connelly & Co Ltd* v *Noble* [1963] 1 All ER 237, [1963] 1 WLR 252; see also the German decision of the Oberlandsgericht München of 29 April 1954, published in Schulze, *Rechtsprechung zum Urheberrecht*, Vol V, No 8, annotated by Ulmer.

[20] See *Redwood Music Ltd* v *Francis, Day & Hunter Ltd and Others* [1978] RPC 429; *Redwood Music Ltd* v *B Feldman & Co Ltd and Others* [1979] RPC 1; consolidated upon appeal as *Redwood Music Ltd* v *B Feldman & Co Ltd and Others* [1979] RPC 385, (CA) and finally decided in the House of Lords as *Chappell & Co Ltd and Others* v *Redwood Music Ltd* and *Redwood Music Ltd* v *Francis, Day & Hunter Ltd and Another* [1981] RPC 337.

[21] This is also implicit in a case where the court determined the applicable law in the absence of a choice by the parties, see the Judgment of the Tokyo High Court of 16 September 1991 (Case NE-619/89), 24 (1993) IIC 391.

[22] See above, p 515.

contract governed by the law of New York. The ghostwriter later claimed part of the royalties and damages for the infringement of her moral right to be identified in France where the book had been published. Various issues arise from these facts. For example, could she assign all or some of her rights? This is a non-contractual issue. What was the exact scope of the rights that were assigned? The latter issue is contractual. Could the parties then choose the applicable law or did French law apply to the publication in France and all contracts in relation to it? In this case, the Court of Appeal in Paris[23] ruled that the parties could choose the applicable law. This meant that French law as the law of the protecting country was used to determine which rights were assignable,[24] but the law of New York as the law of the contract governed the validity and the scope of the actual transfer.[25]

Problems arise also in relation to industrial property rights. For example, a Swiss company has granted a trade mark licence and an exclusive distributorship to a German company for a range of diagnostic products and reagents. This licence contract covers Germany and Austria and it does not contain a clause that determines whether or not the licensee will still be entitled to a certain use of the trade mark once the agreement has been terminated. The latter issue is then to be determined according to the provisions of the applicable law.[26] But is the applicable law the law of the licensor's country, that of the licensee's country or that of either of the countries to which the licence applied and where the trade mark was used?

Other types of contract can be envisaged too. Parties that own potentially confusing trade marks can enter into a delimitation agreement.[27] In such a contract, they can make a choice of law. But is there still a role for the law of the forum, for example to exclude restrictive clauses and provisions, if the law chosen by the parties is applied?

It is to the detailed analysis of the contract choice of law rules that govern these issues that we now turn.

---

[23] Judgment of 1 February 1989, *Anne Bragance* v *Olivier Orban and Michel de Grèce* (1989) 142 *RIDA* 301.
[24] Moral rights were excluded on this basis.
[25] All pecuniary rights had been validly assigned.
[26] See the judgment of 22 November 1994 of the Austrian Supreme Court (Case 4 Ob 118/94), 28 (1997) *IIC* 574.
[27] See *Apple Corps Ltd and Another* v *Apple Computer Inc and Others* [1992] FSR 431.

IV
THE ROME CONVENTION ON THE LAW APPLICABLE TO CONTRACTUAL OBLIGATIONS

1. WHEN DOES THE ROME CONVENTION 1980 APPLY?

The Rome Convention 1980 has been incorporated into English law and brought into force by the Contracts (Applicable Law) Act 1990.[28] The Act applies only to contracts made after 1 April 1991.[29]

Article 1 of the Convention deals with its applicability. The terms of the Article make it clear that the Convention applies to all contractual obligations in any situation involving a choice between the law of different countries. Section 2(3) of the Contracts (Applicable Law) Act 1990 has expanded the applicability of the choice of law rules that are provided for in the Convention to cover purely intra UK choice of law problems, for example, to those involving only English and Scottish law. Some matters, however, have been excluded from the scope of the Convention.[30] Contractual obligations relating to intellectual property rights have not been included in the list in Article 1(2) of the Convention of matters that are excluded from its scope. During the debate on the Contracts (Applicable Law) Bill in the House of Lords, an amendment that would have excluded contracts in relation to intellectual property rights from the scope of the Bill was tabled. This was done on the basis that, due to the complexity of intellectual property, these contracts formed an obvious omission from the list of items that were excluded from the scope of the Rome Convention 1980. The amendment was withdrawn, not because these contracts were not covered by the Convention in the first place, but because it was realised that the United Kingdom could not unilaterally adopt a modified version of the Convention.[31] This means that the Rome Convention 1980 applies to all contractual obligations relating to intellectual property rights, if those obligations arise from contracts that have been concluded after 1 April 1991.[32]

---

[28] See Dicey and Morris, *The Conflict of Laws*, Sweet & Maxwell (12th ed, 1993), Rule 174, at p 1187.
[29] SI 1991/707; The law applicable to contracts made before that date continues to be determined according to the old common law rules (the proper law of the contract doctrine). These rules will not be analysed in detail here.
[30] See in more detail Lagarde, [1991] *Revue Critique de Droit International Privé* 287, at 294–299.
[31] See Hansard (HL) 5 April 1990 vol 517, cols 1544–1547.
[32] See Wadlow, [1997] 1 *EIPR* 11, at 11–12.

2. The Applicable Law

The Convention may lead to the application of any law, even if that is not the law of a Contracting State.[33] The applicable law will, in particular, govern the interpretation of the contract, the performance of the contractual obligations, the various ways of extinguishing these obligations and the issues of the prescription and limitation of actions. The applicable law will also govern the consequences of any breach of a contractual obligation, but this will be done within the limits of the powers conferred on the court by its procedural law. The consequences of any breach will include the assessment of damages in so far as it is governed by rules of law.[34]

(a) THE LAW IS CHOSEN BY THE PARTIES

(i) Contracts made before 1st April 1991

Under traditional common law choice of law rules, the parties were free to choose the applicable law. No specific problems arise from these common law rules in relation to intellectual property rights contracts. It is, therefore, proposed not to analyse these rules in any further detail.[35]

(ii) Contracts made after 1 April 1991

The Rome Convention 1980 recognises, in its Article 3,[36] the freedom of the parties to choose the law applicable to the contract, a principle that is recognised internationally. This rule applies equally to industrial property licence contracts and copyright.[37] So, in the situation where the parties make an express or implied choice of law this choice prevails and no other choice of law problem remains unsolved.[38] The parties are free to choose any law. The applicable law does not need to have a particular connection with the contract.[39] The parties are also free to make alternative choices of law.[40]

According to Article 3, the parties can, first of all, choose the applicable law by making an express choice of law. Such an express choice of law is clearly present if the contract stipulates, for example that it is 'subject to' or 'governed by' a particular law or that it is 'to be construed in accordance with' a particular law. Whether a specific clause amounts to an express

---

[33] Article 2 of the Rome Convention 1980.
[34] Article 10 of the Rome Convention 1980.
[35] See Dicey and Morris, *The Conflict of Laws*, Stevens (11th ed, 1987), chapter 32 and Cheshire and North, *Private International Law*, Butterworths (11th ed, 1987), chapter 18.
[36] [1980] OJ L266/1 f, n 3 above.
[37] See Ulmer, n 3 above, at p 86.
[38] *Ibid*, at 86–87, see also the decision of the German Bundesgerichtshof of 21 October 1964 [1965] *GRUR Int* 504.
[39] See Dicey and Morris, n 28 above, at pp 1213–1214. [40] *Ibid*, at p 1221.

choice of law is a matter of interpretation. This matter should be looked at from a Convention based approach.

In the absence of an express choice, Article 3 allows the choice of the parties to be demonstrated by the terms of the contract or the circumstances of the case. Such a choice has to be demonstrated with reasonable certainty. The intention of the parties is a vital element in this respect. The court will, in the light of all the facts, have to decide whether the parties have made a real choice of law without expressly stating so in the contract. However, the court cannot infer a choice if the parties had no clear intention of making a choice.[41] There are a few good examples of situations in which a choice by the parties may be demonstrated with reasonable certainty.[42] Standard contracts that are known to be governed by a particular system of law are a first example. It is clear, for instance, that a Lloyd's policy of marine insurance is governed by English law. A second example is found in the situation where there is a previous course of dealing between the parties that involved a choice of law. This may, for instance, be the case in a master-contract or in a charterparty under which bills of lading without an express choice of law are issued. A choice of forum clause is a third example of such an implied choice of law.[43] English law did always have a tendency to accept that whoever chooses the forum, also chooses the law of the forum as the applicable law. Fourthly, a reference to particular provisions of a system of law is another example of such a choice of law by the parties. The fifth and last example is when there is an arbitration clause naming the place of arbitration.

In most cases, the choice of law of the parties will cover the whole contract. However, Article 3(1) of the Rome Convention 1980 also allows the parties to select the applicable law for a part of the contract. This may lead to two situations. The parties may have chosen another law that will govern the remainder of the contract, or they may have made no choice of law at all for the remainder of the contract. The rules to determine the applicable law in the absence of a choice by the parties will apply to the remainder of the contract in the latter situation. And finally, the parties are also free to agree at any time to change the law applicable to the contract, as long as the formal validity of the contract and the rights of third parties are not adversely affected by such a change.[44]

Article 3 does not raise any particular problems for contracts in relation to intellectual property rights. Accordingly, our analysis will focus on licence contracts which do not contain a choice of law. It would be wrong to conclude that this analysis is concerned with a problem that can only arise in a marginal number of international licence contracts, because a

---

[41] Giuliano-Lagarde Report, n 11 above, at 17. [42] See *ibid*.
[43] See *Egon Oldendorff* v *Liberia Corpn* [1995] 2 Lloyd's Rep. 64.
[44] Article 3(2) of the Rome Convention 1980.

surprisingly large number of these do not contain a choice of law clause, nor do they imply a choice of law by the licensor and the licensee.[45] The main reason for this perhaps surprising fact, after all most licence contracts are negotiated by experienced lawyers, is simply that the parties were unable to agree on a choice a law. Neither the licensor nor the licensee want to accept the law of the country of the other party out of prestige or because they do not trust the law proposed by the other party, suspecting that it will contain unpleasant surprises.[46]

(b) THE APPLICABLE LAW IN THE ABSENCE OF CHOICE

(i) Contracts made before 1 April 1991

The law applicable to a contract relating to intellectual property that was concluded before 1 April 1991 can, in the absence of a choice of law by the parties, be determined according to two methods. The oldest and most common method involves determining the proper law of the contract. This means an objective test[47] is carried out to locate the contract[48] and to determine the system of law with which the intellectual property contract has the closest and most real connection.[49] This method is used by, eg French,[50] English and Belgian[51] courts. Schnitzer[52] developed the more recent method which relies on the most characteristic performance to determine the law applicable to the licence contract.[53] This method was adopted by the Swiss courts.[54] When applied to international industrial property licences, neither of these methods leads to a clear and uniform solution,[55] as will be seen in the following paragraphs, when the case law and the views of the scholars on this point will be analysed in the light of the determination of the closest connection and the characteristic performance, as required by Article 4 of the Rome Convention 1980.

There are, though, alternative approaches. First, we have to deal briefly with two slightly odd suggestions which do not fit in with the now almost

---

[45] Or assignor and assignee in assignment contracts. On this point, the difference between licences and assignments is irrelevant.
[46] Beier [1983] *Les Nouvelles* 141 at 141 and von Hoffmann (1976) 40 *RabelsZ* 208 at 211.
[47] See *The Assunzione* [1954] 1 All ER 278.
[48] See *Amin Rasheed Corpn v Kuwait Insurance Co* [1984] AC 50 at 61.
[49] *Ibid*, for a more detailed analysis see Cheshire and North *Private International Law*, Butterworths (12th ed 1992), at pp 487–495.
[50] See French Cour de Cassation, 5 December 1910, [1911] Rec Sirey I 129.
[51] See Belgian Hof van Cassatie – Cour de Cassation, 24 February 1938, [1938] Pas I 66.
[52] Schnitzer *Handbuch des internationalen Privatrechts II* Basel (4th ed, 1958) and Schnitzer, [1969] *RabelsZ* 23.
[53] Modiano, *Le contrat de licence de brevet*, Droz (1979), at 127.
[54] See Vischer *Internationales Vertragsrecht* Bern (1962) at 110–111.
[55] Van Hecke and Lenaerts, n 3 above, at p 334.

universally accepted closest connection and characteristic performance approaches.

Bartin suggested a territorial localisation for industrial property rights.[56] Within the same general approach, it could be proposed that one should apply the law of the country of origin, the country where the first patent or industrial design right application was filed, to all issues related to that industrial right. This proposition has never been accepted and both the proper law doctrine and the Rome Convention 1980 prohibit its application to licence contracts. It is also in complete contradiction to every principle of private international law as far as contracts and contractual obligations are concerned. This solution is clearly unacceptable.

Letting the law of the place where the licence contract was made govern the international industrial property licence contract[57] is a solution which is also not acceptable. A first objection is that it is not always easy to determine the place where the contract was made. Not only can a licence contract be sent to the licensee by mail to be signed by the licensee on arrival, but negotiations can take place in various places, the conclusion of such a contract may involve an exchange of letters and/or faxes or the contract can finally be signed at a place where representatives of the parties are present essentially for other purposes. A second, and even more important, objection is that it is impossible to see how the law of the place where the contract is made could by definition be the law of the country with which the licence contract has the closest connection or the law of the country where the contracting party that performs the characteristic performance has its seat.[58] Scholars seem to have completely abandoned this theory.[59]

Secondly, each proposal, which examines and applies these choice of law methods to international contracts relating to intellectual property rights, leads normally to one applicable law, but Diener offers a very different approach based on the balance of interests between licensor and licensee which does not seem to lead directly to one single law being applicable.[60] Rabel and Nussbaum indicate the direction back towards

---

[56] Bartin [1934] *Clunet* 793.

[57] This theory seems to have its roots in France according to Pfaff, [1974] *AWD* 241 at 249; see also Vida, [1964] *Revue Critique de Droit International Privé* 209.

[58] see Troller [1952] GRUR Auslandteil 108 at 120 and Troller *Das internationale Privat- und Zivilprozessrecht im gewerblichen Rechtsschutz und Urheberrecht*, Verlag für Recht und Gesellschaft (1952), at 186.

[59] See Pfaff, n 57 above, at 249, contra: Drobnig's comments during the 'Symposium über die Immaterial güterrechte im internationalen Privatrecht' (AIPPI – Congress Munich 18 April 1975, see the report by M Walter [1975] *GRUR Int* 308) and Drobnig, 40 (1976) *RabelsZ* 189 *et seq*.

[60] See Diener *Contrats internationaux de Propriété industrielle* Litec (1986), also discussed below.

more acceptable solutions by stressing the importance of the application of the law that governs the contractual obligations.[61]

(ii) Article 4 of the Rome Convention 1980

The Rome Convention 1980, in its Article 4, deals with the problem of the applicable law in the absence of a choice of law. The criterion is that of the closest connection. The presumption of the characteristic performance, which is used to determine the closest connection is rebuttable.[62] Although this method is of some help, it does not produce a clear and uniform answer in cases of international intellectual property contracts. It is simply not evident which performance is the characteristic one and almost all these contracts present close connections with more than one legal system. But first, Article 4 itself needs to be looked at a bit more closely.

Article 4 provides an objective test to determine the applicable law. Its aim is to find the country with which the contract is most closely connected. The law of that country will be the applicable law. The intentions of the parties, which played a vital role under Article 3, are of no importance here. What counts are connections linking the contract to a particular country.[63]

A real departure from the common law traditions is found in the fact that the closest connection is, at least in the first instance, not identified through the balancing of the various connecting factors.[64] The Convention starts the identification process in Article 4(2) by applying the rebuttable presumption that the contract is most closely connected with the country in which the party that is to effect the characteristic performance has, at the time of the conclusion of the contract, its habitual residence. The habitual residence is replaced by its central administration if that party is a body corporate or incorporate, and by its principal place of business (or another place of business if the contract stipulates that performance is to be effected through that other place of business) if the party that is to effect the characteristic performance entered into the contract in the course of its trade or profession. Special presumptions apply to contracts in relation to rights in or rights to use immovables and contracts for the carriage of goods. The characteristic performance is normally identified for a certain type of contract and it is accepted that the payment of money cannot be the characteristic performance, as it is an element that is common to many types of contract.[65]

---

[61] Rabel, *The Conflict of Laws*, Chicago (1950), Nussbaum, *Handbuch des internationalen Privatrecht*, Tübingen (1932) and Modiano, n 53 above, at 127.

[62] Articles 4(2) and 4(5) of the Rome Convention 1980 and the Giuliano and Lagarde Report, n 11 above, at 19–23.

[63] Cheshire and North *Private International Law*, Butterworths (12th ed, 1992), at p 487.

[64] See Wadlow, n 32 above, at 13. [65] Giuliano-Lagarde Report, n 11 above, at 20.

The presumption that is contained in Article 4(2) can be rebutted in two situations. These are described in Article 4(5) of the Convention. First, there will be situations in which no single characteristic performance can be determined. The second situation is where it appears from the circumstances as a whole that the contract is more closely connected with another country. In both these situations, there is a return to Article 4(1). This process could be described as the 'roundabout route to the applicable law'.[66] The identification of the applicable law is then dependent upon the outcome of the balancing of the various connecting factors which will identify the country with which the contract has its closest connection. The law of that country will be the applicable law. This technique is almost identical to the old common law system that leads to the identification of the proper law of the contract. Matters such as the place of contracting, the place of performance, the places of residence or business of the parties and the nature and the subject matter of the contract resume their importance at this stage.[67] Article 4(3) contains a special rule for immovable property. This rule is, however, not applicable, because intellectual property rights are to be classified as movables for this purpose.[68]

In exceptional circumstances, a severable part of a contract which has a closer connection with another country may be governed by the law of that country.[69] This option for the court corresponds to the option for the parties to choose the law for a part only of the contract, but it should not be used frequently.

The presumption presents the advantages that uniformity between the courts of the different Member States will be easier to achieve and that the applicable law can be determined even if there is more than one place of performance, but it has also been subjected to a lot of criticism. The presumption applies very well to simple contracts, such as a contract for the sale of goods, but it will be difficult to identify a single characteristic performance in a contract that is of a slightly more complicated nature,[70] especially if it involves mutual obligations of confidence and collaboration. The presumption may also not be the most effective way to determine the closest connection. Is there necessarily such a close link, not with the place where the characteristic performance is to be effected, but with the place of habitual residence of the person that is to effect the characteristic performance? And if the payment of money cannot be the characteristic performance because it is a performance that applies to many types of

---

[66] Wadlow, n 32 above, at 13.   [67] See Dicey and Morris, n 28 above, at p 1232.
[68] See the discussion above, at pp 281–283.
[69] Article 4(1) (second sentence) of the Rome Convention 1980; see also the Giuliano-Lagarde Report, n 11 above, at 23.
[70] See Juenger, in North (ed), *Contract Conflicts*, North-Holland Publishing Company (1982) 295, at p 301.

contracts, does that not unduly and mechanically downgrade the importance of the law of the country of the party that pays for the goods or services?[71]

Before turning to the application of Article 4 to contracts in relation to intellectual property rights, it might be useful to give just a few examples of situations in which Article 4(5) might apply. Many of these reflect the criticisms of the presumption rule. A contract of barter is a good example of a situation where no single characteristic performance can be determined. Any contract that involves mutual obligations that surpass the level of the payment of money could potentially create similar problems. A closer connection with another country could, primarily, be found in a situation where the place of performance differs from the place of business of the party that is to effect the characteristic performance. The contract could in such a situation have a closer link with the country of the place of performance and this could trigger the application of Article 4(5). In certain circumstances, such a closer connection could also be found in a situation where the party that is to effect the characteristic performance has a place of business in the country of the place of performance, whilst having its principal place of business in another country. Such a contract could be more closely connected with the country of the principal place of business.[72]

(iii) Application of Article 4 of the Rome Convention 1980 to contracts in relation to intellectual property rights

(a) *Patent licence and industrial design licence contracts and more general considerations*

(i) *The closest connection*

Typically, a patent licence gives the licensee the right to make the patented product or to use the patented process. An industrial design licence gives the licensee the right to use the design. The licensor develops the technology, the patented product or process or the industrial design, whilst the licensee exploits the technology or the design and pays a royalty for doing so. The licensor often only receives payment if the technology or the design is exploited successfully, because the payment of royalties is linked to the frequency of the use of the technology or the design. The royalty is often expressed as a percentage of the salesprice.

On this basis, a number of countries could claim to have the closest connection with the licence contract. The country of the licensor could rely on

---

[71] For the various criticisms see Collins (1976) 25 *ICLQ* 35, at 47; d'Oliveira (1977) 25 *Am J Comp L* 303, at 326–328; Morse (1982) 2 *Yb Eur L* 107, at 126–131.

[72] See Dicey and Morris, n 28 above, at pp 1237–1238.

the fact that, without the creation and the supply of the technology or the design, nothing would happen. The country of the licensee could rely on the fact that the exploitation of the technology or design involves a major commercial risk and that, without the successful exploitation, the licensor would receive no payment whatsoever. There is, of course, also the country in which the technology or the design is exploited. The exploitation could be seen as the most important element and that country is also the protecting country for the intellectual property rights themselves. A single law would then govern most aspects of both the intellectual property right itself and the contract in relation to the right.

(ii) *The presumption of characteristic performance*

A preliminary point should, briefly, be addressed before turning to the presumption in Article 4(2) of the Convention. Article 4(3) contains a different presumption for immovable property. Are intellectual property rights immovable property for the purposes of the Rome Convention, 1980? It is submitted that they are not. For the purposes of the Convention the term 'immovable property' should be given the narrow sense of land, including buildings, by analogy with the provisions of the Brussels Convention 1968. It has already been seen that, under the latter Convention, intellectual property rights are not to be classified as immovables.[73] Both Conventions are part of the European legal order and any characterisation at that level must prevail. The characterisation of intellectual property rights in domestic law or under the provisions of the *lex situs* are not relevant, since they cannot determine a uniform European meaning which is to be given to these terms for the purposes of both Conventions.[74]

That brings us to Article 4(2) of the Rome Convention 1980. The crucial point here and the one where there could be a difference with other types of contracts is that of the characteristic performance. How will the normal characteristic performance presumption apply to contracts relating to intellectual property rights?

Simple contracts. For a number of simple contracts, the presumption might work rather well. For example, the contract by which an intellectual property right is purely and simply assigned resembles an outright sale of the right. If the assignee pays a lump sum in consideration of the transfer of the right which is effected by the assignor that resemblance is indeed correct. In that case, the assignment is clearly the characteristic performance.[75] The applicable law can then be determined on the basis of the place of habitual residence or business of the assignor, in accordance with Article 4(2). In a second example, the assignment could be replaced by a

---

[73] See chapter 1, p 34–35.　　[74] See Wadlow, n 32 above, at 14.
[75] Wadlow, n 32 above, at 14.

bare licence. If the licence is for a single use, for example a licence to reprint a large passage of a copyright work, and the whole of the consideration is in the form of a lump sum, again there is a resemblance to an outright sale of the right. An approach that favours the identification of the licensor's performance under a licence contract as the characteristic performance of the licence contract has been favoured by some authors. The performance by which the licensor transfers the right is seen by them as the characteristic performance under the licence contract as it is the essential element which enables, and at the same time limits, every activity of the licensee. The obligations of the licensee are subordinated to those of the licensor. Schnitzer argues that the characteristic performance is that of the licensor because the performance of the licensee is nothing but the payment of money, as a lump sum, by means of royalties or as a combination of both. This leads him to consider the licence grant by the licensor as the characteristic performance. Payment of money is considered never to be the characteristic performance, as it is found in many contracts and in exchange for all kinds of specific performances.[76] This systematic preference for the performance which does not involve the payment of a sum of money is also found in the Giuliano and Lagarde Report on the Rome Convention 1980.[77] Lagarde cites a licence contract as an example, which implies that he considers the law of the country of the licensor as the law applicable to the licence contract in the absence of a choice of law in cases involving licence contracts to which the Rome Convention 1980 is applicable.[78] His conclusion corresponds to the Danish pre-Convention position regarding the characteristic performance in intellectual property licence contracts.[79]

Complex contracts. But, 'the more complex a transaction, the less helpful the criterion becomes'.[80] As soon as the simple assignment contract is left behind, things get a lot more complicated. The situation where an assignment or a licence of an intellectual property right is granted in exchange for the payment of royalties rather than for the payment of a lump sum[81] is not at all uncommon. It is almost the standard type of licence contract. In such a situation, the assignee or licensor would also undertake to exploit the right and it accepts the commercial risks that are linked to such an exploitation. Such exploitation could, for example, involve the manufacture, the distribution and the marketing of the licensed articles. In those contracts, the exploitation of the right is, arguably, more important than

[76] Schnitzer, n 52 above, at 597 and Modiano, n 53 above, at 127–128.
[77] Giuliano and Lagarde, n 11 above, at 20.
[78] Lagarde, [1991] *Revue Critique de Droit International Privé* 287, at 307.
[79] See Pfaff, n 57 above, at 247 where he refers to Hjermind 'Dänemark' in Langen, *Internationale Lizenzverträge*, (2nd ed 1958) 93–104.
[80] Juenger, n 70 above, at 301.
[81] In certain contracts, an initial lump sum is combined with the payment of royalties during the exploitation of the intellectual property right. This could complicate things even further.

Exploitation of intellectual property rights: the applicable law

the payment of money, and at least as important as the complete or partial transfer of rights. A single characteristic performance can hardly be identified in these circumstances and it submitted that Schnitzer's view on the matter cannot be readily accepted.

That is also the case for a contract to publish and distribute a book, which could be taken as another example of a more complex contract. Such a contract involves a whole range of performances. The author undertakes to write and deliver the manuscript and to grant a licence to copy his copyright work to the publisher in exchange for a royalty or for a royalty combined with an advance. The publisher's performance lies in the fact that he undertakes to publish and to distribute the work. Paying money or receiving money can be ruled out for the purposes of the identification of the characteristic performance, but it is submitted that the production of the manuscript and the copyright licence on the one hand, and the publication and distribution of the book, on the other hand, are both vital to and characteristic of the contract.[82]

A joint venture contract is probably the most problematic type of contract, especially when joint research and development is envisaged. Typically, such a contract involves the cross licensing of technology and in practice 'the performance by each party seems equally characteristic'.[83]

It is, therefore, submitted that for all but the simplest types of contracts in relation to intellectual property rights, a single characteristic performance cannot be identified. The presumption contained in Article 4(2) of the Rome Convention 1980 cannot be applied successfully in those circumstances. Article 4(5) addresses such a situation by referring back to the closest connection test.

(iii) *Article 4(5)*

The country with which the contract in relation to intellectual property rights has its closest connection needs to be identified in situations where the presumption cannot be applied. The law of that country will be the law applicable to such contracts. Various solutions have been suggested by the caselaw and in scholarly writings. Most of the discussion has centred around licences, as they are the most common type of contract.

The licensor's habitual residence, etc. The first of these solutions proposes the application to the licence contract of the law of the country where the licensor has its habitual residence, place of business or central administration on the basis of the argument that the contract is most closely linked to that country.[84] The arguments in favour of this solution are as follows.

---

[82] See Wadlow, n 32 above, at 14 and Juenger, n 70 above, at 301.
[83] Wadlow, n 32 above, at 14.
[84] See eg the judgment of the Swiss Federal Court [1976] JdT I 519.

First, this solution can be supported on the basis that one can consider the law of the country of the licensor to be the law of the country with which the licence contract has the closest connection. If one prefers this solution, one stresses the connection provided by the invention or the industrial design for which the exclusive right was granted. The country of the licensor is the country where the invention or the industrial design was created. Secondly, it seems equally important that the existence of the whole contract depends on the existence of the exclusive right (and the readiness of the licensor to grant a licence thereof).[85] Only the latter argument is always a valid one. The first argument is not valid if the licensor is in fact granting a sub-licence, being a licensee himself, or if the industrial property right has been assigned to him by the inventor or the creator of the industrial design. Although these arguments can be decisive in some cases if one examines each licence contract separately, they are not convincing enough to prefer systematically the law of the country of the licensor to any other law.

Thirdly, another argument in favour of the law of the country of the licensor is found in the Swiss Private International Law Statute. Article 122(1) reads: 'Contracts on rights in intellectual property are governed by the law of the country where the transferor or licensor has his habitual residence'.[86] The fact that the characteristic performance theory is, in origin, Swiss adds to the value of this argument.[87] Even before the codification of Swiss private international law, the Swiss courts brought the characteristic performance theory into practice. When applied to licence contracts without a choice of law, this resulted in the application of the law of the country of the licensor.[88]

Arguments against the licensor's performance as the characteristic performance are as follows.

One could argue that the determination of the licensor's performance as the characteristic performance of the licence contract does not give a straight answer to the question of which law should be applied. That could still either be the law of the country in which the licensor had to perform

---

[85] See Modiano, n 53 above, at 128.

[86] Swiss Private International Law Statute of 18 December 1987, reproduced in P Karrer and K Arnold, *Switzerland's Private International Law Statute*, Kluwer (1989), the translation is an unofficial one provided by the authors.

[87] Dessemontet suggested that this rule should even apply to non-patented know-how, in *Conflicts and Harmonisation – Mélanges en l'honneur d'Alfred E von Overbeck* 725, at 741.

[88] See the *Togal*-case: judgment of the Swiss Bundesgericht, 22 April 1975, BGE 94 II 362 *et seq.*, [1977] GRUR Int 208 at 209 and M Keller, C Schulze and M Schaetzle, *Die Rechtsprechung des Bundesgerichts im internationalen Privatrecht und die verwandten Rechtsgebieten – Band II – Obligationenrecht*, Schulthess Polygraphischer Verlag (1977), at 300; see also the Swiss case *Stipa v Dixi* BGE 94 II 355f and M Keller, C Schulze and M Schaetzle, *ibid*, at 305 (the law of the country of the licensor can be set aside in exceptional circumstances if the existance of a stronger link with another law is demonstrated).

its characteristic duty, thus normally the law of the protecting country, or the law of the country where the licensor had its seat.[89] The text of Article 4(2) of the Rome Convention 1980 refers only to the latter option, which means that this discussion seems to have become irrelevant. It is submitted, however, that it might resurface in another form. Large multinational companies often centralise the management of their intellectual property rights in a daughter-company that is set up specifically for that purpose. Such a company might be located in a tax haven or at least in a country that has no direct link to the creation of the technology or the intellectual property rights. In such a situation, the application of the second option under Article 4(5) of the Rome Convention 1980 could be triggered, because the link with the country in which the intellectual property management company is established is a very weak one, whilst there is a very strong link with the country in which the licensee is established and in which the licensed right is to be exploited. This is exactly what the Austrian Supreme Court decided in the *Stefanel* case. The law of the Virgin Islands, where the intellectual property management company had been established, was rejected as the applicable law.[90] The law of the country of exploitation is also the law of the protecting country and the law under which the intellectual property right has been registered. This country is also the country where the licensor has to effect its performance under the contract, as the technology has to be made available locally.

Troller was only convinced by the arguments in favour of the law of the country of the licensor if this law was to be applied to a contract in which a licence was granted for several countries. In this type of case, the fact that only one law governs the contract forms an additional advantage.[91]

Ulmer proposes the application of the law of the country of the licensor in the situation where the licence that is granted is neither exclusive nor contains any obligation to exploit the licence.[92] In suggesting this, he clearly has in mind a licence granted to a counterfeiter in a compromise to avoid hard, expensive and protracted litigation. In all other cases, he thinks the effective exploitation by the licensee (in combination with the payment of money) becomes the characteristic performance as the success of the contract depends on this exploitation. Most contracts include a clause which obliges the licensee to pay royalties to the licensor, which means that, even for the licensor, the exploitation becomes the most important point of the contract as its income depends on it.

[89] von Hoffmann, n 46 above, at 213, n 13.
[90] Judgment of 5 May 1987 [1988] GRUR Int 72.
[91] Troller, [1952] *GRUR Auslandteil* 108 at 121, also Vida, n 57 above, Modiano (n 53 above, at 128 and 132) mentions that Troller later reviewed his position by adopting a position similar to that of Ulmer (see below) and she cites: Troller 'Kurzreferat gehalten am Symposium über die Immaterialgüterrechte im internationalen Privatrecht' AIPPI – Congress Munich 18 April 1975.
[92] Ulmer, n 3 above, at 102.

It is clear that the obligation of the licensee does not only imply the payment of money and that, in most cases, the balance between the performances of the parties to the licence contract is more subtle, which means that the main argument in favour of the law of the country of the licensor is no longer valid. One has to conclude that there is no general rule which implies the application of the law of the country of the licensor to the licence contract[93] because its performance is the characteristic one. Only in very specific cases and after individual examination can that law be applied to a licence contract.[94]

The licensee's habitual residence, etc. The second solution proposes the application to the licence contract of the law of the country where the licensee has its habitual residence, place of business or central administration, on the basis of the argument that the contract is most closely linked to that country.[95]

The distinction made by Ulmer, which was mentioned a few paragraphs earlier in this analysis, indicates that he thinks a different solution has certain merits. This solution proposes the law of the country of the licensee as the law applicable to international industrial property licence contracts in the situation where the parties did not choose an applicable law.

Ulmer stresses the link with the country of the licensee, if the licensee has a duty of exploitation or if an exclusive licence is granted.[96] In such a situation, the licensee's performance is the characteristic one. But only a few authors are prepared to accept the applicability of the law of the country of the licensee as a general rule without exceptions.[97]

The arguments in favour of the law of the country of the licensee have been expressed as follows.[98] Whilst Ulmer sees this solution as an exception to the rule that the law of the country of the licensor is the applicable law and Claringbould, on the contrary, sees it as establishing an inflexible rule, the most detailed and reasonable description of this solution and the cases to which it could apply is presented by Giovanna Modiano.[99] In her opinion, the basic option is the applicability of the law of the country of the licensee. Certain cases can, however, present a closer link with another country, in that case the law of that country becomes applicable. The most prominent exception is the case in which the licensee is under no obliga-

---

[93] Contra: Dessemontet, [1978] *Journal of International Law and Economics* 1.
[94] Beier's approach illustrates this; see below and Beier, in Holl and Klinke (eds) *Internationales Privatrecht, Internationales Wirtschaftsrecht*, Carl Heymanns Verlag (1985) p 287 at pp 301–302.
[95] See, eg the judgment of 29 November 1968 of the Obergericht Zürich (Switzerland) 67 (1968) *Blätter für zürcherische Rechtsprechung* 118 (in relation to a trade mark licence).
[96] Ulmer, n 3 above, at 101–102; Troller agreed, earlier he thought the performance of the licensee was the characteristic one in a one country licence contract (above n 91).
[97] Claringbould, *Licenties: Praktische wenken voor de kennishandel*, Kluwer (1982), at p 83.
[98] See generally, Walter, n 4 above, at 59.   [99] Modiano, n 53 above, at 138–141.

tion to exploit the invention or the industrial design and its only obligation consists in the payment of certain sums of money, in which case the applicable law is the law of the country of the licensor.[100]

The Austrian Parliament has favoured the application of the law of the country of the licensee if the licence contract relates to several countries.[101] This means, under Austrian Private International Law, that if one licensee is granted a licence for several countries, the law of the country of the licensee becomes the applicable law, without exceptions, if the parties did not agree on the applicability of the law of another country.[102] In cases of cross-licensing, in which both parties are licensor and licensee for different intellectual property rights, the Austrian statute leads to the application of the law of the country with which the cross-licence contract has the closest connection. In many cases, this is merely restating the problem without suggesting a clear solution.

The starting point of Modiano's defence of the solution which she proposes is the fact that the vast majority of licence contracts are concluded by licensees which are eager to exploit the invention or the industrial design.[103] If one is looking for the characteristic performance, she argues that one has to turn to the licensee. The licensee is investing capital and manpower in the exploitation of the industrial property right. The licensor, in most cases, limits its action to receiving the royalties or any other payments made under the licence contract. In her opinion, technical assistance, quality control and assistance in case of infringement of the right by the licensor cannot change this balance.[104]

There is, however a situation in which these arguments become less convincing, because they are dependent on the fact that the licensee exploits the licence in the country where it is established. There is no apparent reason to apply the law of the country of the licensee, as the law with which the contract has its closest connection, if the licensee exploits the licence in a third country. All the additional efforts of the licensee in exploiting the technology then take place in a third country. If anything, the argument seems to favour the application of the law of the place of exploitation, as the country with which the contract, arguably, has its strongest connection, rather than the law of the country of the licensee.

---

[100] *Ibid* and Modiano, [1981] *Les Nouvelles* 55 at 59–60.
[101] Austrian Federal Statute of 15 June 1978 on Private International Law (IPR–Gesetz), *Bundesgesetzblatt für die Republik Österreich*, 7 July 1978, No 304, 1729 at Para 43(1).
[102] See Köhler and Gürtler, *Internationales Privatrecht – IPR Gesetz*, Druck und Verlag der Österreichischen Staatsdruckerei (1979), at 122–123.
[103] Modiano, n 53 above, at 139, where she reproaches Ulmer for coming to the opposite conclusion without factual grounds.
[104] *Ibid*, at 138–141.

That brings us to the exceptions to the theory that favours the law of the country of the licensee. When it comes to the exceptions to the theory, it should be accepted that the obligation to exploit can be implicit.[105] Ulmer's exception in the situation where the licence is exclusive cannot be endorsed, as there is no evidence that this fact would have any influence on the exploitation so as to render the law of the country of the licensee inapplicable.[106]

Troller does not place the law of the country of the licensee at the heart of his theory, he suggests that the law of the country of the licensee is only appropriate if the licensee, whose licence covers several countries, has a duty to exploit the industrial property right.[107] He sees this situation as being exceptional. But, it is submitted that this is not so. The exploitation of the industrial property right is, in general, the main motivation for the conclusion of a licence agreement.[108] This does not lead to a general preference for the law of the country of the licensee, as the essential fact is the exploitation of the industrial property right and that fact is inevitably linked to the country which grants the protection for it and, as a consequence, becomes the place of exploitation. It is, in truth, only a coincidence that in most cases the licensee also has its seat in the protecting country.

It is clear that, although this theory is workable under Article 4 of the Rome Convention 1980 in several cases, it does not form a solution of general application. The licensee does not always effect the characteristic performance and the licence contract does not in all circumstances have its closest connection with the country in which the licensee is established or has its place of business. The fact that, under the Austrian statute, it is only applied to a specific type of case can be seen as providing additional support for this conclusion.[109]

The law of the protecting country. The third solution proposes the application to the licence contract of the law of the protecting country on the basis of the argument that the contact is most closely linked to that country, as this is also the country where the technology will be exploited.

A solution which is internationally accepted for immovable property prescribes the applicability of the law of the place where the goods are located (*lex rei sitae*). As industrial property rights are a form of property, it could be expected that some authors would try to establish a similar solution in the present context. The *lex rei sitae* (the law of the place where the goods are located), in this case the law of the protecting country, is seen

---

[105] Modiano, n 53 above, at 141 (unclear on this point).
[106] Ulmer, n 3 above, at 102.
[107] Troller, n 91 above, at 121.   [108] See Modiano, n 53 above, at 139.
[109] See above n 101 for the reference to the Statute and below for further details.

as the applicable law by Wolff,[110] Dicey,[111] Schmitthof,[112] Raape,[113] Batiffol,[114] Troller[115] and Beier.[116]

The preference for the law of the country of protection, where the licence will be exercised,[117] is based on the fact that, as far as industrial property rights are concerned, the country of protection is also the country of exploitation.

Several arguments make it possible to see the law of the protecting country as the law of the country with which the licence contract has the closest connection. The element to which most weight is to be given, is the exploitation of the licence.

The first argument in favour of the law of the protecting country is that the objective centre of gravity of the licence contract is found in that country. The contract has the strongest nexus with that country; the industrial property right is located and protected in that country and, in most cases, all or at least the primary exploitation acts are performed there. The latter point is decisive for the determination of the closest connection of the contract since all other elements depend on the exploitation of the invention or the industrial design. The whole idea of industrial property itself depends on the special rights of the inventor or designer and on making the invention or the design available to the public by exploiting it. Exploitation is a necessary requirement for continued protection in most national intellectual property systems. In the authors' view, however, the dominant element is the protection which is granted. This makes it difficult to see the exploitation of the right as 'the' characteristic performance. Beier even sees the fact that the performance of the licensor is the grant of the licence for that country as an additional argument in favour of this solution.[118]

The second argument is that this solution is also the only one which leads to the result that the entire contractual relationship is governed by the same law, because, as demonstrated above,[119] the law which is applied in a compulsory way to certain aspects of the contractual relationship is precisely

---

[110] Wolff, *Private International Law*, Oxford (2nd ed 1950), at 547.
[111] Dicey, *Dicey's Conflict of Laws*, London (7th ed 1958).
[112] Schmithoff, *The English Conflict of Laws*, London (3rd ed 1954).
[113] Raape, *Internationales Privatrecht*, Berlin (5th ed 1961).
[114] Batiffol, *Les Conflits de Lois en Matière de Contrats*, Sirey (1938) and *Traité Elémentaire de Droit International Privé*, LGDJ (3rd ed 1959).
[115] Troller, n 91 above, at 196; for the exceptions which he introduced in his theory at certain stages see above. [116] Beier, n 12 above, at 176; see also below n 127.
[117] See, in this sense District Court of Stuttgart, 14 March 1957, [1956–1957] IPR Rspr No 29; District Court of Düsseldorf, 4 August 1961, [1962] GRUR Int 256 and Court of Appeals of Zürich, 20 November 1968, [1969] AWD 329 (in the latter judgment, the court, equally, indicated that in the absence of a choice of law clause in the licence contract a clause on jurisdiction will amount to a choice of law); all judgments cited by Beier, n 12 above, at 176, n 45.
[118] Beier, n 12 above, at 176.   [119] See above, p 545.

the law of the protecting country.[120] This idea of unity is the major argument advanced in favour of the law of the protecting country by Pfordte.[121] Although this is more a policy argument than one which objectively points towards a legal system, it strengthens the merits of this solution.

The third argument is that, in the majority of cases, the law of the protecting country and the law of the country of the licensee coincide. This reinforces the arguments in favour of the law of the protecting country, but even in the exceptional case where these two indices point to different countries the law of the protecting country should be applied as the arguments in favour of it are the most convincing.[122] As regards a situation where indices point to different countries, Beier[123] gives Ulmer's example of an English firm that grants a licence to a French firm for the Japanese market and refers to the case which came before the District Court of Stuttgart[124] in which a licence contract covering the Dutch market had been concluded between Englishmen and Germans. A different situation is, obviously, presented by a licence for a third country. If the licensor and the licensee have their seat in the same country, such a licence is most closely connected with the country in which both parties have their seat and the characteristic performance presumption in the Rome Convention 1980 is rebutted by this exceptionally close connection (Article 4(5)). The applicable law will be the law of the country in which the parties have their seat.[125]

There are arguments though against the application of the law of the protecting country. First, the application of this law does not seem to be an appropriate solution in the situation where a licence contract for several countries is granted to one licensee, as it could, in such a case, lead to the application of different laws to one contract depending on the country where the problem giving rise to litigation arises. There is, though, an answer to this objection. When a licence for several countries, which is granted to one licensee, involves production (and/or eventually the application of the trade mark to the goods) in the country where the licensee has its seat and the activities of the licensee in all other countries which are covered by the licence are restricted to the marketing and the distribution of the product, the law of the primary country of protection could still be applied to the whole licence contract. Essentially, the exploitation of the industrial property right takes place in that country, and the marketing and distribution in other countries in a later phase does not fundamentally change this.[126]

---

[120] Beier, n 12 above, at 176–177, see also District Court of Stuttgart, 14 March 1957, [1956–1957] IPR Rspr No 29.
[121] Pfordte, [1974] DB 1465 at 1467.
[122] Beier, n 12 above, at 176.   [123] Beier, n 12 above, at 176.   [124] See above, n 117.
[125] See Troller, n 58 *in fine* above, at 199 and Troller, n 91 above, at 121.
[126] Beier, [1983] *Les Nouvelles* 141 at 145.

Exploitation of intellectual property rights: the applicable law 569

The only situation which really presents a problem is the one where the industrial property right is effectively exploited in all countries covered by the licence contract. Here, one could still advocate the application of the law of the protecting country. The parties should have incorporated a choice of law clause in the licence contract if they wanted to subject the licence contract to a single law in all circumstances. But it is suggested that this approach, although correct from an academic point of view, should be replaced by the application of the law of the licensee. The latter option has the advantage that, regardless of the country, one law is applied to all contractual aspects of the licence contract and, in practice, this seems to be the only workable solution where the relationship between the parties is of the one licensor-one licensee-one type. It should, nevertheless, be concluded that the option favouring the law of the (primary) country of protection[127] can successfully be applied to more cases than the solutions previously dealt with and that the arguments in favour of it are rather more convincing.

Secondly, Beier mentions two situations in which the law of the protecting country should be replaced by the law of the country of the licensor or the law common to the licensor and the licensee. It is stressed that these cases only form marginal exceptions and that the Rome Convention 1980 equally recognises this kind of exception where there is a closer connection with another legal system. The first exception arises when a license agreement for a third country is concluded between a licensor and a licensee which have their seat in the same country and thus a common nationality. It is obvious that such a situation is most closely linked with the common law of the parties and that the licence agreement should be governed by the common law of the licensor and the licensee with which they are familiar, rather than by the unfamiliar law of the third, protecting country. The second situation is where there is a very close connection with the law of the country of the licensor. Central to this exception is a transfer of technology license agreement for a completely new technical development, developed unilaterally by the licensor and with which the recipient party has absolutely no experience. The centre of gravity of such an agreement is clearly situated in the country of the licensor if the agreement implies a continuous development of the technology by the licensor and a continuous flow of further know-how and improvements from the licensor to the licensee. Such an agreement should, accordingly, be governed by the law of the country of the licensor.[128]

---

[127] The specific doctrine of the law of the primary country of protection was developed by Beier ('das primäre Schutzland'), see, eg Beier, [1983] Les Nouvelles 141 at 144–145 and Beier, in Holl and Klinke (eds) *Internationales Privatrecht, Internationales Wirtschaftsrecht* Carl Heymanns Verlag (1985) p 287 at pp 296–298 and p 301.
[128] Beier, in Holl and Klinke (eds) *Internationales Privatrecht, Internationales Wirtschaftsrecht* Carl Heymanns Verlag (1985) p 287 at pp 301–302.

It is submitted that, in general terms, the law of the protecting country presents the strongest connection for the purposes of Article 4(5) of the Rome Convention 1980, but, as was made clear above, other conclusions impose themselves in certain situations.

(b) *Contracts in relation to trade marks*

In many respects, contracts in relation to trade marks are similar to those in relation to patents. Generally, the same legal approach can be applied to both types of contract. This uniformity is particularly helpful in the situation where a contract to produce and market a product combines a patent licence with a trade mark licence. The same law will apply to both licences.

Article 4(2) and the characteristic performance presumption will work well with simple contracts. The assignor will effect the characteristic performance in the situation where the trade mark is assigned and a lump sum is paid in consideration of that assignment. This really represents a straightforward sale of the trade mark.

Trade mark licences present more problems. It is submitted that, as a starting point, the approach which we outlined in relation to patent licences ought to be applied. This means that, in most cases, it will not be possible to identify a characteristic performance. This will especially be the case in those situations where the licensee undertakes the production of the labelled product and the marketing of the brand. The creation of the mark by the licensor is then balanced, in terms of characteristic performance, by the marketing and production that is undertaken by the licensee. Both elements are vital to turn the licence into a success. In legal terms, this leads to the application of Article 4(5) of the Rome Convention 1980. The arguments in favour of the various connections have been set out in relation to trade marks and, whilst the strongest connection will have to be determined case by case, it has been concluded that, in the typical case, the closest connection exists with the protecting country.

Some special circumstances can arise, though.[129] Thus, the application of the law of the country of the trade mark owner and licensor is appropriate 'in the case of a well-known trademarked product, protected worldwide, whose marketing through foreign subsidiaries and licensees is directed and controlled from the *situs* of the parent corporation following uniform principles of production, licensing, trademark utilization, and advertising'.[130] In legal terms, this is probably another example of a situation where it is possible to identify the characteristic performance. That characteristic performance is clearly effected by the licensor. It can be added that these exceptional circumstances arise frequently in relation to a franchise contract that includes a trade mark licence.

[129] Beier, [1982] IIC 162 at 163–164.   [130] Beier, n 12 above, at 181.

(c) *Know-how*

Simple assignments of non-patented know-how are rare. Normally, a right to use the secret know-how is granted instead. The latter takes the format of a licence contract. These licence contracts are similar to patent licences. In both cases, a transfer of technology is effected. The involvement of non-patented technology, rather than patented technology, does not have a fundamental impact on the situation. It is, therefore, submitted that the same approach ought, in relation to Article 4 of the Rome Convention 1980, to be taken in relation to both types of licence contract.[131]

As a result, it is suggested that in the situation where a pure know-how licence is granted and where no characteristic performance can be identified under Article 4(2) of the Rome Convention 1980, the applicable law should, equally, be the law of the protecting country.[132] The latter law is the law of the country with which the contract is most closely connected and that criterion is to be used in application of Article 4(5) in such circumstances. The concept of using the same law in relation to patents and know-how has already been advocated by Vida,[133] who suggested that the law of the country of the licensor should be applied to both patent and know-how licence contracts. Returning to the suggestion that the law of the protecting country should apply, a problem seems to arise, however, when the law of the 'protecting' country where the licence will be exercised does not provide any adequate protection for know-how. From a closest connection point of view, the exploitation of the know-how will still be essential and the problem is one of substantive intellectual property law, rather than one of choice of law.

In the situation where the transfer of know-how is part of a more comprehensive deal or contract involving the grant of a licence concerning another industrial property right, eg a combined patent and know-how licence is quite common, the know-how transfer would be governed by the law which governs the licence contract to which it is attached. The whole deal or contract should be seen as a single entity.[134]

An important fact that should be added, and that underlies all suggested solutions concerning industrial property licence contracts, is that the vast majority of contracts are national and regional contracts with a single licensee, the multi-national situation forms the exception, not the rule.[135] This reduces, at least to some extent, the scope of the problems that arise with the approaches advocated above, as these multi-national situations were the most problematic ones. However, this does not necessarily apply to copyright.

[131] See above, p 558 *et seq*.
[132] Beier, n 12 above, at 181.
[133] See n 57 above, at 223.
[134] See also above, p 552.
[135] See Beier, [1983] *Les Nouvelles* 141 at 144.

(d) Copyright

(i) *The closest connection*

Article 4(1) of the Rome Convention 1980 leads immediately to the presumption in Article 4(2) and only becomes relevant again in those case where Article 4(5) is applied. A few preliminary remarks concerning contracts in relation to copyright need, however, to be made.

Many types of contract can be used in relation to copyright. Typically, the owner of the copyright in a work allows someone to do something in relation to the work that would otherwise, normally, amount to an infringement of the copyright in the work. This can be done be means of a licence, for example a licence to copy the work, but it is, in practice, also common to use an assignment. The problem with this assignment is that, often, it does not amount to a sale of the copyright in the work. It can be restricted in scope and in time. It is possible to transfer only part of the right or to stipulate that at the end of a certain period of time the transfer will be undone and that all the rights will return to the original owner of the copyright at that time. For example, the owner of the copyright in a manuscript can assign the right to publish foreign language editions of it to a publisher for a period of 25 years. At the same time, the rights to make a movie on the basis of the manuscript can be assigned to a movie-company that is unrelated to the publisher. These differences in terminology in comparison with patents and trade marks need to be borne in mind. A copyright assignment is not necessarily similar to the sale of the complete right.

More complex contracts can arise. A publishing contract for a book has already been mentioned as an example earlier in this chapter. Similar contracts can be concluded for the production of a video, tailormade software, songs or a TV programme. In these situations, a uniform legal approach seems to be desirable. Contracts to adapt a play for radio broadcasting are yet another example.

Once again, these contracts have, in most cases, connections with many countries. Obvious contenders for the country with which the contract is most closely connected are the country of the author or copyright owner and the country of the publisher, recording company or broadcaster, as well as the protecting country.

(ii) *The presumption of the characteristic performance*

Here, we are again confronted with Article 4(2), which was outlined above.[136] Ulmer set out to determine the characteristic performance in these cases and it is worth giving an overview of his suggestions.[137]

---

[136] See above p 556.   [137] See E Ulmer, n 3 above, at 48–52.

The starting point is the basic proposition that the obligation of the author or his successor in title shall be the characteristic performance.[138] It can be accepted that the countervailing obligation to pay an agreed sum of money, which is an obligation which is found in a great variety of entirely different types of contract, cannot constitute the characteristic performance of a certain (type of) contract. A first example of contracts to which this basic proposition is applicable are agreements by which a collecting society grants permission for the exploitation of its repertoire, particularly exploitation through broadcasting, public performance or mechanical reproduction. The grantee pays a sum of money for a blanket licence, but is not obliged to exploit the works in the repertoire. He just gets the permission to do so should he so wish. He cannot exploit certain parts of the repertoire and exploit other parts repeatedly, etc. A second example is the sale of publication, cinematographic and/or mechanical reproduction rights from one publisher, film producer or manufacturer of sound recordings to another. Again, this is a pure sale under which the buyer's only obligation is to pay the price. The vendor performs the characteristic performance in such a contract.

In Ulmer's view, things change when the grantee undertakes in the contract to exploit the work or to exercise the rights in the work or when exclusive rights are assigned or granted to the grantee in order for the work to be exploited. Here, the grantee determines the exploitation of the work as the essential point. The characteristic performance is performed by the exploiter of the work. The obvious example of such a contract is the publication contract. The publisher undertakes to reproduce and distribute the work and this is the characteristic performance. Another example is where the author assigns his rights to a collecting society which will supervise the exploitation of his rights. In such a case, the collecting society performs the characteristic performance.

The same solution can be applied to those cases where the obligation to exploit is not contained in the contract, but is assumed to exist. If an exclusive reproduction right is granted, for example, in relation to a painting, the obligation to exploit is assumed to exist since the painter would be blocked if no exploitation took place. Exploitation is the only reason why the contract is concluded and the obligation to exploit can, therefore, be assumed. Even in cases where the grant is non-exclusive and without an obligation to exploit, the solution can sometimes be applied. This is so in relation to a work where there are contributions by many authors. A single law of the author, who would perform the characteristic performance, cannot be identified in these cases.

---

[138] See Dessemontet, n 87 above, at 741.

Whilst we accept Ulmer's analysis[139] in those case where the countervailing performance is the payment of money,[140] we do not fully agree with it in relation to contracts where an obligation to exploit is present. The exploitation of the work cannot be seen as the characteristic performance. If no work is created and no right to exploit is granted, there can be no exploitation. On the other hand, the artist needs the exploitation of his work to generate revenue and to keep working. Both aspects are equally important. Ulmer's approach unduly favours the exploiter's side. What is essential to both aspects is the existence of copyright protection. Without the presence of exclusive rights that copyright protection provides the whole contract could not exist. It is, therefore, submitted that the characteristic performance presumption of the Rome Convention 1980 does not apply here as no single characteristic performance can be determined.

(iii) *Article 4(5)*

The impossibility of identifying a single characteristic performance in each contract brings us within the scope of Article 4(5) of the Rome Convention 1980. It is submitted that, for example, cases such as the one where there are contributions by many authors, should be approached as falling under Article 4(5). The characteristic performance presumption needs to lead to the application of a single law, but in this example it would lead to as many laws as there are authors. What remains is that the contract is closely connected with the law of the country in which the publisher is established. One either accepts that the contract is more closely connected with that law than with each of the authors' laws separately, in which case Article 4(5) applies, or one accepts that the closest connection is the one with the country which was covered by the publication contract. It is submitted that the latter view is preferable, because the fact that there is more than one author does, as such, not change the importance of the publisher. Obviously, this solution can only be applied if there exists a single country in respect of which publication rights have been granted.

In more general terms, the strong link with another country which Article 4(5) of the Convention requires is often present. That link exists with the protecting country whose law provides for the essential copyright protection. This leads to the applicability of the law of the protecting country. This approach has as its main advantage the fact that the whole contract, including the transfer of proprietary rights, is governed by the same law. It makes sense to submit, for example, both the contractual obligation to assign the publication rights in a book and the actual assignment to the same law.

---

[139] See Ulmer, n 3 above, at 48–52.
[140] This situation can be compared to the assignment of a trade mark or a patent in exchange for a lump sum. A similar solution applies in all these cases.

Our approach, as outlined above, applies only to those contracts in which right are granted for a single country; it would be impossible to apply at the same time the different laws of all the protecting countries in those situations in which rights are granted in relation to more than one country. When worldwide rights and rights in relation to many countries are granted, Article 4(5) still refers back to the country with which the contract has its closest connection. That country cannot be determined easily. The essential element, in most cases that involve complex copyright contracts, seems to be the exploitation of the copyright work. It is, therefore, submitted that in these cases the closest connection exists between the contract and the country in which the exploiter, ie the publisher, broadcaster, etc, of the work is established.[141]

(e) Distribution agreements

It has been argued that the characteristic performance presumption of Article 4(2) of the Rome Convention 1980 does not even work easily in relation to everyday contracts such as distribution contracts.[142] This type of contract is also, strictly speaking, not a contract in relation to intellectual property rights. It would go beyond the scope of this book to discuss in detail the law applicable to distribution contracts in the situation where the parties did not make a choice of law. A distribution contract could, however, include a patent or a trade mark licence. It is submitted that, if that is the case, the licence part should be dealt with separately for the purposes of choice of law, as it is a severable part of the contract. This might be an example of the sort of exceptional case in which the depeçage option, that is provided for in Article 4, should apply. The inclusion of a licence contract in a distribution agreement does not change the nature of the licence and there is no obvious reason why the licence choice of law rule should no longer be applied to it in these circumstances. All this becomes, of course, only relevant when a law that is different to the law that is applicable to the licence contract would be applicable to the distribution agreement.

(f) A general approach to all industrial property rights

Before reaching a conclusion, some consideration should be given to a general approach to all industrial property rights. It has been suggested by Diener that one should establish a balance of interests between the contracting parties. In doing so, one should focus on the exploitation of the industrial property right; this is the most important element from an

---
[141] See also Walter, n 4 above, at 61 and Plaisant (1962) 35 *RIDA* 63, at 95.
[142] See Juenger, n 70 above, at 301.

economic point of view. This process should indicate which law is the most appropriate one to be applied to the licence contract. The results of this approach vary depending on whether the contract grants an exclusive licence.[143] This approach is not acceptable. It does not fit in with the principles of the Rome Convention 1980. Moreover, it does not present the parties with a clear solution because it relies on a complex balancing act, and accordingly it only creates more uncertainty. Although restricted to patent licences, the latter criticism applies equally to Pfaff's theory,[144] which is also too complex to be workable. This author determines the centre of gravity of the licence contract which is, in his view, the point of contact with the applicable law. He distinguishes between simple licence contracts, to which either the law of the country of protection or the law of the licensor is applicable (this seems to be more about rephrasing the problem than solving it) and exclusive licence contracts, to which the law of the licensee is applicable if it is to supply the economically significant performance and if the licence is granted for several countries or if the licence is granted for one country and the law of the licensee is also the law of the country of protection, but to which the law of the licensor should be applied in all other cases. A workable solution should be based on a few brief rules, leading to a clear and predictable outcome.

(g) *A summary of the position under the Rome Convention 1980*

It is submitted that the foregoing discussion shows clearly that 'there is little unanimity among legal writers as to whose obligation is the most significant in a licensing agreement',[145] but that the arguments in favour of the law of the (primary) country of protection are the most convincing ones, although they do not offer a solution in every case. A similar approach is found in the Austrian Federal Statute of 15 June 1978 on Private International Law.[146]

How does this fit in with the provisions of the Rome Convention 1980? The real starting point is found in Article 4(2), because Article 4(1) amounts, in the first instance, only to a statement of principle.

The above analysis has demonstrated that the characteristic performance presumption works well only in relation to the most simple contracts and, in particular, in relation to those contracts that involve the outright sale of the intellectual property right in exchange for a lump sum. In most other cases, a single characteristic performance cannot be identified. For those cases Article 4(5) refers back to Article 4(1). The country

---

[143] Diener, n 60 above.
[144] Pfaff, [1977] *IIC* 28 at 38.
[145] Modiano, n 53 above, at 57.
[146] IPR – Gesetz, *Bundesgesetzblatt für die Republik Österreich*, 7 July 1978, No 304, 1729 at Para 43; see also G Van Hecke and K Lenaerts, n 3 above, at 334.

with which these contracts in relation to intellectual property rights are most closely connected then needs to be identified. Our analysis led us to emphasise the importance of the exploitation of these rights. That exploitation normally takes place in the protecting country.

Apart from the fact that it is an advantage to be able to apply one single law to all aspects of the industrial property right and its licence, an industrial property licence contract has its closest connection with the protecting country. The protection accorded is the ultimate foundation for the licence contract. Individual cases can, of course, exceptionally, show a particular connection with another country, in which case the application of the law of that country is called for.[147] Some of these cases have been highlighted in the analysis above.

It is, therefore, suggested that, in principle, industrial property contracts should be governed by the law of the protecting country, but that, if a licence for several countries is granted to one licensee and the industrial property right is effectively exploited in all countries covered by the licence contract, the licence contract should be governed by the law of the country of the licensee.

Copyright contracts are subject to similar rules, as demonstrated above. In the situation where the contract grants rights in respect of a single country the closest connection exists with the country of protection. This is, normally, also the country in which the exploitation of the work takes place. But this terminology could become confusing, for example, in those cases where books are printed in third country. Both the printing and the distribution and sale of the books could be seen as a form or aspect of exploiting the work. It is quite common, though, that rights in relation to copyright are granted in respect of more than one country. It is submitted that, in this situation, the essential element is still the exploitation of the work and that this leads to the closest connection being with the country in which the exploiter of the work is established.

3. Limitations on the Applicable Law

(a) MANDATORY RULES

It should also be mentioned that the applicability of the law of the contract is restricted by mandatory provisions of substantive law. Most of these mandatory provisions are found in tax and currency exchange laws and especially in competition law, in cases where industrial property licences are concerned. More generally, they also include all public order provisions.[148] We will now look at the relevant provisions of the Rome Convention 1980 in more detail.

[147] For an example see above n 125.
[148] Beier, n 12 above, at 178 and Modiano *Le contrat de licence de brevet* Droz (1979) at 126.

(i) The relevant provisions of the Rome Convention 1980

The starting point of the Convention is the principle of contractual freedom. The parties are free to choose the applicable law or in the absence of such a choice by the parties the applicable law is determined in an objective way.[149]

There are certain limitations on these principles, though. In certain cases, overriding or mandatory rules replace, or complement, the applicable law. English law was not familiar with the concept of mandatory rules, as such, before they were introduced by the Convention,[150] although similar results were reached in a number of cases.[151] Moreover, English law was familiar with the concept of an overriding English statute,[152] which is effectively the same thing as a mandatory rule of the forum.[153] Given that we are concerned here with an EC Convention our analysis will be comparative in nature, rather than focusing exclusively on English private international law.

(a) *Article 3(3)*

Article 3(3) deals with the narrow case in which all relevant factors point to one country, but in which a foreign law (or forum) has been chosen. In this case, the mandatory rules of that one country will apply and these are defined as the rules one cannot contract out of in a one hundred per cent domestic situation,[154] or in other words 'rules which cannot be derogated from by contract'. This is a reference to the *ius cogens* ('imperative law') and a purely substantive issue is involved. This issue is being dealt with under the criteria of the substantive law, not those of private international law.[155]

(b) *Article 5*

Article 5 deals with consumer contracts that arise in three well defined sets of circumstances.[156] In these cases, the mandatory rules of the country of habitual residence of the consumer cannot be contracted out of, and apply

---

[149] Articles 3 and 4; see Torremans, 25 (1994) *IIC* 390.
[150] Giuliano and Lagarde Report, n 11 above, at 27.
[151] *Ralli Bros* v *Cia Naviera Sota y Aznar* [1920] 2 KB 287, *Foster* v *Driscoll* [1929] 1 KB 470 and *Regazzoni* v *KC Sethia (1944) Ltd* [1956] 2 QB 490.
[152] See Cheshire and North, (11th ed 1987), pp 466–471.
[153] See the discussion of Article 7(2) of the Convention below.
[154] See Cheshire and North, at pp 480–481.
[155] de Boer, 54 (1990) *RabelsZ* 24, at 56.
[156] Briefly, these are: specific publicity and/or a specific invitation was made to the consumer in his country and he accepted there; the other party or his agent received the consumer's order in that country; transborder shopping trips organised by the seller.

in the absence of a choice of law by the parties.[157] This Article may be relevant to certain intellectual property contracts, for example in the case of a software licence if the licensee plans to use the software for private purposes which fall outside his business. Mandatory consumer protection provisions such as Article 5 can also indirectly take on significance in relation to industrial property licence contracts. Beier gives the example that 'they can make it impossible to implement a contract clause obligating a German licensee or subsidiary of a foreign trade mark owner to incorporate a choice of foreign law in its contracts with customers', even if the original licence contract obliged it to do so.[158]

(c) *Article 6*

Article 6 deals with individual employment contracts.[159] The employee is always given the benefit of the mandatory rules of the place where he habitually carries out his work. In the situation where he does not habitually carry out his duties in one country, reference is made to the place of business through which the employee was engaged. This rule may be relevant in relation to intellectual property in the situation where the employee who made an invention applies for compensation.

(d) *Article 7*

Up to now, we have been concerned with mandatory rules as rules one cannot contract out of in a purely domestic situation and a purely domestic contract. Article 7 is radically different because it deals with mandatory rules of the forum or of any third State which are mandatory in an international sense. These rules also want to be applied in an international context.[160] We are concerned here with substantive law rules which are intended to apply, regardless of the law applicable to the contract. In English law, these were known as overriding statutes. It is on these rules that our analysis will focus.

(i) Article 7(1)

Article 7(1) even gives the court a discretionary power to take into account mandatory rules of a foreign country with which the situation has a close connection. Some Contracting States used their right to make a reservation which means Article 7(1) will not be implemented by these countries and

---

[157] See Hartley in North (ed), *Contract Conflicts* North Holland Publishing (1980), at p 111 *et seq*.
[158] Beier, n 12 above, at 169.
[159] See Morse in North (ed), *Contract Conflicts* North Holland Publishing (1980), at p 143 *et seq*.
[160] Cheshire and North, n 63 above, at pp 409–503.

as the UK is amongst these Contracting States we will not discuss Article 7(1) in further detail. Article 7(2), which the UK implemented, as it was required to, deals with mandatory rules of the forum. These rules have to be taken into account as the provision does not give the judge any discretion.

(ii) *Article 7(2)*

Article 7(2) states that: 'Nothing in this Convention shall restrict the application of the rules of the law of the forum in a situation where they are mandatory irrespective of the law otherwise applicable to the contract'. These rules to which Article 7 refers have been described as *règles d'application immédiate*.[161] This means that they override the conflicts process. They are priority rules in the sense that if a certain situation arises, this leads to the application of the mandatory rule before recourse can be had to any normal conflicts rule.[162]

These rules have also been called *lois de police*. Indeed, in the French version of the Convention, this is the term used in the heading to Article 7. This name refers to their imperative character. They want to be applied in a certain situation irrespective of the conflict of law rules.[163] For example, competition law rules often want to be applied when effects of the allegedly anti-competitive conduct are felt within the jurisdiction. Competition law rules are, indeed, the traditional example of mandatory rules. Often this specific category is described as rules which are close to public law, but this description is of little practical use in England as the category of public law is not readily known or used in England in the way that it is on the Continent.

It may be added that the mandatory rules in Article 7(2) refer to overriding the choice of law. They even seem to override the mandatory rules determined by Articles 5 and 6.[164] Another important point is that it has to be 'a situation' where rules are mandatory. Rules are only mandatory in certain situations.

(ii) **How to identify a mandatory rule of the type referred to in Article 7(2)?**

There does not seem to be a general rule or test to determine whether a rule is internationally mandatory. There are only some guiding principles

---

[161] By French and Belgian writers, see, eg Lagarde [1991] *Revue Critique de Droit International Privé* 287.

[162] P Francescakis, *La théorie du renvoi et les conflits de systèmes en droit international privé* Sirey (1958), especially at 11 *et seq* and Francescakis, [1966] *Revue Critique de Droit International Privé* 1.

[163] Vander Elst, *Les Lois de polices et de sûreté* (1956); Loussouarn, 'Cours général de droit international privé', (1973) *Receuil des Cours*, II, at 330–334.

[164] Rinze, [1995] *JBL* 412, at 429; contra: German Bundesgerichtshof, judgment of 26 October 1993, [1994] NJW 262, at 264.

to assist us. Francescakis identifies those laws or rules whose application is necessary to safeguard the political, social and economic structures of a country (the forum for the purposes of Article 7(2)) as mandatory rules.[165]

One should take into account the interests of the forum and the purpose of the rule, as these determine quite often whether or not a rule must be applied in an overriding way or not. De Winter, in a ground breaking work, suggested that we should identify the social aim of the legislation.[166] The purpose of certain harmonising rules could, for example, be to provide legal certainty.[167] The contracting parties need to be able to rely on contractual transactions and this may require the uniform application of certain legal rules in the forum.

Certain statutes indicate whether the rules contained in them are internationally mandatory in nature. This can be done by the inclusion of an express provision, such as the one in the Employment Protection (Consolidation) Act 1978[168] which stated that what matters is that a person ordinarily works in the United Kingdom, whilst it is immaterial whether or not the law governing the contract is the law of a part of the United Kingdom, or the provisions in the Employment Rights Act 1996 which replaced it.[169] It can also be done indirectly by indicating the statute's territorial scope, such as in the Emergency Powers (Defence) Act 1939.[170] Anything that comes within the territorial scope of the Act is affected by its provisions in such a situation, even if English law does not govern the contract. This point might be particularly relevant in relation to intellectual property rights, because most statutory provisions contain such a territorial limitation. Most statutes contain no such indications and leave the decision to the courts. This decision is a complex issue and it would be desirable for new statutes to include express provisions on this.[171]

---

[165] Francescakis, [1966–1969] *Travaux du Comité français de Droit international privé*, at 149 *et seq*.

[166] Barmat de Winter, *De sociale functies der rechtsnormen als grondslag voor de oplossing van internationaal privaatrechtelijke wetsconflicten* Themis (1947), reprinted in Kisch, Dubbink, van Hoogstraaten, Kotting and Jessurun d'Oliveira (eds), *Naar een sociaal IPR: Een keus uit het werk van L I de Winter* Kluwer (1979), at 3–52; de Winter, [1940] *WPNR* 245–249 (No 3675) and 257–261 (No 3676), reprinted in Kisch, Dubbink, van Hoogstraaten, Kotting and Jessurun d'Oliveira (eds), *Naar een sociaal IPR: Een keus uit het werk van L I de Winter* Kluwer (1979), at 164–181 and de Winter, 11 (1964) *Ned T Int R* 329–365, reprinted in Kisch, Dubbink, van Hoogstraaten, Kotting and Jessurun d'Oliveira (eds), *Naar een sociaal IPR: Een keus uit het werk van L I de Winter* Kluwer (1979), at 182–217.

[167] Rinze, n 164 above, at 428.

[168] Sections 141 and 153(5), see Cheshire and North, n 63 above, at p 500.

[169] See ss 196 and 204(1).

[170] Cheshire and North, n 63 above, at 501, see *Boissevain* v *Weil* [1949] 1 KB 482, [1949] 1 All ER 146, affirmed [1950] AC 327, [1950] 1 All ER 728.

[171] See Cheshire and North, n 63 above, at pp 500–502.

The identification of a rule as being an internationally mandatory rule is not necessarily the end of the discussion though. Two further matters arise:[172]

(i) In the pure Romanist civil law view, *lois de police* are applied imperatively, without there being room for any other considerations. This would, for example, be so even if the case has no effects in the forum, while internal harmonisation was the only purpose underlying the rule which made it a mandatory rule. The fact that the aim of the rule is not affected has no impact on the operation of the mandatory rule.

(ii) One could, however, also ask the question whether the purpose of the rule is furthered by its application in a particular case and only apply the mandatory rule of the forum if the answer to this question is in the affirmative. Thus, in the example given above the solution would be different and the mandatory rule would not be applied. This theory finds support in the Dutch *Alnati* case[173] and in de Boer's writings.[174] It would give the forum a certain discretion even in Article 7(2) cases and corresponds perfectly with the negative wording of that Article: 'nothing in this Convention shall restrict'.

(iii) Application to intellectual property statutes

(a) *Are most intellectual property provisions mandatory?*

Two theories, which are rather general in nature, would lead to the identification of most intellectual property provisions as mandatory rules. The first theory is based on the link between competition law and intellectual property law. The second theory is based on the principle of territoriality. These two theories will now be examined.

(i) *An excessively wide scope for competition law*

The first theory takes as its starting point the argument that rules of competition law are always mandatory. As such, this starting point is not objectionable. However, one could develop the theory further by seeing intellectual property as a set of rules regulating competition in the area of creative and innovative products of the mind. This could be supported by analogy with Michael Lehmann's concept of intellectual property as restrictions on competition at the production level in furtherance of com-

---

[172] de Boer, n 155 above, at 58.
[173] *Altnati* judgment of the Hoge Raad (Dutch Supreme Court) of 13 May 1966, [1967] Ned Jur 16 (No 3); see also the discussion in Schultsz, 47 (1983) *RabelsZ* 267, at 273–277.
[174] de Boer, n 155 above.

petition at the innovation level.¹⁷⁵ This would mean that all intellectual property rules regulate competition, for example by determining the scope of the restriction on competition, and would be mandatory. However, such an approach clearly goes too far. The whole concept of intellectual property rights as restrictions on competition in furtherance of competition should only be seen as part of the economic justification for the continuing existence of intellectual property rights in a free market economic system.¹⁷⁶ Lehmann restricted his concept clearly to this area. Not all intellectual property rules regulate competition directly. As a general theory then, the competition law theory is too crude and must be rejected. But it must, on the other hand, be clear that the rules on free movement and competition law, as applied to intellectual property, are mandatory even if, in practice, this restricts substantially the contractual freedom of the licensor and the licensee.¹⁷⁷ An exclusivity clause that would divide the market in two territorial parts, one exclusively reserved for the licensor and one exclusively reserved for the licensee, would, for example, probably be void under the mandatory application of the competition rules. Due to the fact that intellectual property law and competition law are closely linked to each other, there will be a substantial number of intellectual property provisions that will be treated as mandatory rules.

(ii) *The territoriality theory*

The territoriality theory (which is arguably not even wholly supported by the intellectual property Conventions)¹⁷⁸ suggests that intellectual property rules are only applicable within the country of whose intellectual property laws they form part. Whilst this may be true, eg for primary infringement of copyright because the UK legislator has determined the territorial scope of these provisions to infringing acts that occur within the United Kingdom, one cannot bi-lateralise this infringement rule, which would involve the application of the territorial restriction to infringements abroad, and deduce that, inside the territory of a State, these infringement rules are of mandatory application to the exclusion of all other rules. Such an approach may make sense in relation to the property aspects of intellectual property, but one cannot apply this approach generally to all aspects of intellectual property. In the contractual area, this would lead to

---

¹⁷⁵ He refers to intellectual property as restricting competition at the production level in furtherance of competition at the innovation level and in general he works with three levels of competition: innovation, production and consumption; see Lehmann, [1985] *IIC* 525 and [1989] *IIC* 1.

¹⁷⁶ Holyoak and Torremans, *Intellectual Property Law* Butterworths (1995), at pp 13–19.

¹⁷⁷ See, eg the caselaw from the Court of Justice in relation to Articles 30–36, 85 and 86 of the EC Treaty; discussion in Holyoak and Torremans, n 176 above, at 90–116.

¹⁷⁸ See Koumantos' view in 'Copyright and PIL in the Face of the International Diffusion of Works', WIPO Symposium on the Future of Copyright and Neighbouring Rights, 1994, pp 233–234.

the undisputed application of the law of the protecting country to all contractual dealings and we have demonstrated elsewhere[179] that, although there may be a lot of arguments in favour of such an approach in certain circumstances, such a conclusion cannot be justified in other circumstances.[180]

(b) *More specific approaches and examples of mandatory rules*

More specific approaches are likely to be more accurate and helpful. These are based on examples. We will highlight four of these in relation to specific provisions of intellectual property law.

(i) *Article 100A of the European Treaty and rules contained in Directives*

European Directives often cite Article 100A as (part of) their legal basis.[181] This means that the underlying purpose is the creation of the single market in which the application of different rules and the disruption of free competition that follows are no longer possible.[182] This purpose would not be realised if one could contractually tamper with the rules contained in the Directive, since the aim of harmonisation would be obstructed. One could, therefore, conclude that rules such as the right to equitable remuneration[183] and the software decompilation right[184] are mandatory. But one could argue that these mandatory rules require that their effects will be felt in the European Union. Otherwise, they would not lead to the elimination of the normal rules of private international law and then one would be able to contract out of them by choosing a foreign non-EU law as the law applicable to the contract. So these rules might, arguably, not demand their mandatory application if the only effects of the non-application of these rules are found outside the EU. This is fully in line with the idea that rules that are mandatory under Article 7(2) of the Rome Convention 1980 are only mandatory in certain situations.

(ii) *Section 44 Patents Act 1977*

Section 44 deals with restrictive contractual provisions. It states that 'any condition or term of a contract for the supply of a patented product or of

---

[179] Torremans, n 149 above.   [180] See above, pp 576–577.
[181] See, eg The Preamble to Council Directive 92/100 of 19 November 1992 on rental right and lending right and on certain rights related to copyright in the field of intellectual property [1992] OJ L346/61 and the Preamble to Council Directive 91/250 of 14 May 1991 on the legal protection of computer programs [1991] OJ L122/42.
[182] See Rinze, n 164 above, at 428.
[183] Article 4 of Council Directive 92/100 of 19 November 1992 on rental right and lending right and on certain rights related to copyright in the field of intellectual property [1992] OJ L346/61.
[184] Article 6 of Council Directive 91/250 of 14 May 1991 on the legal protection of computer programs [1991] OJ L122/42.

a licence to work a patented invention, or of a contract relating to any such supply or licence, shall be void in so far as it purports' to impose certain undesirable things. The latter are defined, for both types of contract and their related contracts, as an obligation to acquire from the supplier or the licensor anything other than the patented product and as an obligation not to use other articles that are not supplied by the supplier or licensor. In *Chiron v Organon Teknika (No 2)*, the Court of Appeal seems to have decided that Section 44 of the Patents Act 1977 is a mandatory rule.[185] Part of the argument in favour of this conclusion was that contracts which constitute an abuse of the patent right, mainly because they impose obligations and restrictions that are completely unrelated to the patent and its exploitation, are the target of this provision. Abuse of an exclusive right must necessarily infringe competition law and competition law must, in turn, be part of what Francescakis called rules which safeguard the economic structures of a country. Therefore, Section 44 must be a mandatory rule, even if the Court of Appeal phrased it in a slightly different way, without using the the term 'mandatory rules'.[186]

In the *Chiron* case, Chiron brought proceedings for the infringement of its UK patent against Organon Technika and Murex Diagnostics. The defendants sought to rely on Section 44(3) of the Patents Act 1977 to avoid liability. That Section offers a defence in a situation where the restrictive clauses referred to in Section 44(1) are present in a contract that was in force at the time of the alleged infringement. The problem in this case was that the contract was governed by New Jersey law and that no equivalent of Section 44 existed under New Jersey law. Could the English forum mandatorily apply Section 44 of its Patents Act 1977 in such a situation? The Court of Appeal restricted the application of Section 44 to UK patents, but it added that the contract involved need not necessarily be governed by English law. The presence of a restrictive clause makes the contract unenforceable in the United Kingdom, and this result is achieved irrespective of the outcome under the law applicable to the contract. In practical terms, this means that the provision that is contained in Section 44 is mandatory in relation to UK patents. As the rule is already limited territorially, there is no need to impose a further limit by requiring English law to govern the contract.

(iii) *Moral Rights*

Francescakis[187] also pays attention to those rules that are essential to safeguard the social structures of a country. In the droit d'auteur tradition, which stresses the protection of the author, rather than the commercial

---

[185] [1993] FSR 567.
[186] See the note by Moufang in 25 (1994) *IIC* 915, at 922.
[187] See above, notes 162 and 165.

exploitation of the work as the Anglo-Saxon copyright tradition does, one might argue that moral rights to protect the author must form part of that set of rules and be mandatory in nature and that this is especially so after the *John Huston*[188] case, in France. However, if one adopts an entrepreneurial approach to copyright this might be different. One can still argue, as we did before when the *John Huston* case was analysed,[189] that authors should enjoy minimalist moral rights, as a form of fundamental rights, if they are to be found prepared to create more works. And an entrepreneurial system cannot survive without the continuing input of new works. But does that turn our version of moral rights into mandatory rules? It was submitted at that stage that, moral rights ought to be mandatory. Counter-arguments, that could be used to arrive at the opposite conclusion, are the fact that certain moral rights only come into being when asserted by the author and the fact that moral rights can be waived.[190] In private international law terminology, this might equal contracting out of moral rights. It is submitted that such an argument is not correct. Even a right that can be waived must first have been granted. The grant of minimum moral rights is, therefore, mandatory. The United Kingdom might want to take a minimalist approach to moral rights, but even then would the United Kingdom like to see that approach applied, rather than another approach which might, in the United Kingdom's view, grant too much protection for moral rights.

(iv) *Rules relating to employee's inventions*

As regards employee's inventions, one has to turn first of all towards Article 6 of the Rome Convention 1980, because an individual employment contract is involved. This allows us to take into account the internal mandatory rules of the country in which the employee habitually carries out his work in performance of the contract, or those of the country in which the place of business through which the employee was engaged is situated, if there is not any one country in which the employee habitually carries out his work.[191] Whichever option is applicable, if this country is the United Kingdom, then Sections 40–43 of the Patents Act 1977 on compensation of the employee for certain inventions impose their own applicability. This is especially the case for the rules in Section 40(4) and Section 42. Sections 43(2) and (4) make it clear that these rules are also internationally mandatory. Ultimately, Article

---

[188] *Huston v La Cinq*, Judgment of the Cour de Cassation of 28 May 1991, 149 (1991) *RIDA* 197 (with annotations by A Françon); see Ginsburg and Sirinelli, 15 (1991) *Columbia-VLA Journal of Law and the Arts* 135; A Lucas and H J Lucas argue that it should not be taken for granted that moral rights are *lois de police* though (A and H J Lucas, *Traité de la propriété littéraire & artistique* Litec (1994), at 811) and refer to the *Kid* case (Judgment of the French Cour de Cassation of 28 May 1963, [1964] D. 677 and [1964] *Revue Critique de Droit International Privé* 513).

[189] See above, pp 510–511.   [190] See Holyoak and Torremans, n 176 above, chapter 13.

[191] See Morse in North (ed), *Contract Conflicts* North Holland Publishing (1980), at p 143 *et seq*.

7(2) of the Rome Convention 1980 could lead to the application of Sections 40(4) and 42 if the case comes before an English forum, even though Article 6 of the Convention may lead to a foreign applicable law. This Article 7(2) solution might be needed in certain situations because the scope of Section 43(2)(b) does not necessarily correspond to the scope of Article 6. Indeed, attachment to a place of business is not necessarily the same as the place of business through which one was engaged.

(b) MANDATORY RULES: SUMMARY

Whilst it may be clear from the above that mandatory rules play an important part in contracts relating to intellectual property rights, the main difficulty which remains is the identification of rules as being mandatory in nature. It would be wrong to qualify every intellectual property rule as mandatory as neither the territoriality principle nor the link with competition law justifies this. The normal private international law guiding principles will have to lead us to a solution for each individual rule of substantive law. The only difference between intellectual property and other areas of substantive law may be found in the fact that intellectual property and its exclusive rights have a closer link with restrictions on competition than most other areas. So there may, after all, be relatively more mandatory rules in the intellectual property area than in most 'normal' areas of law.

(c) PUBLIC POLICY / ORDRE PUBLIC

This negative principle is found in Article 16 of the Rome Convention 1980 and could be described as the negative other side of the mandatory rule coin. Its application does not change the applicable law or the choice of law rules. It is a general emergency clause which allows the forum not to apply in a particular case the applicable law because that application would create wholly unacceptable consequences from the point of view of the forum's principles of public policy. The applicable law itself, *in abstracto*, is not criticised. While there is no rule of the forum here which overrides the applicable law, the effect can be much the same. If the court finds the foreign rule unacceptable and turns its application down it will fall back on the law of the forum to solve the issue in front of it. The Convention's approach shows strong similarities with the public policy exception that existed under the traditional English rules to deal with obnoxious rules of contract of foreign countries.[192] A reference to these rules is found, as an obiter, in the *Apple* case.[193]

---

[192] See Cheshire and North, n 63 above, at pp 503–504.
[193] *Apple Corps Ltd and Another v Apple Computer Inc and Others* [1992] FSR 431, at 433.

In intellectual property cases, public policy or ordre public could, for example, be invoked in a case where the applicable law would lead to the expropriation of the intellectual property right when a licence contract for a trade mark is not renewed by the holder of the right upon expiry of its term.

4. A Particular Issue: Formal Validity

The material validity of a contract (ie whether or not a valid contract was created) in relation to intellectual property rights is governed by the law that would have been applicable to the contract had it been presumed to be valid. Contracts in relation to intellectual property rights are, in this respect, subject to the same general rule as other contracts. This rule is contained in Article 8 of the Rome Convention. Contracts in relation to the exploitation of intellectual property rights have never given rise to specific problems on this point.[194] The position was, in the past, not necessarily the same in relation to the issue of formal validity.

The issue of formal validity is now governed by Article 9 of the Rome Convention 1980. This Article introduced, in its paragraph 1, a rule involving the alternative application of the law of the place where the contract was concluded, and the law applicable to the contract. And Article 9(2) of the Convention specifies that, if the parties are in different countries while concluding the contract, the contract will present no formal validity problems if the law of the country where the contract is made is replaced either by the law applicable to the contract, as determined under the provisions of the Convention, or by the law of one of the countries in which the parties are at the time of the conclusion of the contract.

Early French caselaw well illustrates this system, which requires that the contract has to meet either the formal requirements of the law applicable to the contract or the formal requirements of the law of the place where the agreement was concluded. The leading case is the *Charlie Chaplin* case. The agreement which gave rise to the litigation was concluded between Charlie Chaplin and an undertaking which was based in Vaduz, Liechtenstein, and which had to be interpreted according to US law. The contract did not comply with the French rules on formal validity and, although France was the protecting country, the French courts assumed that the assignment of copyright was formally valid as it observed the US rules on formal validity. The rules of the *lex contractus*, ie the rules of the law of the country where the contract was concluded, had been observed in this case.[195]

---

[194] *Apple Corps Ltd and Another* v *Apple Computer Inc and Others* (ibid, at 433) is a good example of a pre-Rome Convention case.

[195] Cour de Paris (1959) ICP II 11134 and French Cour de Cassation (1963) ICP II 11134.

As Modiano[196] and Troller[197] point out, there is no reason to depart from the general private international law rule on the formal validity of contracts in the case of contracts in relation to intellectual property rights. According to Modiano, the Rome Convention approach even corresponds to the one taken in relation to intellectual property contracts by the Courts in France[198] and Italy[199] before the Rome Convention 1980 came into force. It may, equally, be added that the Austrian Private International Law Statute contains similar provisions.[200]

The tendency to apply the law of the protecting country, which was found in earlier editions of Dicey and Morris, is, therefore, no longer acceptable, now that the Contracts (Applicable Law) Act 1990 has incorporated the Rome Convention 1980 into English law. It might, indeed, have been an obvious suggestion to apply the law of the protecting country to this issue too. However, this option also has to be rejected on grounds of principle. It would mean, in practice, that a contract which involves rights and their exploitation in two (protecting) countries would, potentially, have to comply with two conflicting sets of formal requirements.

Ulmer also suggested that the law of the protecting country should, equally, be applied to the issue of the formal validity of the industrial property licence contract.[201] Beier accepted the application of the law of the protecting country only 'to the extent that a mandatory provision of one of its statutes requires a particular form'.[202] Beier went on to consider almost every registration or formal requirement regarding the enforceability of the contract in the law of the protecting country as being mandatory.

Whenever certain documents are required for the registration of the licence contract, and that registration is required by the law of the protecting country, a contractual duty to make available the necessary documents

---

[196] Modiano, n 53 above, at 121 and Modiano [1981] *Les Nouvelles* 55 at 56.
[197] Troller [1952] *GRUR Auslandteil* 108 at 118–119 and Troller *Das internationale Privat- und Zivilprozessrecht im gewerblichen Rechtsschutz und Urheberrecht* Verlag für Recht und Gesellschaft (1952) 175 *et seq*.
[198] Cour de Cassation, 1 February 1944, [1944] Rec Sirey I 107 and Tribunal de Grande Instance de la Seine, 18 June 1955, reprinted in [1975] GRUR Int 443 (both case dealt with the assignment of intellectual property rights, but as Modiano ([1981] *Les Nouvelles* 55 at 56), with a reference to P Roubier *Le Droit de la Propriété Industrielle* (1954) at Para 207, suggests, there is no reason to assume that a different approach would be taken in licensing cases, see Modiano, n 53 above, at 124; see also French Cour de Cassation, 28 May 1963, [1964] *Revue Critique de Droit International Privé* 513, with note by Loussouarn.
[199] See the judgment published in [1957] GRUR Int 443, which was cited by Troller 'Kurzreferat gehalten am Symposium über die Immaterialgüterrechte im internationalen Privatrecht' AIPPI – Congress Munich 18 April 1975.
[200] Austrian Federal Statute of 15 June 1978 on Private International Law, (IPR – Gesetz), *Bundesgesetzblatt für die Republik Österreich*, 7 July 1978, No 304, 1729 at Para 8,34 and 43.
[201] Ulmer, n 3 above, at 89 and 101.   [202] Beier, n 12 above, at 178–179.

is placed on the licensor.²⁰³ A mandatory provision of the law of the protecting country can impose a particular form if such a form is required for both the enforceability and the validity of the licence contract. This constitutes the only exception to the rule cited above.²⁰⁴ Under the Rome Convention 1980, such a mandatory provision can overrule the formal validity rule contained in Article 9. This is explained by the general scope of Article 7(2)'s mandatory rule provision. However, in practice, one can only advise the parties to follow the formal requirements of the law of the protecting country unless there is a serious reason not to do so, as it permits them to avoid complications and presents the easiest and safest solution.²⁰⁵

5. Alternative Approaches

The analysis of the operation of the provisions of the Rome Convention 1980 concerning contracts in relation to the exploitation of intellectual property rights has shown clearly that the parties to such contracts must be advised to make a choice of the applicable law. Article 3 does not create problems, but the application of Article 4 is far more problematic. The presumption of characteristic performance only works for a limited number of contracts and the closest connection test that applies in all other situations creates at least some legal uncertainty, even though it has been shown that a rather consistent approach remains possible.

An alternative interpretation of Article 4 of the Rome Convention could, arguably, improve things. It has been shown that complex contracts are almost inevitably subject to the following treatment. Article 4(1) leads to the use of the presumption in Article 4(2) to identify the closest connection. Article 4(2) involves the identification of a single characteristic performance and this is impossible in relation to these complex contracts. Such contracts regularly contain a whole catalogue of performances implementing the various contractual obligations of the parties, that do not involve the bare payment of sums of money. Each party carries out a number of these performances and it is impossible to identify one principal performance. All performances are closely linked to one another and none of them can exist without the others. Article 4(5) leads, in such a situation, back to Article 4(1). Normally, the closest connection for the whole

---

[203] See German Bundesgerichtshof, 21 October 1964, [1965] GRUR Int 504, Ulmer, n 3 above, at 90 and Modiano, n 53 above, at 125 (reference to the Swiss registration practice).

[204] See French Cour de Cassation, 28 May 1963, [1964] *Revue Critique de Droit International Privé* 513, with note by Y Loussouarn.

[205] Beier, n 12 above, at 178–179, as demonstrated above Beier gives a too broad definition of mandatory rules in order to come to an almost permanent application of the law of the protecting country.

contract would then be determined on the basis of Article 4(1). The presumption does not work and Article 4(1) must be used to determine the closest connection.

Would it be possible, though, in the light of the failure to apply Article 4(2) to the whole contract, to split the contract into a number of parts and to restart the application of Article 4 on that basis? It might indeed be possible to identify a single characteristic performance for each part of a complex contract in relation to the exploitation of intellectual property rights.

The messy application of Article 4(5) in combination with Article 4(1) could then be avoided. For each part of the contract, a characteristic performance could be ascertained and the presumption in Article 4(2) could be made to work and would lead to the identification of the applicable law. It is, however, submitted that this alternative approach has one major drawback. It is quite likely that it would lead to the application of a variety of different laws in respect of what is, essentially, a single contract. One applicable law for each obligation under the contract might seem attractive on paper, but, in practice, it would make things unworkable. This alternative must, therefore, be rejected, even if the process of identification of the applicable law under Article 4(2) provides more guidance and legal certainty in advance than the slightly vaguer rule that is found in Article 4(1). This does not exclude the possibility, though, that depeçage might be a helpful tool. For example, a contract that includes a patent and know-how licence, a turn-key contract for the construction of the plant in which the patented product is to be manufactured and a loan agreement to finance the whole deal, could in certain circumstances helpfully be split into its three components for choice of law purposes.

On balance, the approach which was outlined in the first paragraph of this part on alternative approaches might still be the best solution.

V
CONCLUSION

Contracts in relation to the international exploitation of intellectual property rights have always given rise to complex choice of law problems. These problems have, in recent years, been aggravated by the growing importance of this international exploitation. More and more intellectual property rights are granted and are exploited internationally and many of the contracts now cover the worldwide exploitation of the intellectual property right concerned. In this chapter, we had the opportunity to survey these complex choice of law problems and the suggestions that have, in the past, been made to address these problems and to identify an appropriate choice of law rule. Many of these suggestions were made long before the Rome Convention 1980 entered into force, but even in the absence of that Convention and its often somewhat unfamiliar rules, at least as far as most common lawyers are concerned, there was not a single solution that attracted unanimous support.

The Rome Convention 1980 has not solved these problems conclusively either. The very many difficulties that arise when its contract choice of law provisions are applied to international contracts for the exploitation of intellectual property rights have been highlighted on many occasions in this chapter. Our analysis had led to the conclusion though that, in the absence of unanimity and watertight solutions, a workable model for the application in this area of the convention and its provisions can be put forward. In most cases, that model centres around the law of the protecting country. That is where the exploitation of the intellectual property right will take place and that exploitation must be a highly significant performance under the contract. Often, but not always, it will be possible to identify the exploitation of the right as the characteristic performance of the contract. Article 4(2) of the Convention leads, in these situations, to the identification of the law of the protecting country as the law that is applicable to the contract. Other solutions impose themselves in certain circumstances, though, and the operation of mandatory rules and of the provision on public policy should also be taken into account.

It is particularly important to point to complex contracts, as examples of cases where these other solutions are needed. However, there are good reasons to suggest that there is no point in arguing that the only solutions would be the creation of a special convention or of special contract choice of law rules for contracts relating to the international exploitation of intellectual property rights. This is mainly so because identical problems arise in relation to all types of complex contracts. The main problem of the Rome Convention 1980 is that its provisions work very well for normal or simple contracts, but that they do not work well for complex contracts. Contracts in relation to the international exploitation of intellectual property rights are by no means special in this respect. It falls outside the scope of this book to suggest a detailed model for the reform of the provisions of the Rome Convention 1980 and it might, in any case, be extremely difficult to design general rules that can cope effectively with all the different kinds of complex contracts. Such a rule could easily become unduly complicated and unworkable in practice, if it has to take all eventualities into account.

If the problem lies more with the choice of law provisions in general and less with the specific aspects of contracts in relation to the international exploitation of intellectual property rights and if a comprehensive reform of the choice of law provisions seems anything but straightforward, the delicate, but workable way of applying the provisions of the Rome Convention 1980 that has been outlined in this chapter, might be the only realistic solution, although it is in some ways a second best solution.

12

Infringement: The Applicable Law

I	Introduction	595
II	How questions as to the applicable law arise	596
III	The applicable law: the English approach	597
	1. Introduction	597
	2. Mandatory rules of the forum	598
	(a) Mandatory rules in tort cases	598
	(b) Application in infringement cases	599
	3. Tort choice of law rules	606
	(a) Common law rules	606
	(b) The statutory rules	612
	4. Defences	640
	(a) A contractual defence	640
	(b) Invalidity of the right	642
IV	Reform	643
	1. Criticism of the existing law	643
	2. Alternative solutions from abroad	643
	3. Reform of the tort choice of law rules	644
	4. Special rules as to the applicable law in infringement cases	644
	(a) Independent rules or within the framework of existing rules?	645
	(b) Policy considerations when deciding upon the rules	645
	(c) The suggested rules	646

I
INTRODUCTION

In this chapter, the law applicable to infringement will be examined. But first, something needs to be said about how questions as to the applicable law arise.

II
HOW QUESTIONS AS TO THE APPLICABLE LAW ARISE

Such questions arise when the facts of the case involve a relevant foreign element and the substantive law of each country is different. There is a relevant foreign element where one or both of the parties reside abroad or the infringement occurred abroad. There may be an infringement in more than one country. For example, unauthorised copies of a book may be put on sale in all countries of the European Union. Which law will the court with infringement jurisdiction apply, if we assume that England is the country of origin of the work? Can English law be applied to all aspects of the case, or should Belgian copyright law be applied to the infringement in Belgium, Spanish law to the infringement in Spain, Greek law to the infringement in Greece, etc? Or should we turn to the law of the country where the infringing copies were produced? Should we turn to the residence of the parties?

The matter of applicable law is not just an academic one. Important differences between the copyright laws of the Member States continue to exist. The scope of moral rights protection, for example, differs widely. This may result, in certain cases, in a finding of infringement according to the law of one country, whilst there would be no infringement under the law of another country.

If one is inclined to look at intellectual property infringement cases from a damage to property point of view, the fact that patents and trade marks are registered rights provides a first indication that the property may be situated in the country in which it was registered. Registration makes it easier to locate the right and it could lead to an applicable law. National laws in relation to registered rights have also been harmonised to a greater degree than is the case with copyright. All this may appear to reduce the scope for choice of law problems. However, despite this harmonisation differences in interpretation remain and certain auxiliary provisions in the laws of some Member States have no equivalent in the laws of other Member States. In the area of trade marks, a good example is to be found in the harmonised provision that confusion is now to include confusion through association.[1] English judges tend to take the view that this has added nothing to the existing English law,[2] whilst a very different interpretation is suggested by their Benelux counterparts.[3] Patent law offers

---
[1] See the Trade Marks Act 1994, s 10(2).
[2] See the *Wagamama* case [1995] FSR 713.
[3] See, eg *Monopoly/Anti-Monopoly*, Judgment of 24 June 1977 of the Dutch Supreme Court (Hoge Raad), [1978] BIE 39; *Union/Union Soleure*, Judgment of 20 May 1983 of the Benelux

another good example. Historically, English courts tended to interpret patent claims literally in infringement cases. In contrast, German courts applied the purposive interpretation technique. Article 69 of the European Patent Convention and the Protocol to it attempt to solve this problem by instructing the courts to abandon both extremes. However, in cases that come close to the borderline of infringement, the national courts, whilst attempting to apply the harmonised rule, have reached different conclusions. The *Epilady* saga[4] shows this very clearly. Parallel patents existed in many European countries and infringement proceeding were brought in each country in relation to the same type of infringing act. The same device was held to be an infringement in Germany, but not in England.[5] This underlines the practical importance of the applicable law in relation to infringement cases.

Finally, it is important to note that, in infringement cases, a question as to the applicable law can arise even though the substantive laws in question are identical. This comes about because of the principle of territoriality. Take the example of an English resident who infringes the French registered patent belonging to a French resident and does so in France. Under English substantive law, there is no actionability in this situation. English law provides no infringement protection in relation to French patents infringed in France. Under French law, there is actionability. Accordingly, it is vital for an English Court to decide whether to apply English law or French law.

III
THE APPLICABLE LAW: THE ENGLISH APPROACH

1. Introduction

Under English law, there are no special private international law rules dealing with the law applicable to the infringement of intellectual property rights. This means that English private international law rules of general application have to be applied to the specific area of infringement. Two very different sets of rules come into play. The first are tort choice of law rules. The second are the mandatory rules of the forum. The

Court, [1984] BIE 137; *Always/Regina*, Judgment of 27 May 1983 of the Court of Appeal in Brussels, [1993] 4 IER 22. See also C-251/95 *Sabel BV v Puma AG, Rudolf Dassler Sport* [1998] 1 CMLR 445.

[4] See (1993) 24 IIC 803, 823.
[5] *Improver Corpn* v *Remington Consumer Products Ltd* [1989] RPC 69 and [1990] FSR 181.

particular importance of mandatory rules in infringement cases means that this topic will be examined first.

2. Mandatory Rules of the Forum

Much has already been said about the concept of mandatory rules and about how such rules are to be identified.[6] When it comes to the English intellectual property statutes, it has already been seen[7] that they territorially define the scope of their application by only providing redress in respect of UK rights and normally only when these have been infringed in England. This raises the argument that in a number of very common scenarios the UK infringement provisions are intended to apply as mandatory rules, regardless of the law governing the tort of infringement. It is important, therefore, at this early stage of our examination of the applicable law in infringement cases to look in more detail at the concept of mandatory rules of the forum as a limitation on the application of the governing law in tort cases and its application in particular in infringement cases.

(a) Mandatory rules in tort cases

There is a distinct lack of authority in relation to mandatory rules of the forum in tort cases. The reason for this is because under the common law tort choice of law rules there was an automatic reference to English law anyway.

Part III of the Private International Law (Miscellaneous Provisions) Act 1995, which puts tort choice of law rules largely on a statutory basis, preserves the mandatory rules of the forum exception. Section 14(4) states that Part III 'has effect without prejudice to the operation of any rule of law which either has effect notwithstanding the rules of private international law applicable in the particular circumstances or modifies the rules of private international law that would otherwise be applicable'. Even without this provision, English mandatory rules would remain unaffected by Part III since this is only concerned with tort choice of law rules[8] and with the abolition of certain common law rules.[9] Mandatory rules of the forum fall outside both of these. Although Section 14(4) merely preserves the existing position, abolition of the common law double actionability rule and the fact that the mandatory rules of the forum exception has been spelt out in a statute have given new significance to the operation of mandatory rules in tort cases.

---

[6] See above, chapter 11, pp 577–587.   [7] See above, pp 120–121, 125, 131.
[8] See s 9(1), discussed below, p 612.
[9] See ss 10 and 14(2), discussed below, pp 616–617, 618–619.

It has been suggested that Section 1(3) of the Law Reform (Personal Injuries) Act 1948, limiting the effect of certain exclusion clauses in contracts of employment, might operate as a mandatory rule in a negligence action brought by an employee against the employer.[10] It has also been suggested that the provisions in relation to product liability contained in the Consumer Protection Act 1987 could be regarded as having overriding effect.[11] The right to contribution, which can arise between joint tortfeasors, under the Civil Liability (Contribution) Act 1978, has been held to be a matter solely of construction of the language of the Act.[12] The argument, that the Act was only applicable in the first place where the law governing the right to contribution was English law, was rejected. The Act is applicable once liability against joint tortfeasors has been established, applying tort choice of law rules.

There has also been some discussion of mandatory rules of the forum in the context of infringement of intellectual property rights.

(b) APPLICATION IN INFRINGEMENT CASES

The Patents Act 1977 has no express provision as to its overriding effect in infringement cases. When it comes to infringement of copyright, neither has the Copyright, Designs and Patents Act 1988. The same is true when one looks at infringement of registered trade marks under the Trade Marks Act 1994, registered designs under the Registered Designs Act 1949 and unregistered designs under the Copyright Designs and Patents Act 1988. It is a question, therefore, of construing the provisions on infringement contained in these statutes to see whether they are intended to have overriding effect.

The Court of Appeal, in *Chiron Corpn and Others v Organon Teknika Ltd (No 2)*,[13] held that Section 44 of the Patents Act 1977 has overriding effect and applies regardless of whether English law governs the contract. Section 44(1) strikes down certain provisions, whereby a patentee abuses his monopoly of power, in contracts relating to patents. Dillon LJ, who gave the judgment of the Court, pointed out that this subsection is territorially limited to UK patents. Given that there was this one important restriction , the Court was not prepared to add on a further requirement that the contract was governed by English law.

But do the infringement provisions apply regardless of the law governing the tort of infringement?[14] If so, in what circumstances will this

[10] Dicey and Morris, *Fourth Supplement,* p 274.
[11] Morse [1989] *Current Legal Problems* 167. He is not confident that it would be so regarded by the English courts.
[12] *Arab Monetary Fund v Hashim (No 9)* (1994) *Times,* 11 October.   [13] [1993] FSR 567.
[14] The classification of infringement as a tort for choice of law purposes is discussed below, pp 612–616.

happen? It is accepted that the concept of mandatory rules of the forum will come into play in infringement cases.[15] But what is less clear is the precise circumstances when overriding effect should be given to the English provisions on infringement. It is important, in infringement cases, to distinguish four different scenarios, depending on whether it is a UK or foreign right and on whether this was infringed in England or abroad. These four scenarios are as follows: a UK intellectual property right is infringed in England; a UK right is infringed abroad; a foreign right is infringed in England; and a foreign right is infringed abroad.

(i) A UK intellectual property right is infringed in England

It can be stated confidently that, if a UK right is infringed in England, the UK statutory provisions will apply.[16] It matters not that a foreign law is applicable under the tort choice of law rules. Under those rules, doubtless English law will apply anyway in this scenario.[17]

It is right, in principle, that the English statutory provisions on infringement should be construed as having overriding effect in scenario (i). There are, after all, two territorial restrictions on the use of these provisions: protection is only given to the holders of UK rights; and, normally, the infringement must have taken place in England. It would be wrong to add on a further requirement that English law governs under the tort choice of law rules. This was the reasoning adopted in the *Chiron* case[18] and is equally appropriate when discussing tort rather than contract.

Authority in relation to tort, and, in particular, in relation to infringement, can be found in *Mölnlycke AB and Another* v *Procter & Gamble Ltd and Others*.[19] This case concerned an action for infringement of a UK patent. It was said that such an action could only be founded on infringement in England.[20] There was no discussion of whether English law was applicable under the tort choice of law rules; it was assumed that the infringement provisions in the Patents Act 1977 would apply automatically in this scenario.

(ii) A UK right is infringed abroad

(a) *Does UK law operate as a mandatory rule to deny recovery ?*

(i) *The nature of the problem*

This is a much more difficult scenario to deal with. What is clear is that the English intellectual property statutes, normally being territorially limited

---

[15] See below, n 19 and text accompanying.
[16] See Dicey and Morris, *Fourth Supplement*, pp 231, 274; Supplementary Memorandum by Beatson in *HL Paper* 36 (1995), p 62; Annex by Cornish, *ibid* p 64.
[17] See below, pp 618–619.
[18] N 13 above.
[19] [1992] 1 WLR 1112, discussed above, p 147.
[20] *Ibid* at 1118.

to acts of infringement occurring in England,[21] do not protect the holder of a right in this situation, and an action for infringement based on these statutes will fail. However, application of the tort choice of law rules may give a different result. Under these rules, normally, the law of the foreign country where the infringement occurred will apply.[22] Of course, the law of a foreign country is unlikely to provide redress based on the existence of a UK right; it will doubtless only provide protection for the holder of a local right.[23] So the situation under discussion is perhaps a theoretical one. Nonetheless, if this were to occur, would it be possible to base an action in England on actionability under the foreign law of the country where the act of infringement took place?

It has been suggested[24] that the English statutory provisions on infringement have overriding effect in scenario (ii), thereby denying resort to tort choice of law rules and the application of a foreign governing law. The argument for this seems to be based on an assumption that the foreign court would be applying a misplaced view of the ambit of the UK statute.[25] This may or may not be the case. What we are concerned with in scenario (ii) is whether there is actionability under the foreign law, and this will normally arise from the foreign court applying its own statute. But even if this assumption is true, it is not looking at the matter in the right way. The real question is: what did Parliament intend? As has been seen, this intention can be inferred where a statute is territorially limited. What is being suggested, presumably, is that Parliament intended the English statutes to have overriding effect whenever there is an English intellectual property right.

It is submitted that to give overriding effect to the English intellectual property statutes in scenario (ii) is wrong in principle and is not required by the authorities.

(ii) *Arguments of principle*

First, mandatory rules are an exception to the normal application of choice of law rules and a domestic statute should not be given overriding effect unless this is clearly the intention of Parliament.

Secondly, it is, of course, a question of construction whether English statutory provisions on infringement are intended to apply even though a foreign law governs the tort. But what provisions are we talking about?

---

[21] But see *ABKCO Music & Records Inc* v *Music Collection International Ltd and Another* [1995] RPC 657, discussed below pp 603–604.
[22] Private International Law (Miscellaneous Provisions) Act 1995, s 11, discussed below, p 619.
[23] See scenario (iv), discussed below.
[24] See Beatson n 16 above p 63. But compare Dicey and Morris *Fourth Supplement*, pp 231–232.
[25] Beatson, n 16, above, at p 63.

There are no substantive statutory provisions actually stating that the holder of a UK right has no redress under English law in the situation where the right has been infringed abroad. Admittedly, this is implicit from the provisions which provide for redress. But it is hard to accept that the English intellectual property statutes express a strong socio-economic policy to this effect, justifying a departure from the normal application of choice of law rules in a case involving a foreign element, when there is no explicit statement.

Thirdly, the examples given so far of mandatory rules all involve protectionist provisions. There are such provisions in the English intellectual property statutes whereby the holder of a right is protected, but what we are talking about now is an implicit provision denying redress, which is a very different matter.

Fourthly, what we are really concerned with in scenario (ii) is not a concern to uphold English law, which is what mandatory rules are all about, but a disapproval of a foreign law which is prepared to give protection to the holder of a foreign (ie English) right. Public policy,[26] which is a negative concept, should be used to deal with such a case, rather than mandatory rules, which is a positive concept.

(iii) *The authorities*

There is a number of reported cases involving scenario (ii), although in none of them is there an allegation of a foreign law providing for actionability in respect of a UK right.

In the patent infringement case of *The Badische Anilin Und Soda Fabrik* v *The Basle Chemical Works, Bindschedler*,[27] the House of Lords simply considered liability in terms of the English statute, and, since the infringement had taken place abroad, held that the patentee had no right of recovery. There was no mention at all of tort choice of law principles, but this can be explained by the fact that no evidence was given of any actionability under foreign law.

More significant was the judgment of the Vice-Chancellor (Sir Nicholas Browne-Wilkinson) in *Def Lepp Music and Others* v *Stuart-Brown and Others*,[28] which involved infringement of copyright abroad. The claim was for infringement of the UK copyright and, accordingly, failed. It was argued by the plaintiffs that there was a wrong (the nature of which was not specified, there was no evidence that it was breach of copyright) under the laws of Luxembourg and Holland, where the infringements had occurred, and that recourse could be had to the English tort choice of law rules. This submission was rejected. The learned judge said that 'The only wrong under English law that he [counsel for the plaintiffs] can rely on for

[26] Discussed below, pp 634–635.   [27] [1898] AC 200.   [28] [1986] RPC 273.

this purpose is breach of the statutory rights conferred by the Copyright Act 1956 . . . No common law rule of international law can confer on a litigant a right under English law that he would not otherwise possess.'[29] He went on to say, though, that, in any event, the acts were not actionable as a tort in England, as required under the common law tort choice of law rules. The authority of the case is further weakened by the fact that all of these comments were made in the context of jurisdiction where the issue was whether the case was a proper one for service out of the jurisdiction.[30]

In contrast, the High Court of Australia, in *Norbert Steinhardt and Son Ltd v Meth and Another*,[31] applied tort choice of law rules in a case involving a threat of proceedings for infringement of an Australian patent, the infringement having taken place in England. The claim failed because there was no actionability under English law, the law of the State in which the tort was committed. If the Australian statute had been treated as containing mandatory rules which denied recovery in this scenario, it would have been irrelevant what English law said.

Moreover, in the Proceedings of the Special Public Bill Committee[32] concerned with the statutory tort choice of law rules, Lord Wilberforce,[33] relying on Dicey and Morris,[34] thought that tort choice of law rules would apply in this scenario, as do some intellectual property lawyers.[35]

(iv) *Conclusion*

There are strong arguments of principle for not applying the mandatory rules approach in scenario (ii), there are authorities both for and against this approach and they certainly do not dictate its use. Infringements abroad should be treated like other torts and the tort choice of law rules applied to them . This does not mean that an English court has to apply a foreign law which provides redress in respect of infringement of a UK intellectual property right. It is appropriate to refuse to do so on the ground of public policy.[36]

(b) *Does UK law operate as a mandatory rule to provide recovery?*

The Court of Appeal, in *ABKCO Music & Records Inc v Music Collection International Ltd and Another*, in effect, held that a provision in an English intellectual property statute operated as a mandatory rule to provide redress even though a foreign law was applicable according to the tort choice of law rules.[37] The case concerned the liability of a Danish

---

[29] *Ibid*, at 276. [30] See above, p 258. [31] (1960) 105 CLR 440.
[32] HL Paper 36 (1995). [33] *Ibid*, at 53.
[34] At pp 1491–1492. See also Dicey and Morris, *Fourth Supplement*, at pp 231–232.
[35] See Floyd and Purvis [1995] 3 *EIPR* 254 at 111–112.
[36] See below, p 635. [37] [1995] RPC 657, discussed above, p 148 under jurisdiction.

defendant for secondary infringement by authorising in Denmark an infringement of copyright in England. It was held that there was liability under Section 16(2) of the Copyright, Designs and Patents Act 1988. It was enough that the restricted act authorised by the defendant was done within the United Kingdom. Technically, the act of infringement performed by the Danish defendant took place in Denmark. Application of tort choice of law rules, at that time common law rules, would have doubtless meant, according to the second limb of the double actionability rule, that Danish law governed with the result that the plaintiff's claim would have failed. It is important in such a case that Section 16(2) is given an overriding effect and recourse is not had to tort choice of law rules. The situation in *ABKCO* is actually very hard to classify for the purpose of the present discussion. It has much in common with scenario (i) in that for liability under Section 16(2) there has to be authorisation of an act of infringement done in England in respect of a UK copyright.

(iii) A foreign right is infringed in England

The nature of the problem here is very similar to that in scenario (ii). The English intellectual property statutes only protect the holders of UK rights and an action based on such rights will fail. Application of the tort choice of law rules may give a different result. Normally, English law will apply as the law of the country in which the events constituting the tort occurred.[38] There is, though, the possibility of displacing this rule and applying a foreign law,[39] such as that of the country which granted the right.[40] It is possible, albeit perhaps unusual, that this may provide redress, even though the infringement did not occur in that country.[41] The question then arises of whether a successful action can be brought in England based on this foreign law.

It has been suggested[42] that the English statutory provisions have overriding effect not only in scenario (ii) but also in scenario (iii), thereby denying recourse to the tort choice of law rules. It has been argued that 'any other view would mean that there would be two IP rights competing in one country which appears contrary to the principle of national treatment upon which the IP conventions and legislation are based . . .'.[43] Again though, the real question is: what did Parliament intend? The significance of territorial limitations on statutory provisions, as a guide to the inten-

[38] Private International Law (Miscellaneous Provisions) Act 1995, s 11, discussed below p 619.
[39] Private International Law (Miscellaneous Provisions) Act 1995, s 12, discussed below, p 625.
[40] See below, p 632.
[41] English law has been known to do so: see the *ABKCO* case, n 21, above; Copyright Act 1956, ss 1(2) and 31(4), explained below, p 608.
[42] Beatson n 16 above, at p 62.   [43] Beatson, *ibid*.

tions of Parliament, has already been noted. It is, presumably, being suggested, therefore, that Parliament intended the intellectual property statutes to have overriding effect whenever a tort is committed in England. A territorial link based on the act of infringement is certainly no stronger than one based on the grant of the intellectual property right; accordingly, the case for giving overriding effect in scenario (iii) is no stronger than that in scenario (ii).

Moreover, the arguments of principle against the adoption of the mandatory rules approach in relation to scenario (ii) are equally applicable in respect of scenario (iii). When it comes to authorities, there is very little discussion of this scenario in the cases. This is not surprising. Under the common law tort choice of law rules, it was unclear whether English law could ever be displaced by a foreign law in the situation where a tort had been committed in England. The courts would apply English law and an action would fail. Nonetheless, in the *Norbert Steinhardt* case,[44] when discussing the difficulty in operating tort choice of law rules in patent cases, because of the strict territoriality of patents, the High Court of Australia gave, as an example, the fact that 'It is not unlawful to threaten in England to infringe an Australian patent.'[45] It is implicit in the judgment that this scenario is to be dealt with under the tort choice of law rules.

It is submitted that, in scenario (iii), tort choice of law rules should be applied. The application of these rules will be examined later on, but it is worth pointing out at this stage that there may be some difficulty in using the public policy exception in scenario (iii).[46] If so, this could have a knock on effect of English courts being tempted to give overriding effect to English intellectual property statutes to deny recovery as allowed by the foreign law of the country where the infringement occurred.

(iv) A foreign right is infringed abroad

In this scenario, it is absolutely clear that resort should be had to tort choice of law rules. It cannot be argued seriously that Parliament intended the English intellectual property statutes to apply to deny recovery in the situation where there is neither a UK right nor an infringement in England. Moreover, the use of tort choice of law rules in scenario (iv) is supported by leading textbooks on intellectual property[47] and conflict of laws,[48] and by the recent Scots authority of *James Burrough Distillers plc v Speymalt Whisky Distributors Ltd*.[49] In this case, Lord Coulsfield, in the Outer House, applied tort choice of law rules in the situation where an Italian trademark had been infringed in Italy. Application of the common

[44] N 31 above.   [45] *Ibid*, at 444.   [46] See below, p 635.
[47] See Vitoria *et al*, para 10–501.
[48] See Wolff, para 471; Dicey and Morris, p 1516 and *Fourth Supplement*, pp 231–232.
[49] 1989 SLT 561.

law tort choice of law rules in relation to foreign wrongs resulted in the failure of the claim for infringement.[50] Subsequent change to these common law rules, with the introduction of new flexibility following the decision of the Privy Council in *Red Sea Insurance Co Ltd* v *Bouygues SA*,[51] raised the possibility of such a claim succeeding.[52] This is even more likely under the new statutory tort choice of law rules.[53]

3. Tort Choice of Law Rules

These rules will apply in circumstances where the statutory infringement provisions do not operate as mandatory rules of the forum. Part III of the Private International Law (Miscellaneous Provisions) Act 1995 puts tort choice of law rules largely on a statutory basis by abolishing certain common law rules[54] previously applied and by introducing new rules. These statutory rules are based on recommendations from the Law Commissions,[55] but some important amendments were made during the passage of the bill through Parliament. Before examining these new rules, though, it is necessary to look at the common law rules. There are three reasons for this. First, Part III is not retrospective.[56] Secondly, the common law rules still apply in relation to defamation.[57] Thirdly, the scope of Part III is limited to situations where certain common law rules operated.[58]

(a) COMMON LAW RULES

(i) **The rules**

(a) *Torts committed in England*

Where a tort has been committed in England, the courts have always applied English law. It has never been entirely clear under the common law rules whether there is a flexible exception to this rule which would allow the displacement of English law in favour of the application of some more appropriate foreign law. There is such an exception in respect of torts committed abroad but the Court of Appeal has held that the rules in relation to torts committed abroad can be wholly disregarded if the tort

---

[50] See below, p 611.   [51] [1995] 1 AC 190.   [52] See below, p 611.
[53] See Private International Law (Miscellaneous Provisions) Act 1995, s 11, discussed below p 619.
[54] Australian courts still apply common law rules which look to ‚the law of the forum and the law of the place where the wrong was committed: *McKain* v *R W Miller & Co (SA) Pty Ltd* (1991) 174 CLR 1; *Stevens* v *Head* (1993) 176 CLR 433.
[55] Law Com No 193 (1990).   [56] Section 14(1). See below, p 612.
[57] Section 13, discussed below, p 617.
[58] See s 14(2), discussed below, pp 616–617.

was committed in England.[59] In the Privy Council, in the *Red Sea* case,[60] there is no mention at all of the position in relation to torts committed in England; this case was concerned, in effect, with the displacement of English law by that of the foreign law of the place where the tort was committed and not with the displacement of the English law of the place where the tort was committed by a foreign law. Arguably though, the decision raises a question mark over the position in respect of torts committed in England in that it accepts for the first time that a flexible exception may lead to the displacement of English law by a foreign law. Nonetheless, it must remain doubtful whether an exception could ever operate in the situation where a tort is committed in England.

(b) Torts committed abroad

Rule 203 of Dicey and Morris,[61] which is based on *Phillips v Eyre*[62] and *Boys v Chaplin*,[63] states that:

(1) As a general rule, an act done in a foreign country is a tort and actionable as such in England, only if it is both
 (a) actionable as a tort according to English law, or in other words is an act which, if done in England, would be a tort; and
 (b) actionable according to the law of the foreign country where it was done.
(2) But a particular issue between the parties may be governed by the law of the country which, with respect to that issue, has the most significant relationship with the occurrence and the parties.

This statement has been approved by the Privy Council in the *Red Sea* case.[64] Rule 203(1) is a double limbed choice of law rule.[65] It was also held in this case that the exception under (2) can be relied upon to enable a plaintiff to rely on exclusively the foreign law of the place where the tort was committed even if his claim would not be actionable under English law. Previously, the exception had only been used where this led to the application of English law, and so this decision was greeted as introducing new flexibility. Nonetheless, the Privy Council accepted that the exception would not be successfully invoked in every case or even probably in many cases. They approved [66] a statement of Lord Wilberforce in the House of Lords in *Boys v Chaplin*[67] that 'The general rule must apply unless clear and satisfying grounds are shown why it should be departed from . . .'.[68]

---

[59] *Metall und Rohstoff AG v Donaldson Lufkin & Jenrette Inc* [1990] 1 QB 391; overruled on a different point in *Lonrho plc v Fayed* [1991] 3 WLR 188.
[60] N 51 above.   [61] At pp 1487–1488.   [62] (1870) LR 6 QB 1.
[63] [1971] AC 356.   [64] N 51 above.
[65] *Ibid*, at 198. See also *Chaplin v Boys* [1971] AC 356, 385–387 (*per* Lord Wilberforce); *Def Lepp Music v Stuart-Brown* [1986] RPC 273 at 276; Dicey and Morris, pp 1488–1489.
[66] *Ibid* at 939.   [67] [1971] AC 356.   [68] *Ibid* at 391.

(ii) Application in infringement cases

This can be best understood by looking at the same scenarios that were examined in relation to the operation of mandatory rules of the forum.

(a) *A UK right is infringed in England*

It has been seen that, in this scenario, the UK statutory provisions on infringement will apply as mandatory rules of the forum and not the tort choice of law rules.

(b) *A UK right is infringed abroad*

If you apply the common law tort choice of law rules in this scenario, the double actionability requirement set out in Rule 203(1) is not satisfied and the claim will fail. This was said, *obiter*, in the *Def Lepp* case.[69] There was no actionability as a tort under English law, as required by what is now Rule 203(1)(a),[70] since, it was said, the English copyright legislation only gives protection in respect of acts if done in England.[71] It was pointed out by counsel for the plaintiffs that what is now rule 203(1) (a) was phrased in terms that 'in other words is an act which, if done in England, would be a tort'. This looks to be a good argument;[72] it is undeniable that if an infringement of a UK right occurs in England this is a tort. But the Vice-Chancellor brushed this aside, saying that he did not understand what was added by this phrase. What he required was that the acts were actionable as a tort in England.[73]

It is also likely that there will be no actionability according to the law of the foreign country where the act was done, as required by Rule 203(1)(b), because that rule is unlikely to provide redress in respect of what to it is a foreign right. Thus, the High Court of Australia, in the *Norbert Steinhardt* case,[74] held that this requirement was not met where the claim was in respect of a threat of proceedings in England for infringement of an Australian patent. Fullagar J said that 'No action could be maintained in England for an infringement of an Australian patent , or in Australia for an infringement of an English patent'.[75] This was because of the strict territoriality of patents.

This still leaves the possibility of the displacement of the general rule and the application of a foreign law under Rule 203(2). Tort choice of law

---

[69] N 65 above.   [70] At that time Rule 172, which is identically worded.
[71] But see the Copyright Act 1956, ss 1(2) and 31(4), which allowed for actionability for infringement abroad in a country to which provisions of the Act extended. There are no such provisions under the Copyright, Designs and Patents Act 1988.
[72] See Floyd and Purvis [1995] 3 *EIPR* 110 at 111–112.
[73] N 65 above, at 276.   [74] N 31 above.   [75] *Ibid*, at 443.

rules were put on a statutory basis before the courts had been able to absorb the full implications of the *Red Sea* case with its introduction of new flexibility. Nonetheless, two points can be made. First, it is doubtful whether it could really be shown that the law of the country which has the most significant relationship with the occurrence and the parties is that of the foreign country where the tort was committed in a case involving a UK right. One of the most significant, if not the most significant, factors must be that of where the right was created. Secondly, even if a foreign law does apply it is unlikely that there will be actionability under that law in relation to a UK right, as was explained in the *Norbert Steinhardt* case.

(c) *A foreign right is infringed in England*

If you apply the common law tort choice of law rules in this situation, the English courts will apply the law of the forum and the claim will fail. There is no redress under English law in relation to foreign rights. The position is the same in Australia where, according to the *Norbert Steinhardt* case,[76] no action can be maintained for an infringement of an English patent. As has been seen, it is doubtful under the common law rules whether a foreign law could ever displace English law where a tort was committed in England.

(d) *A foreign right is infringed abroad*

(i) *No actionability under English law*

In this fourth scenario, there is no actionability under English law as required under Rule 203(1)(a). Thus, in the *Potter* case,[77] in the Supreme Court of Victoria, Hood J said that, a claim brought in respect of an infringement in New South Wales of New South Wales patent rights, was not actionable under the law of the forum. Similarly, in the *James Burrough* case,[78] a claim brought in Scotland for infringement of an Italian trademark in Italy failed. It was said by Lord Coulsfield that there was no actionability under Scots law in respect of acts of infringement committed abroad. The reasoning is the same as that which comes into play to deny recovery in scenario (b). There is another reason though why there is no actionability under English law in scenario (d), and this different from scenario (b), this is because English law provides no redress in respect of foreign rights. Thus, in *Tyburn Productions Ltd v Conan Doyle*,[79] Vinelott J, relying on the *Def Lepp* case[80] said that 'an infringement of a foreign copyright cannot constitute a tort under English law'.[81]

[76] N 31 above at 443.   [77] [1905] VLR 612 at 631.   [78] N 49 above at 566.
[79] [1991] Ch 75.   [80] N 65 above.
[81] [1991] Ch 75 at 87. See also *LA Gear Inc v Gerald Whelan & Sons Ltd* [1991] FSR 670 at 674. The position is the same in Canada: see McLeod *The Conflict of Laws* (1983), p 560.

The one case that goes against all this is the perplexing decision of Lloyd J in *Pearce v Ove Arup Partnership Ltd and Others*.[82] The case involved the infringement of a Netherlands copyright in the Netherlands. Lloyd J was of the view that if you can overcome the jurisdictional limitation in respect of foreign intellectual property rights, which on the facts you could do because it was a case decided under the Brussels Convention, then this would automatically remove any any problem presented by the double actionability rule. This would appear to be based on the clearly erroneous reasoning that the double actionability rule is equivalent to a jurisdictional rule,[83] when the truth is that this is a double limbed choice of law rule.[84] The non application of a jurisdictional limitation, clearly, cannot satisfy the requirements of a choice of law rule. Moreover, if the double actionability rule is not a choice of law rule, what is the choice of law rule? Lloyd J said that it was the law of the protecting country, copyright arising under which is alleged to have been infringed (*lex protectionis*), in the instant case Dutch law. But there is no authority for this approach.

There will be actionability, though, according to the law of the foreign country where the infringement was done, this is assuming that it was a local right that was infringed there.

(ii) *Getting round the difficulty*

In order to get round the difficulty in scenario (d) of satisfying the requirement that there is actionability under English law, it has been suggested[85] that the locus of the wrongful act should be deemed to be in England as the forum and that the rights themselves which are sought to be protected should be treated as the equivalent English rights. It has been argued that without this the double actionability rule would lose all purpose in the case of territorially defined torts. However, the *Def Lepp* and *James Burrough* cases clearly go against any such suggestion.[86] Even more radically, it has been suggested by the same author that a general tortious remedy should be introduced for the infringement of a foreign trademark, provided that the infringements have occurred in the territory of the conferring State.[87] This has been criticised as 'to invent rights which Parliament has not seen fit to grant and in fact has deliberately refrained from granting'.[88]

---

[82] [1997] 2 WLR 779.
[83] *Ibid* at 790. There is also some misunderstanding of the nature of the subject matter limitation as to jurisdiction.
[84] *Boys v Chaplin* [1971] AC 356, at 385–387 (*per* Lord Wilberforce); *Def Lepp Music v Stuart-Brown* [1986] RPC 273 at 276; Dicey and Morris, pp 1488–1489.
[85] See Kaye [1990] 1 *EIPR* 28.
[86] See Arnold [1990] 7 *EIPR* 254 at 262. [87] Kaye, n 85, above at 30.
[88] Arnold [1990] 7 *EIPR* 254 at 262.

A much more feasible way of obtaining recovery under the common law rules is by the use of the exception contained in Rule 203(2). The *Red Sea* case opened up the distinct possibility that the law of the foreign country in which the infringement took place, and in which the right was created, could be applied as the law of the country which has the most significant relationship with the occurrence and the parties.[89] But as will shortly be seen, the statutory changes to tort choice of law have meant that recovery is now possible in scenario (d) under the statutory general rule without having to have recourse to any such exception to this rule.

(e) Foreign and UK rights infringed abroad

We are concerned here with parallel rights at home and abroad, such as where an inventor obtains a European patent (UK) and a European patent (Germany) for the same invention, in respect of which there has been an infringement abroad. Parallel rights are separate national rights. Even European patents are a bundle of national rights. If a plaintiff relies upon his UK rights the claim will fail: this is scenario (b). If reliance is placed on a foreign right the claim will likewise fail: this is scenario (d). Admittedly, at first glance in scenario (d) there appears to be actionability according to English law in that there is also a UK right[90] but this is a different right from the one relied upon in the action. In the *James Burrough* case,[91] the second petitioners relied upon the infringement of the Italian trademark in Italy. However, the trade mark had been registered not only in Italy but also in the United Kingdom. Nonetheless, Lord Coulson said, *obiter*,[92] that the double actionability requirement would not be satisfied, and that 'the *jus actionis* for breach of an Italian trade mark is a different *jus actionis* from that for breach of a UK trademark. Each *jus actionis* is separately derived from a statutory privilege which the trade mark holder has in the territory in question and is strictly confined to that territory. It follows, in my view, that the fact that a person holds trade marks in each of two separate countries does not satisfy the requirement of double actionability in a case such as the present'.[93] This decision has been the subject of some criticism[94] but does have a ruthless logic. The real fault lies in the requirement of double actionability in the first place.

---

[89] See Floyd and Purvis [1995] 3 *EIPR* 110 at 114; Austin, (1997) 113 *LQR* 321, at 323.
[90] But this would still leave the problem that there has to be an infringement in England, see the *Def Lepp* case discussed at p 608 above.
[91] N 49, above.
[92] The trademarks were held by different persons.
[93] N 49, above, at 566.
[94] See Kaye, n 85, above. See more generally in relation to scenario (e), Floyd and Purvis, n 89, above.

(b) THE STATUTORY RULES

(i) Scope of Part III

(a) *No retrospective effect*

Part III came into force on 1 May 1996.[95] It is not retrospective; it does not apply to 'acts or omissions giving rise to a claim which occur before the commencement of this Part'.[96]

(b) *Tort choice of law*

The rules in Part III 'apply for choosing the law . . . to be used for determining issues relating to tort or (for the purposes of the law of Scotland) delict'.[97] This means: first, there must be a choice of law problem; secondly, there must be an issue relating to tort.

(i) *Choice of law*

Any infringement case involving a relevant foreign element has the potential for raising a question as to the choice of the applicable law. However, it must be recalled that if English law applies as a mandatory rule of the forum no question of choosing the applicable law arises. It follows that in the situation where provisions on infringement in English intellectual property statutes apply as mandatory rules of the forum[98] the position will be unaffected by Part III of the 1995 Act, which will not apply.[99]

(ii) *An issue relating to tort*

This raises a question of characterisation and is much more problematic. Section 9(2) states that 'The characterisation for the purposes of private international law of issues arising in a claim as issues relating to tort or delict is a matter for the courts of the forum.' We know from this that the English courts are to characterise (classify) the issue as one in tort or otherwise, but what criteria are they to apply when doing so? Part III does not say. There is an obvious danger that an English court which does not like a foreign cause of action, unknown in England, might simply characterise it as not being tortious.[100] However, the Law Commissions clearly contemplated that Part III would operate in a case of, for example, invasion of privacy, even though there is no such cause

---

[95] SI 1996/995.
[96] Section 14(1). See *Pearce v Ove Arup Partnership Ltd and Others* [1997] 2 WLR 779 at 782.
[97] Section 9(1). [98] See above, p 600.
[99] See also s 14(2), discussed below, p 616, and s 14(4), discussed below, p 638.
[100] See Carter (1996) 112 *LQR* 190 at 193.

of action under English law.[101] Section 9(2) refers to characterisation 'for the purposes of private international law', which indicates that there does not have to be such a cause of action under English substantive law.[102]

Criteria for characterisation. It is submitted that the following should be used as the criteria in determining the characterisation of a cause of action: the characterisation adopted by English courts for the purposes of choice of law under the common law rules; the characterisation adopted by the English courts for the purposes of jurisdiction; the characterisation adopted in relation to the substantive law. It is also important to mention what should not be used as a criterion. Actionability as a tort by English law has been said to be, in theory at least, a possible criterion.[103] But to introduce this as a requirement would defeat the purpose of Part III, which is concerned with the abolition of the common law rules, including the requirement that actionability under the law of the forum be shown.

Doubtless, the three criteria suggested above will point towards the same characterisation. In the unlikely event of this not being the case, it is submitted that the first criterion is the most important one and should be given priority over the other two criteria, and the second criterion is more important than the third one. Each of these criteria can now be examined.

Characterisation for the purposes of choice of law at common law. It is submitted that if, under the common law choice of law rules, the cause of action has been characterised as tortious and tort choice of law rules applied the same characterisation should be adopted for the purposes of Part III. The corollary to this is that if a non-tortious characterisation has been adopted under the common law choice of law rules, the same should be adopted for the purposes of Part III. In some cases, the English courts may have had to characterise not that precise cause of action but some English equivalent. An example would be a claim brought before the English courts for breach of a foreign law of unfair competition, which in this case takes the form of passing off.[104] There is no English cause of action for unfair competition but there is one for passing-off. If this equivalent has been characterised for choice of law purposes at common law, the same characterisation should be adopted in a claim based on unfair competition under Part III. There may be foreign authority on characterisation for the purposes of choice of law; this constitutes persuasive authority.

---

[101] Clause 1(4) of the Draft Bill, set out in Law Com No 193 (1990) Appendix A, made it clear that such cases can be characterised as tortious. Unfortunately, this wording was not followed.
[102] See Dicey and Morris, *Fourth Supplement*, p 228.
[103] See *HL Paper* 36 (1995), Written Evidence by Briggs, at p 9, and Rogerson, at p 54.
[104] See below, pp 681–682.

Characterisation for the purposes of jurisdiction. If the cause of action has been characterised as tortious for jurisdictional purposes, the same characterisation should be adopted for the purposes of Part III. If a non-tortious characterisation has been adopted for jurisdictional purposes, the same characterisation should be adopted for the purposes of Part III. The characterisation adopted for English equivalents of foreign causes of action should be followed in relation to that foreign cause of action. Foreign authority on characterisation for the purposes of jurisdiction constitutes persuasive authority.

The characterisation adopted in relation to the substantive law. In many cases, particularly where the English court is faced with a cause of action unknown to English law, there will be no authority under the common law rules on characterisation for the purposes of choice of law, or for jurisdictional purposes, and recourse will have to be had to the characterisation adopted in relation to the substantive law.

A number of different situations have to be distinguished. The first is where English law has such a cause of action under its substantive law and characterises it as a tort. In this situation, the answer is clear. A tortious characterisation should be adopted for the purposes of the scope of Part III.

The second situation is where English law has such a cause of action under its substantive law but gives it a non-tortious characterisation. Here too, the answer is clear. The non-tortious characterisation should be adopted for the present purposes and Part III should not apply. This should be so even though the plaintiff relies on a foreign law, which characterises the cause of action as tortious.

The third situation is where English law has such a cause of action under its substantive law but its characterisation is not clear. An example would be an action for non-contractual breach of confidence.[105] An English judge faced with this problem could solve it in one of two ways. The first would be to decide definitively how this should be characterised as a matter of English substantive law, and then allow this to determine the characterisation for the purposes of private international law. The second approach would be to accept that the characterisation, as a matter of English substantive law, is unclear and that no guidance can be gained from this criterion.

The fourth situation is where English law has no such cause of action but has an equivalent. In this situation, the characterisation adopted in respect of this equivalent under the English substantive law should be adopted.

The fifth situation is where English law has no such cause of action or equivalent. In this situation, characterisation is hardest of all. The question has to be asked: if English law had this cause of action , would it be char-

---

[105] See below, pp 699–700.

acterised as tortious? The fact that the foreign country whose law is relied upon regards the cause of action as tortious should be regarded as persuasive evidence to be used by the English courts in favour of adopting a tortious characterisation. This does not mean that this foreign law is being allowed to characterise the issue. The characterisation is still that of the English courts. There is even more persuasive evidence in favour of this tortious characterisation if it can be shown, generally, that other foreign countries that have this cause of action adopt this characterisation. The fact that invasion of privacy, to take an example, is characterised as a tort (or delict) in countries which have this cause of action should be enough to bring it within Part III. This internationalist approach would fit in with the expectations of the Law Commissions that invasion of privacy and other causes of action unknown to English law would come within Part III, would avoid defeating the purpose of Part III, and would fit in with the wording of Section 9(2).

Application in infringement cases. The characterisation of actions for infringement has particularly vexed commentators on Part III. It has been asserted that infringement cases would not be classified as tortious,[106] there are serious doubts whether they can be so classified,[107] it is not clear whether they can be so classified,[108] they are likely to be so classified despite their origins in statute as opposed to the common law,[109] that Part III will apply (without any discussion of the issue of characterisation).[110]

Nonetheless, applying the criteria set out above, the only conclusion that can be reached is that, for the purposes of private international law, infringement should be regarded as raising issues relating to tort. First, at common law, it is tort choice of law rules that have been applied to infringement.[111] Secondly, in the context of jurisdiction, it is well established that the tort rules apply in cases of infringement.[112] Thirdly, in the purely domestic context, it is accepted that infringement is a tort.[113] Fourthly, if infringement is not to be characterised as tortious then there is a very real problem as to how it is to be characterised. It does not fit, for example, into the category of contract or restitution or property.[114] It

---

[106] At least where it is a foreign right that has been infringed in England: Rogerson in *HL Paper* 36 (1995) Written Evidence p 54.

[107] Briggs [1995] *LMCLQ* 519 at 522, pointing unconvincingly to the absence of jurisdiction (but this is only under the traditional rules and is only because of a subject matter limitation and not because of a characterisation point) and because of an erroneous suggestion by Briggs that such claims were not dealt with under the common law rules.

[108] Memorandum by Norton Rose in *HL Paper* 36 (1995) Written Evidence, at 48.

[109] Dicey and Morris, *Fourth Supplement*, p 228. See also Morse, (1996) 45 *ICLQ* 888 at 894.

[110] Supplementary Memorandum from Beatson in *HL Paper* 36 (1995) pp 61–63; Austin, n 89 above, at 323.

[111] See above, pp 608–611.   [112] See above, pp 150, 244.   [113] See above, p 150.

[114] If an issue of ownership of a right arose during infringement proceedings this would be a property matter: see Leslie 1990 SLT 361.

would have to be regarded as *sui generis* and special choice of law rules invented for it.

(c) *Section 14(2)*

Section 14(2) of the 95 Act states that:

Nothing in this Part [Part III] affects any rules of law (including rules of private international law) except those abolished by Section 10 above.

Section 10 abolishes the double actionability rule and exception applied at common law.

(i) *The restriction*

Section 14(2) imposes a further restriction on the scope of Part III. If the common law rules did not require recourse to the double actionability rule or exception, then they are unaffected by Part III, which does not apply. The provision is designed to deal with matters such as maritime torts which have their own special rules at common law;[115] although a tort choice of law problem was raised this was not solved by the application of the double actionability rule and exception. It also repeats the point made elsewhere in Part III, that mandatory rules of the forum are unaffected and continue to apply.

So much can be said with confidence, but what the implications of Section 14(2) are going beyond this is not clear. Does it mean that, for example , a claim for invasion of privacy will fall outside Part III because of an argument that if such a claim had been brought at common law it would have fallen outside the scope of the double actionability rule and exception? This would defeat the expectations of the Law Commissions and the understanding of the overwhelming majority of experts who gave oral and written evidence to the Special Public Bill Committee.[116] Moreover, it is important to note that section 14(2) comes within the ambit of 'savings'. It is an exception to the application of the statutory rules and, as such, should be applied restrictively. This can be done in the following way. Once it is shown that a choice of the applicable law in relation to tort arises, the statutory choice of law rules should be applied, unless it can be established that, at common law, the double actionability rule and exception would not have applied. This will be easy to establish if there is a maritime tort. In contrast, in the case of an invasion of privacy, there is no evidence of special common law choice of law rules or of mandatory rules of the forum. This is not surprising. The double actionability requirement discouraged the bringing of such claims here. The statutory tort choice of

---

[115] See the comments of the Lord Chancellor HL Deb, 6 December 1994.
[116] See *HL Paper* 36 (1995).

law rules would, therefore, be applied, unaffected by Section 14(2). This restrictive approach avoids the courts having to enter into absurd speculative exercises about whether, if such a claim had been brought at common law, it would have been dealt with by special choice of law rules.[117]

(ii) *Application in infringement cases*

In the situation where there are mandatory rules of the forum in respect of infringement,[118] such rules continue to apply by virtue, *inter alia*, of Section 14(2).[119] In the situation where tort choice of law rules apply in infringement cases,[120] Section 14(2) creates no problem. There is no evidence of special common law tort choice of law rules applying in such cases.[121] On the contrary, there are English,[122] Scots[123] and Australian[124] cases applying the double actionability rule in the context of infringement. Of course, the claim failed in these cases, but that is irrelevant for the present discussion. To require there to have been recovery under the double actionability rule would be to reintroduce the double actionability rule by the back door and drive a coach and horses through Part III. In *Pearce* v *Ove Arup Partnership and Others*,[125] Lloyd J clearly thought that following the repeal of the double actionability rule the English courts would be adjudicating on claims, for example, for the infringement of the French law of privacy. One final point to make is that there are well known subject matter limitations in relation to jurisdiction, at least under the traditional rules, in respect of foreign rights and foreign infringements.[126] But this is a very different matter from whether, assuming that there is jurisdiction, the double actionability rule and exception applied at the choice of law stage, and has no relevance in the present context.[127]

(d) *Exclusion of defamation*

Defamation is excluded from the operation of Part III.[128] The choice of law rules in relation to defamation will be examined in the next chapter,[129]

---

[117] As suggested by Briggs [1995] *LMCLQ* 519 at 522.
[118] See scenario (i) above, p 600.
[119] See the Lord Chancellor in *HL Paper* 36 (1995), Part II at col 27; the Informal Briefing from the draftsman in Written Evidence at p 61.
[120] See scenarios (ii)–(iv) above, pp 600–606.
[121] But see the Informal Briefing by the draftsman, *ibid*, at 64.
[122] See the *Def Lepp* case, n 65, above. See also *Pearce* v *Ove Arup Partnership Ltd and Others* [1997] 2 WLR 779.
[123] See the *James Burrough* case, n 49, above.
[124] See the *Norbert Steinhardt* case, n 31, above.
[125] Above n 96, at 789.   [126] See above, pp 279–306.
[127] See, generally, for confusion over jurisdiction and choice of law above, chapter 6 pp 295–298, 305.
[128] Sections 9(3) and 13.   [129] At pp 673–678.

where tortious and other causes of action that are complementary to infringement will be considered.

(e) Events occurring in the forum

Section 9(6) states that 'For the avoidance of doubt (and without prejudice to the operation of Section 14 below) this Part applies in relation to events occurring in the forum as it applies in relation to events occurring in any other country.' The intention is that the statutory choice of law rules will apply in the situation where a tort has been committed in England, and not just where it has been committed abroad.

Unfortunately, Section 9(6) is hard, if not impossible, to square with Sections 10 and 14(2).[130] Section 10 abolishes the double actionability rule and the exception to that rule. That rule applied in relation to foreign torts. Nothing is said in Section 10 in relation to torts committed in England. It follows that the common law rules that applied to such torts have not been abolished, not unless you can regard Section 9(6) as impliedly extending Section 10 to abolish these common law rules as well. Section 14(2) then provides that Part III does not affect any rules other than those abolished by Section 10. In other words, the statutory tort choice of law rules do not apply to torts committed in England!

Section 9(6) was added to the bill, as originally presented to the Lords, because of doubts as to whether the bill applied to torts committed in England.[131] The problem raised by events occurring in the forum should have been dealt with by an addition to Section 10 to include the abolition of the rules relating to torts committed in England.[132] Unsatisfactory drafting should not be allowed to defeat the intentions of Parliament as expressed in Section 9(6), and the statutory rules should be applied to events occurring in England.

(ii) Abolition of certain common law rules

Section 10 abolishes the double actionability rule and the exception to that rule except for claims for defamation. The double actionability rule created considerable injustice. This lay in the fact that plaintiffs were unable to bring successful actions in England and were forced to go abroad where

---

[130] See Briggs [1995] *LMCLQ* 519 at 520 n 18. But see Dicey and Morris, *Fourth Supplement*, p 227 and Morse, (1996) 45 *ICLQ* 888, 890 for an unconvincing attempt to explain the discrepancy on the basis that the *Red Sea* case cast doubt on the *Metall und Rohstoff* case. But there is no suggestion that the *Red Sea* case introduced the double actionability rule and exception in cases involving torts committed in England, yet it is only that rule and the exception to that rule which are abolished by s 10.

[131] See the Lord Chancellor in *HL Paper* 36 (1995), Official Report of the Committee, 1 March 1995, col 27; Oral Evidence by North in *HL Paper* 36 (1995), at 39.

[132] See comments by North, *ibid*.

a less stringent choice of law rule was likely to apply.[133] This injustice was particularly noticeable in infringement cases. It was impossible to satisfy a double actionability rule when applied to a territorially limited substantive law.

(iii) The general rule

(a) *Section 11*

Section 11 distinguishes between cases where elements of the events constituting the tort occur in a single country (single country torts) and those where they occur in different countries (multi-country torts).

(i) *Single country torts*

Section 11(1) states that:

The general rule is that the applicable law is the law of the country in which the events constituting the tort or delict in question occur.

The phrase 'events constituting the tort' is referring to the acts and consequences that make up the tort, which involves looking at the essential elements of the cause of action. For example, in a case of negligent driving, it is the negligent act of driving and the resulting injury to the victim that are the events constituting the tort. On the other hand, the residence and nationality of the parties are not 'events constituting the tort' for these purposes, and are irrelevant when operating this general rule.[134] In most cases, the sequence of events making up the tort occur in a single country.[135] Where this is not so, Section 11(2) will apply.

(ii) *Multi-country torts*

This sub-section is concerned with the situation where elements of the events constituting the tort in question occur in different countries.[136] For example, a product is negligently manufactured in New York but causes injury in England. Section 11(2) sets out three sub-rules to deal with such cases. It provides that:

(2) Where elements of those events occur in different countries, the applicable law under the general rule is to be taken as being –
   (a) for a cause of action in respect of personal injury caused to an individual or death resulting from personal injury, the law of the country where the individual was when he sustained the injury;

---

[133] See the Oral Evidence of Collins in *HL Paper* 36 (1995), at p 67.
[134] Compare the displacement rule in s 12, discussed below, pp 625–626.
[135] The draftsman has suggested that irrelevant connections with another country ought to be ignored: Informal Briefing in Written Evidence in *HL Paper* 36 (1995), at p 63.
[136] See Law Commission Working Paper No 87 (1984), paras 4.61–4.91.

(b) for a cause of action in respect of damage to property; the law of the country where the property was when it was damaged; and
(c) in any other case, the law of the country in which the most significant element or elements of those events occurred.

The Law Commissions have admitted that, in multi-country tort cases, it is fictitious to say that the tort can be localised, on any objective basis, in any one place. Rather, what they are deciding is what country's law they think should apply in such cases.[137] Sub-rules (a) and (b) provide clear answers. Sub-rule (c) applies in cases of, for example, fraudulent misrepresentation, and leaves it to the courts to work out a solution. The court has to look at the events constituting the tort, ie the acts and consequences that make up the tort excluding such matters as the residence and nationality of the parties.[138] There are numerous cases at common law defining the place of the tort in these other cases,[139] and the courts will no doubt look at these cases for guidance. However, they should not feel constrained to follow blindly these decisions. After all, Parliament, in sub-section 2(a), by adopting a place of injury rule, did not follow the common law solution of looking to the place where the negligent act occurred.[140]

(b) *Application in infringement cases*

(i) *The operation of Section 11*
The events constituting the tort. The most obvious event that goes to make up the tort of infringement is that of the act of infringement. The place of the doing of the act has been described as the very essence of the claim.[141] Proof of damage is not required. Infringement is probably best regarded as a single event tort. It is, though, arguable that there is another event that goes to make up the tort. With registered rights this is the registration of the patent, trademark or design. This may have taken place in a country other than the one where the act of infringement occurred, in which case the elements of the events constituting the tort of infringement occur in different countries and resort must be had to Section 11(2). This would certainly complicate matters. Moreover, in so far as evidence to the Special Public Bill Committee refers to infringement there is an assumption that the crucial event is the act of infringement.[142] Indeed, the draftsman thought that Section 11(2) would not operate in infringement cases.[143]

---
[137] Law Commission Working Paper No 87 (1984), para 4.65.
[138] But compare Beatson, n 16 above, at pp 51 and 59.
[139] See Cheshire and North, pp 556–557.   [140] *Ibid* at 554–555.
[141] The *Def Lepp* case, n 65 above, at 276.
[142] See the Supplementary Memorandum from Beatson *HL Paper* 36 (1995) at p 62.
[143] *HL Paper* 36 (1995), Written Evidence at p 64. See also Annex by Cornish to Beatson's Supplementary Memorandum, n 16 above, at p 64.

The great virtue of a rule based on the application of the law of the country where the act of infringement occurred is that this ties in with the territorial basis of the substantive law of infringement, normally only providing redress in relation to local acts, and meets with the approval of intellectual property lawyers.[144]

Section 11(1) requires you to ascertain where the act of infringement occurred. In most cases, there will be no difficulty in this. Normally, it will be obvious where a typical act of infringement, such as marketing goods, takes place. In the *Badische* case,[145] though, there was a difficulty in working out where a vending had occurred. It was held that this was in Switzerland where the Swiss defendants had delivered goods to the Swiss Post Office, which acted as agent for the buyer and not the vendor, and not in England where the goods were ultimately delivered.[146]

In the situation where there are multiple infringements taking place in different countries, it is submitted that each infringement should be treated as a separate tort, with the result that Section 11(1) will apply in respect of each infringement and two or more laws will be applicable.

A multi-country tort – two situations involving multi-country torts. Despite the comments of the draftsman that Section 11(2) would not operate in infringement cases, it is submitted that there are two situations where this provision will operate in such cases. The first is where the act of infringement itself is spread over more than one country. It has already been seen, in the context of jurisdiction,[147] that cases involving infringement of copyright by satellite broadcasting or infringement of copyright, a patent or trade mark over the internet involve a situation where the elements of the events constituting the tort of infringement can occur in different countries. You have a series of elements (an original broadcast which is received in many other countries, or in internet cases uploading of information in one country and its eventual display on a screen in another country going via a number of other countries) that make up the act of infringement, all of which can take place in different countries.[148]

The second situation is where there is a secondary infringement of copyright by authorising a primary infringement. The secondary infringement by authorisation may occur in country A, whereas the primary infringement

---

[144] See Cornish, n 143 above; Floyd and Purvis, n 89 above, at 111. [145] N 27 above.
[146] This was not a case where the elements of the act of infringement took place in different countries. Accordingly, s 11(2) would not apply. Compare the discussion of multi-country torts below.
[147] See above, pp 157–161.
[148] If you regard these cases as single country torts within s 11(1) you would have to localise the act of infringement. This would produce the same result as reached when you apply s 11(2).

may occur in country B. Here too, the elements of the infringement by authorisation occur in more than one country.[149]

Which sub-rule applies? In both situations, it is necessary to apply the appropriate sub-rule under (a), (b) or (c). There is no personal injury or death and so (a) will not apply. Is there 'a cause of action in respect of damage to property' under (b)? It is submitted that, whilst the cause of action is in respect of property, it is not in respect of *damage* to property. Damage is not part of the cause of action.[150] Moreover, it would be exceedingly difficult to apply (b) in a case involving intellectual property, this would involve identifying what the property was that was damaged and where it was when it was damaged.[151] By a process of elimination then, it is necessary to apply (c). This involves identifying the country in which the most significant element or elements of the events constituting the tort of infringement occurred.

The most significant element. As regards the first situation, in a case of infringement of copyright by satellite broadcasting it is submitted that the most significant element is the original transmission of the broadcast rather than its reception in some other country.[152] The upshot is that the law of the country of origin of the broadcast will apply. If the broadcast originated in England, the English court will have jurisdiction[153] and will then apply its own law, a result which is very convenient for the parties. In contrast, application of the law of the country of reception would involve a number of different governing laws. A further advantage of a country of origin rule is that this law determines which country's rules on the protection of copyright should be applied.[154] A country of origin rule also ties in with the jurisdictional rule under which jurisdiction can be asserted on the basis of the origin of the broadcast in the forum.[155] Finally, it ties in with the definition of broadcasting contained in the Satellite Broadcasting Directive.[156]

In a case of infringement over the internet, it is submitted that the most significant element is the uploading of the information that infringes an intellectual property right rather than its eventual downloading. In effect, this is adopting a country of origin rule. The reasons for preferring this are

---

[149] See the *ABKCO* case, n 37 above. This may involve the application of English law as a mandatory rule, above pp 603–604. But not, it is submitted, where the primary infringement occurred abroad or where it is a foreign copyright.

[150] Even where a tort requires damage as part of the cause of action, there is a problem as to whether non-material damage is encompassed within (b). See the discussion of passing-off, below p 660–662.

[151] See above, pp 164–165.   [152] See above.   [153] See above, pp 157–158.
[154] See above, pp 504–506.   [155] See above, chapters 5 and 6 pp 157–158, 248.
[156] EC Council Directive 93/83/EEC of 27 September 1993 on the co-ordination of certain rules concerning copyright and rights related to copyright applicable to satellite broadcasting and cable retransmission, [1993] OJ L248/15, Article 1(2)(b). The definition is set out in chapter 10, p 505 above.

the same ones as were outlined in the previous paragraph and need not be repeated.

The second situation is rather more easy to deal with. If the plaintiff's claim is based upon an act of secondary infringement, it is submitted that the most significant element of the events constituting the tort is the act of secondary infringement itself, rather than the act of primary infringement which has been authorised. Accordingly, the law of the country where the act of authorisation occurred will be applied.

(ii) *The infringement scenarios*

A UK right is infringed in England. The UK statutory provisions on infringement will apply as mandatory rules of the forum.[157] Accordingly, Section 11 will not apply.

A UK right is infringed abroad. It has been argued above[158] that, in this scenario, the tort choice of law rules should apply and the English statutory provisions on infringement law should not operate as mandatory rules of the forum. The law of the foreign country where the infringement occurred will apply by virtue of Section 11. In practice, there is unlikely to be any actionability under this foreign law. The *Norbert Steinhardt* case,[159] decided at common law, illustrates how countries do not provide protection in relation to foreign rights. In the unlikely event of a foreign country providing for actionability in respect of a UK right, it may be possible, in certain circumstances, to displace this law under Section 12.[160] Recourse may also be had to the public policy exception in Section 14.[161]

A foreign right is infringed in the UK. English law applies by virtue of Section 11. Under English law, there is no actionability in this scenario, no protection is provided in respect of foreign rights. Displacement of the general rule may be possible in certain circumstances,[162] but is unlikely to affect the outcome, since the foreign law is unlikely to provide for actionability following an infringement in England. If it were to do so, recourse would have to be had to public policy to avoid the application of that law.[163]

A foreign right is infringed abroad. In this scenario, under the general rule, the law of the foreign country where the act of infringement occurred will apply. If, to take an example, there is an infringement in France , French law will apply and if it is a French right there will be actionability under French law. Section 11 allows an action in England to be based on this.[164] Infringement is a tort where the abolition of the common law rule of double actionability has had a dramatic effect. Thus, if the *James Burrough*

---

[157] See above, p 600.
[158] At pp 600–604.
[159] N 31 above and text accompanying.
[160] Discussed below, pp 631–632.
[161] Discussed below, p 635.
[162] See below, p 632.
[163] For the difficulties involved in using public policy in this situation see below, p 635.
[164] See Floyd and Purvis [1995] 3 *EIPR* 110 at 114. See also Dicey and Morris, *Fourth Supplement*, pp 231–232.

case[165] were to arise now, applying Section 11(1) the plaintiff would be able to bring a successful claim in Scotland based on actionability under Italian law, an act of infringement having taken place there, in respect of the Italian trademark. Even without the introduction of Part III, it may well have been possible, following the *Red Sea* case,[166] for an English court to have applied Italian law under the common law rules.[167] Nevertheless, Part III does improve the position in that a plaintiff can now rely upon a foreign law by virtue of the general rule in Section 11 rather than having to rely upon a common law exception, the scope of which is uncertain.[168]

It is important to note that what is required is actionability under the foreign applicable law. It does not, though, have to be actionable as an infringement. According to the foreign law, it may be some other tort. This does not matter. Thus, if the *Def Lepp* case,[169] which involved infringements in the Netherlands and Luxembourg, were to arise now the plaintiffs would be able to succeed in an action based on proof that there were legal wrongs under the law of those countries, even though there was no evidence that these wrongs consisted of infringement of copyright.[170] Of course, it is necessary that these wrongs can be characterised by the English courts as being tortious for the purposes of private international law.

Multiple infringements. The *Def Lepp* case involved infringements in two countries. Nonetheless, the plaintiffs would be able to succeed in respect of both infringements, provided that there was actionability under both foreign laws. Section 11 opens up tremendous possibilities for the holders of parallel intellectual property rights. For example, a person who holds a European patent (Italy) and a European patent (Germany), which are infringed in those respective countries, will be able to cover both infringements in one action, based on actionability according to the laws of Italy and Germany. It will be necessary, though, for the plaintiff to plead and prove these foreign laws.[171] Of course, there has to be jurisdiction.[172] If the new opportunities opened up by Part III are not to be thwarted it is vital, as suggested above,[173] that the current unwarranted subject matter limitations, under the traditional rules on jurisdiction, in respect of foreign intellectual property rights and foreign infringements, are dropped.[174]

---

[165] N 49 above.
[166] N 51 above.   [167] See Floyd and Purvis [1995] 3 *EIPR* 110 at 113–114.
[168] See generally North, n 131 above, p 37; the Written Evidence of Fentiman, *HL Paper* 36 (1995), pp 19–24. Eg, would you apply French law if there was an infringement there of a French right but both parties were English? The same problem though arises under s 12 of the 1995 Act, see below, p 633.
[169] N 65 above.
[170] See below, chapter 13, for tortious and other causes of action which are complementary to infringement.
[171] For proof of foreign law, see below, pp 636–637.
[172] See above, pp 143, 161–162, 243, 252.   [173] See p 316.
[174] See, generally, Dicey and Morris, *Fourth Supplement*, p 232.

(iv) Displacement of the general rule

(a) Section 12

(i) *The substantially more appropriate test*

Section 12 allows for the displacement of the general rule and the application of the law of some other country. Section 12(1) states that:

(1) If it appears, in all the circumstances, from a comparison of –
  (a) the significance of the factors which connect a tort or delict with the country whose law would be the applicable law under the general rule; and
  (b) the significance of any factors connecting the tort or delict with another country, that it is substantially more appropriate for the applicable law for determining the issues arising in the case, or any of those issues, to be the law of the other country, the general rule is displaced and the applicable law for determining those issues or that issue (as the case may be) is the law of that other country.

This is a complicated test which contains a number of different elements.

The factors. Section 12 is concerned with factors connecting the tort or delict with a country, in other words connecting factors.[175] Section 12(2) states that 'The factors that may be taken into account as connecting a tort or a delict with a country for the purposes of this section include, in particular, factors relating to the parties, to any of the events which constitute the tort or delict in question or to any of the circumstances or consequences of those events'. This is a very wide provision covering four types of factor. First, factors relating to the parties, such as the residence and domicile of the parties. Secondly, factors relating to any of the events which constitute the tort or delict in question. In other words, factors relating to the acts and consequences that make up the tort, such as the place where a negligent act or consequent injury occurred. These have already been examined when discussing Section 11(1).[176] Thirdly, factors relating to any of the circumstances of the events which constitute the tort or delict in question. Fourthly, factors relating to any of the consequences of the events which constitute the tort or delict in question. An example would be where, following direct economic loss in country A, there is, as a consequence, indirect economic loss in the form of loss of profits in country B. This is not a complete list of factors. They are merely examples of things included. Overall, Section 12 factors appear to go wider than the position

---

[175] Compare Fentiman in Written Evidence *HL Paper* 36 (1995) at p 28, who is a little more hesitant but thinks it is likely that this is what s 12(2) is concerned with.
[176] See above p 619.

at common law where the connection was with the occurrence and the parties.[177]

What is not included? Factors are limited to connecting factors and therefore, presumably, do not include policy considerations, such as the fact that the application of one law gives better recovery to the plaintiff than if another is applied, or that the application of English law is particularly convenient because it avoids problems of pleading and proof of foreign law. This contrasts with the position at common law. In *Johnson v Coventry Churchill International Ltd*,[178] the judge, J W Kay QC, in deciding to apply English law, was influenced by the consideration that this 'would afford protection to English workmen required to work abroad for English companies in countries of whose system of law they can be expected to have little knowledge'.[179] He also took into account the fact that the defendants were not likely to be taken unawares by the consequences of the application of English law since they had taken out insurance against such an eventuality.[180] This looks at the expectations of the parties as to what law might apply.[181] Also, presumably, excluded[182] is the question of whether a country is interested in having its law applied. The Law Commissions rejected the use of this American approach to solving choice of law problems.[183] This too contrasts with the position at common law.[184]

The significance of the factors. The courts are required to compare the *significance* of factors connecting the tort with a particular country. This means attaching weight to factors. The courts are given a completely free hand in this.[185] Policy considerations, provided that they go to the weight of a factor, could be taken into account at this stage. For example, in a multi-plaintiff case, the place of injury is particularly important because if you apply that law it ensures evenhanded treatment for all plaintiffs, regardless of their residence. It would not allow in though the sort of policy considerations taken into account in the *Johnson* case.[186] There, the policy considerations operated in favour of applying a particular law rather than a particular connecting factor. Nor would it allow in a consideration of State interests. Under a governmental interest analysis the fact that a State is interested in having its law applied is a reason in itself for apply-

---

[177] See also Law Com Working Paper No 87 (1984), paras 4.122–4.123, 4.140, which followed the common law in this respect.
[178] [1992] 3 All ER 14.   [179] *Ibid* at 25.   [180] *Ibid*.
[181] Fentiman, n 175 above, at p 28 is less sure that the expectations of the parties are excluded under s 12.
[182] Fentiman, *ibid*, is less sure about this.
[183] Law Com Working Paper No 87 (1984), paras 4.36–4.45.
[184] There is support for this approach in the judgment of Lord Wilberforce in *Chaplin v Boys*, n 63 above, at 391–392; and in the *Johnson* case, n 178 above, at 24–25.
[185] See the Memorandum from Mr Justice Jonathan Parker in Written Evidence in *HL Paper* 36 (1995), at pp 49–50.
[186] N 178 above and text accompanying.

ing that State's law, it does not go to the weight of connections. Moreover, as has been mentioned, the Law Commissions have rejected the adoption of this approach.

The process of attaching weight to factors involves the exercise of a certain amount of commonsense. Thus, for example, the weight to be attached to the fact that a company is incorporated in a country is reduced if this is merely a shell company. The weight to be attached to factors will doubtless depend on the tort in question and on the issue that arises in the case. For example, the residence of the parties is particularly important in a case of personal injury where the issue is that of the heads of damages recoverable, for it is in their residence that each party will have to live with the consequences of the accident.[187] On the other hand, if the issue is that of the standard of care, the place where the tort was committed becomes especially relevant.[188]

The comparison. When operating the displacement rule, the courts are required to make a comparison. They must compare, on the one hand, 'the significance of the factors which connect a tort or delict with the country whose law would be the applicable law under the general rule' and, on the other hand, 'the significance of any factors connecting the tort or delict with another country'. What must be compared are not the factors as such but the significance or weight of the factors. The comparison is straightforward where there are only connections with two countries. It is more complex in cases involving three or more countries, for example the law of country A is applicable under the general rule but there are connections with countries B and C. In such a case, two sets of comparisons will have to be made: the significance of the factors connecting the tort with country A compared with country B; the significance of the factors connecting the tort with country A compared with country C.

Substantially more appropriate. If it appears from this comparison that it is substantially more appropriate for the applicable law for determining the issues arising in the case to be the law of the other country, the general rule is displaced and the law of this other country is applied.

It is uncertain whether the use of this 'substantially more appropriate' criterion for displacement and application of the law of another country allows in the consideration of matters which cannot be considered either as 'factors' or as going to the significance of factors for the purposes of Sections 11 and 12. On a strict reading of Section 12, the answer must be that it does not. A court concludes that it is substantially more appropriate for the applicable law to be that of the other country from a comparison of the significance of factors. Moreover, to allow in policy

---

[187] See *Boys v Chaplin* [1971] AC 356, 378–380 (*per* Lord Hodson), 389–393 (*per* Lord Wilberforce).
[188] Morse, pp 291–294.

considerations, which do not go to the significance of factors, or State interests would make Section 12 even more open-ended and uncertain in operation than it is at the moment. There are, though, unfortunate references to State interests in Dicey and Morris,[189] where it is assumed that these can be considered when operating Section 12. It is true that, in two common law cases, the application of the exception was justified, at least in part, on the basis of whether States were interested in having their law applied.[190] But this was an unorthodox way of looking at things even under the common law rules. More importantly, as far as Part III of the 1995 Act is concerned, the draftsman has said that comparisons with the common law exception are unlikely to be of much use.[191] The consideration of State interests is particularly inappropriate given the rejection of this approach by the Law Commissions.[192]

What is clear, under Section 12, is that the requirement that it is 'substantially' more appropriate that the law of the other country applies is a significant one. It introduces a threshold for the operation of the exception so as to avoid the argument in every case that there should be displacement.[193] This is a lower threshold than that provisionally proposed by the Law Commissions in their Working Paper,[194] and means that there can be displacement even where there is a significant connection with the country whose law would be applicable under the general rule.

The importance of the issue. Section 12 is concerned with where it is substantially more appropriate for the applicable law 'for determining the issues arising in the case, or any of those issues,' to be the law of the other country. When operating Section 12, the issue that arises in the case is clearly regarded as being important. It is submitted that the point at which this bites is when attaching weight to particular factors.[195]

(ii) *Examples where the displacement rule will operate*

The Law Commissions gave three examples of where a displacement rule might operate.[196] First, where the law of the place where the tort is committed is fortuitous, such as where a tort is committed wholly aboard a ship in territorial waters. Secondly, where there is a prior existing relationship between the parties, such as where a group of friends, all from England, take a holiday together in Europe. Thirdly, where every factor in a case other than the place of the accident points to a particular system of

---

[189] *Fourth Supplement*, pp 268–269.
[190] See *Boys* v *Chaplin*, n 63 above, at 392 *per* Lord Wilberforce; *Johnson* v *Coventry Churchill International Ltd* [1992] 3 All ER 14 at 24–25.
[191] HL Paper 36 (1995), Written Evidence, at p 63.
[192] See n 183 above and text accompanying.
[193] See Law Com No 193 (1990), para 3.11.
[194] See Law Com Working Paper No 87 (1984), paras 4.122–123.
[195] See above, p 627. [196] Law Com No 193 (1990), para 3.8.

law. What is noticeable about all these examples is that they present easy cases where the connecting factors are polarised so that the overwhelming weight of factors is with a country other than the one whose law is applicable under the general rule.

The last of these examples is based on *Boys* v *Chaplin*,[197] which was decided under the common law rules. However, the few cases applying the exception at common law are not necessarily a reliable guide to the operation of Section 12. First, the general rule to which the exception operates is very different at common law from the one under Section 11.[198] Second, the exception is different. Section 12(2) allows in connecting factors other than the common law ones relating to the occurrence and the parties, but at the same time, seemingly, excludes policy considerations not going to the weight of factors and also excludes the consideration of State interests. Moreover, the exception under Section 12 operates so as to displace the general rule. This means that the *Red Sea* case, in particular, is inappropriate as a guide because it involves the situation where the country whose law was applicable under the exception was also the country where the tort was committed, whereas under Section 12 the exception only operates to displace the law of the place where the tort was committed.

As a final point to note, it is clear that the displacement rule can lead to the application of the law of a third country, ie one that is neither the forum nor the one in which the events constituting the tort occurred. The *Red Sea* case did not deal with this situation and the position in relation thereto was uncertain under the common law rules.

(iii) *How easy will it be to displace the general rule?*

The 'substantially' more appropriate requirement and the nature of the examples given above suggest that it will not be easy to displace the general rule. The less the connection with the country whose law is applicable under the general rule the easier it must be to establish that it is substantially more appropriate that the law of some other country should apply. If it is a multi-country tort,[199] the connections with the country whose law is applicable under the general rule are necessarily attenuated since one or more of the elements that constitute the tort occurred elsewhere. In this situation, it should be easier to operate the displacement rule. This must be so, even where Section 11(2)(c) operates and the law applicable under the general rule is that of the country in which the most significant element(s) of the events constituting the tort occurred.[200]

---

[197] N 63 above.
[198] See the Informal Briefing by the draftsman in Written Evidence in *HL Paper* 36 (1995), at p 63.
[199] See above, pp 619–620.   [200] Compare Dicey and Morris, *Fourth Supplement*, p 268.

(b) Application in infringement cases

Professor Cornish, an eminent intellectual property lawyer, is hostile to the displacement of the general rule in infringement cases on the ground that to apply the law of a country other than the one in which the act of infringement occurred goes against the territorial basis of intellectual property rights.[201] He has said that 'There should be no scope for displacement under cl [Section] 12'.[202] Nonetheless, infringement is not excluded from the scope of Section 12 and so it is necessary to examine how this provision will operate in such cases.

(i) *The operation of Section 12: the factors and their significance*

The key factors in infringement cases are where the act of infringement occurred (a factor relating to the events which constitute the tort) and where the right is created (a factor either relating to the events which constitute the tort or the circumstances of those events). With patents, trademarks and registered designs, the right is created in the country in which it is registered. With copyright, of course, there is more of a problem in identifying where the right is created.[203] Great weight should be attached to the factor of where the act of infringement occurred because it fits in with the territorial principle underlying the substantive law of infringement. Similarly, great weight should be attached to the creation of the right factor: this fits in with the territorial principle underlying the substantive law in that only local rights are protected; if it is a registered right it will be administered in that country;[204] it also means that the same law would govern the issue of infringement of the right as governs the issue of creation.

A further important factor is where the property is situated. This acknowledges that infringement is concerned with the protection of property rights. However, this property, seemingly, will be situated in the same country as that where the right was created.[205]

Another significant factor is that an injunction is sought restraining acts of infringement in a particular country.[206] This latter factor does not appear to come within the four types of factor mentioned in Section 12(2), but this does not set out a complete list of factors.

---

[201] See Cornish in Annex to the Supplementary Memorandum from Beatson in *HL Paper* 36 (1995), at p 64. The draftsman said that he could see no room for the operation of section 12 in infringement cases, see his Informal Briefing in Written Evidence in *HL Paper* 36 (1995), at p 64.

[202] N 201 above, at p 64.   [203] See above, pp 499–501.

[204] See Floyd and Purvis, n 167 above, at p 114. It is also argued there that application of the law of the country of creation would accord with the expectations of the parties, but it is doubtful whether these can be considered under s 12, see above, p 626.

[205] See above, pp 489–496.

[206] See Dyer, (1988) IV *Hague Recueil* 373, 436–439—in relation to unfair competition.

Whilst the residence/domicile of the parties is a factor, it is submitted that it does not have the weight in infringement cases that it has in cases of personal injury.[207] Moreover, in policy terms, there is a great advantage in downgrading the significance to be attached to the residence/domicile of the parties in infringement cases. Such cases are often multi-defendant, with the defendants coming from different countries. The Law Commissions have recommended that the applicable law should be ascertained separately for each pair of opponents and that this 'almost certainly represents the present law'.[208] The application of any approach that puts emphasis on the residence/domicile of the parties is likely to lead to a different governing law for different pairs of opponents, to an unjustifiable lack of evenhandedness in the treatment of the parties.[209]

Another factor of lesser weight is that there is a parallel cause of action, for example for passing-off in a specified country. This is part of the circumstances of the events constituting the tort, which should be regarded as of less weight than the events themselves.

Having examined the factors, and their weight, in infringement cases it is possible to establish whether the law applicable under the general rule can be displaced in such cases.

(ii) *The infringement scenarios*

A UK right is infringed in England. The UK statutory provisions on infringement will apply as mandatory rules of the forum.[210] Accordingly, Section 12 will not apply.[211]

A UK right is infringed abroad. If, for example, a UK trade mark is infringed in Germany, German law will apply under the general rule. A choice of law problem will arise in the unlikely event that Germany provides for recovery in this situation. Can German law be displaced by the application of English law? If all the other factors point to England it is arguable that it can. It looks to be similar to the third of the examples given by the Law Commissions. It is not exactly the same, though. This third example is based on *Boys* v *Chaplin*,[212] which involved one British serviceman injuring another British serviceman in a road accident in Malta. The place of injury was not fortuitous because both parties were stationed in Malta but other crucial factors pointed towards the English system of law. In contrast, in an infringement case, it is arguable, for the reasons outlined above,[213] that the weight to be given to the act of infringement factor should be considerably greater than that to be given to the place of the tort factor in a personal injury case, and the weight to be given to the

---

[207] See Floyd and Purvis, n 167 above.
[208] Law Com No 193 (1990), para 3.53.
[209] See Fawcett (1995) 44 *ICLQ* 744 at 762–766.
[210] See above, p 600.
[211] See Dicey and Morris, *Fourth Supplement*, p 274; Beatson, n 16 above, p 62.
[212] N 63 above.
[213] At p 630.

residence/domicile of the parties should be considerably less in infringement cases than in personal injury ones. Admittedly, it is a UK right that has been infringed and this is an important factor. Nonetheless, on balance it is doubtful whether, in the light of the weight to be given to the factors, it can be said that it is 'substantially' more appropriate for English law to displace that of Germany. Of course, an English court may be tempted to apply Section 12 because of a reluctance to apply a foreign law (in the above example, German law) where it defies internationally accepted views on the territorial scope of intellectual property rights by giving protection to foreign rights. But, if that is the prime concern, it would be better to apply the public policy exception[214] than to strain to bring the case within Section 12.

A foreign right is infringed in England. If, for example, an Italian right is infringed in England, then English law will apply under the general rule. In the unlikely event of Italian law providing redress in this situation, can English law be displaced by Italian law? When it comes to the factors and their weighting, the analysis is exactly the same as that encountered in the second scenario above. In particular, great weight must be given to the fact that the right was infringed in England. The outcome must be the same too. Accordingly, it must be doubtful whether the displacement rule can operate in this scenario. Moreover, there will be a reluctance to apply the exception because it will lead to the application of a foreign law (in the above example, Italian law) which defies internationally accepted views on the territorial scope of intellectual property rights by providing redress in respect of a foreign infringement. However, the answer to this particular concern is the same as in the second scenario above, and the public policy exception should be resorted to, in the very unlikely event of this becoming necessary.

There is, though, one very specialised and unusual situation, technically coming within (this third scenario), where Section 12 should operate. This is the mirror image of the *ABKCO* case.[215] There is the authorisation in England of an act of infringement in Denmark of a Danish copyright. The authorisation can constitute a secondary infringement and, if this is the infringement relied upon by the plaintiff, English law will apply under the general rule. There is no actionability under English law. Let us assume that there is actionability under Danish law.[216] The displacement rule should operate and Danish law should apply. The connection with England is not great; although there is an act of infringement in England, this is of a technical nature and the authorisation has to be of some other infringement, such as by making copies. The connections with Denmark

---

[214] Discussed below, p 635.   [215] N 37 above, discussed above, pp 603–604.
[216] As there is under English law, see above, p 604.

are very strong in that it is a Danish right and there is a primary act of infringement there. There will be no reluctance to apply Danish law, such as could lead to invoking the public policy doctrine, because this is only doing what English law would do in the same circumstances.[217]

A foreign right is infringed abroad. If, for example, a French patent is infringed in France, French law will apply under the general rule. With the two key factors pointing to France, it is submitted that it will not be possible to displace the application of French law. Even if all the other factors pointed to one other country, it would not be possible to say that it is 'substantially' more appropriate for that other law to apply. It is a very different situation from the examples given by the Law Commissions of when the displacement rule will operate. There is no fortuitous place of the tort, no prior existing relationship between the parties and it cannot be said that all the connections are with a country other than the one where the tort was committed.

If there are multiple infringements occurring in different countries, under the general rule there are different applicable laws for each infringement. The displacement rule requires you to look separately at each applicable law and see if it is substantially more appropriate for the law of another country to be applied. What significance is to be given to the fact that there has been an infringement in another country? For example, there has been an infringement in France, but also one in Germany. If the plaintiff relies on the infringement in France, can the defendant displace this by invoking the infringement in Germany factor? It is submitted that the infringement in Germany has little if any relevance to a claim based on an infringement in France and should be given very little, if any, weight.

(v) Savings

Section 14 introduces five savings or exceptions to the rules set out in Part III. The term 'savings' can also refer to preserving something. Section 14 also does this since these five savings are existing exceptions to tort choice of law rules. One of these savings is set out in Section 14(2), which is concerned with the scope of Part III and has already been examined.[218] The remaining four are concerned with: public policy; penal, revenue or other public law; rules of evidence, pleading or practice or procedure; and mandatory rules.

---

[217] See the *ABKCO* case, n 37 above. [218] See above, pp 616–617.

(a) Public Policy

(i) The rule

Section 14(3) states that:

nothing in this Part –
  (a) authorises the application of the law of a country outside the forum as the applicable law for determining issues arising in any claim in so far as to do so –
    (i) would conflict with principles of public policy; ...

It is a well established principle of English private international law that our courts will not apply a foreign law when this would be inconsistent with the fundamental public policy of English law.[219] This principle is exercised sparingly. It is not enough to show that we do things differently in England, the courts 'do not close their doors unless help would violate some fundamental principle of justice, some prevalent conception of good morals, some deep- rooted tradition of the common weal'.[220]

There are numerous examples of the operation of the doctrine in choice of law cases in contract, but there is a dearth of authority in England in relation to torts. The reason for this is not hard to find. The requirement under the common law rules of actionability under English law meant that the English courts seldom got as far as applying a foreign law. With the introduction of Part III, this will change, and doubtless case law will develop on the operation of the doctrine of public policy in the context of tort choice of law.

The Law Commissions[221] envisage that the normal restrictive view of public policy will apply in relation to Part III, as do some of the most eminent commentators,[222] and there is nothing in the wording of Section 14(3)(a)(i) to suggest that some special and different meaning is intended.[223] Any such move would create great uncertainty and would defeat the purpose of Part III. Abolition of the requirement of actionability by English law means that the English courts will not infrequently be

---

[219] See Dicey and Morris, pp 88–96; Cheshire and North, pp 128–137.
[220] *Loucks v Standard Oil Co of New York* 224 NY 99 at 111 (1918) *per* Cardozo J.
[221] Law Com No 193 (1990), para 3.55.
[222] See Dicey and Morris, *Fourth Supplement*, pp 271–272; the Oral Evidence of North in *HL Paper* 36 (1995), at p 43; Collins, *ibid*, at p 72. See also the Lord Chancellor, *ibid*, at p 5. Compare Briggs [1995] *LMCLQ* 519 at 525; Beatson, n 16 above, at p 60; Reed, [1996] *Civil Justice Quarterly* 305, 314–320.
[223] Compare Briggs, *ibid*, who favours a wide view of public policy in relation to Part III and points to the absence of the word 'manifestly' preceding public policy. This word is found in private international law statutes which incorporate international conventions and is there to tell Continental countries, which have a wider view of public policy, to adopt a restrictive view. The word adds nothing as far as English law is concerned, and its omission means nothing.

faced with causes of action that are unknown to English law, if these are routinely struck out as being against public policy it would be as if the common law rules had never been abolished. To take a practical example, it would be very wrong for an English court when faced with a claim for invasion of privacy based on French law to say that the application of such a law is against England's distinctive public policy. We have no such cause of action under English law but there is nothing so extreme or objectionable about this French law as to justify not applying it.[224] Moreover, there is authority in a different context to the effect that public policy cannot be invoked simply on the basis that the foreign cause of action is unknown in England.[225]

(ii) *Application in infringement cases*

There is one situation where it has been suggested above[226] that the application of the foreign law of infringement would be against public policy. This is the, perhaps, theoretical situation where a UK right is infringed abroad (the second scenario) and, unusually, that law provides redress in respect of a foreign (ie English) right. Such a foreign law not only goes against what is, arguably, a fundamental concept of English law but also goes against internationally accepted views on the territorial scope of intellectual property rights. The use of the public policy exception can be justified by analogy with 'the principle of public policy that the courts should give effect to clearly established rules of international law'.[227]

Another situation which would raise the public policy issue is that where a foreign right is infringed in England (the third scenario), and the foreign law is applied under the exception (which is unlikely) and that law provides for actionability even though the infringement occurred abroad (ie in England). The latter is possible, although not likely to happen often. If this were to happen though it is arguable that the public policy exception should operate for the same reasons as given in the previous situation. However, it has to be remembered that an English court, in the *ABKCO* case,[228] provided redress under English law, following a secondary infringement committed abroad. Moreover, under the Copyright Act 1956, infringements of extended copyrights committed abroad were actionable in the UK.[229] In the light of this, it could be said that there is no fundamental provision of English law that is breached by the application of foreign law, and, accordingly, the public policy exception should not operate.

[224] See the oral evidence of Collins in *HL Paper* 36 (1995) at 72.
[225] See *Phrantzes* v *Argenti* [1960] 2 QB 19.   [226] See above, p 623.
[227] Dicey and Morris, p 93 , based on *Re Helbert Wagg & Co Ltd* [1956] Ch 323, 349; *Oppenheimer* v *Cattermole* [1976] AC 249, 278.
[228] N 37 above, discussed at pp 603–604, above.
[229] Sections 1(2) and 31(4); see Arnold, n 86 above, at 262 note 85.

(b) *Penal, revenue or other public law*

Section 14(3)(a)(ii) provides a saving in relation to the application of the law of a country where this 'would give effect to such a penal, revenue or other public law as would not otherwise be enforceable under the law of the forum'. This saving appears to have no particular relevance in infringement cases and so nothing more needs to be said in relation to it.

(c) *Rules of evidence, pleading or practice, or procedure*

Section 14(3) states that:

... nothing in this Part –
   (b) affects any rules of evidence, pleading or practice or authorises questions of procedure in any proceedings to be determined otherwise than in accordance with the law of the forum.

The Law Commissions' Draft Bill merely saved questions of procedure.[230] Part III though also saves rules of evidence, pleading or practice. This addition involves an element of overlap in that one of the well known examples of procedural rules is rules of evidence.

(i) *Evidence, pleading or practice*

Evidence covers the way in which the truth of facts, acts and documents is ascertained; such matters as whether a witness is competent and whether a matter needs to be proved by writing.[231] The addition of the reference to pleading or practice was designed to ensure that the topic of proof of foreign law was covered.[232] It is not entirely clear whether this is covered anyway under the evidence saving. Certainly, aspects of proof of foreign law can be regarded as coming within the topic of evidence and thus within procedure.

Proof of foreign law. There is a well established rule that unless a foreign law is pleaded by a party who wishes to rely on it, it is assumed that it is the same as English law.[233] The onus of proving that it is different lies upon the party who pleads the difference. This means, for example, that a successful negligence action can be brought, based on English domestic law, even though the accident happened in France.[234] However, in the area of passing-off, the courts have not been prepared to grant an injunction preventing acts abroad in the absence of proof as to the local law.[235]

---

[230] Law Com No 193 (1990), Appendix A clause 4(4).
[231] See Cheshire and North, pp 81–85. Presumptions and burden of proof raise particular difficulties, *ibid* at pp 84–85.
[232] *Ibid*, chapter 7.   [233] See Cheshire and North, p 107, and, generally, chapter 7.
[234] See *Schneider* v *Eisovitch* [1960] 2 QB 430.
[235] See *Alfred Dunhill Ltd and Another* v *Sunoptic SA and Another* [1979] FSR 337; discussed below, pp 662–663.

The argument that this was unnecessary because of the presumption that English law was the same as foreign law was rejected in that particular context.

It appears that the same approach is to be applied in infringement cases as has been applied in relation to passing-off. In *International Business Machines Corpn v Phoenix International (Computers) Ltd*,[236] an action for trade mark infringement and passing-off was based on sales in England, Portugal and Denmark. No particulars of the law of the latter two countries was given and Ferris J treated the plaintiff's case as depending solely on a sale effected in England.[237] The question of whether the presumption applies in infringement cases was not discussed. This is not surprising since the question appears to be purely academic. A plaintiff who wishes to obtain an injunction preventing acts of infringement abroad will not wish to rely on English law. The reason for this is obvious: normally, there is no actionability under English law in respect of foreign acts of infringement. The plaintiff will need to rely on actionability under a foreign law and will have to plead and prove this law. There may be a practical problem in adducing evidence of this foreign law if the foreign State has little infringement litigation or has only recently become a party to one of the intellectual property conventions; for example, Portugal, Ireland and Finland have only recently joined the European Patent Convention.[238] In a case of multiple infringements in a number of different foreign countries, proving foreign law will be expensive and inconvenient for the plaintiff, but there does not appear to be any alternative to this, not unless a radical solution is adopted whereby once one foreign law is proved it is assumed that the other foreign laws are the same as the one that has been proven.

(ii) *Procedure*

Section 14(3)(b) preserves the common law rule that matters relating to procedure are governed exclusively by the law of the forum.[239] The Law Commissions gave as examples of procedural matters: the measure of damages (as opposed to the heads of damages); rules of evidence; methods of enforcement; and, generally, the mode of trial and the machinery of justice.[240] The first example is of particular importance in tort choice of law cases and something more needs to be said in relation to this.

The measure of damages. The fact that the measure or assessment of damages in tort has been classified as one of procedure, and, accordingly, English law as the law of the forum will apply to determine this issue,[241]

---

[236] [1994] RPC 251.   [237] *Ibid*, at 266.
[238] See O'Sullivan, [1996] 12 *EIPR* 654, 661.
[239] See, generally, Cheshire and North, chapter 6.
[240] Law Commission Working Paper No 87 (1984) para 4.4.
[241] *Boys v Chaplin* [1971] AC 356 at 378–379, 382–383, 392–393, 394.

creates a practical problem where an action is based on a foreign cause of action that is unknown under English law. For example, how is an English court, applying the law of the forum, going to asses damages for invasion of privacy when there is no such cause of action under English law? The Law Commissions did not think that express guidance need be given on how damages are to be assessed in such cases. They thought that this problem would arise infrequently and the most satisfactory way of dealing with it was to leave the courts to resolve the question on the facts of the dispute before it.[242] In infringement cases, there is no such practical problem since this is a well known cause of action in England and the English courts are used to assessing damages in purely domestic cases of infringement.

(d) Mandatory rules

Section 14(4) states that:

(4) This Part has effect without prejudice to the operation of any rule of law which either has effect notwithstanding the rules of private international law applicable in the particular circumstances or modifies the rules of private international law that would otherwise be so applicable.

(i) *Mandatory rules of the forum*

This topic has already been discussed[243] and nothing more needs to be said in relation to it.

(ii) *Foreign mandatory rules*

Does Section 14(4) cover foreign mandatory rules? The Law Commissions, in their draft bill, made it clear that the saving only referred to the mandatory rules of the forum.[244] Unfortunately, different, and more ambiguous,[245] wording was adopted in the bill that went before Parliament. This has led to the suggestion that there is the possibility of the courts applying the mandatory rules of a foreign country, other than the one whose law is applicable under Sections 11 or 12.[246] The draftsman was aware of this criticism of ambiguity[247] and his failure to clearly restrict the provision to mandatory rules of the forum might suggest an intention to encompass foreign mandatory rules.

---

[242] Law Com No 193 (1990), para 3.38.　　[243] See above, pp 598–606.
[244] Clause 4(3), set out in Law Com No 193 (1990), Appendix A.
[245] See McClean in Written Evidence in *HL Paper* 36 (1995), at 43.
[246] See Rodger in the annotations to the Private International Law (Miscellaneous Provisions) Act 1995 in Current Law Statutes, 42–24.
[247] See the Informal Briefing by the draftsman in Written Evidence in *HL Paper* 36 (1995), at p 64.

Nonetheless, it is submitted that it is unlikely that Parliament intended to introduce a saving in respect of foreign mandatory rules.

First, the Lord Chancellor explained to the Lords that this provision was designed to save the effect of certain mandatory *domestic* rules, as a safeguard for defendants against the application of foreign law.[248]

Secondly, if there had been an intention to introduce a foreign mandatory rules exception, this would surely have specified which country's mandatory rules are to be applied.[249] Is it any country with which the situation has a close connection?[250] Is it the country in which the tortious act took place?[251] Do foreign mandatory have to be applied or is there an element of discretion? If foreign mandatory rules are to be applied under Section 14(4), the courts would have the unenviable task of having to fill in these gaps.

Thirdly, Parliament has specified that Article 7(1) of the Rome Convention of 1980, allowing the application of the mandatory rules of a country other than the one whose law governs the contract, shall not have the force of law in the United Kingdom.[252] Given this attitude towards foreign mandatory rules in contract, it seems unlikely that a different attitude would have been adopted in tort.

Fourthly, unlike in contract,[253] there was no prior common law exception involving application of foreign mandatory rules in tort.

Fifthly, all the other savings in Section 14, including that in respect of the mandatory rules of the forum, preserve existing exceptions, whereas with foreign mandatory rules, Section 14 would be doing something very different: it would be introducing a new exception.

In conclusion, the better view is that Section 14(4) was not intended to introduce a foreign mandatory rules exception and, accordingly, it should not be construed as allowing this.[254]

Application in infringement cases. If there is a saving in respect of foreign mandatory rules, it is possible to think of at least one situation where it could come into play. This is the mirror image of the *ABKCO* case.[255] If a Danish copyright has been infringed in Denmark, this is a situation where the Danish courts may well decide that local law should apply as a mandatory rule, even though there has been an act of secondary infringement in

---

[248] Hansard (HL) 6 December 1994, 833.

[249] Compare Article 7(1) of the Rome Convention, set out in Schedule 1 to the Contracts (Applicable Law) Act 1990. But see Morse, n 109 above, at 901.

[250] See Article 7(1) of the Rome Convention.

[251] See Rodger, above, n 246.   [252] Contracts (Applicable Law) Act 1990, s 2(2).

[253] See the discussion of illegality by the foreign place of performance and of public policy in Cheshire and North, pp 504, 519–520.

[254] See Dicey and Morris, *Fourth Supplement*, p 273. But compare Morse, n 109 above, at 901 who is slightly more hesitant, hoping that it will be confined to mandatory rules of the forum 'so far as possible'.

[255] See above, p 632.

England by way of authorisation of the primary infringement in Denmark. After all, this is what an English court did in the *ABKCO* case[256] itself. If trial takes place in England, the English court, rather than applying English law under Section 11, may wish to give effect to the Danish law. A foreign mandatory rules exception is one way of achieving this. But another more conventional way of achieving the same object in this particular situation is, as suggested above,[257] to apply Danish law under the displacement rule.

4. DEFENCES

(a) A CONTRACTUAL DEFENCE

(i) The nature of the problem

Under English law, an infringement requires an act to be done without consent. If there is a licensing agreement between the parties this will constitute a defence to the infringement action. A question may arise, though, as to the validity of this agreement, and there may be a choice of law problem to be solved. This question arises in the context of a contractual defence to a tort action and thus involves a mixture of tort and contract, the respective choice of law rules of which are very different.[258] Should the question of the validity of the licensing agreement simply be treated as a contractual problem, to be determined by the law applicable to the contract, or as a tortious problem to be determined by the law applicable to the tort? The problem is essentially one of characterisation.

(ii) The solution

(a) *General discussion*

The problem of contractual defences to tort claims is one of the most intractable in private international law and one in respect of which there is very little authority.[259] The Law Commissions were unable to agree on the respective roles of contract and tort in this area and were unable to recommend legislative intervention.[260] Accordingly, Part III is silent on this matter. However, the disagreement was over the issue of whether the effect of a contractual defence, valid under its governing law, should be determined by the law governing the contract or by the applicable law in tort. There appears to have been agreement that the validity of a contrac-

---

[256] See above, pp 603–604.   [257] See above, p 632.   [258] For contract see chapter 11.
[259] But see *Sayers* v *International Drilling Co NV* [1971] 1 WLR 1176; *Brodin* v *A/R Seljan* 1973 SC 213.
[260] See Law Com No 193 (1990), paras 3.49–3.50.

tual term purporting to provide a defence in tort should be decided by the law governing the contract.

But which country's rules on the law governing the contract should be applied? It would be possible to reflect the tortious aspect of the problem by saying that it is the country whose law is applicable in tort whose rules on the law governing the contract should be applied.[261] The Law Commissions discussed this issue in their Working Paper.[262] They reached the provisional conclusion that, on grounds of simplicity and convenience, the forum's contract choice of law rules should be applied, not those of the country whose law is applicable in tort. In so far as this specific issue was mentioned in the Law Commissions' Report, this provisional recommendation seems to have been regarded as being uncontroversial. Moreover, to decide otherwise would involve applying the private international law rules of another country, ie *renvoi*. But this is expressly prohibited by Section 9(5) which states that 'The applicable law to be used for determining the issues arising in a claim shall exclude any choice of law rules forming part of the law of the country or countries concerned'.

(b) *Application in infringement cases*

In infringement cases, the issue that will arise will be as to the validity of the licensing agreement, not as to the effect of a contractual defence. It is submitted that, in the light of the above discussion, the English courts should apply the English rules on the law applicable to the contract to determine this issue of validity.[263] This is what happens in a straight forward contract action: it would be unnecessarily complicated to apply a different rule just because the same issue arises in the context of a defence to an infringement action.

This, in effect, was the approach adopted by the Court of Appeal in *Chiron Corpn and Others* v *Organon Teknika Ltd and Others (No 2)*,[264] although, unfortunately, there was no discussion of the nature of the problem. The defendants pleaded Section 44(3) of the Patents Act 1977 as a defence to an infringement action. This provides a defence where there is a contract relating to the patent containing a term or condition which has been rendered void under Section 44(1) on the basis that the patentee has abused his monopoly of power. As has already been seen,[265] it was held that Section 44(1) applies regardless of whether English law governs the contract. For the present purpose, what is important is that the question of the applicable law in respect of this contractual defence to an infringement

---

[261] See North (1977) 26 *ICLQ* 914 at 927.
[262] Law Commission Working Paper No 87 (1984), paras 6.51–6.53, 2.89–2.101.
[263] See above, chapter 11.
[264] [1993] FSR 567.   [265] See above, pp 585, 599.

action was treated as a contractual matter, to which English rules on the law governing the contract applied.

(b) INVALIDITY OF THE RIGHT

(i) **The nature of the problem**

The defence may be raised that the right which has allegedly been infringed is invalid. Indeed, an infringement action presupposes that there is a valid right. The issue of validity of an intellectual property right, of course, can arise in its own right and not as a defence and, as has been seen,[266] the choice of law rules in relation to validity are very different from those in relation to tort. When invalidity arises as a defence to an infringement action there is a characterisation problem analogous to that examined above where there is a contractual defence. Is the issue basically one of creation of the right, to be determined by the law applicable to the creation of the right, or is it basically a problem of infringement to be determined by the law applicable to the tort? To take a practical example, if the right is created in France but infringed in Italy does the law of France (applicable under the creation rules) or of Italy (applicable under the tort rules) determine the validity of the right?

(ii) **The solution**

It is submitted that the issue of validity of a right when raised as a defence should be determined by the law applicable to the creation of the right and not by the law applicable to the tort. The arguments in favour of this solution are as follows. First, this is analogous to the position in respect of contractual defences. Secondly, there is a strong link between validity and the creation of the right which suggests that the same choice of law rule should apply to both.[267] Thirdly, it makes no sense to apply a different law to validity, depending on whether this issue arises independently or in the context of infringement.[268] This still leaves the problem of which country's rules on the law applicable to creation are to be applied, those of the forum or those of the country whose law is applicable under the tort choice of law rules? Again by analogy with the position in relation to contractual defences, it is submitted that the forum should apply its own rules on the law applicable to creation. The likelihood is that these are not likely to be any different from any other country's rules.

---

[266] See above, pp 508–509, 521–522.
[267] See above, chapter 10 pp 508–509, 521–522.   [268] See above, p 509.

IV
REFORM

1. Criticism of the Existing Law

The existing English law, which has no special rules to deal with the law applicable to infringement, is open to criticism. The major problem encountered when it comes to applying the rules of general application in tort cases to the tort of infringement is that of uncertainty.

First, it is unclear when the English statutory provisions on intellectual property will operate as mandatory rules of the forum. With most other torts, there is no question of English substantive law applying as mandatory rules of the forum.

Secondly, there is uncertainty over the operation of the tort choice of law rules contained in Part III of the 1995 Act in infringement cases. Some of this stems from the unsatisfactory drafting of the Act. Moreover, a general criticism of the statutory tort choice of law rules is that when you come to apply them to anything other than a simple case of negligent driving there is always uncertainty. This is particularly so when applied to infringement cases. There is uncertainty over whether infringement is to be characterised as tortious for the purpose of Part III. What are the events constituting the tort of infringement for the purpose of Section 11? Will there be cases of multi-country infringement under this section? If so, what law will apply? Part III is particularly unclear where there is a multi-country tort and the cause of action is other than in respect of personal injury, death or damage to property. What is the most significant element or elements of the events constituting the infringement, and where does it occur? This is particularly difficult in cases of infringement over the internet or by satellite broadcasting. When will the displacement rule under Section 12 operate in infringement cases? What are the relevant factors in such cases when operating the displacement rule, and what weight should be given to these factors? When will the public policy exception operate in infringement cases? There are few infringement cases decided under the common law tort choice of law rules which can be used as a guide to solving these questions.

Thirdly, there is uncertainty over the position where a contractual defence or invalidity of the right is raised as a defence to infringement. Part III says nothing about contractual defences to tort claims.

2. Alternative Solutions From Abroad

Many countries have adopted special tort choice of law rules for particular torts, such as products liability; traffic accidents; and, most interestingly in the present context, unfair competition.[269] However, this has not happened in infringement cases, and it appears to be the almost universal practice that, in such cases, the tort rules of general application are applied.[270] The Law Commissions were well aware of these foreign tort choice of law rules and approaches, but did not choose to adopt any of them. Indeed, the Law Commissions specifically rejected adoption of the American governmental interest analysis approach as a model for reform of the English and Scottish tort choice of law rules.[271]

3. Reform of the Tort Choice of Law Rules

It has been seen that, in infringement cases, the application of the tort choice of law rules in Part III of the 1995 Act does not work well. It has also been seen that the uncertainty in the law is, in part, due to unsatisfactory drafting of Part III. One option for reform that has to be considered therefore is a redraft of this Act. This could give some guidance on the criteria for characterisation, redraft or abolish Section 14(2), get rid of the inconsistencies between sections that cause real difficulty where events occur in the forum, and make it clear that Section 14(4) only provides a saving for mandatory rules of the forum. Welcome as such reforms would be, not just in infringement cases but in all tort cases, they would not get rid of all the uncertainty that arises in infringement cases. There would still be uncertainty over the operation of the central provisions in Sections 11 and 12. But no redraft of these provisions could provide certainty in relation to every tort and every law fact situation coming before the courts. The only way to provide certainty in relation to the operation of these sections would be to have special rules for special torts, along the lines of the US Restatement, Second, Conflict of Laws.[272] The only special rules coming within the scope of this book, and which, therefore, fall to be discussed, are those relating to infringement and, in the next chapter, complementary torts and other causes of action.

4. Special Rules as to the Applicable Law in Infringement Cases

The introduction of special rules for infringement cases would get rid of the present uncertainty in the law. Nonetheless, this would be a very

---

[269] See below, pp 707–713.
[270] For a comparative survey of tort choice of law rules see *HL Paper* 36 (1995) pp 19–22, and Law Com Working Paper No 87 (1984), Appendix. The Swiss Private International Law Statute of 1987 contains a special chapter on Intellectual Property (chapter 8). Article 110(2), within this chapter, provides that 'As to claims arising from a tortious act, the parties may always agree, after the injurious event, to the application of the law of the forum'.
[271] N 183 above.   [272] Section 145 *et seq*.

different approach from the one applied under the present English law. The Law Commissions considered having special tort choice of law rules for particular torts, including economic torts, but were opposed to this.[273] If such rules were to be introduced, a preliminary question arises of whether these rules should be independent rules, or should operate within the framework of existing rules.

(a) INDEPENDENT RULES OR WITHIN THE FRAMEWORK OF EXISTING RULES?

It would be possible to adopt independent rules for infringement cases, ie rules independent of the existing tort choice of law rules set out in Part III of the 1995 Act. Part III would not apply in infringement cases. There would have to be a new statute dealing with the applicable law in infringement cases, or a new Part added to the 1995 Act. This would be a very radical approach to adopt. Moreover, there are no established precedents which could be used for introducing such rules. There is no Hague Convention on private international law dealing with the law applicable to infringement.[274] Neither are there any national sets of rules abroad which could be adopted.

Alternatively, special rules could be adopted within the framework of the existing tort choice of law rules in Part III. It would be possible to add sub-sections to Sections 11 and 12 of the 1995 Act, clarifying at least some of the present uncertainty in infringement cases. This would be a much less radical approach to adopt and would have the merit of a familiar framework.

(b) POLICY CONSIDERATIONS WHEN DECIDING UPON THE RULES

It is suggested that the following four policy considerations should be borne in mind when determining the content of special rules for infringement cases. First, for reasons of familiarity it is best that they should operate within the framework of existing statutory tort choice of law rules. Secondly, they need to be certain. Thirdly, they need to be compatible, as far as possible, with the jurisdiction rules in infringement cases. Fourthly, they should also be consistent with the tort choice of law rules for the complementary torts, such as unfair competition, examined in the next chapter. This last consideration is particularly important since it is common to

---

[273] Law Commission Working Paper No 87 (1984), paras 5.1–5.70.
[274] See, though, Ginsberg, (1995) 42 *Journal of the Copyright Society of the USA* 318, 337–338 who proposes a combination of choice of law rules for cases of infringement of copyright taking place in a number of countries. This suggestion is influenced by the Hague Products Liability Convention.

have claims based on parallel causes of action, for example trademark infringement and passing-off, and it is convenient if the choice of law rules are such that they lead to the result that the same State's substantive law applies for each cause of action. The fact that these parallel causes of action involve complementary torts justifies the application of the same choice of law rules.[275]

(c) THE SUGGESTED RULES

(i) The special general rule

There should be a special general rule for infringement cases. Section 11 should provide specifically that, in such cases, the law of the country where the act of infringement has been committed or threatened should be applied. There would be no separate provision for multi-country infringement cases. This special provision would make it clear that infringement is to be characterised as a tort for the purpose of Section 11, as well as getting rid of some of the present uncertainty over the operation of that section in infringement cases. There would still be a problem of localising the place where the act of infringement occurred, which is particularly difficult in cases of infringement by satellite broadcasting or over the internet. But this problem has already been encountered in the context of jurisdiction and the same solutions[276] could be applied in the choice of law context. This is one of the great strengths of an act of infringement choice of law rule. It is compatible, as far as possible, with the infringement jurisdiction rules; an English court, that has jurisdiction on the basis of an act of infringement committed or threatened in England, would apply its own law. The proposed rule is also consistent with the tort choice of law rules for complementary causes of action.[277]

The same issue arises in the context of choice of law as arose in jurisdiction cases of whether it is appropriate to base conflict of laws rules on territorial connections in cases of infringement over the internet. Some American writers, when discussing choice of law, have argued that this is not appropriate.[278] Instead, what has been suggested is a whole new approach using Admiralty laws or the *lex mercatoria* or choice of law in Antarctica as the model,[279] or that 'principles of preference' should be developed.[280] However, it has been demonstrated, in the context of jurisdiction, that there are territorial connections in internet cases, and that in such cases it is still appropriate to use a rule which looks to the place

---

[275] Troller, *International Encyclopaedia of Comparative Law* Vol III, chapter 34–14.
[276] See above, pp 236–237, 315–316.   [277] See below, pp 662, 684.
[278] See Burnstein, (1996) 29 *Vanderbilt Journal of Transnational Law* 75; Geller, (1996) 20 *Columbia-VLA Journal of Law and the Arts* 571.
[279] Burnstein, n 278 above.   [280] See Geller, n 278 above.

where the act of infringement occurred, despite the difficulty in localising this place. A choice of law rule based on the same connecting factor is likewise appropriate. Indeed, this would lead to the desirable result that a court which has jurisdiction on the basis that the act of infringement took place there would then be able to apply its own law.

(ii) Displacement of the special general rule

It is submitted that there should remain the possibility of displacement of this general rule. It is not sensible to try to define in advance when this would occur. It would be best to simply retain the flexible wording of Section 12 of Part III. In applying this Section, the same weight should be given to the different types of factor in infringement cases as is suggested above.[281] It will only be in unusual infringement cases that the displacement rule is likely to operate.[282]

(iii) Mandatory rules of the forum

This still leaves the uncertainty over when the English intellectual property statutes apply as mandatory rules of the forum. It should be made clear that the only situation where this will happen is where a UK right has been infringed in England. Section 14(4) of the 1995 Act could set out a special rule to this effect.

(iv) Defences

There is, finally, the uncertainty over the position where a contract or the invalidity of the right is raised as a defence to an infringement action. The whole question of a contractual defence to a tort claim would be much clearer if the provisional conclusion of the Law Commissions in their Working Paper,[283] that the validity of a term in a contract which purports to provide a defence to a claim in tort should be decided by the law governing the contract (to be determined by the forum's contract choice of law rules), had been adopted in the 1995 Act.

---

[281] See above, pp 630–631.   [282] *Ibid*.
[283] Working Paper No 87 (1984), paras 6.51–6.53.

13

Complementary Torts and Other Causes of Action: The Applicable Law

I	Introduction	651
II	Passing-off	652
	1. How choice of law problems arise	652
	2. The applicable law	653
	(a) Introduction	653
	(b) Application of the common law rules in passing-off cases	653
	(c) Application of the statutory rules in passing-off cases	654
III	Malicious falsehood	669
	1. How choice of law problems arise	669
	2. The applicable law	669
	(a) Introduction	669
	(b) Characterisation as malicious falsehood	669
	(c) The exclusion of malicious falsehood from Part III	670
	(d) Application of the common law rules in cases of malicious falsehood	672
IV	Defamation	673
	1. How choice of law problems arise	673
	2. The applicable law	674
	(a) Introduction	674
	(b) Characterisation as defamation	674
	(c) The exclusion of defamation claims from Part III	675
	(d) Application of the common law rules in cases of defamation of a business competitor	676
V	Unfair competition	678
	1. How choice of law problems arise	678
	2. The applicable law	679
	(a) Introduction	679
	(b) Application of the common law rules in unfair competition cases	679
	(c) Application of the statutory rules in unfair competition cases	680
VI	Wider Continental protection in delict	690

		1. How choice of law problems arise	690
		2. The applicable law	690
		(a) Introduction	690
		(b) Application of the statutory rules in cases involving wider continental protection in delict	691
VII	Breach of competition rules		693
	1. How choice of law problems arise		693
	2. The applicable law		694
	(a) Introduction		694
	(b) Application of the statutory rules in breach of competition rules cases		694
VIII	Breach of confidence		697
	1. How choice of law problems arise		697
	2. The applicable law		698
	(a) Introduction		698
	(b) Application of the statutory rules in breach of confidence cases		698
IX	Criticism of the existing law		703
	1. Complexity		703
	2. Uncertainty		703
	3. Inadequate protection		704
	4. Lack of uniformity		704
X	General reform of the tort choice of law rules		704
XI	Special tort choice of law rules		705
	1. The preliminary questions		705
	(a) Rules for the different causes of action or just for unfair competition?		705
	(b) Independent tort choice of law rules or within the framework of existing rules?		706
	2. Independent tort choice of law rules for unfair competition		707
	(a) The Resolution of the Institute of International Law		707
	(b) Article 136 Swiss PIL Statute		711
	(c) A Hague Convention on the law applicable to unfair competition		713
	3. Special tort choice of law rules for the different causes of action		714
	(a) Policy considerations when deciding upon the rules		714
	(b) Suggested rules		714

I
INTRODUCTION

It has already been seen, in the context of jurisdiction, that English substantive law provides a number of different causes of action which are complementary to infringement. These include the torts of passing-off, malicious falsehood, defamation, and causes of action which are more difficult to classify, namely actions for breach of competition rules and breach of confidence. Some other countries provide wider protection, with causes of action in unfair competition, delict or anti-trust. These differences in the substantive law, inevitably, raise questions as to the applicable law.

The applicable law in respect of passing-off, malicious falsehood, defamation, and breach of confidence is, in one respect, a less complex matter that in respect of infringement. The question of whether the substantive English rules should apply as mandatory rules of the forum does not loom as large in this context as it does with infringement. This is because all the aforementioned causes of action derive from case law rather than from statute.[1] Moreover, the substantive law is not subject to the strict territorial limitations on liability which operate in infringement cases.[2] With unfair competition, delict and anti-trust, we are concerned with foreign causes of action, which obviously cannot operate as mandatory rules of the forum. What we are concerned with then are straightforward choice of law problems.

The English approach to solving such problems is to look separately at each cause of action, whether under English law or that of a foreign country, characterise it, and then apply the appropriate choice of law rule for that category. Most of the causes of action which are complementary to infringement are characterised by English law as tortious and, accordingly, the tort choice of law rules are applied. In England, unlike in Switzerland and Austria, which have special tort choice of law rules for unfair competition,[3] there are no special tort choice of law rules for causes of action which are complementary to infringement. The statutory or common law tort choice of law rules, which are of general application, have to be applied.[4] Many other countries adopt the same approach.[5] The

---

[1] For discussion of whether common law rules can operate as mandatory rules of the forum, see below p 668.
[2] There is though a question of territoriality in passing-off cases in respect of goodwill, see above, pp 363–364, 388.
[3] See below, p p 711–713.
[4] With malicious falsehood and defamation there are special tort choice of law rules in the sense that the common law rules apply rather than the statutory ones, see below, pp 670–673, 675–678.
[5] See Dyer, (1988) IV *Hag Rec*, chapter 3.

application of the English tort choice of law rules in relation to the following causes of action will now be considered: passing-off; malicious falsehood; defamation of a business competitor; unfair competition; wider Continental protection in delict; breach of competition rules including anti-trust; and breach of confidence. Alternative tort choice of law solutions will then be considered.

II
PASSING-OFF

1. How Choice of Law Problems Arise

There is a relevant foreign element if one or both of the parties is resident abroad or the passing-off has occurred abroad. The position may become complicated in that some of the acts that lead the plaintiff to bring a case in passing-off may have taken place abroad, others in England. I may be selling my fake advocaat liquor in Britain, but it may have been produced abroad and the label which refers to the collective goodwill of the producers of real advocaat may have been affixed there. There is, of course, a relevant foreign element. But is this a straightforward case where passing-off is to be proven under English law on the basis of the sale in England, or should another law be applied to a certain aspect or to the whole tort because certain acts took place abroad?

The position is also complicated if we look at cases of enabling passing-off. Does English law apply if all I do is enable someone else to pass off goods abroad, for example by supplying the goods? Or should the foreign law apply to the enabling part too? This assumes that the foreign law governs the passing off abroad, but does it? One could indeed argue, as certain Dutch authors seem to do, that these 'enabling' torts are the expression of the general rule that the law of the forum does not allow the encouragement of infringing activity outside the jurisdiction.[6] Or does this principle rely on the existence of a general rule of unfair competition or a general rule that one is liable in tort for the result of one's fault or negligence?[7]

In cases where international goodwill is involved, the issue arises whether this is a matter of fact, or whether the test for goodwill is to be found in the English law of the forum or in the foreign law of the country in which the goodwill is alleged to exist.

When it comes to differences in the substantive law, England has the nominate tort of passing-off, which has no direct equivalent in most other

---
[6] REPdR (1986) 2 *Intellectuele Eigendom & Reclamerecht* 47, with reference to Drion-Martens, *Onrechtmatige Daad*, VI 54 *et seq*.
[7] See, eg Articles 1382 and 1383 of the Belgian and French Civil Code.

countries. The only equivalent is often the wider tort of unfair competition. The prerequisites for and the situations in which both torts apply may well be radically different, although there is bound to be a certain overlap.

2. THE APPLICABLE LAW

(a) INTRODUCTION

Passing-off is a cause of action that is known to English law and so does not present the problems that arise where this is not the case. This is not to say that the discussion of choice of law in respect of passing off is simple. It is complicated by the fact of there being the two very different torts of passing-off, involving very different elements: direct passing-off; and providing the means enabling another to pass off. As has been seen in the previous chapter,[8] the common law tort choice of law rules still have some relevance and so we will start with an examination of their application in passing-off cases.

(b) APPLICATION OF THE COMMON LAW RULES IN PASSING-OFF CASES

The double actionability rule was applied to cases of passing-off committed abroad. Thus, in *James Burrough Distillers plc v Speymalt Whisky Distributors Ltd*,[9] an action was brought in Scotland following a direct passing-off by selling in Italy whisky, bottled by the respondents, as the petitioners' Laphroaig. Lord Coulsfield held, following the petitioners' averments, that the scope and grounds of protection provided by the Italian civil code were broadly similar to those of the delict of passing-off under Scots law. Such a claim should now be based on Italian law and characterised as one of unfair competition.[10] This decision was criticised on the ground that 'the *jus actionis* for passing-off (or equivalent) in Italy involves a misrepresentation which damages goodwill in Italy, whereas the *jus actionis* for passing-off in England involves a misrepresentation which damages goodwill in England. The two are quite distinct'.[11] This criticism is based on the notion that goodwill is territorially limited. Under Scots law, there was no exception to this double actionability rule. In England, there was a flexible exception to this rule, which, in principle, could apply in a passing-off case. However, there does not appear to be a reported instance of this being applied in such a case.

---

[8] See above, p 606. [9] 1989 SLT 561.
[10] For choice of law in relation to unfair competition, see below, pp 679–690.
[11] Arnold [1990] 7 *EIPR* 254 at 262. See also Drysdale and Silverleaf, para 4.55.

The position was different in respect of passing-off committed locally. The double actionability rule did not apply. This was shown in the Scots case of *William Grant & Sons Ltd* v *Glen Catrine Bonded Warehouse Ltd*,[12] which involved enabling passing-off abroad. The instruments of deception were exported from Scotland; accordingly, it was said,[13] the completed wrong took place in Scotland. Scots law was applied. There are numerous other examples of Scots and English courts imposing liability, based on local law, on local defendants for enabling passing off abroad.[14] Under English law, it was never entirely clear whether there was a flexible exception which would allow for the displacement of English law by that of a foreign country.[15] Certainly, there was no such exception under Scots law.

Under the common law rules, it was essential to ascertain where the passing-off was committed. The leading case was *Intercontex* v *Schmidt*,[16] where the plaintiffs, in order to obtain injunctive relief, had to show an arguable case of passing-off. The defendants sent invoices from West Germany to persons outside the UK in respect of publications allegedly passed off as those of the plaintiffs. It was held that the essence of passing-off is misrepresentation and there was no evidence of any act in the UK constituting such misrepresentation. The mere receipt of monies or letters within the UK from persons to whom the misrepresentations were made outside the UK was said to be no part of the tort. The tort was committed abroad and had to satisfy the double actionability rule, it failed to do so because of a lack of evidence of foreign law.[17]

(c) APPLICATION OF THE STATUTORY RULES IN PASSING-OFF CASES

(i) Characterisation as passing-off

When is an action brought before the English courts to be characterised as one of passing-off? This question is an important one because an action for passing-off involves a straightforward application of the statutory tort choice of law rules. If, on the other hand, the action is characterised as unfair competition, there are problems in applying these rules that do not apply in cases of passing-off. The only guidance given in the 1995 Act in respect of characterisation is in connection with the scope of the Act, ie

---

[12] 1995 SLT 936.   [13] *Ibid*, at 942.
[14] For Scots cases see *John Walker & Sons Ltd* v *Douglas McGibbon & Co Ltd* [1975] RPC 506; *John Walker & Sons Ltd* v *Douglas Laing & Co Ltd* 1993 SLT 156. For English cases see *Johnston* v *Orr Ewing* (1882) 7 App Cas 219; *John Walker & Sons Ltd and others* v *Henry Ost & Co Ltd and another* [1970] 2 All ER 106; *White Horse Distillers Ltd* v *Gregson Associates Ltd and Others* 1983 LS Gaz 2844. For an Irish case accepting this principle see *An Bord Trachtala* v *Waterford Foods plc* [1994] FSR 316 at 320.
[15] See above, pp 606–607.   [16] [1988] FSR 575.   [17] See below, p 636.

whether the issue relates to tort.[18] The question being discussed now is a different one, ie which tort is it – passing-off or unfair competition? Nonetheless, it cannot be doubted that this difficult question of characterisation is also one for the English courts to determine. But how are the English courts to decide this question?

It is submitted that the answer lies in the way in which the plaintiff pleads the case.[19] In the situation where reliance is placed on the English or a foreign law of passing-off, there is no difficulty in characterisation. This is undeniably an action in passing-off. In contrast, in the situation where reliance is placed on a foreign law of unfair competition, the characterisation of the action is not so easy. There are different types of unfair competition. If the plaintiff relies on a foreign law of unfair competition, which takes some form other than by means of passing-off, for example it is by improper advertising, then this should be characterised as an action in unfair competition. But what if the plaintiff relies on a foreign law of unfair competition which takes the form of passing-off? This presents a real difficulty in characterisation: is it to be characterised as passing-off or as unfair competition?

In the past, when the common law double actionability rule was applied to torts committed abroad, cases involving the breach of the unfair competition law of a foreign country, taking the form of passing-off, were treated as ones of passing-off.[20] But this is explained by the nature of the common law rule. Applying the first limb of the double actionability rule, the only actionability under English law would be in relation to passing-off. All that was required under the second limb was that there was actionability according to the law of the foreign country where the act was done, and there was no requirement that this was even tortious liability.[21] Now, of course, with the abolition of the first limb of the double actionability rule, by Part III of the Private International Law (Miscellaneous Provisions) Act 1995, there will be cases where a plaintiff relies upon a foreign law of unfair competition, and the characterisation problem has to be squarely faced. It is submitted that cases based on a foreign law of unfair competition by means of passing-off should be characterised as ones of unfair competition. This will have the effect of decreasing the number of passing off cases coming before the English courts and increasing the number of unfair

---

[18] See s 9(2), discussed above, p 612.

[19] This is consistent with the rule that the plaintiff, when he has a choice of suing in tort or contract, is allowed to exercise the option and avail himself of the jurisdiction rules in contract rather than tort: *Matthews* v *Kuwait Bechtel Corpn* [1959] 2 QB 57, discussed below, pp 698–699.

[20] See the *Dunhill* case, n 62 below and text accompanying, and the *James Burrough* case, n 9 above and text accompanying.

[21] See Dicey and Morris, pp 1495–1496. But compare *Def Lepp Music and Others* v *Stuart Brown and Others* [1986] RPC 273 at 277.

competition cases. The arguments in favour of adopting this characterisation are set out below[22] when unfair competition is discussed in detail.

(ii) Does passing-off come within the scope of Part III ?

(a) *Tort choice of law*

In order to ascertain whether, and if so when, passing-off comes within the scope of Part III of the 1995 Act,[23] two separate questions must be addressed: when does passing-off raise a choice of law problem; is passing-off tortious?

(i) *When does passing-off raise a choice of law problem?*
Direct passing-off. In cases of direct passing-off, normally it is going to be easy to see whether there is a relevant foreign element, thereby raising a choice of law problem. For example, if an English plaintiff brings an action based on a direct passing-off committed abroad there is undoubtedly a relevant foreign element. Conversely, there is no such element where a Scots plaintiff brings an action against a Scots defendant before the Scots courts in respect of a direct passing-off committed in Scotland.[24] It is submitted that this is so even where this purely local claim is coupled with separate allegations of a direct passing-off abroad.[25] The different claims should be split up into ones that do and do not involve a choice of law problem. Where there is no choice of law problem, the forum will automatically apply local law as in any other domestic case.

Enabling passing-off. The position is much more difficult in the situation where the passing-off consists of enabling another person to pass off abroad, as in the Scotch whisky cases. It is particularly hard to work out whether there is a foreign element when it is not entirely clear what the elements of this tort are.[26] We know that the tort of passing-off is completed in the forum by supplying another with the means to pass off.[27] In the situation where one of the parties is not local,[28] it can be stated confidently that there is a relevant foreign element. In the situation where both parties are local it could be argued that there is no relevant foreign element. But even in this situation it is submitted that, as a matter of principle, there is a significant foreign element, namely that there has been or will be a passing-off abroad.

---

[22] At pp 680–681.
[23] See above, pp 612–616.
[24] As in the *James Burrough* case, n 9 above.   [25] *Ibid.*   [26] See above, pp 368–369.
[27] *Walker v Ost*, n 14 above, at 116; *An Bord Trachtala v Waterford Foods plc*, n 14 above, at 320. See also the *James Burrough* case, n 9 above, at 564.
[28] See, eg, *Walker v Ost*, n 14 above, where eight of the plaintiffs had registered offices in Scotland and the defendant was English.

Looking at the authorities, the local law has always been applied in cases of enabling passing-off abroad. But it is not clear whether this was because the case was regarded as one where there was no foreign element, which seems the more likely explanation, or because the case was regarded as one involving a foreign element to which local law was applied as the law of the country where the tort was committed. One of the reasons for this uncertainty is that in cases where a tort is committed in England, English courts have always applied English law to the claim, often without discussion of choice of law principles.

A principle akin to that of enabling passing-off abroad was applied in a very different context to that of the Scotch whisky cases in *Fleetwood Mac Promotions Ltd v Clifford Davis Management Ltd*,[29] which illustrates the points made in the above paragraph. The English plaintiff company was granted an interlocutory injunction restraining English defendants from performing as a pop group under the name 'Fleetwood Mac'. It was argued by the defendants that the passing-off went on in the United States and that the plaintiff had not shown any right in respect of passing-off abroad. This was answered by Goff J in terms that the passing-off originated in and was engineered from England where the group was promoted,[30] and, accordingly, there was no need to establish any such right.

Whatever the position in the past under the common law rules, it is submitted that when it comes to the application of Part III there will always be a relevant foreign element in cases of enabling passing-off abroad, even where all the parties are local. What we are now looking for is an element that is relevant for the purpose of the scope of application of Part III. As will be seen,[31] the displacement rule under Section 12 of the Act requires the court to consider a very wide range of connecting factors, including the circumstances and consequences of the events which constitute the tort of passing-off. With the tort of enabling passing-off, this will obviously include the fact that there has been, or will be, a subsequent passing-off abroad. When Section 12 regards this fact as a relevant foreign element it cannot seriously be suggested that enabling passing-off abroad does not come within the scope of Part III.

(ii) *Is passing-off tortious?*

It can be stated confidently that, in an action for passing-off, the issues to be determined by choice of law rules can be characterised, for the purposes of private international law, as ones relating to tort. This was the view of the Law Commissions.[32] Applying the criteria for characterisation set out above,[33] the following points can be made in favour of a tortious

---

[29] [1975] FSR 150; criticised by Wadlow, p 244.   [30] *Ibid*, at 158.
[31] See above, p 664.   [32] See Law Commission Working Paper No 87 (1984), para 5.59.
[33] At pp 613–615.

classification. First, at common law, tort choice of law rules have been applied in passing-off cases;[34] indeed, there was no question of anything other than these rules being applied. Secondly, passing-off is characterised as tortious for the purposes of jurisdiction.[35] Thirdly, it is characterised as tortious under English domestic substantive law. Moreover, other countries also characterise this as a tort under their domestic law.

(b) *The restriction in Section 14(2)*

This restriction, preserving those common law rules which did not require recourse to the double actionability rule or exception, will not apply in passing-off cases. As mentioned above, the double actionability rule was applied in such cases.

(iii) Application of the general rule in passing-off cases

In order to apply in passing-off cases the distinction, found in Section 11, between single country torts (elements of the events constituting the tort in question occur in a single country) and multi-country torts (elements of these events occur in different countries), it is first necessary to determine what the events are that constitute the tort of passing-off.

(a) *The events constituting the tort of passing-off*

The events, ie the acts and consequences, constituting the tort of direct passing-off are well known:[36] goodwill of the plaintiff in his goods; misrepresentation by the defendant leading to confusion; damage to the plaintiff. In the situation where passing-off takes the form of enabling another person to pass off abroad, it is much more difficult to identify the events constituting the tort. It is necessary to look at the elements of the tort and, as has been seen,[37] it is not entirely clear what these are. It is possible though to look at cases, such as *John Walker & Sons Ltd and Others* v *Henry Ost & Co Ltd and Another*,[38] in which the tort was committed.

(b) *Single country passing-off*

(i) *Direct passing-off*

In the great majority of cases of direct passing-off, the three elements that constitute the tort will all occur in the same country. In this situation,

---

[34] See above, pp 653–654.
[35] See *Modus Vivendi Ltd* v *The British Products Sanmex Co Ltd and Another* [1996] FSR 790; discussed above p 374.
[36] See above, pp 361–368.   [37] See above, pp 368–369.
[38] [1970] 2 All ER 106. The facts are set out in chapter 8, p 368.

Section 11(1) provides that 'the applicable law is the law of the country in which the events constituting the tort or delict in question occur'. If these events occur in a foreign country, then Section 11(1) leads to the application of foreign law. The effect of the abolition of the common law double actionability rule is that there is no longer the need to establish that there is actionability as a tort under English law. In passing-off cases, often this was not a problem,[39] although it would have become such if the courts had accepted the argument that the *jus actionis* for passing-off abroad was different from the *jus actionis* for passing-off in England.[40]

If the events constituting the passing-off occur in England, Section 11(1) leads to the application of English law. Part III of the 1995 Act applies in relation to events occurring in the forum as it applies in relation to events occurring in any other country.[41] The facts of *LA Gear Inc v Gerald Whelan & Sons Ltd*[42] illustrate how this would operate. The case concerned a claim for passing-off in respect of the import of footwear into the United Kingdom from Ireland and offers for sale and sales in the United Kingdom. The plaintiff claimed to have a goodwill and reputation in the United Kingdom in respect of these goods. English law would now apply under Section 11(1). Similarly, in the jurisdiction case of *Mecklermedia Corpn and Another v DC Congress GmbH*,[43] there was an allegation of passing-off in England. There was evidence that the plaintiffs had a goodwill in England, the German defendant carried on activities in Germany and Austria which misled the public in England, which in turn caused the plaintiffs damage in England. Once it has been established that these three events constituting the tort occurred in England, English law would apply by virtue of Section 11(1).

(ii) *Enabling another to pass off*

Looking at the facts of *Walker v Ost*, although the case involved a foreign element,[44] it appears that the elements of the events constituting the tort occurred in the same country; the crucial point being that the tort began and was completed in England. The result is that English law would now apply under Section 11(1).

(c) *Multi-country passing-off*

(i) *Examples*

It is only in rare cases that there will be a multi-country tort of passing-off. Two examples can be given. The first one is where, in a case of direct

---

[39] But see the *An Bord Trachtala* case, n 14 above, at 323.
[40] See above, p 653.
[41] Section 9(6), and see, generally, above, p 618.
[42] [1991] FSR 670.
[43] [1997] 3 WLR 479.
[44] See above, p 656.

passing-off, a misrepresentation is made in country A, causing damage to the plaintiff's goodwill in country B. The events and their elements clearly occur in different countries. However, if you accept that there is a concept of world wide goodwill, one consequence is that it is arguable that the misrepresentation and damage to goodwill occur in the same country and there is no multi-country passing-off. The second example is where, again in a case of direct passing-off, the misrepresentation is contained in an invoice and this is sent from one country to another. The elements of one of the requisite events constituting the tort, the act of misrepresentation, can be said to occur in different countries. In the *Intercontex* case, it was not clear from the law report whether the invoices were sent from West Germany to another country, they were definitely not sent to England. In the absence of invoices being sent to another country, it would appear to be a single-country tort for the purpose of Section 11, and paragraph (1) would apply. The fact that cheques were received in England would not make it a multi-country tort since this was said to be no part of the tort. The Law Commissions appear to have assumed that cases which raised the question of where a tort was committed at common law would be multi-country cases under the new law,[45] but if the wording of Section 11 is applied literally it seems that this will not always be so.

It is submitted that, in cases of enabling passing-off abroad, the elements of the events constituting the tort occur in just one country and Section 11(2) will not apply.[46] To be sure, there is a foreign element (namely, that there has been or will be a passing-off abroad) raising a choice of law problem in such cases,[47] but this does not relate to the events constituting the tort, it relates to the circumstances and consequences of those events. One of the parties may be foreign, but again this foreign element does not relate to the events constituting the tort.[48]

It is also submitted that, in the situation where goods are directly passed-off by the defendant in a number of different countries, this should be regarded as a series of separate torts of passing-off, rather than as one passing-off where the elements of the events occur in different countries. Accordingly, Section 11(2) will not apply.

(ii) *Application of Section 11(2) in passing-off cases: does the damage to property sub-rule apply?*

Section 11(2), which deals with the situation where there is a multi-country tort, is particularly difficult to apply in cases of multi-country

---

[45] See Law Commission Working Paper No 87 (1984), paras 4.61–4.91.
[46] But compare Law Commission Working Paper No 87 (1984), para 5.59 where it seems to be assumed that this situation involves a multi-country tort.
[47] See above, p 656.
[48] The requirement sometimes referred to in English cases that the defendant must know and intend the passing-off abroad is not presumably an *event* constituting the tort.

passing-off. This is because it is not entirely clear whether such cases fall within Section 11(2)(b) or 11(2)(c).[49] The former is concerned with a cause of action in respect of damage to property and stipulates that the applicable law is the law of the country where the property was when it was damaged. The latter is concerned with any other case,[50] and stipulates that the applicable law is the law of the country in which the most significant element or elements of the events constituting the tort or delict in question occurred.

The argument in favour of applying the damage to property sub-rule. This is easily stated. In a case of direct passing-off, the cause of action is in respect of damage to property, since this requires damage to the goodwill of the plaintiff in his business, and goodwill is a form of intangible property.[51] The applicable law would then be the law of the country where the goodwill was when it was damaged. It is well established that goodwill is 'inseparable from the business to which it adds value, and . . . exists where the business is carried on'.[52] Where business is carried on in several different countries, goodwill is likewise situated in several different countries.[53]

Arguments against. The Law Commissions regarded passing-off as an economic tort and assumed that, as with other economic torts, sub-rule (2)(c) would apply.[54] There are strong arguments both of principle and policy for adopting this view.

One argument of principle is that the tort of passing-off is not primarily concerned with damage to property, and the special rule applying the law of the country where the property was when it was damaged should only apply to those torts where damage to property is the primary concern. The first half of this argument can be asserted with some degree of confidence. As Gibson J said in the *Intercontex* case, 'The essence of passing-off is misrepresentation'.[55] Likewise, in *Tyburn Productions Ltd* v *Conan Doyle*,[56] Vinelott J said that '. . . although goodwill is local an action for passing-off is an application of the tort of misrepresentation . . .'.[57] The latter half of the argument is perhaps more contentious since sub-rule (2) does not actually say that it only applies to those torts where damage to property is the primary concern. An alternative argument of principle is that sub-rule (2)(b) is solely concerned with material damage to property and so would not

---

[49] See Rodger, 1996 SLT 105, at 107.
[50] Ie other than under s 11(2)(a), cause of action in respect of personal injury or death, or (b), cause of action in respect of damage to property.
[51] See generally, Drysdale and Silverleaf, pp 10–11.
[52] *IRC* v *Muller & Co's Margarine Ltd* [1901] AC 217 at 235. See also *R J Reuter Co Ltd* v *Mulhens* [1954] Ch 50 at 95–96; Dicey and Morris, p 933.
[53] *IRC* v *Muller & Co's Margarine Ltd*, n 52 above.
[54] Law Commission Working Paper No 87 (1984), paras 5.57–5.60.
[55] N 16 above, at 578.   [56] [1991] Ch 75.   [57] *Ibid*, at 87.

apply in respect of intangible property. This appears to have been what the Law Commissions envisaged,[58] although it has to be admitted that the wording of the provision is not so confined.

The arguments of policy in favour of regarding passing-off as coming within sub-rule (2)(c) rather than (2)(b) are as follows. First, to decide otherwise would mean that in proceedings based, as commonly happens, on parallel causes of action for infringement of a trade mark and passing-off, a different sub-rule, and hence possibly a different law, would apply for each cause of action. This would be inevitable since damage is not part of the cause of action for infringement and therefore there is no cause of action in respect of damage to property. Accordingly, sub-rule (2)(b) cannot apply to infringement. Moreover, a different sub-rule would be applicable for passing off than for unfair competition, which would be particularly odd given that one way of committing the tort of unfair competition is by means of passing-off.[59] Secondly, commonly, in passing-off cases, an injunction is sought and this is to prevent acts of passing-off. The choice of law rule should reflect this, rather than the less significant matter of damage to goodwill.

(iii) *Application of the most significant element sub-rule*

When it comes to applying sub-rule 2(c), it is necessary to decide whether the most significant element of the events constituting the tort of direct passing-off is the goodwill of the plaintiff in his goods, the misrepresentation, or the damage to the plaintiff's goodwill. The damage to goodwill occurs where it is situated and so the true choice is between the misrepresentation and the damage. The argument in favour of the latter is that Section 11(2)(a) and (b) focus upon the consequence of the wrongful act rather than upon the act itself and, accordingly, the same should be done under (c).[60] However, what Section 11(2)(c) requires you to do is to focus on the tort and its constituent elements rather than on other sub-rules in that sub-section. If the former is done, the most significant element must be regarded as being the misrepresentation. As has been seen,[61] the misrepresentation is regarded as the essence of the tort. Applying this approach to the two examples of a multi-country tort given above: in the first example, the law of the country where the misrepresentation occurred will be applied. In the second example, there is a question of whether the most significant element is the sending of the misrepresentation or its receipt. In the *Intercontex* case, emphasis was placed on the latter, and it is submitted that this is right.

---

[58] Law Commission Working Paper No 87 (1984), paras 4.78–4.82.
[59] See below, p 707.   [60] See Rodger, n 49 above.   [61] See above, p 654.

(d) Pleading and proof of foreign law

In passing-off cases, the courts have not been prepared to grant an injunction preventing acts abroad in the absence of proof as to the local law. This was decided in *Alfred Dunhill Ltd and Another* v *Sunoptic SA and Another*.[62] An injunction was granted preventing passing-off in Switzerland, following proof that Swiss law would restrain acts likely to cause injurious confusion by passing-off. But an injunction preventing passing-off in certain other countries in which Dunhill traded was refused because of the absence of evidence as to the local law in these other countries. It was argued that the usual presumption that foreign law was the same as English law applied, but this argument was rejected for this type of case. However, it was said that if Dunhill's were to return with a fresh application for an injunction in relation to these other countries 'supported by proper evidence of attempted passing-off in those other countries, of confusion, and all the rest, whatever the local law is, . . .'[63] then a judge might see fit to grant a wider injunction. This was followed in the *Intercontex* case,[64] where an injunction was refused in respect of passing-off abroad since no evidence was produced as to foreign law.

What if the claim is not for an injunction but is only for damages and an account? Presumably, in such a case, the plaintiff can rely upon the normal presumption that foreign law is the same as English law, and the action can succeed without proof of foreign law.

The *Dunhill* and *Intercontex* cases, mentioned above, were decided at common law, but the principle established therein remains good law, despite the introduction of statutory tort choice of law rules, since Part III of the 1995 Act does not affect rules on pleading or proof of foreign law.

(e) Multiple passing-off

The *Dunhill* case involved allegations of passing-off committed by the same defendants in a number of different countries. The plaintiff can in one action claim in respect of each passing-off and will succeed, provided that there is actionability under the law of each country, and also, at least where an injunction is sought, provided that each foreign law is pleaded and proved. Of course, there would have to be jurisdiction against these defendants.

---

[62] [1979] FSR 337.
[63] *Ibid*, at 369.
[64] N 16, above at 578. See also the *Def Lepp* case, n 21 above, at 277.

(iv) Displacement of the general rule

When will the general rule be displaced, by virtue of Section 12,[65] in passing-off cases, ie when is it substantially more appropriate for the applicable law to be that of another country? This involves comparing the significance of the factors connecting the tort of passing-off with the country whose law would be applicable under the general rule and the significance of the factors connecting the tort with another country.

(a) *The factors and their significance in passing-off cases*

Looking at Section 12(2), the relevant factors include the following. First, as with any other tort, factors relating to the parties. Secondly, factors relating to any of the events which constitute the tort of passing off. These events have previously been described.[66] Thirdly, factors relating to any of the circumstances of those events which constitute the passing-off. In a case of direct passing-off, this would include the fact that the activities of the defendant, which led to a misrepresentation and damage in England, took place abroad.[67] In a case of direct passing-off abroad, this would include the fact that this has been made possible by the supply of equipment in England. It would also include the fact that there is a parallel cause of action, such as for infringement of a trade mark in a specified country. This constitutes a connection with the country where the act of infringement occurred and with the country where the trade mark was created. Fourthly, factors relating to any of the consequences of those events which constitute the tort of passing-off. In a case of passing-off by enabling another to pass off abroad, this would include the fact that there has been this passing-off abroad. Section 12(2) makes it clear that this is not an exhaustive list of the types of factor that can be considered. A fifth factor that operates in passing off cases, but which is not within the four types of factor mentioned in Section 12(2), relates to the remedy sought. If an injunction is sought restraining acts of passing-off in a particular country, this constitutes a significant connection with that country. Particular cases may raise further factors.

When it comes to the significance of each of these factors (ie attaching weight to them), it is submitted that, as with infringement,[68] the residence or domicile of the parties does not have the significance in passing-off cases that it has in personal injury cases. This fits in with the position in respect of infringement.[69] On the other hand, it is submitted that the injunction factor should be given considerable weight. It has to be remembered that a law is being chosen for determining issues in a case and a

---

[65] See above, pp 625–629.
[66] See above, p 658.
[67] See the facts of the *Mecklermedia* case, n 43 above.
[68] See above, pp 630–631.
[69] See above, p 631.

crucial issue is whether an injunction will be granted. It is much harder to know what weight to attach to the consequences and circumstances of the passing-off. It is submitted that they should be regarded as being of less weight than the events which constitute the passing-off. Finally, the fact that goodwill is territorially limited means that an argument can be made, analogous to the one in relation to infringement,[70] that it goes against the territorial bias of the substantive law to apply another country's law.

(b) *The operation of the substantially more appropriate test in passing-off cases*

The two different types of passing-off involve very different law/fact scenarios and so it is important to distinguish them for the purpose of the present discussion.

(i) *Direct passing-off*

In a simple case of direct passing-off, ie where there is no additional claim in respect of enabling passing-off abroad, there are relatively few factors to consider and the process of comparing the significance of the factors is fairly straightforward. Thus, in the *Dunhill* case, the factors connecting the tort with Switzerland were that the events constituting the passing-off occurred there and an injunction was sought preventing passing-off there. These are particularly weighty factors. Also the first defendant was Swiss. On the other hand, the plaintiffs and the second defendant were English. It cannot be said in such a case that it is substantially more appropriate for the applicable law to be English. Even if all the parties were English,[71] it is submitted that, given the lack of weight to be attached to the residence/domicile factor, the answer would be the same. It can be stated, in conclusion, that in simple cases of direct passing-off, it must be doubtful whether the displacement rule will operate.

In a more complicated case, ie one involving an additional claim for enabling passing-off abroad, there are more factors to consider and the weighing process is more complicated. As a result, there may be a more persuasive argument for operation of the displacement rule. To illustrate this, one can take the facts of the *James Burrough* case,[72] but with the alteration that the passing-off occurred in Ireland, which has a law of passing-off. Under the general rule, Irish law will apply in respect of the passing-off.[73] Can this be displaced by Scots law? The events which constituted the tort occurred in Ireland. This was not a fortuitous place of the

---

[70] See above, p 630.
[71] See, eg *An Bord Trachtala v Waterford Foods plc* n 14 above, an Irish case where all the parties were Irish.
[72] N 9 above. [73] See above pp 658–659.

tort. Moreover, an injunction was sought preventing this. These are the most significant factors. There was also a parallel cause of action for infringing the second petitioners' Irish trademark in Ireland. On the other hand, the petitioners and respondents came from Scotland. The circumstances involved an earlier tort of enabling passing-off, which was committed in Scotland, and allegations of infringement in the United Kingdom and direct passing-off in Scotland. But the residence of the parties and the circumstances of the tort are of lesser importance. Comparing the significance of the factors connecting the passing-off with Scotland and Ireland, the equation is more evenly balanced than in the *Dunhill* case. Nonetheless, it is submitted that it cannot be said that it is *substantially* more appropriate for the applicable law to be that of Scotland.

(ii) *Enabling passing-off abroad*

In contrast to the position at common law,[74] it is now necessary to determine whether English law will be displaced by a foreign law. In a simple case, where there is no parallel cause of action for direct passing-off abroad, the typical scenario is that found in some of the Scotch whisky cases:[75] the events constituting the tort occurred in Scotland (the forum), an interdict was sought to prevent acts in Scotland and the parties were Scots. It is not even entirely clear that there is a foreign element in such cases.[76] But if, as has been argued above, it is accepted that there is such an element (namely, that there will be or has been a passing-off abroad), it cannot be seriously suggested that this is of sufficient significance to make it substantially more appropriate that Scots law should be displaced by a foreign law.

Even in a more complex case, it is doubtful whether the displacement rule will operate. Take the Scots *James Burrough* case as an example, again substituting Ireland for Italy. Scots law would apply in relation to that part of the claim consisting of allegations in respect of the tort of enabling passing-off abroad. The events constituting the tort occurred in Scotland, and an interdict was sought prohibiting the export of goods from Scotland. These are the most significant factors of all. Other factors pointing to Scotland, albeit of less significance, are that the parties were Scots, an interdict was sought against selling in Scotland, and there was a parallel claim stopping infringement of the first petitioners' trade mark in the United Kingdom. Against this, the consequence of the tort of enabling passing-off abroad was a passing-off in Ireland, and there was a parallel

---

[74] See above, pp 606–607.
[75] See *John Walker & Sons Ltd* v *Douglas McGibbon & Co Ltd*, n 14 above; *William Grant & Sons Ltd* v *Glen Catrine Bonded Warehouse Ltd*, n 12 above. For an English case see *White Horse Distillers Ltd* v *Gregson Associates Ltd and Others*, n 14 above.
[76] See above, p 656.

claim in relation to this. There was also, as part of the circumstances, a parallel claim for infringing the second petitioners' Irish trademark in Ireland. These factors relating to the circumstances and consequences are all factors of less weight than the factor of the events constituting the tort and the interdict factor, all of which point to Scotland. Comparing the significance of these factors, it is submitted that it is not *substantially* more appropriate for the applicable law to be that of Ireland.

(c) *Is there actionability under the law applicable under the displacement rule?*

In the, perhaps, rather unusual situation where the displacement rule does operate in a passing-off case, the question arises of whether there is actionability under the law applicable under this rule. This raises a particular problem where English law displaces that of a foreign country. Is there actionability under English law in respect of a passing-off committed abroad? It has been argued[77] that goodwill is territorially limited and so if the goodwill in question is situated abroad there will be no actionability according to English law. There is, of course, the concept of a world wide goodwill which raises a question over the extent to which goodwill is territorially limited. Moreover, cases decided under the common law rules, including the *James Burrough* case,[78] have accepted that there was actionability under English law, despite the fact that the passing-off occurred abroad and involved foreign goodwill. There is a further difficulty though that, even if there is actionability under English law, there must be some doubt whether the English courts would grant an injunction prohibiting passing-off abroad in relation to foreign goodwill on the basis of this actionability alone. In the common law cases just referred to, there was also actionability under the law of the foreign country where the passing-off occurred.

(v) Savings

(a) *Public policy*

It is hard to see public policy having any part to play in passing-off cases. The English courts are not entitled to invoke public policy so as to refuse to apply a foreign law which allows recovery for passing-off, on the basis that English law would not do so in these circumstances. Nor can one envisage the doctrine being invoked in the converse situation. Differences in the law of passing-off in different countries are inevitable, but there is

---

[77] See Arnold, n 11 above, at 261–262; Drysdale and Silverleaf, para 4.55.
[78] N 9 above, at 563. See also the *Tyburn* case, n 56 above, at 86–87.

nothing so extreme or objectionable in this as to justify the application of the doctrine of public policy.

(b) Mandatory rules

Will the English courts ever apply the English rules on passing-off as mandatory rules of the forum, meaning that these rules will apply notwithstanding that a foreign law is applicable under Sections 11 or 12? It is important to remember that the English law of passing-off is derived from the common law and not from statute. This raises an interesting matter of principle as to whether a common law rule can ever operate as a mandatory rule of the forum. The Law Commissions thought not, and in their draft Bill made this point clear by referring specifically to 'any enactment'.[79] However, Section 14(4) of the 1995 Act is not so confined, referring more generally to 'any rule of law', and the draftsman clearly envisaged that this would encompass both common law and statutory provisions.[80] Nonetheless, instances of common law mandatory rules must be very unusual.[81] It is much more difficult to identify a common law rule as being mandatory than it is to do so with a statutory rule. With the latter, it may be possible to ascertain that it was Parliament's intention that a statutory rule should apply regardless of the law applicable to the tort, by looking at other provisions in the statute imposing a territorial limitation on the scope of the statute or expressly stating that the statute is to have overriding effect. But how is this to be done with a common law rule? What one is talking about is the intention of judges. But which judges, and how is such an intention to be ascertained? Despite these obvious difficulties, there is one situation where it is at least arguable that such an intention can be found. If you accept that goodwill is territorially limited, then it is arguable, by analogy with the position in respect of infringement,[82] that where there is an action based on an act of direct passing-off of goods in England, in respect of which the plaintiff has goodwill in England, then English law should apply even if a foreign law is applicable to the tort by virtue of the displacement rule. However, this scenario is not likely to occur. As has been seen, English law would be applicable in this situation by virtue of Section 11, and the displacement rule would not operate. Accordingly, there would be no need to invoke the mandatory rule of the forum exception in order to avoid the application of the foreign law.

---

[79] Clause 4(3) set out in Appendix A to Law Com Rep No 193 (1990).
[80] *HL Paper* 36 (1995), the Informal Briefing from the Draftsman in Written Evidence at p 64.
[81] See Dicey and Morris, *Fourth Supplement*, p 273.   [82] See above, p 600.

III
MALICIOUS FALSEHOOD

1. How Choice of Law Problems Arise

There will be a relevant foreign element where one or both of the parties is resident abroad or the malicious falsehood occurred abroad. The position is more complicated when only some of the elements of the tort take place abroad. For example, the false statement is made abroad, but it is published or reported in England. There is a relevant foreign element, but such an example raises the question of whether a foreign law of tort could apply to a certain aspect, or to the whole tort, if certain elements take place in England.

As regards differences in the substantive law, most countries do not have a direct equivalent to the English nominate tort of malicious falsehood. Most foreign tort laws are constructed around some wider provisions of a general nature, which might well cover the situations in which English law relies on the tort of malicious falsehood. Different prerequisites might apply, though.

2. The Applicable Law

(a) INTRODUCTION

This cause of action, like passing-off, is one that is known to English law. The notable feature about malicious falsehood is that, although it has much in common with passing-off in that they are both torts providing protection for businesses, it is treated under the statutory tort choice of law rules as having more in common with defamation, which, although it can be used to protect the reputation of a business, is concerned primarily with protecting the reputation of an individual.

(b) CHARACTERISATION AS MALICIOUS FALSEHOOD

The same question of characterisation arises here as has been examined in relation to passing-off:[83] when is an action brought before the English courts to be classified as malicious falsehood? This question is important because malicious falsehood is specifically excluded from the scope of Part III of the 1995 Act and the traditional common law tort choice of law rules will apply. If, on the other hand, the cause of action is characterised as

---
[83] See above, pp 654–655.

unfair competition, the position as regards exclusion from the scope of Part III is less clear. But it is at least arguable that this would come within the scope of Part III with the result that the statutory choice of law rules, which are more favourable to the plaintiff than the common law rules, would apply.

Again, it is submitted that the solution to this problem lies in the way in which the plaintiff pleads the case. In the situation where reliance is placed on the English or a foreign law of malicious falsehood, there is no difficulty in characterisation. This is undeniably an action for malicious falsehood. The difficulty arises in the situation where reliance is placed on a foreign law of unfair competition which takes the form of false and disparaging statements in relation to another's merchandise.[84] It is submitted that such an action should be characterised as one of unfair competition.[85]

(c) THE EXCLUSION OF MALICIOUS FALSEHOOD FROM PART III

(i) The exclusion of 'any defamation claim'

Section 13(1) states that 'Nothing in this Part applies to affect the determination of issues arising in any defamation claim.'

(ii) The wide definition of 'any defamation claim' to include malicious falsehood

Section 13(2) states that 'any defamation claim' means, *inter alia*:

(a) any claim under the law of any part of the United Kingdom for . . . slander of title, slander of goods or other malicious falsehood . . . and
(b) any claim under the law of any other country corresponding to or otherwise in the nature of a claim mentioned in paragraph (a) above.

This definition is a wide one in three respects. First, it goes beyond libel and slander to cover malicious falsehood. Secondly, it covers all the various forms of malicious falsehood found under UK law, ie slander of title, slander of goods or other malicious falsehood. An example of 'other malicious falsehood' would be where false statements are made maliciously about a business rather than its products. Thirdly, it covers claims not only under UK law but also under the law of any other country 'corresponding to or otherwise in the nature of a claim' for malicious falsehood.

Some examples can be given of claims that would be excluded by this definition. A claim for malicious falsehood under English law or for malicious falsehood under Scots law would be excluded by virtue of Section 13(1) and (2)(a). If you take the view that Salmond took, that under English

[84] See, eg Article 3 of the Swiss federal law against unfair competition of 19 December 1986.
[85] See below, pp 680–681.

Complementary torts and other causes of action: the applicable law 671

law passing-off is a type of malicious falsehood,[86] then passing-off would also be excluded. However, it is accepted nowadays that passing-off is a separate tort from malicious falsehood. A claim for malicious falsehood under a foreign law, for example that of New South Wales, would be excluded because of paragraph (2)(b). Such a claim corresponds to one for malicious falsehood under English law, as does a claim for injurious falsehood under the law of New York.[87] The more difficult question is whether unfair competition under a foreign law, which takes the form of a false and disparaging statement, is also excluded on the basis that it is 'in the nature of a claim for' malicious falsehood under English law. Such a claim should be characterised as unfair competition[88] and, accordingly, this question will be examined below when choice of law in relation to unfair competition is considered.[89]

(iii) Why was malicious falsehood excluded?

Defamation was excluded because of a concern with freedom of the press and freedom of the individual, in other words a concern with important policy issues in relation to libel and slander.[90] What is less clear is why this exclusion was extended to malicious falsehood, which is a tort that is different from defamation in numerous ways.[91] The Law Commissions, when putting forward a special rule for defamation[92] (rather than excluding it from Part III altogether), adopted this wide definition[93] without giving any reason for this extension. Presumably, the reason is because malicious falsehood is a parallel tort, protecting the trading reputation of a business and its product, whereas defamation is concerned primarily with protecting the reputation of an individual.

(iv) Was it right to extend the exclusion to malicious falsehood?

Part III of the 1995 Act was introduced to remove the injustice created by the common law tort choice of law rules. This injustice is perpetuated in cases of malicious falsehood. This should only have been done for a very good reason, but no reason has been given for the extension to malicious falsehood. There is, of course, a reason given for the exclusion of libel and slander, but malicious falsehood does not raise the same issues of freedom of speech and freedom of the press. It has more in common with economic torts, such as passing-off and unfair competition, than with defamation. Passing-off and unfair competition were not excluded from Part III and neither should have been malicious falsehood.

[86] See Winfield and Jolowicz on *Tort* (14th ed 1994), p 306, n 3.
[87] See the Restatement, Second, Conflict of Laws, s 151.
[88] See below, pp 680–681.
[89] See below, pp 682–683.
[90] See below, pp 675–676.
[91] See Duncan and Neill on *Defamation* 2nd ed 1983 chapter 2.
[92] See clause 3(2) of the Draft Bill set out in Appendix A to Law Com No 193 (1990).
[93] *Ibid*, at clause 3(5).

(d) APPLICATION OF THE COMMON LAW RULES IN CASES OF MALICIOUS FALSEHOOD

In cases excluded from the scope of Part III, the common law choice of law rules apply.[94] Malicious falsehood is characterised as a tort under English domestic substantive law and so reference has to be made to the tort choice of law rules.

(i) Malicious falsehood committed abroad

In this situation, the double actionability rule will apply as a general rule. The plaintiff has a double hurdle to surmount, which, doubtless, explains the lack of reported cases brought before the English courts in respect of malicious falsehood committed abroad. There is the possibility of applying English law under the exception to this general rule, or, again by virtue of the exception, of applying on its own (without reference to English law) the foreign law of the country where the malicious falsehood was committed. It may also be possible to apply the law of a third country under the exception. The exception allows for a particular issue to be governed by the law of the country which, with respect to that issue, has the most significant relationship with the occurrence and the parties. In the absence of authorities on malicious falsehood, it is difficult to say in what circumstances this exception will come into play. It is submitted, though, that in cases of malicious falsehood, as in cases of passing-off,[95] it is not appropriate to attach the great weight to the residence of the parties that has been attached to this factor in cases of personal injury.

(ii) Malicious falsehood committed in England

In this situation, English law will apply. It is not clear, under the common law rules, whether there is a flexible exception to this rule which would allow for the application of a foreign law. There is, of course, a flexible exception to the general rule in the situation where torts are committed abroad. Moreover, displacement of English law is possible under the statutory tort choice of law rules. It would be increasingly anomalous not to have an exception to the common law rule in the situation where a tort is committed in England.

(iii) Where is malicious falsehood committed?

The test at common law for determining where a tort is committed is clear enough: where, in substance, did this cause of action arise?[96] What is lacking is authority applying this test in cases of malicious falsehood. Looking

---

[94] See above, pp 606–611.
[95] See above, p 664.
[96] *Metall und Rohstoff AG* v *Donaldson Lufkin & Jenrette Inc* [1990] 1 QB 391.

at the elements of the tort – a false statement which is derogatory of the plaintiff's business and goods, made with malice, resulting in damage to the plaintiff – it is submitted that it is the false statement that constitutes the substance of the tort. But is this the making of the statement or its communication to another? The two will often take place in the same country. However, this will not be the case in the situation where the statement is contained in a letter written and posted in country A, but received and read in country B. The argument in favour of the view that malicious falsehood is committed in the country in which the false and disparaging statement is made is that this ties in with the rule that the English courts should have jurisdiction if the statement was made in England.[97] It is submitted that this is the better view. The argument in favour of a place of communication rule is that this is analogous to the place of publication rule adopted in defamation cases,[98] and the 1995 Act treats these two causes of action the same by excluding both from the scope of Part III. Moreover, the American Restatement, Second, Conflict of Laws, adopts the same tort choice of law rules for injurious falsehood as for defamation.[99]

But it has been argued above that malicious falsehood has more in common with economic torts, such as passing-off and unfair competition, than with defamation, and so any argument based on an analogy between the two is rather unconvincing.

Damage cannot be regarded as being the substance of the tort, given that, in most cases, there is no need to prove special damage, ie distinct evidence of harm to the business. Neither should malice be regarded as the substance of the tort, on the pragmatic ground that this requirement of *mens rea* would be difficult to use as a connecting factor.

IV
DEFAMATION

1. How Choice of Law Problems Arise

The choice of law problem arises in analogous circumstances to those described above in relation to malicious falsehood, ie where one or both parties reside abroad or where the defamation occurred abroad. The position is more complicated when only some of the elements of the tort take place abroad. For example, the defamatory statement is made abroad, but it is published or reported in England. There is a relevant foreign element, but this example raises the question of whether a foreign law of tort could apply to a certain aspect, or to the whole tort, if certain elements take place in England.

[97] See above, pp 392–393.   [98] See below, pp 677–678.   [99] See ss 149–151.

As regards differences in the substantive law, the point that immediately attracts attention is the presence, in most countries, of provisions dealing with the invasion of privacy. These provisions cover part of the area that is, under English law, covered by the tort of defamation. There are also differences between the laws of defamation of different common law jurisdictions. For example, in the US, defamation is harder to show, because the plaintiff must amongst other things show the defendant's intent.

2. The Applicable Law

(a) INTRODUCTION

Defamation is a cause of action known to English law. When it comes to defamation of a business competitor this has much in common with economic torts, like passing-off, but is treated, under the statutory tort choice of law rules, as being no different from a straightforward case of defamation.

(b) CHARACTERISATION AS DEFAMATION

It is important to decide when an action brought before the English courts is to be characterised as defamation because, like malicious falsehood, defamation is excluded from the scope of Part III of the 1995 Act and the traditional common law tort choice of law rules will apply. If, on the other hand, the cause of action is characterised as unfair competition, the position as regards exclusion from the scope of Part III is as outlined above.[100]

Applying the suggested criterion of looking at the way in which the plaintiff pleads the action, in the situation where reliance is placed on the English or a foreign law of defamation there is no difficulty in characterisation, even though it is defamation of a business competitor. This is undeniably an action in defamation. The difficulty arises in the situation where reliance is placed on a foreign law of unfair competition which takes the form of defamation or disparagement of a competitor in relation to his business.[101] This may involve what under English law would be classified as defamation. It is submitted that, as with the parallel problem of characterisation in relation to malicious falsehood, such cases should be characterised as unfair competition.[102]

---

[100] See pp 669–670.
[101] See Article I(4) of the Resolution of the Institute of International Law; Article 3 of the Swiss federal law against unfair competition of 19 December 1986.
[102] See below, pp 680–681.

Complementary torts and other causes of action: the applicable law 675

(c) THE EXCLUSION OF DEFAMATION CLAIMS FROM PART III

As has been seen, Section 13(1) of the 1995 Act excludes 'any defamation claim' from the scope of Part III, and the definition of such a claim is, according to Section 13(2), a wide one.

(i) The wide definition of 'any defamation claim'

Section 13(2) states that 'defamation claim' means:

(a) any claim under the law of any part of the United Kingdom for libel or slander ... and any claim under the law of Scotland for verbal injury; and
(b) any claim under the law of any other country corresponding to or otherwise in the nature of a claim mentioned in paragraph (a) above.

The effect of Section 13(1) and (2)(a) is that, for example, a claim brought in England based on libel under English law or based on slander under Northern Ireland law is excluded from the scope of Part III. Paragraph (2)(b) widens the definition to cover a claim brought under a foreign law and would exclude, for example, a claim brought in England based on the libel law of New South Wales. Such a claim should be regarded as one 'corresponding to' a claim mentioned in paragraph (a). More difficult is the question of whether a claim brought under a foreign law of unfair competition law taking the form of defamation or disparagement of a competitor in relation to his business should be regarded as 'in the nature of a claim' for libel or slander under English law. If characterised as defamation, it would come within paragraph (b) and would be excluded. If, as is suggested below,[103] it is characterised as unfair competition the question is less easily answered. This question will be examined later when choice of law in relation to unfair competition is considered.[104]

(ii) Why was defamation excluded?

Defamation was excluded from Part III after a vigorous lobby by the press.[105] English newspapers are sold abroad and there was a concern about the prospect of proceedings being brought in England based on repressive foreign laws without the benefit of defences available under English law.[106] This would act as a fetter on freedom of speech in England. It is arguable that this concern could have been met by use of the doctrine of public policy and by the adoption of the special rule proposed by the Law Commissions, which would have meant that English law applied in cases where a statement published abroad was simultaneously or

---

[103] At pp 680–681. [104] See below, pp 682–683.
[105] See *HL Paper* 36 (1995), Memoranda by the Guild of Editors, pp 79–80, and Whitaker, pp 80–82.
[106] See Lord Lester in Hansard, (HL) 27 March 1995, cols 1410–1413.

previously published in England.[107] Nonetheless, faced with the whole bill being talked out in the Lords, the wish of the press that the common law rules, requiring actionability by English law, should be retained, prevailed.

(iii) Was it right to also exclude defamation of a business competitor?

The exclusion of defamation, naturally, also excludes cases involving defamation of a business competitor. But it is arguable, in the present context, that a very narrow definition of defamation should have been adopted which distinguishes between different types of defamation and does not include defamation of a business competitor. The arguments for this are the same as those put forward in favour of narrowing the existing definition of defamation so as not to include malicious falsehood.[108] Cases involving defamation of a business competitor do not raise issues of freedom of speech and freedom of the press. They have more in common with passing-off and unfair competition than with defamation. Passing-off and unfair competition were not excluded from the scope of Part III and neither should have been defamation of a business competitor. As things stand, the old injustice of the common law tort choice of law rules is perpetuated in such cases, without good reason.

(d) APPLICATION OF THE COMMON LAW RULES IN CASES OF DEFAMATION OF A BUSINESS COMPETITOR

Defamation is characterised as a tort and so the common law tort choice of law rules will apply. There can be no doubt as to this. First, there are authorities at common law applying these rules. Secondly, a tortious characterisation has been applied for jurisdictional purposes. Thirdly, in English substantive law, defamation is characterised as a tort.

(i) Defamation committed abroad

The general rule of double actionability will apply. This will enable a defendant to rely on defences available under English law, such as absolute and qualified privilege, even though such a defence is not available under the law of the foreign country where the tort is committed. Conversely, an action may fail because there may be no actionability under the law of the place where the defamation occurred. For example, as has been mentioned it is much harder to establish defamation under United States law than it is under English law. Despite these difficulties, it may still be possible to satisfy the double actionability rule in a defamation case. *Church of Scientology of California* v *Metropolitan Police Commissioner*[109]

---

[107] See clause 3(2) of the Draft bill set out in Appendix A to Law Com Rep No 193.
[108] See above, pp 669–670.
[109] (1976) 120 Sol Jo 690.

serves as an illustration. The case involved an alleged libel committed in Germany. There was actionability under both English law and German law and the claim succeeded.[110]

As with malicious falsehood,[111] there is the possibility of the flexible exception to the general rule being applied. In applying the most significant relationship test, there is the usual question of the weight to be attached to the residence of the parties. The Law Commissions envisage that considerable weight should be attached to this factor, and that the exception might operate in a defamation case where the parties have a strong personal connection with one country.[112] Whatever the position in a straightforward case of defamation, it must be questioned whether this is right in a case of defamation of a business competitor.

(ii) Defamation committed in England

The position is very much the same as that in relation to malicious falsehood.[113] The leading authority on the rule that, if a tort is committed in England, the English courts will apply English law is a defamation case, *Szalatnay-Stacho v Fink*.[114] The defendant, an official of the Czech government in exile in England, sent documents to the Czech president, who was also in England. These documents were published in England and were defamatory of the plaintiff, the Czech acting Minister in Egypt. The Court of Appeal held that English law was applicable to this tort committed in England.

This case was decided before the introduction of a flexible exception to the double actionability rule. The question now is whether there is such an exception in cases involving torts committed in England. If there is, it will only come into play in rare cases. Not only is the tort committed in England but also this is the forum. It will be difficult to show that the most significant relationship is with some other country. However, the Law Commissions gave the facts of *Fink's* case as an example of circumstances which might justify the application of a foreign law, ie Czech law.[115] What is noticeable about this example is the weight being attached to the personal connection that the parties had with Czechoslovakia. In a case involving defamation of a business competitor, should the same weight be attached to this factor? Arguably not.

(iii) Where is defamation committed?

It is well established that the tort of libel takes place where publication of the libel occurs.[116] In *Church of Scientology v Metropolitan Police*

---

[110] The case raised an issue of vicarious liability, but both laws were satisfied in relation to this issue.
[111] See above, p 672. [112] Law Commission Working Paper No 87 (1984), para 5.91.
[113] See above, p 672. [114] [1947] KB 1.
[115] Law Commission Working Paper No 87 (1984), para 5.91.
[116] Cheshire and North, pp 555–556.

Commissioner,[117] English police officers sent an allegedly libellous report to a German Police Authority. The Court of Appeal regarded the tort as having been committed in Germany. In a case of alleged slander by remarks broadcast in the United States and heard in Ontario, it was held that the tort alleged had been committed in Ontario.[118] In a case of defamation by satellite broadcasting, the libel will be published where the broadcast is received. In a case of defamation over the internet, it will, presumably, be where the information is retrieved, ie is downloaded, or, in cases where retrieval is not necessary,[119] where it is received.

V
UNFAIR COMPETITION

1. How Choice of Law Problems Arise

As regards a relevant foreign element, one or both of the parties may be resident abroad, or the unfair competition may have occurred abroad. The position is more complicated where elements of the activity that amounts to unfair competition have taken place in various countries. The strategy may have been devised in one country, the goods involved may have been produced or altered in a second country and the marketing of the goods may take place in a third country. There is, of course, a relevant foreign element. It is unreasonable to apply the law of various countries in such a case, but how is the one applicable law to be chosen? Should priority be given to the country where the effects of the activity on competition in the market are felt,[120] or should priority be given to the law of the country in which the most important element of the act of unfair competition took place? Should recourse be had to the residence of the parties?

As regards substantive law differences, the provisions of the countries that have laws of unfair competition are far from identical. Discriminatory pricing, unauthorised use of unregistered trade marks and issues of consumer protection are a few examples of areas that are covered, but not all national laws of unfair competition deal with all of these. Even when they do, the prerequisites and requirements for a successful action may well be

---

[117] N 109 above.
[118] *Jenner v Sun Oil Co* [1952] 2 DLR 526. This was a jurisdiction case but is, nonetheless, regarded as a good authority in relation to choice of law.
[119] See generally, Perritt, (1996) 41 *Villanova L Rev* 1 at 20–24.
[120] English law does not contain a tort of unfair competition, but this principle finds support under German law, which does include a tort of unfair competition. See Drobnig, *American-German Private International Law*, Oceana, (2nd ed, 1972), chapter XII, at 306–309 and Sandrock [1985] *GRUR Int* 507.

different. And, of course, English law does not have the tort of unfair competition at all.

2. THE APPLICABLE LAW

(a) INTRODUCTION

The question of the law applicable to unfair competition is particularly difficult to answer. There are two reasons for this. First, there is no general theory and no cause of action for unfair competition under English law. Secondly, unfair competition under foreign law can take a wide variety of different forms, some of which are equivalent to the various English nominate torts examined above, ie passing-off, malicious falsehood and defamation. The particular difficulties arising in unfair competition cases will be examined when looking at the application of the statutory rules in such cases. But first, something needs to be said about the application of the common law rules.

(b) APPLICATION OF THE COMMON LAW RULES IN UNFAIR COMPETITION CASES

Unfair competition is a good area to look at to see the injustice created by the common law tort choice of law rules.[121] The requirement of actionability by English law under the first limb of the double actionability rule meant that an action based on the unfair competition law of a foreign country could well fail because of the absence of this cause of action under English law. It is true that England does have the various nominate torts mentioned above, but these do not provide as ample a protection for the rights of injured traders as Continental laws of unfair competition.[122] Even where the form of unfair competition looks to be equivalent to one of these English torts, such as in a case of unfair competition by passing-off, there could be argument over whether the two laws were sufficiently similar to satisfy the double actionability rule.[123] Moreover, at common law, such a case would be regarded as one of passing-off rather than as one of unfair competition.[124] The upshot is that, under the common law rules, the English courts were not squarely faced with unfair competition choice of law cases. Under the statutory tort choice of law rules, they will be.

---

[121] See Collins in *HL Paper* 36 (1995), Oral Evidence at p 67.
[122] See *An Bord Trachtala* v *Waterford Foods plc*, n 14 above, at 321 in relation to passing-off.
[123] See the *James Burrough* case, n 9 above.   [124] See above, p 655.

(c) APPLICATION OF THE STATUTORY RULES IN UNFAIR COMPETITION CASES

When it comes to applying the statutory tort choice of law rules in unfair competition cases, the fact that there is no English cause of action for unfair competition and that this foreign cause of action can take a wide variety of different forms lead to special difficulties in relation to deciding when a cause of action is to be characterised as unfair competition; whether unfair competition should be characterised as a tort; whether certain types of unfair competition are excluded from the scope of Part III; what the elements of the tort are for the purposes of the general rule and displacement rule; whether the application of a foreign law of unfair competition is against public policy. These special difficulties, as well as the usual difficulties, in applying the statutory rules will now be examined.

(i) Characterisation as unfair competition

The problem of determining when a cause of action is to be characterised as unfair competition is particularly difficult to solve. This question is of great importance because of the fact that if the cause of action is characterised as malicious falsehood or defamation it is excluded from the scope of Part III. Unfair competition taking these forms is, arguably, not excluded. Moreover, if it is characterised as passing-off, this would involve a straightforward application of the rules in Part III, whereas there are special difficulties if Part III is applied to unfair competition.

There are two possible approaches that could be adopted towards this question of characterisation. The first is to characterise actions based on a foreign law of unfair competition according to their English equivalents. This would still leave some instances of unfair competition where there is no English equivalent, such as where there is the sale of a competitor's goods under the representation that these are one's own.[125] It would mean, though, that there would be relatively few cases characterised as unfair competition coming before the English courts.

The second, and it is submitted better, approach would be to characterise the action as unfair competition whenever the plaintiff relies upon a foreign law of unfair competition, regardless of the form that this takes. Unfair competition in the form of passing-off, or false and disparaging statements about another's merchandise, or defamation or disparagement of a competitor in relation to his business, or violation of manufacturing or business secrets[126] would all be characterised as unfair competition. The arguments in favour of adopting this approach are as follows. First, the

---

[125] See Article I(2) of the Resolution of the Institute of International Law.
[126] See the discussion of breach of confidence, below pp 698–699.

plaintiff is basing his action upon the foreign law. There is some logic then in an English court, when characterising the cause of action, accepting the characterisation adopted under that law. When, according to that law, the cause of action is accepted as one of unfair competition it would be odd for the English courts to re-classify it as passing-off, or malicious falsehood, or defamation. Secondly, if the English courts were to re-classify the cause of action, this would have to be on the basis that the foreign tort is equivalent to an English tort. To determine this would require a detailed examination of the foreign law and a comparison with English law. What if, on examination, some element of the two torts is found to be different? For example, an action based on foreign law in respect of a false and disparaging statement may not require the same elements as malicious falsehood under English law. This would raise the question of just how close a resemblance the two laws would have to have to allow for re-classification. Thirdly, this solution has the merit of simplicity. Fourthly, it avoids having to differentiate between different types of unfair competition. This is important because the plaintiff may base a claim on more than one type of unfair competition under the law of a foreign country. Fifthly, this fits in with the EC jurisdiction rules, in relation to which it has been argued[127] that with passing-off under English law, the rules should be interpreted in the same way as in cases of unfair competition. Sixthly, the result of re-classifying as malicious falsehood or defamation would be to exclude such claims from the scope of Part III. The reason for excluding 'defamation claims' was not prompted by a concern for cases involving a business competitor, and, accordingly, a characterisation should be adopted which avoids exclusion.

(ii) Does unfair competition come within the scope of Part III?

(a) *Tort choice of law*

Is unfair competition tortious? This question of characterisation is much more difficult to answer in the case of unfair competition than in the case of passing-off, malicious falsehood or defamation. With these last three, there is a cause of action under English domestic law and this is undeniably tortious. The problem with unfair competition is that of having to characterise a cause of action when there is no such cause of action under English law. Of course, this is not fatal to characterising unfair competition as a tort. Characterisation is carried out for 'the purposes of private international law', which contemplates that causes of action unknown under English substantive law can be characterised as tortious. Collins appears to assume, and Morse suggests, that unfair competition will come within

[127] See above, p 371.

the scope of Part III.[128] Not surprisingly, the same thing is suggested in Dicey and Morris.[129] What is more, the Law Commissions failed to distinguish between unfair competition and breach of competition law, but said, seemingly in respect of both, that it would not be safe to assume that tort choice of law rules would never apply in such cases.[130]

If the criteria for characterisation suggested above are applied,[131] it is clear that a tortious characterisation should be adopted. First, the common law tort choice of law rules were applied in cases involving the breach of foreign laws of unfair competition,[132] albeit cases which were regarded by the English courts as ones of passing-off. Moreover, other countries, it has been said without exception,[133] characterise unfair competition as tortious for choice of law purposes. Secondly, unfair competition is characterised as a tort for jurisdictional purposes.[134] Thirdly, under English law, the equivalent causes of action to unfair competition, such as passing-off and malicious falsehood, are torts. When it comes to unfair competition itself, it is accepted by both civil and common lawyers that such rules form part of the law of tort.[135] Finally, there is one further argument, one of policy, in favour of a tortious characterisation. A claim based on unfair competition under a foreign law is likely to be coupled with claims in tort for passing-off or infringement. It would be very inconvenient to have different choice of law rules applying for parallel claims in a single action.

(b) *The restriction in Section 14(2)*

Unfair competition has been cited as an illustration of the uncertainty created by Section 14(2).[136] However, this is not a good example. The double actionability rule was applied in the *James Burrough*[137] and *Dunhill* cases,[138] which involved unfair competition under the laws of, respectively, Italy and Switzerland. It follows that the restriction in Section 14(2) has no application in cases of unfair competition.

---

[128] Collins, n 121 above at 67; Morse, (1996) 45 *ICLQ* 888, 894. But compare Lord Wilberforce in the Official Report of the Committee on the Bill in *HL Paper* 36 (1995), p 11.
[129] *Fourth Supplement*, at p 229.
[130] Law Commission Working Paper No 87 (1984), para 5.62, more generally para 5.57 *et seq*.
[131] See above, pp 613–615.
[132] See the *James Burrough* case, n 9 above, and the *Dunhill* case, n 62 above.
[133] See Dyer, n 5 above, at p 408.   [134] See above, pp 410–411.
[135] See Troller, *International Encyclopaedia of Comparative Law* Vol III, at 34–4.
[136] See Briggs, [1995] *LMCLQ* 519, at 522.
[137] N 9 above.   [138] N 62 above.

(c) *Are certain types of unfair competition excluded from Part III?*

If you characterise unfair competition in the form of false and disparaging statements about another's merchandise, or in the form of defamation or disparagement of a competitor in relation to his business as, respectively, malicious falsehood and defamation, both torts will be excluded from the scope of Part III by virtue of Section 13, which excludes 'any defamation claim' (defined to include malicious falsehood). However, even if you accept the argument, put forward above, that these are best characterised as unfair competition, it is arguable that both types of unfair competition are still excluded from the scope of Part III by virtue of Section 13. It will be recalled that 'any defamation claim' is widely defined to encompass any claim under the law of any country other than the United Kingdom 'corresponding to or otherwise in the nature of' a claim for malicious falsehood, libel or slander. It is not clear what is required for a claim under a foreign law to be said to correspond to or otherwise be in the nature of a claim under the law of any part of the United Kingdom. A claim for unfair competition under a foreign law when it takes the form of a false and disparaging statement about another's merchandise could be said to be equivalent to one of malicious falsehood under English law. But what if no malice is required under the foreign law, does it really correspond to the English tort? With no requirement of malice, it is at least arguable that the nature of the tort is different.

Moreover, there are strong policy reasons, in general, for cutting back the width of the exclusion in cases of ambiguity and, in particular, for not excluding unfair competition in the form of a false and disparaging statement about another's merchandise or in the form of defamation or disparagement of a competitor in relation to his business. First, excluding torts from the scope of Part III would mean subjecting them to the common law rules and all the injustice that this entails.[139] This should only be done for good reason. The reason for the exclusion of defamation claims was a concern with issues of freedom of speech and freedom of the press, a concern that arises in relation to libel and slander. In cases of ambiguity involving other torts, this should be resolved against exclusion. The exclusionary rule was not prompted by a concern with foreign laws of unfair competition or with the reputation of businesses and their products. There is ambiguity in the operation of Section 13(2) in cases of unfair competition and this should be resolved against exclusion. Secondly, this avoids having to differentiate between different forms of unfair competition. This is a very real problem, given that a plaintiff may base his action on several different forms of unfair competition.

[139] See above, pp 606–611.

(iii) Application of the general rule in unfair competition cases

(a) *What are the events constituting the tort?*

How are the English courts to identify, for the purposes of Section 11,[140] the events that constitute the tort of unfair competition when there is no such cause of action under English law? Speaking generally, unfair competition is no different from most other torts in that it has as its elements an act and consequent damage.[141] However, to identify what the elements of the tort are in terms of a precise act and damage is more difficult. Yet we need to know this. Which country's definition of unfair competition is to be used? The tort may have connections with two or more countries. Once the right definition has been identified you may be faced with a long list of different forms of unfair competition. Which form of unfair competition is to be examined for its elements? The only practicable answer to both questions is to concentrate on the law of the country which the plaintiff relies upon, and, looking at that country's definition, on the form of unfair competition relied upon.

Doing this, it is easy enough to identify the wrongful act. As has been seen,[142] national definitions of unfair competition set out lists of specific acts of unfair competition, such as passing-off, false and disparaging statements, misleading advertising.

However, it is much more difficult to identify the damage.[143] It has been seen, in the context of jurisdiction, that there is a very real definitional problem in relation to the 'damage' in unfair competition cases. This could be referring to the place where damage to a particular relationship was sustained; or, the direct economic loss to the victim; or, the indirect economic loss to the victim by way of loss of profits. This last option cannot be used as a basis of jurisdiction under the Brussels Convention and so should not be used as the definition for choice of law purposes. This is because it is desirable that an English court which has jurisdiction on the basis of damage should be then able to apply local law. This may not happen if the last option were to be adopted. In the context of jurisdiction, there are authorities supporting the direct economic loss solution and it is submitted that the same definition should be adopted in the present context. An English court, having jurisdiction on this basis, can then apply English law. The nature of the direct economic loss, and hence the place where this occurs, will vary with the form of unfair competition being relied upon by the plaintiff.[144] Where this takes the form of passing-off or improper advertising, this will be the loss of sales. Where it takes the form

---

[140] See above, pp 619–620.
[141] See Troller, n 135 above, at 34–6.
[142] See above, pp 409–410.
[143] See Stromholm, *Torts in the Conflict of Laws*, p 129.
[144] See the discussion in the context of jurisdiction, above p 413.

of disparagement resulting in the loss of a supplier, it will be the economic cost of loss of the supplier.

(b) *Single country unfair competition*

Doubtless, in many cases of unfair competition, the elements of the events constituting the tort, ie the act and the damage, will occur in the same foreign country. For example, there is an act of unfair competition in the form of passing-off in New York leading to damage by way of lost sales in New York. The law of that country will then apply by virtue of Section 11(1). The facts of *Alfred Dunhill Ltd and Another* v *Sunoptic SA and Another*[145] provide a simple illustration. A Swiss company advertised and sold sunglasses and spectacle frames in Switzerland under the trademark of CD Christopher Dunhill-London. The plaintiffs, a UK company which carried on their business under the name and trademark 'Dunhill', traded in Switzerland and alleged that injurious confusion was created there. This was a case decided at common law. Swiss law would now apply to such facts by virtue of Section 11(1).

(c) *Multi-country unfair competition*

Such cases will arise whenever the act of unfair competition and the damage occur in different countries. In such cases, the cause of action is not in respect of personal injury or death and so Section 11(2)(a) will not apply.

Is the cause of action in respect of damage to property, and thus within Section 11(2)(b)? There is an argument that it is. This is founded on the theory, used in Germany, that the basis of unfair competition is that property rights have been invaded by the competitor in question.[146] If you accept this view, the cause of action is in respect of property, and because damage is part of the cause of action, it is in respect of damage to property.[147] However, there are much stronger arguments against this. First, there is a competing theory, prevalent in France and Switzerland, that the basis of unfair competition is the abuse of the right to compete in the market.[148] Secondly, if an English court looks at the English equivalents, such as passing-off, these are not regarded as coming within Section 11(2)(b). Thirdly, there would be the problem of identifying what the property was that was damaged and where it was when damaged. Fourthly, if Section 11(2)(b) does not apply, the result is that (2)(c) will apply instead. This is the rule that should apply in respect of infringement.[149] It is desirable that the same rule should apply in relation to the complementary tort of unfair

---

[145] N 62 above.　　　　　　　　　　[146] See Dyer, n 5 above, at pp 384–386.
[147] Compare the position in respect of infringement, above p 622.
[148] See Dyer, n 5 above, at pp 386–387.　　[149] See above, p 622.

competition, particularly when there may well be parallel causes of action for infringement and unfair competition.

Under Section 11(2)(c), the applicable law will be that of the country in which the most significant element or elements of the events constituting the unfair competition occurred. As has been seen, it is not easy to identify precisely the events constituting a foreign law of unfair competition, neither is it going to be easy for an English court to ascertain the most significant element of those events. Is this the act or the damage?

It can be argued that the place of acting assumes particular importance for five reasons. First, the place where the competition is influenced by the act is, normally, determined deliberately by the tortfeasor in advance.[150] Secondly, there is the definitional problem over what the damage is in cases of unfair competition,[151] so that it is harder to identify the damage than the wrongful act in such cases. Thirdly, unfair competition is unusual in that some of its forms, such as appropriation of trade secrets or trade disparagement, involve an act committed in one country but which has an impact in a number of different countries.[152] Fourthly, in a case of unfair competition by means of passing-off, the English equivalent is passing-off and the most significant element of this tort is the act of misrepresentation.[153] Where the English equivalent is malicious falsehood or defamation, the substance of the tort is also an act rather than the consequent damage.[154] Fifthly, in a case of unfair competition arising out of a television broadcast, such as one involving improper advertising, it would look to be more appropriate to apply the law of the country where the broadcast originated than the law of the country where the damage occurred. A place of acting rule would allow this, whereas a place of damage rule would not.[155]

The same point can be made in relation to improper advertising over the internet, where it would look more appropriate to apply the law of the country of uploading than that of the country where the damage occurred. A place of acting rule would allow this, whereas a place of damage rule would not.

The arguments in favour of adopting a place of damage solution for unfair competition are as follows. First, in those provisions where Section 11(2) chooses between the place of acting and the place of injury or damage, it favours the latter.[156] However, this is not a strong argument since it has to be admitted that what Section 11(2)(c) requires you to do is to con-

---

[150] See Troller, n 135 above, at 34–6; Stromholm, n 143 above, at p 129.
[151] See the discussion in relation to jurisdiction, above pp 412–414.
[152] Rappeport, (1958) 20 *Univ Pittsburgh L Rev* 1, at 29–30.   [153] See above, p 662.
[154] See above, pp 672–673, 677–678.
[155] See *Hague Conference on private international law* Prel Doc No 5 of May 1995, 'Update on civil liability for unfair competition'.
[156] See s 11(2)(a) and (b), discussed above at pp 619–620.

centrate on the tort and its constituent parts rather than upon other sub-rules in that sub-section. Secondly, it has been pointed out that there is evidence of a movement away from a place of acting rule if you look at choice of law rules for products liability.[157] Thirdly, support for a place of damage rule is to be found in certain special tort choice of law rules for unfair competition.[158] Fourthly, the latter solve the definitional problem.[159] Fifthly, the place of acting can be fortuitous.[160] Examples would be: the place where an improper advertisement was posted, or the place where an employee was induced to disclose a secret. Sixthly, the place of acting is not easy to localise in cases of unfair competition by satellite broadcasting and over the internet.

The arguments are fairly evenly balanced, but it is submitted that those in favour of a place of damage rule outweigh those in favour of a place of acting rule. Accordingly, in cases of multi-country unfair competition, the applicable law should be that of the country where the direct economic loss to the victim occurs.

(iv) Displacement of the general rule

The most obvious problem in operating the displacement rule in unfair competition cases is in relation to the factors and their significance. One of the factors is the events which constitute the tort in question. With unfair competition, there will be the same problem in identifying this in this context as there is when operating the general rule. Other factors will include the residence of the parties and the fact that an injunction is sought preventing conduct in a particular country. If you accept the idea that the theoretical basis of unfair competition is the protection of industrial property, then another factor will be where the property is situated. But the difficulty in identifying this and the fact that there is disagreement over the theoretical basis of unfair competition raises a question as to whether this should be considered at all.

When it comes to attaching weight to the different types of factor, it would be possible to look at the equivalent English tort and apply the weighting adopted for this tort. For example, in a case of unfair competition by means of passing-off, the same weighting would be adopted as in cases of passing-off.[161] Thus, the significance attached to the residence or domicile of the parties would be much less than in personal injury cases. On the other hand, the injunction factor would be given considerable weight.[162] The consequences and circumstances of the unfair competition

---

[157] Dyer, n 5 above, at pp 415–417. He mentions the Hague Convention on the law applicable to products liability of 1972.
[158] See below, pp 708, 711.
[159] See below, pp 708, 711.
[160] See Troller, n 135 above, at 34–10.
[161] See above, pp 664–665.
[162] See Dyer, n 5 above, at pp 436–439.

would be given less weight than the events constituting the unfair competition. So the fact that there is a parallel action would be of lesser significance than the events constituting the unfair competition itself. In the situation where there is no English equivalent, the same weight could be attached to these different types of factor as in passing-off cases.

The uncertainty in relation to the operation of a displacement rule makes it worth looking at when other countries allow displacement of a general rule in cases of unfair competition. The Swiss special tort choice of law rules for unfair competition do not allow for the displacement of the general rule by the law of the parties' common habitual residence, whereas this would happen in a case of personal injury.[163] On the other hand, the German courts have applied German law of unfair competition as the law of the parties' common nationality even though the act of unfair competition was committed abroad.[164] In the United States, it is suggested in the Second Restatement that in cases of unfair competition the most significant factor is not the place of injury, as it is in personal injury cases, but the place of the defendant's conduct.[165]

(v) Savings

(a) *Public policy*

Whenever an English court is faced with a claim based on a foreign cause of action which is unknown to English law, as it will be now under the statutory rules, the question inevitably arises of whether application of that foreign law would conflict with principles of public policy. Giving public policy its normal restrictive meaning, it is submitted that there is nothing so extreme or objectionable about a foreign law of unfair competition as to justify not applying it on this basis. Indeed, there are the English equivalents of a number of the various forms of unfair competition. Moreover, when it cannot be seriously suggested that the application of a foreign law of passing off as found in a common law jurisdiction is against public policy, it also cannot be seriously suggested that a foreign law of unfair competition by means of passing-off is against public policy either.

---

[163] See Articles 133(1) and 136, the latter is discussed below, pp 711–712.
[164] BGH 20 Dec 1963, BGHZ 40, 391 with note *Wengler*, JZ 1964, 372, IPRspr 1962/63 no 161. See also Troller, n 135 above, at 34–11.
[165] Restatement, Second, Conflict of Laws S 145, comment f.

(b) Rules of evidence, pleading or practice, or procedure

(i) Evidence, pleading or practice

Proof of foreign law. It is submitted that, in unfair competition cases, the courts should not grant an injunction preventing acts abroad in the absence of proof as to the local law. This is the position in relation to passing-off, established by the *Dunhill* case.[166] The facts of that case should be characterised now as involving unfair competition under Swiss law rather than as passing-off.[167] If proof is to be required for unfair competition by means of passing-off it would be inconsistent not to also require it for other forms of unfair competition.

(ii) Procedure

Measure of damages. The rule that characterises the issue of the assessment or quantification of damages as a procedural matter, and, therefore, to be determined by the application of English law, is one that is not easy to apply in relation to unfair competition. There is a very real practical problem of how an English court is to assess damages for unfair competition when we do not have this cause of action ourselves.[168] One solution would be to look at the English equivalent and be guided by the way in which we assess this tort. Obviously, this would not work where there is no such equivalent. Another solution would be to produce evidence as to quantification under the relevant foreign law. The English courts could adopt the same principles on which damages are quantified abroad. At first sight, there would appear to be a problem with American unfair competition law because of the award of punitive damages by their courts.[169] However, an award of punitive damages is best regarded as a matter of substance, and thus for the choice of law rules, rather than as one of procedure.[170] Adopting the principles applied by the foreign courts does not mean that it would be right in a case involving, for example, unfair competition under Italian law to award one million lira on the basis that this would be the sum awarded by an Italian court in an unfair competition case.

---

[166] N 62 above. See also *International Business Machines Corpn and Another* v *Phoenix International (Computers) Ltd* [1994] RPC 251, 266–a passing-off case concerning an application to strike out a defence.
[167] See above, pp 680–681.
[168] See generally, the comments of Norton Rose in *HL Paper* 36 (1995), Written Evidence at p 48.
[169] See *Texaco Inc* v *Pennzoil* 729 SW 2d 768– award of 10 billion dollars for compensatory and punitive damages. See generally Noton Rose, n 168 above.
[170] See *Waterhouse* v *Australian Broadcasting Corpn* (1989) 86 ACTR 1 – exemplary damages classified as a matter of substance.

(c) *Mandatory rules*

With no English cause of action for unfair competition, there can be no question of English law applying as a mandatory rule of the forum. With unfair competition, what we are concerned with are foreign laws, and Part III should not be construed as allowing for the application of mandatory rules of a foreign law.

VI
WIDER CONTINENTAL PROTECTION IN DELICT

1. How Choice of Law Problems Arise

There will be a relevant foreign element if one or both of the parties reside abroad or if the delict occurred abroad. The issue of the choice between the laws of various countries will also, obviously, arise when some of the elements of the delict take place abroad. An example can be found in the facts of a Dutch case[171] in which the Dutch court ordered a Dutch company to stop trading in boxes for cheese that were to be marketed in Germany and would give rise to an infringement of an intellectual property right under German law. Which law did the court apply? In this case, it can be argued that the court applied Dutch law. There is indeed some support for the argument that Dutch law contains a rule that enabling the infringement abroad of a foreign intellectual property right amounts to a tort under Dutch law, whilst not being an infringement under their intellectual property laws, and that Dutch law will be applicable if the enabling activity takes place in the Netherlands.[172] Alternatively, the law of the country where the 'enabled' infringement takes place could be applied.

As regards differences in substantive law, suffice it to say that some of the continental provisions are clearly wider in scope than our intellectual property infringement provisions, whilst there are also differences between the provisions of the various continental legal systems.

2. The Applicable Law

(a) INTRODUCTION

What we are concerned with here are foreign causes of action that are unknown to English law and also have no English equivalent. The fact that

---

[171] *Baars Kaas/Westland*, [1986] BIE, No 21.
[172] See REPdR, (1986) 2 *Intellectuele Eigendom & Reclamerecht*, 47.

the cause of action is unknown causes some of the same difficulties encountered in cases of unfair competition.

(b) APPLICATION OF THE STATUTORY RULES IN CASES INVOLVING WIDER CONTINENTAL PROTECTION IN DELICT

(i) Characterisation as wider Continental protection in delict

There is no difficulty in relation to this. There is no such English cause of action or equivalent, which could be used as a basis for re-classification. Accordingly, the cause of action should be characterised as involving wider Continental protection in delict whenever the plaintiff relies upon a foreign law which provides such protection.

(ii) Does wider Continental protection in delict come within the scope of Part III?

(a) *Is it tortious?*

In this most difficult of all situations as regards characterisation, ie where there is no such English cause of action and no equivalent, it has been suggested above[173] that the fact that the foreign country whose law is relied upon regards the cause of action as delictual should be regarded as persuasive evidence to be used by the English courts in favour of adopting a tortious characterisation. There is even more persuasive evidence in favour of this tortious characterisation if it can be shown, generally, that other Continental countries that provide this wider protection adopt this characterisation. In the present instance, it is hard to see what other characterisation could be adopted.

(b) *The restriction in Section 14(2)*

You would not expect to find authorities under the common law tort choice of law rules applying the double actionability rule in a case where there is no cause of action or equivalent under English law (ie there is no actionability under English law). In the absence of such authorities, there is a problem with the restriction in Section 14(2). However, in *Def Lepp Music and Others* v *Stuart-Brown and Others*,[174] the double actionability rule was applied in circumstances involving an allegation that the making of records and their sale abroad constituted unspecified legal wrongs under the law of Luxembourg and Holland. Even without this authority, there is no evidence of any special tort choice of law rule being adopted at

---

[173] At pp 614–615.   [174] [1986] RPC 273.

common law; it follows that it cannot be established that the double actionability rule and exception would not have applied. Accordingly, Section 14(2) should not operate as a restriction on the scope of Part III in cases of wider Continental protection in delict.

(iii) Application of the general rule in cases involving wider Continental protection in delict

(a) *What are the events constituting the tort?*

The same problem arises as with unfair competition. There is no such cause of action under English law and so recourse has to be made to the law which the plaintiff relies upon to ascertain what the events constituting the tort are.

(b) *Single country delicts*

In most cases, all the elements of the events constituting the foreign delict will occur in the same foreign country, with the result that the law of that country will apply. The facts of the *Def Lepp* case, decided under the common law tort choice of law rules, provide an example. The plaintiffs claimed to be owners of the UK copyright in a tape recording which it was alleged the defendants had pirated. It was further alleged that the sixth defendant, a company incorporated and resident in Luxembourg, had manufactured records from the tape recording, and sold these to the eighth defendant, a Dutch company. The latter, allegedly, sold some of the records in the Netherlands to the ninth defendant who imported a number into the United Kingdom. The plaintiffs claimed that under the law of Luxembourg and the Netherlands, the making of the records and their sale constituted legal wrongs. Luxembourg and Dutch law would now be applied by virtue of Section 11(1). Doubtless, before an injunction could be granted, there would need to be proof as to the foreign law.[175]

When it comes to applying the foreign law, the precise nature of the delict according to Luxembourg or Dutch law does not matter. All that is required for a successful action is that there is actionability under that law. It does not even have to be actionable as a delict according to the foreign law, provided, of course, that the cause of action is classified by the English courts, for the purposes of private international law, as tortious. Thus, in *Walker v Ost*,[176] it was alleged that a quasi-delict had been committed in Ecuador. A successful action could now be brought based on the wrong under Ecuador law. The circumstances involved what under English law would be passing-off and so the wrong would be charac-

---

[175] See above, pp 662–663.   [176] N 14 above.

(c) Multi-country delicts

In such cases, Section 11(2)(c) will apply. The same problem arises as with unfair competition, ie ascertaining the most significant element or elements of the events constituting the tort when the cause of action relied upon is a foreign one which is unknown under English law. It is submitted that the same solution should be adopted as in cases of unfair competition. Accordingly, the most significant element should be regarded as being the damage.[177]

(d) Multiple delicts

The *Def Lepp* case involved allegations of delicts committed in Luxembourg and Holland, of separate wrongs under two different laws. Part III enables a plaintiff to claim in one action in respect of both delicts.

(iv) Displacement of the general rule

The same problem of determining the events constituting the tort arises when this has to be considered as a factor under the displacement rule. There is also the problem of attaching weight to factors when there is no equivalent English cause of action.[178] The same weight should be given to the different types of factor, mentioned in Section 12(2) of the 1995 Act, as in cases of direct passing-off.[179] This is important because a claim based on wider Continental protection in delict may well be coupled with one for direct passing-off.

VII
BREACH OF COMPETITION RULES

1. How Choice of Law Problems Arise

The issue of the choice between the law of various countries once more arises where one or both of the parties reside abroad or the breach of competition law occurred abroad. The position becomes complicated where only some of the elements of the activity that amounts to a breach of competition law take place abroad. For example, the infringing agreement has

---

[177] This assumes that the foreign law requires damage; if not, the most significant element would have to be an act.
[178] See above, p 688.
[179] See above, pp 664–666.

been concluded abroad, but is implemented in England. There is, of course, a relevant foreign element. One could apply the law of the country where the effect of the anti-competitive conduct is felt, or the law of the country where the essential element of the tort takes place or the law of the parties' residence. In any case, more that one law could, potentially, be applicable and a choice of law rule needs to be identified.

As regards differences in substantive law, national competition rules are not necessarily a copy of Articles 85 and 86 EC. The latter provisions have been used as a source of inspiration in many cases, but the outcome is quite different from country to country. US competition law is even more different, for example through the specific way in which the rule of reason has been incorporated into it.

2. The Applicable Law

(a) INTRODUCTION

Determination of the applicable law in respect of breach of competition rules is complicated by the fact that within the broad umbrella of competition rules can come national and EC competition rules, rules on restrictive practices and anti-trust legislation. Some of the problems in applying the statutory tort choice of law rules to cases in respect of breach of competition rules are familiar from the earlier discussion of other causes of action. Is the cause of action tortious? Is Section 14(2) satisfied? What are the events constituting the tort? There is then one problem which is unique to this cause of action. Does an action for breach of US anti-trust legislation fall within the principle that the English courts will not entertain an action for the enforcement, whether directly or indirectly, of a foreign penal, revenue or other public law?

(b) APPLICATION OF THE STATUTORY RULES IN BREACH OF COMPETITION RULES CASES

(i) No exclusion of breach of competition rules from Part III

The Law Commissions considered whether torts based on competition, restrictive practices or anti-trust law should be expressly excluded altogether from the new choice of law rules.[180] One of the objections made in the past to foreign anti-trust law was that it involved the extra-territorial application of law by the foreign court . This objection does not apply where it is the English court that is applying the foreign law. No such rec-

---

[180] Law Commission Working Paper No 87 (1984), para 5.65.

ommendation for exclusion was made and the statutory rules will apply in the normal way rather than the traditional common law rules.[181]

(ii) Characterisation as breach of competition rules

With breach of competition rules, there is not the problem that you have with unfair competition over a possible re-classification according to English equivalents which are different torts and raise separate problems when it comes to applying the rules in Part III. It is submitted that a cause of action is to be characterised as breach of competition rules whenever a plaintiff relies upon English or foreign competition law. The practical point of difficulty is that it is not always easy to determine whether a foreign cause of action is, on the one hand, for breach of competition rules or, on the other hand, for unfair competition.

(iii) Do breach of competition rules come within the scope of Part III?

(a) *Is it tortious?*

The Law Commissions thought it possible that a claim based on what they referred to as breach of foreign competition, restrictive practices, or anti-trust legislation might not be governed by the tort choice of law rules but by some other choice of law rules instead.[182] They pointed out that a claim for breach of US anti-trust legislation brought in the United States courts in the *Laker Airways* litigation[183] was pleaded separately from a claim in tort. Nonetheless, they concluded that it was not safe to assume that in a claim based on foreign competition, restrictive practices or anti-trust law our tort choice of law rules would never apply.[184]

There are good arguments in favour of characterising such claims as tortious. First, applying the characterisation criteria set out above, a breach of Community competition law is characterised as tortious for jurisdictional purposes, both under the EC and traditional English rules.[185] The same characterisation should be adopted for choice of law purposes and for the breach of all types of competition law, including US anti-trust legislation.

Secondly, there is the view that any breach of Community law, including its competition law, which gives rise to a claim for damages, is tortious.[186] It would be possible to have a different characterisation for the breach of a different type of competition law, such as anti-trust legislation. But this would be unnecessarily complicated.

---

[181] But see the discussion, below, pp 696–697, in relation to savings.
[182] Law Commission Working Paper No 87 (1984), paras 5.61–5.62.
[183] See *British Airways Board* v *Laker Airways Ltd* [1984] QB 142, Appendix to the CA judgment.
[184] N 182 above, at para 5.62.   [185] See above, pp 423, 425.   [186] See above, p 423.

Thirdly, as a matter of policy, the same tortious characterisation should be adopted as for unfair competition given the uncertainty that sometimes exists, when you look at the foreign law, in determining which of the two it is.

(b) *The Restriction in section 14(2)*

There does not appear to be any authority applying the double actionability rule in relation to a claim based on the breach of foreign competition rules. More importantly, there is no evidence of special tort choice of law rules having been adopted at common law for such cases, as happened with maritime torts. Applying a restrictive interpretation of this provision,[187] as befits the fact that it involves an exception to the application of the statutory tort choice of law rules contained in Part III, it cannot be established that the double actionability rule and exception would not have applied. Accordingly, Section 14(2) should not operate as a restriction on the application of Part III in breach of competition rules cases.

(iv) Application of the general rule in breach of competition rules cases

Where reliance is placed on foreign competition law, there may be a problem in identifying what the events are that constitute the tort. If you take the example of a claim based on US anti-trust legislation, there is no such cause of action under English law. The events constituting the tort can only be identified with the necessary precision by looking at the requirements for a successful action under US law.

(v) Displacement of the general rule

The same problem of identifying the events constituting the tort arises when considering this factor under the displacement rule as it does under the general rule. The same weight should be given to the different types of factor as for cases of direct passing-off.

(vi) Savings

(a) *A foreign penal, revenue or other public law*

The Law Commissions thought it possible that a civil action under foreign anti-trust legislation might fall within the principle that the English courts will not entertain an action for the enforcement, whether directly or indirectly, of a penal, revenue or other public law. This principle is, of course, preserved under the Act.[188] Dicey and Morris regards such legislation as

---

[187] See above, p 616. [188] Section 14(3)(a)(ii), discussed above p 636.

falling within 'other public law'.[189] If correct, and the Law Commissions regard the position as being unclear,[190] this means that the English courts will not entertain such an action.

The Law Commissions went on to point out that even if the English courts were to entertain actions based on US anti-trust legislation, the remedy of multiple damages under that law would be regarded as penal and unenforceable by an English court. There are statements to this effect from English judges in the *Laker Airways* litigation. Accordingly, an English court would not grant multiple damages in a case based on US anti-trust law. That this is undoubtedly the position is supported by the fact that a US judgment for such damages is unenforceable in England.[191] For an English court directly to apply the US law, arguably, would be against public policy.[192]

(b) *Mandatory rules*

In a claim for damages following a breach of Article 85 or 86 of the Treaty of Rome, the English courts will apply these provisions as mandatory rules of the forum.

VIII
BREACH OF CONFIDENCE

1. How Choice of Law Problems Arise

Access to the confidential information may have been gained in country A, whilst the wrongful disclosure of the information may take place in country B. The effects of that wrongful disclosure may be felt in country C. The fact that elements that are relevant for the action for breach of confidence take place in more than one jurisdiction, obviously, raises problems of choice of law. As with the other complementary causes of action, there would also be a choice of law question where one or both of the parties reside abroad, or where all the elements of the breach of confidence occurred abroad.

The substantive law of breach of confidence is also different in the various legal systems. This is another point where choice of law questions arise. Many civil law systems rely on the general tort rule which involves liability based on fault or negligence and back that up with criminal law

[189] Dicey and Morris, p 108.
[190] Law Commission Working Paper No 87 (1984), para 5.62.
[191] Protection of Trading Interests Act 1980, s 5(2).
[192] Law Commission, n 190 above, at para 5.63.

provisions. The requirements for a successful action are often quite different from those that are found in the English breach of confidence action.

2. THE APPLICABLE LAW

(a) INTRODUCTION

Breach of confidence is a cause of action that is known to English law and so does not present the sort of problems that you encounter where this is not the case. The position is complicated though by the fact that it can take both contractual and non-contractual forms. As regards the latter, there is a real problem over whether this is to be characterised as a tort for the purposes of private international law. If the statutory tort choice of law rules are applied, there is a lack of authority under the common law rules to assist in answering the many questions that arise concerning their application.

(b) APPLICATION OF THE STATUTORY RULES IN BREACH OF CONFIDENCE CASES

(i) Characterisation as breach of confidence

The characterisation as breach of confidence and the borderline with unfair competition raises the same difficulty as has been encountered in relation to passing-off.[193] There is no problem whenever a plaintiff relies upon English or a foreign law of contractual or non-contractual breach of confidence. The problem comes whenever the plaintiff relies upon a foreign law of unfair competition which takes a form such as that of violation of manufacturing or business secrets,[194] or improper appropriation of a competitor's efforts.[195] Is this breach of confidence or unfair competition? It is submitted that, consistently with what has been argued elsewhere in this chapter,[196] cases of unfair competition in such forms should be characterised as ones of unfair competition. This means, of course, the application of tort choice of law rules. If it is a case involving a contract between the parties, such as where a former employee misuses confidential information this may seem a rather curious result.[197] In this situation, Swiss law applies the contract choice of law rules rather than the special tort ones for unfair competition.[198] Nonetheless, the approach being suggested is supported by the English rule in a case involving a contract of employment,

---

[193] See above, pp 654–655.
[194] See Article 6 of the Swiss federal law against unfair competition of 19 December 1986.
[195] See Article I(2) of the Resolution of the Institute of International Law; Article 5(a) of the Swiss federal law against unfair competition of 19 December 1986.
[196] See above, pp 655, 670, 674, 680–681.
[197] See, generally, the discussion by Dyer, n 5 above, at pp 429–431.
[198] Article 133(3) of the Swiss Private International Law Statute, discussed below, p 712.

(ii) Does breach of confidence come within the scope of Part III?

(a) *Is it tortious?*

(i) *Contractual breach of confidence*

It is important, from the outset, to distinguish between contractual breach of confidence and non-contractual. If the cause of action is based on the former, contract choice of law rules[200] will apply. If, on the other hand, the cause of action is based on the breach of a non-contractual duty of confidence, the characterisation of this cause of action is much more difficult. The latter situation will now be considered.

(ii) *Non-contractual breach of confidence*

The problem of characterisation. Characterisation of non-contractual breach of confidence for the purposes of the scope of Part III is exceptionally difficult. With the other causes of action, examined above, the application of the suggested criteria for characterisation provides an answer. But this is not the case with this cause of action. There are, seemingly, no English authorities at common law on characterisation for the purposes of choice of law. The characterisation for the purposes of jurisdiction is not clear.[201] Normally, this would still leave the characterisation for the purposes of the substantive law as a possible criterion. This is a cause of action known to English law and so you would have thought that this would provide an answer. But, of course, what is unusual about non-contractual breach of confidence is the fact that its characterisation, as a matter of English substantive law, is particularly unclear.[202]

Deciding the characterisation under the English substantive law. An English judge faced with this uncertainty could decide definitively how non-contractual breach of confidence should be characterised as a matter of English substantive law, and then allow this to determine the characterisation for the purposes of private international law. If this is characterised as tortious as a matter of substantive law, and there is much to be said for this,[203] then the statutory tort choice of law rules will apply. However, if confidential information is regarded as being a form of property the position is more complicated. Do the property choice of law rules apply? The answer is, presumably, no. There is no proprietary issue to be settled.

---

[199] *Matthews v Kuwait Bechtel Corpn* [1959] 2 QB 57.
[200] See above, chapter 11.
[201] See above, pp 433, 444–445.
[202] See above, pp 430–431.
[203] See above, pp 430–431.

What is involved is damage to property and if you characterise the cause of action as being tortious what you have is tortious damage to property. Another option would be to characterise non-contractual breach of confidence as being a cause of action in equity, but it is not clear what law applies to such a cause of action. The same is true if you characterise the cause of action as being *sui generis*. Where there are no existing choice of law rules, the courts would, presumably, have to invent them.

The alternative, and, it is submitted, much better approach would be to accept that the characterisation as a matter of English substantive law is unclear and that no guidance can be gained from this. This does not mean, though, that Part III cannot be applied.

A tortious characterisation for the purposes of private international law. Ultimately, what we are concerned with is characterisation 'for the purposes of private international law', ie for the purposes of the scope of Part III. There is an important point that can be made in favour of giving non-contractual breach of confidence a tortious characterisation for these purposes. Normally, if this is done, the choice of law position is clear, Part III will apply. If Part III does not apply, it is not clear which choice of law rules will apply. This will, presumably, necessitate a characterisation of the substantive law, with the problem, noted above, that for some of the possible characterisations there are no choice of law rules.

It is submitted that, for the purposes of the scope of Part III, a tortious characterisation should be adopted for non-contractual breach of confidence. This appears to have been the view of Lord Lester during the passage of the Private International Law (Miscellaneous Provisions) Bill through the Lords. He sought an amendment to the bill so as to exclude not only defamation but also claims characterised as tortious based upon a law for the protection of confidentiality.[204] If claims for breach of confidence were not capable of being characterised as tortious there would be no need for such an exclusion.[205]

(b) *The restriction in Section 14(2)*

The position is essentially the same as that in relation to breach of competition rules. There is no authority on the application of the double actionability rule in relation to non-contractual breach of confidence.[206] Nevertheless, there is no evidence of special common law tort choice of law rules for non-contractual breach of confidence and, accordingly, the restriction on the scope of Part III contained in Section 14(2) should not operate.

---

[204] Hansard, (HL) 27 March 1995 cols 1410–1414.
[205] This amendment was in fact withdrawn and Lord Lester accepted that it went too far in referring to confidentiality.
[206] See Briggs, n 136 above, at 522.

(iii) Application of the general rule in cases of non-contractual breach of confidence

(a) *The events constituting the cause of action*

What are the events, ie the acts and consequences, constituting a cause of action for breach of confidence? This, of course, involves looking at the essential elements or requirements of this cause of action. The requirement that the information has the necessary quality of confidence about it cannot be regarded as an event, being neither an act nor a consequence of an act. Accordingly, the three events constituting the cause of action are: the imparting of information in circumstances importing an obligation of confidence; the unauthorised use of that information; and, seemingly, the detriment to the confider of the information from this unauthorised use.

(b) *Single country non-contractual breach of confidence*

No doubt, in the great majority of cases, the elements of these events will occur in the same country and the law of that country will apply. Indeed, in the situation where the detriment is the mere unauthorised disclosure of the information, then this detriment will occur in the same country as that where the unauthorised use, ie by disclosure, of the information occurred. Nonetheless, it is possible to envisage examples of multi-country breach of confidence.

(c) *Multi-country non-contractual breach of confidence*

An example would be where information is imparted in England but used in Japan. Section 11(2) will then come into play. Another example would be where confidential information is used in Japan but causes detriment in the form of financial loss to the confider in England.

Does the damage to property sub-rule apply? If confidential information is regarded as a form of property, then the cause of action can be said to be tortious damage to property and the law of the country where the property was when it was damaged will apply by virtue of Section 11(2)(b). This would then raise the question of where the confidential information is situated. However, the better view is that, as a matter of substantive law, confidential information should not be regarded as a form of property.[207]

If confidential information is not regarded as a form of property, the result is that the most significant element sub-rule contained in Section

---

[207] See above, p 430.

11(2)(c) would apply. This requires identification of the most significant element or elements of the events constituting the breach of confidence. There are no tort choice of law cases decided at common law to provide guidance on this. Is the most significant element the imparting of the information, its use, or the detriment? The imparting of the information is not a wrongful act of the defendant, being neither wrongful nor an act of the defendant. Accordingly, this should not be regarded as the most significant element. The choice is between the unauthorised use of the confidential information and the consequent detriment. Two points can be made in favour of the former. First, this fits in well with the jurisdiction rules. Jurisdiction is available under the Brussels Convention in the Contracting State in which the confidential information has been used in an unauthorised way. Admittedly, jurisdiction is also available in the Contracting State in which the damage occurred, but, as has been seen,[208] there is some uncertainty over what the damage is for jurisdictional purposes. Secondly, as a matter of English substantive law the requirement of detriment is not as firmly or long established as the other requirements. There is also, perhaps, more uncertainty over what constitutes detriment than there is in relation to the other requirements. It is submitted, therefore, that in a multi-country case, the law of the country in which the confidential information has been used in an unauthorised way should be applied.

(iv) Displacement of the general rule

The absence of cases decided under the common law tort choice of law rules makes it difficult to know what weight to attach to each of the relevant factors. However, it is submitted that the same weight should be given to the different types of factor as in cases of direct passing-off.

(v) Savings

(a) *Public policy*

The position is very much the same as for passing-off. It is hard to see public policy having any part to play in cases of non-contractual breach of confidence when this is a cause of action known to English law.

(b) *Mandatory rules*

Non-contractual breach of confidence is derived from the common law and instances of such rules operating as mandatory rules of the forum are going to be extremely rare. In the specific case of non-contractual breach of confidence, it is hard to think of a situation where this would happen.

---

[208] See above, pp 440–441, 444.

IX
CRITICISM OF THE EXISTING LAW

Having examined the various tortious and other causes of action which are complementary to infringement, it can be seen that the existing law leads to complexity, uncertainty, inadequate protection, and a lack of uniformity.

1. COMPLEXITY

This can be illustrated by two examples. First, the same tort choice of law rules are not applied for all the causes of action which are complementary to infringement. The common law rules apply for malicious falsehood and defamation; whereas the statutory rules apply for the other causes of action in tort. Secondly, when it comes to applying the statutory tort choice of law rules, there are different problems in respect of each cause of action. Thus, for example, with passing-off, which is a cause of action known to English law, the problems are very different from those in relation to unfair competition, a cause of action unknown to English law.

2. UNCERTAINTY

A general criticism of the statutory tort choice of law rules is that when you come to apply them to anything other than negligent driving there is always uncertainty. But this is particularly so when applied to the various causes of action that are complementary to infringement. There is a number of reasons for this.

First, the English courts will be faced with claims based on a foreign law of unfair competition, delict or anti-trust. These are causes of action unknown to English law and raise questions in relation to the application of Part III that are extremely difficult to answer. Is the foreign cause of action tortious? Does the reservation in Section 14(2) apply? What are the events constituting the tort for the purposes of the general rule and the displacement rule? Is it against public policy to apply this foreign law? Does the application of the foreign law infringe the principle that an English court will not enforce a foreign revenue, penal or other public law? These questions do not cause the same difficulty in respect of causes of action which are known to English law.

Secondly, the fact that English law has separate torts of passing-off, malicious falsehood, and defamation, whereas many other countries have a wide all embracing cause of action for unfair competition means that the question looms large of when an action is to be characterised, on the one hand, as unfair competition and, on the other hand, according to its English equivalent of passing-off, malicious falsehood, or defamation. Part III gives no answer as to how this question is to be answered.

Thirdly, even where the cause of action is known to English law there can be uniquely difficult problems in this area. Non-contractual breach of confidence is extremely difficult to characterise (ie is it a tort for the purposes of private international law?) because of the uncertainty over its characterisation in the English substantive law.

Fourthly, Part III is particularly unclear where there is a multi-country tort and the cause of action is other than in respect of personal injury, death or damage to property. It is not clear whether passing-off is a cause of action in respect of property. All the other causes of action, though, are not in respect of property and so fall within that unfortunate category where, in effect, Part III does not provide an answer.

Fifthly, apart from actions for passing-off or defamation, there are few cases decided under the common law tort choice of law rules which can be used as a guide to solving some of the questions arising under the statutory rules. Questions, such as determining when there is a multi-country tort under the general rule, and what weight is to be attached to the different types of factor under the displacement rule.

3. Inadequate Protection

The protection of the reputation of a business and its products is greatly weakened by the unjustified exclusion of malicious falsehood and defamation from the scope of Part III, thereby subjecting them to the common law tort choice of law rules, with all the injustice that this entails.

4. Lack of Uniformity

There is a lack of uniformity in having different tort choice of law rules applying for different causes of action, despite the fact that they are all complementary to the tort of infringement and may be relied upon as parallel causes of action in the same proceedings.

X
GENERAL REFORM OF THE TORT CHOICE OF LAW RULES

It has already been seen, in the context of infringement, that, although general reform of the tort choice of law rules has a role to play, what are also needed, if you want certainty, are special choice of law rules for particular torts. This need is reinforced when you look at complementary torts and other causes of action. The criticisms made above show the unique problems that arise in relation to these particular torts. No general redraft of the tort choice of law rules is going to solve these problems.

XI
SPECIAL TORT CHOICE OF LAW RULES

The defects in the existing English law could be cured by having special tort choice of law rules for causes of action that are complementary to infringement. Before looking at the content of such rules two preliminary questions must be answered. First, should there be special tort choice of law rules for each of these different causes of action or just for unfair competition, which could be widely defined to include nearly all of these causes of action? Secondly, should the special tort choice of law rules be independent of the normal tort choice of law rules, or should they operate within the framework of these rules.

1. The Preliminary Questions

(a) rules for the different causes of action or just for unfair competition?

Retaining the existing framework of different causes of action has the great merit of familiarity. As far as English law is concerned, there is a psychological hurdle to be surmounted if tort choice of law rules are to be introduced just for unfair competition. It is particularly difficult for any country which does not have a law of unfair competition as part of its substantive law to accept this wide category for the purposes of tort choice of law. Moreover, unfair competition would have to be defined, although, as will be seen, this is not as difficult as might be thought.[209]

In countries which have a substantive law of unfair competition, there has been considerable discussion of special tort choice of law rules for this cause of action. There are well established precedents that could be followed. There is the Resolution of the Institute of International law and Article 136 of the Swiss Private International Law Statute. The great advantage for England of adopting special tort choice of law rules for unfair competition is that it is possible to define this concept in such a way

---

[209] See Article I of the Resolution of the Institute of International Law, discussed below, pp 707–708. But compare Law Commission Working Paper No 87 (1984), para 5.58.

as to encompass many of the English and foreign causes of action that are complementary to infringement,[210] including passing-off, malicious falsehood, defamation, unfair competition, wider Continental protection in delict, and non-contractual breach of confidence.[211] There would then be uniform tort choice of law rules for all of these causes of action. This is desirable for four reasons. First, it recognises that all of these causes of action have something in common: they are all complementary to the tort of infringement. Secondly, it is consistent with the law of jurisdiction where this wide category of unfair competition is likely to be adopted by the Court of Justice in cases under the Brussels Convention.[212] Thirdly, it is convenient that the same choice of law rule should apply, regardless of which cause of action is relied upon, particularly when a claim may be based upon parallel causes of action. Fourthly, it avoids the difficult question of characterisation of whether, for example, an action for unfair competition in the form of passing-off is one of passing-off or unfair competition.

(b) INDEPENDENT TORT CHOICE OF LAW RULES OR WITHIN THE FRAMEWORK OF EXISTING RULES?

This question is very closely related to the previous one. If it is decided to adopt a radical approach and introduce special tort choice of law rules for unfair competition, it is likely that this would also involve an equally radical introduction of independent tort choice of law rules. This is what has happened in the Resolution of the Institute of International Law and in Article 136 of the Swiss Private International Law Statute, and is the form that any future Hague Convention on the law applicable to unfair competition would take. Unfair competition, if this concept is very widely defined, is a complex area and is probably best served by having a whole set of independent rules, rather than by merely tinkering within the existing framework of tort choice of law rules, as has happened in a number of countries, such as Germany.[213]

On the other hand, if it is decided to introduce special tort choice of law rules for the different causes of action, this is likely to lead to the adoption of rules based on the existing framework of tort choice of law rules contained in Part III of the 1995 Act. The best argument for retaining the existing causes of action for the purposes of tort choice of law is that of familiarity. Familiarity would also suggest that the existing framework of

---

[210] But not breach of competition rules, which are discussed below at pp 718–719.
[211] It could also include inducement of breach of contract, see Article I (6) of the Resolution of the Institute of International Law, discussed below at p 708.
[212] See above, pp 371–372, 410.
[213] See Troller, n 135 above, at 34–11. See also Wengler, (1955) 4 *Am J Comp Law* 167, 174. *seq.*

tort choice of law rules should be retained. It would be a formidable task to invent a whole series of independent tort choice of law rules for all the different causes of action that are complementary to infringement. For some of these causes of action, such as passing-off, there are no foreign precedents for such independent rules. However, precedents are available for malicious falsehood, defamation, unfair competition and breach of competition rules.[214]

In practical terms then, the choice is between, on the one hand, independent tort choice of law rules for unfair competition and, on the other hand, special tort choice of law rules for the different causes of action, which would normally operate within the framework of existing tort choice of law rules. These two alternatives will now be considered.

2. Independent Tort Choice of Law Rules for Unfair Competition

This would be a very radical approach for English law to adopt in so far as it would involve both recognising a broad concept of unfair competition for the purposes of tort choice of law and introducing independent tort choice of law rules which would replace Part III of the 1995 Act entirely. There are though precedents that could be followed: there is the Resolution of the Institute of International Law; and Article 136 of the Swiss Private International Law Statute.

(a) THE RESOLUTION OF THE INSTITUTE OF INTERNATIONAL LAW

The Institute of International Law, at the Cambridge Session in 1983, adopted a Resolution on the Conflict of Laws Rules on Unfair Competition. Although the tort choice of law rules proposed in the Resolution are independent, when it comes to looking at the actual content of these rules they are surprisingly similar to those put forward by the Law Commissions for tort choice of law generally in their Working Paper,[215] in that there is, effectively, a general rule which looks to the place of injury, and a most significant relationship exception.

(i) The scope of the Resolution

Article I defines the area covered by the Resolution, adopting Article 10bis of the Paris Convention for the Protection of Industrial Property, as 'any act of competition contrary to honest practice in industrial or commercial matters'. It goes on to particularise acts so covered by giving as examples: passing-off one's goods as those of another; improper appropriation of a

---

[214] Discussed below, at pp 716–719.   [215] Working Paper No 87 (1984), see Model I.

competitor's efforts, including improper appropriation and disclosure of trade secrets; improper advertising; defamation or disparagement of a competitor in relation to his products or business; unfair price competition; improper interference with a competitor's business, as for example by inducing breach of a competitor's contract. This is an extremely wide definition. However, it does not cover, and this is deliberate, trade mark, patent and copyright infringement on the basis that, except where otherwise provided by treaty, statutes providing such protection are not given extraterritorial effect. Nor does it cover restrictive or monopolistic practices since they are seen as presenting special problems.

(ii) The general rules

Article II provides that:

(1) Where injury is caused to a competitor's business in a particular market by conduct which could reasonably have been expected to have that effect, the internal law of the State in which that market is situated should apply to determine the rights and liabilities of the parties, whether such conduct occurs in that State or in some other State or States.

(2) Where conduct causes injury to a Competitor's business in a number of markets situated in different States, the applicable law should be the internal law of each State where such a market is situated.

Paragraph (1) favours a place of injury rule over a place of acting rule. It gets over the definitional uncertainty in relation to the place of injury by making it clear that what is being referred to is the injury to a competitor's business in a particular market. The applicable law is that of the State in which that market is situated. A 'market' refers to the territory of a single State.[216] This rule is concerned with the immediate impact upon a competitor's business. Thus, if goods are passed off or advertised in State A causing injury to a competitor's business there, the law of that State will apply, even if that competitor is incorporated and has its principal place of business in State B.[217] It is required that injury to a competitor's business is reasonably foreseeable. In the situation where injury is not reasonably foreseeable, the applicable law is determined by Article IV, discussed below.

Another problem with a place of injury rule is that injury in unfair competition cases can occur in several States. Paragraph (2) makes it clear that where injury is caused to a competitor's business in a number of markets situated in different States, the applicable law should be the internal law of each State where such a market is situated. It is very inconvenient to have to apply several different laws and there is much to be said for trying to identify one single law in this situation. This is an argument for adopt-

---

[216] See the note accompanying Article II.   [217] Ibid.

ing a proper law of unfair competition solution.[218] As will be seen, the Resolution allows for the displacement of these general rules in exceptional circumstances, which it is contemplated include those where injury is suffered in so many States as to render impossible the application of the internal law of each place of injury.[219]

(iii) The exceptions

There are two provisions, both of which are concerned with the significance of the relationship with the parties, their conduct and the injury, which operate by way of exception to the general rules. Article III deals with the situation where the law applicable under the general rules has an insufficiently significant relationship with the parties, their conduct and the injury. Article IV deals with situations not covered by the rules stated in Article II. It is not entirely clear whether these Articles represent two exceptions to the general rule or merely one exception which applies in two different situations. These two provisions will now be examined.

(a) *Article III*

This states that:

In exceptional situations in which the State whose internal law would be applicable under the rules stated in Article II does not have a sufficiently significant relationship with the parties, their conduct and the injury, the internal law of the State indicated by the most relevant connecting factor, or by the majority of the relevant connecting factors, should be applied.

Like the flexible exception originally recommended by the Law Commissions, but not adopted in Part III of the 1995 Act, this exception has a threshold requirement whereby it is only triggered where the law that would be applicable under the general rules does not have a sufficiently significant relationship with the parties, their conduct and the injury. Reference to the significance of the relationship with the parties, their conduct and the injury is to be found in American law in the Restatement Second, Conflict of Laws.[220] In determining whether a State has a sufficiently significant relationship, the court should take into account all the material factors. This still leaves some uncertainty over when the relationship can be regarded as being not 'sufficiently' significant for these purposes. The note accompanying Article III gives as an example the situation, previously mentioned, in which injury is suffered in so many States as to render impracticable the application of the internal law of each place of injury.

---

[218] See generally Troller, n 135 above, at 34–11 et seq.
[219] See Article III discussed below. [220] Section 145.

This still leaves the question of identifying the law which is to displace the general rules. This is the law of the State indicated by the most relevant connecting factor, or by the majority of the relevant connecting factors. It is by no means obvious which State is so indicated. The accompanying note envisages that this would normally be the State 'where the defendant's conduct had the greatest immediate impact upon the plaintiff's business'. If it is not possible to identify such a State, the law of the State indicated by the most relevant connecting factor would usually be 'the internal law of the State of the plaintiff's principal place of business'.

(b) *Article IV*

This states that:

Rights and liabilities resulting from unfair competition in situations that are not covered by the rules stated in Article II should be determined by the internal law of the State which has the most significant relationship with the parties, their conduct and the injury.

Examples of situations not covered by Article II include[221] where the place of injury cannot be identified;[222] or no market is involved, as where a competitor's employee is enticed to leave his employment; or the defendant establishes that he could not reasonably have foreseen that he would by his conduct have caused injury to the plaintiff's business in a particular State. In each of these situations, the applicable law is that of the State which has the most significant relationship with the parties, their conduct and the injury. The 'most significant relationship' is determined in the same way as for Article III.

(iv) Public policy

Article VII provides that the rules in the Resolution 'need not be applied if they would lead to a result which would be manifestly incompatible with the public policy of the forum'.

(v) Preparations for an act of unfair competition

Article V provides that 'preparations for an act of unfair competition may be restrained by injunction under the law of the State where those preparations are made'. This is a welcome provision. It is analogous to the English and Scots position at common law in cases of enabling passing-off.[223] This would cover the sorts of preparatory acts found in the Scotch

---

[221] See the note accompanying the Article.
[222] Dyer gives as an example a case of inducement of breach of contract affecting the bank balance of a company, n 5 above, at p 434.
[223] See above, p 654.

whisky cases, but it has also been suggested that it would encompass the situation where deceptive advertising is being broadcast from one country to another.[224] The fact that there is no exception to this Article brings welcome certainty to the law.[225]

(b) ARTICLE 136 SWISS PIL STATUTE

(i) The scope of the provision

This provision is intended to encompass what is regarded as unfair competition under the substantive law of Switzerland.[226] The Swiss federal law against unfair competition of 19 December 1986 gives a wide definition to this concept. However, the provision is also intended to apply to claims brought under foreign laws of unfair competition which may be wider than Swiss law.[227]

(ii) The general rule

Article 136(1) states that 'Claims of unfair competition are governed by the law of the country in whose market the unfair act has its effect'. Essentially, the same provision is to be found in the Austrian Federal Law on Private International Law of 15 June 1978.[228] Moreover, there are some choice of law cases in the United States which, in effect, apply this rule.[229] The terminology used in Article 136(1) is different from that under the general rule contained in Article II(1) of the Resolution of the Institute of International Law.[230] However, it is doubtful whether it leads to the application of any different law from that applicable under the Resolution. The effect on a market of an act of unfair competition presumably is to cause injury to a competitor's business in that particular market. Concentration, for choice of law purposes, on the effects of acts of unfair competition is also a common theme in German literature and case law.[231] The Law Commissions have described this general rule as '... in theory, attractive ...'.[232] However, they point out that more than one market might be affected and that the market affected might be a truly supra-national one.[233]

---

[224] See Dyer, n 5 above, at p 439.
[225] Compare the position under the statutory tort choice of law rules in relation to enabling passing-off, discussed above, pp 666–667.
[226] See Imhoff-Scheier and Patocchi, *Torts and Unjust Enrichment in the New Swiss Conflict of Laws*, pp 155–156.
[227] Ibid.
[228] Article 48, para 2.   [229] See Scoles and Hay, *Conflict of Laws* (2d ed), pp 629–630.
[230] Discussed above.   [231] See Troller, n 135 above, at 34–11.
[232] Law Commission Working Paper No 87 (1984), para 5.58.
[233] Ibid.

(iii) The exceptions

(a) Article 136(2)

This provides that:

> If the unlawful act is directed exclusively against operational interests of the damaged or injured party, the applicable law will be that of the country in which the establishment concerned is located.

Article 136(2) draws a distinction between whether the unlawful act is directed exclusively against operational interests of the damaged or injured party or not, and applies in the former case. This is not an easy distinction to apply. It has been suggested that operational interests are ones affecting the internal interests of an enterprise, but not directly its relations with the public.[234] In line with this, it has been commented that 'Operational interests are violated in case of sabotage, economic espionage, or inducement to breach of contract'.[235] On the other hand, it has been said that such interests would not be violated in cases involving negative advertising or unfair comparison.[236] Nor, presumably, would they be in a case of unfair competition by passing-off.

(b) Article 133(3)

Article 133 subsection 3 of the PIL Statute is reserved. This provides that '. . . when a tortious act violates a pre-existing legal relationship between the tortfeasor and the injured party, the claims based on this act are governed by the law applicable to that legal relationship'. What is noticeable about this provision is its narrowness. It is confined to where a pre-existing relationship is violated. This would cover a contractual relationship between the parties, but it is arguable that it would extend to the situation where the parties are merely negotiating and, for example, confidential information is passed on giving rise to a legal relationship between the parties by way of a duty of confidence. This would leave the question to be answered: what law is applicable to that legal relationship? This is easy enough if the relationship is contractual, it is the law governing the contract. But what if the relationship is non-contractual, what law governs the duty to maintain a confidence?

---

[234] See Troller, n 135 above, at 34–12.
[235] Karrer and Arnold, *Switzerland's Private International Law Statute* 2nd ed, p 124. see also Troller, n 135 above, at 34–12.
[236] Karrer and Arnold, n 235 above.

(c) Article 15

Article 15 is a general provision in relation to the applicable law under the statute. It provides in paragraph 1 that:

1. The law applicable under the provisions of this Act shall exceptionally not be applied where, in view of the circumstances as a whole, the situation clearly appears to have only a loose connection with that system of law and a much closer connection with another system.

This is similar to Article III of the Resolution of the Institute of International Law. It too has a threshold requirement, in this case that there is only 'a loose connection' with the law applicable under Article 136 and a much closer connection with another system. However, unlike Article III, it does not actually say what law does apply. It is implicit, though, that this must be the law of the system with which there is a much closer connection. A possible example of a situation where this provision would operate is that where the unfair act has its effect in country A but an injunction is sought preventing a preparatory act in country B. It has been suggested that the law of country B would apply under this exception.[237] It has also been suggested that Article 15 can displace the law applicable under Article 133(3).[238]

It is important to note that the normal tort choice of law rule under the Statute, that the law of the parties' common habitual residence is applied,[239] does not operate in cases of unfair competition.

(d) Public policy, mandatory rules

The general exceptions in the Statute relating to public policy[240] and the mandatory provisions of Swiss law[241] and of foreign law[242] will apply equally to unfair competition as to any other tort.

(e) A HAGUE CONVENTION ON THE LAW APPLICABLE TO UNFAIR COMPETITION

The Hague Conference on Private International Law has this topic on its agenda, and a considerable amount of preliminary work has been done.[243] However, there is not thought to be a pressing need for a Convention, and so other topics have been given priority on the agenda.

---

[237] See Dyer, n 5 above, at pp 436–439.
[238] Imhoff-Scheier and Patocchi, n 226 above, at pp 177–179.
[239] Article 133(1).
[240] Article 17.
[241] Article 18.
[242] Article 19.
[243] See Prel Doc No 2 November 1987 'Exploratory Study on the Law Applicable to Unfair Competition'.

714   *Intellectual Property and Private International Law*

3. Special Tort Choice of Law Rules for the Different Causes of Action

This is a much less radical approach in that it would retain, for tort choice of law purposes, the separate causes of action protecting the business and goods of competitors, and the basic framework of the statutory tort choice of law rules. Even so, it is a very different approach from the one applied under the present English law. The Law Commissions considered having special tort choice of law rules for particular torts, including economic torts, but were opposed to this.[244] Nonetheless, introducing separate special tort choice of law rules for each cause of action protecting the business and goods of competitors would provide an answer to many of the unanswered questions that arise when the statutory tort choice of law rules are applied to these causes of action.

(a) POLICY CONSIDERATIONS WHEN DECIDING UPON THE RULES

The policy considerations that should be borne in mind when determining the content of special tort choice of law rules for complementary torts are, by and large, the same as for infringement.[245] First, for reasons of familiarity, it is best that they operate within the framework of existing statutory tort choice of law rules. Secondly, they need to be certain. Thirdly, they need to be compatible, as far as possible, with the jurisdiction rules for that particular cause of action. Fourthly, they should be consistent with the tort choice of law rules for infringement. Fifthly, and this is different from infringement, the separate special tort choice of law rules for one cause of action that is complementary to infringement need to be consistent with the rules for other complementary causes of action.

(b) SUGGESTED RULES

(i) Passing-off

Although the Law Commissions were opposed to having special rules for particular torts, they acknowledged that passing-off was one area in which it might seem possible to have such a special provision, and that it might be suggested that the, *prima facie*, applicable law 'should be that of the country in which the product was passed off'.[246] Nonetheless, they decided not to recommend this rule because of a concern that it could lead to the courts being no longer able to apply English law under the doctrine

---
[244] Law Commission Working Paper No 87 (1984), paras 5.1–5.70.
[245] See above, pp 645–646.
[246] Law Commission Working Paper No 87 (1984), para 5.59.

Complementary torts and other causes of action: the applicable law 715

of enabling passing-off abroad. This concern is unjustified, given that enabling passing-off is a separate tort from direct passing-off. The adoption of a special rule for direct passing-off can have no effect on this other tort. Moreover, it is perfectly possible to adopt two special rules: one for enabling passing-off; the other for direct passing-off. [247]

(a) *Enabling passing-off abroad*

The present uncertainty can be ended by having a special rule that, in a case of enabling passing-off abroad, the applicable law should be that of the country where the act of enabling was committed. There should be no displacement of this rule. This would turn the clock back to the position at common law. The approach adopted at common law has been described by the Law Commissions as being convenient.[248] In cases involving acts of enabling in England, normally there will be no difficulty in asserting jurisdiction since the defendant will usually be domiciled/resident in England.[249] The English court will then apply English law.

(b) *Direct passing-off*

A lot of the present uncertainty can be ended by having a general rule that, with direct passing-off, the applicable law should be that of the country where the misrepresentation was made. This would be compatible with the choice of law rule for infringement, according to which the law of the country where the act of infringement occurred is, normally, applied.[250] The misrepresentation is likely to take place in the same country, with the result that the same law will apply to both causes of action. The suggested rule also fits in with jurisdiction rules in so far as that in those cases where jurisdiction is based on an act of misrepresentation in England the court will end up applying English law. Naturally, it is not possible to fit in with all the many different bases of jurisdiction. It is submitted that there should remain the possibility of displacement of this general rule, since there is this possibility in infringement cases. It is not possible to define in advance when displacement should operate. It would be best to simply retain the flexible wording of Section 12 of Part III. In applying this section, the same weight should be given to the different types of factor as has been suggested above when discussing the present law in relation to direct passing-off.[251] As with the present law, it is doubtful whether, in practice, the displacement rule will operate in simple cases of direct passing-off, or even in complex cases.

[247] See the Resolution of the Institute of International Law, discussed above, pp 708–711.
[248] Law Commission Working Paper No 87 (1984), para 5.59.
[249] See above, pp 371, 381.   [250] See above, pp 620–621.   [251] See pp 664–666.

(ii) Malicious falsehood

The common law tort choice of law rules should not operate. Instead, there should be special tort choice of law rules operating within the framework of the statutory tort choice of law rules. For the reasons given above,[252] it would be best not to adopt the American precedent of the special rules for injurious falsehood found in the Restatement, Second, Conflict of Laws. As a general rule, the applicable law should be that of the country where the false statement was made. This would follow what is probably the position at common law and would be compatible with the special tort choice of law rules suggested for the complementary torts of passing-off and infringement. As with these other causes of action, there should remain the possibility of displacement under Section 12, with the weighting to be attached to the different types of factor as suggested above in cases of direct passing-off.[253]

(iii) Defamation of a business competitor

Here too, the common law tort choice of law rules should not operate. There should be special tort choice of law rules operating within the framework of the statutory tort choice of law rules. As a general rule, the applicable law should be that of the country where the publication occurred. This follows the position at common law and that adopted under the American Restatement, Second, Conflict of Laws.[254] This rule would apply equally to defamation over the internet. As with passing-off, malicious falsehood and infringement, there should remain the possibility of displacement under Section 12, with the weighting to be attached to the different types of factor as suggested above in cases of direct passing-off.

(iv) Unfair competition

We are concerned here with claims characterised as unfair competition under the present English law.[255] Much has been written by both civil and common lawyers in relation to special tort choice of law rules for unfair competition and a number of alternative solutions have been put forward. The key question is the familiar one of whether such rules should operate within the framework of existing tort choice of law rules, as is the case with the other causes of action considered above, or whether they should be independent.

---

[252] At pp 706–707.   [253] At pp 664–666.
[254] Section 149. Section 150 is concerned with multi-State defamation, ie where publication occurs in two or more States. Normally, the law of the plaintiff's domicile will apply, provided that there was publication in that State.
[255] See above, pp 680–681.

(a) Keeping within the framework of existing statutory tort choice of law rules

This would involve having a general rule and an exception.

(i) The general rule

There is a wide variety of different formulations that could be adopted as a general rule. However, the real choice is between looking at the act of unfair competition and the effects of that act. The arguments in favour of a place of injury rule in preference to a place of acting rule have already been considered[256] and need not be repeated. It would be best, though, not to refer in the rule to 'damage' as such, because of the definitional problem inherent in this. Instead, a formulation should be adopted which is based on the idea of the market where the parties compete with each other. The precise terms of the rule could follow any one of three different formulations.

First, the applicable law should be the law of the market where the competing interests collide. This follows Continental case law.[257] Moreover, the International League Against Unfair Competition, at its Nice Congress in 1967, adopted a motion in favour of applying the law of the place where the tort was committed, defining this place as that where the collision of interests occurs.[258]

Secondly, the applicable law should be the law of the country where the market, in which injury to a competitor's business has been caused, is situated. This is based on Article II(1) of the Resolution of the Institute of International Law.[259]

Thirdly, the applicable law should be the law of the country in whose market the unfair act of competition has its effect. This is the rule contained in Article 136(1) of the Swiss Private International Law Statute.[260]

It would not appear to matter which formulation is adopted in terms of the result produced. It is submitted, though, that the second formulation is the easiest to understand and is therefore preferable to the other two formulations. This rule would apply equally to unfair competition over the internet.

(ii) The exception

As with the above causes of action, there would remain the possibility of displacement under Section 12, with the weighting to be attached to the different types of factor mentioned in Section 12(2) of the 1995 Act, as suggested above.[261]

---

[256] See above, pp 686–687.
[258] See Dyer, n 5 above, at pp 417–418.
[260] See above, p 711.
[257] See Troller, n 135 above, at 34–11.
[259] See above, p 708.
[261] At pp 687–688.

(b) Independent tort choice of law rules

The alternative would be to apply independent tort choice of law rules for unfair competition which could be taken from the Resolution of the Institute of International law or from Article 136 of the Swiss Private International Law Statute. This would be a more radical approach, involving taking both the general rule and the exception from these sets of independent rules. However, unlike under these independent rules, unfair competition would have to be narrowly defined to only cover actions characterised as unfair competition under the present English law.

(v) Wider Continental protection in delict

Given that what is involved is a cause of action unknown to English law, the problem in devising a suitable general rule is essentially the same as that for unfair competition. It is more appropriate to focus upon the damage than the wrongful act for the reasons outlined in relation to unfair competition. Accordingly, the applicable law should be that of the country where damage is caused to a competitor's business. As with the above causes of action, there should be the possibility of displacement under Section 12, with the weighting to be attached to the different types of factor as suggested above.[262]

(vi) Breach of competition rules

The key decision in devising suitable special tort choice of law rules is the same as that encountered in relation to unfair competition. A choice has to be made between keeping within the framework of the normal statutory tort choice of law rules and adopting independent rules.

(a) *Keeping within the framework of existing statutory tort choice of law rules*

(i) *The general rule*

It would be possible to invent a rule, adopting the same solution as for the general rule for unfair competition.[263] For example, the applicable law could be that of the country where damage is caused to a competitor's business.

(ii) *The exception*

There would remain the possibility of displacement under Section 12, with the weighting to be attached to the different types of factor, as suggested above.[264]

---

[262] At p 693. [263] See above, p 717. [264] At pp 687–688.

(iii) *Savings: a foreign penal, revenue or other public law*
What has been said earlier[265] on this topic, in the context of the current law, is equally applicable in the present context.

(b) Independent tort choice of law rules

The alternative would be to look at what other countries do and apply their independent tort choice of law rules for breach of competition rules. The Swiss Private International Law Statute has such rules. Article 137 provides that:

1. Claims of restraint of competition are governed by the law of the country in whose market the restraint directly affects the damaged or injured party.

2. If claims of restraint of competition are governed by foreign law, no damages can be awarded in Switzerland beyond those that would be awarded under Swiss law in case of an unlawful restraint of competition.

This provision applies to what is regarded as breach of competition under the substantive law of Switzerland, but is intended also to apply to claims brought under foreign laws of unfair competition.[266]

The general rule is set out in paragraph 1. This rule is similar to the Swiss general rule for unfair competition, and shows a willingness to apply foreign anti-trust laws. There is though a requirement that the effect on the market be 'direct'.

The first exception to this general rule is contained in paragraph 2, which limits the damages that may be awarded where a foreign law is applied to what would be awarded under Swiss law.[267] The second exception is Article 15 of the Statute, which will apply in this context as it does in relation to unfair competition.[268]

Other exceptions are to be found in the general provisions under the Statute: ie, public policy;[269] mandatory provisions of Swiss law (which can be used to uphold Swiss cartels);[270] mandatory provisions of foreign law.[271]

(vii) Breach of confidence

Special tort choice of law rules would resolve any uncertainty over the characterisation of non-contractual breach of confidence. This is a cause of action known to English law. Accordingly, as with most other such causes of action, the general rule should be based on the wrongful act. It is submitted that the applicable law should be that of the country in which the

---

[265] At pp 696–697. [266] See Imhoff-Scheier and Patocchi, p 159.
[267] An analogous provision is found in relation to product liability, see Article 135(2).
[268] See above, p 713. [269] Article 17. [270] Article 18.
[271] Article 19.

confidential information has been used in an unauthorised way. If the unauthorised use takes place in England, the English courts have jurisdiction and will end up applying English law.[272] There should be the possibility of displacement under Section 12 of the 1995 Act, with the weighting to be attached to the different types of factor, as suggested above.[273]

[272] See Article 5(3) of the Brussels Convention, discussed above, pp 439–440.
[273] At pp 664–666.

SECTION III

RECOGNITION AND ENFORCEMENT OF FOREIGN JUDGMENTS

Preliminary Remarks

The first two stages of a private international law case, ie jurisdiction and choice of law, have already been examined. There is, though, a third stage, namely that of the recognition and enforcement of the judgment. It may be possible to enforce the judgment in the State in which the action was brought, but where this is not possible it is necessary to recognise and enforce the judgment in some other State in which the defendant has assets.

Intellectual property is exploited internationally in most cases. Infringement of parallel rights often takes place in more than one country at the same time and in the same way. If a single court is to deal with the infringement case, its judgment will often need to be recognised and enforced in all other countries concerned. The recognition and enforcement of interim orders can, in this respect, create particularly complicated problems. On top of these special situations, there are, obviously, those intellectual property related cases where a judgment needs to be recognised and enforced abroad in those countries where the defendant has assets, if no assets are to be found in the forum.

The national and territorial character of intellectual property rights may give rise to problems. National courts may see it as their exclusive prerogative to deal with national intellectual property rights, and especially with their validity, and they may refuse the recognition and enforcement of foreign judgments that dealt with their national rights.

The rules on recognition and enforcement of foreign judgments apply to all judgments. Judgments in relation to intellectual property are not subject to special rules. Most of the rules do not create specific problems for judgments in relation to intellectual property. However, it is fair to say that the rules on recognition and enforcement have, in the past, not been used extensively in relation to these judgments. As we discussed above, intellectual property lawyers experienced serious problems in relation to jurisdiction in relation to foreign intellectual property rights when bringing a case in the English courts. The impression was created that each intellectual property right was only dealt with in the country in which it had been created. That meant that few attempts were made to have foreign intellectual property related judgments recognised and enforced in any part of the United Kingdom. Hence the reduced importance of the rules on recognition and enforcement of foreign judgments in this context. It is submitted, though, that that importance will grow in the future. We have demonstrated, in the first two parts of this book, that many of the restrictions on jurisdiction and choice of law have been or ought to be removed.

This should lead to an increase of English judgments dealing with foreign intellectual property rights and a similar tendency is already showing abroad. This will inevitably give rise to attempts to recognise foreign intellectual property related judgments in one or more parts of the United Kingdom.

We will not attempt to deal with every single aspect of the issues raised by the recognition and enforcement of foreign judgments. We will rather focus our attention on those issues that are particularly relevant in relation to intellectual property rights.

14

Recognition and Enforcement of Foreign Judgments Relating to Intellectual Property

I	Introduction		724
II	How problems arise in intellectual property cases		724
III	The Brussels Convention		725
	1. The scope of the Convention		725
		(a) A judgment given in a Contracting State	725
		(b) The type of jurisdiction rule is irrelevant	726
		(c) The judgment is given in respect of a civil and commercial matter	726
		(d) *Ex parte* orders are not covered	726
	2. Recognition of the foreign judgment		727
		(a) An essential first step	727
		(b) The rebuttable presumption in favour of recognition	727
		(c) Defences against recognition	728
	3. Enforcement of the foreign judgment		732
IV	The Lugano Convention		733
V	The Common Law system		733
	1. Requirements		734
		(a) The jurisdiction of the foreign court	734
		(b) The finality of the foreign judgment	735
		(c) The judgment must be for a fixed sum of money	735
		(d) No examination of the merits	735
	2. Defences against recognition and enforcement		736
		(a) Fraud	736
		(b) Public policy	736
		(c) A foreign penal law	737
		(d) The Protection of Trading Interests Act 1980	737
		(e) The natural justice defence	738
		(f) Cause of action estoppel	738
		(g) The foreign judgment is in breach of a dispute settlement agreement	738
VI	Enforcement of foreign judgments by statute		739
VII	Decisions in relation to supranational or semi-supranational rights		740

I
INTRODUCTION

Under English law, the recognition and enforcement of foreign judgments is complicated by the fact that there is a wide variety of different sets of rules dealing with this topic. A basic distinction can be made though between recognition and enforcement under the EC/EFTA rules, and recognition and enforcement under the traditional English rules. Both systems will be examined in this chapter. We will also, briefly, turn our attention to the special rules that exist in relation to supranational or semi-supranational intellectual property rights. It is submitted as a preliminary comment that intellectual property related cases give rise to few special problems as regards recognition and enforcement of foreign judgments, hence the relative brevity of this chapter.

II
HOW PROBLEMS ARISE IN INTELLECTUAL PROPERTY CASES

The first set of problems arises out of the territorial and exclusive nature of intellectual property rights and their close link with competition law. The country that grants the intellectual property right typically also deals with its validity. However, there might be occasions where a foreign court, for example in infringement proceedings, has determined the validity of a foreign intellectual property right. Will an English court recognise the foreign judgment and authorise its enforcement in such a situation? And is it only the validity point that creates these problems? Arguably, a territorial right applies only in the country that granted it and maybe its infringement should exclusively be dealt with by the courts of the granting country. Would that mean that a foreign judgment would not be recognised and enforced even if it deals only with the infringement issue? Would any other solution offend against public policy?

A second set of problems surrounds the recognition and enforcement of foreign interim orders. Should an English court recognise and enforce such an order which was, for example, granted by a Dutch court in a case of alleged infringement of Dutch, English and French parallel patents? The Dutch court may have taken jurisdiction to grant an extraterritorial interim order on a basis which is not readily accepted by the English courts. Does that influence the decision at the recognition and enforcement stage?

In contrast, few problems arise when foreign judgments that deal with disputes in relation to contracts concerning the commercial exploitation of intellectual property rights need to be recognised and enforced in England. This is because of the straightforwardly contractual nature of such disputes.

III
THE BRUSSELS CONVENTION

The Brussels Convention on Jurisdiction and the Enforcement of Judgments in Civil and Commercial Matters 1968, as amended, contains one of the main systems of rules for the recognition and the enforcement of foreign judgments. However, since the Convention does not cover all foreign judgments, its scope will have to be defined precisely and the systems that apply to judgments that fall outside its scope will be discussed later on in this chapter. The Brussels Convention contains separate rules on recognition and enforcement. They will be analysed in as far as they apply to intellectual property related cases. Interim orders and revocation orders are obvious examples of 'judgments' arising in such cases.

The Convention's aim is that judgments should circulate freely within the Community, so as not to cause any disturbance to economic life. To achieve this, the Convention provides an almost automatic recognition mechanism and a simplified and rather procedural enforcement mechanism. These have only become possible as a result of the harmonisation of the bases on which the courts take jurisdiction in the first place. The controls could only be relaxed at the recognition and enforcement stage, because strict and uniform controls have been introduced at the jurisdictional stage.

1. THE SCOPE OF THE CONVENTION

(a) A JUDGMENT GIVEN IN A CONTRACTING STATE

According to the Convention,[1] its rules on recognition and enforcement will apply to the exclusion of all other rules where the judgment concerned has been given in a Contracting State. Article 25 defines the term 'judgment' widely as 'any judgment given by a Court or Tribunal in a Contracting State'. Courts at all levels are covered by this provision and the use of the words 'any judgment' signals that the rules will apply irrespective of the type of judgment, order, decree, decision etc. There is no

---
[1] Articles 26 and 31.

726   *Intellectual Property and Private International Law*

requirement that the judgment is a final one.[2] As far as intellectual property cases are concerned, an injunction can come within Article 25, as can an interim order.

(b) THE TYPE OF JURISDICTION RULE IS IRRELEVANT

As long as recognition and enforcement is sought in relation to a judgment that has been given by a court or a tribunal in a Contracting State, the Convention applies irrespective of the basis on which that court or tribunal took jurisdiction. It is by no means necessary that the court or the tribunal took jurisdiction on the basis of a jurisdictional rule that is contained in the Brussels Convention.[3] It could have taken jurisdiction on the basis of a traditional national rule.

(c) THE JUDGMENT IS GIVEN IN RESPECT OF A CIVIL AND COMMERCIAL MATTER

This is the point where the scope of the Convention is restricted. The Convention's rules on recognition and enforcement will only be applicable if the judgment is given in respect of a matter coming within the scope of the Convention. The Convention's definition of civil and commercial matters does not need to be repeated here, suffice it to say that the same definition applies in relation to jurisdiction and recognition and enforcement. This matter is always raised at the recognition and enforcement stage and the court that is asked to recognise and to enforce a judgment is obliged to take a fresh look at the matter. Irrespective of the outcome at the jurisdictional stage, it has to examine whether or not the matter falls within the scope of the Convention. Only a positive answer will lead to the application of the Convention's rules on recognition and enforcement[4].

(d) *EX PARTE* ORDERS ARE NOT COVERED

The Convention's automatic recognition and enforcement system applies on the assumption that the final judgment will only be handed down after both parties have been notified of the proceedings and were given the opportunity to put their case to the court. Proceedings which by their nature exclude that are not covered.[5] *Ex parte* orders, where the defendant was unaware of the proceedings and only the plaintiff's arguments were

---

[2] See Case 143/78 *De Cavel* v *De Cavel* [1979] ECR 1055.
[3] See Case 178/83 *Firma P* v *Firma K* [1984] ECR 3033.
[4] See Giardina (1978) 27 *ICLQ* 263, at 275.   [5] See Article 27(2) of the Convention.

before the court, cannot be recognised or enforced under the Convention's system of rules.[6]

Ex parte orders are often applied for in intellectual property infringement cases and especially in relation to copyright. The fact that they cannot be recognised and enforced within the European Community under the simplified Convention system creates a serious hurdle and it may oblige the plaintiff to apply for a separate order in each of the countries involved. This was demonstrated in a case involving EMI Records, where enforcement of a German *ex parte* permanent injunction was refused, because the defendant had not been served with process in the judgment granting State and had not been given an opportunity to be heard before the order was made. The fact that the defendant was given a reasonable opportunity at a later date prior to the enforcement of the judgment to apply to the court that made the order to have it set aside does not remove the *ex parte* character of the order.[7]

2. Recognition of the Foreign Judgment

(a) an essential first step

No foreign judgment can be enforced until it has been recognised. Recognition is an essential first step towards the enforcement of the foreign judgment. Enforcement will not always follow though. If the judgment is simply to be used as a defence in a new action its recognition will be sufficient. And finally, recognition can also operate on its own, for example to establish a title to property or by way of a set-off.

(b) the rebuttable presumption in favour of recognition

Article 26 of the Convention stipulates that 'a judgment given in a Contracting State shall be recognised in the other Contracting States without any special procedure being required'. No requirements and procedures are added to this rule. A foreign judgment should automatically be given the same effects in the recognising State as it has in the State in which it was given.[8] However, the automatic recognition is in reality nothing more than a rebuttable presumption that judgments are to be recognised.[9] This must be the logical consequence of the fact that the Convention also

---

[6] Case 125/79 *Denilauler* v *Couchet Frères* [1981] ECR 1553.
[7] *EMI Records Ltd* v *Modern Music Karl-Ulrich Walterbach GmbH* [1992] 1 QB 115, [1992] 1 All ER 616, [1991] 3 WLR 663.
[8] Case 145/86 *Hoffmann* v *Krieg* [1988] ECR 645.
[9] See the opinion of the Advocate General in Case 42/76 *De Wolf* v *Cox* [1976] ECR 1759, [1977] 2 CMLR 43.

lists a number of defences against the recognition of foreign judgments. The presence, in practice, of any of these defences will rebut the presumption and block the recognition of the foreign judgment.[10]

(c) DEFENCES AGAINST RECOGNITION

(i) Public policy

The main defence against the recognition of a foreign judgment is the fact that such recognition would be contrary to public policy in the State in which recognition is sought.[11] This defence should not be used to dispute the merits of the original decision. Differences between the substantive law or in the rules on private international law applied by the court that gave the judgment and the law or the rules that would have been applied by the court that is asked to recognise the judgment if it had considered the case, should not trigger the operation of the public policy defence and neither should, as such, the absence of reasons in the original judgment. The defence only operates if the recognition rather than the judgment itself is contrary to public policy. Another way of putting it is that the recognition should produce results in the recognising country which cannot be reconciled with its public policy. Clearly, such a defence will only apply in exceptional circumstances. Arguably,[12] public policy can only be invoked if the decision of the foreign court was reached on the basis of proceedings that deviate from the basic principles of the recognising country's procedural law to such an extent that, according to the law of the recognising country, the decision cannot have been reached in regular and constitutional proceedings.[13] Recognising such a judgment would have unacceptable results in the recognising country. The situation where the defendant is given notification of the institution of the original action, but is then denied a reasonable opportunity to present his case, is a good example of this.[14] It is submitted that there may be other extreme cases in which the defence could be applied outside the purely procedural field, as long as recognition would produce harmful and totally unacceptable results in the recognising country. Examples are the situation where the recognition of the foreign judgment would be unconscionable because of the outrageous character of the substantive rule[15] that was applied by the original court, and the situation where recognition of the judgment would put the economic and foreign policy of the United Kingdom at risk. Finally, fraud can also be brought under the public policy heading.[16] However, this can only

---

[10] See, eg Article 27.
[11] Article 27(1) of the Convention.
[12] Bertrams, (1995) 26 *IIC* 618, at 631.
[13] Kropholler, *Europäisches Zivilprozessrecht*, Heidelberg, (1993), Article 27, No 7.
[14] See Article 27(2) of the Convention.   [15] Eg leading to payment for illegal activities.
[16] See *Interdesco SA v Nullifire Ltd* [1992] 1 Lloyd's Rep 180.

be done if a number of requirements are met. First, the foreign court should not have ruled on the precise matters which the defendant seeks to raise. Secondly, the defendant should, first of all, pursue any available remedy in the country in which the judgment that is allegedly tainted by fraud was given. And thirdly, a challenge to the foreign judgment should only be entertained if a challenge to an English judgment would be permitted in similar circumstances.

When it comes to intellectual property rights, difficult problems may arise because of the territorial character of such rights. This has led to the assumption that the courts of the granting country will have exclusive competence to deal with these rights and especially with their validity. If a foreign court dealt with these rights, and their validity in particular, it could be argued that the domestic court could refuse recognition on the basis that this would be contrary to its public policy. However, this line of argument cannot be accepted. This will become clear when we examine by way of illustration what would happen if the foreign court concluded that the intellectual property right was invalid and granted a revocation order. The question then arises whether a revocation order granted by a court in the Contracting State with infringement jurisdiction will be recognised in other Contracting States. Clearly, it will not be in the situation where the courts of another Contracting State have exclusive jurisdiction under Article 16(4), but this is a matter for Article 28 of the Convention[17] rather than for the public policy defence. However, even where this is not the situation, recognition could, arguably,[18] be refused on the ground of public policy.[19] Against this, it should be noted that this concept is only used in exceptional cases,[20] and normally (Article 16 is an exception) cannot be used to review the jurisdiction of the judgment granting State. It cannot be used to review an assertion of jurisdiction. It is submitted that any use of the public policy defence in this context can not be justified. Article 27(1) should not be used to check whether the substance of the foreign judgment can be reconciled with the public policy of the recognising country.[21] The question is whether recognition as a judicial decision is reconcilable with that public policy. The court can check whether the foreign decision is of such a nature that it can be treated as the equivalent of a domestic judgment. Criteria such as proper notice of the proceedings and time and opportunity to present one's arguments become relevant here, but apart from these marginal aspects of natural justice, the foreign procedure cannot be tested in the light of the public policy of the recognising country.[22] Whilst made by way of illustration in the context of a revocation order,

---

[17] See below, pp 731–732.
[18] Wadlow, (1985) 10 *ELR* 305 at 313.
[19] Article 27(1).
[20] Case 145/86 *Hoffmann* v *Krieg* [1988] ECR 645.
[21] See *SISRO* v *Ampersand Software BV* [1994] ILPr 55 (CA).
[22] See Court of Appeal Paris, judgment of 28 January 1994, *Braillecellen II*, [1994] BIE 395.

these comments are of general application whenever the public policy defence is invoked. This was also the view of the Court of Appeal in Paris[23] when it was asked to recognise a Dutch intellectual property related decision.

This decision needs to be applauded, but it also brings us to the difficult and more specialised issue of interim measures, as the Dutch decision was an interim one. This was the first occasion on which a foreign court had to decide whether or not to recognise Dutch extraterritorial interim measures granted in the context of a Kort Geding. Will such an injunction be recognised and enforced in other Contracting States? Under the Brussels and Lugano Conventions, judgments granted in one Contracting State are recognised in other Contracting States on a semi-automatic basis. A 'judgment', for these purposes, includes an injunction. The Dutch Kort Geding procedure is not an *ex parte* one and so the rule which precludes the recognition of *ex parte* orders will not operate. Would recognition of a cross-border injunction be contrary to public policy in the State in which recognition is sought? This defence to recognition is only to be used in exceptional cases and it is submitted that this is not such a case. This is supported by the decision of the Paris Court of Appeals which has held that recognition of a Dutch cross-border injunction would not be contrary to public policy.[24] In the view of the French court, the Dutch decision comes under the normal rules on recognition and is treated like any other decision. This means that the reasoning which was explained in the previous paragraph applies and the defence cannot apply in this type of case.

(ii) Natural justice

The impact of the absence of proper notice of the proceedings, etc[25] was discussed above in relation to the scope of the Convention. The defendant must have received proper notice and he must have been given the time and the opportunity to defend himself in court. This rule applies to any type of proceedings. There is no need to add anything else at this stage and this defence does not raise any special problems in relation to intellectual property related cases.

(iii) Irreconcilable judgment in the recognising State

A judgment that has been given in the State in which recognition is sought operates as a defence against the recognition of the foreign judgment.[26] Such a judgment can be given before or even after the foreign judgment.

---

[23] See Court of Appeal Paris, judgment of 28 January 1994, *Braillecellen II*, [1994] BIE 395, with comment by Verkade, see also [1995] 3 *EIPR* D-73.

[24] *Ibid*. It should be noted that the French Courts were not in a position to grant measures similar to those granted by the Dutch Courts.

[25] Article 27(2) of the Convention. [26] Article 27(3) of the Convention.

On top of that, the two judgments must be irreconcilable. This latter requirement has been held to mean that they should entail legal consequences that are mutually exclusive.[27]

This defence can be applied in intellectual property cases in the situation where the party that has been successful in an infringement action in the defendant's State seeks to have that judgment recognised in the State in which the intellectual property right is registered and is confronted in that State with a domestic judgment (obtained by the defendant in the infringement action) that revokes the right.[28] The consequences of these two judgments mutually exclude each other and the foreign infringement judgment will not be recognised.

(iv) Preliminary questions

Article 27(4) provides that a foreign judgment shall not be recognised 'if the court of the State of origin, in order to arrive at its judgment, has decided a preliminary question concerning the status or legal capacity of natural persons, rights in property arising out of a matrimonial relationship, wills or succession in a way that conflicts with a rule of the private international law of the State in which recognition is sought, unless the same result would have been reached by the application of the rules of private international law of that State'.

This defence will hardly ever be relevant in intellectual property related cases, except perhaps in some of those copyright cases where the rights of the decendants of the author or copyright owner are at issue.

(v) An irreconcilable judgment in a non-Contracting State

A foreign judgment will also not be recognised if it is irreconcilable with a judgment given by a court in a non-Contracting State. There are two requirements for this defence to apply.[29] The judgment in a non-Contracting State must be an earlier judgment and the two judgments must be irreconcilable in the sense that they should entail legal consequences that are mutually exclusive.

(vi) Conflict with Article 16(4)

Article 28 of the Convention has the effect that a foreign judgment will not be recognised if it conflicts with the provisions of Article 16(4). A case that is concerned principally with the validity or the registration procedure of a registered intellectual property right comes within the exclusive jurisdiction of the court of the country in which registration takes place. If a foreign court has, nevertheless, taken jurisdiction in breach of that provision,

---

[27] Case 145/86 *Hoffmann* v *Krieg* [1988] ECR 645.
[28] Tritton and Tritton, [1987] 12 *EIPR* 349, at 351.
[29] Article 27(5) of the Convention.

its judgment will not be entitled to recognition under the Brussels Convention.[30]

3. Enforcement of the Foreign Judgment

A foreign judgment that has been recognised can subsequently be enforced in the recognising State. This shall be done upon an *ex parte* application for registration for enforcement having been filed by any interested party.[31] The judgment must also be enforceable in the State of origin. The application is submitted to the court specified in Article 32 of the Convention. That court gives its decision without being able to review the substance of the foreign judgment.[32] The decision can be either to authorise or to refuse enforcement. A refusal can only be based on the fact that the requirements for recognition contained in Articles 27 and 28 have not been met, that the judgment is not enforceable in its State of origin, or that the requirements of Articles 32 and 33 (right court and procedure when applying) have not been met. Article 40 *et seq* give the unsuccessful applicant a right of appeal against a refusal to enforce the foreign judgment.

Once the enforcement has been authorised on the basis of an *ex parte* application, the party against whom it has been authorised can, within the prescribed time limit, bring an appeal to oppose the authorisation to enforce the foreign judgment.[33] These *inter partes* proceedings are heard by the court designated in Article 37(1) of the Convention. As long as such an appeal can be launched, and during the appeal, the effective enforcement of the judgment is suspended, but the applicant can take protective measures against the property of the person against whom enforcement is sought.[34] The appeal court can review the decision that was reached on the basis of the *ex parte* application on substance. The same provisions will be used in the review, but Article 38 gives the appeal court two additional options on top of the possibility of authorising or refusing the recognition of the foreign judgment. It can, first of all, stay the proceedings if two cumulative conditions are met. The applicant must have applied for such a stay, and he can do so even though he is unable to rely on one of the grounds for refusing enforcement provided for in Articles 27 and 28. On top of that, an 'ordinary' appeal must have been brought against the original foreign judgment in the State of origin of the judgment, or such an appeal must still be capable of being brought. A refusal to stay the enforcement of the judgment in its State of origin does not dictate the way in which the discretion to stay the proceedings should be exercised,[35] but

---

[30] See also Tritton and Tritton, above, n 28, at 351.
[31] Article 31 of the Convention. [32] Article 34 of the Convention.
[33] Article 36 of the Convention. [34] Article 39 of the Convention.
[35] See *SISRO v Ampersand Software BV* [1994] ILPr 55 (CA).

it may nevertheless be relevant in that respect.[36] And secondly, the appeal court can make enforcement of the foreign judgment conditional on the provision of security.

In a final stage of the enforcement procedure, an appeal on a point of law can be launched against the judgment on appeal. Some doubt has arisen as to whether a decision based on the two latter options in Article 38 should be treated as a judgment on appeal against which an appeal on a point of law is possible. It seems to be the case that, in this context, the court can only rule on challenges relating to the incorrect application of the law, and not on appeals against decisions refusing to stay the proceedings or lifting a stay previously ordered.[37]

The application of these provisions in intellectual property related cases does not seem to cause any special problems.

IV
THE LUGANO CONVENTION

Judgments granted in EFTA Contracting States will be recognised and enforced under the Lugano Convention. The provisions on recognition and enforcement that are contained in this Convention are, in most respects, identical to those contained in the Brussels Convention.[38]

V
THE COMMON LAW SYSTEM

There are, obviously, many foreign judgments that cannot be recognised and enforced under the Brussels or Lugano Convention. Judgments rendered by a court in a non-Contracting State and judgments in matters that fall outside the scope in point of subject matter of the Convention, or that fall outside the scope of the Convention because they come under the provisions of a specialist Convention, come within this category.[39] These judgments are recognised and enforced under the English traditional rules. In this section, we will examine briefly recognition and enforcement at common law. Enforcement of foreign judgments by statute will be mentioned briefly in the next section.

---

[36] Opinion of Advocate General Léger in Case C-432/93 *SISRO* v *Ampersand Software BV*.
[37] Ibid.
[38] For the tiny differences see Cheshire and North, *Private International Law*, Butterworths, (12th ed, 1992), 442–444.
[39] And *ex parte* orders, as these are also excluded by the Convention.

For recognition and enforcement at common law, a number of requirements have to be satisfied and a number of defences can be raised. The rules on recognition and enforcement at common law will have to be used in cases where there is no bilateral or multilateral agreement with the country concerned.

1. REQUIREMENTS

(a) THE JURISDICTION OF THE FOREIGN COURT

This is an essential requirement and one that is often difficult to satisfy. The foreign court that gave the judgment that is to be recognised and enforced in England must have had jurisdiction over the defendant in an international sense. That jurisdiction must have existed from the point of view of English law.[40] In practice, two alternatives are available. The defendant may have submitted to the jurisdiction of the foreign court or he may have been present in the jurisdiction. No other grounds of jurisdiction, such as domicile or nationality, can be taken into account.

(i) Presence in the jurisdiction

A natural person that is present in the foreign jurisdiction can validly be sued in the foreign court in the eyes of English law.[41] For a corporate defendant, the equivalent of presence in the jurisdiction is the possession of a fixed place of business for more than a minimal amount of time, provided that the corporate defendant's business has been transacted from that place of business.[42]

(ii) Submission to the jurisdiction of the foreign court

The jurisdiction of the foreign court is also validly established if it can be demonstrated that the party concerned has submitted to the jurisdiction of the foreign court. This can be done in three ways. First, the party that is the plaintiff in the foreign action has necessarily submitted itself to the jurisdiction of the foreign court.[43] The intellectual property right owner who sues abroad for the alleged infringement of his right, submits to the jurisdiction of the foreign court. He cannot object to the recognition and enforcement of the foreign judgment on grounds of jurisdiction if the foreign court dismisses his claim and gives judgment in favour of the defendant. Secondly, any party can agree to submit to the jurisdiction of the

---

[40] See *Pemberton v Hughes* [1899] 1 Ch 781 at 790 *et seq* and *Salvesen v Administrator of Austrian Property* [1927] AC 641 at 659.
[41] See *Carrick v Hancock* (1895) 12 TLR 59.
[42] See *Adams v Cape Industries plc* [1990] Ch 433 at 503–531.
[43] *Novelli v Rossi* (1831) 2 B & Ad 757 and *Schibsby v Westenholz* (1870) LR 6 QB 155 at 161.

foreign court.⁴⁴ However, such an agreement, probably, cannot be implied.⁴⁵ For example, a licensee will have submitted to the jurisdiction of the foreign court if the licence agreement contained a jurisdiction clause whereby the parties agreed to submit all disputes to the foreign court. And thirdly, any party that enters a voluntary appearance before the foreign court submits to its jurisdiction.⁴⁶ Such an appearance must be in order to fight the case on its merits. Appearances to dispute the jurisdiction of the court, even when accompanied by a substantive argument in the alternative, are to be disregarded.

(b) THE FINALITY OF THE FOREIGN JUDGMENT

Only final and conclusive judgments that determine all controversies between the parties can be recognised and enforced in England. The foreign judgment must be *res judicata* by the law of the country in which it was given.⁴⁷ However, the fact that an appeal can be lodged against the judgment in the foreign country does not mean that the judgment is not final and conclusive. The English court does have a discretion to stay the execution of the foreign judgment in the situation where an appeal is pending abroad.

(c) THE JUDGMENT MUST BE FOR A FIXED SUM OF MONEY

The English courts will only recognise and enforce foreign judgments *in personam* that are judgments for a fixed sum of money.⁴⁸ Judgments for specific performance will not be entitled to recognition and enforcement. Whilst this does not create problems for the standard intellectual property infringement case where damages have been awarded, it is clear that an injunction to stop the infringement will not be entitled to recognition and enforcement. In the latter case, the plaintiff will have to apply afresh for an injunction in front of an English court.

(d) NO EXAMINATION OF THE MERITS

A foreign judgment that meets the above requirements is not impeachable on its merits. The English court is not allowed to reopen the discussion in

---

⁴⁴ See the patent assignment case of *Feyerick v Hubbard* (1902) 71 LJKB 509.
⁴⁵ See *Copin v Adamson* (1874) LR 9 Ex Ch 345 and *Vallée v Dumergue* (1849) 4 Exch 290.
⁴⁶ Section 33 of the Civil Jurisdiction and Judgments Act 1982; *Henry v Geoprosco* [1976] QB 726, [1975] 2 All ER 702 and *Tracomin SA v Sudan Oil Seeds Co Ltd* [1983] 3 All ER 137, [1983] 1 WLR 1026; Cheshire and North, pp 353–358.
⁴⁷ See *Nouvion v Freeman* (1889) 15 App Cas 1 and *Blohn v Desser* [1962] 2 QB 116, [1961] 3 All ER 1.
⁴⁸ *Sadler v Robins* (1808) 1 Camp 253.

relation to the facts, the law (including aspects of English law as applied by the foreign court) or the procedure that has been applied. The only exception to this rule is the internal competence of the foreign court. A judgment that is a nullity in the foreign country in which it was given, is not entitled to recognition and enforcement in England. Apart from this obvious point, the English court will not reopen the case at the recognition and enforcement stage. Any defence that is available abroad has to be raised there in the main proceedings.

2. Defences Against Recognition and Enforcement

(a) FRAUD

A foreign judgment that has been obtained by fraud will not be entitled to recognition and enforcement in England.[49] Examples of fraud are the situation where the foreign court has been imposed upon by a trick that was not apparent at the trial or the situation where the foreign court acted in a fraudulent way. The fraud defence can always be raised at the recognition and enforcement stage, even if the argument has already been raised and rejected in the main proceedings. The only exception to this rule is the situation where the issue of fraud has been the subject of a separate trial.[50] The English court will, inevitably, go into the detail of the merits of the foreign judgment when it examines the allegation of fraud if the latter is raised again at the recognition and enforcement stage. The application of the fraud defence in intellectual property related cases does not seem to create any special problems.

(b) PUBLIC POLICY

This is the standard emergency safety valve in any system of private international law. Foreign judgments that are contrary to English public policy are not entitled to recognition and enforcement. No action will be sustainable on such a foreign judgment.[51] Whenever possible, this defence must be raised in the course of the main proceedings.

Whilst it serves no special purpose to list all known occasions on which the defence has been successful, it may be useful, in this context, to mention again the territorial character of intellectual property rights. Many cases in which a foreign court has dealt with the infringement of an English intellectual property right will fall foul of the jurisdiction require-

[49] See Cheshire and North, pp 377–380.
[50] *House of Spring Gardens Ltd* v *Waite* [1991] 1 QB 241, [1990] 2 All ER 990.
[51] See *Israel Discount Bank of New York* v *Hadjipateras* [1984] 1 WLR 137 and *Vervaeke* v *Smith* [1983] 1 AC 145.

ment. However, if we assume that the defendant was either present in the foreign jurisdiction or has submitted to the jurisdiction of the foreign court, could the public policy defence still stop the recognition and enforcement of such a judgment? In other words, does the territorial character of the right and the fact that it has been granted nationally as an exclusive right mean that any interference with it by the foreign court would necessarily be objectionable on public policy grounds?

Traditionally, English courts have always adopted the view that English courts deal with English intellectual property rights, whilst foreign courts deal with foreign intellectual property rights. It is submitted that a foreign judgment should be refused recognition and enforcement on public policy grounds if it deals with an English intellectual property right, especially if it invalidates the right. The recent judgments allowing the English courts to try infringement actions involving foreign intellectual property rights seem to be based entirely on the compulsory nature of the Brussels Convention.[52] It is submitted that the position remains unchanged outside the scope of that Convention.

(c) A FOREIGN PENAL LAW

This defence renders any foreign judgment that imposes a criminal sanction upon the infringer of an intellectual property right unenforceable in England. This is a straightforward application in the field of intellectual property of the general private international law rule that foreign revenue, penal or other public laws will not be applied in England.[53] Judgments that purport to do that will not be recognised or enforced.

(d) THE PROTECTION OF TRADING INTERESTS ACT 1980

This specific defence was not designed with intellectual property in mind. There is no doubt, however, that it will block the recognition and enforcement of any foreign judgment that sets out to apply a foreign anti-trust law extraterritorially in those cases where the anti-trust infringement is based on an intellectual property right. Section 5(2) of the Act may apply in these cases.

---

[52] See *Pearce v Ove Arup Partnership Ltd and Others* [1997] 3 All ER 31, [1997] 2 WLR 779; *Coin Controls v Suzo International* [1997] 3 All ER 45; *Fort Dodge Animal Health Ltd and Others v Akzo Nobel NV and Another* [1998] FSR 222.
[53] See *US v Inkley* [1989] QB 255, [1988] 3 All ER 144 and Cheshire and North, pp 381–382.

(e) THE NATURAL JUSTICE DEFENCE

Recognition and enforcement in England will be denied to a foreign judgment that is contrary to natural justice.[54] It is submitted that this defence operates almost independently from the subject matter of the case. Whether or not an intellectual property related matter is at issue will not have any significance. In general terms, the defendant will need to have been given due notice and a proper opportunity to be heard in such a case, just as in any other case. The defence can also be used in those cases where a procedural defect resulted in a breach of substantial justice, in the view of the English court.[55] The latter would, for example, be the case if the damages for the infringement of an intellectual property right were assessed on an average basis rather than taking into account the particular circumstances of the case.

(f) CAUSE OF ACTION ESTOPPEL

A prior decision on the same matter by an English court prevents the matter from being raised again before another English court. A prior decision by an English court will stop an action for the recognition and enforcement in England of a foreign judgment, because there will be a cause of action estoppel.[56] The matter at issue could, for example, involve the breach of a patent licence contract.

The position where there is a later English decision is more uncertain, but it can be assumed that such a decision would also give rise to a cause of action estoppel, since the House of Lords in the leading case of *Vervaeke v Smith*[57] did not specify that the English judgment had to be the earlier judgment. Moreover, the reasoning in that case applies equally well to a later English judgment.

(g) THE FOREIGN JUDGMENT IS IN BREACH OF A DISPUTE SETTLEMENT AGREEMENT

The parties are bound by their dispute settlement agreement. Section 32 of the Civil Jurisdiction and Judgments Act 1982 makes it clear that a foreign judgment, that has been obtained as a result of a breach by one of the parties of an agreement on jurisdiction or arbitration, will not be recognised or enforced in England. Three conditions need to be satisfied. First, there must be an agreement on jurisdiction (a court in a country other than the

---

[54] *Jacobson v Frachon* (1928) 138 LT 386.   [55] *Adams v Cape Industries plc* [1990] Ch 433.
[56] See *Vervaeke v Smith* [1983] 1 AC 145 and *E D & F Mann (Sugar) Ltd v Yani Haryanto (No 2)* [1991] 1 Lloyd's Rep 429.
[57] [1983] 1 AC 145.

one in which the proceedings were eventually brought) or arbitration. Secondly, the person against whom the foreign decision was given neither brought the proceedings, nor did he agree to them. Thirdly, the person against whom the foreign judgment was given did not make a counter-claim or otherwise submit to the jurisdiction of the foreign court. This defence might well come into play in litigation in relation to agreements concerning the commercial exploitation of intellectual property rights.

VI
ENFORCEMENT OF FOREIGN JUDGMENTS BY STATUTE

A number of Statutes deal specifically with the recognition and enforcement of foreign judgments granted by the courts of certain countries. The Civil Jurisdiction and Judgments Act 1982 deals with recognition and enforcement within the United Kingdom. Provision is made in the Administration of Justice Act 1920 for the enforcement of judgments obtained in a superior court of any part of the Commonwealth. And finally, the Foreign Judgments (Reciprocal Enforcement Act) 1933, which applies a registration system, as does the 1920 Act, will be used to enforce foreign judgments that have as their country of origin a country to which the registration scheme has been extended by Order in Council. Such an extension will be granted on a reciprocal basis. Both the 1920 and the 1933 Acts include a requirement that the foreign country is prepared to afford substantial reciprocity of treatment to judgments that have been obtained in the United Kingdom.[58]

It is not necessary, for our current purposes, to deal in detail with the requirements for and the defences against enforcement under the 1920 and 1933 Acts, as on these points the statutory provisions largely copy the provisions at common law. Moreover, the application of these statutory regimes to intellectual property related cases does not give rise to any special problems.

---

[58] See Cheshire and North, pp 392–405.

VII
DECISIONS IN RELATION TO SUPRANATIONAL OR SEMI-SUPRANATIONAL RIGHTS

The recognition and enforcement of most supranational intellectual property rights, such as the Community trade mark, are governed by the Brussels Convention.[59] The special rules in Title X of the Community Trade Mark Regulation[60] and in the other instruments that create these supranational rights deal with jurisdiction, rather than with recognition and enforcement of foreign judgments.

However, there is an exception to this in the European Patent Convention. Judgments that decide the issue of the right to the grant of a European Patent are subject to a separate recognition system that could be described as a simplified version of the Brussels Convention system. This separate system is contained in the Protocol on Recognition.[61] If such a decision is final under the law of the Contracting State in which it has been given, it shall be recognised in all other Contracting States without requiring any special procedure.[62] Specifically, the jurisdiction of the foreign court should not be reviewed.[63] However, this special recognition procedure does not apply where 'an applicant for a European Patent who has not contested a claim proves that the document initiating the proceedings was not notified to him regularly and sufficiently early for him to defend himself'[64] or where 'an applicant proves that the decision is incompatible with another decision given in a Contracting State in proceedings between the same parties which were started before those in which the decision to be recognised was given'.[65] These two situations could be characterised as natural justice and issue estoppel respectively. They are standard defences that are also found in all general systems of recognition and enforcement of foreign judgments.

The Protocol does not specify what happens in cases where one of these two defences applies. It would be logical to assume that the normal rules on recognition and enforcement of foreign judgments of the Contracting State concerned would apply in the situation where the special Protocol system is inapplicable due to the operation of the defence.

---

[59] See, eg Article 90 of Council Regulation 40/94 on the Community Trade Mark [1994] OJ L11/1.
[60] See above, pp 532–533.
[61] Protocol on Jurisdiction and the Recognition of Decisions in respect of the Right to the Grant of a European Patent.
[62] Article 9(1) of the Protocol.
[63] Article 9(2) of the Protocol.
[64] Article 10(a) of the Protocol.
[65] Article 10(b) of the Protocol.

However, that would not lead to the recognition and enforcement in England of the disputed decision, because the defence has its counterpart under English law. Accordingly, those decisions that involve the defences that are provided by the Protocol will simply not be recognised and enforced in England.

Selected Bibliography

Annand and Norman *Blackstone's Guide to the Trade Marks Act 1994*, by R Annand and H Norman (London: Blackstone Press, 1994).

Anton *Private International Law: A treatise from the standpoint of Scots law*, by A E Anton, 2nd ed (Edinburgh: W Green, 1990).

Anton & Beaumont *Civil Jurisdiction in Scotland*, by A E Anton and P Beaumont (Edinburgh: W Green, 1995).

Batiffol *Les Conflits de Lois en Matière de Contrats*, by H Batiffol (Paris: Sirey, 1938)

—— *Traité Elémentaire de Droit International Privé*, by H Batiffol, 3rd ed (Paris: LGDJ, 1959).

Bergé *La Protection Internationale et Communautaire du Droit d'Auteur*, by J-S Bergé (Paris: LGDJ, 1996).

Blakeney *Legal Aspects of the Transfer of Technology to Developing Countries*, by M Blakeney (London: ESC Publishing, 1989).

—— *Trade Related Aspects of Intellectual Property Rights: A Concise Guide to the TRIPs Agreement*, by M Blakeney (London: Sweet & Maxwell, 1996).

Carey Miller and Beaumont *The Option of Litigation in Europe*, ed by D L Carey Miller and P R Beaumont (London: British Institute of International and Comparative Law, 1993).

Cheshire and North *Private International Law*, by P M North and J J Fawcett, 12th ed (London: Butterworths, 1992).

Claringbould, *Licenties: Praktische wenken voor de kennishandel*, by H Claringbould (Deventer: Kluwer, 1982).

Coleman *The Legal Protection of Trade Secrets*, by A Coleman (London: Sweet and Maxwell, 1992).

Collins *The Civil Jurisdiction and Judgments Act 1982*, by L A Collins (London: Butterworths, 1983).

—— Essays, *Essays in International Litigation and the Conflict of Laws* by L A Collins (Oxford: Oxford University Press, 1994).

Copinger and Skone James *Copinger and Skone James on the Law of Copyright*, by E P Skone James, J J Mummery, J Rayner James, K M Garnett, 13th ed (London: Sweet & Maxwell, 1991).

Cornish, *Intellectual Property* by W R Cornish, 3rd ed (London: Sweet & Maxwell, 1995).

Desbois, Françon and Kerever *Les Conventions internationales du droit d'auteur et des droits voisins*, by K Desbois, A Françon and A Kerever (Paris: Dalloz, 1976).

Dicey *Dicey's Conflict of Laws*, by A Dicey and J Morris, 7th ed (London: Stevens, 1958).

Dicey and Morris *The Conflict of Laws*, by L A Collins and others, 12th ed (London: Sweet and Maxwell, 1993).

Diener *Contrats internationaux de Propriété industrielle*, by M Diener (Paris: Litec, 1986).

Doutrelepont *Le droit et l'objet d'art: le droit de suite des artistes plasticiens dans l'union européenne. Analyse juridique, approche économique*, by C Doutrelepont (Brussels and Paris: Bruylant and LGDJ, 1996).
Drobnig *American-German Private International Law*, by U Drobnig, 2nd ed (Dobbs Ferry (NY): Oceana, 1972).
Drysdale and Silverleaf, *Passing Off: Law and Practice*, by J Drysdale and M Silverleaf, 2nd ed (London: Butterworths, 1995).
Fawcett *Declining Jurisdiction*, ed by J J Fawcett (Oxford: Oxford University Press, 1995).
Francescakis *La théorie du renvoi et les conflits de systèmes en droit international privé*, by P Francescakis (Paris: Sirey, 1958).
Franzosi *European Design Protection: Commentary to Directive and Regulation Proposals*, ed by M Franzosi (Deventer: Kluwer Law International, 1996).
Goff and Jones *Restitution*, by G Jones, 4th ed (London: Sweet & Maxwell, 1993).
Gothot et Holleaux *La Convention de Bruxelles du 27 Septembre 1968*, by P Gothot and D Holleaux (Paris: Jupiter, 1985).
Hartley *Civil Jurisdiction and Judgments*, by T C Hartley (London: Butterworths, 1984).
Holl and Klinke *Internationales Privatrecht, Internationales Wirtschaftsrecht*, ed by W Holl and U Klinke (Köln: Carl Heymanns Verlag, 1985).
Holleaux, Foyer and de la Pradelle *Droit International Privé*, by D Holleaux, A Foyer and G De Geouffre de la Pradelle (Paris: Masson, 1987).
Holyoak and Torremans *Intellectual Property Law*, by J Holyoak and P Torremans (London: Butterworths, 1995).
Imhoff-Scheier and Patocchi *Torts and Unjust Enrichment in the New Swiss Conflict of Laws*, by A-C Imhoff-Scheier and P-M Patocchi (Zurich: Schulthess Polygraphischer Verlag, 1990).
Karrer and Arnold *Switzerland's Private International Law Statute*, by P Karrer and K Arnold (Deventer: Kluwer, 1989).
Kaye *Civil Jurisdiction and Enforcement of Foreign Judgments*, by P Kaye (Abingdon: Professional Books Ltd, 1987).
Keller, Schulze and Schaetzle *Die Rechtsprechung des Bundesgerichts im internationalen Privatrecht und die verwandten Rechtsgebieten – Band II – Obligationenrecht*, by M Keller, C Schulze and M Schaetzle (Zurich: Schulthess Polygraphischer Verlag, 1977).
Kisch, Dubbink, van Hoogstraaten, Kotting and Jessurun d'Oliveira *Naar een sociaal IPR: Een keus uit het werk van L I de Winter* ed by Kisch, Dubbink, van Hoogstraaten, Kotting and Jessurun d'Oliveira (Deventer: Kluwer, 1979).
Köhler and Gürtler *Internationales Privatrecht – IPR Gesetz*, by H Köhler and G Gürtler (Vienna: Druck und Verlag der Österreichischen Staatsdruckerei, 1979).
Kropholler *Europäisches Zivilprozessrecht: Kommentar zum EuGVU*, by J Kropholler (Heidelberg: Recht und Wirtschaft, 1996).
Ladas *The International Protection of Literary and Artistic Property*, by S P Ladas (1938).
Laddie, Prescott and Vitoria *The Modern Law of Copyright*, by H Laddie, P Prescott and M Vitoria, 2nd ed (London: Butterworths, 1995)
Langen *Internationale Lizenzverträge*, by E Langen and H-U Wilke, 2nd ed (Weinheim: Chemie Weinheim, 1958).

Locher *Das Internationale Privat-und Zivilprozessrecht der Immaterialgüterrechte aus urheberrechtlicher Sicht*, by F Locher (Zurich: Schulthess Polygraphischer Verlag, 1993).
Lucas and Lucas *Traité de la propriété littéraire et artistique* , by A and H-J Lucas (Paris: Litec, 1994).
McLachlan and Nygh *Transnational Tort Litigation; Jurisdictional Principles*, ed C McLachlan and P E Nygh (Oxford: Oxford University Press, 1996).
McLeod *The Conflict of Laws*, by J G Mcleod (Calgary, Alberta: Carswell Legal Publications, 1983).
Morse *Torts in Private International Law*, by C G J Morse (Amsterdam: North Holland Publishing, 1978).
North *Contract Conflicts*, ed by P M North (Amsterdam: North Holland Publishing Co, 1982).
Nussbaum *Handbuch des internationalen Privatrecht*, by A Nussbaum (Tübingen: Mohr, 1932).
Nygh *Conflict of Laws in Australia*, by P E Nygh, 6th ed (Sydney: Butterworths, 1995).
O'Malley and Layton *European Civil Practice*, by S O'Malley and A Layton (London: Sweet and Maxwell, 1989).
Park and Cromie *International Commercial Litigation*, by Park and Cromie (London: Butterworths, 1990).
Raape *Internationales Privatrecht*, by L Raape, 5th ed (Berlin: Vahlen, 1961).
Rabel *The Conflict of Laws: A Comparative Study*, by E Rabel (Chicago: Callaghan, 1950).
Raynard *Droit d'auteur et conflits de lois*, by J Raynard (Paris: Litec, 1990).
Ricketson *The Berne Convention for the Protection of literary and Artistic Works: 1886–1986*, by S Ricketson (Deventer: Kluwer, 1987).
Roubier *Le Droit de la Propriété Industrielle*, by P Roubier (Paris: Sirey, 1954).
Schack *Zur Anknüpfung des Urheberrechts im internationalen Privatrecht*, by H Schack (Berlin: Duncker & Humblot, 1979).
Schmithoff *The English Conflict of Laws*, by C M Schmithoff, 3rd ed (London: Stevens, 1954).
Schnitzer *Handbuch des internationalen Privatrechts II*, by A Schnitzer, 4th ed (Basel: Verl. für Recht und Gesellschaft, 1958).
Scoles and Hay *Conflict of Laws*, by E F Scoles and P Hay, 2nd ed (St Paul, Minnesota: West Publishing, 1992).
Terrell *Terrell on the Law of Patents*, by D Young, A Watson, S Thorley and R Miller, 14th ed (London: Sweet and Maxwell, 1994).
Tritton, *Intellectual Property in Europe*, by G Tritton (London: Sweet & Maxwell, 1996).
Troller *Das internationale Privat-und Zivilprozessrecht im gewerblichen Rechtsschutz und Urheberrecht*, by A Troller (Basel: Verl für Recht und Gesellschaft, 1952).
Ulmer *Intellectual Property Rights and the Conflict of Laws*, by E Ulmer (Deventer: Kluwer, 1978).
Vander Elst *Les Lois de polices et de sûreté*, by R Vander Elst (Paris: Sirey, 1956).
Van Hecke and Lenaerts *Internationaal Privaatrecht*, by G Van Hecke and K Lenaerts, 2nd ed (Brussels: Story-Scientia, 1989).

Vischer *Internationales Vertragsrecht*, by F Vischer (Bern: Stämpfli, 1962).
Vitoria et al *Encyclopedia of UK and European Patent Law*, by M Vitoria, R Jacob, W R Cornish, F Clark, D Alexander (London: Sweet & Maxwell).
Whish *Competition Law*, by R Whish, 3rd ed (London: Butterworths, 1993).
Winfield and Jolowicz *Winfield and Jolowicz on Tort*, by W V H. Rodgers, 14th ed (London: Sweet and Maxwell, 1994).
Wolff *Traité élémentaire du droit international*, by M Wolff
—— *Private International Law*, by M Wolff, 2nd ed (Oxford: Oxford University Press, 1950).
X *Festschrift G S Marikadis*, by X (Athens: Sakoulas, 1966).

Index

abuse of process
  infringement proceedings 176
Article 16(4) Brussels and Lugano Conventions 15–27
  allocation of jurisdiction within United Kingdom 26–7
  allocation to courts of contracting state in which deposit or registration has been applied for 22–3
  application in relation to European patents 24
  deposit or registration applied for 21
  EC/EFTA contracting state 22
  European patents 20–1
  exclusive jurisdiction 22
  interpretation 16
  justification 15–16
  parallel applications 23–4
  patents, trade marks, designs, or other similar rights required to be deposited or registered 20
  proceedings concerned with registration or validity 17–20
    meaning 17–18
    what is covered 18–19
    what is not covered 19
  regardless of domicile 16–17
  scope 16–22
  service out of jurisdiction 25–6
Article 109 Swiss PIL statute 46–8, 71
  bases of jurisdiction 46–7
  comparison with traditional English rules 47–8
  scope 46
  subject matter limitation on jurisdiction 47

Berne Convention 1886 462–75
  alternative interpretation 472–5
  bilateralisation of unilateral conflict rules 472–3
  connecting factor which takes priority 464–5
  determination of applicable law 467–8
  first publication of work in Member State 463–4
  headquarters or habitual residence of architects 464
  headquarters or habitual residence of maker of cinematographic work 464
  how choice of law problems arise 465–6
  law applying to qualifying works 466–8
  minimum protection granted by substantive rules 471–2
  national treatment 468–9
  nationality 462–3
  qualification rules 462–6
  relevant connecting factors 462–4
  restrictions on application of law of protecting country 469–72
  restrictive interpretation of Article 5(2) 473–5
    arguments against 474–5
    arguments in favour 473–4
  role for law of country of origin 469–71
  scope 462–5
  whether qualification rule includes choice of law 466–7
breach of competition rules 416–26, 693–7
  action within scope of Article 5(3), whether 423
  actions 421–2
  applicable law 694–7
    application of general rule 696
    chacterisation 695
    displacement of general rule 696
    foreign penal, revenue or other public law 696–7
    mandatory rules 697
    no exclusion from Part III 694–5
    Part III, scope of 695–6
      restriction in section 14(2) 696
      tortious, whether 695–6
    savings 696–7
    statutory rules 694–7
  Article 85 416–19
    analysis of provision 417–19
    application to intellectual property agreements 419
    paragraph 1 417–18
    paragraph 2 418
    paragraph 3 418–19
    provision 416–17
  Article 86 419–21
    abuse of dominant position 419–20
    application in context of intellectual property 420–1
  EC/EFT rules 423–5
  how choice of law problems arise 693–4
  how judicial problems arise 422–3

breach of competition rules (*cont.*):
  jurisdictional provisions 423–6
    place of event giving rise to damage 424
    place where damage has occurred 424–5
    substantive law 416–22
    traditional rules 425–6
breach of confidence 426–47, 697–702
  applicable law 427–8, 698–702
    application of general rule 701–2
      events constituting cause of action 701
        multi-country non-contractual breach of confidence 701–2
        single country non-contractual breach of confidence 701
    chacterisation 698–9
    displacement of general rule 702
    mandatory rules 702
    Part III, scope of 699–700
      contractual breach 699
      non-contractual breach 699–700
      tortious characterisation for purposes of private international law 700
    public policy 702
    restriction in section 14(2) 700
    savings 702
    statutory rules 698–702
  Article 2 431
  Article 5 432–41
  Article 5(1) 432–4
    matters relating to contract 432–3
    place of performance of obligation 433
  Article 5(3) 433–41
    confidentiality of plaintiff's information 440–1
    direct economic loss 441
    effect on plaintiff's commercial interests 441
    place where damage occurred 440
    place where harmful event occurred 439–41
    scope 433–9
    uncertainty in England 434–8
  Article 17 442
  classification 430–1
  confidential information passing between employer and employee 428–9
  consolidating litigation 442–3
    Article 2 442
    Article 6(1) 442
    Article 17 442–3
  EC/EFTA rules 431–43
  elements of action 426–30
  forum conveniens discretion 447
  heads of Order 11, rule 1(1) 443–7
    both contractual and non-contractual obligations 446–7
    constructive trustee head 446
    contractual obligation 443–4
    injunction 445–6
    multi-defendant head 445
    non-contractual obligation 444–6
    tort head 444–5
  how choice of law problems arise 697–8
  how jurisdictional problems arise 431
  jurisdictional provisions 431–47
  occasion of confidence 427–9
  substantive law 426–31
  suggested rules 453
  traditional rules 443–7
  unauthorised use of confidential information 429–30
  when information confidential 427
Brussels Convention 725–33
  enforcement of foreign judgment 732–3
  ex parte orders not covered 726–7
  judgment given in contracting state 725–6
  judgment given in respect of civil and commercial matter 726
  jurisdiction 2
  recognition of foreign judgment 727–32
    conflict with Article 16(4) 731–2
    defences 728–32
    essential first step 727
    irreconcilable judgment in non-contracting state 731
    irreconcilable judgment in recognising state 730–1
    natural justice 730
    preliminary questions 731
    public policy 728–30
    rebuttable presumption in favour of recognition 727–8
  scope 725–7
  type of jurisdiction rule irrelevant 726
business reputation
  applicable law 526–7

choice of law
  alternative approaches 538–41
  Berne Convention 1886 462–75 *see also* Berne Convention 1886
  elements in intellectual property convention 460–81
    no straightforward answers 461–2
    reasons for looking at 460–1
  how issues arise 460
  international co-operation agreements 479
  Paris Convention *see* Paris Convention for the Protection of Industrial Property 1883

Rome Convention 1961 *see* Rome
    Convention 1961
  rules 455–6
  supra-national intellectual property
    rights 479–80
  TRIPS Agreement *see* TRIPS Agreement
Community design right
  applicable law 535–7
Community patent 535
  applicable law 535
Community plant variety right
  applicable law 537–8
Community rights
  applicable law 532–8
Community trade mark 532–5
  applicable law 532–5
  Article 14 532
  national law provisions 534–5
  substantive rules in regulation 533–4
  Title X 532–3
**contracts in relation to exploitation of
    intellectual property rights** 73–117
  anti-trust issues 113
  applicable law 543–93
  Article 5(1), Brussels and Lugano
    Conventions 77–90
    application to intellectual property
      contracts 79–89
    assignments 89
      assignee's obligations 89
      assignor's obligations 89
    distribution agreements 81–8
      distributor's obligations 81–3
      grantor's obligations 83
      negative obligation 84–6
      obligation to continue 87
      obligation to give reasonable notice
        before terminating agreement
        86–7
      obligation to supply 83–4
      obligations of grantor 88
    employment contracts 90
    licences 79–81
      licensee's obligations 79
      licensor's obligations 79–81
    provision 77–8
  Article 16(4), Brussels and Lugano
    Conventions 91–4
    counterclaim for revocation 92–3
    invalidity defence 91–2
    normal position 91
    separate revocation proceedings 93
    validity of agreement contested 93–4
  Article 17, Brussels and Lugano
    Conventions 94
  declining jurisdiction 95–6
    Brussels and Lugano Conventions 95

EC/EFTA rules 76–96
  bases of jurisdiction 76–94
  consumer contracts 90
  general jurisdiction 76–7
  special jurisdiction: Articles 5 and 6 77
forum non conveniens 95–6
how jurisdictional problems arise 75–6
how questions of applicable law arise
  549–50
jurisdiction 73–117
jurisdictional provisions 76–113
limitations on jurisdiction 111–12
  Article 16(4), Brussels and Lugano
    Conventions 112
  state immunity 112
  subject matter 111–12
reform 113–17
  Article 5(1) 113–14
    reform 115–16
  EC/EFTA Rules 113–17
    Article 5(1) 113–14
    excessively wide choice of fora 114
    uncertainty 113
  operation in cases of exploitation
    116–17
  traditional rules 117
restraining foreign proceedings 96
Rome Convention 1980 551–91 *see also*
  Rome Convention on the Law
  Applicable to Contractual
  Obligations
service of writ out of jurisdiction 97–106
  complexity arising from different
    standards of proof for merits and
    heads 101–3
  establishing liability 103
  exercise of discretion 103–6
  forum conveniens 103–5
  heads of Order 11, rule 1(1) 97–101
    contract heads 97–8
    injunction head 100–1
    multi-defendant head 99–100
    serious issue to be tried 101–3
    significance of particular head 105–6
substantive law background 74–5
traditional rules 97–113
  bases of jurisdiction 97–106
  declining jurisdiction 106–8
    arbitration agreements 108
    foreign jurisdiction clauses 107–8
    forum non conveniens 106–7
  restraining foreign proceedings
    109–11
    invasion of legal or equitable right
      not to be sued abroad 110
    trial available in alternative form
      abroad 110

contracts in relation to exploitation of intellectual property rights (*cont.*):
  traditional rules (*cont.*):
    restraining foreign proceedings (*cont.*):
      trial available in England and abroad 109–10
      unconscionable proceedings 111
    service of writ out of jurisdiction 97–106
    service of writ within jurisdiction 97
  transfer of technology contracts 112–13
copyright 498–517
  applicable law 498–517
  authorship:
    applicable law 509–11
  broadcasting:
    applicable law 504
  civil remedies:
    applicable law 506
  contracts relating to:
    applicable law 547–9
  creation 7
    applicable law 499–501
  exceptions to rights 506
  first ownership:
    applicable law 511–13
  fixation in material form 500
  formalities 501
  infringement *see* infringement
  moral rights:
    applicable law 502–4
  qualification requirement 501
  satellite broadcasting:
    applicable law 504–6
  scope:
    applicable law 501–6
  termination of right:
    applicable law 507–8
  transferability of right:
    applicable law 515–17
  types of works protected 500
  validity of right:
    applicable law 508–9
  works created by employees:
    applicable law 513–15
creation and validity of intellectual property rights 6–48
  Article 2, Lugano Convention 33
  Article 5(1), Brussels and Lugano Conventions 33–4
  Article 5(5), Brussels and Lugano Conventions 34
  Article 16(1), Brussels and Lugano Conventions 34–5
  Article 16(4) Brussels and Lugano Conventions 15–27 *see also* Article 16(4) Brussels and Lugano Conventions
  Article 17, Brussels and Lugano Conventions 36
  Article 18, Brussels and Lugano Conventions 36
  Article 21, Brussels and Lugano Conventions 36–7
  Article 109 Swiss PIL statute 46–8 *see also* Article 109 Swiss PIL statute
  Articles 5 and 6, Brussels and Lugano conventions 33–4
  EC/EFTA rules 30–9
    bases of jurisdiction 32
    civil and commercial matter 30–1
    declining jurisdiction 36–8
    lis pendens 36–7
    patents registered outside EC/EFTA states 31–2
    subject matter limitation on jurisdiction 38–9
    using doctrine of *forum non conveniens* 38
    when applicable 30–2
  European Patent Convention 1973 27–8
  jurisdiction 6–48
  jurisdictional problems 10–11
  jurisdictional provisions 11–45
  jurisdictional rules of general application 28–45
    application 28–9
    foreign created rights 29–30
    locally created rights 29
  service of writ out of jurisdiction 40–2
    exercise of discretion 41–2
    heads of Order 11, rule 1(1) 40–1
    serious issue to be tried 41
  special jurisdictional rules 11–28
    intellectual property conventions 12–15
    recourse to rules of private international law 14
    rejection of traditional law 12–14
    restriction on 14–15
    traditional view 12
  substantive law background 6–10
  traditional rules on jurisdiction 39–45
    application 39–40
    bases of jurisdiction 40
    criticism of 45
    declining jurisdiction 42–3
    foreign rights, and 43–5
    service of writ out of jurisdiction 40–2
    service of writ within jurisdiction 40
    state immunity 45
    subject matter limitations on jurisdiction 43–5

creation, scope and termination of intellectual property rights
  applicable law 484–541
  choice of law problems 486–7

databases
  sui generis right in relation to 528–9
defamation 394–409, 673–8
  applicable law 674–8
    characterisation 674
    committed abroad 676–7
    committed in England 677
    common law rules 676–8
    exclusion of claims from Part III 675–6
      'any defamation claim' 675–6
      business competitor 676
    place where committed 677–8
  discretionary element 406–9
    applicable law 407–8
    avoidance of multiplicity of actions in different states 408
    connections with alternative fora 406–7
    multi-state reputation 407
    no reputation in England 406
    no subject matter limitations on jurisdiction 408–9
    place where tort committed 407
  EC/EFTA rules 396–402
    business competitor 401–2
    complex defamation 399–400
    defamation rules 396–401
    simple defamation 400–1
  elements 394–5
  how choice of law problems arise 673–4
  how jurisdictional problems arise 396
  jurisdictional provisions 396–409
  no territorial limits on harmful activity 395
  protection of professional or business reputation 395–6
  recent example 394
  substantive law 394–6
  tort head of Order 11 402–6
    act committed within jurisdiction 404–5
    application of *Shevill* case 403–4
    damage sustained within jurisdiction 405–6
    inappropriate test 403
    new head 403–6
    old head 402–3
  traditional rules 402–9
delict 415–16, 690–3
  applicable law 690–3
    application of general rule 692–3
      displacement 693
      events constituting tort 692
    multi-country 693
    multiple delicts 693
    single country 692–3
  Part III, scope of 691–2
    restriction in section 14(2) 691–2
    tortious characterisation 691
  statutory rules 691–3
  EC/EFTA rules 415–16
  how choice of law problems arise 690
  how jurisdictional problems arise 415
  jurisdictional provisions 415–16
  substantive law 415
  traditional rules 416
design right
  creation 8
designs 342–4
  how jurisdictional problems arise 342–3
  infringement *see* infringement
  jurisdictional provisions 343–4
  registered 7
  substantive law background 342

European Community rights
  jurisdictional issues 317–58
European Patent Convention 1973 27–8
  applicable law 530–1
  judicial system 27–8
forum shopping
  infringement, and *see* infringement
  trade mark infringement 330–1

goodwill
  situs 526–7
grant and ownership of intellectual property rights 49–71
  Article 5(1), Brussels and Lugano Conventions 63–4
  Article 16(4), Brussels and Lugano Conventions 61–2
  Article 17, Brussels and Lugano Conventions 64–5
  Article 109 Swiss PIL Statute 71
  declining jurisdiction 69
  EC/EFTA rules 63–6
    bases of jurisdiction 63–5
    declining jurisdiction 65
    subject matter on jurisdiction 65–6
    using doctrine of *forum non conveniens* 65
  foreign rights 69–70
  how disputes arise 50
  how jurisdictional problems arise 50–1
  jurisdiction 49–71
  jurisdictional provisions 51–70
  jurisdictional rules of general application 62–70
    application 62–3

grant and ownership of intellectual property rights (*cont.*):
  limitations on jurisdiction 69–70
  Protocol on Recognition attached to European Patent Convention 52–61
    allocation of jurisdiction to German courts 59
    applicant's residence in contracting state 56–7
    application 52–4
    bases of jurisdiction 55–60
    complex rules 55
    contracting state where employee mainly employed 57–8
    declining jurisdiction 60–1
    examination of jurisdiction 59–60
    five different situations 55
    five rules 56–9
    hierarchy of rules 59
    jurisdiction agreements 58–9
    no definition of residence/principal place of business 60
    regardless of residence of applicant 54
    relationship with Brussels and Lugano Conventions 54
    residence within one of contracting states of party claiming right to grant of European patent 57
    right to grant of European patent 52–4
  service of writ out of jurisdiction 67–9
    exercise of discretion 68–9
    heads of Order 11, rule 1(1) 67–8
    serious issue to be tried 68
  special jurisdictional rules 52–62
  state immunity 70
  traditional rules on jurisdiction 66–70
    application 66
    criticism of 70
    service of writ out of jurisdiction 67–9
    service of writ within jurisdiction 66

industrial property rights 545–7
  contractual aspects of transfer 546–7
  formalities 547
  issues relating to 545–6
  restrictions for transfer 547
infringement 119–37
  abroad 299–306
    Australian authority 302
    authorities 300–3
    confusion between jurisdiction and choice of law 305
    Def Lepp case 301
    forum non conveniens 304–5
    Morocco Bound case 300–1
    New Zealand authority 302
    policy considerations 303–4
    successful action, whether 305–6
    Tyburn case 302
    US authority 302–3
  abuse of process 176
  act of 131
  applicable law 595–647
    alternative solutions from abroad 643–4
    criticisms of existing law 643
    English approach 597–642
    how questions arise 596–7
    independent rules 645
    policy considerations 645–6
    reform 643–7
    reform of tort choice of law rules 644
    special rules in infringement cases 644–5
    suggested rules 646–7
      defences 647
      displacement of special general rule 647
      mandatory rules of forum 647
      special general rule 646–7
  Article 5, Brussels and Lugano Conventions 149–70
    Article 5(3) 149–69
    Article 5(5) 169–70
    denial of existence of tort 150–1
    place where harmful event occurred 152–69
      act of infringement 156–61
      copyright 156–8
      definitional problem 152–3
      event giving rise to damage 156–63
      infringement actions 153–6
      infringement cases 164–7
      internet 158–61
      multiple acts 161–2
      multiple damage 167–8
      patents 156
      place where damage occurred 163–4
      solution provided by Court of Justice 152–3
      special definition for infringement cases 168–9
      where defendant has establishment 162–3
    scope of Article 5(3) 150
    threatened wrongs 151–2
  Article 6, Brussels and Lugano Conventions 170–5
    additional requirements 174–5
    European patents 173–4
    joint tortfeasors 172
    multiple infringements 172–3
    parallel rights 173
    reasons for multi-defendant litigation 171

Index

requirements 172–5
requisite connection between various actions 172–4
bases of jurisdiction 241–66
copyright 124–7
  primary infringement 124–6
    basic rule 124–5
    territorial scope 125
  secondary 127
  specific forms 126
criticism of existing law 314–15
cross-border injunctions 218–28
  Brussels Convention 221–5
  Dutch position 218–20
    foreign reaction 220–1
    willingness to grant 220
  enforcement 225
  English courts, and 225–8
  English position 225–8
  extra-territorial effect of provisional measure 224–5
  Kort-Geding procedure 219–20
  provisional measure within Article 24, whether 222–4
    importance 222
    references to Court of Justice 223–4
    queries 222–3
  recognition 225
databases 130–1
  copyright aspect 130–1
  sui generis aspect 131
declining jurisdiction 266–79
defences 640–2
  contractual 640–2
    nature of problem 640
    solution 640–2
  invalidity of right 642
    nature of problem 642
    solution 642
designs 127–30
  infringing article 129
  primary 128
  registered 129–30
  secondary 128–9
  unregistered 127–8
elements 131–4
  definition by English law 133–4
exclusive jurisdiction: Article 16 175–6
foreign immovable property 280–3
  arguments of principle and policy 281–2
  case law 282–3
  classification of intellectual property rights 281–3
  exclusionary rule 280–1
foreign intellectual property rights 283–99

confusion between jurisdiction and choice of law 295–8
  examples 295–7
  reasons for 297
development of limitation 282–90
English limitation 284–90
extension to Australia of exclusionary rule to patents 283–4
forum non conveniens, and 293–5
infringements abroad 299–306
origin of limitation 283–90
treatment of different issues 299
treatment of different rights 298–9
Tyburn case 284–90
critique of decision 286–90
forum non conveniens 267–74, 293–5
  act of infringement, place of 270–1
  another available forum 268–9
  clearly more appropriate forum abroad 268–71
  justice, requirements of 271–2
  multiplicity of proceedings 273–4
  principles to be applied when exercising discretion 267–72
  role 267
  stay pending decision abroad in relation to validity 272–3
forum shopping 196–201, 306–7
  advantages to be obtained 198–201, 307
  choice of fora 197–8
  outside Europe 307
  personal advantage 198
  procedural advantages 198–9
  substantive law advantage 199–200
  tort choice of law rules 200
  within Europe 306–7
how jurisdictional problems arise 134–5
interim relief 312–13
international discovery 228–30, 313–14
  determining which company to join 229
  difficulties involved 229–30, 314
  establishing liability 229–30
  need to join foreigner as substantive defendant 228–9, 313
  satisfying jurisdictional criteria 230
jurisdiction under EC/EFTA rules 141–237
  alternative solution 232
  application of rules 141–2
  bases 142–76
  criticism of existing law 231
  declining jurisdiction 177–90
    Article 22(2) 185–6
    forum non conveniens 186–8
      altering facts 187–8

infringement (*cont.*):
  jurisdiction under EC/EFTA rules (*cont.*):
    forum non conveniens (*cont.*):
      Re Harrods (Buenos Aires) Ltd 186–7
    general: Article 2 142–3
      advantages 143
      disadvantages 143
    independent jurisdictional rules 233
    infringements committed outside
      EC/EFTA contracting states 195
    internet, and 236–7
    invalidity, defence of 202–10
      argument based on wording of
        conventions 203
      Articles 19 and 16(4), effect 202–8,
        210–11, 213–14
      Coin Controls Ltd case 204–6
      decision of Court of Justice, need for
        208
      Fort Dodge case 206–7
      J A Motte v Tecno Spa 207–8
    lis pendens 177–82
      court second seized giving way to
        first seized 182
      same cause of action 177–81
      same parties 181–2
    no subject matter limitations on jurisdic-
      tion 190–6
      Coin Controls case 193
      difficulties in establishing basis of
        jurisdiction against person 196
      foreign rights created outside
        EC/EFTA contracting states 193–6
      Fort Dodge case 193
      judicial misunderstanding 191
      Pearce case 192–3
      position under Conventions 190
    provisional measures 214–18
      infringement cases 217–18
    reform 231–7
    reform of jurisdictional rules of general
      application 232–3
    related actions 182–6
      exercise of discretion to stay 185
      expedient to hear and determine two
        actions together 184–5
      risk of irreconcilable judgments
        183–4
      stay of proceedings 182–3
    restraining foreign proceedings
      188–90
      contracting state 189–90
      non-contracting state 188–9
    special jurisdictional rules 233–7
    suggested additions to Article 5(3)
      234–6
    suggested rules 234–6

validity, and 201–14
  basis of jurisdiction necessary,
    whether 208–9
  counterclaim for revocation 210–13
  necessity of basis of jurisdiction
    211–12
  recognition of revocation order 212–13
  invalidity, defence of 202–10
  nature of problem 201–2
  separate revocation proceedings
    210, 213–14
jurisdiction under traditional rules
  241–315
mandatory rules of forum 598–606
  application 599–606
  foreign right infringed abroad 605–6
  foreign right infringed in England
    604–5
  tort cases 598–9
  UK intellectual property right
    infringed in England 600
  UK law operating to provide recovery
    603–4
  UK right infringed abroad 600–3
no requirement of damage 132
parallel rights 135–7
  old fashioned view 135–6
  same essential content 136–7
patents 120–2
  basic rule 120
  defences 121
  purposive interpretation 121–2
  territorial requirement 120–1
performances, rights in 127
performing, rights in 127
preliminary matters 119–37
prevention of allegations 132–3
reform 314–16
  general rules 315
  special rules 315–16
restraining foreign proceedings 266–79
  bringing of proceedings abroad is
    invasion of legal or equitable right
    not to be sued there 277
  bringing of proceedings abroad would
    be unconscionable 277
  infringement of foreign intellectual
    property right 277–8
  infringement of parallel rights 278–9
  infringement of UK intellectual
    property right 278
  trial available in alternative fora
    abroad 276–7
  trial available in England and abroad
    275–6
section 14(2), Act of 1995 616–18
  application 617

Index

defamation, exclusion of 617
  events occurring in forum 618
  restriction 616–17
service of writ out of jurisdiction 243–66
  act from which damage resulted
    committed in England 244–9
    copyrights 247–8
    infringement over internet 248–9
    patents 244–7
  damage sustained in England 249–52
    considerations when fixing upon
      definition 250–1
    nature of problem 249–52
    options 251–2
  exercise of discretion 259–66
    alternative forum abroad 260–1
    applicable law 262
    appropriate forum 261–3
    consolidation of litigation in multi-
      defendant cases 262
    convenience 261
    expense 261
    forum conveniens 259–60
    general considerations 259–66
    injustice abroad 263–4
    parallel proceedings 263
    significance of particular head of
      Order 11 264–6
    witnesses 261–2
  foreign intellectual property right 266
  heads of Order 11, rule 1(1) 244–56
    injunction head 254–6
      application in infringement cases
        254–5
      use in infringement cases 255–6
    multi-defendant head 253–4
    tort head 244–53
  multiple acts of infringement and
    damage 252
  serious issue to be tried 256–8
    establishing liability 257–8
    injunction head 257
    multi-defendant head 257
    standard of proof 256–7
    tort head 257
  threatened wrongs 252–3, 256
service of writ within jurisdiction 241–3
  advantages 243
  presence within jurisdiction 241–3
special jurisdiction: Articles 5 and 6
  144–75
  act of infringement 145
  applicable law 145
  English law applies 145–8
  establishing liability 145–9
  foreign law applies 148–9
  serious issue on merits 144–5

territorial limitation on liability 145–8
threshold requirement 144–9
validity of right 149
state immunity 279
statutory rules for tort choice of law
  612–40
  abolition of certain common law rules
    618–19
  application in infringement cases
    615–16
  characterisation for purposes of
    jurisdiction 614–15
  choice of law 612
  criteria for characterisation 613
  displacement of general rule 625–33
  evidence, pleading or practice, rules of
    636–7
  general rule 619–24
  issue relating to tort 612–16
  mandatory rules 638–40
    foreign 638–40
  no retrospective effect 612
  penal law, and 636
  procedure, rules of 637–8
  public law, and 636
  public policy 634–5
    application in infringement cases
      635
    rule 634–5
  revenue law, and 636
  savings 633
  section 11 619–24
    infringement scenario 623–4
    multi-country torts 619–20
    operation 620–3
  section 12 625–33
    displacing general rule 629
    examples where displacement rule
      will operate 628–9
    factors and their significance 630–1
    infringement scenarios 631–3
    operation 630–1
    single country torts 619
    substantially more appropriate test
      625–8
subject matter limitations in relation to
  jurisdiction 279–306
  foreign immovable property 280–3
  foreign intellectual property right
    283–99
  infra-UK cases 306
policy considerations 290–3
substantive law 120–34
territorial limitation on liability 131
tort choice of law rules 606–40
  foreign and UK rights infringed abroad
    611

infringement (*cont.*):
  tort choice of law rules (*cont.*):
    foreign right infringed abroad 609–11
    foreign right infringed in England 609
    statutory rules 612–40
    torts committed abroad 607
      torts committed in England 606–7
      UK right infringed abroad 608–9
      UK right infringed in England 608
  torts, comparison with 449
  trade marks 122–4
    basic rule 122–3
    Community trade mark 124
    comparative advertising 123–4
  validity, and 307–12
    Article 16(4) 307–8
    counterclaim for revocation 311–12
    foreign intellectual property rights, and 310–11
    invalidity, defence of 308–11
    present law 308–10
    separate revocation proceedings 312
intellectual property
  choice of law rules 489–98
  property, as 487–98
  property characterisation 488–9
intellectual property rights 6–48
  choice of law
    alternative approaches 538–41
  contrasts in relation to exploitation *see* contracts in relation to exploitation of intellectual property rights
  creation 6–48 *see also* creation and validity of intellectual property rights
  grant *see* grant and ownership of intellectual property rights
  jurisdictional problems 10–11
  jurisdictional provisions 11–45
  litigation 8–10
    infringement linked 9–10
    registration linked 8–9
    revocation linked 9
  methods of creation 6–10
  nature of 496–7
  negative declaration 10
  ownership *see* grant and ownership of intellectual property rights
  property rules not sufficient 497–8
  registration 6–7
    revocation 8
  situs 489–96
    alternative approach 494–6
    copyright 493–4
    Dicey and Morris approach 489–90
    exercise 495–6
    patents 490–2

  law governing creation of right 491–2
  transfer of right 490–1
  registered designs 492
  registration 495–6
  restrictions on competition, and 494–5
  trade marks 492–3
  special jurisdictional rules 11–28
  tortious protection 525–7
  validity 6–43 *see also* creation and validity of intellectual property rights
  widening categories 525
international co-operation agreements 479
internet
  infringement over 158–61, 248–9

jurisdiction
  applicable law, and 3–4
  application of traditional rules 3
  Brussels Convention 2
  EC/EFTA rules 1–3
  Lugano Convention 3
jurisdictional issues 3

Lugano Convention 733
  jurisdiction 3

malicious falsehood 388–94, 669–73
  act committed within jurisdiction 393
  applicable law 669–73
    characterisation 669–70
    committed abroad 672
    committed in England 672–3
    common law rules 672–3
    exclusion from Part III 670–1
      'any defamation claim' 670–1
      reason for 671
    place where committed 672–3
  Article 5(3) 392–3
    place of event giving rise to damage 392
    place where damage occurred 392–3
  damage 391
  damage sustained within jurisdiction 393–4
  derogatory statement 390
  EC/EFTA rules 392–3
  false statement 389–90
  how choice of law problems arise 669
  how jurisdictional problems arise 391
  jurisdictional problems 392–4
  malice 390–1
  substantive law 389–91
  traditional rules 393–4
mandatory rules of the forum 456–7

Index

moral rights
  applicable law 502–4

Paris Convention for the Protection of Industrial Property 1883 477–8
  law of protecting country 477–8
  national treatment 477
passing off 361–87, 652–68
  applicable law 652–68
    application of general rule 658–63
      direct passing-off 658–9
      enabling another to pass off 659
      events constituting tort 658
      multi-country passing off 659–62
      multiple passing-off 663
      pleading and proof of foreign law 662–3
      single country passing-off 658–9
    characterisation 654–5
    common law rules 653–4
    displacement of general rule 663–7
      actionability, and 667
      factors 664
    substantially more appropriate test 665–7
    mandatory rules 668
    Part III, Act of 1995 656–8
      choice of law problems 656–7
      passing-off tortious, whether 657–8
      restriction in s.14(2) 658
      tort choice of law 656–8
    public policy 667
    savings 667–8
    statutory rules 654–68
  Articles 5(3) and 6(1) 371–8
    damage to goodwill 375–7
    multiple acts 378
    place of event giving rise to damage 374–5
    place where business lost 377
    place where damage occurred 375
    place where harmful event occurred 373–4
    scope of Article 5(3) 372–3
    threshold requirement 372
    threatened passing-off 373
    unfair competition 371–2
  bases of jurisdiction 381–4
    act committed within jurisdiction 381–2
    damage sustained within jurisdiction 382
    discretionary element 384–6
    forum conveniens 384–5
      applicable law 384–5
      multiple acts of passing-off 385
      place where goodwill situated 385
      relief sought 385

  injunction head 384
  multiple damage 382–3
  multi-defendant head 383
  multiple acts 382–3
  restraining foreign proceedings 385–6
  threatened passing off 381
  tort head 381–3
  damage 367–8
  declining jurisdiction 379–80
    lis pendens 379–80
      cause of action and subject matter the same 379–80
      parties the same, whether 380
    related actions 380
  EC/EFTA rules 370–80
    application of Brussels and Lugano Conventions 370
    bases of jurisdiction 370–8
  enabling 368–9
  goodwill 363–5
    collective 365
    existence 363
    geographical extent 363–4
    less obvious types 365
    location 363–4
    trade-related 364
  how choice of law problems arise 652–3
  how jurisdictional problems arise 369–70
  jurisdictional provisions 370–88
  misrepresentation 365–7
    different version of original product 367
    intention not required 367
    name as source of confusion 366
    use of similar get-up 365–6
  no subject matter limitations in relation to jurisdiction 386–8
    authorities 387
    consolidation of litigation 387
    different treatment 388
  substantive law 361–9
  traditional rules 381–8
Patent Co-operation Treaty
  applicable law 530
patents 344–9, 517–25
  applicable law 517–25
  application 6–7
  how jurisdictional problems arise 344–5
  infringement *see* infringement
  jurisdictional provisions 345–9
  law of protecting country 519–22
  ownership of rights
    applicable law 522–5
  Part VI, Community Patent Convention 346–9
    allocation of jurisdiction within UK 348

patents (*cont.*):
  Part VI, Community Patent Convention (*cont.*):
    bases of jurisdiction 347–8
    Brussels Convention, and 348
    compulsory licences 347
    exclusive jurisdiction 347
    German courts 348
    relationship with Brussels Convention 347
    right to patent 347–8
    scope 346–7
    stay of proceedings 348–9
    validity 349
  Protocol on Litigation 345–6
  registration system
    applicable law 517–18
  substantive law 344
performances, rights in
  infringement 127
plant variety rights 349–58
  bases of jurisdiction 352–5
    Articles 5(1), 17 and 18, Lugano Convention 354–5
    Brussels Convention 355
    courts for place where harmful event occurred 354
    defendant's domicile/an establishment 352–3
    Lugano Convention 354–5
    Member States in which seat of Office located 353–4
    plaintif's domicile/an establishment 353
  Brussels Convention 352
  declining jurisdiction 356–7
  how jurisdictional problems arise 350
  infringements committed abroad 355–6
  invalidity, plea of 356
  jurisdictional provisions 350–8
  Lugano Convention 351–2
  proceedings 351
  protective measures 357
  provisional measures 357
  stay of proceedings 356–7
  substantive law background 349–50
  summary of similarities and differences between rules 357–8

recognition and enforcement of foreign judgments 721–41
  Brussels Convention 1968 *see* Brussels Convention
  cause of action estoppel 738
  common law system 733–9
  decisions in relation to supranational or semi-supranational rights 740–1
  defences 736–9
  European Patent Convention 740–1
  finality of foreign judgment 735
  foreign judgment in breach of dispute settlement agreement 738–9
  foreign penal law 737
  fraud 736
  how problems arise in intellectual property cases 724–5
  judgment must be for fixed sum of money 735
  jurisdiction of foreign court 734–5
    presence in jurisdiction 734
    submission to 734–5
  Lugano Convention 733
  natural justice defence 738
  no examination of merits 735–6
  Protection of Trading Interests Act 1980 737
  public policy 736–7
  requirements 734–6
  statute 739
rights created by international conventions 529–31
  applicable law 529–31
Rome Convention on the Law Applicable to Contractual Obligations 476–7, 551–91
  alternative approaches 590–1
  applicable law 552–77
  applicable law in absence of choice 554–77
    Article 4 556–8
    contracts made before April 1 1991 554–5
  application 551
  application of Article 4 to contracts 558–77
    Article 4(5) 561–9
    contracts in relation to trade marks 570
    copyright 572–5
      Article 4(5) 574–5
      closest connection 572
      presumption of characteristic performance 572–4
    distribution agreements 575
    general approach to all industrial property rights 575–6
    know-how 570–1
    law of protecting country 566–9
    licences 558–69
      closest connection 558–9
      presumption of characteristic performance 559–61
    licensee's habitual residence 564–6
    licensor's habitual residence 561–4

Article 3(3) 578
Article 5 578–9
Article 6 579
Article 7 579–82
Article 7(1) 579–80
Article 7(2) 580–2
formal validity 588–90
law chosen by parties 552–4
  contracts made after 1 April 1991 552–4
  contracts made before 1st April 1991 552
law of protecting country 476–7
limitations on applicable law 577–88
mandatory rules 577
  application to intellectual property statutes 582–7
  Article 100A European Treaty 584–5
  excessively wide scope for competition law 582–3
  moral rights 585–6
  ordre public 587–8
  public policy 587–8
  rules relating to employee's inventions 586–7
  section 44 Patents Act 1977 584–5
  summary 587
  territoriality theory 583–4
national treatment 476–7
qualification 476
state immunity 45, 70, 112
infringement, and 279

torts
applicable law 651–720
  suggested rules 714–20
    breach of competition 718–19
    breach of confidence 719–20
    defamation of business competitor 716
    delict 718
    keeping within framework of existing rules 717
    malicious falsehood 716
    passing-off 714–15
    unfair competition 716–18
  choice of law rules
    general reform 704–5
  criticism of existing law 448–9, 703–4
    complexity 703
    inadequate protection 704
    lack of uniformity 704
    uncertainty 703
  infringement, comparison with 449
  reform 447–53
    independent rules or within framework of existing rules 451

rules for different causes of action or just for unfair competition 449–50
special jurisdiction rules 449–53
reform of general jurisdictional rules 449
special choice of law rules 705–20
  Article 136 Swiss PIL Statute 711–13
    exceptions 712–13
    general rule 711
    mandatory rules 713
    public policy 713
    scope 711
  Hague Convention on Law Applicable to Unfair Competition 713
  independent or within framework of existing rules 706–7
  independent rules for unfair competition 707–20
  Resolution of Institute of International Law 707–11
    exceptions 709–10
    general rules 708–9
    preparations for act of unfair competition 710–11
    public policy 710
    scope 707
  rules for different causes of action or for unfair competition 705–6
special tort choice of law rules for different causes of action 714–20
policy considerations 714
trade marks 318–41, 517–25
applicable law 517–25
application 7
disputes other than in relation to infringement 320–1
  Brussels Convention 320–1
  provisions applying 321
how jurisdictional problems arise 318–19
infringement 321–41 *see also* infringement
  allocation of jurisdiction within UK 328
  Articles 17 and 18, Brussels Convention 324–5
  bases of jurisdiction 323–6
  bases of jurisdiction contained in Brussels Convention 326
  Brussels Convention 322
  Community trade mark courts 322
  counterclaims 331–3
  declining jurisdiction 334–9
    Articles 21 and 22, Brussels Convention 334–5
    Community trade marks 334–6
    discretionary power 335–6
    related actions 334

trade marks (*cont.*):
  infringement (*cont.*):
    declining jurisdiction (*cont.*):
      simultaneous and successive civil actions 336–9
    defendant's domicile/an establishment 323–4
    definition of domicile/an establishment 322–3
    extent of jurisdiction 326–8
    forum shopping 330–1
    invalidity 331–3
    invalidity as defence 333
    jurisdiction based on Article 93(1) to (4) 327
    jurisdiction based on Article 93(5) 327–8
    local act 325–6
    plaintiff's domicile/an establishment 324
    procedure for service of writ 341
    protective measures 339–41
    provisional measures 339–41
    Regulation compared with Brussels convention 328–30
    residual jurisdiction based on Brussels Convention 328
    revocation 331–3
    safeguarding rights of defendant 341
    sanctions 341
    seat of office 324
  jurisdictional provisions 319–41
  law of protecting country 519–22
  ownership of rights
    applicable law 522
  registration system
    applicable law 517–18
  substantive law background 318
TRIPS Agreement 480–1
  national treatment 480–1

unfair competition 409–14, 678–90
  applicable law 679–90
    application of general rule 684–7
    displacement of general rule 687–8
    events constituting tort 684–5
    multi-country 685–7
    single country 685
  characterisation 680–1
  commmon law rules 679
  mandatory rules 690
  measure of damages 689
  Part III 681–3
    exclusions 682–3
    restrictions in section 14(2) 682
    tort choice of law 681–2
  procedure, rules of 689
  public policy 688
  rules of evidence, pleading or practice 689
  savings 688–90
  statutory rules 680–90
  Article 5(3) 410–14
    place of event giving rise to damage 411–12
    place where damage occurred 412–14
    place where damage to particular relationship was sustained 412
    place where direct economic loss to plaintiff was sustained 413–14
  EC/EFTA rules 410–14
  how choice of law problems arise 678–9
  how jurisdictional problems arise 410
  jurisdictional provisions 410–14
  passing-off, and 371–2
  substantive law 409–10
  suggested rules 452–3
  traditional rules 414